PUBLIC PAPERS OF THE PRESIDENTS

OF THE UNITED STATES

PUBLIC PAPERS OF THE PRESIDENTS

OF THE UNITED STATES

Richard Nixon

Containing the Public Messages, Speeches, and

Statements of the President

1972

UNITED STATES GOVERNMENT PRINTING OFFICE

WASHINGTON : 1974

PUBLISHED BY THE
OFFICE OF THE FEDERAL REGISTER
NATIONAL ARCHIVES AND RECORDS SERVICE
GENERAL SERVICES ADMINISTRATION

For sale by the Superintendent of Documents, U.S. Government Printing Office
Washington, D.C. 20402 - Price $18.55
Stock Number 2203-00900

FOREWORD

IN THIS published record of Presidential speeches, messages, and other communications, the casual reader and serious scholar alike will find a verbal outline of a year rich in the stuff of history.

Nineteen hundred seventy-two witnessed the closing chapter of our long struggle for an honorable settlement in Vietnam. It saw America successfully building a global structure of lasting peace by forging new international relationships and strengthening old ones. And, at home, it saw the emergence of a broad-based consensus for governmental reform, economic restraint and responsibility, and national renewal.

The sweep of events spanned continents. For the first time, a President of the United States was welcomed in the capitals of two nations which have been our most powerful adversaries. In Moscow, Peking, and other global nerve centers, American initiatives laid the groundwork for an era of reduced tensions and greater international understanding.

Within our own borders, a surging national economy turned more fully from the works of war to the challenges of peace. For the first time in a generation, Government and people could dedicate themselves to the goal of a prosperity unblemished by war or inflation.

Finally, in November of 1972, the American people were offered the clearest electoral choice in a century—a choice between two sharply contrasting sets of policies and philosophies of government. Statement by statement, issue by issue, the papers in this volume define the policies and philosophies for which I stood in that election, policies and philosophies which provide the goals for my Administration during its second term.

It is obvious that no collection of public papers, however encyclopedic, can paint the full picture of the many events it recounts. The intricate play of personalities, the subtleties of planning, timing, and execution defy precise description; the thousand random factors that can change even the most carefully charted course do not lend themselves to easy portrayal on paper.

Yet by reviewing the materials assembled here, readers should be able to sense both the broad strokes and the fine shadings which shaped our national policies in 1972. And in the laws, treaties, and executive actions that grew out of these events, we can see the tangible effects of these sometimes intangible forces.

Each document in this volume, long or short, marks an aspiration conceived, achieved or frustrated. And if, as the Athenian historian Thucydides maintained, history is philosophy taught by example, then each document is also part of a lesson as useful to posterity as it was instructive to those who lived it.

Every generation views history through lenses of its own making. The same picture constantly alters in hue and perspective and the relative importance of its individual parts forever fluctuates. Sometimes the result is greater clarity. At other times it is only fresh distortion. But in all cases, a full written transcript of the past can serve as a steadying focal point, a beacon pointing the way to sound interpretation and reevaluation.

The stronger the beacon—and the physical bulk of this volume attests to its strength in the case of 1972—the clearer the illumination it can throw on what is past and the brighter the light it can cast toward future horizons.

Richard Nixon

PREFACE

IN THIS VOLUME are gathered most of the public messages and statements of the 37th President of the United States that were released by the White House in 1972. Similar volumes are available covering the Administrations of Presidents Truman, Eisenhower, Kennedy, and Johnson.

The series was begun in 1957 in response to a recommendation of the National Historical Publications Commission. Until then there had been no systematic publication of Presidential papers. An extensive compilation of the messages and papers of the Presidents, covering the period 1789 to 1897, was assembled by James D. Richardson and published under Congressional authority between 1896 and 1899. Since then various private compilations have been issued but there was no uniform publication comparable to the *Congressional Record* or the *United States Supreme Court Reports*. Many Presidential papers could be found only in mimeographed White House releases or as reported in the press. The National Historical Publications Commission therefore recommended the establishment of an official series in which Presidential writings and utterances of a public nature could be made promptly available.

The Commission's recommendation was incorporated in regulations of the Administrative Committee of the Federal Register issued under section 6 of the Federal Register Act (44 U.S.C. 1506). The Committee's regulations, establishing the series and providing for the coverage of prior years, are reprinted as Appendix F.

CONTENT AND ARRANGEMENT

The text of this book is based on Presidential materials issued during the period as White House releases and on transcripts of news conferences. Original source materials, where available, including tape recordings, have been used to protect against errors in transcription.

The dates shown at the end of item headings are White House release dates. In instances where the date of the document differs from the release date that fact is shown in the note immediately following the item. Textnotes, footnotes, and cross references have been supplied where needed for purposes of clarity. In this volume, for the first time, an effort has been made to annotate those occasions when the President spoke from a prepared text and when he spoke without referring to notes.

Remarks or addresses were delivered in Washington, D.C., unless otherwise indicated. Similarly, statements, messages, and letters were issued from the White House in Washington unless otherwise indicated. All times shown are local time.

Items published in this volume are presented in chronological order, rather than being grouped in classes. Most needs for a classified arrangement are met by the subject index. For example, a reader interested in veto messages sent to Congress during 1972 will find them listed in the index under the heading "Veto messages and memorandums of disapproval."

Appendixes A through E have been provided to deal with special categories of Presidential issuances and actions, as noted below.

White House releases not included as items in this volume and not appearing in later appendixes are listed in Appendix A.

Items of general interest announced by the White House during 1972 and not noted elsewhere in the volume are listed in Appendix B.

Though not all proclamations, Executive orders, and similar documents required by law to be published in the *Federal Register* and *Code of Federal Regulations* were issued as White House releases during 1972, a complete listing of these documents by number and subject appears in Appendix C.

The President is required by statute to transmit numerous reports to the Congress. Those transmitted during the period covered by this volume are listed in Appendix D.

Appendix E is a feature unique to the 1972 volume and includes announcements of decisions on personnel changes for President

Nixon's second term, as made public by the White House Press Secretary in the weeks following the election.

This series is under the direction of Fred J. Emery, Director, and Ernest J. Galdi, Deputy Director, of the Office of the Federal Register. Editors of the present volume were Jean T. Eisinger and Ruth C. Pontius, assisted by other members of the Presidential and Government Manual Branch.

White House assistance in selection and annotation of the documents was provided by Raymond K. Price, Jr., Special Consultant to the President, David R. Gergen, Special Assistant to the President, Cecilia Bellinger, Staff Assistant for Research, and John J. Ratchford, Executive Clerk of the White House.

The photographic portfolio was prepared with the help of Ollie Atkins, Personal Photographer to the President, and Robert J. McKendry, Superintendent, Division of Typography and Design, United States Government Printing Office. The Government Printing Office was also responsible for the typography, design, and production of the volume.

JAMES B. RHOADS
Archivist of the United States

ARTHUR F. SAMPSON
Administrator of General Services
January 1974

CONTENTS

LIST OF ITEMS

List of Items

List of Items

List of Items

List of Items

List of Items

List of Items

List of Items

Richard Nixon

1972

"A Conversation With the President," Interview With Dan Rather of the Columbia Broadcasting System.
January 2, 1972

THE PRESIDENT. Good evening, ladies and gentlemen. I wish to welcome all of you to this interview in the Oval Office of the President, and, Mr. Rather, we will go right to your questions.

QUESTIONS

DECISION ON CANDIDACY

[1.] MR. RATHER. Thank you, Mr. President, and for myself and on behalf of my colleagues in the White House press corps, Happy New Year to you.

Since this is a new year, may we assume that you are a candidate for reelection?

THE PRESIDENT. That is not an unexpected question.

MR. RATHER. I wouldn't think so.

THE PRESIDENT. I will answer it simply by saying that before the 14th of January I will have to make a decision and announce that decision with regard to candidacy, because that is the time that I will have to decide whether to enter the New Hampshire primary.

I will be making a decision. I will be announcing it by the 14th. As far as candidacy is concerned, while I cannot, and therefore will not, announce it on this program—I think I should save that for all your colleagues—I will say that I have decided already what I will do during the period of the campaign.

Whatever my decision is, I have decided that I will engage in no public partisan activities until after the Republican Convention. The problems of the Presidency, the problems of this office in which we sit, in this year 1972, are so great that it will not be possible to take time off for partisan politics.

ATTORNEY GENERAL MITCHELL AND THE CAMPAIGN

[2.] MR. RATHER. Mr. President, someone will have to run your campaign, and it is widely assumed that Attorney General Mitchell will be leaving. Could you tell us when he will be leaving?

THE PRESIDENT. Well, you are getting me right into the question that I just refused to answer, but I understand that. If I make the decision to become a candidate—and there is, of course, good reason to think that I might make the decision in that direction, although there is always the possibility that one might change his mind—but if I make that decision, the man who is best qualified to run the campaign is Attorney General Mitchell.

The only problem I have with that is that he is also, in my opinion, the best qualified to be Attorney General of the United States. I haven't crossed that bridge yet. That is one of the hard decisions I am going to have to make in the event that we come down affirmatively to enter the New Hampshire primary.

CIRCUMSTANCES AFFECTING CANDIDACY

[3.] MR. RATHER. Mr. President, under what circumstances would you not be a candidate for reelection?

THE PRESIDENT. Well, it would depend, Mr. Rather, on circumstances that none of us might foresee at this point. I have often said that it is not well to be coy about this business of candidacy. Most assume that a man who has served in the office of President will be a candidate for reelection if the Constitution allows him to do so.

You may recall, however, that President Johnson, when he was faced with this difficult choice, decided not to be a candidate.

MR. RATHER. Frankly, I was thinking of that when I asked you.

THE PRESIDENT. I do not anticipate that events such as led President Johnson to his decision may affect my decision; however, I do know that it is always wise to delay until the last possible moment any very important decision, and, of course, making the decision to be a candidate for President—as I know better than anybody else—is a very important decision.

VICE PRESIDENT AGNEW

[4.] MR. RATHER. Mr. President, can you give us assurances categorically and unequivocally that if you are a candidate that you want to run again with Vice President Agnew and that he will be your running mate, if you have anything to do with it?

THE PRESIDENT. Well, Mr. Rather, with regard to the Vice Presidency, the decision will be made at the convention, as will be the case with the candidate for President.

However, to give you an inkling as to my own thinking with regard to that decision—and if I am a candidate, I obviously will have something to say about it—my view is that one should not break up a winning combination. I believe that the Vice President has handled his difficult assignments with dignity, with courage. He has, at times, been a man of controversy, but when a man has done a good job in a position, when he has been part of a winning team, I believe that he should stay on the team. That is my thinking at this time.

BOMBING RESUMPTION AND TROOP WITHDRAWALS

[5.] MR. RATHER. Mr. President, as you enter this election year, there are quite obviously two central themes that you have been emphasizing. You have stated them over again in the phrases, "a generation of peace" and "a prosperity without war."

I would like to take advantage of this opportunity to examine in some detail and some depth the concepts beneath those phrases.

First, on a generation of peace. On everyone's mind is the resumption of the widespread bombing of North Vietnam. Other than what we already know from the authorities in Saigon and what Secretary Laird has said, could you assess the military benefits of that?

THE PRESIDENT. With regard to the military benefits, let me say first why we did it. You were present in the White House Press Room, as you always are, when I was there making the last troop withdrawal announcement [1] which will bring the troops down to 139,000 by the first of February. And, at that time, I said that in the event that the enemy stepped up its infiltration, or engaged in other activities which imperiled, in my opinion,

----

[1] See 1971 volume, Item 356 [1.].

our remaining forces as our forces were becoming less, that I would take action to deal with the situation.

Most of you reported it. And most of the reporters also wrote it. I meant exactly what I said. The enemy did step up its infiltration. They violated the understanding of 1968, when the bombing halt was agreed to, with regard to firing on our unarmed reconnaissance planes. They shelled Saigon on December 19.

Under those circumstances, I had no other choice but to bomb, in this case, selected military targets and supply buildup areas. Those were the only areas that were hit.

The results have been very, very effective, and I think that their effectiveness will be demonstrated by the statement I am now going to make.

Before the first of February, well before the first of February, I will make another withdrawal announcement. Our withdrawal will continue on schedule, at least at the present rate, possibly at somewhat a larger rate. I will not make the decision with regard to the rate at this point, but the withdrawal can go forward on schedule and as far as our American casualties are concerned, which, as you know, as reported on Thursday of last week on CBS and other networks, were one—the lowest in 6 years.

MR. RATHER. That included a truce period for Christmas, did it not?

THE PRESIDENT. It included a truce period, but as you know they have averaged less than 10 for 3 months, whereas they were averaging 300—up to 300 a week when we came into office. But our casualties as a result of these activities, I believe, can be kept at this very low level.

AMERICAN INVOLVEMENT IN VIETNAM

[6.] MR. RATHER. Mr. President, you were quoted in a Time magazine interview this past week—and I want to get the direct quotation if I may—saying, "The issue of Vietnam will not be an issue in the campaign as far as this Administration is concerned, because we will have brought the American involvement to an end."

Now, may one properly assume from that, that by Election Day there will be no Americans, land, sea, or air, no residual force, fighting in support of Laotians, Cambodians, or South Vietnamese?

THE PRESIDENT. Mr. Rather, that depends on one circumstance, which is very much in my mind, and in the minds I know of all of our listeners and viewers. That is the situation with regard to our POW's. First, as far as American involvement is concerned, we are still pursuing the negotiating track. There is a possibility—I know many believe there is no possibility, but I believe there is some—and we are continuing to pursue it with the meeting resuming next week, of ending the war through negotiation. We have offered, as you know, a cease-fire throughout Indochina, including Laos and Cambodia. We have offered a total withdrawal of all outside forces. We would offer an exchange of POW's, and under these circumstances, we believe that this is a time that those offers should seriously be considered.

In the event that no progress is made on the negotiating front, then we will have to continue on what we call the Vietnamization front. Now it is quite obvious, if you look at the numbers, if we are down to 139,000 by the first of February, if I make another announcement of approximately the same level or at an even somewhat higher level for a period in the future, that the number of Americans in Vietnam will be down to a very low level well before the election.

Now, the question arises then, can the President of the United States, sitting in this office, with the responsibility for 400 POW's and 1,500 missing in action throughout Southeast Asia, because they are also potential POW's, can he withdraw all of our forces as long as the enemy holds one American as a prisoner of war? The answer is no.

So I would have to say that with regard to the statement that I made to Time magazine, our goal is to end the American involvement in Vietnam before the end of this year, and before the election, not just because it is an election, but because these are the ways our plans are working out. Our preference is to end it by negotiation. If that does not work we will do it by withdrawal through Vietnamization. But if POW's are still retained by North Vietnam, in order to have any bargaining position at all with the Vietnamese, North Vietnamese, we will have to continue to retain a residual force in Vietnam, and we will have to continue the possibility of air strikes on the North Vietnamese.

MR. RATHER. If you have to continue both of those—and the likelihood at the moment concerning the negotiating posture of both sides in Paris is that that is very likely—if you have to maintain a residual force and keep open at least the threat of additional air strikes, then how can you campaign saying you have ended the American involvement?

THE PRESIDENT. Well, the important thing is not how I can campaign with

regard to the American involvement, but the important thing is whether the American people are convinced that the President of the United States has done everything that he can to bring this desperately difficult war to an end, and that he is doing everything that he can in view of dealing with international outlaws to protect American men and to get back Americans who are held, as are our Americans who are POW's at the present time.

Now, let's look at the situation when we came into office. I remember the first day I sat in this room. I looked at the number of Americans in Vietnam, 539,000. I looked at the casualty rates, averaging as high as 300 a week. I saw that there was no plan to bring any home. There was no negotiating plan on the table at Paris. And what has happened?

Well, we have brought 400,000 home. As we have already indicated, the rate of withdrawal will continue throughout the next few months. We have reduced the casualties from 300 a month—last week to one—to an average of less than 10 over the past 3 months. Now, that is too many— one American dying in war anyplace in the world is too many as far as I am concerned—but that is a considerable achievement.

As far as the POW problem is concerned, that is one that we unfortunately are confronted with. But let me just give this much hope to our POW people. I believe that as the enemy looks at the alternatives that they may decide, as they see the American involvement ending, that it would be well for them not to retain our POW's and run the risk that it would be necessary for the United States to stay in Vietnam.

I know sometimes you and some of your colleagues have pointed out, and with very

4

good reason, that if when we had 540,000 in Vietnam that had no effect in getting the enemy to negotiate on POW's, why would having 25 or 35 thousand as a residual force have any effect? And the answer is: Does the enemy want the United States to withdraw from Vietnam, or doesn't it?

PRISONER-OF-WAR NEGOTIATIONS

[7.] MR. RATHER. Mr. President, speaking of POW families, a lady from Florida called in this afternoon and asked that I ask you this question. She is Mrs. Gerald Gartley, from Florida, who is the mother of a 27-year-old Navy lieutenant who is a prisoner. Her question, which I take this opportunity to ask on her behalf, is: Have we ever asked the North Vietnamese and the Provisional Revolutionary Government if they will release the POW's and guarantee the safety of our withdrawing troops if we set a date for withdrawal of all U.S. forces from South Vietnam? Have we ever asked them that?

THE PRESIDENT. Mr. Rather, that particular matter has been one that has been under discussion at various times in the Paris peace talks, but you yourself recall, because you reported it, or at least your Paris correspondent reported it on CBS, and I think even NBC and ABC had this as well, that when that was floated out this fall, the North Vietnamese totally rejected it.

In other words, that is the deal of saying that if we set a deadline, then they will give us back our POW's——

MR. RATHER. Excuse me, that was publicly done, Mr. President?

THE PRESIDENT. That was publicly done, that is correct. You remember the

United States Senator had met, he said, with some of the people from North Vietnam.[2] He was convinced that in the event that we set a deadline, that that would mean that they would release the prisoners. The North Vietnamese said deadline for prisoners was no deal. That was publicly stated.

Under those circumstances, this, of course, is a very cruel action on their part, to reject out of hand even the possibility of that kind of discussion.

I would say this, looking to the future, that as I have just pointed out, that when we come down to the end, as far as our own involvement in Vietnam is concerned, the question of whether or not they will return our prisoners in exchange for a total American withdrawal is one that they will have a chance to answer.

And I could also point out that we have participated in a great number of discussions other than those public discussions in Paris. Sitting right here in this room—as a matter of fact, you are sitting in my chair, Mr. Gromyko was sitting in this chair—I raised the subject of POW's with him. Dr. Kissinger raised the subject with Chou En-lai on both of his visits to the People's Republic of China.

MR. RATHER. Excuse me, Mr. President. Did we do that before——

THE PRESIDENT. In the event that at the time of the meetings that I will have in China and later on in the Soviet Union, we have not made progress in this area, the subjects will again be raised.

Now, I am not suggesting—because, be-

[2] On September 12, 1971, Senator George McGovern of South Dakota announced he had met in Paris on September 10 and 11 with representatives of North Vietnam and the Provisional Revolutionary Government.

lieve me, it is a heartrending matter to read the letters from the POW wives and their next of kin in other ways, to read those letters and to realize how their hopes have been dashed year after year. But I can tell you that we have pursued every negotiating channel; that we have made a number of offers in various channels and that when the total record is published, and it will be published in due time, at an appropriate time, our lady from Florida and the others will realize that we have gone the extra mile as far as POW's are concerned. I do not want to disclose any further details because negotiations are underway.

MR. RATHER. I am sorry to interrupt you and I was going to ask whether there would be something on your agenda in Peking and Moscow, and you have answered the question in your answer saying so.

THE PRESIDENT. It will be on the agenda, I emphasize, provided it is still a live question, because we are, naturally, hoping that in both of these cases we can go forward.

Now, let me point out, we should not give the impression that because we raised the subject with the Chinese, we raised it with the Soviet Union, that that is going to mean action, because we have raised it at other levels already.

I would point out one slightly hopeful note: the fact that the Chinese, after holding two Americans prisoner for many years, released them, as you know, about 2 or 3 weeks ago. At least their attitude toward prisoners seems to be much more civilized than that of the North Vietnamese. Whether they can influence the North Vietnamese toward a similar attitude, however, remains to be seen.

TIMING OF THE PRESIDENT'S ACTIONS

[8.] MR. RATHER. Mr. President, you have raised the subject of China, and I am sure it comes as no surprise to you that I would like to talk with you about that. Everyone is interested. You have also mentioned that you hope to reach your goals in the war this year, 1972; that everything seems to have been pointed in the direction of climaxing in this election year: besides your ultimate goals in the war, victory over inflation, driving down unemployment, agreement for the strategic arms limitations, trips to Peking and Moscow.

Is all of this coincidental, the timing, or is it, as some of even your friends say, some of the timing must be politically motivated?

THE PRESIDENT. Well, that is a very legitimate question, and I understand why many would feel that it was politically motivated. After all, when you look at the bombing halt of 1968, I know many on our side felt that that was politically motivated, at least the timing of it. I, of course, never made such a charge, and would not, and I don't think you would, because I think President Johnson was interested in doing everything that he could while he was President, and before the election, to start some negotiations in Paris.

But I realize that anyone who sits in this office is one that is going to be charged with having a political motivation for everything that he does. But just let me point this out: Let me say that if I could have ended the war the day I came into office, in a way that would not have encouraged that kind of aggression in other parts of the world, that would not have resulted in what I would have thought—and I thought then and think now—would have been a disastrous blow to America's foreign policy leadership in the world, believe me, I would have done it.

Anyone who signs, as the President does, letters to the next of kin of men killed in war has, as his constant thought in his mind, the first time he wakes up in the morning and the last time as he goes to sleep at night, when he goes to bed—he has in mind what can he do to bring that war to an end in a way that isn't going to bring on other wars, or in a way that will discourage other wars.

So as far as the timing on this is concerned, we haven't, as one Senator even had the temerity to suggest, delayed the ending of the war until the election year. If we could end it tomorrow, we would end it.

Now, as far as the Peking visit and the Moscow visit are concerned, we could have had a Moscow summit when we first came into office. It would have been a failure, just as the Glassboro summit was a failure. When summits are not well planned, when they have for their purpose just cosmetics, they raise great hopes, and then there is a great thud when they fall down.

In the case of the Soviet summit, both the Soviet leaders and I—and I have been in direct correspondence, as you know, with Mr. Brezhnev on this for some time, as well as discussions with Gromyko and Dobrynin—were convinced that until we had items for the agenda which would lead to possible substantive agreements, we should not have a summit.

What broke the back as far as having the Moscow summit was concerned, and what brought this timing, was the Berlin agreement. That historic agreement indi-

cated that the United States and the Soviet Union, agreeing on that critical area, might find a possibility of agreeing on other problems, where our interests might run in conflict—possibly the Mideast, possibly arms limitation, certainly trade and other areas. That is why the Moscow summit is timed at this point.

Now, the Chinese summit is one that I, as you may recall, wrote about in 1967. You may not recall it, because in 1967 there weren't many who thought I would be sitting here now, and certainly I wasn't sure.

MR. RATHER. Frankly, I didn't think you would be.

THE PRESIDENT. And that makes you not a bad prophet, either. But looking at the situation in 1967, I wrote an article for Foreign Affairs. As you know, I traveled very extensively while I was out of office, and much more freely than I can travel now. But in that article, I raised the lid on what many think was the biggest surprise in history when I made the 90-second announcement that we were going to go to China.[8]

I said then that the United States, looking to the future, had to find a way to open communications with the leaders of 750 million people who lived in Mainland China, and so the long process began. If we could have had it in 1969 or 1970, if it could have been properly prepared, we would have done so; but I can assure you it wasn't delayed because I was thinking, "Well, if I could just have it before the New Hampshire primary, in the year 1972, what a coup."

And the other side of that is, you see, it takes two to work out this neat little conspiracy that someone set up. Does any-

---

[8] See 1971 volume, Item 231.

body suggest the Soviet Union is interested in my reelection; that the Chinese would set their summit so that I could do well at that time of year?

MR. RATHER. Well, I don't know——

THE PRESIDENT. The answer, of course, is that I would doubt if that were the case. I don't mean that they would be against my reelection; but I am simply suggesting that those of us who make decisions in offices like this, certainly we think politically. We have that responsibility. We are leaders of our party; we are leaders of our country. But the country comes first.

I can assure you ending the war in Vietnam, building a lasting peace through opening to China, limiting tensions between the United States and the Soviet Union—those decisions have no political connotations whatever. If we could have done it earlier, we would have done it. And if this is not the right time to do it, we would have postponed it.

SUMMITRY

[9.] MR. RATHER. Well, that raises the question, Mr. President, that has always bothered me about summitry and I know from your writings before you became President, just before you came to this office, about the dangers of summitry. Doesn't it give the Communists in both capitals, Peking and Moscow, a bargaining advantage to bargain with you at the summit in the middle of an American election year? Wouldn't it have been better to say we either have the summits in both cases before our election year starts or postpone them a few months until after the election so as not to give the Communists this bargaining advantage?

THE PRESIDENT. Well, first, peace is

too important to postpone, and I will elaborate on that for just a moment if I can, after I cover the second part of the question. The second part of the question deals with the whole problem of summitry and whether or not it is a good idea. You raised that point, and I think I should respond to it. Summits which are held for the sake of having summits are a very bad idea, but when you are dealing with governments which have basically one-man rule—and that is true of the Soviet Union, it is true of the People's Republic of China—then for the major decisions summitry sometimes becomes a necessity. I became convinced that with regard to China and with regard to the Soviet Union that it would serve our interests and their interests in avoiding those confrontations that might lead to war, in building a world of peace, to meet, and the timing was such that it had to be now. To postpone it might have meant that something could have occurred in between so it would not be held at all. And as I have already pointed out, we could not arrange to have it earlier.

Now, second, with regard to the bargaining position, let me make one thing— it seems to me in that connection [there] is very possibly a misunderstanding. Let me get that misunderstanding out of the way. When I go to meet with the leaders of the People's Republic of China, with Mr. Chou En-lai, Mr. Mao Tse-tung, and later on with Mr. Brezhnev and Mr. Kosygin, I can assure you that there is not going to be any bargaining advantage due to my desire to affect our election campaign. And I say that not to be sanctimonious, not to be pious, but because I know what is riding. What is riding here is the future for generations to come, and the wrong kind of an agreement with the Soviet Union, one, for example, in the arms control field that would give them an advantage and make us the second strongest nation in the world, the wrong kind of an agreement with the Chinese, one that would discourage our friends in non-Communist Asia, that kind of an agreement, and so forth, would be one that simply would not be worth making.

Let me say, any President—it would not be just me, any President—would not want to win an election at that cost, and I certainly will not. I am going into these meetings, I can assure you, well prepared, and I will go well prepared and I will go there to defend the interest of the United States, to negotiate as well as I can, to reduce the differences, recognizing that there are basic philosophical differences between us and the two Communist powers. But unless we talk about those differences eventually we may end up fighting about them, and that will be the end of civilization as we know it.

RELATIONS WITH CHINA

[10.]   MR. RATHER. Mr. President, one other question about China, and I would again like to refer to a direct quotation. As late as March of 1971 you said, and I quote, "Under no circumstances will we proceed with the policy of normalizing relations with Communist China if the cost of that policy is to expel Taiwan from the family of nations."

Now we have proceeded with the policy of normalizing relations with China; Taiwan has been expelled from the United Nations. Isn't that a contradiction?

THE PRESIDENT. It is a contradiction, but not the way we planned it. As far as our normalization of relations is concerned, I should point out they are not

yet normalized. I should also point out that when we do have our meeting in February, beginning on February 21, in the People's Republic of China, that recognition in the conventional sense will not be one of the results. They do not expect that. We do not expect that. The reason it cannot be one of the results is that as long as we continue to recognize Taiwan, which we do, as long as we continue to have our defense treaty with Taiwan, which we will, the People's Republic will not have diplomatic relations in the conventional sense with that country. So we are not going to have that kind of normalization. However, we will have normalization—because it is fair, and I know this is certainly the intent with which you ask the question—we will have normalization in terms of setting up some method of communication better than we currently have, because nations that do not have diplomatic relations in the conventional sense can have relations and that is one thing that we will be able to do.

Now, as far as our having that kind of normalization, at the time that Taiwan was expelled from the community of nations is concerned, we fought hard to avoid Taiwan being expelled. We thought it was a mistake, but being a member of the community of nations, we believed that we had to accept the verdict. Under the circumstances, however, we will go to the People's Republic, we will have this relationship normalized on the basis that I have just described, but we will continue also our relations with Taiwan, and we will continue our defense agreement.

MR. RATHER. Are we beginning to withdraw American forces from Taiwan?

THE PRESIDENT. Not at this point.

MR. RATHER. Mr. President, why is it necessary——

THE PRESIDENT. I know, incidentally, Mr. Rather, that that question is raised because there have been reports to the effect, because when Dr. Kissinger was there—I didn't want you to raise the question without pointing up that I knew there was good reason to—that when Dr. Kissinger was there, that he had made some deal with Mr. Chou En-lai that if we had the meeting in China, that we would withdraw some forces before I got there. Let me just set the record straight.

He has said, and I have said it, I can say it, too—and I have read every word of the transcript of those long, long sessions he had with Mr. Chou En-lai, as I am sure Chou En-lai has read them—there were no conditions on our side and no conditions on their side.

This will be tough, hard bargaining between people who have very great differences, but people who have one thing in common, and that is that we had better talk about differences or we may end up fighting about them.

Let me just point up one other thing, too, in that respect. We have been talking about Vietnam. I think many of our viewers may not realize that in the two terribly difficult wars, little wars they call them, that the United States has been engaged in, in the last 20 years, both of them are wars in the rimland of Asia. Both of them are wars in which the Chinese were involved: directly in Korea, where, as you know, there were thousands of Chinese volunteers involved in fighting Americans; and indirectly in South Vietnam where the Chinese militarily, insofar as supplies are concerned, are supporting the North Vietnamese.

So, as you look at the past history where the United States in 20 years has had to fight in two wars, where the People's Republic of China was involved on the other side, and you look at the possibilities of the future when the People's Republic, which is now a weak nuclear power, compared to us, would be a very substantial nuclear power 15 or 20 years from now, it is imperative that we find a way to settle our differences better than we have had in the past.

That is why the communication must come. And anyone who sits in this office at this time cannot just think of the next year, the next 2 years, the problems—and there are many problems that are caused by this move toward China, problems with our friends, and it causes them concern—but no one can sit in this office and allow hanging over the world and hanging over the United States for the future this great danger of the most populous nation in the world becoming a major nuclear power and outside the world community, with no contact with the United States of America.

That is why I made the decision to go to China, and this trip, of course, will have as its major purpose setting up that long dialogue which may avert what would otherwise be an inevitable clash.

CUBA

[11.] MR. RATHER. Why is it vital or necessary, I think you used the word, to reestablish a diplomatic dialogue with Communist China, and continue to ignore a Communist country in our own backyard, Cuba?

THE PRESIDENT. The situation is quite different. Our policy toward Cuba, Mr. Rather, is directly related to what Cuba's policy is toward us. Cuba is a Communist country. What Cuba has in terms of its internal policy is Cuba's business, although we would prefer our system and I think many Cubans would as well.

But, on the other hand, Cuba is engaged in a constant program of belligerence toward the United States and also toward its neighbors in the inter-American community.

Now, I suppose it could be said, what about China? We point to the Korean war, we point to what is going on now in North Vietnam. The difference is that at this particular time, we have some evidence that the Chinese are now ready to talk about their role in Asia and our role in Asia. We think it is well to talk about it. There has been no indication whatever that Castro will recede one inch from his determination of exporting Castro-type revolution all over the hemisphere. As long as he is engaged in that kind of operation, our policy isn't going to change.

MR. RATHER. If he gave you such an indication, would you move to reestablish a dialogue with Cuba as you have with China?

THE PRESIDENT. We have no expectation whatever of that. We follow Mr. Castro's activities, his public speeches and the like, very, very closely. And he thrives, since he has made virtually a basket case of Cuba economically, in stirring up trouble in other countries. He couldn't possibly survive, in my opinion, unless he had this policy of "foreign devils."

MR. RATHER. Mr. President, I am afraid in one respect you and I are alike. That is, we like to talk about foreign policy. But time moves on and I may be looking for work tomorrow if we don't begin talking about some domestic affairs.

THE PRESIDENT. And also, if you don't ask me those questions, they will say I am not interested in it.

JETS FOR ISRAEL

[12.] MR. RATHER. But I can't leave—with your permission, I think we have to do it fairly quickly—leave without asking at least one question about the Middle East. There have been widespread reports that you have agreed in principle to sell additional Phantom jets to Israel. Is that true?

THE PRESIDENT. We have made a decision, Mr. Rather, implementing a policy that I have long announced, that we will not allow the balance, the military balance, in the Mideast to be shifted.

Now the Soviet Union has been sending in very significant arms shipments to the U.A.R. In view of those shipments, as that continues to escalate, we have had to consider the requests of Israel for planes in order to see that the balance does not shift.

We have made a commitment in principle. As far as implementing that commitment is concerned, however, I—this is not, of course, the time to go into it.

PUBLIC OPINION AND THE PRESIDENT

[13.] MR. RATHER. Mr. President, shifting now to domestic affairs, and before we went into this broadcast, I sought questions from many of my colleagues in the White House press corps, and I think I should tell you that the following question was among the most popular of those submitted.

THE PRESIDENT. Popular with them.

MR. RATHER. Popular with them. And I hope it will be with you.

Public opinion polls, the Harris poll was the last one, the Gallup polls before, indicated that the American people, in overwhelming majority, give you high marks for decisiveness, for willingness to change. But, in the case of the Harris poll, about 50 percent said that you had failed to inspire confidence and faith and lacked personal warmth and compassion. Why do you suppose that is?

THE PRESIDENT. Well, it is because people tell the pollsters that, of course. So, that is what the people must believe.

But, on the other hand, without trying to psychoanalyze myself, because that is your job, I would simply answer the question by saying that my strong point is not rhetoric, it isn't showmanship, it isn't big promises—those things that create the glamour and the excitement that people call charisma and warmth.

My strong point, if I have a strong point, is performance. I always do more than I say. I always produce more than I promise. Oh, I don't mean that from time to time I may not have made promises that I was unable to keep, but generally speaking, whether it is in the foreign field, or in the domestic field, I believe that actions are what count. And also, I think that is what the country needs.

At this particular point, I think we have to realize that when I took office in 1968 [1969], not only were 300 Americans a week being killed in Vietnam, and there were 539,000 there, but we had riots in most of our cities; the President, as you recall at that time, could not safely travel to most of the cities, and I have been to most of the States and cities since that time, incidentally. That is no reflection on him. It means that times have changed some. The campuses were in great turmoil.

At that particular point, I could have moved with a great deal of flamboyance and showmanship and the rest, but I think what got us into the trouble that we

reaped in 1968, and a lot of it carried over in 1969, was hot rhetoric, big promises, and then failure to come through on them.

I feel that when the trouble of a nation has been caused by too much rhetoric, the cure for that trouble is not more rhetoric. What I think, therefore, is needed at this time, in order to gain the confidence of the people and, let me put it more directly, in order to give the people of this country confidence in their government, is for their government to do something, to produce something.

That is why I want this Administration, in the brief time that I am here, I want this Administration to be one that will bring an end of American involvement in Vietnam, that will look beyond, however, simply ending one war, building a lasting peace, and that is what China and Russia, those visits, are all about; keeping it cool in the Mideast if we possibly can, moving not only to maintain the balance but possibly negotiation in that area—and then on the domestic front, an historic reform of government, welfare reform, revenue sharing, government reorganization, an attack on the drug problem, all of these things.

Now, these are big programs. I think, however, that performing in some of these fields will have a very great effect on the attitude of the American people toward— if I could put it in a general sense—maybe not toward this President as a person, but toward the Presidency. The Presidency is what is on the line here.

When the Presidency fails to come through, people lose confidence in government. They lose confidence in Congress. They lose confidence in the courts. As a matter of fact, I saw a poll the other day where the people had a very low opinion of confidence as far as the media was concerned. That is not good.

What we have to do, what you have to do, what I have to do, all of us in a position of responsibility in our society, is to restore confidence that this is a good country, that our government can produce, and the way to do that is to set our sights high, but make our promises realistic and then get some performance. I think that at the conclusion of my term, I am going to have quite a bit of performance.

[14.] MR. RATHER. Mr. President, as a journalist, I know that one of the greatest problems is trying to explain how you made a mistake, how you got a fact wrong, how you made a wrong analysis on a particular problem. And for anyone in politics—this applies, of course, to previous Presidents as well—one of the problems, as you mentioned, was promises unkept.

This gets, I think, to the core of your dissertation on the need for confidence and what we are going through as a people in terms of confidence with the media, with the Presidency, and with a lot of things. Yet the same Harris poll indicated that only about a third of the people thought that you had kept your campaign promises.

Now, I think you will agree that anyone in politics should be held accountable. I, as a journalist, think that everyone in politics should be given an opportunity to explain. So would you explain—obviously as briefly as possible, but as fully as you think necessary—in 1968 you said, "I pledge to redress the present economic imbalance without increasing unemployment." That is a direct quotation.

Now, unemployment was, I believe, 3.6

when you came in. It is at or near 6 percent for the last several months.

THE PRESIDENT. Let's take that one first, yes, please.

Unemployment was 3.6 when I came in, at a cost of 300 casualties a week in Vietnam. Since I have come in, we have brought 400,000 people home from Vietnam. There are 2 million people who have been let out of defense plants and out of the armed services as a result of our winding down the war in Vietnam, and if those people were still in the defense plants and still in Vietnam, unemployment would still be 3.6. That is too high a cost.

MR. RATHER. But wasn't that foreseeable, Mr. President?

THE PRESIDENT. That was foreseeable. But my point is, what I was saying was that we should have a combination—a combination of bringing a war to an end and then moving from there to a kind of prosperity of high employment and low unemployment that we haven't had since President Eisenhower was President in this room in 1957. That was the only time it was less than 5 percent.

In all the years of the sixties, unemployment averaged 5.8, except in the war years. Now, we can do better than that, and as we move from war to peace in the year 1972, we are going to bring the unemployment rate below that.

[15.] MR. RATHER. Now, another September 1968 quotation: "Seventy-four percent of farm parity is intolerable. I pledge that in my administration farmers will have better." Farm parity is at or near 70 now, has not been back up to even 74 percent through most of your Administration.

THE PRESIDENT. Well, let's look at the farm parity in terms of another factor: Farm income, which is what farmers really

13

care about a great deal, as you know, because it was also reported on CBS just 2 weeks ago, came up sharply in the last month.

I look for the year 1972 to be a very good year as far as the farmers are concerned in terms of their income, and also in terms of parity. And I should point out that in this instance, here is where we are going to get one of the benefits of our new international economic policy. As you know, Secretary Connally has bargained very hard. He has been criticized for bargaining too hard, for getting some kind of trade agreements in return for what the United States is doing in certain other fields.

Now, this will not come easy, but in dealing with the European Community, and in dealing with Japan and other countries, we believe that one of the areas where we can get greater trade opportunities is in the field of agriculture. That, of course, will mean more farm income. It will deal more effectively with the parity problem.

We are not satisfied with that number. Right today we are trying to do better, and we will do better.

[16.]   MR. RATHER. Can we agree that broken promises, like a bad story, are pretty hard to explain, and hurt confidence, whether it is a journalist who doesn't deliver on his story, or whether it is a man in political office who is unable, for whatever reason, to deliver on a pledge?

THE PRESIDENT. Certainly, that is true, and the difference, of course, is that the journalist really doesn't have to retract his story, as you know.

MR. RATHER. But he should, when he is wrong.

THE PRESIDENT. A few do, and many

would like to. But it is difficult, because it destroys your credibility. But let me say that in this respect, that I think the important thing for the man sitting in this office is that he must never be satisfied—never be satisfied with what he is doing.

As far as I see it, at the present time, it could perhaps well be said that if you cooled the country, and we have; if we can now see the end of our involvement in Vietnam, and we do; that we should set these particular goals as being a pretty good accomplishment, particularly when we combine it with a new economic policy which has cut the rate of inflation, and we believe it will continue to during the next year.

That has resulted in the first real increase in income due to the fact that with the inflation rate cut down, and our wages, of course, going up, we find for the first time, wage earners who were on a treadmill for 4 years, from 1967 to 1970, now, in the year 1971, for the first time in 5 years, began to make some headway.

When we see all of these things, I think we could well say that that is a pretty good record. That isn't enough, though. It isn't enough.

As I tried to say a moment ago, in the short time that any man is in this office, he has got to look down that road. He has got to look down 25 years from now. I get back to the real reason for the China move. The real reason is that despite the fact it would be easier—it is easier not to raise difficult problems with our friends, and I have been criticized very strongly from people of my own party on the China move, with our friends in the world community, the Japanese and others who have been concerned about it—it would have been easier simply to continue the line that we have been taking with regard to China and not attempt to open this dialogue, recognizing how great the risks were.

But looking down that road, any man sitting in this office, as President of the United States, who failed to seize the moment, the chance—the chance that was offered to me, as a result of planning, I must say, on our part, too—failed to seize that moment, he would have to answer to future generations.

Now, it may be too soon, if we are talking about in terms of the next election, for people to give credit to the President, or to blame him for the success or failure of what happens on this movement to China, but if 25 years from now, as a result of what we have done now, we avert a confrontation with China, it will all be worth it.

THE ECONOMY

[17.] MR. RATHER. Mr. President, a couple of questions on the economy, if I may. It occurs to me that your, until recently, Chairman of the Council of Economic Advisers, Dr. Paul McCracken, said a few days ago that government controls on the economy would be "necessary long past this year," I believe was his phrase. Is that true?

THE PRESIDENT. Well, Chairman McCracken is reflecting the view that in some areas controls may be necessary. I would put it another way, without disagreeing with Chairman McCracken. We will keep controls on only as long as we need them, and we are going to decontrol just as fast as we can, as the inflation psychology runs its course.

Let us take just one example. Take rent controls. We found for example that in certain areas of the country, a major city, there was a very high number of vacancies. Well, that area should be decontrolled right now, because when you have a high number of vacancies, you don't need control. The competition controls the rents. So it is in certain other areas.

I do not believe in a controlled economy. I believe that we had to have these controls in order to break an inflationary psychology which had been fueled by war, and which apparently was not going to be broken unless we took the very hard action that we did take. But having taken it, we are now going to see it through. We want to reach our goal, and we believe that we will achieve our goal of keeping inflation at the 2 to 3 percent level for the year 1972, which will be a major achievement. That is half of what it was last year.

MR. RATHER. I gather the answer to the question then is "perhaps." The question was whether controls may be necessary beyond this year.

THE PRESIDENT. Perhaps, but I would emphasize very strongly, because I would not want to mislead you and all others who have to comment on this, and then to say that I have changed my mind, "perhaps," except that if the program of controls is successful, as successful as we would hope that it would be, the amount of controls that we have toward the end may be far less than the statement by Chairman McCracken implied.

I see the decontrol coming perhaps at a faster pace, but we will keep them on if they are necessary.

BLACKS IN AMERICA

[18.] MR. RATHER. Mr. President, you were quoted in a recent interview as saying, and again I quote, "Black people are different from white people." I don't understand what you mean by that. Exactly what did you mean by that? How are black people different from white people?

THE PRESIDENT. Well, the main way to answer that question is to talk to black people, as I do, to black people on my staff, to black people that I have gone to school with. An individual who grows up in America as a black has, whenever he talks very frankly with you, the inevitable memory of what has happened to his people through the years. He looks back to the days of slavery. He looks back to the days of prejudice. He knows that some of that prejudice is still there. He realizes therefore that when he is in school, when he is looking for a job, whatever the case might be, that he is different, he is different from the white person, and for that reason he therefore has problems that the white person does not have. And I think unless we recognize that fact, we are not going to do the right kind of job that we should in handling black-white relations.

GOVERNOR GEORGE WALLACE

[19.] MR. RATHER. Mr. President, do you consider Governor George Wallace and what he stands for a threat to holding this society together?

THE PRESIDENT. Well, I noted at the moment that he has decided to enter the Democratic primaries, and I really think that that question should be directed to the Democratic candidate when you have him on the equal time that I am sure is going to be requested after this program.

MR. RATHER. I would like very much to ask the Democratic candidate that, when it is decided who he shall be. But the question was put directly to you.

THE PRESIDENT. It is not the problem here of our party. As far as Mr. Wallace is concerned, he is now seeking the Democratic nomination, and that is one that

is going to have to be worked out within their own party.

AMNESTY FOR DRAFT EVADERS

[20.] MR. RATHER. Mr. President, recently you were asked a question about amnesty. You were asked if you foresaw any possibility of granting amnesty to those young men who have fled the country to avoid the draft, and you had a one-word answer, which was "No."

Since then some Congressmen, among others, have proposed allowing those young men who want to come back, who are willing to do it, to come back without punishment, if they will take alternative service, 2 years, 4 years. Is there no amount of alternative service under which you could foresee granting amnesty?

THE PRESIDENT. No. The question that I was answering in that conference that you referred to, as you recall, followed one where I had talked about the withdrawal of our forces, and the question was prefaced with that, as I recall.

MR. RATHER. Correct. It was.

THE PRESIDENT. In view of the withdrawal of forces, how about amnesty? And I said, "No." The answer is at this time "No." As long as there are Americans who chose to serve their country rather than desert their country—and it is a hard choice—and they are there in Vietnam, there will be no amnesty for those who deserted their country. As long as there are any POW's held by the North Vietnamese, there will be no amnesty for those who have deserted their country.

Just let me say, Mr. Rather, on that score, I don't say this because I am hardhearted. I say it because it is the only right thing to do. Two and a half million young Americans had to make the choice when they went to serve in Vietnam. Most of them, I am sure, did not want to go. It is not a very pleasant place. I have been there a number of times; nice people, but it is not a pleasant place for an American to serve, and particularly in uniform.

I imagine most of those young Americans when they went out there did so with some reluctance, but they chose to serve. Of those that chose to serve, thousands of them died for their choice, and until this war is over, and until we get the POW's back, those who chose to desert their country, a few hundred, they can live with their choice. That is my attitude.

Mr. RATHER. But, at some future time, the door might be opened?

THE PRESIDENT. We always, Mr. Rather, under our system, provide amnesty. You remember Abraham Lincoln in the last days of the Civil War, as a matter of fact just before his death, decided to give amnesty to anyone who had deserted if he would come back and rejoin his unit and serve out his period of time. Amnesty, of course, is always in the prerogative of the Chief Executive. I, for one, would be very liberal with regard to amnesty, but not while there are Americans in Vietnam fighting to serve their country and defend their country, and not while POW's are held by the enemy. After that we will consider it, but it would have to be on a basis of their paying the price, of course, that anyone should pay for violating the law.

ROLE OF WOMEN

[21.] Mr. RATHER. I understand, Mr. President, we have only about a minute and a half left. I am going to be in trouble at home if I don't ask this question. Some political leaders——

THE PRESIDENT. You mean with CBS?

Mr. RATHER. No, I mean with Mrs. Rather. Some political leaders and some others have taken to not addressing women by "Miss" or "Mrs." They have gone to the "Ms." Why not do that with White House letters?

THE PRESIDENT. I guess I am a little old-fashioned, but I rather prefer the "Miss" or "Mrs." But if they want to do it the other way, of course, we accept it. I can assure you some of the things that have come in letters are quite amusing.

Mr. RATHER. Mr. President, are there any aspects of the Presidency that are better suited to a man than to a woman?

THE PRESIDENT. I would say that, as we consider the role of women in American political life, that a woman could serve in this office. I am not suggesting that that is going to happen soon. I am suggesting, however, that, looking to the future, as the place of women as executives in our society is recognized, as women develop respect for themselves as executives rather than as women, that their place in political life is going to be recognized more and more.

Now, I want to help with Mrs. Rather when you go home and simply say, as far as I am concerned, I have the greatest respect for women in both capacities, those who are homemakers, and those who decide to go into politics or into business, but let us have freedom of choice for women.

Mr. RATHER. Thank you, Mr. President.

NOTE: The hour-long interview began at 9:30 p.m. in the Oval Office at the White House. It was broadcast live on radio and television. The President spoke without referring to notes.

2   Remarks to Workers at the National Steel and Shipbuilding Company in San Diego, California. *January 4,* 1972

Mr. Banks, Secretary Gibson, Mayor Wilson, and men and women of National:

It is a very great privilege for me to be here today. I just flew in from Washington last night, and it is good to be here on this beautiful California day, right here in San Diego. And it is particularly good to be here because of the reason that I am coming here.

I am not going to bore you with the statistics and with a lot of history about how it came about that these ships are going to be built here in this yard, but I think just to give you a feeling of what it means, of how important this moment is to you, to those of you who have jobs, to this yard and its future, and to this country, I think it is well perhaps to spend just a moment on what this occasion is and how it came about.

In 1968, when I was speaking in Seattle at a yard—a pretty empty yard, as a matter of fact—I spoke about the U.S. merchant marine and, you know, when you make a speech, you do a little studying to find out a little about the subject, because you figure the people you are talking to know more about it than you do, and they usually do.

What I found was that at that particular time, the United States merchant marine was in very great trouble. I found, for example, that three-fourths of all American-built ships then in use were more than 20 years of age, whereas, only one-fourth of all ships in the world then in use were more than 20 years of age.

In that kind of competition, we were a born loser, because our ships were too old,

they were too inefficient, and new nations—as a matter of fact, some of the nations with whom we had been allies in World War II and who had been our enemies in World War II—had built these ships that were now driving us into a second-class position around the world.

I felt that we ought to do something about it. When I was elected I made a proposal in 1969 about the American merchant marine. In 1970, the Congress in a bipartisan action, Republicans and Democrats joining together because they could see that this was bigger than any partisanship, overwhelmingly approved that proposal.

In 1971, the plans went forward under men like Mr. Gibson, Secretary Stans, and all the others in Government interested in this, until we are now beginning to let the contracts. As a matter of fact, some have already been let.

Today, $54 million in contracts will be signed by Mr. Gibson for here, the Todd Shipyards in Long Beach will have $60 million worth of contracts, and others will follow in other parts of the country.

Now, just let me say a word about what this all means, and why it is important. I know that it is kind of fashionable sometimes these days to say, "What difference does it make whether the United States is number one in air transport, or number one in the merchant marine," or what have you.

The answer is: It makes a good deal of difference. We don't have to be number one in everything, but we have to try to be. Because whenever a nation or a person quits trying to be number one, he ceases, or that nation ceases, to be a great nation. We want America to try to be number one, and that is one of the reasons we are doing this in this area.

Now, the second point I would like to make is that this comes as we are ending a very long and difficult war, and as we enter what we hope will be a period of negotiation and peace for the United States.

But even that shows the importance of what we are doing today because the peacetime competition is going to be even more difficult than the kind of competition we had in war.

The nations that previously were engaged in war activities now are competing with us, and competing with us very, very hard. We welcome that. We accept competition, but it means we have got to do better. And that, of course, is why we are able to come here for these contracts today.

We are doing better. Costs are being cut down. I have been talking to my old friend Jesse Calhoun [president, National Marine Engineers Beneficial Association] about that problem. I have been talking, of course, to the people in management about that problem.

Costs have come down almost 50 percent, and that means that as the costs come down, as we build more efficient ships, there will be more jobs and America will get back into the position of being the leading maritime nation of the world. We can do it.

We can't do it without your help and we know and I know, as I look at this great group of people here, that we are going to be able to do it, because we Americans are a people who don't like to

be number two. We Americans are a people who like to be the best in anything that we do and that is what we are going to do in this instance.

Finally, I would just like to leave one thought with you. As we go forward on these ships, I think it is interesting for you to know that the three that are built in this yard are the first three of this kind ever to be built in the United States of America, so you are doing something that has never been done before.

The reason they have never been built in the United States of America before is that the United States wasn't able to compete, but now we can. The better job that you do here, now, on these ships, the more opportunities we are going to have to have more jobs like this in the future.

VOICE FROM THE CROWD. We can do it.

THE PRESIDENT. You bet you can.

And so, I simply want to conclude with a very old story, one that many of you, I am sure, have heard.

During the Middle Ages, two stonemasons were asked what they were doing as they were working on their jobs. One looked down, and he said, "I'm shaping stones." And the other looked up, and he said, "I'm building a cathedral."

And today, all of the thousands of men and women here are going to be doing jobs, and you can look down at that job— it is important, of course, just for the sake of what it is doing, what it produces in the way of an income and the rest.

But I hope all of you, from time to time, look up, and say, "I'm not just building a ship; I'm building America. I am making sure my country is going to be number one insofar as its merchant marine is concerned."

Thank you.

NOTE: The President spoke at 10:36 a.m. at the shipyard of the company. He spoke without referring to notes.

John V. Banks was executive vice president, National Steel and Shipbuilding Company; Andrew E. Gibson was Assistant Secretary of Commerce for Maritime Affairs; and Pete Wilson was mayor of San Diego.

On the same day, the White House released a fact sheet on the contracts awarded to the company to build three new bulk carriers for the United States merchant marine.

3   Statement Announcing Decision To Proceed With Development of the Space Shuttle.   *January* 5, 1972

I HAVE decided today that the United States should proceed at once with the development of an entirely new type of space transportation system designed to help transform the space frontier of the 1970's into familiar territory, easily accessible for human endeavor in the 1980's and 1990's.

This system will center on a space vehicle that can shuttle repeatedly from earth to orbit and back. It will revolutionize transportation into near space by routinizing it. It will take the astronomical costs out of astronautics. In short, it will go a long way toward delivering the rich benefits of practical space utilization and the valuable spinoffs from space efforts into the daily lives of Americans and all people.

The new year 1972 is a year of conclusion for America's current series of manned flights to the moon. Much is expected from the two remaining Apollo missions—in fact, their scientific results should exceed the return from all the earlier flights together. Thus they will place a fitting capstone on this vastly successful undertaking. But they also bring us to an important decision point—a point of assessing what our space horizons are as Apollo ends, and of determining where we go from here.

In the scientific arena, the past decade of experience has taught us that spacecraft are an irreplaceable tool for learning about our near-earth space environment, the moon, and the planets, besides being an important aid to our studies of the sun and stars. In utilizing space to meet needs on earth, we have seen the tremendous potential of satellites for intercontinental communications and worldwide weather forecasting. We are gaining the capability to use satellites as tools in global monitoring and management of natural resources, in agricultural applications, and in pollution control. We can foresee their use in guiding airliners across the oceans and in bringing televised education to wide areas of the world.

However, all these possibilities, and countless others with direct and dramatic bearing on human betterment, can never be more than fractionally realized so long as every single trip from earth to orbit remains a matter of special effort and staggering expense. This is why commitment to the space shuttle program is the right next step for America to take, in moving out from our present beachhead in the sky to achieve a real working presence in space—because the space shuttle will give us routine access to space by sharply reducing costs in dollars and preparation time.

The new system will differ radically from all existing booster systems, in that most of this new system will be recovered and used again and again—up to 100 times. The resulting economies may bring operating costs down as low as one-tenth of those for present launch vehicles.

The resulting changes in modes of flight and reentry will make the ride safer and less demanding for the passengers, so that men and women with work to do in space can "commute" aloft, without having to spend years in training for the skills and rigors of old-style space flight. As scientists and technicians are actually able to accompany their instruments into space, limiting boundaries between our manned and unmanned space programs will disappear. Development of new space applications will be able to proceed much faster. Repair or servicing of satellites in space will become possible, as will delivery of valuable payloads from orbit back to earth.

The general reliability and versatility which the shuttle system offers seems likely to establish it quickly as the workhorse of our whole space effort, taking the place of all present launch vehicles except the very smallest and very largest.

NASA and many aerospace companies have carried out extensive design studies for the shuttle. Congress has reviewed and approved this effort. Preparation is now sufficient for us to commence the actual work of construction with full confidence of success. In order to minimize technical and economic risks, the space agency will continue to take a cautious evolutionary approach in the development of this new system. Even so, by moving ahead at this time, we can have the shuttle in manned flight by 1978, and operational a short time later.

It is also significant that this major new national enterprise will engage the best

efforts of thousands of highly skilled workers and hundreds of contractor firms over the next several years. The amazing "technology explosion" that has swept this country in the years since we ventured into space should remind us that robust activity in the aerospace industry is healthy for everyone—not just in jobs and income, but in the extension of our capabilities in every direction. The continued preeminence of America and American industry in the aerospace field will be an important part of the shuttle's "payload."

Views of the earth from space have shown us how small and fragile our home planet truly is. We are learning the imperatives of universal brotherhood and global ecology—learning to think and act as guardians of one tiny blue and green island in the trackless oceans of the universe. This new program will give more people more access to the liberating perspectives of space, even as it extends our ability to cope with physical challenges of earth and broadens our opportunities for international cooperation in low-cost, multi-purpose space missions.

"We must sail sometimes with the wind and sometimes against it," said Oliver Wendell Holmes, "but we must sail, and not drift, nor lie at anchor." So with man's epic voyage into space—a voyage the United States of America has led and still shall lead.

NOTE: The statement was released at San Clemente, Calif.

On the same day, the White House released a fact sheet and the transcript of a news briefing on the space shuttle. Participants in the news briefing were James C. Fletcher, Administrator, and George M. Low, Deputy Administrator, National Aeronautics and Space Administration.

4 Remarks on Departure of Prime Minister Eisaku Sato of Japan From the Western White House. *January 7, 1972*

Mr. Prime Minister and ladies and gentlemen:

We have just concluded a series of meetings in which the Prime Minister and I have had a far-ranging and very comprehensive discussion of a number of issues.

I think it can be safely said that this is the most comprehensive discussion which has ever taken place between the Prime Minister of Japan and the President of the United States. It has also been a very constructive discussion, as will be indicated by the press statement which will be jointly issued, and also by the statements that will be made after this meeting by the Prime Minister.

We have found that on many major issues we have substantial agreement. What this meeting particularly has brought home to the Prime Minister and to me is that there is what I would term a natural interdependence between Japan and the United States. We both are nations of the Pacific. We are nations who have the responsibility for peace in the Pacific, and peace in the Pacific, of course, is indispensable if we are to have peace in the world.

I should point out that this is the last of a series of meetings that I have had with major free world leaders. The fact that it was the last one gave the Prime Minister and me an opportunity to discuss the results of the previous meetings, and also to particularly concentrate on problems of the Pacific area, in which we have a common interest.

Then, finally, what was different and significant about this meeting was that it was the first occasion that I was honored to have the head of state, the head of government of another country, on a state visit as a guest in my home. That, of course, tells us something about the very close relationship between Japan and the United States, and between the Prime Minister of Japan and the President of the United States and our colleagues who are standing here beside me.

So with that, Mr. Prime Minister, we thank you for coming so far for these talks. We know that they will contribute to peace in the Pacific and we wish you well on your return journey to Tokyo.

NOTE: The President spoke at 1:30 p.m. at the Western White House in San Clemente, Calif. He spoke without referring to notes.

Following the President's remarks, Prime Minister Sato spoke in Japanese. His remarks were translated by an interpreter as follows:

I wish to express my heartfelt appreciation for the opportunity given me to renew my long, personal friendship with President Nixon during the 2-day talks with him. I am confident that these meetings have contributed to strengthen the unshakable relationship of mutual trust and interdependence between the peoples of the United States and Japan.

On behalf of the Japanese delegation, I would like to express my sincere thanks for the warm hospitality extended to us by President Nixon.

I would also like to extend to President Nixon my best wishes for his health, and hope that his forthcoming visits to Peking and Moscow will bring about fruitful achievements for the peace and prosperity of the world.

I thank you.

On January 6, 1972, the President greeted Prime Minister Sato in a ceremony at the Western White House and hosted a working dinner for the Prime Minister that evening.

5   Joint Statement Following Meetings With Prime Minister Sato of Japan.   *January* 7, 1972

PRIME Minister Sato and President Nixon, meeting in San Clemente on January 6 and 7, 1972 had wide-ranging and productive discussions that reflected the close, friendly relations between Japan and the United States. They covered the general international situation with particular emphasis on Asia including China, as well as bilateral relations between Japan and the United States.

The Prime Minister and the President recognized that in the changing world situation today, there are hopeful trends pointing toward a relaxation of tension, and they emphasized the need for further efforts to encourage such trends so as to promote lasting peace and stability. These efforts would involve close cooperation between the two governments and with other governments. They also recognized that the maintenance of cooperative relations between Japan and the United States is an indispensable factor for peace and stability in Asia, and accordingly they confirmed that the two Governments would continue to consult closely on their respective Asian policies.

The Prime Minister and the President, recalling the more than one hundred years of association between the two countries, emphasized the importance of U.S.-Japanese relations being founded on mutual trust and interdependence. In this connection, they highly valued the important role played by the Treaty of Mutual Cooperation and Security between Japan and the United States.

The Prime Minister and the President discussed the problems relating to the return of Okinawa as contemplated in the Joint Communiqué of November 21, 1969. They were gratified that the Reversion Agreement signed on June 17, 1971 had received the support of the respective legislatures, and decided to effect the return of Okinawa to Japan on May 15, 1972. The President indicated the intention of the United States Government to confirm upon reversion that the assurances of the United States Government concerning nuclear weapons on Okinawa have been fully carried out. To this the Prime Minister expressed his deep appreciation. The Prime Minister explained to the President why he felt it necessary that, after reversion, the facilities and areas of the United States armed forces located in Okinawa be realigned or reduced to the extent possible, particularly those in areas densely populated or closely related to industrial development. The President replied that these factors would be taken fully into consideration in working out after reversion mutually acceptable adjustments in the facilities and areas consistent with the purpose of the Treaty of Mutual Cooperation and Security.

Recognizing that the further strengthening of the already close economic ties between Japan and the United States was of vital importance to the overall relations between the two countries as well as to the expansion of the world economy as a whole, the Prime Minister and the President expressed their satisfaction that significant progress was being made, particularly since the meeting of the Japan-United States Committee on Trade and Economic Affairs last September, towards improvement of trade conditions and economic relations between the two countries.

They shared the expectation that the international currency realignment of last December would provide a firm basis on which to chart future development of the world economy, and stated their determination to exert renewed efforts, in combination with other countries, towards improved monetary arrangements, expanded world trade and assisting developing countries. In this connection they affirmed the importance of conditions that facilitate the flow of both public assistance and private capital.

The Prime Minister and the President reaffirmed the basic view that Japan and the United States, jointly ascribing to the principles of freedom and democracy, would cooperate closely with each other in all areas such as the political, cultural, economic, scientific and technological fields to achieve the common goals of maintaining and promoting peace and prosperity of the world and the well-being of their countrymen.

They agreed that the two Governments would expand cooperation in the fields of environment, of the peaceful uses of atomic energy and the peaceful exploration and use of outer space. They further agreed that experts of the two countries would examine concrete steps in this regard. They also agreed that steps be taken to increase cultural exchanges and in this regard the President welcomed the explanation given on the contemplated establishment of a Japanese cultural exchange program.

NOTE: The joint statement was released at San Clemente, Calif.

On January 6, 1972, the White House released the transcript of a news briefing by Secretary of the Treasury John B. Connally on a meeting with Mikio Mizuta, Japanese Minister of Finance, Kakuei Tanaka, Japanese Minister of International Trade and Industry, and Maurice H. Stans, Secretary of Commerce. The White House also released the transcript of a news briefing by Secretary of State William P. Rogers on his meeting with Japanese Foreign Minister Takeo Fukuda. The transcripts are printed in the Weekly Compilation of Presidential Documents (vol. 8, pp. 29 and 32).

6   Letter Announcing Candidacy for Renomination and Reelection. *January 7,* 1972

Dear Lane:

Thank you for your generous letter, and for the petitions you have filed entering my name in the New Hampshire primary.

It was in New Hampshire that I began my campaign for the Presidency four years ago, and I remember well the opportunity that campaign provided to visit so much of the State and to meet so many of its people. I have tried to be true to the trust they expressed, and to carry forward the effort we began in New Hampshire in

1968: to bring peace and progress both abroad and at home, and to give America the leadership it needs for a new era of national greatness.

We have made significant beginnings in these past three years. I want to complete the work that we have begun, and therefore I shall be a candidate for re-nomination and re-election. I deeply appreciate the confidence expressed by those who signed the petitions, and I shall do all in my power to be worthy of that confidence.

In addition to New Hampshire, I shall also permit my name to be entered in the other primaries. As I am sure you will understand, however, it will not be possible for me to campaign actively and personally in any of the primary elections. I feel it is essential, particularly in this year when events of such importance to the world's future are taking place, that at least until the Republican Convention the President should refrain from public partisan activities in order to conduct the business of government with the minimum intrusion of purely political activity.

On my behalf, therefore, please express to the people of New Hampshire my warm greetings, my gratitude for their past courtesies, and my hope that together we can work toward a national renewal that will make the anniversary year of 1976 as proud a milestone for America as was 1776.

Sincerely,

RICHARD NIXON

[Mr. Lane Dwinell, New Hampshire Committee for Re-election of the President, The New Hampshire Highway Hotel, Concord, New Hampshire 03301]

NOTE: The letter, dated January 5, 1972, was made available to the press on January 7.

7 Remarks on Mrs. Nixon's Return From Africa. *January* 9, 1972

Mr. Vice President, Congressman Ford, members of the Cabinet, and all of you who have been so very kind to come to the airport here today on this rainy night:

First, I want to thank you for wishing me a happy birthday, and I know that it was hard for you to come. But I think perhaps the best birthday present, and the greatest sacrifice, was made by Mrs. Nixon: She flew 4,000 miles for my birthday party tonight.

Now I am in a bit of an awkward position, because I have to welcome her back officially, and I also have to welcome her back personally. I asked our Chief of Protocol, Ambassador Mosbacher, how I should address her, and so he wrote me a memorandum. He said, "You could call her Mrs. Nixon, or you could call her Madam Ambassador." But I guess I will just call her "Pat." Welcome home, Pat. We are glad you are here.

Now, if I could just spend a moment to tell you how this trip came about, and why

I think the choice that was made was a good one. My very dear and old friend, President Tolbert of Liberia, wrote me a personal note inviting me to his inauguration. We have very much in common. We both served as Vice Presidents during the same period of time, and he became President of his country, as I have had the honor of becoming President of the United States. And he is the President of the oldest republic in Africa and, of course, the United States is the oldest republic in the American Continent.

So I wanted to go, but I could not because of some of the demands of the schedule here at that time. So I wrote him back a personal note and said that while I could not come, I would try to send a very good substitute. Now, since the trip began, I have been reading the newspapers and, Mr. Vice President, also watching television, and as I watched the television and read the newspapers, of the welcomes that Mrs. Nixon received in Liberia and Ghana and Ivory Coast, I realized that the substitute was doing a much better job than the principal would have done.

I simply want to say that this trip meant a great deal to us, the fact that Mrs. Nixon could go there. We have some very special memories of Africa. As Vice President, in 1957 we attended the ceremonies in which the first of the new black African countries received its independence: Ghana. I have been back several times since then, but now, on this occasion, this opportunity to go to the inauguration of President Tolbert, and then to be received again in Ghana and then in Ivory Coast, what this trip really demonstrates is this:

We have a very good, friendly, government-to-government relationship with the countries of Africa. But we, in America, also have a very deep, personal interest in those countries, and by Mrs. Nixon going there, she was demonstrating what I know every person in this country would want to: that we have a feeling of friendship and affection for the millions of people that live in this very old continent, but with many new countries and with great, great hopes for the future. And for that reason, the trip was taken and, of course, I thought it was a success.

Now, I had a lot more written down, but anything I said about what Mrs. Nixon did on this trip, people would attribute to bias, and they would be right. Now I was trying to think of somebody who could speak in welcoming Mrs. Nixon and could appraise the trip in a very honest way. The Vice President always says just what he thinks. [*Laughter*] However, before giving him this microphone, I want to remind him: I have the last word, and so does Mrs. Nixon. [*Laughter*]

Mr. Vice President.

THE VICE PRESIDENT. *Mr. President, Mrs. Nixon:*

Mr. President, this is a wonderful way for us to assist you in celebrating your birthday and welcoming back our very gracious First Lady from this very effective and wonderful trip that she made to three African nations, a trip that took some 8 days, and which, Mr. President, we all followed with great interest, just as you did, via the newspapers and television.

Now, Mr. President, I am not sure I am fully qualified to speak frankly on this occasion, because I must admit to some bias myself where Mrs. Nixon is concerned. And I think most of the people in this country, and indeed, just about everyone that I have talked to in my trips wherever I go in the world, is aware of the fact that Mrs. Nixon has discharged her duties as America's First Lady with distinction and grace. And the welcome that was given her in the African nations that she visited, the warmth of that reception and her gracious and generous response to it, made all of us very proud of you, Mrs. Nixon.

I think that we can simply say that even though it is the President's birthday, we all are the recipients of a present by having you back among us tonight, and we hope that this will be not your sole exercise in foreign affairs, but this may be the beginning of other and more enjoyable and more fruitful enterprises that you may undertake. And who knows, the reason I say more enjoyable and more fruitful is simply because in recognition of the times as they exist today, women seem to be doing more things and perhaps someday you may visit these countries taking along the President as simply ancillary baggage. [*Laughter*]

We are glad to have you back.

THE FIRST LADY. Before my husband grabs the microphone, I do want to thank all of you for coming out to the airport and welcoming me home.

I really had a wonderful journey. The people in the three countries I visited— Liberia, Ghana, and Ivory Coast—could not have been more friendly or more gracious or more hospitable. In fact, their hospitality was boundless and they all sent greetings, the leaders and the people in all walks of life, to you here in the United States.

They are proud of the partnership with the United States, and this partnership is built on equality, mutual respect, and friendship. I hope that it will always remain that way.

Thank you, again.

THE PRESIDENT. And thank you, ladies and gentlemen, all of our very good friends who have come out here today, and thank you, Madam Ambassador.

NOTE: The exchange of remarks began at 6:04 p.m. at Andrews Air Force Base, Md.

8 Statement on the Appointment of Arthur S. Flemming as Special Consultant to the President on Aging. *January 11, 1972*

THIS Administration's commitment to forging a new national policy of respect for, and service to, older Americans is significantly forwarded today by the appointment of Dr. Arthur S. Flemming as my Special Consultant on Aging. I am delighted to be gaining the services of this distinguished public servant, who was an able Secretary of Health, Education, and Welfare under President Eisenhower, who has been a leader in American education for many years, and whose energetic direction as Chairman contributed so much to the success of the 1971 White House Conference on Aging.

I am determined, as I said in my address to that Conference last month, that the voice of older Americans will be heard in the White House when matters that affect the interests of older Americans are being discussed. No one in the United States today is better qualified to raise that voice, forcefully and persuasively, than Arthur Flemming. He will advise me on the whole range of concerns relating to older persons; he will pursue aggressively, as my representative, the goals of better implementation and tighter coordination of all Federal activities in the field of aging; he will continue as a member of our Cabinet-level Domestic Council Committee on Aging; and he will also continue as Chairman of the White House Conference on Aging during the crucial post-conference year—the year of action. His responsibilities in this area will include appointing and heading up the activities of a post-conference board to act as agent for the delegates in following up their proposals.

In the early days of the Administration I asked John B. Martin, Commissioner of the Administration on Aging in the Department of Health, Education, and Welfare, to take on the additional responsibilities of a new post as Special Assistant to the President on Aging. His very effective service in that post has not only meant better representation for older citizens at the highest level of government; it has also revealed that the dimensions of the job to be done are such that another good man is needed. Now, with Arthur Flem-

ming's arrival as John Martin's teammate, "senior power" doubles its forces at the White House. Better Federal assistance to the aging should be the result.

9   Remarks at the Swearing In of Arthur S. Flemming as Special Consultant to the President on Aging. *January 11, 1972*

Ladies and gentlemen:

I welcome Dr. Flemming as an old friend in swearing him in today. I recall during the years he served on President Eisenhower's Cabinet how ably he served his country. As I bring him into this special position, I should point out to those members of the press corps who did not follow him then that he had several attributes: One, he is a man who is tremendously popular in the Government, and two, despite that very calm exterior he has, he is enormously tenacious. Once he starts working on something, he keeps working until the job is done. Three, he believes very deeply in matters before he takes on an assignment.

I know his heart is deeply committed, as is his mind, to the problems of the elderly. I know that as he travels around the country and sees the problems, that he will come with his recommendations to this office. He will not pound the desk, but he can be even more effective than that in his quiet, effective way.

I think the elderly have in him one who will very effectively present a point of view that needs to be represented here in the highest office of the White House, eloquently, as he does. Also, I believe that we have in him the man who has the experience and the background to take this particular issue, to analyze all its parts, and

to make recommendations, not for the sake of their being particularly melodramatic, but for the sake of getting things done in this critical area for our senior citizens across the land.

Now we will have the swearing-in ceremony. I will give the Bible to Mrs. Flemming and Judge Flannery will swear him in.

[At this point, Thomas A. Flannery, United States District Judge for the District of Columbia, administered the oath of office. The President then resumed speaking.]

Dr. Flemming, you will have other occasions when you can talk at greater length, but now you are recognized for one minute, if you like.

NOTE: The President spoke at 12:05 p.m. in the Oval Office at the White House. He spoke without referring to notes.

Dr. Flemming responded as follows:

Mr. President, first of all, may I express to you my very deep appreciation for the opportunity that you are affording me to work in behalf of the older citizens of this country. I am very, very grateful for the opportunity of, in this way, becoming a part of your Administration.

You have made very clear to me the duties and the responsibilities of this position. I feel that our Nation must accept the concept of the dignity and worth of every older citizen and I think it must reflect the acceptance of that concept by what we do, rather than by what we say.

It is in that spirit that I accept the position to which you have appointed me, and it is in that spirit that I will endeavor to discharge the duties and responsibilities of the office.

I make that commitment, and I am happy to have the opportunity to make it.

10   Statement About Pay Adjustments for Federal Blue-Collar Employees. *January* 11, 1972

I HAVE taken two actions today which directly affect all blue-collar employees of the Federal Government:

—First, I have authorized an immediate resumption of wage surveys for blue-collar workers, which will lead to pay increases for those workers where the surveys indicate that adjustments are needed. This action is consistent with the pay hikes granted to white-collar workers this month under provisions of the Economic Stabilization Act Amendments of 1971.

—Secondly, I have signed an Executive order [11639] directing the Civil Service Commission to issue instructions to executive agencies on fixing the rates of basic pay for blue-collar employees. These instructions will limit pay adjustments for these workers to guidelines established by the Pay Board in the same way that adjustments are now circumscribed for Federal white-collar workers.

Together, these measures are designed to insure that Federal workers—white- and blue-collar—receive similar treatment with regard to pay adjustments, and that this is consistent with Pay Board policies.

11   Memorandums About Pay Adjustments for Federal Blue-Collar Employees. *January* 11, 1972

Memorandum for Honorable Robert E. Hampton, Chairman, United States Civil Service Commission:

SUBJECT: Federal wage increases

In August and September 1971, actions were initiated to defer for six months expected pay increases for both white-collar and blue-collar Federal employees. These actions provided similar pay treatment for both groups of employees.

Under the provisions of the Economic Stabilization Act Amendments of 1971, pay for white-collar Federal employees under the statutory systems will be adjusted at the beginning of the first pay period in January 1972.

In order to provide, insofar as practicable, similar treatment of future pay adjustments for white- and blue-collar employees, my memorandum of September 1, 1971, directing the deferment of Federal blue-collar wage adjustments, is hereby rescinded.

To accomplish this action I have addressed the attached memorandum to the heads of executive departments and agencies. As indicated therein, this memorandum assigns to you, as Chairman of the Civil Service Commission, responsibility to take necessary actions to expedite wage surveys which have been delayed so that new wage schedules can be issued as soon as possible. The normal wage survey cycle should be resumed as soon as practicable.

RICHARD NIXON

Memorandum for the Heads of Executive Departments and Agencies:

SUBJECT: Federal Wage and Salary Increases

In August and September, 1971, actions were initiated to defer for six months expected pay increases for both white-collar and blue-collar Federal employees. These actions provided similar pay treatment for both groups of employees.

Under the provisions of the Economic Stabilization Act Amendments of 1971, pay for white-collar Federal employees under the statutory systems will be adjusted at the beginning of the first pay period in January 1972.

In order to provide, insofar as practicable, similar treatment of future pay adjustments for white- and blue-collar employees, my memorandum of September 1, 1971, directing the deferment of Federal blue-collar wage adjustments, is hereby rescinded. The Chairman of the Civil Service Commission is being directed to take necessary actions to expedite wage surveys which have been delayed so that new wage schedules can be issued as soon as possible.

Heads of executive agencies are authorized to adjust by administrative action the rates of pay which are subject to the provisions of section 5307 of Title 5 of the United States Code, consistent with the adjustments effected by Executive Order No. 11637 of December 22, 1971. Such adjustments shall also be consistent with the policies and pay increase guidelines issued by the Pay Board established under Executive Order No. 11627 of October 15, 1971.

RICHARD NIXON

---

12   Remarks Announcing Withdrawal of Additional United States Troops From Vietnam.   *January* 13, 1972

Ladies and gentlemen:

I am announcing today the withdrawal of an additional 70,000 [troops] from Vietnam over the next 3 months.

This means that our troop ceiling by May 1 will be down to 69,000. This withdrawal has the approval of the Secretary of Defense, the Chairman of the Joint Chiefs of Staff, and the Government of South Vietnam.

There will be another announcement that will be made before May 1 with regard to a further withdrawal.

The Secretary of Defense will brief you on the details of the announcement.

NOTE: The President spoke at 11:06 a.m. in the Briefing Room at the White House. He spoke without referring to notes.

On the same day, the White House released the transcript of a news briefing by Secretary of Defense Melvin R. Laird on the withdrawal of United States troops. The transcript is printed in the Weekly Compilation of Presidential Documents (vol. 8, p. 50).

13   Statement Announcing United States Policy on
Economic Assistance and Investment Security
in Developing Nations.   *January* 19, 1972

WE LIVE in an age that rightly attaches very high importance to economic development. The people of the developing societies in particular see in their own economic development the path to fulfillment of a whole range of national and human aspirations. The United States continues to support wholeheartedly, as we have done for decades, the efforts of those societies to grow economically—out of our deep conviction that, as I said in my Inaugural Address, "To go forward at all is to go forward together"; that the well-being of mankind is in the final analysis indivisible; and that a better fed, better clothed, healthier, and more literate world will be a more peaceful world as well.

As we enter 1972, therefore, I think it is appropriate to outline my views on some important aspects of overseas development policy. I shall discuss these matters in broader compass and greater detail in messages to be transmitted to the Congress in the coming weeks. Nineteen seventy-one saw great changes in the international monetary and trade fields, especially among the developed nations. A new economic policy was charted for the United States and a promising beginning was made on a broad reform of the international monetary system, starting with a realignment of international exchange rates. Now, in 1972, the problem of how best to assist the development of the world's emerging nations will move more to the forefront of our concern.

Any policy for such assistance is prompted by a mutuality of interest. Through our development assistance pro-grams, financing in the form of taxes paid by ordinary Americans at all income levels is made available to help people in other nations realize their aspirations. A variety of other mechanisms also serves to transfer economic resources from the United States to developing nations.

Three aspects of U.S. development assistance programs received concentrated attention during the past year. These were:

—Continuing a program of bilateral economic assistance
—Meeting our international undertakings for the funding of multilateral development institutions
—Clarifying the role of private foreign investment in overseas development and dealing with the problem of expropriations.

As to our bilateral economic program, it is my intention to seek a regular and adequate fiscal year 1972 appropriation to replace the present interim financing arrangement which expires February 22. I urge that this be one of the first items addressed and completed by the Congress after it reconvenes. Looking beyond this immediate need, I hope the Congress will give early attention to the proposals which I submitted last year to reform our foreign assistance programs to meet the challenges of the seventies.

In regard to our participation in multilateral institutions, I attach the highest importance to meeting in full the financial pledges we make. In 1970, the United States agreed with its hemispheric partners on replenishing the Inter-American

Development Bank. Our contributions to this Bank represent our most concrete form of support for regional development in Latin America. While the Congress did approve partial financing for the Bank before the recess, it is urgent that the integrity of this international agreement be preserved through providing the needed payments in full.

These Inter-American Bank contributions—together with our vital contributions to the International Development Association, the World Bank, and the Asian Development Bank—are the heart of my announced policy of channeling substantial resources for development through these experienced and technically proficient multilateral institutions. These latter contributions also require prompt legislative action, and I look to the Congress to demonstrate to other nations that the United States will continue its long-standing cooperative approach to international development through multilateral financial mechanisms.

I also wish to make clear the approach of this Administration to the role of private investment in developing countries, and in particular to one of the major problems affecting such private investment: upholding accepted principles of international law in the face of expropriations without adequate compensation.

A principal objective of foreign economic assistance programs is to assist developing countries in attracting private investment. A nation's ability to compete for this scarce and vital development ingredient is improved by programs which develop economic infrastructure, increase literacy, and raise health standards. Private investment, as a carrier of technology, of trade opportunities, and of capital itself, in turn becomes a major factor in promoting industrial and agricultural development. Further, a significant flow of private foreign capital stimulates the mobilization and formation of domestic capital within the recipient country.

A sort of symbiosis exists—with government aid efforts not only speeding the flow of, but actually depending for their success upon, private capital both domestic and foreign. And, of course, from the investor's point of view, foreign private investment must either yield financial benefits to him over time, or cease to be available. Mutual benefit is thus the *sine qua non* of successful foreign private investment.

Unfortunately, for all concerned, these virtually axiomatic views on the beneficial role of and necessary conditions for private capital have been challenged in recent and important instances. United States enterprises, and those of many other nations, operating abroad under valid contracts negotiated in good faith, and within the established legal codes of certain foreign countries, have found their contracts revoked and their assets seized with inadequate compensation, or with no compensation.

Such actions by other governments are wasteful from a resource standpoint, shortsighted considering their adverse effects on the flow of private investment funds from all sources, and unfair to the legitimate interests of foreign private investors.

The wisdom of any expropriation is questionable, even when adequate compensation is paid. The resources diverted to compensate investments that are already producing employment and taxes often could be used more productively to finance new investment in the domestic economy, particularly in areas of high social priority to which foreign capital does not always flow. Consequently, countries that expropriate often postpone the attainment of their own development goals. Still more unfairly, expropriations in one developing country can and do impair the investment climate in other developing countries.

In light of all this, it seems to me imperative to state—to our citizens and to other nations—the policy of this Government in future situations involving expropriatory acts.

1. Under international law, the United States has a right to expect:

—that any taking of American private property will be nondiscriminatory;

—that it will be for a public purpose; and

—that its citizens will receive prompt, adequate, and effective compensation from the expropriating country.

Thus, when a country expropriates a significant U.S. interest without making reasonable provision for such compensation to U.S. citizens, we will presume that the United States will not extend new bilateral economic benefits to the expropriating country unless and until it is determined that the country is taking reasonable steps to provide adequate compensation, or that there are major factors affecting U.S. interests which require continuance of all or part of these benefits.

2. In the face of the expropriatory circumstances just described, we will presume that the U.S. Government will withhold its support from loans under consideration in multilateral development banks.

3. Humanitarian assistance will, of course, continue to receive special consideration under such circumstances.

4. In order to carry out this policy effectively, I have directed that each potential expropriation case be followed closely. A special interagency group will be established under the Council on International Economic Policy to review such cases and to recommend courses of action for the U.S. Government.

5. The Departments of State, Treasury, and Commerce are increasing their interchange of views with the business community on problems relating to private U.S. investment abroad in order to improve government and business awareness of each other's concerns, actions, and plans. The Department of State has set up a special office to follow expropriation cases in support of the Council on International Economic Policy.

6. Since these issues are of concern to a broad portion of the international community, the U.S. Government will consult with governments of developed and developing countries on expropriation matters to work out effective measures for dealing with these problems on a multilateral basis.

7. Along with other governments, we shall cooperate with the international financial institutions—in particular the World Bank Group, the Inter-American Development Bank, and the Asian Development Bank—to achieve a mutually beneficial investment atmosphere. The international financial institutions have often assisted in the settlement of investment disputes, and we expect they will continue to do so.

8. One way to make reasonable provision for just compensation in an expropriation dispute is to refer the dispute to international adjudication or arbitration. Firm agreement in advance on dispute settlement procedures is a desirable means of anticipating possible disagreements between host governments and foreign investors. Accordingly, I support the exist-

ing International Center for the Settlement of Investment Disputes within the World Bank Group, as well as the establishment in the very near future of the International Investment Insurance Agency, now under discussion in the World Bank Group. The Overseas Private Investment Corporation will make every effort to incorporate independent dispute settlement procedures in its new insurance and guarantee agreements.

I announce these decisions because I believe there should be no uncertainty regarding U.S. policy. The adoption by the U.S. Government of this policy is consistent with international law. The policy will be implemented within the framework of existing domestic law until the Congress modifies present statutes, along the lines already proposed by this Administration. The United States fully respects the sovereign rights of others, but it will not ignore actions prejudicial to the rule of law and legitimate U.S. interest.

Finally, as we look beyond our proper national interests to the larger considerations of the world interest, let us not forget that only within a framework of international law will the developed nations be able to provide increasing support for the aspirations of our less developed neighbors around the world.

NOTE: On the same day, the White House released the transcript of a news briefing on the President's policy statement by Peter G. Peterson, Executive Director, Council on International Economic Policy.

14   Address on the State of the Union Delivered Before a Joint Session of the Congress.   *January* 20, 1972

Mr. Speaker, Mr. President, my colleagues in the Congress, our distinguished guests, my fellow Americans:

Twenty-five years ago I sat here as a freshman Congressman—along with Speaker Albert—and listened for the first time to the President address the State of the Union.

I shall never forget that moment. The Senate, the diplomatic corps, the Supreme Court, the Cabinet entered the Chamber, and then the President of the United States. As all of you are aware, I had some differences with President Truman. He had some with me. But I remember that on that day—the day he addressed that joint session of the newly elected Republican 80th Congress, he spoke not as a partisan, but as President of all the people—calling upon the Congress to put aside partisan considerations in the national interest.

The Greek-Turkish aid program, the Marshall Plan, the great foreign policy initiatives which have been responsible for avoiding a world war for over 25 years were approved by the 80th Congress, by a bipartisan majority of which I was proud to be a part.

Nineteen hundred seventy-two is now before us. It holds precious time in which to accomplish good for the Nation. We must not waste it. I know the political pressures in this session of the Congress will be great. There are more candidates for the Presidency in this Chamber today than there probably have been at any one time in the whole history of the Republic. And there is an honest difference of opinion, not only between the parties, but within each party, on some foreign policy issues and on some domestic policy issues.

However, there are great national problems that are so vital that they transcend partisanship. So let us have our debates. Let us have our honest differences. But let us join in keeping the national interest first. Let us join in making sure that legislation the Nation needs does not become hostage to the political interests of any party or any person.

There is ample precedent, in this election year, for me to present you with a huge list of new proposals, knowing full well that there would not be any possibility of your passing them if you worked night and day.

I shall not do that.

I have presented to the leaders of the Congress today a message of 15,000 words discussing in some detail where the Nation stands and setting forth specific legislative items on which I have asked the Congress to act. Much of this is legislation which I proposed in 1969, in 1970, and also in the first session of this 92d Congress and on which I feel it is essential that action be completed this year.

I am not presenting proposals which have attractive labels but no hope of passage. I am presenting only vital programs which are within the capacity of this Congress to enact, within the capacity of the budget to finance, and which I believe should be above partisanship—programs which deal with urgent priorities for the Nation, which should and must be the subject of bipartisan action by this Congress in the interests of the country in 1972.

When I took the oath of office on the steps of this building just 3 years ago today, the Nation was ending one of the most tortured decades in its history.

The 1960's were a time of great progress in many areas. But as we all know, they were also times of great agony—the agonies of war, of inflation, of rapidly rising crime, of deteriorating cities, of hopes raised and disappointed, and of anger and frustration that led finally to violence and to the worst civil disorder in a century.

I recall these troubles not to point any fingers of blame. The Nation was so torn in those final years of the sixties that many in both parties questioned whether America could be governed at all.

The Nation has made significant progress in these first years of the seventies:

Our cities are no longer engulfed by civil disorders.

Our colleges and universities have again become places of learning instead of battlegrounds.

A beginning has been made in preserving and protecting our environment.

The rate of increase in crime has been slowed—and here in the District of Columbia, the one city where the Federal Government has direct jurisdiction, serious crime in 1971 was actually reduced by 13 percent from the year before.

Most important, because of the beginnings that have been made, we can say today that this year 1972 can be the year in which America may make the greatest progress in 25 years toward achieving our goal of being at peace with all the nations of the world.

As our involvement in the war in Vietnam comes to an end, we must now go on to build a generation of peace.

To achieve that goal, we must first face realistically the need to maintain our defense.

In the past 3 years, we have reduced the burden of arms. For the first time in

20 years, spending on defense has been brought below spending on human resources.

As we look to the future, we find encouraging progress in our negotiations with the Soviet Union on limitation of strategic arms. And looking further into the future, we hope there can eventually be agreement on the mutual reduction of arms. But until there is such a mutual agreement, we must maintain the strength necessary to deter war.

And that is why, because of rising research and development costs, because of increases in military and civilian pay, because of the need to proceed with new weapons systems, my budget for the coming fiscal year will provide for an increase in defense spending.

Strong military defenses are not the enemy of peace; they are the guardians of peace.

There could be no more misguided set of priorities than one which would tempt others by weakening America, and thereby endanger the peace of the world.

In our foreign policy, we have entered a new era. The world has changed greatly in the 11 years since President John Kennedy said in his Inaugural Address, ". . . we shall pay any price, bear any burden, meet any hardship, support any friend, oppose any foe to assure the survival and the success of liberty."

Our policy has been carefully and deliberately adjusted to meet the new realities of the new world we live in. We make today only those commitments we are able and prepared to meet.

Our commitment to freedom remains strong and unshakable. But others must bear their share of the burden of defending freedom around the world.

And so this, then, is our policy:

—We will maintain a nuclear deterrent adequate to meet any threat to the security of the United States or of our allies.

—We will help other nations develop the capability of defending themselves.

—We will faithfully honor all of our treaty commitments.

—We will act to defend our interests, whenever and wherever they are threatened anyplace in the world.

—But where our interests or our treaty commitments are not involved, our role will be limited.

—We will not intervene militarily.

—But we will use our influence to prevent war.

—If war comes, we will use our influence to stop it.

—Once it is over, we will do our share in helping to bind up the wounds of those who have participated in it.

As you know, I will soon be visting the People's Republic of China and the Soviet Union. I go there with no illusions. We have great differences with both powers. We shall continue to have great differences. But peace depends on the ability of great powers to live together on the same planet despite their differences.

We would not be true to our obligation to generations yet unborn if we failed to seize this moment to do everything in our power to insure that we will be able to talk about those differences, rather than to fight about them, in the future.

As we look back over this century, let us, in the highest spirit of bipartisanship, recognize that we can be proud of our Nation's record in foreign affairs.

America has given more generously of itself toward maintaining freedom, preserving peace, alleviating human suffering around the globe, than any nation has ever done in the history of man.

We have fought four wars in this century, but our power has never been used to break the peace, only to keep it; never been used to destroy freedom, only to defend it. We now have within our reach the goal of insuring that the next generation can be the first generation in this century to be spared the scourges of war.

Turning to our problems at home, we are making progress toward our goal of a new prosperity without war.

Industrial production, consumer spending, retail sales, personal income all have been rising. Total employment, real income are the highest in history. New homebuilding starts this past year reached the highest level ever. Business and consumer confidence have both been rising. Interest rates are down. The rate of inflation is down. We can look with confidence to 1972 as the year when the back of inflation will be broken.

Now, this a good record, but it is not good enough—not when we still have an unemployment rate of 6 percent.

It is not enough to point out that this was the rate of the early peacetime years of the sixties, or that if the more than 2 million men released from the Armed Forces and defense-related industries were still in their wartime jobs, unemployment would be far lower.

Our goal in this country is full employment in peacetime. We intend to meet that goal, and we can.

The Congress has helped to meet that goal by passing our job-creating tax program last month.

The historic monetary agreements, agreements that we have reached with the major European nations, Canada, and Japan, will help meet it by providing new markets for American products, new jobs for American workers.

Our budget will help meet it by being expansionary without being inflationary— a job-producing budget that will help take up the gap as the economy expands to full employment.

Our program to raise farm income will help meet it by helping to revitalize rural America, by giving to America's farmers their fair share of America's increasing productivity.

We also will help meet our goal of full employment in peacetime with a set of major initiatives to stimulate more imaginative use of America's great capacity for technological advance, and to direct it toward improving the quality of life for every American.

In reaching the moon, we demonstrated what miracles American technology is capable of achieving. Now the time has come to move more deliberately toward making full use of that technology here on earth, of harnessing the wonders of science to the service of man.

I shall soon send to the Congress a special message proposing a new program of Federal partnership in technological research and development—with Federal incentives to increase private research, federally supported research on projects designed to improve our everyday lives in ways that will range from improving mass transit to developing new systems of emergency health care that could save thousands of lives annually.

Historically, our superior technology and high productivity have made it possible for American workers to be the highest paid in the world by far, and yet for our goods still to compete in world markets.

37

Now we face a new situation. As other nations move rapidly forward in technology, the answer to the new competition is not to build a wall around America, but rather to remain competitive by improving our own technology still further and by increasing productivity in American industry.

Our new monetary and trade agreements will make it possible for American goods to compete fairly in the world's markets—but they still must compete. The new technology program will put to use the skills of many highly trained Americans, skills that might otherwise be wasted. It will also meet the growing technological challenge from abroad, and it will thus help to create new industries, as well as creating more jobs for America's workers in producing for the world's markets.

This second session of the 92d Congress already has before it more than 90 major Administration proposals which still await action.

I have discussed these in the extensive written message that I have presented to the Congress today.

They include, among others, our programs to improve life for the aging; to combat crime and drug abuse; to improve health services and to ensure that no one will be denied needed health care because of inability to pay; to protect workers' pension rights; to promote equal opportunity for members of minorities, and others who have been left behind; to expand consumer protection; to improve the environment; to revitalize rural America; to help the cities; to launch new initiatives in education; to improve transportation, and to put an end to costly labor tie-ups in transportation.

The west coast dock strike is a case in point. This Nation cannot and will not tolerate that kind of irresponsible labor tie-up in the future.

The messages also include basic reforms which are essential if our structure of government is to be adequate in the decades ahead.

They include reform of our wasteful and outmoded welfare system—substitution of a new system that provides work requirements and work incentives for those who can help themselves, income support for those who cannot help themselves, and fairness to the working poor.

They include a $17 billion program of Federal revenue sharing with the States and localities as an investment in their renewal, an investment also of faith in the American people.

They also include a sweeping reorganization of the executive branch of the Federal Government so that it will be more efficient, more responsive, and able to meet the challenges of the decades ahead.

One year ago, standing in this place, I laid before the opening session of this Congress six great goals. One of these was welfare reform. That proposal has been before the Congress now for nearly 2½ years.

My proposals on revenue sharing, government reorganization, health care, and the environment have now been before the Congress for nearly a year. Many of the other major proposals that I have referred to have been here that long or longer.

Now, 1971, we can say, was a year of consideration of these measures. Now let us join in making 1972 a year of action on them, action by the Congress, for the Nation and for the people of America.

Now, in addition, there is one pressing

need which I have not previously covered, but which must be placed on the national agenda.

We long have looked in this Nation to the local property tax as the main source of financing for public primary and secondary education.

As a result, soaring school costs, soaring property tax rates now threaten both our communities and our schools. They threaten communities because property taxes, which more than doubled in the 10 years from 1960 to '70, have become one of the most oppressive and discriminatory of all taxes, hitting most cruelly at the elderly and the retired; and they threaten schools, as hard-pressed voters understandably reject new bond issues at the polls.

The problem has been given even greater urgency by four recent court decisions, which have held that the conventional method of financing schools through local property taxes is discriminatory and unconstitutional.

Nearly 2 years ago, I named a special Presidential commission to study the problems of school finance, and I also directed the Federal departments to look into the same problems. We are developing comprehensive proposals to meet these problems.

This issue involves two complex and interrelated sets of problems: support of the schools and the basic relationships of Federal, State, and local governments in any tax reforms.

Under the leadership of the Secretary of the Treasury, we are carefully reviewing all of the tax aspects, and I have this week enlisted the Advisory Commission on Intergovernmental Relations in addressing the intergovernmental relations aspects.

I have asked this bipartisan Commission to review our proposals for Federal action to cope with the gathering crisis of school finance and property taxes. Later in the year, when both Commissions have completed their studies, I shall make my final recommendations for relieving the burden of property taxes and providing both fair and adequate financing for our children's education.

These recommendations will be revolutionary. But all these recommendations, however, will be rooted in one fundamental principle with which there can be no compromise: Local school boards must have control over local schools.

As we look ahead over the coming decades, vast new growth and change are not only certainties, they will be the dominant reality of this world, and particularly of our life in America.

Surveying the certainty of rapid change, we can be like a fallen rider caught in the stirrups—or we can sit high in the saddle, the masters of change, directing it on a course we choose.

The secret of mastering change in today's world is to reach back to old and proven principles, and to adapt them with imagination and intelligence to the new realities of a new age.

That is what we have done in the proposals that I have laid before the Congress. They are rooted in basic principles that are as enduring as human nature, as robust as the American experience; and they are responsive to new conditions. Thus they represent a spirit of change that is truly renewal.

As we look back at those old principles, we find them as timely as they are timeless.

We believe in independence, and self-reliance, and the creative value of the competitive spirit.

We believe in full and equal opportunity for all Americans and in the protection of individual rights and liberties.

We believe in the family as the keystone of the community, and in the community as the keystone of the Nation.

We believe in compassion toward those in need.

We believe in a system of law, justice, and order as the basis of a genuinely free society.

We believe that a person should get what he works for—and that those who can, should work for what they get.

We believe in the capacity of people to make their own decisions in their own lives, in their own communities—and we believe in their right to make those decisions.

In applying these principles, we have done so with the full understanding that what we seek in the seventies, what our quest is, is not merely for more, but for better—for a better quality of life for all Americans.

Thus, for example, we are giving a new measure of attention to cleaning up our air and water, making our surroundings more attractive. We are providing broader support for the arts, helping stimulate a deeper appreciation of what they can contribute to the Nation's activities and to our individual lives.

But nothing really matters more to the quality of our lives than the way we treat one another, than our capacity to live respectfully together as a unified society, with a full, generous regard for the rights of others and also for the feelings of others.

As we recover from the turmoil and violence of recent years, as we learn once again to speak with one another instead of shouting at one another, we are regaining that capacity.

As is customary here, on this occasion, I have been talking about programs. Programs are important. But even more important than programs is what we *are* as a Nation—what we mean as a Nation, to ourselves and to the world.

In New York Harbor stands one of the most famous statues in the world—the Statue of Liberty, the gift in 1886 of the people of France to the people of the United States. This statue is more than a landmark; it is a symbol—a symbol of what America has meant to the world.

It reminds us that what America has meant is not its wealth, and not its power, but its spirit and purpose—a land that enshrines liberty and opportunity, and that has held out a hand of welcome to millions in search of a better and a fuller and, above all, a freer life.

The world's hopes poured into America, along with its people. And those hopes, those dreams, that have been brought here from every corner of the world, have become a part of the hope that we now hold out to the world.

Four years from now, America will celebrate the 200th anniversary of its founding as a Nation. There are those who say that the old Spirit of '76 is dead—that we no longer have the strength of character, the idealism, the faith in our founding purposes that that spirit represents.

Those who say this do not know America.

We have been undergoing self-doubts and self-criticism. But these are only the other side of our growing sensitivity to the persistence of want in the midst of plenty, of our impatience with the slowness with which age-old ills are being overcome.

If we were indifferent to the shortcomings of our society, or complacent about our institutions, or blind to the lingering inequities—then we would have lost our way.

But the fact that we have those concerns is evidence that our ideals, deep down, are still strong. Indeed, they remind us that what is really best about America is its compassion. They remind us that in the final analysis, America is great not because it is strong, not because it is rich, but because this is a good country.

Let us reject the narrow visions of those who would tell us that we are evil because we are not yet perfect, that we are corrupt because we are not yet pure, that all the sweat and toil and sacrifice that have gone into the building of America were for naught because the building is not yet done.

Let us see that the path we are traveling is wide, with room in it for all of us, and that its direction is toward a better Nation and a more peaceful world.

Never has it mattered more that we go forward together.

Look at this Chamber. The leadership of America is here today—the Supreme Court, the Cabinet, the Senate, the House of Representatives.

Together, we hold the future of the Nation, and the conscience of the Nation in our hands.

Because this year is an election year, it will be a time of great pressure.

If we yield to that pressure and fail to deal seriously with the historic challenges that we face, we will have failed the trust of millions of Americans and shaken the confidence they have a right to place in us, in their Government.

Never has a Congress had a greater opportunity to leave a legacy of a profound and constructive reform for the Nation than this Congress.

If we succeed in these tasks, there will be credit enough for all—not only for doing what is right, but doing it in the right way, by rising above partisan interest to serve the national interest.

And if we fail, more than any one of us, America will be the loser.

That is why my call upon the Congress today is for a high statesmanship, so that in the years to come Americans will look back and say because it withstood the intense pressures of a political year, and achieved such great good for the American people and for the future of this Nation, this was truly a great Congress.

NOTE: The President spoke at 12:34 p.m. in the House Chamber at the Capitol, after being introduced by Carl Albert, Speaker of the House of Representatives. The address was broadcast live on radio and television.

The President spoke from a prepared text. An advance text of his address was released on the same day.

---

15   Annual Message to the Congress on the State of the Union. *January* 20, 1972

To the Congress of the United States:

It was just 3 years ago today that I took the oath of office as President. I opened my address that day by suggesting that some moments in history stand out "as moments of beginning," when "courses are set that shape decades or centuries." I went on to say that "this can be such a moment."

Looking back 3 years later, I would suggest that it was such a moment—a time in which new courses were set on which we now are traveling. Just how profoundly these new courses will shape our decade or our century is still an unanswered question, however, as we enter the fourth year of this administration. For moments of beginning will mean very little in history unless we also have the determination to follow up on those beginnings.

Setting the course is not enough. Staying the course is an equally important challenge. Good government involves both the responsibility for making fresh starts and the responsibility for perseverance.

The responsibility for perseverance is one that is shared by the President, the public, and the Congress.

—We have come a long way, for example, on the road to ending the Vietnam war and to improving relations with our adversaries. But these initiatives will depend for their lasting meaning on our persistence in seeing them through.

—The magnificent cooperation of the American people has enabled us to make substantial progress in curbing inflation and in reinvigorating our economy. But the new prosperity we seek can be completed only if the public continues in its commitment to economic responsibility and discipline.

—Encouraging new starts have also been made over the last 3 years in treating our domestic ills. But continued progress now requires the Congress to act on its large and growing backlog of pending legislation.

America's agenda for action is already well established as we enter 1972. It will grow in the weeks ahead as we present still more initiatives. But we dare not let the emergence of new business obscure the urgency of old business. Our new agenda will be little more than an empty gesture if we abandon—or even de-emphasize—that part of the old agenda which is yet unfinished.

GETTING OURSELVES TOGETHER

One measure of the Nation's progress in these first years of the seventies is the improvement in our national morale. While the 1960's were a time of great accomplishment, they were also a time of growing confusion. Our recovery from that condition is not complete, but we have made a strong beginning.

Then we were a shaken and uncertain people, but now we are recovering our confidence. Then we were divided and suspicious, but now we are renewing our sense of common purpose. Then we were surrounded by shouting and posturing, but we have been learning once again to lower our voices. And we have also been learning to listen.

A history of the 1960's was recently published under the title, *Coming Apart*. But today we can say with confidence that we are coming apart no longer. The "center" of American life has held, and once again we are getting ourselves together.

THE SPIRIT OF REASON AND REALISM

Under the pressures of an election year, it would be easy to look upon the legislative program merely as a political device and not as a serious agenda. We must resist this temptation. The year ahead of us holds precious time in which to accomplish good for this Nation and we must not, we dare not, waste it. Our progress depends on a continuing spirit of partnership between the President and the Congress, between the House and the Senate, between Republicans and Democrats.

That spirit does not require us always to agree with one another but it does require us to approach our tasks, together, in a spirit of reason and realism.

Clear words are the great servant of reason. Intemperate words are the great enemy of reason. The cute slogan, the glib headline, the clever retort, the appeal to passion—these are not the way to truth or to good public policy.

To be dedicated to clear thinking, to place the interests of all above the interests of the few, to hold to ultimate values and to curb momentary passions, to think more about the next generation and less about the next election—these are now our special challenges.

Ending the War

The condition of a nation's spirit cannot be measured with precision, but some of the factors which influence that spirit can. I believe the most dramatic single measurement of the distance we have traveled in the last 36 months is found in the statistics concerning our involvement in the war in Vietnam.

On January 20, 1969 our authorized troop ceiling in Vietnam was 549,500. And there was no withdrawal plan to bring these men home. On seven occasions since that time, I have announced withdrawal decisions—involving a total of 480,500 troops. As a result, our troop ceiling will be only 69,000 by May 1. This means that in 3 years we will have cut our troop strength in Vietnam by 87 percent. As we proceed toward our goal of a South Vietnam fully able to defend itself, we will reduce that level still further.

In this same period, expenditures connected with the war have been cut drastically. There has been a drop of well over 50 percent in American air activity in all of Southeast Asia. Our ground combat role has been ended. Most importantly, there has been a reduction of 95 percent in combat deaths.

Our aim is to cut the death and casualty toll by 100 percent, to obtain the release of those who are prisoners of war, and to end the fighting altogether.

It is my hope that we can end this tragic conflict through negotiation. If we cannot, then we will end it through Vietnamization. But end it we shall—in a way which fulfills our commitment to the people of South Vietnam and which gives them the chance for which they have already sacrificed so much—the chance to choose their own future.

The Lessons of Change

The American people have learned many lessons in the wake of Vietnam—some helpful and some dangerous. One important lesson is that we can best serve our own interests in the world by setting realistic limits on what we try to accomplish unilaterally. For the peace of the world will be more secure, and its progress more rapid, as more nations come to share more fully in the responsibilities for peace and for progress.

At the same time, to conclude that the United States should now withdraw from all or most of its international responsibilities would be to make a dangerous error. There has been a tendency among some to swing from one extreme to the other in the wake of Vietnam, from wanting to do too much in the world to wanting to do too little. We must resist this temptation to over-react. We must stop the swinging pendulum before it moves to an opposite position, and forge instead an attitude toward the world which is balanced and sensible and realistic.

America has an important role to play in international affairs, a great influence to exert for good. As we have throughout this century, we must continue our profound concern for advancing peace and freedom, by the most effective means possible, even as we shift somewhat our view of what means are most effective.

This is our policy:

—We will maintain a nuclear deterrent adequate to meet any threat to the security of the United States or of our allies.

—We will help other nations develop the capability of defending themselves.

—We will faithfully honor all of our treaty commitments.

—We will act to defend our interests whenever and wherever they are threatened any place in the world.

—But where our interests or our treaty commitments are not involved our role will be limited.

—We will not intervene militarily.

—But we will use our influence to prevent war.

—If war comes we will use our influence to try to stop it.

—Once war is over we will do our share in helping to bind up the wounds of those who have participated in it.

OPENING NEW LINES OF COMMUNICATION

Even as we seek to deal more realistically with our partners, so we must also deal more realistically with those who have been our adversaries. In the last year we have made a number of notable advances

toward this goal.

In our dealings with the Soviet Union, for example, we have been able, together with our allies, to reach an historic agreement concerning Berlin. We have advanced the prospects for limiting strategic armaments. We have moved toward greater cooperation in space research and toward improving our economic relationships. There have been disappointments such as South Asia and uncertainties such as the Middle East. But there has also been progress we can build on.

It is to build on the progress of the past and to lay the foundations for greater progress in the future that I will soon be visiting the capitals of both the People's Republic of China and the Soviet Union. These visits will help to fulfill the promise I made in my Inaugural address when I said "that during this administration our lines of communication will be open," so that we can help create "an open world—open to ideas, open to the exchange of goods and people, a world in which no people, great or small, will live in angry isolation." It is in this spirit that I will undertake these journeys.

We must also be realistic, however, about the scope of our differences with these governments. My visits will mean not that our differences have disappeared or will disappear in the near future. But peace depends on the ability of great powers to live together on the same planet despite their differences. The important thing is that we talk about these differences rather than fight about them.

It would be a serious mistake to say that nothing can come of our expanded communications with Peking and Moscow. But it would also be a mistake to expect too much too quickly.

It would also be wrong to focus so much

attention on these new opportunities that we neglect our old friends. That is why I have met in the last few weeks with the leaders of two of our hemisphere neighbors, Canada and Brazil, with the leaders of three great European nations, and with the Prime Minister of Japan. I believe these meetings were extremely successful in cementing our understandings with these governments as we move forward together in a fast changing period.

Our consultations with our allies may not receive as much attention as our talks with potential adversaries. But this makes them no less important. The cornerstone of our foreign policy remains—and will remain—our close bonds with our friends around the world.

A STRONG DEFENSE: THE GUARDIAN OF PEACE

There are two additional elements which are critical to our efforts to strengthen the structure of peace.

The first of these is the military strength of the United States.

In the last 3 years we have been moving from a wartime to a peacetime footing, from a period of continued confrontation and arms competition to a period of negotiation and potential arms limitation, from a period when America often acted as policeman for the world to a period when other nations are assuming greater responsibility for their own defense. I was recently encouraged, for example, by the decision of our European allies to increase their share of the NATO defense budget by some $1 billion.

As a part of this process, we have ended the production of chemical and biological weaponry and have converted two of our largest facilities for such production to

humanitarian research. We have been able to reduce and in some periods even to eliminate draft calls. In 1971, draft calls—which were as high as 382,000 at the peak of the Vietnam war—fell below 100,000, the lowest level since 1962. In the coming year they will be significantly lower. I am confident that by the middle of next year we can achieve our goal of reducing draft calls to zero.

As a result of all these developments, our defense spending has fallen to 7 percent of our gross national product in the current fiscal year, compared with 8.3 percent in 1964 and 9.5 percent in 1968. That figure will be down to 6.4 percent in fiscal year 1973. Without sacrificing any of our security interests, we have been able to bring defense spending below the level of human resource spending for the first time in 20 years. This condition is maintained in my new budget—which also, for the first time, allocates more money to the Department of Health, Education, and Welfare than to the Department of Defense.

But just as we avoid extreme reactions in our political attitudes toward the world, so we must avoid over-reacting as we plan for our defense. We have reversed spending priorities, but we have never compromised our national security. And we never will. For any step which weakens America's defenses will also weaken the prospects for peace.

Our plans for the next year call for an increase in defense spending. That increase is made necessary in part by rising research and development costs, in part by military pay increases—which, in turn, will help us eliminate the draft—and in part by the need to proceed with new weapon systems to maintain our security at an adequate level. Even as we seek with

45

the greatest urgency stable controls on armaments, we cannot ignore the fact that others are going forward with major increases in their own arms programs.

In the year ahead we will be working to improve and protect, to diversify and disperse our strategic forces in ways which make them even less vulnerable to attack and more effective in deterring war. I will request a substantial budget increase to preserve the sufficiency of our strategic nuclear deterrent, including an allocation of over $900 million to improve our sea-based deterrent force. I recently directed the Department of Defense to develop a program to build additional missile launching submarines, carrying a new and far more effective missile. We will also proceed with programs to reoutfit our Polaris submarines with the Poseidon missile system, to replace older land-based missiles with Minuteman III, and to deploy the SAFEGUARD Antiballistic Missile System.

At the same time, we must move to maintain our strength at sea. The Navy's budget was increased by $2 billion in the current fiscal year, and I will ask for a similar increase next year, with particular emphasis on our shipbuilding programs.

Our military research and development program must also be stepped up. Our budget in this area was increased by $594 million in the current fiscal year and I will recommend a further increase for next year of $838 million. I will also propose a substantial program to develop and procure more effective weapons systems for our land and tactical air forces, and to improve the National Guard and Reserves, providing more modern weapons and better training.

In addition, we will expand our strong program to attract volunteer career soldiers so that we can phase out the draft. With the cooperation of the Congress, we have been able to double the basic pay of first time enlistees. Further substantial military pay increases are planned. I will also submit to the Congress an overall reform of our military retirement and survivor benefit programs, raising the level of protection for military families. In addition, we will expand efforts to improve race relations, to equalize promotional opportunities, to control drug abuse, and generally to improve the quality of life in the Armed Forces.

As we take all of these steps, let us remember that strong military defenses are not the enemy of peace; they are the guardians of peace. Our ability to build a stable and tranquil world—to achieve an arms control agreement, for example—depends on our ability to negotiate from a position of strength. We seek adequate power not as an end in itself but as a means for achieving our purpose. And our purpose is peace.

In my Inaugural address 3 years ago I called for cooperation to reduce the burden of arms—and I am encouraged by the progress we have been making toward that goal. But I also added this comment: ". . . to all those who would be tempted by weakness, let us leave no doubt that we will be as strong as we need to be for as long as we need to be." Today I repeat that reminder.

A REALISTIC PROGRAM OF FOREIGN ASSISTANCE

Another important expression of America's interest and influence in the world is our foreign assistance effort. This effort has special significance at a time when we are reducing our direct military presence abroad and encouraging other countries to assume greater responsibilities. Their growing ability to undertake these responsibilities often depends on America's foreign assistance.

We have taken significant steps to reform our foreign assistance programs in recent years, to eliminate waste and to give them greater impact. Now three further imperatives rest with the Congress:

—to fund in full the levels of assistance which I have earlier recommended for the current fiscal year, before the present interim funding arrangement expires in late February;

—to act upon the fundamental aid reform proposals submitted by this administration in 1971;

—and to modify those statutes which govern our response to expropriation of American property by foreign governments, as I recommended in my recent statement on the security of overseas investments.

These actions, taken together, will constitute not an exception to the emerging pattern for a more realistic American role in the world, but rather a fully consistent and crucially important element in that pattern.

As we work to help our partners in the world community develop their economic potential and strengthen their military forces, we should also cooperate fully with them in meeting international challenges such as the menace of narcotics, the threat of pollution, the growth of population, the proper use of the seas and seabeds, and the plight of those who have been vic-timized by wars and natural disasters. All of these are global problems and they must be confronted on a global basis. The efforts of the United Nations to respond creatively to these challenges have been most promising, as has the work of NATO in the environmental field. Now we must build on these beginnings.

AMERICA'S INFLUENCE FOR GOOD

The United States is not the world's policeman nor the keeper of its moral conscience. But—whether we like it or not—we still represent a force for stability in what has too often been an unstable world, a force for justice in a world which is too often unjust, a force for progress in a world which desperately needs to progress, a force for peace in a world that is weary of war.

We can have a great influence for good in our world—and for that reason we bear a great responsibility. Whether we fulfill that responsibility—whether we fully use our influence for good—these are questions we will be answering as we reshape our attitudes and policies toward other countries, as we determine our defensive capabilities, and as we make fundamental decisions about foreign assistance. I will soon discuss these and other concerns in greater detail in my annual report to the Congress on foreign policy.

Our influence for good in the world depends, of course, not only on decisions which touch directly on international affairs but also on our internal strength—on our sense of pride and purpose, on the vitality of our economy, on the success of our efforts to build a better life for all

47

our people. Let us turn then from the state of the Union abroad to the state of the Union at home.

THE ECONOMY: TOWARD A NEW PROSPERITY

Just as the Vietnam war occasioned much of our spiritual crisis, so it lay at the root of our economic problems 3 years ago. The attempt to finance that war through budget deficits in a period of full employment had produced a wave of price inflation as dangerous and as persistent as any in our history. It was more persistent, frankly, than I expected it would be when I first took office. And it only yielded slowly to our dual efforts to cool the war and to cool inflation.

Our challenge was further compounded by the need to reabsorb more than 2 million persons who were released from the Armed Forces and from defense-related industries and by the substantial expansion of the labor force.

In short, the escalation of the Vietnam war in the late 1960's destroyed price stability. And the de-escalation of that war in the early 1970's impeded full employment.

Throughout these years, however, I have remained convinced that both price stability and full employment were realistic goals for this country. By last summer it became apparent that our efforts to eradicate inflation without wage and price controls would either take too long or—if they were to take effect quickly—would come at the cost of persistent high unemployment. This cost was unacceptable. On August 15th I therefore announced a series of new economic policies to speed our progress toward a new prosperity without inflation in peacetime.

These policies have received the strong support of the Congress and the American people, and as a result they have been effective. To carry forward these policies, three important steps were taken this past December—all within a brief 2-week period—which will also help to make the coming year a very good year for the American economy.

On December 10, I signed into law the Revenue Act of 1971, providing tax cuts over the next 3 years of some $15 billion, cuts which I requested to stimulate the economy and to provide hundreds of thousands of new jobs. On December 22, I signed into law the Economic Stabilization Act Amendments of 1971, which will allow us to continue our program of wage and price restraints to break the back of inflation.

Between these two events, on December 18, I was able to announce a major breakthrough on the international economic front—reached in cooperation with our primary economic partners. This breakthrough will mitigate the intolerable strains which were building up in the world's monetary and payments structure and will lead to a removal of trade barriers which have impeded American exports. It also sets the stage for broader reforms in the international monetary system so that we can avoid repeated monetary crises in the future. Both the monetary realignment—the first of its scope in history—and our progress in readjusting trade conditions will mean better markets for American goods abroad and more jobs for American workers at home.

A BRIGHTER ECONOMIC PICTURE

As a result of all these steps, the economic picture—which has brightened steadily during the last 5 months—will, I believe, continue to grow brighter. This is not my judgment alone; it is widely shared by the American people. Virtually every survey and forecast in recent weeks shows a substantial improvement in public attitudes about the economy—which are themselves so instrumental in shaping economic realities.

The inflationary psychology which gripped our Nation so tightly for so long is on the ebb. Business and consumer confidence has been rising. Businessmen are planning a 9.1 percent increase in plant and equipment expenditures in 1972, more than four times as large as the increase in 1971. Consumer spending and retail sales are on the rise. Home building is booming—housing starts last year were up more than 40 percent from 1970, setting an all-time record. Interest rates are sharply down. Both income and production are rising. Real output in our economy in the last 3 months of 1971 grew at a rate that was about double that of the previous two quarters.

Perhaps most importantly, total employment has moved above the 80 million mark—to a record high—and is growing rapidly. In the last 5 months of 1971, some 1.1 million additional jobs were created in our economy and only a very unusual increase in the size of our total labor force kept the unemployment rate from falling.

But whatever the reason, 6 percent unemployment is too high. I am determined to cut that percentage—through a variety of measures. The budget I present to the Congress next week will be an expansionary budget—reflecting the impact of new job-creating tax cuts and job-creating expenditures. We will also push to increase employment through our programs for manpower training and public service employment, through our efforts to expand foreign markets, and through other new initiatives.

Expanded employment in 1972 will be different, however, from many other periods of full prosperity. For it will come without the stimulus of war—and it will come without inflation. Our program of wage and price controls is working. The consumer price index, which rose at a yearly rate of slightly over 6 percent during 1969 and the first half of 1970, rose at a rate of only 1.7 percent from August through November of 1971.

I would emphasize once again, however, that our ultimate objective is lasting price stability without controls. When we achieve an end to the inflationary psychology which developed in the 1960's, we will return to our traditional policy of relying on free market forces to determine wages and prices.

I would also emphasize that while our new budget will be in deficit, the deficit will not be irresponsible. It will be less than this year's actual deficit and would disappear entirely under full employment conditions. While Federal spending continues to grow, the rate of increase in spending has been cut very sharply—to little more than half that experienced under the previous administration. The fact that our battle against inflation has led us to adopt a new policy of wage and price restraints should not obscure the continued importance of our fiscal and monetary policies in holding down the cost of living. It is most important that the Congress join now in resisting the temptation to overspend and in accepting the dis-

cipline of a balanced full employment
budget.

I will soon present a more complete
discussion of all of these matters in my
Budget Message and in my Economic
Report.

A NEW ERA IN INTERNATIONAL ECONOMICS

Just as we have entered a new period
of negotiation in world politics, so we have
also moved into a new period of negotiation on the international economic front.
We expect these negotiations to help us
build both a new international system for
the exchange of money and a new system
of international trade. These accomplishments, in turn, can open a new era of
fair competition and constructive interdependence in the global economy.

We have already made important
strides in this direction. The realignment
of exchange rates which was announced
last month represents an important forward step—but now we also need basic
long-range monetary reform. We have
made an important beginning toward al-
tering the conditions for international
trade and investment—and we expect further substantial progress. I would emphasize that progress for some nations in
these fields need not come at the expense
of others. All nations will benefit from the
right kind of monetary and trade reform.

Certainly the United States has a high
stake in such improvements. Our international economic position has been slowly
deteriorating now for some time—a condition which could have dangerous implications for both our influence abroad and
our prosperity at home. It has been estimated, for example, that full employment
prosperity will depend on the creation of

some 20 million additional jobs in this
decade. And expanding our foreign markets is a most effective way to expand
domestic employment.

One of the major reasons for the weakening of our international economic position is that the ground rules for the exchange of goods and money have forced
us to compete with one hand tied behind
our back. One of our most important accomplishments in 1971 was our progress
in changing this situation.

COMPETING MORE EFFECTIVELY

Monetary and trade reforms are only
one part of this story. The ability of the
United States to hold its own in world
competition depends not only on the fairness of the rules, but also on the competitiveness of our economy. We have made
great progress in the last few months in
improving the terms of competition. Now
we must also do all we can to strengthen
the ability of our own economy to
compete.

We stand today at a turning point in
the history of our country—and in the
history of our planet. On the one hand,
we have the opportunity to help bring a
new economic order to the world, an open
order in which nations eagerly face outward to build that network of interdependence which is the best foundation for
prosperity and for peace. But we will also
be tempted in the months ahead to take
the opposite course—to withdraw from
the world economically as some would
have us withdraw politically, to build an
economic "Fortress America" within
which our growing weakness could be
concealed. Like a child who will not go out
to play with other children, we would
probably be saved a few minor bumps and

bruises in the short run if we were to adopt this course. But in the long run the world would surely pass us by.

I reject this approach. I remain committed to that open world I discussed in my Inaugural address. That is why I have worked for a more inviting climate for America's economic activity abroad. That is why I have placed so much emphasis on increasing the productivity of our economy at home. And that is also why I believe so firmly that we must stimulate more long-range investment in our economy, find more effective ways to develop and use new technology, and do a better job of training and using skilled manpower.

An acute awareness of the international economic challenge led to the creation just one year ago of the Cabinet-level Council on International Economic Policy. This new institution has helped us to understand this challenge better and to respond to it more effectively.

As our understanding deepens, we will discover additional ways of improving our ability to compete. For example, we can enhance our competitive position by moving to implement the metric system of measurement, a proposal which the Secretary of Commerce presented in detail to the Congress last year. And we should also be doing far more to gain our fair share of the international tourism market, now estimated at $17 billion annually, one of the largest factors in world trade. A substantial part of our balance of payments deficit results from the fact that American tourists abroad spend $2.5 billion more than foreign tourists spend in the United States. We can help correct this situation by attracting more foreign tourists to our shores—especially as we enter our Bicentennial era. I am therefore requesting that the budget for the United States Travel Service be nearly doubled in the coming year.

THE UNFINISHED AGENDA

Our progress toward building a new economic order at home and abroad has been made possible by the cooperation and cohesion of the American people. I am sure that many Americans had misgivings about one aspect or another of the new economic policies I introduced last summer. But most have nevertheless been ready to accept this new effort in order to build the broad support which is essential for effective change.

The time has now come for us to apply this same sense of realism and reasonability to other reform proposals which have been languishing on our domestic agenda. As was the case with our economic policies, most Americans agree that we need a change in our welfare system, in our health strategy, in our programs to improve the environment, in the way we finance State and local government, and in the organization of government at the Federal level. Most Americans are not satisfied with the status quo in education, in transportation, in law enforcement, in drug control, in community development. In each of these areas—and in others—I have put forward specific proposals which are responsive to this deep desire for change.

And yet achieving change has often been difficult. There has been progress in some areas, but for the most part, as a nation we have not shown the same sense of self-discipline in our response to social challenges that we have developed in meeting our economic needs. We have not been as ready as we should have been to compromise our differences and to build a broad coalition for change. And so we often have found ourselves in a situation of stalemate—doing essentially nothing even though most of us agree that nothing is the very worst thing we can do.

Two years ago this week, and again one year ago, my messages on the state of the Union contained broad proposals for domestic reform. I am presenting a number of new proposals in this year's message. But I also call once again, with renewed urgency, for action on our unfinished agenda.

WELFARE REFORM

The first item of unfinished business is welfare reform.

Since I first presented my proposals in August of 1969, some 4 million additional persons have been added to our welfare rolls. The cost of our old welfare system has grown by an additional $4.2 billion. People have not been moving as fast as they should from welfare rolls to payrolls. Too much of the traffic has been the other way.

Our antiquated welfare system is responsible for this calamity. Our new program of "workfare" would begin to end it.

Today, more than ever, we need a new program which is based on the dignity of work, which provides strong incentives for work, and which includes for those who are able to work an effective work requirement. Today, more than ever, we need a new program which helps hold families together rather than driving them apart, which provides day care services so that low income mothers can trade dependence on government for the dignity of employment, which relieves intolerable fiscal pressures on State and local governments, and which replaces 54 administrative sys-

tems with a more efficient and reliable nationwide approach.

I have now given prominent attention to this subject in three consecutive messages on the state of the Union. The House of Representatives has passed welfare reform twice. Now that the new economic legislation has been passed, I urge the Senate Finance Committee to place welfare reform at the top of its agenda. It is my earnest hope that when this Congress adjourns, welfare reform will not be an item of pending business but an accomplished reality.

REVENUE SHARING: RETURNING POWER TO THE PEOPLE

At the same time that I introduced my welfare proposals 2½ years ago, I also presented a program for sharing Federal revenues with State and local governments. Last year I greatly expanded on this concept. Yet, despite undisputed evidence of compelling needs, despite overwhelming public support, despite the endorsement of both major political parties and most of the Nation's Governors and mayors, and despite the fact that most other nations with federal systems of government already have such a program, revenue sharing still remains on the list of unfinished business.

I call again today for the enactment of revenue sharing. During its first full year of operation our proposed programs would spend $17.6 billion, both for general purposes and through six special purpose programs for law enforcement, manpower, education, transportation, rural community development, and urban community development.

As with welfare reform, the need for

revenue sharing becomes more acute as time passes. The financial crisis of State and local government is deepening. The pattern of breakdown in State and municipal services grows more threatening. Inequitable tax pressures are mounting. The demand for more flexible and more responsive government—at levels closer to the problems and closer to the people—is building.

Revenue sharing can help us meet these challenges. It can help reverse what has been the flow of power and resources toward Washington by sending power and resources back to the States, to the communities, and to the people. Revenue sharing can bring a new sense of accountability, a new burst of energy and a new spirit of creativity to our federal system.

I am pleased that the House Ways and Means Committee has made revenue sharing its first order of business in the new session. I urge the Congress to enact in this session, not an empty program which bears the revenue sharing label while continuing the outworn system of categorical grants, but a bold, comprehensive program of genuine revenue sharing.

I also presented last year a $100 million program of planning and management grants to help the States and localities do a better job of analyzing their problems and carrying out solutions. I hope this program will also be quickly accepted. For only as State and local governments get a new lease on life can we hope to bring government back to the people—and with it a stronger sense that each individual can be in control of his life, that every person can make a difference.

OVERHAULING THE MACHINERY OF GOVERNMENT: EXECUTIVE REORGANIZATION

As we work to make State and local government more responsive—and more responsible—let us also seek these same goals at the Federal level. I again urge the Congress to enact my proposals for reorganizing the executive branch of the Federal Government. Here again, support from the general public—as well as from those who have served in the executive branch under several Presidents—has been most encouraging. So has the success of the important organizational reforms we have already made. These have included a restructured Executive Office of the President—with a new Domestic Council, a new Office of Management and Budget, and other units; reorganized field operations in Federal agencies; stronger mechanisms for interagency coordination, such as Federal Regional Councils; a new United States Postal Service; and new offices for such purposes as protecting the environment, coordinating communications policy, helping the consumer, and stimulating voluntary service. But the centerpiece of our efforts to streamline the executive branch still awaits approval.

How the government is put together often determines how well the government can do its job. Our Founding Fathers understood this fact—and thus gave detailed attention to the most precise structural questions. Since that time, however, and especially in recent decades, new responsibilities and new constituencies have caused the structure they established to expand enormously—and

53

in a piecemeal and haphazard fashion.

As a result, our Federal Government today is too often a sluggish and unresponsive institution, unable to deliver a dollar's worth of service for a dollar's worth of taxes.

My answer to this problem is to streamline the executive branch by reducing the overall number of executive departments and by creating four new departments in which existing responsibilities would be refocused in a coherent and comprehensive way. The rationale which I have advanced calls for organizing these new departments around the major purposes of the government—by creating a Department of Natural Resources, a Department of Human Resources, a Department of Community Development, and a Department of Economic Affairs. I have revised my original plan so that we would not eliminate the Department of Agriculture but rather restructure that Department so it can focus more effectively on the needs of farmers.

The Congress has recently reorganized its own operations, and the Chief Justice of the United States has led a major effort to reform and restructure the judicial branch. The impulse for reorganization is strong and the need for reorganization is clear. I hope the Congress will not let this opportunity for sweeping reform of the executive branch slip away.

A NEW APPROACH TO THE DELIVERY OF
SOCIAL SERVICES

As a further step to put the machinery of government in proper working order, I will also propose new legislation to reform and rationalize the way in which social services are delivered to families and individuals.

Today it often seems that our service programs are unresponsive to the recipients' needs and wasteful of the taxpayers' money. A major reason is their extreme fragmentation. Rather than pulling many services together, our present system separates them into narrow and rigid categories. The father of a family is helped by one program, his daughter by another, and his elderly parents by a third. An individual goes to one place for nutritional help, to another for health services, and to still another for educational counseling. A community finds that it cannot transfer Federal funds from one program area to another area in which needs are more pressing.

Meanwhile, officials at all levels of government find themselves wasting enormous amounts of time, energy, and the taxpayers' money untangling Federal red tape—time and energy and dollars which could better be spent in meeting people's needs.

We need a new approach to the delivery of social services—one which is built around people and not around programs. We need an approach which treats a person as a whole and which treats the family as a unit. We need to break through rigid categorical walls, to open up narrow bureaucratic compartments, to consolidate and coordinate related programs in a comprehensive approach to related problems.

The Allied Services Act which will soon be submitted to the Congress offers one set of tools for carrying out that new approach in the programs of the Department of Health, Education, and Welfare. It would strengthen State and local planning and administrative capacities, allow for the transfer of funds among various HEW programs, and permit the waiver of certain cumbersome Federal requirements. By streamlining and simplifying the delivery of services, it would help more people move more rapidly from public dependency toward the dignity of being eself-sufficient.

Good men and good money can be wasted on bad mechanisms. By giving those mechanisms a thorough overhaul, we can help to restore the confidence of the people in the capacities of their government.

PROTECTING THE ENVIRONMENT

A central theme of both my earlier messages on the state of the Union was the state of our environment—and the importance of making "our peace with nature." The last few years have been a time in which environmental values have become firmly embedded in our attitudes—and in our institutions. At the Federal level, we have established a new Environmental Protection Agency, a new Council on Environmental Quality and a new National Oceanic and Atmospheric Administration, and we have proposed an entire new Department of Natural Resources. New air quality standards have been set, and there is evidence that the air in many cities is becoming less polluted. Under authority granted by the Refuse Act of 1899, we have instituted a new permit program which, for the first time, allows the Federal Government to inventory all significant industrial sources of water pollution and to specify required abatement actions. Under the Refuse Act, more than 160 civil actions and 320 criminal actions to stop water pollution have been filed against alleged polluters in the last 12 months. Major programs have also been launched to build new municipal waste

treatment facilities, to stop pollution from Federal facilities, to expand our wilderness areas, and to leave a legacy of parks for future generations. Our outlays for inner city parks have been significantly expanded, and 62 Federal tracts have been transferred to the States and to local governments for recreational uses. In the coming year, I hope to transfer to local park use much more Federal land which is suitable for recreation but which is now underutilized. I trust the Congress will not delay this process.

The most striking fact about environmental legislation in the early 1970's is how much has been proposed and how little has been enacted. Of the major legislative proposals I made in my special message to the Congress on the environment last winter, 18 are still awaiting final action. They include measures to regulate pesticides and toxic substances, to control noise pollution, to restrict dumping in the oceans, in coastal waters, and in the Great Lakes, to create an effective policy for the use and development of land, to regulate the siting of power plants, to control strip mining, and to help achieve many other important environmental goals. The unfinished agenda also includes our National Resource Land Management Act, and other measures to improve environmental protection on federally owned lands.

The need for action in these areas is urgent. The forces which threaten our environment will not wait while we procrastinate. Nor can we afford to rest on last year's agenda in the environmental field. For as our understanding of these problems increases, so must our range of responses. Accordingly, I will soon be sending to the Congress another message on the environment that will present further administrative and legislative initiatives. Altogether our new budget will contain more than three times as much money for environmental programs in fiscal year 1973 as we spent in fiscal year 1969. To fail in meeting the environmental challenge, however, would be even more costly.

I urge the Congress to put aside narrow partisan perspectives that merely ask "whether" we should act to protect the environment and to focus instead on the more difficult question of "how" such action can most effectively be carried out.

ABUNDANT CLEAN ENERGY

In my message to the Congress on energy policy, last June, I outlined additional steps relating to the environment which also merit renewed attention. The challenge, as I defined it, is to produce a sufficient supply of energy to fuel our industrial civilization and at the same time to protect a beautiful and healthy environment. I am convinced that we can achieve both these goals, that we can respect our good earth without turning our back on progress.

In that message last June, I presented a long list of means for assuring an ample supply of clean energy—including the liquid metal fast breeder reactor—and I again emphasize their importance. Because it often takes several years to bring new technologies into use in the energy field, there is no time for delay. Accordingly, I am including in my new budget increased funding for the most promising of these and other clean energy programs. By acting this year, we can avoid having to choose in some future year between too little energy and too much pollution.

KEEPING PEOPLE HEALTHY

The National Health Strategy I outlined last February is designed to achieve one of the Nation's most important goals for the 1970's, improving the quality and availability of medical care, while fighting the trend toward runaway costs. Important elements of that strategy have already been enacted. The Comprehensive Health Manpower Training Act and the Nurse Training Act, which I signed on November 18, represent the most far-reaching effort in our history to increase the supply of doctors, nurses, dentists and other health professionals and to attract them to areas which are experiencing manpower shortages. The National Cancer Act, which I signed on December 23, marked the climax of a year-long effort to step up our campaign against cancer. During the past year, our cancer research budget has been increased by $100 million and the full weight of my office has been given to our all-out war on this disease. We have also expanded the fight against sickle cell anemia by an additional $5 million.

I hope that action on these significant fronts during the first session of the 92nd Congress will now be matched by action in other areas during the second session. The Health Maintenance Organization Act, for example, is an essential tool for helping doctors deliver care more effectively and more efficiently with a greater emphasis on prevention and early treatment. By working to keep our people healthy instead of treating us only when we are sick, Health Maintenance Organizations can do a great deal to help us reduce medical costs.

Our National Health Insurance Partnership legislation is also essential to assure that no American is denied basic medical care because of inability to pay. Too often, present health insurance leaves critical outpatient services uncovered, distorting the way in which facilities are used. It also fails to protect adequately against catastrophic costs and to provide sufficient assistance for the poor. The answer I have suggested is a comprehensive national plan—not one that nationalizes our private health insurance industry but one that corrects the weaknesses in that system while building on its considerable strengths.

A large part of the enormous increase in the Nation's expenditures on health in recent years has gone not to additional services but merely to meet price inflation. Our efforts to balance the growing demand for care with an increased supply of services will help to change this picture. So will that part of our economic program which is designed to control medical costs. I am confident that with the continued cooperation of those who provide health services, we will succeed on this most important battlefront in our war against inflation.

Our program for the next year will also include further funding increases for health research—including substantial new sums for cancer and sickle cell anemia—as well as further increases for medical schools and for meeting special problems such as drug addiction and alcoholism. We also plan to construct new veterans hospitals and expand the staffs at existing ones.

In addition, we will be giving increased attention to the fight against diseases of the heart, blood vessels and lungs, which presently account for more than half of all the deaths in this country. It is deeply disturbing to realize that, largely because of heart disease, the mortality rate for men under the age of 55 is about twice as great in the United States as it is, for example, in some Scandinavian countries.

I will shortly assign a panel of distinguished experts to help us determine why heart disease is so prevalent and so menacing and what we can do about it. I will also recommend an expanded budget for the National Heart and Lung Institute. The young father struck down by a heart attack in the prime of life, the productive citizen crippled by a stroke, an older person tortured by breathing difficulties during his later years—these are tragedies which can be reduced in number and we must do all that is possible to reduce them.

NUTRITION

One of the critical areas in which we have worked to advance the health of the Nation is that of combating hunger and improving nutrition. With the increases in our new budget, expenditures on our food stamp program will have increased ninefold since 1969, to the $2.3 billion level. Spending on school lunches for needy children will have increased more than sevenfold, from $107 million in 1969 to $770 million in 1973. Because of new regulations which will be implemented in the year ahead, we will be able to increase further both the equity of our food stamp program and the adequacy of its benefits.

COPING WITH ACCIDENTS—AND
PREVENTING THEM

Last year, more than 115,000 Americans lost their lives in accidents. Four hundred thousand more were permanently disabled and 10 million were tem-

57

porarily disabled. The loss to our economy from accidents last year is estimated at over $28 billion. These are sad and staggering figures—especially since this toll could be greatly reduced by upgrading our emergency medical services. Such improvement does not even require new scientific breakthroughs; it only requires that we apply our present knowledge more effectively.

To help in this effort, I am directing the Department of Health, Education, and Welfare to develop new ways of organizing emergency medical services and of providing care to accident victims. By improving communication, transportation, and the training of emergency personnel, we can save many thousands of lives which would otherwise be lost to accidents and sudden illnesses.

One of the significant joint accomplishments of the Congress and this administration has been a vigorous new program to protect against job-related accidents and illnesses. Our occupational health and safety program will be further strengthened in the year ahead—as will our ongoing efforts to promote air traffic safety, boating safety, and safety on the highways.

In the last 3 years, the motor vehicle death rate has fallen by 13 percent, but we still lose some 50,000 lives on our highways *each year*—more than we have lost in combat in the entire Vietnam war.

Fully one-half of these deaths were directly linked to alcohol. This appalling reality is a blight on our entire Nation—and only the active concern of the entire Nation can remove it. The Federal Government will continue to help all it can, through its efforts to promote highway safety and automobile safety, and through stronger programs to help the problem drinker.

YESTERDAY'S GOALS: TOMORROW'S ACCOMPLISHMENTS

Welfare reform, revenue sharing, executive reorganization, environmental protection, and the new national health strategy—these, along with economic improvement, constituted the six great goals I emphasized in my last State of the Union address—six major components of a New American Revolution. They remain six areas of great concern today. With the cooperation of the Congress, they can be six areas of great accomplishment tomorrow.

But the challenges we face cannot be reduced to six categories. Our problems—and our opportunities—are manifold, and action on many fronts is required. It is partly for this reason that my State of the Union address this year includes this written message to the Congress. For it gives me the chance to discuss more fully a number of programs which also belong on our list of highest priorities.

ACTION FOR THE AGING

Last month, I joined with thousands of delegates to the White House Conference on Aging in a personal commitment to make 1972 a year of action on behalf of 21 million older Americans. Today I call on the Congress to join me in that pledge. For unless the American dream comes true for our older generation it cannot be complete for any generation.

We can begin to make this a year of action for the aging by acting on a number of proposals which have been pending since 1969. For older Americans, the most significant of these is the bill designated H.R. 1. This legislation, which also contains our general welfare reform measures, would place a national floor under the income of all older Americans, guarantee inflation-proof social security benefits, allow social security recipients to earn more from their own work, increase benefits for widows, and provide a 5-percent across-the-board increase in social security. Altogether, H.R. 1—as it now stands—would mean some $5.5 billion in increased benefits for America's older citizens. I hope the Congress will also take this opportunity to eliminate the $5.80 monthly fee now charged under Part B of Medicare—a step which would add an additional $1.5 billion to the income of the elderly. These additions would come on top of earlier social security increases totalling some $3 billion over the last 3 years.

A number of newer proposals also deserve approval. I am requesting that the budget of the Administration on Aging be increased five-fold over last year's request, to $100 million, in part so that we can expand programs which help older citizens live dignified lives in their own homes. I am recommending substantially larger budgets for those programs which give older Americans a better chance to serve their countrymen—Retired Senior Volunteers, Foster Grandparents, and others. And we will also work to ease the burden of property taxes which so many older Americans find so inequitable and so burdensome. Other initiatives, including proposals for extending and improving the Older Americans Act, will be presented as we review the recommendations of the White House Conference on Aging. Our new Cabinet-level Domestic Council Committee on Aging has these recommendations at the top of its agenda.

We will also be following up in 1972 on one of the most important of our 1971 initiatives—the crackdown on substandard nursing homes. Our follow-through will give special attention to providing alternative arrangements for those who are victimized by such facilities.

The legislation I have submitted to provide greater financial security at retirement, both for those now covered by private pension plans and those who are not, also merits prompt action by the Congress. Only half the country's work force is now covered by tax deductible private pensions; the other half deserve a tax deduction for their retirement savings too. Those who are now covered by pension plans deserve the assurance that their plans are administered under strict fiduciary standards with full disclosure. And they should also have the security provided by prompt vesting—the assurance that even if one leaves a given job, he can still receive the pension he earned there when he retires. The legislation I have proposed would achieve these goals, and would also raise the limit on deductible pension savings for the self-employed.

The state of our Union is strong today because of what older Americans have so long been giving to their country. The state of our Union will be stronger tomorrow if we recognize how much they still can contribute. The best thing our country can give to its older citizens is the chance to be a part of it, the chance to play a continuing role in the great American adventure.

EQUAL OPPORTUNITY FOR MINORITIES

America cannot be at its best as it approaches its 200th birthday unless all Americans have the opportunity to be at their best. A free and open American society, one that is true to the ideals of its founders, must give each of its citizens an equal chance at the starting line and an equal opportunity to go as far and as high as his talents and energies will take him.

The Nation can be proud of the progress it has made in assuring equal opportunity for members of minority groups in recent years. There are many measures of our progress.

Since 1969, we have virtually eliminated the dual school system in the South. Three years ago, 68 percent of all black children in the South were attending all black schools; today only 9 percent are attending schools which are entirely black. Nationally, the number of 100 percent minority schools has decreased by 70 percent during the past 3 years. To further expand educational opportunity, my proposed budget for predominantly black colleges will exceed $200 million next year, more than double the level of 3 years ago.

On the economic front, overall Federal aid to minority business enterprise has increased threefold in the last 3 years, and I will propose a further increase of $90 million. Federal hiring among minorities has been intensified, despite cutbacks in Federal employment, so that one-fifth of all Federal employees are now members of minority groups. Building on strong efforts such as the Philadelphia Plan, we will work harder to ensure that Federal contractors meet fair hiring standards. Compliance reviews will be stepped up, to a level more than 300 percent higher than in 1969. Our proposed budget for the Equal Employment Opportunity Commission will be up 36 percent next year, while our proposed budget for enforcing fair housing laws will grow by 20 percent. I also support legislation to strengthen the enforcement powers of the

EEOC by providing the Commission with authority to seek court enforcement of its decisions and by giving it jurisdiction over the hiring practices of State and local governments.

Overall, our proposed budget for civil rights activities is up 25 percent for next year, an increase which will give us nearly three times as much money for advancing civil rights as we had 3 years ago. We also plan a 42 percent increase in the budget for the Cabinet Committee on Opportunities for the Spanish Speaking. And I will propose that the Congress extend the operations of the Civil Rights Commission for another 5-year period.

SELF-DETERMINATION FOR INDIANS

One of the major initiatives in the second year of my Presidency was designed to bring a new era in which the future for American Indians is determined by Indian acts and Indian decisions. The comprehensive program I put forward sought to avoid the twin dangers of paternalism on the one hand and the termination of trust responsibility on the other. Some parts of this program have now become effective, including a generous settlement of the Alaska Native Claims and the return to the Taos Pueblo Indians of the sacred lands around Blue Lake. Construction grants have been authorized to assist the Navajo Community College, the first Indian-managed institution of higher education.

We are also making progress toward Indian self-determination on the administrative front. A newly reorganized Bureau of Indian Affairs, with almost all-Indian leadership, will from now on be concentrating its resources on a program of reservation-by-reservation development, including redirection of employment assistance to strengthen reservation economies, creating local Indian Action Teams for manpower training, and increased contracting of education and other functions to Indian communities.

I again urge the Congress to join in helping Indians help themselves in fields such as health, education, the protection of land and water rights, and economic development. We have talked about injustice to the first Americans long enough. As Indian leaders themselves have put it, the time has come for more rain and less thunder.

EQUAL RIGHTS FOR WOMEN

This administration will also continue its strong efforts to open equal opportunities for women, recognizing clearly that women are often denied such opportunities today. While every woman may not want a career outside the home, every woman should have the freedom to choose whatever career she wishes—and an equal chance to pursue it.

We have already moved vigorously against job discrimination based on sex in both the private and public sectors. For the first time, guidelines have been issued to require that Government contractors in the private sector have action plans for the hiring and promotion of women. We are committed to strong enforcement of equal employment opportunity for women under Title VII of the Civil Rights Act. To help carry out these commitments I will propose to the Congress that the jurisdiction of the Commission on Civil Rights be broadened to encompass sex-based discrimination.

Within the Government, more women have been appointed to high posts than ever before. As the result of my directives issued in April 1971 the number of women appointed to high-level Federal positions has more than doubled—and the number of women in Federal middle management positions has also increased dramatically. More women than ever before have been appointed to Presidential boards and commissions. Our vigorous program to recruit more women for Federal service will be continued and intensified in the coming year.

OPPORTUNITY FOR VETERANS

A grateful nation owes its servicemen and servicewomen every opportunity it can open to them when they return to civilian life. The Nation may be weary of war, but we dare not grow weary of doing right by those who have borne its heaviest burdens.

The Federal Government is carrying out this responsibility in many ways: through the G.I. Bill for education—which will spend 2½ times more in 1973 than in 1969; through home loan programs and disability and pension benefits—which also have been expanded; through better medical services—including strong new drug treatment programs; through its budget for veterans hospitals, which is already many times the 1969 level and will be stepped up further next year.

We have been particularly concerned in the last 3 years with the employment of veterans—who experience higher unemployment rates than those who have not served in the Armed Forces. During this past year I announced a six-point national program to increase public awareness of this problem, to provide training and counseling to veterans seeking jobs and to help them find employment opportunities.

61

Under the direction of the Secretary of Labor and with the help of our Jobs for Veterans Committee and the National Alliance of Businessmen, this program has been moving forward. During its first five months of operation, 122,000 Vietnam-era veterans were placed in jobs by the Federal-State Employment Service and 40,000 were enrolled in job training programs. During the next six months, we expect the Federal-State Employment Service to place some 200,000 additional veterans in jobs and to enroll nearly 200,000 more in manpower training programs.

But let us never forget, in this as in so many other areas, that the opportunity for any individual to contribute fully to his society depends in the final analysis on the response—in his own community—of other individuals.

GREATER ROLE FOR AMERICAN YOUTH

Full participation and first class citizenship—these must be our goals for America's young people. It was to help achieve these goals that I signed legislation to lower the minimum voting age to 18 in June of 1970, and moved to secure a court validation of its constitutionality. And I took special pleasure a year later in witnessing the certification of the amendment which placed this franchise guarantee in the Constitution.

But a voice at election time alone is not enough. Young people should have a hearing in government on a day-by-day basis. To this end, and at my direction, agencies throughout the Federal Government have stepped up their hiring of young people and have opened new youth advisory channels. We have also convened the first White House Youth Conference—a wide-open forum whose recommendations have been receiving a thorough review by the Executive departments.

Several other reforms also mean greater freedom and opportunity for America's young people. Draft calls have been substantially reduced, as a step toward our target of reducing them to zero by mid-1973. The lottery system and other new procedures and the contributions of youth advisory councils and younger members on local boards have made the draft far more fair than it was. My educational reform proposals embody the principle that no qualified student who wants to go to college should be barred by lack of money— a guarantee that would open doors of opportunity for many thousands of deserving young people. Our new career education emphasis can also be a significant springboard to good jobs and rewarding lives.

Young America's "extra dimension" in the sixties and seventies has been a drive to help the less fortunate—an activist idealism bent on making the world a better place to live. Our new ACTION volunteer agency, building on the successful experiences of constituent units such as the Peace Corps and Vista, has already broadened service opportunities for the young— and more new programs are in prospect. The Congress can do its part in forwarding this positive momentum by assuring that the ACTION programs have sufficient funds to carry out their mission.

THE AMERICAN FARMER

As we face the challenge of competing more effectively abroad and of producing more efficiently at home, our entire Nation can take the American farmer as its model. While the productivity of our non-farm industries has gone up 60 percent during the last 20 years, agricultural productivity has gone up 200 percent, or nearly 3½ times as much. One result has been better products and lower prices for American consumers. Another is that farmers have more than held their own in international markets. Figures for the last fiscal year show nearly a $900 million surplus for commercial agricultural trade.

The strength of American agriculture is at the heart of the strength of America. American farmers deserve a fair share in the fruits of our prosperity.

We still have much ground to cover before we arrive at that goal—but we have been moving steadily toward it. In 1950 the income of the average farmer was only 58 percent of that of his non-farm counterpart. Today that figure stands at 74 percent—not nearly high enough, but moving in the right direction.

Gross farm income reached a record high in 1971, and for 1972 a further increase of $2 billion is predicted. Because of restraints on production costs, net farm income is expected to rise in 1972 by 6.4 percent or some $1 billion. Average income per farm is expected to go up 8 percent—to an all-time high—in the next 12 months.

Still there are very serious farm problems—and we are taking strong action to meet them.

I promised 3 years ago to end the sharp skid in farm exports—and I have kept that promise. In just 2 years, farm exports climbed by 37 percent, and last year they set an all-time record. Our expanded marketing programs, the agreement to sell 2 million tons of feed grains to the Soviet Union, our massive aid to South Asia under Public Law 480, and our efforts to halt transportation strikes—by doing all we can under the old law and by proposing a new and better one—these efforts and others are moving us toward our $10 billion farm export goal.

I have also promised to expand domestic markets, to improve the management of surpluses, and to help in other ways to raise the prices received by farmers. I have kept that promise, too. A surprisingly large harvest drove corn prices down last year, but they have risen sharply since last November. Prices received by dairy farmers, at the highest level in history last year, will continue strong in 1972. Soybean prices will be at their highest level in two decades. Prices received by farmers for hogs, poultry and eggs are all expected to go higher. Expanded Government purchases and other assistance will also provide a greater boost to farm income.

With the close cooperation of the Congress, we have expanded the farmers' freedom and flexibility through the Agricultural Act of 1970. We have strengthened the Farm Credit System and substantially increased the availability of farm credit. Programs for controlling plant and animal disease and for soil and water conservation have also been expanded. All these efforts will continue, as will our efforts to improve the legal climate for cooperative bargaining—an important factor in protecting the vitality of the family farm and in resisting excessive Government management.

DEVELOPING RURAL AMERICA

In my address to the Congress at this time 2 years ago, I spoke of the fact that one-third of our counties had lost population in the 1960's, that many of our rural areas were slowly being emptied of their people and their promise, and that we should work to reverse this picture by including rural America in a nationwide program to foster balanced growth.

It is striking to realize that even if we had a population of one billion—nearly five times the current level—our area is so great that we would still not be as densely populated as many European nations are at present. Clearly, our problems are not so much those of numbers as they are of distribution. We must work to revitalize the American countryside.

We have begun to make progress on this front in the last 3 years. Rural housing programs have been increased by more than 450 percent from 1969 to 1973. The number of families benefiting from rural water and sewer programs is now 75 percent greater than it was in 1969. We have worked to encourage sensible growth patterns through the location of Federal facilities. The first biennial Report on National Growth, which will be released in the near future, will further describe these patterns, their policy implications and the many ways we are responding to this challenge.

But we must do more. The Congress can begin by passing my $1.1 billion program of Special Revenue Sharing for Rural Community Development. In addition, I will soon present a major proposal to expand significantly the credit authorities of the Farmers Home Administration, so that this agency—which has done so much to help individual farmers—can also help spur commercial, industrial and community development in rural America. Hopefully, the FHA will be able to undertake this work as a part of a new Department of Community Development.

In all these ways, we can help ensure that rural America will be in the years ahead what it has been from our Nation's beginning—an area which looks eagerly to the future with a sense of hope and promise.

A COMMITMENT TO OUR CITIES

Our commitment to balanced growth also requires a commitment to our cities— to old cities threatened by decay, to suburbs now sprawling senselessly because of inadequate planning, and to new cities not yet born but clearly needed by our growing population. I discussed these challenges in my special message to the Congress on Population Growth and the American Future in the summer of 1969— and I have often discussed them since. My recommendations for transportation, education, health, welfare, revenue sharing, planning and management assistance, executive reorganization, the environment—especially the proposed Land Use Policy Act—and my proposals in many other areas touch directly on community development.

One of the keys to better cities is better coordination of these many components. Two of my pending proposals go straight to the heart of this challenge. The first, a new Department of Community Development, would provide a single point of focus for our strategy for growth. The second, Special Revenue Sharing for Urban Community Development, would remove the rigidities of categorical project grants which now do so much to fragment planning, delay action, and discourage local responsibility. My new budget proposes a $300 million increase over the full year level which we proposed for this program a year ago.

The Department of Housing and Urban Development has been working to foster orderly growth in our cities in a number of additional ways. A Planned Variation concept has been introduced into the Model Cities program which gives localities more control over their own future. HUD's own programs have been considerably decentralized. The New Communities Program has moved forward and seven projects have received final approval. The Department's efforts to expand mortgage capital, to more than double the level of subsidized housing, and to encourage new and more efficient building techniques through programs like Operation Breakthrough have all contributed to our record level of housing starts. Still more can be done if the Congress enacts the administration's Housing Consolidation and Simplification Act, proposed in 1970.

The Federal Government is only one of many influences on development patterns across our land. Nevertheless, its influence is considerable. We must do all we can to see that its influence is good.

IMPROVING TRANSPORTATION

Although the executive branch and the Congress have been led by different parties during the last 3 years, we have cooperated with particular effectiveness in the field of transportation. Together we have shaped the Urban Mass Transportation Assistance Act of 1970—a 12-year, $10 billion effort to expand and improve our common carriers and thus make our cities more livable. We have brought into effect a 10-year, $3 billion ship construction program as well as increased research efforts and a modified program of operating subsidies to revamp our merchant marine. We have accelerated efforts to improve air travel under the new Airport and Airway Trust Fund and have been working in fresh ways to save and improve

our railway passenger service. Great progress has also been made in promoting transportation safety and we have moved effectively against cargo thefts and skyjacking.

I hope this strong record will be even stronger by the time the 92nd Congress adjourns. I hope that our Special Revenue Sharing program for transportation will by then be a reality—so that cities and States can make better long-range plans with greater freedom to achieve their own proper balance among the many modes of transportation. I hope, too, that our recommendations for revitalizing surface freight transportation will by then be accepted, including measures both to modernize railway equipment and operations and to update regulatory practices. By encouraging competition, flexibility and efficiency among freight carriers, these steps could save the American people billions of dollars in freight costs every year, helping to curb inflation, expand employment and improve our balance of trade.

One of our most damaging and perplexing economic problems is that of massive and prolonged transportation strikes. There is no reason why the public should be the helpless victim of such strikes—but this is frequently what happens. The dock strike, for example, has been extremely costly for the American people, particularly for the farmer for whom a whole year's income can hinge on how promptly he can move his goods. Last year's railroad strike also dealt a severe blow to our economy.

Both of these emergencies could have been met far more effectively if the Congress had enacted my Emergency Public Interest Protection Act, which I proposed in February of 1970. By passing this legislation in this session, the Congress can give us the permanent machinery so badly needed for resolving future disputes.

Historically, our transportation systems have provided the cutting edge for our development. Now, to keep our country from falling behind the times, we must keep well ahead of events in our transportation planning. This is why we are placing more emphasis and spending more money this year on transportation research and development. For this reason, too, I will propose a 65 percent increase—to the $1 billion level—in our budget for mass transportation. Highway building has been our first priority—and our greatest success story—in the past two decades. Now we must write a similar success story for mass transportation in the 1970's.

PEACE AT HOME: FIGHTING CRIME

Our quest for peace abroad over the last 3 years has been accompanied by an intensive quest for peace at home. And our success in stabilizing developments on the international scene has been matched by a growing sense of stability in America. Civil disorders no longer engulf our cities. Colleges and universities have again become places of learning. And while crime is still increasing, the rate of increase has slowed to a 5-year low. In the one city for which the Federal Government has a special responsibility—Washington, D.C.—the picture is even brighter, for here serious crime actually fell by 13 percent in the last year. Washington was one of 52 major cities which recorded a net reduction in crime in the first nine months of 1971, compared to 23 major cities which made comparable progress a year earlier.

This encouraging beginning is not something that has just happened by itself—I believe it results directly from strong new crime fighting efforts by this administration, by the Congress, and by State and local governments.

Federal expenditures on crime have increased 200 percent since 1969 and we are proposing another 18 percent increase in our new budget. The Organized Crime Control Act of 1970, the District of Columbia Court Reform Act, and the Omnibus Crime Control Act of 1970 have all provided new instruments for this important battle. So has our effort to expand the Federal strike force program as a weapon against organized crime. Late last year, we held the first National Conference on Corrections—and we will continue to move forward in this most critical field. I will also propose legislation to improve our juvenile delinquency prevention programs. And I again urge action on my Special Revenue Sharing proposal for law enforcement.

By continuing our stepped up assistance to local law enforcement authorities through the Law Enforcement Assistance Administration, by continuing to press for improved courts and correctional institutions, by continuing our intensified war on drug abuse, and by continuing to give vigorous support to the principles of order and respect for law, I believe that what has been achieved in the Nation's capital can be achieved in a growing number of other communities throughout the Nation.

COMBATING DRUG ABUSE

A problem of modern life which is of deepest concern to most Americans—and of particular anguish to many—is that of drug abuse. For increasing dependence on drugs will surely sap our Nation's strength and destroy our Nation's character.

Meeting this challenge is not a task for government alone. I have been heartened by the efforts of millions of individual Americans from all walks of life who are trying to communicate across the barriers created by drug use, to reach out with compassion to those who have become drug dependent. The Federal Government will continue to lead in this effort. The last 3 years have seen an increase of nearly 600 percent in Federal expenditures for treatment and rehabilitation and an increase of more than 500 percent in program levels for research, education and training. I will propose further substantial increases for these programs in the coming year.

In order to develop a national strategy for this effort and to coordinate activities which are spread through nine Federal agencies, I asked Congress last June to create a Special Action Office for Drug Abuse Prevention. I also established an interim Office by Executive order, and that unit is beginning to have an impact. But now we must have both the legislative authority and the funds I requested if this Office is to move ahead with its critical mission.

On another front, the United States will continue to press for a strong collective effort by nations throughout the world to eliminate drugs at their source. And we will intensify the world-wide attack on drug smugglers and all who protect them. The Cabinet Committee on International Narcotics Control—which I created last September—is coordinating our diplomatic and law enforcement efforts in this area.

We will also step up our program to curb illicit drug traffic at our borders and within our country. Over the last 3 years Federal expenditures for this work have more than doubled, and I will propose a further funding increase next year. In addition, I will soon initiate a major new program to drive drug traffickers and pushers off the streets of America. This program will be built around a nationwide network of investigative and prosecutive units, utilizing special grand juries established under the Organized Crime Control Act of 1970, to assist State and local agencies in detecting, arresting, and convicting those who would profit from the misery of others.

STRENGTHENING CONSUMER PROTECTION

Our plans for 1972 include further steps to protect consumers against hazardous food and drugs and other dangerous products. These efforts will carry forward the campaign I launched in 1969 to establish a "Buyer's Bill of Rights" and to strengthen consumer protection. As a part of that campaign, we have established a new Office of Consumer Affairs, directed by my Special Assistant for Consumer Affairs, to give consumers greater access to government, to promote consumer education, to encourage voluntary efforts by business, to work with State and local governments, and to help the Federal Government improve its consumer-related activities. We have also established a new Consumer Product Information Coordinating Center in the General Services Administration to help us share a wider range of Federal research and buying expertise with the public.

But many of our plans in this field still await Congressional action, including measures to insure product safety, to fight consumer fraud, to require full disclosure in warranties and guarantees, and to protect against unsafe medical devices.

67

REFORMING AND RENEWING EDUCATION

It was nearly 2 years ago, in March of 1970, that I presented my major proposals for reform and renewal in education. These proposals included student assistance measures to ensure that no qualified person would be barred from college by a lack of money, a National Institute of Education to bring new energy and new direction to educational research, and a National Foundation for Higher Education to encourage innovation in learning beyond high school. These initiatives are still awaiting final action by the Congress. They deserve prompt approval.

I would also underscore my continuing confidence that Special Revenue Sharing for Education can do much to strengthen the backbone of our educational system, our public elementary and secondary schools. Special Revenue Sharing recognizes the Nation's interest in their improvement without compromising the principle of local control. I also call again for the enactment of my $1.5 billion program of Emergency School Aid to help local school districts desegregate wisely and well. This program has twice been approved by the House and once by the Senate in different versions. I hope the Senate will now send the legislation promptly to the conference committee so that an agreement can be reached on this important measure at an early date.

This bill is designed to help local school districts with the problems incident to desegregation. We must have an end to the dual school system, as conscience and the Constitution both require—and we must also have good schools. In this connection, I repeat my own firm belief that

educational quality—so vital to the future of all of our children—is not enhanced by unnecessary busing for the sole purpose of achieving an arbitrary racial balance.

FINANCING OUR SCHOOLS

I particularly hope that 1972 will be a year in which we resolve one of the most critical questions we face in education today: how best to finance our schools.

In recent years the growing scope and rising costs of education have so overburdened local revenues that financial crisis has become a way of life in many school districts. As a result, neither the benefits nor the burdens of education have been equitably distributed.

The brunt of the growing pressures has fallen on the property tax—one of the most inequitable and regressive of all public levies. Property taxes in the United States represent a higher proportion of public income than in almost any other nation. They have more than doubled in the last decade and have been particularly burdensome for our lower and middle income families and for older Americans.

These intolerable pressures—on the property tax and on our schools—led me to establish the President's Commission on School Finance in March of 1970. I charged this Commission with the responsibility to review comprehensively both the revenue needs and the revenue resources of public and non-public elementary and secondary education. The Commission will make its final report to me in March.

At the same time, the Domestic Council—and particularly the Secretaries of the Treasury and of Health, Education, and Welfare—have also been studying this difficult and tangled problem. The entire question has been given even greater urgency by recent court decisions in California, Minnesota, New Jersey, and Texas, which have held the conventional method of financing schools through local property taxes discriminatory and unconstitutional. Similar court actions are pending in more than half of our States. While these cases have not yet been reviewed by the Supreme Court, we cannot ignore the serious questions they have raised for our States, for our local school districts, and for the entire Nation.

The overhaul of school finance involves two complex and interrelated sets of problems: those concerning support of the schools themselves, and also the basic relationships of Federal, State and local governments in any program of tax reform.

We have been developing a set of comprehensive proposals to deal with these questions. Under the leadership of the Secretary of the Treasury, we are carefully reviewing the tax aspects of these proposals; and I have this week enlisted the Advisory Commission on Intergovernmental Relations in addressing the intergovernmental relations aspects. Members of the Congress and of the executive branch, Governors, State legislators, local officials and private citizens comprise this group.

Later in the year, after I have received the reports of both the President's Commission on School Finance and the Advisory Commission on Intergovernmental Relations, I shall make my final recommendations for relieving the burden of property taxes and providing both fair and adequate financing for our children's education—consistent with the principle of preserving the control by local school boards over local schools.

A NEW EMPHASIS ON CAREER EDUCATION

Career Education is another area of major new emphasis, an emphasis which grows out of my belief that our schools should be doing more to build self-reliance and self-sufficiency, to prepare students for a productive and fulfilling life. Too often, this has not been happening. Too many of our students, from all income groups, have been "turning off" or "tuning out" on their educational experiences. And—whether they drop out of school or proceed on to college—too many young people find themselves unmotivated and ill equipped for a rewarding social role. Many other Americans, who have already entered the world of work, find that they are dissatisfied with their jobs but feel that it is too late to change directions, that they already are "locked in."

One reason for this situation is the inflexibility of our educational system, including the fact that it so rigidly separates academic and vocational curricula. Too often vocational education is foolishly stigmatized as being less desirable than academic preparation. And too often the academic curriculum offers very little preparation for viable careers. Most students are unable to combine the most valuable features of both vocational and academic education; once they have chosen one curriculum, it is difficult to move to the other.

The present approach serves the best interests of neither our students nor our society. The unhappy result is high numbers of able people who are unemployed, underemployed, or unhappily employed on the one hand—while many challenging jobs go begging on the other.

We need a new approach, and I believe

the best new approach is to strengthen Career Education.

Career Education provides people of all ages with broader exposure to and better preparation for the world of work. It not only helps the young, but also provides adults with an opportunity to adapt their skills to changing needs, changing technology, and their own changing interests. It would not prematurely force an individual into a specific area of work but would expand his ability to choose wisely from a wider range of options. Neither would it result in a slighting of academic preparation, which would remain a central part of the educational blend.

Career Education is not a single specific program. It is more usefully thought of as a goal—and one that we can pursue through many methods. What we need today is a nationwide search for such methods—a search which involves every area of education and every level of government. To help spark this venture, I will propose an intensified Federal effort to develop model programs which apply and test the best ideas in this field.

There is no more disconcerting waste than the waste of human potential. And there is no better investment than an investment in human fulfillment. Career Education can help make education and training more meaningful for the student, more rewarding for the teacher, more available to the adult, more relevant for the disadvantaged, and more productive for our country.

MANPOWER PROGRAMS: TAPPING OUR
FULL POTENTIAL

Our trillion dollar economy rests in the final analysis on our 88 million member labor force. How well that force is used today, how well that force is prepared for tomorrow—these are central questions for our country.

They are particularly important questions in a time of stiff economic challenge and burgeoning economic opportunity. At such a time, we must find better ways to tap the full potential of every citizen.

This means doing all we can to open new education and employment opportunities for members of minority groups. It means a stronger effort to help the veteran find useful and satisfying work and to tap the enormous talents of the elderly. It means helping women—in whatever role they choose—to realize their full potential. It also means caring for the unemployed—sustaining them, retraining them and helping them find new employment.

This administration has grappled directly with these assignments. We began by completely revamping the Manpower Administration in the Department of Labor. We have expanded our manpower programs to record levels. We proposed—and the Congress enacted—a massive reform of unemployment insurance, adding 9 million workers to the system and expanding the size and duration of benefits. We instituted a Job Bank to match jobs with available workers. The efforts of the National Alliance of Businessmen to train and hire the hard-core unemployed were given a new nationwide focus. That organization has also joined with our Jobs for Veterans program in finding employment for returning servicemen. We have worked to open more jobs for women. Through the Philadelphia Plan and other actions, we have expanded equal opportunity in employment for members of minority groups. Summer jobs for disadvantaged youths went up by one-third last summer. And on July 12 of last year I signed the Emergency Employment Act of 1971, providing more than 130,000 jobs in the public sector.

In the manpower field, as in others, there is also an important unfinished agenda. At the top of this list is my Special Revenue Sharing program for manpower—a bill which would provide more Federal dollars for manpower training while increasing substantially the impact of each dollar by allowing States and cities to tailor training to local labor conditions. My welfare reform proposals are also pertinent in this context, since they are built around the goal of moving people from welfare rolls to payrolls. To help in this effort, H.R. 1 would provide transitional opportunities in community service employment for another 200,000 persons. The Career Education program can also have an important long-range influence on the way we use our manpower. And so can a major new thrust which I am announcing today to stimulate more imaginative use of America's great strength in science and technology.

MARSHALLING SCIENCE AND TECHNOLOGY

As we work to build a more productive, more competitive, more prosperous America, we will do well to remember the keys to our progress in the past. There have been many, including the competitive nature of our free enterprise system; the energy of our working men and women; and the abundant gifts of nature. One other quality which has always been a key to progress is our special bent for technology, our singular ability to harness the discoveries of science in the service of man.

At least from the time of Benjamin Franklin, American ingenuity has enjoyed a wide international reputation. We have been known as a people who could "build a better mousetrap"—and this capacity has been one important reason for both our domestic prosperity and our international strength.

In recent years, America has focused a large share of its technological energy on projects for defense and for space. These projects have had great value. Defense technology has helped us preserve our freedom and protect the peace. Space technology has enabled us to share unparalleled adventures and to lift our sights beyond earth's bounds. The daily life of the average man has also been improved by much of our defense and space research—for example, by work on radar, jet engines, nuclear reactors, communications and weather satellites, and computers. Defense and space projects have also enabled us to build and maintain our general technological capacity, which— as a result—can now be more readily applied to civilian purposes.

America must continue with strong and sensible programs of research and development for defense and for space. I have felt for some time, however, that we should also be doing more to apply our scientific and technological genius directly to domestic opportunities. Toward this end, I have already increased our civilian research and development budget by more than 40 percent since 1969 and have directed the National Science Foundation to give more attention to this area.

I have also reoriented our space program so that it will have even greater domestic benefits. As a part of this effort, I recently announced support for the development of a new earth orbital vehicle that promises to introduce a new era in

71

space research. This vehicle, the space shuttle, is one that can be recovered and used again and again, lowering significantly both the cost and the risk of space operations. The space shuttle would also open new opportunities in fields such as weather forecasting, domestic and international communications, the monitoring of natural resources, and air traffic safety.

The space shuttle is a wise national investment. I urge the Congress to approve this plan so that we can realize these substantial economies and these substantial benefits.

Over the last several months, this administration has undertaken a major review of both the problems and the opportunities for American technology. Leading scientists and researchers from our universities and from industry have contributed to this study. One important conclusion we have reached is that much more needs to be known about the process of stimulating and applying research and development. In some cases, for example, the barriers to progress are financial. In others they are technical. In still other instances, customs, habits, laws, and regulations are the chief obstacles. We need to learn more about all these considerations—and we intend to do so. One immediate step in this effort will be the White House Conference on the Industrial World Ahead which will convene next month and will devote considerable attention to research and development questions.

But while our knowledge in this field is still modest, there are nevertheless a number of important new steps which we can take at this time. I will soon present specific recommendations for such steps in a special message to the Congress. Among these proposals will be an increase next

year of $700 million in civilian research and development spending, a 15 percent increase over last year's level and a 65 percent increase over 1969. We will place new emphasis on cooperation with private research and development, including new experimental programs for cost sharing and for technology transfers from the public to the private sector. Our program will include special incentives for smaller high technology firms, which have an excellent record of cost effectiveness.

In addition, our Federal agencies which are highly oriented toward technology—such as the Atomic Energy Commission and the National Aeronautics and Space Administration—will work more closely with agencies which have a primary social mission. For example, our outstanding capabilities in space technology should be used to help the Department of Transportation develop better mass transportation systems. As has been said so often in the last 2 years, a nation that can send three people across 240,000 miles of space to the moon should also be able to send 240,000 people 3 miles across a city to work.

Finally, we will seek to set clear and intelligent targets for research and development, so that our resources can be focused on projects where an extra effort is most likely to produce a breakthrough and where the breakthrough is most likely to make a difference in our lives. Our initial efforts will include new or accelerated activities aimed at:

—creating new sources of clean and abundant energy;

—developing safe, fast, pollution-free transportation;

—reducing the loss of life and property from earthquakes, hurricanes and other natural disasters;

—developing effective emergency

health care systems which could lead to the saving of as many as 30,000 lives each year;
—finding new ways to curb drug traffic and rehabilitate drug users.

And these are only the beginning.

I cannot predict exactly where each of these new thrusts will eventually lead us in the years ahead. But I can say with assurance that the program I have outlined will open new employment opportunities for American workers, increase the productivity of the American economy, and expand foreign markets for American goods. I can also predict with confidence that this program will enhance our standard of living and improve the quality of our lives.

Science and technology represent an enormous power in our life—and a unique opportunity. It is now for us to decide whether we will waste these magnificent energies—or whether we will use them to create a better world for ourselves and for our children.

A Growing Agenda for Action

The danger in presenting any substantial statement of concerns and requests is that any subject which is omitted from the list may for that reason be regarded as unimportant. I hope the Congress will vigorously resist any such suggestions, for there are many other important proposals before the House and the Senate which also deserve attention and enactment.

I think, for example, of our program for the District of Columbia. In addition to proposals already before the Congress, I will soon submit additional legislation outlining a special balanced program of physical and social development for the Nation's capital as part of our Bicentennial

celebration. In this and other ways, we can make that celebration both a fitting commemoration of our revolutionary origins and a bold further step to fulfill their promise.

I think, too, of our program to help small businessmen, of our proposals concerning communications, of our recommendations involving the construction of public buildings, and of our program for the arts and humanities—where the proposed new budget is 6 times the level of 3 years ago.

In all, some 90 pieces of major legislation which I have recommended to the Congress still await action. And that list is growing longer. It is now for the Congress to decide whether this agenda represents the beginning of new progress for America—or simply another false start.

The Need for Reason and Realism

I have covered many subjects in this message. Clearly, our challenges are many and complex. But that is the way things must be for responsible government in our diverse and complicated world.

We can choose, of course, to retreat from this world, pretending that our problems can be solved merely by trusting in a new philosophy, a single personality, or a simple formula. But such a retreat can only add to our difficulties and our disillusion.

If we are to be equal to the complexity of our times we must learn to move on many fronts and to keep many commitments. We must learn to reckon our success not by how much we start but by how much we finish. We must learn to be tenacious. We must learn to persevere.

If we are to master our moment, we must first be masters of ourselves. We must respond to the call which has been a central theme of this message—the call to reason and to realism.

To meet the challenge of complexity we must also learn to disperse and decentralize power—at home and abroad—allowing more people in more places to release their creative energies. We must remember that the greatest resource for good in this world is the power of the people themselves—not moving in lockstep to the commands of the few—but providing their own discipline and dis-

covering their own destiny.

Above all, we must not lose our capacity to dream, to see, amid the realities of today, the possibilities for tomorrow. And then—if we believe in our dreams—we also must wake up and work for them.

RICHARD NIXON

The White House,

January 20, 1972.

NOTE: The President handed his written message on the State of the Union to Speaker of the House Albert and President of the Senate Agnew at the conclusion of his spoken address.

16   Letter to the Chairman of the Advisory Commission on Intergovernmental Relations About a School Finance Study.   *January* 20, 1972

Dear Bob:

One of the greatest challenges this Nation faces today is the need to reform our system of financing public education which, as you know, primarily depends on local property taxes. The President's Commission on School Finance, which I appointed in 1970, will be transmitting its recommendations to me in March on the over-all directions in which we should be moving.

Any major shift in current reliance on local school property taxes is likely to have a significant effect on the relationships among the Federal government, the states, and local governments. In our discussion last week with Neil McElroy,[1] I requested the Advisory Commission on Intergovernmental Relations to undertake a study on this subject.

In particular, I would like the Commission to examine:

(1) the impact on intergovernmental relations of a tax reform proposal which would replace residential school property taxes with a Federal value added tax;

(2) whether a Federal value added tax is the best substitute for residential school property taxes;

(3) if a value added tax is to be utilized as a substitute for residential school property taxes (a) what should be the size and nature of the base of expenditures subject to the tax, and (b) what should be the type of income tax credit or other method which is utilized to eliminate otherwise regressive aspects of the tax;

[1] On January 13, 1972, the President and the Vice President met with Robert Merriam, Chairman, Advisory Commission on Intergovernmental Relations, Neil H. McElroy, Chairman, President's Commission on School Finance, and Elliot L. Richardson, Secretary, and Sidney P. Marland, Jr., Commissioner of Education, Department of Health, Education, and Welfare, to discuss school finance recommendations.

(4) the best method for providing renter relief under a proposal which replaces residential school property taxes; and

(5) the best means of insuring, under a system of school finance in which the states have primary financing responsibility, that local school districts will be able to retain control of basic education decisions, including the provision of local programs of educational enrichment.

The problems are pressing, and I have asked you to complete such a study as soon as possible, and to keep me advised in the interim as to the progress of your study. You will have the complete cooperation and assistance of the Vice President, Secretary Connally and Secretary Richardson, as well as of the Domestic Council.

I very much appreciate the willingness of the Commission to undertake this effort.

Sincerely,

RICHARD NIXON

[Mr. Robert Merriam, Chairman, Advisory Commission on Intergovernmental Relations, 726 Jackson Place, N.W., Washington, D.C.]

17   Special Message to the Congress Transmitting Proposed Legislation To Arbitrate the West Coast Dock Strike and Urging Passage of the Crippling Strikes Prevention Act. *January* 21, 1972

To the Congress of the United States:

The Nation is faced today with yet another transportation strike which is intolerable in its effect upon millions of Americans, and I am determined that we shall end it at once.

The dock dispute on the West Coast has been festering for over a year, but because a few have been insensitive to the harm they are inflicting upon the many who are not a party to it, no reasonable settlement has been reached. Now this work stoppage, renewed after an injunction under the Taft-Hartley Act has expired, again threatens the Nation's health and safety. Those of us in public office must act swiftly and responsibly to avert its damaging consequences.

Because all other Government remedies have been exhausted, I am proposing to the Congress today special legislation to set up immediately a three-member arbitration board. This board, to be appointed by the Secretary of Labor, would hear and settle all issues in this dispute. No strike or lockout would be permitted from the day this legislation is enacted until the day that the arbitration board makes its determinations. The board's determinations would be made within 40 days and would be binding upon the parties for a definite period of time—at least 18 months.

Let there be no mistake about the urgency of this legislation. This is a vital matter to the people of this country, and the Nation can afford no delay. I earnestly implore the Congress to have this resolution on my desk by the end of next week.

This is an unusually pressing request for the opening days of a new session of the Congress, but let there also be no mistake about the dimensions of destruction which this strike is wreaking upon its victims:

—Before I invoked the Taft-Hartley in-

75

junction in an earlier attempt to settle this dispute, thousands of farmers reaped a harvest of despair as their export crops were blocked by closed ports and could not reach waiting customers overseas. Hundreds of millions of dollars were lost. Because the strike has now resumed, these farmers are again victimized.

—There is an increasing danger that some of these trade losses will become permanent, as foreign purchasers come to believe that our farmers and businessmen cannot provide dependable deliveries. Japan, a billion-dollar market for agricultural imports, has already asked other suppliers to step up production so that it can lessen its dependence on American exports.

—Layoffs, reduced operations, and even business failures also hang over the heads of many other Americans who engage directly or indirectly in exports. Some areas are especially vulnerable, such as the State of Hawaii, which has been hit by shortages of vital supplies, mounting food costs and unemployment rates unmatched for half a generation. Also hard pressed are California, Oregon and Washington.

I cannot emphasize too strongly that all of these people—and, indeed, our national economy—have been made hostage to the interests of those few who persist in prolonging this dispute. These men and women who are hurt so unfairly cannot accept the fact that a dispute in which they play no part can destroy them—nor can you and I. There is no justification for waiting any longer.

It is with extreme reluctance that I propose this legislation, for as I have stressed to the Congress before, I firmly believe that governmental intervention in the collective bargaining process should be as limited as possible. Compulsory arbitration is not generally a satisfactory method of resolving labor disputes. Under the present, deplorable circumstances, however, there is no remaining alternative.

As this resolution is considered, there is one very tough question before us to which reasonable Americans deserve an answer: Why have we once again reached the flash point?

Let there be no mistake about the facts. For two long years, the Congress has had before it comprehensive proposals which I submitted and have repeatedly urged that it pass for the resolution of emergency transportation disputes. This legislation still languishes unenacted.

These proposals, which should best be called the "crippling strikes prevention act" in the future, would have avoided the present crisis, and if enacted will avert what will otherwise be the inevitability of similar crises in the future. They would encourage the parties to bargain more responsibly, and in the event that no settlement is reached, would establish a workable mechanism for resolving the dispute without Congressional action.

Our present legislative tools are plainly inadequate. Four times since I called for these comprehensive measures, it has been necessary for the Congress to enact special legislation to deal with disputes in the troubled transportation industry.

The present dock dispute is perhaps the best illustration of how futile Government actions can be under present law. Bargaining between the parties began in November 1970. After six months of negotiations, the parties gave up their attempt to reach early agreement and suspended their talks until the contract deadline approached. On July 1, 1971 the longshoremen went out on strike, creating a shipping paralysis on the west coast which reverberated throughout our economy.

The resources of the Federal Government, including exhaustive mediation efforts by the Director of the Federal Mediation and Conciliation Service, proved to be of no avail in resolving the dispute. With grave concern, I watched the crisis broaden and deepen, and I personally met with the parties in an attempt to find some way to end this bitter impasse.

By October 1971, it became evident that collective bargaining had failed in this dispute and that action had to be taken to protect the national health and safety. Thus on October 4, I invoked the national emergency provisions of the Taft-Hartley Act which resulted in an 80-day cooling-off period.

Unfortunately, the lengthy negotiations during this period and thereafter did not result in the hoped-for settlement.

The history of this dispute and the bargaining posture of the parties provide no hope that a further extension of time would be useful, or that it would bring the parties any closer to a resolution of this matter. They compel me to submit this special legislation to the Congress and to appeal once more for legislative action that will enable us to deal with future emergency transportation disputes without the necessity of this sort of *ad hoc* legislation that can never undo the damage already done.

I proposed new, comprehensive legislation in February 1970, and there was no Congressional action that year. I resubmitted the measure in February 1971, and hearings were held, but there was no appreciable action. On December 15, 1971, I reminded the Congress that a renewed work stoppage was possible on the west coast and that statutory remedies were desperately needed. The Congress recessed without any response.

As soon as the Congress enacts the special legislation before it today, I urge in the most emphatic terms that it turn its attentions immediately to the Crippling Strikes Prevention Act.

RICHARD NIXON

The White House,
    January 21, 1972.

NOTE: The text of the message was released at Key Biscayne, Fla.

On the same day, the White House released the text of a proposed joint resolution providing for arbitration of the west coast dock strike and the transcript of a news briefing by Under Secretary of Labor Laurence H. Silberman on the President's message.

On January 17, 1972, the White House released the transcript of a news briefing by Under Secretary Silberman on the dock strike.

18   White House Statement About a Treaty Admitting New Members Into the European Economic Community.
January 22, 1972

THE PRESIDENT welcomes the signing today in Brussels of the treaty enlarging the European Community to include the United Kingdom, Ireland, Denmark, and Norway.

The United States has always supported the strengthening and enlargement of the European Community. Upon the occasion of this historic act, the President wishes to emphasize that this support is as strong as ever. The development of European unity will enable the peoples of Europe more effectively to contribute to the enhancement of world peace, security, and prosperity.

The President reaffirms that the closest cooperation between the U.S. and the emerging Europe is a cornerstone of our foreign policy.

NOTE: The statement was made available to the press at Key Biscayne, Fla.

19   Annual Budget Message to the Congress, Fiscal Year 1973. *January 24, 1972*

To the Congress of the United States:

The Budget of the United States for the fiscal year 1973 has as a central purpose a new prosperity for all Americans without the stimulus of war and without the drain of inflation.

To provide for the needs of our people by creating new peacetime jobs and revitalizing the economy, we are spending $38.8 billion more in the current (1972) fiscal year than our receipts.

I make that estimate fully aware that it is a large deficit, but one that is necessary in a year of reduced receipts, as we increase jobs and bring the economy back toward capacity.

I am able to project a 1973 budget, with rising revenues, that cuts this year's actual deficit by $13½ billion and brings us strongly forward toward our goal of a balanced budget in a time of full employment.

If we were to spend less, we would be "too little and too late" to stimulate greater business activity and create more jobs; if we were to spend more, we would be spending "too much, too soon" and thereby invite a renewal of inflation. Instead, we must spend "enough and on time" to keep the economy on a steadily upward peacetime course while providing jobs for all who want them and meeting the urgent needs of the American people.

The budget for fiscal 1972 reflects this Government's confidence in the American economy's ability and capacity to respond to sensible stimulation. The budget for 1973, held to full-employment balance, diminishes stimulation as the new prosperity takes hold and, by so doing, acts as a barrier against the renewal of inflationary pressure.

I strongly urge the Congress to respect the full-employment spending guideline this year, just as business and labor are expected to respect wage and price guidelines set forth to protect the earning and buying power of the American worker and consumer. In the long run, only the intelligent application of responsible fiscal and monetary policies, coupled with the breaking of inflationary expectations, will bring about peacetime prosperity without rising prices in a free market economy.

Deficit spending at this time, like temporary wage and price controls, is strong but necessary medicine. We take that medicine because we need it, not because we like it; as our economy successfully combats unemployment, we will stop taking the medicine well before we become addicted to it.

Preparing the Federal budget forces us to face up to the choices and challenges before us—to decide what national interests take priority.

The budget is a superb deflator of

rhetoric because it calls to account the open-ended promises heard so often in an election year. Proposals, no matter how attractive, must be paid for, and when spending is proposed that takes us beyond full employment balance, that payment must either be in the form of new taxes or rising prices. As the budget submitted herewith proves, I intend to resist the kind of spending that drives up taxes or drives up prices.

One priority that most Americans will agree upon is the return of power to people, after decades of the flow of power to Washington. One good way of turning rhetoric into reality is to put that principle into practice in the tax area.

Power in its most specific sense is spending power. My own choice between Government spending and individual spending has been clear and consistent: I believe some of that power should be taken from the Federal Government and returned to the individual.

Accordingly, over the past 3 years, *the rate of increase in Government spending has been cut nearly in half* compared to the 3 comparable years before this Administration took office.

From 1965 to 1968, Federal spending increased by 51%—an annual average of 17%; over the 3-year period 1969–72, spending rose by 28%—an average of 9% per year. The increase from 1972 to the spending level proposed in this budget

is only 4.1%. This slash in the momentum of Federal spending is all the more dramatic when you consider that 71% of Federal spending is "uncontrollable"— that is, locked into the budget by previous congressional decisions.

By putting the brakes on the increase in Government spending, we have been able to leave more spending power in the hands of the individual taxpayer. *In 1973, individuals will pay $22 billion less in Federal income taxes than they would if the tax rates and structure were the same as those in existence when I took office.* To a family of four that earns $7,500 a year, that means a reduction of Federal income taxes of $272 this calendar year. I believe that the members of that family can use that money more productively for their own needs than Government can use it for them.

The basic shift in the Government's fiscal philosophy has gone relatively unnoticed. The upward curve of Federal spending is beginning to flatten out, while the Federal income tax "bite" out of the individual paycheck is becoming measurably less. This change in direction is as remarkable as it has been unremarked. We are not only talking about returning power—economic power, real power—to people and localities, we are doing something about it.

Throughout this budget, a clear trend can be seen that is designed to return

FEDERAL INCOME TAX REDUCTIONS FOR MARRIED COUPLE WITH 2 CHILDREN, 1969–72

[Calendar year]

	Taxes paid		Reduction between 1969 and 1972	
Wage income	1969	1972	Amount	Percentage
$5,000...............................	$290	$98	$192	66
$7,500...............................	756	484	272	36
$10,000...............................	1,225	905	320	26
$15,000...............................	2,268	1,820	448	20

79

power to people—in real terms, in dollars-and-cents terms. It is a trend which is expressed by Federal income tax cuts, by more State and local participation in program administration, and by more Federal funds going to State and local governments without restrictions.

This is the right course for the American people; it reflects their will; I remind the Congress of its power and responsibility to make revenue sharing and other returns of power to people a reality in this current session.

Another priority—one upon which so much of our progress at home depends—is to create a peaceful world order. We could never fulfill our hopes for a full generation of peace from a position of weakness; we can only negotiate and maintain peace if our military power continues to be second to none.

A demagogue may find it easy enough to advocate that we simply allocate necessary defense dollars to social programs, but a responsible Congress and a responsible President cannot afford such easy answers.

Our success in reducing our involvement in Vietnam by 480,000 men before May 1, 1972, and comparable materiel reductions will help enable us—for the first time—to spend more in the Department of Health, Education, and Welfare than we spend in the Department of Defense.

But it would be foolhardy not to modernize our defense at this crucial moment. Accordingly, and still within our full-employment guideline, I propose a $6.3 billion increase in budget authority for military programs, including vitally needed additions to our strategic forces and our naval strength.

In the 1972 defense appropriation bill, which the Congress did not pass until De-

cember of 1971, the Congress cut my appropriation request by $3 billion. My 1971 defense request was cut by the Congress by $2.1 billion. These were costly cuts, especially in the field of research and development.

We must be prudent in our defense spending, making certain we get the best defense for each taxpayer dollar spent. Productivity here too must be increased, but we cannot afford to be "penny-wise and pound-foolish." *Nothing could be more wasteful than to have to pay the price of weakness.* It costs far less to maintain our strength than it would cost to fall behind and have to catch up, even if that could be done. I urge the Congress not to make the costly mistakes it has made in previous years in its defense cuts; the budget as submitted represents America's actual military needs, and offers the best means to secure peace for the coming generation.

Another priority of this budget is to direct the resources of the Federal Government toward those needs the American people most want met and to the people who are most in need.

Welfare Reform, with training and work incentives, with a new fairness toward the working poor and a minimum income for every dependent family, is a good idea whose time has come. It has been proposed and studied; it has been refined and improved upon; it is ripe for action now. Further delay in enactment would not only be unwise in fiscal terms, but cruel in human terms. The proposed program is infinitely better than the wasteful, demeaning system that now calls itself welfare. This budget proposes appropriation of $450 million to start the replacement of welfare with "workfare."

Revenue Sharing has been debated at

length. Each day and each State's experience only confirms the inescapable fact that it is wanted and needed—now. The States and cities urgently require this aid; individual Americans need it for everything from improved law enforcement to tax relief. This budget allocates $2.5 billion in 1972 and $5.3 billion in 1973 to make General Revenue Sharing a reality now.

Schools need emergency assistance now to make necessary adjustments to provide equal educational opportunity. This budget allocates $500 million in 1972 and $1 billion in 1973 for this purpose.

Government reorganization is needed now, to deliver more services for each tax dollar collected. The pain this change will bring to special interests and bureaucracies is less important than the pain existing bureaucratic arrangements now cause the people. A reorganized government will be a better, more efficient government.

Health care must be improved and made available to all Americans, without driving up medical costs. This budget provides for legislative actions and necessary funding to make better health care available on the most widespread basis, to emphasize preventive medicine, and to pursue an all-out campaign to eliminate cancer and sickle cell anemia.

Drug abuse prevention must be intensified to curb narcotics trafficking and to expand Federal drug rehabilitation efforts coordinated by the White House Special Action Office. The budget allocates $594 million to these and other drug abuse prevention campaigns.

A new commitment to the aging is long overdue to add dignity and usefulness to their lives. This budget provides for total spending of $50 billion on behalf of the aging, $16 billion more than in 1969. Most importantly, $5½ billion will be added to the incomes of older Americans when proposed social security and Welfare Reform legislation is fully in effect. In addition, service initiatives will be launched that will focus on better nutrition and other services designed to help the elderly live independently in their own homes.

Scientific research and technology, so essential to our national security, also must focus more directly on solving our domestic problems, increasing our productivity, and improving our competitive position in international trade. The budget allocates $17.8 billion for this, an increase of $1.4 billion over 1972.

Veterans of the Nation will receive the special consideration they deserve, with particular emphasis on those reentering civilian life after service in Vietnam. This budget provides more than $12 billion in budget authority for veterans benefits, with an increase of over $1 billion for modernization, replacement, and record staffing of VA hospitals, higher compensation for disabled veterans, and enhanced job training opportunities, higher GI bill allowances, and other improved services.

Details on each of these proposals are given later in this Budget Message.

ECONOMIC SETTING AND FISCAL POLICY

ECONOMIC SETTING.—In January 1969, the Nation's chief economic problem was mounting inflation.

Anti-inflationary policies that we adopted began gradually to lower the rate of price increases. However, progress was slower than we had hoped and was accompanied by an unacceptable increase in unemployment. This increase was in part a result of the transition of 2½ million people from wartime to peacetime activities.

During 1970 and 1971, responsible economic policies provided stimulus to expand the economy. The budgets for these years had actual deficits of $2.8 billion and $23 billion, but full-employment surpluses of $3.1 billion and $4.9 billion.

As a result of these policies, progress was made in moderating inflation and in expanding real output in the first half of calendar year 1971. However, inflation and unemployment continued to be unacceptably high. Meanwhile, a deterioration in the trade and balance of payments position of the United States, caused in part by the inflationary pressures of the latter half of the 1960's and aggravated by weaknesses in international monetary and trading arrangements, required decisive corrective action.

Action was called for and action was taken.

On August 15, 1971, I announced a new economic policy that:

—imposed a 90-day freeze on wage and price increases;

—proposed a job development tax credit to increase employment by stimulating investment;

—recommended repeal of the automobile excise tax and an early increase in the personal tax exemption, which together would provide an extra $8 billion of stimulus to the economy over a 3-year period;

—reduced planned Federal spending in 1972 by $5 billion; and

—suspended the convertibility of the dollar into gold and other reserve assets and imposed a temporary 10% import surcharge, thereby laying the foundation for improved trade performance and for basic changes in the international economic system.

The public responded to the new economic policy with the widespread support essential to its success.

This policy has begun to move the economy toward full employment without inflation and without war, a condition we have not experienced in this generation. The consumer price index rose only 1.7% at an annual rate from August to November—the lowest rate of increase for a comparable period in 4½ years. From August to December, industrial wholesale prices rose only 0.5% at an annual rate, after increasing at a 4.6% annual rate during the first 8 months of the year.

Now we have moved beyond the wage and price freeze into a transitional period of flexible wage and price controls and on the way to a return to reasonable stability under free markets.

The proposed tax reductions were part of the Revenue Act of 1971, which became law on December 10. Because of the general expectation that the Congress would approve them, the economic effect of these reductions began to be felt immediately after August 15. Automobile sales soared to a record rate in October, interest rates declined, and business investment plans—after some hesitation—are being revised upward. Taken together, these results will create many of the new jobs needed for full employment.

Negotiations with our international trading partners produced a major agreement in mid-December. Exchange rates were realigned through a devaluation of the dollar and revaluation of the currencies of some of our major trading partners. The 10% surcharge on imports was removed as promised. That agreement will improve the competitive position of U.S. industry and agriculture and permit us to move forward in negotiations on fundamental reform of the international monetary system and on elimination of barriers to expanded international trade.

Each element of the new economic policy has a vital role in sustaining the momentum of our economy. The 1973 budget carries out a fiscal policy that is responsive to the needs of the Nation and responsible in holding down inflation.

BUDGET POLICY.—The full-employment budget concept is central to the budget policy of this Administration. Except in emergency conditions, *expenditures should not exceed the level at which the budget would be balanced under conditions of full employment.* The 1973 budget conforms to this guideline. By doing so, it provides necessary stimulus for expansion, but is not inflationary.

We have planned the 1973 expenditures to adhere to the full-employment budget concept, even though this has required making many difficult decisions. It now appears that the 1972 full-employment budget will be $8.1 billion in deficit. While our economy can absorb such a deficit for a time, the experience of the late 1960's provides ample warning of the danger of continued, and rising, full-employment deficits. The lesson of 1966–68, when such deficits led to an intolerable inflation, is too clear and too close to permit any relaxation of control of Government spending.

Keeping the 1973 budget in full-employment balance will not be easy. The tax changes that have been made during my Administration have reduced 1973 full-employment revenue by a net total of $20 billion. This reduction has been good for the economy, and has given each of us more freedom to decide how he will spend his money and live his life. However, the lower receipts and the need to balance the

1973 full-employment budget require that the Congress carefully consider the Nation's priorities, as I have done in preparing this budget. The task is made harder by the fact that the growth of programs— especially, uncontrollable programs, which now account for 71% of total outlays—could easily lead to another full-employment deficit in 1973 if the Congress adds to my recommendations for domestic spending as it did last year.

The simple fact is that not all programs can or should grow. I urge the Congress to face squarely the difficult questions involved in setting priorities within the overall constraint of a full-employment balance, and not to take the dangerous course of trying to match domestic spending increases with cuts in vitally needed defense funds.

SUMMARY OF THE 1973 BUDGET

For 1973, the Federal budget at full-employment is approximately in balance.

Budget receipts in 1973 are estimated to be $220.8 billion, which is $23 billion higher than in 1972. If the economy were operating at full employment throughout the year, the revenues produced would be $245 billion.

Estimated receipts for 1973 reflect a reduction of $6.9 billion as a result of the tax cuts proposed in the new economic policy and incorporated in the Revenue Act of 1971. About $5 billion of this reduction is in individuals' taxes. The resulting increase in consumers' purchasing power will be a major source of strength in the economy.

Budget outlays in the coming year are expected to be $246.3 billion, an increase of $9.6 billion over the current year. This

THE BUDGET TOTALS

[Fiscal years. In billions]

Description	1971 actual	1972 estimate	1973 estimate
Budget receipts...	$188.4	$197.8	$220.8
Budget outlays..	211.4	236.6	246.3
Deficit (—)..	—23.0	—38.8	—25.5
Full-employment receipts............................	214.1	225.0	245.0
Full-employment outlays [1]............................	209.2	233.1	244.3
Full-employment surplus or deficit (—)..................	4.9	—8.1	0.7
Budget authority......................................	236.4	249.8	270.9

	1970 actual		
Outstanding debt, end of year:			
Gross Federal debt.....................	$382.6	$409.5	$455.8	$493.2
Debt held by the public.................	284.9	304.3	343.8	371.3
Outstanding Federal and federally assisted credit, end of year:			
Direct loans [2].........................	51.1	53.2	50.7	51.4
Guaranteed and insured loans [3]...........	105.4	118.7	136.8	158.6
Direct loans by Government-sponsored agencies......................	37.5	38.8	54.6	65.8

[1] These estimates reflect the fact that under conditions of full employment outlays for unemployment insurance benefits and the Emergency Employment Act program would be lower. Spending under other programs are also affected by employment conditions. For example, outlays for food stamps, social security benefits, public assistance, and veterans' pensions would also be lower under conditions of full employment, and interest would be higher. If adjustments were feasible for all such items, full employment outlays probably would be lower.

[2] Including loans in expenditure account.

[3] Excluding loans held by Government or Government-sponsored agencies.

outlay increase will also help provide jobs and business investment in the year ahead, while remaining within the limit set by full-employment budget guidelines. If the economy were operating at full employment throughout the year, outlays for unemployment insurance benefits and the Emergency Employment Act—and outlay totals—would be lower than the amounts included in the 1973 budget.

This budget requests $271 billion of *budget authority*—the right to make commitments to spend—in 1973. About $185 billion of this amount will require new action on the part of the Congress.

STRATEGY FOR PEACE

The highest priority of my Administration is to bring about an era of peace and prosperity. We are pursuing this goal through partnership with our allies, military strength adequate to deter aggression, negotiations with those with whom we differ, and foreign assistance that encourages self-sufficiency.

We seek peace to reduce the human suffering that is an inevitable part of war. With peace we can release energies and resources that can be used to improve the quality of life everywhere. We have accomplished much of this high purpose during the past 3 years—particularly as a result of the Vietnamization program.

• South Vietnamese forces have assumed the responsibility for ground combat operations. Vietnamization is moving forward in other areas as well. As a result:
—U.S. casualties due to hostilities have been averaging less than 10 per week, as compared with 300 per week in 1968;
—the authorized troop level in South Vietnam will have been reduced from 549,500 in January 1969 to 69,000 as of May 1, 1972; and
—draft calls have been reduced from a Vietnam war high of 382,000 to 94,000 in calendar year 1971, as we move toward the goal of zero draft calls.

• Negotiations with the Soviet Union on strategic arms limitations are progressing.

• Agreement has been reached with NATO members on a 5-year plan to strengthen their defenses, with a substantial increase in their financial contribution.

• Security assistance programs are being planned with a view toward better coordinating them with our overall security effort. In some cases, this may permit additional reductions in U.S. manpower needs overseas.

Our efforts toward peace have not been—and will not be—at the expense of our military strength. Indeed, measures to maintain that strength are a vital part of our peace efforts. Accordingly, this budget proposes a substantial increase in defense programs to provide for the following improvements:

—additional resources for our strategic forces to increase emphasis on our sea-based strategic deterrent force and to continue modernization of present offensive and defensive forces;

—a major increase in shipbuilding, reflecting the high priority I place upon modernizing our naval forces;

—a sizable increase in research and development to assure continuation of our technological superiority;

—newer equipment, higher manning levels, and further training to improve the ability of the National Guard and Reserves to supplement the Active Forces;

—continued development and procurement of more effective weapons systems for the land and tactical air forces; and

—a major effort to achieve an all-volunteer force. Toward this end, a career in the Armed Forces was made more attractive by doubling the basic pay of first time enlistees in November 1971. Other increases in military pay are budgeted for January 1972 and 1973.

Strong foreign assistance programs are also an essential part of our strategy for peace, serving to:

—implement the Nixon Doctrine by helping foreign nations assume a greater share of the responsibility for their defense;

—strengthen the economies of developing nations; and

—provide humanitarian assistance and relief.

85

We must be steadfast in our foreign assistance. We are moving from an era of confrontation to an era of negotiation and increased reliance on our allies to defend themselves. In this setting, I have carefully weighed our basic assistance requirements against our domestic priorities, and now submit a program based on a thorough assessment of what is essential. We must not undercut the efforts of developing nations to stand on their own. Nor can we shortchange the nations now shouldering the burden of their own defense after they—and we—have given so much.

MEETING HUMAN NEEDS

My Administration has begun widespread reform and has sought to take new directions in Federal human resources programs. From 1969 to 1972, outlays for these purposes grew by 63%, while total budget outlays grew by only 28%. This increase is designed to buy such real improvements as:
- —greater benefits for the aged and other beneficiaries under social security;
- —additional training opportunities for the disadvantaged;
- —reform of the food stamp program to establish national standards and to give more help to the most needy;
- —better health care for millions of low-income persons and for the aged;
- —expanded and improved veterans programs;
- —increased educational opportunities for students from lower income families; and
- —extension of unemployment insurance coverage to more Americans.

As a result, human resources spending will be 45% of the 1973 budget, while defense programs will be 32%. Our policy of ending our involvement in the Vietnam war has helped make this possible by freeing resources to keep us strong externally as well as internally. This exactly reverses the priorities of the prior administration. In 1968, the defense share was 45% and the human resources share was 32%.

While this is a substantial record of progress, our work is far from complete.

This budget recommends new initiatives and emphasizes many reforms proposed last year—*on which the Congress has yet to complete action.* These proposals are a necessary part of my efforts to return more of the power to the people, to strengthen the capacity of State and local governments to govern, and—especially by assuring the civil rights of all our citizens—to contribute to personal freedom and human dignity.

To help overcome the fragmentation in human services, which so often loses sight of the whole person and the family, I am proposing Allied Services legislation that would assist State and local governments to respond to human needs more efficiently, more flexibly, and more comprehensively. The legislation would authorize the transfer of Federal funds between Department of Health, Education, and Welfare programs not included in revenue sharing, the waiver of cumbersome Federal program requirements, and limited funding for planning and administrative costs.

WELFARE REFORM.—Almost four decades of experience with the present welfare system is more than enough to teach us that the system has failed.
- It takes away the incentive to work.
- It lacks adequate job opportunities and child care services that would en-

86

courage and assist recipients to become self-supporting.

- Its benefits are inadequate to the needs of its recipients.
- It encourages families to break up so that they might qualify for assistance.
- Its 54 different systems with diverse standards defy efficient administration and create severe inequities.

I urge that the Congress approve promptly the Administration's Workfare legislative proposal. My proposal would remove the greatest evils of the present system by:

—emphasizing work incentives, work requirements, job training and public employment opportunities, child care, and reform of social service programs to encourage families to become and remain self-supporting;

—providing benefits for the first time to families with fathers who work but who do not earn enough to provide a decent standard of living for the family;

—setting a national minimum income standard for all families with children in America;

—establishing uniform national eligibility standards;

—reducing the fiscal pressure on States caused by rapidly rising welfare expenditures; and

—raising income limits to allow retired persons to earn more without loss of benefits.

NUTRITION FOR THE NEEDY.—This Administration has taken decisive steps to feed the hungry and eliminate malnutrition in America. Most importantly, major reforms of the Food Stamp program that I proposed are now in operation. New regulations will:

—establish uniform eligibility standards that equal or exceed the present State standards in all States;

—concentrate benefits on those most in need;

—guarantee family stamp allotments for the needy large enough to purchase a nutritionally adequate diet, with increases tied to the cost of living; and

—provide a work requirement for those able to work.

As a result of these and earlier Administration actions, we have provided more benefits to more people in need than ever before. Food stamp outlays have increased ninefold from 1969 to 1973—reaching an estimated $2.3 billion in benefits for 13 million poor in 1973.

In addition, there will be nearly a threefold increase between 1969 and 1973 in the number of needy schoolchildren receiving subsidized lunches.

A NEW DIGNITY FOR THE AGING.—Last November, I convened the White House Conference on Aging to develop proposals for improving the lives of our senior citizens. The recommendations of the Conference clearly indicate that programs to aid the aged should serve two essential purposes.

- They should provide the aged with sufficient income and necessary services to permit them to remain independent.
- They should assist aged citizens to live active and useful lives.

This budget is responsive to these recommendations. In 1973, the Federal Government will spend nearly $50 billion to assist the Nation's 21 million aged persons. This is $16 billion more than the amount spent to assist the aging in 1969.

Several major proposals in this budget are responsive to the special needs of the aged:

—social security and workfare legislation that will add $5.5 billion to the income of the elderly when it is fully in effect and provide an income floor for older Americans;

—elimination of the monthly premium for supplementary medical insurance in Medicare that will save the elderly $1.5 billion in the first full year;

—$100 million, a fivefold increase over the amount budgeted last year, for the Administration on Aging to provide additional homemaker services, home health aides, transportation, and nutrition services to help older Americans remain in their homes;

—a tripling of the retired senior volunteer program, a doubling of the foster grandparents programs, and a doubling of jobs programs for older persons with low incomes from the levels budgeted last year to enable more of the aged to engage in useful community projects; and

—tax incentives that will broaden the coverage of private pension plans.

The Congress has not yet acted on the major reform in the social security system that I proposed last year—providing automatic adjustments for increases in the cost of living. The older Americans who depend on their social security checks have waited long enough. I urge the Congress to act promptly on this reform and, in addition to:

—raise benefits by 5%, effective July 1, 1972, making the cumulative increase more than one-third in less than 3 years;

—allow recipients to earn more money from wages without losing their benefits; and

—increase widows' benefits up to the level their deceased husbands would have received.

IMPROVING HEALTH CARE.—Almost a year ago, I submitted a health message to the Congress establishing a National Health Strategy for the 1970's. This strategy was directed toward three objectives: prevention of health problems, assured access to medical care, and greater efficiency within the health care system.

To achieve these objectives, I urge the Congress to act promptly on the pending National Health Insurance Standards Act, the proposed Family Health Insurance Plan, and legislation to support the development of health maintenance organizations.

In addition, in 1973, I propose further actions that are essential to my national health strategy, including:

—a substantial increase in funds for the attacks on cancer and sickle cell anemia;

—continued financial support to our health manpower training institutions and to their students;

—expanded efforts to develop health maintenance organizations as a model of improved health care delivery;

—significant increases for protecting consumers from hazardous food and products;

—expanded community programs to deal with special health problems, such as drug addiction and alcoholism;

—improvement of the Medicare program by eliminating the monthly premium for physician services; and

—substantial increases in medical personnel at veterans' hospitals and in funds for constructing new and better hospital facilities for veterans.

DRUG ABUSE PREVENTION.—Last summer, I emphasized the need for a coordinated attack on drug abuse and drug dependency in this country and created the Special Action Office for Drug Abuse Prevention and the Cabinet Committee on International Narcotics Control to monitor and coordinate a concerted Federal effort. Legislation to give the Special Action Office a statutory base was proposed by the Administration more than 7 months ago and should be approved promptly.

In 1973, I am proposing an increase in program levels of $120 million for treatment, rehabilitation, and law enforcement programs, including control of illicit supplies. Funds for research, education, prevention, treatment, and rehabilitation will increase from $310 million in 1972 to $365 million in 1973 while obligations for law enforcement activities will grow from $164 million in 1972 to $229 million in 1973. Under the direction of a Special Consultant to the President, we are mounting a coordinated attack on dope sellers in 24 cities throughout the country.

GUARANTEEING CIVIL RIGHTS.—All of our citizens should expect a first priority of government to be protection of their civil rights. My Administration is committed to a course of action to insure that people can share fully in the benefits of our society regardless of race, sex, religion, or national origin. Significant accomplishments have been made. Much remains to be done:
- We will continue the increase in minority hirings in the Federal service, especially in professional and supervisory positions, despite cutbacks

in Federal employment. More than 13,000 minority employees were hired between November 1969 and May 1971, and minority increases in upper and middle grade levels occurred at much faster rates than for non-minorities. Minorities now constitute approximately one-fifth of all Federal employees.
- We will continue to press efforts to assure that women will hold more jobs with greater responsibilities than ever before. Between October 31, 1970 and October 31, 1971, women holding Federal positions at levels GS–13 and above increased by 7%.
- We will continue the upgrading of efforts to open opportunities for Spanish-speaking Americans. The budget of the Cabinet Committee on the Spanish-Speaking will be increased by 42%.
- We will step up our efforts to promote self-determination for Indians on reservations and to assist them in their economic development. For example, legislation to establish an Indian Trust Counsel Authority has been proposed to guarantee that the rights of the Indian people in natural resources are—at last—effectively defended. Outlays for programs benefiting Indians on reservations will reach $1.2 billion in 1973.
- We will double our resources and our efforts to assure that Federal contractors meet the commitments of their affirmative minority hiring plans. Compliance reviews will increase to 52,000 compared to 12,300 in 1969.
- We will continue to accelerate Federal financial aid and technical assistance to increase minority business

opportunities in America. Outlays for these programs have grown from $213 million in 1969 to $716 million in 1973.

• We will continue our efforts to help with the problems of school desegregation and upgrade our assistance to black colleges and other developing institutions of higher education. The Emergency School Act will provide $1.5 billion over a two-year period to assist in school desegregation.

• We will add to our efforts to eradicate unlawful discrimination in the sale, rental, or financing of housing. Expenditures for these programs will increase 20% in 1973 to $11 million.

• We will increase the outlays of the Equal Employment Opportunity Commission from $22 million to $30 million to enhance their capability to end discrimination in the private sector.

To carry out these plans, I have recommended total expenditures of $2.6 billion for Federal civil rights activities in 1973. This compares with $911 million in 1969. Outlays will increase by 25% between 1972 and 1973.

VETERANS BENEFITS.—In moving toward a generation of peace, we will provide improved benefits for the men and women who have helped obtain that peace through military service and great sacrifice. For the returning veteran, this budget demonstrates our concern by providing greater opportunities for entry into jobs, education, and training. For those who have been disabled in service, this budget provides medical care of high quality that is better tailored to their needs— together with greater benefits for rehabilitation and compensation. For the widows

and children of those who did not return, this budget provides additional dependents' compensation, education, and training. Budget authority for these and other benefits and services will be increased by $1 billion in 1973—to $12.4 billion.

Marked benefit improvements will include:

—an increase of 10,000 in average employment in VA medical facilities, raising the staff to patient ratio for VA hospital care to a record 1.5 to 1;

—a 66% increase in budget authority for construction of new and better hospital facilities, including seven new replacement hospitals;

—improvements in the structure and levels of veterans compensation benefits, to insure more adequate benefits for the most seriously disabled; and

—an increase in the monthly individual benefit payment for the GI bill from $175 to $190, linked with other program improvements I have proposed.

EDUCATION AND MANPOWER TRAINING.—The need for reform in Federal education and manpower training programs has not diminished since last year, but the reforms I recommended then are *still awaiting action by the Congress.*

We must reform these programs so that people can achieve their potential intellectual and occupational skills. For this reason, I again emphasize the need for action on proposals to:

—substitute special revenue sharing programs for categorical grant programs in both of these areas;

—assist school districts in desegregation efforts;

—establish a National Institute of Education to support research and experimentation and a National

Foundation on Higher Education to promote reforms in our colleges and universities;

—provide additional training opportunities and strong incentives under Welfare Reform for welfare recipients to undertake suitable employment or job training;

—assure the returning veteran greater opportunities for jobs, education, and training; and

—reform student aid programs for higher education to increase their effectiveness and direct more aid to students from lower income families.

Let me use that last proposal as an example. I believe that no qualified student should be denied a college education because he cannot afford to pay for it. Most Americans and most Congressmen agree. I have proposed the legislation that will make this a reality. I am ready to sign that legislation. But there it sits, in Congress, while thousands of young people miss their chance.

FIGHTING CRIME

When I took office, the safety and health of our citizens were menaced by rising crime. Violent crimes and illegal traffic in narcotics and dangerous drugs were threatening to get out of control. A crisis existed, and prompt action was called for. I directed that a national strategy to combat crime be developed and promptly put into effect.

Any successful strategy to combat crime must recognize that State and local governments are responsible for most law enforcement in the United States. Such a strategy must also provide for the prevention of crime and for the rehabilitation of criminals.

I took action early to strengthen the hand of State and local government law enforcement agencies.

• Outlays for law enforcement assistance were increased substantially. They will total $595 million in 1973, nearly 18 times the $33½ million of 1969.

• Law enforcement special revenue sharing was proposed to give State and local governments increased flexibility to use Federal funds in ways that are best suited to solving local crime problems. *The Congress should act on this proposal.*

Federal law enforcement activities are also an essential part of our efforts to combat crime—especially organized crime and traffic in narcotics and dangerous drugs. In 1973, we will:

—step up our attack against the criminal systems that import and distribute narcotics and dangerous drugs; and

—continue to enforce vigorously the Organized Crime Control Act of 1970.

Outlays for law enforcement activities will be $2.3 billion in 1973, an increase of $1.7 billion over 1969.

My Administration has given priority to combating crime in our Nation's Capital, where the Federal Government has a special responsibility. These efforts have been successful. Serious crime in the District of Columbia in 1971 was approximately 14% below the level of the previous calendar year.

IMPROVING THE ENVIRONMENT

Protecting and improving our environment is a never-ending job. The basic responsibility rests with States and local governments, industry, and the public. However, the Federal Government must provide leadership.

In 1970, the Environmental Protection Agency was established to improve our pollution control efforts, and the Council on Environmental Quality was established to advise on problems and policies related to environmental quality.

Now, new initiatives are being undertaken.

- To clean our air, we have:
  —set national standards for the six major air pollutants and guidelines for State implementation plans to meet these standards;
  —set pollution abatement standards for new facilities in five industrial categories;
  —recommended a sulfur emissions tax to encourage reductions in this major source of pollution; and
  —supported research and development to provide a low-pollution alternative to the conventional internal combustion engine and to provide means to reduce pollution from burning coal and oil.
- To clean our water, we have:
  —required permits under the Refuse Act to control discharges of industrial pollutants into our waterways;
  —proposed legislation to control dumping into oceans, coastal waters, and the Great Lakes; and
  —initiated a 3-year, $6 billion program to assist State and local governments in building sewage treatment facilities.
- To reduce noise pollution, we have proposed legislation to regulate and to set labeling requirements for major sources of noise.

- To improve and protect health, we have proposed new legislation on pesticides to regulate their use and to strengthen and coordinate Federal and State control efforts.
- To use our lands more wisely, we have proposed legislation on power-plant siting, mined area protection, and land use regulation.

Many of the proposals that I have submitted to the Congress have not yet been enacted. Our Nation cannot make the major efforts that are needed to protect and improve the environment unless Congress will respond to the urgent need for this legislation. *I urge rapid approval by the Congress of these pending environmental proposals.* With the passage of this legislation—and the additional proposals that I will submit to Congress in a special environmental message in February—we will be able to move forward vigorously in all areas of environmental quality.

The outlays requested for major environmental programs in 1973 are $2.5 billion, *more than three times the 1969 level.* These funds will support expanded efforts in all major environmental programs. For example, Federal programs have assisted in increasing the population served by secondary sewage treatment from 91 million in 1969 to 115 million in 1973, and in removing 27% more pollution from municipal sewage effluent than was removed in 1968.

PARKS AND OPEN SPACES.—As our expanding economy provides higher standards of living and increased opportunity for leisure, our citizens will want additional parks and other recreational facilities, especially in and near cities. We also want to assure the preservation of nationally important natural and historic areas.

This budget provides for meeting these future needs.

I am proposing that the Land and Water Conservation Fund annual authorization be fully funded to provide:

—$197 million in grants for State and local governments to assist them to acquire and develop lands for recreation and parks; and

—$98 million for the acquisition of nationally significant natural or historic areas by Federal agencies.

In the period 1970–73, this program will have provided over $1.1 billion, compared to $535 million provided for this purpose in 1966–69.

The budget also proposes to continue, under the Legacy of Parks program, the transfer of surplus Federal property to State and local governments for recreation facilities, parks, and historic sites. In 1973, over 20,000 acres, with a market value of $120 million, will be transferred under this program. For the period 1969–73, a total of 47,000 acres of land with a market value of $245 million will have been provided to State and local governments.

COMMUNITY DEVELOPMENT AND HOUSING.—During the past 3 years, solid progress has been made toward providing decent, safe, and sanitary housing for every American. In calendar year 1971, the volume of new housing construction—more than 2 million new starts—was the highest in the history of this country. The construction of Government-assisted housing for low- and moderate-income families has also been increased to record high levels over the past 3 years.

This Administration has taken steps to decentralize Federal programs that assist community development and housing activities to make them more responsive to local needs and preferences.

Our efforts to aid community development and to provide better housing are still not as productive as they can be. I have proposed major reforms that would make them more so:

—a program of urban community development revenue sharing that would replace five categorical grant programs and provide State and local governments $2.3 billion in 1973;

—a Department of Community Development that would consolidate in one organization the many programs and activities that are essential to community development;

—legislation that would simplify and consolidate housing programs; and

—a new planning and management assistance program that would help States and localities improve their executive management capabilities.

These reforms, pending before the Congress, should be enacted promptly.

AGRICULTURE AND RURAL DEVELOPMENT.—This Administration has made major improvements in programs to help farmers share equitably in the Nation's progress. In addition, I have proposed a new program for rural community development through revenue sharing. I urge the Congress to enact this program in time to be effective on July 1, 1973.

I will shortly recommend further legislation to:

—improve the availability of credit for both farmers and rural residents; and

—give greater emphasis to our efforts to encourage community and industrial development in rural areas.

My budget proposals for 1973 will also

further our goal of making all rural residents first-class citizens living in first-class communities. Specifically, we will:
- —expand the availability of rural housing;
- —strengthen farm incomes through orderly handling of the bumper 1971 grain crop; and
- —help finance critically needed waste disposal and water supply systems for nearly 500,000 rural families.

SCIENCE AND TECHNOLOGY IN THE SERVICE OF MAN

In this year's budget, and subsequently, I shall propose how we can accelerate the effort I began 3 years ago to turn science and technology to the service of man.

Research and development have been critical elements of our national life since World War II. They have been the key to our national security and health and instrumental in the solution of many important civilian problems. Research and development also have made significant contributions to our economy in terms of jobs, productivity, and foreign trade.

This Administration has continuously searched for more effective ways to turn science and technology to the service of man. Since 1969, funds for civilian R & D have increased 65%. We have started new programs and strengthened others to help focus R & D on priority human needs.

We have been reordering our research and development investments in defense and space. We have reassessed the space program and placed it on a firm future footing with increased attention to practical and economical applications of space and reductions in the cost of manned space flight.

At the same time we have strengthened our defense research and development capability to insure that the country will not face the possibility of technological surprise or lack the deterrent power necessary to protect our national security. To provide this assurance, budget authority for Department of Defense research, development, test, and evaluation is being increased $838 million to an all-time high of $8.5 billion in 1973.

To emphasize this Administration's strong belief that science and technology can make significant contributions to the quality of American life and to economic growth, I propose additional steps in 1973 to:
- —secure the contributions that science and technology can make to our national life;
- —initiate a series of experiments to find better ways to encourage private investment in R & D, including investment by small entrepreneurial R & D firms, which have made significant contributions to the generation and exploitation of innovative ideas;
- —draw more directly on the capabilities of those agencies which have created the technologies that harnessed the atom and conquered space. AEC and NASA will increasingly use their talents on such problems as clean, economical energy, and clean, safe, and fast transportation systems. For example, this year we shall have the agency which sent men to the moon and back begin to assist the Department of Transportation in finding better ways to send people downtown and back; and
- —review carefully our policies in areas of economic regulation, which may unnecessarily restrict wider utiliza-

tion or development of new technical advances.

I am also initiating new programs and strengthening research and development aimed at three important objectives:

—protecting man and nature from each other;

—using the resources of nature to serve mankind's needs; and

—pioneering new and improved human services.

The overall result of our efforts to strengthen science and technology in the national interest is reflected in the 1973 increase of $1.4 billion in obligations to a total of $17.8 billion. I firmly believe this large increase is vital to the security, welfare, and economic well-being of our country.

IMPROVING GOVERNMENT

Improved efficiency and responsiveness at all levels of government is a major objective of this Administration. One of my first acts as President was to direct that an intensive review be made of our Federal system of government. We found that the executive branch was badly organized to accomplish domestic objectives. We found that State and local governments were often unable to meet the needs of their citizens because of a fiscal crisis that was steadily worsening. And we also found that Federal programs to assist State and local governments had become a maze of separate programs, understood only by members of a new profession—grantsmanship specialists.

The Administration has developed a comprehensive strategy for dealing with these problems. This strategy includes:

• *Revenue sharing*—an important element of the strategy—to provide fiscal relief and to strengthen State and local governments;

• *Reorganization of the executive branch* to create four new departments structured around the basic domestic activities of government;

• *Federal Assistance Review (FAR)* to strengthen delivery of Federal assistance to State and local governments;

• *Regional councils* to help in our program of returning power to the people;

• *Technical assistance* to help State and local governments improve their organizational structures and management processes; and

• *Budget reform* to enable the executive branch and the Congress better to serve the people.

REVENUE SHARING.—A year ago I proposed to the Congress a General Revenue Sharing program and six special revenue sharing programs to relieve the fiscal crisis of State and local governments and to eliminate some of the problems of the present categorical grant system. No action has yet been taken on these proposals. I *again* urge that Congress enact these proposals.

If enacted to become effective January 1, 1972, as I am proposing, the General Revenue Sharing program would:

—provide $2.5 billion of budget authority in fiscal year 1972 and $5.3 billion in fiscal year 1973 to help relieve the fiscal plight of State and local governments;

—enable those units of government closest to the people to determine how the funds would be spent to meet local needs and priorities; and

—reduce pressures to raise State and local taxes.

The special revenue sharing programs

95

would provide assistance to State and local governments for six broad purposes, with discretion in the use of these funds to be left primarily to State and local governments. The following table shows the categories proposed and the first full year budget authority that would be provided for each one:

REVENUE SHARING PROPOSAL FOR FIRST FULL YEAR

Description	Billions
General revenue sharing	$5. 3
Special revenue sharing:	
Urban community development.	2. 3
Rural community development..	1. 1
Education	3. 2
Manpower training	2. 0
Law enforcement	0. 9
Transportation	2. 8
Total	17. 6

In total, these revenue sharing proposals would provide $17½ billion to State and local government in their first full year of operation. The magnitude of the fiscal crisis and the inefficiency and unresponsiveness of the present grant system make favorable action during this session of Congress an urgent need. We can ill-afford further delay.

REORGANIZATION OF THE EXECUTIVE BRANCH.—In my 1971 State of the Union message, I proposed reform of the executive branch by regrouping functions now scattered among seven cabinet departments and several independent agencies into four new departments organized around the major domestic purposes of government: Community development, natural resources, human resources, and economic affairs.

In my message on departmental reorganization, which I transmitted to the Congress on March 25, 1971, I described in detail the need for a comprehensive restructuring of the domestic executive departments to equip them to serve our Nation in the last third of this century. I cited the fragmentation of Federal responsibility for education matters, for manpower programs, for the development and conservation of water resources, for the management of public lands, and for assisting communities in meeting their needs for water and sewer services.

Typically, three or four separate departments or agencies are now engaged in administering overlapping or conflicting programs concerned with a single government objective. This dispersion and duplication of related functions has increased the costs of administration, generated interagency conflict and rivalry, weakened the departmental secretary as a leader in program development and execution, and imposed inexcusable inconvenience on the public being served. The excessive number of departments and agencies independently pursuing related goals has also frustrated able officials at all levels, impeded the decentralization of Federal operations, and made the coordination of administration in the field inordinately difficult.

By pulling together under each secretary the bulk of the programs which contribute to the achievement of a stated departmental mission, we can assure the prompt decisionmaking, the improvement of procedures, and the integration of Federal activities which we need for effective government.

Legislation and detailed plans for the reorganization have been transmitted to the Congress. I urge the early enactment of these basic proposals. They are vital elements of my strategy to narrow the gap between what the Federal Government promises and what it delivers.

FEDERAL ASSISTANCE REVIEW (FAR).—In 1969, I initiated the Federal Assistance Review program to streamline the Federal grant system. Primary emphasis was placed on improving the operation of Federal programs to strengthen the capacity of State and local governments. Achievements include:

—standardization of regional boundaries;

—simplification of Federal review procedures for grant applications;

—substantial delegation of authority to Federal field offices;

—a system for informing Governors and State legislatures of approval action on all Federal grants;

—a Project Notification and Review System, utilizing State and regional clearinghouses to facilitate State and local review of Federal grant applications at the formative stage;

—a pilot integrated grant administration program, enabling State and local governments to apply for several Federal assistance grants through a single application; further consolidation and joint funding authority is being sought under proposed legislation; and

—more participation by State and local officials in determining how Federal funds are used to respond to local needs.

FEDERAL REGIONAL COUNCILS.—As part of the FAR effort, Federal Regional Councils, consisting of the regional directors of the major human resources agencies, were established in each of the 10 regions. The Councils have now demonstrated considerable potential for increasing Federal responsiveness and coordination at the State and local level.

I shall shortly constitute the Councils formally as bodies within which regional directors of the major grant agencies develop common strategies and mechanisms for program delivery, review program plans jointly with Governors and mayors, and resolve regional interagency issues expeditiously.

TECHNICAL ASSISTANCE.—Since 1969, the Federal Government has offered broad-based organization and management assistance to State and local governments who have requested it. The assistance has taken the form of a review of the organizational structures and the major management processes of each requesting government. Improvements are then suggested. Subsequently, technical and other assistance is available to help the governments implement improvements they think are important. Even though resources are limited, I intend to encourage this form of technical assistance.

REFORMING THE BUDGET PROCESS.— The American people deserve, and our Government requires, a more orderly and more rational budget process.

The preparation of this budget, like those of other recent years, has been handicapped by the delays in enactment of appropriations for the fiscal year which began last July 1. *There is still one 1972 appropriation bill which has not been enacted* even as I write this, 12 months after I submitted the 1972 budget. Moreover, the uncertainties and hesitation caused by these delays in congressional action have hindered the orderly management of the Government.

There has been excessive attention to details and virtually no attention paid to overall totals or the effect of individual irresponsible acts of spending on the budget totals. Any procedural reform that encouraged the Congress to be aware of

97

the overall effect of their individual actions would have substantial benefits for us all.

There have been delays of many months in the enactment of regular appropriation bills, and there have also been periods in which temporary appropriations have been permitted to expire, leaving some agencies with no authority to continue operations.

Changes in the way the Congress conducts its business are its business. But, in the matter of the budget process, the results of the present methods have seriously affected how well I can administer and manage the executive branch.

THE LONGER VIEW

In 1976, our Nation will celebrate its 200th birthday. Three basic questions must be answered as we look toward a proper celebration of our bicentennial.

* How can we best achieve our great national goals?
* What role should the Federal Government have in this effort?
* How can we best rededicate ourselves to the ideal of personal freedom?

In considering these questions, we cannot ignore the hard fact that the increase in uncommitted resources between now and 1976 will be small in comparison with the magnitude of the tasks, forcing us to make difficult decisions about priorities.

My basic preferences in allocating our national resources are clear.

First, I believe that to avoid permanent inflation and waste we should assure that we count the costs before we make spending decisions. We can do that by adhering to the principle that spending must not exceed the level at which the budget would be balanced if the economy were at full employment.

Second, I believe that an increasing share of our national resources must be returned to private citizens and State and local governments to enable them—rather than the Federal Government—to meet individual and community needs.

RESPONSIBLE BUDGETING.—The first principle—the full employment budget principle—imposes a necessary discipline on Federal spending.

Last year, the budget margin projected for 1976—the potential Federal budget surplus, *assuming full employment and only the programs and tax structure in existence or proposed then (1971)*—was $30 billion. Actions taken in the last 12 months and those proposed in this budget will reduce that margin to only $5 billion. This margin is less than $25 for each man, woman, and child in the expected 1976 population, and is less than 1.6% of projected 1976 budget receipts. And yet, it must be sufficient to cover the 1976 costs of all new proposals not included in this budget.

The moral is clear. A strong fiscal discipline will be necessary in the years ahead if we are to preserve the buying power of the dollar. New spending programs must be evaluated against the most stringent of standards: *do they have enough merit to warrant increases in taxes or elimination of existing programs?*

This Administration has measured its proposals against this standard. I have made the hard choices necessary to assure that they can be financed within a full-employment budget policy.

I urge the Congress to engage in a similar self-discipline in making the hard choices that will be required during the next few years. This Administration will vigorously oppose irresponsible and short-sighted spending proposals that would commit large sums of Federal money to schemes that are politically attractive but would endanger an inflation-free prosperity.

CONCLUSION

There will be those who contend that in this budget their favorite programs are not financed, or are not financed as much as they want them to be.

They will be absolutely right.

Government expenses increase each year because special interest groups, representing only those who stand to benefit from their program, persuade decision-makers that more resources are needed for those programs without regard to the effect on the total budget. The cost is multiplied by geometric progression when this tactic is repeated for literally hundreds of programs. Seldom do any of these groups recommend additional taxes to finance their proposed spending.

Then inflationary factors, frequently induced by the large total volume of spending resulting from individual decisions made without consideration of the larger picture, force the cost of these programs upward. At the same time the special constituency benefiting from the program is enlarged and strengthened, its demands are correspondingly increased, and the cycle continues to feed upon itself.

Taken together, what is good for all the special interests is bad for the public interest. Our strength is in our ability to act as one nation, not as a conglomerate of warring and greedy factions.

For this reason my 1973 budget, large as it is, will not be large enough to satisfy many. However, I hope the American people will make their desire for less pervasive government known in unmistakable terms to their elected representatives. It is essential to preserve the private enterprise system, with its competitive spirit and its work ethic, which has done so much to inspire the independent and help the dependent and which has made this Nation the economic example to the rest of the world.

That system has enabled us to secure, for our people, a far higher standard of living than any experienced, or even envisioned, by the rest of the civilized world.

I do not wish it said of my Administration that we furthered or encouraged the process of discarding that heritage. So, I have emphasized fiscal responsibility and downward pressure on Federal expenditures, rather than simply accept all requests of all special groups and hope that the inevitable need for new taxes could be delayed as long as possible.

I am not averse to a day of reckoning, but when it comes, I want it to be said that this Administration foresaw the danger, held spending to amounts that could be paid from full-employment revenues, and took all steps possible to reduce the need for raising taxes so that the Federal Government plays a smaller, not a larger, role in the life of each of us. In this way, every citizen will have a larger share of the fruits of his labor to spend the way he or she freely chooses.

RICHARD NIXON

January 24, 1972.

NOTE: The message as sent to the Congress included illustrative diagrams which have not been reproduced in this volume.

The President signed the message in a ceremony in the Cabinet Room at the White House.

20   Statement Urging the Congress To Enact a Ceiling on Government Spending.   *January 24, 1972*

THE BUDGET I send to the Congress requires spending more than we will collect in taxes.

It will be a job-creating budget and a noninflationary budget only if spending is limited to the amount the tax system would produce if the economy were operating at full employment.

Those who increase spending beyond that amount will be responsible for causing more inflation.

It is vital that the Executive and the Congress act together to stop raids on the Treasury which would trigger another inflationary spiral.

In submitting this budget I am therefore urging the Congress, before it considers any appropriations bills, to enact a rigid ceiling on outlays that will prevent the Government spending more than the $246 billion requested in this budget. That ceiling on expenditures should apply equally to the Congress and to the executive branch.

We urgently need an absolute limit on Government spending. Only thus can we end inflation, stabilize the economy, and provide employment and real prosperity for all.

NOTE: On the same day, the White House released the transcript of a news briefing by George P. Shultz, Director, Office of Management and Budget, on the President's statement.

21   Address to the Nation Making Public a Plan for Peace in Vietnam.   *January 25, 1972*

Good evening:

I have asked for this television time tonight to make public a plan for peace that can end the war in Vietnam.

The offer that I shall now present, on behalf of the Government of the United States and the Government of South Vietnam, with the full knowledge and approval of President Thieu, is both generous and far-reaching.

It is a plan to end the war now; it includes an offer to withdraw all American forces within 6 months of an agreement; its acceptance would mean the speedy return of all the prisoners of war to their homes.

Three years ago when I took office, there were 550,000 Americans in Vietnam; the number killed in action was running as high as 300 a week; there were no plans to bring any Americans home, and the only thing that had been settled in Paris was the shape of the conference table.

I immediately moved to fulfill a pledge I had made to the American people: to bring about a peace that could last, not only for the United States, but for the long-suffering people of Southeast Asia.

There were two honorable paths open to us.

The path of negotiation was, and is, the path we prefer. But it takes two to negotiate; there had to be another way in case the other side refused to negotiate.

That path we called Vietnamization. What it meant was training and equipping the South Vietnamese to defend themselves, and steadily withdrawing Americans, as they developed the capability to do so.

The path of Vietnamization has been successful. Two weeks ago, you will recall, I announced that by May 1, American forces in Vietnam would be down to 69,000. That means almost one-half million Americans will have been brought home from Vietnam over the past 3 years. In terms of American lives, the losses of 300 a week have been reduced by over 95 percent—to less than 10 a week.

But the path of Vietnamization has been the long voyage home. It has strained the patience and tested the perseverance of the American people. What of the shortcut, the shortcut we prefer, the path of negotiation?

Progress here has been disappointing. The American people deserve an accounting of why it has been disappointing. Tonight I intend to give you that accounting, and in so doing, I am going to try to break the deadlock in the negotiations.

We have made a series of public proposals designed to bring an end to the conflict. But early in this Administration, after 10 months of no progress in the public Paris talks, I became convinced that it was necessary to explore the possibility of negotiating in private channels, to see whether it would be possible to end the public deadlock.

After consultation with Secretary of State Rogers, our Ambassador in Saigon, and our chief negotiator in Paris, and with the full knowledge and approval of President Thieu, I sent Dr. Kissinger to Paris as my personal representative on August 4, 1969, 30 months ago, to begin these secret peace negotiations.

Since that time, Dr. Kissinger has traveled to Paris 12 times on these secret missions. He has met seven times with Le Duc Tho, one of Hanoi's top political leaders, and Minister Xuan Thuy, head of the North Vietnamese delegation to the Paris talks, and he has met with Minister Xuan Thuy five times alone. I would like, incidentally, to take this opportunity to thank President Pompidou of France for his personal assistance in helping to make the arrangements for these secret talks.

This is why I initiated these private negotiations: Privately, both sides can be more flexible in offering new approaches and also private discussions allow both sides to talk frankly, to take positions free from the pressure of public debate.

In seeking peace in Vietnam, with so many lives at stake, I felt we could not afford to let any opportunity go by— private or public—to negotiate a settlement. As I have stated on a number of occasions, I was prepared and I remain prepared to explore any avenue, public or private, to speed negotiations to end the war.

For 30 months, whenever Secretary Rogers, Dr. Kissinger, or I were asked about secret negotiations we would only say we were pursuing every possible channel in our search for peace. There was never a leak, because we were determined not to jeopardize the secret negotiations. Until recently, this course showed signs of yielding some progress.

Now, however, it is my judgment that the purposes of peace will best be served by bringing out publicly the proposals we have been making in private.

Nothing is served by silence when the other side exploits our good faith to divide America and to avoid the conference table. Nothing is served by silence when it misleads some Americans into accusing their own government of failing to do what it has already done. Nothing is served by silence when it enables the other side to imply possible solutions publicly that it has already flatly rejected privately.

The time has come to lay the record of our secret negotiations on the table. Just as secret negotiations can sometimes break a public deadlock, public disclosure may help to break a secret deadlock.

Some Americans, who believed what the North Vietnamese led them to believe, have charged that the United States has not pursued negotiations intensively. As the record that I now will disclose will show, just the opposite is true.

Questions have been raised as to why we have not proposed a deadline for the withdrawal of all American forces in exchange for a cease-fire and the return of our prisoners of war; why we have not discussed the seven-point proposal made by the Vietcong last July in Paris; why we have not submitted a new plan of our own to move the negotiations off dead center.

As the private record will show, we have taken all these steps and more—and have been flatly rejected or ignored by the other side.

On May 31, 1971, 8 months ago, at one of the secret meetings in Paris, we offered specifically to agree to a deadline for the withdrawal of all American forces in exchange for the release of all prisoners of war and a cease-fire.

At the next private meeting, on June 26, the North Vietnamese rejected our offer. They privately proposed instead their own nine-point plan which insisted that we overthrow the Government of South Vietnam.

Five days later, on July 1, the enemy publicly presented a different package of proposals—the seven-point Vietcong plan.

That posed a dilemma: Which package should we respond to, the public plan or the secret plan?

On July 12, at another private meeting in Paris, Dr. Kissinger put that question to the North Vietnamese directly. They said we should deal with their nine-point secret plan, because it covered all of Indochina including Laos and Cambodia, while the Vietcong seven-point proposal was limited to Vietnam.

So that is what we did. But we went even beyond that, dealing with some of the points in the public plan that were not covered in the secret plan.

On August 16, at another private meeting, we went further. We offered the complete withdrawal of U.S. and allied forces within 9 months after an agreement on an overall settlement. On September 13, the North Vietnamese rejected that proposal. They continued to insist that we overthrow the South Vietnamese Government.

Now, what has been the result of these private efforts? For months, the North Vietnamese have been berating us at the public sessions for not responding to their side's publicly presented seven-point plan.

The truth is that we did respond to the enemy's plan, in the manner they wanted us to respond—secretly. In full possession of our complete response, the North Vietnamese publicly denounced us for not having responded at all. They induced many Americans in the press and the Congress into echoing their propaganda—Americans who could not know they were being falsely used by the enemy to stir up divisiveness in this country.

I decided in October that we should

make another attempt to break the deadlock. I consulted with President Thieu, who concurred fully in a new plan. On October 11, I sent a private communication to the North Vietnamese that contained new elements that could move negotiations forward. I urged a meeting on November 1 between Dr. Kissinger and Special Adviser Le Duc Tho, or some other appropriate official from Hanoi.

On October 25, the North Vietnamese agreed to meet and suggested November 20 as the time for a meeting. On November 17, just 3 days before the scheduled meeting, they said Le Duc Tho was ill. We offered to meet as soon as he recovered, either with him, or immediately with any other authorized leader who could come from Hanoi.

Two months have passed since they called off that meeting. The only reply to our plan has been an increase in troop infiltration from North Vietnam and Communist military offensives in Laos and Cambodia. Our proposal for peace was answered by a step-up in the war on their part.

That is where matters stand today.

We are being asked publicly to respond to proposals that we answered, and in some respects accepted, months ago in private.

We are being asked publicly to set a terminal date for our withdrawals when we already offered one in private.

And the most comprehensive peace plan of this conflict lies ignored in a secret channel, while the enemy tries again for military victory.

That is why I have instructed Ambassador Porter to present our plan publicly at this Thursday's session of the Paris peace talks, along with alternatives to make it even more flexible.

We are publishing the full details of our plan tonight. It will prove beyond doubt which side has made every effort to make these negotiations succeed. It will show unmistakably that Hanoi—not Washington or Saigon—has made the war go on.

Here is the essence of our peace plan; public disclosure may gain it the attention it deserves in Hanoi.

Within 6 months of an agreement:
—We shall withdraw all U.S. and allied forces from South Vietnam.
—We shall exchange all prisoners of war.
—There shall be a cease-fire throughout Indochina.
—There shall be a new presidential election in South Vietnam.

President Thieu will announce the elements of this election. These include international supervision and an independent body to organize and run the election, representing all political forces in South Vietnam, including the National Liberation Front.

Furthermore, President Thieu has informed me that within the framework of the agreement outlined above, he makes the following offer: He and Vice President Huong would be ready to resign one month before the new election. The Chairman of the Senate, as caretaker head of the Government, would assume administrative responsibilities in South Vietnam, but the election would be the sole responsibility of the independent election body I have just described.

There are several other proposals in our new peace plan; for example, as we offered privately on July 26 of last year, we remain prepared to undertake a major reconstruction program throughout Indochina, including North Vietnam, to help all these peoples recover from the ravages of a generation of war.

We will pursue any approach that will speed negotiations.

We are ready to negotiate the plan I have outlined tonight and conclude a comprehensive agreement on all military and political issues. Because some parts of this agreement could prove more difficult to negotiate than others, we would be willing to begin implementing certain military aspects while negotiations continue on the implementation of other issues, just as we suggested in our private proposal in October.

Or, as we proposed last May, we remain willing to settle only the military issues and leave the political issues to the Vietnamese alone. Under this approach, we would withdraw all U.S. and allied forces within 6 months in exchange for an Indochina cease-fire and the release of all prisoners.

The choice is up to the enemy.

This is a settlement offer which is fair to North Vietnam and fair to South Vietnam. It deserves the light of public scrutiny by these nations and by other nations throughout the world. And it deserves the united support of the American people.

We made the substance of this generous offer privately over 3 months ago. It has not been rejected, but it has been ignored. I reiterate that peace offer tonight. It can no longer be ignored.

The only thing this plan does not do is to join our enemy to overthrow our ally, which the United States of America will never do. If the enemy wants peace, it will have to recognize the important difference between settlement and surrender.

This has been a long and agonizing

struggle. But it is difficult to see how anyone, regardless of his past position on the war, could now say that we have not gone the extra mile in offering a settlement that is fair, fair to everybody concerned.

By the steadiness of our withdrawal of troops, America has proved its resolution to end our involvement in the war; by our readiness to act in the spirit of conciliation, America has proved its desire to be involved in the building of a permanent peace throughout Indochina.

We are ready to negotiate peace immediately.

If the enemy rejects our offer to negotiate, we shall continue our program of ending American involvement in the war by withdrawing our remaining forces as the South Vietnamese develop the capability to defend themselves.

If the enemy's answer to our peace offer is to step up their military attacks, I shall fully meet my responsibility as Commander in Chief of our Armed Forces to protect our remaining troops.

We do not prefer this course of action.

We want to end the war not only for America but for all the people of Indochina. The plan I have proposed tonight can accomplish that goal.

Some of our citizens have become accustomed to thinking that whatever our Government says must be false, and whatever our enemies say must be true, as far as this war is concerned. Well, the record I have revealed tonight proves the contrary. We can now demonstrate publicly what we have long been demonstrating privately—that America has taken the initiative not only to end our participation in this war, but to end the war itself for all concerned.

This has been the longest, the most

difficult war in American history.

Honest and patriotic Americans have disagreed as to whether we should have become involved at all 9 years ago; and there has been disagreement on the conduct of the war. The proposal I have made tonight is one on which we all can agree.

Let us unite now, unite in our search for peace—a peace that is fair to both sides—a peace that can last.

Thank you and good night.

NOTE: The President spoke at 8:30 p.m. in the Oval Office at the White House. The address was broadcast live on radio and television.

Before delivering the address, he met with the bipartisan leadership of the Congress.

The President spoke from a prepared text. An advance text of his address was released on the same day, as well as the text of the joint U.S.-South Vietnam peace proposal which read as follows:

1. There will be a total withdrawal from South Vietnam of all U.S. forces and other foreign forces allied with the Government of South Vietnam within 6 months of an agreement.

2. The release of all military men and innocent civilians captured throughout Indochina will be carried out in parallel with the troop withdrawals mentioned in point 1. Both sides will present a complete list of military men and innocent civilians held throughout Indochina on the day the agreement is signed. The release will begin on the same day as the troop withdrawals and will be completed when they are completed.

3. The following principles will govern the political future of South Vietnam:

The political future of South Vietnam will be left for the South Vietnamese people to decide for themselves, free from outside interference.

There will be a free and democratic Presidential election in South Vietnam within 6 months of an agreement. This election will be organized and run by an independent body representing all political forces in South Vietnam which will assume its responsibilities on the date of the agreement. This body will, among other responsibilities, determine the qualification of candidates. All political forces in South Vietnam can participate in the election and present candidates. There will be international supervision of this election.

One month before the Presidential election takes place, the incumbent President and Vice President of South Vietnam will resign. The Chairman of the Senate, as caretaker head of the Government, will assume administrative responsibilities except for those pertaining to the election, which will remain with the independent election body.

The United States, for its part, declares that it:

—will support no candidate and will remain completely neutral in the election,

—will abide by the outcome of this election and any other political processes shaped by the South Vietnamese people themselves,

—is prepared to define its military and economic assistance relationship with any government that exists in South Vietnam.

Both sides agree that:

—South Vietnam, together with the other countries of Indochina, should adopt a foreign policy consistent with the military provisions of the 1954 Geneva Accords.

—Reunification of Vietnam should be decided on the basis of discussions and agreements between North and South Vietnam without constraint and annexation from either party, and without foreign interference.

4. Both sides will respect the 1954 Geneva Agreements on Indochina and those of 1962 on Laos. There will be no foreign intervention in the Indochinese countries and the Indochinese peoples will be left to settle their own affairs by themselves.

5. The problems existing among the Indochinese countries will be settled by the Indochinese parties on the basis of mutual respect for independence, sovereignty, territorial integrity, and non-interference in each other's affairs. Among the problems that will be settled

is the implementation of the principle that all armed forces of the countries of Indochina must remain within their national frontiers.

6. There will be a general cease-fire throughout Indochina, to begin when the agreement is signed. As part of the cease-fire, there will be no further infiltration of outside forces into any of the countries of Indochina.

7. There will be international supervision of the military aspects of this agreement including the cease-fire and its provisions, the release of prisoners of war and innocent civilians, the withdrawal of outside forces from Indochina, and the implementation of the principle that all armed forces of the countries of Indochina must remain within their national frontiers.

8. There will be an international guarantee for the fundamental national rights of the Indochinese peoples, the status of all the countries in Indochina, and lasting peace in this region.

Both sides express their willingness to participate in an international conference for this and other appropriate purposes.

_____

On January 26, the White House released the transcript of a news briefing on the secret negotiations in Paris by Henry A. Kissinger, Assistant to the President for National Security Affairs. Dr. Kissinger's news briefing is printed in the Weekly Compilation of Presidential Documents (vol. 8, p. 126). On the same day, the White House also released the transcript of a news briefing on the President's plan for peace by Republican Congressional Leaders Senator Hugh Scott and Representative Gerald R. Ford following a meeting with the President.

22 Statement About the Death of Former Senator Carl Hayden. *January 26, 1972*

FOR 57 years, the energy and devotion of Carl Hayden strengthened and enriched the Congress of the United States. In the Congress—and in the country—he helped to keep alive the spirit and the character of the old West.

Senator Hayden told generations of newcomers to the Congress that it was better to be a workhorse than a showhorse—and he followed that adage in every aspect of his life. As a result, his influence for good reached into every corner of our national experience. Quietly, but firmly, he made his lasting imprint on our history.

Carl Hayden entered the Congress a year before I was born. The first man to represent Arizona in the House of Representatives, his name became synonymous with the development of that State. With his death, Arizona and the Nation have lost another great link with our pioneering past.

Carl Hayden became a legendary figure for his countrymen even before his active years were over. Today, the entire Nation mourns his passing. But we know that as long as the Nation lives his legend will live on.

NOTE: Senator Hayden, 94, died after a prolonged illness in Mesa, Ariz., on January 25, 1972.

He served in the House of Representatives from 1912 to 1927, and in the Senate from 1927 to 1969 when he retired. He was President pro tempore of the Senate from January 1957 until his retirement.

Deputy Attorney General Richard G. Kleindienst represented the President at the funeral services.

23   Remarks Announcing Changes in the Cabinet and the Executive Office of the President.   *January 27, 1972*

Ladies and gentlemen:

As you can see from the three men who surround me, this announcement is not a surprise. Having read many of your columns and dope stories I know that you have been speculating about the change that would be made in the office of the Secretary of Commerce.

Secretary Stans is leaving the Cabinet, and his resignation, of course, will be completed when his successor is approved. In his leaving the Cabinet, I, of course, have very deep regrets, because of all the people in our official family, Secretary Stans is one of my closest personal, as well as political, friends. He has served splendidly in the position of Secretary of Commerce. He has initiated a number of new programs which have been covered in the 15,000-word report that I presented to the Congress just a few days ago. And he, I know, in any position that he undertakes, can be expected to do a very, very competent job.

As you know, I have known him through the years of the Eisenhower Administration, and then in California when we worked together in an unsuccessful political campaign, and then finally in 1968 when he was helpful in our campaign to a very great degree, and then through 3 years in the Cabinet family.

Due to the fact that I do have this rule that I have announced that I will not discuss partisan matters until after the convention, I will not announce directly the position that he is going to undertake. I will simply say that the Secretary of Commerce, once his successor is approved, will become the chancellor of the exchequer of one of the two major parties.[1] I am sure he will be very successful in that operation as he has always been in handling fundraising activities in the past.

As a successor, we have Pete Peterson. One who is known so well to you, who leaves his present position, I am sure, with regret, but who will be able to carry on many of the ideas that he has worked on in the Council on International Economic Policy, to carry them on as Secretary of Commerce.

He is a young man, remarkably successful in business, one who has an understanding of world affairs, international affairs and also what makes the business community tick. I think—and Secretary Stans and I both agreed on this when we selected his successor—we believe we have here a man who can move into this position and will do a very outstanding job as the new Secretary of Commerce.

And then to replace him, we have another Pete, Pete Flanigan, who has been on the White House Staff and one of our closest associates going back over 15 years. He has a great deal of experience in private business in the international economic field.

I should say also that the position that he undertakes is undertaken with the total approval of the various Cabinet officers who will be working with him, the Secretary of the Treasury, the Secretary of State, the Secretary of Commerce, and others.

---

[1] On February 15, 1972, Maurice H. Stans became chairman of the Finance Committee to Re-Elect the President.

And in discussing this matter just recently with Secretary Connally, we felt that there couldn't be a better replacement for Mr. Peterson as Chairman of this extremely important Council at this time when so many international economic problems would be before us, than Peter Flanigan.

So with that, I will leave these three gentlemen to say whatever they like to the members of the press at this point and we will turn the meeting over first, of course, to Secretary Stans. And I express my thanks to him for his past service to this Government, in political campaigns, and for the future service which I know he will render to one of the two major parties.

NOTE: The President spoke at 11:25 a.m. in the Briefing Room at the White House. He spoke without referring to notes.

The remarks of Secretary Stans, Mr. Peterson, and Mr. Flanigan were as follows:

SECRETARY STANS. Mr. President, thank you very much. Thank you.

I don't think I will make a very long pitch here, because I don't see any potential large contributors in the room anywhere, at least not in money terms. [*Laughter*]

I think it is well known that I leave the Department of Commerce with some reluctance, because we had a great many things going on there that I think were very successful, and others which were about to come to fruition. But I really and sincerely feel in my personal dedication to President Nixon that I can serve my country best by working for his reelection so that he can carry out for another 4 years the programs that he has instituted in these 4 years.

From the time that he lost the election in 1960, I believe that Richard Nixon had the capability to be a great President. I worked for him in campaigns in 1962, 1966, 1968, and I am going to do it again in 1972 for the reason I have already described.

I am extremely pleased that Pete Peterson will be my successor. I have worked with him since he has been in the White House as head of the Council on International Economic

Policy. I have found him extremely able, affable, and a person who has a great many constructive ideas. I think that he will make a great Secretary of Commerce.

I want to say, too, that I am very proud of the organization that I leave to him in the Department of Commerce. The career people and the non-career people have done a great job of carrying out the President's policies, and my objectives, and I think we have a momentum and a respect for the Department that hasn't existed for a long time. I hope that is true and I hope that is your finding.

So of all the people that I know, I am particularly pleased that Pete Peterson is the one who has been chosen by the President.

I will say the same thing for Peter Flanigan. I worked with him even longer in some of the political campaigns before 1969, and since he has been in the White House since the beginning of 1969. We have had a great many difficult matters to cope with, and I have had nothing but great respect for his tremendous mental capabilities, his resourcefulness, and ingenuity in difficult issues.

So I leave the Cabinet, of course, as anyone does, with great reluctance, but for a purpose which I think is a very important one.

Next Tuesday I plan to hold a press conference at the Department of Commerce to deal with the individual issues and specifics of our programs as we leave them, and of course, will be delighted to see any of you there.

MR. PETERSON. I am obviously flattered by the President's generous offer to serve as the Secretary of Commerce. I am very inspired, Maury Stans, by your record.

I am also impressed with my successor. I think Peter will obviously out-perform his predecessor, and I am very much looking forward, Peter, to working with you, but as a member of the Council that you will be the Executive Director of.

We have started some important programs on the Council. I know Peter will do a fine job of carrying on.

The President has asked me if I wouldn't devote a good deal of my energy to the whole question of America's competitive position, its program for increasing its productivity, because however necessary it is that we get an improved monetary system, an improved trading system, ultimately how we fare in the seventies and eighties is going to depend upon how successfully we can compete and how productive we can become.

As impressed as I am by both my predecessor and my successor, I must say I am much less impressed with our ability to keep a secret, at least in this particular instance. Now I would like to introduce Peter Flanigan to you. Congratulations, Pete.

MR. FLANIGAN. Thank you, Pete.

I am apparently the "Chance" in this Tinker to Evers to Chance, or as I am following Pete Peterson, maybe I am the "repeat." [*Laughter*]

I am also told that Pete can't answer questions because he is subject to confirmation and because of protocol, I can't either, therefore. I am happy to say I don't have to be confirmed for this job, but nevertheless, those are the rules that Ron [Ziegler] laid down. [*Laughter*]

I look forward, of course, to working with Pete Peterson. We will miss the Secretary here in the business of government, but I know from experience how effective he is in the business of politics, and nothing could be more important than what he is doing there.

At this moment, this point in our national life when international economic competition has become a major force, both for the health of our economy at home and in our relations with countries abroad, I am honored and flattered that the President has asked me to carry on the outstanding work that Pete Peterson started as Director of the Council on International Economic Policy.

And the end of that effort, the entire purpose, is to be sure that we get fair treatment for American workers and American industry in international trade and in that way contribute to the President's quest for a peaceful and a prosperous world. Certainly the groundwork that has been laid at the Council and the successes to date are effective. I look forward to trying to match that record. Thank you very much.

24   Letter Accepting the Resignation of Maurice H. Stans as Secretary of Commerce. *January 27, 1972*

Dear Maury:

I have your letter of January 17 tendering your resignation as Secretary of Commerce, and I will, as you have requested, accept it effective on or about February 15, 1972. I do this with a sense of both great regret and profound gratitude—regret because you are leaving a post in which you have served with the utmost distinction and gratitude because you will be playing a key role in the forthcoming campaign.

Your three years of leadership at the Department of Commerce have been a source of the highest satisfaction to me, as you have given that vital arm of the national government a new spirit of purpose and urgency to match the needs of America and its free enterprise system. When I nominated you as Secretary of Commerce, I did so because I knew our country demanded the experience and direction which you were uniquely equipped to offer. This you have done in the fullest measure. Your superb work and unswerving dedication have contributed in large measure to the fact that the United States is now well on the road to a new era of prosperity, without the artificial stimulus of a war-time economy.

For many years you have been by my side, ever a loyal friend and wise counselor, and I am deeply pleased and honored that you will continue to be there.

As you leave public office, you can do so with the knowledge that you have served your President, your country, and your fellow citizens with the highest skill and devotion, just as you did for more than five years under President Eisenhower.

Every American who values the very best in government has reason to be thankful for your participation.

With my warmest personal regards to Kathleen and to you,

Sincerely,

RICHARD NIXON

[Honorable Maurice H. Stans, Secretary of Commerce, Washington, D.C. 20230]

NOTE: Mr. Stans' letter of resignation, dated January 17, 1972, and released with the President's letter, read as follows:

Dear Mr. President:

By this letter I tender to you my resignation as Secretary of Commerce, effective on or about February 15.

My three years in the Department of Commerce have been most gratifying. I believe that the organization and services of the Department have been significantly improved and that it is today far more responsive to public needs.

Because there are, as always, important and interesting items of unfinished business, I leave with some reluctance. However, I am resigning to assist in the campaign for your reelection, and I believe that in this way I can best serve the interests of the country in 1972.

I am grateful for the privilege of having been a member of the Cabinet under your inspiring and effective leadership.

Respectfully yours,

MAURICE H. STANS

[The President, The White House, Washington, D.C.]

25 Statement on Nominating Peter G. Peterson To Be Secretary of Commerce. *January* 27, 1972

I AM today nominating Peter G. Peterson to be Secretary of Commerce.

Mr. Peterson has, since February of 1971, served as my Assistant for International Economic Affairs as well as Executive Director of the Council on International Economic Policy. His chief responsibility to the President has been to review and analyze the world's changing economic conditions and to translate his findings into recommended international economic policies for the decade ahead.

Prior to Mr. Peterson's undertaking this important mission he was chief executive of Bell and Howell, where he was active in all aspects of the commercial sector, both foreign and domestic.

His experience in government and his previous industrial experience in the management of businesses that are both in technological and competitive fields equip him well for the broader responsibilities to which I am nominating him.

I have proposed formation of a new Department of Economic Affairs where all of the various economic activities of the executive branch can be brought together. One of Mr. Peterson's assignments will be to bring leadership to this reorganization effort. I know he shares my concern for the success of this undertaking.

Because the competition in today's world is so intense and so demanding of domestic economic dynamism, I am asking Mr. Peterson, as the new Secretary of Commerce, to focus major attention and energy on the ways in which America's competitiveness and productivity can be improved in the years ahead. Toward that goal, I am asking him to assume the chairmanship of the National Commission on Productivity.

Facing, as we are, a new competition in a new world, we can be satisfied with nothing less than a new prosperity—without inflation, without war, with high productivity and full employment. It will not be easy but, with a revitalization of America's competitive spirit, it can and will be done. I have every confidence that Mr.

Peterson will do much to help bring our Nation closer to these goals.

NOTE: On February 29, 1972, Mr. Peterson was sworn in as Secretary of Commerce in a ceremony at the White House.

26   Annual Message to the Congress: The Economic Report of the President. *January* 27, 1972

To the Congress of the United States:

The American economy is beginning to feel the effects of the new policies launched last August.

I undertook the New Economic Policy because it was becoming clear that not enough was being done to meet our ambitious goals for the American economy. The new measures are designed to bring the Nation to higher employment, greater price stability, and a stronger international position.

The essence of the New Economic Policy is not the specific list of measures we announced on August 15; it is the determination to do all that is necessary to achieve the Nation's goals.

Nineteen hundred and seventy-one was in many ways a good economic year. Total employment, total output, output per person, real hourly earnings, and real income after tax per person all reached new highs. The inflation which had plagued the country since 1965 began to subside. In the first 8 months of the year the rate of inflation was 30 percent less than in the same months of 1970.

But I did not believe this was enough to meet the Nation's needs. Although the rate of inflation had declined before August, it was still too high. Although unemployment stopped rising, it remained near 6 percent. In the first part of the year, our international balance-of-payments deficit—the excess of our payments

to the rest of the world over their payments to us—had risen far too high.

The conditions called for decisive actions. On August 15, I announced these actions.

First, I imposed a 90-day freeze on prices, wages, and rents.

Second, I suspended conversion of dollars into gold and other reserve assets.

Third, I imposed a temporary surcharge on imports generally at the rate of 10 percent.

Fourth, I proposed a number of tax changes intended to stimulate the economy, including repeal of the excise tax on automobiles, a tax credit for investment, and reduction of income taxes on individuals. At the same time I took steps to keep the budget under control.

The package of measures was unprecedented in scope and degree. My Administration had struggled for 2½ years in an effort to check the inflation we inherited by means more consistent with economic freedom than price-wage controls. But the inflationary momentum generated by the policy actions and inactions of 1965–68 was too stubborn to be eradicated by these means alone. Or at least it seemed that it could only be eradicated at the price of persistent high unemployment—and this was a price we would not ask the American people to pay.

Similarly, more than a decade of balance-of-payments deficits had built up an overhang of obligations and distrust which no longer left time for the gradual methods of correction which had been tried earlier.

The measures begun on August 15 will have effects continuing long into the future. They cannot be fully evaluated by what has happened in the little over 5 months since that date. Still the results up to this point have been extremely encouraging.

The freeze slowed down the rate of inflation dramatically. In the 3 months of its duration the index of consumer prices rose only 0.4 percent, compared to 1.0 percent in the previous 3 months. The freeze was a great testimonial to the public spirit of the American people, because that result could have been achieved with the small enforcement staff we had only if the people had been cooperating voluntarily.

The freeze was followed by a comprehensive, mandatory system of controls, with more flexible and equitable standards than were possible during the first 90 days. General principles and specific regulations have been formulated, staffs have been assembled and cases are being decided. This effort is under the direction of citizens on the Price Commission and Pay Board, with advice from other citizens on special panels concerned with health services, State and local government, and rent. These citizens are doing a difficult job, doing it well, and the Nation is in their debt.

While this inflation-control system was being put in place, vigorous action was going forward on the international front. The suspension of the convertibility of the dollar was a shock felt around the world. The surcharge emphasized the need to act swiftly and decisively to improve our position. Happily, the process of adjustment

began promptly, without disrupting the flow of international business. Other currencies rose in cost relative to the U.S. dollar. As a result, the cost of foreign goods increased relative to the cost of U.S. goods, improving the competitive position of American workers and industries. International negotiations were begun to stabilize exchange rates at levels that would help in correcting the worldwide disequilibrium, of which the U.S. balance-of-payments deficit was the most obvious symptom. These negotiations led to significant agreements on a number of points:

1. Realignment of exchange rates, with other currencies rising in cost relative to the dollar, as part of which we agreed to recommend to Congress that the price of gold in dollars be raised when progress had been made in trade liberalization.

2. Commitment to discussion of more general reform of the international monetary system.

3. Widening of the permitted range of variation of exchange rates, pending other measures of reform.

4. Commitment to begin discussions to reduce trade barriers, including some most harmful to the United States.

5. Assumption of a larger share of the costs of common defense by some of our allies.

6. Elimination of the temporary U.S. surcharge on imports.

The third part of the August 15 action was the stimulative tax program. Enactment of this package by Congress, although not entirely in the form I had proposed, put in place the final part of my New Economic Policy.

In part as a result of this program, economic activity rose more rapidly in the latter part of the year. In the fourth quarter real output increased at the annual rate of 6 percent, compared with about 3 percent in the 2 previous quarters. Employment rose by about 1.1 million from July to December, and only an extraordinarily large rise of the civilian labor force—1.3 million—kept unemployment from falling.

Nineteen hundred and seventy-two begins on a note of much greater confidence than prevailed 6 or 12 months ago. Output is rising at a rate which will boost employment rapidly and eat into unemployment. There is every reason to expect this rate of increase to continue. The Federal Government has contributed impetus to this advance by tax reductions and expenditure increases. The Federal Reserve has taken steps to create the monetary conditions necessary for rapid economic expansion.

The operation of the new control system in an economy without inflationary pressure of demand holds out great promise of sharply reducing the inflation rate. We are converting the fear of perpetual inflation into a growing hope for price stability. We are lifting from the people the frustrating anxiety about what their savings and their income will be worth a year from now or 5 years from now.

For the first time in over a decade the United States is moving decisively to restore strength to its international economic position.

The outlook is bright, but much remains to be done. The great problem is to get the unemployment rate down from the 6-percent level where it was in 1971. It was reduced from that level in the sixties by a war buildup; it must be reduced from that level in the seventies by the creation of peacetime jobs.

It is obvious that the unemployment problem has been intensified by the reduction of over 2 million defense-related jobs and by the need to squeeze down inflation. But 6 percent unemployment is too much, and I am determined to reduce that number significantly in 1972.

To that end I proposed the tax reduction package of 1971. Federal expenditures will rise by $25.2 billion between last fiscal year and fiscal 1972. Together these tax reductions and expenditure increases will leave a budget deficit of $38.8 billion this year. If we were at full employment in the present fiscal year, expenditures would exceed receipts by $8.1 billion. This is strong medicine, and I do not propose to continue its use, but we have taken it in order to give a powerful stimulus to employment.

We have imposed price and wage controls to assure that the expansion of demand does not run to waste in more inflation but generates real output and real employment.

We have suspended dollar convertibility and reduced the international cost of the dollar which will help restore the competitive position of U.S. workers and thereby generate jobs for them.

We have instituted a public service employment program to provide jobs directly for people who find it especially hard to get work.

We have expanded the number of people on federally assisted manpower programs to record levels.

We have established computerized Job Banks to help match up jobseekers and job vacancies.

We have proposed welfare reform to increase incentives to employment.

We have proposed special revenue sharing for manpower programs, to make them more effective.

We have proposed revision of the minimum wage system to remove obstacles to the employment of young and inexperienced workers.

We expect that these measures, and others, will contribute to a substantial reduction of unemployment.

In addition to getting unemployment down, a second major economic task before us is to develop and apply the price-wage control system, which is still in its formative stage, to the point where its objective is achieved. The objective of the controls is a state of affairs in which reasonable price stability can be maintained without controls. That state of affairs can and will be reached. How long it will take, no one can say. We will persevere until the goal is reached, but we will not keep the controls one day longer than necessary.

The success of the stabilization program depends fundamentally upon the cooperation of the American people. This means not only compliance with the regulations. It means also mutual understanding of the difficulties that all of us—working people, businessmen, consumers, farmers, Government officials—encounter in this new and complicated program. Our experience in the past few months convinces me that we shall have this necessary ingredient for success.

We embarked last year on another great task—to create an international economic system in which we and others can reap the benefits of the exchange of goods and services without danger to our domestic economies. Despite all the troubles in this field in recent years both the American people and our trading partners are enjoying on a larger scale than ever before what is the object of the whole international economic exercise—consumption of

foreign goods that are better or cheaper or more interesting than domestic goods, as well as foreign travel and profitable investment abroad.

We don't want to reduce these benefits. We want to expand them. To do that, we in the United States must be able to pay in the way that is best—chiefly by selling abroad those things that we produce best or more cheaply, including the products of our agriculture and our other high-technology industries. This is our objective in the international discussions launched by our acts of last year and continuing this year.

These tasks, in which Government takes the lead, are superimposed on the fundamental task of the American economy, upon which the welfare of the people most depends and which is basically performed by the people and not by the Government. That fundamental task is the efficient and innovative production of the goods and services that the American people want. That is why I have emphasized the need for greater productivity and a resurgence of the competitive spirit.

The outstanding performance of the American economy in this respect provides a background of strength which permits the Government to face its economic problems with confidence and to bring about a new prosperity without inflation and without war.

RICHARD NIXON

January 27, 1972.

NOTE: The President's message, together with the Annual Report of the Council of Economic Advisers, is printed in the "Economic Report of the President, Transmitted to the Congress January 1972" (Government Printing Office, 1972, 304 pp.).

The President signed the Economic Report in a ceremony in the Cabinet Room at the White House.

27   Statement on the Death of Mahalia Jackson. *January* 27, 1972

AMERICA and the world, black people and all people, today mourn the passing of Mahalia Jackson. She was a noble woman, an artist without peer, a magnetic ambassador of goodwill for the United States in other lands, an exemplary servant of her God. All her years she poured out her soul in song and her heart in service to her people. Millions of ears will miss the sound of that great rich voice "making a joyful noise unto the Lord," as she liked to call her work—yet her life story itself sings the Gospel message of freedom, and will not cease to do so.

NOTE: Mahalia Jackson, 60, died after a prolonged illness at the Little Company of Mary Hospital in Evergreen Park outside of Chicago, Ill.

Sammy Davis, Jr., represented the President at the funeral in Chicago on February 1, 1972

28   Statement on Establishing the Office for Drug Abuse Law Enforcement.   *January* 28, 1972

DRUG abuse—as I said 7 months ago— is America's "public enemy number one." It is an all-pervasive and yet an elusive enemy. I am convinced that the only effective way to fight this menace is by attacking it on many fronts—through a balanced, comprehensive strategy.

For the past 3 years, this Administration has been working to carry out such a strategy. We have moved to eliminate dangerous drugs at their source, to cut their international flow, to stop them from entering our country, and to intercept them after they do. We have been educating our people to understand the drug problem more completely. We have expanded significantly our efforts to prevent drug addiction and to treat and rehabilitate those who have become drug-dependent.

A NEW INITIATIVE

Today our balanced, comprehensive attack on drug abuse moves forward in yet another critical area as we institute a major new program to drive drug traffickers and drug pushers off the streets of America.

I have signed today an Executive order [11641] establishing a new Office for Drug Abuse Law Enforcement in the Department of Justice. This Office will marshal a wide range of government resources— including new authorities granted in the Organized Crime Control Act of 1970— in a concentrated assault on the street-level heroin pusher. Working through nine regional offices, our new program will use special grand juries to gather extensive new information concerning drug traffickers and will pool this intelligence for use by Federal, State, and local law enforcement agencies. It will draw on the Department of Justice and the Department of the Treasury to assist State and local agencies in detecting, arresting, and prosecuting heroin traffickers.

I am pleased to announce that the new Office for Drug Abuse Law Enforcement will be headed by Myles J. Ambrose, who has been serving as our Commissioner of

Customs. Mr. Ambrose will also serve as my own Special Consultant for Drug Abuse Law Enforcement, advising me on all matters relating to this important subject.

PROGRAMS ALREADY IN OPERATION

This effort to meet the drug menace directly on the streets of America—an effort which I promised in my message on the State of the Union—complements our other drug-related initiatives.

—*The Special Action Office for Drug Abuse Prevention,* established on an interim basis last June and headed by Dr. Jerome Jaffe, is already beginning to have an impact in the fields of drug abuse education, treatment, rehabilitation, and prevention. The Office is working to coordinate programs which are spread through nine Federal agencies and to develop a national strategy to guide these efforts. Drawing on private and public expertise, the Special Action Office has spurred new research, gathered valuable information, planned for a new drug training and education center, and helped in setting up a major program to identify and treat drug abuse in the armed services.

The Special Action Office—which has already done so much—can do much more if the Congress will promptly give it the authority and the funds I have requested for it.

—*The Cabinet Committee on International Narcotics Control,* established last September and chaired by Secretary Rogers, is taking the lead in our efforts to fight the international drug traffic and to eliminate drugs at their source. We have appointed Narcotics Control Coordinators in all affected American embassies around the world and have been working closely with other governments to strengthen drug control efforts. We were especially gratified when Turkey announced last summer a total ban on the growing of the opium poppy.

—Drug dependence in the Armed Forces and among veterans is being reduced considerably by *expanded drug treatment and rehabilitation programs in the Department of Defense and in the Veterans Administration.* Drug identification and detoxification programs, which began in Vietnam, have been expanded to include all military personnel in the United States who are being discharged, sent abroad, or are returning from overseas duty. In the year ahead the Veterans Administration will offer treatment and rehabilitative service to an estimated 20,000 addicts. It will expand its drug dependence units by as many as 12, creating a total of up to 44 such units.

—We have also been moving ahead with a range of other activities. The Comprehensive Drug Abuse Prevention and Control Act of 1970—which I proposed in July of 1969—was passed by the Congress and signed into law in October of 1970. The model State narcotics legislation which I also recommended has been adopted by 26 States and is being considered in 15 others.

Tens of thousands of teachers, students, and community leaders have been trained under our National Drug Education Training Program. A new National Clearinghouse for Drug Abuse Information has been established. Some 25 million pieces of drug education information have been distributed by the Federal Government. We have established a Federal Drug Abuse Prevention Coordinating Committee at the interagency level and a number of White House conferences on drug abuse have been conducted.

In addition, the Federal Government is carrying out a number of major research programs to help us better to identify and analyze drugs and more fully to understand how they are moved about the country and around the world. I have also recommended the creation of a United Nations Fund for Drug Control—to which we have already contributed $1 million and pledged $1 million more—and have recommended several steps to strengthen international narcotics agreements.

In the enforcement field, the number of authorized new positions in the Bureau of Narcotics and Dangerous Drugs and in the Bureau of Customs has jumped by more than 2,000 in the past year alone. We are expanding our program to train State prosecutors to handle cases under the newly enacted Uniform Controlled Dangerous Substances Act. We are stepping up the work of the Joint State-Federal Narcotics Task Force in New York City.

It is estimated that the amount of heroin which will be seized in the current fiscal year will be more than four times what was seized in fiscal year 1969. Since that time, the number of drug-related arrests has nearly doubled.

Overall Expenditures

Perhaps the most dramatic evidence of our stepped-up campaign against drug abuse lies in the budget figures for various aspects of our effort. In the last 3 years, for example, Federal obligations for drug treatment and rehabilitation have increased *nearly sevenfold*, from $28 million to $189.6 million, and we have proposed

a further increase of $40.6 million for next year. Obligations for research, education, training, and prevention activities have also grown *nearly sevenfold*, from $17.5 million in fiscal year 1969 to $120.5 million this year, and our new budget calls for a further increase of $14.5 million.

This means that we will be obligating more than eight times as much for treatment, rehabilitation, research, education, training, and prevention in the coming fiscal year as we were when this Administration took office.

As far as law enforcement obligations relating to drug abuse are concerned, the level has increased more than eightfold in our first 3 years in office—from $20.2 million to $164.4 million. We plan to increase this figure by another $64.6 million next year to the $229 million level.

A Balanced and Comprehensive Program

The central concept behind all of these programs is that our overall approach to the drug menace must be balanced and comprehensive—fighting those who traffic in drugs, helping those who have been victimized by drugs, and protecting those who have not yet been threatened. The new initiative I have launched today in the area of law enforcement is aimed against those who would profit from the misery of others. It will confront the street-level heroin pusher with a dedicated group of lawyers and investigators intent upon exposing and eliminating retail sales of heroin. At the same time, however, we must be sure that we have sufficient treatment facilities to handle any increase in the number of addicts seeking treatment because of the disruption of heroin trafficking. The Special

117

Action Office for Drug Abuse Prevention, which helped in the development of this new law enforcement program, has assured me that we will be able to meet an increased demand in the treatment field if the Congress passes its new legislation.

Drug abuse, as I said in my message on the State of the Union, saps our Nation's strength and destroys our Nation's character. The Federal Government cannot meet this menace alone—but it can take a strong leadership position. I believe we have developed a Federal program for combating drug abuse which is both firm and compassionate. With the cooperation of the Congress, the State and local governments, and the American people, that program will continue to grow in effectiveness.

NOTE: On the same day, the White House released a fact sheet and the transcript of a news briefing on the new drug abuse law enforcement program. Participants in the news briefing were John N. Mitchell, Attorney General, and Myles J. Ambrose, Special Assistant Attorney General, Office for Drug Abuse Law Enforcement, Department of Justice.

29   Remarks on Presenting the Presidential Medal of Freedom to DeWitt and Lila Acheson Wallace.   *January* 28, 1972

Mr. and Mrs. Wallace and ladies and gentlemen:

This is a birthday party, as you all know, for the Reader's Digest, which is 50 years old. We have tried to pay a tribute to the Digest and to the founders of the Digest a little earlier in the State Dining Room, but since we have some special guests who were not able to join us there, but who we understand were able to be with us at another room that was available and also some special guests from the press, I think that all of us in this room would like to pay tribute to our honored guests.

I do not want to repeat here what I said in the Dining Room. And I have been trying to think of something that would perhaps express the feelings of everybody here who knows the Wallaces on this special day.

I think of the Digest, the years that I have read it and all the special articles, "How to Increase Your Word Power," "Life in These United States," but I think of all the special articles that I remember, the features, the one that perhaps made the most indelible impression was the series, "The Most Unforgettable Character I Ever Met."

Tonight we could speak of Lila and DeWitt Wallace in terms of by far the biggest circulation of any publication in the world. We could speak of them as having created a publication that is now read by over 100 million people in the world. We could speak of them also as people who have created a publication which has perhaps, in the deepest sense, done more good in creating a feeling of idealism in this country and among people abroad, understanding of this country, than any publication we have ever had.

All of those things have been said and can be said by anyone. But I think for us, and everybody in this room is in that category tonight, who consider ourselves to be the Wallaces' special friends, I think we would say that in that 50 years of that wonderful series, "The Most Unforgettable Character I Ever Met," the Digest made two great mistakes. The Digest never had Lila Wallace in it or DeWitt Wallace, and they both should have been in it.

Now Hobart Lewis [1] is the only one who could rectify that mistake, but Wally wouldn't let him do it if he tried.

So, tonight in the White House, in this room, in this company, before those who are friends of the Wallaces, friends of the Digest, contributors to it, readers of it, I, speaking for all of the United States and for readers of the Digest around the world, would like to rectify that error, one of the few the Digest has made. And if Mrs. Nixon would escort our two honored guests here, I will rectify it properly tonight.

The highest honor that can be given to a civilian in this country is the Medal of Freedom and it is one of those few discretionary powers that the United States President has in terms of honors, to determine who receives the Medal of Freedom. I have not often exercised that power and I think I, in this instance, have made a selection that millions of Americans and millions around the world will applaud.

Tonight, I first want to present a Medal of Freedom to DeWitt Wallace. The citation reads as follows:

"To DeWitt Wallace: The co-founder with Lila Acheson Wallace of The Reader's Digest and partner in its direction for half a century, he has made a towering contribution to that freedom of the mind from which spring all our other liberties. This magazine has become a monthly university in print, teaching 100 million readers worldwide the wonder of common

___
[1] President and editor-in-chief of the Reader's Digest.

life and the scope of man's potential. In DeWitt Wallace, America has a son to be deeply proud of—one whose lifework shows American enterprise at its creative best, and the American ethic in its fullest flower."

I used the word partner deliberately in that citation, because of all the great business enterprises and publishing enterprises in this country, none has been a partnership from the beginning and throughout its existence more than the Reader's Digest. It began that way, it remains that way, and this wonderful partnership in their home, that some of us have had the privilege of visiting, and in this publication, is an example for all Americans and people around the world.

So the second citation reads:

"To Lila Acheson Wallace: Co-founder with DeWitt Wallace of The Reader's Digest half a century ago and partner with him in its direction ever since, Lila Wallace has helped make all America better read. Her vision and drive have given wings to the workhorse printed word, fashioning a Pegasus of a magazine that carries American insights to 100 million readers worldwide. Her gracious touch at Pleasantville has shown the way to infusing industrial settings with culture and the joy of work."

NOTE: The President spoke at 10:48 p.m. in the East Room at the White House. He spoke without referring to notes.

On the same day, the White House released a fact sheet on the Presidential Medal of Freedom.

Following the President's remarks, Mr. Wallace responded as follows:

I am absolutely flabbergasted. I am sure Lila is, too. We rather suspected some shenanigans might be going on, but I thought at most it might be a carving set or something of that sort.

I can't for the life of me understand why there is such a shindig, such a glorious shindig, because a magazine is still in its infancy. I am sure it is going to have a long life, and normally we don't have these pow-wows for an infant that is still in its swaddling clothes.

Actually, I think the infant is so precocious that I am hopeful it will even skip entirely the trying period of adolescence.

By the way, I do not understand why the President and Secretary Connally do not provide a round-trip 3-month ticket around the world for all these youngsters who are having this poor, sufferingness period of adolescence.

But we—Lila and I—will certainly remember this occasion as long as we live, and hopefully, far longer. I say that and I hope that Billy Graham and Norman Peale noted that.

I thank you, thank you, thank you.

30 Remarks on Intention To Nominate Marina von Neumann Whitman To Be a Member of the Council of Economic Advisers. *January* 29, 1972

MRS. WHITMAN must be confirmed by the Senate, so she will not be able to say anything on her own behalf today, but we are delighted that she has accepted the appointment of the nomination to the Council of Economic Advisers. And as our chitchat here indicates, while I am sure most stories, as I know from the inspired lead which appeared in the papers this morning indicated, this is very important, because this is the first time a woman has ever been a member of the Council. So be it. That is important.

But what is more important, I think, is that of those who were considered for this post, that Herb Stein had Mrs. Whitman first on his list and this is an indication of our concern. I think it is the feeling of this Administration and I think of most people in the Government, Democrats and Republicans, when we look for quality, particularly where brains are concerned, and achievement, that we are not concerned about color, we are not concerned about race, we are not concerned about religion, we are not concerned about sex, we are concerned about quality.

And you don't have to feel—I always say this about people—[*laughter*]. But, in any event, in this field, we have now added to the Council an experienced, despite her young years, and also an intellectual ability of the first magnitude, and that is what Mr. Stein wants and Ezra Solomon wants. You are outnumbered. It is two to one.

MRS. WHITMAN. That is right.

THE PRESIDENT. But not in terms of brains. So, we are very pleased. You can say a word. Your main problem I think was bringing your children downtown this morning.

MRS. WHITMAN. I guess the family logistics were a little complicated, but that seems to have been straightened out with great success.

Thank you. I guess I can say how very, very pleased I am to be here and how pleased and honored and excited I am to be coming and to be given a chance to tackle some of the most exciting and important and difficult, challenging problems that are in this country today.

One of the things about being an economist is that unlike doctors and lawyers and so forth, we very seldom get a chance to practice our profession as well as to teach. So, it is a very unique, really, opportunity to be given this chance to practice, I hope, in the highest sense, my profession.

Also, I was on the Council's staff last year and I left Friday, August 13, which was, for many, many reasons, a bad time to leave. [*Laughter*] In fact, may I tell you a little story about that?

THE PRESIDENT. Sure.

MRS. WHITMAN. When I was just packing up, I left the Council and had a call from a member of the Council staff on Sunday the 15th, saying, "Be sure and watch your television set tonight, because the President is really going to drop a bomb." My 8-year-old daughter said, "He is? Where?" I just wish all bombs could be as productive as that particular one.

In any case, I really feel I am coming home to work again with Herb and Ezra Solomon and I am very grateful to you, Mr. President, for inviting me back.

THE PRESIDENT. Well, we are happy to have you and I think this is, first, a very important assignment as the Council's work this year, which must be not only a very good year, but also it is a period in which we feel that it is very important to get on the Council a variety of experience,

a broad base of experience and that we are accomplishing.

MR. STEIN. Marina will work in two of the most vital areas for this year. She will do our international economics and with the experience she has, she will conduct our relations mainly with the price-wage control system, on which she is now an expert, since she has been a member of the Price Commission for 3 months and that is more experience than anybody else has. So, she has a lot to do and we are counting very heavily on her.

THE PRESIDENT. Thank you very much.

NOTE: The President spoke at 10:14 a.m. in the Oval Office at the White House. He spoke without referring to notes.

A White House announcement containing biographical information on Mrs. Whitman was released on the same day and is printed in the Weekly Compilation of Presidential Documents (vol. 8, p. 150). The White House also released the transcript of a news conference by Herbert Stein, Chairman, Council of Economic Advisers, Mrs. Whitman, and Barbara H. Franklin, Staff Assistant to the President for Executive Manpower, on the nomination.

On March 13, 1972, Mrs. Whitman was sworn in as a member of the Council in a ceremony at the White House.

---

31 Remarks at a Dinner Honoring Robert J. Brown, Special Assistant to the President. *January 30, 1972*

Mr. Mason, and all of the distinguished guests at the head table:

There are as many at the head table as there are in the audience, believe me— look at that.

I know this is an interruption of this beautiful dinner tonight. Although I had another engagement for which I was already dressed when I got the call from Don Rumsfeld and Maurice Stans that

they were honoring Bob Brown, I said, "I will come over." And I am glad to be here.

Everybody in this audience rightly figures that whenever the President of the United States makes a speech, he probably had it all figured out in advance. I can tell you that tonight this is off the cuff; it is from the heart. And I want to say a few things about Bob Brown, about those who honor him here, and about this audience.

First, I asked Sammy [Davis] to come over for a reason. He has probably forgotten this, but I will always remember it. Seventeen years ago, on one of the few evenings when I was Vice President when we had a little time off in New York, we went over to the Copacabana Restaurant. He was performing then. He was a young star. And he performed, I remember, with his father and his uncle.

Afterwards, I went backstage and I met the three of them—this wonderful family. And I said to them, "This has to be the very best that possibly could be done in the field of entertainment."

And Sammy said, "Well, you're probably right." [*Laughter*]

No, he didn't say that, because he is a man who knows how good he is, but he also is a very humble man. But he appreciated the fact that I came back with my wife, and believe me, I appreciated the fact that he was a great star, a star then and a star now.

I thought back on that time, and I thought also of the present time, and this brings me to Bob Brown.

In the field of music, in the field of art, in the field of athletics, we all know that as far as ability is concerned, it is recognized; it knows no color, it knows no religion. If a man or a woman has it, he or she goes to the top, and that is the way it ought to be.

And what Bob Brown stands for in this White House of ours is this: Bob Brown is a rather quiet kind of a man, but he is the most tenacious fellow I ever knew, believe me. But the point that he makes over and over again in my office is this: that not just in the field of music, or in the field of art or the field of athletics where

we have learned that any kind of a difference with regard to color denies us the ability that can see us the perfection, the very best, he says, "You know, we have got to be sure that in every field of life in America, when a man or woman has got it, he or she has got to be able to go to the top." That is what he stands for.

Now I said that I was going to speak directly to you and from the heart. That isn't true in America today, not completely. It perhaps will never be true, because we will never be perfect. But it is better than it was, and it is going to be better, and we have got to make it better, because what we have to do is to provide the opportunities in this country that every individual, if he wants to go to the top in Government, he can go to the top.

Let me tell you something. Why does Ed Brooke win overwhelmingly for Attorney General and for Senator in the State of Massachusetts? Not because he has got the black vote, but because he is the best there is in that State. That is why he goes to the top.

So in the field of government, so it must be in the field of business. I know that there are many in this audience that rather wonder whether our whole program of minority business enterprise means anything. It looks like sort of tokenism and symbolism. But it is a beginning, and we have to have a situation in which people can go to the top, because if one group of people are forever going to be confined to doing tasks that are not those that are administrative or executive, that is not right. We have got to be sure that if an individual really has it, he has the chance to go to the top.

And that is one of the things Bob Brown

has fought for, that he has talked for, and that we are trying to work for. We haven't done as well as we would like to do, but we want your help, the help of everybody in this audience, black or white, to see that we reach that great goal, that everybody can go to the top in America.

And now, just a personal word about Bob Brown, if I may. We have something in common. I was delighted to meet his grandmother tonight. She really looks like his mother, believe me, or his sister, for that matter. But whatever the case might be, we both were educated in North Carolina. I spent 3 years there and Bob spent most of his life there. So when we first met, just a few years ago, we reminisced about that State and about the things we had learned together. And I was delighted that he would come to us at the White House and work in this cause, work quietly, but very, very effectively for the ideals that he believed in and that I believed in.

And I simply want to say that I don't think of any better tribute to Bob than what you have done tonight. When I checked a little before this meeting, I said, "What are they doing, are they just giving this for Bob Brown, a testimonial for him?" I said, "Who is going to get the money?" And I asked Mr. Mason, "Is this house paid?" And he said, "Yes." And that of course is good, too.

Paid for what? And then I thought what a wonderful tribute to a man. Not for himself—he isn't going to get anything out of this except a picture, which I hope they print in the paper, incidentally.

But when I think of the cause of sickle cell anemia, when I think of the cause of foster children, when I think of the cause

of the Mississippi project, I realize that all of the 2,000 people in this room say, "This is a nice dinner." It was nice because Bob Brown and Sally, his wife, are honored, and his wonderful grandmother, and Sammy Davis, with his magnificent entertainment, along with the other stars who are here.

But also it was a nice dinner and an event we will never forget, because of what you have contributed, by what you have paid to come to this dinner. You will help particularly young people, young people that might otherwise never have had a chance, young people that didn't have enough nutrition, young people that didn't have enough guidance, young people that might have gotten off on the wrong track, and you have helped them by what you did tonight.

Let me say, speaking now, and I trust that I speak for all of you, whatever our backgrounds, whether we come from poor families, as I did, as did Bob, or wealthy families, whether we are black or white, whatever our religion, let us be thankful tonight that when it comes to the young of America, whatever they are, when we can all go forward together in helping those young people have a chance to go to the top if they have got it, it is a wonderful cause and I am glad to be here with you.

Thank you.

NOTE: The President spoke at approximately 8:45 p.m. in the Main Ballroom of the Washington Hilton Hotel. He spoke without referring to notes.

Willie C. Mason was chairman of the dinner.

In addition to honoring Mr. Brown, the dinner was a benefit for the Sickle Cell Anemia Fund, the Social Services Administration for Foster Children of D.C., the Howard University Mississippi Project, and the United Negro College Fund.

32   Remarks at the National Prayer Breakfast.
February 1, 1972

Congressman Quie, and all of our distinguished guests:

Perhaps at no time or no place in America could we find a gathering which more symbolized the strength of America than this meeting this morning.

Perhaps it says it best in the Pledge of Allegiance to the Flag, as amended, ". . . one Nation under God, indivisible, with liberty and justice for all."

Look across this room, look at this head table, remember those who have spoken and you will see those words all represented right here in this meeting this morning—one Nation under God. There are different parties here, there are different faiths, there are different races and different colors, there are different philosophies, but it is still one Nation, and it is under God, with liberty and justice for all.

Then as we hear those words, we realize that words can mean nothing unless our thoughts go with them. "Words without thoughts never to heaven go."

So, we think of our thoughts, and we realize that, as Mayor Washington[1] has so eloquently indicated, we have made great progress, but we have a long way to go. "Liberty and justice for all" is a magnificent ideal. America has come further perhaps than most of the nations of the world. We would like to say perhaps we have come further than any other nation. But we also need humility in order to understand how much further we have to go.

But what is very important about this

gathering is that we would not be here unless we all recognized in our hearts that we were not perfect, that we were seeking to do the very best that we can in our brief stay on this earth to achieve goals that are bigger than all of us, bigger than our differences, differences between parties and faiths and philosophies, all the rest of which we are aware in this great cosmopolitan country of ours.

And now that brings us to the moment that we have now very great responsibility for.

I spoke at this breakfast 3 years ago and 2 years ago and now this year. Each year then, you remember, I spoke of peace, peace at home and peace in the world. The year 1972 is the year of opportunity for peace such as America has never had in its whole history. I say "never had." There might have been a time when America could have exerted its power for peace in a very aggressive way.

One of our very distinguished guests today is the Secretary General of NATO, the former Foreign Minister of Holland, Mr. Luns. As I was talking to him yesterday, he remarked about the fact that immediately after World War II the United States, because it had a monopoly on nuclear weapons, could have imposed its will on any nation, any place in the world. It did not do so.

We helped our former enemies until today they are our major competitors in the free world. We helped our allies and we poured out our wealth, too, to all of the underdeveloped countries of the world.

We shouldn't stand and brag about

---

[1] Walter E. Washington, mayor of the District of Columbia.

that in terms that make the others feel inferior. We shouldn't stand here and expect that they should say thank you. Because it was right to do so, we thought. We thought it then, we think it now. That is our way. That is our way to show our dedication to what the Nation has stood for from the beginning: liberty and justice for all, not just in America, but throughout the world.

Mention has been made of the fact that I shall be traveling on two long journeys with Mrs. Nixon, one to Peking and one to Moscow. And all of the people in this room are aware of the fact that while these journeys have never before been undertaken by a President of the United States, this does not mean that we are going to find that instant peace will follow from them.

We have to realize that we have great differences, differences between our Government and that of the Government of Mainland China, the People's Republic of China, differences between our Government and the Government of the Soviet Union. And it is naive to think, or even to suggest, that those differences will evaporate if we just get to know each other better. I wish it were so, but it is not so; it has never been so.

In fact, the differences that we have with those great powers, their governments that is, is not because we do not know them or they know us, but because we do know them and they know us. The philosophic gulf is enormous. It will continue.

But there is, on the other hand, another factor, a very pragmatic one, which brings us together. We all realize that because of the new sources of power that have been unleashed in the world that we all must learn either to live together or we shall die together.

That is putting it in its most negative and harsh terms. I could perhaps put it in other terms.

I recall the many visits I have made to countries around the world and what impressed me the most: the great leaders, the historical monuments, all those things that impress a visitor from abroad. And then when Mrs. Nixon came back from Africa, it came to me again what impressed me, and what, of course, had impressed her on her visits.

She told me about the leaders, impressive men and women working in these countries for liberty and justice for all in their way—far from it in many instances, but trying.

But what impressed her the most were the children—children, eyes wide with wonder and hope, love, very little hate. Oh, differences, of course, because children have their differences as we know. But those children—they happened to be black—the children that I have seen, Chinese children, Russian children, by the hundreds of thousands in capitals around the world, make us all realize that that is what it is all about.

In this country, before we can help to bring peace to the world, we, of course, must have peace among ourselves, and Mayor Washington has so eloquently addressed himself to that subject. And as we have peace among ourselves, then perhaps we can play a role, imperfect though it may be, at this historic moment in the history of nations, to bring a period of peace between great nations that are very different, not just racially but, more important and more deeply, philosophically.

Then before we become too arrogant with the most deadly of the seven deadly sins, the sin of pride, let us remember that the two great wars of this century, wars which cost 20 million dead, were fought between Christian nations praying to the same God.

Let us remember now that fortunately Christian nations in the world live in peace together, and we trust will in the future. Let us remember that as a Christian nation, but also as a nation that is enriched by other faiths as well, that we have a charge and a destiny.

No longer do we have a monopoly on nuclear weapons, but the United States has this great asset as a nation that may be able to play the role of peacemaker in this last generation of the 20th century: We want nothing from any other nation. We want to impose our will on no other nation. We do not want their economic subversion or even submission. We want for them what we have, in their way as we have in our way, and try to have in our way, one nation, with liberty and justice for all.

They will all not have it, just as we have not had it perfectly. But our role may be to help build a new structure of peace in the world, where peoples with great differences can live together, talk about those differences, rather than fight about them.

Do it because we fear to die, but do it also because we think of those children—black children, yellow children, white children, brown children—over half the world is less than 20 years of age—and we think: Let us leave the world one in which they can have what we have never had,

a full generation of peace.

In the great agony of the War Between the States, which Abraham Lincoln so eloquently expressed in his Second Inaugural, he pointed out that devout men on both sides prayed to the same God. And in pointing it out, he, of course, expressed what all of us need to understand here today: that because of our faith we are not perfect, because of our faith we are not superior. Only the way we live, what we do, will deserve the plaudits of the world or of this Nation or even of our own self-satisfaction.

In that same period, as the war was drawing to an end, a man came to Lincoln and said, "Is God on our side?" And Lincoln's answer, you will all remember, was, "I am more concerned not whether God is on our side, but whether we are on God's side."

Virtually everyone this morning who has prayed, has prayed for the President of the United States, and for that, as a person, I am deeply grateful. But as you pray in the future, as these journeys take place, will you pray primarily that this Nation, under God, in the person of its President, will, to the best of our ability, be on God's side.

NOTE: The President spoke at 9:05 a.m. in the International Ballroom of the Washington Hilton Hotel. He spoke without referring to notes.

Representative Albert H. Quie of Minnesota presided at the 20th annual breakfast, sponsored by the United States Senate and House Prayer Breakfast Groups.

More than 3,000 guests, including representatives from government, the diplomatic corps, industry, labor, and the academic community, attended the breakfast.

33   Special Message to the Congress on Rural Development.
February 1, 1972

To the Congress of the United States:

From the very beginnings of our history, the vitality of rural America has been at the heart of our Nation's strength. It is essential that we preserve and expand that vitality in the years ahead. For America will not be able to look eagerly to the future with a sense of promise and hope unless those who live in its rural areas are able to share in this vision. To help improve the quality of life in the American countryside, I am today presenting a series of proposals designed to marshal more effectively the energies of the private sector and of government at all levels in a cooperative program of rural development.

THE PROBLEMS OF RURAL AMERICA

All Americans have a high stake in rural development. For the problems which many rural areas are now experiencing are directly linked to those of our cities and suburbs. Changing patterns of life in rural America have changed the pattern of life in all of America.

A central cause of these changing patterns has been the increasing mechanization of agriculture and of other natural resource industries such as mining and lumber—a process which has resulted in a substantial reduction in jobs in these occupations in recent years. While employment opportunities in other occupations have more than offset these declines, the overall growth of economic opportunity in rural America has lagged far behind that of our urban areas. Today, dramatic disparities exist between metropolitan and rural areas in such indices as per capita income, housing standards, educational attainment and access to medical care.

At the same time, political institutions designed to deal with simpler problems in simpler times have frequently been unable to cope with these new challenges. The Federal Government often finds that it is too remote and too unwieldy to respond with precision to State and local needs. State and local governments are frequently too impoverished or too fragmented to undertake the necessary planning and development activities. Their problems are accentuated by the fact that widely dispersed rural population inevitably means a higher expenditure per person for most government programs.

One result of all these factors is that semi-deserted country towns—once centers of life for the surrounding countryside—stand today as stark reminders of unused and abandoned rural resources. In each of the three decades since 1940, half of our counties (not always the same ones) have lost population. Two out of every five of our counties lost population in all three decades. As I said in my State of the Union Message two years ago, many of our rural areas are being emptied of their people and their promise.

In many cases, those who have left the countryside have simply taken their problems with them. Indeed, many have seen their problems intensify as they have settled in over-crowded urban areas.

It is striking to realize, as I noted in this year's Message on the State of the Union, that even if we had a population of one billion—nearly five times the current level—our area is so great that we would still not be as densely populated as many

European nations are at present. Our problems are not so much those of numbers as of distribution. And their solution requires the revitalization of the American countryside.

CHANGING OUR APPROACH

In seeking to solve the problems of rural areas, we must not simply seek more money from the Congress and the taxpayers. In the past decade we have seen the folly of pouring money into projects which were ill-considered and lacking in local support. What we must now seek instead is a fundamental change in the way government approaches the entire developmental challenge.

The Federal Government has spent considerable sums on rural development. Programs which we have recommended for inclusion in our rural development Revenue Sharing plan alone are spending almost $1 billion this year and this is only a small part of our overall rural development spending. And yet, despite this substantial funding, the problems have continued to grow. What is it that has been missing from our rural development programs?

MORE CONTROL AT THE STATE AND LOCAL LEVEL

I believe that a major missing ingredient has been effective control of development programs at lower levels of government. Because we have relied so exclusively on Federal funds—handed out through bureaucratic processes and through narrow categorical grants—too many decisions have been made in Washington and too few have been made in rural America. I believe this is wrong. I believe we should return power to officials who are selected at the State and local levels.

As long as the Federal Government sets rigid rules, both through legislative and administrative guidelines, there is little room for local initiative. Under our present system, a project that does not meet Federal standards does not get funded. This means that the talents of local government officials, of leaders in the private sector, and of public-spirited citizens cannot be fully utilized. Almost all of the success stories that can be found in rural economic development have occurred because local officials and private leaders have entered into a public-spirited partnership and have taken the initiative. We must do all we can to encourage such partnerships.

IMPROVED PLANNING

Even as we seek to decentralize, we must also work to improve planning. In many respects these goals represent two sides of the same coin. For plans which are developed at levels close to the people are likely to be more realistic, more imaginative and more useful than abstract blueprints which are drawn up far away from the scene of the action or which are altered to meet rigid Federal rules. Effective development does not require plans that can survive the scrutiny of Washington. Effective development requires plans that people believe in and will work to accomplish.

MORE ADEQUATE PUBLIC AND PRIVATE RESOURCES

More adequate development also requires more adequate resources. This does not simply mean more Federal money; it also means that Federal funds now available must be freed from the inhibiting restrictions within which they are now entangled. Funds which are free of these restrictions can be used in each locality where the needs are greatest, eliminating a great deal of inefficiency and waste.

But Federal grant money provides only a part of the Federal contribution to rural America. Adequate credit resources can also be extremely important in developing community facilities and in attracting private investment. In the end it is not Federal money, nor even the vast sums spent by State and local governments, which hold the key to rural development. The private sector has an enormous role to play and public efforts must keep this fact centrally in mind.

HELPING THE FARMER AND PROTECTING THE ENVIRONMENT

Rural America cannot move forward effectively into the future unless it respects those elements which have been the base of its strength in the past. We cannot build a stronger rural economy, for example, unless we also build a stronger agricultural economy. While we must work to change the American countryside, we must never do so at the expense of those who produce our food and fiber. We must work to create a better life for American farmers even as we provide an expanded range of opportunities for those who are no longer needed on the farm.

Even as we do more to promote agricultural prosperity, so we must do more to protect the rural environment. Just as development must not come at the expense of the farmer, so it must not come at the expense of environmental concerns. We cannot fully develop the American countryside if we destroy the beauty and the natural resources which are so much a part of its essential value.

BASIC PRINCIPLES

These then are the basic principles which should guide our new approach to rural community development:

We must treat the problems of rural America as a part of a general strategy for balanced growth.

We must reverse the flow of power to the Federal Government and return more power to State and local officials.

We must fight the rigidities of narrowly focused categorical grants.

We must facilitate more adequate advance planning.

We must reorganize the Federal Government so that it can more effectively support planning and execution at the State and local level.

We must provide adequate resources and credit, in ways which attract greater private resources for development.

We must develop rural America in ways which protect agriculture and the environment.

On the basis of these principles, we have prepared the following recommendations for action—including proposals which have been submitted earlier and a number of new initiatives.

PROPOSALS ALREADY SUBMITTED TO THE CONGRESS

DEPARTMENT OF COMMUNITY DEVELOPMENT

One of the most significant barriers to effective planning and coordination in rural areas has been the fragmentation of

Federal efforts. Too many programs which should be closely related are operating as very separate entities. As a result, State and community leaders must often run a complex obstacle course in order to obtain development assistance. Frequently there is poor coordination and wasteful duplication and in some cases the action of one Federal agency actually conflicts with that of another.

The principal reason for this fragmentation has been the failure of the Government to recognize the inter-relationship among rural, suburban and urban problems and the need to strengthen the essential social and economic partnership between rural America and our great metropolitan centers.

I believe the proper solution to this problem is to gather the principal Federal programs which support community development within a single new Department of Community Development.

This new department would both simplify and expedite the tasks of State and local governments through a broad range of program and technical support efforts. Because fewer questions would have to be resolved in Washington at the interagency level, the new department would also expedite the decentralization of Federal decision-making which this administration has already begun. The new Department of Community Development would take over most of the functions now performed by the Department of Housing and Urban Development; some of the functions of the Department of Transportation, the Office of Economic Opportunity and the Small Business Administration; and the responsibilities of the Department of Commerce with respect to the Title V regional commissions.

Under our revised plan for executive reorganization, the Department of Agriculture would remain as a separate department focusing on the needs of farmers. But a number of present Department of Agriculture development functions would be moved to the new Department of Community Development, including the Farmers Home Administration loan and grant programs for rural community water and sewer systems and for rural housing; the Rural Electrification Administration loan programs for electric and telephone systems; the recently established Rural Telephone Bank; research programs related to rural community development conducted by the Economic Development Division of the Economic Research Service; and the programs of the recently established Rural Development Service.

Comprehensive reorganization would mean that every Federal dollar spent on rural development could have a far greater impact. I again call on the Congress to establish this new department, which would be uniquely capable of launching a well-developed, well-coordinated campaign to achieve the nation's community development goals.

A REVENUE SHARING PLAN FOR RURAL AMERICA

Our revenue sharing plan for rural America proposes to unite the funding for a number of existing programs into a single more flexible resource for rural community development. Our proposed program would add $179 million to the various programs to be consolidated, bringing the total annual program to a level of $1.1 billion. Each State would receive at least as much under revenue sharing as it receives under the current system of categorical grants. The program would take effect at the beginning of Fiscal Year 1974.

Rural community development revenue sharing funds would be paid out to the States and to Puerto Rico, the Virgin Islands and Guam according to a formula which takes three factors into account: the State's rural population, the State's rural per capita income in comparison to the national average, and the State's change in rural population compared to the change in population in all States. In addition, every State would receive a minimum amount to assure that all States participate in the program.

The revenue sharing proposal incorporates a requirement for statewide development plans to ensure that activities carried on under the rural community development revenue sharing program could be coordinated with activities under the other general and special revenue sharing proposals, including those for urban community development and for transportation. Each year the States would prepare a comprehensive statewide development plan which would outline spending intentions for programs in rural areas and smaller cities, as well as in metropolitan and suburban areas. It would be the responsibility of the Governor of each State to draw up this statewide plan. This process would be supported by another major administration initiative, our proposed $100 million planning and management grant program.

The development plan would be formulated through a consultative process which would consider plans submitted by multijurisdictional planning districts, which the Governors could establish with rural revenue sharing funds. These local planning organizations would be composed of local elected officials and would be established in all areas of the State. One member from each of these district planning bodies would sit on a panel to assist the Governor in the comprehensive planning process.

This process for developing a statewide plan would ensure that public officials and the general public itself would focus attention on the inter-relationships between rural and urban development within each State. The plan would identify potential growth areas and development sites as well as areas which are of special environmental concern. The plan could also take into account interstate projects and programs developed through the regional commission mechanism.

The rural community development revenue sharing program represents a reaffirmation of faith in State and local governments. It is based on the concept that local people have the best understanding of local problems and on the belief that they have the will and the ability to move vigorously and intelligently to solve them. The revenue sharing approach removes the often stifling and always frustrating strictures which require that Federal grants be used for narrow purposes. It provides the flexibility which State and local governments need in order to fund those projects which they themselves believe would best ensure rational development in their areas and most effectively enhance the quality of life.

The development plans drawn up under this program would cover an entire State. Rural revenue sharing funds would be spent largely outside metropolitan areas while urban revenue sharing funds would be used within those areas. It is important to note, however, that rural areas include almost 2800 of the more than 3100 counties in the United States.

Last March, when I submitted the rural community development revenue sharing proposal for the first time, I said that "the major challenge facing rural America is to diversify its economy and to provide full opportunity for its people to enjoy the benefits of American life." I still believe that revenue sharing can do a great deal to help rural America meet that challenge.

NEW PROPOSALS

Revenue sharing and reorganization can have a great long-range significance for rural America. But we must also take a number of other steps which I am outlining today, including two major new proposals. The first involves a new approach to rural financial assistance. The second concerns added authorities for improving the environment and attaining conservation objectives in rural America.

EXPANDED CREDIT FOR RURAL AMERICA

I am recommending today a new rural community development credit sharing authority which would give the Secretary of Agriculture and the State Governors new tools to help revitalize rural areas. Under this proposal, a new Rural Development Credit Fund would be established to provide loans, loan insurance and loan guarantees to the States for their use in assisting development. This credit would be made available through the Farmers Home Administration for up to 80 percent of the cost of establishing or improving businesses which help create economic growth in rural areas. This fund would also make loans and guarantees for sewer and water facilities and other public works and community facilities, such as industrial parks and community centers,

which work directly or indirectly to improve employment opportunities.

Loans and guarantees would be made in accordance with the State development plan required under rural revenue sharing. The States would select specific projects which are consistent with this development plan.

A significant new feature of this credit-sharing proposal is the requirement that most of the authorizations be divided among the States according to the same formula established for rural community development revenue sharing. Specifically, 80 percent of the loan funds for commercial and industrial development and for community facilities would be allocated to the States on a formula basis. The remaining 20 percent of loan authorities would be administered by the Secretary of Agriculture. A large portion of the authorization—65 percent in each fiscal year—would be reserved for commercial and industrial development uses and the remainder would be available for community development purposes. Each State would know in advance the amount of grants and credit it could commit according to its plan each year.

This proposal would involve private lending institutions as fully as possible in the rural revitalization effort. Financial assistance would not be provided under the program unless it was clear that firms and communities could not obtain credit elsewhere. Fully three-quarters of each year's authorization would have to be in the form of a guarantee of loans made by private financial institutions. Hopefully, almost all loans could be made by this sector of our economy. In addition to the direct involvement of private banks, this program would also emphasize loans to private entrepreneurs for job creation through commercial and industrial development. Since some equity would be required, these business decision-makers would be far more likely to make realistic, workable development decisions than far-removed Federal bureaucrats can now do. It is also likely that these market-oriented decisions would provide sounder, long-term employment opportunities. This combination of Federal funding, local initiative and statewide planning utilizing the private market economy should produce a far more productive use of our resources.

I am proposing an authorization level for this credit-sharing program, which includes the existing Farmers Home Administration water and sewer program, of $1.3 billion in fiscal year 1974.

My new proposals also involve additional features and technical improvements which would streamline and improve the effectiveness of farm and rural loan programs now administered by the Department of Agriculture. Among these are proposals to increase the farm operating loan limit to $50,000 and to increase the limit on new loans to be held in the agricultural credit insurance fund from $100 million to $500 million. This latter provision would provide adequate levels to ensure that the expanded loan and guarantee program would have a substantial impact on rural areas.

In summary, this new approach to credit assistance contains several advantageous features:

(1) It would establish a direct link between credit assistance and revenue sharing since both programs would be administered according to the same statewide plan.

(2) It would expand the role of private lending institutions. Firms otherwise unable to obtain credit would have a chance to mature under this plan so that they could borrow from private lending institutions at a later time without Federal guarantees.

(3) The plan could work through a delivery system for servicing loans which is already in operation—the Farmers Home Administration, which has offices in more than 1,700 counties. There is an office within a relatively short distance of practically every rural community in the United States. This whole system, moreover, could be readily transferred to a new Department of Community Development.

(4) Projects could be jointly financed by a number of Federal agencies, such as Small Business Administration, the Department of Housing and Urban Development, and the Environmental Protection Agency, as well as by other private and public State and local agencies.

(5) Improved planning and program coordination would be possible under statewide plans which grow out of the needs and suggestions of multi-jurisdictional planning districts already established in more than half of the States. These planning bodies would also provide expertise for communities that are too small to employ their own development experts.

IMPROVING THE RURAL ENVIRONMENT

To help carry out our environmental concerns, I propose that the Secretary of Agriculture be authorized to share the costs of long-term conservation in watershed areas. Such an authorization has worked most successfully under the Great Plains program. This measure would foster the orderly establishment of needed land treatment measures within the small watershed areas of the country.

In addition, technical and cost-sharing assistance should be authorized within watershed areas for the improvement of water quality. This would mean that, for the first time, Federal cost-sharing would be made available to improve water quality on a year-round basis. Such technical and cost-sharing assistance should also be provided in Resource Conservation and Development Project areas.

Finally, the Secretary of Agriculture should be authorized to inventory and to monitor soil, water, and related resources and to issue a national land inventory report at five-year intervals. Such data could be used at all levels of government in land use policy planning.

All these proposals would broaden the dimensions of Federal service and would give new impetus to the entire rural development task. But I would emphasize again that this task must be one in which the people themselves are directly involved—and it must begin in rural America. Our proposals would provide rural people and communities with the tools they need to achieve their goals and I hope these recommendations will receive early and favorable consideration.

RESULTS OF OUR INCREASED EMPHASIS
ON RURAL DEVELOPMENT

These essential steps now depend on action by the Congress. But while action on past proposals has been pending, we have also been taking a number of administrative steps to improve our rural development programs and have substantially increased program funding. For example:

—The funding of principal rural development programs in the Department of Agriculture this year ($2.8 billion) is more than four times that of fiscal year 1961 and twice that of fiscal year 1969. Twenty-nine of the thirty-four rural development programs in that department have been expanded since 1969.

—Since 1969, the Department of Housing and Urban Development has nearly tripled its grants for non-metropolitan planning districts. It funded 155 districts which received $3.4 million in grants in the last complete fiscal year.

—Rural housing assistance, with an emphasis on low and moderate income families, has reached a record level of $1.6 billion under the Farmers Home Administration program—more than triple the 1969 level.

—Research on rural development and housing is estimated at $9 million this year, more than double that of 1969.

—Funding for community sewer and water facilities has reached a record high level of $300 million in loans, plus $42 million in direct grants. This represents an increase of almost 80 percent over the level provided two years ago.

—Soil Conservation Service resource conservation and development, flood prevention, and watershed programs have expanded from $103 million in fiscal year 1969 to an estimated $156 million this year.

—With the recent release of an additional $109 million in funds for rural electrification, total available funds for the Rural Electrification Administration have been increased to $438 million for the current fiscal year. REA loans from 1969 to 1971 totaled more than $1.4 billion. Since 1969, REA-financed systems connected 700,000 new electric services and 420,000 telephone users—the largest three-year growth since the 1950's.

—The Rural Telephone Bank, with an initial Federal subscription of $60 million in the first two years, has been established to provide new credit resources for telephone cooperatives seeking to improve rural communications.

—Extension Service community development activities this year attained a funding level estimated at $12.7 million, an increase of $3.7 million over 1969 levels.

—To broaden the role of the employment service in serving our rural population, a Rural Manpower Service has been established in the Department of Labor.

—A cooperative program called Concerted Services in Training and Education has involved several Federal agencies as well as local organizations in helping individuals better utilize Federal programs.

—A special office has been created within the Department of Health, Education, and Welfare to focus on special problems of human resource development in rural areas.

This expansion of Federal efforts to stimulate the development of rural communities has been paralleled by the increased efforts of individual citizens, civic organizations, private enterprise and government at the State, county and municipal level. There are many evidences of the resulting overall progress.

—Outmigration from rural communities slowed from 4.6 million during the 1950's to 2.4 million during the 1960's. Most of the population losses during the 1960's occurred in the Great Plains and inter-mountain areas of the West, but gains were realized in parts of the Southern Piedmont, the middle Tennessee Val-

ley, eastern Oklahoma, and northern and western Arkansas. This is evidence that the migratory tide can be slowed—and in some instances even reversed.

—Income per capita in rural America is growing faster than in metropolitan America, though it still remains below the urban level.

—While the incidence of poverty is greater in rural than in urban America, its reduction rate is nearly twice as fast.

—Non-farm employment outside the metropolitan centers has generally grown at a slightly faster rate than employment in metropolitan areas. Manufacturing employment is expanding more rapidly in rural areas than in the large cities.

—Although rural America still contains about two-thirds of our inadequate housing, the ratio of inadequate to adequate rural housing units has been reduced from one-third to one-seventh in recent years. Rural electric and telephone services have improved; more than 98 percent of America's farms are now electrified.

—During the past three years, per capita farm income has averaged about 75 percent that of non-farm workers. This is still too low, but it represents a significant improvement over the past decade.

—The median years of school completed by persons 25 to 29 years of age is now about the same—12 years plus—in metropolitan and non-metropolitan areas.

All of these signs of progress are most encouraging. But this record is not something to stand on—it is something to build on. Much significant work has already been done—but the most important tasks are still before us.

The longer we put off these tasks the more difficult they will be. With the cooperation of the Congress we can promptly take up this work, opening new doors of opportunity for all who seek a better life in rural America.

RICHARD NIXON

The White House,
  February 1, 1972.

NOTE: On the same day, the White House released a fact sheet and the transcript of a news briefing on the message. Participants in the news briefing were George W. Romney, Secretary of Housing and Urban Development; and Earl L. Butz, Secretary, and Joseph D. Coffey, Acting Deputy Under Secretary for Rural Development, Department of Agriculture.

34 Message to the Congress Transmitting Annual Report of the National Endowment for the Humanities. *February* 1, 1972

To the Congress of the United States:

In transmitting this Sixth Annual Report of the National Endowment for the Humanities, I particularly commend to your attention the new programs begun by the Endowment during fiscal year 1971. These programs, created in order to broaden the uses of the humanities by the American public, include an experimental program on a statewide basis for informal adult education in the humanities and the Jefferson Lecture on the Humanities, a national series which will bring humanistic learning directly to bear on public affairs.

These new programs and the expansion of existing programs described in this report were made possible by the strong support in increased funding given by the Congress to the Endowment at my request. Both the executive and legislative branches have now recognized that the humanities—languages, history, philosophy, literature and ethics among others—are an essential tool for restoring contemporary problems and that the Endowment can eventually place this tool within the grasp of more Americans than ever before.

Federal support of the National Endowment for the Humanities has had the desired effect of stimulating private giving and private initiative. I am therefore happy to report that in fiscal year 1971 the Endowment received a total of 517 separate gifts, about four times the number received the previous year. These gifts or pledges, amounting to $2.5 million, made it possible for the Endowment for the second year in a row to draw the full amount of Federal matching funds appropriated for that purpose.

It is my pleasure, too, to note that the Humanities Endowment's Sixth Annual Report is printed on recycled paper as a part of this Federal Agency's effort to make use of the Nation's natural resources.

RICHARD NIXON

The White House,
  February 1, 1972.

NOTE: The 127-page report is entitled "National Endowment for the Humanities, Sixth Annual Report."

35 Statement About an Explosion in East St. Louis, Illinois, and the Use of Planned Variations Funds. *February 1, 1972*

I WAS most distressed to learn of the chemical car explosion on January 22 which caused such great damage in East St. Louis, Ill. My thoughts have been with those who have been injured or left homeless by this tragedy and with all who were affected by the damage to schools and streets and by interruptions in the water and electric supply. I want the Federal Government to do everything it can to help during this difficult time.

Often tragedies of this sort are compounded when the delivery of resources needed for recovery is obstructed or delayed. Fortunately, this will not be the case in East St. Louis. For under a new Administration program, substantial Federal resources are available to East St. Louis without redtape—to be used as the local officials think best.

This new flexibility has been achieved through the Planned Variations project, which we have been carrying out under the Model Cities program in the Department of Housing and Urban Development. This project began last July when I announced that 20 cities—including East St. Louis—would participate in an intensive effort to demonstrate what local governments can accomplish with Federal money when they are given greater freedom from Federal regulations.[1]

In spending Planned Variations money, a city can decide for itself which problems are most pressing and how they can best be attacked. And when a city's needs shift, as they have in the wake of the East St.

Louis explosion, local officials can quickly shift their programs to meet those needs, without having to obtain Washington's approval for every detail of their new approach.

East St. Louis has recently received $760,000 under the Planned Variations program—the first installment of the $3.8 million it will eventually receive. I am pleased to note that the city has decided to direct a portion of these funds to provide shelter for those whose homes were damaged and destroyed in the recent explosion and to repair needed public facilities, including four badly damaged schools. This action was taken this past Saturday by the mayor and city council of East St. Louis. It was concurred in by the Model City Agency in East St. Louis at its meeting just last night. This prompt action would not have been possible if these monies were encumbered by strict Federal guidelines and restraints.

The Federal Government has also been able to provide the city with technical assistance in planning the recovery effort and has made available some 200 temporary housing units for those who have been displaced from their homes.

The advantages of local control, so dramatically evident in this particular case, could be experienced on a regular basis in all of our communities if the revenue sharing programs which I have recommended to the Congress were put into effect. The Planned Variations program was designed as a test of what cities and States could accomplish under the revenue sharing approach. I believe that the

---

[1] See 1971 volume, Item 241.

prompt actions which have been taken to meet pressing human needs in East St. Louis are evidence of the soundness of that approach.

I am pleased that the Federal Government could be of assistance in this time of emergency and that the local govern-ment was in a position to use that assistance with the greatest possible effectiveness. I hope and trust that the neighborhood affected by the tragedy of January 22 will now experience a quick recovery and a healthy development.

36   Special Message to the Congress Urging Passage of the West Coast Dock Strike Resolution and the Crippling Strikes Prevention Act.   *February 2, 1972*

To the Congress of the United States:

As the dock strike on the West Coast continues to impose a cruel and intolerable burden upon the American people, I appeal once again to the Congress for emergency action to end these transportation disputes.

There are now two bills before the Congress dealing with transportation stoppages, and immediate action is urgently required on both:

—S.J. Resolution 187, which would quickly halt the West Coast strike and lead to a fair and early settlement under binding arbitration.

—And the Crippling Strikes Prevention Act, S. 560, which would grant the executive branch sufficient authority so that future disruptions in the transportation industry could be averted.

The American public is rightly frustrated today by the inaction of Congress in ending the West Coast strike. Some crops are rotting while others are stalled in their bins, export customers are looking for more dependable trading partners, and jobs and businesses are threatened with extinction. Tens of thousands of people, who share no part of this dispute, are suffering needlessly.

Yet our Government stands idly by, paralyzed because the executive branch has exhausted all available remedies and a majority in the Congress has been unwilling to enact necessary legislation. This failure to act in time of need speaks directly to the question of why some Americans have lost confidence in their government.

We must act now, swiftly and decisively. Twelve days ago I proposed special legislation to end this strike and asked for enactment within a week. That deadline has passed without a response, and I must report to the American people today that I cannot predict when relief will come. To say that I am disappointed is to state the case in its mildest terms.

For those who argue that the Government should not interfere with collective bargaining, the short answer is that the bargaining in this case has thus far failed—and failed badly for 15 months. I share the belief that Government ordinarily should not tamper with the freedom of bargaining, but when the processes have broken down and the Nation's health and safety are at stake we in public office have no right to turn our heads.

I am also aware that some members of Congress believe this strike will soon be settled at the bargaining table. I sincerely hope they are right, and I urge the parties to continue their bargaining, but the 15 months of fruitless bargaining which have already passed convince me that we cannot depend on this solution.

ISSUES OF GREAT URGENCY

In the absence of an agreement, the critical question is whether all of us in Washington sense the urgency of these issues. I can assure you that the farmer whose grain is wasting away and the exporter who has lost his contract regard this strike as a matter of utmost urgency, and I plead with the Congress to recognize their plight.

For two years I have been trying to impress upon the Congress the need for new legislation in this field. In 1970, during the 91st Congress, and again in 1971 during the 92nd Congress, I proposed the comprehensive crippling strikes prevention program so that future transportation stoppages could be resolved. There has been precious little affirmative response. Yet I am confident that if the Congress had enacted those measures, there might have been no strike on the West Coast and the issues in dispute would have been fairly settled.

Let us resolve that this stoppage on the West Coast will be the last of its kind. The Congress should act immediately to end the West Coast strike and, with utmost dispatch, pass the Crippling Strikes Prevention Act.

THE CRIPPLING STRIKES PREVENTION ACT

Certainly the more far-reaching of the two proposals on which I am seeking action is the Crippling Strikes Prevention Act. It would give the President additional—and, in my opinion, essential—new authority to deal with emergency disputes in the railroad, airline, maritime, longshore, and trucking industries.

First, it would discontinue the emergency strike provisions of the Railway Labor Act of 1926 and provide that all transportation disputes be settled under the Taft-Hartley Act. Currently, disputes in the railroad and airline industries are subject to the Railway Labor Act while all other emergency transportation disputes are governed by the Taft-Hartley Act. Of the two acts, the railway labor law is clearly the inferior. Under it, the President can delay a strike or lockout for 60 days by appointing an Emergency Board to study the issues and recommend a settlement. Unfortunately, these provisions only seem to discourage hard bargaining because the parties are hesitant to compromise their position before the Board is appointed, and then, recognizing that the Board will probably seek a middle position, the parties tend to adopt a more extreme stance in order to pull the Board in their direction. Thus the gap widens between the disputants and because neither the Board nor the President has any additional authority, strikes often resume at the end of the 60-day period. These resumptions have occurred at the rate of more than one per year since 1947, and four times during this administration alone I have been forced to ask Congress for special legislation. This is a sorry record, best consigned to our history books.

THREE NEW OPTIONS

Secondly, I propose a major revision of the Taft-Hartley Act to give the President three new options in the case of all emergency disputes in the transportation industry. Under current provisions of this Act, the President may appoint a Board of Inquiry when he believes that a work stoppage imperils the Nation's health or safety. Upon receiving a report from the Board on the status of the strike, the President may direct the Attorney General to petition a Federal District Court to enjoin the strike for an 80-day "cooling-off" period. But there the formal authority of the Federal Government ends: the Board of Inquiry may issue no recommendation on a settlement and the President has no additional options when the 80-day period elapses except to ask for emergency legislation. On nine of 30 occasions when this machinery has been invoked since 1947, a strike or lockout has resumed after the 80-day period, as it has now on the West Coast.

To permit a more flexible Federal response, I propose that the President be granted three options when the "cooling-off" period fails to produce a settlement:

—First, he could extend the period for 30 days, a most useful device if the dispute seems to be near an end.

—Secondly, he could require partial operation of the troubled industry, so that those segments essential to the national health or safety could be kept in operation for an additional 180 days.

—Or thirdly, he could invoke a "final offer selection" procedure whereby the final offers of each party would be submitted to a neutral panel. This panel would select, without amendment, the most reasonable of the offers as the final and binding contract between the parties. Unlike bargaining which now occurs under the Railway Labor Act or under arbitration, this approach would en-

courage the parties to narrow their positions so that they could persuade the panel of their reasonableness. Thus genuine negotiations and settlement would be encouraged automatically.

Among the additional features of this proposal is the establishment of a National Special Industries Commission to conduct a two-year study of labor relations in industries which are especially subject to national emergency disputes.

As I informed the Congress two years ago, the Crippling Strikes Prevention Act creates a balance between two cherished but sometimes inconsistent principles: the protection of the national health and safety against damaging work stoppages, and the protection of collective bargaining from interference by the Government. "Ideally," I said then, "we would provide maximum public protection with minimum Federal interference."

Without doubt, my proposal would tip the present scales back in the direction of greater protection for the public, but we must face up to the hard realities that the old way simply has not worked. The scales, in fact, have been heavily weighted against the public. The actions I propose would not only correct the balance but would also preserve and enhance the processes of collective bargaining.

THE WEST COAST DISPUTE

The present tie-up on the West Coast vividly illustrates why we need the Crippling Strikes Prevention Act. Both the failure of negotiations and the resulting economic losses have been a painful lesson for us all.

Talks and negotiations between the parties have dragged on for 15 months, and I have used every remedy at my command, but to no avail. The Taft-Hartley machinery has been tried, and it has failed. Two extensions in time have been arranged by Government mediators, and twice the mediators' efforts have fallen short. And I have met personally with the parties. Yet this strike has resumed. In my view, it is abundantly clear that present legislation is inadequate and that we need comprehensive solutions.

Only now are we beginning to realize the full damages of the first 100-day strike which closed down the West Coast ports between July 1 and October 9, 1971. I recounted some of these losses to the Congress in my message 12 days ago, but the facts bear emphasis:

—It is estimated that American exports would have been $600 million higher during this 100-day period except for the work stoppage.

—The strike was particularly hard on our farmers, who have been exporting the product of one cropland acre out of four. During the June–September period, farm exports from the West Coast dropped from $288 million in the same period in 1970 to $73 million in 1971.

—Wheat farmers suffered the worst calamities of all, as their sales to major Far Eastern markets fell off drastically. Japan, for instance, purchases over 50 percent of her wheat from the United States. Since April, we have lost sales to Japan of at least 25 million bushels of wheat valued at $40 million. Ominously, the day after the strike resumed last month, the Japanese purchased 8.7 million bushels of wheat for a spring delivery, but only 1.6 million bushels were bought from the United States.

—Our merchant fleet also sustained heavy losses, as did exporters of vegetables, rice, cotton, and livestock, and wood products, and numerous related industries.

APPALLING HUMAN COSTS

Overall, the 100-day strike thrust a spike into our progress toward economic recovery, threatened our balance of payments, and undermined the confidence of foreign buyers who need to rely upon dependable deliveries. But the most appalling costs were in human terms—those tens of thousands who were not parties to the dispute but suffered because of it.

Those same people are suffering needlessly again, as the costs of resuming the strike begin to mount. I met yesterday with the Governors of California and Washington, whose States along with Oregon lost an estimated total of $23.5 million a day during the 100-day strike, and they have reported to me that the cost of this resumption is intolerable to their economies. The State of Hawaii is also beginning to feel the punishment. If the strike persists for several weeks, we can anticipate a significant increase in unemployment on the West Coast and huge financial losses for many people across the country.

We can and must end this dispute. Because the parties have already been bargaining under different ground rules for many months, I do not think it would be fair or wise in this case to impose the "final offer selection" solution which I am proposing in the more comprehensive Crippling Strikes Prevention Act. I also see no merit in another "cooling-off" extension, because it offers little hope of resolution and it only increases the uncertainty in foreign markets. Instead, I urge the adoption of a plan for settlement by arbitration. As I explained to the Congress 12 days ago, I am asking that a three-member arbitration board be appointed by the Secretary of Labor to hear all the issues and then issue a settlement that would be binding for at least 18 months. No strike or lockout would be permitted from the day this legislation is enacted until the expiration of the binding settlement established by the board.

I strongly favor free collective bargaining, but the time has come for decisive action. I call upon the Congress to take

such action on both this emergency bill and the Crippling Strikes Prevention Act.

RICHARD NIXON

The White House,
    February 2, 1972.

NOTE: On the same day, the White House released a fact sheet and the transcript of a news briefing on the message. Participants in the news briefing were Laurence H. Silberman, Under Secretary of Labor, and Clark Mac-Gregor, Counsel to the President for Congressional Relations.

On February 1, 1972, the White House released the transcript of a news briefing by Governors Ronald Reagan of California and Daniel J. Evans of Washington and Secretary of Labor James D. Hodgson on the dock strike and the proposed legislation, after the Governors had met with the President.

37 Message to the Senate Transmitting Convention on the Illicit Movement of Cultural Property. *February 2, 1972*

To the Senate of the United States:

With a view to receiving the advice and consent of the Senate to accession, I transmit herewith the Convention on the Means of Prohibiting and Preventing the Illicit Import, Export and Transfer of Ownership of Cultural Property.

The illicit movement of national art treasures has become a matter of serious concern in the world community. Many countries have lost important cultural property through illegal exportation. The theft of art objects from museums, churches and collections is increasing. Rising prices for antiquities stimulate looting of archaeological sites, causing the destruction of irreplaceable resources for scientific and cultural studies. In addition, the appearance in the United States of important art treasures of suspicious origin gives rise to problems in our relations with other countries.

The Convention, adopted on November 14, 1970, by a vote of 77 to 1 with 8 abstentions at the Sixteenth General Conference of the United Nations Educational, Scientific and Cultural Organization, is a significant effort at multilateral cooperation to help preserve the cultural resources of mankind. Under the Convention, each state undertakes to protect its own cultural heritage and agrees to cooperate in a number of important but limited respects to help protect the cultural heritage of other states. Perhaps the heart of the Convention from the standpoint of the United States is Article 9, which establishes an important new framework for international cooperation. Under this Article, the states parties undertake to participate in a concerted international effort to determine and to carry out the necessary corrective measures in cases in which a state's cultural patrimony is in jeopardy from pillage of archaeological or ethnological materials.

The Convention also requires states parties to prohibit the import of cultural property stolen from museums, public monuments or similar institutions and to take appropriate steps, upon request, to recover and return such cultural property. In addition, they pledge to take what measures they can, consistent with existing national legislation, to prevent museums and similar institutions within their territory from acquiring cultural property originating in another state party which has been illegally exported after entry into force of the Convention.

I am enclosing the report of the Secretary of State, which more fully explains the Convention and the reservation and understandings we recommend. Certain provisions of the Convention will require implementing legislation, which the Executive Branch will be prepared to discuss during the Senate's consideration of the Convention.

I believe international cooperation is required in order to preserve the priceless heritage of humanity, and I urge the Senate to give prompt advice and consent to United States accession to this Convention, subject to the reservation and understandings recommended in the report of the Secretary of State.

RICHARD NIXON

The White House,
    February 2, 1972.

NOTE: The text of the convention and the report of the Secretary of State are printed in Senate Executive B (92d Cong., 2d sess.).

38   Remarks on Presenting the Heart-of-the-Year Award to Pearl Bailey.   *February* 2, 1972

I AM very happy to present this award to Pearl Bailey. I have presented awards to her before. Pearl Bailey has been here as our guest at the White House. She has also taken on a capacity, unpaid, as a volunteer ambassador at large for the United States in countries throughout the world. For that we are very grateful.

I think in presenting this award, I should say two things. It is significant to note that two Presidents before I was here had heart disease, and yet in this, which is supposed to be the most burdensome and wearing job in the world, they were able to carry on the duties of this office. It does prove that heart disease is not a barrier.

But I also know from having seen Pearl Bailey in "Dolly" and the rest and seen her magnificent ability to raise an audience with her radiant personality, that if she has any restrictions because of heart disease, it doesn't show. You compensate in other ways.

I also would like to say that when we speak of the Heart-of-the-Year Award, I guess, first, we think of the heart physically. A big heart physically, I understand, is bad for you. But also we speak of the heart in the sense of the poet and in that respect, a big heart is something that we all admire.

I believe we could say with regard to Pearl Bailey, she, from the standpoint of emotion, from the standpoint of poetry, from the standpoint of love—all of these things that the heart symbolizes—she has a big heart which is demonstrated by her great audience and we appreciate that and we present this award to her in that spirit.

NOTE: The President spoke at 12:17 p.m. in the Oval Office at the White House. He spoke without referring to notes.

The President presented the Heart-of-the Year Award to Pearl Bailey on behalf of the American Heart Association. The award is given annually to a "distinguished American whose faith and courage in meeting the personal challenge of heart disease have inspired people throughout the Nation with confidence in the objectives and program of the American Heart Association."

On the same day, the President signed Proclamation 4104, designating the month of February as American Heart Month.

39   Remarks to Athletes Attending a White House Sponsored Conference on Drug Abuse. *February 3, 1972*

Ladies and gentlemen:

I would like to begin this White House briefing with a confession that perhaps doesn't need to be made before this distinguished audience. It has been rather well publicized that I am somewhat of a sports fan. As a matter of fact, I have not been able to demonstrate that too much over the past year. I have seen only one baseball game—incidentally, the Senators won that one, too—and no football games, but several on television, baseball, football. The only basketball game I saw, incidentally, was when the [Los Angeles] Lakers lost to the [Milwaukee] Bucks in that great game out there in Milwaukee a few weeks ago.

But in the course of seeing games and, of course, commenting upon them and picking plays—usually ones that didn't work—I have learned a lot about the game, about the men in it, and what they have contributed to this country. As one who sees sports almost exclusively on television, I want you to know that the worst part of it is the commercials, except for one kind of commercial. I think it is one of the most exciting ventures in the whole field of sports, and also in the field of television broadcasting.

When I saw the breaks come, you know, in the timeout or whatever the case might be, and then on would come what you thought was an instant replay, and then it was a commercial—a commercial by a man that you admired, admired as a fine athlete on the field or on the basketball court, as the case might be, or the baseball diamond. He would come on and he would talk very effectively, very eloquently, about the subject of drug abuse in the United States. I realized as I saw those commercials, first, that we were getting—"we," I mean by that the United States Government, because we asked that those for whom you are playing, that they cooperate, and the networks, of course, have cooperated, and a number of other agencies—you wonder how effective they have been.

Let me tell you we have a little proof. Many of you will know that at the end of the commercials, there is a little sign that goes on, "If you want information about drug abuse, write to the National Drug Abuse Clearinghouse in Washington, D.C." Since those commercials began, there have been over 100,000 requests that have come in. That means you got through. People were listening. They were paying attention.

What I am saying to you is that, as a sports fan, I admire those here for your great achievements in your chosen professions at this time in your lives; but as an American, I am just deeply grateful for this free time you have been giving, because you can command a little pay for that time—don't give it away free, incidentally, except to us—for the free time you have been giving in making these commercials, in getting at a subject in which every American concerned about the future of his country, and particularly the future of our children, has a very, very great interest.

Now, as far as the briefing is concerned, to show you how broad our interest is, and how we are attempting to wage a battle against drug abuse, which is not limited to just one section, but it is total, it is what we might describe as total warfare against drug abuse in the United States and in the world.

An indication of how it is total are the people who will be addressing you: John Ehrlichman, the head of our domestic staff, will be the master of ceremonies. But we have the Secretary of State, the top ranking member of the Cabinet. Why is he here? Because we want to try to stop drugs coming into this country at the source. We don't produce heroin, for example, in the United States. They do produce it—the poppy that grows heroin—in Turkey. They produce it in some parts of Southeast Asia. We have made remarkable progress in this respect. And this is a result of the cooperation of the State Department, our ambassadors abroad working with the Governments of Turkey, France, and several other foreign governments. The Secretary of State will fill you in on those activities: stopping drugs from coming in at the source, making it more difficult for them to come in.

Of course, any program is not going to be completely successful. Some are going to get in. They are smuggled in, and there are a variety of ways they can get around anything that we do.

The other thing that we have been trying to do, and this is the second phase of the program, is: Once they get in, then we want to have laws effectively enforced that will punish the pushers. Now, we have set up several programs in this field, the Congress has cooperated, and you are going to be briefed by the top people in our Government who have the responsibility for law enforcement at the Federal level and who, of course, are working with State and local and city governments in seeing that we punish the pushers.

There are many reprehensible crimes, in my opinion, in this country. I can think of no crime, including even the crime of murder, burglary—you name it—which is more reprehensible than for an individual to destroy the life of a young person by pushing drugs. It is a terrible thing to do. We are having an all-out offensive waged all over this country to punish the pushers.

Now, there is another side to it. You know, many times in the field of crime— and I speak now as a lawyer and, of course, the Secretary of State is a lawyer, and so is John Ehrlichman, we all will have this same view—many times in the field of crime there is a tendency to think all you need is a law with a strong enough penalty and there will be no crime. Not true, because that is only one side of it. No matter how strong the penalty is, there are some who are going to break the law.

Once they break the law, particularly

in the field of dangerous drugs, then you have to have some compassion; then you have to take care of the addicts. That doesn't mean you excuse them from breaking the law. It does mean that once they break the law, you have to find a way to get them back into productive society, to take what would otherwise be a totally destroyed human being and make him or her whole again.

That is why we have Dr. Jaffe here, who is the top expert in this country in the field of the treatment of drug addicts. He will tell you something about what we are doing, about how we treat them; not only prevent it, but then, once a person becomes addicted, to treat that particular situation.

So we have named three of the great offensives: One, stop it at the source. That is the Secretary of State's primary responsibility, and, of course, the Secretary of the Treasury, through the Customs and the rest, works in this field as well.

Second, we have the law enforcement, and that is, punish the pushers and the peddlers, and there you will hear from the responsible people in that area.

Then, third, you have the treatment of people once they go over the wall and finally become addicts. Dr. Jaffe and others will talk to you about that.

But now comes your part. The law can be the best enforced law; we can try to stop it at the source; and we can treat the addicts. But most important, what we have to do is to try to educate, particularly, young Americans, so that there won't be the demand. We have to stop them before they start. And that, of course, is where you—the champions on the football field and the baseball field and the basketball court—where you have really done a marvelous job, a job which we

could not possibly pay you for adequately if we had to pay your television fees commercially. But you have done a marvelous job of handling this problem.

I know, incidentally, having done a little television myself through the years, and having done a few spots, what a chore it must have been; you know, they keep going over it, "Another take, please, another take." And you must have said, "Oh, why do I have to do it again? Is it worthwhile?"

I just want you to know, and I want your wives to know, who are here with you: We have looked at the situation, we have looked at the results; I know of no program that has paid off more, that has been more effective, than what the athletes of America have done in this field, and we are here to thank you for it.

Later, at 5 o'clock, when the briefings are completed, Mrs. Nixon will be downstairs and we would like to welcome all of you and your wives in the dining room for some refreshments and meet and greet you each personally.

At this time I will turn the program over to the experts, and will simply close by saying: As a sports fan I admire what you have done in the sports field, but also, as one who has the responsibility to do everything that I can to deal with one of the major problems America faces today, drug abuse, we want to thank people who can reach young people such as a preacher can't reach them, a politician can't reach them, a teacher can't reach them. You can, because they admire you. They respect you. They want to be like you, and that is why you get across.

Thank you very much.

NOTE: The President spoke at 2:10 p.m. in the East Room at the White House. He spoke without referring to notes.

Those attending the conference included college and professional athletes, the commissioners and heads of the professional sports leagues, network officials, and representatives of the Advertising Council, Inc.

40   Special Message to the Congress Outlining Plans for the Bicentennial Observance in the District of Columbia. *February 4, 1972*

To the Congress of the United States:

"Seafaring is necessary," says the Latin inscription on an old building in one of the great European port cities; "mere living is not." This same spirit of movement, venture, and quest animates the whole sweep of America's story—from its discovery by men who lived for sailing, to its founding as a nation by men who lived for liberty, to its modern maturity as the world's preeminent power—and it will do so still, 4 years hence, when we observe the Bicentennial of American independence. The Nation could not if it wanted to, and should not if it could, drop anchor somewhere in 1976 and savor the occasion at leisure. By its very nature it can only speed through the year as through any other, under full sail, on into a new century.

The central challenge of our Bicentennial preparations, therefore, is to plan for an observance "on the move." Many groups—public and private, national and local—have already devoted several years of creative thought and effort to meeting this challenge. The common goal to which all subscribe has nowhere been stated better than in the 1970 report of the celebration's official planning and coordinating body, the American Revolution Bicentennial Commission (ARBC): "to forge a new national commitment—a new Spirit for '76—a commitment which will unite the nation in purpose and dedication to the advancement of human welfare as we move into Century III of American National Life."

We can best forge such a spirit, the Commission went on to recommend, by approaching the Bicentennial as an occasion both for understanding our heritage better and for quickening the progress toward our horizons—not just in one chosen location or a few, but in every State, city, and community. The Commission's goal and the principles deriving from it have my strongest support, and I have followed with interest the ARBC's further work as well as that of the individual Bicentennial Commissions already set up or now being formed by each State and territory, Puerto Rico, and the District of Columbia.

THE BICENTENNIAL IN WASHINGTON

Since the Federal Government has special responsibility for District of Columbia affairs, my closest contact has been with the planning effort now underway here in the District—and I have found its progress thus far most impressive. And so it should be. For while no one city will dominate this truly national anniversary, Washington—which was built to be the Capital of the Republic born in 1776 and seat of the Government constituted in 1787, and which has been in many ways a center of the hopes of all Americans in all generations since—has a unique role to play. As its plans are made known, they may well serve as a stimulus and an example for the equally important plans being made in thousands of other communities. *Both to ensure that Washington itself is ready for 1976 and to spur Bicentennial activity all across the country, I shall outline to the Congress today an action plan for Federal partnership in the District of Columbia's Bicentennial observance.*

My proposals follow two basic themes. One is the quest for quality of life—today's name for the age-old aspiration which Jefferson at the Nation's birth called "the pursuit of happiness." Here is the very essence of a Bicentennial celebrated "on the move." The past success of this quest, its present vigor, and its future prospects will provide a telling measure for our self-assessment as the great milestone nears. Such a theme's immediacy will call up exertion as well as congratulation—not only a birthday party but an actual rebirth.

The second theme which I would stress is dual excellence for Washington. In choosing which Bicentennial projects to pursue among myriad worthy possibilities, an old question arises again and again: Washington for Washingtonians, or Washington for all Americans? A kind of civic schizophrenia has troubled this city from the earliest days of its double existence as both a national capital and a community in its own right. Solutions going to both extremes have had their advocates—yet there is a better answer than either making thousands of people reside neglected in a strictly Federal city that is "a nice place to visit," or making millions of other people receive their governance from a narrowly provincial and self-centered capital where officials and visitors are classed as outsiders.

The Bicentennial Era, I am convinced, is the right time for Washington to gain a new and more expansive sense of itself, and to find in its dual identity an opportunity for dual excellence unparalleled among American cities. The seat of government can excel as an exemplary living city, at the same time the home of 750,000 local residents excels as a gracious host to fellow citizens and foreign visitors who may number 40 million during 1976 alone.

The projects proposed in this message, then, treat quality of life in the Nation's Capital as indivisible. They aim for dual excellence, in the conviction that a more liveable city is a more visitable one, and vice versa. For the most part, they emphasize physical construction—not by any means because public works are the sum total of our Bicentennial intentions for the District, but only because building time is already becoming critically short. Activities of many other types, such as commemorative events, pageantry, and social and cultural programs, which will of course be essential to the human dimension of the Bicentennial but which require somewhat shorter lead-times, are also being planned. Reports on these activities and, in many cases, requests for approval and funding will be submitted to the Congress as we move toward 1976.

One further note on Bicentennial concerns not mentioned here but certainly not forgotten: It is my feeling that nothing we could do for the District of Columbia during the next 4 years would be more meaningful or more appropriate to the Spirit of '76 than granting this city and its people first-class status: voting representation in the Congress. I am encouraged by the apparently warmer climate for this reform on Capitol Hill in 1972, and it will continue to have my support.

FORT LINCOLN NEW TOWN

Speaking at the National Archives last summer in a ceremony inaugurating the Bicentennial Era, I described an unusual painting which hangs in the Roosevelt Room across from the Oval Office in the White House. The scene portrayed is the signing of the Declaration of Independence—but for some reason the canvas was never finished, and many of the figures in the crowded hall are just sketched in, or left blank. The symbolism of this, I said, is that "the American Revolution is unfinished business, with important roles still open for each of us to play." A broad cross-section of District of Columbia citizens have now begun playing their roles in the continuing drama by serving on Mayor Washington's recently formed Bicentennial Assembly and Bicentennial Commission. We in the administration found the work of the old local Commission quite valuable in formulating our own plans for 1976, and we look forward to working closely with the reorganized, two-level planning group in the future.

One of the strongest strains of community opinion identified by local representatives like these is a commitment to revitalizing the urban heart of this Washington area. This, not flight to the suburbs or complacent satisfaction with the status quo, seems to arouse hope and determination at the neighborhood level. At the same time it seems a most appropriate cornerstone for a Bicentennial program designed to lift the quality of Washington life.

Accordingly, I shall initiate immediate Federal action to move ahead on plans for building a new town at Fort Lincoln in Northeast Washington. Fort Lincoln, over 300 acres of open land which received its name as a military post a century ago and which was long the site of the National Training School for Boys, offers an ideal chance to create not just another urban project where homes are razed and the human factor is designed out, but a totally new community planned around people. More than 4,000 dwellings for families of varied incomes are envisioned—three-quarters of them owner-occupied, to provide an anchor of stability in the development.

Innovative public transportation and communications systems and experimental educational programs would help knit the community together. Both the installation of these features and the construction work itself would be used as demonstration settings for some of the social-benefit technology applications which I proposed in my State of the Union message. Also integral to the new town would be a Federal employment center for 5,000 to 10,000 employees, and a possible satellite campus for the Federal City College. The development would be financed through public-private partnership, with the initial Federal investment (supplemented by District contributions which will need approval by the Congress) likely to be matched several times over in related private investment.

"The city lives!"—a rallying cry which meets with considerable skepticism in some quarters today—would be the assurance forcefully offered to Washingtonians and the world by a Fort Lincoln town occupied and operating in 1976. We are determined to make it happen.

NEIGHBORHOOD SOCIAL DEVELOPMENT

The Fort Lincoln idea is not new, but the impetus behind it is—a neighborhood, community-based impetus, with which I am delighted to associate this administration. *In order to demonstrate our support for this kind of bootstrap Bicentennial initiative, we shall ask the Congress to make available several million dollars in Federal funds to supplement the local funds set aside to carry out the social development project proposals which will be gathered by the local Bicentennial Commission and Assembly in neighborhoods all over Washington beginning this spring.* None of these latter projects will approach the scale of Fort Lincoln, but most will be no less soundly rooted in ordinary people's knowledge of their own needs. The process of listening and response, as well as the project implementation itself, will make for a healthier and more progressive city.

We are also increasing our efforts to assist in redevelopment of the inner-city areas devastated by the riots of April 1968. Two recent groundbreakings give evidence that the work is moving ahead, but also remind us of how much is left to do. The job, of course, is not the Federal Government's alone, but we must and shall contribute our full share and see the obligation through at an accelerated pace.

MORE COMMUNITY PARKS

One frequently voiced need is for more parkland—not just in the ceremonial center of the city, but out in the residential sections as well. *Planning is now underway for a joint Federal-District park development program focusing on underused, publicly owned land near the Anacostia River, close to some of the District's most crowded neighborhoods.* New recreational facilities will be constructed, to permit intensive use of the sorely needed

new parks by Anacostia residents. Also within the Anacostia Basin, improvements will be carried out at the National Arboretum. *Another major green-space project planned for completion by 1976 is the Fort Circle Parks, 17 outposts of the Army's old defensive system around the periphery of the District of Columbia, some dating back as far as the War of 1812.* Strips of parkland are to link all the forts into a continuous belt containing bike trails, hiking paths, community recreation facilities, and campsites. Further, the District and the Interior Department will cooperate in rehabilitating and upgrading smaller parks in many areas of the city. I ask the Congress to approve the funds requested in my 1973 budget to move all of these projects forward on schedule.

A NEW DOWNTOWN CENTER

I also support, as vital to the kind of development momentum Washington must have to hold its head up among American cities in the Bicentennial Era, the District government's intention to construct a major convention center-sports arena complex near Mount Vernon Square.

This project would help to counter the centrifugal forces which are pushing both the leisure activities of local people and the major gatherings of out-of-town visitors away from the centers of many major cities. It would mean new business and investments and jobs for blocks around. And it would inject new life into nearby neighborhoods—provided, of course, that the legitimate concerns of merchants, working people, and residents in those neighborhoods receive fair consideration in the planning and location process. The scope of Federal assistance, however, should be appropriately limited, since I believe that a development largely local in function and benefits should have substantial local financing as well.

FOLLOWING THROUGH: EDUCATION AND TRANSPORTATION

New communities, new parks, new focal points for downtown business—all will help Washington carry through the ARBC's "Horizons '76" theme of honoring our founding principles by forging a better future with them. So too will two other ongoing District efforts, for which congressional assistance requested during the last session is still much needed: our public colleges and our METRO subway system.

Washington Technical Institute is proceeding with plans for buildings at its new permanent location on the north side of the former Bureau of Standards site in Northwest Washington. Federal City College remains in scattered lease space throughout the city despite explosive enrollment growth in the past 4 years; it hopes to occupy a campus of its own in and around the old District Library building north of Mount Vernon Square, as well as satellite locations elsewhere. *The Congress can help to expedite these campus development efforts by enacting the D.C. Capital Financing Act, which makes special provision for funding college construction through direct Federal grants rather than through Treasury loans as at present.*

In my D.C. message urging this action last April, I noted that WTI and the new International Center which is to share the Bureau of Standards site will in the future symbolize "side by side the Capital City's dedication to human development and to international understanding." Action by the Congress late in 1971 cleared the way for actual sale to foreign governments of lots at the International Center to begin last week. By 1976 the cluster of new chanceries there will be a pride to Americans and foreign guests alike. Let us now make sure that the District's public colleges will also be a showplace in the Bicentennial year. Ample and balanced opportunities in higher education are essential, if we are to convince millions of 1976 student visitors that the District takes care of its own.

METRO, and all of the other elements which with it will comprise a balanced modern transportation system for greater Washington, are central to Bicentennial plans for the District. We need the pride of achievement in areawide cooperation which the system will give all communities taking part. We need its people-moving capacity to cope with visitor traffic which may average up to 100,000 people daily throughout the anniversary year. *I am today renewing the commitment of all the agencies and resources of the Federal Government toward maximum progress on the entire transportation system—subway, freeways, bridges, parking, and support facilities—before 1976.* The action of the Congress in December to support continued METRO funding was enormously heartening to the people of the Capital region; it gave, in fact, a glimmer of hope to beleaguered commuters everywhere. The grim Thanksgiving prospect of a great many excavated streets to fill back in has now become the far brighter prospect of at least 24 miles of operating subway— the most modern anywhere—by 1976. *Urgently needed now is prompt approval by the Congress of Federal guarantees for*

METRO revenue bonds—the next essential step to getting the trains running.

TO WELCOME 40 MILLION GUESTS

Both the sheer visitor volume anticipated at the height of the bicentennial observance, and the important goal of eliminating a "them and us" polarity between city residents and their guests from around the world, dictate that past patterns which have made the Mall and its immediate environs a sort of "tourist ghetto" must now go. All of Washington must be made not only hospitable and attractive to the visitor—which the proposals just outlined should go far toward achieving—but easily accessible as well. *I have directed the Secretary of Transportation to coordinate interagency action plans for supplementing those subway lines in service by 1976 with a coordinated network of other public transportation on which visitors can move from fringe parking areas (to be developed under these plans) to points of interest nearer the city center.*

At the hub of this network should be a new National Visitors Center in and around Union Station. Such a facility, desirable for all years, becomes indispensable as we look to the Bicentennial. *I have therefore charged the Secretary of the Interior, in consultation with the Secretary of Transportation, to take immediate action to move the National Visitors Center out of the talk stage, and to prepare new proposals for bringing it to completion by 1976.* When Union Station was built early in this century at the height of the railroad era, one of its express purposes was to permit removal of an unsightly terminal and tracks from the east end of the Mall. Its rehabilitation in the seventies as the Capital's principal reception and orientation point for travelers on all modes of ground transportation would be most appropriate, and would once again relieve the Mall and downtown areas of much traffic congestion. An "air rights" parking garage for buses and visitors' cars, convenient public transit connections, and a central information facility tied in with a citywide tourist guidance and information system would be the major features of the project.

Here is an opportunity for public and private resources to combine to fill a Bicentennial need. Notwithstanding the collapse of previous railroad financing plans for the Center at the time of the Penn Central bankruptcy, I have asked Secretaries Morton and Volpe to seek substantial railroad participation as they formulate the new proposals. I shall submit these to the Congress as soon as possible, with hopes of rapid approval.

Another step which should promote smoother tourist flow to major attractions is construction of a METRO station at Arlington National Cemetery. This station, for which planning funds are requested in my new budget, would speed movement from Washington over to the Arlington shrine, which by 1976 will be enhanced with numerous improvements including a new Memorial Chapel and columbarium. At the same time it would offer the arriving visitor one more convenient transfer point from private to public transportation on the way into the Capital itself.

BICENTENNIAL GARDENS

Moving in toward the center of the city, what will the 1976 visitor find along the Mall? *Most strikingly new and charm-*

ing, perhaps, would be a park and recrea-tion center called Bicentennial Gardens, which I propose be developed in the open land along Constitution Avenue between the Washington Monument and Lincoln Memorial. Since the last of the old World War I "tempos" were removed from the West Mall in 1970, we have explored many alternative plans for developing in their place facilities for people of all ages, incomes, and interests, residents and tour-ists alike, to enjoy.

The Bicentennial Gardens plan, which will soon be ready to present in detail but which of course remains open to the ideas and desires of those for whom it is in-tended, might be called an American cousin of Copenhagen's beloved Tivoli. It follows the present contours of the land on a low profile in keeping with other Mall developments. A restaurant, smaller eating areas, an open-air theater, a band-shell, an area for ice skating, a children's play area, fountains, gardens, a boating lake, and walking paths are examples of the kind of features that might be in-cluded. There could be underground parking to accommodate tour buses, a terminal for the tourist trams, and a visi-tors center in the middle of the Gardens. With such a development, the Mall's at-tractions would be better balanced and dispersed, evening activities now concen-trated in the Smithsonian Quadrangle would have a second focal point, and mingling of Washingtonians and visitors in a pleasant year-round setting would be encouraged. Quality of life for everyone in the Capital would be enhanced.

THE MALL IN 1976

The three major monuments and me-morials in easy reach of Bicentennial Gardens are to be renovated and im-proved in a 4-year Park Service program beginning with this year's budget now be-fore the Congress. Another facelifting project along the whole length of the Mall, and on the Ellipse as well, will re-construct roadways, add walks, bikeways, plantings, and fountains, and provide for a new Ceremonial Drive. This work too is budgeted for fiscal year 1973 and be-yond, to be completed by 1976.

The Mall east of the Washington Mon-ument should also have a new look for the Bicentennial. Besides the Hirshhorn Mu-seum and National Gallery of Art addi-tion which are now being constructed, there will be a handsome new building for one of the Mall's oldest tenants, the Smithsonian Institution. *This structure, which will house the National Air and Space Museum with exhibits ranging from Kitty Hawk to Hadley Rille and with a former astronaut in charge, can be ready in 1976 if the Congress will move now to approve FY 1973 construction funds for it; the plans are nearly complete.* The Smithsonian also plans restoration of the historic Arts and Industries Building to its original 1880s appearance, as a fit setting for the Nation's Centennial ex-hibits which it displayed following the Philadelphia Exposition nearly a century ago and will display again for the Bicen-tennial, and construction of a major new "Nation of Nations" exhibit in the Mu-seum of History and Technology to illus-trate America's multi-cultural tradition. Both projects are the subject of FY 1973 budget requests.

A fourth important undertaking by the Smithsonian—not on the Mall but rather a part of the effort to give the Bicenten-nial activities metropolitan scope—is the Bicentennial Outdoor Museum planned for old Fort Foote, Maryland, on the Potomac in Prince Georges County. The restored fort is to serve as the scene for re-creation of Revolutionary events such as encampments, war-time life, and parades for 1976. *I ask prompt congressional action on legislation to approve the Bicentennial Outdoor Museum and to authorize appropriations for planning it.*

REALIZING A VISION: PENNSYLVANIA AVENUE

As L'Enfant's majestic expanse of Mall provides an axis along which Washington visitors can honor and relive the American past, so Pennsylvania Avenue, leaving the Mall by the new reflecting pool in front of the Capitol and angling away from it a long mile up to the White House, forms the main axis of government activity shaping the American present and future. This avenue, then, also demands attention as we move to dress up the heart of the city for our two hundredth birthday. *By 1976, let us complete the great Federal Triangle office complex in the spirit of the McMillan Commission's original vision 70 years ago. Let us build at its center a Grand Plaza worthy of the name, by transforming what is now a parking lot into a people-oriented park for government workers and visitors to enjoy.* (Visitors will also benefit from the new information and orientation center to be opened in the Great Hall of the Commerce Building by 1976, intended to introduce citizens to the activities of all the executive departments and agencies.) I have requested funds in my budget for fiscal year 1973 to move forward on the Federal Triangle and Grand Plaza projects; with the cooperation of the Congress the work will begin in the near future.

The north side of Pennsylvania Avenue, and with it many blocks of the downtown area, can also be revitalized or well on the way by the time we celebrate the Bicentennial. The FBI building now rising north of the Avenue symbolizes half of the answer—Federal construction—and can stand completed and in use by 1976 with continued congressional support. A further appropriation for this project is included in my new budget requests.

The other half of the answer for Pennsylvania Avenue is coordinated development planning which will mobilize the private sector and help bring commercial and residential activity back to this part of the city. The heart of Washington must not become so dominated by Federal buildings that it sits abandoned and lifeless on evenings and weekends. The two Presidents before me initiated steps to prevent this, and to make the Avenue instead a corridor of lively and varied activity, public and private—and my Administration has continued to press this effort. In September 1970 I announced my strong support for a legislative proposal to establish a development corporation to accomplish the needed revitalization. Since then the proposal has been substantially modified in a good faith effort to accommodate all interests and segments of opinion. *Once again, I urge the Congress to act quickly and favorably on the Pennsylvania Avenue Bicentennial Development Corporation bill.*

When I first expressed support for the

corporation plan nearly 17 months ago, I called it "an opportunity to fulfill, in this city, at this time, a magnificent vision of the men who founded our Nation, and at the same time to create a standard for the rest of the Nation by which to measure their own urban achievement, and on which to build visions of their own." It is not an opportunity that waits forever, though; of the time available between that 1970 statement and the beginning of the Bicentennial year, more than a fourth is already gone. Every month that passes without this legislation further dims our chances of giving all Americans one birthday present they ought to have—a Capital "main street" to be proud of.

THE NEXT FOUR YEARS

Both local and Federal plans for the Bicentennial celebration here in the Nation's Capital are far from complete at present. It is right that they should continue to evolve and expand as we move toward 1976. This message, however, attempts to set the tone and theme for Federal participation over the course of the next 4 years, and also to convey some of the aspirations of Washingtonians themselves without presuming to dictate what those aspirations should be.

The various levels and jurisdictions of government in the Washington area are well organized to follow through on the proposals I make today and to supervise further planning. The American Revolution Bicentennial Commission, with its distinguished bipartisan membership headed by David J. Mahoney, continues to provide excellent national leadership.

The District government is well served by the responsive local Assembly and Commission structure to which I referred above; Mayor Washington is also establishing liaison with suburban planning bodies and with State officials of both Virginia and Maryland. The massive and diverse physical construction effort outlined in this message has been coordinated through a full-time District of Columbia bicentennial task force within the General Services Administration, until recently headed with great skill by Administrator Robert Kunzig. Now that Mr. Kunzig has become a Federal judge, I shall ensure that this coordination work is carried forward at the same high standard.

Under such direction and with the support of the Congress, we can achieve our Bicentennial goal of dual excellence in the District of Columbia, and we can realize by 1976 a dramatic improvement in the quality of Washington life for all whose physical or spiritual home this great Capital is. And by so doing we can help to inspire and encourage the preparations of other communities all across the country for a truly magnificent Bicentennial.

RICHARD NIXON

The White House,
  February 4, 1972.

NOTE: On the same day, the White House released the transcript of a news briefing on plans for the Bicentennial observance in the District of Columbia. Participants in the news briefing were Walter E. Washington, mayor of the District of Columbia, Robert L. Kunzig, Associate Judge, United States Court of Claims, Egil Krogh, Jr., Deputy Assistant to the President for Domestic Affairs, and Theodore C. Lutz, Budget Examiner, Office of Management and Budget.

41   Message to the Congress Transmitting First Annual Report
of Activities Under the Uniform Relocation Assistance
and Real Property Acquisition Policies Act of 1970.
February 4, 1972

To the Congress of the United States:

In accordance with Section 214 of Public Law 91–646, I am transmitting today the first annual report of each Federal agency whose activities are governed, in part, by the Uniform Relocation Assistance and Real Property Acquisition Policies Act of 1970.

The agency reports describe initial steps which have been taken under the Act to provide for the uniform and equitable treatment of persons displaced from homes, businesses or farms by Federal and federally assisted programs and to establish uniform and equitable real property acquisition policies for these programs. The reports cover the period January 2, 1971 through June 30, 1971.

To assure equitable treatment and essential uniformity in administering the law, I requested in a letter to Federal agencies, dated January 4, 1971, that a number of actions be taken. First, the Office of Management and Budget was asked to chair an interagency task force to develop guidelines for all agencies to follow in the issuance of regulations and procedures implementing the Uniform Relocation Assistance Act. The Departments of Justice, Transportation, Defense, and Housing and Urban Development, and the General Services Administration were requested to assist in this development. These guidelines were issued February 27, 1971, and supplemental instructions were issued on August 30, 1971. As noted in the attached reports, the agencies have now

promulgated regulations and procedures to implement the act pursuant to the guidelines.

Secondly, I requested Federal agencies administering mortgage insurance programs to determine whether guarantees could be given to individuals who were displaced and might otherwise be ineligible because of age, physical, or other conditions. Studies completed early in 1971 indicated that such guarantees could be made, and I am advised that these agencies are now fully implementing Section 203(b) of the Act.

Thirdly, I directed the Secretary of Housing and Urban Development to develop criteria and procedures whereby all Federal and federally assisted programs could use the authority provided by Section 206(a) of the Act to construct replacement housing as a last resort. These criteria and procedures to assure uniform and equitable policies and practices by all agencies have been published in the Federal Register, and the Department is evaluating comments received for consideration in the preparation of final instructions on this subject.

The Department of Housing and Urban Development, pursuant to my request, is also developing criteria and procedures for implementing section 215 of the act. That section concerns loans for planning and other preliminary expenses necessary for securing federally insured mortgage financing for the rehabilitation or construction of housing for displaced persons. These procedures and criteria should be issued shortly.

I also directed the Office of Management and Budget to form and to chair a Relocation Assistance Advisory Committee. This Committee includes representatives of the Departments of Agriculture; Defense; Health, Education, and Welfare; and Transportation; the General Services Administration; the Office of Economic Opportunity; and the United States Postal Service.

This Committee will continually review the Government's relocation program for the purpose of making recommendations to the Office of Management and Budget for improvements in the guidelines and for new legislation. In the interests of uniform and equitable administration of the law, it will also provide a vehicle for co-ordinating the relocation programs of each of the agencies.

Executive branch review of the relocation assistance program and of the provisions of the Uniform Relocation Assistance and Real Property Acquisition Policies Act of 1970 has disclosed a number of problem areas which require legislative consideration. The principal areas identified are detailed as enclosure 4 of this report, while other problem areas are identified in individual agency reports. Corrective legislation will be submitted to the Congress.

RICHARD NIXON

The White House,
    February 4, 1972.

NOTE: The text of the message was released at Key Biscayne, Fla.

42   Statement About National Crime Prevention Week, 1972. *February 4, 1972*

LAW enforcement is not a job for the police officer alone. To be effective law enforcement must be backed by the understanding and support of an informed citizenry. It gives me pleasure, therefore, to salute the members of the National Exchange Club and commend them on their annual sponsorship of National Crime Prevention Week.

The twenty-fifth anniversary of this observance comes at a time when crime still poses a major threat to our way of life and to the well-being of our people. But at the same time, encouraging statistics for 1971 tell us that the rate of increase in criminal offenses has been slowed to its lowest rate in five years. In fifty-two American cities crime is currently on the decrease, as compared to only twenty-three such cities a year ago. In our Nation's Capital the number of crimes in the past year was thirteen percent below 1970.

These results did not just happen. They stem from strong new measures adopted by this Administration, by the Congress, by state and local governments and by outstanding civic organizations such as the National Exchange Club.

I welcome this opportunity to pledge my Administration's continuing efforts to expand and intensify crime prevention programs, through both direct Federal activity and Federal aid to local law enforcement.

As one example of recent Federal action, we have introduced special strike-forces which are proving to be useful deterrents to organized crime in our large urban areas. We will now use a similar approach in our all-out drive against drug traffickers and pushers who corrode our national life. On the local level we have made a grant of $160 million to strengthen the fight against serious crime in our major metropolitan centers. We will continue to extend this kind of aid through the Law Enforcement Assistance Administration, and through Revenue Sharing when it is approved by the Congress.

These are just two examples of our full-scale commitment to back up the police officer in a task that is of such critical concern to every citizen. I am especially grateful to the public-spirited members of the National Exchange Club for the initiative and encouragement they have given to this effort in the last quarter-century. I look forward to our continuing cooperation in the years ahead.

RICHARD NIXON

NOTE: The statement was made available to the press at Key Biscayne, Fla., in connection with the observance of National Crime Prevention Week, February 6–12, 1972.

43   Statement About a Special Message to the Congress on Special Revenue Sharing for Manpower. *February 5, 1972*

THROUGH the efforts of all its people, America is making great progress in the fight against inflation. At the same time, the American economy is also doing remarkably well at producing new jobs. Since I announced the new economic policy less than 6 months ago, more than a million new jobs have been generated. This is a good record. Though unemployment remains unacceptably high, it gives promise of further progress toward our goal of full employment without war and without inflation.

One of the greatest challenges of this industrial transition from war to peace has been the need to absorb more than 2 million workers from the Armed Forces and defense-related jobs into the civilian economy. Yet, it is not enough to point out that if they were still in their wartime jobs the rate of unemployment would be far lower. Nor is it enough to point to the large number of new young workers who have gone out in search of their first jobs.

This is not an acceptable answer for an unemployed worker wondering why he has no job. Though we are making progress, we must do better still and we shall.

We have taken many new measures to cut unemployment, and most are just beginning to take hold on the economy— and to have their effect in expanding employment. Among these have been:

—A tax program calculated to expand employment even more significantly during 1972.

—An economic stabilization program to ensure that the economic expansion we are developing is not lost in inflated wages and prices, but is directed toward producing more jobs.

—A transitional public service employment program to give meaningful work to the thousands of jobless Americans in the hardest hit areas.

—New international monetary and trade policies which will improve the competitive position of American industry and produce jobs for American workers.

—Expansionary budget policies for fiscal years 1972 and 1973 to help move us toward full employment.

There is more that can and should be done: One thing needed is to improve the quality of our manpower development programs, and to make them more responsive to the particular needs of particular localities.

On Monday, I will be sending to the Congress a message on manpower special revenue sharing. In that message I will again propose a way to improve the training and job placement service which we can offer to the unemployed American.

For too long there has been a gap between Federal manpower programs' promise and their performance for the jobless individual. It is time that we give our communities the flexibility they need to design programs better suited to their own special employment conditions. The Manpower Revenue Sharing Act which I will again propose in my message on Monday can help to do all of these things. It is clearly time that we do a better job of getting the jobless worker trained and a better job of getting him off the unemployment rolls and onto a payroll.

NOTE: The statement was released at Key Biscayne, Fla.

44 Statement About the Death of Marianne Moore. *February* 6, 1972

MRS. NIXON and I join the Nation today in mourning the loss of one of our most distinguished poets, Marianne Moore. Admired for her imaginative style and adored for her love of man and animal, she was an endearing companion to her readers for a half century. In her, as she said there should be in all poetry, was truly "a place for the genuine."

We can be grateful that the splash of color and enchantment which she added to the Western World will brighten our landscape for many years to come.

NOTE: Miss Moore, 84, died in her sleep at her home in New York City on February 5, 1972.

The statement was made available to the press at Key Biscayne, Fla.

45 Special Message to the Congress on Special Revenue Sharing for Manpower. *February* 7, 1972

To the Congress of the United States:

There are few issues of greater concern today, to the Congress and to the President, than the state of the American economy. We are passing from a period when the economy was inflated by the strains of war to a time when it will be challenged by the needs of peace.

Adding to the inevitable problems of transition has been the increasingly vigorous economic competition of other countries. We welcome this competition, but we must also realize that it requires us to give renewed attention to increasing American productivity—not only to ensure the continued improvement in our own standard of living, but also to keep our Nation's goods competitive in the world's markets, thereby providing jobs for American workers.

During the late fifties and early sixties our annual rate of increase in labor productivity averaged 3.4 percent. But by the mid-sixties it had begun its drop to an average of only 1.8 percent.

We are taking important steps to revive the productivity of American labor. Our New Economic Policy is shrinking the bulge of inflation. We are proposing a new program to promote technological progress—for advances in research and development are essential ingredients of rising productivity. But technological advance is not the whole story: increases in the skills of our labor force also play a large part.

We are not interested in the competitiveness of our labor force for its own sake. We are concerned about the individual American—concerned that he learn the skills to gain employment or learn more skills to gain better employment. We are concerned about the health of our economy, knowing that a strong, highly productive economy is the individual American's best insurance against unemployment. This is why the Federal Government provides manpower training—to increase the opportunities of jobless Americans to share in the abundance of America.

Today, I again urge that the Congress enable us to improve our manpower programs by enacting the Manpower Revenue Sharing Act.

Ten years ago, the Congress recognized Federal responsibility for comprehensive manpower training by passing the Manpower Development and Training Act of 1962. The MDTA and the Economic Opportunity Act of 1964 have grown to include over a dozen separate, narrow grant programs, each with its own purposes. Yet, even though manpower programs have grown in number, the need for manpower training has outpaced the capability of these older programs to provide services. Our commitment is strong, but we have not bridged the gap between the promises and the performance of Federal manpower programs. Something better is needed—on this we can all agree.

THE OLD WAY: A NEED FOR REFORM

Like the field of manpower training, many other areas of Federal assistance are suffering from a hardening of governmental arteries. Federal programs are meant to meet the needs of individual citizens living in 50 States and in thousands of communities, but those diverse needs are not being met by rigid, standardized Federal programs. Instead, the pressure on State and local resources is building to the breaking point. The traditional answer would be the establishment of even more separate categories of Federal aid.

Federal aid is needed, but the proliferation of Federal plans, programs, categories, and requirements has compounded the individual problems faced by American communities today. Frequently, Federal involvement has merely generated a false sense of security—a security which has been betrayed by the continuing multiplication of communities' social needs and the failure of government to meet those needs.

Federal aid outlays account for 21 percent of State and local revenues today, but many Federal grants require State and local officials to match some percentage of Federal aid with local money which could be better spent in other ways to solve local problems. In many cases, State and local officials must decide either to accept Federal aid with its accompanying allocation of State and local funds or to receive no Federal aid at all.

Federal maintenance of effort provisions further distort local priorities by requiring State and local governments to continue projects irrespective of their effectiveness in meeting their own needs. Once again, our communities lose more of the flexibility which would enable them to meet what they consider their most pressing needs.

Frustrating and time-consuming project approval requirements, a jungle of red tape, often make it impossible for State and local governments to count on having Federal money when it is needed. No matter how pressing some needs may be, communities must wait, sometimes months or even years, for the slowly grinding wheels of bureaucracy to consider each grant in minute detail.

The real problem lies not with the Federal Government's intentions, but with how it tries to meet communities' needs—by undertaking one narrow, inflexible program after another. The number of separate categories has grown until no one is sure of their boundaries. In 1963, there were only 160 individual grant programs amounting to about $8.6 billion, but now there are over 1,000 such programs amounting to almost $40 billion. Each rigid category of additional aid reflects the worst kind of arrogance: the presumption that only the Federal Government

knows local needs and how to meet them.

If we have faith in the American people—and I for one do—then we must recognize that in thousands of communities, each with its own problems and priorities, there live people quite capable of determining and meeting their own needs and in all probability doing a better job of it than the Washington bureaucracy. Quite simply, today's local needs are likely to be met best by local solutions.

The time has clearly come to reform the way in which the Federal Government aids local and State authorities. The time has clearly come when those who serve at the State and local level and are charged with the responsibility for finding workable solutions to State and local problems should be given a chance. Clearly, it is time that Federal aid became truly that, aid, not rigid and often confusing control.

Waste, confusion, and inefficiency are too often the price paid by local and State governments for Federal aid under the present system. Last year the Federal Government discovered the following cases, to cite just a few examples:

—One Northcentral State had 93 people on its government payroll to do nothing but apply for Federal *education* grants.

—A study of grant programs in one Western city revealed that only 15 percent of the Federal funds to that city went through its mayor or elected government.

—Federal demands on the time and attention of local officials is particularly serious. In one small Midwestern city, a part-time mayor had to attend sixteen separate evening meetings per month, one with Federal officials from each of the sixteen separate grant programs in which his small city participates.

THE NEW WAY: SPECIAL REVENUE SHARING

In a series of special messages to the Congress last year, I proposed Special Revenue Sharing, a new system of Federal aid which would serve the purposes of our State and local governments better than the system of narrow Federal grant programs now operating. I proposed that funds be made available to States and localities for six broad purposes—manpower, law enforcement, education, transportation, urban community development, and rural community development—to be used, for each of these purposes, as they see fit to meet their particular needs. Those proposals, if enacted, would consolidate over 130 separate programs into six general purpose areas. Under our Special Revenue Sharing proposals, in the first full year of operation, $12.3 billion in Federal funds would be provided to States and localities for those six broad purposes. These funds would be free from matching requirements, maintenance of effort restrictions, presently rigid prior Federal project approval requirements, and, best of all, inflexible Federal plans. But there are two major stipulations: (1) the money is subject to all the civil rights requirements of Title VI of the Civil Rights Act of 1964, and (2) no government unit would receive less money under these proposals than it did under the old system of narrow Federal grants.

Special Revenue Sharing is not a wholesale dismantling of the Federal grants system, as some critics have charged. It is a careful effort to decide which level of government can best deal with a particular problem and then to move the necessary funds and decision-making power to that level of government. When a Federal approach is needed we should take that road, but when a local approach is better we should move the resources and power to that level.

I realize that these are challenging concepts, which have major implications for the structure of American government—Federal, State and local—and for the effectiveness with which government serves the people. They require us in Washington to give up some of our power, so that more power can be returned to the States, to the localities, and to the people, where it will be better used. It is appropriate, therefore, that the Congress give full consideration to all of these proposals for fundamental reform and move rapidly to create effective programs to meet today's needs.

MANPOWER SERVICES FOR THE SEVENTIES

I recognize that it is incumbent upon those who propose change to justify the changes. I believe our experience with Federal manpower programs over the last 10 years justifies the changes we are proposing.

All those represented in the current array of patchwork manpower programs—the schools, private employers, public agencies, nonprofit groups, not to mention the unemployed workers—know that the present system is not delivering the jobs, the training, and the other manpower services that this Nation needs and has a right to expect.

As we begin the second decade of comprehensive manpower assistance for our unemployed and underemployed citizens we know we must do better, and we can do better. It is time for a change.

Manpower experts throughout the Nation agree that the necessary reform of the Nation's system of manpower training should have as its three basic goals the decategorization, the decentralization, and the consolidation of existing manpower development efforts.

The Manpower Revenue Sharing Act that I have proposed would allow us to achieve those goals. It would benefit citizens in every corner of the Nation and offer renewed hope to members of our society who have lacked opportunity— hope for jobs, for advancement, and for a better standard of living. It would establish a new framework of constructive partnership for manpower training among Federal, State, and local governments. Its principles are simple and fundamental, yet far-reaching.

THE PRINCIPLES OF MANPOWER SPECIAL REVENUE SHARING

First, the Manpower Revenue Sharing Act does *not mandate* any existing categorical program or guarantee its perpetuation—irrespective of its performance—in any community. However, it would *not prohibit* the continuation of any project which a particular locality feels effectively serves its own and its workers' needs. It is time to end the restrictiveness of the old, narrow programs which have frustrated communities' efforts to develop manpower programs geared to their own needs and circumstances.

In its first full year of operation, the Manpower Revenue Sharing Act would provide $2 billion for manpower purposes, of which $1.7 billion would be divided

among State and local units of government—without unnecessary red tape— using a formula based on the size of their labor force and the numbers of unemployed and disadvantaged. The remainder would be used by the Secretary of Labor to meet the generalized national needs of this new system.

It would authorize a broad range of services, including:
—classroom instruction in both remedial education and occupational skills;
—training on the job with both public and private employers, aided by manpower subsidies;
—job opportunities, including work experience and short-term employment for special age groups and the temporarily unemployed, and transitional public service employment at all levels of government.

These services, all designed to help move people toward self-supporting employment, augmented by temporary income support, relocation assistance, child care and other supportive services authorized by the Act, would make it possible for our communities to mount integrated manpower development programs truly responsive to their own priority needs.

The *second* major goal of Manpower Special Revenue Sharing is to increase substantially reliance upon State and local governments to manage major manpower activities. Local governments are often powerless when jobs are not to be had. It is time we equipped our local governments with the resources and decision-making power to meet their responsibilities.

The Manpower Revenue Sharing Act meets this objective. It would provide communities with the resources they need to help get people into jobs and job-training. Decisions on what needs to be done to improve specific local manpower conditions cannot and should not be made in Washington. They should be delegated to the area where the unemployed person lives and wants to work.

The *third* way to move toward a new era in manpower development is through consolidation of the multiple, frequently inconsistent, funding authorizations for manpower activities. Even members of the congressional Appropriations Committees frequently chafe under the unmanageable task of sorting out the confusing array of alphabetical "programs" created by existing manpower enactments. While a good deal of untangling has been done by administrative action, the only durable solution is an overall reform.

The Manpower Revenue Sharing Act would replace the two major pieces of legislation which have spawned most of the acronym programs—the Manpower Development and Training Act and Title I of the Economic Opportunity Act—with a single statute which incorporates the flexibility needed by State and local government.

The Manpower Revenue Sharing Act submitted to the Congress in March of 1971 incorporates all three of these vital concepts. I believe that the application of these principles in the Manpower Revenue Sharing Act is sound, but the principles are more important than the details. Reasonable men may disagree on the specifics of any important legislation, but there comes a time when its principles must be earnestly debated and decisions made. For the principles of Manpower Special Revenue Sharing, that time has come. The fine points of this legislation, which were discussed in my message of March 4, 1971, are open to refinement,

but I believe the principles of Special Revenue Sharing are too important to be eviscerated.

Our country needs new manpower legislation. Let us now write a new charter for the second decade of manpower development that will produce solid performance—for the economy, for the unemployed and underemployed, and for government itself.

RESTORING THE AMERICAN SPIRIT

The Special Revenue Sharing approach to providing Federal help would enable us to deal more effectively with many of this Nation's most pressing problems. But it would do much more. It would help to restore the American spirit.

In recent years many Americans have come to doubt the capacity of government—at all levels—to meet the needs of an increasingly complex Nation. They have watched as the power to effect change in their communities has moved gradually from the local level, with the reality of friends and community, to the national center, to Washington. There was a time when the increasing centralization of government fostered a greater sense of national purpose. But more recently, the weight of unfulfilled promises reinforced by the growing complexity of social problems has caused many Americans to doubt the capability of our system of government.

By providing new resources to the levels of government closest to the problems and closest to the people involved—people who may see their problems in a different light than the Federal Government—both General and Special Revenue Sharing will do much to revive the confidence and spirit of our people. A free and diverse Nation needs a diversity of approaches; a free Nation should invest its faith in the right and ability of its people to meet the needs of their own communities. No greater sense of confidence can be found than that of a community which has solved its own problems and met its own needs.

Confidence in government is nowhere under greater challenge than among the young, yet the future of America depends upon the involvement of our young in the day-to-day business of governing this land. By making resources available to the more localized units of government, where more people can play a more direct role—and by placing the power of decision where the people are—I hope that many of the young will come to realize that their participation can truly make a difference. This purpose—this philosophy—is at the heart of Special Revenue Sharing.

The people's right to change what does not work is one of the greatest principles of our system of government—and that principle will be strengthened as the governments closest to the people are strengthened. Though the Federal Government has tried with intelligence and vigor to meet the people's needs, many of its purposes have gone unfulfilled for far too long. Now, let us help those most directly affected to try their hand. American society and American government can only benefit from ensuring to our citizens the fullest possible opportunity to make their communities better places, for themselves, for their families, and for their neighbors.

RICHARD NIXON

The White House,
    February 7, 1972.

NOTE: On the same day, the White House released two fact sheets on special revenue sharing for manpower and the transcript of a news briefing by Secretary of Labor James D. Hodgson on the message.

46   Statement on Signing the Federal Election Campaign Act of 1971.   *February 7, 1972*

WHEN I vetoed the bill to limit expenditures on political broadcasting in October of 1970, I pointed out that the goal of controlling campaign expenditures was a highly laudable one. The chief problem with the bill then before me was that it did not limit overall costs but applied only to radio and television. As I put it then, it plugged "only one hole in a sieve."

Since that time, the House and Senate have worked to design a better bill. I believe they have succeeded in that endeavor. S. 382, the Federal Election Campaign Act of 1971, limits the amount candidates for Federal elective offices may spend on advertising, not just on radio and television, but through all communications media. It limits contributions by candidates and their families to their own campaigns. It provides for full reporting of both the sources and the uses of campaign funds, both after elections and during campaigns. By giving the American public full access to the facts of political financing, this legislation will guard against campaign abuses and will work to build public confidence in the integrity of the electoral process.

The Federal Election Campaign Act of 1971 is a realistic and enforceable bill, an important step forward in an area which has been of great public concern. Because I share that concern, I am pleased to give my approval to this bill.

NOTE: As enacted, S. 382 is Public Law 92–225 (86 Stat. 3).

On the same day, the White House released an announcement summarizing the provisions of the act.

47 Statement About the Death of Ambassador Llewellyn E. Thompson. *February 7, 1972*

THE DEATH of Ambassador Llewellyn E. Thompson deprives the Nation—and, indeed, the entire world—of one of its wisest and most experienced counselors in statecraft.

He served a succession of Presidents with consummate skill in the arts of diplomacy.

I was particularly indebted to him when he came out of well-earned retirement to advise me personally, on the crucial SALT talks, and to participate in the early negotiating sessions as a member of the U.S. Delegation.

I deeply regret the passing of this great public servant, who contributed so much to the successes of American foreign policy over the past generation.

Mrs. Nixon and I join Ambassador Thompson's wife and children—and his many friends, colleagues, and admirers in Washington and around the world—in mourning this grave loss to the Nation.

NOTE: Ambassador Thompson, 67, died of cancer at the Clinical Center of the National Institutes of Health, Bethesda, Md., on February 6, 1972. He had served as Ambassador to the Soviet Union from 1957 to 1962 and from 1967 to 1969, Ambassador at Large, Department of State, from 1962 to 1967, and member of the United States delegation to the strategic arms limitation talks from 1969 to 1972.

Secretary of State William P. Rogers represented the President at funeral services for the Ambassador.

48 Statement on Signing the Foreign Assistance Act of 1971. *February 7, 1972*

I HAVE today signed S. 2819, the Foreign Assistance Act of 1971. That act authorizes appropriations for our international development assistance programs until June 30, 1973, and for the remainder of foreign aid activities, including international security assistance programs, through June 30, 1972.

Viewed against the vital national objectives which our foreign assistance programs are designed to pursue, the act is a great disappointment. It severely cuts the amounts requested by the Administration for development assistance and security assistance and is below minimum acceptable levels. It does not include the major reform proposals that I sent to the Congress in April of last year.

Moreover, the bill reaches my desk more than halfway through the fiscal year, delayed by legislative entanglements resulting from the attachment in committee of an unprecedented number of restrictive and non-germane amendments, some of which raise grave constitutional questions. While many were modified or removed in the long months of debate, the final product adds significant additional restrictions and limitations to those already in law which have hampered the efficient administration of foreign aid and the effective conduct of foreign affairs.

The foreign assistance programs of the United States constitute a fundamental element of our strategy for peace. While these programs have had a troubled his-

tory and have sometimes been unpopular, their role in maintaining the security of our Nation is indispensable. I call upon this session of the 92d Congress to restore a comprehensive security and development assistance program through legislation equal to the challenges and the opportunities for peace which lie before us.

NOTE: As enacted, S. 2819 is Public Law 92–226 (86 Stat. 20).

49   Remarks to the White House Conference on the "Industrial World Ahead: A Look at Business in 1990." *February* 7, 1972

Secretary Stans, members of the Cabinet, all of the distinguished guests here at this Conference:

After that rather lengthy introduction, I shall try to respond in kind. I was expecting that Maurice Stans, my longtime friend from Washington, California, and now Washington days, would perhaps find something he could say. [*Laughter*]

Could I just say a word, however, about him? As you probably have noted in the press—and this report in the press is accurate [*laughter*]—Secretary Stans is completing his service as Secretary of Commerce and then will be taking on a new position. Since this is a nonpartisan group, he is going to be the chancellor of the exchequer of one of the two major parties.

But I think all of you should know that the idea of this Conference, the concept, was his. He has been a splendid Secretary of Commerce in this Administration. In so many fields that are not well known, like minority business enterprise and others, he has done an outstanding job. He is a man, pragmatist though he is, who has vision, who sees the future. I remember

his coming to me many, many months ago, talking about this Conference, developing its concepts.

I cannot think of any more effective way that a man could leave the position of Secretary of Commerce on a higher note than a conference of this type, which was his idea.

I appreciate the fact that all of you—representatives of business, representatives of labor and of government—have participated in the Conference, and will be doing so in the next 2 days.

My remarks today, I am sure, will be somewhat anticlimactic after some of the things you heard this morning about the future of the United States and what it holds. Perhaps I can put that future, however, in the context of the world I understand best, the context of politics in its broadest sense, of world politics, and then, of course, relate it to the problems of American business and American labor.

In the current issue of Fortune, the story is told of three men on a desert island who spotted a tidal wave headed their way. The first man decided to use the time remaining on wine, women, and song. The second man chose to get down on his knees and pray. The third man—and I am sure he was an American businessman—got busy trying to figure out how to breathe under water.

Now, as we look ahead to the industrial world of the future at this White House Conference, it is well to remember that there is something to be said for enjoying life, the power of prayer is very important, but as we face the future, we must also get ready to live in it.

In the course of this Conference, you will be exploring the exciting prospects that lie ahead for the workingman and the businessman, and the workingwoman and businesswoman of America. You will be examining the new social responsibilities of business, the challenges of the new technology so vital to the betterment of the lives of our people, the future of the economy.

There has really never been a time when a hard, searching look ahead has been more essential for America than it is today.

We cannot really plan for the industrial world ahead without considering the total picture of the world of the future. We have to ask ourselves which way the world is heading; what we, as a Nation, must do to influence the course of history toward more freedom, toward a generation of peace; and what kind of people we will have to be to make a difference in our children's lives and in the world of tomorrow.

These are profound questions, and the kind that all too many people consider themselves just too busy to deal with. But the American dream is too important to be left to the dreamers, and that is no reflection on your morning speakers. Practical men have to examine their ideals and shape the future in the image of their hopes.

The people of the United States of America, as we all know, make up approximately 6 percent of the population of the world. Let's consider what that figure means.

First, it means that we have a great deal to be proud of. When 6 percent of the people of the world produce one-fifth of the world's steel, one-third of its electric power, one-third of all automobiles, then even our most severe critics will have to admit that the American economic system must be doing something right.

The fact that we number only six out of every 100 people in the world means something else that must give us pause, however. It means that we, who believe in majority rule, are a minority group in the world. If we are to lead, we cannot lead by force of arms or by weight of numbers; we can lead only by the force of our example and the quality of our vision.

What is it that has brought this 6 percent, this minority of the world that calls itself America, to the highest standard of living, the highest expression of human freedom?

What is it that will propel this Nation forward in the coming generation to lead mankind in its search for a better life in a world of peace?

I am convinced that the answer lies in a real but intangible quality called the American spirit.

In today's world, that spirit is being tested. America is being tested.

We have got to learn once again to compete in the world—and the only way we can compete is on the basis of our own productivity.

In the past, America has been able to pay the highest wages in the world, to enjoy the highest standard of living in the world, and still compete in the world's markets because we had the best technology and the highest productivity.

But in recent years, while other nations have been modernizing, while others have been spurting ahead in productivity, in America we have let productivity slip; we have neglected capital investment; we have fallen behind other nations in the attention and support we give to applied science and to advances in technology.

We can be proud, as Americans, of our record of generosity in the 25 years since World War II. With your help, the help of business and labor, this great, productive American economy made it possible. Old enemies as well as old friends have gotten back on their feet, and new nations have been started on the long road to prosperity.

This help has been good, certainly, for other nations. It has been good for the world, and in the long run I believe it has been good for America.

But let us see where we are now. During the decade of the sixties, exports of American manufactured goods increased by 110 percent.

During the same 10 years, exports of German manufactured goods rose by 200 percent, Canada's by 285 percent, Japan—now the second greatest producer in the non-Communist world—increased her exports of manufactured goods in the past 10 years by 400 percent.

Now, this is just one measure of the competition we face. It is one of the reasons why last year, for the first time since 1888, we had our first unfavorable trade deficit.

Nations never stand still. They go forward or they fall backward.

Other nations in the world today are going forward—some of them rapidly forward. And America has to exert itself, we have to be at our very best, if we are to remain competitive in the world.

In business and in life, there is a time when tough decisions have to be made. In this Administration, we made some tough decisions in order to help get the economy back on its feet in the transition from war to peace, to get it back on a stable basis, with full employment, moving forward in a sustainable way.

I believe in discussing these tough decisions. I am going to talk about my philosophy and some of the things, very candidly, that I have had to do.

I believe in economic freedom. I believe the best economy for America is a free market economy. But faced with the choice of temporary wage and price controls or continued inflation, I chose temporary controls to curb inflation.

I believe in balanced budgets, but faced with the choice between budget deficits and unemployment, I chose deficits to help create more jobs.

In the long run, our goal is to remove the controls, get rid of the deficits—once we have brought about price stability and full employment.

But in the short run, there is going to be a lot of complaining, and I understand that. I am prepared to take the heat because I believe that in the position I hold, I have to put first things first, and full employment without inflation in a period of peace must come first for America.

Now, I talked about some of my hard decisions. Let me talk about some of yours. Are you going to crawl into a shell and demand protection from world competition; or are you going to roll up your sleeves and increase productivity?

Are you going to expend your energy

complaining about controls; or are you going to adopt wage and price policies that will remove the pressure of inflation and the need for controls?

Now I am convinced I made the right decisions. I am convinced you will make the right decisions as well—right for yourselves and right for our country.

I recognize that there are many people around who are uncertain about whether we can really cut the rate of inflation. Well, there are two answers to these doubts. First, the record: Consumer prices rose 3.4 percent in 1971, too much; but that is compared to 5.5 the year before. That is the right direction—down. That shows that it can be done.

And second, we are determined to keep pushing down the rate of inflation. We have made a commitment; we have proved the lengths we are prepared to go to keep our commitments. We will see this fight against rising prices through to stability.

Just as controls and our other policies, we believe, are going to work to stop inflation, our policies to create more jobs are going to work.

You all know that in the past 6 months, civilian employment has increased by over a million jobs. Yet that surge has not made nearly enough of a dent in the unemployment figures. This we all agree. In the most recent quarter, real output rose at a rate double that of the preceding two quarters. Now, that is a basis for real confidence—the confidence that should generate further expansion and more jobs. Nobody says the road to full employment is quick and easy; but I believe, based on the record, that we are on that road.

Now we come to the key to it all. What enables each worker to get more out of his work, each investor to get more out of his investment, and the Nation to get more out of its economy? The answer is productivity.

You as businessmen, as labor leaders, all have said this. For a long time in America we were able to take productivity increases for granted. We just assumed it was going to happen, and it did. We rather imagined a sort of technological cornucopia that promised increasing abundance every year without any extra effort on our part—and this made us somewhat complacent. We tended to imagine that more was our due—regardless of what we did; whether we did more, there was going to be more.

But now the new situation in the world has changed all that.

Even if we were content just to fight with one another for a bigger slice of the same old pie, instead of making the pie bigger, this would no longer be enough. Our markets would disappear; and not only would we no longer sell abroad, but we could no longer afford to buy from abroad; and America would stagnate.

But we are not going to stagnate. We still have the American spirit. But having the spirit is not enough; we have to use it.

If we are to maintain our leadership in the world of the future, it will not be by force of arms. It will be by the strength of our spirit, backed by the vigor of our economy—which is the greatest asset we have in world affairs today. If we slip back as an economic power, then we will slip also as a moral force in the world, for it will have been because we ceased to try, because we ceased to compete, because we gave up on ourselves and the world.

I do not believe that America has given up, that it will give up. Nor do I believe that we in America, because of the competition we face, will try to build a wall around ourselves.

If we were ever to permit this Nation to turn isolationist in its foreign policy, we would be inviting another war or the destruction of our freedom.

If we were to let this Nation turn protectionist in its economic policy, we would be inviting a trade war—and like the other kind of war, every nation on this planet would lose.

We are not going to let either of these things happen. We are not going to become isolationist in our foreign policy and we are not going to become protectionist in our economic policy. We are not about to forget the secret of the world's highest standard of living—a competitive spirit that results in rising productivity.

That is what America has stood for for almost 200 years. It is what has made us the economic wonder of the world today.

After years of lagging productivity, which I just referred to, we made a comeback last year—back to a 3.6 percent rise. Now we have momentum—and we must never again forget the secret of American success.

For too long, I think, we have to recognize that too many of us in this country, too many businessmen, too many workingmen, thought of the American economy as a kind of giant turtle. It may have been fat and lazy, but it had a protective shell that seemed impregnable.

But let me point out to you that nature played a trick on the turtle. The only way he can move forward is to stick his neck out.

Well, the time has come for that turtle, this great, giant American economy which you represent, the leadership of which is in this room tonight, the time has come for this turtle to stick its neck out and get moving.

As it does, it will show that America's competitive spirit is alive and healthy, ready to lead the world into the new prosperity.

As all of you in this room are aware, 2 weeks from now I will be in Mainland China. And then, a few months from now, I will be in the Soviet Union. Both of these trips of course have created great interest in America and in the world.

As I have often said, neither should raise any illusions about what can be accomplished. Because of the differences in our systems of government and our attitude toward the world, there will be great differences after the trips as well as before.

The goal is, of course, to try to develop a dialogue, a communication, a process through which it may be possible in the next generation and a generation after that, that instead of fighting about those differences that we will continue to have, we will talk about them. This is a goal worth journeying halfway around the world to achieve.

I do not mean to suggest to this audience or any in the world that we are going to have instant peace as a result of these two journeys. But I do know what our hopes are—that it will be possibly a safer world and that it may be possibly a more open world, and that our children may live possibly in a world of peace, with different systems of government, talking rather than fighting, and that they will live in an open world, able to move more or less freely around the world, to know its excitement, the interest, wherever people may live, any place on this planet.

That, I would trust, would be a contribution that I might be able to make, not by myself, but at least make a beginning in these two journeys that I will be taking.

But I ought to say that the other side

of that coin is that to the extent we are able to succeed, to the extent that the dangers of war in the world become less, the challenges of peace will become greater.

Let's look at the world again. Look at it in terms of where we are and what the competition will be. Twenty-five years ago the United States, economically, as everybody in this room knows, had no competitors whatever. We were only competing against ourselves. Because of the destruction in Europe and in Asia, because none of the other nations in the world were in our league, we were, in effect, able to lead the world just as fast as we wanted to. No one else was pressing us.

Let me use a favorite example from the world of sports. Many of you have been watching the Winter Olympics. I remember the first Olympics that I read about, in the year 1928. Some of you are old enough to remember it, too. The great miler of the twenties was Paavo Nurmi of Finland. He was probably the greatest miler who ever lived. He never broke 4 minutes, however.

You also remember that when he ran, he ran with a wristwatch and he timed himself on each lap because there was no one who could compete with him and press him. In order even to get as close to 4 minutes as he did, he had to run against the clock.

Twenty-five years ago, economically, America was running against the clock. That is not true today. We have the new Europe with Britain in the Common Market. We have the Soviet Union now the second power economically in the world. We have Mainland China with all of its potential in the future. We have Japan, the second most productive non-Commu-

nist economy in the world. We have also the future possibilities in Latin America, and Asia, the Mideast, and Africa.

So, here we see America looking forward to that target date of ours and of this Conference, the year 1990. We see an America no longer running against the clock, an America still ahead, but an America having to do its best in order to maintain its leadership.

What I am saying to this audience today is very simply this: In the position that I hold I want to do everything that I can to seize the moment to make the world safer, to make it a more peaceful world, to make it a more open world.

In the position that you have, as business leaders and labor leaders, you will determine whether the America in that new world with all those new competitors is going to slide back and let the others who are stronger, have a greater spirit, a greater sense of destiny, pass us by, or whether that spirit that has made this country as great as it is, still exists in the hearts and minds of our people.

Among those who compete with us, a government edict, a pronouncement by one leader or a bureaucracy can whip a people into some kind of productivity. That is not true in this country. The future of the American economy can be affected by government, and I say thank God for this. However, the future of the American economy is determined not by a few government officials, but by the decisions of a million decisionmakers throughout this country in business and in labor.

That is why, Mr. Secretary, in this historic Conference, as we look down toward the end of the century, let us hope and pray it will be a more peaceful world, that it will be a more open world. And let us do everything that we can, each in our individual ways, to see that America remains competitive economically by not running, as we had to after World War II, only against the clock, but doing our best. And our best will be good enough.

Thank you.

NOTE: The President spoke at 9:22 p.m. in the Ballroom of the Sheraton-Park Hotel.

He spoke from a prepared text. An advance text of his remarks was released on the same day.

The 3-day Conference was attended by 1,500 representatives of business, labor, the academic community, and government.

50   Statement on Transmitting a Special Message to the Congress Outlining the 1972 Environmental Program. *February 8, 1972*

EACH of us, all across this great land, has a stake in maintaining and improving environmental quality: clean air and clean water, the wise use of our land, the protection of wildlife and natural beauty, parks for all to enjoy.

These are part of the birthright of every American. To guarantee that birthright, we must act, and act decisively. It is literally now or never.

During the past 3 years, we have made a good start. We have passed new laws to protect the environment, and we have mobilized the power of public concern. But there is much yet to be done.

Eighteen of the major environmental proposals which I put forward a year ago have still not received final action by the Congress. I repeat today my urgent request for Congressional action on this much needed legislation, and I am also presenting a number of new proposals.

The environmental agenda now before the Congress includes laws to deal with water pollution, pesticide hazards, ocean dumping, excessive noise, careless land development, and many other environmental problems. These problems will not stand still for politics or for partisanship. They demand to be met now. By meeting them now, we can make 1972 the best year ever for environmental progress.

The time has come for man to make his peace with nature. Let us renew our commitment. Let us redouble our effort. The quality of our life on this good land is a cause to unite all Americans.

NOTE: The President read the statement in the Family Theater for sound and film recording.

51   Special Message to the Congress Outlining the 1972 Environmental Program. *February 8, 1972*

To the Congress of the United States:

From the very first, the American spirit has been one of self-reliance and confident action. Always we have been a people to say with Henley "I am the master of my fate . . . the captain of my soul"— a people sure that man commands his own destiny. What has dawned dramatically upon us in recent years, though, is a new recognition that to a significant extent man commands as well the very destiny of this planet where he lives, and the destiny of all life upon it. We have even begun to see that these destinies are not many and separate at all—that in fact they are indivisibly one.

This is the environmental awakening. It marks a new sensitivity of the American spirit and a new maturity of American public life. It is working a revolution in values, as commitment to responsible partnership with nature replaces cavalier assumptions that we can play God with our surroundings and survive. It is leading to broad reforms in action, as individuals, corporations, government, and civic groups mobilize to conserve resources, to control pollution, to anticipate and prevent emerging environmental problems, to manage the land more wisely, and to preserve wildness.

In messages to the Congress during 1970 and 1971 I proposed comprehensive initiatives reflecting the earliest and most visible concerns of the environmental awakening. The new cast of the public mind had to be translated into new legislation. New insights had to have new governmental forms and processes through which to operate. Broadly-based problems—such as air pollution, water pollution and pesticide hazards—had to be dealt with first.

The necessary first steps in each of these areas have now been taken, though in all of them the work is far from completed. Now, as we press on with that work in 1972, we must also come to grips with the basic factors which underlie our more obvious environmental problems—factors like the use of land and the impact of incentives or disincentives built into our economic system. We are gaining an increasingly sophisticated understanding of the

way economic, institutional, and legal forces shape our surroundings for good or ill; the next step is learning how to turn such forces to environmental benefit.

Primary responsibility for the actions that are needed to protect and enhance our environment rests with State and local government, consumers, industry, and private organizations of various kinds—but the Federal Government must provide leadership. On the first day of this decade I stated that "it is literally now or never" for true quality of life in America. Amid much encouraging evidence that it can and will be "now," we must not slacken our pace but accelerate it. Environmental concern must crystallize into permanent patterns of thought and action. What began as environmental awakening must mature finally into a new and higher environmental way of life. If we flag in our dedication and will, the problems themselves will not go away. Toward keeping the momentum of awareness and action, I pledge my full support and that of this Administration, and I urgently solicit the continuing cooperation of the Congress and the American people.

Two Years' Agenda

FROM CONSIDERATION TO ACTION

In my 1971 environmental message, just one year ago today, I sent to the Congress a comprehensive program designed to clean up the problems of the past, and to deal with emerging problems before they become critical. These proposals included:

Regulation of toxic substances
Comprehensive improvement in pesticide control authority
Noise control

Preservation of historic buildings

Power plant siting

Regulation of environmental effects of surface and underground mining

Ocean dumping regulation

More effective control of water pollution through a greatly expanded waste treatment grant program and strengthened standard-setting and enforcement authorities

A National Land Use Policy Act

Substantial expansion of the wilderness system

Expanded international cooperation

To date, most of the legislation on this list has been the subject of congressional hearings; most of it has attracted heartening interest and support; but none of it has yet received final congressional action. Last year was, quite properly, a year of consideration of these measures by the Congress. I urge, however, that this be a year of action on all of them, so that we can move on from intention to accomplishment in the important needs they address. Passage of these measures and creation of the unified Department of Natural Resources which I also proposed in 1971—by this 92nd Congress—will be essential if we are to have an adequate base for improving environmental quality.

BUILDING ON THE BASE

As that base is being established, we must move ahead to build wisely and rapidly upon it. I shall outline today a plan for doing that, with initiatives and actions in the following areas:

—Tightening pollution control

A Toxic Wastes Disposal Control Act

Legislation to control sediment from construction activities

An emissions charge to reduce sulfur oxide air pollution

Clean energy research and energy conservation measures

—Making technology an environmental ally

Integrated pest management

Stepped-up research on noise control

Stepped-up research on air pollution effects and measurement

—Improving land use

Expansion and strengthening of the National Land Use Policy Act

Protection of wetlands

—Protecting our natural heritage

A ban on use of poisons for predator control on public lands

A stronger law to protect endangered species of wildlife

Big Cypress National Fresh Water Reserve

National Recreation Areas around New York Harbor and the Golden Gate

Conversion of 20 additional Federal properties to recreational use

18 new Wilderness Areas

Regulation of off-road vehicles on Federal lands

—Expanding international cooperation on the environment

Establishment of a United Nations Fund for the Environment

Further measures to control marine pollution

—Protecting children from lead-based paint

—Enlisting the young
President's Environmental **Merit**
Awards Program for high schools
Youth opportunities in the Depart-
ment of Agriculture Field Scout
program.

TIGHTENING POLLUTION CONTROL

The legislative framework for dealing with our major air pollution problems has become law, and I have made comprehensive recommendations regarding water pollution control. But several problems remain to be addressed which are difficult to deal with under the general pollution control authorities.

DISPOSAL OF TOXIC WASTES

Increasingly strict air and water pollution control laws and their more effective enforcement have led to greater reliance on land—both surface and underground—for disposal of waste products from the toxic substances being used in ever greater volume and variety in our society. Without adequate controls, such waste disposal may cause contamination of underground and surface waters leading to direct health hazards.

—I propose a Toxic Wastes Disposal Control Act, under which the Environmental Protection Agency would establish Federal guidelines and requirements for State programs to regulate disposal on or under the land of those toxic wastes which pose a hazard to health. The act would provide for Federal enforcement action if a State should fail to establish its own program.

SEDIMENT CONTROL

Sediment, small particles of soil which enter the water, is the most pervasive water pollution problem which does not come primarily from municipal or industrial sources. Heavy loads of sediment interfere with many beneficial uses of water, such as swimming and water supply, and can change the entire character of an aquatic environment. Many of our great waterways are afflicted with this problem. In our urban areas, a significant amount of sediment comes from construction. However, if proper construction practices are followed, sediment runoff from this source can be greatly reduced.

—I propose legislation calling upon the States to establish, through appropriate local and regional agencies, regulatory programs to control sediment affecting water quality from earth-moving activities such as building and road construction.

The Environmental Protection Agency, together with other Federal agencies, would develop Federal guidelines for appropriate control measures. Federal enforcement would take place in situations where a State failed to implement such a program.

SULFUR OXIDES EMISSIONS CHARGE

In my 1971 Environmental Message, I announced plans to ask for imposition of a charge on sulfur oxides emissions, one of the air pollutants most damaging to human health and property, and vegetation. The Council on Environmental Quality, the Treasury Department and the Environmental Protection Agency have now completed their studies on this measure and have developed the details of an emission charge proposal.

—I propose a charge on sulfur emitted into the atmosphere from combustion, refining, smelting, and other processes.

This charge would begin in 1976 and apply in all regions where the air quality does not meet national standards for sulfur oxides during 1975. The charge would be 15¢ per pound on sulfur emitted in regions where the primary standards—which are designed to be protective of public health—have not been met within the deadline for achievement prescribed in the Clean Air Act. In regions where air quality met the primary standard but exceeded the secondary national standard—designed to protect property, vegetation, and aesthetic values—a charge of $.10 per pound of sulfur emitted would apply. Areas which reduce emissions sufficiently to meet both primary and secondary air quality standards would be exempt from the emission charge.

This charge is an application of the principle that the costs of pollution should be included in the price of the product. Combined with our existing regulatory authority, it would constitute a strong economic incentive to achieve the sulfur oxides standards necessary to protect health, and then further to reduce emissions to levels which protect welfare and aesthetics.

CLEAN ENERGY GENERATION AND
CONSERVATION

Ours is an energy-based economy, and energy resources are the basis for future economic progress. Yet the consumption of energy-producing fuels contributes to many of our most serious pollution problems. In order to have both environmental quality and an improving standard of living, we will need to develop new clean energy sources and to learn to use energy more efficiently.

Our success in meeting energy needs while preventing adverse environmental effects from energy generation and transmission will depend heavily on the state of available technology. In my message to the Congress on energy of last June, I announced a series of steps to increase research on clean and efficient energy production. But further action is needed.

—As part of my new commitment to augment Federal research and development and target it more effectively on solving domestic problems, I have requested in the 1973 budget an additional $88 million for development of a broad spectrum of new technologies for producing clean energy.

In addition to carrying forward the priority efforts I have already announced—the liquid metal fast breeder reactor, pipeline quality gas from coal, and sulfur oxide control technology—the budget provides funds for new or increased efforts on fusion power, solar energy, magneto-hydrodynamics, industrial gas from coal, dry cooling towers for power plant waste heat, large energy storage batteries and advanced underground electric transmission lines. These new efforts relate to both our immediate and our future energy problems, and are needed to assure adequate supplies of clean energy.

My message on energy also announced several steps that would be taken by the Federal Government to use energy more efficiently and with less environmental harm. One of these steps was issuance by the Secretary of Housing and Urban Development of revised standards for insulation in new federally insured houses. The new standards for single-family structures, which have now been issued through the Federal Housing Administration, reduce the maximum permissible heat loss by about one-third for a typical home. The fuel savings which will result from the application of these new standards will, in an average climate, exceed in one year the cost of the additional insulation required.

—*I am now directing the Secretary of Housing and Urban Development to issue revised insulation standards for apartments and other multifamily structures not covered by the earlier revision. The new rules will cut maximum permissible heat loss by 40%.*

The savings in fuel costs after a 5-year period will on the average more than offset the additional construction costs occasioned by these revised standards.

These stricter insulation standards are only one example of administrative actions which can be taken by the Federal Government to eliminate wasteful use of energy. The Federal Government can and must provide leadership by finding and implementing additional ways of reducing such waste.

—*I have therefore instructed the Council on Environmental Quality and the Office of Science and Technology, working with other Federal agencies, to conduct a survey to determine what additional actions might be taken to conserve energy in Federal activities.*

This survey will look at innovative ways to reduce wasteful consumption of energy while also reducing total costs and undesirable environmental impact.

RECYCLING

Recycling—the technique which treats many types of solid wastes not as pollutants but as recoverable and reusable "resources out of place"—is an important part of the answer to the Nation's solid waste burden. Last year, at my direction, the General Services Administration began reorienting government procurement policies to set a strong Federal example in the use of recycled products.

—*Because Federal tax policy should also offer recycling incentives, the Treasury Department is clarifying the availability of tax exempt treatment industrial revenue bond financing for the construction of recycling facilities built by private concerns to recycle their own wastes.*

THE ENVIRONMENTAL TRANSITION

Many environmental problems are influenced by the way our economy operates. Conversely, efforts to improve environmental quality have an impact on the economy. Our national income accounting does not explicitly recognize the cost of pollution damages to health, materials, and aesthetics in the computation of our economic well-being. Many goods and services fail to bear the full costs of the damages they cause from pollution, and hence are underpriced.

Environmental quality requirements will affect many of our industries by imposing new costs on production. We know that these impacts fall unevenly on industries, new and old firms, and on communities, but little concrete data has been available. Contract studies have recently been performed for the Council on Environmental Quality, the Environmental Protection Agency, and the Department of Commerce, under the policy guidance of the Council of Economic Advisers. These initial studies suggest that pollution control costs will result in some price increases, competitive trade disadvantages, and employment shifts. The major impact of these costs will be on older, and usually smaller plants.

As long as we carefully set our environmental goals to assure that the benefits we achieve are greater than the social and economic costs, the changes which will occur in our economy are desirable, and we as a Nation will benefit from them.

MAKING TECHNOLOGY AN ENVIRONMENTAL ALLY

The time has come to increase the technological resources allocated to the challenges of meeting high-priority domestic needs. In my State of the Union Message last month, I announced an expanded Federal research and development commitment for this purpose. There is great potential for achievement through technology in the fight against pollution and the larger drive for quality in our environment.

The temptation to cast technology in the role of ecological villain must be resisted—for to do so is to deprive ourselves of a vital tool available for enhancing environmental quality. As Peter Drucker has said, "the environment is a problem of [the] success" [1] of technological society, by no means a proof of its failure. The difficulties which some applications of technology have engendered might indeed be rectified by turning our backs on the 20th

---

[1] Peter F. Drucker, "The Age of Discontinuity: Guidelines to Our Changing Society" (Harper and Row, 1969).

century, but only at a price in privation which we do not want to pay and do not have to pay. There is no need to throw out the baby with the bath water. Technology can and must be wisely applied so that it becomes environmentally self-corrective. This is the standard for which we must aim.

INTEGRATED PEST MANAGEMENT

Chemical pesticides are a familiar example of a technological innovation which has provided important benefits to man but which has also produced unintended and unanticipated harm. New technologies of integrated pest management must be developed so that agricultural and forest productivity can be maintained together with, rather than at the expense of, environmental quality. Integrated pest management means judicious use of selective chemical pesticides in combination with nonchemical agents and methods. It seeks to maximize reliance on such natural pest population controls as predators, sterilization, and pest diseases. The following actions are being taken:

—I have directed the Department of Agriculture, the National Science Foundation, and the Environmental Protection Agency to launch a large-scale integrated pest management research and development program. This program will be conducted by a number of our leading universities.

—I have directed the Department of Agriculture to increase field testing of promising new methods of pest detection and control. Also, other existing Federal pesticide application programs will be examined for the purpose of incorporating new pest management techniques.

—I have directed the Departments of

Agriculture and of Health, Education, and Welfare to encourage the development of training and certification programs at appropriate academic institutions in order to provide the large number of crop protection specialists that will be needed as integrated pest management becomes more fully utilized.

—I have authorized the Department of Agriculture to expand its crop field scout demonstration program to cover nearly four million acres under agricultural production by the upcoming growing season.

Through this program many unnecessary pesticide applications can be eliminated, since the scouts will be used to determine when pesticide applications are actually needed.

In my message on the environment last February, I proposed a comprehensive revision of our pesticide control laws—a revision which still awaits final congressional action. Also essential to a sound national pesticide policy are measures to ensure that agricultural workers are protected from adverse exposures to these chemicals.

—I am directing the Departments of Labor and Health, Education, and Welfare to develop standards under the Occupational Safety and Health Act to protect such workers from pesticide poisoning.

NOISE CONTROL RESEARCH

Scientific findings increasingly confirm what few urban dwellers or industrial workers need to be told—that excessive noise can constitute a significant threat to human well-being. The Congress already has before it a comprehensive noise control bill, which I proposed a year ago. A quieter environment cannot simply be legislated into being. We shall also need to develop better methods to achieve our goal.

—I have requested in my 1973 budget a $23 million increase in research and development funds for reducing noise from airplanes. I have also requested new funds for research and development for reducing street traffic noise.

RESEARCH ON AIR POLLUTION EFFECTS
AND MEASUREMENT

Our pollution control efforts are based largely on the establishment of enforceable standards of environmental quality. Initial standards have often been based on incomplete knowledge because the necessary information has not been available. Also, the lack of adequate instruments to measure pollution and of models of how pollutants are dispersed has made it difficult to know exactly how much pollution must be controlled in a particular area. We need added research and development to make more precise judgments of what standards should be set and how we can most practically achieve our goals.

—I have requested in my 1973 budget an additional $12 million to increase research on the health effects of air pollution, on regional air pollution modeling, and on improved pollution instrumentation and measurement.

IMPROVING LAND USE

In recent years we have come to view our land as a limited and irreplaceable resource. No longer do we imagine that there will always be more of it over the horizon—more woodlands and shorelands and wetlands—if we neglect or overdevelop the land in view. A new maturity is giving rise to a land ethic which recognizes that improper land use affects the public interest and limits the choices that we and our descendants will have.

Now we must equip our institutions to carry out the responsibility implicit in this new outlook. We must create the administrative and regulatory mechanisms necessary to assure wise land use and to stop haphazard, wasteful, or environmentally damaging development. Some States are moving ahead on their own to develop stronger land-use institutions and controls. Federal programs can and should reinforce this encouraging trend.

NATIONAL LAND USE POLICY ACT

The National Land Use Policy Act, which I proposed to the Congress last year, would provide Federal assistance to encourage the States, in cooperation with local governments, to protect lands which are of critical environmental concern and to control major development. While not yet enacted, this measure has been the subject of much useful debate.

—*I propose amendments to this pending National Land Use Policy legislation which would require States to control the siting of major transportation facilities, and impose sanctions on any State which does not establish an adequate land use program.*

Under these amendments, the State programs established pursuant to the act would not only have to embody methods for controlling land use *around* key growth-inducing developments such as highways, airports, and recreational facilities; the States would also have to provide controls over the actual *siting* of the major highways and airports themselves. The change recognizes the fact that these initial siting decisions, once made, can often

trigger runaway growth and adverse environmental effects.

The amendments would further provide that any State that had not established an acceptable land use program by 1975 would be subject to annual reductions of certain Federal funds. Seven percent of the funds allocated under sections of the Airport and Airways Development Act, the Federal-Aid Highway Acts including the Highway Trust Fund, and the Land and Water Conservation Fund, would be withheld in the first year. An additional 7 percent would be withheld for each additional year that a State was without an approved land use program. Money thus withheld from noncomplying States would be allocated among States which did have acceptable programs.

These strong new amendments are necessary in view of the significant effect that Federal programs, particularly transportation programs, have upon land use decisions.

PROTECTION OF WETLANDS

The Nation's coastal and estuarine wetlands are vital to the survival of a wide variety of fish and wildlife; they have an important function in controlling floods and tidal forces; and they contain some of the most beautiful areas left on this continent. These same lands, however, are often some of the most sought-after for development. As a consequence, wetland acreage has been declining as more and more areas are drained and filled for residential, commercial, and industrial projects.

My National Land Use Policy Act would direct State attention to these important areas by defining wetlands among the "environmentally critical areas" which it singles out for special protection, and by giving priority attention to the coastal zones. I propose to supplement these safeguards with new economic disincentives to further discourage unnecessary wetlands development.

—*I propose legislation to limit applicability of certain Federal tax benefits when development occurs in coastal wetlands.*

MANAGEMENT OF PUBLIC LANDS

During 1971, I acted to strengthen the environmental requirements relating to management and use of the Nation's vast acreage of federally-owned public lands administered by the Department of the Interior. I proposed new legislation to establish an overall management policy for these public lands, something which we have been without for far too long. This legislation, still pending before the Congress, would direct the Secretary of the Interior to manage our public lands in a manner that would protect their environmental quality for present and future generations. The policy which it would establish declares the retention of the public lands to be in the national interest except where disposal of particular tracts would lead to a significant improvement in their management, or where the disposal would serve important public objectives which cannot be achieved on non-public lands.

PROTECTING OUR NATURAL HERITAGE

Wild places and wild things constitute a treasure to be cherished and protected for all time. The pleasure and refreshment which they give man confirm their value to society. More importantly per-

haps, the wonder, beauty, and elemental force in which the least of them share suggest a higher right to exist—not granted them by man and not his to take away. In environmental policy as anywhere else we cannot deal in absolutes. Yet we can at least give considerations like these more relative weight in the seventies, and become a more civilized people in a healthier land because of it.

PREDATOR CONTROL

Americans today set high value on the preservation of wildlife. The old notion that "the only good predator is a dead one" is no longer acceptable as we understand that even the animals and birds which sometimes prey on domesticated animals have their own value in maintaining the balance of nature.

The widespread use of highly toxic poisons to kill coyotes and other predatory animals and birds is a practice which has been a source of increasing concern to the American public and to the federal officials responsible for the public lands.

Last year the Council on Environmental Quality and the Department of the Interior appointed an Advisory Committee on Predator Control to study the entire question of predator and related animal control activities. The Committee found that persistent poisons have been applied to range and forest lands without adequate knowledge of their effects on the ecology or their utility in preventing losses to livestock. The large-scale use of poisons for control of predators and field rodents has resulted in unintended losses of other animals and in other harmful effects on natural ecosystems. The Committee concluded that necessary control of coyotes and other predators can be accomplished by methods other than poisons.

Certainly, predators can represent a threat to sheep and some other domesticated animals. But we must use more selective methods of control that will preserve ecological values while continuing to protect livestock.

—I am today issuing an Executive Order [11643] barring the use of poisons for predator control on all public lands. (Exceptions will be made only for emergency situations.) I also propose legislation to shift the emphasis of the current direct Federal predator control program to one of research and technical and financial assistance to the States to help them control predator populations by means other than poisons.

ENDANGERED SPECIES

It has only been in recent years that efforts have been undertaken to list and protect those species of animals whose continued existence is in jeopardy. Starting with our national symbol, the bald eagle, we have expanded our concern over the extinction of these animals to include the present list of over 100. We have already found, however, that even the most recent act to protect endangered species, which dates only from 1969, simply does not provide the kind of management tools needed to act early enough to save a vanishing species. In particular, existing laws do not generally allow the Federal Government to control shooting, trapping, or other taking of endangered species.

—I propose legislation to provide for early identification and protection of en-dangered species. My new proposal would make the taking of endangered species a Federal offense for the first time, and would permit protective measures to be undertaken before a species is so depleted that regeneration is difficult or impossible.

MIGRATORY SPECIES

The protection of migratory species, besides preserving wildlife values, exemplifies cooperative environmental effort among the United States, Canada, and Mexico. By treaties entered into among these three countries, migratory species are protected. New species may be added by common agreement between the United States and Mexico.

—I have authorized the Secretary of State, in conjunction with the Secretary of the Interior, to seek the agreement of the Mexican Government to add 33 new families of birds to the protected list.

Included in the proposal are eagles, hawks, falcons, owls, and many of the most attractive species of wading birds. I am hopeful that treaty protection can be accorded them in the near future.

BIG CYPRESS NATIONAL FRESH WATER RESERVE

After careful review of the environmental significance of the Big Cypress Swamp in Florida, particularly of the need for water from this source to maintain the unique ecology of Everglades National Park, I directed the Secretary of the Interior to prepare legislation to create the Big Cypress National Fresh Water Reserve. This legislation, which has now been submitted to the Congress, will empower the Federal Government to acquire the requisite legal interest in 547,000 acres of Big Cypress.

NEW PARKLANDS AT THE GATEWAYS

The need to provide breathing space and recreational opportunities in our major urban centers is a major concern of this Administration. Two of the Nation's major gateways to the world—New York City and San Francisco—have land nearby with exceptional scenic and recreational potential, and we are moving to make that land available for people to enjoy. In May of 1971, I proposed legislation to authorize a Gateway National Recreation Area in New York and New Jersey. This proposal would open to a metropolitan region of more than 14 million people a National Recreation Area offering more than 23,000 acres of prime beaches, wildlife preserves, and historical attractions including the nation's oldest operating lighthouse.

On our western shore lies another area uniquely appropriate for making recreational and scenic values more accessible to a metropolitan community.

—I propose legislation to establish a Golden Gate National Recreation Area in and around San Francisco Bay.

This proposal would encompass a number of existing parks, military reservations, and private lands to provide a full range of recreation experiences. Altogether, the area would encompass some 24,000 acres of fine beaches, rugged coasts, and readily accessible urban parklands, extending approximately 30 miles along some of America's most beautiful coastline north and south of Golden Gate Bridge. Angel and Alcatraz Islands in the bay would be within the boundaries of the National

Recreation Area, as would a number of properties on the mainland which afford magnificent views of the city, the bay and the ocean. As part of this plan, I am directing that the Presidio at San Francisco be opened for dual military and civilian recreational uses.

CONVERTING FEDERAL PROPERTIES TO PARKS

Among the most important legacies that we can pass on to future generations is an endowment of parklands and recreational areas that will enrich leisure opportunities and make the beauties of the earth and sea accessible to all Americans. This is the object of our Legacy of Parks program, initiated early in 1971. As part of this program, I directed the Property Review Board to give priority to potential park and recreation areas in its search for alternative uses of federally held real property. The results of this search so far have been most encouraging. To the original 40 properties which I announced in my Environmental Message of 1971 as being well suited for park use, another 111 prospects have been added. And from this total of 151 prospective parklands, 63 have already been made available.

—Today I am pleased to announce that 20 more parcels of Federal land are being made available for park and recreation use.

These newest parcels, combined with those which have been announced over the past year, provide a legacy of 83 parklands for America which comprise 14,585 acres in 31 States and Puerto Rico. The estimated fair market value of these properties is over $56 million. In the months to come, every effort will be made to extend this legacy to all 50 States. The green spaces and natural retreats that we tend to take for granted will not be available for future enjoyment unless we act now to develop and protect them.

WILDERNESS AREAS

One of the first environmental goals I set when I took office was to stimulate the program to identify and recommend to the Congress new wilderness areas. Although this program was behind schedule at that time, I am now able to report that the September, 1974 statutory deadline for reviews can and will be met.

The Wilderness Act of 1964 set aside 54 areas, consisting of about 9.1 million acres, as the nucleus of our wilderness system. Since then, 33 new areas totalling almost 1.2 million acres within National Forests, National Parks, and National Wildlife Refuges have been added to the system. Thirty-one areas totalling about 3.6 million acres, including 18 areas submitted by this Administration, have been proposed to the Congress but have yet to be acted upon. One of the most significant elements of this process has been the active participation by the public in all of its phases. At public wilderness hearings held all across the country, fair consideration has been given to all interests and points of view, with constructive citizen involvement in the decision-making process.

—I am today proposing 18 new wilderness areas which, when approved, will add another 1.3 million acres to the wilderness system.

Eight of these proposals are within the National Forests, four are within National Park areas, and six are in National Wildlife Refuges.

Of these areas, 1.2 million acres would be in the following National Forests: Blue Range National Forest, Arizona and New Mexico; Agua Tibia and Emigrant National Forests, California; Eagles Nest and Weminuche National Forests, Colorado; Mission Mountains National Forest, Montana; Aldo Leopold National Forest, New Mexico; and Glacier National Forest, Wyoming.

A total of 40,000 acres would be in our National Park system in the following locations: Black Canyon of the Gunnison National Monument, Colorado; Bryce Canyon National Park, Utah; Chiricahua National Monument, Arizona; Colorado National Monument, Colorado.

Finally, a total of 87,000 acres would be in areas administered by the Fish and Wildlife Services of the Department of the Interior in the following locations: St. Marks, National Wildlife Refuge, Florida; Wolf Island, National Wildlife Refuge, Georgia; Moosehorn National Wildlife Refuge, Maine; San Juan Islands, National Wildlife Refuge, Washington; Cape Romain, National Wildlife Refuge, South Carolina; and Bosque del Apache, National Wildlife Refuge, New Mexico.

The year 1972 can bring some of the greatest accomplishment in wilderness preservation since passage of the Wilderness Act in 1964. I urge prompt and systematic consideration by the Congress of these 18 new proposals and of the 31 currently pending before it. Approval of all 49 additions would bring the system up to a total of over 15 million acres.

Unfortunately, few of these wilderness areas are within easy access of the most populous areas of the United States. The major purpose of my Legacy of Parks program is to bring recreation opportunities closer to the people, and while wilderness is only one such opportunity, it is a very important one. A few of the areas proposed today or previously are in the eastern sections of the country, but the great majority of wilderness areas are found in the West. This of course is where most of our pristine wild areas are. But a greater effort can still be made to see that wilderness recreation values are preserved to the maximum extent possible, in the regions where most of our people live.

—I am therefore directing the Secretaries of Agriculture and the Interior to accelerate the identification of areas in the Eastern United States having wilderness potential.

OFF-ROAD VEHICLES

A recent study by the Department of the Interior estimated that Americans own more than 5 million off-road recreational vehicles—motorcycles, minibikes, trail bikes, snowmobiles, dune-buggies, all-terrain vehicles, and others. The use of these vehicles is dramatically on the increase: data show a three-fold growth between 1967 and 1971 alone.

As the number of off-road vehicles has increased, so has their use on public lands. Too often the land has suffered as a result. Increasingly, Federal recreational lands have become the focus of conflict between the newer motorized recreationist and the traditional hiker, camper, and horseback rider. In the past, Federal land-management agencies have used widely varying approaches to dealing with this conflict. The time has come for a unified Federal policy toward use of off-road vehicles on Federal lands.

—I have today signed an Executive Order [11644] directing the Secretaries of Agriculture, Interior, Army and the Board of Directors of the Tennessee Valley Authority to develop regulations providing for control over the use of off-road vehicles on Federal lands.

They will designate areas of use and non-use, specify operating conditions that will be necessary to minimize damage to the natural resources of the Federal lands, and ensure compatibility with other recreational uses, taking into account noise and other factors.

EXPANDING INTERNATIONAL COOPERATION ON THE ENVIRONMENT

We are now growing accustomed to the view of our planet as seen from space—a blue and brown disk shrouded in white patches of clouds. But we do not ponder often enough the striking lesson it teaches about the global reach of environmental imperatives. No matter what else divides men and nations, this perspective should unite them. We must work harder to foster such world environmental consciousness and shared purpose.

UNITED NATIONS CONFERENCE ON THE HUMAN ENVIRONMENT

To cope with environmental questions that are truly international, we and other nations look to the first world conference of governments ever convened on this subject: the United Nations Conference on the Human Environment, to be held in Stockholm, Sweden, in June of this year. This should be a seminal event of the international community's attempt to cope with these serious, shared problems of global concern that transcend political differences.

But efforts to improve the global environment cannot go forward without the means to act.

—To help provide such means, I pro-

pose that a voluntary United Nations Fund for the Environment be established, with an initial funding goal of $100 million for the first 5 years.

This Fund would help to stimulate international cooperation on environmental problems by supporting a centralized coordination point for United Nations activities in this field. It would also help to bring new resources to bear on the increasing number of worldwide problems through activities such as monitoring and cleanup of the oceans and atmosphere.

—If such a Fund is established, I will recommend to the Congress that the United States commit itself to provide its fair share of the Fund on a matching basis over the first 5 years.

This level of support would provide start-up assistance under mutually agreed-upon terms. As these programs get underway, it may well be that the member nations will decide that additional resources are required. I invite other nations to join with us in this commitment to meaningful action.

CONTROL OF MARINE POLLUTION

Ocean pollution is clearly one of our major international environmental problems. I am gratified that in the past year the Congress has taken several steps to reduce the risks of oil spills on the high seas. However, further congressional action is needed to ratify several pending international conventions and to adopt implementing legislation for the various oil-spill conventions which have been ratified or which are awaiting approval.

Action on these recommendations will complete the first round of international conventions to deal with marine pollution. We have taken initiatives in three inter-

national forums to develop a second and more sophisticated round of agreements in this area. We are preparing for a 1973 Intergovernmental Maritime Consultative Organization (IMCO) Conference to draft a convention barring intentional discharges to the sea of oil and hazardous substances from ships. In conjunction with the Law of the Sea Conference scheduled for 1973, we are examining measures to control the effects of developing undersea resources. And, in the preparatory work for the 1972 U.N. Conference on the Human Environment, progress has been made on an agreement to regulate the ocean dumping of shore-generated wastes, and further work in this area has been scheduled by IMCO. We hope to conclude conventions in each of these areas by 1973.

PROTECTING CHILDREN FROM LEAD-BASED PAINT

To many Americans, "environment" means the city streets where they live and work. It is here that a localized but acutely dangerous type of "pollution" has appeared and stirred mounting public concern.

The victims are children: the hazard is lead-based paint. Such paint was applied to the walls of most dwellings prior to the 1950's. When the paint chips and peels from the walls in dilapidated housing, it is frequently eaten by small children. This sometimes results in lead poisoning which can cause permanent mental retardation and occasionally death. We can and must prevent unnecessary loss of life and health from this hazard, which particularly afflicts the poorest segments of our population.

To help meet the lead-paint threat, the

Department of Health, Education, and Welfare will administer grants and technical assistance to initiate programs in over 50 communities to test children in high-risk areas for lead concentrations. In addition, these programs will support the development of community organization and public education to increase public awareness of this hazard. Other Federal agencies are also active in the effort to combat lead-based paint poisoning. ACTION and other volunteers will assist city governments to help alleviate lead paint hazards. The Department of Housing and Urban Development is engaged in research and other actions to detect and eliminate this hazard.

The resources of the private sector should also be utilized through local laws requiring owners of housing wherever possible to control lead paint hazards.

ENLISTING THE YOUNG

The starting point of environmental quality is in the hearts and minds of the people. Unless the people have a deep commitment to the new values and a clear understanding of the new problems, all our laws and programs and spending will avail little. The young, quick to commit and used to learning, are gaining the changed outlook fastest of all. Their enthusiasm about the environment spreads with a healthy contagion: their energy in its behalf can be an impressive force for good.

Four youth participation programs of mutual benefit to the young and the Nation are now planned or underway:

Last October, I initiated the Environmental Merit Awards Program. This program, directed by the Environmental Protection Agency in cooperation with the U.S. Office of Education, awards national recognition to successful student projects leading to environmental understanding or improvement. Qualifications for the awards are determined by a local board consisting of secondary school students, faculty, and representatives of the local community. Already more than 2,000 high schools, representing all 50 States, have registered in the program.

The Department of Agriculture's expanded field scout demonstration program, designed to permit more effective pest control with less reliance on chemical pesticides, will employ thousands of high school and college students. These young people will be scouting cotton and tobacco pests in the coming growing season, and the program will be expanded to other crops in future years.

The Environmental Protection Agency has recently initiated in its Seattle regional office a pilot program using young people to assist the agency in many of its important tasks, including monitoring. EPA is working with State and local pollution control agencies to identify monitoring needs. ACTION and the youth training programs are providing the manpower. If this initial program proves successful, the concept will be expanded.

ACTION volunteers and young people employed through the Neighborhood Youth Corps, Job Corps, and college work-study programs will work with city governments to help alleviate lead paint hazards, gaining experience in community health work as they give urgently needed aid to inner-city families.

Young people working on environmental projects, learning the skills necessary for a particular job, must also understand how their work relates to the environmental process as a whole. Thus, all of these activities must be supplemented by continued improvement in many aspects of environmental education to help all of our citizens, both young and old, develop a better awareness of man's relation to his environment. In my first Environmental Quality Report, I stressed the importance of improving the Nation's "environmental literacy." This goal remains as important as ever, and our progress toward it must continue.

ONE DESTINY

Our destiny is one: this the environmental awakening has taught America in these first years of the seventies. Let us never forget, though, that it is not a destiny of fear, but of promise. As I stated last August in transmitting the Second Annual Report of the Council on Environmental Quality: "The work of environmental improvement is a task for all our people . . . The achievement of that goal will challenge the creativity of our science and technology, the enterprise and adaptability of our industry, the responsiveness and sense of balance of our political and legal institutions, and the resourcefulness and the capacity of this country to honor those human values upon which the quality of our national life must ultimately depend." We shall rise to the challenge of solving our environmental problems by enlisting the creative energy of all of our citizens in a cause truly worthy of the best that each can bring to it.

While we share our environmental problems with all the people of the world, our industrial might, which has made us the leader among nations in terms of material well-being, also gives us the responsibility of dealing with environmental problems first among the nations. We can be proud that our solutions and our performance will become the measure for others climbing the ladder of aspirations and difficulties; we can set our sights on a standard that will lift their expectations of what man can do.

The pursuit of environmental quality will require courage and patience. Problems that have been building over many years will not yield to facile solutions. But I do not doubt that Americans have the wit and the will to win—to fulfill our brightest vision of what the future can be.

RICHARD NIXON

The White House,
  February 8, 1972.

NOTE: On the same day, the White House released a fact sheet and the transcript of a news briefing on the message. Participants in the news briefing were Rogers C. B. Morton, Secretary of the Interior, Russell E. Train, Chairman, Council on Environmental Quality, and William D. Ruckelshaus, Administrator, Environmental Protection Agency.

---

52 Letter to the President of the Senate and the Speaker of the House Transmitting Proposals for 18 Additional National Wilderness Areas. *February 8, 1972*

PURSUANT to the Wilderness Act of September 3, 1964, I am pleased today to transmit proposals for 18 additions to the National Wilderness Preservation System.

The proposed new wilderness areas, which cover 1.3 million acres in all, are enumerated in my Special Message on the Environment of today's date. Two other possibilities considered by the Secretary of the Interior in his review of roadless areas of 5,000 acres or more—Martin National Wildlife Refuge, Maryland, and Wupatki National Monument, Arizona—were found to be unsuitable for inclusion in the Wilderness System. I concur in this finding and in the 18 favorable recommendations of the Secretaries of the Interior and of Agriculture, all of which are transmitted herewith.

Timely and farsighted action is impera-

tive if we are to preserve America's irreplaceable heritage of wildness as part of our legacy to the future. I urge that protected status be promptly extended to the lands covered by these proposals and by the 31 previous wilderness recommendations already pending before the Congress.

Sincerely,

RICHARD NIXON

NOTE: This is the text of identical letters addressed to the Honorable Spiro T. Agnew, President of the Senate, and the Honorable Carl Albert, Speaker of the House of Representatives.

---

53 Message to the Congress Transmitting a Report of Negotiations With Canada on Reconstruction of the Alaska Highway. *February* 8, 1972

To the Congress of the United States:

I hereby submit to the Congress a Report of the negotiations with the Government of Canada concerning the reconstruction of the Alaska Highway between Dawson Creek, Canada, and the Alaska border. Pursuant to Section 119 of Public Law 91–605, these negotiations were held in the summer and fall of 1971 between representatives of our Departments of State and Transportation and officials of the respective Canadian Ministries.

Based upon these discussions, the Secretaries of Transportation and State have concluded, and I have agreed, that a U.S. offer to Canada to undertake this project on a cost-sharing basis would not be justified at this time. Our negotiations closed with an understanding that this would be the United States position. The Canadian Government has also indicated that it

does not wish to undertake such a project with its own resources.

Underlying these conclusions are the facts that alternative transportation routes are now being developed, especially in British Columbia, and that anticipated traffic volume on the Alaskan Highway should not be sufficiently heavy to warrant reconstruction and paving. The enclosed Report, submitted in response to Section 119(b) of the Federal-Aid Highway Act of 1970 (P.L. 91–605), spells out these findings in greater detail.

As a result of these conclusions, no further action seems necessary at this time.

RICHARD NIXON

The White House,

February 8, 1972.

NOTE: The report is entitled "Alaska Highway Report" (13 pp. plus attachments).

54   Radio Address About the Third Annual Foreign Policy Report to the Congress.   *February 9, 1972*

Good morning:

Today I have submitted to the Congress my third annual report on United States foreign policy. I want to share my thoughts with you now on some of the highlights of that report.

For the first time in a generation, the most powerful nation in the world and the most populous nation in the world, the United States and the People's Republic of China, have begun a process of communication.

For the first time in a generation, we have taken a series of steps that could mean a new relationship with the Soviet Union.

For the first time in a generation, our alliances with the nations of Europe, Japan, and other nations have been re-shaped to reflect their new capacity to assume a greater responsibility for their own defense.

For the first time in a generation, we have laid a new basis for fair competition in world trade that will mean more jobs for American workers.

These are great changes. They have brought the world closer to a stable peace. They did not happen by accident. These breakthroughs toward peace took place in the past year for good reason.

Three years ago we stopped reacting on the basis of yesterday's habits and started acting to deal with the realities of today and the opportunities of tomorrow.

Where has this new attitude taken us?

In our relations with the Soviet Union, these were the elements of the breakthrough that took place over the past 12 months.

We broke the deadlock in the arms limitation negotiation and agreed on a framework for progress in the SALT talks.

We agreed on a treaty barring weapons of mass destruction from the ocean floor, and on another treaty to remove the threat of germ warfare.

We agreed on a more reliable "hot line" between Washington and Moscow, and found new ways to consult each other in emergencies which will reduce the risk of accidental nuclear war.

And in a step of the greatest importance, we reached an agreement on Berlin. If there was one city where World War III could have broken out in the past 20 years, it was Berlin. This new agreement reduces the danger of the super powers in direct confrontation.

There are other areas where we have had, and continue to have, serious differences with the Soviet Union. On balance, however, I have concluded that Soviet willingness to take positive steps toward peace in the past year makes a meeting at the highest level timely, particularly in arms limitation and economic cooperation.

And that is why, for the first time, a President of the United States will visit Moscow. I will go to that meeting in May with no naive illusions, but with some reasonable expectations.

Our relations with the Soviet Union were helped by the fact that our two nations have had long-established communications. Because we deeply understood what our real differences were, we could move to negotiate them.

When it came to dealing with the People's Republic of China, 25 years of hostility stood in the way. Accordingly, I began what is now 3 years of the most painstaking and necessarily discreet preparation for an opening to the world's most populous nation.

In 2 weeks, I shall begin my journey for peace to Peking. The agreement to meet, and the mutual trust needed to make the arrangements for the first American state visit to the People's Republic of China is a breakthrough of great importance.

We do not expect instant solutions to deep-seated differences. But the visit is a beginning. Now, in the relations between our countries, the old exchange of denunciations can be replaced with a constructive exchange of views.

Just as we have established a creative relationship with our adversaries, we have developed a more balanced alliance with our friends.

Not so long ago, our alliances were addressed exclusively to the containment of the Soviet Union and the People's Republic of China. But now there has to be more to our alliance. It is fairly simple to unite about what you are against. It is a lot more complicated to hold together an alliance on the basis of what you are for.

We do not shy away from this complexity because now, in this time of breakthroughs, there has never been a greater need for a sense of common purpose among the non-Communist nations. There is no requirement that we all march in lockstep; but there is a need to move forward in the same direction.

And that is why we encourage initiative and self-reliance on the part of our allies.

That is why our alliance is becoming what we need in the real world of the seventies—a dynamic coalition of self-assured and independent nations.

Our former dependents have become our competitors. That is good for them, and it is also good for us.

But as the roles change, the rules change. The old international monetary and trading system had become unfair to the American workers and to American business. Facing vigorous, healthy competitors, the United States could no longer be expected to compete with one hand tied behind its back.

Nothing would have happened unless we made it happen. Last August, we took action to stimulate a worldwide settlement of the problem. Within a few months, a general realignment of currencies took place, the first step toward complete reform.

We succeeded in moving the non-Communist world away from the constant state of monetary crisis of the past decade, and we removed a danger to the unity of the free world.

Let me turn now to Vietnam. This has been America's longest and most difficult war. It began long before I became President. And I have been doing everything I can honorably do to end it.

I have brought almost one-half million men home from Vietnam. As high as 300 a week were being killed in action when I took office. This week there were two. We have reduced air sorties, budget costs, and draft calls. And we have made the most generous peace offer in the history of warfare.

I have no complaint over the fact that during this period, when I have been ending a war I did not begin, I have been subjected to vigorous criticism. I do not question the patriotism or the sincerity of those who disagree with my policies to bring peace, but as I said in 1968 when I was a candidate for President, we have only one President at a time, and only the President can negotiate an end to the war.

There should always be free debate and criticism, so that our policy will represent the best thinking of our Nation, but a candidate for President has a higher responsibility than the ordinary critic. A candidate should make any criticism he believes would contribute to bringing an honorable peace. But I would hope that anyone seeking the Presidency would examine his statements carefully to be sure that nothing he says might give the enemy an incentive to prolong the war until after the election.

Trust in the United States among the 45 nations with which we have treaty commitments is essential if peace and freedom are to be preserved in the world. Let us end our involvement in the war in Vietnam in a way which will not destroy that trust.

Looking ahead on the world scene, how can we move ahead to make the most of the breakthroughs of the past year? We must advance the delicate process of creating a more constructive relationship between ourselves and the People's Republic of China.

We must bring the arms race under control, and by so doing, lay the basis for other major steps toward peace that can be taken together by the United States and the Soviet Union. And equally important, we must continue to strengthen the partnership with our friends. We must work with friends and adversaries to build an international structure of peace which everyone will work to preserve because each nation will realize its stake in its preservation.

We must continue the process of reforming the world's financial and trading systems so that workers and consumers can benefit in America and in every country that has a competitive spirit.

Those are by no means the only items on our international agenda. We want to see the cease-fire in the Middle East, which we initiated, moved toward a more secure and permanent peace. We want to work out with our friends in Latin America, Africa, and non-Communist Asia new ways of helping them help themselves. We want to shore up the eroding confidence in the United Nations.

There is much unfinished business. But there is a new awareness of reality growing in the world. Movement and progress can be felt today where there was stagnation and frustration before.

By facing the realities of the world today—as this breakthrough year has shown we are capable of doing—we can make peace a reality in the generation ahead.

Thank you and good morning.

NOTE: The President spoke 11:05 a.m. in a room adjoining the Oval Office at the White House. His remarks were broadcast live on nationwide radio.

He spoke from a prepared text. An advance text of his remarks was released on the same day.

55   Message to the Congress Transmitting Third Annual Report on United States Foreign Policy.
February 9, 1972

To the Congress of the United States:

As I prepare to set out on my summit trips to Peking and Moscow, it is especially timely for the American people and the Congress to have available a basis for understanding the Government's policies and broad purposes in foreign affairs. That is the function of this, my third annual report.

These annual reports trace the evolution of our policies over the years of our term of office and describe our responses to new problems and issues as they have arisen. They provide an insight into our philosophy of foreign policy and our new approaches to peace.

The broad framework presented here will be filled out in two other major documents: the Secretary of State's second annual report, which will describe in detail our relations with individual countries and set forth the major public documentation of our policy, and the annual Defense Report of the Secretary of Defense.

RICHARD NIXON

The White House,

February 9, 1972.

56   Third Annual Report to the Congress on United States Foreign Policy.   *February* 9, 1972

CONTENTS

PART I: 1971—THE WATERSHED
YEAR—AN OVERVIEW

This is the third Report of this kind which I have made to the Congress. It comes after a year of dramatic developments. The earlier Reports set forth fully this Administration's analysis of the world situation. They expressed the conviction that new conditions required fundamental changes in America's world role. They expounded our conception of what that role should be.

In short, they foreshadowed a transformation of American foreign relations with both our friends and our adversaries.

For three years, our policies have been designed to move steadily, and with increasing momentum, toward that transformation.

1971 was the watershed year. The foundation laid and the cumulative effect of the actions taken earlier enabled us to achieve, during the past year, changes in our foreign policy of historic scope and significance:

—An opening to the People's Republic of China;
—The beginning of a new relationship with the Soviet Union;
—The laying of a foundation for a healthier and more sustainable relationship with our European allies and Japan;
—The creation of a new environment for the world's monetary and trade activities.

This Report is addressed to those and other developments. It is, however, a companion piece to the two earlier Reports, for without an understanding of the philosophical conception upon which specific actions were based, the actions themselves can neither be adequately understood nor

fairly judged. This account of a year of intense action, therefore, properly begins with a brief review of the intellectual foundation on which those actions rest.

A Changed World

In the first two Reports, I stressed the fact that the postwar period of international relations had ended, and that it was the task of this Administration to shape a new foreign policy to meet the requirements of a new era. I set forth at some length the changes in the world which made a new policy not only desirable, but necessary.

1. The recovery of economic strength and political vitality by Western Europe and Japan, with the inexorable result that both their role and ours in the world must be adjusted to reflect their regained vigor and self-assurance.

2. The increasing self-reliance of the states created by the dissolution of the colonial empires, and the growth of both their ability and determination to see to their own security and well-being.

3. The breakdown in the unity of the Communist Bloc, with all that implies for the shift of energies and resources to purposes other than a single-minded challenge to the United States and its friends, and for a higher priority in at least some Communist countries to the pursuit of national interests rather than their subordination to the requirements of world revolution.

4. The end of an indisputable U.S. superiority in strategic strength, and its replacement by a strategic balance in which the U.S. and Soviet nuclear forces are comparable.

5. The growth among the American people of the conviction that the time had

come for other nations to share a greater portion of the burden of world leadership; and its corollary that the assured continuity of our long term involvement required a responsible, but more restrained American role.

THE PHILOSOPHY OF A NEW AMERICAN FOREIGN POLICY

The earlier Reports also set forth the philosophical convictions upon which this Administration was proceeding to reshape American policies to the requirements of the new realities. The core principles of this philosophy are:

—A leading American role in world affairs continues to be indispensable to the kind of world our own well-being requires.

—The end of the bipolar postwar world opens to this generation a unique opportunity to create a new and lasting structure of peace.

—The end of bipolarity requires that the structure must be built with the resources and concepts of many nations—for only when nations participate in creating an international system do they contribute to its vitality and accept its validity.

—Our friendships are constant, but the means by which they are mutually expressed must be adjusted as world conditions change. The continuity and vigor of our alliances require that our friends assume greater responsibilities for our common endeavors.

—Our enmities are not immutable, and we must be prepared realistically to recognize and deal with their cause.

—This requires mutual self-restraint and a willingness to accommodate conflicting national interests through negotiation rather than confrontation.

—Agreements are not, however, an end in themselves. They have permanent significance only when they contribute to a stable structure of peace which all countries wish to preserve because all countries share its benefits.

—The unprecedented advances in science and technology have created a new dimension of international life. The global community faces a series of urgent problems and opportunities which transcend all geographic and ideological borders. It is the distinguishing characteristic of these issues that their solution requires international cooperation on the broadest scale.

—We must, therefore, be willing to work with all countries—adversaries as well as friends—toward a structure of peace to which all nations contribute and in which all nations have a stake.

THE BREAKTHROUGH—ACTIONS WE HAVE TAKEN

This Report is an accounting of the application of that philosophy to American foreign policy. It is beyond dispute that we have made signal progress. Taken together, the initiatives of 1971 constitute a profound change in America's world role.

The heart of our new conception of that role is a more balanced alliance with our friends—and a more creative connection with our adversaries.

BREAKTHROUGH WITH OUR ADVERSARIES. Toward our two principal adversaries, the People's Republic of China and the Soviet Union, we faced dissimilar problems. With China, the task was to establish a civilized discourse on how to replace estrangement with a dialogue serving to benefit both countries. With the Soviet Union, we already had the discourse. We had examined at great length the general principles upon which the policies of both countries must be based, if we were to move from the mere assertion to the harmonization of conflicting national interests. The task was to make this discourse fruitful by moving to the achievement of concrete arrangements of benefit both to the Soviet Union and ourselves.

We have, in 1971, made striking progress toward both goals:

1. The People's Republic of China. We have ended a 25-year period of implacable hostility, mutually embraced as a central feature of national policy. Fragile as it is, the rapprochement between the most populous nation and the most powerful nation of the world could have greater significance for future generations than any other measure we have taken this year.

This initiative was the fruit of almost three years of the most painstaking, meticulous, and necessarily discreet preparation. It is an essential step in tempering animosities which have their roots in the past and which stand in the way of our hopes for the future.

My visit to Peking in February will certainly not bring a quick resolution of the deep differences which divided us from the People's Republic of China. But it will be a beginning, and it will signal the end of a sterile and barren interlude in the relationship between two great peoples. Finally, it will represent a necessary and giant step toward the creation of a stable structure of world peace.

2. The Soviet Union. We have succeeded in giving a new momentum to the prospects for more constructive relations through a series of concrete agreements which get at the cause of the tension between our two countries. The agreements vary in importance, but together provide serious grounds for believing that a fundamental improvement in the U.S.-Soviet relationship may be possible.

—In February, we agreed on a treaty barring weapons of mass destruction from the ocean floor.

—In May, we broke the deadlock which had developed in the talks on limiting strategic arms, and agreed on a framework which made it possible to resume progress.

—In September, we agreed on a draft treaty prohibiting the production or possession of biological and toxic weapons.

—In September, we and our British and French allies reached an agreement with the Soviet Union on Berlin to end the use of the citizens of West Berlin as Cold War hostages, and to reduce the danger of Berlin once again becoming the focus of a sharp and dangerous international confrontation.

—In September, we agreed on a more reliable "Hot Line" communication between Washington and Moscow, and on measures for notification and consultation designed to reduce the risk of an accidental nuclear war.

—In November, the visit of the American Secretary of Commerce to Moscow was the beginning of conversations looking toward a general normalization of economic relations.

These steps can represent the start of a new relationship with the Soviet Union. There were, however, other developments in 1971 which make it unclear whether we are now witnessing a permanent change in Soviet policy or only a passing phase concerned more with tactics than with a fundamental commitment to a stable international system. Soviet weapons development and deployment activity, Soviet arms policy in the Middle East, Soviet behavior during the India-Pakistan crisis and the expansionist implications of Soviet naval activities, all raise serious questions.

Nonetheless, the number and scope of the positive developments led us to conclude that a meeting at the highest level was appropriate and might provide the stimulus for additional progress, particularly in the fields of arms limitation and economic cooperation. Thus, in May, for the first time in our history, the President of the United States will visit Moscow. We go to that meeting with hope and determination to succeed.

BREAKTHROUGH WITH OUR ALLIES. With our principal allies in Western Europe and Japan, the need was to shape our relationship into a more mature political partnership. Our alliances must now be flexible enough to permit members to pursue autonomous policies within a common framework of strategic goals. Our allies are no longer willing to have the alliance rest only on American prescriptions—and we are no longer willing to have our alliances depend for their potency and sustenance primarily on American contributions.

European unity, and Japan's status as the third greatest industrial power, lead inevitably to economic competition between us. We recognize also the necessity and right of a reinvigorated Europe and Japan to pursue their own political initiatives, just as we wish to pursue ours.

Our alliances, therefore, can no longer draw their cohesion only from our agreement on what we are against. We need instead a clearer focus on what we are for.

Our alliances are no longer addressed primarily to the containment of the Soviet Union and China behind an American shield. They are, instead, addressed to the creation with those powers of a stable world peace. That task absolutely requires the maintenance of the allied strength of the non-Communist world.

Within that framework, we expect and welcome a greater diversity of policy. Alliance does not require that those tendencies be stifled, but only that they be accommodated and coordinated within an overall framework of unity and common purpose.

In 1971, important actions were taken to put that theory into fruitful practice.

1. The removal of the economic threat to allied unity. The old international monetary and trading system had begun to undermine our alliance system. It had become unfair, in one aspect or another, both for us and our major trading partners and allies.

—It led inevitably to recurrent international monetary crises.

—Its dependence on the dollar as a reserve currency was seen by others as enabling us to escape monetary and fiscal discipline in domestic policy.

—Its rigidity limited our ability to redress our imbalance of payments, while enabling others to alter their currencies to improve their own trading position.

—It contributed to a chronic U.S. imbalance of payments.

—It placed severe strains on our political relations with some of our closest friends and allies.

Both political and economic common sense dictated vigorous action—in our own national interest, in that of our allies, and in our shared interest in allied unity. What we needed was not a patchwork adjustment, but a more fundamental change in the manner in which the non-Communist world's economy is managed.

Despite the general dissatisfaction, the inertia of the existing system and the conventional opposition to drastic change were tremendous. Hard steps were necessary to bring home to other countries that we were serious, and that reform of the international trade environment and a general realignment of currency values could no longer be delayed.

We, therefore, took drastic unilateral measures on August 15. Paradoxically, these were taken in order to stimulate a multilateral settlement of the problem. We did not in the period that followed resort to bilateral agreements. We sought instead a new international agreement which all would participate in creating.

In December of 1971, the general realignment of currencies took place. That was the necessary first step. With our partners we will, over the next year or two, pursue a more balanced monetary system and a more equitable trading environment. Most important of all, we have acted together to meet our economic problems in a way which strengthens our unity and guarantees our continued cooperation. We have, therefore, put behind us the imminent danger that conflicting economic interests would lead to the unravelling of free world cohesion.

2. *The evolution of our political and defense relationships.* Our partnerships today comprise a varied and dynamic coalition of self-assured and independent states. In this Administration, the United States has shifted from the predominant role it played in the postwar period to a new role of accepting and encouraging initiative and leadership from our allies. Our basic common interests establish the requirement, and maturity and statesmanship furnish the tools, for the preservation of the basic harmony of our policies.

In consonance with our new approaches to China and the Soviet Union, we supported a series of measures by our allies looking toward more autonomous policies. Both our initiatives and theirs were confirmed and coordinated at the end of the year in a series of meetings with the leaders of our principal allies.

—We welcomed the British decision to join the movement of European integration. A stronger Europe and more dynamic Britain are in the common interest of the West. I discussed with Prime Minister Heath at Bermuda the implications of that decision for the traditional special U.S.-U.K. relationship, and we reached agreement on how to harmonize our continuing friendship with Britain's new policies.

—We recognized France's special concerns as to the nature of the exchange rate adjustment. We met with President Pompidou in the Azores and agreed to a mutual adjustment that made possible the association of all major allies in the ensuing solution.

—We reaffirmed our acceptance of West Germany's desire for a more normal relationship with her Eastern neighbors. At Key Biscayne, we met with Chancellor Brandt and agreed upon the crucial and central role that Germany's participation in the Atlantic Alliance plays in Germany's future, including her future hopes for further improvement in her relations with Eastern Europe.

—With all our European allies we have stressed that the justification for the continued American military presence in Europe can only come from a clear and well-thought-out common strategy, and a consensus on how to to share its responsibilities more equitably.

—We met with Prime Minister Sato at San Clemente, and agreed to the expedited return of Okinawa to Japan. This removes from our agenda an issue of vast potential for the disruption of the U.S.-Japanese friendship. We also indicated that we would regard a larger Japanese role in the economic and political affairs of Asia not as a substitute for or interference with our role, but as natural, necessary and proper. We clarified the fact that our initiative toward China is consistent with the continuity of the close U.S.-Japanese relationship.

The Problem of Timing

These were the most dramatic manifestations of our new policy toward both friends and adversaries. In the nature of things, progress in all areas could not be achieved simultaneously—and this led for a time to understandable concern that our interests in some areas were being sacrificed to the need for progress in others. Our approach to China had an impact on Japan, as did our negotiations with the Soviet Union on our friends in Western Europe. Our unilateral economic measures affected both. As a result, our relations with our allies appeared for a period of several months to be somewhat out of phase with the innovations taken in our relations with our adversaries.

By the end of the year, however, it was clear that our initiatives toward both our friends and our adversaries were in basic harmony. Progress in each contributed to progress in the other. In phase, each reinforced and gave added momentum to the other.

The total effect was an integrated and consistent adjustment of U.S. foreign policy to the requirements of a changed world.

Other Areas of Progress

There were other areas in which important, if quieter, progress was made in 1971 toward shaping the new American role in the world.

In our relations with all countries we proceeded to give effect to our new policy of insisting that the United States has neither the prescriptions nor the resources for the solution of problems in which ours is not the prime national interest. It is coming to be widely understood that we are in earnest when we say that it is for others to formulate solutions to these problems, and that our contribution should be viewed as a supplement to the application of major resources from those primarily at interest.

LATIN AMERICA. We have looked to our Latin American neighbors for their initiatives and leadership. We are encouraging them to shape the political and economic framework in which our own contribution to common aims can be most effective.

ASIA. We have helped our Asian allies create a greater capability to meet their own defense needs. This has enabled us to reduce substantially our military presence there, without abandoning our commitments to those steadfast friends. Indeed, by adhering to this pattern of building greater local capability, we have in three years reduced the American military presence in Asia from almost 800 thousand to less than 300 thousand without endangering the stability of the area or abandoning our commitments to our friends.

AFRICA. We have followed a deliberate policy of restraint in involvement in the political problems of Africa, while increasing our contribution to worthy African-initiated development activities.

NEW DIMENSION OF DIPLOMACY. We have taken the initiative in stimulating international action on many of the issues which constitute the new dimension of diplomacy.

—We are making a major effort to reach worldwide agreement in 1973 on a new Law of the Sea. Such an agreement is needed to ensure that the vast potential of the ocean and its resources serves to benefit mankind rather than becoming a new source of conflict between nations.

—We have taken the lead in organizing a concerted international effort to control narcotics.

—We have helped in persuading the world community to recognize the dangers of, and take effective measures to control, excessive population growth.

—We are participating in a major effort to focus the world's attention and resources constructively on the threat to the global environment.

—We have consistently asserted and worked to stimulate the general world interest in space exploration and global communications.

—We have provided leadership in the efforts of the world community to meet the challenge of air piracy.

OUR BASIC NATIONAL PURPOSE—AND VIETNAM

Each of the initiatives described is significant in itself. But their true significance lies in the fact that they are all part of a whole, each contributing to our basic purpose of building a stable peace.

During much of the previous decade, our national effort to reach that goal had been disrupted by our concentration on the war in Southeast Asia. We therefore faced the exigent need to reshape the American role in Vietnam so that it contributed to, rather than inhibited, progress toward the national goal of secure world peace.

We promised to end the conflict, but in a way that did not mock our effort to bring about a stable peace. On January 25, 1972 I described our thirty-month effort to reach peace through secret negotiations. I also presented our new proposals which clearly make possible a peaceful settlement which entrusts the political future of South Vietnam to the South Vietnamese. Alternatively, as we offered to do over nine months ago, we are ready to conclude a settlement of military issues only. To date, however, our earnest efforts to end the war for all participants through negotiations have foundered on Communist obstinacy. That has left us no choice but to move toward ending the war for America through Vietnamization of the conflict.

We have come a long way. In Vietnam, we have changed the very nature of the U.S. involvement. Our ground combat role has effectively ended. When I came into office, the American troop ceiling in Vietnam was 549,500, and we were suffering an average of more than 1,000 casualties a month. As I write this Report, our

troop level has dropped below 139,000—
and will be no higher than 69,000 by the
first day of May. In December 1971 our
combat deaths were down to 17. Air sorties, budget costs, draft calls—all have
sharply declined.

Those facts represent the transformation of the American role in Vietnam. We
have done this, as we promised to do,
without abandoning our commitments to
our allies. As our role has diminished,
South Vietnam has been able increasingly
to meet its own defense needs and provide
growing security to its people.

PROGRESS WAS TEMPERED BY DISAPPOINTMENTS

During the year there were several
sharp disappointments.

—The greatest was the failure of our
intense public and private efforts to
end the Vietnam War through a
negotiated settlement. Such a settlement continues to be available to our
enemy whenever he is prepared to
negotiate in earnest. The only serious
barrier to a settlement which remains
is the enemy's insistence that we
cooperate with him to force on our
ally at the negotiating table a solution
which the enemy cannot force upon
him in the field, and is unwilling to
entrust to a political process. That we
are not willing to do. We are ready
to reach an agreement which allows
the South Vietnamese to determine
their own future without outside interference. This goal can be reached
whenever Hanoi distinguishes between a settlement and a surrender.

—In South Asia, we made a determined year-long effort to prevent a
war. We did not succeed. Our deep

interest in the well-being of both
India and Pakistan compounded our
disappointment. We attempted to
moderate the crisis with a massive
relief effort and with an intense diplomatic campaign to promote a
political solution. But war had its
own momentum. The violation of
peace in South Asia had ominous
implications for the stability of other
areas of tension in the world and for
our efforts to establish a more hopeful
relationship with our adversaries.

—In the Middle East, we were unable
to make a breakthrough toward
peace. Although the ceasefire resulting from our initiative in 1970 was
maintained, it did not prove possible
to engage the parties in negotiations,
and consequently no progress was
made toward the essential requirement of Middle-Eastern peace: an
arrangement which rests the security
of all on something more reliable
than the good will of a nation's
adversaries.

—In Latin America, we have yet to
work out with our friends a solution
of the conflict between their desire
for our help and their determination
to be free of dependence upon us.
The thrust for change in Latin
America, and our response to it, have
yet to shape themselves into a pattern
permitting us to make as full a contribution as we wish and as our
hemisphere friends expect.

—In Africa, we have witnessed the
growing maturity of the newly independent states, and the increasing
concentration of their governments
on the hard tasks of internal development. This is a heartening process,
and it is one which deserves our en-

couragement. It is, therefore, a sharp disappointment, both to us and to our African friends, that our shrinking aid appropriations may prevent us from matching our expressions of good will with the material assistance which African countries want and need.

—In the United Nations we were unable to preserve a place for the Republic of China.

Unfinished Business

In 1971, we passed a critical point in creating a new world role for the United States. But we are far from having completed the task. In almost every case, a listing of what we have done serves as an illustration of how far we still have to go. Our accomplishments as well as our disappointments define the agenda for the future. In all candor, I must say that the salient feature of the current state of U.S. foreign policy is the need for more progress on a whole series of pressing problems.

—We need to prove, through additional concrete accomplishments, the benefit to both the Soviet Union and ourselves of mutual self-restraint and willingness to accommodate rather than merely assert our respective national interests.

—We need to continue the hopeful but delicate process of creating a better relationship between ourselves and the People's Republic of China.

—We need to bring the arms race under control. Nothing would do more for our material and psychological well-being than to lighten this burden. It is axiomatic that it cannot be done at the sacrifice of our na-

tional security; but if it can be done without such a sacrifice, nothing would contribute more to our national security.

—We need to find the most effective way to help the poorer nations. Yet we now find ourselves in national disarray regarding our approach to economic assistance. Our wealth, our humanitarian traditions, and our interests dictate that we have an active foreign assistance program. The world looks to us for help in this area, and it is right that we should respond. I am prepared to work with the Congress to that end.

—We need to finish the construction with our partners of a reformed trade and monetary system which sustains our unity by encouraging the economic well-being of all.

—We need to continue, with both our friends and our adversaries, to build an international system which all will work to preserve because all recognize their stake in its preservation.

—We need to deal realistically with the fact that the United Nations is facing what I can only call a crisis of confidence. Whatever its current weaknesses, the UN makes an essential contribution to the structure of world peace and thus to mankind's future.

This Report is, therefore, presented with a very sober awareness of how great a task still lies before the nation. We are still engaged in the essential job of redefining our role in the world. It must do justice to our capacity and obligation for leadership. It must also recognize our limitations. Above all, it must be based on a solid consensus of American public understanding and support. It is my hope that this Report will help engender that support among the people of the nation and the Congress which represents them.

We believe the direction we have established and the actions we have taken commend themselves to such support.

PART II: AREAS OF MAJOR CHANGE

—The Soviet Union
—China
—Europe and the Atlantic Alliance
—Japan
—International Economic Policy

THE SOVIET UNION

". . . one of the paramount problems of our time is that we must transcend the old patterns of power politics in which nations sought to exploit every volatile situation for their own advantage or to squeeze the maximum advantage for themselves out of every negotiation.

". . . The profoundest national interest of our time—for every nation—is not immediate gain, but the preservation of peace."

Address to the United Nations
October 23, 1970

Since the nuclear age began, both the world's fears of Armageddon and its hopes for a stable peace have rested on the relationship between the United States and the Soviet Union. For most of that period, the policies of both countries have been directed more to the fearful possibility than to the larger hope.

But it is not inevitable that our relationship with the Soviets be dominated by an incessant and dangerous contest made all the more ominous by an occasional, but always brief and unproductive, oscillation

toward detente. The true interests of neither country require such a relationship. The needs of neither are served by the restrictions it places on the intercourse between our two great peoples.

It has been the purpose of this Administration to transform the U.S.-Soviet relationship so that a mutual search for a stable peace and security becomes its dominant feature and its driving force. If the ultimate prospect for a stable world peace requires accommodation between China and the United States, both the immediate and the long term hopes for world stability rest on a more decent and mutually beneficial relationship between ourselves and the Soviet Union.

Such a vision is not quixotic. It has been rendered possible by the end of the bipolar rigidity which characterized the postwar world. It is sustained by the desire of the Soviet people for the benefits which would be theirs if their government could reduce the vast investment of resources in international competition with us. And it is countenanced by the readiness of the American people to search for a new and just approach to lasting peace.

For the three years of this Administration, we have, therefore, worked to establish a more positive relationship with the Soviet Union.

Paradoxically, this required that we put aside the temptations of immediate, but shallow, "accomplishments" such as unprepared and unproductive summit meetings. A constructive relationship with the Soviet Union cannot be built merely by mutual assertions of good intentions or assurances of good will. History has amply shown how barren such gestures are of genuine and lasting result.

The issues which divide the United States and the Soviet Union are real and serious. They are at the heart of the security and well-being of both countries. They are not, therefore, susceptible to solution by resort to mere atmospherics. They require, instead, concrete agreements on the specific problems which cause the tension between our two countries.

Such agreements can be obtained only by a careful and painstaking effort by both countries. It requires each to exercise restraint, to recognize and accept the legitimate interests of the other, and to negotiate realistically to accommodate conflicting views. For our part, we are committed to such an approach. We are convinced that it can serve the best interests of the American and Soviet peoples and the peoples of the world.

That is the burden of the message which, in various ways, we have been conveying to the Soviet leaders for the past three years. We hope that what has been accomplished will prove to be the beginning of a transformation of the relationship between ourselves and the Soviet Union.

The first requirement for such a transformation is that we understand clearly the sources of our differences. They are profound and they do not spring from transitory causes, or from personalities, or from some historical accident. Rather, they are rooted in the different ways our two countries have developed. They are exacerbated by tendencies which spring from our national personalities and our differing approaches to the conduct of international affairs.

—Americans consider tensions in international relations abnormal, and yearn to see them resolved as quickly as possible. We tend to believe that good will is a principal ingredient for their resolution, and that our own good will is beyond question. We assume that if tensions persist, it is proof that our adversary is implacably hostile to us. The application of these attitudes to relations with the Soviet Union has led us to excessive and unjustified optimism during periods of detente, and to uncritical acceptance of inevitable and unbounded hostility during periods of tension.

—The USSR tends to view external tensions as the inevitable corollary of conflicting social systems. Soviet diplomacy therefore is prepared to accept international tension as normal, and, too often, to view negotiations with the United States as a form of harsh competition from which only one side can possibly gain advantage. In the past, this attitude has often tempted the Soviets to treat the occasional improvement in our relations as a transitory opportunity to achieve narrow tactical advantages. It has led the Soviets to consider the intervening periods of hostility as inevitable, and the causes of that hostility as beyond resolution.

—Both these attitudes reflect the national experiences of the United States and the Soviet Union, and have worked for two decades to frustrate a better relationship between our two countries. They cause periods of detente to founder, and they protract and intensify the periods of hostility.

It is, of course, true that there are deep concerns that divide us. The beginning of a process of accommodation is to recognize them for what they are.

—We are ideological adversaries, and will remain so.

—We are political and military com-

87–234—74——17

petitors, and neither can be indifferent to advances by the other in either field.

—We each stand at the head of a group of countries whose association we value and are not prepared to sacrifice to an improvement in Soviet-American relations.

—We each possess an awesome nuclear force created and designed to meet the threat implicit in the other's strength.

—We both conduct global policies. Unless prudence is used, this can create new tensions and areas of conflict in our relations.

—Both our peoples are acutely conscious of almost half-a-century of sharp hostility. This historic fact conditions efforts to move toward a better relationship.

The essence of this Administration's approach to the Soviet Union has been to concentrate on the substance rather than the climate of our relationship and to confront squarely the serious issues which divide us. This required the careful and unemotional examination with the Soviet Union of the specific problems which appeared susceptible of resolution and of the general approach which both countries must take to those problems and to the overall conduct of our relationship, if progress were, in fact, to be obtained.

Our determination to pursue this approach was reinforced by changes in the international scene affecting Soviet interests and the USSR's position in the world. There were ambiguous tendencies in Soviet policy; the same factors that might lead the USSR toward greater hostility also suggested the opportunity for a relaxation of tension. The task of American policy was to recognize the persist-

ence of this ambiguity and to take action to strengthen the more positive tendencies.

—Sharp rivalries had grown up within the Communist world and had become an important influence on Soviet foreign policy. They created some immediate pressures to compete for the mantle of militancy. In some areas—especially in Asia—Communist competition actually sharpened conflicts. The breakup of a single Communist entity, however, relaxed some of the ideological inhibitions against dealing with the U.S. and forced the Soviet Union to reevaluate its security concerns. This suggested that the Soviet Union might seek a reduction of tensions with the U.S. and its Atlantic allies.

—The Soviet Union had created a nuclear force comparable to ours. The magnitude of Soviet strategic programs and their accelerating pace opened up both opportunities and dangers that had not existed before; the USSR might be tempted by the possibility of gaining a dominant position, even though it should be clear that neither side would permit the other to develop a decisive strategic advantage. On the other hand, it was possible that for the first time, strategic conditions freed the USSR from some of its own fears and might permit serious arms limitations at no disadvantage to either side.

—The expansion of Soviet military and economic resources has made feasible a steady expansion of the Soviet presence in the Middle East, in South Asia, and in other areas. As it increases its influence, however, the Soviet Union also acquires responsibilities, and hopefully a new interest in regional stability. To the degree the USSR exercises its influence in the interest of restraint, the USSR and the U.S. could act on parallel courses.

—The Soviet Union has created a mature industrialized economy. The continued growth of that economy made it possible to sustain a major arms program and increasingly serve civilian needs. On the other hand, the satisfaction of the growing expectations of the Soviet people for consumer benefits provides an incentive for a more normal relationship with the industrial powers of the non-Communist world.

We have sought to encourage those tendencies in Soviet policy which suggested a readiness to seek change through an evolutionary process. Thus, at the outset of this Administration, I stated publicly that our goal was to move from confrontation to negotiation, and that in pursuing that policy, our relations with the Soviet Union would be governed by four principles.

—We would judge Soviet policy by its actions on the key issues which divide us. In negotiations we would adopt a conciliatory posture, but our positions would be affected only by concrete measures, not by assumptions regarding Soviet intentions.

—Our objective was significant progress on divisive issues, rather than superficial changes in the climate of the U.S.-Soviet relationship. On March 4, 1969, I suggested Berlin, limitations on strategic arms, the Middle East, and Vietnam as areas where progress should be made.

—We would set no preconditions. We would judge each issue on its merits. Nevertheless, we recognized that accommodation is a process, and that the settlement of a major issue could not fail to improve the prospect for the settlement of others, just as failure would cloud the prospects of broad progress.

—A broad and mutual self-restraint was essential. If either side sought to gain significant advantage over the other, it would inevitably lead to counteractions aimed at redressing the balance. That in turn would jeopardize any progress that had already been achieved, and make infinitely more difficult the task of reaching agreements on the specific issues which divide us.

In 1969, a beginning was made. Negotiations were initiated on Berlin and on the limitation of strategic arms. Discussions took place on the Middle East situation.

Progress, however, came slowly, when it came at all. The conflicting tendencies in Soviet policy were evident. The Soviets sought detente in Europe without a relaxation of hostility toward the United States. They encouraged a favorable turn in Soviet-German relations, while taking an adamant stand in the Four-Power negotiations on Berlin. Under those conditions a broad discussion of European security could not take place; repeated Soviet calls for such a discussion appeared to be more a maneuver to divide the West than a reflection of a desire to resolve conflicting interests.

In 1970, tensions began to heighten once more. There was a sharp crisis in the Middle East. The fragile ceasefire achieved in August, to which we attached great value and for which we had labored long, was almost killed in its infancy. The cause was a rash and provocative Soviet and Egyptian missile buildup along the Suez Canal. Soviet-supported Syria attacked and, for a short time, threatened the survival of Jordan, a good friend of the United States. The Soviets appeared to be attempting to build a submarine base in Cuba, which would have violated the understanding which ended the Cuban missile crisis, and could have posed a threat to peace. The initial progress in the arms limitation talks gave way to an impasse. The talks on Berlin stagnated.

By the fall of 1970 we seemed on the verge of a new, perhaps prolonged, and certainly fruitless and dangerous period of tension. The Soviet Union did not seem to share our interest in better relations, nor was there evidence that it was resolved to practice the self-restraint essential to such relations.

At the same time, there were other trends that led us to conclude that a more personal and direct approach to the Soviet leaders might be timely and productive, despite the apparent deterioration in our relations. They might have their own reasons for second thoughts. The crises in the Middle East and the Caribbean had underlined once again the dangers of unmitigated competition between us. There were new stresses in Eastern Europe which might give the Soviets a reinvigorated desire for a reduction of East-West tensions in Europe. The approach of the Soviet Party Congress ensured that Soviet leaders were reexamining their policies and the prospects they offered. They might be attracted to alternatives which carried greater promise.

We were approaching a turning point. I felt an obligation to convey to the Soviet leaders my conviction that an improvement in relations was still a distinct possibility, and that the alternative to it was a sharp deterioration dangerous for both of us and bereft of promise to either.

I invited Foreign Minister Gromyko to Washington on October 22, 1970, and we discussed at some length the general prospects for Soviet-American relations and the status of specific issues.

On the following day I went to New York and spoke to the United Nations General Assembly. That speech was addressed primarily to the leaders of the Soviet Union:

"The issue of war and peace cannot be solved unless we in the United States and the Soviet Union demonstrate both the will and the capacity to put our relationship on a basis consistent with the aspirations of mankind. . . . In the world today we are at a crossroads. We can follow the old way, playing the traditional game of international relations, but at ever-increasing risk. Everyone will lose. No one will gain. Or we can take a new road.

"I invite the leaders of the Soviet Union to join us in taking that new road . . ."

Shortly thereafter I initiated a confidential and ultimately productive exchange directly with the Soviet leaders.

In all of these initiatives I stressed the need for concrete progress, and pointed to the Berlin and arms limitation talks as ideal candidates for a successful accommodation of our interests. Both negotiations were at an impasse. Both required bold initiatives.

The talks on the limitation of strategic arms had reached a point of fundamental conflict beyond the ability of the negotiators to resolve. The Soviet Union wished to work toward an initial agreement limited solely to anti-ballistic missiles. We considered that so narrow a solution would risk upsetting the strategic balance, and might put a premium on the further development of offensive weapons. Each view was held firmly and was reinforced by the national view of the imperatives of security in a nuclear age. The impasse could be resolved only at the highest political level, and only by an agreement which somehow took into account the concerns reflected in both positions.

My exchanges with the Soviet leaders were addressed to this problem. A mutual interest in compromise was developed and both sides made a positive contribution. As a result we were able to agree upon a basis which permitted the negotiations to resume their momentum and their progress. We agreed that first priority in the talks would go to defensive systems, but that the final conclusion of such an agreement would take place simultaneously with an agreement on limitations on offensive weapons. Thus the assured and essential linkage was preserved between offensive and defensive limitations.

In the same period, in consultation with our allies, I approved a more intense program for the Berlin talks, which had been discussed with Foreign Minister Gromyko. Those negotiations, too, were stalled. Neither side would abandon legal and political principles to which they had adhered for two decades. Nonetheless, both sides were prepared for an agreement, though for different reasons. The Soviets recognized that the ratification of the West German-Soviet treaty would be impossible if there were no Berlin agreement. We wanted to remove Berlin as a perennial source of conflict and tension. We agreed, therefore, to lay aside the legal and political issues and to seek an accord on and a clarification of West Germany's ties to West Berlin.

In this period, there were other evidences of a spirit of reciprocity on the Soviet side. The position taken by Secretary Brezhnev at the Soviet Party Congress in March 1971 was encouraging. We felt that the Soviet leaders, in effect, had publicly accepted the offer of the new road in Soviet-American relations which I had suggested in my UN speech. This impression was confirmed in various private exchanges. Most important of all, it was reflected in the concrete progress made during 1971 on a wide range of issues.

—On May 20, 1971 I announced that the impasse in the SALT negotiations had been broken. Vigor and promise were restored to the talks.

—In August, the Ambassadors of the United Kingdom, France, the Soviet Union, and the United States reached an agreement on Berlin which was approved by their governments and signed on September 3. This agreement guarantees that access to the Western sectors of Berlin from West Germany will be unimpeded, and that West Berliners will be able to travel to East Berlin and East Germany on the same basis as any other persons.

—In September, the United States and the Soviet Union agreed at the Geneva disarmament talks to a draft treaty banning the development, production, or possession of biological and toxin weapons. The treaty was submitted to the UN and endorsed in December.

—In September, the SALT talks resulted in two new agreements. The first will improve the reliability of direct communications between the heads of the Soviet and American governments—the "Hot Line"—by the use of satellite communications. The second involves the exchange of certain information to reduce the risk of an accidental nuclear war.

—In November our Secretary of Commerce visited the Soviet Union and initiated a series of discussions with Soviet leaders looking toward the normalization of our economic relations. He was received with marked cordiality. His discussions with Premier Kosygin opened a broad vista for an expansion of mutually beneficial economic contacts between ourselves and the Soviet Union.

In addition to these major developments, there was a series of agreements on additional measures striking both in their diversity and in their promise of mutual advantage.

—In January, representatives of the National Aeronautics and Space Administration and the Soviet Academy of Sciences discussed cooperation in space research. This followed an agreement the previous October to study measures which would permit Soviet space craft to dock with our own.

—In May we agreed to the participation of American firms in a large Soviet manufacturing project on the Kama River. This will lead to substantial American sales.

—In May the Surgeon General of the United States and his Soviet counterpart discussed the establishment of a joint health policy board which would meet annually to cooperate in research on cancer and heart disease.

—In October, an American delegation went to Moscow to discuss measures to reduce the chances of incidents at sea between our Navy and that of the Soviet Union. Initial understandings were reached, and the talks will continue with the aim of a formal and broad agreement to reduce the potential for a dangerous but unintended confrontation.

—In November we agreed with the Soviet Union to discuss changes in our maritime regulations to facilitate the use by the ships of each side of the port facilities of the other.

THE MEETING AT THE SUMMIT

By the fall of 1971 it was beyond dispute that marked progress had been made, both on broad international issues, and in our bilateral relationship with the Soviet Union.

Thus the conditions had been created which justified a meeting between myself and the Soviet leaders. The progress that had been made gave promise that such a meeting could be successful and lead to additional progress. It ensured that a summit would not be an empty and self-deluding exercise in atmospherics.

On October 12, 1971, I announced:

"The leaders of the United States and the Soviet Union, in their exchanges during the past year, have agreed that a meeting between them would be desirable once sufficient progress had been made in negotiations at lower levels.

"In light of the recent advances in bilateral and multilateral negotiations involving the two countries, it has been agreed that such a meeting will take place in Moscow in the latter part of May, 1972.

"President Nixon and the Soviet leaders will review all major issues, with a view towards further improving their bilateral relations and enhancing the prospects of world peace."

In Moscow, we will have three central objectives. We want to complete work on those issues which have been carried to the point of final decision. We want to establish a political framework for dealing with the issues still in dispute. And we want to examine with the Soviet leaders the further development of the U.S.-Soviet relationship in the years ahead.

The tasks ahead arise logically from the present state of relations:

—An accord on an initial strategic arms limitation agreement, or on the issues to be addressed in the second stage of the SALT negotiations.

—A discussion of the problem of the Middle East and the reasons for the failure to reach a peaceful settlement there.

—A discussion of the problem of European security in all its aspects and the identification of mutually shared objectives which will provide a basis for further normalization of intercourse between Eastern and Western Europe. No agreements in this area, however, will be made without our allies.

—An exploration of our policies in other areas of the world and the extent to which we share an interest in stability.

—An examination of the possibility of additional bilateral cooperation. The steps taken so far have been significant, but are meager, indeed, in terms of the potential. There are a variety of fields in which U.S.-Soviet cooperation would benefit both. Our economic relations are perhaps the most obvious example. Bilateral coopera-

tion will be facilitated if we can continue to make progress on the major international issues.

We do not, of course, expect the Soviet Union to give up its pursuit of its own interests. We do not expect to give up pursuing our own. We do expect, and are prepared ourselves to demonstrate, self-restraint in the pursuit of those interests. We do expect a recognition of the fact that the general improvement in our relationship transcends in importance the kind of narrow advantages which can be sought only by imperiling the cooperation between our two countries.

One series of conversations in Moscow cannot be expected to end two decades' accumulation of problems. For a long period of time, competition is likely to be the hallmark of our relationship with the Soviet Union. We will be confronted by ambiguous and contradictory trends in Soviet policy. The continuing buildup of Soviet military power is one obvious source of deep concern. Soviet attitudes during the crisis in South Asia have dangerous implications for other regional conflicts, even though in the end the USSR played a restraining role. Similarly, the USSR's position in the Middle East reflects a mixture of Soviet interest in expansionist policies and Soviet recognition of the dangers of confrontation.

In the past year, however, we have also had evidence that there can be mutual accommodation of conflicting interests, and that competition need not be translated into hostility or crisis. We have evidence that on both sides there is an increasing willingness to break with the traditional patterns of Soviet-American relations. A readiness to capitalize on this momentum is the real test of the summit.

The USSR has the choice: whether the

current period of relaxation is to be merely another offensive tactic or truly an opportunity to develop an international system resting on the stability of relations between the superpowers. Its choice will be demonstrated in actions prior to and after our meetings.

For our part, we are committed to a new relationship. I made this commitment in my Inaugural Address, at the United Nations, and in my exchanges with the Soviet leaders. Our actions have demonstrated our seriousness. We have the opportunity to usher in a new era in international relations. If we can do so, the transformation of Soviet-American relations can become one of the most significant achievements of our time.

CHINA

Few events can be called historic. The announcement which I read on July 15 merits that term:

"Premier Chou En-lai and Dr. Henry Kissinger, President Nixon's Assistant for National Security Affairs, held talks in Peking from July 9 to 11, 1971. Knowing of President Nixon's expressed desire to visit the People's Republic of China, Premier Chou En-lai on behalf of the Government of the People's Republic of China has extended an invitation to President Nixon to visit China at an appropriate date before May 1972.

"President Nixon has accepted the invitation with pleasure.

"The meeting between the leaders of China and the United States is to seek the normalization of relations between the two countries and also to exchange views on questions of concern to the two sides."

This announcement could have the most profound significance for future generations. The course leading up to it

was carefully navigated; the opening we have made is still fragile; the immediate concrete achievements may be limited. But our purpose, and now our potential, is to establish contact between the world's most powerful nation and the world's most populous nation, and to confine our future confrontations to the conference table. Contact now might help avert a disastrous catastrophe later. It should serve to enrich the lives of our two peoples. And it could lead to cooperative ventures between our countries in the future.

THE HISTORICAL SETTING

My meetings with the leaders of the People's Republic of China will be unprecedented.

The earliest Sino-American contacts developed in the early 1800's. At that time the ancient Chinese empire, secure and preeminent, was just beginning the painful process of adapting itself to the outside world. With the world's longest history of self-government, and as the dominant political and cultural force in their region, the Chinese were self-confident and self-contained as the "Middle Kingdom" of the world. Nevertheless they were exploited by technologically superior foreign powers. The United States—isolationist and bending its energies to national development—favored the territorial integrity of China; but our "open door" doctrine of equal treatment for all foreigners carried ambiguity in Chinese eyes.

The Communist leaders thus inherited a tradition marked by both pride and humiliation; the Chinese experience had not been one of dealing with the outside world as equals but one of their Chinese superiority or foreign exploitation. In recent years China has passed through a period of domestic turmoil and shifts in external relationships. China's leaders have decided to break the isolation that was partly self-chosen, to explore more normal relations with other countries, and to take their place in the international dialogue.

While the Chinese Revolution ran its long and tortured course the United States ended a long history of isolationism and plunged with zeal and idealism into worldwide responsibilities. We alone among the major powers emerged relatively unscathed from the Second World War. We provided the bulk of both the plans and resources for security and development around the globe. And we perceived the Communist countries, including China, as a monolithic bloc with central direction.

Today, two and a half decades after the war, new realities are reflected in a new American approach to foreign policy. The growing strength and self-confidence of others allow them to assume greater responsibilities and us to shift to a more restrained role. And with the time long past when one nation could speak for all Communist countries, we deal with individual nations on the basis of their foreign, and not their domestic, policy.

Thus, in February of 1972, after many vicissitudes, many achievements and our separate evolution, the U.S. and China enter this dialogue on a fresh foundation of national equality and mutual respect. We are both turning a new page in our histories.

Despite this hopeful beginning, we remain separated by profound differences in principle and the suspicions of decades. Until 1971 we had had little meaningful contact for most of a generation. The People's Republic's critical public statements and interpretations of history are well known to us. We have also made our position clear.

It serves no purpose to gloss over these sources of division. Neither side pretended during preparations for my journey, and neither will pretend afterwards, that we have solved our basic problems. We can expect our talks to be marked by the directness and candor which best serve leaders whose differences are deep but whose policies are rooted in realism.

A NEW APPROACH

My journey to the People's Republic of China marks both an end and a beginning. It is the culmination of three years of patient mutual effort to pierce the isolation of decades. And it represents the launching of a new process.

The July 15, 1971 statement on my trip was sudden and dramatic, but it was preceded and produced by a carefully developed series of steps. In fact, no other U.S. foreign policy move in the past three years has been approached more meticulously.

As far back as October 1967, I had written in the journal *Foreign Affairs* that "any American policy toward Asia must come urgently to grips with the reality of China," while pointing out that bold new initiatives without preparation were inappropriate.

In January 1969 I entered office convinced that a new policy toward the People's Republic of China was an essential component of a new American foreign policy. I was, of course, fully aware of the profound ideological and political differences between our countries, and of the hostility and suspicion to be overcome. But I believed also that in this era we

213

could not afford to be cut off from a quarter of the world's population. We had an obligation to try to establish contact, to define our positions, and perhaps move on to greater understanding.

Recalling our historical experience and contemplating tomorrow's world, I saw the present period as a unique moment. The shifting tides in international relations, our new foreign policy perspectives, the changing face of China—these were the factors, at work in Peking as well as Washington, that beckoned our two nations toward a dialogue.

The following considerations shaped this Administration's approach to the People's Republic of China.

—Peace in Asia and peace in the world require that we exchange views, not so much despite our differences as because of them. A clearer grasp of each other's purposes is essential in an age of turmoil and nuclear weapons.

—It is in America's interest, and the world's interest, that the People's Republic of China play its appropriate role in shaping international arrangements that affect its concerns. Only then will that great nation have a stake in such arrangements; only then will they endure.

—No one nation should be the sole voice for a bloc of states. We will deal with all countries on the basis of specific issues and external behavior, not abstract theory.

—Both Chinese and American policies could be much less rigid if we had no need to consider each other permanent enemies. Over the longer term there need be no clashes between our fundamental national concerns.

—China and the United States share many parallel interests and can do much together to enrich the lives of our peoples. It is no accident that the Chinese and American peoples have such a long history of friendship.

On this basis we decided that a careful search for a new relationship should be undertaken. We believed that the Chinese could be engaged in such an effort.

THE UNFOLDING OF U.S. POLICY

Both political and technical problems lay in the way of such a search. When this Administration assumed responsibility, there had been virtually no contact between mainland China and the American people for two decades. This was true for our governments as well, although sterile talks in Geneva and Warsaw had dragged on intermittently since 1955. A deep gulf of mistrust and noncommunication separated us.

We faced two major questions. First, how to convey our views privately to the authorities in Peking? Second, what public steps would demonstrate our willingness to set a new direction in our relations?

Within two weeks of my inauguration we moved on both of these fronts. I ordered that efforts be undertaken to communicate our new attitude through private channels, and to seek contact with the People's Republic of China.

This process turned out to be delicate and complex. It is extremely difficult to establish even rudimentary communications between two governments which have been completely isolated from one another for twenty years. Neither technical nor diplomatic means of direct contact existed. It was necessary to find an intermediary country which had the full trust of both nations, and could be relied upon to promote the dialogue with discretion, restraint, and diplomatic skill.

The two sides began clarifying their general intentions through mutually friendly countries. After a period of cautious exploration and gathering confidence, we settled upon a reliable means of communication between Washington and Peking.

In February 1969, I also directed that a comprehensive National Security Council study be made of our policy toward China, setting in motion a policy review process which has continued throughout these past three years. We addressed both the broader ramifications of a new approach and the specific steps to carry it out.

Drawing on this analysis, we began to implement a phased sequence of unilateral measures to indicate the direction in which this Administration was prepared to move. We believed that these practical steps, progressively relaxing trade and travel restrictions, would make clear to the Chinese leaders over time that we were prepared for a serious dialogue. We had no illusion that we could bargain for Chinese good will. Because of the difficulties in communication we deliberately chose initiatives that could be ignored or quietly accepted; since they required no Chinese actions, they were difficult to reject. We purposely avoided dramatic moves which could invoke dramatic rebukes and set back the whole carefully nurtured process.

Throughout 1969 and 1970 we underlined our willingness to have a more constructive relationship.

—In July 1969, we permitted noncommercial purchases of Chinese goods without special authorization by American tourists, museums and others. We also broadened the categories of U.S. citizens whose passports would be validated automatically for travel to China.

—In December 1969, we allowed subsidiaries of American firms abroad to engage in commerce between mainland China and third countries.

—In January and February 1970, the two sides held Ambassadorial meetings in Warsaw, which in turn had been set through private exchanges. These sessions underlined the handicaps of this formal discourse. The two sides' representatives had minimum flexibility; they could do little more than read prepared statements and refer back to their capitals for instructions for the next meeting. This cumbersome exchange between wary adversaries reinforced the need for a new approach.

—In March 1970, we announced that U.S. passports would be validated for travel to mainland China for any legitimate purpose.

—In April 1970, we authorized selective licensing of non-strategic U.S. goods for export to mainland China.

—In August 1970, we lifted certain restrictions on American oil companies operating abroad so that most foreign ships could use American-owned bunkering facilities on trips to and from mainland Chinese ports.

By the end of 1970, therefore, we had laid out a careful record of unilateral initiatives. Throughout these two years we had accompanied these steps with a series of public statements which delineated our general attitude.

—Secretary Rogers in a speech in Canberra, Australia on August 8, 1969, noted the barriers between our countries but added, "We nonetheless look forward to a time when we can enter into a useful dialogue and to a reduction of tensions."

—In my February 1970 Foreign Policy Report, I stated that ". . . it is certainly in our interest, and in the interest of peace and stability in Asia and the world, that we take what steps we can toward improved practical relations with Peking. . . . we will seek to promote understandings which can establish a new pattern of mutually beneficial actions."

—On October 26, 1970, in a toast to visiting President Ceausescu of Romania, I deliberately used Peking's official title, "the People's Republic of China". This was the first time an American President had ever done so.

By the time of my second Foreign Policy Report in February 1971, we had reason to believe that our moves were being noted and evaluated by the Chinese. In that Report, I cited the importance of China's participation in world affairs, reiterated that we were ready for a dialogue with Peking, and stated that we hoped to see the People's Republic of China assume a constructive role in the family of nations. I looked toward the immediate future:

"In the coming year, I will carefully examine what further steps we might take to create broader opportunities for contacts between the Chinese and American peoples, and how we might remove needless obstacles to the realization of these opportunities. We hope for, but will not be deterred by a lack of, reciprocity."

THE BREAKTHROUGH

By the fall of 1970, in private and reliable diplomatic channels, the Chinese began to respond. Both sides were now working to launch a process. The spring of 1971 saw a series of orchestrated public and private steps which culminated in Dr. Kissinger's July trip to Peking and the agreement for me to meet with the leaders of the People's Republic of China.

—On March 15, 1971 we announced that U.S. passports no longer needed special validation for travel to mainland China.

—On April 6, 1971, in Nagoya, Japan, the U.S. table tennis team competing in the world championships received an invitation from the Chinese team to visit mainland China. This was accepted the next day. The Chinese also granted visas to seven Western newsmen to cover the team's tour. The U.S. team traveled extensively in China, and was received on April 14 by Prime Minister Chou En-lai, who told them: "with your acceptance of our invitation, you have opened a new page in the relations of the Chinese and American people."

—On that same day, we moved to further the momentum that had clearly developed. I decided on the following measures which had been under governmental study since December 1970:

• We would expedite visas for visitors from the PRC;

• U.S. currency controls would be relaxed to permit the PRC to use dollars;

• Restrictions on U.S. oil companies

providing fuel to ships or aircraft en route to or from China (except those bound to or from North Korea, North Vietnam and Cuba) were eliminated;

• U.S. vessels or aircraft would be permitted to carry Chinese cargoes between non-Chinese ports, and U.S.-owned foreign-flag carriers could call at Chinese ports; and

• A list of items of a non-strategic nature would be compiled for direct export to the PRC.

—In the April 30 issue of *Life* magazine, the author, Edgar Snow, reported a conversation he had had earlier with Chairman Mao Tse-tung which confirmed private signals we had already received of Chinese interest in my visiting China.

—On May 7, 1971 we removed U.S. controls on dollar transactions with China (except those in previously blocked accounts) and certain controls on U.S. bunkering facilities and flagships.

—On June 10, 1971 we announced the end of the twenty-one year embargo on trade with the PRC. We issued a general export license for a long list of nonstrategic items for China and designated other items to be considered on a case-by-case basis. Restrictions on the import of Chinese goods were simultaneously lifted.

The stage was thus set for Dr. Kissinger's secret visit to Peking. From July 9 to July 11, Dr. Kissinger held very extensive and important discussions with Premier Chou En-lai which produced the agreement that I would visit China before May 1972.

From October 20 to 26, Dr. Kissinger again visited Peking to reach agreement on the major arrangements for my trip. Further lengthy talks with Prime Minister Chou En-lai and other Chinese officials produced the basic framework for my meetings with the leaders of the People's Republic of China—including the February 21, 1972 date, the duration and itinerary, the broad agenda, and the approximate composition and facilities for the accompanying party and representatives of the media. The major elements were announced at the end of November.

On December 13, 1971 the Chinese released two Americans whom they had been holding prisoner, and commuted the life sentence of a third American to five more years. This welcome gesture came after Dr. Kissinger transmitted my personal concern during his two visits to Peking. It was both a concrete result of our efforts to establish a dialogue and a hopeful sign for future progress in our relations.

INTERNATIONAL IMPACT

No major step in international relations is taken without some painful adjustments and potential costs. Indeed, the tendency is to focus on the risks that might flow from a departure from familiar patterns and to lose sight of its possible benefits. It is precisely this tendency that inhibits major initiatives and perpetuates established policies which sustain the status quo.

We undertook our initiatives toward the People's Republic of China aware of the problems as well as the opportunities. Such a dramatic move was bound to stir great changes in the world. The news of my forthcoming trip had an expectedly galvanic impact and set in motion new currents in international relations.

We were able to inform our friends only shortly before this announcement, and we understand the complications this caused for them. There were overriding reasons for keeping Dr. Kissinger's July visit secret. We could not risk advance public disclosure of these conversations whose outcome we could not predict. This would have risked disillusionment by inflating expectations which we could not be certain of meeting. And it would have created pressures on both the Chinese and American sides, forcing both of us to take public positions which could only have frozen discussions before they began. Moreover, we knew the July discussions would not settle anything directly concerning third parties; neither we nor Peking would set or accept any preconditions.

Regardless of how it was achieved, the change in the U.S.-Chinese relationship after 20 years of animosity was bound to be unsettling. Indeed, once Peking had decided to improve relations with the U.S., it had the capability to shake our relations with our friends through its own unilateral moves; the mere invitation to an American table tennis team had major repercussions.

The price we paid for secrecy was therefore unavoidable. It should prove transitory. The important task was to move swiftly to explain our purposes to our friends and to begin meaningful exchanges about the prospects for the future.

This we have done. Since July we have consulted with interested nations, outlining our objectives and expectations, and making clear we would not negotiate to the detriment of their interests. Secretary Rogers was extremely active in explaining our China policy to Foreign Ministers and other leaders of foreign countries. Secre-

tary Connally and Governor Reagan traveled through Asia as my personal representatives, and carried my views on our China initiative and Asian policies in general. I sent personal messages to many of our friends and allies. Our Ambassadors were instructed to explain our views and solicit those of their host governments. The prospects of my meetings in Peking and in Moscow were among the primary topics of my series of talks with allied leaders in December 1971 and January of this year.

We shall continue this process of consultation as we move forward in our relationship with the People's Republic of China. Our talks with our friends have focused on the longer term implications for U.S. policy. Questions have been raised which we have been careful to address publicly as well as privately.

How should our Asian friends interpret this initiative in terms of our commitments and their direct interests? There are, first of all, some general principles which apply to our relations with all concerned countries. Neither we nor the People's Republic asked, or would have accepted, any conditions for the opening of our dialogue. Neither country expects the other to barter away its principles or abandon its friends. Indeed, we have moved jointly in the conviction that more normal relations between us will serve the interests of all countries and reduce tensions in the Far East.

My conversations with the Chinese leaders will focus primarily on bilateral questions. Either side is free to raise any subject it wishes, and, of course, issues affecting the general peace are of bilateral concern. But we have made it clear to our Asian friends that we will maintain our commitments and that we will not negotiate on behalf of third parties. We cannot set out to build an honorable relationship of mutual respect with the PRC unless we also respect the interests of our long term friends.

Should our moves be read as shifting our priorities from Tokyo to Peking? They should not. With the Chinese we are at the beginning of a long process. With the Japanese we have enjoyed over two decades of the closest political and economic cooperation. It would be shortsighted indeed to exchange strong ties with a crucial ally for some mitigation of the hostility of a dedicated opponent. But it would be equally shortsighted not to seek communication and better understanding with a quarter of the world's people. We see no conflict in these two aims.

The preservation of our close relationship with Japan during this effort to broaden communications with China will call for wisdom and restraint on all sides. Each of us will have to avoid temptations to exacerbate relations between the other two. Despite the uneasy legacies of history, there can be more room for progress through cooperative interchange than through destructive rivalry.

What are the implications for our longstanding ties to the Republic of China? In my address announcing my trip to Peking, and since then, I have emphasized that our new dialogue with the PRC would not be at the expense of friends. Nevertheless, we recognize that this process cannot help but be painful for our old friend on Taiwan, the Republic of China. Our position is clear. We exerted the maximum diplomatic efforts to retain its seat in the United Nations. We regret the decision of the General Assembly to deprive the Republic of China of its representation although we welcomed the admission of

the People's Republic of China. With the Republic of China, we shall maintain our friendship, our diplomatic ties, and our defense commitment. The ultimate relationship between Taiwan and the mainland is not a matter for the United States to decide. A peaceful resolution of this problem by the parties would do much to reduce tension in the Far East. We are not, however, urging either party to follow any particular course.

What does our China initiative mean for our relations with the Soviet Union? Our policy is not aimed against Moscow. The U.S. and the USSR have issues of paramount importance to resolve; it would be costly indeed to impair progress on these through new antagonisms. Nevertheless some observers have warned that progress toward normalization of relations with Peking would inevitably jeopardize our relations with its Communist rival. There is no reason for this to be the case. Our various negotiations with the Soviet Union, for example on Berlin and SALT, made major progress subsequent to the July 15 announcement; and the agreement to meet with the Soviet leadership in May 1972 was announced on October 12, 1971.

Others have suggested that we should use our opening to Peking to exploit Sino-Soviet tensions. We have consistently explained to all parties that we will not attempt to do so because it would be self-defeating and dangerous. We did not create the differences between the two Communist powers. They disagree over the proper interpretation of Communist philosophy, a subject in which we have no competence and little interest. And they dispute the lines of their common border, which can hardly be susceptible to our manipulation. In any event we will try to have better relations with both countries. In pursuing this objective we will conduct our diplomacy with both honesty and frankness.

THE JOURNEY TO PEKING

The record of the past three years illustrates that reality, not sentimentality, has led to my journey. And reality will shape the future of our relations.

I go to Peking without illusions. But I go nevertheless committed to the improvement of relations between our two countries, for the sake of our two peoples and the people of the world. The course we and the Chinese have chosen has been produced by conviction, not by personalities or the prospect of tactical gains. We shall deal with the People's Republic of China:

—Confident that a peaceful and prospering China is in our own national interest;

—Recognizing that the talents and achievements of its people must be given their appropriate reflection in world affairs;

—Assured that peace in Asia and the fullest measure of progress and stability in Asia and in the world require China's positive contribution;

—Knowing that, like the United States, the People's Republic of China will not sacrifice its principles;

—Convinced that we can construct a permanent relationship with China only if we are reliable—in our relations with our friends as well as with China;

—Assuming that the People's Republic of China will shape its policy toward us with a reciprocal attitude.

These principles will guide my approach to my forthcoming conversations with Chairman Mao Tse-tung and Premier Chou En-lai. The tenor of these discussions and of our future relations, of course, does not depend on us alone. It will require a mutual understanding of perspectives and a mutual willingness to combine a principled approach with a respect for each other's interests.

At this point in history we need talks at the highest level. Eighteen years of desultory ambassadorial discussions in Geneva and Warsaw demonstrated that subsidiary problems could not be cleared away at lower levels. Authoritative exchanges between our leaders, however, now hold hope of genuine communication across the gulf and the setting of a new direction.

The trip to Peking is not an end in itself but the launching of a process. The historic significance of this journey lies beyond whatever formal understandings we might reach. We are talking at last. We are meeting as equals. A prominent feature of the postwar landscape will be changed. At the highest level we will close one chapter and see whether we can begin writing a new one.

Both sides can be expected to state their principles and their views with complete frankness. We will each know clearly where the other stands on the issues that divide us. We will look for ways to begin reducing our differences. We will attempt to find some common ground on which to build a more constructive relationship.

If we can accomplish these objectives, we will have made a solid beginning.

Over the longer term, we will see whether two countries—whose histories and cultures are completely different, whose recent isolation has been total, whose ideologies clash, and whose visions of the future collide—can nevertheless move from antagonism to communication to understanding.

On January 20, 1969 in my Inaugural Address, I defined our approach toward all potential adversaries:

"After a period of confrontation, we are entering an era of negotiation.

"Let all nations know that during this Administration our lines of communication will be open.

"We seek an open world—open to ideas, open to the exchange of goods and people—a world in which no people, great or small, will live in angry isolation.

"We cannot expect to make everyone our friend, but we can try to make no one our enemy."

When I spoke those lines, I had the People's Republic of China very much in mind. It is this attitude that shaped our policy from the outset and led to the July 15, 1971 announcement. It is in this spirit that I go to Peking.

EUROPE AND THE ATLANTIC ALLIANCE

"As Britain goes into Europe, there will be a new Europe. The United States is, at the present time, embarked on creating what is really a new America, and we do live at a time when because of the fast changing events in the world, we live in a new world. It is essential that the new Europe and the new America, together with the other nations in the world . . . work together."

> Remarks following Meetings with
> Prime Minister Heath in Bermuda
> December 21, 1971

In 1971, several of the fundamental goals of United States policy in Europe came measurably closer.

—The unification of Western Europe made a major advance, as the decisive steps were taken last year toward the membership of Britain, Ireland, Denmark, and Norway in the European Community.

—The major Atlantic nations and Japan reached agreement in December on a realignment of exchange rates. This laid the ground for new international monetary arrangements reflecting a more balanced long term relationship between the U.S. and its economically strong partners.

—Our allies strengthened their force contribution to the common defense and took up a greater share of the collective burden.

—The Four Powers reached an agreement on Berlin, designed to end the perennial postwar crises over the city and to improve the situation of the brave people of West Berlin in concrete ways.

—The prospect arose, for the first time, of concrete discussions with the East on other unresolved issues of security and cooperation in all of Europe.

—The new, more mature political relationship between the United States and its partners was symbolized by my unprecedented series of summit meetings with Alliance leaders at the end of the year.

The flourishing of the Atlantic world, the security of the Atlantic Alliance, and the relaxation of East-West tension have been the broad purposes of United States policy in Europe for 27 years. I came into office at an historical turning point, when new conditions emerging in Europe offered unique opportunities for progress toward these goals. In three years, much of this promise has been fulfilled. The accomplishments of 1971 were break-throughs.

When Great Britain, Ireland, Norway, and Denmark signed the treaty enlarging the European Community on January 22, I issued a strong statement welcoming it and emphatically reaffirming our tradi-tional support for the advancement of European unity. In two previous Foreign Policy Reports, I expressed this support in similarly categorical terms—but I also pointed to the problems which European integration implied for the United States and for our political and economic rela-tions with our allies across the Atlantic. The events of the past year have now brought these problems dramatically to the fore.

In the 1940's and into the 1950's, West-ern Europe was prostrate—politically, economically, and militarily. The United States, preeminent in the world, had only just emerged from its isolationist tradi-tion. In this environment, our allies shifted the responsibility for major decisions to us. In their eyes, the overriding purpose of the new arrangements—for defense, economic policy, and foreign policy—was to link us to Europe in tangible ways on a long term peacetime basis. They therefore deferred to our prescriptions and wel-comed our lead—even on formulas for European integration.

Both to us and to them the advantages of European unification were unambig-uous. It would help dispel the internecine hatreds of the recent past; it would maxi-mize the effectiveness of U.S. assistance; it would hasten Western Europe's political and economic recovery and thereby en-hance its security. These were common interests, and no inconsistency was seen between European unity and broader Atlantic unity. Cooperation came so easily that it was widely assumed for years in the United States that a strong and united Europe would readily take up a large part of the American burden, while still accept-ing American leadership.

But a self-respecting nation or group of nations will take up a burden only if it sees it as its own burden. By the 1960's Europe was in a position to do more for itself and for the Alliance. Nevertheless, old habits on both sides of the Atlantic persisted and inhibited the development of a more balanced relationship.

—Their economies thriving, their social cohesion and institutions restored, our allies were acting more and more self-confidently and independently on the world stage. The United States continued to lead in tutelary fashion, however, looking for allied endorsement of U.S. prescriptions.

—Our allies fluctuated between taking the U.S. commitment to Europe for granted, and panicking at the thought of U.S. withdrawal. We would not withdraw from Europe. But the Atlantic community was *their* community, too: all allies had to feel a stake in and responsibility for the achievement of common purposes.

As Prime Minister Heath has stated, four new members will now be joining with others in Europe "to work out the common European policies . . . govern-ing our dealings with the rest of the world, our trade, our finance and eventually our defense." A Western European summit meeting may be held in the coming year, giving further impetus and direction to the emerging European identity. This will mark a striking change in political as well as economic relations across the Atlantic.

The United States is realistic. This change means the end of American tutelage and the end of the era of automatic unity. But discord is not inevitable either. The challenge to our maturity and political skill is to establish a new practice in Atlantic unity—finding common ground in a consensus of independent policies instead of in deference to American prescriptions.

This essential harmony of our purposes is the enduring link between a uniting Europe and the United States. This is why we have always favored European unity and why we welcome its growth not only in geographical area but also into new spheres of policy.

We continue to feel that political and defense cooperation within Europe will be the fulfillment of European unity. European and American interests in defense and East-West diplomacy are fundamentally parallel and give sufficient incentive for coordinating independent policies. Two strong powers in the West would add flexibility to Western diplomacy, and could increasingly share the responsibilities of decision.

Competitive habits within the Atlantic world are most natural in the economic sphere—precisely the field in which integration in Europe has come first. While reduction of trade barriers is a major goal of the Community, this has progressed more rapidly within the Community than between it and the outside world. So far, in practice, protection of certain special interests within Europe has been a major concern in the Community's collective decisions; this is the easiest course for an economic union that has yet to develop

the political unity needed to make hard decisions taking account of interests outside the Community. As this political will develops, it will facilitate cooperation in the wider Atlantic relationship.

Europe's economic recovery has, of course, been of enormous benefit to U.S. trade. But it means, also, that the postwar economic imbalance across the Atlantic has been redressed. We now face the additional prospect of a 10-nation European Community—a giant concentration of economic power—with a common external tariff and an expanding network of preferential trading arrangements with other countries in Europe, Africa, and Asia. This cannot fail to have an impact on the trading position of the United States.

There is only one constructive solution: to face up to the political necessity of accommodating conflicting economic interests. In the postwar period this came easily; today, it will come only with effort. Inertia, which may seem comfortable to one side, will only lead to strains in our relations. We must both keep our eyes on our fundamental shared interest in freer and expanded trade across the Atlantic, a foundation of our mutual prosperity. Last June, under the leadership of Secretary Rogers, the leading industrialized nations in the OECD embarked on a major collective effort to address the many trade and related issues. This will require determined statesmanship and hard political decisions. We are prepared.

The 1971 international economic crisis was a facet of the same problem, and an example of how cooperation can work. Twenty years had eroded the predominance of the U.S. economy and U.S. dollar upon which the trading and monetary system had been built. In new conditions, the system was structurally unsound. In two previous Foreign Policy Reports and in many forums I called for basic reform. Progress was slow. Then last August, we faced an emergency; I acted decisively to put our own house in order and to turn the crisis into an opportunity for the West to put the international monetary house in order as well. We brought home to our partners that we were serious.

There were temptations for the United States then to make separate bilateral arrangements with selected countries in order to bring pressure on our other trading partners for a solution most economically advantageous to us. However, the political unity of the Atlantic world was of paramount importance to the United States, and we had to reach a solution in a manner that fostered it.

My summit meetings with allied leaders in December and January laid the political basis for a broad cooperative solution. I was able to assure Prime Minister Trudeau of Canada—our most important trading partner—that we understood the strong impact of our New Economic Policy on Canada and were eager to reinforce our close friendship with Canada. I then made an approach to the ally whose views on the economic question differed most from ours—President Pompidou of France. Our meeting at the Azores produced an agreement in principle on major points, which opened the way for the multilateral consensus achieved in December at the Smithsonian meeting of the Group of Ten. This development is discussed in greater detail in the International Economic Policy chapter.

There were important concessions on all sides; the result was a tremendous gain for the whole free world.

ALLIANCE DEFENSE

Western collective defense in Europe has deterred war for more than two decades and provided the essential condition of security in which free European institutions could revive and flourish. Today, the military balance underpins the overall stability on the Continent which makes detente feasible in the 1970's. East-West diplomacy in Europe is more active today than at any time since the Second World War; new hopes and new complexities are emerging. This is hardly the time for the West to abandon the very cohesion and stability that have brought these new opportunities about.

But this makes it more, not less, important for the Alliance to face up to the basic security question confronting it: do we have a clear rationale for our force deployments today, or are they the vestige of military and political conditions of two decades ago?

NATO Strategy and Forces. The function of our military forces is to deter war—and to defend our nations if war breaks out. As strategic conditions change, we have to ensure that our strategies and deployments fulfill these functions in the new environment. The Alliance conducted such a review in 1970. Together we asked some basic questions:

—What military threats were most likely in the 1970's?

—What military strategy would be most likely to deter aggressive actions and provide forces for a viable defense?

—What relationship between strategic nuclear, theater nuclear, and conventional forces would best support our strategy?

—How should the responsibilities of

decision and effort be shared within the Alliance?

—What specific improvements in our force posture were required to make it effective for our strategy?

From our review, we concluded that for the foreseeable future a major war in Europe was unlikely. But it was evident that Europe was still prone to crises as long as East-West political issues were unresolved, and that the confrontation of opposing forces raised a risk of conflict unless NATO's forces were clearly sufficient to deter and defend. Soviet military power in Europe had grown, not diminished, over the decade, and was now being projected beyond the Soviet periphery into the Mediterranean, the North Atlantic, and elsewhere.

In an era of strategic balance between the U.S. and USSR, the more plausible threats were those below the threshold of strategic nuclear war. The Alliance therefore reaffirmed its consensus that it needed a flexible strategy, resting on the deployment of appropriate forward defenses. We could not afford to be dependent solely upon conventional forces, because these might be inadequate to prevent defeat of our armies or loss of territory. Sole reliance upon early resort to nuclear weapons, on the other hand, would leave us no option between capitulation and risking all-out mutual destruction.

Twenty years ago, ironically, when our conventional forces returned to Europe in strength, the U.S. enjoyed a nuclear monopoly and had perhaps less military need of a massive conventional presence. Today, when we no longer have this unilateral nuclear advantage, a NATO conventional option is needed as never before. The nuclear forces of the United States, supplemented by the nuclear forces of our allies, remain the backbone of our deterrent. But in today's strategic conditions, our willingness to defend ourselves is made most credible by our willingness and ability to resist at every level of force or threat of force.

Our Alliance review also determined that improvements in NATO's ground, air, and naval forces and logistical infrastructure were essential to maintain the balance with the Warsaw Pact's theater forces. Our European allies, on their own initiative, have launched high-priority programs to make some of the specific improvements required:

—For example, Warsaw Pact strength in Central Europe rests primarily on a superiority in tanks. Our allies plan to add more than 1,100 new main battle tanks and 700 medium-range anti-tank weapons in 1971 and 1972, and an additional 600 tanks and more than 8,500 anti-tank weapons in coming years.

—Additional European programs will contribute more than 300 self-propelled heavy artillery pieces, 600 other combat vehicles, over 400 modern combat aircraft and helicopters, and 20 ships in 1971–72, and an additional 3,500 combat vehicles, over 500 modern combat aircraft and helicopters, and 53 ships in the future.

NATO's Nuclear Planning Group has made important progress in its review of key questions of nuclear doctrine. Some doctrinal issues have required reexamination in the light of new strategic conditions; a joint and better Alliance understanding of the complexities inherent in nuclear defense now permits the refinement of other elements of our doctrine. Our review will continue. These are difficult and crucial issues, on which there are some divergencies of view. We will not impose our view, but doctrines cannot be improvised in times of crisis and left to chance. An allied consensus is needed, and achievable.

U.S. Forces in Europe. It is proper for the Congress to examine whether U.S. troop deployments in Europe have a rational basis that justifies their cost. No number has merit in the abstract; our force level is essential for the support of the agreed defense strategy that maintains our cohesion and the stable military balance in contemporary conditions. To undermine either for budgetary reasons would be false economy and foolish policy.

Therefore, given the existing strategic balance and a similar effort by our allies, it is the policy of this Government to maintain and improve our forces in Europe and not reduce them except through reciprocal reductions negotiated with the Warsaw Pact. With such mutual reduction now on the agenda of East-West diplomacy, this is precisely the moment *not* to make unilateral cuts in our strength.

Moreover, major unilateral reductions by the United States would upset the balance of conventional forces in Central Europe and leave NATO with no options in a crisis other than capitulation or immediate resort to nuclear weapons. This would undermine the strategy that the Alliance has accepted as the most rational for the contemporary military balance. American forces should not be reduced to the role of a hostage, triggering automatic use of nuclear weapons, at the very time when the strategic equation makes such a strategy less and less plausible.

If the U.S. did not carry *its* crucial share of the common burden, there would be no prospect of our allies' making up the difference. Not only would they lose confidence in our pledges; they would lose confidence in the very possibility of Western European defense. Our allies would feel themselves increasingly alone. Atlantic cohesion would weaken. In the shadow of Soviet power, Western Europe would be drawn, against its will, away from its Alliance ties.

Thus, in the absence of a negotiated mutual reduction, the Soviet Union has little incentive to reciprocate a U.S. withdrawal. Soviet troops are not deployed in Europe just to match ours. They secure Soviet hegemony over Eastern Europe; most importantly, perhaps, they embody the Soviet Union's permanent presence as a power in the European sphere. The Soviet Union would be unlikely to forgo the political advantage it would gain if Western military power in Europe weakened unilaterally.

Steps to relax tensions in Europe, in my view, must be steps which increase security, not insecurity.

As Chancellor Brandt has pointed out emphatically on several occasions, Western cohesion underpinned by the visible and substantial commitment of American power in Europe is the essential condition that makes efforts at detente possible today. With East-West diplomacy more complex and relationships more fluid than ever before in 20 years, unilateral American withdrawals from Europe would undermine stability. Today's conditions, not those of 20 years ago, make America's strength in Europe absolutely essential. I therefore intend to maintain it.

Sharing the Defense Burden. The Alliance's 1970 strategic review brought the rationale of our defense efforts into clear focus and brought home to every ally its own strong interest in the success of the common strategy. A significant result has been an increase in burden sharing.

—In December 1970, our allies' European Defense Improvement Program committed an additional $1 billion to modernizing NATO communications, accelerating construction of shelters for NATO aircraft, and improving their own national forces.

—In December 1971, they announced further increases of about $1 billion to their defense contribution in 1972. This took the form of the significant additions to the Alliance's armory of tanks, anti-tank weapons, artillery, combat aircraft, helicopters, and ships, as described above.

Another aspect of the burden sharing problem—the balance of payments costs of U.S. forces in Europe—has not yet been solved. Our payments deficits attributable to our defense commitments distort both the international monetary system and our military planning. A substantial portion of our NATO expenditures in local currency is offset by financial arrangements with the Federal Republic of Germany, where most of our forces are concentrated; the new agreement for 1972–73 is for $2 billion, including $183 million for renovating facilities housing our forces. These agreements are testimony to cooperation. They are not a long term solution, however, and they strain Alliance relations each time they come up for renewal.

In this matter, we should work toward arrangements whereby the United States could maintain its forces in Europe with balance of payments consequences no different from those of maintaining the same forces in the United States. This would neutralize the balance of payments issue

and allow the Alliance to plan its forces on security criteria.

EAST-WEST RELATIONS IN EUROPE

This Administration has regarded a resolution of the political issues dividing Europe as a paramount objective of our foreign policy. Three years ago, East-West relations were virtually frozen. Relatively few East-West negotiations were taking place; little or no progress had been made in addressing the major issues. A slight improvement in the atmosphere of relations in 1967–68 was quickly dispelled by the invasion of Czechoslovakia. There was no firm basis for movement toward detente.

Some of our allies were pursuing detente in bilateral contacts with the East, but it was clear that most bilateral questions were part of a wider web of European security issues. The Soviet Union could not be given the opportunity to offer selective detente, smoothing relations with some Western nations but not others.

Thus, Western cohesion must be the bedrock of our pursuit of detente. We and our allies have a responsibility to consult together in sufficient depth to ensure that our efforts are complementary and that our priorities and broad purposes are essentially the same.

There are bilateral negotiations between the U.S. and USSR—SALT and my forthcoming summit, for example. But, as I have stressed since I came into office, coordination with our allies is an essential precondition of bilateral U.S.-Soviet negotiations which affect their interests. On SALT, we have consulted scrupulously with our allies at every stage. After the announcement of the Moscow and Peking summits, my summit meetings with allied leaders ensured the harmony of our diplomacy in advance of these trips. Our allies have no veto over U.S. policy, just as we have no veto over theirs, but I was able to reassure them that I would be making no agreements at their expense.

Another principle I have long emphasized is that detente will not come about except through negotiation on concrete problems. A cordial atmosphere is not enough. Political conflicts left unresolved would inevitably flare up again to poison it. As I said at the 20th anniversary meeting of the North Atlantic Alliance in April 1969: "It is not enough to talk of European security in the abstract. We must know the elements of insecurity and how to remove them."

We allies have therefore addressed the main issues of East-West relations in Europe.

—The Alliance proposed that the prospects for detente could be radically improved if we could alleviate the tensions surrounding Berlin—a focus of perennial crisis since 1948.

—We agreed that a more constructive Soviet-American relationship was an integral part of a relaxation of European tension; thus the U.S. began negotiations on SALT, against a background of close allied consultation.

—NATO again proposed negotiation on mutual balanced force reductions in Europe, and began the careful and vital preparatory work of analyzing the issues involved.

—The Alliance consulted on whether and how a comprehensive European conference, as proposed by the Warsaw Pact, could be used as a forum for constructively addressing the substantive problems of European security.

Germany and Berlin. Previous periods of European detente proved illusory either because nations failed to deal with the central questions of the division of Germany and Berlin, or because the attempts to deal with them created further stalemate and confrontation. If a relaxation of tension was to come about in the 1970's—and I was convinced it could—it would be tested in new efforts to address these issues. On my visit to West Berlin in February 1969, therefore, I called for an end to the tensions over Berlin. Chancellor Brandt has proposed to normalize his country's relations with its Eastern neighbors through new treaty relationships.

It was for the West German government in the first instance to work out an approach to the German national problem. At the same time, issues related to the division of Germany were of natural and direct concern to all European powers; the U.S., the U.K., France, and the USSR, in particular, have special rights and responsibilities regarding Berlin. The two key problems—West Germany's relations with its Eastern neighbors and the Four-Power relationship in Berlin—were thus related organically. The Soviet-German treaty of 1970 could not in itself normalize the situation in Central Europe if Berlin were ignored.

The Berlin negotiators faced a tangle of two decades' accumulation of conflicting legal arguments, administrative practices, and political and economic interests. The ideal solution—reunification of Berlin—was not feasible. On the other hand, it was unacceptable to us to treat West Berlin as a separate political entity deprived of its natural ties to the Federal Republic or the security guarantee of the three Western powers.

The parties broke through the impasse in 1971 by putting aside the arguments over the political or juridical status of the city and concentrating instead on new practical arrangements to improve conditions for West Berliners and remove specific irritants. The Four-Power agreement on Berlin, signed on September 3, 1971, was a milestone achievement.

—The Soviet guarantee of unimpeded and preferential civilian traffic between the Western sectors of Berlin and the Federal Republic is a central fact of the agreement and a major improvement.

—There is no change in the legal status of the Western sectors of Berlin: they remain under the authority of the three powers, who share with the USSR responsibility for the city as a whole, and they continue, as in the past, not to be regarded as a constituent part of the Federal Republic. At the same time, the Soviet Union has formally accepted that the vital ties between West Berlin and the Federal Republic will be maintained and developed.

—The Soviet Union has accepted that communications between West Berlin and East Berlin and the German Democratic Republic, and West Berliners' visiting rights, will be improved. It has further been agreed that, where the security and status of the city are not involved, the Federal Republic may represent the Western sectors of Berlin abroad and that international agreements and arrangements entered into by the Federal Republic may be extended to the Western sectors.

—The three Western allies have authorized the establishment of a Soviet Consulate General and additional Soviet commercial offices in the Western sectors, accredited to the appropriate authorities of the three Western powers. No change in Berlin's status is implied; the Soviet presence in the Western sectors will still be subject to allied authority.

Conference on Security and Cooperation in Europe. When the Berlin accord comes into force with the signing of the final Four-Power protocol, this will unlock a diplomatic process. A Berlin agreement, in the view of the Western powers, is a prerequisite to any broader European negotiation: it could smooth the way toward possible accommodations on other European security issues, which are all affected by the Berlin situation; it would also imply a willingness on the Soviet side to reach concrete settlements.

A question now facing the West is the Soviet proposal of a conference of all European countries, plus the United States and Canada, to discuss security and cooperation in Europe.

If such a conference is carefully prepared and will address substantive issues, the United States favors it. It is in the long term interest of the Soviet Union, too, I believe, that a conference be used productively in this way and not be merely a forum for speeches and friendly atmosphere. It is essential that we have a clear picture of what issues a conference can address and what concrete contribution to security it can make.

We therefore intend to discuss the relevant issues of European security and cooperation fully with our allies, and to develop coordinated Western positions. Then, if the Berlin accord has already been consummated, we will be prepared to move to multilateral exploratory talks with other prospective participants.

The conference as defined by the Warsaw Pact would address two subjects: a joint declaration against the use or threat of force, and an agreement to expand cooperation in scientific, cultural, and economic areas.

The mere atmosphere of detente, in our view, is insufficient—not only because this is not durable, but also because it is difficult to evaluate measures proposed in the name of so vague an objective. Moreover, general declarations open to major disputes over interpretation are of illusory benefit, and possibly even dangerous. It is not enough to agree on cooperation in the abstract. How will cooperation be implemented in practice? Will it include freer intercourse among the European peoples, East and West? How would a conference promote economic relations other than through existing institutions and means?

Real progress, in short, requires pursuing detente in ways that will make it real and lasting, even though this may take more time and more effort.

Mutual and Balanced Force Reductions (MBFR). NATO first proposed mutual and balanced force reductions in the summer of 1968. When I took office in 1969, I found the Alliance in need of fuller preparation and analysis of the technical and political complexities involved.

Before we negotiate, we have to be clear about the rationale for mutual reductions. Some see it as a response to domestic budgetary pressures in the U.S. for unilateral reductions; some support it as a substitute for a Conference on European Security;

others seek an accord on MBFR as a demonstration of political detente.

None of these approaches helps us answer the principal question: What kind of MBFR agreement do we want? We are dealing here with the heart of the security problem in Europe; we therefore have no responsible choice but to judge an agreement by the criterion of undiminished security. In this way, we truly contribute to detente. There would be little value in token reductions that have no military significance, or in an MBFR agreement that only magnifies insecurity. We must do the hard work of finding formulas that offer real and fair reductions.

Our analyses within the U.S. Government, which we are now sharing with our allies, are described in the Arms Control chapter of this Report. The Alliance will work through this preparation together. There will be no bilateral negotiation on MBFR between the U.S. and USSR.

Relations With Eastern Europe. The joint statement after my meeting with President Tito in Washington on October 30, 1971 declared our strong belief that "a firm peace and true security are indivisible and can be attained only in Europe as a whole, and not in only one or another part of it."

Through most of the postwar period, relations between Eastern and Western Europe were limited. Relationships with Eastern Europe were inhibited by our conflicts with the USSR. This was unnatural. The nations of Europe have long-standing political, economic and cultural ties with each other.

As the forces of change have begun to loosen postwar political rigidities, new expectations and aspirations have arisen in both Western and Eastern Europe. The benefits of relaxation must extend to both.

The Soviet Union has a right to its own security. But neither a durable peace nor an era of cooperation in Europe can be built on principles that divide the continent and violate the sovereignty of its nations and the freedom of its peoples.

Our approach is based on these general principles:

—Every nation in Europe has the sovereign right to conduct independent policies and therefore to be our friend without being anyone else's enemy.

—The use or threat of force by the Soviet Union in Eastern Europe can only lead to European crises. It is therefore incompatible with detente in Europe and detente in U.S.-Soviet relations.

—We do not want to complicate the difficulties of East European nations' relations with their allies; nevertheless there are ample opportunities for economic, technical, and cultural cooperation on the basis of reciprocity. The Eastern European countries themselves can determine the pace and scope of their developing relations with the United States.

We have demonstrated these principles in new constructive relationships between the United States and Eastern Europe. I was the first American President ever to visit Romania and Yugoslavia. We base our ties with both these countries on mutual respect, independence, and sovereign equality. We share the belief that this should be the basis of relations between nations regardless of divergence or similarity in social, economic, or political systems:

—Our relations with non-aligned *Yugoslavia* are a factor for peace and stability in Europe, the Mediterranean, and the Middle East. In 1971, President Tito made his first State visit to the United States. We resolved to continue our high-level exchanges and to broaden the scope of our economic relations.

—We are supporting legislation to grant Most Favored Nation tariff treatment to *Romania*. Our Export-Import Bank credits and Romania's new membership in GATT will facilitate our economic relations.

—Our first exchange of cabinet-level visits with *Poland* took Secretaries Volpe and Stans to Warsaw and brought Polish Science Minister Kaczmarek to Washington. Postmaster General Blount visited *Hungary,* as part of our developing contacts.

—Our trade with Eastern Europe since 1968 has substantially increased, and we expect it to continue to grow. Trade provides a material foundation for further development of normal relations.

ISSUES FOR THE FUTURE

Intellectually and culturally, the winds are blowing from the West in Europe. Western economic and political institutions are flourishing. Western libertarian values are revered perhaps more strongly in the East where they are suppressed than in the West where they are taken for granted.

The historic duty of the leaders of the Western Alliance is to preserve the conditions that underpin our successes. The past year has shown us the hopeful prospects for the future—the strengthening of European unity, new economic arrangements, the resolution of East-West issues, a new mature political relationship among us. If we allow the independent vigor of our separate states to pull us apart, if we neglect the prerequisites of security that have sustained us and kept the peace for 27 years, if we pursue illusory forms of de-

231

tente instead of the substance—then the coming decade will bring new dangers instead of new triumphs.

With our partners we face specific tasks, building on what we have achieved:

—To face squarely the economic issues between a 10-nation European Community and the United States;

—To carry through, vigorously and cooperatively, the reform of the international monetary and trading system;

—To intensify our efforts in NATO's Committee on the Challenges of Modern Society and bring other nations into a joint attack on the environmental and social problems of the modern world;

—To finish the job of making the force improvements and equitable sharing arrangements that will sustain our common defense;

—To draw upon our unity and security to engage the East in the building of a broader structure of reconciliation and peace in all of Europe.

JAPAN

"My Administration shares with the Government of Japan the conviction that our relationship is vital to the kind of world we both want. We are determined to act accordingly. But the future will require adjustments in the U.S.-Japanese relationship, and the issues involved are too important and their solutions too complicated to be viewed with any complacency on either side."

U.S. Foreign Policy for the 1970's
Report to the Congress
February 25, 1971

Japan is our most important ally in Asia. It is our second greatest trading partner. It is an essential participant, if a stable world peace is to be built. Our security, our prosperity, and our global policies are therefore intimately and inextricably linked to the U.S.-Japanese relationship. The well-being of both countries requires cooperation and a shared commitment to the same fundamental goals.

Last year was critical for our relationship. It was a year both of stress and of progress. It brought a sharp awareness of the divergence of some of our interests— and in its wake, a better understanding of the need for the mature and equitable management of those divergences.

Our China and economic initiatives were a shock to the U.S.-Japanese relationship. Both grew out of the new realities of a changed world situation. For precisely that reason, they had an unsettling effect upon Japan, which had become accustomed to a U.S.-Japanese relationship rooted in the postwar period and based on a bipolar concept of world power. That relationship, however, had already been overtaken by time and Japan's phenomenal economic growth. The shocks of 1971, therefore, only accelerated an evolution in U.S.-Japanese relations that was in any event, overdue, unavoidable, and in the long run, desirable.

The U.S.-Japanese relationship is in the process of inevitable change, not because the alliance of the past decades has failed, but because it has succeeded.

—Asian stability was bolstered by our pledge to work together in the common defense. Our defense postures together provided the fabric of Japan's security, while our forward basing in the area contributed to regional defense.

—Asian development was symbolized by Japan's economic resurgence and encouraged by our fruitful economic links.

As Japan gained in strength, our parallel development assistance efforts nourished a broader regional advance.

—Asian political freedoms were strengthened by the process of Japan's recovery under a democratic system of government. The health of political ties between our democracies served as an example to the democratic experiment elsewhere in Asia.

This relationship stands out as a major success of American postwar diplomacy. Its purpose was to provide the sustenance and security which Japan required for economic and psychological recovery from the trauma of World War II. That recovery is complete.

In a remarkable display of disciplined energy, the Japanese people have again placed their nation firmly in the front rank of international powers. Our relationship now requires greater reciprocity.

Japan's history reinforces the inevitability of this change. For it testifies eloquently to Japan's national pride and capacity to respond to changing conditions in its external surroundings. As an island power, Japan's participation in broad regional or global alliances has traditionally been limited and intermittent. As its recovery proceeded, it was certain that Japan would play a more autonomous role in world affairs. In retrospect, the last two decades will be seen as a transitional period in which Japan, while relying on U.S. economic support and military protection, reestablished its inner cohesion as a society, and defined a more independent national role for itself. That is as it should be.

By 1969, the cumulative strains imposed on the U.S.-Japanese relationship were considerable and evident.

—We needed to face the political and psychological implications of Japan's growing strength and pride. The Japanese island of Okinawa had been under American administration for more than 25 years. Okinawa's status would disrupt and embitter the U.S.-Japanese friendship unless it were changed to reflect the new realities.

—We needed to adjust our economic relations to reflect the fact that Japan had become the world's third greatest industrial power. Japan provided the largest overseas market for American goods as well as formidable competition to us in both our domestic and world markets. Japan also benefited greatly from the liberal trade policies of the United States. But Japan's insistence on restricting its own markets contributed to a growing imbalance in our trade, and was an anachronism, inconsistent with its economic strength and symbolizing a lack of economic reciprocity which could not be long sustained.

—We both needed to bring into better balance our contributions to Asian development. Japan's political cohesion and economic prowess gave it the capacity to make a major contribution—and its commerce and investments in Asia gave Japan a clear interest in the region's stability.

—Signs that China was moving toward more constructive contacts with other nations would impel the issue of China policy to the fore for both countries. Eventually, we would have to face the problem of harmonizing our changing national perspectives towards China.

—Japan had long since acquired the industrial and technological strength to assume responsibility for its own conventional defense. However,

Japan continued to rely on American nuclear power for strategic security. It was, moreover, prevented by constitutional, political, and psychological factors, and by the attitudes of its Asian neighbors, from projecting military power beyond its own borders. Thus the Mutual Security Treaty continued to serve Japan's interests, as well as our own. Still it was clear that changes would come in our defense relationship as Japan regained its strength and pride.

We faced, then, not a desire for change but the dynamics of change. The question was not whether to maintain the partnership which had served us both so well. The question was how to inject into our relationship the characteristics of equality and reciprocity without which it could not be sustained.

We began with Okinawa. In November 1969, I met with Prime Minister Sato and we agreed on the broad principles which should govern the reversion of Okinawa to Japanese administration. The problems were many and difficult. Our military installations on Okinawa were central to the security shield which we helped provide to the free nations of East Asia, including Japan. The quarter-century of American administration had created a web of political and economic problems to resolve before reversion. But in 1971, our negotiations resulted in a treaty which terminated this last administrative vestige of the Second World War. We retain our military installations in Okinawa, but on the same basis as those in the Japanese home islands. Early this year, at Prime Minister Sato's request I agreed to speed up the final reversion. Thus, our recognition of Japan's needs for political self-

assertion has enabled us to remove this long-standing irritant in our friendship.

Japan now plays a major and steadily increasing role in assisting other Asian nations with their development needs. After years of U.S. leadership in this field we greatly welcome Japan's increasing contribution—which reflects Japan's realization that its own interests require it to participate in shaping the environment of Asia. Japan has pledged one per-cent of its gross national product to assisting less developed countries. That goal is already being approached, although we would hope to see a greater Japanese use of grants and concessional loans rather than commercial credits. The Japanese are playing a particularly prominent role in the Asian Development Bank and in the international groupings providing assistance to Indonesia and the Philippines.

Japan is developing plans to strengthen its conventional defense capabilities over the next few years. This is a reflection of heightened Japanese self-reliance and readiness to assume greater responsibilities. This welcome trend has been accompanied by a consolidation of our own military facilities and a reduction of our forces in both Japan and Okinawa.

There has, therefore, been steady progress in recent years in the assumption by Japan of a role in world affairs more consistent with its power. However, there has been less progress in reshaping our bilateral relations along more reciprocal lines. Until this year, the Japanese still tended to consider that their dependence upon us limited independent political initiatives of our own, while their political problems commended some independence of initiative on their part. Similarly, in our economic relationship, it was evident that Japan, like our European allies, tended to take our commitment to a liberal trading system for granted without extending equivalent access to its own market.

Both these attitudes were understandable. But both stood in the way of the necessary task of creating a more mature basis for the continuation of U.S.-Japanese cooperation. In 1971, both also proved to be incorrect.

I knew that the July 15 announcement of my forthcoming visit to Peking would have a profound impact on Japan. It brought China policy and Japan's own future role in a changing Asia abruptly to the forefront of our relationship. The issue of China policy is, if anything, even more important for Japan than for the United States. Geography, culture, history, and trade potential make it a central issue in Japanese domestic politics as well as a key aspect of Japan's foreign policy. On a matter of such intrinsic importance, Japan could not fail to be disturbed at any implication that our policies, which had been so closely aligned, were diverging.

It was also clear, however, that we shared a fundamental interest in improved relations with China. We both have an enormous stake in ending the era of confrontation in Asia. Japan is already China's largest trading associate, and for some time has had not only economic ties but trade representation in the People's Republic of China.

The issue between us, then, is not whether the opening to China is desirable—but the need to harmonize our sometimes differing perspectives and interests in a common strategic conception and a shared overall goal.

For our part, we have made it clear that our aim in Peking is to establish a better mutual understanding of one another's policies. We will not seek or discuss bilateral arrangements that could adversely affect the interests of our allies. We have no interest in arrangements which would sacrifice our friendship with a long-standing ally to the need for better communication with a long-standing adversary.

Therefore, there is no cause for either Japan or the United States to feel a lack of trust concerning our parallel policies toward China. In the chapter of this Report concerning China we have set forth the reasons why it was impossible for us to consult with our allies prior to the public announcement of the Peking visit. We have since that time consulted very widely. We have made particular efforts to assure Japan of the basic harmony which clearly exists between a lessening of Asian tensions and the health of the U.S.-Japanese friendship.

My recent meeting with Prime Minister Sato at San Clemente permitted the full review of our policies and purposes and was an integral part of my preparation for the talks in Peking.

We are not on a divergent course, and autonomous policies need not create strains in our relationship so long as we both recognize the need to mesh those policies. Both the autonomy and the basic harmony of our actions are implicit and essential elements in the new relationship of equality and reciprocity which we seek with Japan. We are not involved—and must not become involved—in a competitive race toward accommodation. But in a changing world, we are both concerned with the removal of old animosities. Our alliance must now serve as the firm foundation of a stable Asia upon which both of us can confidently seek a more balanced and productive relationship with our adversaries.

Last year also brought an economic shock to the U.S.-Japanese relationship. In last year's Report, I expressed satisfaction that Japan recognized the need to liberalize its controls on imports and foreign investment, and confidence that in the months ahead we would be able to resolve our bilateral economic difficulties. Our experience in the first half of 1971, however, showed that progress would be slower than we had hoped. In the meantime, the need for greater reciprocity in our economic relationship became ever more urgent and necessary. By the middle of 1971, adjustments in our vast economic relationship had become a pressing requirement of U.S. national policy. They could no longer be delayed.

In the International Economic Policy chapter of this Report, I have described the underlying problems inherent in world trading and monetary arrangements which had been created in an era of unchallenged U.S. economic superiority. The regained economic vigor of our allies had created unavoidable pressures for reform. To our allies, including Japan, the shortcomings in the existing system appeared less significant than the hazards of changing it. To the U.S., our deteriorating trade and payments situation left no choice but to take the steps necessary to bring about a multilateral settlement of outstanding issues. Our imbalances with Japan were by no means unique, but they did reflect the magnitude of our concern.

—By midyear, Japan's favorable trade balance with the U.S. had reached a rate double that of any earlier year, accounting for a significant measure of our payments problems and threatening further difficulties for our domestic economy.

—Impelled by an increasingly anachronistic exchange rate, Japan's soaring global trade surplus exceeded half a billion dollars each month from March to August. Substantial adjustment in the parity of the yen, set in 1949, seemed to us indispensable.

Our efforts to persuade our allies of the need for reform had been patient—and unfruitful. On August 15 we announced a series of unilateral measures. They were harsh, but they were required in order to establish the basis for a multilateral solution to what had become an intolerable problem.

We recognized that these measures would have a great impact on all of our major trading partners. We knew that the impact would be particularly strong in Japan, because of the dimensions of our commerce with each other and because of Japan's strong dependence on foreign trade. However, it was for precisely those reasons that we could no longer delay in working out together a more equitable monetary and trading relationship.

The past six months have brought substantial progress toward that goal. In December, a fundamental and general realignment of currency values took place, and Japan made a major contribution to that essential step. In a series of bilateral talks—particularly the September meeting of the Japan-United States Committee on Trade and Economic Affairs—progress was made toward reducing trade barriers. These discussions are continuing.

In October, we passed a milestone in our trade relations with Japan by the agreement to moderate—but still permit—the growth of Japanese synthetic textile sales in the U.S. market. This issue, which had important political and economic aspects in both of our countries, had become a serious irritant in our relations. After many months of hard negotiations which admittedly had an adverse effect on the general atmosphere between us, the agreement of October 15 resolved this vexing issue.

Last year therefore dramatized for both Japan and the United States the two truths which must be recognized if our relationship is to continue to prosper. We have a need to adjust our relationship—and we have the ability to do it in a way that serves the interests of both of our countries. The future health of our friendship is not served by ignoring our differences. Nor is it served by expectations that either country will subordinate its interests in order to maintain an atmosphere of perfect amity. The continuity of our relationship is too important to both of us to permit such a concentration on its atmosphere rather than its substance.

We recognize that some of our actions during the past year placed the Japanese Government in a difficult position. We recognize that our actions have accelerated the Japanese trend toward more autonomous policies. We regret the former, but could not do otherwise. We welcome the latter as both inevitable and desirable—inevitable because it reflects the reality of Japanese strength in the 1970's—desirable because it is a necessary step in the transformation of our relationship to the more mature and reciprocal partnership required in the 1970's.

We intend that Japan shall remain our most important Asian ally. We expect that the future will bring an even greater degree of interdependence between us. We believe the vitality of our friendship and our cooperation in international matters is essential to the stable Asia we both require—and to the peaceful world we both seek.

These are the convictions which led me to travel to Alaska to welcome to American soil the Emperor and Empress of Japan on the first visit abroad of a reigning Japanese monarch. These are the convictions which underlie the extensive and unique network of official contacts which we have established between Japanese Government officials and our own. For example, in September we had a joint meeting in Washington of seven Japanese Cabinet officers and their American counterparts, for a very wide-ranging and authoritative examination of our relationship.

It was to ensure the harmony of our policies that Prime Minister Sato and I met in San Clemente in January. We reviewed all aspects of the events of the previous year, and examined the tasks which lie before us. I stressed that the adjustments we seek in our relationship demonstrate our recognition of Japan's new status—not doubts about the value of our alliance. On their part, Prime Minister Sato and his colleagues left me confident that they, too, consider a sound political relationship between us as essential to Japanese interests and to our shared goals in Asia and the world.

The process of adjustment will sometimes be arduous. But in 1971 we proved that it can be done by making the necessary adjustments in several of the most important issues on our agenda. The unjustified complacency of the recent past has been replaced with a greater awareness of the task which we both face. That fact constitutes a solid basis for renewed confidence in the future of U.S.-Japanese cooperation, with all that such cooperation promises for the mutual benefit of our two peoples, and for the world's hopes for a stable structure of peace and prosperity.

INTERNATIONAL ECONOMIC POLICY

"What has happened here is that the whole free world has won, because as a result of this agreement, we will have, from a financial and monetary standpoint, a more stable world."

> Remarks Announcing the
> Monetary Agreement of the
> Group of Ten
> December 18, 1971

The year 1971 marked a turning point in the world economy. We undertook a series of far-reaching measures which revitalized our foreign economic policy and set the stage for fundamental and long term reforms in the international economic system.

THE SETTING FOR CHANGE

In the immediate postwar period new arrangements and institutions to govern the international economic system were established. At that time the United States was the preeminent economic power in the world and assumed primary responsibility for the economic viability and security of much of the non-Communist world. We launched the Marshall Plan to help Europe get back on its feet. We assisted in the economic recovery of Japan. We encouraged European economic cooperation.

Along with other nations, we helped

to establish the International Monetary Fund (IMF) to promote world monetary cooperation; the General Agreement on Tariffs and Trade (GATT) to create a code and a mechanism for the orderly conduct of international trade; and the World Bank to assist reconstruction in Europe and provide assistance to the less developed nations. These formed the institutional basis of an international economic system which promoted the expanding flow of commerce and resources needed to restore free world prosperity.

Since those institutions were established, the world economy has undergone major structural changes. Both the volume of commerce and the transfer of financial resources have increased greatly. The industrial capacities of Europe, Japan, and Canada have grown rapidly, and each is now a strong trading and financial power. These new realities needed to be reflected in both our foreign economic relationships and international institutions and arrangements. In 1971 our policies were directed at achieving that objective.

INTERNATIONAL MONETARY POLICY

After two decades of stability and progress, a series of crises beginning in the late 1960's had shown that the international monetary system could not cope adequately with the scale and severity of contemporary world monetary problems. In 1971 the situation reached critical proportions.

Monetary crises in May and August, and our deteriorating balance of payments position, convinced me that a major realignment of currencies and reform of the international monetary system were necessary. On August 15, I instituted a series of measures—including a suspension of dollar convertibility—which dramatically focused international attention and energies on achievement of these goals.

It is important to understand the circumstances that led to these decisions.

Developing Strain. At the Bretton Woods Conference in 1944, to help achieve our objective of rebuilding the free world through the expansion of trade and rapid economic reconstruction, we took the lead in the creation of a new international monetary system. We hoped that this system would avoid the restrictions and competitive devaluations which characterized the 1930's, and would enhance the ability of countries to rebuild their own economies. This system permitted parity adjustments, which were expected to be used when countries were in fundamental balance of payments disequilibrium. Exchange rate stability was to be enhanced by enabling countries to draw on a pool of currencies established in the IMF to supplement their own gold and foreign exchange reserves, and thus tide them over temporary or cyclical balance of payments difficulties. These alternatives were provided to enable countries to avoid having to depart from sound domestic economic policies or impose controls to correct balance of payments problems.

The Bretton Woods system, our assistance, and the strong efforts made by other nations to rebuild their economies helped to bring about a period of vigorous and sustained economic expansion. Our reconstruction assistance and persistent balance of payments deficits provided substantial liquidity to countries whose reserves had been depleted. Their holdings of both dollars and gold increased substantially. In

the immediate postwar era this enabled many nations to support the large flow of imports required for their reconstruction.

In the 1960's, however, the international monetary system showed increasing strain. The persistent U.S. deficits, once unambiguously helpful to other countries as a source of liquid reserves, led to an increasing imbalance between U.S. liquid assets and liabilities. Eventually, doubts began to arise concerning the ability of the U.S. to maintain convertibility of the dollar into gold or other reserve assets. A supplementary source of reserves was clearly needed, and agreement was reached within the International Monetary Fund in 1969 to create an alternative source of international liquidity in the form of Special Drawing Rights (SDR's).

This reform did not, however, deal with other sources of stress. In the face of large and continuing balance of payments problems, countries were compelled to alter the value of their exchange rates, usually after long delay and in an atmosphere of crisis. Such adjustments were made with increased frequency in the late 1960's. They were necessarily large in magnitude, psychologically destabilizing, and politically disruptive in the adjusting country.

Furthermore, pressure to adjust did not apply equally to all countries. Those countries with a significant balance of payments surplus and undervalued currencies felt little pressure to revalue (increase the value of) their currencies. Indeed, they felt an incentive not to do so. Undervalued exchange rates enabled them to achieve the large trade surpluses which some considered desirable in order to enhance the rates of their domestic economic growth and employment and to protect their external financial positions. But countries with overvalued exchange rates eventually had to devalue to correct their balance of payments deficits and halt the drain on their reserves. Thus, devaluations were more frequent than revaluations.

The dollar, as the world's major reserve and transaction currency, was the linchpin of the international economic system. While other nations were free to change the value of their currencies in relation to the dollar, the U.S. played a passive role. During the 1960's, changes in the values of other currencies tended to push higher the average exchange value of the dollar. This aggravated a relative loss of American economic competitiveness as foreign countries completed their postwar reconstruction, achieved high levels of productivity, and proved extremely adept at developing export markets. Our domestic inflation in the late 1960's seriously accelerated this trend.

The key role of the dollar made it difficult to correct this situation through a devaluation, since the stability and liquidity of the system was based on the maintenance of a stable dollar. Even if we had wished to devalue in terms of gold, it would have had no effect on our balance of payments unless other nations agreed not to devalue as well.

These strains in the system led to a series of crises. In November 1967, following a major speculative assault on the pound, the United Kingdom and a number of other countries were forced to devalue. The subsequent crisis of confidence in currency markets engendered mass purchases of gold by speculators. The gold reserves of central banks were being drained until the introduction of the two-tier system in March, 1968 isolated private gold trading from international monetary transactions. From the spring of 1968, the franc was recurrently subject to speculative attack. France, along with the Franc Area, devalued in August of the following year. A major influx of currency into Germany led to revaluation of the mark in October 1969.

In 1970, although a major crisis was avoided, a decline in U.S. interest rates relative to rates in major European countries drove large amounts of dollars abroad and complicated European attempts to achieve domestic monetary stability.

The situation worsened in 1971. Accelerated monetary growth in this country and an outflow of short-term capital, accompanied by a deficit in our balance of trade, caused dollars to flow abroad in record amounts. As a result Europe and Japan took in billions of dollars. In May, Germany decided to float the mark. Speculation continued and extraordinarily large sums were traded in world currency markets.

The August 1971 Measures. By August, the situation was clearly no longer sustainable. Mainly due to a sharp deterioration in our trade position, the underlying payments position of the United States had turned sharply adverse. It was clear that the dollar was overvalued, while the currencies of certain of our trading partners were manifestly undervalued. Our remaining reserves were being seriously depleted, and the amount of dollars held by foreign central banks rapidly increased. Intense speculation was shaking the foundations of the international monetary system.

If we had permitted this situation to continue, our balance of payments would have deteriorated further, speculation would have intensified, and distortions in the international economic system would have become even more difficult to correct. Domestic pressure for precipitate withdrawals of our troops in Europe would have increased, and the risk of a relapse into short-sighted protectionism would have become overwhelming. It would have caused enormous economic uncertainty and instability in the free world and seriously threatened the prosperity of many nations.

If we had chosen merely to continue to patch up the system, the strong domestic measures I took on August 15 might have ended the crisis for the moment. But then we certainly would have been faced with the recurrence of such crises in the future.

We concluded, after full review, that these alternatives were unacceptable. Strong unilateral measures were required to address both the immediate crisis and the fundamental structural problems of the system. On August 15 I suspended convertibility of the dollar into gold and other reserve assets. At the same time I imposed a temporary 10 percent surcharge on dutiable imports to raise their price and thereby reduce their level. And I specified that while the surcharge remained in effect, the Job Development Credit which I was proposing to the Congress was not to be applied to give tax credit for imported capital goods.

My objectives were to create conditions for a realignment of exchange rates and to stimulate progress in the areas of trade and burden sharing—in order to bring about a sustained turn-around in our balance of payments. And I wanted to set the stage for negotiations leading to a reformed international monetary order.

The August 15 measures were not in themselves a lasting solution. Such a solution would depend on two factors. First, we would need major improvements in our domestic economy. The wage/price freeze and subsequent controls are measures which we expect to reduce our high rate of inflation. The Job Development Credit and other tax reductions which I proposed are designed to stimulate domestic growth and productivity, reduce unemployment, and encourage new investments which will make U.S. industry more competitive.

Second, we needed a major international cooperative effort to help us improve our balance of payments position, and ultimately to reform the system itself. When some countries are in balance of payment disequilibrium because of deficit, others are in disequilibrium on the surplus side. What we faced, therefore, was an international problem requiring a multilateral solution.

The Road to Agreement. The strong August 15 measures were necessary to emphasize the seriousness of the problem and the urgent need for international action. There was a temptation then for us to approach a multilateral solution primarily by making advantageous separate arrangements with particular nations and then putting pressure on certain others. But we chose another course. We placed paramount importance on avoiding tactics which would weaken confidence and political unity among free world nations. It was essential that the final outcome be arrived at in a spirit of international unity and cooperation and serve the interests of all concerned. Only such a solution would be durable. For these reasons, we gave priority to international forums and multilateral discussions.

In the weeks following August 15, we

set out to clarify the dimensions of the problem. In mid-September, Secretary Connally, at the London meeting of the Group of Ten—the Finance Ministers and Central Bank Governors of the major industrialized nations of the free world—spelled out our objectives and stressed the necessity for action.

During the same period several countries allowed their currencies to float. Depending on the degree of intervention and exchange restriction by the particular country, this would permit market forces to play a significant role in determining its currency's value. Had all currencies been permitted to float freely, without government intervention or restriction, the process of currency realignment might have been facilitated. As an incentive Secretary Connally proposed at the annual meeting of the IMF at the end of September that, if other governments would allow their currencies to float freely for a transitional period—and if tangible progress toward the removal of certain barriers to trade could be made—we would immediately remove the surcharge. This approach met with little response. Many countries were reluctant to allow market forces to determine the value of their currencies and attached priority to a return to fixed rates. But there were grounds for optimism in the fact that some currencies were approaching more realistic exchange rates.

At the Group of Ten Meeting in Rome in early December, possible avenues for resolving the immediate problems were clarified and developed. The United States had strongly opposed any change in the official dollar price of gold, out of concern that such a change might feed hopes or expectations that gold might achieve and maintain a more important role in the monetary system, contrary to our intentions. Nevertheless, Secretary Connally, on behalf of the United States, explored the extent to which a formal devaluation of the dollar in terms of gold might help to bring about a satisfactory comprehensive agreement. It was particularly necessary to determine whether a realignment of satisfactory magnitude could be agreed upon, and what contributions other nations would make to it.

An adequate realignment required the participation of all major industrialized nations. The failure of one nation to participate would have made it more difficult for others to agree to a significant revaluation vis-a-vis the dollar. The participation of France, in particular, was important because of the significance certain other countries attached to the exchange rate between their currencies and the franc. We recognized France's strong interest in its competitive position in Europe and in maintaining the gold parity of the franc at the level established in 1969.

In mid-December in the Azores, President Pompidou and I reached an agreement in principle on our joint contribution to an overall solution. We agreed to work toward a prompt multilateral realignment of exchange rates through a devaluation of the dollar and a revaluation of some other currencies.

At the Group of Ten Meeting at the Smithsonian in Washington, the negotiations bore fruit. On December 18, Secretary Connally, who chaired the Group during this significant series of meetings, reported to me that a satisfactory agreement had been reached. It covered a new pattern of exchange rate relationships, involving both revaluations and devaluations. The Group also recognized that trade arrangements were important to assuring a new and lasting equilibrium in the international economy. To facilitate the realignment, we agreed that as soon as the related trade measures were available for Congressional scrutiny, we would propose legislation to devalue the dollar in terms of gold. The U.S. also agreed to remove the import surcharge and the "buy American" provisions of the Job Development Credit. I announced implementation of this decision at my meeting in Bermuda with Prime Minister Heath.

The Smithsonian agreement—unlike the arrangements decided on at Bretton Woods, when the United States was the predominant nation—was fashioned by relatively coequal economic powers. It was the first time in history that nations had negotiated a multilateral realignment of exchange rates. Significantly, the participating nations also agreed that discussions should be undertaken promptly to consider reform in the international monetary system over the longer term.

The December realignment decreases the price in foreign currencies of American exports, making them more competitive in foreign markets. It raises the price of foreign imports in our domestic market. This will help us to improve substantially our balance of trade and payments position, although we should not expect an immediate turn-around. It will help stimulate domestic employment, especially in the export sector.

We and our partners also established the concept of wider bands—allowing exchange rates to fluctuate over a wider range around the newly established rates. This, plus the more realistic exchange rates, should dampen future speculation caused by the expectation of major changes in currency values.

Future Reforms. This realignment must be only the first step toward more funda-mental reform. We must see to it that the rigidities and imbalances of the old system give way to a greater adaptability and resilience to ensure lasting stability. We must develop reasonable rules of the road, adhered to by all, and recognize that cooperative multilateral management must remove the disproportionate burden of responsibility for the system from this country's shoulders.

I believe recent developments have reinforced an old truth: changes in exchange rates are demonstrably matters of concern to many nations. The failure of countries to make appropriate adjustments, thereby perpetuating imbalances, is also of international concern. The need and disciplines for adjustments should bear on surplus countries and deficit countries alike.

The amount of international liquidity affects many nations. In 1969 the world took a giant step toward improving the international system by agreeing to create Special Drawing Rights in the International Monetary Fund. Over $9 billion of this international money has been created. Experience with this asset will be invaluable in finding appropriate ways to diminish the role of gold and to avoid the excessive reliance on reserve currencies that had become characteristic of the system.

In 1972 I expect progress toward the development of arrangements with other nations which ensure that the monetary system is responsive to our common interest and that it provides a more durable framework for further expansion of trade and investment.

INTERNATIONAL TRADE POLICY

In 1971 we took strong measures to reverse our declining trade position, focused

243

international attention on the fundamental problems confronting the world trading system, and moved ahead with a major effort to improve our competitive position.

The Setting. World trade affects the standard of living and the welfare of citizens of this and every other country. For this reason, the removal of barriers to the free exchange of goods in the international market has been a major cornerstone of U.S. policy since the 1930's.

The results have been impressive. Tariffs of industrialized countries have been reduced to roughly one-third of their immediate postwar level. Between 1950 and 1970, U.S. exports quadrupled from $11 billion to $43 billion. U.S. workers, farmers, and businesses have gained greater access for their products in world markets, while American consumers have benefited from an increasingly wide variety of products from other nations. The postwar prosperity of this country and its allies has been enhanced by a rapid growth in trade between us. These trading relationships have provided a solid underpinning for our strong political bonds.

In recent years, however, international trading relationships have changed significantly. The European Community and Japan are now centers of economic power and strong international competitors. The Community is today the largest trading area in the world. Japan has made rapid advances in productivity and become a vigorous exporter. But discriminatory trading arrangements are assuming greater importance. Additional trade barriers have been erected. And past reductions in tariffs have exposed other barriers to trade, which have not been adequately addressed.

Within the world trading system, the United States recently has experienced its own particular problems. The productivity of American labor and industry has not increased as rapidly as that of some of our important trade partners; our rate of inflation in recent years has been unacceptably high; and the dollar had become overvalued. The combined effect has been a reduction in the competitiveness of American products in domestic and foreign markets. Our balance of trade has eroded to the point that in 1971—for the first time since 1893—we experienced a trade deficit. Our problems have been complicated by the fact that our major trading partners maintain barriers—in many cases both unwarranted and outmoded—which are detrimental to our exports. These have been focal points of political friction and have held back growth in employment in specific U.S. industries.

Trade Policy. Our objectives in 1971 were:

—To curb inflation and realign exchange rates, thereby increasing the competitiveness of American products;

—To seek removal of specific barriers to U.S. exports;

—To set the stage for further international negotiations leading to a more fundamental attack on trade barriers;

—To strengthen the export competitiveness of American industry;

—To facilitate adjustment of domestic industries to the pressures of excessively rapid import increases, and to assist in some cases with measures to cushion the impact of these pressures;

—To broaden and increase opportunities for trade with Communist countries.

The Measures of August 15. Our comprehensive program of August 15 has achieved significant success in dealing with the root causes of our trade problem:

—The December realignment has corrected a major problem. The previously overvalued dollar had made American products artificially more expensive than competing products in foreign and domestic markets. Conversely, the products of countries with undervalued exchange rates were relatively less expensive both at home and in other markets. The appreciation of other currencies relative to the dollar, by adjusting this situation, should substantially improve our export performance and dampen the increase of imports.

—The wage-price freeze, and the subsequent restraints of Phase II, should enable us to check inflation. The high rate of inflation that became entrenched in the latter part of the 1960's exacerbated the problems caused by the overvalued dollar. Reducing inflation will increase the competitiveness of American products and thereby strengthen our export performance. It will make our products a better buy for our own consumers.

—We have made positive progress in resolving a number of trade issues, which will result in the removal of certain restrictions against American exports. We look forward to reaching agreement with our trading partners to bring about major multilateral negotiations in 1972–73 on more basic trade issues, with a view to a general expansion of world trade including improved access for American products to foreign markets.

Trade Negotiations. There is a deep

and growing consciousness in the United States that international trade is important to our domestic economy, and that some of our major trading partners are following certain trade policies which adversely affect us. In recent years trade issues have been focal points for domestic political and protectionist pressures. They have been major irritants in our relations with other nations. Particularly worrisome are new preferential trading arrangements being entered into by the European Community, which encourage the development of a world divided into discriminatory trading blocs. This in turn would constrain worldwide trade opportunities, including our own, weaken seriously the multilateral basis of international economic relations and raise the risk of political tensions. Progress in dealing with these points of friction would reinforce political support in this country for an expanded European Community and for our strong ties with Japan, Canada, Europe and our other allies.

But trade, like monetary issues, is a multilateral problem which must be addressed in a spirit of multilateral cooperation. Today the European Community, Japan, the United States and other nations maintain trade barriers which adversely affect each other's exports. The Community maintains an agricultural policy which is highly detrimental to the agricultural exports of the United States and other efficient producers, as well as a number of special restrictions on industrial products from Japan and East Asia. Japan retains a variety of barriers which restrict imports from this country, Europe and Canada. The United States too has import restrictions which affect the trade of other nations.

Bilateral negotiations alone cannot resolve these issues. Because of the importance of international cooperation in this area, at the June Ministerial meeting of the Organization for Economic Cooperation and Development (OECD), Secretary Rogers took the lead in establishing a small, high-level group of experts to consider how best to deal with world trade problems. I have designated my Special Representative for Trade Negotiations, Mr. William D. Eberle, to represent this country.

Discussions within that group, and the trade talks we have had in the last several months, have led us to conclude that the time has come to begin moving toward a major series of international negotiations for reduction of trade barriers. A compelling case for such an effort was made in the report of my Commission on International Trade and Investment Policy, chaired by Mr. Albert L. Williams. A sustained and reciprocal reduction of trade barriers is needed—to reverse the movement toward discriminatory trading blocs and to remove the restrictions in each country which others use to justify the imposition of their own new restrictions. Only an international trading system which is mutually advantageous to the major trading nations and has their confidence and support is sustainable over the long run. We are prepared to move in unison with other major trading nations toward this end.

U.S. Domestic Measures. The long term solution to our trade problem does not lie solely in the removal of trade barriers by other nations. A more competitive and productive American economy, particularly in the export sector, is vitally important. The Job Development Tax Credit should stimulate new investment and thereby increase productivity. And

we will institute programs to develop new technologies which will increase our competitiveness and enhance export possibilities.

In addition, the Council on International Economic Policy (CIEP) which began operations in February 1971 under my Assistant for International Economic Affairs, Mr. Peter G. Peterson, is developing long range programs to improve U.S. competitiveness and strengthen U.S. export performance—thereby stimulating employment in our export industries—and to improve programs of domestic adjustment to foreign competition.

My first assignment to Mr. Peterson was to prepare a comprehensive briefing on the changed world economy and this country's position in it. His briefing was presented to the Cabinet, members of the Congress, and other interested groups. In December, Mr. Peterson made public a report, based on his analysis, which cautioned against erecting new barriers to imports. It called instead for a firm negotiating posture to assure our products equal access to world markets and, to take advantage of such access, for a positive program to build on America's strengths and increase our international competitiveness. I fully endorse this view and will strongly support our efforts to implement it. Accordingly, I have directed the CIEP to consider closely the recommendations contained in the report of the Williams Commission. That report contains creative and far-reaching proposals to increase the strength and resilience of our economy, stimulate vigorous export growth, improve the technical capability that supports U.S. export performance, and ease the adjustment problem posed by import competition.

Because of the importance I attach to

expanding U.S. exports, I proposed, and the Congress passed, legislation permitting the establishment of the Domestic International Sales Corporation (DISC). This will provide limited tax deferral for income from export sales, thus according it treatment similar to that accorded income of U.S.-owned production and sales subsidiaries abroad. This reduces an unintended tax incentive to produce overseas, instead of domestically, products for sale abroad. This Administration also strongly supported legislation, which I signed into law in August, permitting the Export-Import Bank to expand its program and thereby provide increased assistance in financing U.S. exports.

Along with these measures to promote our trade interests abroad and boost our exports we took actions in 1971 to meet concerns of important elements within this country through methods other than restrictive trade legislation:

—We negotiated a voluntary textile restraint agreement with the four major textile exporters in the Far East: Japan, Korea, the Republic of China and Hong Kong. This will moderate the recent rapid rate of growth of woolen and man-made textile imports from these countries, which has had a disruptive effect on jobs in the U.S. textile industry.

—We invoked the multilateral Long-Term Arrangement on Cotton Textiles where necessary to restrain rapid growth in imports of those products.

—We negotiated for an improvement of the Voluntary Steel Arrangement in order to limit exports of steel mill products from Japan and members of the European Community to the U.S.

—We continued to enforce anti-dumping laws to protect American industries from being injured by unfair pricing by foreign competitors.

—Adjustment assistance, which provides financial and technical aid to individual firms and workers injured by imports, has been made available in a number of areas. I have directed that an interagency effort be made to improve the effectiveness and timeliness of such assistance.

Trade with Communist Countries. In 1971, opportunities for trade with Communist countries were broadened and increased. This was both consistent with the evolution of our foreign policy, and of significant benefit to our trading interests. Although trade with these nations is less than one percent of our exports at present, they are an important potential market for our products. As relations have improved, trade has grown. As the former continues, so will the latter.

Among the major steps this past year were the following:

—We supported Romania's accession to the GATT and supported Congressional action to authorize Most Favored Nation tariff treatment for that country. Following the recent liberalization of legislative restrictions on the Export-Import Bank's providing credits for exports to Communist countries, I authorized that these facilities be provided for our exports to Romania.

—In April I relaxed the currency controls which had prevented the use of dollars in transactions with the People's Republic of China. At the same time I relaxed restrictions on provision of fuel to ships and aircraft

247

going to or from China, and permitted U.S. vessels to carry Chinese cargoes between non-Chinese ports.

—In June I removed trade controls on a wide range of non-strategic U.S. products to permit their export to the People's Republic of China without a license. The effect of these measures has been to end the 21-year embargo on direct trade with the People's Republic of China.

—Secretary Stans' visit to the Soviet Union and Poland, and the large number of licenses issued for American exporters wishing to sell to these countries, should enhance the possibility of increased trade.

—In November we concluded a sale of approximately $136 million of grains to the Soviet Union, which will be of significant benefit to American farmers.

—We further facilitated trade with Communist countries by reducing the number of goods requiring licenses without weakening effective control over the export of strategic commodities.

Future Progress. In 1971 we took actions to remove restrictions against our exports and to encourage renewed international efforts to remove trade barriers. A broad international assault on such barriers is necessary. The only sustainable system for the future must be one seen to be of mutual advantage for all. A retreat by any nation or group of nations into protectionism, or attempts to gain advantage over others by means of neomercantilist policies, will deal a severe blow to the international cooperation which underlies the strength and prosperity of all nations.

FOREIGN ASSISTANCE

1971 was a year of crisis for foreign assistance. The changes in the postwar world and our experience in this area called for a new approach. On April 21 I submitted to the Congress legislation embodying such an approach, and proposing a major reform to carry it out.

The Changed Setting. The United States first undertook to provide economic assistance to foreign nations in the aftermath of World War II. At that time we alone possessed the resources necessary to rebuild devastated countries. The Marshall Plan was a major element in the economic recovery of Europe. Subsequently, we undertook to assist the less developed nations of Africa, Asia, and Latin America. In the 1950's and most of the 1960's, we provided well over half of all development assistance.

This situation has changed. Other nations, to whose reconstruction we contributed in substantial measure, have assumed greater responsibility for providing assistance to the less developed countries. Multilateral institutions which we played a major role in helping to establish today provide a strong international focus on development. They provide an institutional structure for improved planning and execution, and a broader sharing of responsibility, in the development assistance effort.

In substantial part because of this effort, significant progress has been made. Many lower income countries long burdened with stagnant economies are now attaining growth rates of over five percent per year, significantly increasing their food production, improving the health of their citizens, and expanding educational facilities for their children. The lower income countries today are meeting the major part of their development needs through their own resources. And, although continuing to need foreign assistance, most are now highly effective in setting their own development priorities and in utilizing the aid they receive.

When this Administration assumed office, we undertook a thorough reexamination of our foreign assistance program. We needed an accurate picture of what we wanted aid to achieve. And we needed a clear concept of how our foreign assistance program should be restructured to meet our objectives in the 1970's.

During the latter part of 1969 and the beginning of 1970, my Task Force on International Development, chaired by Mr. Rudolph Peterson, undertook a comprehensive study of our entire foreign assistance program. Subsequently, other government agencies studied that group's report and provided their own views. After close review of these, I proposed legislation embodying a new approach to foreign assistance.

A New Approach for the 1970's. The first step was to understand clearly the objectives of our foreign assistance effort. Under the existing structure, development, humanitarian, and security assistance had been combined under the Foreign Assistance Act. Economic and social objectives had tended to become entwined with security objectives. Some attempted to justify development assistance on the grounds that it could win friends, convert nations to our way of thinking, and thereby serve our security needs. Others justified security assistance on developmental, as well as security, grounds. And while there are situations in which these justifications have merit, pres-

entation of the program in this way confused their main purposes.

There are three types of foreign assistance, which can effectively serve three main objectives.

—Security assistance (including military aid and economic supporting assistance) is vital to help friendly countries develop the capability to defend themselves.

—Humanitarian assistance helps countries struck by natural disasters or the human consequences of political upheaval.

—Economic aid assists lower income countries in their efforts to achieve economic and social progress.

In order to enable us to distinguish between these objectives and fix program responsibility for each, it was essential to present them clearly and establish an administrative and policy structure for each. In my April 21 message to the Congress, therefore, I proposed two bills: one for International Security Assistance and the other for International Development and Humanitarian Assistance—thereby separating them for the first time. To assure more effective policy control and management, I proposed that a Coordinator of Security Assistance be established in the Department of State, and that responsibility also be centralized for coordinating humanitarian assistance programs.

Development Assistance. The most detailed and comprehensive proposals in my April 21 message pertained to development assistance. Reform was clearly called for.

The Agency for International Development was established at a time when it was incumbent upon the United States to play the major role in the foreign assistance effort. That Agency's past leadership

249

of the international development process should be a source of pride to Americans. It pioneered many of the innovations in foreign assistance which are accepted as having been critical to the success of development in certain nations. It has trained and brought together a large number of individuals extremely skilled in solving the problems of the developing countries. It has been looked to by many nations not only to provide them with aid but also to help them determine their development priorities. It compiled information and technical data on which other nations and the international development institutions relied heavily.

But today's changed setting requires a new approach.

—Because multilateral institutions enable us to contribute to development on a broad scale, our bilateral aid can and should be focused on countries in which we have a special interest and on problems where it can do the most good.

—Because developing nations themselves are increasingly able to set their development priorities and plans, and to determine their most urgent assistance needs, the U.S. should play a less direct role in this phase of development, and decrease the number of personnel stationed abroad for this purpose.

—Because a number of other donors, along with the multilateral institutions, now provide substantial sums of aid, our bilateral assistance should be coordinated with theirs. And the multilateral institutions should take the lead in providing information and data to all donor nations, and in integrating their assistance.

Based on this approach, I proposed a set of reforms including the creation of two new development institutions: one to provide capital development loans and the other to provide technical assistance. I hope that in 1972 the Congress will give closer consideration to these proposals and the approach of which they are a part. I regard them as the basis for discussion with the Congress aimed at formulating a program which effectively pursues this country's national and international interests and merits the bipartisan support foreign assistance has enjoyed in the past.

In an effort to improve our program based on this approach, major changes have been effected:

—AID has separated the administration of its economic security assistance programs from that of its development assistance programs.

—AID's technical assistance program is concentrating on major development priorities, including food production, education and health, with emphasis on the application of innovative techniques to solve crucial problems common to many lower income countries.

—AID is strengthening its population and humanitarian assistance programs to provide immediate help in disasters and to improve its capacity to deal with the vital problems of hunger and population.

—AID has launched a systematic effort to engage American private organizations more effectively in the application of technical and scientific capabilities to help the developing countries.

—AID, by concentrating its activities in major priority areas, has been able to reduce its staff by approximately 30 percent since 1969 and the number of its overseas officials to the lowest level since the Agency was founded.

—The Overseas Private Investment Corporation came into being in January 1971. Through its insurance services and other investment incentives, it has stimulated investment by U.S. firms in constructive projects in the developing countries.

These changes have significantly improved our foreign assistance program, and AID will institute further reforms during 1972. I am pleased by this progress and believe it merits strong support.

I was distressed by the Congressional action on foreign assistance during the latter part of last year. The 10 percent reduction in foreign aid which I ordered in August was effected as a budgetary measure at a time when Americans also were asked to sacrifice. It did not signal a renunciation of the commitment of this Administration to assist the developing countries. It did not justify the action taken by the Senate in November which almost abolished our entire aid program. This action, subsequent Congressional treatment of the aid program, and the large cuts in the aid levels I requested are of serious concern to those of us who realize the importance of this program, and to friendly nations who look to us for assistance. The vital role of foreign assistance and the progress which is being made deserve the support of the American people and the Congress.

Expropriation. Because of the significance of this issue, I recently clarified our policy on the protection of U.S. private investment overseas. Henceforth, should an American firm be expropriated without reasonable steps to provide prompt, adequate and effective compensation, there

is a presumption that the expropriating country would receive no new bilateral economic benefits until such steps have been taken, unless major factors affecting our interests require us to do otherwise. Similarly, we would withhold our support for loans to that country in multilateral development institutions, under the same presumption. And, because expropriation is a concern of many countries, we are placing greater emphasis on the use of multilateral mechanisms for dealing with this problem. We urge greater use of the International Center for the Settlement of Investment Disputes and support fully the early establishment of the International Investment Insurance Agency.

Multilateral Assistance. A necessary complement to the more effective bilateral program we are attempting to build, and a major element in my new approach to foreign assistance, is a broader international sharing of responsibility for the development assistance effort.

We will need the same degree of international cooperation in development assistance as is necessary in the areas of monetary and trade policy. We fully support a strengthened international effort for development through our membership in the multilateral development institutions and various consortia and consultative groups, through United Nations specialized agencies and the United Nations Development Program, and through our continued participation in the Development Assistance Committee of the OECD.

The assistance we provide through the multilateral institutions is of special importance to the development effort. These institutions have made outstanding progress in providing vitally needed aid and in assuming an effective leadership role. We are committed to continue to provide assistance through these institutions as they continue to progress. I have requested, and I urge the Congress to provide, $320 million per annum over the next three years for the International Development Association of the World Bank. These funds—which are more than equaled by contributions from other countries—enable the Bank to provide low interest loans to the poorest of the developing countries.

I have also urged the fulfillment of our commitment to the Fund for Special Operations of the Inter-American Development Bank and the soft loan window of the Asian Development Bank. The funds channeled through these institutions represent an important contribution to regional development in these areas and to assisting their poorest countries. Work continues to go forward on creation of the African Development Bank's Special Fund. And the hard loan funds which I have requested for the World Bank and the regional banks will enable these institutions to balance their lending by making long term loans on terms closer to commercial rates to countries which can afford them.

Further, we have agreed with other industrialized nations to institute a system of generalized tariff preferences for imports from the lower income countries. The European Community, Japan, Britain, and others have already instituted their generalized preferential arrangements. After our meetings with the British in Bermuda, Secretary Rogers announced that we expect to submit legislation to the Congress.

Outlook. This year could prove to be decisive for foreign assistance. Will the United States continue to provide meaningful amounts of development assistance? Will we continue to participate constructively in an international effort which has, in large part because of our past leadership, played such a major role in bringing about progress in the developing world?

This Administration will work cooperatively with the Congress with a view to reaching affirmative answers to these questions. The failure of this, the world's richest nation, to assist adequately the world's poor nations in their development efforts today and in the decade ahead would be one of the great human tragedies of history. Just as would a failure to confront poverty, hunger, and disease in our own country, it could not but make this a less desirable world. This nation has the resources and the know-how to make a vital contribution to the efforts of developing nations to improve the quality of life of their people. At a time when we are asking all nations to share in the responsibility for building world peace, we must do our part to ensure that all nations share in the world's prosperity.

ISSUES FOR THE FUTURE

In 1971 we set the stage for fundamental and long term reforms in the international economic system. 1972 will be a critical year in determining whether the nations of the free world can display in other areas the same strong international cooperation which it took to reach the December monetary agreement. It will test whether we in this nation can address these problems with the same spirit of competitiveness and cooperation which has been the basis of our prosperity for so many years.

Our goals will be to:

—Begin discussions with other nations to reform the international monetary system so that it can better cope with the needs of the international community in the future.

—Work in cooperation with our major trading partners to set the stage for major international negotiations leading to a mutual reduction in trade barriers.

—Continue our efforts to hold down inflation, to increase the productivity of our domestic economy and export sector, and to strengthen our adjustment assistance effort.

—Work toward an improved foreign assistance program which will merit increased domestic support and will enable us to adequately contribute, along with other industrialized nations, to an international assistance effort which will ensure that the development progress made in the 1950's and 1960's can continue in this decade.

—Address, and develop effective methods of dealing with, potential issues such as the role of the multinational corporation, foreign investment policy, and the effects of environmental control on international trade and investment patterns.

This is a challenging agenda. Our ability to deal effectively with the issues it poses will have a profound bearing on our future prosperity. It will play a major role in determining the directions of the world economy and the prospects for political cooperation in this decade.

PART III: AREAS OF CONTINUING TRANSITION

—East Asia
—Latin America
—Africa

EAST ASIA

". . . the new strength in Asia is a fact, and it requires a different and more restrained American approach, designed to encourage and sustain Asian regionalism, Asian self-reliance, and Asian initiatives. For those characteristics are essential to the construction of a stable international order in the region."

U.S. Foreign Policy for the 1970's
A Report to the Congress
February 25, 1971

Our substantial interests and our deep historic involvement in Asia assure that the U.S. will continue to be a Pacific power. But there is an evident need for a new form of American participation in Asian affairs that reflects the growing national vigor and self-confidence of our friends. It is no longer either feasible or desirable that American resources, plans, and forces be considered the principal means of guaranteeing Asian security and progress. It is essential that the currents of change in Asia be channeled in a positive direction. It is certain that each of the major powers concerned with Asia—the U.S., the USSR, Japan, and the People's Republic of China—will play a role in shaping a new structure of regional stability. I am convinced that an active American contribution will hasten that achievement.

For the past three years, this Administration has applied these concepts to the challenge of building peace in Asia.

Today, our Asian and Pacific allies are acting with a new self-assurance. Japan and Australia are strengthening their contribution to the economic foundation of Asian stability. Among the developing states of Asia, a new level of regional collaboration is taking root. Collectively as well as individually, our Asian friends are assuming a growing role in shaping a structure of security and progress.

Today, a strong and prosperous Japan recognizes, as we do, that a more mature political relationship between us is an inevitable and desirable result of its dramatic reemergence as a major power. The sometimes difficult adjustments in our relations challenge the creativity of our statesmanship. Both governments are convinced of our capacity to harmonize different but basically parallel policies. Indeed, transitory strains have proved incapable of disrupting the growing web of ties linking the United States and Japan.

Our historic initiative toward the People's Republic of China contains the potential for a new era in which Asia's major powers can act with restraint and respect for the legitimate interests of others. Our allies know that this initiative owes much to the past success of our joint policies—and that we could not and will not build for the future at the expense of the commitments that have bolstered Asian stability for a generation. This effort to ease tensions in Asia, by working for understanding with its most populous nation, can in the long run enhance our allies' security, much as U.S. defense commitments do today. The latter, in any event, remain valid.

Our progress in bringing to an end American involvement in the Vietnam war—without abandoning a nation counting on our support—reinforces the integrity of our commitments elsewhere in Asia. Our diminishing role in Vietnam has also reduced the domestic strains that could otherwise have weakened the basis for American participation in building Asia's future. Our progress in transferring the combat burden to South Vietnam's own forces bears witness to the vital role of local self-reliance, while it underscores the need for substantial American economic and military assistance as American direct involvement declines.

Our policies correspond to the realities of change and to the growing capabilities of our partners in Asia. They are serving as a catalyst for the emergence of a new structure of relationships. Its ultimate shape is not yet fixed. To create a lasting peace, the other major powers must demonstrate the necessary maturity and restraint and the developing states must act with the requisite enterprise and self-confidence. But we have laid a basis for a new and sustainable form of U.S. participation in that effort. Elsewhere in this Report I have described this Administration's policies toward the great powers concerned with Asia. In this chapter, I will describe our relations with the other, increasingly self-reliant, states of East Asia.

TOWARD FULLER PARTICIPATION BY ASIANS

Although the policies of the major powers can and should provide a framework for regional stability and economic advance, only the active participation of all states in Asia can give that framework vitality, flexibility, and the strength to endure. In 1971—a year of momentous developments in relations with our principal allies and adversaries—Asian nations made quiet progress by relying increasingly on themselves and working together for shared goals.

We welcome this trend. We look forward to an Asia in which the task of ensuring security, development, and political consolidation can be carried primarily by the governments and peoples of Asia. Similarly, we believe they have an indispensable role to play in creating effective mechanisms of regional collaboration and in shaping the broader structure of international relations in Asia.

The situation now confronting the developing states in Asia justifies both deep concern and high hope. Insurgency and political violence, often abetted from outside, continue to plague the nations of Southeast Asia. Communist pressures still combine with historic antagonisms and cultural differences to check the advance to stability. In some countries the demands of national security and the constraints of tradition continue to hamper economic growth.

But much has been, and is being, achieved. The world's most exciting records of economic development are being written by the nations of free Asia, whose regional rate of advance approached seven percent last year. The Republic of China, the Republic of Korea, Singapore, and Hong Kong are exceeding this growth rate; Malaysia and the Philippines follow closely.

The economic record of the Republic of China attracts special notice. The island has become a model for economic development. Last year its gross national product rose by over 11 percent, per capita income by 13 percent, and exports by 33

percent. Its worldwide trading relations continue to expand, despite the regrettable loss of its rightful place in the United Nations.

The outlook in Asia is brightened by the emergence of a stable Indonesia—one-half of Southeast Asia in both area and population—whose enlightened economic policies and active diplomacy promise benefits to its neighbors as well as its own people. The election last year of Foreign Minister Malik as President of the United Nations General Assembly was a symbol of Indonesia's enhanced stature. In July, the holding of free national elections—the first in 16 years—dramatized the advance of political freedom and thus strengthened the government's base of domestic support. In the economic sphere, a healthy growth in exports, investment and rice production continued, while the rate of inflation dropped to less than 4 percent from 9 percent in 1970 and 650 percent in 1966. The American contribution to Indonesia's development effort amounted to nearly $215 million, or about one-third of the total provided through the aegis of the Inter-Governmental Group on Indonesia, which links the major donor nations, as well as the World Bank and International Monetary Fund. We also continued a modest security assistance program.

The Philippines, which pioneered the "Green Revolution" with the development of miracle rice, pushed its economic growth rate to 6.5 percent in 1971. Continuing an effort begun two years ago, the Philippines has made headway on a nagging balance of payments problem by strengthening its exports and tightening its fiscal discipline. It is well on the way to becoming a showcase of population control, with a well-organized and innovative program which it is expanding to cover the widely scattered islands of the archipelago. The Philippines continues to be a mainstay of regional cooperation.

A central purpose of the new partnership we are building with Asian states is to nurture a growing sense of regional identity and self-confidence. Without it, a vital impetus for cooperation would be lost, and individual nations would be obliged to choose between an inward-looking nationalism, and excessive reliance on the initiative of others to bring coherence and stability to the area. Working together, however, smaller powers can gain the influence needed to mold their own futures, while their efforts provide a natural focus for assistance and cooperation from others.

The past three years have seen a noteworthy advance of the spirit of regionalism in Asia. Formal political associations such as the Asian and Pacific Council (ASPAC) and the Association of Southeast Asian Nations (ASEAN) have demonstrated the utility of periodic consultations on major regional issues, and have served as a forum for the resolution of differences between participants. Most recently, the ASEAN Foreign Ministers, meeting at Kuala Lumpur in November 1971, declared their intention to consult with other Southeast Asian states and outside powers on long term means to strengthen the region's security and independence. Their expressed interest in an eventual neutralization of the area bears witness to their readiness to discuss even the most difficult issues of common interest. Our own dialogue with the ASEAN member states also demonstrates a sober awareness that much remains to be done before such an objective can be realized: the secure independence of sovereign Southeast Asian nations is its essential precondition.

Just as significant to Asia's peaceful development is the contribution of regional economic organizations. In recent years, the Asian Development Bank has grown to become a major source of the area's development and technical assistance. By the end of 1971 it had approved 85 loans to 16 developing nations in Asia, totaling some $639 million. It is particularly heartening that the advantaged nations of Asia have played an active role in these achievements. Though I attach great importance to our continued financial support for Asian development—including Congressional approval of soft loan funds for the Asian Development Bank—there are welcome signs that others recognize the limits of our resources and the need for a broader effort.

Japan's leading role in Asian development efforts is well known. Less widely recognized, however, is the contribution of Australia, which now ranks as the world's third largest aid donor in terms of the percentage of its GNP earmarked for this purpose. While Papua/New Guinea has been the principal recipient, Australia has made substantial grants to Indonesia, Vietnam, Cambodia, and the South Pacific Commission as well. New Zealand has also channeled increased aid to Southeast Asia and the Pacific area.

The World Bank, the International Monetary Fund, and the nations of Europe have pooled their efforts with our own and with those of Asian states in a growing number of international consortia established to assist such nations as Indonesia, Korea, the Philippines, and Thailand. This arrangement not only maximizes resources, but also ensures their coordinated use for priority needs.

MEETING THE REQUIREMENTS OF
SECURITY

Economic progress and political stability must rest on a foundation of security. The central role we have played in providing the margin of security for the nations of East Asia has enabled development to proceed and national self-confidence to thrive. Therefore, as we shaped a new Asian role for ourselves, we recognized a need to help create a greater indigenous capability to ensure security.

In July 1969, I set forth at Guam my concept of a new direction for our defense policy.

First, I emphasized that the United States would keep its treaty commitments, while relating our concrete contributions of troops and resources to changing conditions in the area. To abandon the structure so painfully built up over the past 25 years would only invite new conflict or induce sudden and unforeseeable shifts in alignments. Henceforth, however, we would carefully weigh our interests in undertaking new commitments, and we would shun a reflexive response to threats and conditions in the variegated context of modern Asia.

Second, I affirmed our intention to provide a shield if a nation allied with us or vital to our security were threatened by a nuclear power. Here, too, we were convinced of the need to forestall upheaval in the international relations of Asia and elsewhere. Our course would be to preclude nuclear blackmail while discouraging nations from developing their own nuclear capability.

Finally, I stated our intention to help meet other forms of aggression by providing military and economic assistance, while looking primarily to the threatened nation to provide the manpower for its own defense.

These principles have stood the test of experience, and I am confident that Asians themselves have welcomed them. By our actions as well as our words, we have demonstrated that America remains committed in Asia and determined to participate in building its future.

—Our bilateral security treaties with Japan, the Republic of China, the Philippines, and the Republic of Korea remain the touchstones of regional stability. Similarly, our multilateral security pacts—ANZUS and SEATO—have made a valued contribution to peace. They have been and will be honored. In meetings this past year we joined our partners in the Southeast Asia Treaty Organization (SEATO) and the ANZUS Pact in noting encouraging trends in the region, while reiterating the continued importance of cooperation and consultation in the common defense. These alliances have helped provide the measure of strength that now enables us to move toward a dialogue with the Communist powers.

—We will continue to maintain sufficient U.S. forces in the region to permit us to meet our commitments. Adjustments in our own military deployments in Asia have come only after thoroughgoing reviews with our partners. If this country is to move to a more balanced participation in Asian affairs, it is essential that we proceed from a shared understanding of where we are going and how we will get there.

—Our provision of substantial—and in some cases increased—security and economic assistance is indispensable

257

to support the transition to self-reliance in Asia. I am convinced that the Congress and the American people will continue to prefer this course over a retreat from Asian problems— and from our responsibility to help provide Asians with the vital resources needed to meet them.

There are tangible grounds for hope. The South Vietnamese, with our support, have demonstrated their ability to assume a rapidly growing share of the combat burden. The record also is encouraging elsewhere.

—We were heartened at the decision of Australia, New Zealand, and the United Kingdom, in April, to join Malaysia and Singapore in a new Five Power arrangement for cooperation in the defense of Malaysia and Singapore. It facilitates continuing stability in that area, and symbolizes the feasibility of a broad regional approach among concerned nations.

—Korea's remarkable economic growth—averaging over 10 percent annually in recent years—and the increased strength and competence of its armed forces suggested that adjustments in U.S. deployments were feasible. We reached joint agreement in early 1971 on a program to modernize the Korean armed forces as our own forces in Korea were reduced by one-third. The Koreans, on their part, have undertaken to increase their own self-sufficiency in defense. At the same time, the Republic of Korea is maintaining a significant contribution to the allied effort in South Vietnam. Last August, South Korea took the initiative to begin discussions with North Korea on ways to alleviate the plight of families separated by war two decades ago. This is a hopeful sign that tensions on the Korean Peninsula may be reduced.

—In cooperation with Thailand, we have focused on economic and military assistance to support Thai efforts to meet their security needs without sacrificing the nation's economic growth. We have reaffirmed our intention to continue our aid and maintain our SEATO security commitment. For its part, Thailand has demonstrated determination to deal with its externally-aided insurgency. Our close consultations on ways to achieve shared objectives in Indochina remain an important factor in the Nixon Doctrine's success in Southeast Asia.

American military retrenchment in Asia has not been—and cannot be—an end in itself. New doctrines and new ways of relating joint efforts serve the basic purpose of bringing our posture into harmony with a transitional era. It is perhaps inevitable that the most widely noted result of the Nixon Doctrine has been the reduction, by nearly 460,000 men, in our military presence in Asia. This Administration and all Americans can take satisfaction in the fact that it has been possible to reduce our deployments without jeopardizing our tangible national interests or broad strategic objectives.

THE ROAD AHEAD

In the years to come we must continue to tailor our policies to a new pattern of leadership in a changing Asia. The policies of the four major powers concerned with Asia will profoundly influence its future structure; the individual and collective endeavors of all Asian states will give that structure substance and durability.

I am convinced that the United States can set itself no more worthy goal than fostering in Asia the self-reliance that made our own nation great. National and regional cohesion among these nations is the natural companion—as well as the precondition—of restraint by the major powers. If the transition to a new structure of peace is not to founder, we must meet the challenge of relating our efforts to Asia's needs. To do otherwise would mock our sacrifices in Vietnam, discourage the parallel efforts of our Japanese and Australian allies, and make irrelevant our effort to build a bridge with our adversaries.

LATIN AMERICA

"The destiny of every nation within our inter-American system remains of foremost concern to the United States."

Message to the
Inter-American Press Association
October 25, 1971

Our association with our sister republics of the Western Hemisphere has always been unique in our foreign relations. Geography, history, a common heritage of self-government, and shared interests in the world at large have traditionally given our hemisphere relations a special durability.

When I came into office, however, the premises of our Latin American policy in the postwar period could no longer be uncritically accepted. The easy assumption of hemispheric community—reinforced by shared experience in the Second World War and by the new inter-American system—was being severely challenged by the new intensity of nationalism, pluralism, and pressures for change. The ambitious U.S. undertaking to lead the whole continent to democracy and progress—exemplified by our directive role in the Alliance for Progress—could not be sustained in a new period of accelerating expectations and greater assertion by Latin Americans themselves of their right and capacity to determine their own future.

These challenges were inherent in the new political environment of the 1970's. United States policy was hardly responsible for all the problems our relationship faced; nor could a new U.S. policy solve them. This, in fact, was one of the most obvious lessons we had to learn from our postwar experience. But the United States needed a new approach to hemispheric policy in order to respond to new conditions constructively and to lay the basis of a more mature political relationship with Latin American nations.

We needed, and we undertook, a fundamental rethinking of our premises.

We concluded, first, that geography and history and U.S. interests did give our relationship with Latin America a special—and continuing—importance. We could not treat Latin America as simply another region of the developing world. The hemisphere is unique and our political ties in it are unique.

We could see also that the growing sense of national and regional identity in Latin America was expressing itself increasingly in terms of differentiation from the United States. Henceforth a sense of hemisphere-wide community could be sustained only on a new, more realistic basis. The problems in our relationship were, at their roots, political. Solutions would be found in reconciliation of basic interests, not merely in economic programs. Of course, because of the central importance of development as a common objective, our assistance in that effort would be an essential ingredient in our relationship. In the long run, we hoped that the achievement of progress would boost national self-assurance and reduce the need for foreign scapegoats. Nevertheless, we had to understand that the mobilization of national energies and the frustrations of the development process could be accompanied by greater anti-U.S. sentiment, not less.

In recent years, U.S. policy had fluctuated between taking our neighbors for granted and launching ambitious crusades in which we promised a transformation of the continent. The penalties for taking our neighbors for granted were obvious. Our political ties to our own hemisphere would erode. The United States would become a target, rather than an ally, of legitimate national aspirations. Extremist methods would gain wider acceptance. We would have betrayed our own humanitarian traditions and our national commitment to freedom and human dignity.

The penalties for attempting ambitious crusades were less obvious but almost as serious. Enthusiasm was no substitute for concrete achievement. Pious exhortations for a massive U.S. effort would serve no purpose when the U.S. Congress was barely willing to preserve, let alone increase, our foreign assistance program. Raising unrealistic expectations would ultimately end only in greater frustration and bitterness. History had taught us, moreover, that progress toward development and democracy depended in the first instance upon indigenous capacities, traditions, and leadership. Latin Americans understood this, and so should we.

Therefore, this Administration has adopted a new approach to hemispheric policy, more consistent with modern reality. It reflects the new thrust of United States foreign policy under the Nixon Doctrine. We have changed the manner of our participation in both bilateral and collective efforts. We pretend no monopoly on ideas, but elicit and encourage the initiatives of our partners. The concrete economic steps the United States has taken to assist Latin America have been responses to their ideas and their concerns. We give our active support where it is wanted and where it makes a difference.

Ironically, in an area where the pervasiveness of change is a cliche of political rhetoric, old notions of expected U.S. behavior are proving difficult to throw off. United States performance is still to some extent being measured inappropriately by the yardsticks of the past. We are inevitably a leader, and hemispheric unity remains a fundamental principle. But a hemisphere of nations increasingly assertive of their individual identities is less amenable to U.S. direction and less likely to achieve cohesion automatically. Latin American nations vigorously mobilizing themselves for development should be less dependent on U.S. prescriptions.

This is a more mature relationship.

Our adjustment is thus a positive development of great importance. The United States has assumed a new role of leadership and support that we can sustain over the long term. It does justice to the national dignity of our partners. It is the only basis on which genuine progress in the hemisphere can be achieved.

Our policies over the past three years reflect four positive themes:

—A wider sharing of ideas and responsibility in hemispheric collaboration;

—A mature U.S. response to political diversity and nationalism;

—A practical and concrete U.S. contribution to economic and social development;

—A humanitarian concern for the quality of life in the hemisphere.

SHARING IDEAS AND SHARING RESPONSIBILITY

The nations of Latin America are our partners, not our dependents.

A tutelary style of United States leadership is unsuited to today's political conditions. The most effective form of hemispheric collaboration in the 1970's is based on a wider sharing of ideas and a wider devolution of initiative.

In this regard, my face-to-face consultations with Latin American leaders over the past three years have been especially valuable. This past December, I conferred in Washington with President Medici of Brazil, as part of my consultation with our allies and friends in advance of my summit vists to Peking and Moscow. We had an important exchange of views on major issues of global as well as hemispheric concern. In spite of some current disagreements between us, on territorial waters and fishing rights, for example, our discussions confirmed a broad area of shared purposes. I have had important talks also with Presidents Lleras of Colombia, Caldera of Venezuela, and Somoza of Nicaragua, in addition to my frequent meetings with Presidents Diaz Ordaz and Echeverria of Mexico.

This is one function of consultation—to foster a sense of shared objectives and help achieve them. Hemispheric enterprises are most effective—and best help Latin America realize its great promise—when Latin Americans themselves play the major part in designing them. This strengthens the hemisphere-wide community.

However, it has long been obvious to our Latin American neighbors that within the wider community they share certain major interests and viewpoints as a group vis-a-vis the United States. The United States gains nothing by ignoring this or trying to deny it. The differences between us are apparent. What will preserve the hemisphere-wide community is practical cooperation among nations which have much to offer one another.

This Latin American sense of regional identity is now increasingly reflected in hemispheric practice, particularly on economic questions. In the Special Committee on Consultation and Negotiation, for example, a body in the Inter-American Economic and Social Council (IA-ECOSOC) for dealing with trade issues, the Latin Americans increasingly consult among themselves before discussions with the United States. Latin American nations have also formed, on their own, the Special Coordinating Commission for Latin America (CECLA), for concerting their positions on political and economic issues vis-a-vis the United States and the rest of the industrialized world. This group produced the Consensus of Vina del Mar—the set of proposals to the United States which contributed valuably to the program I announced in October 1969.

This new practice of Latin American consultation can be a constructive force for cohesion in the hemisphere as a whole; it can make cooperation between the U.S. and Latin America more effective and more responsive. It will be a challenge to statesmanship to ensure that it never degenerates into hostile confrontation, which would be an obstacle to achievement, and thus self-defeating.

COMMUNITY, DIVERSITY, AND NATIONALISM

The hemisphere community took shape historically as an association of free republics joining together against domination and interference from tyrannies across the ocean. This sense of unity was reinforced by the Second World War and was embodied in the new institutions and instruments of the inter-American system.

Our cohesion has served many other common purposes since then. It has provided forums for multilateral consideration of issues facing us all. It has afforded mechanisms for peaceful settlement of disputes within the hemisphere. It has enabled Latin Americans to express a collective voice in discussions with the United States and the rest of the world.

In the 1970's, this cohesion is being tested by rapid and turbulent change—more intense nationalism, accelerating expectations, new ideologies and political movements, a new diversity of political systems and expanding ties between Latin American countries and the rest of the world. These new conditions are bound to transform our political relationships.

Our task is to respond constructively with a realistic set of objectives and principles for United States policy. We have done so.

There are hemispheric questions on which our judgments differ from those of some of our partners. As I said in October 1969: "partnership—mutuality—these do not flow naturally. We have to work at them." I do not believe that frank

discussion and fair settlements between sovereign nations are inconsistent with national dignity.

Our especially close relationship with Mexico provides striking examples of problems resolved systematically by self-respecting states who feel a preeminent interest in good relations. The closeness reflected in my several meetings in 1969 and 1970 with Presidents Diaz Ordaz and Echeverria resulted in specific agreements on such matters as narcotics control, boundaries, civil air routes, agricultural imports, Colorado River salinity, joint flood control projects, and the return of archaeological treasures.

In addition, in 1971 the United States and Nicaragua abrogated the Bryan-Chamorro Treaty, relinquishing canal-construction rights in Nicaragua which we no longer require. Presidential Counsellor Finch, visiting six Latin American nations on my behalf in November 1971, signed an agreement recognizing Honduran sovereignty over the Swan Islands. We have entered new negotiations with Panama to achieve a mutually acceptable basis for the continuing efficient operation and defense of the Panama Canal.

Our mutual interest also requires that we and our neighbors address in this same cooperative spirit the two significant disputes which flared up last year in our relations with Latin America—the fisheries dispute and the problem of expropriation. Let me state frankly the United States view on these unsettled questions.

In 1971, Ecuador seized and fined a great number of U.S.-owned tuna boats fishing within its claimed 200-mile territorial sea. United States law required me to suspend new military sales and credits to Ecuador as a result; seizures have continued nevertheless. Disagreements over the fisheries question have also arisen with Peru and Brazil.

The technical issue is a dispute over the legal definition of the territorial sea. The central issue is political—how to reconcile conflicting interests in an environment in which national pride and nationalist emotions exacerbate our differences. Fundamental security interests of the United States are involved. We do not believe that a continuing cycle of seizures and sanctions serves anyone's interest. We therefore consider it essential to negotiate at least an interim solution: to halt the seizures and sanctions while preserving the juridical positions of both sides until the 1973 UN Conference on the Law of the Sea, which we hope will reach an international consensus. Counsellor Finch reopened talks on this issue on his visit to Ecuador and Peru, and we have also discussed the problem with Brazil.

Major differences have also arisen in the past three years between the United States and some Latin American countries over expropriation of foreign private investments.

International law permits non-discriminatory nationalization of property for public purposes but it also requires reasonable provision for prompt, adequate, and effective compensation. Although mutually acceptable compensation agreements are negotiated in the majority of instances in Latin America, there have been important cases in which the legitimate interests of private investors have been treated arbitrarily and inequitably.

In our view this only jeopardizes the achievement of the goals in whose name these actions are taken. Latin America needs external capital, because internal savings are simply insufficient for develop-ment needs. While every country has the right to determine its own conditions for private investment, a government that rejects or discourages private capital cannot realistically assume that foreign public capital will make up the difference. What is needed now is a frank understanding which protects the legitimate interests of private investors, while being fair to the countries in which they invest. This would restore mutual confidence and maintain the flow of needed resources.

In January of this year, I announced the principles that shall govern U.S. Government policy on this matter worldwide. This policy is set forth in the International Economic Policy chapter of this Report.

In our view, the hemisphere community is big enough, mature enough and tolerant enough to accept a diversity of national approaches to human goals. We therefore deal realistically with governments as they are—right and left. We have strong preferences and hopes to see free democratic processes prevail, but we cannot impose our political structure on other nations. We respect the hemispheric principle of non-intervention. We shape our relations with governments according to their policies and actions as they affect our interests and the interests of the inter-American system, not according to their domestic structures.

Our relations with Chile are an example. Chile's leaders will not be charmed out of their deeply held convictions by gestures on our part. We recognize that they are serious men whose ideological principles are, to some extent, frankly in conflict with ours. Nevertheless, our relations will hinge not on their ideology but on their conduct toward the outside world. As I have said many times, we are prepared to have the kind of relationship with the Chilean Government that it is prepared to have with us.

In this context, its actions thus far on compensation for expropriated U.S.-owned copper companies are not encouraging. The application ex post facto of unprecedented legal rules which effectively nullify compensation is, in our view, inconsistent with international law. We and other public and private sources of development investment will take account of whether or not the Chilean Government meets its international obligations.

The integrity of international law, moreover, is not something only the United States has an interest in. On the contrary, it is a world interest. Smaller nations in particular are the beneficiaries of the restraints and obligations which international law seeks to impose on the conduct of states.

It is a challenge to statesmanship to see to it that nationalism works as a positive force and not as an obstacle to mutually beneficial relations between states.

Confrontation and extremism are destructive. For this reason the United States continues to assist the efforts of its partners to combat subversive violence, both with material and training support for security programs and with support for building the institutions and processes of democratic, social and economic progress.

Regrettably, Cuba has not abandoned its promotion of subversive violence. There has been some moderation of its rhetoric and more selectivity in its approach to exporting revolution, but these seem to be only a shift in tactics prompted by the consistent failures of its domestic policy and revolutionary adventures. Cuba continues to furnish money, weapons, train-

ing, and ideological leadership to revolutionary and terrorist groups. Similarly, Cuba has increased, not diminished, its military ties with the USSR—its receipt of arms and provision of facilities—and thus invited a permanent Soviet military presence into the hemisphere. Cuba isolates itself by these policies, which are an obvious and direct threat to the rest of the community. The United States will consider supporting a change in the OAS sanctions against Cuba only when the evidence demonstrates a real change in Cuba's policies.

A PROGRAM OF ACTION FOR DEVELOPMENT

A hemisphere divided by a yawning gulf between wealth and squalor is no community. The commitment of the United States to human dignity implies a commitment to help our neighbors achieve their overriding national objective—economic and social development.

There is no certainty that development contributes directly or immediately to democracy, or peace, or friendlier relations with the United States. In the long run, we hope it will. We will assist in the hemispheric effort with realistic expectations and with a realistic program of action that will have an impact.

Trade opportunities are crucial to Latin American development. Export earnings are the most important long term source of foreign exchange; they are a means of financing development without dependence on external aid and without the real or imagined infringement of national sovereignty that so often complicates bilateral and even multilateral lending and investment.

The growth of these earnings, however,

is dependent upon long term trends in world demand for Latin America's raw materials and semi-processed goods. Today, the trends in demand are far from adequate to provide the earnings needed. This has been a major burden on Latin American development and one of our partners' most urgent concerns.

The United States, for its part, has taken steps to provide access for such Latin American products as sugar, coffee and meat to our own market. But the problem is greater than this and has to be attacked on a worldwide basis. Latin America was not included in the arrangements by which many industrialized nations gave preferential treatment to selected countries or regions in the developing world. The answer to this—which the U.S. championed—was to press for a generalized system by which industrial countries gave preferential treatment to the products of all developing countries. We made great progress. The European Community, Japan, and other nations have put generalized tariff preference schemes into effect. As Secretary Rogers announced in December, we expect to submit our own generalized preference legislation to the Congress.

For the past three years, in addition, the United States has maintained the average annual level of development assistance of the first ten years of the Alliance for Progress. I have urged the Congress to move quickly and favorably on our new appropriations, particularly for bilateral aid and for the Inter-American Development Bank (IDB), the principal regional entity for development lending. Over the past three years, this Administration has responded to Latin American proposals and taken concrete steps to assist their efforts for development. For example:

—In my October 1969 address, I announced a milestone reform: the relaxation of restrictions which "tied" U.S. loans to Latin America to the purchase of U.S. exports.

—We have given financial and technical support to enhance the effectiveness of multilateral institutions like IA–ECOSOC, CIAP, and IDB as vehicles for Latin American leadership in planning development assistance and setting development priorities.

—I exempted the hemisphere from the ten percent reduction of bilateral foreign aid which was a part of our August 15 emergency New Economic Policy.

—We have supported efforts to develop capital markets, tourism, and export promotion, and to facilitate the transfer of technology for development needs.

—We have given assistance to the Central American Bank for Economic Integration and the Caribbean Development Bank.

—The U.S. signed agreements with Panama and Colombia on the financing of the last unfinished link of the Pan American Highway—the Darien Gap. Construction can now begin this year.

THE QUALITY OF LIFE
IN THE HEMISPHERE

Our ties with Latin America at the people-to-people level are a tradition unto themselves. They cover the range of human and institutional activities—educational, cultural and professional exchanges; volunteer and other humanitarian programs; counterpart contacts between schools, industries, labor unions, credit unions, foundations, cooperatives, and other non-governmental institutions. These people-to-people contacts have the advantage that they are less politically sensitive and generally can survive uncertainties and fluctuations in official relations. In 1970, the United States created the Inter-American Social Development Institute to assist the growth of non-governmental institutions in Latin America. This is a contribution to pluralism and to the kinds of social organization by which people and communities participate directly in improving their own lives.

The government and people of the United States contribute to human betterment in Latin America in other ways. Our public and private assistance to victims of natural disaster is a well-known and longstanding tradition. Our aid to Peru after the 1970 earthquake, and Mrs. Nixon's visit to the scene, were symbolic of our concern.

THE HEMISPHERIC FUTURE

The United States cannot be indifferent to the hemisphere in which it lives. But geography alone does not make a community. Our association will thrive only if our common purposes do. The United States believes it has much to contribute, as well as much to gain, in a continuing close relationship with its fellow inhabitants of the Western Hemisphere. We recognize nevertheless that the difficulties facing United States policy will grow, rather than diminish, as the decade unfolds; there will inevitably be strains and

disappointments. This will test our compassion, our tolerance and our maturity.

The new United States policy I first announced in October 1969 was a statement of a new philosophy and a blueprint for concrete action. Our philosophy is one of realism and restraint. This is the approach best suited to the realities of the new era and to history's lesson that we in the U.S., whatever our good intentions, cannot mold the continent to our preferred image. Our program of concrete action, designed for effectiveness rather than glamor, is directly responsive to Latin American ideas and needs.

To realize our purposes, these will be our tasks in the years ahead:

To share initiative and responsibility more widely in collective enterprises. This is a constructive way of responding to a radically new political environment in which our partners are more assertive of their right and capacity to determine their own future. The inter-American system and its practices should reflect this more balanced relationship.

To demonstrate in word and deed the vitality of the common aspirations of the hemisphere. We are realistic. Differences in interest and perspective are natural. We need to discuss differences and negotiate solutions, as is proper among sovereign states who share an interest in preserving a constructive relationship.

To make an effective contribution to economic development in Latin America. We cannot allow the ferment of the age to immobilize us. We can be responsive to good programs in many practical ways— even given the broad limits on what the United States is capable of providing or accomplishing by itself. We will move forward with our program of action.

To tap the humanitarian concern of the people of the United States for the betterment of people's lives in the hemisphere. This humane concern for people and people's lives is an enduring commitment and a vast resource. It runs far deeper than foreign policies and political relations, and sustains them all.

AFRICA

"The potential of Africa is great, but so are its problems. We view Africa with the strongest of goodwill, tempered by the sober recognition of the limits of the contribution which we can make to many of its problems. We look to African leadership to build the framework within which other nations, including the United States, can fully contribute to a bright African future. A peaceful, progressive, and just Africa is an exciting and worthy goal. We hope by our policies to facilitate economic progress in one part of Africa, human and social justice in the other, and peace in both."

U.S. Foreign Policy for the 1970's
A Report to the Congress
February 25, 1971

We owe it to ourselves and to Africa to define clearly and to state candidly American interests, aims and possibilities in the African Continent. We owe it to ourselves and to the Africans to understand clearly their aims and priorities.

Our African diplomacy, including my own meetings these past three years with the leaders of 14 African nations, has been directed to the establishment of an honest relationship with the peoples and governments of the continent.

Africa is in its second decade of emancipation from colonial rule and the achievements of independent Africa have been impressive:

—Despite great obstacles, African states have maintained their political independence and territorial integrity.

—Though progress was uneven, a number of African states have taken significant strides to broaden their economic base and to develop untapped resources.

—In the face of overwhelming domestic strains, African leaders in the main have succeeded in moving toward internal consolidation.

—Despite great ethnic diversity and unnatural geographic divisions, Africans have created new regional institutions to grapple with common problems.

Africans, however, still face two awesome problems:

—The hope for modernization is spreading across Africa more rapidly than the means to assure its realization. The problems created by slender resources of capital and skilled manpower are aggravated by the narrow scope of national economies. Many African countries face a harsh choice between policies involving cooperation with others which hold realistic promise of growth—and the jealous guarding of unmitigated sovereignty.

—The quest of southern Africa's black majorities for full participation in their countries' political and economic life continues to meet minority intransigence and repression, and to divert African attention from the problems of development.

AMERICA'S INTERESTS IN AFRICA

Historically, U.S. interests derive from the many American citizens of African descent, and the long involvement of American churchmen, educators, and businessmen with Africa. In the last two decades, Africa's drive for independence stimulated our interest, and commanded our understanding and our support. The creation of new independent governments in Africa gave a new focus to our relationship and opened new opportunities for fruitful contacts between us. The special identification of black Americans with their African heritage adds intensity to our inherent interest in demonstrating that men of all races can live and prosper together.

One-third of the world's independent nations are in Africa. Their voice and views are increasingly important in world affairs. Our global responsibilities require that we seek their understanding and diplomatic support for a wide range of policies.

In the economic sphere our common interests are substantial and growing. African leaders look to the United States for help primarily in meeting their development objectives. The American interest in a fruitful relationship with the African Continent commands that we, along with others, respond. On our part, we consider this an area particularly appropriate for an active U.S. role in African affairs. As African countries diversify their economic relationships, our own economic interests and opportunities in Africa expand. Our interest in African trade and investment opportunities matches the African interest in American goods and their desire for American technology.

THE NEED FOR MUTUAL RESPECT AND
RESTRAINT

If these American interests in Africa provide a firm basis for relations of mutual benefit—and I believe they do—I am equally convinced that both African and American interests are served by political restraint in our policy toward Africa.

We have made preeminently clear our respect for the diversity and independence of African nations. For historical and geographical reasons, Africa is resistant to involvement in alien conflicts and controversies. This accords with our purposes as well as Africa's. As Secretary of State Rogers stated following his February 1970 trip to Africa:

"We have no desire for any special influence in Africa except the influence that naturally and mutually develops among friends . . . we do not believe that Africa should be the scene of major power conflicts. We on our part do not propose to make it so."

Restraint must be mutual to be effective. Non-African powers should not seek, nor Africans provide, opportunities for exploiting local conflicts. Africans have demonstrated, in their drive for autonomy and self-reliance, their ability to solve their problems without outside interference.

Mutual respect in relations with the United States also includes African recognition of our non-interference in African political affairs. We expect African nations to resist the temptation to serve domestic political purposes by making unsubstantiated charges of American interference in their affairs. Such charges appeared in a few places in Africa in 1971, particularly in Madagascar and Guinea.

American restraint accords with the

natural pride of new nations molding their own future after generations of foreign rule. It is precisely what we demanded of others after we had obtained our own independence. The United States cannot, and will not, therefore, attempt to define Africa's goals, nor determine how they should be met. We will not recommend internal political arrangements to Africans—though we naturally prefer open and tolerant systems. But we can and we will support African commitments to the values we share.

THE DIMENSIONS OF COOPERATION

The United States responded, in 1971, to the special and priority concerns of Africans. This Administration was able, even in the face of declining worldwide aid resources, to increase U.S. support for African development. Our development loans to African nations increased 30 percent and Export-Import Bank activity rose 140 percent. In addition, we provided almost 40 percent of the total cost of multilateral assistance programs in Africa. Last year the Peace Corps maintained 2,500 volunteers in 25 African countries, providing teacher training and vocational skills. American assistance to Africa totaled about $550 million last year, compared to $450 million in 1970.

This record speaks for itself. We have been increasingly active in precisely that area in which Africa expects and wants an American contribution.

Private American investment in Africa is growing at an annual rate of 14 percent, a fact of the greatest promise for Africa's economic future. Private investment will undoubtedly play a major role in providing the Continent with the capital and technology it needs. We will continue to make every effort to encourage private investment in Africa. It will benefit not only Africa, but the world, to encourage efficient development of Africa's resources of petroleum, mineral, and agricultural products. American companies will also continue to help create new manufacturing enterprises and to facilitate expanded trade and tourism by working to build ports and railroads, air links and hotels.

U.S. private investment in Africa now totals about $3.5 billion, and continues to grow rapidly. Americans are participating in important new enterprises started last year in Nigeria and Zaire. The Export-Import Bank and the Overseas Private Investment Corporation stand ready to facilitate such ventures where our participation is wanted and where it can take place on a footing of mutual benefit. Africans who want this participation must, of course, create a hospitable climate for private investment. Kenya, Ivory Coast, Liberia, Nigeria, and Zaire are examples of the benefits which flow from such a climate.

Our growing trade with Africa yielded the United States a 1971 trade surplus of about $400 million, while providing Africans with expanded markets for the exports so vital to their growth. 1971 saw the opening of our sugar market to Malawi and Uganda for the first time, and an increase in our quotas for Madagascar, Mauritius, and Swaziland. Despite our own economic difficulties, we exempted many African raw material exports from the temporary import surcharge imposed from August to December. We have announced our intention to submit to the Congress legislation to implement a system of generalized preferences for the exports of developing areas, including Africa. This year we will open in Nigeria

269

our first Regional Trade Center in Africa. It should lead to a further expansion of African-American trade.

No one's interest is served by underestimating the magnitude of the task ahead, or by exaggerating the contribution outsiders are able or willing to make to the realization of Africa's aspirations. The earlier era of euphoria is over. If Africa is to move ahead in the 1970's, it must be largely on the basis of its own efforts and its own prescriptions. Assistance from others will supplement, but will not replace, the need for the application of major resources from the African nations themselves. There is no need to hesitate in expressing that fact. Africans know it, and say it, for it has been a recurring theme in my many private discussions with African leaders.

THE SOUTHERN AFRICAN DILEMMA

For more than a decade, leading Americans in all fields have expressed this nation's profound concern over racial injustice in southern Africa, and decried the serious potential of the issue for bringing large scale conflict to this region. As I have repeatedly made clear, I share the conviction that the United States cannot be indifferent to racial policies which violate our national ideals and constitute a direct affront to American citizens. As a nation, we cherish and have worked arduously toward the goal of equality of opportunity for all Americans. It is incumbent on us to support and encourage these concepts abroad, and to do what we can to forestall violence across international frontiers.

The United States can take pride in the measures it has taken to discourage a military buildup in the areas of minority rule.

We have maintained our arms embargoes in those areas. We have stressed the need for self-determination in colonial areas. We have facilitated contact between the races, and underlined the fact that greater political and economic opportunity for Africans serves the true interests of all races. I detailed the steps we have taken in last year's Report. It is a record second to none among the major powers.

Americans alone, however, cannot solve the racial problems of southern Africa. The notion that one nation, however powerful or well-intentioned, can master the most intractable issues plaguing foreign societies belongs to a past era.

For our part, we look toward black and white *in Africa* to play the primary role in working toward progress consistent with human dignity. We support their efforts by:

—Encouraging communication between the races in Africa, and between African peoples and our own.
—Making known directly to the parties involved our views on their actions. My Administration will not condone recourse to violence, either as a means of enforcing submission of a majority to a minority or as a formula for effecting needed social change.

The situation today offers no grounds for complacency about the imminence of racial justice in southern Africa. It is, therefore, important that we continue to do everything we can to encourage respect for human dignity.

In South Africa, men continue to be demeaned for reason of their race, and to be detained and harassed for their views about official policy. But the outside world is witnessing with sober hope the suggestions of change inside South Africa, where questioning voices are being raised, examining both the premises and the results of that country's policies. Private companies, many of them American, are considering new ways to open opportunities for African workers. There is an imbalance between the needs of South Africa's active economy and her adherence to racial policies which deprive her of the growing pool of human talent which that economy requires. There is some hope in that anomaly.

In Southern Rhodesia, after six years of economic sanctions designed to end the rebellion against Britain, Rhodesian and British negotiators reached agreement in November on the terms of a proposed settlement. These are now being put before the people of Rhodesia whose choice it is whether to accept or reject them. We hope this process will set Rhodesia on the path toward racial equality.

In the Portuguese territories, development in some areas is overshadowed by guerrilla warfare and repression. By our words and actions, we have made clear our view that progress toward self-determination offers the best hope of a permanent and profitable Portuguese-African relationship.

In Namibia, South Africa continues to resist the efforts of the United Nations on behalf of self-determination. It rejects the 1971 holding of the International Court of Justice that South Africa is obliged to quit Namibia. We accept that holding and continue to discourage U.S. investment in Namibia. We seek to encourage peaceful ways of realizing and protecting the rights of the people of Namibia.

Some call for the United States to take the prime responsibility for the racial problems of southern Africa. Some want the United States to force upon the minority governments of southern Africa immediate and, if need be, violent change. I have indicated why I reject that position. Southern Africa contains within itself the seeds of change. We can and will work with others to encourage that process.

OUR EXPANDING RELATIONS WITH AFRICA

There is a growing depth and breadth to our relations with the Continent. Today, the unprecedented frequency of personal contact between American and African leaders reflects that fact. I visited Africa four times before becoming President, and was able to study at first hand and in considerable detail the problems as well as the progress being achieved. Since 1969, I have met personally with the leaders of 14 African states. Both Vice President Agnew and Secretary of State Rogers have made extensive visits to Africa and have had contacts with African leaders that have been invaluable in setting the course of our African policies. A very special event occurred in January when, for the first time, the wife of an American President visited Africa officially. I was deeply gratified at the warmth of her reception in Liberia, Ghana, and Ivory Coast.

These exchanges have enabled me to confirm that a policy based on economic support, political restraint, and mutual respect serves us well. It accords with the high priority African leaders place on developing their economies. It accords with Africa's desire to be free of foreign political influence and Africa's need to avoid the diversion of resources inevitable if conflict comes to the continent. Finally, it accords with the growing realization of

271

Africa's leaders and people that their destiny is in their own hands, where they
want it and where it should be.

PART IV: AREAS OF TURBULENCE
AND CHALLENGE

—Indochina
—Middle East
—South Asia

INDOCHINA

VIETNAM

"To end this war—but to end it in a
way that will strengthen trust for America
around the world, not undermine it; in a
way that will redeem the sacrifices that
have been made, not insult them; in a way
that will heal this Nation, not tear it
apart."

Address to the Nation
April 7, 1971

The essential international challenge
when this Administration took office was
to shape a new American role in the world,
to share responsibilities in creative partnerships with our friends, and to move
from confrontation to negotiation with
our opponents. But as we set out on this
road in January 1969, we faced the hard
realities of a seemingly open ended war in
Indochina.
  —Five years of steadily rising American
  troop levels in Vietnam had brought
  our authorized strength there to
  549,500.
  —American combat deaths during 1968
  had averaged 278 weekly.
  —Americans were flying about 33,000
  tactical air sorties each month in
  Indochina, including 18,500 in South
  Vietnam.

—U.S. monthly draft calls in 1968 averaged over 30,000.
—In mid-1969, roughly 40 percent of
South Vietnam's rural population
was under government control, with
50 percent contested and 10 percent
under the control of the other side.
As the enemy's general offensives of
1968 demonstrated, the urban population of 6 million was by no means
secure from attack.
—Straining under the burdens of war,
the South Vietnamese economy was
wracked by inflation running at a
rate of 35–40 percent. There was little planning to overcome this problem, let alone to provide for long
range economic development.
—The additional costs of the Vietnam
War to the United States had reached
$22 billion a year.
—There was no comprehensive plan
for lowering American involvement
and no suggestion that American
troop levels could be reduced. Indeed
in September 1968, the then Secretary of Defense stated: "We have not
yet reached the level of 549,500 in
South Vietnam. We intend to continue to build toward that level. We
have no intention of lowering that
level, either by next June or at any
time in the foreseeable future."
—The expanded Paris peace talks were
just beginning and had settled only
on procedures. There were no negotiating proposals on the conference
table to end the conflict.
—Our domestic fabric was severely
strained by dissent over the conflict,
and increasing numbers of Americans
were pressing for the extreme solutions of escalation or immediate
disengagement.

How we dealt with this issue would be crucial to our efforts to shape a new role for America in the 1970's and beyond. Obviously we wanted to end the war. But we knew that the way we ended the war, or our involvement in it, would fundamentally affect our broader international effort.

There were no easy choices. Further escalation of our military efforts would deepen the divisions in our society, could not assure success in a conflict which was as much political as military, and could risk a wider war.

Continuing on the same path offered no clear prospect either of ending American involvement or of ending the war. Such a course could not have commanded American domestic support.

Precipitate disengagement, without regard to consequences, would have made impossible our efforts to forge a new foreign policy. It might have been domestically popular for a short term, but as its consequences became clear, the agony of recrimination would have replaced the agony of war. Overseas, this course would have shaken the trust of our friends and earned the contempt of our adversaries. We could not begin to build new partnerships by turning our back on people who had come to count on our support. And we could not set out to negotiate with adversaries by abandoning allies.

There were, however, two possible courses of action that would be internationally responsible and responsive to domestic opinion. The fastest and most decisive course was to negotiate a settlement to end the war for all participants. We progressively defined the terms of a settlement publicly and privately to Hanoi. This effort culminated in the comprehensive U.S.-South Vietnamese proposal which I made public on January 25, 1972.

However, we could not afford to rely solely on North Vietnamese willingness to reach a settlement. We needed an alternative. Thus we launched the process of progressively turning over defense responsibilities to the South Vietnamese and thereby reducing U.S. involvement. We also hoped this course would stimulate negotiation.

Progress in Vietnamization

We have come a long way.

—There has been a steady decline in American forces over the past three years, with over 400,000 of our troops withdrawn. The authorized American troop level on February 1, 1972 was 139,000. On January 13, 1972 I announced a further withdrawal which by May 1, 1972 will bring our forces down to 69,000, or an 87 percent reduction from the authorized level this Administration inherited.

—American combat deaths averaged 278 per week in 1968. In 1971, they were down to an average of 26, and in the last six months of 1971 were 11 per week. Close to 60 percent of all U.S. casualties during this Administration occurred in 1969, including 40 percent during the first six months—before our programs had a chance to take hold. Despite its vastly greater role in the war, South Vietnam's casualties have also dropped from the 1968 level.

—In 1971 Americans flew a monthly average of 11,000 attack sorties in Indochina, including only 1,500 in South Vietnam, representing declines of about 70 percent and 90 percent respectively of the comparable 1968 figures.

—Average monthly U.S. draft calls declined to 7,500 in 1971, one-fourth the 1968 figure.

—During 1971 the South Vietnamese army, up to 1.1 million from the 1968 level of 800,000, conducted twenty major combat engagements for every one involving U.S. forces. By year's end U.S. forces had shifted essentially to a defensive and base security role.

—In the countryside, at the close of 1971 approximately 73 percent of the rural population was under South Vietnamese government control, with 24 percent contested and 3 percent still in enemy hands. Added to the now secure urban population of 6 million, this represents over 80 percent of the total South Vietnamese population under GVN control.

—South Vietnamese economic reforms have reduced inflation to 15 percent annually, turned over more than 800,000 acres of land to tenant farmers, and laid the grounds for long range economic development.

—The additional costs of the war have steadily dropped and total $8 billion in the current fiscal year, down by almost 65 percent from the costs three years ago.

This is the record of our Vietnamization policy. It has now effectively concluded the U.S. ground combat responsibility. Our other activities are being transferred to the South Vietnamese. We are ending American involvement in the war while making it possible for those who do not wish to be dominated by outside forces to carry on their own defense.

Negotiations

We would greatly prefer to see the conflict end for Asians as well as for Americans. Thus we have pressed intensive secret negotiations since August 1969. The thirty-month record of these negotiations and the comprehensive peace plan that I announced on January 25, 1972, underline a fundamental aspect of our Vietnam policy: our first priority and our preferred solution has always been a negotiated settlement of the conflict.

Together with the South Vietnamese, we have always been prepared to make a generous settlement. We have hoped that the steady success of Vietnamization and the prospect of South Vietnamese self-reliance would give the other side an incentive to negotiate. Our objective has been to convince Hanoi that it had better prospects at the conference table than on the battlefield.

We knew from the beginning that the negotiations faced formidable obstacles. The North Vietnamese view negotiations as an alternative route to victory, not a compromise with opponents. For them, negotiations are a continuation of the military struggle by other means, rather than an effort to bridge the gap between positions.

The North Vietnamese have also calculated that they could achieve their aims through military pressures that would eventually cause the collapse of American domestic support and the unraveling of the political fabric in South Vietnam.

The gathering momentum of Vietnamization clearly faces our adversaries with the prospect of an increasingly stronger and self-reliant South Vietnam. Yet Hanoi chooses to fight on instead of seeking a negotiated settlement. Our sweeping proposals offer them a fair chance to compete for political power in South Vietnam. Yet they maintain their patently unacceptable demand that we guarantee a Communist takeover.

Unilateral Initiatives for Peace. Both the Communist side and other parties have suggested a long series of measures the U.S. should take to launch meaningful negotiations. We have taken nearly all of them. But each move on our part has only brought fresh demands from the other side.

—Thus, the bombing halt and the agreement to expand the Paris Peace Talks in 1968 were made on the assumption that genuine negotiations would take place at the talks. They never have.

—Thus, the U.S. not only agreed to the principle of withdrawal but actually began withdrawals of American troops. The response was that more substantial withdrawals were required.

—Thus, the U.S. continued withdrawals and has now brought home over three-quarters of our men. The response was that we should remove *all* our troops.

—Thus, we have agreed to remove all U.S. forces as part of an overall settlement. The response was that we should do so unconditionally.

—Thus, we offered an immediate cease-fire throughout Indochina which would end all U.S. military activities in the region. There has never been any positive response to this proposal.

Public Initiatives for Peace. In addition to these various unilateral measures, we have publicly offered a series of increasingly comprehensive negotiating proposals for an overall solution to the war.

On May 14, 1969 I proposed that all outside forces be removed from South Vietnam and that the South Vietnamese

be allowed freely to choose their future through internationally supervised elections.

On July 11, 1969 President Thieu offered elections, with all parties including the NLF free to participate and to sit on a Mixed Electoral Commission.

On April 20, 1970 I spelled out the principles for a fair political solution.

—It must reflect the will of the South Vietnamese people and allow them to determine their own future without outside interference.

—It should reflect the existing relationship of political forces within South Vietnam.

—We will abide by the outcome of any political process agreed upon.

On October 7, 1970 in the hope of stimulating genuine negotiations, I presented a comprehensive proposal for an overall settlement.

—An internationally supervised cease-fire-in-place throughout Indochina.

—An Indochina Peace Conference.

—The withdrawal of all American forces from South Vietnam on a schedule to be worked out as part of an overall settlement.

—A political settlement in South Vietnam based on the principles that I had outlined on April 20.

—The immediate unconditional release of all prisoners of war.

Secret Initiatives for Peace. We were determined not to pass up any opportunity—public or private—to negotiate a settlement. Early in this Administration, after ten months of no progress in the plenary sessions at Paris, I decided to establish a private and secret channel so that both sides could talk frankly, free from the pressures of public debate.

With the full knowledge and approval

275

of President Thieu, my Assistant for National Security Affairs, Dr. Kissinger, traveled to Paris for secret meetings with the North Vietnamese on twelve occasions between August 1969 and September 1971. He met seven times with both Le Duc Tho, of Hanoi's political leadership, and Minister Xuan Thuy, head of the North Vietnamese delegation in Paris. He had five additional meetings with Minister Xuan Thuy.

The tone and spirit of our approach to these meetings were carefully designed to establish a framework for agreement. We made no take-it-or-leave-it proposals. We stressed our interest in a settlement they would genuinely want to keep. And, as our talks proceeded, we shaped our offers in response to their expressed preference for a comprehensive settlement. The following chronology is illustrative.

—On May 31, 1971 we offered a total U.S. withdrawal in return for a prisoner exchange and an Indochina ceasefire, leaving the other outstanding issues for subsequent resolution among the Indochinese parties themselves.

—In their response, the North Vietnamese insisted that political questions had to be incorporated in any settlement.

—On June 26, therefore, they tabled their own nine point plan, which included the demand for the removal of the Government of the Republic of Vietnam as part of any settlement. In order to speed negotiations, we agreed to depart from the approach of our May 31 proposal and to deal with the political as well as the military issues. In effect, we accepted their nine points as a basis for nego-

tiation; and from that time, every American proposal has followed both the sequence and subject matter of the North Vietnamese plan.

—Five days later, on July 1, at the Paris Peace talks, the other side *publicly* presented another set of proposals— the National Liberation Front's Seven Points. On a number of issues the substance was the same, although the formulations were different. However, there were some points in each plan which were not in the other. The NLF plan focused on issues pertaining to South Vietnam, while Hanoi's secret proposal dealt with all of Indochina.

—We were thus faced with a secret proposal in a private channel, and a different public proposal in the open negotiations. On July 12 we asked the North Vietnamese which plan they wanted us to address. They replied they wished us to respond to their secret proposal. We did so, and also incorporated in our reply some aspects of the public seven points which were not covered in the secret nine points.

—On July 12, and again on July 26, we went through each of the nine points, item by item, seeking to bridge the gap between our positions. We sought to shape an agreement in principle which both sides could sign, and then introduce into the public talks as the the basis for a detailed negotiation of a final agreement.

In pursuing this goal, on August 16, we tabled a new eight point proposal:

—We offered to withdraw all U.S. and allied forces within 9 months of the date of an agreement. We suggested a terminal date of August 1, 1972, provided an agreement was signed by November 1, 1971.

—We made specific proposals to ensure a fair political process in South Vietnam based on a number of political principles meeting both North Vietnamese and NLF concerns. These included (1) total U.S. neutrality in Vietnamese elections; (2) acceptance of the outcome of their results; (3) limitations on foreign military aid to South Vietnam if North Vietnam would accept similar restrictions; (4) nonalignment for South Vietnam together with the other countries of Indochina; and (5) reunification on terms for the North and South to work out.

—I also gave my personal undertaking to request from the Congress, immediately after the signing of an agreement in principle, a five-year reconstruction program for Indochina.

—At the next secret meeting, on September 13, Hanoi turned down our proposal. They cited two main reasons. First, they said the interval before total withdrawal (9 months) was too long, and that we had been unclear about how we defined total withdrawal. Secondly, they rejected our political principles as insufficient. They repeated their demand that we replace the Thieu government.

We reflected on these two issues and consulted closely with President Thieu. On October 11, we conveyed to the North Vietnamese a new proposal in one more attempt to break the deadlock. We proposed a November 1 meeting with Mr. Le Duc Tho, or any other appropriate North Vietnamese political leader, together with Minister Xuan Thuy. They countered with a proposal for a November 20 meeting. We accepted.

On November 17, just three days before the scheduled meeting, the North Vietnamese advised us that Mr. Le Duc Tho was unable to attend the meeting. We responded that we stood ready to meet at any time with Mr. Tho or any other member of Hanoi's political leadership, together with Minister Xuan Thuy.

Since that time there has been no response to our October 11 proposal or a suggestion for a meeting. It was that fact which finally led me to make our proposals public. We owed the American people an account of where we stood.

For we had paid a considerable price all those months for respecting the confidential nature of our private talks. The North Vietnamese themselves constantly berated us in public for not responding to the NLF's public proposal, even though they had asked us instead to respond to their private proposal, and we had done so. This propaganda tactic created a serious divergence between American public understanding and the factual situation. It led some Americans into believing that their Government was not doing all it should to reach a negotiated settlement.

Continued silence on our part would only have perpetuated the domestic confusion concerning our negotiating position and efforts. Moreover, by committing ourselves publicly and formally to a new plan, we could also erase any possible doubts Hanoi might have about our willingness to back up our private offers.

Our Eight Point Proposal. On January 25, President Thieu and I publicly offered a new eight point peace proposal which was presented in detail at the Paris Peace Talks two days later. Its main elements provide that, *within six months* of an agreement, there shall be:

—A complete withdrawal of all U.S. and allied forces from South Vietnam;

—An exchange of all prisoners throughout Indochina;

—A cease fire throughout Indochina;

—A new presidential election in South Vietnam.

The proposal also calls for respect for the Geneva Accords of 1954 and the Laos agreements of 1962; settlement by the Indochinese parties themselves of problems existing between them, including the role of North Vietnamese forces; international supervision, as necessary, of the agreement; and an international guarantee which could involve an international conference. I also reaffirmed our willingness to undertake a reconstruction program for Indochina, including North Vietnam.

The provisions of our proposal regarding the presidential election in Vietnam deserve special attention.

—The election would be organized and conducted by an independent body representing all political forces in South Vietnam, including the National Liberation Front. This body would begin its work the day an agreement was signed.

—One month before the election, President Thieu and Vice President Huong would resign. The Chairman of the Senate would assume the administrative responsibilities of the government except for those pertaining to the election, which would remain with the independent election body.

—The election would be internationally supervised.

—All U.S. troops would be out of South Vietnam before the election. We would remain completely neutral and support no candidate in the election. We would abide by its result, or the outcome of any other political process shaped by the South Vietnamese people themselves.

Because some elements could prove more difficult to negotiate than others, we indicated our willingness to proceed with the implementation of certain military aspects while negotiations continue on other issues. Thus, we are prepared to begin troop withdrawals and prisoner exchanges immediately upon signature of an agreement in principle, and to complete that process within the specified six-month period, provided final agreement has been reached on the other aspects of an overall settlement.

Alternatively we remain willing, as we proposed secretly last May, to settle only the military issues and leave the political issues to be resolved separately. Under this approach we would withdraw all U.S. and allied forces within six months, in exchange for an Indochina-wide ceasefire and the release of all prisoners.

The choice is up to Hanoi.

Our Peace Plan Is New, Comprehensive, and Flexible. Since the last private meeting in September we have essentially met all of Hanoi's proposals on military issues except the requirement that we withdraw equipment and cease our aid to South Vietnam. We and the South Vietnamese have offered every reasonable means of ensuring that the political process will be fair to all parties, and that the incumbent government will have no undue advantage. Past statements of principle have now been made specific. We have designed our formulations to meet the stated requirements of the other side; and we have made clear in our communications that we remain prepared to listen to additional suggestions from them. The following are *new elements* of our proposal.

  —The U.S. and the other countries allied with the Republic of Vietnam offer a fixed date of six months for total withdrawal either as part of an overall agreement or an agreement on military issues alone.

  —These withdrawals would take place *before* the withdrawal of other outside forces and *before* the new presidential election.

  —President Thieu's secret offer to step down one month before the new presidential election is unprecedented; his willingness to make that offer public is an important political fact in itself.

  —We are ready to accept limitations on military and economic aid to South Vietnam if North Vietnam will accept limitations on the nearly one billion dollars of aid it receives annually from its allies.

  —We are prepared to undertake a massive 7½ billion dollar five-year reconstruction program in conjunction with an overall agreement, in which North Vietnam could share up to two and a half billion dollars.

I believe the record of secret negotiations and our new peace proposals make unmistakably clear that we have been and are ready to conclude a fair settlement. The stubborn reality is that the North Vietnamese have blocked all possible openings so far. They have continued to insist not only that we withdraw unconditionally but that as we do we replace the present leadership in South Vietnam.

They offer no political process except one that will ensure in advance that the Communists rule the South.

In our view, there is only one fundamental issue left—*will we collude with our enemies to overturn our friends? Will we impose a future on the Vietnamese people that the other side has been unable to gain militarily or politically? This we shall never do.*

So long as the other side insists on a settlement that is a thinly veiled formula for their takeover with our assistance, negotiations cannot succeed. If instead they are willing to compete fairly in the political arena in South Vietnam, they will find our side forthcoming in meeting their concerns.

Prisoners of War

No single issue has received greater attention or been the subject of more intense efforts in this Administration than the plight of our prisoners of war in Indochina.

About 1,500 of our armed forces and some 40 U.S. civilians remain captured or missing in territory held by North Vietnam and its allies. The other side is holding the prisoners of war under circumstances which violate humanitarian principles and the Geneva Conventions on POW's agreed to by North Vietnam. The enemy has refused to allow international inspection of its prisoner camps. It has refused to furnish to the International Red Cross or to other impartial agencies complete lists of the prisoners it holds. Moreover, it has provided no lists at all for the prisoners it holds in South Vietnam, Laos and Cambodia. It has curtailed the regular flow of mail between the men and their families.

At the end of 1971 the other side finally

released a large number of letters. They included the first evidence ever received that some of our men held in South Vietnam were still alive. While we welcomed this development, it also underlined the cruel and unnecessary anguish caused to American families by Hanoi's withholding for so long the fact that these men were alive.

Neither identifying all of our men held by the Communists nor providing their total numbers could have any military significance. It is their suffering and the anguish of their families which give them value as hostages for Hanoi and its allies. The requirements of international law and decency are clear; the Communist side stands in violation of universally accepted standards. Their policy has set a grim precedent.

This Administration has moved on many fronts to deal with this problem. Our basic position is that this issue should be treated on a humanitarian basis and separated from other military and political issues in the conflict. As I said in my peace initiative of October 7, 1970:

"The immediate release of all prisoners of war would be a simple act of humanity. But it could serve even more. It could serve to establish good faith, the intent to make progress, and thus to improve the prospects for negotiation."

The plight of our prisoners has aroused the widest concern. There have been hearings and resolutions in the Congress. The International Red Cross has made known its concern. The United Nations has adopted a strong resolution calling for compliance with the Geneva Convention, and specifically proposing that seriously sick and wounded prisoners, and those held for long periods, be interned in neutral nations. Many governments have publicly offered such neutral internment, subject to the agreement of both sides. We regret North Vietnam's failure to respond constructively to these humanitarian moves.

In addition to our formal initiatives, the South Vietnamese have, with our support, taken a long series of unilateral steps in an attempt to prompt the early release of prisoners. Over the past five years they have released over 4,000 POW's in South Vietnam and some 250 to North Vietnam. Just in the last year and a half alone, South Vietnam initiated the following moves.

—On July 8, 1970 it returned 62 North Vietnamese sick and wounded prisoners to North Vietnam, along with 24 North Vietnamese fishermen who had been rescued in South Vietnamese waters.

—On October 8, 1970 the Government of South Vietnam joined in the U.S. proposal for the total and prompt release of all prisoners of war held by all sides.

—On December 10, 1970 it proposed the release of all North Vietnamese prisoners it holds in return for the release of all U.S. and free world prisoners and all South Vietnamese prisoners of war held outside South Vietnam.

—On January 24, 1971 it released 35 more North Vietnamese prisoners of war.

—On January 26, 1971 it offered to repatriate all sick and wounded POW's and called for similar action by the other side.

—On April 8, 1971 South Vietnam proposed that sick and wounded prisoners as well as prisoners held in captivity for a long period of time be interned in a neutral country, a proposal supported by the U.S. Government on the same date at the Paris Peace Talks.

—On April 29, 1971 South Vietnam offered to return 570 sick and wounded North Vietnamese prisoners to North Vietnam and to intern in a neutral country 1,200 North Vietnamese prisoners held four years or longer.

—On November 1, 1971 on the occasion of President Thieu's inauguration, it announced the freeing of almost 3,000 Viet Cong prisoners of war in South Vietnam.

We have reinforced these initiatives: special envoys, such as Astronaut Frank Borman and Postmaster General Blount, have gone abroad to seek support for proper POW treatment; a dramatic rescue attempt was made at Son Tay in November 1970.

We have explored all possible channels and all responsible means of gaining freedom for the men. I have reaffirmed my personal commitment. In meeting with a group of POW/MIA families on September 28, 1971, I told them:

". . . I have considered the problem of obtaining the release of our POW's and missing in action as being one that has Presidential priority.

"I can assure you that every negotiating channel . . . including many private channels that have not yet been disclosed, have been pursued, are being pursued, and will be pursued. . . ."

Despite the other side's behavior thus far, this Administration will continue to use every means to press for proper treatment and prompt release of all Americans held in captivity. I have said that Americans in significant numbers will remain in South Vietnam until we secure the release of our imprisoned men.

At the same time, we will continue to work for a responsible settlement to the Indochina conflict which will give the people of that area the opportunity to determine freely their own future and speed the return of all our men to their families.

South Vietnam's Growing Capacity To Protect Itself

Public attention naturally has focused on the withdrawal of American forces, the transfer of combat responsibilities to the South Vietnamese and the resulting decline in American involvement. But this is only one aspect of Vietnamization; there are psychological, political, and economic dimensions as well as military ones.

The Vietnamization program in its broadest sense means establishing security and winning allegiance in the countryside; developing responsive political institutions; managing a war-torn economy and steering it toward longer range development. Progress in these efforts will determine South Vietnam's future.

As the withdrawal of most American forces from Vietnam has proceeded, we have seen to it that those remaining are not jeopardized by North Vietnamese efforts to build up their strength and launch new offensives. We continue to work closely with the other countries who have had troops in Vietnam: Australia, Korea, New Zealand, and Thailand. These nations are also withdrawing their forces as South Vietnam's defense capabilities grow.

Much of the progress in 1971 can be traced to the disruption of the enemy's network in southern Laos a year ago, just as similar operations in Cambodia two years ago accelerated Vietnamization in 1970.

Last year I recalled the purposes and the results of the joint U.S.-South Vietnamese operations against the North Vietnamese bases in Cambodia in the spring of 1970. They greatly reduced American casualties, inflicted extensive material and manpower losses on the enemy, ended the concept of immune sanctuaries, dislocated enemy supply lines and strategy, ensured the continuance of our troop withdrawal program, and bought time and confidence for the South Vietnamese armed forces.

In many respects the South Vietnamese incursions into Southern Laos, or LAMSON 719, in early February 1971 paralleled the Cambodian sanctuary operations of the previous year.

—Both operations were defensive in nature. The South Vietnamese pursued North Vietnamese forces only where they had been camped for years, attacking South Vietnam without fear of reprisal.

—On both occasions the purpose of the sweep was to cut enemy communications, destroy enemy supplies, and thus blunt the possibility of future enemy offensives during the following months. Without these operations the Communists would have had the option of launching major attacks on South Vietnamese and U.S. forces in 1970 and 1971.

—In both cases the very substantial impact was measured in following months by reduced enemy military activity in South Vietnam, accelerated Vietnamization and increased U.S. withdrawals. And on both occasions U.S. casualties declined sharply after the operations. During the six months before the Cambodian opera-

tions U.S. combat deaths averaged 93 a week; in the six months after they were 51. U.S. combat deaths before LAMSON 719 averaged 44 a week; afterward they averaged 26.

The one major difference between the Cambodian and Laos operations reflects the success of Vietnamization. Unlike the 1970 Cambodian sweeps, which included U.S. combat troops, LAMSON 719 was entirely conducted by South Vietnamese ground forces, with the U.S. strictly in a supporting role. The South Vietnamese mounted complex multidivision operations in difficult terrain, in adverse weather and against a well-prepared enemy.

LAMSON 719 thus underlined major progress. Three years previously the South Vietnamese were fighting enemy units in and close to South Vietnam's own population centers. Now they were dealing with the enemy threat in remote sanctuary areas, without the support of U.S. ground combat forces or advisers, and keeping their own territory pacified at the same time. I summed up the impact of the Laotian operations in my April 7 address to the Nation when I announced that the American withdrawal rate would be increased and that 100,000 more American troops would be brought home from South Vietnam by December 1.

The trends in South Vietnam since that time have remained positive. American casualties have declined further. We continued to step up the rate of American withdrawals during 1971. Enemy offensive activity in South Vietnam stayed low. The situation in the countryside has continued to show progress.

In coming months the enemy can be expected to pose maximum challenges to Vietnamization. At the turn of the year there were many signs that the enemy was preparing for major offensives, especially in the northern half of South Vietnam. As U.S. withdrawals cut our presence down to a minimum level, Hanoi would still like to discredit the record of these past three years and shake the widespread confidence that the South Vietnamese can defend themselves.

Our friends are bound to suffer some isolated setbacks. But these should not distort the overall picture of growing self-sufficiency and security. We and the South Vietnamese are both confident of their ability to handle the North Vietnamese challenge.

By the close of 1971 the U.S. ground combat role was effectively completed. The year saw a constant advance toward the goal I discussed on April 7:

"As you can see from the progress we have made to date and by this announcement tonight, the American involvement in Vietnam is coming to an end. The day the South Vietnamese can take over their own defense is in sight. Our goal is a total American withdrawal from Vietnam. We can and will reach that goal through our program of Vietnamization if necessary."

The Situation in the Countryside

No aspect of the conflict, and no measure of Vietnamization, is more important than the relentless, if unpublicized, struggle for the South Vietnamese living in the countryside, commonly called pacification.

Pacification involves the situation in rural areas in all its dimensions—physical security, popular allegiance, and the military, administrative, and political effectiveness of both sides. A successful pacification effort permits the villager to return to his land and improve his farm, confident that he will be able to harvest and market his crops in security.

During the past year, the South Vietnamese faced a crucial challenge: to keep up the momentum of pacification, while simultaneously taking over an increasing share of combat responsibilities as U.S. and other allied forces rapidly withdrew. In most areas, this challenge was met successfully.

To measure progress in the countryside we developed in 1969 complex criteria which weigh various factors indicative of control. The basic criterion, which we measure rigidly, is whether a hamlet has adequate defense and a fully functioning government official resident both day and night. Throughout this Administration we have also sent teams from Washington to South Vietnam to make candid on-the-scene assessments and verify reports from the field.

In mid-1969, our indicator showed roughly 40 percent of the rural population under South Vietnamese control, 50 percent contested, and 10 percent under the control of the other side. By the end of 1970 these percentages were respectively 65, 30, and 5.

We did not expect pacification to progress at the same rate in 1971. The remaining contested areas are those in which the other side is most firmly rooted, where the Communist infrastructure has been established for as long as two decades, and where enemy bases and infiltration routes are closest to the rural population. Nevertheless, in 1971 the South Vietnamese Government increased its control over the rural population from 65 percent to 73 percent. At year's end the Government's control was under 60 percent in only seven of the 44 provinces, compared with 15 provinces in December 1970. Government control was over 80 percent in 20 provinces compared with nine a year earlier.

Over 80 percent of the total population of South Vietnam, including the six million urban dwellers and eight million in rural areas, is under effective Government control.

Despite the substantial overall progress in pacification, there were also some setbacks. The percentage of the rural population under uncontested Government of Vietnam control declined in five of the seven most northern provinces, closest to the enemy's staging areas in North Vietnam and Laos. We hope that the formation of an additional division in the northern sector and other recent steps by the Government will reverse that trend.

More South Vietnamese now receive government protection and services than at any time in the past decade. A majority of the population has participated in national and local elections. Rice production has risen to the highest level in history. A major land reform program has resulted in distribution of more than 850,000 acres of land to over 275,000 farm families.

And perhaps most significantly of all, the government has the confidence to hand over nearly 600,000 weapons to peasants who serve as a local militia, the People's Self-Defense Forces. A government unpopular with its people would never dare to arm them.

These are the actions of a government that is increasingly sure of allegiance and taking the steps to deserve that allegiance.

Political Development

In last year's Report I pointed out that the political dimension was crucial for South Vietnam's future and would take on increasing importance as the military

efforts wound down. Noting the upcoming Presidential and lower house elections, I said that, "1971 will show the extent of political development in South Vietnam."

The results this past year have been mixed. There are areas in which political freedom and development still need to be advanced in South Vietnam. And the cohesiveness of the non-Communist political forces remains to be tested.

But this should not obscure some fundamental facts. In just a few short years, South Vietnam has made remarkable progress building toward democracy in the midst of a war. The past four years have been characterized by basic political stability in South Vietnam rather than the turbulence of the previous period. The Constitution is proving effective, and participation in the political process is broadening.

A consistent political evolution has taken place in the period since the election of a Constitutional Assembly in 1966 and of the President and a National Assembly in 1967. The numbers of voters and candidates participating has been exceptionally high in the numerous national and local elections held during the last five years, despite the announced Communist intent to disrupt elections and to attack candidates. Over 95 percent of the elections for hamlet chiefs and village councils have been completed. Councils have been elected in all provinces and municipalities.

This trend was furthered in the August 1971 national elections for South Vietnam's lower house. There was lively competition, and 78 percent of the eligible voters turned out. As in the Senate elections a year earlier, where an opposition slate led the returns, groups critical of the Government won significant victories and increased their substantial representation in the Legislature, a fact that attests to the fairness of these contests.

More international attention was devoted to the South Vietnamese presidential election in October 1971. We hoped that this election would be vigorously contested. We have stressed the concept of free choice in South Vietnam. We believed that a contested election would leave the resulting South Vietnamese Government in a stronger position than an unopposed victory. We had an obligation to make our views known, publicly and privately. We emphasized our view that there should be more than one candidate, and we worked diligently to encourage opponents of President Thieu to remain in the race.

But at this stage in South Vietnam's political development, a contested election depends upon the personal motives and calculations of individuals. South Vietnam lacks well established political parties capable of guaranteeing alternative candidates. The interplay of personalities and circumstances in South Vietnam last year simply failed to produce a contest. Some observers believed that President Thieu's use of governmental powers was primarily responsible. Others believed that opponents deliberately chose to embarrass President Thieu rather than contest an election they expected to lose in any case.

We were disappointed that the election was uncontested; but we rejected the view that we should intervene directly or cut off aid to South Vietnam. In the final phases of American involvement, we were determined to avoid the practices which helped produce our involvement in the first place.

We thus preferred the disappointment of an uncontested election to the probably fatal mistake of attempted manipulation of the South Vietnamese political scene. In the final analysis, it is to the credit of the South Vietnamese—opponents as well as supporters of the regime—that they emerged from a trying and uncertain summer with their political stability and constitutional structure intact. Despite its remaining problems, South Vietnam's political development contrasts favorably, indeed, with North Vietnam, where there are no true elections at all.

Economic Development

A sound Vietnamese economy is crucial for political stability and a viable government. Last year I recounted the successful efforts of the South Vietnamese to brake the rampant inflation that had plagued that nation for years. This effort was continued in 1971. Further actions were taken to lay the groundwork for long range economic development.

The achievements in 1971 were especially striking, in view of the need to support a large military establishment and the dislocations resulting from large U.S. troop withdrawals.

—Domestic tax receipts increased 25 percent.

—Prices increased less than 15 percent.

—Production of rice, lumber, fish and textiles rose.

—New plants were built to produce textiles, plywood, electric power, plastic products and flour.

On November 15, in his first address to the legislature after his inauguration, President Thieu made economic development and eventual economic self-sufficiency major national goals. He announced comprehensive economic reforms to increase savings and investment, to raise domestic tax collections, and to encourage exports, industrialization and private foreign investment. The program included a major devaluation of the piaster, a difficult but essential step.

It is a courageous undertaking to move forward rapidly on development when almost half of the country's able-bodied men are needed for the military effort and the costs of security impose a tremendous burden on the economy. The Vietnamese look to their friends to assist them in their development efforts.

We had hoped to respond promptly by diverting some assistance funds in 1972 to support Vietnamese development. The unwise Congressional reduction of foreign assistance funds has hampered this effort. In the current budget, I am requesting funds specifically for economic development in Vietnam.

South Vietnam will continue to need substantial U.S. support to fill the gap between government revenues and defense costs. This form of U.S. assistance can be reduced over the next several years as the program for internal development takes hold and the economic and tax reforms yield larger revenues. We must not expect instantaneous results, however, so long as the South Vietnamese are forced to devote a major portion of their national effort to defending against North Vietnamese aggression.

South Vietnam has been plagued with war for three and a half decades. It remains a poor country with per capita income of less than $150. But it has rich potential and an industrious people. The ending of hostilities would allow the full utilization of these resources. We stand ready to assist all Vietnamese in peaceful development.

Remaining Problems

Each of the past three years has shown accelerating progress in Vietnam. However, we are under no illusions about the stubbornness and gravity of the remaining problems.

—*Breaking the Negotiating Impasse.* A negotiated settlement remains the quickest and most humane way to end the conflict. It holds out the only real promise that the war will soon cease for Asians as well as for Americans, for Laos and Cambodia as well as for Vietnam. However, three years of unilateral moves, secret talks, negotiating proposals, and Vietnamization progress have failed to induce the other side to join with us in settling the struggle at the conference table. We have reduced the issues to a single crucial question: will the political future of South Vietnam be imposed by outsiders or will it be competitively shaped by the South Vietnamese? The other side has consistently been unyielding on this political issue. We will nevertheless continue our efforts, in any promising forum.

—*Retrieving Our Men.* Either as part of an overall settlement, or through other means, we shall secure the release of American prisoners held throughout Indochina. The other side continues to exploit this issue and to manipulate the sentiments of the American people. Hanoi has demonstrated that it will try to extract maximum advantages by using our men as bargaining pawns. So long as they hold our men there will be American forces in South Vietnam. We will pursue every honorable path until we succeed in returning these prisoners to their families.

—*Completing the Transfer of Defense Responsibilities.* Last year brought the effective conclusion of the American ground combat role in South Vietnam. The South Vietnamese assumed that burden, and a steadily increasing share of all other responsibilities in the conflict. The remaining problems include completion of the transfer of air and logistic support to the South Vietnamese; improving the pacification situation in the northern provinces; building more cohesive non-Communist political forces; and setting in train the long term development of South Vietnam.

Major tests can be expected in coming months. Only the sustained will of the South Vietnamese can meet that challenge. As we complete the Vietnamization process, we will need the continued understanding of the American people to finish the process which has brought us so far, to redeem our sacrifices, and to contribute to the building of a more stable peace.

LAOS AND CAMBODIA

Vietnam is the central theater in what is, in fact, a wider war. For Hanoi has made the war an Indochina conflict by spreading its troops throughout the peninsula.

In 1971, with their position deteriorating in South Vietnam itself, the North Vietnamese continued, and have now stepped up, their aggression in Laos and Cambodia. Hanoi maintains over 60,000

troops in Cambodia and more North Vietnamese troops in Laos, some 100,000, than in South Vietnam.

The situations in Laos and Cambodia are similar in many respects:

—Both of these countries have totally defensive military establishments; neither poses any conceivable threat to North Vietnam.

—The neutrality, independence, and territorial integrity of both countries have been inscribed in international agreements which Hanoi signed, but contemptuously ignores.

—North Vietnamese troops for years have used both countries as infiltration corridors, staging bases, and sanctuaries for attacks against South Vietnam.

—North Vietnam continues to threaten the legitimate governments in both countries in order to further its attacks on South Vietnam, but also perhaps with the intention of taking Laos and Cambodia themselves.

—The overwhelming numbers of North Vietnamese troops in both countries strip away any pretense that the conflicts in Laos and Cambodia are civil wars.

The Lao and Cambodian governments have tried to restore their independence and neutrality through diplomatic means; failing that, they have been forced to turn to their friends for support of their defense. The United States and other nations have responded to their requests for assistance. We have supported both diplomatic efforts to bring peace to Laos and Cambodia, and defensive military efforts in the absence of a settlement.

On the diplomatic front, we have always backed the efforts of Lao Prime Minister Souvanna Phouma—the neutralist leader supported by Hanoi at the time of the 1962 Geneva Accords—to reinstitute those Accords. In Cambodia we long tolerated a difficult military situation and we encouraged negotiations when Prince Sihanouk was first deposed by the National Assembly in March 1970.

Our negotiating proposals on Vietnam have consistently been addressed to the broader Indochina context. In the face of North Vietnam's refusal to address these problems at the conference table, we have continued the policies of previous Administrations in extending military and economic support to the Royal Lao Government. We have provided military assistance for Cambodia since the spring of 1970, when North Vietnamese troops moved out of the border sanctuaries and extended their operations into broader areas of Cambodia.

Our constant objectives in both countries have been to ensure the momentum of Vietnamization and our withdrawals, to protect American and allied lives, and to help maintain the precarious balance within these two countries as they fight to restore their independence and neutrality.

In both countries our activities are limited, requested, supportive, and defensive.

Laos and Cambodia Provide for Their Own Defense. In Laos, government forces continue to offer a tenacious defense despite years of combat against a numerically superior enemy. The struggle there ebbs and flows on a seasonal basis. The Laotian conflict is, in effect, two wars. In the north, North Vietnamese troops maintain pressure on the very government which Hanoi helped to create in 1962. In the south, the enemy concentrates on expanding and protecting the

Ho Chi Minh trail complex which is vital to its military strength in South Vietnam and Cambodia.

The Cambodian Government, faced with the assault on its independence, has rallied the population to the cause of national survival. From a lightly-equipped and largely ceremonial force of 35,000 men in 1970, the Cambodian army has now grown to approximately 200,000, for the most part volunteers.

The army has fought bravely, but it lacks training, equipment, and experience. And it faces over 60,000 well-equipped North Vietnamese troops, hardened and experienced by years of war.

Despite the measures which they are taking in their own defense, these two countries are clearly no match for a much larger North Vietnam, and they must have external assistance to survive. It would be a grim development indeed if these two small nations, so clearly the victims of external aggression, were overwhelmed because of restrictions placed on American and other allied aid while North Vietnam continued to receive the full backing of its own allies.

Neither country has requested the deployment of U.S. troops. They are manning the front lines. Thus, there are not—and there will not be—any U.S. ground combat troops in either country.

Together With Other Countries, We Provide Military And Economic Assistance. In Laos, this remains as outlined in my comprehensive report of March 1970—military aid for regular and irregular Lao forces when requested by the Lao Government; reconnaissance flights and air operations to interdict North Vietnamese troops and supplies on the Ho Chi Minh Trail; logistic and air support for Lao forces when requested by the Government. We also provide economic assistance to control inflation, support essential Government services, and assist economic development.

In Cambodia, we have given military assistance since April 1970 and economic assistance and PL 480 programs since March 1971. With the approval of the government we are also conducting air interdiction missions against enemy personnel and supplies that are, or can be, used in offensives against American and allied forces in South Vietnam.

South Vietnam Has Mounted Defensive Operations Against North Vietnamese Forces in Their Laotian and Cambodian Base Areas. I have already described the purposes of these operations and noted the increasing South Vietnamese capabilities that they have demonstrated. In Cambodia, operations are at the request of the Government and serve to relieve enemy pressures against Cambodia as well as South Vietnam. In Laos, the South Vietnamese operations were strictly limited in objective and duration.

It is senseless to claim that these operations against enemy sanctuaries serve to widen the Vietnam war. Not a single South Vietnamese soldier has gone anywhere except where tens of thousands of North Vietnamese troops have been entrenched for years, violating one country's territory to attack another. It is Hanoi which widened the conflict long ago.

As I said in last year's Foreign Policy Report:

"The arguments against South Vietnam's defensive actions suggest that Hanoi has the right—without provocation and with complete immunity—to send its forces into Laos and Cambodia, threaten

their governments, and prepare to bring its full strength to bear on South Vietnam itself.

"The choice for South Vietnam is not between limiting and expanding the war. It is between what it is doing in self-defense and passively watching the menace grow along its borders."

The presence and activities of North Vietnamese troops in Laos and Cambodia are indefensible. Nevertheless, we can expect the Lao and Cambodian peoples to be subjected to additional attacks as Hanoi pursues its aims in the region. These countries ask nothing but to be left alone to shape their own destinies. They have demonstrated their courage, and their determination to try to provide for their own defense. Together with others, we shall continue to provide the support that will help to sustain them in their struggle.

I once again appeal to the other side to join in the search for peace in Indochina. Proposals now on the negotiating table could end this conflict on a basis that would respect the sacrifices of all participants.

It is long past time to still the sound of war, to return the men of both sides to their families, and to devote the energies of all to the fruitful tasks of peace.

MIDDLE EAST

"What I am saying to you today is not that I predict a Mideastern settlement. I do say that it is in the interests of both major powers, the Soviet Union and the United States, not to allow that very explosive part of the world to drive them into a confrontation that neither of them wants, although our interests are very diametrically opposed in that part of the world—except our common interest in not becoming involved in a war."

Media Briefing
Rochester, New York
June 18, 1971

Soon after taking office, I pledged that we would "pursue every possible avenue to peace in the Mideast that we can."

An end to the perpetual state of crisis in the Middle East would be a major contribution to the stability of global peace. It would free energies and resources for the building of a better life for the people of the area. It would reduce the danger of a new clash and spreading war. It would remove a major obstacle to the fuller development of productive ties between the countries of the region and the outside world.

I also pledged that the United States would now assume the initiative. Inaction was unlikely to promote peace; it was more likely to allow the situation to deteriorate once again into war as it did in 1967. It was our responsibility to engage actively in the search for a settlement, in full awareness of the difficulties we would face.

In 1971, the danger of war was contained, although the risk remained high. New approaches to a settlement were explored, although up to now without result.

—The ceasefire between Israel and its neighbors, brought about by our initiative the previous year, endured through 1971. It has now lasted 18 months. It was in the interest of each side to maintain it, and to make it possible for the other side to do so.

—Efforts to achieve an overall Arab-Israeli settlement lost momentum. Egypt and Israel, with our help, then explored the possibility of an interim agreement—a set of concrete steps toward peace which did not require addressing all the issues of a comprehensive settlement at the outset.

—Despite our restraint in our military supply policy, substantial new Soviet pledges and shipments of arms to Egypt continued the arms race. At the end of the year I felt obliged to reiterate that the United States would not allow the military balance to be upset.

—The USSR continued to build up its own military facilities in Egypt and to station increasingly sophisticated weaponry there.

In the Middle East, as elsewhere in Asia and Africa, the essential problem of peace in the 20th century has been to shape new patterns of order. The postwar period—the first generation of independence in most of the Middle East—has seen continual turmoil. If this is to give way to a new era of stability, new relationships must be shaped—accommodating national aspirations, fulfilling hopes for social progress and providing a structure of security.

The obstacles today are many.

Local tensions in the Middle East periodically threaten to break into open conflict. The Arab-Israeli conflict is foremost among these. But there are others. In the Persian Gulf, the special treaty relationships between Britain and some of the sheikhdoms ended in 1971; the stability of new political entities and structures remains to be consolidated. On Cyprus, the Greek and Turkish Cypriot communities have still not found a durable formula of reconciliation. Rivalries—personal, religious, ethnic, economic, ideological, and otherwise—divide the Islamic world. The Palestinian people, dispersed throughout the Arab world, continue to press their struggle for a homeland on the consciences and policies of Arab governments, exacerbating tensions within and among Arab countries and with Israel. Stable and moderate governments are threatened by subversive movements, some aided and supported from outside.

The competitive interests of the great powers are a further source of tension, adding to local instabilities and posing the risk of wider and more dangerous conflict. As I wrote in February 1970: "One of the lessons of 1967 was that local events and forces have a momentum of their own, and that conscious and serious effort is required for the major powers to resist being caught up in them." There must be understandings on the part of the great powers, tacit or explicit, on the limits of acceptable behavior.

In the Middle East, new relationships with the world outside are developing. There are temptations for some great powers to exploit these relationships, to increase their military involvement or to obstruct peacemaking efforts in the quest for unilateral political advantage in the region. This only fuels local tensions, with consequences transcending the issues in the local dispute. But there are also opportunities for the great powers to contribute cooperatively to the search for Middle East peace, and thereby to further the constructive trends in their own global relations.

A secure peace in the Middle East requires stable relations on both levels— accommodation within the region and a balance among the powers outside.

ARAB-ISRAELI SETTLEMENT

The greatest threat to peace and stability in the Middle East remains the Arab-Israeli conflict. Last year saw a new approach to beginning negotiations. This negotiating process has not yet produced results. But the United States undertook its major diplomatic effort of the past three years with no illusions about the obstacles in the way of a settlement.

It is one of the ironies of history that the 20th century has thrown together into bitter conflict these two peoples who had lived and worked peacefully side by side in the Middle East for centuries. In the last fifty years, and particularly since independence, they have been locked in incessant struggle. The Arabs saw the new State of Israel as an unwanted intruder in an Arab world and the plight of the Palestinian refugees as an historic injustice; to the Israelis, refugees of a holocaust, survival was more than a cliche of political rhetoric. To negotiate a peace between these two peoples requires overcoming an extraordinary legacy of mutual fear and mistrust.

The Israelis seek concrete security. To them this means more than an Arab offer of formal peace; it means Arab willingness to let Israel exist on terms which do not leave it vulnerable to future reversals of Arab policy. To Israel, security will require changes in its pre-1967 borders, as well as such additional protection as demilitarization and international guarantees might provide. Israel points out—and cites the recent war in South Asia as an example—that a formal state of peace does not by itself assure security, and that international guarantees are no substitute for the physical conditions and means for security. In the absence of a settlement negotiated by the parties without pre-conditions, Israel continues to hold the territories captured in the 1967 war.

The Arabs, on the other hand, want advance assurance that all the captured territories will be returned. They also seek a just settlement of the grievances of the Palestinians. Some Arab governments have said that they are prepared to accept Israel as it was between 1949 and 1967, but that any enlargement of Israel beyond that is intolerable and implies Israeli expansionist designs. Thus they resist any changes in the pre-war borders. In the meantime, the Arabs feel they cannot allow the situation to become frozen; they stress their determination to struggle as long as Israel holds Arab lands.

This seemingly vicious circle is the objective difficulty which has stood in the way of a settlement. Two approaches to break this impasse have been tried.

—One way has been to attempt to gain all the major mutual assurances required—peace for Israel, the territories for the Arabs—as the first stage in a negotiation. This approach has characterized most of the peace efforts since 1967. Some outside party or group—Ambassador Jarring, the special representative of the UN Secretary General; the Four Powers; or the U.S. and USSR—has tried to develop formulae containing sufficient commitments by each side to give the other hope of achieving what it wants in a negotiation.

—A second route, tried for the first time in 1971, is to begin a process of negotiation without pre-arranged commitments on the fundamental issues. The hope would be that an interim agreement, or the momentum of the bargaining process itself, would create conditions facilitating the more basic settlement.

The Search for a Comprehensive Solution. From 1969 to early 1971, the quest for peace in the Middle East was a search for a formula for a comprehensive political solution. The agreed and accepted framework was, and remains, UN Security Council Resolution 242 of November 22, 1967. The effort went through two distinct phases.

In 1969 the United States first undertook to engage other powers in the negotiating effort. We did not feel that the U.S. alone should assume exclusive responsibility for making and keeping peace in the Middle East. First responsibility, of course, lay with the parties to the conflict. But it was also true that the Soviet Union and other powers with interests in the region would have to accept some responsibility, or else no structure of peace would last. We therefore conducted talks bilaterally with the USSR, and at the UN together with the USSR, Britain, and France, searching for a formula which all sides could accept as a starting point for negotiation. The Soviets turned that effort aside at the end of 1969. Tensions in the area increased sharply in the spring of 1970, with frequent and serious military clashes between Israel and Egypt and stepped-up activity by Palestinian guerrillas.

In the second phase, in response to that renewed tension and to the Soviet Union's apparent loss of interest in further cooperative effort, the U.S. decided by June 1970 that it had no responsible choice but to try on its own to break the spiral of violence. We could not stand by and watch the situation deteriorate into war. We therefore took a major initiative. We invited Israel and the Arabs to "stop shooting and start talking." We proposed a ceasefire and military standstill, to pave the way for a renewed effort at negotiation. The parties accepted our proposal in August. The autumn of 1970, however, was absorbed in dealing with new conflicts—the Soviet-Egyptian violations of the standstill agreement, and the breakdown of domestic order in Jordan and the invasion of Jordan by Syrian forces in September.

In January 1971, Ambassador Jarring finally began discussions with both Israel and Egypt on launching negotiations. He sought assurance from Egypt and Israel that negotiations could proceed on the basis of (a) an Israeli "commitment to withdraw its forces from occupied United Arab Republic territory to the former international boundary between Egypt and the British mandate of Palestine," and (b) an Egyptian "commitment to enter into a peace agreement with Israel." Egypt gave a qualified commitment to this effect. Israel was willing to enter talks looking toward agreement on secure and recognized borders but not to agree in advance to withdraw to the former international border. Ambassador Jarring's effort lost momentum at the end of February.

The Search for an Interim Agreement. Attention then turned to another approach—an interim step toward peace in the form of an agreement for reopening the Suez Canal and a partial withdrawal of Israeli troops. This idea, which had been suggested publicly by both Israeli and Egyptian officials, was explored by the Secretary of State in May 1971 during his trip to the area and through subsequent diplomatic contacts. By autumn we had identified six principal issues in this negotiation:

—The relationship between an interim agreement and an overall settlement;
—Duration of the ceasefire to preserve a tolerable climate for ongoing talks;
—The extent of withdrawal of military forces from the Canal;
—The nature of supervisory arrangements;
—The nature of the Egyptian presence east of the Canal; and
—The use of the Canal by Israel during the period of an interim agreement.

These were not technical questions. To the parties, they went to the heart of the basic issues of security and peace. An interim agreement, for example, is acceptable to Egypt only to the extent that it implies or is linked to final recovery of all the occupied territories. But to Israel an interim agreement is acceptable only if it does not confirm that territories will be restored without negotiation on secure borders. The interim approach, however, offers hope only if it can make progress on concrete steps. But it can make such progress only if it can somehow put aside temporarily the two sides' fundamental differences regarding the final settlement. The more ambitious the proposed formula for an interim agreement, the more it risks foundering over those very differences.

Throughout all these negotiations, each side has sought to influence the other's negotiating position by increasing its own military strength. I have stated on several occasions in the past year that an arms balance is essential to stability but that military equilibrium alone cannot produce peace. The U.S. has demonstrated its commitment to maintaining a military balance that can serve as a foundation for negotiation, but we have also made intensive efforts to start peace negotiations.

We have no other choice. A settlement is in the basic interest of both sides, of the United States, and of world peace.

THE NEED FOR GREAT POWER RESTRAINT

The Arab-Israeli conflict is not in the first instance a U.S.-Soviet dispute, nor can it be settled by the global powers. But it is clear that the posture of the major powers can facilitate or inhibit agreement. Their arms can fuel the conflict; their diplomatic positions can make it more intractable; their exploitation of tension for unilateral gain can foment new crises. Hopes for peace will be undermined if either the U.S. or the USSR feels that the other is either using a negotiation or delaying a settlement to improve its political position at the expense of the other.

In this regard, the Soviet Union's effort to use the Arab-Israeli conflict to perpetuate and expand its own military position in Egypt has been a matter of concern to the United States. The USSR has taken advantage of Egypt's increasing dependence on Soviet military supply to gain the use of naval and air facilities in Egypt. This has serious implications for the stability of the balance of power locally, regionally in the Eastern Mediterranean, and globally. The Atlantic Alliance cannot ignore the possible implications of this move for the stability of the East-West relationship.

This is but one example of the consequences of the failure of the U.S. and USSR to reach some general understanding on the basic conditions of stability in the Middle East. Fundamental interests of the major powers are involved and some measure of disagreement is inevitable. Neither great power would succeed

in helping the parties reach a settlement if its efforts ran counter to the interests of the other, or if the other refused to cooperate.

This was the rationale of our dialogue with the USSR on the Middle East in 1969. Those talks unfortunately foundered because of two developments.

—The Soviet Union tried to draw a final political and territorial blueprint, including final boundaries, instead of helping launch a process of negotiation. We envisioned that boundaries could be drawn in the course of such a process to make them more secure, though it was our view that changes would not be substantial. In the fall of 1969, we reached an understanding with the USSR on a possible procedure for indirect Arab-Israeli talks. In December 1969, the Soviet Union changed its mind on this understanding.

—The Soviet Union applied its energies in early 1970 to a major military buildup in Egypt, which further delayed negotiation. Egypt's "war of attrition" along the Suez Canal had grown in intensity and Israel had responded with air raids deep into Egypt. The Soviets thereupon deployed in Egypt some 80 surface-to-air missile installations, several squadrons of combat aircraft with Soviet pilots, 5,000 missile crew members and technicians, and about 11,-000 other advisers. This buildup continued through the summer of 1970, and Soviet personnel were directly involved in violations of the standstill agreement of August 7. Israel refused to negotiate until the violations were rectified. The U.S. provided Israel with means to cope with this situation. The Soviets since that time have introduced into Egypt SA–6 mobile surface-to-air missiles and the FOXBAT and other advanced MIG aircraft. Most recently they have reintroduced TU–16 bombers equipped with long-range air-to-surface missiles. Much of this equipment was operated and defended exclusively by Soviets.

The Soviet Union has an interest in avoiding major conflict in the Middle East. We hope the Soviet Union understands that it can serve this interest best by restraint in arms supply, refraining from the use of this dispute to enhance its own military position, and encouraging the negotiation of a peace.

ISSUES FOR THE FUTURE

The urgent necessity, of course, is to find a way to an Arab-Israeli settlement.
—At a minimum, the ceasefire must be maintained if the climate for negotiations is to be preserved. Progress in negotiations, in turn, would provide valuable additional incentive for choosing political instead of military solutions.
—The military balance must not be allowed to tempt one side to seek an easy victory or panic the other side into a move of desperation. An end to the arms race, of course, would be the best hope for a stable balance over the longer term.
—Maintaining the military balance, however, is not by itself a policy which can bring peace. The search for an overall Arab-Israeli settlement will continue under Ambassador Jarring's auspices. Our efforts to help the parties achieve an interim agreement will also continue, as long as the parties wish. The interim approach, if it is to succeed, must find a way to make progress on practical and partial aspects of the situation without raising all the contentious issues that obstruct a comprehensive solution.
—The U.S. and the USSR can contribute to the process of settlement by encouraging Arabs and Israelis to begin serious negotiation The great powers also have a responsibility to enhance, not undermine, the basic conditions of stability in the area. Injecting the global strategic rivalry into the region is incompatible with Middle East peace and with detente in U.S.-Soviet relations.

Peace would free the energies and resources of the Middle East for the more fruitful enterprises of economic and social development. The United States looks hopefully toward a new era of constructive and mutually beneficial relations with all the nations and people of the area. The realization of these hopes—theirs and ours—depends on the achievement of peace.

SOUTH ASIA

"I shall never forget the conversation I had with Prime Minister Nehru . . . when I was Vice President. On that trip around the world of 73 days, in 20 countries, I asked every head of government and state what he wanted most for his country. Some said roads; others said industrial development; others said better agricultural development; others said education. Prime Minister Nehru did not answer in that way. He thought a moment, and he said, 'What India needs, what the world needs, is a generation of peace.' "

> Remarks at a Dinner Honoring
> the Prime Minister of India.
> November 4, 1971

The United States made a determined effort throughout 1971 to prevent a war in South Asia and to encourage a political solution. We did not succeed.

A year ago I described the broad objectives of United States policy in South Asia:

"Our aim is a structure of peace and stability within which the people of this region can develop its great potential and their independent vision of the future. Our policy is to help these nations deal with their own problems, and to bring our activity into a stable balance with that of the other major powers with interests in the area."

This structure of regional peace broke down in 1971.

The United States has had an enduring interest in the security, independence, and progress of both India and Pakistan. On my visits to their capitals in the summer of 1969, in my two previous Foreign Policy Reports, and on many other occasions, I have expressed my strong personal interest in warm relations with both countries. There have been fluctuations in our political relationships over the years—from our earliest ties with Pakistan in SEATO and CENTO, to our defense cooperation with India after the 1962 border war with China, to the Nixon Doctrine's posture of balance and restraint. But our fundamental interests and ties have been constant.

—India is a great country, a free and democratic nation, in whose future as a model of progress for the developing world the United States has invested its hopes and resources. India has been by far the principal beneficiary of U.S. development assistance—to the extent of approximately $10 billion since its independence. In Fiscal Year 1971, this Administration provided $540 million, or approximately two-thirds of the world's net development aid to India.

—The United States has long maintained a close tie also with Pakistan. Since its independence we have contributed almost $4 billion to its economic development.

In 1971, these constructive relationships and shared hopes for progress were shaken by war.

UNITED STATES POLICY IN THE EMERGING CRISIS

The crisis began as an internal conflict in Pakistan. Pakistan's elections in December 1970 gave a majority in the National Assembly to the Awami League, a movement seeking substantial autonomy for the Bengalis of East Pakistan. When negotiations between the Government and the League on a formula for autonomy broke down at the end of March 1971, the Government ordered the army to suppress all separatist opposition. The League was banned; its leader, Sheikh Mujibur Rahman, was jailed for treason. As the army's campaign advanced in East Pakistan through spring and summer of 1971, countless thousands were killed, civil administration crumbled, famine threatened, and millions left their homes and fled to India.

The United States did not support or

condone this military action. Immediately, in early April, we ceased issuing and renewing licenses for military shipments to Pakistan, we put a hold on arms that had been committed the year before, and we ceased new commitments for economic development loans. This shut off $35 million worth of arms. Less than $5 million worth of spare parts, already in the pipeline under earlier licenses, was shipped before the pipeline dried up completely by the beginning of November.

The crisis quickly acquired an international character. The flood of refugees was a tremendous burden on India's scarce resources and a threat to political stability in the Indian states into which the refugees poured. With support from India, a guerrilla movement developed in East Pakistan. Both countries moved their military forces to their common borders, and tensions mounted dangerously between them.

It was a foregone conclusion that if war broke out, India would win. But in our view war was neither inevitable nor acceptable.

We realized full well that there were objective limits to what the United States could do. South Asia was a region in which we had no preeminent position of influence. Tensions between Hindus and Moslems, and among the many feuding ethnic groups in this subcontinent of 700 million people, had endured for centuries. Nevertheless, because of our ties with both countries, in 1971 we were the only great power in a position to try to provide a political alternative to a military solution.

There were three levels of the crisis, and the United States addressed them all:
—The humanitarian problem of the Bengali refugees in India and the millions who remained in East Pakis-

tan facing chaos and the threat of famine;
—The problem of political settlement between East and West Pakistan—the basic issue of the crisis;
—The danger of war between India and Pakistan, which grew week by week.

On May 28, I expressed our concerns in letters to the leaders of both Pakistan and India. To President Yahya, I wrote:

"I feel sure you will agree with me that the first essential step is to bring an end to the civil strife and restore peaceful conditions in East Pakistan. Then full-scale efforts can go forward within an international framework to help your government provide relief assistance to the people who need it. . . .

"While this is being done, it will, of course, be essential to ensure that tensions in the region as a whole do not increase to the point of international conflict. I would be less than candid if I did not express my deep concern over the possibility that the situation there might escalate to that danger point. I believe, therefore, that it is absolutely vital for the maintenance of peace in the Subcontinent to restore conditions in East Pakistan conducive to the return of refugees from Indian territory as quickly as possible. I urge you to continue to exercise restraint both along your borders with India and in your general relations with that country. We are counseling the Government of India to do the same.

"It is only in a peaceful atmosphere that you and your administration can make effective progress toward the political accommodation you seek in East Pakistan."

To Prime Minister Gandhi, I wrote:

"We share your government's hope that

peace and stability can be restored in the subcontinent and that all the countries of the area can develop democratic systems of government consistent with their own traditions and history.

"The United States Government has not been a passive observer of these events. We have under active and continuous review two elements of the situation which we regard as particularly urgent: the human suffering and dislocation which has taken place and the basic political cause of this suffering and dislocation.

* * *

"In regard to the basic cause of this human suffering and dislocation, my government has also been active. We have chosen to work primarily through quiet diplomacy, as we have informed your Ambassador and Foreign Minister. We have been discussing with the Government of Pakistan the importance of achieving a peaceful political accommodation and of restoring conditions under which the refugee flow would stop and the refugees would be able to return to their homes. . . .

"I am also deeply concerned that the present situation not develop into a more widespread conflict in South Asia, either as a result of the refugee flow or through actions which might escalate the insurgency which may be developing in East Pakistan. The problems involved in this situation can and should be solved peacefully. As you know, in recent months we have been impressed by the vitality of Indian democracy and the strength of purpose which your government has shown in meeting the complex social and economic problems which India faces. India's friends would be dismayed were this progress to be interrupted by war. As one of Asia's major powers, India has a

special responsibility for maintaining the peace and stability of the region."

Throughout the summer, we refrained from public declarations but continued to express our concerns privately to all parties. It would have served neither Indian nor Bengali interests for us to alienate ourselves from the Government of Pakistan, whose policy and action were at the heart of the problem. This was explained again to the Government of India in July; its response was to express hope that our influence would produce results.

The three problems—the humanitarian, the political, and the danger of war—were obviously interlinked. The tragedy was that they could not all be resolved within the same time-frame. The humanitarian problem was monumental and immediate. A political settlement would take time. The threat of war, tragically, had its own momentum.

We responded to the *humanitarian emergency* with an urgent and massive program of relief, in the framework of a United Nations effort. We were ready to provide $500 million in cash or commodities, nearly twice as much as the rest of the world combined. We committed $91 million through the UN for the support of the nearly ten million refugees in India and $158 million both through the UN and bilaterally for the 60–70 million people in East Pakistan to help avert famine and stem the further outflow of refugees. I asked the Congress for $250 million more, and stated that more food would be provided if needed. We financed the chartering of vessels to transport grain into the interior of East Pakistan. We gave financial and technical support to the whole UN program. Although pockets of need remained, by November province-wide famine had been averted in East

Pakistan. The refugees in India were sustained at least above the level of starvation.

But we knew that *political settlement* between East and West Pakistan was the key to ending the crisis. Our relief program was an effort to gain the needed time for a political process to work. Direct relief to the refugees in India was essential if India were to manage their support; famine in East Pakistan would have made impossible any restoration of normal life or civil peace, redoubling the flood of refugees and further inflaming tensions between Pakistan and India.

It was obvious to us that a lasting political solution could be found only on the basis of some form of autonomy for East Pakistan. Over the summer, in contacts in Washington as well as in their capitals, we made clear to all parties that we favored such a solution. We sought to set in motion a process of accommodation.

We obtained assurance from President Yahya that Sheikh Mujibur Rahman would not be executed. At our urging, Pakistan agreed to an internationalized relief presence in East Pakistan. We urged an amnesty for refugees of all creeds, replacement of the military governor of East Pakistan by a civilian, and a timetable for return to full civilian rule. Pakistan took all these steps. Return to civilian rule was pledged for the end of December and could have increased the chances for a political settlement and the release of Sheikh Mujib. Meanwhile, in August, we established contact with Bengali representatives in Calcutta. By early November, President Yahya told us he was prepared to begin negotiation with any representative of this group not charged with high crimes in Pakistan, or with Awami League leaders still in East Pakistan. In mid-

November, we informed India that we were prepared to promote discussion of an explicit timetable for East Pakistani autonomy.

India was kept fully informed of all these developments at every stage. It indicated little interest. Meanwhile, India expanded its support of the guerrillas, and hostilities escalated along the eastern border.

The United States cannot be certain that the steps it proposed would have brought about a negotiation, or that such a negotiation would have produced a settlement. But it is clear that a political process was in train, which could have been supported and facilitated by all the parties involved if they had wished. This is the basis for the profound disappointment we felt and expressed when war erupted.

We had known the *danger of war* would increase toward the end of 1971, as weather conditions and India's military readiness improved and as the guerrilla forces completed training. In addition to humanitarian and political steps to provide alternatives to war, we sought directly to ease the military confrontation. In contacts in Washington and other capitals, in letters and face-to-face meetings with heads of government, foreign ministers, and ambassadors, we exerted our influence for restraint.

—To the Soviet Union, we made the point repeatedly over the summer that it behooved the two superpowers to be forces for peace. We asked the Soviet Union for its ideas on possible joint action.

—We continued to urge Pakistan to restore normal life in the East, and to put together a program of administrative and political steps that could stem the tide of refugees and lay a basis for a constitutional settlement.

—We told India that we attached the greatest importance to close U.S.-Indian relations, would do all we could to help with the burden of the refugees, but could only regard an Indian resort to armed attack as a tragic mistake. As early as August 11, Secretary Rogers told the Indian Ambassador that the Administration could not continue economic assistance to a nation that started a war.

As the tension along the border intensified in the fall, the United States proposed that both Indian and Pakistani troops pull back from the borders. Pakistan accepted this proposal; India turned it down. UN Secretary General Thant placed his good offices at the disposal of both. Pakistan responded favorably, and in addition suggested the dispatch of UN observers to both sides of the border. India refused the Secretary General's offer, and declined to accept UN observers. The United States then proposed to Pakistan that it pull its forces back from the borders unilaterally, as a first step toward a mutual pullback. Pakistan accepted this idea, provided India would give some assurance that it would eventually reciprocate. India would not.

Time had run out on a peaceful solution. In late November, open war on a broad front erupted between India and Pakistan.

The United States had sought for many years to establish conditions of stability which would have made this war less likely. We had observed an embargo on heavy arms to both sides since their 1965 war over Kashmir. Our military deliveries to both, amounting to only $70 million over six years, were restricted to non-lethal equipment and spare parts for equipment previously supplied. We concentrated instead on assistance for economic development. Our economic aid to India in those six years totaled some $4.2 billion. We provided over $1.3 billion in economic assistance to Pakistan over the period—with an increasing concentration on promoting development in East Pakistan.

Over the six years of our embargo, however, the Soviet Union and its Eastern European allies sharply expanded their military supply to India and furnished over $730 million of arms—including tanks, combat aircraft, artillery, surface-to-air missiles, submarines, missile boats, and other heavy equipment. Our six-year arms embargo had a much greater impact on Pakistan than on India. India's total military procurement after 1965—not a period of increasing tension with China—was more than four times that of Pakistan. While China supplied Pakistan with $133 million in arms over the period, India obtained from abroad almost twice the quantity of arms as Pakistan. Moreover, at the same time India built up its capacity to produce its own heavy arms—a capacity which Pakistan did not have. As a result, the military balance shifted decisively toward India between 1966 and 1971.

THE OUTBREAK AND CONTAINMENT
OF WAR

When war erupted toward the end of November, the world community was close to unanimous that there was one urgent necessity—to stop it.

On December 4, the United States requested an urgent session of the UN Security Council, which voted, 11 to 2, for an immediate ceasefire and withdrawal of foreign forces. The USSR vetoed this and a second resolution soon after. A similar resolution then passed on December 7 in the General Assembly by 104 to 11, with 10 abstentions. Of all the nations of the UN, only the USSR, some of its East European allies, India, and Bhutan opposed it; our position was supported by the overwhelming majority of the nations of the world. The Soviet Union blocked international action until the capture of East Pakistan was a *fait accompli.*

Then, during the week of December 6, we received convincing evidence that India was seriously contemplating the seizure of Pakistan-held portions of Kashmir and the destruction of Pakistan's military forces in the West. We could not ignore this evidence. Nor could we ignore the fact that when we repeatedly asked India and its supporters for clear assurances to the contrary, we did not receive them. We had to take action to prevent a wider war. On December 12 we called for another emergency session of the UN Security Council. We declared:

"With East Pakistan virtually occupied by Indian troops, a continuation of the war would take on increasingly the character of armed attack on the very existence of a member state of the U.N. All permanent members of the Security Council have an obligation to end this threat to world peace on an urgent basis."

The Soviet Union vetoed again. Intensive exchanges took place with the Soviet leaders. A ceasefire, however, was not agreed to until December 17.

The U.S. had two choices when the war broke out.

We could take a stand against the war and try to stop it, or we could maintain a "neutral" position and acquiesce in it. The former course meant strains in our relations with India, as well as as the risk of failure. But the latter course, I concluded, ran even greater risks. Acquiescence had ominous implications for the survival of Pakistan, for the stability of many other countries in the world, for the integrity of international processes for keeping the peace, and for relations among the great powers. These risks were unacceptable.

We did not act out of bias, or in ignorance of India's agony under the burden of the refugees, or in sympathy with Pakistani actions that had generated the crisis. As Ambassador Bush stressed in the Security Council on December 4, the United States "values its close relations with both India and Pakistan." He continued:

"We recognize that a fundamental political accommodation still has not been achieved in East Pakistan. . . . this body cannot accept recourse to force to solve this problem. . . . The very purpose which draws us together here—building a peaceful world— will be thwarted if a situation is accepted in which a government intervenes across its borders in the affairs of another with military forces in violation of the United Nations Charter."

If we had not taken a stand against the war, it would have been prolonged and the likelihood of an attack in the West greatly increased. It was not my view in the first place that war was the solution to a humanitarian problem. The complete disintegration by force of a member state was intolerable and could not be acquiesced in by the United Nations. The war had to be brought to a halt.

The global implications of this war were clear to the world community. The resort to military solutions, if accepted,

301

would only tempt other nations in other delicately poised regions of tension to try the same. The credibility of international efforts to promote or guarantee regional peace in strife-torn regions would be undermined. The danger of war in the Middle East, in particular, would be measurably increased. Restraints would be weakened all around the world.

Internal ethnic conflicts and separatist strains, moreover, are a phenomenon of the contemporary world. India, more than most, has a heavy stake in the principle that such instabilities should not be exploited by other countries through subversion or resort to arms. The alternative is a formula for anarchy. The unanimity of Third World countries against this war was testimony to the universality of this concern.

Beyond this, there were implications for great-power relations.

Soviet policy, I regret to say, seemed to show the same tendency we have witnessed before in the 1967 Middle East war and the 1970 Jordanian crisis—to allow events to boil up toward crisis in the hope of political gain. The Soviet Union assured us that its August treaty of friendship with India was designed to strengthen its influence for peace. Whatever the intent, in retrospect it appears that the treaty, together with new arms deliveries and military consultations, gave India additional assurance of Soviet political support as the crisis mounted.

The United States, under the Nixon Doctrine, has struck a new balance between our international commitments and the increasing self-reliance of our friends; the Soviet Union in the 1970's is projecting a political and military presence without precedent into many new regions of the globe. Over the past three years, we

have sought to encourage constructive trends in U.S.-Soviet relations. It would be dangerous to world peace if our efforts to promote a detente between the superpowers were interpreted as an opportunity for the strategic expansion of Soviet power. If we had failed to take a stand, such an interpretation could only have been encouraged, and the genuine relaxation of tensions we have been seeking could have been jeopardized.

Finally, it was our view that the war in South Asia was bound to have serious implications for the evolution of the policy of the People's Republic of China. That country's attitude toward the global system was certain to be profoundly influenced by its assessment of the principles by which this system was governed— whether force and threat ruled or whether restraint was the international standard.

These were our overwhelming concerns. They underlay our efforts to prevent war and our efforts to stop war when it broke out. They went to the heart of our responsibility as a great power.

WHERE DO WE GO FROM HERE?

The crisis of 1971 transformed South Asia. We enter 1972 acutely aware of the challenges the new conditions present.

Pakistan remains a close friend. Its people face the ordeal of rebuilding the society and economy of a shattered state. The United States stands ready to help. Our concern for the well-being and security of the people of Pakistan does not end with the end of a crisis.

Our relief effort in East Bengal will continue. The authorities face the grim challenge of creating a viable political structure and economy in one of the most impoverished—and now newly devastated—areas of the world. We have never been hostile to Bengali aspirations. Our aid program in the 1960's increasingly concentrated on development in East Bengal. We provided two-thirds of the world's emergency aid to the province in 1971. We would expect other nations to bear a proportionate share of that responsibility in the future, but as the United States strengthens new relationships in Asia, we have no intention of ignoring these 70 million people.

The United States, of course, has a tradition of friendship with India as well as with Pakistan. Our strong interest in Indian democracy and progress is not diminished.

It makes no sense to assume, however, that a country's democratic political system—or its size—requires our automatic agreement with every aspect of its foreign policy. We have our views and concerns in the world, just as India has its own. We disagreed with specific Indian actions in November and December, and we said so.

We did not expect this to be popular in India. Great nations like our two nations, however, do not make their policy on so ephemeral a basis. For this reason, we could not accept the argument that our criticism would drive India into the arms of the Soviet Union. India itself, we knew, had the strongest interest of all in its own democracy and nonalignment. And India and the Soviet Union already had a political tie of a kind that the U.S. would not attempt to match. This tie—inherent in the expanding Soviet-Indian military supply relationship after 1965—originated long in advance of the November war, the August treaty of friendship, our July China initiative, or the March crisis in Pakistan. When the August treaty was signed, both sides told us that it had been in preparation for more than two years. Beyond this, in the 1971 crisis, the Soviet Union was willing to veto UN action and to make military moves to deter China on India's behalf. For the United States to compete with the Soviet Union in fueling an arms race, obstructing UN efforts to stop a war, and threatening China, was out of the question.

We are prepared now for a serious dialogue with India on the future of our relations. We look forward to a fruitful discussion. This will depend not on an identity of policies, but on respect for each other's views and concerns. This should go both ways.

Just as the success of Indian democracy and progress is important to us, we also have a continuing interest in India's independence and nonalignment. Thus our political as well as our economic relationship will naturally be the subject of our dialogue. If India has an interest in maintaining balanced relationships with all major powers, we are prepared to respond constructively. Of interest to us also will be the posture that South Asia's most powerful country now adopts toward its neighbors on the subcontinent.

I know that India will have its own issues to add to the agenda. India's basic policy choices are India's to make. We both, nevertheless, have an interest in finding common ground. We can search out ways of transcending our recent differences and resuming our traditionally close relationship.

What will be the role of the great powers in the subcontinent's future? The 1971 crisis was bound to affect great-power relations. After my July 15 Peking summit announcement, and also during the diplomacy of the South Asian crisis, there was fanciful speculation of a U.S.-

Chinese alignment. There is no such alignment; neither of my summit meetings is directed against any other nation. And there were ample opportunities for the Soviet Union to help prevent the Pakistani political conflict from being turned into an international war.

A more constructive approach to great-power relations in South Asia—and elsewhere—will be one of the goals I hope to further in my discussions in both Peking and Moscow.

A tragic irony of 1971 was that the conflict in South Asia erupted against a background of major developments, global and regional, which had offered unprecedented hope:

—Globally, we could see the beginnings of a new relationship between the United States and the People's Republic of China; concrete progress on important issues in U.S.-Soviet relations; a maturing relationship between the U.S. and East Asia as the Nixon Doctrine took effect and the U.S. sharply reduced its military involvement in Vietnam; the increasing contribution of Japan in Asian affairs; and efforts among industrialized nations to create new economic relationships increasing the trade opportunities of the developing world.

—Regionally, there were breakthroughs in economic development. The "Green Revolution" in agriculture was laying the basis for industrial development and steady growth. Trade earnings were financing an increasing proportion of development needs, strengthening economic and political self-reliance.

Our purpose now will be to recapture the momentum of these positive developments. The 700 million people of the sub-continent deserve a better future than the tragedy of 1971 seemed to portend. It is for them to fashion their own vision of such a future. The world has an interest in the regional peace and stability which are the preconditions for their achieving it.

PART V: THE IMPERATIVE OF SECURITY

—Strategic Policy and Forces
—General Purposes Forces
—Security Assistance
—Arms Control

ASSURING NATIONAL SECURITY

"We do not seek power as an end in itself. We seek power adequate to our purpose, and our purpose is peace."

> Address To The
> Naval Officer Candidate School
> March 12, 1971

National security is the paramount responsibility of any American President. There has always been an essential continuity between administrations in meeting this responsibility. Just as long range decisions of previous Presidents have shaped present capabilities, the choices I make today will be crucial to our future security.

Security issues in the 1970's are more complex than ever before.

—The fundamental requirements for our security are not as obvious today as they were in the earlier bipolar era when threats were less complex.

—Many citizens and legislators are understandably concerned over the high cost of modern weapons systems, and over the size of the U.S. share of the heavy security burdens borne by us and our increasingly prosperous allies.

—The Vietnam experience has left some Americans skeptical concerning defense issues.

—The current strategic balance with the Soviet Union creates new conditions which could provide additional incentives for negotiations on limiting armaments, but could also lead to localized conflicts below the level of strategic nuclear war.

To meet our security requirements under the Nixon Doctrine and a national strategy of realistic deterrence, we must harmonize our essential strategic objectives, our general defense posture, and our foreign policy requirements with the resources available to meet our security and domestic needs. Our military program must not absorb resources beyond those essential to meet foreseeable dangers. Nevertheless, I recognize that there is a prudent minimum below which we cannot go without jeopardizing the nation's fundamental security interests. If this were allowed to happen, we would lose control over our destiny both at home and abroad.

In this Administration, we have been able, for the first time in twenty years, to spend more on domestic social programs than on defense. The total defense budget is today a smaller portion of the Federal Budget and a smaller portion of our Gross National Product than at any time since the Korean War. Measured in terms of constant dollars our defense spending is already down to the pre-Vietnam War level. It will remain so next year, even though overall defense spending will be increased in order to maintain our security at an adequate level.

American strength is essential if we are to move from an era of confrontation toward an era of negotiation. As the world's strongest power, this nation has important responsibilities to its friends as well as unique opportunities for improving global stability. American weakness would make no contribution to peace. On the contrary, it would undermine prospects for peace.

We have taken a number of steps to nurture an international climate in which progress in arms control is possible. In the past year we have moved forward in bilateral discussions with the Soviet Union on strategic arms limitations and in multilateral efforts to provide a firm basis for control of both nuclear and conventional weapons. We have made important advances toward achieving strategic stability, but there also have been disturbing developments. While engaged in the strategic arms negotiations we have witnessed a continuing Soviet buildup in nearly every major category of military power.

An agreement to limit strategic weapons would be an unprecedented achievement. Our goal is to stabilize the strategic balance through mutual restraint and agreements which provide no unilateral advantage. We recognize that only a mutually designed balance of strategic armaments can establish a shared basis for security. On the other hand, if the Soviet Union attempts to extend its strategic buildup beyond equality, the United States will have no choice but to initiate compensating actions.

The new strategic environment increases the importance of maintaining a full range of credible options to meet our international commitments and the requirements of our own defense. With USSR general purpose forces expanding, modernizing, and projecting Soviet power in new areas of the globe, we have taken steps to strengthen American and allied capabilities.

In ensuring the continuing viability of our national defense, we are establishing a sound basis for our strategic and general purpose forces that is compatible with our arms control efforts, our political objectives, and the potential threats to our security.

The chapters that follow set forth our defense policies and the challenges we face.

STRATEGIC POLICY AND FORCES

"We must be more resourceful than ever in the pursuit of peace, and at the same time more determined than ever in the maintenance of our defenses. For even as many things are changing in the world of the 1970s, one fact remains: American strength is the keystone in the structure of peace."

Address to the
U.S. Military Academy
May 29, 1971

Of the many elements that constitute military power in the nuclear age, strategic nuclear forces are most crucial. Strategic forces:

—Are the primary deterrent to nuclear attacks against the United States or its allies;

—Compel an aggressor contemplating less than all-out attacks to recognize the unacceptable risk of escalation; and

—Reduce the likelihood of intimidation or coercion of the U.S. or its allies.

When this Administration took office, the United States for the first time faced the prospect of a rough parity with the USSR in strategic forces. While the Soviet Union had moved forward with great energy, the U.S. had held its strategic missile launchers at existing levels for nearly four years.

Assessing the implications of the emerging balance was an urgent task. Rather than simply adding up the relative size or capabilities of Soviet and American strategic forces, we had to address broader underlying questions.

—Would parity in strategic power increase or decrease the probability of nuclear war?

—Would the continuing momentum of Soviet strategic programs give them political advantages?

—What actually were the new capabilities of our adversaries? What trends in deployments and doctrines were implicit? What were their strategic alternatives?

Only by examining such questions could we make rational decisions on the size and composition of American strategic forces and evaluate the alternative postures we might adopt in the future.

A fundamental factor in determining the quantitative and qualitative characteristics of our strategic posture was the development of a doctrine for employment of these forces in the environment of the 1970's. In the 1950's, when the U.S. had a near monopoly in strategic nuclear forces, it was felt that deterrence could be maintained by a doctrine of all-out massive response.

As Soviet strategic capabilities developed early in the last decade, a more flexible range of responses was believed necessary. Emphasis was placed on the ability to destroy selectively an enemy's military forces while sparing the civilian population by withholding attacks against cities.

The variety and size of Soviet strategic forces increased further during the last Administration and complicated the American problem of destroying Soviet offensive forces remaining after a Soviet first strike. The earlier doctrines no longer seemed credible, and the doctrine of "assured destruction" gained wide acceptance. Under this concept, deterrence was believed guaranteed by maintaining the capability to destroy a sizable percentage of an adversary's industrial capacity and population even following an all-out attack on our own strategic forces. Under this theory, a buildup of the other side's strategic forces was not considered critical as long as we maintained enough invulnerable forces.

After reviewing various concepts for our strategic forces, I decided that our forces should be based on a doctrine of "strategic sufficiency" which takes into account political factors and a broader set of military factors than did the "assured destruction" concept. In last year's Report I described this doctrine as follows:

"In its narrow military sense, it means enough force to inflict a level of damage on a potential aggressor sufficient to deter him from attacking. Sole reliance on a 'launch-on-warning' strategy, sometimes suggested by those who would give less weight to the protection of our forces, would force us to live at the edge of a precipice and deny us the flexibility we wish to preserve.

"In its broader political sense, sufficiency means the maintenance of forces adequate to prevent us and our allies from being coerced. Thus the relationship between our strategic forces and those of the Soviet Union must be such that our ability and resolve to protect our vital security interests will not be underestimated."

Sufficiency requires forces that are adequate in quantity and have the qualitative characteristics to maintain a stable strategic balance despite technological change. Capabilities of both the U.S. and USSR have reached a point where our programs need not be driven by fear of minor quantitative imbalances. The Soviet Union cannot be permitted, however, to establish a significant numerical advantage in overall offensive and defensive forces.

Our forces must be maintained at a level sufficient to make it clear that even an all-out surprise attack on the United States by the USSR would not cripple our capability to retaliate. Our forces must also be capable of flexible application. A simple "assured destruction" doctrine does not meet our present requirements for a flexible range of strategic options. No President should be left with only one strategic course of action, particularly that of ordering the mass destruction of enemy civilians and facilities. Given the range of possible political-military situations which could conceivably confront us, our strategic policy should not be based solely on a capability of inflicting urban and industrial damage presumed to be beyond the level an adversary would accept. We must be able to respond at levels appropriate to the situation. This problem will be the subject of continuing study.

Faced with a potential Soviet threat to the sufficiency of our forces, I directed in the first year of my Administration:

—Initial deployments of an anti-ballistic missile system.

—Research on new long range submarine-launched ballistic missile systems.

—The equipping of existing missiles

with multiple warheads that could attack a number of targets.

—The addition of air-to-surface missiles to strategic bombers for better penetration of air defenses and the development of an improved strategic bomber.

—Continued research and development programs to improve the quality of our forces and to ensure that advances in technology would not place us in a disadvantageous position.

Our actions have been designed primarily to guarantee the continuing survivability of our retaliatory forces. These improvements in our existing forces and the development of new programs are not incompatible with negotiations to limit strategic arms. They complement the broad effort of this Administration to guarantee the security of the United States while moving toward a structure of greater international stability and restraint. We have been conscious of the opportunities provided in the Strategic Arms Limitation Talks to add a vital dimension of stability to our competitive relationship with the USSR.

THE STRATEGIC BALANCE—1972

Last year there were uncertainties in our appraisal of Soviet strategic forces. Some of these uncertainties have now been removed, unfortunately not in a reassuring way. Others remain. At this time last year it appeared that the Soviets might have slowed and perhaps ceased deployment of land-based strategic missiles. It was hoped that this was an indication of self-restraint. It was not. Since that time the overall Soviet strategic program has continued to move ahead.

—The pause in construction of ICBM silos was apparently related to the introduction of major improvements or the deployment of a totally new missile system. There is evidence that two new or greatly modified ICBM systems are being developed.

—Nearly 100 new ICBM silos are being constructed. Some of these silos are for large modern missiles such as the SS–9, which, because of their warhead size and potential accuracy, could directly threaten our land-based ICBMs.

—The multiple warhead version of a second ICBM system has already been extensively tested.

—An improved submarine-launched ballistic missile is also being perfected, and ballistic missile submarine production has increased significantly. The Soviet Union now has operational or under construction more modern ballistic missile submarines than does the United States. In the near future the USSR will have achieved parity in nuclear-powered ballistic missile submarines while additionally maintaining some 100 SLBM launchers on older submarines.

—A new Soviet bomber is being flight tested.

—ABM construction has resumed around Moscow; new types of ABM radars and ballistic missile interceptor systems are being tested.

In short, in virtually every category of strategic offensive and defensive weapons the Soviet Union has continued to improve its capability.

These collective developments raise serious questions concerning Soviet objectives. The Soviet Union is continuing to create strategic capabilities beyond a level which by any reasonable standard already seems sufficient. It is therefore inevitable that we ask whether the Soviet Union seeks the numbers and types of forces needed to attack and destroy vital elements of our own strategic forces.

The following table illustrates the relative growth of operational Soviet strategic missile forces.

Operational U.S. and USSR Missile Launchers

	Mid-1965	End 1969	End 1970	End 1971
ICBMs				
U.S.........	934	1,054	1,054	1,054
USSR.......	224	1,190	1,440	1,520
SLBMs				
U.S.........	464	656	656	656
USSR.......	107	240	350	500

We cannot know the intentions of the Soviet leadership, but we must assume that this trend reflects a calculated policy within the framework of an overall strategic rationale. While it seems unlikely that the Soviet Union would actually plan to use these forces in an all-out manner, their existence is a disturbing reality which has compelled me to request the funding of additional offsetting measures.

Our forces are currently sufficient, but we have acted with great restraint. The number of missile launchers in the U.S. strategic force has not changed for five years. We have improved the retaliatory capability of each missile with added warheads, but we have not provided our missiles with the combined numbers, accuracy and warhead yield necessary to threaten Soviet forces with a disarming strike. The Soviets have the technical capability to develop similarly sophisticated systems but with greater warhead yields and consequently greater capability for a disarming strike.

We are approaching a crucial turning point in our strategic arms programs. If the Soviet Union continues to expand strategic forces, compensating U.S. programs will be mandatory. The preferable alternative would be a combination of mutual restraint and an agreement in SALT. But under no circumstances will I permit the further erosion of the strategic balance with the USSR. I am confident that the Congress shares these sentiments.

THE FORCES FOR SUFFICIENCY

As Soviet strategic forces have developed over the past three years, we have taken actions to preserve the sufficiency of our forces. The primary objective of these improvements has been to decrease the potential vulnerability of our deterrent forces. Given the size and sophistication of Soviet weapons, arguments based on arithmetical computations that our destructive capability is excessive are simplistic. We must retain the capability to deter or to retaliate if necessary, even if one element or substantial portions of our mix of bombers, land-based ICBMs, and submarine-launched missiles become vulnerable. At the same time we have exercised restraint consistent with stability and the discussions in SALT.

Thus, in light of growing Soviet strategic capabilities, we have taken certain measured steps to strengthen our defensive position by improving the prospects for survival of our forces.

—We have continued to increase the hardness of our Minuteman ICBM silos, making them less vulnerable to attack. This contributes to stability by decreasing the prospect of a successful disarming attack by a potential aggressor.

309

—We are continuing our program to put multiple independently targetable warheads on strategic missiles. This ensures a credible capability to retaliate. With these warheads, the missiles which survive an initial attack will still be able to strike large numbers of targets and complicate an enemy's defensive problems. They also serve as insurance against increasingly sophisticated missile defenses.

—We are continuing development of a new manned bomber to replace the aging B–52s. This is an important element in the mix of retaliatory forces which provides assurance against technological breakthroughs and complicates an enemy's offensive and defensive problems. We are also improving penetration aids for our strategic bomber force.

—We are decreasing the time it takes our bomber force to leave the ground on warning of an attack. We also are relocating these bombers to bases further from the coast to reduce the threat from Soviet ballistic missile submarines.

—We are designing a new long range submarine-launched missile system (ULMS—Undersea Long Range Missile System). This system will allow our submarines to operate in a larger ocean area where they will be even less vulnerable to enemy anti-submarine forces. The first version of this missile can be placed in existing submarines. We are also initiating a program to build additional missile submarines. This is particularly important at a time of increasing threat to our land-based missiles.

—We are continuing an active research program to ensure the survivability of our forces over the long term.

—We are prepared to take additional actions to increase quickly the capabilities of our strategic forces should unabated Soviet deployments continue.

In considering the overall strategic balance, our ballistic missile submarine force currently provides a compensating factor. Although the Soviet sea-based ballistic missile force is approaching numerical parity, our missiles have longer range and are being equipped with multiple independently targetable warheads. Moreover, our new submarines are now superior in quality.

Thus our forces meet the test of sufficiency.

BALLISTIC MISSILE DEFENSE

In announcing the Safeguard ABM program, I promised to review each phase of the deployment to ensure that we were doing no more than the existing threat required. We have measured progress of the program against the background of SALT, our strategic policy, changes in Soviet capabilities, and the development of Chinese forces.

—Soviet strategic forces, even at current levels, have the potential of threatening our land-based ICBMs if the Soviets choose to make certain qualitative improvements. They have the necessary technological base.

—The Chinese are continuing to develop a strategic offensive capability.

—The possibility of accidental attacks remains.

These facts confirm the wisdom of the decision to begin Safeguard deployment. However, we may soon complete a

SALT agreement with the USSR which will limit ABM deployments. From the beginning of SALT negotiations it has been implicit that we would be willing to forego extensive ABM protection in return for the greater stability offered by an equitable limit on both offensive and defensive strategic forces. In deploying Safeguard we have taken only those steps that are essential while preserving the option for an agreement on ABM limitations. These actions have given the Soviet Union an incentive for concluding an agreement controlling defensive deployments. Our future actions will continue to reflect progress made in SALT.

In our decisions on deployments of strategic systems, on qualitative improvements and on SALT, our objective has been to act with restraint while preserving the security of the United States and its allies. Our present strategic forces are sufficient and we are moving toward an agreement which should stabilize the strategic balance and foreclose future rounds of arms competition. If, however, important systems are not constrained by agreements and the Soviet Union continues to build up its strategic forces, I will continue to take actions necessary to protect the national security.

GENERAL PURPOSE FORCES

"The strength that commands respect is the only foundation on which peace among nations can ever be built."

> Remarks to the
> VFW Convention at Dallas
> August 19, 1971

At no other time in the nuclear era has it been so essential to maintain a full range of credible options for defending Ameri-can interests. Approaching strategic parity with the Soviet Union and the developing Chinese nuclear capability may have reduced the range of conflicts deterred by strategic forces alone. If, in these circumstances, allied general purpose forces are weak, aggression by conventional means or attempts at political coercion might seem more inviting.

In 1969 we undertook a comprehensive assessment of military requirements for the 1970's. We concluded that general purpose forces must be capable of meeting a major threat to American and allied interests in Europe or Asia and of simultaneously coping with a minor contingency elsewhere. The prospect of a two-front coordinated attack in Europe and Asia was considered remote because of the risks of nuclear war and the improbability of Sino-Soviet cooperation. The likelihood of that cooperation has now receded even further.

Nevertheless, the presence of potentially hostile countries in both Asia and Europe requires counterposing allied forces capable of maintaining a successful defense in either theater until reinforced.

Approaching strategic parity also means that the probability of challenges below the level of full-scale nuclear or conventional war has increased. During this Administration, the United States has been involved in crises in the Middle East, Asia, and elsewhere. The Jordanian crisis of 1970 demonstrated the importance of being able to employ forces to stabilize a local situation involving great power interests.

The emerging Soviet capability to apply military leverage in remote areas has further underlined the need for countervailing American forces. In the first years of this decade there have been:

—Soviet treaties with Egypt and India and Soviet claims to be protecting the interests of an increasing number of nations;

—Soviet pilots in Egypt in combat against Israeli aircraft, the deployment of a sophisticated air defense system to Egypt, and the use of Egyptian airfields for Soviet missions; and

—Increased Soviet naval presence in the Mediterranean, the Indian Ocean and the Western Hemisphere, particularly in the Caribbean.

Obviously, even with this expanding Soviet capability to combine military with economic and political pressures, not all potential challenges to our interests involve the USSR or other major powers directly. The need for American military forces in situations not involving other nuclear powers should lessen over time with the success of our cooperative efforts under the Nixon Doctrine to strengthen allied national and regional defense forces.

SHAPING OUR COMMON DEFENSE

Drawing on studies completed in the first years of the Administration, our efforts in 1971 concentrated on designing U.S. forces and encouraging development of allied forces to meet more effectively the threats to security in Europe, Asia, and other areas of the world.

In *Europe* we and our allies have undertaken new initiatives to strengthen NATO. These include:

—Fortifying NATO defenses by constructing aircraft shelters, improving NATO troop mobility, increasing defenses against armored attack, and strengthening allied naval forces.

—Utilizing men in command and support functions more effectively.

—Improving allied reserve force readiness, mobilization capabilities, and American ability to lift forces to Europe rapidly in a crisis.

We have also continued consultations on arrangements to reduce balance of payments and other costs of maintaining U.S. forces in Europe. These developments are discussed in this Report's chapter on Europe.

This year our allies will continue to implement their $1 billion five-year European Defense Improvements Program which will further strengthen NATO air defense, communications, mobilization, armor, anti-tank, and naval capabilities. In addition, our NATO allies are spending more than $3 billion in 1972 for major military equipment which will further modernize their forces.

We will continue to maintain forces in Europe that provide a credible capability to defend our interests.

In 1971 we also concentrated on a thorough analysis of possible threats, necessary improvements in allied defenses, and those American forces required to support our *Asian* strategy in this decade. The review covered the full range of U.S. force options. The following are some preliminary conclusions.

—The U.S. nuclear shield will be maintained to protect our Asian allies from attack or coercion by a nuclear power.

—It will continue to be essential to maintain strong forward American deployments, while also providing appropriate military and economic assistance.

—Allied military capabilities, especially in ground forces, are expected to improve substantially, making possible some further adjustments in U.S. deployments.

—Subversion and guerrilla warfare remain a potent danger to our friends in Asia. While the threat should be dealt with primarily by indigenous forces, we must continue to provide military and economic assistance to supplement local efforts.

Thus, while helping our Asian friends improve their forces, we will maintain our own peacetime land, sea, and air deployments in Asia at a level which provides assurance to our allies of continuing U.S. support and demonstrates our ability and determination to meet our commitments.

In addition to examining our continuing political and military requirements in Europe and Asia, we have made similar studies of other areas of the world. In the process we have assessed potential challenges to our interests. We are designing flexible general purpose forces which will permit us to respond as necessary to threats to those interests.

EMERGING FORCE STRUCTURE

Having assessed the fundamental elements of a rational strategy for the 1970's within the framework of the Nixon Doctrine, we have been able to refine planning for forces to meet post-Vietnam requirements. Alternative force structures have been examined both in terms of capabilities to carry out missions and in terms of cost implications. We have also reviewed tactical nuclear weapons planning for both Europe and Asia. In addition, a number of specific issues concerning the composition of our forces have been addressed.

—With regard to *land forces,* the major issue in the Fiscal Year 1973 program was the number of Army divisions necessary to support our post-Vietnam strategy. After reviewing the effect on allied capabilities in Europe and Asia of an Army ranging between 11 and 14 divisions, I concluded that 13 U.S. Army divisions were needed to support NATO effectively and to retain the capability to reinforce adequately our Asian allies.

Another issue concerned the best combination of armored/mechanized divisions, most essential to the defense of NATO, and lighter divisions which are needed in both NATO and Asia. We decided on a mix of 7⅔ armored/mechanized divisions and 5⅓ infantry, airborne, and airmobile divisions.

—The review of *naval* requirements considered alternative levels of fleet deployments including the specific numbers of aircraft carriers, escorts, submarines, and support ships needed to control the seas in a major conflict and meet our commitments throughout the globe. We considered aircraft carrier levels ranging from 13 to 17. In view of the need to keep carriers continuously in the Atlantic, Mediterranean and Pacific, and also available for a range of other contingencies, I concluded that 16 carriers would be required in FY 1973.

—We will retain the flexibility and mobility provided by our three *Marine Corps* divisions and three air wings by maintaining them in a high state of readiness.

—The effectiveness of our *tactical air force* in meeting defense commitments is measured not only by the numbers of aircraft available, but by the level of pilot proficiency and equipment readiness. After considering a range of aircraft levels and degrees of readiness we found that our requirements to deter or to respond immediately to attacks could best be met by maintaining about 22 Air Force wings at a high state of readiness.

Because of the priority of Vietnam requirements, some essential modernization programs have been deferred. We cannot relinquish the essential advantage which superior equipment affords. Accordingly, we are putting renewed emphasis on modernizing our forces.

The military command structure must also be kept under review to assure that it reflects the changing character and disposition of our forces. Last year I approved certain changes, proposed by the Secretary of Defense, designed to streamline the command organization and to bring theater responsibilities more in line with requirements of the 1970's. The most significant step was the disestablishment of the U.S. Strike Command which was responsible both for a geographical area, now assigned to other commands, and for training of certain land and air forces. The Readiness Command was created to consolidate control of the strategic reserve of combat units based in the United States ready to reinforce other commands.

With these improvements, the force posture we have designed will continue to meet the needs of our national strategy.

MANAGING DEFENSE RESOURCES

In order to realize the full effectiveness of our forces we must assure that all resources provided for defense are efficiently employed. The need to improve management practices is especially acute in the areas of manpower and weapons development. Personnel costs now absorb over half of the defense budget; by the middle of this decade these costs may rise to well over 60 percent. At the same time, the costs of new weapons systems have generally been two to three times the costs of those they replace, largely due to increasing complexity. The combination of these two effects may by the mid-1970's seriously limit our ability to finance forces to meet our anticipated security requirements. The imaginative and forceful management initiatives now being undertaken by the Secretary of Defense will continue to provide the key to solving these problems.

In the manpower area we have concentrated on efforts to eliminate the draft by attracting more volunteers with increased pay and other financial benefits. These measures have temporarily contributed to the increase in personnel costs. But the success of these programs and the reduction of our forces in Vietnam have produced significantly lower draft levels. Last year we drafted only one-third as many men as were drafted in the year before I took office.

We plan to eliminate draft calls altogether by July 1973. To reach that goal there are problems which must be resolved.

—We need to enlist men with the ability to operate and repair the sophisticated weaponry of modern warfare.

—We must enhance the attractiveness of service careers while building a disciplined and effective force.

I am confident that we will solve these problems and that we will be able to end reliance on the draft without sacrificing military readiness.

Nothing will be more essential to the maintenance of our strength in the remainder of the 1970's than the quality and dedication of the men who choose a military career. In order to attract men who meet the highest standards, we must strengthen the vitality of the armed forces. This is the responsibility of every service. We must also bolster respect for the military profession in our society. This is the responsibility of every citizen.

SECURITY ASSISTANCE

"These security assistance programs . . . critically affect our ability to meet our bilateral and collective security commitments. They are central to the achievement of major objectives of U.S. national security and foreign policy."

> Message to Congress on the
> U.S. Foreign Assistance Program
> April 21, 1971

Security assistance is a cornerstone of our foreign policy and of Free World security, as it has been ever since the early days of the Second World War. Our programs have adapted to changing circumstances, but our purpose has remained steadfast—to assist those willing to work for peace and progress. Our friends are demonstrating the ability and willingness to shoulder a larger share of the common effort, but their material resources frequently are inadequate. They do not seek American forces; they do ask for the equipment and supplies which they themselves cannot provide.

In the first of these foreign policy statements two years ago I spoke of three basic principles of our foreign policy: partnership, strength, and a willingness to nego-

tiate. It was with these principles in mind that in July 1969, at Guam, I enunciated the policy which has come to be known as the Nixon Doctrine. The essence of this approach is that the U.S. will fulfill its commitments, while looking to its friends and allies to play a greater role in providing for their own defense.

The effectiveness of local deterrence and defense is, in the last analysis, measured by the will and effort of the threatened country. For unless a country mobilizes its own psychological, human, and material resources, our assistance cannot be effective. Given that will and effort, however, our assistance can make the critical difference—to the security of the threatened nation and to world stability and peace. This is especially significant in areas where the United States is reducing its military presence. Part of the role of deterrence and defense which our forces have long filled is now being assumed by local or regional forces. But to do so, they must have our help.

Some of our friends do not have resources sufficient for both development and defense. They face a dilemma: to devote scarce resources to defense and thereby sacrifice development progress— or to emphasize economic development, hoping their security will not be threatened or that others will defend them. Our assistance can help these countries through this difficult stage until their own hard work and determination—supplemented by our economic and security aid—enable them to assume the costs of both dependable defense and steady development. To encourage others to make such efforts while refusing to provide the resources they require to stand on their own would be both illogical and self-defeating. The purpose of U.S. security assistance, therefore, is to ease and to speed the transition to greater national self-reliance.

We know from experience that such a transition is possible. A number of countries which were once dependent on large amounts of U.S. aid have achieved or are nearing self-reliance. Others are progressing toward that goal, but need our support if they are to reach it in safety.

We know also that until other nations are more self-reliant, our common objectives of partnership, strength, and international cooperation cannot be realized. If both we and our friends are to be secure, we must have a program of action. If we are to ask others to assume an increasing share of their own and free world defense, then we must share the skills, equipment and technology which will allow them to share the burden.

—Cambodia is a striking example. The Cambodian people have rallied to resist the occupation of their homeland by a determined and stronger enemy. Assisted with U.S. equipment, the Cambodian Army has grown from 30,000 to approximately 200,-000 within less than 24 months. They have greatly complicated the enemy's efforts to supply its forces operating against South Vietnam; and they have strengthened their cooperation with their neighbors as they seek to meet the common threat.

—The Republic of Korea prospers with a flourishing economy and a high rate of growth. Behind the shield provided by its own forces and the United Nations command, U.S. forces have been reduced and no longer man major defenses along the DMZ. Our military assistance program is making it possible for Korea to complete the modernization of its forces which is essential if Korea is to provide for its own defense.

Security assistance also provides a means whereby we can influence others to limit arms races. Some maintain that if we refused to provide military assistance or to sell weapons, arms competition would diminish in many areas. If we were the only source of modern weapons, that argument would be valid. But other countries which are sources of military arms have not shown restraint. If we refuse military assistance programs, we forsake the opportunity such programs afford to counsel moderation in arms acquisition. Countries which perceive threats to their security can and do acquire the weapons they want elsewhere.

Our security assistance, like our other programs, reflects our vision of a future structure of peace in a world in which independent states cooperate for mutual benefit. Our friends can be assured that we will continue to help them meet their defense needs through a well managed and flexible security assistance program.

ARMS CONTROL

"I decided early in the Administration that we should seek to maintain our security whenever possible through cooperative efforts with other nations at the lowest possible level of uncertainty, cost, and potential violence."

> U.S. Foreign Policy for the 1970's
> Report to the Congress
> February 18, 1970

The nuclear era places on the two preponderant powers a unique responsibility to explore means of limiting military competition. Never before have weapons so fundamental to national security become the subject of negotiations between competing powers. Agreement to limit strategic nuclear weapons would be an unprecedented achievement not only in the field of arms control, but also in the evolution of political relations.

The limitation of armaments is an essential element in the larger political process of building a more stable international system. By contributing to international stability and restraint, arms control agreements can provide a greater measure of security than could be achieved by relying solely on military power. A mutual willingness to curb arms competition indicates constructive intentions in political as well as strategic areas. Progress in controlling arms can reinforce progress in a much wider area of international relations.

This Administration has made a determined effort to negotiate equitable strategic arms agreements with the Soviet Union. Our efforts at arms control, moreover, have not been confined to bilateral strategic negotiations, but have encompassed a variety of weapons and international forums. The process of developing agreements has proceeded in three separate but related areas:

—First, and of overriding importance, has been the effort to control strategic arms competition between the United States and the Soviet Union.

—Second, in regions where major powers confront each other, as in Central Europe, we have explored means for establishing a more stable military balance at reduced force levels.

—Finally, on the broad international front, arms control measures such as elimination of biological and toxin weapons and restrictions on the deployment of nuclear weapons in vari-

ous environments have been undertaken with the participation of nuclear and non-nuclear powers.

In each of these areas, the United States has taken important initiatives in the interest of international stability and peace. Three years of intense efforts have produced significant progress.

STRATEGIC ARMS LIMITATION
TALKS (SALT)

From the beginning of this Administration, issues related to strategic arms limitations have been given the highest priority. I recognized that even a modest success in such an endeavor could break the pattern of seemingly endless and increasingly dangerous competition.

In order to have maximum flexibility in negotiations with the Soviet Union, we began our preparations for strategic arms talks with a systematic examination of the issues. By analyzing every combination of weapons systems that might conceivably be subject to limitation and by examining measures that could be used to verify compliance in any agreement, we developed a sound basis for moving negotiations in the direction most likely to lead to an equitable agreement. In the ensuing discussions with the Soviet Union, we were determined not to be restricted to a fixed position which would have to be renegotiated internally every time there was a change of position. It was anticipated that our new approach might forestall the early stalemates which had characterized previous arms control negotiations when opening positions inevitably differed.

We recognized that negotiations would be especially complicated because of the difficulty of establishing equivalence between Soviet and American weapon systems that differed not only in number but in characteristics and capabilities. Moreover, both nations were at different stages in key weapons programs.

—The Soviet intercontinental ballistic missile arsenal had continued to grow while the U.S. had ceased deployment of ICBMs. In addition, American ICBMs consisted almost entirely of medium size missiles, while the USSR had deployed a variety of sizes. One Soviet system, the SS–9 ICBM, carried a much larger warhead and had no American counterpart. Although U.S. missiles were smaller, they were more sophisticated and had a capability for multiple independently targeted warheads. The larger Soviet missiles, however, had the capacity to carry a greater number of these warheads if developed along lines similar to our program.

—The United States had not built ballistic missile submarines since 1967; the Soviet program, although begun later, was expanding at an accelerated rate in 1969.

—In 1964 the USSR began deploying an anti-ballistic missile system to protect its capital; our Safeguard ABM program, begun only in 1969, was designed to protect our land-based retaliatory forces, to defend against attacks by a small number of missiles, and to protect against an accidental attack.

Thus, even an agreement in principle to limit certain strategic systems would have left open major questions of defining precise limits without creating an advantage for one side.

Despite these problems, the approaching strategic parity provided an opportunity to achieve an overall agreement that would yield no unilateral advantage and could contribute to a more stable strategic environment. For the first time it was possible to conceive of agreements reflecting a genuine balance.

Meticulous preparations enabled us to begin negotiations in November 1969 with an understanding of the full range of issues, and to move efficiently from preliminary explorations of strategic principles to concrete proposals.

By late 1970, several phases of negotiations had isolated the key differences.

—We disagreed on the kinds of weapons systems that would be limited in an agreement. The U.S. preferred to cover all major strategic systems— land and sea-based ballistic missiles, heavy bombers, and anti-ballistic missiles; the USSR defined "strategic" to include certain U.S. air and naval deployments abroad, while excluding various systems of their own, including medium range missiles.

—We had not been able to agree on an equitable basis for limiting individual offensive systems that differed in numbers or capabilities.

—The scope of an initial agreement was undetermined. The USSR proposed that it limit defensive forces alone; the U.S. felt it must encompass both offensive and defensive forces.

These differences meant that negotiating a comprehensive agreement would be very complicated and necessarily time-consuming.

As negotiations entered their second year, the continuing buildup of Soviet strategic systems was of particular concern. During the first year of negotiations the Soviets had increased their total arsenal of intercontinental ballistic missile launchers by nearly one-fourth and submarine launchers by nearly one-half.

At that time, I concluded that four principles were fundamental to our position.

— First, the strategic balance would be endangered if we limited defensive forces alone and left the offensive threat unconstrained. An essential objective of the negotiations would be defeated by unchecked deployments of offensive systems. For example, with only defensive forces limited by an agreement, the continued expansion of Soviet offensive forces, especially the large SS–9 ICBMs if armed with multiple warheads, could eventually give the USSR a capability for seriously threatening our land-based strategic forces.

— Second, it would be dangerous if, while constraining offensive forces, strategic defenses were allowed to increase without limit. In sufficient numbers and sophistication, ABM systems deployed to defend cities can reduce capabilities to retaliate. Thus, unlimited ABM expansion ultimately would force an offensive buildup.

— Third, if we could not devise satisfactory formulas for limiting all major weapon systems, we should concentrate on those of primary importance in the strategic balance which if unchecked would become most threatening to overall strategic equilibrium.

— Finally, if we could not find technical solutions for limiting systems that already differed in numbers and capabilities, an interim step might be a freeze at current levels on deploy-

ments of the most destabilizing offensive weapons.

These conclusions were the basis for my personal intervention with the Soviet leaders. Recognizing that only by establishing a political commitment at the highest level could we make significant progress on the range of technical issues that still confronted the negotiators, I attempted to create a new negotiating framework in which both sides could proceed. This overture, followed by several months of intensive negotiations, ultimately produced the breakthrough announced on May 20, 1971:

"The Governments of the United States and the Soviet Union, after reviewing the course of their talks on the limitation of strategic armaments, have agreed to concentrate this year on working out an agreement for the limitation of the deployment of antiballistic missiles systems (ABMs). They have also agreed that, together with concluding an agreement to limit ABMs, they will agree on certain measures with respect to the limitation of offensive strategic weapons.

"The two sides are taking this course in the conviction that it will create more favorable conditions for further negotiations to limit all strategic arms. These negotiations will be actively pursued."

In essence, this new understanding involved elements that bridged the concerns of both sides.

— An ABM agreement would have initial priority in further discussions. Since most progress had been made in this area, we would concentrate during the remainder of 1971 on negotiating an agreement on limiting defensive systems.

— The essential linkage between agreements to limit offensive and defensive systems would be preserved, and the two agreements would be concluded simultaneously.

—The impasse over the composition of strategic offensive weapons was resolved by concentrating on an initial agreement for those offensive systems having the major impact on the strategic balance.

The breakthrough on May 20 revitalized the negotiations. It was followed by progress in related areas. On September 30, 1971, the U.S. and USSR signed two agreements which had been worked out in parallel with the main arms negotiations.

—The first established agreed measures that each side would adopt to reduce the risk of nuclear war occurring as a result of an accident or unauthorized acts.

—The second provided that the direct communications link (Hot Line) between the U.S. and the USSR would be made more secure and less vulnerable by employing satellites in the communications system.

These agreements demonstrated a mutual willingness to deal seriously with other strategic issues.

The exact scope of the agreements derived from the commitment of May 20 is still under negotiation, and I am obliged to protect the confidentiality of these talks. I can report that a consensus is developing on certain essential elements which provide a basis for further movement toward an agreement that accommodates concerns expressed by each side.

—Comprehensive limitations should be placed on ABM systems. Deployments should neither provide a defense of the entire national territory

nor threaten the overall strategic balance. However, reaching agreement has been complicated because the existing Soviet system is designed to protect Moscow in contrast with our initial ABM deployments which defend ICBMs located in less populous areas.

—Since an ABM agreement will cover all aspects of limitations on ABM defensive systems, it should be a long term commitment formalized in a treaty.

—There should be an interim solution to the question of offensive controls. Certain offensive weapons should be frozen to prevent widening of numerical differentials to a point which would necessitate additional American countermeasures. An interim agreement would not be as comprehensive as the ABM Treaty and further offensive limitations would be considered in a second phase of negotiations. Because it is only an interim measure, it is more appropriately concluded in a formal agreement of a different type.

—An essential linkage between the substance and duration of the documents dealing with offensive and defensive aspects must be preserved.

The extent of the interim offensive agreement is still under intensive negotiation, reflecting the greater complexity of questions related to offensive systems. We must weigh the advantages of prolonging the current stage of negotiations in order to reach agreements on every offensive system against the consequences of allowing the current Soviet buildup to continue, perhaps for a considerable period. Considering the overall balance of offensive systems, including our program of multiple warhead deployment, there will be no disadvantage for the U.S. in an interim freeze of certain systems. Moreover, Soviet willingness to limit the size of its offensive forces would reflect a desire for longer term solutions rather than unilateral efforts to achieve marginal advantages.

Achieving initial agreements to limit both offensive and defensive strategic programs will be a major step in constraining the strategic arms race without compromising the security of either side. On the other hand, if negotiations are protracted while the Soviets continue offensive missile deployments and development of new systems, the U.S. has no choice but to proceed with major new strategic programs. This is a reality of our competitive relationship. The SALT negotiations offer a constructive alternative to unlimited competition. I am confident that agreements limiting strategic arms are feasible and in the interests of both nations. Equitable agreements can only enhance mutual security. They would represent an enormous change in the course of our postwar competition.

MUTUAL AND BALANCED FORCE REDUCTIONS (MBFR)

Although negotiations to limit strategic arms are of fundamental significance to U.S.-USSR relations, the existence of large military forces in Central Europe provides another opportunity for increasing international stability by negotiated reductions. This issue, of course, is not primarily between the U.S. and USSR; it involves the vital interests of our allies and states of the Warsaw Pact.

The possibility of mutual and balanced force reductions was first raised by NATO in 1968, but thus far has elicited no spe-

cific reply from the USSR or the other Warsaw Pact countries. Not until the spring of 1971 did the Soviet leaders even acknowledge this Western initiative directly. Nevertheless, this Administration has conducted an intensive analysis of the issues in order that we and our NATO partners will be in the best possible position should negotiations develop.

We found that attitudes toward force reductions in Central Europe often reflected certain abstract assumptions that needed more extensive analysis. For example, there was the view that reductions could be primarily a means of political detente because it was believed that the military balance would not be affected as long as both sides were reduced by equal percentages. Therefore, the size of reductions could be determined on the basis of what proved negotiable, since an equal percentage reduction presumably would not alter the balance of forces. On the other hand, there were arguments that no reductions of any size should be considered because the USSR's geographic advantage enables the Warsaw Pact to reinforce forces more rapidly than NATO, and thus quickly compensate for earlier reductions.

In addition, there were also important technical questions to be resolved: how to establish criteria for equating the forces and equipment of several different countries; how to compensate for the fact that our forces would be withdrawn to the continental United States while Soviet forces withdrawn would return to the USSR, only a few hundred miles distant; and how to verify reductions, particularly smaller ones. Other forces might be disbanded within national territory, which would pose quite different problems of verification. Constraints would have to be introduced to verify that reduced levels were not exceeded, or that withdrawn forces were not being covertly brought back into the zone of reductions, and to provide confidence in the stability of the entire process by enhancing warning of any buildup of forces.

Obviously, a large number of questions needed detailed evaluation before concrete proposals could be developed. In close consultation with our allies, we initiated a systematic study. Our aim was to clarify common objectives within the Alliance in preparation for eventual negotiations with the other side.

In the first phase of our analysis we examined each individual element of force reductions: the forces of each nation, the various weapons systems, the variants in geographical areas, the constraints on reduced forces, and the requirements for verifying different increments of reductions of both national and foreign forces.

Subsequent phases have become more detailed and specific. We have used the analyses of the individual elements of reductions to develop illustrative models of agreements that reflect different concepts. Thus, two broad approaches to reductions have been examined:

—Proportionately equal ones applying the same percentage of reductions to both sides.

—Asymmetrical ones in which reductions would be made in differing amounts in various categories.

Having established a conceptual approach, we proceeded to evaluate the existing military balance in Central Europe. We then compared it with various alternatives to determine the military implications of a new balance of forces resulting from reductions. These analyses included:

—An examination of the changing ratio

of forces as general mobilization proceeded.

—A determination of requirements to insure verification of an agreement.

—Development of a general sequence for negotiation. In this way the major effects were highlighted and the merits of each model could be compared with greater precision.

Certain tentative findings have emerged at this stage of preparations:

—Small reductions, on the order of ten percent or less, cannot be confidently verified to assure that reductions have actually taken place, especially those forces demobilized within national territories.

—Larger reductions can be verified, provided they are made under certain conditions and accompanied by measures to ensure continuing compliance.

—The USSR can mobilize and reinforce its forces in Central Europe much more rapidly than NATO. Therefore, an agreement to reduce forces simply on an equal percentage basis is inherently unfavorable to NATO, and the larger the percentage, the greater the inequity.

The results of our preliminary work have been furnished to NATO. Along with Alliance studies, it has facilitated internal NATO discussion on the direction of further analysis. We and our allies concluded last year that preparations had advanced to a point where it would be advantageous to discuss certain preliminary principles with the USSR. An exploratory mission, which would be led by former Secretary General of NATO Manlio G. Brosio, was proposed. The USSR, however, has not yet accepted this proposal.

Issues that could be usefully explored include the exact geographical area for reductions, whether to reduce both foreign and national forces, and how the entire process of reduction could be balanced in a way that would create no military advantages for either side. Already, the extensive studies completed have laid a promising foundation for constructive discussions once the interest of NATO nations is reciprocated by members of the Warsaw Pact.

Undiminished military security for NATO is the only rational criterion for establishing force reductions. Thus, the process of reducing forces in Central Europe must create no unilateral military advantages. For this reason, we are examining alternative approaches. It may be possible to offset the Warsaw Pact's advantages under equal percentage reductions by reaching a more comprehensive agreement. Critical elements in such an agreement would include adequate verification provisions and effective constraints on the movement of forces. We are also evaluating the possibility of asymmetrical but equitable reductions which would preserve the overall military balance. Our analytical work will continue to concentrate on both of these alternative approaches.

PROGRESS IN INTERNATIONAL AGREEMENTS

Concern about arms control has not been restricted to the major powers. In recognition of this the United States a decade ago was instrumental in establishing a representative international forum for examination of arms control issues. The Conference of the Committee on Disarmament (CCD) has gradually become an important instrument for developing an international consensus.

This Administration has played an active role in this forum. As a result of our initiatives and in cooperation with other participants, some significant achievements have been recorded.

Biological and Chemical Arms Control. Early in this Administration we began a comprehensive review of biological and chemical weapons policy and programs.

—In following through on my declaration that the United States totally renounced the use and possession of biological and toxin weapons, we began a program for safe destruction of existing stocks that is scheduled to be completed this summer. We are converting facilities previously used for biological warfare research to major health and environmental safety missions. The sophisticated scientific facilities at Fort Detrick, Maryland, for example, will become a leading research center in the war against cancer; those at Pine Bluff Arsenal, Arkansas, are being turned into a new national research center to examine the biological effects on the environment of a number of chemical substances.

—With our clear example and strong support, the CCD agreed last September on the draft of an international treaty banning the development, production and stockpiling of biological and toxin weapons and requiring destruction of existing stocks. This international commitment is a unique milestone. Following its signature, I intend to submit this treaty to the U.S. Senate for its advice and consent to ratification this year.

323

Seabeds. A treaty banning weapons of mass destruction from the seabeds was signed in Washington on February 11, 1971 and subsequently submitted to the Senate. This is a significant achievement. The major powers have agreed not to place nuclear weapons on the ocean floor, an area which encompasses about 70 percent of the earth's surface. It has already been signed by more than 80 states.

Nuclear Non-Proliferation. Further progress has been made in restricting the spread of nuclear weapons to new regions. Following a unanimous vote of advice and consent by the Senate, the U.S. ratified on May 12, 1971 Additional Protocol II to the Treaty for the Prohibition of Nuclear Weapons in Latin America. Under this Protocol, the United States agreed to respect the nuclear-free zone created by the treaty, which is now in force for seventeen of our Latin American neighbors and applies to an area of over 2½ million square miles containing a population of more than 100 million persons.

NEW AREAS FOR PROGRESS

New areas for progress in controlling arms demand attention.

—In the *Middle East* the U.S. is committed to maintaining a military balance. Our fundamental position, however, is that the U.S. and USSR have a special responsibility to restrain the flow of armaments.

—In *South Asia* outside powers should assume a similar responsibility. Attempts to strengthen local forces through supply of major armaments have exacerbated tensions inherent in the political situation.

—*Different forums,* such as a world conference or a five power nuclear conference, have been suggested for dealing with arms control issues. The United States is willing to consider these and other efforts. However, rather than searching for new mechanisms or institutions, we believe that the primary challenge for the present is to complete the work already begun in the UN, in the CCD at Geneva, in regional arrangements, and, above all, in Soviet-American discussions.

CONCLUSION

Advances in arms control have enhanced prospects for a new era of greater mutual security in the world. The progress already achieved has helped provide a basis for new opportunities in 1972 to discuss constructively a broad range of differences with potential adversaries. Increased security will become a reality if together we can create a new structure of international understanding, stability and restraint.

In this period of transition, we cannot ignore the potential security threats to this nation and its allies or our obligation to maintain a credible and effective American military position. We are committed to progress in arms control, but I will not allow negotiations to become a subterfuge by which potential adversaries obtain military advantages. The continuing sufficiency of our strength is not incompatible with our arms control efforts; on the contrary, it helps create the conditions that make equitable settlements of political differences possible.

Consistent with the Nixon Doctrine, we will maintain those forces essential to deal with the challenges of the 1970's, and we will develop a solid foundation for strength over the long term to ensure against potential dangers in the future. Our security assistance programs will contribute to the strengthening of our allies and a more equitable sharing of defense burdens in our common interest.

This is a year of historic new opportunities for building a more stable world. The continuing cohesiveness of our alliances and the continuing strength of our common defense are essential to achieving this goal.

PART VI: THE IMPERATIVE OF GLOBAL COOPERATION

—The United Nations
—The New Dimensions of Diplomacy

THE UNITED NATIONS

"With the world in urgent need of a dynamic, effective international organization, it is appropriate for us as a people and as individuals to renew our sense of tough-minded dedication to making the UN work."

Proclamation of
United Nations Day
July 9, 1971

The United Nations is an experiment in cooperation among nations. It is a mistake to assume that its success is foreordained or its ultimate result altogether predictable. It is a mistake either to exaggerate its capability or to underestimate its potential.

No one knows what role time and success might bring to the United Nations. It is conceivable that it may ultimately come to play a definitive role in the settlement of international disputes. But that is for the future to determine.

We have reached a point at which it is no service to the idea of the United Nations and no contribution to its future to blink at its limitations. We believe the United Nations is now entering a crucial period. A pervasive skepticism concerning the UN is widespread, and was reflected in the speeches made in the recent General Assembly session and in several actions taken by the Congress of the United States. Our obligation to the future requires that we face that fact squarely. We believe that the time has come for a large dose of realism and candor in United States policy toward the United Nations.

The United Nations is not a world government, rendering and enforcing sovereign judgments on conflicts between its members. Rather, it is itself a collection of sovereign states, and the unique virtue on which it must rely is the ability to encourage accommodation of conflicting sovereign interests. It has only limited authority to do more. It is unlikely to grow in authority if it does less.

This Administration will, therefore—as it has since its beginning—strive to focus the United Nations constructively on the tasks it does best. They are many and they are important. We will, above all, conduct our UN activities in such a way as to preserve and enhance the potential of the world organization to grow, as the world grows, toward understanding, tolerance and the sublimation of national conflicts of interest.

This requires that we be frank in assessing the weaknesses in the current UN structure and performance, and in asserting the need for improvements. We will do this not only because the UN's health is essential to the present, but because we attach profound importance to its future.

Many important reforms are needed. Secretary General Waldheim has indicated that he is aware of the need for reform and for actions to strengthen the United Nations. We fully support him in his determination to come to grips with the UN's problems.

MAJOR PROBLEMS OF THE
UNITED NATIONS

The United Nations now faces four problems upon which progress must be made if the organization is not to suffer, perhaps grievously.

1. Preserving the World Peace. This is the UN's fundamental purpose. Two things are equally clear about its performance to date. It has been far short of satisfactory—and it has been far better than nothing.

By its mere existence, the UN serves as a constant forum-in-being in which resolutions of conflicts can be sought. It thereby makes an essential and irreplaceable contribution to the machinery of peacekeeping.

The peoples of the world, however, expect more of the UN than merely to furnish an institutional device for facilitating negotiations between conflicting parties. People expect the UN, as an institution, to act as a force for peace. It is, therefore, a matter of grave concern that the members of the UN have too often and too consistently prevented it from doing so.

That is why it was a severe blow to the moral authority of the UN that it was unable even to moderate the India-Pakistan conflict. The foremost function of the Security Council should be to prevent the use of military force by one UN member against another. In this crisis, the Soviet veto rendered the Security Council im-

potent, and thereby depreciated that body and had the paradoxical effect of confirming the new conditions created by the resort to military force.

It is a bleak truth that on that occasion a call for a ceasefire and withdrawal was vetoed by a great power whose forces were not involved in the dispute. The veto had been used only once before in the history of the UN in that way—that time also by the Soviet Union. That use of UN machinery is not consistent with the obligations of a great power.

Clearly, the UN depends upon the cooperation of its member states—particularly the permanent members of the Security Council—to realize its potential for keeping the peace. Clearly, that fact limits the UN's peacekeeping ability. It need not, however, lead to paralysis as it did in the India-Pakistan crisis.

Precisely because the major powers carry the prime responsibility for world peace, they also carry the responsibility for ensuring the creative and realistic use of the world organization's potential for contributing to peace.

There are four primary methods by which the UN, acting as an institution, can attempt to keep the peace. The first is through recommendations or mandatory decisions of the Security Council. The second is through resolutions embodying the will of the General Assembly. The third is through peacekeeping missions sent into conflict-ridden areas. The fourth is the voluntary resort by states in dispute to resolution of their conflict either by an ad hoc authority or by the International Court of Justice.

The current situation with respect to all four of these mechanisms is not encouraging, as the India-Pakistan crisis made clear. The Secretary General's offer of good offices was not accepted by India. Following the outbreak of hostilities, resort to the veto thwarted Security Council efforts to prevent the use of military force by one state to change the internal structure of another. Although the General Assembly voted overwhelmingly for a ceasefire and withdrawal, resolutions by that body are not mandatory and are therefore effective only to the extent that they constitute an impressive expression of world public opinion. Even then, they have effect only if the conflicting parties are sensitive to such an expression. India, in fact, ignored the General Assembly resolution.

It is in the dispatch of peacekeeping missions to strife-torn areas (the Middle East, Kashmir, Cyprus, the former Congo) that the UN has, in the past, been able to make major contributions. We are concerned that the use of this device for controlling international conflict has become increasingly difficult.

The crux of the problem has been the insistence of the Soviet Union that the Security Council should exercise direct, detailed, and day-to-day control over peacekeeping missions. Such an arrangement would, of course, subject to the veto almost any aspect of the organization, operation, or activities of a UN peacekeeping mission.

We think such an arrangement would be so cumbersome as to preclude effective operations. We agree with the Soviet Union that the Security Council should maintain overall supervision and furnish policy guidance for peacekeeping missions. But we think it essential that the Secretary General have sufficient authority to handle day-to-day problems effectively as they arise.

Our earnest efforts to resolve this problem have, thus far, been fruitless. Over the course of the next year we will make a further effort to work out a solution. The presence of the People's Republic of China in the Security Council will obviously affect the chances for success, but it is too early at this stage to know whether the Chinese presence will facilitate, or constitute an additional serious barrier to, a solution.

Nations have shown little willingness to seek voluntary adjudication of their disputes. In 1971, for example, the International Court had before it only two cases, and one of those for an advisory opinion.

Despite the apathy shown at the last General Assembly on this matter, there may also be an opportunity to reinvigorate the role of the International Court of Justice. In the coming year, the United States will be alert for disputes to which we are a party which might be resolved through the use of the International Court. We are, for example, prepared to place before the World Court our dispute with Ecuador over fishing rights. It may thus be possible, by example, to strengthen this potentially important aspect of the UN system's dispute-settlement machinery.

2. Confrontation versus Negotiation. The effectiveness of the UN continued to be impaired this year by an excessive resort to the politics of confrontation by members who placed group solidarity above the need for a realistic consensus. Political debates continued to be long on rhetoric and short on concrete accomplishment.

When views are strongly held and widely shared among members, it is natural and right that they find expression. It is true that countries will naturally attempt to further their national objectives inside the UN as well as out. It is also true that violence of language is preferable to violence of action.

But the world does not need, and the United Nations was not created to serve as, a cockpit in which conflicting national positions can be made irreconcilable. Nor is it the purpose of the United Nations to award "victories" or register "defeats". It is, rather, the business of the United Nations to serve as a forum for moderating disputes, for asserting the larger world interest in the pacific resolution of conflict.

As we pursue the path of negotiation rather than confrontation in our national policies, we shall work in the United Nations for a spirit of accommodation and an atmosphere of civility, which even among enemies encourages reconciliation.

A case in point was the UN's handling of the Chinese representation issue. A continuing and consistent policy of this Administration has been to encourage the People's Republic of China to play a constructive role in the community of nations. The time had clearly arrived to welcome them in the United Nations, and we ourselves put forward a resolution which would have accomplished this.

At issue, however, was the status of the Republic of China, which has a population larger than two-thirds of the UN members, and had been a constructive and valuable member of the organization since its founding. We did not believe that the UN needed to take a position on the juridical relationship between the People's Republic of China and the Republic of China. That could, and should, have been left to them to work out.

The United States understands majority rule, and accepts the UN decision. But that does not change our view that it was unnecessary and unfortunate that the UN closed its eyes to one reality, at the very moment when it was recognizing another.

3. The UN Financial Crisis. The United Nations is on the edge of bankruptcy. The basic cause of this deepening financial crisis is the long-standing refusal of the Soviet Union, France, and several other countries to pay their share of the cost for UN peacekeeping missions sent to the Congo and the Middle East. These same countries also refuse to pay their share of related "peacekeeping" items in the regular annual budget of the UN, primarily retirement of the bonds that the UN was forced to issue in 1962 to pay its peacekeeping debts. In addition, the Soviet Union and some of the East European nations persist in paying their annual assessed share of the UN's regular technical assistance programs in rubles, most of which cannot be utilized by the UN and must therefore be carried as arrearages. South Africa also has withheld payment of its share of certain UN activities which it opposes.

These practices have created a serious deficit for the organization, and the simple fact is that for some years the UN has not received sufficient revenues to meet its voted budgets and authorized expenditures. As a result, the UN's working capital fund has been exhausted and the organization has become increasingly dependent on emergency stop-gap measures to meet its daily operating expenses. In the coming months, even such desperate measures may not be sufficient.

This is an intolerable situation. The immediate need is to take steps to prevent further growth of the deficit. During the past session of the General Assembly, the United States delegation proposed a series of measures to prevent UN expenditures from exceeding cash income. We welcome

Secretary General Waldheim's decision to take a number of austerity measures as one of his first acts upon taking office. Austerity will lead to criticism, but it should not be directed at the Secretary General but at those UN members whose failure to meet their obligations has made it necessary.

Urgent as it is, however, the prevention of the further growth of the deficit is not a sufficient response to the UN's financial problems. As long as the accumulated deficit remains, the day-to-day financing of UN operations must be considered precarious.

The solution should go beyond the immediate problem to the reconstruction of an effective instrument of international cooperation deserving our confidence. The United States is prepared to play a constructive role in the search for such a solution. We will not, however, take the initial or major responsibility for making up a deficit created by the policies of other countries.

4. The Need for a Wider Sharing of the Costs of the UN. There is another aspect of the UN financial arrangements which requires candor. It is fashionable to dismiss the cost of the United Nations as a pittance compared with the cost of other activities, such as defense. However, this does not relieve us of responsibility to scrutinize those expenditures carefully to determine that the costs are equitably shared and that the benefits justify them. The total expenditures of the UN system in 1971, including the Specialized Agencies and voluntary programs, exceeded $1.1 billion. The contribution from U.S. public funds was $462 million (including about $150 million for East Pakistan relief). It is self-evident that expenditures and budgets of such magnitude must be subject to the same careful review which other uses of public money undergo.

The UN's regular assessed budget is about one-fifth of the costs of the whole UN system. The General Assembly decides both the size of this budget and the percentage which each member state is required to contribute. This percentage is based primarily on capacity to pay. When the UN was founded, the U.S. yearly assessment would have been about 49 percent on a strict capacity-to-pay basis. We thought then, and we think now, that it is unhealthy for a world organization to be excessively dependent upon the financial contribution of any one member state. Accordingly, the first U.S. assessment was set at 39 percent, and over the years we have succeeded in reducing our assessed contribution to its current level of 31.52 percent.

Last year, I appointed a distinguished group of Americans under the chairmanship of our former Ambassador to the UN, Henry Cabot Lodge, to study U.S. participation in the UN. Among its recommendations to improve the UN and our role in it, the Commission concluded that the United States should seek to reduce its contribution to not more than 25 percent of the assessed budget of the United Nations, using this saving to increase our voluntary contributions to other UN programs.

We are fully aware that an assessed contribution of that level would mean that many UN member states would be paying a greater proportion of their Gross National Product to the UN than would the United States. Indeed that is the case now, and has been since the foundation of the United Nations. However, the implications for the health of the organization and the views of the American public and the Congress regarding the proper size of the U.S. contribution to the UN budget cannot be ignored. Capacity to pay is a valid general guide to assessments, but it is not the only guide. Prudence and political realism dictate that no one country should be assessed a disproportionate share of the expenses of an organization approaching universality in which each member, large or small, has but one vote. That is particularly true when experience has shown that the major contributing countries are unable to exercise effective control over the UN budget.

It is, therefore, the policy of this Administration to negotiate with other UN member states an arrangement by which the U.S. contribution to the assessed budget of the United Nations and its Specialized Agencies will be brought down to the level of 25 percent. In view of the UN's current financial difficulties, and of the requirements of international law, we must proceed in an orderly way in reaching this goal. It is unrealistic to expect that it can be done immediately.

This 25 percent limitation should not and will not apply to the voluntary contributions upon which many of the more important UN functions are now dependent. Current UN activities financed by voluntary national contributions include such activities as narcotics control, disaster relief, major economic assistance activities (the United Nations Development Program), population control, etc. All these are activities to which individual nations contribute, or not, as each sees fit. The size of each nation's contribution is determined by its own interest in the program. In most instances, the U.S. share of the cost of these programs is larger than our assessed share of the regular UN budget. That is a matter of national choice. The United States will continue to make generous contributions to activities of this kind which we have a particular interest in encouraging.

THE FUNDING OF TECHNICAL ASSISTANCE

In a number of the Specialized Agencies of the United Nations and in the UN itself a substantial portion of their assessed budgets is being devoted to economic or technical assistance projects for less developed countries. Given the voting realities in these organizations, this means simply that the United States and other major contributors have very limited control over the degree of financial support which they are required to give to such activities.

While the funding of such assistance out of assessed contributions may have been understandable before the UN Development Program was established, it can no longer be justified. We believe that the assessed contribution of the UN Specialized Agencies should relate to the administration of the organizations themselves and to activities of common benefit. Assistance which benefits only some countries, however desirable, should properly be funded through voluntary national contributions, thus permitting each country to determine for itself the amount of its own national resources which should be applied to these purposes.

We recognize the hope among some developing nations that their voting strength in UN organizations can be used to force an increase in the economic assistance which they receive from the developed countries. The aim is not unworthy. But the means can easily become self-defeating.

Economic aid programs depend upon

political support in the developed countries, whose taxpayers are the ultimate donors. This support cannot be compelled. Attempts to use the one nation-one vote principle to do so will, in the long run, endanger this whole important area of UN activity.

THE DECLINE IN CONGRESSIONAL SUPPORT FOR THE UN

During the past year, the United States Congress took four actions which require mention in this report:

—The House of Representatives, although the action is not final, for the first time refused to provide a voluntary contribution to the UN Development Program (UNDP).

—For the second year in a row, the Congress refused to pay the United States assessed dues to the International Labor Organization.

—The Congress failed to provide the U.S. contribution to the expansion of the UN Headquarters facilities in New York City.

—The Congress exempted strategic and critical materials, notably chrome, from the U.S. implementation of the mandatory UN sanctions on imports from Rhodesia.

It would be a mistake to conclude that these actions were motivated by Congressional hostility to the United Nations. These were not concerted actions, and they took place for a variety of reasons. But it would also be a mistake not to recognize the implications of these actions. They could hardly have taken place if the UN, as an entity, enjoyed stronger support in the Congress and among the American people. That fact is, I believe,

far more significant than the individual arguments upon which the Congress based its decisions.

A reduction of U.S. support for the UNDP would be particularly unfortunate. The UN system has gradually become a major instrument for encouraging economic and social progress in the developing countries, and the UNDP is the primary instrument by which the UN fills this role. The United States has been the major contributor of funds to the UNDP, and since its inception the UNDP has been headed by a distinguished American, Paul Hoffman.

Last year there were several developments which should reconfirm the American attachment to this program. Progress continued in making the UNDP's machinery more efficient. The contributions to the UNDP from other countries were significantly increased. And when Paul Hoffman retired at the end of the year, the UN chose another outstanding American, Rudolph Peterson, as his successor. The UNDP deserves our continuing support.

During its current session, the Congress must also face the problem of American participation in the ILO. The United States is now almost two years in arrears, and therefore on the verge of losing its vote under the ILO rules. There were cogent reasons behind the Congressional dissatisfaction with the ILO. During the past two years, however, the ILO has responded to our efforts to revitalize its tripartite structure and procedures. It is simply not consistent with our national dignity to attempt to maintain influence and membership in the ILO if we are not prepared to pay our dues. This Administration will, therefore, have no choice but to give notice of withdrawal from the ILO unless the Congress sees fit to provide our assessed contributions to that organization.

AN AREA OF PROGRESS—THE NEW DIMENSION IN DIPLOMACY

A candid recognition of the problems which we see in some aspects of the current UN performance should not lead us to lose sight of the fact that it continues, in other areas, to make significant progress and to contribute mightily to the well-being of mankind.

General public knowledge of the UN is limited to the major conflicts in which it becomes involved. But the UN is also deeply engaged in a wide range of constructive activities in what I have called the "quiet side" of the UN. These activities never make headlines, but that is no measure of their importance. The UN is irreplaceable and indefatigable in fostering international cooperation in science, health, agriculture, navigation, communications, and many other fields. The fact, for example, that we no longer need smallpox vaccinations is largely due to the patient, worldwide work of the World Health Organization.

In earlier reports to the Congress and in my appearances before the UN General Assembly, I have commended to the attention of the UN a series of urgent global problems. This is the new dimension of diplomacy, brought about by the technological revolution. It consists of problems which by their very nature involve all the nations of the world, and can be satisfactorily met only in a context of the broadest international cooperation and agreement. All men share an interest in clean air and water, though they may differ on how the costs of achieving these benefits should be allocated. The vast majority of men wish to preserve themselves and their fellowmen from drug addiction and to protect international travel from air piracy. They wish to see the frontiers of space and ocean so regulated as to minimize the potentialities for human conflict, and to see an effective organization to provide disaster relief.

These problems constitute a major opportunity for the United Nations system. At a time when political realities inhibit the UN's ability to meet some of its original purposes, the new dimension of diplomacy gives to the UN an agenda of urgent tasks. Their successful accomplishment will not only be a significant contribution to the well-being of mankind, but will also serve to inculcate and nurture among nations the habit of cooperation for the general good—and for the ultimate acceptance of the rule of law to govern international relations. That, after all, is the heart of the purpose for which the UN was founded.

The UN possesses special and unique capacities for dealing with these problems. It has in being a trained Secretariat. It can attract the expert talent required. It can direct attention to the transcendent global interest in these problems, to which national interests must be accommodated. Finally, it can use its moral authority to stimulate international action.

The progress made in the past year is described in the following chapter of this message, but it is gratifying to report here that the world community has begun to act vigorously in these areas, and that the United Nations is playing a central role.

THE ESSENTIAL TASK OF THE UN

Ours is the age when man has first come to realize that he can in fact destroy his own species. Ours is the age when the problems and complexities of technological revolution have so multiplied that coping with them is, in many ways, clearly beyond the capacities of individual national governments. Ours, therefore, must be the age when the international institutions of cooperation are perfected. The basic question is—can man create institutions to save him from the dark forces of his own nature and from the overwhelming consequences of his technological successes?

I believe profoundly that the answer is yes, and that a healthy and increasingly vigorous United Nations is essential to success. But the task is too important for mere sentimentality. We cannot afford to confuse good intentions with genuine accomplishment. That is why we shall pursue the goal of an effective United Nations with the same hardheaded realism and dedication that we devote to our other national goals.

NEW DIMENSIONS OF DIPLOMACY

"Thus there has come into being a new dimension in the foreign policy of the United States, not as a matter of choice and deliberate action on our part, but as a reflection of the demanding realities of the world in which we live."

> U.S. Foreign Policy for 1970's
> Report to the Congress
> February 25, 1971

The rise of modern science and the technological revolution it has brought in train have been monuments to the creativity of man and powerful catalysts to a betterment of the human condition. Yet man cannot escape the irony of history—solutions to old problems spawn new ones.

—In our time, man has mastered distance as it is measured on this planet. But modern transport and communications can lead to poisoned air, polluted water, the dissemination of corrupting and dangerous drugs, and air piracy for personal or political advantage.

—Man is rapidly developing the ability to exploit the new twin frontiers of the ocean and outer space. However, being rich in potential benefits, these frontiers are also potential sources of international dispute.

—Man is on the threshold of ending his vulnerability to pestilence and famine. But one of the results of this boon is a new specter of uncontrollable population growth.

We have no choice but to cope with the new problems of technological civilization. Individual governments must do what they can, but in a world grown small, these issues must be recognized for what they are—problems of the human species to be addressed on a global scale.

This is one of the great challenges of our time. Human rationality enables us to see the need clearly, but it is sobering to reflect that in the past it has always been more effective when applied to nature than when directed to the intractable difficulties of getting man to cooperate with man.

I have in the past called on the international community to focus attention and energy on these problems. I am happy to say that the response has, in general, been

333

vigorous. The global challenge has been accepted and the new tasks for diplomacy are being addressed.

THE OCEANS

Future generations may well look back upon the 1970's as the decade in which the nations of the world made the fundamental decisions regulating the use of over two-thirds of our planet.

The task is urgent. Technological advances have made all nations increasingly aware of the new benefits which the ocean can yield. Competition among nations for control of the ocean's resources, and the growing divergence of national claims, could constitute serious threats to world peace.

The United States relies upon the seas to meet its global responsibilities. Our security, and that of our friends, depends upon freedom of navigation and overflight of the high seas, and on free movement through and over international straits. A significant portion of our strategic deterrent is seaborne. The trend to more extensive territorial sea claims by other nations thus threatens very directly our national security.

Shortly after taking office, this Administration began what is probably the most comprehensive review of U.S. oceans policy in our history. Several conclusions emerged.

First, multilateral agreement is essential. Nations have interests in the seas which differ widely and result in different national priorities. Unilateral claims to the sea or its resources force other nations to make a stark choice between confrontation and acquiescence in situations prejudicial to their interests. Neither result contributes to stable world peace.

Second, freedom of navigation and overflight must be protected. Any significant diminution of such freedoms beyond a narrow territorial sea would fundamentally affect international security and trade. The basic political decision, made centuries ago, that nations would not interfere with each other's rights to communicate by sea must be preserved. We need, however, to reconcile traditional uses of the seas with their new potential.

Third, an equitable system must be established for regulating the exploitation of the resources of the ocean and seabeds beyond national jurisdiction. The value of the resources ensures that exploitation will follow promptly the development of the necessary technology. Therefore, it is essential to set up a system under which the exploitation will contribute to, rather than endanger, peace among nations. No state should be permitted to treat these resources as an exclusive national property or to exploit them in a manner harmful to the interests of other states or the global environment. Moreover, the smaller and poorer nations of the world should be given a fair share of the benefits from these resources, which are the common heritage of mankind. While nations with long coastlines can acquire this share from resources solely off their own coasts, others with short coastlines or none at all must look to a reasonable international system if they are to receive a fair portion of the ocean's wealth. A system which permits a just allocation of ocean resources is, therefore, an important ingredient of a stable arrangement which all nations will support because all have a stake in its preservation.

Fourth, it is not possible for any nation, acting unilaterally, to ensure adequate protection of the marine environment.

334

Unless there are firm minimum international standards, the search for relative economic advantage will preclude effective environmental protection.

These principles underlie the new U.S. oceans policy which I announced in May 1970 and the detailed proposals we have made to the world community since then.

Our initiatives have received a ready response. Following considerable discussion in the fall of 1970, the UN General Assembly called for a comprehensive international conference for 1973. A multination UN Seabed Committee was given the job of drafting, in the interim, the agreement required to assure the success of that conference.

The U.S. has put forward four detailed proposals—on the seabeds, the breadth of the territorial sea, transit through straits, and living resources. The first of these proposals was given to the UN in August 1970 in the form of a draft United Nations convention on the international seabed area. I described its essentials in last year's Report to the Congress.

On August 3, 1971 we supplemented this initiative by putting forward proposals on the breadth of the territorial sea, on free transit through and over international straits, and on carefully defined preferential rights over fisheries.

Breadth of Territorial Sea. The U.S. has adhered to a three-mile territorial sea for almost two centuries. The claims of other states vary widely, ranging to a maximum of 200 miles. There is a clear need for a uniform territorial sea and a general sentiment in the international community that it should be somewhat broader than three miles. We therefore proposed that the maximum breadth of the territorial sea be set at 12 miles.

Straits. Since many straits used for international navigation, however, are less than 24 miles wide, and thus would be completely overlapped by a 12-mile territorial sea, the U.S. put forward, as a condition to our agreement to a 12-mile territorial sea, a provision for a new right of "free transit."

That provision is essential because the ambiguous doctrine of "innocent passage" would otherwise apply, and states bordering straits would be required to decide which ships and planes should, and which should not, pass. Domestic and international pressures could be brought to bear on every decision. The oceans are too vital a highway of communication, and guaranteed passage through straits is too essential to our security, to be subject to such uncertainty. At the same time, the U.S. recognizes that adjacent coastal states do have legitimate concerns about traffic safety regulations and pollution, and has indicated its willingness to accommodate these concerns in a manner not prejudicing the basic right of free transit.

Living Resources. The question of fisheries management and conservation is intimately associated with the world's food needs. Fish are a primary source of protein for nations with low nutritional levels, and they make the difference between starvation and survival for millions of human beings. Modern fishing methods and careless conservation practices have now made it painfully clear that international and regional cooperation is urgently needed to maintain the productivity of this valuable, self-replenishing resource. There is, however, an inherent conflict between the interests of those who fish off the coasts of other countries, and the coastal states themselves. The former seek to protect what they consider traditional rights. The latter seek recognition of their

335

priority interest in the resources off their own coasts.

The U.S. proposal on fisheries offered a pragmatic solution based on sound conservation practices. Appropriate worldwide or regional fisheries organizations would be established to regulate the harvest of the living resources of the high seas. Coastal states would be recognized as having a priority interest based on their actual fishing capacity. Traditional fishing rights would be a matter of negotiation between the coastal and distant-water fishing states most concerned. All states would be eligible to fish for the remainder of the allowable catch. Special provisions would be made for highly migratory stocks and anadromous species, for enforcement procedures, and for compulsory dispute settlement.

In summary, the U.S. is deeply engaged in an international effort to write a new law of the sea. We have put forth comprehensive proposals designed to harmonize the multiple uses of the oceans. There is no inherent incompatibility between proper utilization of ocean resources and traditional freedoms of the sea. But territorial concepts such as absolute sovereignty cannot be applied either to seabed resources beyond the limits of national jurisdiction or to international navigation rights. Modified maritime doctrines and rules are needed to accommodate the diverse interests involved. The time has arrived for monumental decisions on the law of the sea, and the U.S. has acted forthrightly to meet the challenge.

CONTROL OF DRUG ABUSE

Narcotics addiction continues to spread at an alarming rate, in the United States and elsewhere. In my message to the Congress on June 17, 1971 I said that the problem had assumed the proportions of a national emergency, and I committed this Administration to the leadership of an intense international attack on the supply, demand, and illicit traffic in narcotics and other dangerous drugs.

In August, I established a Cabinet Committee on International Narcotics Control under the chairmanship of the Secretary of State. This committee is charged with the formulation and coordination of all policies of the Federal Government relating to the goal of curtailing the flow of narcotics and other dangerous drugs into the United States.

Turkey has been the single most important source of the opium which is converted to heroin marketed in the U.S. Therefore, it was a signal achievement when, on June 30, 1971 the Prime Minister of Turkey announced that Turkey will ban all production of opium after the 1972 crop is harvested. We must now be particularly vigilant against others stepping in to replace the illicit heroin supplies which formerly originated in the Turkish poppy fields.

Southeast Asia is another major source of illicit drugs, and during the past year important steps were taken to tighten controls in that area. In September, the United States agreed to support Thailand's efforts to suppress the supply and trafficking in illicit narcotics and dangerous drugs. In November, the Government of Laos put into effect a tough new narcotics law banning the manufacture, trading, and transportation of opium and its derivatives, including heroin. Subsequently Laos placed strict controls on the importation and distribution of acetic anhydride, a key ingredient in the production of heroin. In addition, President Thieu has sent an antinarcotics law to the Vietnamese National Assembly. During November the Government of Australia sponsored a meeting of regional narcotics officials to discuss and develop regional approaches to the drug problem in Asia.

These actions will contribute positively to combating the drug problem in Southeast Asia, and, in particular, to reducing the flow of heroin to American servicemen in the area.

On February 26, 1971 the Attorney General and the French Minister of the Interior signed an agreement for the detailed coordination of our two governments' attack on the illicit drug traffic. The primary objective of this joint effort is the discovery and destruction of heroin conversion laboratories in southern France, and the interception of the illicit heroin traffic from France to North America. The Canadian authorities have also joined in this endeavor. Seizures and destruction of illegal narcotics shipments in the France-North America channel increased during the past year in the wake of this combined effort.

The Governments of the United States and Mexico have been cooperating closely in narcotics control since 1969. That effort has resulted in the seizure by Mexican authorities of hundreds of pounds of crude opium, heroin, and cocaine and the destruction of over 12,000 fields of marijuana and opium poppy. Mexican officials have also intercepted large quantities of psychotropic substances intended for illegal sale in the United States.

At United States initiative, a United Nations Fund for Drug Abuse Control was established in March to finance a concerted worldwide action program. We made the initial pledge to the fund of $2 million, which has been augmented by pledges from several other countries including substantial amounts from Canada, Germany, and France. We are encouraging more countries to contribute, and we will seek additional U.S. contributions from the Congress when required. The fund will assist UN members to reduce both the illegal demand for and supply of dangerous drugs.

In March 1971, we also proposed amendments to increase the effectiveness of the 1961 Single Convention on Narcotic Drugs. Under the Convention's present terms, parties are committed to restrict the production, manufacture, export and import of narcotic drugs so that they will be used exclusively for legitimate medical and scientific purposes. Compliance with these undertakings, however, is essentially voluntary. Our amendments are designed to tighten compliance, and we are conducting extensive diplomatic consultations throughout the world to support this objective. An international conference will be held in Geneva in March 1972 to consider these and other proposals to amend the Convention.

Cooperation in control of dangerous drugs works both ways. While the sources of our chief narcotics problem are foreign, the United States is a source of illegal psychotropic drugs—such as LSD and other hallucinogens, the amphetamines, barbiturates, and tranquilizers—which afflict other nations. If we expect other governments to help stop the flow of heroin to our shores, we must act with equal vigor to prevent equally dangerous substances from going into their nations from our own. Accordingly, following the signature last year by the United States and 22 other nations in Vienna of a Convention on Psychotropic Substances, I sent it to the Senate for its early advice and consent to ratification. This is the first international agreement to combat the abuse of psychotropic substances. It will bring these drugs under rigorous controls similar to those envisaged for narcotic drugs under a strengthened Single Convention.

In summary, during the past year our Government has made an intense effort to widen and strengthen controls over narcotic and other dangerous drugs, both domestically and internationally. It is gratifying to report that these efforts are enlisting increasing international support.

AIRCRAFT HIJACKING AND SABOTAGE

The growth of air transportation has brought the people of the world in closer contact with each other. Perhaps it was inevitable that some would find the means of preying upon this bounty. If so, it is equally inevitable that the world must protect itself against air hijacking and sabotage. It is doing so.

The aircraft hijacking convention, negotiated in The Hague in December 1970, requires contracting states to extradite or prosecute hijackers apprehended on their territory. More than 80 states have signed the convention thus far. In September a companion convention was concluded at Montreal on suppression of other unlawful acts against civil aviation, notably sabotage. This agreement, too, provides for the prosecution or extradition of offenders.

These two conventions will increase the likelihood that hijackers, saboteurs, and persons committing other attacks against civil aircraft will be punished—regardless of the motive, where the act took place, or where the criminal is found. Universal ratification would ensure that air pirates could find no place to hide.

We intend to press for wide adherence to these agreements and for continued international cooperation, including exchanges of information on security measures. We will also continue to urge international agreement to suspend air services to countries which refuse to cooperate in the release of hijacked aircraft and in the punishment of hijackers.

POPULATION GROWTH

The worldwide population growth rate is still explosive. It implies vastly larger numbers of people in each future decade—numbers far beyond the capacities of most countries to educate, employ, house decently, or even feed adequately. This is a problem of the greatest urgency. The international community must give priority to the task of preventing these potential tragedies from becoming realities.

Last year, we continued to encourage and support United Nations leadership in this field. We pledged to match the contributions of other countries to the United Nations Fund for Population Activities, which has grown with a speed which demonstrates that the world community realizes the exigent nature of the problem. In only its second year of existence, the fund was able to provide $31.6 million to the population control activities of UN agencies and 58 countries. At the same time, our Agency for International Development contributed funds, training and technical support to the population control programs of 33 countries. AID also provided support for several lines of research which hold considerable promise for greatly improved means of fertility control.

PROTECTION OF THE ENVIRONMENT

The earth's resources of air and water are not—as we used to think—unlimited. There is a common requirement of mankind for fresh air, clean water, and uncontaminated soil. This interest is threatened, and the international community must respond to the challenge. Discussions were held in a variety of forums last year, and we should expect soon to see results beginning to emerge.

Preparations are well underway for the UN Conference on the Human Environment to be held in Stockholm this June. We expect the Conference to encourage global monitoring of the oceans, the atmosphere, and the ecological systems. The Conference will also focus attention on such immediate practical problems as managing urban areas, providing potable water, and disposing of solid waste.

As a contribution toward specific accomplishment, the United States has introduced a draft convention on ocean dumping and is participating in the development of a World Heritage Trust Convention, both for possible completion at Stockholm. We hope the Stockholm Conference will also bring greater support for an international agreement to protect endangered species.

Cooperation on the pressing problems of modern society has become an important third dimension of the Atlantic Alliance. NATO's Committee on the Challenges of Modern Society (CCMS), established at our suggestion in 1969, continues to develop new initiatives in such fields as advanced health care services, waste treatment, and urban problems. As a result of a CCMS road safety project, all major automobile producing countries are now developing experimental safety vehicles designed to reduce auto injury rates worldwide. Agreement has been reached on a systems approach to air pollution problems, including jointly developed air quality criteria based on health factors, and the CCMS initiative to eliminate oil spills has stimulated broader international attention to that problem.

An Environmental Committee of the Organization of Economic Cooperation and Development was established in 1970. The United States has taken the lead in seeking guidelines that would avoid trade problems that could result from national measures to abate pollution. The Committee has also arranged for systematic consultation on government action to control the use of chemicals, including pesticides, and is now considering general guidelines for government policies in this field.

The Economic Commission for Europe held a symposium on the environment in Prague last May, and took steps to promote East-West cooperation to deal with common environmental problems.

Significant progress was made last year to combat the oil pollution of the world's oceans and shorelines. In October, the major maritime nations adopted regulations on the size of tanks in oil tankers, which will reduce the spillage of oil as a result of accidents. We are negotiating actively on a new convention to ban all intentional discharges from vessels. And we have successfully concluded two conventions which will provide rapid and certain compensation, on a strict liability basis, to victims damaged by oil spills.

In addition to these multilateral efforts,

the U.S. has broadened bilateral discussions with our immediate neighbors, Canada and Mexico, and with Japan, Argentina, Italy, and others, to solve certain basic environmental problems of particular concern to us.

We are, therefore, rapidly overcoming the initial lack of recognition of the need for international cooperation to protect the environment. However, the world community now faces a more difficult problem, that of determining how the cost of remedial action is to be assigned. We believe that a keystone in the effort to develop compatible national approaches should be the principle that the polluter pays for the economic costs of environmental control. It is the objective of this Administration that the costs of pollution control be allocated in a uniform manner among different countries. Otherwise, international trade patterns would be distorted, and we do not think economic disadvantages should accrue to nations because of efforts made in a common cause.

OUTER SPACE

As our astronauts have seen, the unity of the Earth is experienced most vividly from outer space. And conversely, seen from our planet, space itself is a frontier to mankind as a whole, not merely to individual nations. Space is, therefore, an unparalleled field for cooperation among nations.

As we move into the second decade of space exploration, the U.S. is committed to work with others in space for the benefit of all mankind. We are taking whatever steps can reasonably and properly be taken to work with other countries in the development of their space skills.

Specifically, we have assured the Euro-pean Space Conference that its member countries may obtain our assistance in launching satellites which are for peaceful purposes and which are consistent with international obligations embodied in such agreements as the Outer Space Treaty and the arrangements for the International Telecommunication Satellite Consortium (INTELSAT). We are prepared to consider such assistance to other interested countries. In addition, we are working closely with the Europeans on the concepts and design of a reusable space transportation system.

Over the past year, NASA has agreed with the Soviet Academy of Sciences to significant cooperation in specific space tasks, and in the exchange of information and plans concerning our respective space programs. We have exchanged samples of lunar soil. We are examining together the means to enable Soviet manned spacecraft and our own to rendezvous and dock in space. Joint expert groups have been meeting to arrange details of further collaboration in space meteorology, biology, and medicine, in the study of the natural environment, and in exploration of the moon and planets.

In 1971, after years of negotiation in which the United States has played a leading role, the United Nations General Assembly approved an Outer Space Liability Convention. The Convention, when it enters into force, will provide for the payment of compensation for damage caused by space activities.

Last year also brought a new definitive charter for the operation of INTELSAT. When ratified and signed by two-thirds of the 80 member countries, sometime this year, this will replace the interim arrangements under which INTELSAT has been operating since 1964.

DISASTER RELIEF

Each year, the sudden, savage violence of natural and man-made disasters strikes at millions of our fellowmen. Despite the certainty that disasters will continue to occur, the world community has been very slow in establishing a central mechanism to plan for and coordinate disaster relief.

We have encouraged the United Nations to meet this need. Last year, the General Assembly voted to create a co-ordinator for disaster relief. He will have a small staff—rapidly expandable in emergencies—to undertake his vital task. I applaud this development.

Even before it accepted the new role of coordinating disaster relief, the UN last year showed its ability to mount a very impressive large-scale relief effort to assist the refugees and to avert famine during the crisis in South Asia. The job was effectively done—although interrupted by the India-Pakistan war—and our Government supported it with large financial contributions.

———

These, then, are beginnings the international community has made in addressing the new tasks for diplomacy. Our country is in the forefront of these efforts, and we will continue to be. But these are world challenges, and nothing less than a global response can suffice. Thus far, the response is heartening.

PART VII: THE POLICY-MAKING PROCESS: THE NSC SYSTEM

"If our policy is to embody a coherent vision of the world and a rational conception of America's interests, our specific actions must be the products of rational and deliberate choice."

U.S. Foreign Policy for the 1970's
A Report to the Congress
February 18, 1970

My Reports in 1970 and 1971 described in detail the structure of the National Security Council system and how it works. Its function is so central to the conception and development of our national security policy, however, that it is well to look again briefly at the purposes and role of the system.

THE TASK WE FACED

At the time of my inauguration, it was clear that we were on the threshold of momentous decisions in our foreign policy. The postwar era in international relations was fast disappearing, and with it many of the fundamental assumptions underpinning our policy for the past generation. In order to redefine the nature of American participation in world affairs, we needed to ask the kinds of basic questions that Americans have not had to face for many years. Moreover, we would be examining these questions during a period of growing debate over national priorities and competing claims for the resources available to support our global posture.

It was imperative that I have at my disposal an effective mechanism for policy review and decision making. Before my election, I stated my firm conviction that the foreign policy successes of the Eisenhower period were in part attributable to the careful planning and regular review of policy issues carried out by the National Security Council. I pledged to restore the NSC to its preeminent position in na-

341

tional security planning. The basic issues we faced demanded a system which ensured the most careful analysis of all relevant facts and views.

—It was essential that my senior advisers and I have the full benefit of a full and fair presentation of the views of all agencies within the foreign affairs community.

—I wanted procedures which enabled us to concentrate first on basic purposes over the long term and, only then, on the operational questions of how to proceed.

—We sought to stimulate creativity in our foreign policy by requiring that alternative courses of action be identified and assessed at every stage of the process of policy review.

—We needed a systematic planning effort to lay the groundwork for the actions that could be required in a future crisis.

—Our system had to overcome distortion in the policy review process by ensuring that our analyses proceeded from a common appreciation of the facts.

THE APPROACH WE TOOK

One of my first acts as President was to reaffirm the role of the National Security Council as the principal forum for Presidential review, coordination, and control of U.S. Government activity in the field of national security and foreign affairs. To support the Council we established a system of committees, each with specific responsibilities and each including representatives of all Government agencies concerned with the problem at hand. All parts of the NSC system have as their common purpose to provide me with a clear statement of the issues, realistic options for dealing with them, and the implications of each option for our long term objectives. A second purpose of the system is to ensure that after a decision is made, it is communicated to the agencies involved with precision and implemented effectively by them.

The apex of the system is the *National Security Council* itself. Its statutory members are the President, the Vice President, the Secretary of State, the Secretary of Defense, and the Director of the Office of Emergency Preparedness. The Secretary of the Treasury, the Attorney General, the Director of Central Intelligence, and the Chairman of the Joint Chiefs of Staff regularly attend Council meetings, as well as others at my invitation. So far, during my Administration, the Council has met 73 times. The Council does not, of course, make decisions. Its discussions put the issues and choices in sharp focus and give me the counsel of my senior advisers as the final step in a process of comprehensive review before I make a decision.

Supporting and assisting the National Security Council are six senior bodies, each at the Under Secretary level. Though they have slightly different membership, the primary differences among them lie in their authority and function, and in the experts on whom they rely. Each has representation from the interested agencies. These groups ensure that each agency's views are fully and fairly presented, that dissent is not stifled, and that differences are not compromised away before being presented to me. They ensure that I get the views of each agency, refined by the analysis and criticism of the other concerned agencies. No President could carry out his responsibilities if offered only a single recommendation devised to achieve a bureaucratic consensus.

Three of these groups have the purpose of preparing policy issues for my consideration, either at a National Security Council meeting, or by memorandum if the issue is susceptible to full presentation in that manner. No issue is handled by memorandum if any Cabinet officer desires its consideration at a Council meeting.

—The *Senior Review Group* is the workhorse of the system, and handles the great majority of the policy issues brought to me for decision. Interdepartmental Groups, chaired by Assistant Secretaries of State, prepare the initial studies, which are then reviewed by the SRG to ensure that the issues, options, and agency views are fully presented. During my Administration the Senior Review Group has met 130 times.

—*The Defense Program Review Committee* analyzes the choices inherent in defense budget decisions, relating alternative levels of defense expenditure to other national priorities, both domestic and foreign.

—The *Verification Panel* is charged with the painstaking technical analysis of arms control issues, including the verification requirements which must accompany arms limitations and the capabilities of weapons systems whose limitation is being considered. The Verification Panel also advises me on negotiating options in SALT, and on considerations involved in proposals for MBFR.

The National Security Council *Intelligence Committee* has been added to this

level of the system during the past year. It advises me on the quality, scope, and timeliness of the intelligence input to Presidential decisions, and on the steps to improve it.

Two additional groups are charged with the implementation of decisions. In a Government as large as ours, this requires careful, deliberate, and coordinated effort. These groups do not develop or recommend policy courses except where there may be a need for clarification of specific aspects of a broad decision already reached.

—The *Under Secretaries Committee,* chaired by the Under Secretary of State, is the basic instrument for ensuring effective and uniform execution of foreign policy decisions throughout the Government. It has submitted over 75 memoranda setting forth detailed options, programs, and recommendations to implement policy decisions.

—The *Washington Special Actions Group* is charged with meeting the special need for coordination in crisis situations. Not a decision making body, the WSAG serves as a management team assuring flexible and timely actions by the responsible departments in the context of Presidential decisions and the developing situation. It also is responsible for anticipating future crises, for reviewing contingency plans prepared by the Interdepartmental Groups, and for developing options for NSC consideration. In times of crisis, it is supported by a special inter-agency task force established in the Department of State. There have been 94 meetings of the WSAG during my Administration, usually during crises, and typically following meetings of the National Security Council from which basic decisions emerged. I have personally met with the WSAG on a number of occasions.

In every policy review or crisis situation, the range of the NSC system is brought to bear. This ensures extensive and continuing review of policy and operational choices on all major issues. For example:

—In connection with SALT, the Verification Panel has met 22 times and the NSC 8 times.

—On European issues, including Berlin, MBFR, and the proposed Conference on European Security and Cooperation, the SRG has met 20 times, the Verification Panel 5 times and the NSC 8 times.

—During the Jordan crisis in 1970, the WSAG met 12 times, the SRG 5 times, and the NSC 4 times.

—Between March and December 1971 the NSC met 3 times, the SRG met 4 times, and the WSAG met 18 times on the situation in South Asia.

The National Security Council system draws on the entire machinery of the executive branch of the Government. The extensive network of interdepartmental study groups exists for a single purpose: to ensure that the entire wealth of imagination, expert knowledge, and experience available in the Government is brought to bear on the issues on which I must make a decision.

I rely heavily on the advice and judgment of the Secretary of State, my senior foreign policy adviser, but clearly there must be a means by which I can secure the views of all agencies concerned with national security affairs and foreign policy. There can be no question of the right and obligation of each agency to present its views. The NSC system exists to assure and protect that right. There is no more cogent demonstration of this than the fact that for the first time, through the Defense Program Review Committee, the broad foreign policy judgment of the Department of State is actively sought in the planning of the defense budget.

The emphasis at all levels in the policy formulation process is, as it must be, on candor. Precisely for this reason the right and ability of all senior advisers and their assistants to give their views and recommendations and to comment on those of others candidly throughout the deliberative process must be assured. Only in this way can the President and the National Security Council have the benefit of the widest range of thought and the clearest expression of opinion.

This Administration will be judged by the substance of its policies, not by the instruments chosen to devise them. But at no time in our history was the need for rigorous and systematic review of our policies more urgent. I was determined that our system of decision making be responsive to my need for a statement of clearcut alternatives and their costs and consequences, from which I could select the course to be pursued. The NSC system has provided me with that range of choice. The candor with which my advisers have expressed their views on all of the significant issues we have faced has been a hallmark of the system and essential to its success. The accomplishments of this Administration stand as a measure of the success of that system as an effective vehicle for the creative and orderly formulation and execution of our foreign policy.

PART VIII: CONCLUSION

I have stated many times that we seek a generation of peace. That is the goal of this Administration, and it is against that standard that the initiatives of 1971 should be judged.

In the last analysis, only the future will tell whether or not the developments of the past year have truly brought us closer to that goal. All we can say with certainty now is that a generation of peace is a more credible goal at the end of 1971 than it appeared to be at its beginning. It may still appear to be distant. It does not, however, still appear fanciful and utopian.

That fact in itself is important. Both this country and the world need a brighter vision than managing crises and aiming only at staving off the ultimate conflagration. The influence which history and our own efforts have given this Nation can—and must—be used for something more than an organization of world affairs which aims merely at keeping international animosities in some sort of tenuous, fragile and constantly endangered balance. The containment of enmity is better than its release. But it is not enough as a permanent goal.

For too long, American policy consisted of reacting to events. We had a sense of mission, but rarely a clear definition of our purpose. We were drawn into situations, responding tactically, without a clear perception of where we would end up. When we were not forced by events, we seldom struck out along new paths because we had no positive conception of where we wanted to go.

Our times demand more. A durable peace is a set of conditions and requires a conscious effort to create those conditions. Peace will not come about by itself, with us passively looking on or striking moralistic poses. Nor will it come about automatically with the ending of a war. How many wars in this century have ended without bringing a lasting peace because statesmen failed to shape a durable peace out of the conditions which emerged from the conflict? This is why it makes a difference *how* we liquidate the vestiges of an earlier era as we move into the new. The future of peace—in Asia, in the Middle East, in Europe—depends in large measure upon the steadfastness and purposefulness of American policy all around the world.

Today the United States is once again acting with assurance and purpose on the world stage.

Vietnam no longer distracts our attention from the fundamental issues of global diplomacy or diverts our energies from priorities at home.

Our dramatic departures of the past year—the fruits of our planning and policies over three years—reflect the historical conditions we see today and the historic possibilities we see for tomorrow. They were momentous steps, accelerating the very process of change which they addressed. The world—and we ourselves—are still in the process of adjusting to the developments we have set in train. But we know where we are going. We are moving with history, and moving history ourselves.

There will always be conflict in the

world, and turbulent change and international rivalries. But we can seek a new structure of global relationships in which all nations, friend and adversary, participate and have a stake. We can seek to build this into a world in which all nations, great and small, can live without fear that their security and survival are in danger, and without fear that every conflict contains for them the potential for Armageddon. In such a structure of peace, habits of moderation and compromise can be nurtured, and peoples and nations will find their fullest opportunities for social progress, justice, and freedom.

This is what we mean by a generation of peace.

NOTE: The text of the above item was issued by the White House in the form of a 215-page booklet entitled "U.S. Foreign Policy for the 1970's: The Emerging Structure of Peace; A Report to the Congress by Richard Nixon, President of the United States, February 9, 1972."

On the same day, the White House released the transcripts of two news briefings on the President's report. The briefings were held by Henry A. Kissinger, Assistant to the President for National Security Affairs, on February 7 and 9.

57 Message to the Congress Transmitting Annual Report of the United States Arms Control and Disarmament Agency. *February* 10, 1972

To the Congress of the United States:

Pursuant to the Arms Control and Disarmament Act as amended (P.L. 87–297), I herewith transmit the Eleventh Annual Report of the U.S. Arms Control and Disarmament Agency. I am also pleased to report to the Congress that this document reflects appreciable progress in the disarmament field during calendar year 1971.

Our progress has been especially significant in the Strategic Arms Limitation Talks with the Soviet Union. In May 1971, I was able to announce that a deadlock had been broken. We reached an understanding with the Soviet leadership to concentrate on working out an accord to limit the deployment of defensive anti-ballistic missile systems (ABMs), and to conclude it simultaneously with an agreement on certain measures limiting offensive strategic weapons. This joint understanding reinforces my firm commitment to reach an equitable agreement limiting both offensive and defensive strategic nuclear weapons.

Another highlight of 1971 occurred when the American and Soviet SALT Delegations reached two collateral agreements that were signed in Washington on September 30. The first dealt with measures to be taken by each country to reduce the risk of accidental nuclear war, while the second provided for improvements in the reliability of the Washington-Moscow Direct Communications Line, or "Hot Line", by using satellite communications systems.

In Geneva, at the Conference of the Committee on Disarmament, the United

States was also among the principal architects of a convention banning the development, production and stockpiling of biological weapons and toxins. The presence of these weapons in the arsenals of any civilized nation is no longer justified.

As 1972 opens, I am determined to maintain American leadership in achieving arms control measures which will enhance both national and world security and contribute to a lasting peace.

RICHARD NIXON

The White House,

February 10, 1972.

NOTE: The message is printed in the report entitled "Arms Control Report: 11th Annual Report to the Congress, U.S. Arms Control and Disarmament Agency; January 1–December 31, 1971" (44 pp. plus appendixes).

58   The President's News Conference of *February* 10, 1972

THE PRESIDENT'S TRIP TO CHINA

THE PRESIDENT. [1.] Ladies and gentlemen, before going to your other questions, I would like to make an announcement with regard to the details of the trip to Mainland China. This will not cover all the details, but it will at least cover those that we can announce at this time.

The official party will be announced from Florida, Key Biscayne, on Saturday the 12th. Of course, as you know, we have already announced that Dr. Kissinger, the Secretary of State, Mrs. Nixon, and I will be going, and the other members of the official party at that time will be announced from Washington.

On Monday [February 14], I have an event that I think has already been announced, a meeting with André Malraux, and I am giving a dinner that night for him to which several Congressional leaders will be invited, as well as members of the official party, the Secretary of State, Dr. Kissinger.

In mentioning André Malraux, I do not want to reflect on many of the other experts—and there are many experts in this field of China—whose books have been brought to my attention. I do not want to indicate I have read them all but I have been exposed to a great number. I asked him to come because there was an interesting coincidence.

In 1969, when I met with President de Gaulle in Paris, Mr. Malraux at that time was the Minister of Culture in the de Gaulle Cabinet. We had a discussion prior to the dinner on the subject of China generally, and I was particularly impressed with his analysis of the leaders. His book, at least the one I have read—he's written many—but his book, the one I particularly refer to was his "Anti-Memoirs." I would commend it to you not only for what it tells about China and its leaders, but also about France, its problems, and the whole World War II and post-World War II era.

I give you this only to indicate the breadth of the kind of briefings that all of us who are going to participate in the talks are trying to undertake. It is very different from the other meetings that we have had at the highest level with other governments. I have visited virtually all of the other countries, just as I, of course, have visited the Soviet Union.

But here it is essential to do an enormous amount of homework just to come up to the starting line. I don't want to say that after having read as much as I have, and as much as I will be reading between now and the time we arrive, that I will be an expert, but at least I will be familiar with the men that we will be meeting and the problems that may be discussed.

Tuesday and Wednesday will be used primarily to finish up on many of the domestic matters that are, of course, the subject of matters that I will be discussing with Secretary Connally and Mr. Ehrlichman over this weekend, and also for further briefings from members of the NSC staff and the State Department on the China trip.

The time of departure has now been set. It will be 10 o'clock, Thursday morning the 17th, from Andrews. We will fly directly to Hawaii. We will spend Thursday night and all day Friday in Hawaii.

The following morning, Saturday morning, on the 19th, the press plane will go directly to Mainland China, stopping at Shanghai first, and arriving in Peking. The Chinese Government is arranging this so that the members of the press can be on the ground prior to the time that I will be arriving.

On that same day, Saturday, the 19th, the Presidential plane, the Spirit of '76, will fly to Guam, and we will overnight in Guam and then take off the next day, Sunday, for Shanghai and Peking, arriv-

ing in Peking Sunday morning at approximately 10 or 10:30, eastern time, U.S.[1] The date, of course, is the 21st there and the 20th here. As you know, we cross the International Date Line on the way.

A couple of other points that I know have been raised in briefings and that I can only cover generally:

With regard to agenda, both governments have decided that we will not make any announcements on agenda items prior to the meetings. The agenda will be covered by a joint communique that will be issued at the conclusion of our talks and consequently, questions on agenda, what will be discussed and so forth, on the part of both sides, will not be answered either before we get there or during the course of the meetings, unless the two sides decide, while we are meeting, that an agenda item can properly be discussed or disclosed.

With regard to this itinerary itself, the itinerary, generally as you know, has been announced for three cities. With regard to what we do in each city, it is being kept flexible and no final decisions have been made and none will be announced at this time.

Mrs. Nixon's itinerary will be much more public than mine. And she will have an opportunity, which I hope many of you also will have, those of you who are going, to visit a number of institutions, places of interest in Peking, Hangchow, and Shanghai. She, having, as you know, traveled to perhaps more countries than any First Lady, is looking forward to this with a great deal of interest and, I think, as she

---

[1] The arrival in Peking was scheduled for 11:30 a.m., Monday, Peking time, which is 10:30 p.m., Sunday, e.s.t.

demonstrated on her trip to Africa, her events, I think, will be worth covering.

One side note is that, and I am sure all of you who have been studying, as I have, will have noted this, is that one development in 20th century China that is very significant, is the enormous elevation in the status of women. Total equality is now recognized and looking back over Chinese history, that is, of course, a very significant change.

Consequently, I think Mrs. Nixon's activities will be significant for them. It will be, of course, very significant for us in the United States to see their schools and the other institutions and how they compare with ours and the other countries that we will visit.

As far as my agenda is concerned, there will not be a great deal of what I would call public—well, to put it perhaps rather plainly—sightseeing. There will be some. I mean actually I would hope to see some of the points of interest and the Chinese Government is arranging for some. But we have both agreed that this visit is one, taking place as it does at this time, in which first priority must be given to our talks, and sightseeing and protocol must come second. And consequently, we have agreed that we will not get frozen in to any extended travel within the cities which we will be visiting, in the event that that might interfere with an extended conversation that might be taking place.

I do not want to suggest here what the length of the talks will be but, necessarily, because we are in truth at a beginning, they will be much longer, both with Mr. Chou En-lai and with Mr. Mao Tse-tung than with the leaders of other governments that we have visited. Because there

we are not starting at the beginning—we had the opportunity to come immediately to matters of substance.

Finally, in order to perhaps put the trip in context, you have heard me discuss it in various speeches that I have made generally. I haven't really much to add, because as I pointed out, the agenda items will be decided at the beginning of the meetings, but they will be published at the end of our meetings and by communique.

But I think we could say this: This trip should not be one which would create very great optimism or very great pessimism. It is one in which we must recognize that 20 years of hostility and virtually no communication will not be swept away by one week of discussion.

However, it will mark a watershed in the relations between the two governments; the postwar era with respect to the People's Republic of China and the United States, that chapter now comes to an end from the time that I set foot on the soil of Mainland China, and a new chapter begins.

Now, how the new chapter is written will be influenced, perhaps influenced substantially, by the talks that will take place. On our side and, we believe, also on their side, we hope that the new chapter will be one of more communication and that it will be a chapter that will be marked by negotiation rather than confrontation and one that will be marked by the absence of armed conflict. These are our hopes.

We, of course, will now see to what extent those hopes can be realized in this first meeting.

I will go to any other questions.

QUESTIONS

MEETINGS WITH CHINESE LEADERS

[2.] Q. Mr. President, Mr. Malraux has been quoted as having said that he is sure that the first question that Mao will ask you is, "Will you provide aid for China?" and that the rest of the trip, the success of the talks, will be determined by your answer. Can you give us any indication that if that is true what you will say?

THE PRESIDENT. That gets into the area that I will decline to comment upon, because it involves the agenda items. I cannot really predict with as much confidence as Mr. Malraux perhaps can, as to what Mr. Mao Tse-tung's questions will be.

So, consequently, I don't believe it would be proper to comment now on a question that has not yet been asked by him. If it is asked, I will have an answer.

Q. Mr. President, do you look upon these talks—do you look upon your meeting with Chou En-lai and Mao Tse-tung as dialogue or negotiation?

THE PRESIDENT. They will be primarily dialogue. Here a very subtle but definite distinction is made between the talks that will take place in Peking and the talks that will take place in Moscow.

In the talks in Moscow there are certain subjects that we have been negotiating about and those subjects, therefore, will be negotiated, although, of course, there will be dialogue as well. Dialogue is an essential part of negotiation.

In the case of Peking, there will necessarily have to be a substantial amount of dialogue before we can come to the point of negotiating on substantive matters. I should emphasize, too, that it has already been pointed out by Dr. Kissinger when he returned, that when we speak of these matters that they will be primarily bilateral matters. Beyond that, however, I will not go.

CRITICISM OF POLICIES

[3.] Q. Mr. President, Mr. Haldeman [2] has had very strong words for critics of your peace proposal, saying that they are consciously aiding and abetting the enemy. Your statement was somewhat softer. The Democrats do not seem to still think it is enough. Do you think that Mr. Haldeman's statement, since he is so close to you and a lot of people interpret his thinking as very close to yours, should be left to lie as it is or is there something further that you should say?

THE PRESIDENT. There is nothing further that I should say. I think Mr. Ziegler covered the situation with regard to Mr. Haldeman and you ladies and gentlemen pressed him very hard on that on Monday.

I stated my position very clearly yesterday in my summary of the state of the world speech. We have here a situation where there is a difference of opinion among various candidates for the Presidency as to how they should conduct themselves at this time.

As I pointed out, I considered it a matter of judgment. I do not question the patriotism, I do not question the sincerity of people who disagree with me, because a lot of people do disagree with me on this and other issues as well.

Perhaps to put it in a clearer context, I was a very vigorous critic of the policies that got us into Vietnam. I was a critic, for example, of the settlement which resulted in the partition of Laos, which

---

[2] H. R. Haldeman, Assistant to the President.

opened the Ho Chi Minh Trail and paved the way for the invasion of the South by the North Vietnamese troops.

I was a critic of the policies and the actions which, I think most observers would agree, contributed to the assassination of Diem [3] and the succession of coups which then brought on further armed conflict. I was a strong critic of the conduct of the war before I was a candidate and after I was a candidate. But once I became a candidate and once President Johnson announced he would no longer be a candidate, and the peace talks began, I said then that as far as I was concerned, as a man seeking the Presidency, I would say nothing that would, in any way, jeopardize those peace talks.

So there is in my view—and I do not ask others to hold it, I ask them to consider it—there is, in my view, a very great difference between criticizing policies that got us into war and criticizing the conduct of war and criticisms by a Presidential candidate of a policy to end the war and to bring peace.

What we have here is a situation, as Secretary Rogers has pointed out, a situation where within one week after a very forthcoming peace proposal has been made, various Presidential candidates sought to propose another settlement which went beyond that.

My own candid judgment is that that kind of action has the effect, as I implied in my remarks yesterday, it has the effect of having the government in Hanoi consider at least that they might be well advised to wait until after the election rather than negotiate.

So my view is that as far as I was con-

cerned that is why I did not criticize when I was a candidate for President, after President Johnson started the negotiation. I thought it was good judgment then.

As far as others are concerned, they have to consult their own consciences. They apparently have determined that they wish to take another course of action. I disagree with the course of action. I would strongly urge at this point that all candidates for President, Republican and Democrat, review their public statements and really consider whether they believe they are going to help the cause of peace or hurt it, whether they are going to encourage the enemy to negotiate or encourage him to continue the war.

I have stated my position very categorically. It is different from others. I respect the other opinions. You will have to let the people judge as to which is right.

PRESIDENT THIEU AND THE PEACE
PROPOSALS

[4.] Q. Mr. President, is there real flexibility in this country on the question of when President Thieu should resign and inflexibility in Saigon? Is there a real difference and are you going to do anything about it?

THE PRESIDENT. Well, I noticed the flap that has occurred from President Thieu's statement today, and based on his interpretation of what Secretary Rogers had said. I think the misunderstanding can be cleared up by what I now say.

Every proposal we have made in Paris has been a joint proposal by the Government of South Vietnam and the Government of the United States. Every proposal that we have made has been after consultation with and after receiving suggestions from the Government of South

---

[3] Ngo Dinh Diem, President of the Republic of Vietnam, 1955–63.

Vietnam, as well as the Government of the United States.

The best example of that is the proposal that I announced on January 25 and which we had presented on October 11. The offer on the part of President Thieu to resign a month before the election was his idea. And we included it in the proposal. It was a very, in my opinion, a very statesmanlike thing for him to do and showed his devotion to the proposition of trying to find a way to break the political deadlock which has deadlocked these talks all along.

Now, at this point, I can say that any future proposals we make will be joint proposals of the Government of South Vietnam and the Government of the United States. As far as we are concerned, we have made an offer. It is forthcoming. Many have said it is as far as we should go. We are ready to negotiate on that offer, we and the Government of South Vietnam, but under no circumstances are we going to make any further proposals without the consultation with and the agreement of the Government of South Vietnam, particularly on political issues, because the political issues are primarily theirs to decide rather than ours.

And I would say also, that under no circumstances are we going to negotiate with our enemy in a way that undercuts our ally.

We are not going to negotiate over the heads of our ally with our enemies to overthrow our ally. As I said in my speech on January 25, we are ready to negotiate a settlement, but we are not going to negotiate a surrender either for the United States, nor are we going to negotiate the surrender of 15 million people of South Vietnam to the Communists.

So, as far as President Thieu and his Government is concerned, and our Government is concerned, the proposal that we have made is a joint proposal. If there are to be any changes in that proposal—and we don't intend to make any unless and until there is some indication that the enemy intends to negotiate in good faith—it will be a joint proposal.

The next step is up to the enemy. Our proposal is on the table and it is going to stand there until we get a reply from them.

VIETNAM AS AN ISSUE

[5.] Q. Mr. President, you have said in the past that if the Democrats hope to make an issue of Vietnam, that the rug would be pulled out from under them. I think that is a fairly accurate quote. Do you feel that that issue now remains a live issue, and are you disappointed that it does still remain a part of the public dialogue in so intense a way?

THE PRESIDENT. I am very disappointed that the enemy has refused to negotiate and I, as you know, have always pointed out that we have a two-track approach to ending the American involvement. Our favorite track is negotiation. That could have ended it in '69, '70, '71. We made various proposals we think were the basis for negotiation.

The longer track is Vietnamization. That will end the American involvement in a predictable time, as I think most of us can see.

As far as pulling the rug out from under those who criticize—and it is not a partisan issue; there are Republicans as well as Democrats who have disagreements on this; I respect those disagreements—as far as pulling the rug out is concerned, I would say that I think any American would be delighted to have the rug pulled out from under him on this issue if it brings peace and an end to the killing. That is what we are trying to do.

I would hope that Presidential candidates, particularly, would consult their consciences before they make proposals which might be misread—might be—they would not intend it, I am sure—but might be misread by the enemy and thereby encourage them to wait until after the election before even discussing a very forthcoming proposal.

PRESIDENTIAL NEWS CONFERENCES

[6.] Q. Mr. President, why are you not, sir, holding news conferences with very much regularity or frequency? And what, in particular, do you have against televised news conferences? I believe it has been more than 8 months since you have held one of those.

THE PRESIDENT. Well, I will hold news conferences whenever I believe that they will serve the public interest.

As far as televised news conferences are concerned, I find that the ladies and gentlemen in the press corps have a very vigorous difference of opinion as to which is the more valuable forum.

I remember the last time, or a few months ago, that I was in this office, the first time I had an in-office conference. Mr. Bailey [Charles W. Bailey 2d, Minneapolis Tribune and Minneapolis Star], the former head of the White House Correspondents, said, "This is the best kind of press conference." I am sure Mr. Rather [Dan Rather, CBS News] thinks the best kind of press conference is one with him alone. [*Laughter*]

So I will have Q&A with one commentator. I have had questions and answers with some members of the press, as you know, alone. I will have in-office press conferences. Sometimes I have walked out into the room there, as I did when I announced the Soviet summit, and have a press conference in the press room, so that whoever wants to may film it, and on other occasions we may have a televised press conference.

I would only say, finally, with regard to the televised press conference, it is no more work than one like this, and I would suggest that I do follow the columns and the commentators pretty well, and I noted that there was considerable—I wouldn't call it criticism—but eyebrow-raising with regard to "Why has the President been on television so much? He had 'A Day in the Life of the President,' and that took an hour of prime time. He had a half-hour the night before Christmas, CBS. Then he had an hour with Rather, another CBS. Then he had a State of the Union Message, and he took prime time for the purpose of making announcements on Vietnam in addition to all the rest."

Let me say, I think television has probably had as much of the President as it wants at this point, and that is why you are getting this kind of a conference today.

PRESIDENTIAL ASSISTANT HALDEMAN

[7.] Q. Mr. President, you had some public advice today and yesterday about how critics of the war should conduct themselves. Do you have any public advice for Mr. Haldeman?

THE PRESIDENT. I have answered the question. Anything further?

CONSULTATION WITH PRESIDENT THIEU

[8.] Q. Mr. President, you have left open the question of your flexibility on President Thieu. He is upset. We have had these running stories from Saigon. In effect, you have said the policy is flexible. But do you plan to consult with him at some early point to soothe his feelings?

THE PRESIDENT. We already have. We are in constant consultation. I have discussed the matter with Ambassador Bunker. President Thieu knows, first, as he said in his own statement—because if you will read it carefully, he pointed out that he felt that we had consulted him— he knows, first, that we have never made a proposal except when it was a joint proposal. He knows now there will be no new proposals made unless it is a joint proposal and I trust that this press conference that I am having now with you ladies and gentlemen will reassure not only him, but the people of South Vietnam as well on that point.

As far as flexibility is concerned, what Secretary Rogers was referring to was what we have always said, that we have put a proposal on the table; we are ready to negotiate on it.

Now, that does not mean, however, that after having made such a proposal that 2 weeks later we are going to go a step further and say that we will go further than we have in that proposal. At this point, I emphasize here today we have made a proposal. We think it is reasonable. The enemy has not responded to it. Until the enemy does respond to it, there will be no further proposals and no further concessions on our part.

RECOGNITION OF BANGLADESH

[9.] Q. Mr. President, you spoke in your foreign policy report about sympathy for the aspirations of the East Bengali people. Could you give us some idea of the factors and perhaps the timing of your decision on the recognition of Bangladesh?

THE PRESIDENT. With regard to the problem of the Bengali people, first, let me say that on the humanitarian side, as you know, both before the war, during the war, and after the war, the United States has been the most generous of all of the nations. We will continue to be. That is separate from the political side.

With regard to the political side, we have under study our whole relationship with the subcontinent and as part of that relationship, of course, the 70 million people in Bangladesh are involved. We have not yet made a decision with regard to recognition and you should not expect a decision prior to the time that I return from China.

CONSTITUTIONAL AMENDMENTS ON
BUSING

[10.] Q. Mr. President, what are your views on the constitutional amendments on busing now before the House and the Senate?

THE PRESIDENT. Which one?

Q. Well, the amendments have to do with——

THE PRESIDENT. There are several. Let me get at it this way. My views on busing are well known. I favor the neighborhood school. I favor local control of local schools. I oppose busing for the purpose of racial balance. Those are my views which have been stated on many occasions.

The problem we have now is that some courts have handed down decisions which seem to differ from those views. And so the question arises as to whether legislation or a constitutional amendment is necessary if we are to see that those views that I have just enunciated can properly be held and implemented.

Because if the courts, acting under the Constitution, decide that the views that I have held are unconstitutional, I, of course, will have to follow the courts.

Under these circumstances, therefore, I have ordered a study of the legislative route and of the constitutional amendments. And, as part of that study, I have asked that Senator Brock and Senator Baker in the Senate and Congressman Steed and Congressman Lent in the House, come to the White House on Monday for the purpose of discussing their amendments. The purpose of this discussion is to see whether the constitutional amendment approach is the best approach to this problem.

After I have met Monday, I will be glad to have Mr. Ziegler brief you on what the next step will be. I have not made a decision on it but the matter is under consideration.

NEIGHBORHOOD LEGAL SERVICES

[11.] Q. Mr. President, what is your position on civil suits filed in the names of indigents by Neighborhood Legal Services lawyers against local and State governments? Is that a legitimate function of Neighborhood Legal Services offices?

THE PRESIDENT. I am not going to get into that at this point.

TAX REFORM PROPOSALS

[12.] Q. Mr. President, on another Congressional matter, you have been receiving strong suggestions from Congressional Democrats on the proposed tax reform program. How do you intend to respond?

THE PRESIDENT. I didn't hear the first part of the question.

Q. The proposal for tax reforms, the suggestion that you submit a program for tax reform, has been broached by the Democrats. How do you intend to respond?

THE PRESIDENT. First, there will be no increase in taxes this year. It is obvious that even if the Administration were to recommend tax reform this year, it would be impossible for the Congress, particularly the Ways and Means Committee, as much as it has on its plate, and the Finance Committee, with welfare reform, revenue sharing, and the rest, ever to get to it.

So there will be no tax increase this year.

Second, I pointed out in the State of the Union Message that we are studying the problem of the property tax. We are studying it, first, because it is the most regressive of all taxes and, second, because in those States, and that is most of the States, where the property tax is the primary source for financing public education, recent court decisions indicate it may be unconstitutional.

Under these circumstances, that is why I have asked the McElroy Commission [4] and the Commission on Intergovernmen-

---

[4] Neil H. McElroy was Chairman of the President's Commission on School Finance.

tal Relations to study this problem as to how general tax reform might be undertaken which would meet the objections to the property tax and perhaps mitigate the inequities and find another source of revenue to replace it.

Now we come to the value-added tax. The value-added tax should be put in perspective. We have not recommended a value-added tax and at the present time it is one of a number of proposals being considered by the Treasury Department, by the Domestic Council, and the others with responsibility, as part of a general tax reform.

But one point that should be made is this: The property tax is regressive. In the event that we finally decide, after hearing from these two Commissions, that tax reform is necessary for the future, and it will have to be next year and not this, we are certainly not going to replace one regressive tax with another regressive tax.

That is why when you discuss value-added—and Secretary Connally and I have had a long discussion about this just 2 days ago and we are going to discuss it again in Florida tomorrow, along with other problems of that type—when you discuss value-added, it can't even be considered unless the formula can be found to remove its regressive features, if you had it across the board. I don't know whether such a formula can be found.

But to sum up, we have made no decision with regard to a value-added tax. At the present time, we have not yet found a way, frankly, that we could recommend it to replace the property tax. But, with the obligation to face up to the need to reduce or reform property taxes, the Treasury Department necessarily is considering other methods of taxation.

And I emphasize again, there will be no new taxes this year and, second, whenever any tax reform is recommended by this Administration, it will not be one which will replace one form of regression with another form of regression. It will not be one that increases the tax burden for Americans. It will be one that simply reforms it and makes it more equitable.

FRANK CORMIER (Associated Press). Thank you, Mr. President.

Q. Mr. President, we haven't had a press conference with you for 3 months. I wonder if we could have one or two more questions.

THE PRESIDENT. Oh, sure. Go ahead.

U.S. POSITION ON INDIA-PAKISTAN WAR

[13.] Q. I would like to ask you, Mr. President, about the statements that were made by the Administration officials during the India-Pakistan war. Mr. Kissinger told us, during that war, that this Administration had no bias toward India. Subsequently, papers came to light quoting Mr. Kissinger saying that he was getting hell from you every half hour because the Government wasn't——

THE PRESIDENT. Every hour. [*Laughter*]

Q. ——because the Government wasn't tilting enough toward Pakistan.

THE PRESIDENT. Keep your good humor, otherwise you lose your colleagues.

Q. I am wondering from a credibility standpoint, how do you reconcile these two things?

THE PRESIDENT. I remember being in this office on what I think was one of the saddest days of President Eisenhower's Presidency. At the time we had come out against the British, the French, and the Israelis in the Suez crisis. We did so because we were against the war, not because we were anti-British, anti-French, or anti-

Israeli. As a matter of fact we were pro-British and pro-French and pro-Israeli, but we were against war more.

As far as India is concerned, for 25 years—and those of you who have followed me in the House will know this, as a Member of the House, a Member of the Senate, as Vice President, when I was out of office, and now as President—I have supported every Indian aid program. I believe it is very important for the world's largest non-Communist country to have a chance to make a success of its experiment in democracy, in comparison with its great neighbor to the north, which is the world's largest Communist country. That and, of course, other reasons, of course, are involved.

But as far as being anti-Indian is concerned, I can only say I was antiwar. We did everything that we could to avoid the war, as I pointed out. At this point, we are going to do everything that we can to develop a new relationship with the countries on the subcontinent that will be pro-Indian, pro-Bengalese, pro-Pakistan, but mostly pro-peace.

That is what that part of the world needs. A million were killed in the war of partition. That is probably a modest figure. And then they went through the terrible agony again in 1965, and now they have gone through it again.

It was Prime Minister Nehru who told me that more than anything else what the subcontinent needed was a generation of peace. That is where I got the phrase.

Now as far as we were concerned, I believed that our policies—certainly, we may have made mistakes—but our policies had the purpose of avoiding the war, of stopping it once it began, and now of doing everything we can to heal up the wounds.

ANDERSON PAPERS

[14.] Q. Mr. President, has the Administration discovered, sir, who was the source of the papers that were leaked to Mr. Anderson,[5] and are you planning any action against that person if you know who it is?

THE PRESIDENT. Well, first, we have a lot of circumstantial evidence. Second, as a lawyer, I can say that we do not have evidence that I consider adequate or that the Attorney General considers adequate to take to court. You can be sure that the investigation is continuing. If the investigation gets a break which provides the kind of evidence which will stand up in court, we will present it, but we cannot go to court on circumstantial evidence.

EXPRESSION OF VIEWS BY CANDIDATES

[15.] Q. Mr. President, a few moments ago you discussed your stand in 1968 in regard to the peace negotiations. We know now that there was really very little possibility——

THE PRESIDENT. As a matter of fact, you know it now, but I said it then, over and over again, to those who had to listen to my speech—I only had one in 1968, as you recall. [*Laughter*] That is what you wrote anyway.

But I pointed out that I thought there was very little chance, but I said as long—and this was my phrase, I just read it this morning—as long as there was any chance whatever—and I could not be sure, be-

[5] Jack N. Anderson, columnist, Bell-McClure Syndicate, published four columns on January 9–12, 1972, disclosing information from confidential meetings of the Washington Special Actions Group about Administration policy on the India-Pakistan war.

357

cause I wasn't being consulted—for a breakthrough at the peace table, I was going to say nothing that might destroy that chance. That was my view. It may have been wrong.

Q. Could I take sort of a different tack?

THE PRESIDENT. Sure, any way you want.

Q. As a consequence of your position in 1968, you were promising to end the war, but because of the negotiations that were going on, you felt yourself unable to tell the American people how you proposed to do it once elected President.

Now, it is almost 4 years since these negotiations, in a way, began with President Johnson's announcement of March 31, 1968. Do you think that under these circumstances it is fair to the American people and to your rivals and to this Nation for those who seek the highest office and who have views on the war not to say how they would proceed if they were to become the next President?

THE PRESIDENT. All the candidates for the Presidency have a right to say what they want. They must determine whether

they believe it is right to say it. I concluded in 1968 that, as one who was a potential President, and that was particularly true after I received the nomination, that while I had a right to criticize, it was not right to do so.

Now, each of these candidates may feel that the peace proposal that we have made is one that they don't think goes far enough. They may feel that we should make one that would overthrow the Government of South Vietnam, or some other proposal that will satisfy the enemy. They have a right to say that. The American people then will have to judge.

But I am suggesting now that we have made a proposal that is fair, it is forthcoming, it should be negotiated on, and the responsibility for the enemy's failing to negotiate may have to be borne by those who encourage the enemy to wait until after the election.

MR. CORMIER. Thank you again, Mr. President.

NOTE: President Nixon's twenty-second news conference was held at 4 p.m. in the Oval Office at the White House on Thursday, February 10, 1972. He spoke without referring to notes.

59   Remarks at the First Annual Awards Dinner of the National Center for Voluntary Action. *February* 10, 1972

Mr. Etherington, Mr. Ford,[1] *the award winners, all of the distinguished guests:*

I will not delay your dinner too long, because I know that I am just the first course and that more is to come. But I

---

[1] Henry Ford II was the retiring chairman of the board of directors of the National Center for Voluntary Action. Edwin D. Etherington, who had served as president of the Center from March 1971, was the new chairman.

did want the opportunity to visit the awards dinner and not only to be honored to participate in the presentation of plaques, but also to say something to you, the 400 in this room—this is really the 400 believe me, right here, from all over America—but to say something to you about volunteerism, something that will not be new, but something that constantly needs to be reemphasized in America. I think we saw something about volunteerism in the awards that were just presented; more will be said about them later.

As I understand, I gave them a plaque and somebody else gives them a $5,000 check and certainly that tells us something too. You could not possibly buy what they have been able to give with $5,000, because as Ted Etherington has indicated, what really distinguishes volunteerism is that it provides services; it brings forth efforts that money simply could not buy.

It is true all over this country, not just thousands or tens of thousands or hundreds of thousands, but millions of volunteers are represented in various organizations. It is a very distinctive feature of American life. De Tocqueville noticed it 100 years ago as he traveled through America. He said what really distinguished this country, whether it was in the East, or what was then the very primitive Midwest, was the multiplicity of volunteer organizations, overlapping each other, but all working toward a common objective of making their communities or their States and their Nation a better place.

And most recently, Willy Brandt, the Nobel Peace Prize winner, after our meeting in Miami, Florida, spent 2 weeks in Florida. He had a press conference. He was very generous in his comments about the United States and its people. He said what impressed him the most about the American people was volunteerism. He said, "We in Europe do not really know this country as we should," because naturally people in other countries know us by our Government or by our Ambassadors and others, and we try to do the best we can, but that is highly impersonal. It is even impersonal when we provide foreign aid, when we help in other ways.

But as Willy Brandt pointed out, as he saw in the areas that he visited in his 2 weeks' stay in Florida, hundreds of people, helping in hospitals and schools and other agencies, it gave him a different feeling about America than he had ever had before and he, of all the foreign leaders, knows us as well as almost any.

So, it shows that you do represent something that is very special about this country, something that is worth preserving, and something that is worth nurturing because it needs to grow. It presents America at its best. It presents America at its best at home; it also presents America at its best abroad. Because when we do things as a government abroad, that is rather expected to have a selfish interest—sometimes it does; sometimes it is solely humanitarian.

But when we do things as volunteers, whether it is in the Peace Corps or other areas, it has a different connotation, it moves from people to people.

So, here tonight, we honor volunteers.

I think perhaps the best way I can put it is to go back to something that Walt Whitman said. He said what really distinguished America was that this was the country in which the President took off his hat to the people rather than where the people took off their hats to the President.

Tonight I take off my hat to the volunteers of America, to this group, to all that have worked in it. Any President would. And he would do so because he is very proud, speaking for all the Nation, to thank people who give of their time and their efforts and their hearts in good causes.

We have seen two groups represented here and they tell us something too. The organization SERVE is, as you know, one of senior citizens. I have spoken to numbers of senior citizens' groups recently and Arthur Flemming[2] and I have often talked about it. This is the impression that constantly comes through.

When a person retires he no longer has business responsibilities. He just doesn't want to be fed, housed, taken care of. He or she wants to be useful, wants to do something. And volunteerism is a wonderful way for older people who have retired. Let us be thankful that we have such people as that.

Now a word about Mrs. Giles. Here we really feel it. You think of those 40 children who, except for her, might not have had a chance. But they did have a chance, and she did it. You are probably wondering what I was talking to her about. I was just asking her, now how could you have done this for 50 years? Mrs. Giles said to me, "I am only 71." And that tells us something else, if you want to keep looking young, be a volunteer. Mrs. Giles is the best proof of that.

Now, could I say a word about our retiring chairman, Henry Ford. He flew from London to come here and tomorrow he flies back to London and then on to other stops around the world.

I thought of what he represented. Here is a man that we all know is enormously successful in business. He is a man we all know who has contributed, not thousands, or hundreds—which is about as much as we can do—but millions and millions of dollars to good causes around the world, and in America. We are thankful for him, his organization, his people, for what they have done. But then we see something else about him.

---

[2] Chairman of the 1971 White House Conference on Aging and Special Consultant to the President on Aging.

Here is a man who could have said, "Well, I have given these huge checks, millions of dollars, so I have done my part." But he goes further, he gives of himself. He gives us executive talent and leadership that money could not possibly buy. What a great credit it is to the American free enterprise system that one of our top businessmen is not satisfied with just giving his money, he gives of himself. That is the kind of example we like in America and we thank Henry Ford for providing it.

Now, finally, I would like to leave this thought with all of you. We would all wish that more who have worked could be personally awarded. But let this be a symbol of how we all so deeply feel, the fact that you are here, the fact that you will go back to your organizations and tell about this dinner—this, I hope, will give a new lift to volunteerism in your communities and in your States.

I can assure you, that as far as the government of this country is concerned— and I say this in a totally nonpartisan, bipartisan way, whether it is a Republican administration or a Democratic administration, this is something we are not divided on. We are for it because it is good for America. I think that this is something that brings Americans together.

We can have religious differences, we can be of different colors, we can be of different generations, but when it comes to working to help people, retarded children, older people who are shut-ins, sick people, whatever the case might be, that is something that brings us together, and that is why I consider it a very great privilege to speak at such a dinner as this. I consider it a very great privilege to honor those who have been honored tonight and I consider it also a privilege to thank all of you for all that you have done through the years.

A final thought: When I announced to the press today some of the items of the schedule that we will be undertaking in the trip to Mainland China, which will begin next Thursday, I pointed out that my schedule would necessarily be very flexible because of the extensive talks I would be having with the leaders of that government and that those talks had to take priority over protocol or seeing those points of interest that anyone would want to see in a country he had not visited before.

But I also pointed out that Mrs. Nixon would not have those inhibitions, that she would have the privilege, and it will be a privilege for her, as it was when she visited Africa just a few weeks ago, and as it has been as she has visited so many countries all over the world during the years we have been in and out of public life. She will have the opportunity to, in this country, the most populous of all the nations of the world, to visit their schools, their hospitals, to see their people.

We know there are great differences in our philosophies. There are great differences between our governments and they are not going to be washed away by simply a week's discussions, particularly since there has been 20 years in which we have had hostility and virtually no communication.

But of this thing I am sure: If, on such a trip, there can be just the opening of communication, if the people of China could only feel that the people of America want peace with all people in the world, that when children are concerned we care about them, no matter what their government may be, that where people who are in distress are concerned, we care about

them, no matter what differences we may have in foreign policy—this is what America really wants to convey to peoples around the world. We believe that that may be possible, at least steps can be taken in that direction in the brief time that we are there.

But the main point that I make is this: I look over this audience. About half are women and half are men. Among the leaders in volunteerism here, in addition to the men who will all be properly recognized, we have Eunice Kennedy Shriver, who has been so active in volunteerism for so many years, and Mrs. Romney,[3] who has been, also, so very active in volunteerism. And this tells us something else.

An interesting point that I have found and that any of you who have studied recent Chinese history will find, is that perhaps one of the most significant changes that has occurred in the 20th century in that huge country that we know so little about has been that women have changed insofar as their status is concerned. I am not suggesting in this respect that this would not have happened had there not been changes in government and so forth such as have occurred there, but I do say that for us in the United States to recognize that in many parts of the world women are now reaching a new state of recognition and that we on our part should demonstrate that we also have that same standard, that this is a message on a people-to-people basis that is enormously important to get across.

I think that one of the most striking things and the encouraging things about volunteerism in America is that really,

[3] Lenore Romney, member of the Center's board of directors and wife of George W. Romney, Secretary of Housing and Urban Development.

there are more women in it than men. Part of it is the fact that women may have more time, but part of it might be the fact that they may have more heart. But for whatever the reason, it is America at its best.

I know many times when I write a speech and make one my secretary will say, "Now be sure you don't refer to men doing this and that; you've got to say 'men and women'." I suppose she is thinking of women's lib and all that. All that I know is this: She is right. She is right because, as this banquet so well illustrates, there is no area in which the women of America can render greater service to their country and their community than in the field of volunteerism.

So we are proud of what the men have done, people like Henry Ford and Ted Etherington. But we recognize that they stand up here and they make the speeches and they may take some of the bows, but the women do the work, and we thank you for doing it.

Thank you.

NOTE: The President spoke at 7:13 p.m. at the John F. Kennedy Center for the Performing Arts. He spoke without referring to notes.

He presented plaques to the winners of the 1971 National Volunteer Awards. The group category award went to SERVE (Serve and Enrich Retirement by Volunteer Experience) of New York City, one of the pioneer groups in mobilizing elderly and retired persons for volunteer work. Winner in the individual category was Mrs. Arnette Giles of Pearlington, Miss., the wife of a small-town minister, who has raised more than 40 retarded, abandoned, and needy children in addition to five of her own. She also works at a retarded children's school and helps the elderly in her community.

60   Letter to Representative Robert McClory of Illinois on the Occasion of Lincoln's Birthday.   *February* 12, 1972

Dear Bob:

When you represent me at the wreath-laying ceremony at the Lincoln Memorial, I hope you will convey my best wishes to all who pay tribute to the leadership which this strong yet simple man brought to a divided nation over a century ago.

He was an open man, genuine, rough-hewn and full of hope for America. His abiding faith in God and in the ultimate wisdom and goodness of the common people guided him all the years of his life and touched the soul of the land. His forthright and honest words sank deep into the understanding of every listener, and what he said of Henry Clay, a man he deeply admired, could well be applied to Lincoln himself:

He loved his country partly because it was his own country, but mostly because it was a free country; and he burned with a zeal for its advancement, prosperity and glory, because he saw in such, the advancement, prosperity and glory of human liberty, human right and human nature. He desired the prosperity of his countrymen partly because they were his countrymen, but chiefly to show to the world that free-men could be prosperous.

Now, one hundred and twenty years

later, we work in a divided world to establish a peace to end all wars, and we seek to move America forward here at home bringing its people together and building a new and lasting prosperity. We need more than ever the qualities of Lincoln to inspire us and give us confidence to do our duty as we understand it, to serve America better so that America may better serve mankind.

Sincerely,

RICHARD NIXON

[Honorable Robert McClory, House of Representatives, Washington, D.C. 20515]

NOTE: The letter, dated February 7, 1972, was released at Key Biscayne, Fla., on February 12.

61 Statement About the Cost of Living Council's Quarterly Report on the Economic Stabilization Program. *February* 12, 1972

TODAY'S report by the Cost of Living Council shows that we have made an important beginning to our national effort against inflation.

The battle has not yet been won. But we are on the way toward winning it.

The 90-day wage-price freeze that I imposed on August 15 met its objectives of braking the rise in wages and prices, of turning around the inflationary psychology that had gripped the Nation, and of making it possible to establish the machinery for post-freeze stabilization.

The controls established by the Cost of Living Council are now in place, and public support and cooperation for them continues.

In the months ahead, the Council, the Pay Board, the Price Commission, and all those associated with the stabilization program will face many tough decisions. They will have to be persistent in their efforts, keeping the public interest first in making those decisions. They will need the help and support of the American people.

This Administration is determined to defeat inflation. I am confident that the American people share that determination.

NOTE: The report, covering the period August 15 through December 31, 1971, is entitled "Economic Stabilization Program Quarterly Report: Executive Office of the President—Cost of Living Council" (Government Printing Office, 164 pp.).

62 Letter Accepting the Resignation of John N. Mitchell as Attorney General. *February* 15, 1972

Dear John:

As you have requested in your letter of February 15, I accept your resignation as Attorney General effective March 1, 1972. I do so on a note of the utmost regret—but a regret compensated by a sense of personal and heartfelt gratitude on behalf of myself and all Americans.

As chief legal advisor to the President, and as the leader of our fight against crime and lawlessness, you have left a permanent imprint for the better on our Nation of which I am immensely proud. You have made this a time of historic accomplishment in expanding and intensifying the Federal Government's anti-crime efforts, in launching new and more effective efforts to combat drug abuse, in improving the system of justice for all, and, not least, in developing greater public support for the forces of law and justice throughout the country. You have given the American people new—and newly justified—confidence in their ability to halt the spiral of crime, and to restore domestic peace.

Your consistently wise advice and counsel have been of immense value to me throughout the course of our Administration, and I know I can speak for all of your colleagues in saying we shall greatly miss you around the Cabinet table.

As you leave our official family, you do so with the warmest of good wishes and with deep thanks for a difficult task superbly done.

Sincerely,

RICHARD NIXON

[The Honorable John N. Mitchell, The Attorney General, Department of Justice, Washington, D.C.]

63   Memorandum About the Federal Summer Employment Program for Youth.   *February 17, 1972*

Memorandum for Heads of Executive Departments and Agencies:

For many young Americans, particularly needy students, summer jobs can be the decisive factor in the completion of their education. This year, the Federal agencies can once again make that all-important difference, offering sound guidance on the choice of future careers for all who participate in the Federal Summer Employment Program for Youth.

Those who are engaged in this year's program can also gain practical work experience and a better understanding of how their Government serves the people. Agencies, in turn, can benefit from the contributions made by these enthusiastic, energetic young summer workers.

This year, many students will be employed as a result of successful competition in a nationwide summer employment examination, under merit staffing programs developed by agencies, and under the Federal Summer Intern Program. In addition, we must continue to provide opportunities for needy youths: therefore we have set once again the general goal successfully met last summer—employment of one needy youth for every 40 regular employees on your payroll.

I have asked the Chairman of the Civil Service Commission to again provide the leadership and guidelines for summer employment and to report to me on the accomplishments of the 1972 program; and I ask each of you to give personal support to this important investment in our future.

RICHARD NIXON

NOTE: On March 7, 1972, at the direction of the President, a meeting to launch the 1972 summer employment program for youth was held at the White House, with the Vice President as Chairman. Mayors of nine cities and representatives of the U.S. Conference of Mayors, National League of Cities, and National Alliance of Businessmen attended the meeting. On the same day, the White House released the transcript of a news briefing on the summer employment program by Laurence H. Silberman, Under Secretary, and Malcolm R. Lovell, Jr., Assistant Secretary for Manpower, Department of Labor.

63A   Chronology of Visit to the People's Republic of China. *February* 17–28, 1972

EDITOR'S NOTE: The following chronology of events was prepared from White House announcements and outlines public activities of the President and Mrs. Nixon during their visit to the People's Republic of China.

Thursday, February 17

After a departure ceremony on the South Lawn of the White House, the President and Mrs. Nixon went by helicopter to Andrews Air Force Base for the flight to Hawaii, en route to the People's Republic of China.

Arriving at Kaneohe Marine Corps Air Station, Oahu, Hawaii, the President and Mrs. Nixon motored to the residence of the Commanding General, First Marine Brigade, where they remained until Saturday afternoon, February 19, reading and preparing for the China visit.

Saturday, February 19–Sunday, February 20

The President and Mrs. Nixon boarded the Spirit of '76 at Kaneohe Marine Corps Air Station for the 8-hour flight to Guam. Crossing the International Date Line en route, they arrived at Guam International Airport shortly after 5 p.m. on Sunday, February 20, Guam time. They spent the night at Nimitz Hill, the residence of the Commander, Naval Forces, Marianas.

Monday, February 21

At 7 a.m., Guam time, the President and Mrs. Nixon left Guam International Airport for Shanghai, their first stop in the People's Republic of China. They arrived, after a 4-hour flight, at Hung Chiao (Rainbow Bridge) Airport, Shanghai, at 9 a.m., China time, where they were greeted by officials of the People's Republic, headed by Vice Minister of Foreign Affairs Ch'iao Kuan-hua. After refreshments and a tour of the terminal, the Presidential party again boarded the Spirit of '76, accompanied by Vice Minister Ch'iao, Chang Wen-chin and Wang Hai-jung of the Foreign Ministry, a Chinese navigator, radio operator, and

three interpreters, for the final leg of the flight to Peking.

At about 11:30 a.m., China time, the party arrived at Capital Airport near Peking. Premier Chou En-lai greeted the President and members of his party, stood with the President for the playing of the national anthems of the two countries, and accompanied the President in a review of the troops.

The Premier then accompanied the President in a motorcade to Peking, to Taio Yu Tai (Angling Terrace), the guest house where the President and Mrs. Nixon would stay during their visit.

In the afternoon, the President met for an hour with Chairman Mao Tse-tung at the Chairman's residence and for an hour with Premier Chou and other officials in plenary session at the Great Hall of the People.

The President and Mrs. Nixon were guests of Premier Chou at a banquet in the Great Hall of the People in the evening.

Tuesday, February 22

After a morning of staff meetings and attention to other White House business, the President met for 4 hours with Premier Chou in the Great Hall.

The First Lady visited the kitchen of the Peking Hotel, where she toured food preparation and cooking areas, and talked with cooks and helpers. She was accompanied by Mme. Lin Chia-mei, wife of Vice Premier Li Hsien-nien, Mme. Chi P'eng-fei, wife of the Minister of Foreign Affairs, and Sun Hsin-mang, head of the revolutionary committee of the hotel. During the tour, Mrs. Nixon told reporters of plans for the People's Republic to present to the people of America two giant pandas, in appreciation for the two musk oxen which were to be given to the Peking Zoo on behalf of the people of the United States.

In the afternoon, Mrs. Nixon visited the Summer Palace, an imperial residence and garden during the Ching Dynasty. She toured rooms used by the Empress Tzu Hsi and walked in the gardens, viewing the lake Kun Ming and Longevity Hill. She then went to the Peking Zoo and saw the zoo's pandas.

In the evening, the President and First Lady attended a cultural program with Premier and Madame Chou and Chiang Ch'ing, the wife of Chairman Mao Tse-tung. They saw a performance of the ballet, "The Red Detachment of Women."

Wednesday, February 23

The President and Premier Chou met in the afternoon for 4 hours of discussions at the guest house where the President was staying.

The First Lady visited the Evergreen People's Commune on the west edge of Peking. In her hour-long tour, she visited the commune's clinic, where she observed acupuncture treatments, second- and third-grade classrooms, a commune home, agricultural areas and greenhouses, and a dry goods store.

In the afternoon, Mrs. Nixon visited the Peking Glassware Factory and talked with workers making glass flowers and animals.

In the evening, with Premier Chou En-lai, the President and Mrs. Nixon attended a public exhibition of gymnastics, badminton, and table tennis at the Capital Gymnasium.

Thursday, February 24

The President and Mrs. Nixon, accompanied by Vice Premier Li Hsien-nien, drove 35 miles north of Peking to visit the Ba Da Ling portion of the Great Wall of China, and then the tombs of the emperors of the Ming Dynasty.

In the afternoon, the President and Premier Chou met again for 3 hours of discussion. The President and Mrs. Nixon later attended an informal private dinner hosted by Premier Chou in the Great Hall.

Friday, February 25

In the morning, the President and Mrs. Nixon went to the Forbidden City, the site in Peking of the residence of the emperors for some 800 years prior to the early 20th century. They were accompanied by Marshal Yeh

Chien-ying, Vice Chairman of the Military Affairs Commission.

In the afternoon, the President met again with Premier Chou for an hour.

The First Lady toured the Peking Children's Hospital.

Marking the final evening of their Peking stay, the President and the First Lady hosted a banquet honoring Premier Chou and other Chinese officials in the Great Hall.

Saturday, February 26

At the Peking Airport, the President and Premier Chou and other officials of the United States and the People's Republic met in plenary session for approximately one hour.

The President and the First Lady, with Premier Chou, then boarded the Premier's plane for the flight to Hangchow, People's Republic of China. From Hangchow Airport, they drove to a guest house on West Lake, a park and recreational site, where they were to spend the night.

In the afternoon, they joined in a walking tour of Flower Fort Park and a boat tour of West Lake, stopping briefly at the Island of Three Towers Reflecting the Moon. Mrs. Nixon also visited the Temple of the Great Buddha.

They were entertained in the evening at a banquet given by the Chekiang Province Revolutionary Committee.

Sunday, February 27

With Premier Chou, the President and the First Lady flew in the Premier's plane from Hangchow Airport to Shanghai. From Shanghai Airport, they motorcaded to the Shanghai Industrial Exhibition, where, with Premier Chou, they toured exhibits of heavy machinery and electronic equipment, handicrafts, surgical techniques, textiles, light industry, musical instruments, toys, and arts and crafts.

Mrs. Nixon also visited the Shanghai Municipal Children's Palace, where she watched demonstrations of dancing, gymnastics, a puppet show, theatrics, swordplay, and art by students at the center. Her guide was Chang Hong, a fifth-grade student.

In the late afternoon, the joint communique agreed upon by the President and Premier Chou was released.

In the evening, the President and First Lady were guests at a banquet in the Shanghai Exhibition Hall hosted by the Shanghai Municipal Revolutionary Committee. Premier Chou and Committee Chairman Chang Ch'un-ch'iao then accompanied the President and Mrs. Nixon to a cultural program of acrobatics in the Exhibition Hall.

Monday, February 28

Premier Chou visited with the President for an hour at the Ching Kiang guest house and then accompanied the Presidential party to the airport for official farewells before the takeoff for the return flight at 10 a.m.

Crossing the International Date Line, the Spirit of '76 arrived at Elmendorf Air Force Base, Anchorage, Alaska, at midnight on Sunday, February 27, Alaska time. The President and the First Lady spent the night at the residence of the Commanding General and left for the final leg of the flight to Washington at 9:40 a.m. on Monday, February 28, Alaska time.

The official party arrived at Andrews Air Force Base near Washington at 9:15 p.m., e.s.t.

64   Remarks on Departure From the White House for a State Visit to the People's Republic of China. *February* 17, 1972

Mr. Vice President, Mr. Speaker, Members of the Congress, and members of the Cabinet:

I want to express my very deep appreciation to all of you who have come here to send us off on this historic mission, and I particularly want to express appreciation to the bipartisan leadership of the House and Senate who are here.

Their presence and the messages that have poured in from all over the country to the White House over the past few days, wishing us well on this trip, I think, underline the statement that I made on July 15, last year, when I announced the visit.

That statement was, as you will recall, that this would be a journey for peace. We, of course, are under no illusions that 20 years of hostility between the People's Republic of China and the United States of America are going to be swept away by one week of talks that we will have there.

But as Premier Chou En-lai said in a toast that he proposed to Dr. Kissinger and the members of the advance group in October, the American people are a great people. The Chinese people are a great

people. The fact that they are separated by a vast ocean and great differences in philosophy should not prevent them from finding common ground.

As we look to the future, we must recognize that the Government of the People's Republic of China and the Government of the United States have had great differences. We will have differences in the future. But what we must do is to find a way to see that we can have differences without being enemies in war. If we can make progress toward that goal on this trip, the world will be a much safer world and the chance particularly for all of those young children over there to grow up in a world of peace will be infinitely greater.

I would simply say in conclusion that if there is a postscript that I hope might be written with regard to this trip, it would be the words on the plaque which was left on the moon by our first astronauts when they landed there: "We came in peace for all mankind."

Thank you and goodby.

NOTE: The President spoke at 10:10 a.m. on the South Lawn at the White House. He spoke without referring to notes. The departure ceremony was broadcast live on radio and television.

The President had met with the Bipartisan leaders of the Congress prior to the departure ceremony.

On February 12, 1972, the White House released a list of the members of the official party and biographical data on each member. The list is printed in the Weekly Compilation of Presidential Documents (vol. 8, p. 444).

65 Statement on Signing a Bill To Arbitrate Settlement of the West Coast Dock Strike. *February* 21, 1972

THE SECRETARY of Labor has informed me today that an agreement has now been reached in the west coast dock strike and the workers have returned to their jobs.

While this contract will still be subject to approval by the Pay Board, the entire Nation can be gratified by the willingness of the parties to settle their differences voluntarily. For thousands of Americans whose livelihoods have been threatened, this strike has been a painful experience and its end is most welcome.

For several days, I have delayed action on S.J. Res. 197, a bill to end the strike by arbitration, in the hope that the pending legislation would encourage the parties to reach a voluntary accord. Today, as this legislation takes effect with my signature, I am pleased to note that the arbitration machinery will no longer be needed.

I must point out, however, that our agenda on transportation strikes is not yet clear. Repeatedly over the past 2 years I have urged the Congress to act on a comprehensive measure to avoid future strikes of this kind, and yet the Crippling Strikes Prevention Act still awaits action. The Congress did approve special legislation for this west coast strike, and I appreciate the significance of that action. The other shoe must now drop, however, or the Nation can only hobble into the future.

NOTE: The statement was released at Peking, People's Republic of China, where the President signed the bill. As enacted, S.J. Res. 197 is Public Law 92–235 (86 Stat. 40).

On the same day, the White House released the transcript of a news briefing by Secretary of Labor James D. Hodgson on the act and on the agreement reached in the dock strike.

On February 7, 1972, the White House released a statement by Secretary Hodgson on a proposed settlement of the dock strike. On February 8, the White House released the transcript of a news briefing by Secretary Hodgson on further progress toward settlement of the strike.

66 Toasts of the President and Premier Chou En-lai of the People's Republic of China at a Banquet Honoring the President in Peking. *February* 21, 1972

Mr. Prime Minister and all of your distinguished guests this evening:

On behalf of all of your American guests, I wish to thank you for the incomparable hospitality for which the Chinese people are justly famous throughout the world. I particularly want to pay tribute, not only to those who prepared the magnificent dinner, but also to those who have provided the splendid music. Never have I heard American music played better in a foreign land.

Mr. Prime Minister, I wish to thank you for your very gracious and eloquent remarks. At this very moment, through the wonder of telecommunications, more people are seeing and hearing what we say than on any other such occasion in the whole history of the world. Yet, what we say here will not be long remembered. What we do here can change the world.

As you said in your toast, the Chinese people are a great people, the American people are a great people. If our two peoples are enemies the future of this world we share together is dark indeed. But if we can find common ground to work together, the chance for world peace is immeasurably increased.

In the spirit of frankness which I hope will characterize our talks this week, let us recognize at the outset these points: We have at times in the past been enemies. We have great differences today. What brings us together is that we have common interests which transcend those differences. As we discuss our differences, neither of us will compromise our principles. But while we cannot close the gulf between us, we can try to bridge it so that we may be able to talk across it.

So, let us, in these next 5 days, start a long march together, not in lockstep, but on different roads leading to the same goal, the goal of building a world structure of peace and justice in which all may stand together with equal dignity and in which each nation, large or small, has a right to determine its own form of government, free of outside interference or domination. The world watches. The world listens. The world waits to see what we will do. What is the world? In a personal sense, I think of my eldest daughter whose birthday is today. As I think of her, I think of all the children in the world, in Asia, in Africa, in Europe, in the Americas, most of whom were born since the date of the foundation of the People's Republic of China.

What legacy shall we leave our children? Are they destined to die for the hatreds which have plagued the old world, or are they destined to live because we had the vision to build a new world?

There is no reason for us to be enemies. Neither of us seeks the territory of the other; neither of us seeks domination over the other; neither of us seeks to stretch out our hands and rule the world.

Chairman Mao has written, "So many deeds cry out to be done, and always urgently. The world rolls on. Time passes. Ten thousand years are too long. Seize the day, seize the hour."

This is the hour, this is the day for our two peoples to rise to the heights of greatness which can build a new and a better world.

In that spirit, I ask all of you present to join me in raising your glasses to Chairman Mao, to Prime Minister Chou, and to the friendship of the Chinese and American people which can lead to friendship and peace for all people in the world.

NOTE: The President spoke at 8:55 p.m. in the Great Hall of the People. He spoke from a prepared text in response to a toast proposed by Premier Chou. The exchange of toasts was broadcast live on television via satellite.

The Premier spoke in Chinese. His remarks were translated by an interpreter as follows:

Mr. President and Mrs. Nixon, ladies and gentlemen, comrades and friends:

First of all, I have the pleasure on behalf of Chairman Mao Tse-tung and the Chinese Government to extend our welcome to Mr. President and Mrs. Nixon and to our other American guests.

I also wish to take this opportunity to extend on behalf of the Chinese people cordial greetings to the American people on the other side of the great ocean.

President Nixon's visit to our country at the invitation of the Chinese Government provides the leaders of the two countries with an opportunity of meeting in person to seek the normalization of relations between the two countries and also to exchange views on questions of concern to the two sides. This is a positive move in conformity with the desire of the Chinese and American peoples and an event unprecedented in the history of the relations between China and the United States.

The American people are a great people. The Chinese people are a great people. The peoples of our two countries have always been friendly to each other. But owing to reasons known to all, contacts between the two peoples were suspended for over 20 years. Now, through the common efforts of China and the United States, the gate to friendly contacts has finally been opened. At the present time it has become a strong desire of the Chinese and American peoples to promote the normalization of relations between the two countries and work for the relaxation of tension. The people, and the people alone, are the motive force in the making of world history. We are confident that the day will surely come when this common desire of our two peoples will be realized.

The social systems of China and the United States are fundamentally different, and there exist great differences between the Chinese Government and the United States Government. However, these differences should not hinder China and the United States from establishing normal state relations on the basis of the Five Principles of mutual respect for sovereignty and territorial integrity, mutual nonaggression, noninterference in each other's internal affairs, equality and mutual benefit, and peaceful coexistence; still less should they lead to war. As early as 1955 the Chinese Government publicly stated that the Chinese people do not want to have a war with the United States and that the Chinese Government is willing to sit down and enter into negotiations with the United States Government.

This is a policy which we have pursued consistently. We have taken note of the fact that in his speech before setting out for China President Nixon on his part said that "what we must do is to find a way to see that we can have differences without being enemies in war." We hope that, through a frank exchange of views between our two sides to gain a clearer notion of our differences and make efforts to find common ground, a new start can be made in the relations between our two countries.

In conclusion, I propose a toast

—to the health of President Nixon and Mrs. Nixon,

—to the health of our other American guests,

—to the health of all our friends and comrades present, and

—to the friendship between the Chinese and American peoples.

67 Exchange With Reporters at the Great Wall of China. *February 24, 1972*

THE PRESIDENT. I can only say to the media, who, like myself, have never seen the Great Wall before, that it exceeds all expectations. When one stands there and sees the Wall going to the peak of this mountain and realizes that it runs for hundreds of miles, as a matter of fact thousands of miles, over the mountains and through the valleys of this country, that it was built over 2,000 years ago, I think that you would have to conclude that this is a great wall and that it had to be built by a great people.

Many lives, of course, were lost in building it because there was no machinery or equipment at the time. It had to all be done by hand. But under the circumstances, it is certainly a symbol of what China in the past has been and of what China in the future can become. A people who could build a wall like this certainly have a great past to be proud of and a people who have this kind of a past must also have a great future.

My hope is that in the future, perhaps as a result of the beginning that we have made on this journey, that many, many Americans, particularly the young Americans who like to travel so much, will have an opportunity to come here as I have come here today with Mrs. Nixon and the others in our party, that they will be able to see this Wall, that they will think back as I think back to the history of this great people, and that they will have an opportunity, as we have had an opportunity, to know the Chinese people, and know them better.

What is most important is that we have an open world. As we look at this Wall, we do not want walls of any kind between peoples. I think one of the results of our trip, we hope, may be that the walls that are erected, whether they are physical walls like this or whether they are other walls, ideology or philosophy, will not divide peoples in the world; that peoples, regardless of their differences and backgrounds and their philosophies, will have an opportunity to communicate with each other, to know each other, and to share with each other those particular endeavors that will mean peaceful progress in the years ahead.

So, all in all, I would say, finally, we have come a long way to be here today, 16,000 miles. Many things that have occurred on this trip have made me realize that it was worth coming, but I would say, as I look at the Wall, it is worth coming 16,000 miles just to stand here and see the Wall.

Do you agree, Mr. Secretary?

SECRETARY ROGERS. I certainly do, Mr. President. It really is a tremendous privilege we have all had to be here today.

THE PRESIDENT. And I really didn't need the coat.

TRANSLATOR. No, this is great weather.

THE PRESIDENT. It's marvelous. And nobody is ever going to see the hat that I brought. I didn't need it. And my ears are not nearly as cold as they get when I walk sometimes on the streets of New York—in those side streets that go, you know, through the middle of Manhattan and down through those tall buildings—and the wind blows. It's much colder than this.

TRANSLATOR. The Vice Premier says that Mr. President has given a very good speech. [*Laughter*]

THE PRESIDENT. I was supposed to just say a word. The Vice Premier has climbed to the top. But we both decided that this was a job really for Foreign Ministers and not for the Vice Premier and myself.

But I would simply conclude, because I know we have to go on, that while we will not climb to the top today, we are already meeting at the summit in Peking.

Let me ask the members of the press, do you think it was worth coming?

REPORTERS. Yes, sir.

THE PRESIDENT. You know, you are lucky, and my wife is lucky: You get out to see the great points of interest. She gives me a report every night. Of course, I would not trade. My talks are very interesting, too.

Q. Are you finding, Mr. President, the afterhours events as entertaining as we are, such as the athletic events?

THE PRESIDENT. Fantastic. I thought not only the ballet was great, Tom [Jarriel, ABC News], but I also thought that the athletic event last night was just superb. As you know, I have a rather casual interest in athletics, and it has been so reported. But the gymnastic events—I have never seen a tumbler like the last one. I have never seen that move made by a tumbler before. I didn't think it was possible to make that move. Then, of course, the ping pong players, unbelievable, particularly the young ones, those little girls, those teenaged boys! I used to play a little ping pong years ago—I thought I played it. Now I realize I was playing another game, except for the score.

Then too, the ballet, of course, as we all know, had its message and that was one of its purposes but also, while it was a powerful message and intended for that, it was also very dramatic and excellent theater, excellent dancing, excellent music, and really superb acting. I was very impressed.

I have seen ballets all over the world, including the Soviet Union and the United States. This is certainly the equal of any ballet that I have seen, in terms of production. I thought some of the production effects were very dramatic, too—the scene where they showed the guerrilla forces going across the stage at the end at great speed in the dark. I can't describe it, but certainly people who had a chance to see it on television will remember it. And I thought another thing was the vivid effect, when they had the rifle fire, of having the gunpowder smoke float back into the audience so that we could smell it. You had a feel there of realism that was quite vivid.

REPORTER. Thank you very much.

NOTE: The exchange began at approximately 10 a.m. following the President's tour of the Ba Da Ling portion of the Great Wall.

68   Exchange With Reporters at the Tombs of the Emperors of the Ming Dynasty. *February* 24, 1972

THE PRESIDENT. I have not had an opportunity, of course, to see this before. The only thing I think is comparable to it in the world is the Valley of Kings in Egypt. That is a very different time, of course, and a different country.

But when one sees these tombs, while this does not go back very far in China's history—its history goes back thousands of years rather than hundreds—it is again, of course, a reminder that they are very proud in terms of cultural development and the rest, a rich history of the Chinese people.

As I said earlier, it is worth coming 16,000 miles to see the Wall, and it is worth coming that far to see this, too.

Q. Will you be recommending that Americans apply for visas to have an op-portunity to be tourists in China?

THE PRESIDENT. I won't comment on that question at this point. When we complete our meetings, we will see what kind of recommendations will be made in that respect. Certainly speaking in a general sense, I think it would be very valuable and worthwhile for Americans and, for that matter, people in all countries, to be able to visit China. It is a great and old civilization, these people who have given so much to the world in terms of culture and development in many ways.

It is important as we think of ourselves as members of the family of man, that we know them and know them better, and I would hope that in the future that my children, and their children as well, would have the opportunity to come here.

I would put it this way: That when we think of the world, most of us think of our own countries, some even our own States, and some just our cities. We should think of the whole world, and we have not known Asia well enough. And when you speak of Asia, the great country of China is a country we have not known long enough. That communication has been cut for the last 20 years, and in the future I would hope one of the developments that would occur as a result of our trip is that apart from the relations between governments, that people will be able to come here and that, of course, Chinese people would be able to come to the United States.

I don't mean to suggest that that exchange of people solves the problems of the world or problems between governments. But it so enriches the lives of people to know other civilizations and not to live simply on their own little island.

That is why this experience, I am sure, is not only an interesting experience for us but for the members of the press. I think it reminds us that all of us must work for an open world where people of different cultures, different philosophies, and so forth, may at least have an opportunity to know each other.

NOTE: The exchange began at approximately 1 p.m. following the President's tour of the Ming Tombs.

69   Toasts of the President and Premier Chou En-lai of China at a Banquet Honoring the Premier in Peking. *February* 25, 1972

Mr. Prime Minister and our very distinguished guests from the People's Republic of China and the United States of America:

It is a great privilege while we are guests in your country to be able to welcome you and the Chinese who are present here as our guests this evening.

On behalf of Mrs. Nixon and all of the members of our official party, I want to express our deep appreciation for the boundless and gracious hospitality which you have extended to us.

As you know, it is the custom in our country that the members of the press have the right to speak for themselves and that no one in government can speak for them. But I am sure that all those from the American press who are here tonight will grant me the rare privilege of speaking for the press in extending their ap-

preciation to you and your government for the many courtesies you have extended to them.

You have made it possible for the story of this historic visit to be read, seen, and heard by more people all over the world than on any previous occasion in history.

Yesterday, along with hundreds of millions of viewers on television, we saw what is truly one of the wonders of the world, the Great Wall. As I walked along the Wall, I thought of the sacrifices that went into building it; I thought of what it showed about the determination of the Chinese people to retain their independence throughout their long history; I thought about the fact that the Wall tells us that China has a great history and that the people who built this wonder of the world also have a great future.

The Great Wall is no longer a wall

373

dividing China from the rest of the world, but it is a reminder of the fact that there are many walls still existing in the world which divide nations and peoples.

The Great Wall is also a reminder that for almost a generation there has been a wall between the People's Republic of China and the United States of America.

In these past 4 days we have begun the long process of removing that wall between us. We began our talks recognizing that we have great differences, but we are determined that those differences not prevent us from living together in peace.

You believe deeply in your system, and we believe just as deeply in our system. It is not our common beliefs that have brought us together here, but our common interests and our common hopes, the interest that each of us has to maintain our independence and the security of our peoples and the hope that each of us has to build a new world order in which nations and peoples with different systems and different values can live together in peace, respecting one another while disagreeing with one another, letting history rather than the battlefield be the judge of their different ideas.

Mr. Prime Minister, you have noted that the plane which brought us here is named the Spirit of '76. Just this week, we have celebrated in America the birth of George Washington, the Father of our Country, who led America to independence in our Revolution and served as our first President.

He bade farewell at the close of his term with these words to his countrymen: "Observe good faith and justice toward all nations. Cultivate peace and harmony with all."

It is in that spirit, the spirit of '76, that I ask you to rise and join me in a toast to Chairman Mao, to Premier Chou, to the people of our two countries, and to the hope of our children that peace and harmony can be the legacy of our generation to theirs.

NOTE: The President spoke at 9:05 p.m. in the Great Hall of the People. He spoke from a prepared text. The exchange of toasts was broadcast live on television via satellite.

Premier Chou responded in Chinese. His remarks were translated by an interpreter as follows:

Mr. President and Mrs. Nixon, ladies and gentlemen, comrades and friends:

First of all, on behalf of all my Chinese colleagues here and in my own name, I would like to express appreciation to President and Mrs. Nixon for inviting us to this banquet.

The President and his party are leaving Peking tomorrow to visit southern parts of China. In the past few days President Nixon met with Chairman Mao Tse-tung and our two sides held a number of further talks in which we exchanged views on the normalization of relations between China and the United States and on other questions of concern to the two sides.

There exist great differences of principle between our two sides. Through earnest and frank discussions a clearer knowledge of each other's positions and stands has been gained. This has been beneficial to both sides.

The times are advancing and the world changing. We are deeply convinced that the strength of the people is powerful and that whatever zigzags and reverses there will be in the development of history, the general trend of the world is definitely towards light and not darkness.

It is the common desire of the Chinese and American peoples to enhance their mutual understanding and friendship and promote the normalization of relations between China and the United States. The Chinese Government and people will work unswervingly towards this goal.

I now propose a toast to the great American people, to the great Chinese people, to the friendship of the Chinese and American peo- ples, to the health of President Nixon and Mrs. Nixon, and to the health of all the other American guests present.

70   Toasts of the President and Chairman Nan P'ing at a Banquet in Hangchow. *February* 26, 1972

Mr. Chairman, Mr. Prime Minister, and all of our friends from China and the United States:

When we were planning the schedule for our visit to the People's Republic of China, the Prime Minister determined what cities we would visit. Our time would only permit Peking, of course, and two other cities in this great country. And the Prime Minister naturally said one city must be Shanghai, the biggest city in China. And then, out of all of the other great cities in China, he said the other city must be Hangchow.

Now that we have been here, now that we have seen the splendor of this city, we realize why it has been said that heaven is above and beneath are Hangchow and Soochow. I am sure that the proud citizens of this province would say that Peking is the head of China, but Hangchow is the heart of China.

Tonight I wish to express appreciation on behalf of all of our party for this wonderful banquet and particularly for the beautiful decorations that we see here and on these tables which are a tribute to the great sense of beauty for which Hangchow is famous all over the world.

I think that since we have applauded the Chairman of the Revolutionary Committee and others, that all of us, too, would like to join in applause for those who prepared this wonderful banquet, who prepared these beautiful decorations, and who served us so beautifully tonight.

Mr. Chairman, Mr. Prime Minister, I propose tonight a toast to the health of Chairman Mao Tse-tung, to the health of Premier Chou, to the friendship between the Chinese people and the American people, and to our children and their children. May their future be as bright as the beauty of Hangchow.

On this informal occasion, may I express my appreciation to my Chinese voice, to Mrs. Chang. I listened to her translation. She got every word right.

NOTE: The President spoke at approximately 9:20 p.m. in the Hangchow Hotel. He spoke from a prepared text in response to a toast proposed by Nan P'ing, Chairman of the Chekiang Province Revolutionary Committee.

Mrs. Chang Fan-chih served as interpreter for both the President and Chairman Nan. She translated Chairman Nan's remarks, delivered in Chinese, as follows:

Mr. President and Mrs. Nixon, ladies and gentlemen, comrades, and friends:

We feel happy that President Nixon and Mrs. Nixon and all our other American guests have come here to Hangchow today for a visit. I would like to express welcome to you on behalf of the Revolutionary Committees of Chekiang Province and Hangchow City.

I would also like to take this opportunity to express thanks to President Nixon because the precious gift that has been given to the leaders and people of our country by Mr. President, the redwood trees, are planted here in our city, and we hope that they will continuously grow taller and stronger as a symbol of the friendship between the Chinese and American people.

Hangchow is a scenic spot of well-known fame in China, and we hope that aside from your busy work, you will be able to get some good rest during your stay here.

I propose a toast to the health of President Nixon and Mrs. Nixon, to the health of all our other American guests, to the health of all our friends and comrades present here, and to the friendship between the peoples of China and the United States.

71 Joint Statement Following Discussions With Leaders of the People's Republic of China. *February* 27, 1972

PRESIDENT Richard Nixon of the United States of America visited the People's Republic of China at the invitation of Premier Chou En-lai of the People's Republic of China from February 21 to February 28, 1972. Accompanying the President were Mrs. Nixon, U.S. Secretary of State William Rogers, Assistant to the President Dr. Henry Kissinger, and other American officials.

President Nixon met with Chairman Mao Tse-tung of the Communist Party of China on February 21. The two leaders had a serious and frank exchange of views on Sino-U.S. relations and world affairs.

During the visit, extensive, earnest, and frank discussions were held between President Nixon and Premier Chou En-lai on the normalization of relations between the United States of America and the People's Republic of China, as well as on other matters of interest to both sides. In addition, Secretary of State William Rogers and Foreign Minister Chi P'eng-fei held talks in the same spirit.

President Nixon and his party visited Peking and viewed cultural, industrial and agricultural sites, and they also toured Hangchow and Shanghai where, continuing discussions with Chinese leaders, they viewed similar places of interest.

The leaders of the People's Republic of China and the United States of America found it beneficial to have this opportunity, after so many years without contact, to present candidly to one another their views on a variety of issues. They reviewed the international situation in which important changes and great upheavals are taking place and expounded their respective positions and attitudes.

The U.S. side stated: Peace in Asia and peace in the world requires efforts both to reduce immediate tensions and to eliminate the basic causes of conflict. The United States will work for a just and secure peace: just, because it fulfills the aspirations of peoples and nations for freedom and progress; secure, because it removes the danger of foreign aggression. The United States supports individual freedom and social progress for all the peoples of the world, free of outside pressure or intervention. The United States believes that the effort to reduce tensions is served by improving communication between countries that have different ideologies so as to lessen the risks of confrontation through accident, miscalculation or misunderstanding. Countries should treat each other with mutual respect and be willing to compete peacefully, letting performance be the ultimate judge. No country should claim infallibility and each country should be prepared to re-examine its own attitudes for the common good. The United States stressed that the peoples of Indochina should be allowed to determine their destiny without outside intervention; its constant primary objective has been a negotiated solution; the eight-point proposal put forward by the Republic of Vietnam and the United States on January 27, 1972 represents a basis for the attainment of that objective; in the absence of a negotiated settlement the United States envisages the ultimate withdrawal of all U.S. forces from the region consistent with the aim of self-determination for each country of Indochina. The United States will maintain its close ties with and support for the Republic of Korea; the United States will support efforts of the Republic of Korea to seek a relaxation of tension and increased communication in the Korean peninsula. The United States places the highest value on its friendly relations with Japan; it will continue to develop the existing close bonds. Consistent with the United Nations Security Council Resolution of December 21, 1971, the United States favors the continuation of the ceasefire between India and Pakistan and the withdrawal of all military forces to within their own territories and to their own sides of the ceasefire line in Jammu and Kashmir; the United States supports the right of the peoples of South Asia to shape their own future in peace, free of military threat, and without having the area become the subject of great power rivalry.

The Chinese side stated: Wherever there is oppression, there is resistance. Countries want independence, nations want liberation and the people want revolution—this has become the irresistible trend of history. All nations, big or small, should be equal; big nations should not bully the small and strong nations should not bully the weak. China will never be a superpower and it opposes hegemony and power politics of any kind. The Chinese

side stated that it firmly supports the struggles of all the oppressed people and nations for freedom and liberation and that the people of all countries have the right to choose their social systems according to their own wishes and the right to safeguard the independence, sovereignty and territorial integrity of their own countries and oppose foreign aggression, interference, control and subversion. All foreign troops should be withdrawn to their own countries.

The Chinese side expressed its firm support to the peoples of Vietnam, Laos, and Cambodia in their efforts for the attainment of their goal and its firm support to the seven-point proposal of the Provisional Revolutionary Government of the Republic of South Vietnam and the elaboration of February this year on the two key problems in the proposal, and to the Joint Declaration of the Summit Conference of the Indochinese Peoples. It firmly supports the eight-point program for the peaceful unification of Korea put forward by the Government of the Democratic People's Republic of Korea on April 12, 1971, and the stand for the abolition of the "U.N. Commission for the Unification and Rehabilitation of Korea." It firmly opposes the revival and outward expansion of Japanese militarism and firmly supports the Japanese people's desire to build an independent, democratic, peaceful and neutral Japan. It firmly maintains that India and Pakistan should, in accordance with the United Nations resolutions on the India-Pakistan question, immediately withdraw all their forces to their respective territories and to their own sides of the ceasefire line in Jammu and Kashmir and firmly supports the Pakistan Government and people in their struggle to preserve their independence and sovereignty and the people of Jammu and Kashmir in their struggle for the right of self-determination.

There are essential differences between China and the United States in their social systems and foreign policies. However, the two sides agreed that countries, regardless of their social systems, should conduct their relations on the principles of respect for the sovereignty and territorial integrity of all states, non-aggression against other states, non-interference in the internal affairs of other states, equality and mutual benefit, and peaceful coexistence. International disputes should be settled on this basis, without resorting to the use or threat of force. The United States and the People's Republic of China are prepared to apply these principles to their mutual relations.

With these principles of international relations in mind the two sides stated that:
—progress toward the normalization of relations between China and the United States is in the interests of all countries;
—both wish to reduce the danger of international military conflict;
—neither should seek hegemony in the Asia-Pacific region and each is opposed to efforts by any other country or group of countries to establish such hegemony; and
—neither is prepared to negotiate on behalf of any third party or to enter into agreements or understandings with the other directed at other states.

Both sides are of the view that it would be against the interests of the peoples of the world for any major country to collude with another against other countries, or for major countries to divide up the world into spheres of interest.

The two sides reviewed the long-standing serious disputes between China and the United States. The Chinese side reaffirmed its position: The Taiwan question is the crucial question obstructing the normalization of relations between China and the United States; the Government of the People's Republic of China is the sole legal government of China; Taiwan is a province of China which has long been returned to the motherland; the liberation of Taiwan is China's internal affair in which no other country has the right to interfere; and all U.S. forces and military installations must be withdrawn from Taiwan. The Chinese Government firmly opposes any activities which aim at the creation of "one China, one Taiwan," "one China, two governments," "two Chinas," and "independent Taiwan" or advocate that "the status of Taiwan remains to be determined."

The U.S. side declared: The United States acknowledges that all Chinese on either side of the Taiwan Strait maintain there is but one China and that Taiwan is a part of China. The United States Government does not challenge that position. It reaffirms its interest in a peaceful settlement of the Taiwan question by the Chinese themselves. With this prospect in mind, it affirms the ultimate objective of the withdrawal of all U.S. forces and military installations from Taiwan. In the meantime, it will progressively reduce its forces and military installations on Taiwan as the tension in the area diminishes.

The two sides agreed that it is desirable to broaden the understanding between the two peoples. To this end, they discussed specific areas in such fields as science, technology, culture, sports and journalism, in which people-to-people contacts and exchanges would be mutually beneficial. Each side undertakes to facilitate the further development of such contacts and exchanges.

Both sides view bilateral trade as another area from which mutual benefit can be derived, and agreed that economic relations based on equality and mutual benefit are in the interest of the people of the two countries. They agree to facilitate the progressive development of trade between their two countries.

The two sides agreed that they will stay in contact through various channels, including the sending of a senior U.S. representative to Peking from time to time for concrete consultations to further the normalization of relations between the two countries and continue to exchange views on issues of common interest.

The two sides expressed the hope that the gains achieved during this visit would open up new prospects for the relations between the two countries. They believe that the normalization of relations between the two countries is not only in the interest of the Chinese and American peoples but also contributes to the relaxa-

tion of tension in Asia and the world.

President Nixon, Mrs. Nixon and the American party expressed their appreciation for the gracious hospitality shown them by the Government and people of the People's Republic of China.

NOTE: The joint statement was released at Shanghai, People's Republic of China.

On the same day, the White House released a statement by Press Secretary Ronald L. Ziegler and the transcript of a news briefing on the joint statement. Participants in the news briefing were Henry A. Kissinger, Assistant to the President for National Security Affairs, and Marshall Green, Assistant Secretary of State for East Asian and Pacific Affairs. The statement and the transcript are printed in the Weekly Compilation of Presidential Documents (vol. 8, pp. 480 and 476).

On February 14, 1972, the White House released a statement by Press Secretary Ziegler on further relaxation of trade with the People's Republic of China. The statement is printed in the Weekly Compilation of Presidential Documents (vol. 8, p. 438).

On February 21, the White House released a statement and the transcript of a news briefing by Press Secretary Ziegler on the President's meeting with Chairman Mao Tse-tung. The statement is printed in the Weekly Compilation of Presidential Documents (vol. 8, p. 466).

72   Toasts of the President and Chairman Chang Ch'un-ch'iao at a Banquet in Shanghai. *February* 27, 1972

Mr. Prime Minister, Chairman Chang, and our Chinese and American friends:

This magnificent banquet marks the end of our stay in the People's Republic of China. We have been here a week. This was the week that changed the world.

As we look back over this week, we think of the boundless hospitality that has been extended to all of us by our Chinese friends.

We have, today, seen the progress of modern China. We have seen the matchless wonders of ancient China. We have seen also the beauty of the countryside, the vibrancy of a great city, Shanghai. All this we enjoyed enormously.

But most important was the fact that we had the opportunity to have talks with Chairman Mao, with Prime Minister Chou En-lai, with the Foreign Minister and other people in the government.

The joint communique which we have issued today summarizes the results of our talks. That communique will make headlines around the world tomorrow. But what we have said in that communique is not nearly as important as what we will do in the years ahead to build a bridge across 16,000 miles and 22 years of hostility which have divided us in the past.

What we have said today is that we shall build that bridge. And because the Chinese people and the American people, as the Prime Minister has said, are a great people, we can build that long bridge.

To do so requires more than the letters, the words of the communique. The letters and the words are a beginning, but the actions that follow must be in the spirit which characterized our talks.

With Chairman Mao, with the Prime Minister, and with others with whom we have met, our talks have been characterized by frankness, by honesty, by determination, and above all, by mutual respect.

Our communique indicates, as it should, some areas of difference. It also indicates some areas of agreement. To mention only one that is particularly appropriate here in Shanghai, is the fact that this great city, over the past, has on many occasions been the victim of foreign aggression and foreign occupation. And we join the Chinese people, we the American people, in our dedication to this principle: That never again shall foreign domination, foreign occupation, be visited upon this city or any part of China or any independent country in this world.

Mr. Prime Minister, our two peoples tonight hold the future of the world in our hands. As we think of that future, we are dedicated to the principle that we can build a new world, a world of peace, a world of justice, a world of independence for all nations.

If we succeed in working together where we can find common ground, if we can find the common ground on which we can both stand, where we can build the bridge between us and build a new world, generations in the years ahead will look back and thank us for this meeting that we have held in this past week. Let the great Chinese people and the great American people be worthy of the hopes and ideals of the world, for peace and justice and progress for all.

In that spirit, I ask all of you to join in a toast to the health of Chairman Mao, of Prime Minister Chou En-lai, and to all of our Chinese friends here tonight, and our American friends, and to that friendship between our two peoples to which Chairman Chang has referred so eloquently.

NOTE: The President spoke at approximately 8:30 p. m. in the Shanghai Exhibition Hall. He spoke from a prepared text in response to a toast proposed by Chang Ch'un-ch'iao, Chairman of the Shanghai Municipal Revolutionary Committee.

Chairman Chang spoke in Chinese. His remarks were translated by an interpreter as follows:

Mr. President and Mrs. Nixon, ladies and gentlemen, friends and comrades:

After having visited Peking and Hangchow, President Nixon and Mrs. Nixon and our other American guests have today come to Shanghai. On behalf of the Shanghai Municipal Revolutionary Committee, I extend our welcome to all of you.

I would like to take this opportunity to extend to the great American people the good wishes and cordial greetings of the people of Shanghai.

During his current visit to our country, President Nixon had a meeting with Chairman Mao Tse-tung and held many talks with Premier

Chou En-lai. The two sides had a serious and frank exchange of views on the normalization of the relations between China and the United States and on matters of interest to the two sides.

We people of Shanghai, like the people throughout our country, welcome this positive action which conforms to the common desires of the peoples of China and the United States. And we are glad that it is in Shanghai today that we have reached agreement on the joint communique after the discussions which took place over the past few days.

Shanghai is a city where our people have relatively a lot of contacts with peoples from other countries. In the 23 years since the liberation of this city in 1949, fundamental changes have taken place and our city has now been preliminarily transformed and built into a comprehensive socialist industrial base of our country, but this means that we have only completed the first step of our long march and at present the industry of Shanghai is not yet very advanced and in some aspects it is still rather backward.

More heavy and arduous tasks still await us, and the working class and the people of the entire Shanghai municipality are continuing to work hard under the leadership of the Communist Party of China along the road charted by Chairman Mao Tse-tung, the road of maintaining independence and keeping the initiative in our own hands and relying on our own efforts.

On the eve of the departure from our country for home of Mr. President and Mrs. Nixon, and our other American guests, I would like to propose a toast to the health of President Nixon and Mrs. Nixon, to the health of our other American guests, and to the friendship between the great Chinese people and the great American people.

73   Remarks at Andrews Air Force Base on Returning From the People's Republic of China.   *February* 28, 1972

Mr. Vice President, Members of the Congress, members of the Cabinet, members of the diplomatic corps, and ladies and gentlemen:

I want to express my very deep appreciation, and the appreciation of all of us, for this wonderfully warm welcome that you have given us and for the support that we have had on the trip that we have just completed from Americans of both political parties and all walks of life across this land.

Because of the superb efforts of the hardworking members of the press who accompanied us—they got even less sleep than I did—millions of Americans in this past week have seen more of China than I did. Consequently, tonight I would like to talk to you not about what we saw but about what we did, to sum up the results of the trip and to put it in perspective.

When I announced this trip last July, I described it as a journey for peace. In the last 30 years, Americans have in three different wars gone off by the hundreds of thousands to fight, and some to die, in Asia and in the Pacific. One of the central motives behind my journey to China was to prevent that from happening a fourth time to another generation of Americans.

As I have often said, peace means more than the mere absence of war. In a technical sense, we were at peace with the People's Republic of China before this trip, but a gulf of almost 12,000 miles and 22 years of noncommunication and hostility separated the United States of America from the 750 million people who live in the People's Republic of China, and that is one-fourth of all the people in the world.

As a result of this trip, we have started the long process of building a bridge across that gulf, and even now we have something better than the mere absence of war. Not only have we completed a week of intensive talks at the highest levels, we have set up a procedure whereby we can continue to have discussions in the future. We have demonstrated that nations with very deep and fundamental differences can learn to discuss those differences calmly, rationally, and frankly, without compromising their principles. This is the basis of a structure for peace, where we can talk about differences rather than fight about them.

The primary goal of this trip was to reestablish communication with the People's Republic of China after a generation of hostility. We achieved that goal.

Let me turn now to our joint communique.

We did not bring back any written or unwritten agreements that will guarantee peace in our time. We did not bring home any magic formula which will make unnecessary the efforts of the American people to continue to maintain the strength so that we can continue to be free.

We made some necessary and important beginnings, however, in several areas. We entered into agreements to expand cultural, educational, and journalistic contacts between the Chinese and the American people. We agreed to work to begin and broaden trade between our two countries. We have agreed that the communications that have now been established between our governments will be strengthened and expanded.

Most important, we have agreed on some rules of international conduct which will reduce the risk of confrontation and war in Asia and in the Pacific.

We agreed that we are opposed to

domination of the Pacific area by any one power. We agreed that international disputes should be settled without the use of the threat of force and we agreed that we are prepared to apply this principle to our mutual relations.

With respect to Taiwan, we stated our established policy that our forces overseas will be reduced gradually as tensions ease, and that our ultimate objective is to withdraw our forces as a peaceful settlement is achieved.

We have agreed that we will not negotiate the fate of other nations behind their backs, and we did not do so at Peking. There were no secret deals of any kind. We have done all this without giving up any United States commitment to any other country.

In our talks, the talks that I had with the leaders of the People's Republic and that the Secretary of State had with the office of the Government of the People's Republic in the foreign affairs area, we both realized that a bridge of understanding that spans almost 12,000 miles and 22 years of hostility can't be built in one week of discussions. But we have agreed to begin to build that bridge, recognizing that our work will require years of patient effort. We made no attempt to pretend that major differences did not exist between our two governments, because they do exist.

This communique was unique in honestly setting forth differences rather than trying to cover them up with diplomatic doubletalk.

One of the gifts that we left behind in Hangchow was a planted sapling of the American redwood tree. As all Californians know, and as most Americans know, redwoods grow from saplings into the giants of the forest. But the process is not one of days or even years; it is a process of centuries.

Just as we hope that those saplings, those tiny saplings that we left in China, will grow one day into mighty redwoods, so we hope, too, that the seeds planted on this journey for peace will grow and prosper into a more enduring structure for peace and security in the Western Pacific.

But peace is too urgent to wait for centuries. We must seize the moment to move toward that goal now, and this is what we have done on this journey.

As I am sure you realize, it was a great experience for us to see the timeless wonders of ancient China, the changes that are being made in modern China. And one fact stands out, among many others, from my talks with the Chinese leaders: It is their total belief, their total dedication, to their system of government. That is their right, just as it is the right of any country to choose the kind of government it wants.

But as I return from this trip, just as has been the case on my return from other trips abroad which have taken me to over 80 countries, I come back to America with an even stronger faith in our system of government.

As I flew across America today, all the way from Alaska, over the Rockies, the Plains, and then on to Washington, I thought of the greatness of our country and, most of all, I thought of the freedom, the opportunity, the progress that 200 million Americans are privileged to enjoy. I realized again this is a beautiful country. And tonight my prayer and my hope is that as a result of this trip, our children will have a better chance to grow up in a peaceful world.

Thank you.

NOTE: The President spoke at 9:30 p.m. at Andrews Air Force Base, Md. He spoke from a prepared text. Vice President Spiro T. Agnew had welcomed the President as follows:

Mr. President, Mrs. Nixon, distinguished guests, ladies and gentlemen:

For more than a week we have witnessed through the miracle of satellite television, the sights and sounds of a society that has been closed to Americans for over two decades. We have been made aware of many new things in that society through this visit, Mr. President. We have witnessed much of what you have done with feelings of pride and pleasure and an immense curiosity that has certainly not been diminished by the amount of attention paid by the media to this visit.

I must confess that we have been surprised to some extent by your facility with chopsticks, Mr. President, and by the equal facility of the Chinese orchestra which rendered "America the Beautiful."

But I will say that the week's undertakings were intensively covered—I think that is the understatement of this week, Mr. President—and we enjoyed every minute of it as we watched with pride and approval the way you and the members of your party and our gracious First Lady conducted yourselves.

Speaking of our First Lady, I don't think I can let this occasion pass without reminding you that I predicted what a tremendous asset she would be in the future to American diplomacy and she didn't let me down a bit. As a matter of fact, she did an absolutely outstanding job under the most difficult, unpredictable circumstances.

Mr. President, just before you left to go to China, you stated that although the Chinese and the American people were separated by a vast ocean and by great differences of philosophy, there was no reason why with effort we could not undertake to diminish the tensions between our countries. I believe you have crossed that ocean in a successful effort to do just that.

Because of your visit, the Chinese and the American people stand further removed from the kind of confrontation that the world has feared for many decades. And we, the American people, are tremendously grateful for that effort on your part.

With due regard to the lateness of the hour and the fatigue that you must feel after so much intensive discussion, preparation, and the time changes and the long flight, I think I can close by simply saying that we are glad to have you back, and we feel easier tonight because of the trip that you took.

74 Special Message to the Congress on Health Care. *March 2, 1972*

To the Congress of the United States:

An all-directions reform of our health care system—so that every citizen will be able to get quality health care at reasonable cost regardless of income and regardless of area of residence—remains an item of highest priority on my unfinished agenda for America in the 1970s.

In the ultimate sense, the general good health of our people is the foundation of our national strength, as well as being the truest wealth that individuals can possess.

Nothing should impede us from doing whatever is necessary to bring the best possible health care to those who do not now have it—while improving health care quality for everyone—at the earliest possible time.

In 1971, I submitted to the Congress my new National Health Strategy which would produce the kind of health care Americans desire and deserve, at costs we all can afford.

Since that time, a great national debate over health care has taken place. And both branches of the Congress have conducted searching examinations of our health needs, receiving and studying testimony from all segments of our society.

The Congress has acted on measures advancing certain parts of my National Health Strategy:

—The Comprehensive Health Manpower Training Act of 1971 and the Nurse Training Act of 1971, which I signed last November, will spur the greatest effort in our history to expand the supply of health personnel. Additionally and importantly, it will attract them to the areas of health care shortages, helping to close one of the most glaring gaps in our present system.

—The Congress also passed the National Cancer Act which I proposed last year. This action opens the way for a high-intensity effort to defeat the No. 2 killer and disabler of our time, an effort fueled by an additional $100 million in the last year. A total of $430 million is budgeted for cancer programs in fiscal year 1973, compared to $185 million in fiscal year 1969.

—The Congress responded to my statement of early 1970 on needed improvements in veterans medical care by authorizing increased funds in 1971 and 1972, increases which have brought the VA hospital-to-patient ratios to an all-time high and have provided many additional specialty and medical services, including increased medical manpower training.

—The Congress also created a National Health Service Corps of young professionals to serve the many rural areas and inner city neighborhoods which are critically short on health care. By mid-summer, more than 100 communities around the Nation will be benefiting from these teams.

These are important steps, without doubt, but we still must lay the bedrock foundations for a new national health care system for all our people.

The need for action is critical for far too many of our citizens.

The time for action is now.

I therefore again urge the Congress to act on the many parts of my health care program which are still pending so that we can end—at the earliest possible time—the individual anguishes, the needless neglects and the family financial fears caused by the gaps, inequities and maldistributions of the present system.

The United States now spends more than $75 billion annually on health care—and for most people, relatively good service results.

Yet, despite this huge annual national outlay, millions of citizens do not have adequate access to health care. Our record in this field does not live up to our national potential.

That sobering fact should summon us to prompt but effective action to reform and reorganize health care practices, while simultaneously resisting the relentless inflation of health care costs.

MORE THAN MONEY IS NEEDED

When the subject of health care improvements is mentioned, as is the case with so many other problems, too many people and too many institutions think first and solely of money—bills, payments, premiums, coverages, grants, subsidies and appropriations.

But far more than money is involved in our current health care crisis.

More money is important—but any attempted health care solution based primarily on money is simply not going to do the job.

In health care as in so many other areas, the most expensive remedy is not necessarily the most effective one.

One basic shortcoming of a solution to health care problems which depends entirely on spending more money, can be seen in the Medicare and Medicaid programs. Medicare and Medicaid did deliver needed dollars to the health care problems of the elderly and the poor. But at the same time, little was done to alter the existing supply and distribution of doctors, nurses, hospitals and other health resources. Our health care supply, in short, remained largely the same while massive new demands were loaded onto it.

The predictable result was an acute price inflation, one basic cause of our health economic quandary of the past 11 years.

In this period, national health expenditures rose by 188 percent, from $26 billion in fiscal 1960 to $75 billion in fiscal 1971. But a large part of this enormous increase in the Nation's health expenditure went, not for more and better health care, but merely to meet price inflation.

If we do not lessen this trend, all other reform efforts may be in vain.

That is why my National Health Strategy was designed with built-in incentives to encourage sensible economies—in the use of health facilities, in direct cost-control procedures, and through more efficient ways to bring health care to people at the community level. That is also why we have given careful attention to medical prices in Phase II of the Economic Stabilization Program.

Several months ago, the Price Commission ruled that increases in physician fees must be kept to within 2½ percent. Rules also were issued to hold down runaway price increases among hospitals, nursing homes and other health care institutions. All of these efforts were directed toward our goal of reducing the previous 7.7 percent annual price increase in total health care costs to half of that level, 3.85 percent this year.

These actions should buy us some time. But they are, at best, a temporary tourniquet on health care price inflation.

We must now direct our energies, attentions and action to the long-range factors affecting the cost, the quality and the availability of medical care.

My overall program, of course, is one that would improve health care for everyone. But it is worthy of special note that these recommendations have a particular importance and a high value for older Americans, whose health care needs usually rise just as their incomes are declining.

We Should Build on Present Strengths

When we examine the status of health care in America, we always must be careful to recognize its strengths. For most Americans, more care of higher quality has been the result of our rising national investment in health, both governmental and private.

We lead the world in medical science, research and development. We have obliterated some major diseases and drastically reduced the incidence of others. New institutions, new treatments and new drugs abound. There has been a marked

and steady gain in the number of people covered by some form of health insurance to 84 percent of those under 65, and coverages have been expanding. Life expectancy has risen by 3.4 percent since 1950 and the maternal death rate has declined 66 percent. Days lost from work in the same period are down 3.5 percent and days lost from school have declined 7.5 percent—both excellent measures of the general good state of our health.

All of this is progress—real progress.

It would be folly to raze the structure that produced this progress—and start from scratch on some entirely new basis—in order to repair shortcomings and redirect and revitalize the thrust of our health system.

To nationalize health care as some have proposed, and thus federalize medical personnel, institutions and procedures—eventually if not at the start—also would amount to a stunning new financial burden for every American taxpayer.

The average household would pay more than $1,000 a year as its share of the required new Federal expenditure of more than $80 billion each and every year. Such a massive new Federal budget item would run counter to the temper of the American taxpayer.

Also, such a massive new Federal budget item would run counter to the efforts of this Administration to decentralize programs and revenues, rather than bring new responsibilities to Washington.

And, finally, such a massive new Federal budget requirement would dim our efforts to bring needed Federal actions in many new areas—some of which bear directly on health, such as environmental protection.

Clearly we must find a better answer to

the deficiencies in our health care system. Unfortunately, such deficiencies are not difficult to identify:

—In inner cities and in many rural areas, there is an acute shortage of physicians. Health screening under various government programs has found that appalling percentages of young people, mostly from deprived areas, have not seen a doctor since early childhood, have never seen a dentist and have never received any preventive care.

—General practitioners are scarce in many areas and many people, regardless of income or location, have difficulty obtaining needed medical attention on short notice.

—Our medical schools must turn away qualified applicants.

—While we emphasize preventive maintenance for our automobiles and appliances, we do not do the same for our bodies. The private health insurance system, good as it is, operates largely as standby emergency equipment, not coming into use until we are stricken and admitted to the most expensive facility, a hospital.

—Relative affluence is no ultimate protection against health care costs. A single catastrophic illness can wipe out the financial security of almost any family under most present health insurance policies.

To remedy these problems, however, will require far more than the efforts of the Federal Government—although the Federal role is vital and will be met by this Administration.

It is going to take the complementing efforts of many other units, of government at the State and local levels; of educational and health organizations and institutions of all kinds; of physicians and other medical personnel of all varieties; of private enterprise and of individual citizens.

My National Health Strategy is designed to enlist all those creative talents into a truly national effort, coordinated but not regimented by four guiding principles:

Capitalizing on existing strengths: We resolve to preserve the best in our existing health care system, building upon those strong elements the new programs needed to correct existing deficiencies.

Equal access for all to health care: We must do all we can to end any racial, economic, social or geographical barriers which may prevent any citizen from obtaining adequate health protection.

Balanced supply and demand: It makes little sense to expand the demand for health care without also making certain that proper increases take place in the numbers of available physicians and other medical personnel, in hospitals and in other kinds of medical facilities.

Efficient organization: We must bring basic reorganizations to our health care system so that we can cease reinforcing inequities and relying on inefficiencies. The exact same system which has failed us in many cases in the past certainly will not be able to serve properly the increased demands of the future.

Major Actions Awaited

Three major programs, now awaiting action in the Congress after substantial hearings and study, would give life to these principles.

—The National Health Insurance Partnership Act,

—The Health Maintenance Organization Assistance Act,

—and H.R. 1, my welfare reform bill

which also would amend Medicare and Medicaid in several significant ways.

THE NATIONAL HEALTH INSURANCE
PARTNERSHIP ACT

This proposal for a comprehensive national health insurance program, in which the public and private sector would join, would guarantee that no American family would have to forego needed medical attention because of inability to pay.

My plan would fill gaps in our present health insurance coverage. But, beyond that, it would redirect our entire system to better and more efficient ways of bringing health care to our people.

There are two critical parts of this Act:

1. *The National Health Insurance Standards Act* would require employers to provide adequate health insurance for their employees, who would share in underwriting its costs. This approach follows precedents of long-standing under which personal security—and thus national economic progress—has been enhanced by requiring employers to provide minimum wages and disability and retirement benefits and to observe occupational health and safety standards.

Required coverages would include not less than $50,000 protection against catastrophic costs for each family member; hospital services; physician services both in and out of a hospital; maternity care; well-baby care (including immunizations); laboratory expenses and certain other costs.

The proposed package would include certain deductibles and coinsurance features, which would help keep costs down by encouraging the use of more efficient health care procedures.

It would permit many workers, as an alternative to paying separate fees for services, to purchase instead memberships in a Health Maintenance Organization. The fact that workers and unions would have a direct economic stake in the program would serve as an additional built-in incentive for avoiding unnecessary costs and yet maintaining high quality.

The national standards prescribed, moreover, would necessarily limit the range within which benefits could vary. This provision would serve to sharpen competition and cost-consciousness among insurance companies seeking to provide coverage at the lowest overall cost.

Any time the Federal Government, in effect, prescribes and guarantees certain things it must take the necessary follow-through steps to assure that the interests of consumers and taxpayers are fully protected.

Accordingly, legislative proposals have been submitted to the Congress within recent weeks for regulating private health insurance companies, in order to assure that they can and will do the job, and that insurance will be offered at reasonable rates. In addition, States would be required to provide group-rate coverage for people such as the self-employed and special groups who do not qualify for other plans.

2. Another vital step in my proposed program is the *Family Health Insurance Plan (FHIP)* which would meet the needs of poor families not covered by the National Health Insurance Standards Act because they are headed by unemployed or self-employed persons whose income is below certain levels. For a family of four, the ceiling for eligibility would be an annual income of $5,000. FHIP would replace that portion of Medicaid designed

to help such families. Medicaid would remain for the aged poor, the blind, the disabled and some children.

HEALTH MAINTENANCE ORGANIZATIONS

Beyond filling gaps in insurance coverage, we must also turn our attention to how the money thus provided will be spent—on what kind of services and in what kind of institutions. This is why the Health Maintenance Organization concept is such a central feature of my National Health Strategy.

The HMO is a method for financing and providing health care that has won growing respect. It brings together into a single organization the physician, the hospital, the laboratory and the clinic, so that patients can get the right care at the right moment.

HMO's utilize a method of payment that encourages the prevention of illness and promotes the efficient use of doctors and hospitals. Unlike traditional fee-for-service billing, the HMO contracts to provide its comprehensive care for a fixed annual sum that is determined in advance.

Under this financial arrangement, the doctors' and hospitals' incomes are determined not by how much the patient is sick, but by how much he is well. HMO's thus have the strongest possible incentive for keeping well members from becoming ill and for curing sick members as quickly as possible.

I do not believe that HMO's should or will entirely replace fee-for-service financing. But I do believe that they ought to be everywhere available so that families will have a choice between these methods. The HMO is no mere drawing-board concept—more than 7 million Americans

are now HMO subscribers and that number is growing.

Several pieces of major legislation now before the Congress would give powerful stimulus to the development of HMO's:

1. *The Health Maintenance Organization Assistance Act* would provide technical and financial aid to help new HMO's get started, and would spell out standards of operation;

2. *The National Health Insurance Partnership Act* described above requires that individuals be given a choice between fee-for-service or HMO payment plans;

3. H.R. 1 contains one provision allowing HMO-type reimbursement for Medicare patients and another that would increase the Federal share of payments made to HMO's under State Medicaid programs.

I urge that the Congress give early consideration to these three measures, in order to hasten the development of this efficient method for low-cost, one-stop health service. Meantime, the Administration has moved forward in this area on its own under existing legislative authorities.

Last year, while HMO legislation was being prepared, I directed the Department of Health, Education, and Welfare to focus existing funds and staff on an early HMO development effort. This effort has already achieved payoffs:

To date, 110 planning and development grants and contracts have been let to potential HMO sponsors and some 200,000 Medicaid patients are now enrolled in HMO-type plans. Also, in a few months, 10 Family Health Centers will be operating with federally-supported funds to provide prepaid health care to persons living in underserved areas. Each of these

Centers can develop into a full-service HMO. I have requested funds in 1973 to expand this support.

To keep this momentum going, I have included in the fiscal year 1972 supplemental budget $27 million for HMO development, and requested $60 million for this purpose in fiscal year 1973.

I will also propose amendments to the pending HMO Assistance Act that would authorize the establishment of an HMO loan fund.

THE NATIONAL NEED FOR H.R. 1

One of the greatest hazards to life and health is poverty. Death and illness rates among the poor are many times those for the rest of the Nation. The steady elimination of poverty would in itself improve the health of millions of Americans.

H.R. 1's main purpose is to help people lift themselves free of poverty's grip by providing them with jobs, job training, income supplements for the working poor and child care centers for mothers seeking work.

For this reason alone, enactment of H.R. 1 must be considered centerpiece legislation in the building of a National Health Strategy.

But H.R. 1 also includes the following measures to extend health care to more Americans—especially older Americans— and to control costs:

Additional Persons Covered:

—Persons eligible for Part A of Medicare (hospital care) would be automatically enrolled in Part B (physician's care).

—Medicare (both Parts A and B) would be extended to many disabled persons not now covered.

H.R. 1 as it now stands, however, would

still require monthly premium payments to cover the costs of Part B. I have recommended that the Congress eliminate this $5.80 monthly premium payment and finance Medicare coverage of physician services through the social security payroll tax. This can be done within the Medicare tax rate now included in H.R. 1. If enacted, this change would save $1.5 billion annually for older Americans and would be equivalent to a 5 percent increase in social security cash benefits.

Cost Control Features:

—Medicare and Medicaid reimbursement would be denied any hospital or other institution for interest, depreciation and service charges on any construction disapproved by local or regional health planning agencies. Moreover, to strengthen local and regional health planning agencies, my fiscal year 1973 budget would increase the Federal matching share. In addition, grants to establish 100 new local and 20 new State planning agencies would bring health planning to more than 80 percent of the Nation's population.

—Reviews of claim samples and utilization patterns, which have saved much money in the Medicare program, would be applied to Medicaid.

—The efficiency of Medicaid hospitals and health facilities would be improved by testing various alternative methods of reimbursing them.

—Cost sharing would be introduced after 30 days of hospitalization under Medicare.

—Federal Medicaid matching rates would decline one-third after the first 60 days of care.

—Federal Medicaid matching rates would be increased 25 percent for services for which the States contract with HMO's or other comprehensive health care facilities.

These latter three revisions are aimed at minimizing inefficient institutional care and encouraging more effective modes of treatment.

RESEARCH AND PREVENTION PROGRAMS

My overall health program encompasses actions on three levels: 1) improving protection against health care costs; 2) improving the health care system itself; and 3) working creatively on research and prevention efforts, to eradicate health menaces and to hold down the incidence of illnesses.

A truly effective national health strategy requires that a significant share of Federal research funds be concentrated on major health threats, particularly when research advances indicate the possibility of breakthrough progress.

Potentially high payoff health research and prevention programs include:

HEART DISEASE

If current rates of incidence continue, some 12 million Americans will suffer heart attacks in the next 10 years.

I shortly will assign a panel of distinguished professional experts to guide us in determining why heart disease is so prevalent and what we should be doing to combat it.[1] In the meantime, the fiscal

[1] On March 24, 1972, the President announced that he had asked Dr. John S. Millis, president and director of the National Fund for Medical Education, to head the Advisory Panel on Heart Disease. A White House announcement of the membership of the Panel was released on April 4 and is printed in the Weekly Compilation of Presidential Documents (vol. 8, p. 724).

year 1973 budget provides funds for exploring:

—the development of new medical devices to assist blood circulation and improved instruments for the early detection of heart disease; and

—tests to explore the relationship of such high-risk factors as smoking, high blood pressure and high blood fats to the onset and progression of heart disease.

CANCER

The National Cancer Act I signed into law December 23, 1971, creates the authority for organizing an all-out attack on this dread disease. The new cancer program it creates will be directly responsive to the President's direction.

This new program's work will be given further momentum by my decision last October to convert the former biological warfare facility at Fort Detrick, Maryland into a cancer research center.

To finance this all-out research effort, I have requested that an additional $93 million be allocated for cancer research in fiscal year 1973, bringing the total funding available that year to $430 million.

In the past two and one-half years, we have more than doubled the funding for cancer research, reflecting this Administration's strong commitment to defeat this dread killer as soon as humanly possible.

ALCOHOLISM

One tragic and costly illness which touches every community in our land is alcoholism. There are more than 9 million alcoholics and alcohol abusers in our Nation.

The human cost of this condition is incalculable—broken homes, broken lives and the tragedy of 28,000 victims of alcohol-related highway deaths every year.

The recently established National Institute of Alcohol Abuse and Alcoholism will soon launch an intensive public education program through television and radio and will continue to support model treatment projects from which States and communities will be able to pattern programs to fight this enemy.

Meanwhile, the Department of Health, Education, and Welfare and the Department of Transportation are funding projects in 35 States to demonstrate the value of highway safety, enforcement and education efforts among drinking drivers. The Veterans Administration will increase the number of its Alcohol Dependence Treatment Units by more than one-third, to 56 units in fiscal year 1973.

DRUG ABUSE

Drug abuse now constitutes a national emergency.

In response to this threat and to the need for coordination of Federal programs aimed at drug abuse, I established the Special Action Office for Drug Abuse Prevention within the Executive Office of the President. Its special areas of action are programs for treating and rehabilitating the drug abuser and for alerting our young people to the dangers of drug abuse.

I have proposed legislation to the Congress which would extend and clarify the authority of this Office. I am hopeful that Senate and House conferees will soon be able to resolve differences in the versions passed by the two branches and emerge with a single bill responsive to the Nation's needs.

The new Special Action Office, however, has not been idly awaiting this legislation. It has been vigorously setting about the task of identifying the areas of greatest need and channelling Federal resources into these areas.

The Department of Defense, for example, working in close coordination with the Special Action Office, has instituted drug abuse identification, education, and treatment programs which effectively combatted last year's heroin problem among our troops in South Vietnam. Indications are that the corner has been turned on this threat and that the incidence of drug dependence among our troops is declining.

The Veterans Administration, again in coordination with the Special Action Office, has accomplished more than a six-fold increase in the number of drug dependency treatment centers in fiscal year 1972, with an increase to 44 centers proposed in fiscal year 1973.

In fiscal year 1972, I have increased funds available for the prevention of drug abuse by more than 130 percent. For fiscal year 1973, I have requested over $365 million to treat the drug abuser and prevent the spread of the affliction of drug abuse.

This is more than eight times as much as was being spent for this purpose when this Administration took office.

SICKLE CELL DISEASE

About one out of every 500 black infants falls victim to the painful, life-shortening disease called sickle cell anemia. This inherited disease trait is carried by about two million black Americans.

In fiscal year 1972, $10 million was allocated to attack this problem and an advisory committee of prominent black leaders was organized to help direct the effort. This committee's recommendations are in hand and an aggressive action program is ready to start.

To underwrite this effort, I am proposing to increase the new budget for sickle cell disease from $10 million in fiscal 1972 to $15 million in fiscal 1973.

The Veterans Administration's medical care system also can be counted on to make an important contribution to the fight against sickle cell anemia.

Eight separate research projects concerning sickle cell anemia are underway in VA hospitals and more will be started this year. All 166 VA hospitals will launch a broad screening, treatment and educational effort to combat this disease.

On any given day, about 17,000 black veterans are in VA hospitals and some 116,000 are treated annually.

All these expanded efforts will lead to a better and longer life for thousands of black Americans.

FAMILY PLANNING SERVICES

Nearly three years ago, I called for a program that would provide family planning services to all who wanted them but could not afford their cost. The timetable for achieving this goal was five years.

To meet that schedule, funding for services administered by the National Center for Family Planning for this program has been steadily increased from $39 million in fiscal year 1971 to $91 million in fiscal year 1972. I am requesting $139 million for this Center in fiscal year 1973.

Total Federal support for family planning services and research in fiscal 1973 will rise to $240 million, a threefold increase since fiscal year 1969.

VENEREAL DISEASE

Last year, more than 2.5 million venereal disease cases were detected in the United States. Two-thirds of the victims were under 25.

A concentrated program to find persons with infectious cases and treat them is needed to bring this disease under control. I am, therefore, recommending that $31 million be allocated for this purpose in fiscal year 1973, more than two and one-half times the level of support for VD programs in 1971.

HEALTH EDUCATION

Aside from formal treatment programs, public and private, the general health of individuals depends very much on their own informed actions and practices.

Last year, I proposed that a National Health Education Foundation be established to coordinate a nationwide program to alert people on ways in which they could protect their own health. Since that time, a number of public meetings have been held by a committee I established then to gather views on all aspects of health education.[2] The report of this committee will be sent to me this year.

The committee hopes to define more explicitly the Nation's need for health education programs and to determine ways of rallying all the resources of our society to meet this need.

CONSUMER SAFETY

More than a half century has passed since basic legislation was enacted to en-

---

[2] President's Committee on Health Education.

sure the safety of the foods and drugs which Americans consume. Since then, industrial and agricultural revolutions have generated an endless variety of new products, food additives, industrial compounds, cosmetics, synthetic fabrics and other materials which are employed to feed, clothe, medicate and adorn the American consumer.

These revolutions created an entirely new man-made environment—and we must make absolutely certain that this new environment does not bring harmful side-effects which outweigh its evident benefits.

The only way to ensure that goal is met is to give the agency charged with that responsibility the resources it needs to meet the challenge.

My budget request for the Food and Drug Administration for fiscal year 1973 represents the largest single-year expansion in the history of this agency—70 percent. I believe this expansion is amply justified by the magnitude of the task this agency faces.

In the past year, the foundations for a modern program of consumer protection have been laid. The FDA has begun a detailed review of the thousands of non-prescription drug products now marketed. The pharmaceutical industry has been asked to cooperate in compiling a complete inventory of every drug available to the consumer.

Meanwhile, I have proposed the following legislation to ensure more effective protection for consumers:

—A wholesome fish and fish products bill which provides for the expansion of inspections of fish handlers and greater authority to assure the safety of fish products.

—A Consumer Product Safety bill which would authorize the Federal Government to establish and enforce new standards for product safety.

—Medical device legislation which would not only authorize the establishment of safety standards for these products, but would also provide for premarketing scientific review when warranted.

—A drug identification bill now before the Congress would provide a method for quickly and accurately identifying any pill or tablet. This provision would reduce the risk of error in taking medicines and allow prompt treatment following accidental ingestion.

—The Toxic Substances Control Act that I proposed last year also awaits action by the Congress. This legislation would require any company developing a new chemical that may see widespread use to test it thoroughly beforehand for possible toxic effects.

NURSING HOMES

If there is one place to begin upgrading the quality of health care, it is in the nursing homes that care for older Americans. Many homes provide excellent care and concern, but far too many others are callous, understaffed, unsanitary and downright dangerous.

Last August I announced an eight-point program to upgrade the quality of life and the standards of care in American nursing homes. The Federal interest and responsibility in this field is clear, since Federal programs including Medicare and Medicaid provide some 40 percent of total nursing home income nationally.

That HEW effort is well underway now:

Federal field teams have surveyed every State nursing home inspection program, and as a result 38 of 39 States found to have deficiencies have corrected them. The 39th is acting to meet Federal standards. To help States upgrade nursing homes, I have proposed legislation to pay 100 percent of the costs of inspecting these facilities.

Meanwhile, at my direction, a Federally-funded program to train 2,000 State nursing home inspectors and to train 41,000 nursing home employees is also underway. The Federal field force for assisting nursing homes is being augmented and fire, safety and health codes have been strengthened.

One way to measure the results of these efforts is to learn how patients in nursing homes feel about the care they are given. We have therefore also begun a program to monitor the complaints and suggestions of nursing home residents.

APPLYING SCIENCE AND TECHNOLOGY

In my State of the Union message, I proposed a new Federal partnership with the private sector to stimulate civilian technological research and development. One of the most vital areas where we can focus this partnership—perhaps utilizing engineers and scientists displaced from other jobs—is in improving human health. Opportunities in this field include:

1. *Emergency Medical Services:* By using new technologies to improve emergency care systems and by using more and better trained people to run those systems, we can save the lives of many heart attack victims and many victims of auto accidents every year. The loss to the Nation represented by these unnecessary deaths cannot be calculated. I have already allocated $8 million in fiscal year 1972 to develop model systems and training programs and my budget proposes that $15 million be invested for additional demonstrations in fiscal year 1973.

2. *Blood:* Blood is a unique national resource. An adequate system for collecting and delivering blood at its time and place of need can save many lives. Yet we do not have a nationwide system to meet this need and we need to draw upon the skills of modern management and technology to develop one. I have therefore directed the Department of Health, Education, and Welfare to make an intensive study and to recommend to me as soon as possible a plan for developing a safe, fast and efficient nationwide blood collection and distribution system.

3. *Health Information Systems:* Each physician, hospital and clinic today is virtually an information island unto itself. Records and billings are not kept on the same basis everywhere, laboratory tests are often needlessly repeated and vital patient data can get lost. All of these problems have been accentuated because our population is so constantly on the move. The technology exists to end this chaos and improve the quality of care. I have therefore asked the Secretary of Health, Education, and Welfare to plan a series of projects to demonstrate the feasibility of developing integrated and uniform systems of health information.

4. *Handicapping Conditions:* In America today there are half a million blind, 850,000 deaf and 15 million suffering paralysis and loss of limbs. So far, the major responses to their need to gain self-sufficiency, have been vocational rehabilitation and welfare programs. Now the skills that took us to the moon and back need to be put to work developing devices to help the blind see, the deaf hear and the crippled move.

TOWARD A BETTER HEALTH CARE
SYSTEM

Working together, this Administration and the Congress already have taken some significant strides in our mutual determination to provide the best, and the most widely available, health care system the world has ever known.

The time now has come to take the final steps to reorganize, to revitalize and to redirect American health care—to build on its historic accomplishments, to close its gaps and to provide it with the incentives and sustenance to move toward a more perfect mission of human compassion.

I believe that the health care resources of America in 1972, if strengthened and expanded as I have proposed in this Message, will be more than sufficient to move us significantly toward that great goal.

If the Administration and the Congress continue to act together—and act on the major proposals this year, as I strongly again urge—then the 1970s will be remembered as an era in which the United States took the historic step of making the health of the entire population not only a great goal but a practical objective.

RICHARD NIXON

The White House,
March 2, 1972.

NOTE: The text of the message was released at Key Biscayne, Fla.

On the same day, the White House released a fact sheet and the transcript of a news briefing on the message. The news briefing was held by Dr. Merlin K. DuVal, Assistant Secretary of Health, Education, and Welfare for Health and Scientific Affairs.

---

75 Memorandum Establishing a Council on International Economic Policy Special Working Group for Textile Trade Policy. *March 3, 1972*

Memorandum for:
 The Secretary of State
 The Secretary of the Treasury
 The Secretary of Agriculture
 The Secretary of Commerce
 The Secretary of Labor
 The Director, Office of Management and Budget
 The Chairman, Council of Economic Advisers
 The Assistant to the President for National Security Affairs
 The Executive Director of the Domestic Council
 The Special Representative for Trade Negotiations

 The Executive Director of the Council on International Economic Policy
 The Honorable David M. Kennedy

Pursuant to my memorandum of January 18, 1971, establishing the Council on International Economic Policy, this memorandum establishes a Special Working Group of the Council for textile trade policy.

The Special Working Group will be chaired by Ambassador [at Large] Kennedy and will in addition consist of the Assistant Secretaries of State, the Treasury, Agriculture, Commerce, and Labor, the Special Representative for Trade Negotiations, and the Executive Director of the Council on International Economic Policy.

The duties of the Special Working Group are these:

1. Advise generally with respect to policies affecting actions by the United States concerning international trade in textiles and textile products under Section 204 of the Agricultural Act of 1956 and other laws.

2. Establish procedures by which the Committee for the Implementation of Textile Agreements shall, under the policy guidance of the Special Working Group, take actions with respect to the rights and obligations of the United States under Articles 3 and 6 of the Long Term Ar-

rangement Regarding Trade in Cotton Textiles.

3. Develop policy proposals with respect to the negotiation of additional bilateral and multilateral textile trade agreements.

The Committee for the Implementation of Textile Agreements will submit to the Special Working Group such reports and recommendations concerning textile trade policy and the implementation of textile trade agreements as the Special Working Group may request.

RICHARD NIXON

NOTE: The memorandum was released at Key Biscayne, Fla.

On the same day, the President signed Executive Order 11651 establishing the Committee for the Implementation of Textile Agreements.

76   Statement About the Death of William H. Lawrence. *March 3,* 1972

BILL LAWRENCE was one of the most independent and highly respected members of the national political press corps, always tough-minded in his search for the facts.

His death was most untimely and tragic, but it came on an assignment symbolic of his long career—in the snows of New Hampshire covering the start of yet another national political campaign. He will

be greatly missed by all who have followed his reports over the years.

NOTE: Mr. Lawrence, 56, died of a heart attack in Bedford, N.H., on March 2, 1972.

He was a reporter for the New York Times for 20 years before joining the American Broadcasting Company in 1961 as White House correspondent. He was national affairs editor for ABC News from 1968 until his death.

The statement was released at Key Biscayne, Fla.

77   Memorandum Urging Support of the Red Cross. *March 4,* 1972

Memorandum for Heads of Executive Departments and Agencies:

This March the Nation will once again observe Red Cross Month—a traditional time when the American National Red Cross seeks the support of every Ameri-

can citizen for its humanitarian services.

The historic record of mercy and service of the Red Cross needs no detailed explanation. Its efforts this past year have alleviated the suffering of disaster victims at home and abroad, trained hundreds of

397

thousands to deal effectively in matters of health and safety, and through its blood donor program, saved the lives of untold numbers. These contributions are practical manifestations of the very best in the human spirit.

As President of the United States and Honorary Chairman of the American National Red Cross, I extend my warm personal support to its varied activities on behalf of mankind in need.

I know that all of you will join me in this support, and that you will take an affirmative lead in seeing that every Federal employee and every member of the Armed Services is made aware again of the many ways in which they can help the Red Cross stand fully equipped to help them. It is essential to the Nation that the Red Cross continue to receive that wide public support, both in funds and in manpower, that permits it to wage its creative attack.

Let us all respond generously.

RICHARD NIXON

NOTE: The memorandum, dated March 1, 1972, was released on March 4 at Key Biscayne, Fla.

On February 16, the President signed Proclamation 4110, designating March as Red Cross Month.

78   Remarks at the Veterans of Foreign Wars Congressional Banquet.   *March 7, 1972*

Commander Vicites, all of the distinguished guests and all of the very honored winners of the Voice of Democracy Contest who are here tonight, and my friends, and I can say also my comrades, of the Veterans of Foreign Wars:

I am honored to be here for two very important reasons: first with regard to the Veterans of Foreign Wars, and the second with regard to the honored guests tonight.

Your Commander has spoken very generously of my participation over many years, not only as a member but also as a speaker on many occasions before various meetings of the Veterans of Foreign Wars, including, of course, several conventions and several dinners of this type. I would like to say a word to those who are members of the Veterans of Foreign Wars, those who are leaders from all over the United States.

I want to tell you something about what your support has meant to the man, whoever that man is, who happens to be President of the United States. The man who is President of the United States has to make many difficult decisions. Some of them are decisions that have to do with domestic affairs in which there is legitimate controversy and in which men and women of good will can have very vigorous differences of opinion.

Others are matters that affect the security of the Nation in which there are also differences of opinion. But also, there are some issues in which whoever happens to be President of the United States must have assistance far beyond his party; he must have assistance from the Nation, from people of both parties, from men and women who put the country first and the party second.

Over the past 3 years there have been numbers of occasions when I have had to make some decisions in the field of foreign policy that were somewhat controversial. I remember on many of those occasions that I have asked for the assistance of and the support of the Veterans of Foreign Wars, and whatever that decision was, whether it was a decision that was necessary to keep America strong through developing a system of defense against nuclear weapons, whether it was a decision to defend American men who were fighting abroad by taking action that was terribly difficult but terribly important for their survival, whatever the decision was, I can say that on occasion after occasion when I have talked to whoever happened to be the Commander of the Veterans of Foreign Wars, whether it was Chief Rainwater or Commander Vicites, I have asked them and never have the Veterans of Foreign Wars been found wanting when the chips were down.

The Commander has referred to the fact that I have returned from a journey. That journey, to many people, meant perhaps more than a realist would recognize that it should mean, and that is that because a trip has been taken, because the leader of a very powerful nation, the United States of America, was meeting with a leader of the most populous nation of the world, that this meant that peace was going to be something that we could assume, something that now made it no longer necessary for us to maintain the strength, the strength in arms, even more important, the strength in character which America has had in the past and which it needs at the present time.

Let me put that trip, perhaps, in its proper perspective in just a moment. The trip was necessary, necessary because, as we look at the history of this organization, I think of the fact that most of us who are members were veterans of World War II. I think of the fact that for the veterans of World War II, their younger brothers fought in Korea and their sons fought in Vietnam, and the great question of our time is simply this: Are their grandchildren, are those who sit here, these winners, are they and their children going to fight in another war?

We look at those wars: World War II, Korea, Vietnam. It is most significant to note that each of them, for the United States, came from the Pacific. World War II began in the Pacific for America. Korea came from the Pacific, and Vietnam, of course, came from the Pacific. So the great question is: Can we, those of us who have positions of leadership, develop a new policy, a new relationship, which will not guarantee peace, because that can never be sure, but which will provide a better chance that we can have peace in the future?

As I said over and over again on this recent journey, there is no question about the differences that we have with the leaders of the most populous nation in the world, differences that are deep in philosophy, and very deep in terms of our views about the world. But there is also no question about this: that is, that if the most populous nation in the world and the nation at the present time that is the most powerful nation in the world, if they do not communicate, the chances of our having peace in the Pacific and peace in the world are very dim.

If, on the other hand, we can establish a process by which we can talk about our differences, rather than fight about our differences, the chance that these young people in front of us can grow up in a period which we did not enjoy, a generation of peace, is infinitely better. That is why the trip was necessary, and that is why we took it.

I do not hold out any false hopes. I would only say that in this period when we are entering negotiations with those who could be our enemies, not only there but in other parts of the world, the need for the United States of America to maintain its strength—its military strength, its economic strength, and above all its moral and spiritual strength, its faith in this country, its belief in America—has never been greater. Because if we are to have peace in this period ahead, it will not come if America, with all of its power and all of its wealth, withdraws into itself and refuses to play the role that it must play, play it not for purposes of conquest and not for purposes of domination, but for purposes of using our power so that the world may be one in which nations and peoples with different philosophies can live together, rather than die together.

And so at this particular instant, there has never been a time when we needed in this country more men and women like the men and women who proudly belong to the Veterans of Foreign Wars, who believe in this country, who recognize the need for strength, who also appreciate the necessity for negotiation. There has never been a time when we needed people who thought along those lines more.

I remember talking with President Eisenhower once, and he said something very significant, very early in his Administration. He said, "There is no one who hates war more than someone who has seen a lot of it." Of course, he was a great example of that truth.

That could be said of all of the Veterans

of Foreign Wars. And yet you, as Veterans of Foreign Wars, you know that if we are to have peace, it will not come through weakness, and on the other side it will not come through belligerence, but it will come through strength, and the willingness to negotiate a new era in which we can have peace, peace through strength and conciliation at the very highest level.

That brings me to our honored guest tonight. I have been thinking of these dinners I have attended. I have been thinking of the men I have appeared with on the occasion of these dinners, appeared for and spoken in behalf of.

Senator Jackson, who is a man who, when all these great issues have come before the Senate, stood very firm for the cause of a strong United States, for putting the country above party.

I think of Congressman Arends. Congressman Arends, a man who could always be counted upon through all the years that I have known him—I have not known him quite as long as he has been in the Congress, but almost—but a man who always, like Senator Jackson, put the country first and his party second.

And I think tonight of Doc Morgan. Now, Doc Morgan is going to follow me, so I had better say nice things about him. In speaking of Doc Morgan, I want to speak of the House of Representatives because he, as you know, is the chairman of the Foreign Affairs Committee of the House of Representatives. I think of Doc Morgan, of Speaker Carl Albert, Chairman George Mahon, who is here tonight, of the Appropriations Committee, of "Tiger" [Olin E.] Teague, the chairman of the Veterans' Affairs Committee. It occurred to me, as I mentioned those names, they are all Democrats. As I mentioned those names, it occurs to me, too, that the immediate past Commander of the VFW and the present Commander of the VFW are Democrats. So why am I here?

I am here for this reason: One of the most eloquent of all the men who have served in American political life was a Senator from Indiana around the turn of the century. All of you have read about him; you have read Bower's life of Beveridge. This great Indiana Senator made perhaps some of the greatest speeches ever heard in the Senate or in this country. He once said something that I thought was very simple but very eloquent. That was that one who is a partisan of principle is a prince of statesmanship. Those are the men we honor tonight.

I could speak of Doc Morgan in terms of his years of service on the Foreign Affairs Committee, chairman of that committee since 1959. I know that every time I, in my 3 years in this office, have called upon him, he has not been found wanting. I know that whether we speak, and

I now mention those in the House of Representatives with whom he has worked, whether it is Speaker Albert, or the former Speaker, Speaker McCormack, or George Mahon, or Tiger Teague, and let's get one Republican in it, or Les Arends, that whenever an issue came up that involved this Nation, its security, its strength, the peace that we all want, he was a man who was a partisan, a strong partisan, but a partisan for principle, and therefore a prince of statesmanship.

I honor him tonight as a prince of statesmanship.

NOTE: The President spoke at 8:52 p.m. in the Ballroom of the Sheraton-Park Hotel. He spoke without referring to notes.

Representative Thomas E. Morgan of Pennsylvania received the organization's Congressional Award at the banquet.

Following his remarks, the President greeted the 53 winners of the Voice of Democracy contest, sponsored annually by the Veterans of Foreign Wars. The winners, high school students from the 50 States, the District of Columbia, the Canal Zone, and Pacific areas, had written brief radio scripts on the theme, "My Responsibility to Freedom."

---

79 Statement on Establishing a New System for Classification and Declassification of Government Documents Relating to National Security. *March 8, 1972*

I HAVE today signed an Executive order [11652] establishing a new, more progressive system for classification and declassification of Government documents relating to national security. This reform springs from a review that I initiated almost 14 months ago and represents the first major overhaul of our classification procedures since 1953.

By a separate action, I have also directed the Secretary of State to accelerate publication of the official documentary series, "Foreign Relations of the United States," so that historians and others will have more rapid access to papers created after World War II.

Both of these actions are designed to lift the veil of secrecy which now enshrouds altogether too many papers written by employees of the Federal establishment—

and to do so without jeopardizing any of our legitimate defense or foreign policy interests.

SHORTCOMINGS OF PRESENT CLASSIFICATION SYSTEM

Unfortunately, the system of classification which has evolved in the United States has failed to meet the standards of an open and democratic society, allowing too many papers to be classified for too long a time. The controls which have been imposed on classification authority have proved unworkable, and classification has frequently served to conceal bureaucratic mistakes or to prevent embarrassment to officials and administrations.

Once locked away in Government files, these papers have accumulated in enormous quantities and have become hidden from public exposure for years, for decades—even for generations. It is estimated that the National Archives now has 160 million pages of classified documents from World War II and over 300 million pages of classified documents for the years 1946 through 1954.

The many abuses of the security system can no longer be tolerated. Fundamental to our way of life is the belief that when information which properly belongs to the public is systematically withheld by those in power, the people soon become ignorant of their own affairs, distrustful of those who manage them, and—eventually—incapable of determining their own destinies.

Yet since the early days of the Republic, Americans have also recognized that the Federal Government is obliged to protect certain information which might otherwise jeopardize the security of the country. That need has become particularly acute in recent years as the United States has assumed a powerful position in world affairs, and as world peace has come to depend in large part on how that position is safeguarded. We are also moving into an era of delicate negotiations in which it will be especially important that governments be able to communicate in confidence.

Clearly, the two principles of an informed public and of confidentiality within the Government are irreconcilable in their purest forms, and a balance must be struck between them.

REVIEW ORDERED IN JANUARY 1971

In order to strike that balance in favor of more complete public disclosure and in keeping with my pledge to create an open Administration, I directed on January 15, 1971, that a review be made of security classification procedures now in effect. An interagency committee was set up to study the existing system, to make recommendations with respect to its operation, and to propose steps that might be taken to provide speedier declassification. I later directed that the scope of the review be expanded to cover all aspects of information security.

The Executive order I have signed today is based upon the results of this study, as well as on our own operational experiences under current rules, on findings of similar studies in the past growing out of Congressional hearings, and on a reexamination of the rationale underlying the Freedom of Information Act.

BASIS FOR OPTIMISM

We cannot be assured of complete success in this endeavor. In such a complex field, rules can never be airtight and we must rely upon the good judgment of individuals throughout the Government. Yet I believe that our new approach does provide a basis for considerable optimism. The full force of my office has been committed to this endeavor. The rules have been tightened with great care. In addition, in a critically important shift, we have reversed the burden of proof: For the first time, we are placing that burden—and even the threat of administrative sanction—upon those who wish to preserve the secrecy of documents, rather than upon those who wish to declassify them after a reasonable time.

The new system will become effective on June 1, 1972. Among its most significant features are these:

—The rules for classifying documents are more restrictive.

—The number of departments and people who can originally classify information has been substantially reduced.

—Timetables ranging from 6 to 10 years have been set for the automatic declassification of documents. Exceptions will be allowed only for such information as falls within four specifically defined categories.

—Any document exempted from automatic declassification will be subject to mandatory review after a 10-year period. Thus, for the first time, a private citizen is given a clear right to have national security information reviewed on the basis of specified criteria to determine if continued classification is warranted, so long as the document can be adequately identified and obtained by the Government with a reasonable amount of effort.

—If information is still classified 30 years after origination, it will then be automatically declassified unless the head of the originating department determines in writing that its continued protection is still necessary and he sets a time for declassification.

—Sanctions may be imposed upon those who abuse the system.

—And a continuing monitoring process will be set up under the National Security Council and an Interagency Classification Review Committee, whose Chairman is to be appointed by the President.

These rules are explained in greater detail below.

ELEMENTS OF THE NEW SYSTEM

1. *Tighter Rules for Classification.*

Under the new order, materials can be classified Top Secret, Secret, or Confidential only if their unauthorized disclosure *"could reasonably be expected"* to cause, respectively, exceptionally grave damage, serious damage, or damage to the national security. Heretofore, material could be classified if the originator had any expectation of such damage however remote. This new test is intended to reduce the amount of protected information. In addition, the order explicitly directs that the "Top Secret" stamp must be used with "utmost restraint" while "Secret" shall be used "sparingly."

2. *Reduction in Classification Authority.*

The new order also substantially reduces the number of agencies in the Government authorized to classify information and material. Under current rules, 24

Federal departments and agencies outside the Executive Office of the President have broad classification authority, while several others have more restricted powers. Under the new system, only 12 departments and agencies and such offices in the Executive Office as the President may designate will have authority to originally classify information "Top Secret" and 13 others will have authority to stamp materials "Secret" and "Confidential."

In the principal departments concerned with national security, namely State, Defense, and the CIA, the number of individuals who may be authorized to classify material "Top Secret" is also drastically reduced from 5,100 to approximately 1,860. This authority may be exercised only by the heads of the departments and agencies and certain high officials within their organizations whom the heads must designate in writing. Reductions in classification authority are also being made at the "Secret" and "Confidential" levels.

It is anticipated that by reducing the number of agencies with classification powers as well as the number of people within those agencies who have personal classification authority, we can sharply reduce the quantity of material which enters the Government's classified files.

3. *Precise Identification of Classified Information.*

A major source of unnecessary classification under the old Executive order was the practical impossibility of discerning which portions of a classified document actually required classification. Incorporation of any material from a classified paper into another document usually resulted in the classification of the new document, and innocuous portions of neither paper could be released.

To the extent practicable, each classified document under the new system will be marked to show which portions are classified, at what level, and which portions are unclassified.

4. *Rules for Declassifying Documents.*

Perhaps the most innovative and crucial aspect of the Executive order I have signed today is the procedure it establishes for the downgrading and declassification of documents. Aside from a small amount of documents which are subject to declassification after a 12-year period as specified by existing regulations, the vast majority of documents classified since World War II have never been given a rigorous declassification review and they remain classified to this day. I believe we can cure these ills under the new order.

A. Documents Classified After May 31, 1972

Unless specifically exempted, all documents classified after May 31, 1972, are to be automatically downgraded *and* declassified. "Top Secret" information is to be downgraded to "Secret" after 2 years, to "Confidential" after 2 more years, and declassified after a total of 10 years. "Secret" information is to be downgraded to "Confidential" after 2 years and declassified after a total of 8 years. "Confidential" documents are to be declassified after 6 years.

Information may be exempted from the automatic process only by an official with "Top Secret" classification authority and that official must specify in writing in which of four specific exemption categories the material falls and, where possible, he must also indicate when declassification will in fact occur. The four exemption categories are:

404

—Classified information furnished in confidence by a foreign government or international organization;

—Classified information covered by statute, or pertaining to cryptography, or disclosing intelligence sources or methods;

—Classified information disclosing a system, plan, installation, project or specific foreign relations matter the continued protection of which is essential to the national security;

—Classified information which, if disclosed, "would place a person in immediate jeopardy." The jeopardy intended here is physical harm, not personal embarrassment or discomfiture.

Upon request from anyone, including a member of the general public, exempted material is subject to mandatory review by the originating Department after 10 years from the date of origin so long as (a) the request describes the record with sufficient particularity that it may be identified, and (b) the record can be obtained with a reasonable amount of effort.

If material is still classified 30 years after the date of its original classification, it shall then be automatically declassified. Classification may be further extended only if the head of the originating Department personally determines in writing that its continued protection is essential to national security or that its disclosure would place a person in immediate jeopardy. In these instances—and I am encouraged to believe that they will be limited in number—the Department head must also specify the period of continued classification.

B. Documents Classified Before June 1, 1972

Essentially these same standards will be applied to materials classified prior to the effective date of this order, but in view of their vast quantity, the 6–10 year rule for automatic declassification can only be applied to those documents already subject to a 12-year declassification under current procedures. All others will be subject to the mandatory review process at any time after 10 years from the date of origin, provided the particularity and reasonable effort tests are met. After 30 years all remaining classified information shall be systematically reviewed for declassification by the Archivist of the United States. The Archivist shall continue the protection of this material after the 30-year deadline only if the head of the originating Department so specifies in writing under conditions noted above.

This new responsibility for the Archivist is tailored to fit with Administration plans for an immediate and systematic declassification of World War II documents. On August 3, 1971, I asked the Congress for a supplemental appropriation of $636,000 so that we could begin this project under the direction of the National Archives and Records Service of the General Services Administration. The Congress has not yet responded to this request, but I am hopeful of action this year.

5. *Sanctions Against Over-Classification.*

Unlike the current system, in which officials find it in their own best interest to classify all materials of a questionable nature, I am hopeful that the new Executive order will encourage them to exercise their authority with restraint. The order explicitly states that information shall never be classified "in order to conceal inefficiency or administrative error . . . or to prevent for any other reason the release of information which does not require protection in the interest of national

405

security." More than that, each agency is to provide a means of identifying the classifying authority for each document and each official is to be held personally responsible for the propriety of the classifications attributed to him. Repeated abuse of the process through excessive classification shall be grounds for administrative action.

6. *Monitoring the New System.*

Of critical importance to the effectiveness of my Executive order will be the new administrative machinery designed to ensure that its provisions are not allowed to become mere meaningless exhortations. The National Security Council will monitor compliance with the Executive order. In addition, the order creates a small Interagency Classification Review Committee with extensive powers to oversee agency implementation of the new system, and to take action on complaints both from within and from outside the Government on the administration of the order.

ACCELERATING PUBLICATION OF FOREIGN RELATIONS SERIES

My second action today was to direct an acceleration in the publication by the Department of State of the official documentary series, "Foreign Relations of the United States." Since 1861, that series has been an invaluable resource for historians and others interested in our past. For many years each publication contained documents written only a few years before, but soon after the Second World War, when Government files were bulging with war papers, a 20-year lag developed between origination and publication. Now, however, the lag has stretched to 26 years and the Department of State is presently publishing materials relating to events of 1946. This delay is too long, and I have directed the Secretary of State to institute immediately a program to reduce this time lag to 20 years, and to accomplish this mission within 3 years. I have also instructed the Secretary of Defense, the Director of Central Intelligence, and my Assistant for National Security Affairs to cooperate fully with this effort.

NOTE: On the same day, the White House released the transcript of a news briefing on the new classification and declassification system by John D. Ehrlichman, Assistant to the President for Domestic Affairs, and David R. Young, Executive Director, Interagency Classification Review Committee.

On August 3, 1972, the White House released an announcement of a report by John S. D. Eisenhower, Chairman, Interagency Classification Review Committee, on progress made in the new classification and declassification system. A fact sheet and chart on the progress in carrying out the provisions of Executive Order 11652 were also released. The announcement is printed in the Weekly Compilation of Presidential Documents (vol. 8, p. 1199).

80   Order Designating Authority To Classify Information or Material Within the Executive Office of the President. *March 8, 1972*

PURSUANT to Section 2(A) of the Executive Order of March 8, 1972, entitled Classification and Declassification of National Security Information and Material, I hereby designate the following offices in the Executive Office of the

President as possessing authority to originally classify information or material
"Top Secret" as set forth in said Order:

The White House Office
National Security Council
Office of Management and Budget
Domestic Council
Office of Science and Technology
Office of Emergency Preparedness
President's Foreign Intelligence Ad-
visory Board

Council on International Economic
Policy
Council of Economic Advisers
National Aeronautics and Space
Council
Office of Telecommunications Policy

RICHARD NIXON

The White House,
March 8, 1972.

---

81   Memorandums About Acceleration of Publication of
"Foreign Relations of the United States" Series.
March 8, 1972

Memorandum for the Secretary of State:

SUBJECT: Acceleration of Publication of
"Foreign Relations" Series

The official documentary series "Foreign Relations of the United States," published by the Department of State, has for
many years provided the American public
with an indispensable perspective on our
Nation's history. The materials now being
published, however, relate to the events
of 1946, and I think that in the interests
of a better informed public the length of
time between event and publication
should be shortened. Accordingly, I ask
that, without impairing the quality and
comprehensive nature of the series, you
immediately institute a program to reduce
this time lag to 20 years. Your objective
should be to make this reduction within
the next 3 years and to keep the publication point at 20 years from then on.

In order to achieve this goal in the most
expeditious manner, I am today instructing the Secretary of Defense, the Director
of Central Intelligence, and the Assistant
to the President for National Security Af-

fairs to cooperate fully with you in collecting and declassifying the appropriate
materials to the maximum extent consistent with the requirements of national
security.

RICHARD NIXON

Memorandum for:
The Secretary of Defense
The Director of Central Intelligence
The Assistant to the President for Na-
tional Security Affairs

SUBJECT: Acceleration of Publication of
"Foreign Relations" Series

I have today instructed the Secretary
of State to institute a program to reduce
the time lag of the official documentary
series "Foreign Relations of the United
States," published by the Department of
State, from 26 to 20 years.

The Department of State, in carrying
out this instruction, will be seeking the assistance of your department or agency in
the collection and declassification of the
material in question. I ask that you coop-

erate fully with the Secretary of State to meet the above objectives in the most expeditious manner and to the maximum extent consistent with the requirements of national security.

RICHARD NIXON

82 Message to the Congress Transmitting Annual Report of the United States-Japan Cooperative Medical Science Program. *March* 9, 1972

To the Congress of the United States:

I am pleased to send to the Congress the Fifth Annual Report of the United States-Japan Cooperative Medical Science Program.

This joint research effort in the medical sciences, undertaken in 1965 following a meeting between the Prime Minister of Japan and the President of the United States, continues its sharp focus upon widespread diseases of great importance in Asian nations: cholera, leprosy, malnutrition, the parasitic diseases filariasis and schistosomiasis, tuberculosis and certain viral diseases.

During 1971 several reports were published marking this program's first 5 years of research progress. Following careful planning and a review of objectives, it has been decided to expand the program scope to include research concerned with pollutant induced cancer, birth defects and related abnormalities.

This effort remains directed primarily toward diseases in Asia, however, the research results are clearly relevant to a much broader human spectrum. I am particularly heartened by the mutuality of this joint activity which has been undertaken so successfully by biomedical scientists in Japan and the United States. We can find few satisfactions greater than working effectively together with other nations for the ultimate benefit of all mankind.

RICHARD NIXON

The White House,
   March 9, 1972.

NOTE: The 12-page report is entitled "Fifth Annual Report to Congress: United States-Japan Cooperative Medical Science Program."

83 Statement About Air Transportation Safety. *March* 9, 1972

THREE times in the past 48 hours, tragedies that could have taken hundreds of lives have been narrowly averted. An explosive device was found aboard a passenger aircraft at New York's Kennedy Airport Tuesday night and defused only minutes before it was due to explode. Early yesterday morning, a bomb shattered a jetliner on the ground at Las Vegas. Fortunately, no one was aboard; had the plane been in flight, it would surely have been lost with all aboard. Then, later yesterday, a third bomb was discovered on another jet at Seattle.

Eighteen months ago, I ordered comprehensive, forceful action to halt the wave of criminal incidents on U.S. flag aircraft. The sky marshal and passenger screening programs conducted jointly by the Government and the airlines since that time have progressively reduced the hijacker's chances of success. From a onetime high of 83 percent, the success average of hijacking attempts diminished to 44 percent last year and now to only 25 percent thus far in 1972. Our efforts will continue until we reduce that rate to zero.

Now, however, our air transportation system faces a new threat, in the form of vicious extortion plots like the ones which have been directed at air traffic across the country this week. We must not be intimidated by such lawlessness. Rather we must and will meet this blackmail on the ground as vigorously as we have met piracy in the air.

As the attempt to create a crisis situation has emerged over the past several days, I have mobilized all appropriate security forces and resources of the Federal Government under the overall command of the Secretary of Transportation. This includes the Departments of State, Transportation, Defense, Treasury, and Justice—particularly the FAA, LEAA, Bureau of Customs, U.S. Marshals Service, and FBI. With this assistance we have so far rendered the plot a failure; no lives have been lost; the brazen ransom demands have been resisted. The Federal mobilization will continue, and will be augmented as necessary, until the current threat is crushed.

I have today ordered Secretary Volpe to take a series of measures aimed at better protecting against such incidents in the future.

The Federal Aviation Administration's new security regulations for air carriers, published in the Federal Register March 7, will take effect at once; we can no longer afford the 90-day implementation period previously stipulated for them. These regulations mandate immediate steps by every carrier to prevent or deter carriage of weapons or explosives aboard its aircraft; to prevent or deter unauthorized access to its aircraft; to tighten its baggage check-in procedures; and to improve the security of its cargo and baggage loading operations.

The Department of Transportation will expedite final rulemaking action for new security regulations governing airport operators, to complement the measures now required of the airline companies. The effect of these regulations will be to enforce the strict separation of operating areas at airports from public areas, thereby tightening the control of physical access to the former so that a security envelope is created around the aircraft and their supporting systems and personnel.

There is no time to lose. I have asked Secretary Volpe to convene a meeting as soon as possible with leaders of the aviation community to check on the followup of the steps we are taking today. He will continue to monitor progress of these efforts closely, and will keep me continuously informed.

Commercial aviation in the United States has built a commendable record of service and safety. I mean to do all in my power to help protect that record, by preventing air travel from becoming a vehicle for traffic in terrorism. We shall keep our airports, our airways, and our air travelers safe.

NOTE: On the same day, the White House released the transcript of a news briefing on the President's statement by Lt. Gen. Benjamin O. Davis, Jr., Assistant Secretary for Safety and Consumer Affairs, and Richard F. Lally, Director, Office of Transportation Security, Department of Transportation.

84   Statement on Signing Bills Authorizing United States Contributions to Multilateral Development Institutions.   *March 10, 1972*

TODAY I have signed into law three bills which are of special importance to our relations with the developing nations of Latin America, Asia, and Africa. These bills authorize significant United States contributions to three multilateral development institutions—the Inter-American Development Bank, the International Development Association, and the Asian Development Bank.

The activities of these institutions over the past decade have clearly demonstrated how much can be accomplished by great multilateral endeavors toward constructive and peaceful goals. Their increasing capacity to deal with the complex problems of development promises even greater achievements during this decade. It is for these reasons that I have given my strong support to legislation increasing the resources of these international development lending organizations. And I believe that it is for these same reasons that the Congress approved my requests by substantial bipartisan majorities.

The reasons which underlie our support for the international financial institutions are well known; they include: the international burden sharing that these institutions make possible, the experience and expertise that these institutions bring to development, and the very substantial long-range benefits to the United States from expanding markets and sources of supply in the developing countries.

These factors are consistent with the evolving world role I see for the United States in the decade ahead. They are the counterpart in the development field of the new approach we are charting in world monetary and trade policies—an approach which calls upon all partners to contribute their fair share to a balanced international economy. This legislation reaffirms the willingness of the United States to play a constructive leadership role within that context.

The bill providing $900 million of additional authority for the Fund for Special Operations of the Inter-American Development Bank is an important expression of our continued commitment to development in the Western Hemisphere. This action completes the authorizing phase of the arrangements which we and our Latin American partners worked out at Punta del Este in April of 1970. It clearly recognizes the high degree of importance which we and the Latin American people attach to this hemispheric institution and its work.

The funds authorized for the International Development Association of the World Bank will help that institution continue its work of providing credits to the poorest of the developing nations on suitable terms. The funds we provide to the IDA are essential to a broad international sharing of responsibility for the development effort, since other developed countries will provide more than 1½ times the amount that we contribute. Prompt appropriation of our contributions is especially important at this time, when funds available for new lending by this important institution have been virtually exhausted.

For Asia, the authority that becomes effective today will provide an initial United States contribution to the special funds of the Asian Development Bank. This money will be especially important in the evolving pattern of United States relations with Asia, helping Asian nations to become economically self-sufficient. Other countries have already contributed substantial amounts to this institution, but our resources are needed to continue the momentum that has been established.

The legislation which I sign today is evidence of the willingness of the United States to provide the funds required to carry out these programs. The amounts called for are within our capabilities.

They are consistent with and have been taken into account in our budgetary planning. They are essential if the idea of multilateral assistance is to remain a viable concept. And they are necessary if we are to continue to participate constructively in an international effort which has, in large part because of our past leadership, played such a major role in fostering progress in the developing world.

I urge that the Congress act promptly in appropriating the full amounts authorized by this legislation.

NOTE: The President signed the bills in a ceremony in the Cabinet Room at the White House. As enacted, S. 748, relating to the Inter-American Development Bank, is Public Law 92–246 (86 Stat. 59); S. 2010, relating to the International Development Association, is Public Law 92–247 (86 Stat. 60); and S. 749, relating to the Asian Development Bank, is Public Law 92–245 (86 Stat. 57).

85 Statement Urging Continuation of Radio Free Europe and Radio Liberty. *March* 11, 1972

I AM deeply concerned at the imminent prospect that Radio Free Europe and Radio Liberty may be compelled to shut down. With the support of the American government and people, these two unique voices of freedom have for many years been a vital source of uncensored news and commentary for tens of millions of people in Eastern Europe and the Soviet Union.

In this country, we have always set great store by freedom of communication. It is therefore only natural that the

American press and the American people, as represented by the overwhelming majority of the Congress, should have expressed strong backing for Radio Free Europe and Radio Liberty. Large majorities in both the House of Representatives and the Senate have affirmed their support for a continuing role for these two international broadcasting efforts. It would be a tragedy if their light should now be extinguished because of a parliamentary impasse between the two Houses.

86   Special Message to the Congress Transmitting Proposed Legislation for Funding of Foreign Assistance Programs in Fiscal Year 1973. *March 14, 1972*

To the Congress of the United States:

Today I am transmitting to the Congress legislation which would authorize funding for my foreign aid proposals for the coming fiscal year. This draft bill, which is entitled the Foreign Assistance Act of 1972, also contains provisions to make our military assistance more effective.

As I have often indicated, our foreign assistance programs are a central element in our foreign policy for the 1970s. For it is as dangerous for this Nation to ignore the problems of poverty and hunger and the need for security in other nations as it is to ignore our own domestic needs.

The Congress, acting after two-thirds of the current fiscal year had already passed, drastically reduced my foreign assistance requests for fiscal year 1972. In my judgment, the amounts appropriated for both security and development assistance in fiscal year 1972 are below the minimum level required to attain our foreign policy and national security goals. These reductions have created difficult problems in essential programs and in our relations with several countries. A repetition of these reductions and delays in 1973 would call into serious question the firmness of our commitments abroad and could have a destabilizing effect at a time when calm confidence in our support and perseverance will be critically needed. I therefore urge the Congress to act promptly to authorize and appropriate the full amounts requested for foreign assistance in fiscal year 1973.

In forwarding the Foreign Assistance Act of 1972, I would also underscore the points I made in my message to the Congress on April 21, 1971. In that message I addressed the need for fundamental reform of foreign assistance and recommended a major reorganization of these programs. I hope that the Congress will give closer consideration to these proposals in this session, and that together we can develop the most effective program possible, one that truly merits the broad bipartisan support that foreign aid has enjoyed in the past.

SECURITY ASSISTANCE

As I pointed out in my annual Report to the Congress on Foreign Policy last month: "Security assistance is a cornerstone of our foreign policy and of Free World security. . ." We live today in a period of transition in world affairs, in a time in which the United States is taking bold initiatives to build a new structure of peace, while asking our friends and allies to assume a greater responsibility for their own defense.

As we begin to make adjustments in our international role, it is especially critical that we maintain a firm United States commitment to an adequate level of security assistance. For without such adequate levels, our friends and allies will lack the confidence required for successful international cooperation in an era of negotiations. And without adequate security assistance, we cannot safely reduce our military presence abroad.

I am therefore requesting authorizations for security assistance programs totalling $2,151 million in fiscal year 1973: $780 million for grant military assistance, $527 million for military credit sales, and $844 million for security supporting assistance, of which an estimated $50 million is intended for Israel.

NARCOTICS CONTROL

I am requesting that a separate appropriation of $42.5 million be authorized for the support of international narcotics control activities. Control of illicit drug production and trafficking is one of the highest priorities of my Administration. I believe the authorization and appropriation of funds specifically for this purpose is essential to clearly demonstrate the determination of the Administration, the Congress, and the American people to overcome this serious menace.

SOUTH ASIA RELIEF AND RECONSTRUCTION ASSISTANCE

I am also proposing the authorization of $100 million in fiscal year 1973 for refugee relief and humanitarian assistance in South Asia. This sum would be in addition to the $200 million appropriated for this purpose for the current fiscal year.

The damage and destruction growing out of the war between India and Pakistan has truly been immense. We have indicated our willingness to work with other donors under the auspices of the United Nations to provide relief and rehabilitation to those in need.

The Secretary General of the United Nations has issued an assessment of these needs and a special appeal for support. We have already made an initial contribution to this effort and will continue to contribute in the light of the efforts of others and further assessments of need. The $100 million which I am requesting would enable us to continue to participate generously, along with other nations, in this important work.

RICHARD NIXON

The White House,
    March 14, 1972.

87   Message to the Congress Transmitting Annual Manpower Report of the President. *March* 15, 1972

To the Congress of the United States:

This is the tenth annual Manpower Report of the President and the third of my Administration. The information in this volume, as in its predecessors, will help to deepen the Nation's understanding of manpower problems and issues and to point the way toward achievement of our human resources development goals.

The second decade of an active manpower policy, which begins in March of this year, is dedicated to attaining full opportunity for all American workers.

Our tactics for pursuing this objective are twofold: First, to accomplish much needed and long overdue reform of the manpower programs set up under the Manpower Development and Training

Act and subsequent legislation and thus increase their effectiveness in enhancing the employability of jobless workers; and, second, to move toward a broader national manpower policy which will be an important adjunct of economic policy in achieving our Nation's economic and social objectives.

My Administration has made substantial progress in improving the operation of manpower programs under existing legislative authorizations, as described in this report. Fundamental reform of these programs, however, requires new legislation. For this reason, in the recent Special Message to the Congress which forms the first part of this volume I again urged speedy enactment of a Manpower Revenue Sharing Act, to make possible coordinated and flexible manpower programs administered by local governments in accordance with local needs.

The need for a comprehensive national manpower policy which is sensitive to the manpower implications of government actions in many fields is also documented in this report. There is hardly any major aspect of government policy which does not significantly affect the utilization, size, and skills of the country's work force.

Yet during the 1960's, efforts to appraise the employment impact of new and changing policies and programs were fragmentary, at best—leading to avoidable inefficiencies in program operations and unnecessarily severe adjustments for workers, industries, and local communities.

Both the efficiency of our economy and the well-being of the country's workers will be served by more systematic assessment of the manpower consequences of government policies and programs. Ac-

cordingly, I am instructing the Secretary of Labor to develop for my consideration recommendations with respect to the most effective mechanisms for achieving such an assessment and for assuring the findings receive appropriate attention in the government's decision making processes.

The upturn in employment late in 1971, in response to the New Economic Policy which I announced in August, is another subject discussed in this report. The outlook is now favorable for economic and employment expansion. However, as I said in my Economic Report in January, unemployment must be further reduced. This will be accomplished by the stimulus given to employment through our fiscal and monetary policies and by a number of special measures discussed in the present record, among them:

—The expansion in enrollments in federally assisted manpower programs to record figures, providing a substantial increase in opportunities for Negroes and other minorities;

—The new program of public service employment which serves two purposes simultaneously—opening transitional jobs for unemployed workers and filling unmet needs for essential public services;

—Better matching of workers and jobs through computerized Job Banks; and

—Special programs to aid the reemployment of veterans and persons displaced because of cutbacks in the defense and aerospace programs.

Teenage workers have by far the highest jobless rate of any group—more than four times the rate for adult workers in 1971. The remedial action underway and needed to meet their special problems is discussed in depth in this report. In particular, we propose a special, lower, youth minimum wage to help overcome employers' reluctance to hire inexperienced young workers.

A new approach to career education in the public schools is also being developed. This would give young people more realistic career preparation and help to build an easier, more effective school-to-work transition, paving the way toward a real solution to the problems of jobless youth.

The final focus of the report is on the professions. Scientists and engineers, teachers, doctors, and other professional and technical personnel represent only about one out of every seven workers, but they carry a responsibility for the country's economic and social well-being, its defense and position of world leadership, out of all proportion to their numbers.

We have two major objectives with respect to professional personnel. In the immediate future, we must promote full utilization of their talents and training, and we are moving strongly toward that goal through the special programs we have undertaken to aid the reemployment of the relatively small numbers of scientists

and engineers now out of work or underemployed.

In the longer view, we must assure a supply of new entrants into the professions adequate to meet national needs. As the findings of this report indicate, this objective is in process of accomplishment in the major professional fields, including the health professions. With the increased Federal funds for medical and nursing education that I have recommended to implement the new 1971 health manpower legislation, rapid progress will be possible in achieving a better standard of health care for all Americans.

I am pleased to transmit herewith a report on manpower requirements, resources, utilization and training as required under the Manpower Development and Training Act.

RICHARD NIXON

The White House,
   March 15, 1972.

NOTE: The message is printed in the report entitled "Manpower Report of the President Including a Report on Manpower Requirements, Resources, Utilization, and Training by the United States Department of Labor" (Government Printing Office, 284 pp.).

88   St. Patrick's Day Message.
March 16, 1972

ST. PATRICK'S Day lifts the spirit not only of Irish Americans, but of all Americans who cherish those qualities of heart and soul that are so characteristic of the Irish: warmth and wit, originality and openness of heart, faith and fortitude. There is a little bit of the Celt in all of us. That is why Americans of every na-

tionality join in St. Patrick's Day festivities, especially "the wearin' o' the green."

Ireland has invigorated our American way of life—in government, journalism, science, commerce, education; through its music, drama and poetry. Irish charm is found everywhere.

Mrs. Nixon and I value our own Irish

heritage and we take special pleasure in greeting our fellow citizens of Hibernian descent—and all those who, on St. Patrick's Day, celebrate America's gratitude for what Erin has given us.

RICHARD NIXON

NOTE: The message was made available to the press.

On March 17, 1972, Ambassador and Mrs. William Warnock of Ireland called on the President at the White House to present the traditional St. Patrick's Day gift of shamrocks in a Waterford crystal vase.

89   Special Message to the Congress on Science and Technology.   *March 16, 1972*

To the Congress of the United States:

The ability of the American people to harness the discoveries of science in the service of man has always been an important element in our national progress. As I noted in my most recent message on the State of the Union, Americans have long been known all over the world for their technological ingenuity—for being able to "build a better mousetrap"—and this capacity has undergirded both our domestic prosperity and our international strength.

We owe a great deal to the researchers and engineers, the managers and entrepreneurs who have made this record possible. Again and again they have met what seemed like impossible challenges. Again and again they have achieved success. They have found a way of preventing polio, placed men on the moon, and sent television pictures across the oceans. They have contributed much to our standard of living and our military strength.

But the accomplishments of the past are not something we can rest on. They are something we must build on. I am therefore calling today for a strong new effort to marshal science and technology in the work of strengthening our economy and improving the quality of our life. And I am outlining ways in which the Federal Government can work as a more

effective partner in this great task.

The importance of technological innovation has become dramatically evident in the past few years. For one thing, we have come to recognize that such innovation is essential to improving our economic productivity—to producing more and better goods and services at lower costs. And improved productivity, in turn, is essential if we are to achieve a full and durable prosperity—without inflation and without war. By fostering greater productivity, technological innovation can help us to expand our markets at home and abroad, strengthening old industries, creating new ones, and generally providing more jobs for the millions who will soon be entering the labor market.

This work is particularly important at a time when other countries are rapidly moving upward on the scientific and technological ladder, challenging us both in intellectual and in economic terms. Our international position in fields such as electronics, aircraft, steel, automobiles and shipbuilding is not as strong as it once was. A better performance is essential to both the health of our domestic economy and our leadership position abroad.

At the same time, the impact of new technology can do much to enrich the quality of our lives. The forces which threaten that quality will be growing at a dramatic pace in the years ahead. One of the great questions of our time is whether our capacity to deal with these forces will grow at a similar rate. The answer to that question lies in our scientific and technological progress.

As we face the new challenges of the 1970's, we can draw upon a great reservoir of scientific and technological information and skill—the result of the enormous investments which both the Federal Government and private enterprise made in research and development in recent years. In addition, this Nation's historic commitment to scientific excellence, its determination to take the lead in exploring the unknown, have given us a great tradition, a rich legacy on which to draw. Now it is for us to extend that tradition by applying that legacy in new situations.

In pursuing this goal, it is important to remember several things. In the first place, we must always be aware that the mere act of scientific discovery alone is not enough. Even the most important breakthrough will have little impact on our lives unless it is put to use—and putting an idea to use is a far more complex process than has often been appreciated. To accomplish this transformation, we must combine the genius of invention with the skills of entrepreneurship, management, marketing and finance.

Secondly, we must see that the environment for technological innovation is a favorable one. In some cases, excessive regulation, inadequate incentives and other barriers to innovation have worked to discourage and even to impede the entrepreneurial spirit. We need to do a better job of determining the extent to which such conditions exist, their underlying causes, and the best ways of dealing with them.

Thirdly, we must realize that the mere development of a new idea does not necessarily mean that it can or should be put into immediate use. In some cases, laws or regulations may inhibit its implementation. In other cases, the costs of the process may not be worth the benefits it produces. The introduction of some new technologies may produce undesirable side effects. Patterns of living and human behavior must also be taken into account. By realistically appreciating the limits of technological innovation, we will be in a better position fully to marshal its amazing strengths.

A fourth consideration concerns the need for scientific and technological manpower. Creative, inventive, dedicated scientists and engineers will surely be in demand in the years ahead; young people who believe they would find satisfaction in such careers should not hesitate to undertake them. I am convinced they will find ample opportunity to serve their communities and their country in important and exciting ways.

The fifth basic point I would make concerning our overall approach to science and technology in the 1970's concerns the importance of maintaining that spirit of curiosity and adventure which has always driven us to explore the unknown. This means that we must continue to give an important place to basic research and to exploratory experiments which provide the new ideas on which our edifice of technological accomplishment rests. Basic research in both the public and private sectors today is essential to our continuing progress tomorrow. All departments and agencies of the Federal Government will continue to support basic research which can help provide a broader range of future development options.

Finally, we must appreciate that the progress we seek requires a new partnership in science and technology—one which brings together the Federal Government, private enterprise, State and local governments, and our universities and research centers in a coordinated, cooperative effort to serve the national interest. Each member of that partnership must play the role it can play best; each must respect and reinforce the unique capacities of the other members. Only if this happens, only if our new partnership thrives, can we be sure that our scientific and technological resources will be used as effectively as possible in meeting our priority national needs.

With a new sense of purpose and a new sense of partnership, we can make the 1970's a great new era for American science and technology. Let us look now at some of the specific elements in this process.

STRENGTHENING THE FEDERAL ROLE

The role of the Federal Government in shaping American science and technology is pivotal. Of all our Nation's expenditures on research and development, 55 percent are presently funded by the Federal Government. Directly or indirectly, the Federal Government supports the employment of nearly half of all research and development personnel in the United States.

A good part of our Federal effort in this field has been directed in the past toward our national security needs. Because a strong national defense is essential to the maintenance of world peace, our research and development in support of national security must always be sufficient to our needs. We must ensure our strategic deterrent capability, continue the modernization of our Armed Forces, and strengthen the overall technological base that underlies future military systems. For these reasons, I have proposed a substantial increase for defense research and development for fiscal year 1973.

In this message, however, I would like to focus on how we can better apply our scientific resources in meeting civilian needs. Since the beginning of this Administration, I have felt that we should be doing more to focus our scientific and technological resources on the problems of the environment, health, energy, transportation and other pressing domestic concerns. If my new budget proposals are accepted, Federal funds for research and development concerning domestic problems will be 65 percent greater in the coming fiscal year than they were in 1969.

But increased funding is not the only prerequisite for progress in this field. We also need to spend our scarce resources more effectively. Accordingly, I have moved to develop an overall strategic approach in the allocation of Federal scientific and technological resources. As a part of this effort, I directed the Domestic Council last year to examine new technology opportunities in relation to domestic problems. In all of our planning, we have been concentrating not only on *how much* we spend but also on *how* we spend it.

My recommendations for strengthening the Federal role in science and technology have been presented to the Congress in my State of the Union message, in my budget for fiscal year 1973, and in individual agency presentations. I urge the Congress to support the various elements of this new Federal strategy.

1) We are reorienting our space pro-

gram to focus on domestic needs—such as communications, weather forecasting and natural resource exploration. One important way of doing this is by designing and developing a reusable space shuttle, a step which would allow us to seize new opportunities in space with higher reliability at lower costs.

2) We are moving to set and meet certain civilian research and development targets. In my State of the Union Message, my Budget Message and in other communications with the Congress, I have identified a number of areas where new efforts are most likely to produce significant progress and help us meet pressing domestic needs. They include:

—Providing new sources of energy without pollution. My proposed budget for fiscal year 1973 would increase energy-related research and development expenditures by 22 percent.

—Developing fast, safe, pollution-free transportation. I have proposed spending 46 percent more in the coming fiscal year on a variety of transportation projects.

—Working to reduce the loss of life and property from natural disasters. I have asked, for example, that our earthquake research program be doubled and that our hurricane research efforts be increased.

—Improving drug abuse rehabilitation programs and efforts to curb drug trafficking. Our budget requests in this critical area are four times the level of 1971.

—Increasing biomedical research efforts, especially those concerning cancer and heart disease, and generally providing more efficient and effective health care, including better emergency health care systems.

3) We will also draw more directly on the capabilities of our high technology agencies—the Atomic Energy Commis-

sion, the National Aeronautics and Space Administration and the National Bureau of Standards in the Department of Commerce—in applying research and development to domestic problems.

4) We are making strong efforts to improve the scientific and technological basis for setting Federal standards and regulations. For example, by learning to measure more precisely the level of air pollution and its effects on our health, we can do a more effective job of setting pollution standards and of enforcing those standards once they are established.

5) I am also providing in my 1973 budget for a 12 percent increase for research and development conducted at universities and colleges. This increase reflects the effort of the past 2 years to encourage educational institutions to undertake research related to important national problems.

6) Finally, I believe that the National Science Foundation should draw on all sectors of the scientific and technological community in working to meet significant domestic challenges. To this end, I am taking action to permit the Foundation to support applied research in industry when the use of industrial capabilities would be advantageous in accomplishing the Foundation's objectives.

SUPPORTING RESEARCH AND DEVELOPMENT IN THE PRIVATE SECTOR

The direction of private scientific and technological activities is determined in large measure by thousands of private decisions—and this should always be the case. But we cannot ignore the fact that Federal policy also has a great impact on what happens in the private sector. This influence is exerted in many ways—including direct Federal support for such research and development.

In general, I believe it is appropriate for the Federal Government to encourage private research and development to the extent that the market mechanism is not effective in bringing needed innovations into use. This can happen in a number of circumstances. For example, the sheer size of some developmental projects is beyond the reach of private firms particularly in industries which are fragmented into many small companies. In other cases, the benefits of projects cannot be captured by private institutions, even though they may be very significant for the whole of society. In still other cases, the risks of certain projects, while acceptable to society as a whole, are excessive for individual companies.

In all these cases, Federal support of private research and development is necessary and desirable. We must see that such support is made available—through cost-sharing agreements, procurement policies or other arrangements.

One example of the benefits of such a partnership between the Federal Government and private enterprise is the program I presented last June to meet our growing need for clean energy. As I outlined the Federal role in this effort, I also indicated that industry's response to these initiatives would be crucial. That response has been most encouraging to date. For example, the electric utilities have already pledged some $25 million a year for a period of 10 years for developing a liquid metal fast breeder reactor demonstration plant. These pledges have come through the Edison Electric Institute, the American Public Power Association, and the National Rural Electric Cooperative As-

sociation. This effort is one part of a larger effort by the electrical utilities to raise $150 million annually for research and development to meet the growing demand for clean electric power.

At the same time, the gas companies, through the American Gas Association, have raised $10 million to accelerate the effort to convert coal into gas. This sum represents industry's first year share in a pilot plant program which will be financed one-third by industry and two-thirds by the Federal Government. When it proves feasible to proceed to the demonstration stage, industrial contributions to this project will be expected to increase.

APPLYING GOVERNMENT-SPONSORED
TECHNOLOGIES

An asset unused is an asset wasted. Federal research and development activities generate a great deal of new technology which could be applied in ways which go well beyond the immediate mission of the supporting agency. In such cases, I believe the Government has a responsibility to transfer the results of its research and development activities to wider use in the private sector.

It was to further this objective that we created in 1970 the new National Technical Information Service in the Department of Commerce. In addition, the new incentives programs of the National Science Foundation and the National Bureau of Standards will seek effective means of improving and accelerating the transfer of research and development results from Federal programs to a wider range of potential users.

One important barrier to the private development and commercial application of Government-sponsored technologies is the lack of incentive which results from the fact that such technologies are generally available to all competitors. To help remedy this situation, I approved last August a change in the Government patent policy which liberalized the private use of Government-owned patents. I directed that such patents may be made available to private firms through exclusive licenses where needed to encourage commercial application.

As a further step in this same direction, I am today directing my Science Adviser and the Secretary of Commerce to develop plans for a new, systematic effort to promote actively the licensing of Government-owned patents and to obtain domestic and foreign patent protection for technology owned by the United States Government in order to promote its transfer into the civilian economy.

IMPROVING THE CLIMATE FOR INNOVATION

There are many ways in which the Federal Government influences the level and the quality of private research and development. Its direct supportive efforts are important, but other policies—such as tax, patent, procurement, regulation and antitrust policies—also can have a significant effect on the climate for innovation.

We know, for instance, that a strong and reliable patent system is important to technological progress and industrial strength. The process of applying technology to achieve our national goals calls for a tremendous investment of money, energy and talent by our private enterprise system. If we expect industry to support this investment, we must make the most effective possible use of the incentives which are provided by our patent system.

The way we apply our antitrust laws can also do much to shape research and development. Uncertain reward and high risks can be significant barriers to progress when a firm is small in relation to the scale of effort required for successful projects. In such cases, formal or informal combinations of firms provide one means for hurdling these barriers, especially in highly fragmented industries. On the other hand, joint efforts among leading firms in highly concentrated industries would normally be considered undesirable. In general, combinations which lead to an improved allocation of the resources of the nation are normally permissible, but actions which lead to excessive market power for any single group are not. Any joint program for research and development must be approached in a way that does not detract from the normal competitive incentives of our free enterprise economy.

I believe we need to be better informed about the full consequences of all such policies for scientific and technological progress. For this reason, I have included in my budget for the coming fiscal year a program whereby the National Science Foundation would support assessments and studies focused specifically on barriers to technological innovation and on the consequences of adopting alternative Federal policies which would reduce or eliminate these barriers. These studies would be undertaken in close consultation with the Executive Office of the President, the Department of Commerce and other concerned departments and agencies, so that the results can be most expeditiously considered as further Government decisions are made.

There are a number of additional steps which can also do much to enhance the climate for innovation.

1) I shall submit legislation to encourage the development of the small, high technology firms which have had such a distinguished pioneering record. Because the combination of high technology and small size makes such firms exceptionally risky from an investment standpoint, my proposal would provide additional means for the Small Business Investment Companies (SBICs) to improve the availability of venture capital to such firms.

a. I propose that the ratio of Government support to SBICs be increased. This increased assistance would be channeled to small business concerns which are principally engaged in the development or exploitation of inventions or of technological improvements and new products.

b. I propose that the current limit on Small Business Administration loans to each SBIC be increased to $20 million to allow for growth in SBIC funds devoted to technology investments.

c. I propose that federally regulated commercial banks again be permitted to achieve up to 100 percent ownership of an SBIC, rather than the limited 50 percent ownership which is allowed at present.

d. To enhance risk-taking and entrepreneurial ventures, I again urge passage of the small business tax bill, which would provide for extending the eligibility period for the exercise of qualified stock options from 5 to 8 or 10 years, reducing the holding period for non-registered stock from 3 years to 1 year, and extending the tax-loss carry-forward from 5 to 10 years. These provisions would apply to small firms, as defined in the proposed legislation.

2) I have requested in my proposed budget for fiscal year 1973 that new programs be set up by the National Science Foundation and the National Bureau of Standards to determine effective ways of stimulating non-Federal investment in research and development and of improving the application of research and development results. The experiments to be set up under this program are designed to test a variety of partnership arrangements among the various levels of government, private firms and universities. They would include the exploration of new arrangements for cost-sharing, patent licensing, and research support, as well as the testing of incentives for industrial research associations.

3) To provide a focal point within the executive branch for policies concerning industrial research and development, the Department of Commerce will appraise, on a continuing basis, the technological strengths and weaknesses of American industry. It will propose measures to assure a vigorous state of industrial progress. The Department will work with other agencies in identifying barriers to such progress and will draw on the studies and assessments prepared through the National Science Foundation and the National Bureau of Standards.

4) To foster useful innovation, I also plan to establish a new program of research and development prizes. These prizes will be awarded by the President for outstanding achievements by individuals and institutions and will be used especially to encourage needed innovation in key areas of public concern. I believe these prizes will be an important symbol of the Nation's concern for our scientific and technological challenges.

5) An important step which could

be of great significance in fostering technological innovations and enhancing our position in world trade is that of changing to the metric system of measurement. The Secretary of Commerce has submitted to the Congress legislation which would allow us to begin to develop a carefully coordinated national plan to bring about this change. The proposed legislation would bring together a broadly representative board of private citizens who would work with all sectors of our society in planning for such a transition. Should such a change be decided on, it would be implemented on a cooperative, voluntary basis.

STRONGER FEDERAL, STATE AND LOCAL PARTNERSHIPS

A consistent theme which runs throughout my program for making government more responsive to public needs is the idea that each level of government should do what it can do best. This same theme characterizes my approach to the challenges of research and development. The Federal Government, for example, can usually do a good job of massing research and development resources. But State and local governments usually have a much better "feel" for the specific public challenges to which those resources can be applied. If we are to use science and technology effectively in meeting these challenges, then State and local governments should have a central role in the application process. That process is a difficult one at best; it will be even more complex and frustrating if the States and localities are not adequately involved.

To help build a greater sense of partnership among the three levels of the Federal system, I am directing my Science Adviser, in cooperation with the Office of Intergovernmental Relations, to serve as a focal point for discussions among various Federal agencies and the representatives of State and local governments. These discussions should lay the basis for developing a better means for collaboration and consultation on scientific and technological questions in the future. They should focus on the following specific subjects:

1) Systematic ways for communicating to the appropriate Federal agencies the priority needs of State and local governments, along with information concerning locally-generated solutions to such problems. In this way, such information can be incorporated into the Federal research and development planning process.

2) Ways of assuring State and local governments adequate access to the technical resources of major Federal research and development centers, such as those which are concerned with transportation, the environment, and the development of new sources of energy.

3) Methods whereby the Federal Government can encourage the aggregation of State and local markets for certain products so that industries can give government purchasers the benefits of innovation and economies of scale.

The discussions which take place between Federal, State and local representatives can also help to guide the experimental programs I have proposed for the National Science Foundation and the National Bureau of Standards. These programs, in turn, can explore the possibilities for creating better ties between State and local governments on the one hand and local industries and universities on the other, thus stimulating the use of research and development in improving the efficiency and effectiveness of public services at the State and local level.

WORLD PARTNERSHIP IN SCIENCE AND TECHNOLOGY

The laws of nature transcend national boundaries. Increasingly, the peoples of the world are irrevocably linked in a complex web of global interdependence—and increasingly the strands of that web are woven by science and technology.

The cause of scientific and technological progress has always been advanced when men have been able to reach across international boundaries in common pursuits. Toward this end, we must now work to facilitate the flow of people and the exchange of ideas, and to recognize that the basic problems faced in each nation are shared by every nation.

I believe this country can benefit substantially from the experience of other countries, even as we help other countries by sharing our information and facilities and specialists with them. To promote this goal, I am directing the Federal agencies, under the leadership of the Department of State, to identify new opportunities for international cooperation in research and development. At the same time, I am inviting other countries to join in research efforts in the United States, including:

—the effort to conquer cancer at the unique research facilities of our National Institutes of Health and at Fort Detrick, Maryland; and

—the effort to understand the adverse health effects of chemicals, drugs and pollutants at the new National Center for Toxicological Research at Pine Bluff, Arkansas.

These two projects concern priority problems which now challenge the whole world's research community. But they are only a part of the larger fabric of cooperative international efforts in which we are now engaged.

Science and technology can also provide important links with countries which have different political systems from ours. For example, we have recently concluded an agreement with the Soviet Union in the field of health, an agreement which provides for joint research on cancer, heart disease and environmental health problems. We are also cooperating with the Soviet Union in the space field; we will continue to exchange lunar samples and we are exploring prospects for closer cooperation in satellite meteorology, in remote sensing of the environment, and in space medicine. Beyond this, joint working groups have verified the technical feasibility of a docking mission between a SALYUT Station [1] and an Apollo spacecraft.

One result of my recent visit to the People's Republic of China was an agreement to facilitate the development of contacts and exchanges in many fields, including science and technology. I expect to see further progress in this area.

The United Nations and a number of its specialized agencies are also involved in a wide range of scientific and technological activities. The importance of these tasks—and the clear need for an international approach to technical problems with global implications—argues for the most effective possible organization and coordination of various international agencies concerned. As a step in this direction, I proposed in a recent message to the Congress the creation of a United

---

[1] A Soviet orbital space laboratory station.

Nations Fund for the Environment to foster an international attack on environmental problems. Also, I believe the American scientific community should participate more fully in the science activities of international agencies.

To further these objectives, I am taking steps to initiate a broad review of United States involvement in the scientific and technological programs of international organizations and of steps that might be taken to make United States participation in these activities more effective, with even stronger ties to our domestic programs.

Finally, I would emphasize that United States science and technology can and must play an important role in the progress of developing nations. We are committed to bring the best of our science and technology to bear on the critical problems of development through our reorganized foreign assistance programs.

A NEW SENSE OF PURPOSE AND A NEW SENSE OF PARTNERSHIP

The years ahead will require a new sense of purpose and a new sense of partnership in science and technology. We must define our goals clearly, so that we know where we are going. And then we must develop careful strategies for pur-

suing those goals, strategies which bring together the Federal Government, the private sector, the universities, and the States and local communities in a cooperative pursuit of progress. Only then can we be confident that our public and private resources for science and technology will be spent as effectively as possible.

In all these efforts, it will be essential that the American people be better equipped to make wise judgments concerning public issues which involve science and technology. As our national life is increasingly permeated by science and technology, it is important that public understanding grow apace.

The investment we make today in science and technology and in the development of our future scientific and technical talent is an investment in tomorrow—an investment which can have a tremendous impact on the basic quality of our lives. We must be sure that we invest wisely and well.

RICHARD NIXON

The White House,
　March 16, 1972.

NOTE: On the same day, the White House released a fact sheet and the transcript of a news briefing on the message. Participants in the news briefing were Dr. Edward E. David, Jr., Director, Office of Science and Technology, and Alan K. McAdams, Senior Staff Economist, Council of Economic Advisers.

90　Address to the Nation on Equal Educational Opportunities and School Busing. *March* 16, 1972

Good evening:

Tonight I want to talk to you about one of the most difficult issues of our time—the issue of busing.

Across this Nation—in the North, East,

West, and South—States, cities, and local school districts have been torn apart in debate over this issue.

My own position is well known. I am opposed to busing for the purpose of achieving racial balance in our schools. I have spoken out against busing scores of times over many years.

And I believe most Americans, white and black, share that view.

But what we need now is not just speaking out against more busing. We need action to stop it. Above all, we need to stop it in the right way—in a way that will provide better education for every child in America in a desegregated school system.

The reason action is so urgent is because of a number of recent decisions of the lower Federal courts. Those courts have gone too far—in some cases beyond the requirements laid down by the Supreme Court—in ordering massive busing to achieve racial balance. The decisions have left in their wake confusion and contradiction in the law; anger, fear, and turmoil in local communities; and, worst of all, agonized concern among hundreds of thousands of parents for the education and the safety of their children who have been forced by court order to be bused miles away from their neighborhood schools.

What is the answer?

There are many who believe that a constitutional amendment is the only way to deal with this problem. The constitutional amendment proposal deserves a thorough consideration by the Congress on its merits. But as an answer to the immediate problem we face of stopping more busing now, the constitutional amendment approach has a fatal flaw: It takes too long.

A constitutional amendment would take between a year and 18 months, at the very least, to become effective. This means that hundreds of thousands of schoolchildren will be ordered by the courts to be bused away from their neighborhood schools in the next school year, with no hope for relief.

What we need is action now—not action 2, 3, or 4 years from now. And there is only one effective way to deal with the problem now. That is for the Congress to act. That is why I am sending a special message to the Congress tomorrow urging immediate consideration and action on two measures.

First, I shall propose legislation that would call an immediate halt to all new busing orders by Federal courts—a moratorium on new busing.

Next, I shall propose a companion measure—the Equal Educational Opportunities Act of 1972.

This act would require that every State or locality grant equal educational opportunity to every person, regardless of race, color, or national origin. For the first time in our history, the cherished American ideal of equality of educational opportunity would be affirmed in the law of the land by the elected representatives of the people in Congress.

The act would further establish an educational bill of rights for Mexican-Americans, Puerto Ricans, Indians, and others who start their education under language handicaps, to make certain that they, too, will have equal opportunity.

The act I propose would concentrate Federal school aid funds on the areas of greatest educational need. That would mean directing over $2½ billion in the next year mainly towards improving the education of children from poor families.

This proposal deals directly with the problem that has been too often overlooked. We all know that within the central cities of our Nation there are schools so inferior that it is hypocritical even to suggest that the poor children who go there are getting a decent education, let alone an education comparable to that of children who go to schools in the suburbs. Even the most extreme proponents of busing admit that it would be years before programs could be set up and financed which would bus a majority of these children out of these central city areas to better schools in the suburbs. That means that putting primary emphasis on more busing, rather than on better education, inevitably will leave a lost generation of poor children in the central cities, doomed to inferior education.

It is time for us to make a national commitment to see that the schools in the central cities are upgraded so that the children who go there will have just as good a chance to get quality education as do the children who go to school in the suburbs.

What I am proposing is that at the same time we stop more busing, we move forward to guarantee that the children currently attending the poorest schools in our cities and in rural areas be provided with education equal to that of good schools in their communities.

Taken together, the two elements of my proposal—the moratorium on new busing and the Equal Educational Opportunities Act, would focus our efforts where they really belong: on better education for all of our children, rather than on more busing for some of our children.

In addition, I am directing all agencies and departments of the Federal Government at every level to carry out the spirit as well as the letter of the message in all of their actions. I am directing that the Justice Department intervene in selected cases where the lower courts have gone

beyond the Supreme Court's requirements in ordering busing.

These are the highlights of the new approach I propose. Let me now go to the heart of the problem that confronts us. I want to tell you why I feel that busing for the purpose of achieving racial balance in our schools is wrong, and why the great majority of Americans are right in wanting to bring it to an end.

The purpose of such busing is to help end segregation. But experience in case after case has shown that busing is a bad means to a good end. The frank recognition of that fact does not reduce our commitment to desegregation; it simply tells us that we have to come up with a better means to that good end.

The great majority of Americans, white and black, feel strongly that the busing of schoolchildren away from their own neighborhoods for the purpose of achieving racial balance is wrong.

But the great majority, black and white, also are determined that the process of desegregation must go forward until the goal of genuinely equal educational opportunity is achieved.

The question, then, is "How can we end segregation in a way that does not result in more busing?" The proposals I am sending to the Congress provide an answer to that question.

One emotional undercurrent that has done much to make this issue so difficult is the feeling that some people have that to oppose busing is to be antiblack. This is dangerous nonsense.

There is no escaping the fact that some people do oppose busing because of racial prejudice. But to go on from this to conclude that "antibusing" is simply a code word for prejudice is a vicious libel on millions of concerned parents who oppose

427

busing not because they are against desegregation, but because they are for better education for their children.

They want their children educated in their own neighborhoods. Many have invested their life's savings in a home in a neighborhood they chose because it had good schools. They do not want their children bused across the city to an inferior school just to meet some social planner's concept of what is considered to be the correct racial balance or what is called "progressive" social policy.

There are right reasons for opposing busing, and there are wrong reasons—and most people, including large and increasing numbers of blacks, oppose it for reasons that have little or nothing to do with race. It would compound an injustice to persist in massive busing simply because some people oppose it for the wrong reasons.

There is another element to consider, and this is the most important one of all. That is the human element which I see reflected in thousands of letters I have received in my mail from worried parents all over the country, North, East, West, and South. Let me give you some examples.

I believe it is wrong when an 8-year-old child who was once able to walk to a neighborhood school is now forced to travel 2 hours a day on a bus.

I believe it is wrong when a working mother is suddenly faced with three different bus schedules for her children and that makes it impossible for her to continue to work.

I believe it is wrong when parents are burdened with new worries about their children's safety on the road and in the neighborhoods far from home.

I believe it is wrong when a child in a poor neighborhood is denied the extra personal attention and financial support in his school that we know can make all the difference.

All these individual human wrongs add up to a deeply felt and growing frustration. These are wrongs that can be and must be set right.

That is the purpose of the legislation I am sending to Congress tomorrow.

I submit these proposals to the Congress, and I commend them to all of you listening tonight, mindful of the profound importance and the special complexity of the issues they address. The key is action, and action now. And Congress holds that key. If you agree with the goals I have described tonight—to stop more busing now and provide equality of education for all of our children—I urge you to let your Congressman and Senators know your views so that Congress will act promptly to deal with this problem.

Let me close with a personal note. This is a deeply emotional and divisive issue. I have done my very best to undertake to weigh and respect the conflicting interests, to strike a balance which is thoughtful and just, to search for answers that will best serve all of our Nation's children.

I realize the program I have recommended will not satisfy the extremists on the one side who oppose busing for the wrong reasons.

I realize that my program will not satisfy the extreme social planners on the other side who insist on more busing, even at the cost of better education.

But while what I have said tonight will not appeal to either extreme, I believe I have expressed the views of the majority of Americans. Because I believe that the majority of Americans of all races want more busing stopped and better education started.

Let us recognize that the issue of busing divides many Americans. But let us also recognize that the commitment to equal opportunity in education unites all Americans.

The proposals I am submitting to Congress will allow us to turn away from what divides us and to turn toward what unites us.

The way we handle this difficult issue is a supreme test of the character, the responsibility, and the decency of the American people.

Let us handle it in a way we can be proud of—by uniting behind a program which will make it possible for all the children in this great and good country of ours to receive a better education and to enjoy a better life.

Thank you. Good night.

NOTE: The President spoke at 10 p.m. from the Oval Office at the White House. His address was broadcast live on radio and television.

The President spoke from a prepared text. An advance text of his address was released on the same day.

---

91   Special Message to the Congress on Equal Educational Opportunities and School Busing.   *March* 17, 1972

To the Congress of the United States:

In this message, I wish to discuss a question which divides many Americans. That is the question of busing.

I want to do so in a way that will enable us to focus our attention on a question which unites all Americans. That is the question of how to ensure a better education for all of our children.

In the furor over busing, it has become all too easy to forget what busing is supposed to be designed to achieve: equality of educational opportunity for all Americans.

Conscience and the Constitution both require that no child should be denied equal educational opportunity. That Constitutional mandate was laid down by the Supreme Court in *Brown* v. *Board of Education* in 1954. The years since have been ones of dismantling the old dual school system in those areas where it existed—a process that has now been substantially completed.

As we look to the future, it is clear that the efforts to provide equal educational opportunity must now focus much more specifically on education: on assuring that the opportunity is not only equal, but adequate, and that in those remaining cases in which desegregation has not yet been completed it be achieved with a greater sensitivity to educational needs.

Acting within the present framework of Constitutional and case law, the lower Federal courts have ordered a wide variety of remedies for the equal protection violations they have found. These remedies have included such plans as redrawing attendance zones, pairing, clustering and consolidation of school districts. Some of these plans have not required extensive additional transportation of pupils. But some have required that pupils be bused long distances, at great inconvenience. In some cases plans have required that children be bused away from their neighborhoods to schools that are inferior or even unsafe.

The maze of differing and sometimes inconsistent orders by the various lower courts has led to contradiction and uncer-

429

tainty, and often to vastly unequal treatment among regions, States and local school districts. In the absence of statutory guidelines, many lower court decisions have gone far beyond what most people would consider reasonable, and beyond what the Supreme Court has said is necessary, in the requirements they have imposed for the reorganization of school districts and the transportation of school pupils.

All too often, the result has been a classic case of the remedy for one evil creating another evil. In this case, a remedy for the historic evil of racial discrimination has often created a new evil of disrupting communities and imposing hardship on children—both black and white—who are themselves wholly innocent of the wrongs that the plan seeks to set right.

The 14th Amendment to the Constitution—under which the school desegregation cases have arisen—provides that "The Congress shall have power to enforce, by appropriate legislation, the provisions of this article."

Until now, enforcement has been left largely to the courts—which have operated within a limited range of available remedies, and in the limited context of case law rather than of statutory law. I propose that the Congress now accept the responsibility and use the authority given to it under the 14th Amendment to clear up the confusion which contradictory court orders have created, and to establish reasonable national standards.

The legislation I propose today would accomplish this.

It would put an immediate stop to further new busing orders by the Federal courts.

It would enlist the wisdom, the re-

sources and the experience of the Congress in the solution of the vexing problems involved in fashioning school desegregation policies that are true to the Constitutional requirements and fair to the people and communities concerned.

It would establish uniform national criteria, to ensure that the Federal courts in all sections and all States would have a common set of standards to guide them.

These measures would protect the right of a community to maintain neighborhood schools—while also establishing a shared local and Federal responsibility to raise the level of education in the neediest neighborhoods, with special programs for those disadvantaged children who need special attention.

At the same time, these measures would not roll back the Constitution, or undo the great advances that have been made in ending school segregation, or undermine the continuing drive for equal rights.

Specifically, I propose that the Congress enact two measures which together would shift the focus from more transportation to better education, and would curb busing while expanding educational opportunity. They are:

1. *The Equal Educational Opportunities Act of 1972.* This would:

—Require that no State or locality could deny equal educational opportunity to any person on account of race, color or national origin.

—Establish criteria for determining what constitutes a denial of equal opportunity.

—Establish priorities of remedies for schools that are required to desegregate, with busing to be required only as a last resort, and then only under strict limitations.

—Provide for the concentration of Federal school-aid funds specifically on the areas of greatest educational need, in a way and in sufficient quantities so they can have a real and substantial impact in terms of improving the education of children from poor families.

2. *The Student Transportation Moratorium Act of 1972.*

—This would provide a period of time during which any future, new busing orders by the courts would not go into effect, while the Congress considered legislative approaches—such as the Equal Educational Opportunities Act—to the questions raised by school desegregation cases. This moratorium on new busing would be effective until July 1, 1973, or until the Congress passed the appropriate legislation, whichever was sooner. Its purpose would not be to contravene rights under the 14th Amendment, but simply to hold in abeyance further busing orders while the Congress investigated and considered alternative methods of securing those rights—methods that could establish a new and broader context in which the courts could decide desegregation cases, and that could render busing orders unnecessary.

Together, these two measures would provide an immediate stop to new busing in the short run, and constructive alternatives to busing in the long run—and they would give the Congress the time it needs to consider fully and fairly one of the most complex and difficult issues to confront the Nation in modern times.

Busing: the Fears and Concerns

Before discussing the specifics of these proposals, let me deal candidly with the controversy surrounding busing itself.

There are some people who fear any curbs on busing because they fear that it would break the momentum of the drive for equal rights for blacks and other minorities. Some fear it would go further, and that it would set in motion a chain of reversals that would undo all the advances so painfully achieved in the past generation.

It is essential that whatever we do to curb busing be done in a way that plainly will not have these other consequences. It is vitally important that the Nation's continued commitment to equal rights and equal opportunities be clear and concrete.

On the other hand, it is equally important that we not allow emotionalism to crowd out reason, or get so lost in symbols that words lose their meaning.

One emotional undercurrent that has done much to make this so difficult an issue is the feeling some people have that to oppose busing is to be anti-black. This is closely related to the arguments often put forward that resistance to any move, no matter what, that may be advanced in the name of desegregation is "racist." This is dangerous nonsense.

There is no escaping the fact that some people oppose busing because of racial prejudice. But to go on from this to conclude that "anti-busing" is simply a code word for prejudice is an exercise in arrant unreason. There are right reasons for opposing busing, and there are wrong reasons—and most people, including large and increasing numbers of blacks and other minorities, oppose it for reasons that have little or nothing to do with race. It would compound an injustice to persist in massive busing simply because some people oppose it for the wrong reasons.

431

For most Americans, the school bus used to be a symbol of hope—of better education. In too many communities today, it has become a symbol of helplessness, frustration and outrage—of a wrenching of children away from their families, and from the schools their families may have moved to be near, and sending them arbitrarily to others far distant.

It has become a symbol of social engineering on the basis of abstractions, with too little regard for the desires and the feelings of those most directly concerned: the children, and their families.

Schools exist to serve the children, not to bear the burden of social change. As I put it in my policy statement on school desegregation 2 years ago (on March 24, 1970):

"One of the mistakes of past policy has been to demand too much of our schools: They have been expected not only to educate, but also to accomplish a social transformation. Children in many instances have not been served, but used—in what all too often has proved a tragically futile effort to achieve in the schools the kind of multiracial society which the adult community has failed to achieve for itself.

"If we are to be realists, we must recognize that in a free society there are limits to the amount of Government coercion that can reasonably be used; that in achieving desegregation we must proceed with the least possible disruption of the education of the Nation's children; and that our children are highly sensitive to conflict, and highly vulnerable to lasting psychic injury.

"Failing to recognize these factors, past policies have placed on the schools and the children too great a share of the burden of eliminating racial disparities throughout our society. A major part of this task falls to the schools. But they cannot do it all or even most of it by themselves. Other institutions can share the burden of breaking down racial barriers, but only the schools can perform the task of education itself. If our schools fail to educate, then whatever they may achieve in integrating the races will turn out to be only a Pyrrhic victory."

The Supreme Court has also recognized this problem. Writing for a unanimous Court in the *Swann* case last April, Chief Justice Burger said:

"The constant theme and thrust of every holding from *Brown I* to date is that state-enforced separation of races in public schools is discrimination that violates the Equal Protection Clause. The remedy commanded was to dismantle dual school systems.

"We are concerned in these cases with the elimination of the discrimination inherent in the dual school systems, not with myriad factors of human existence which can cause discrimination in a multitude of ways on racial, religious, or ethnic grounds. The target of the cases from *Brown I* to the present was the dual school system. The elimination of racial discrimination in public schools is a large task and one that should not be retarded by efforts to achieve broader purposes lying beyond the jurisdiction of school authorities. One vehicle can carry only a limited amount of baggage. . . .

"Our objective in dealing with the issues presented by these cases is to see that school authorities exclude no pupil of a racial minority from any school, directly or indirectly, on account of race; it does not and cannot embrace all the problems of racial prejudice, even when those problems contribute to disproportionate racial concentrations in some schools."

In addressing the busing question, it is important that we do so in historical perspective.

Busing for the purpose of desegregation was begun—mostly on a modest scale—as one of a mix of remedies to meet the requirements laid down by various lower Federal courts for achieving the difficult transition from the old dual school system to a new, unitary system.

At the time, the problems of transition that loomed ahead were massive, the old habits deeply entrenched, community resistance often extremely strong. As the years wore on, the courts grew increasingly impatient with what they sometimes saw as delay or evasion, and increasingly insistent that, as the Supreme Court put it in the *Green* decision in 1968, desegregation plans must promise "realistically to work, and . . . to work *now*."

But in the past 3 years, progress toward eliminating the vestiges of the dual system has been phenomenal—and so too has been the shift in public attitudes in those areas where dual systems were formerly operated. In State after State and community after community, local civic, business and educational leaders of all races have come forward to help make the transition peacefully and successfully. Few voices are now raised urging a return to the old patterns of enforced segregation.

This new climate of acceptance of the basic Constitutional doctrine is a new element of great importance: for the greater the elements of basic good faith, of desire to make the system work, the less need or justification there is for extreme remedies rooted in coercion.

At the same time, there has been a marked shift in the focus of concerns by blacks and members of other minorities.

Minority parents have long had a deep and special concern with improving the quality of their children's education. For a number of years, the principal emphasis of this concern—and of the Nation's attention—was on desegregating the schools. Now that the dismantling of the old dual system has been substantially completed there is once again a far greater balance of emphasis on improving schools, on convenience, on the chance for parental involvement—in short, on the same concerns that motivate white parents—and, in many communities, on securing a greater measure of control over schools that serve primarily minority-group communities. Moving forward on desegregation is still important—but the principal concern is with preserving the principle, and with ensuring that the great gains made since *Brown*, and particularly in recent years, are not rolled back in a reaction against excessive busing. Many black leaders now express private concern, moreover, that a reckless extension of busing requirements could bring about precisely the results they fear most: a reaction that would undo those gains, and that would begin the unraveling of advances in other areas that also are based on newly expanded interpretations of basic Constitutional rights.

Also, it has not escaped their notice that those who insist on system-wide racial balance insist on a condition in which, in most communities, every school would be run by whites and dominated by whites, with blacks in a permanent minority—and without escape from that minority status. The result would be to deny blacks the right to have schools in which they are the majority.

In short, this is not the simple black-white issue that some simplistically present it as being. There are deep divisions of opinion among people of all races—with recent surveys showing strong opposition to busing among black parents as well as among white parents—not because they are against desegregation but because they are for better education.

In the process of school desegregation, we all have been learning; perceptions have been changing. Those who once said "no" to racial integration have accepted the concept, and believe in equality before the law. Those who once thought massive busing was the answer have also been changing their minds in the light of experience.

As we cut through the clouds of emotionalism that surround the busing question, we can begin to identify the legitimate issues.

Concern for the quality of education a child gets is legitimate.

Concern that there be no retreat from the principle of ending racial discrimination is legitimate.

Concern for the distance a child has to travel to get to school is legitimate.

Concern over requiring that a child attend a more distant school when one is available near his home is legitimate.

Concern for the obligation of government to assure, as nearly as possible, that all the children of a given district have equal educational opportunity is legitimate.

Concern for the way educational resources are allocated among the schools of a district is legitimate.

Concern for the degree of control parents and local school boards should have over their schools is legitimate.

In the long, difficult effort to give life to what is in the law, to desegregate the Nation's schools and enforce the principle

of equal opportunity, many experiments have been tried. Some have worked, and some have not. We now have the benefit of a fuller fund of experience than we had 18 years ago, or even 2 years ago. It has also become apparent that community resistance—black as well as white—to plans that massively disrupt education and separate parents from their children's schools, makes those plans unacceptable to communities on which they are imposed.

Against this background, the objectives of the reforms I propose are:

—To give practical meaning to the concept of equal educational opportunity.

—To apply the experience gained in the process of desegregation, and also in efforts to give special help to the educationally disadvantaged.

—To ensure the continuing vitality of the principles laid down in *Brown* v. *Board of Education.*

—To downgrade busing as a tool for achieving equal educational opportunity.

—To sustain the rights and responsibilities vested by the States in local school boards.

THE EQUAL EDUCATIONAL OPPORTUNITIES ACT

In the historic effort since 1954 to end the system of State-enforced segregation in the public schools, all three branches of Government have had important functions and responsibilities. Their roles, however, have been unequal.

If some of the Federal courts have lately tended toward extreme remedies in school desegregation cases—and some have—this has been in considerable part because the work has largely gone forward in the courts, case-by-case, and because the courts have carried a heavy share of the burden while having to operate within a limited framework of reference and remedies. The efforts have therefore frequently been disconnected, and the result has been not only great progress but also the creation of problems severe enough to threaten the immense achievement of these 18 difficult years.

If we are to consolidate our gains and move ahead on our problems—both the old and the new—we must undertake now to bring the leaven of experience to the logic of the law.

Drawing on the lessons of experience, we must provide the courts with a new framework of reference and remedies.

The angry debate over busing has at one and the same time both illuminated and obscured a number of broad areas in which realism and shared concern in fact unite most American parents, whatever their race. Knowledge of such shared concerns is the most precious product of experience; it also is the soundest foundation of law. The time is at hand for the legislative, executive and judicial branches of Government to act on this knowledge, and by so doing to lift the sense of crisis that threatens the education of our children and the peace of our people.

The Equal Educational Opportunities Act that I propose today draws on that experience, and is designed to give the courts a new and broader base on which to decide future cases, and to place the emphasis where it belongs: on better education for all of our chidren.

EQUAL OPPORTUNITY: THE CRITERIA

The act I propose undertakes, in the light of experience, both to prohibit and to define the denial of equal educational opportunity. In essence, it provides that:

—No State shall deny equal educational opportunity to any person on account of race, color or national origin.

—Students shall not be deliberately segregated either among or within the public schools.

—Where deliberate segregation was formerly practiced, educational agencies have an affirmative duty to remove the vestiges of the dual system.

—A student may not be assigned to a school other than the one nearest his home, if doing so would result in a greater degree of racial segregation.

—Subject to the other provisions of the act, the assignment of students to their neighborhood schools would not be considered a denial of equal educational opportunity unless the schools were located or the assignment made for the purpose of racial segregation.

—Racial balance is not required.

—There can be no discrimination in the employment and assignment of faculty and staff.

—School authorities may not authorize student transfers that would have the effect of increasing segregation.

—School authorities must take appropriate action to overcome whatever language barriers might exist, in order to enable all students to participate equally in educational programs. This would establish, in effect, an educational bill of rights for Mexican-Americans, Puerto Ricans, Indians, and others who start under language handicaps, and ensure at last that they too would have equal opportunity.

—Through Federal financial assistance

435

and incentives, school districts would be strongly encouraged not only to avoid shortchanging the schools that serve their neediest children, but beyond this to establish and maintain special learning programs in those schools that would help children who were behind to catch up. These incentives would also encourage school authorities to provide for voluntary transfers of students that would reduce racial concentrations.

Thus, the act would set standards for all school districts throughout the Nation, as the basic requirements for carrying out, in the field of public education, the Constitutional guarantee that each person shall have equal protection of the laws. It would establish broad-based and specific criteria to ensure against racial discrimination in school assignments, to establish the equal educational rights of Mexican-Americans, Puerto Ricans and others starting with language handicaps, to protect the principle of the neighborhood school. It would also provide money and incentives to help ensure for schools in poor neighborhoods the fair treatment they have too often been denied in the past, and to provide the special learning and extra attention that children in those neighborhoods so often need.

DENIAL OF EQUAL OPPORTUNITY: THE
REMEDIES

In the past, the courts have largely been left to their own devices in determining appropriate remedies in school desegregation cases. The results have been sometimes sound, sometimes bizarre—but certainly uneven. The time has come for the Congress, on the basis of experience, to provide guidance. Where a violation exists, the act I propose would provide that:

—The remedies imposed must be limited to those needed to correct the particular violations that have been found.

—School district lines must not be ignored or altered unless they are clearly shown to have been drawn for purposes of segregation.

—Additional busing must not be required unless no other remedy can be found to correct the particular violation that exists.

—A priority of remedies would be established, with the court required to use the first remedy on the list, or the first combination of remedies, that would correct the unlawful condition. The list of authorized remedies—in order—is:

(1) Assigning students to the schools closest to their homes that provide the appropriate level and type of education, taking into account school capacities and natural physical barriers;

(2) Assigning students to the schools closest to their homes that provide the appropriate level and type of education, considering only school capacities;

(3) Permitting students to transfer from a school in which their race is a majority to one in which it is a minority;

(4) Creation or revision of attendance zones or grade structures without necessitating increased student transportation;

(5) Construction of new schools or the closing of inferior schools;

(6) The use of magnet schools or educational parks to promote integration;

(7) Any other plan which is educationally sound and administratively feasible. However, such a plan could not require increased busing of students in the sixth grade or below. If a plan involved additional busing of older children, then: (a) It could not be ordered unless there was clear and convincing evidence that no other method would work; (b) in no case could it be ordered on other than a temporary basis; (c) it could not pose a risk to health, or significantly impinge on the educational process; (d) the school district could be granted a stay until the order had been passed on by the court of appeals.

—Beginning with the effective date of the act, time limits would be placed on desegregation orders. They would be limited to 10 years' duration—or 5 years if they called for student transportation—provided that during that period the school authorities had been in good-faith compliance. New orders could then be entered only if there had been new violations.

These rules would thus clearly define what the Federal courts could and could not require; however, the States and localities would remain free to carry out voluntary school integration plans that might go substantially beyond the Federal requirements.

This is an important distinction. Where busing would provide educational advantages for the community's children, and where the community wants to undertake it, the community should—and will—have that choice. What is objec-

tionable is an arbitrary Federal requirement—whether administrative or judicial—that the community must undertake massive additional busing as a matter of Federal law. The essence of a free society is to restrict the range of what must be done, and broaden the range of what may be done.

EQUAL OPPORTUNITY: BROADENING THE SCOPE

If we were simply to place curbs on busing and do nothing more, then we would not have kept faith with the hopes, the needs—or the rights—of the neediest of our children.

Even adding the many protections built into the rights and remedies sections of the Equal Educational Opportunities Act, we would not by this alone provide what their special needs require.

Busing helps some poor children; it poses a hardship for others; but there are many more, and in many areas the great majority—in the heart of New York, and in South Chicago, for example—whom it could never reach.

If we were to treat busing as some sort of magic panacea, and to concentrate our efforts and resources on that as the principal means of achieving quality education for blacks and other minorities, then in these areas of dense minority concentration a whole generation could be lost.

If we hold massive busing to be, in any event, an unacceptable remedy for the inequalities of educational opportunity that exist, then we must do more to improve the schools where poor families live.

Rather than require the spending of scarce resources on ever-longer bus rides for those who happen to live where busing is possible, we should encourage the putting of those resources directly into education—serving all the disadvantaged children, not merely those on the bus routes.

In order to reach the great majority of the children who most need extra help, I propose a new approach to financing the extra efforts required: one that puts the money where the needs are, drawing on the funds I have requested for this and the next fiscal year under Title I of the Elementary and Secondary Education Act of 1965 and under the Emergency School Aid Act now pending before the Congress.

As part of the Equal Educational Opportunities Act, I propose to broaden the uses of the funds under the Emergency School Aid Act, and to provide the Secretary of Health, Education, and Welfare with additional authority to encourage effective special learning programs in those schools where the needs are greatest.

Detailed program criteria would be spelled out in administrative guidelines— but the intent of this program is to use a major portion of the $1.5 billion Emergency School Aid money as, in effect, incentive grants to encourage eligible districts to design educational programs that would do three things:

—Assure (as a condition of getting the grant) that the district's expenditures on its poorest schools were at least comparable to those on its other schools.

—Provide, above this, a compensatory education grant of approximately $300 per low-income pupil for schools in which substantial numbers of the students are from poor families, if the concentration of poor students exceeds specified limits.

—Require that this compensatory grant be spent entirely on basic instructional programs for language skills and mathematics, and on basic supportive services

such as health and nutrition.

—Provide a "bonus" to the receiving school for each pupil transferring from a poor school to a non-poor school where his race is in the minority, without reducing the grant to the transferring school.

Priority would be given to those districts that are desegregating either voluntarily or under court order, and to those that are addressing problems of both racial and economic impaction.

Under this plan, the remaining portion of the $1.5 billion available under the Emergency School Aid Act for this and the next fiscal year would go toward the other kinds of aid originally envisaged under it.

This partial shift of funds is now possible for two reasons: First, in the nearly 2 years since I first proposed the Emergency School Aid Act, much of what it was designed to help with has already been done. Second, to the extent that the standards set forth in the Equal Educational Opportunities Act would relieve desegregating districts of some of the more expensive requirements that might otherwise be laid upon them, a part of the money originally intended to help meet those expenses can logically be diverted to these other, closely related needs. I would stress once again, in this connection, the importance I attach to final passage of the Emergency School Aid Act: those districts that are now desegregating still need its help, and the funds to be made available for these new purposes are an essential element of a balanced equal opportunity package.

I also propose that instead of being terminated at the end of fiscal 1973, as presently scheduled, the Emergency School Aid Act continue to be authorized at a $1 billion annual level—of which I would expect the greatest part to be used for the purposes I have outlined here. At the current level of funding of Title I of the Elementary and Secondary Education Act of 1965, this would provide a total approaching $2.5 billion annually for compensatory education purposes.

For some years now, there has been a running debate about the effectiveness of added spending for programs of compensatory or remedial education. Some have maintained there is virtually no correlation between dollar input and learning output; others have maintained there is a direct correlation; experience has been mixed.

What does now seem clear is that while many Title I experiments have failed, many others have succeeded substantially and even dramatically; and what also is clear is that without the extra efforts such extra funding would make possible, there is little chance of breaking the cycle of deprivation.

A case can be made that Title I has fallen short of expectations, and that in some respects it has failed. In many cases, pupils in the programs funded by it have shown no improvement whatever, and funds have frequently been misused or squandered foolishly. Federal audits of State Title I efforts have found instances where naivete, inexperience, confusion, despair, and even clear violations of the law have thwarted the act's effectiveness. In some instances, Title I funds have been illegally spent on unauthorized materials and facilities, or used to fund local services other than those intended by the act, such as paying salaries not directly related to the act's purposes.

The most prevalent failing has been the spending of Title I funds as general revenue. Out of 40 States audited between

1966 and 1970, 14 were found to have spent Title I funds as general revenue.

Too often, one result has been that instead of actually being concentrated in the areas of critical need, Title I moneys have been diffused throughout the system; and they have not reached the targeted schools—and targeted children—in sufficient amounts to have a real impact.

On the positive side, Title I has effected some important changes of benefit to disadvantaged children.

First, Title I has encouraged some States to expand considerably the contributions from State and local funds for compensatory education. In the 1965–66 school year, the States spent only $2.7 million of their own revenues, but by the 1968–69 school year—largely due to major efforts by California and New York—they were contributing $198 million.

Second, Title I has better focused attention on pupils who previously were too often ignored. About 8 million children are in schools receiving some compensatory funds. In 46 States programs have been established to aid almost a quarter of a million children of migratory workers. As an added dividend, many States have begun to focus educational attention on the early childhood years which are so important to the learning process.

Finally, local schools have been encouraged by Title I to experiment and innovate. Given our highly decentralized national educational system and the relatively minor role one Federal program usually plays, there have been encouraging examples of programs fostered by Title I which have worked.

In designing compensatory programs, it is difficult to know exactly what will work. The circumstances of one locality may differ dramatically from those of other localities. What helps one group of children may not be of particular benefit to others. In these experimental years, local educational agencies and the schools have had to start from scratch, and to learn for themselves how to educate those who in the past had too often simply been left to fall further behind.

In the process, some schools did well and others did not. Some districts benefited by active leadership and community involvement, while others were slow to innovate and to break new ground.

While there is a great deal yet to be learned about the design of successful compensatory programs, the experience so far does point in one crucial direction: to the importance of providing sufficiently concentrated funding to establish the educational equivalent of a "critical mass," or threshold level. Where funds have been spread too thinly, they have been wasted or dissipated with little to show for their expenditure. Where they have been concentrated, the results have been frequently encouraging and sometimes dramatic.

In a sample of some 10,000 disadvantaged pupils in California, 82 percent of those in projects spending less than $150 extra per pupil showed little or no achievement gain. Of those students in projects spending over $250 extra per pupil, 94 percent gained more than one year per year of exposure; 58 percent gained between 1.4 and 1.9 years per year of exposure. Throughout the country States as widely separated as Connecticut and Florida have recognized a correlation between a "critical mass" expenditure and marked effectiveness.

Of late, several important studies have supported the idea of a "critical mass"

compensatory expenditure to afford disadvantaged pupils equal educational opportunity. The New York State Commission on the Quality, Cost, and Financing of Elementary and Secondary Education, the National Educational Finance Project, and the President's Commission on School Finance have all cited the importance of such a substantial additional per pupil expenditure for disadvantaged pupils.

The program which I propose aims to assure schools with substantial concentrations of poor children of receiving an average $300 compensatory education grant for each child.

In order to encourage voluntary transfers, under circumstances where they would reduce both racial isolation and low-income concentration, any school accepting such transfers would receive the extra $300 allotted for the transferring student plus a bonus payment depending on the proportion of poor children in that school.

One key to the success of this new approach would be the "critical mass" achieved by both increasing and concentrating the funds made available; another would be vigorous administrative follow-through to ensure that the funds are used in the intended schools and for the intended purposes.

THE STUDENT TRANSPORTATION
MORATORIUM ACT

In times of rapid and even headlong change, there occasionally is an urgent need for reflection and reassessment. This is especially true when powerful, historic forces are moving the Nation toward a conflict of fundamental principles—a conflict that can be avoided if each of us does his share, and if all branches of Government will join in helping to redefine the questions before us.

Like any comprehensive legislative recommendation, the Equal Educational Opportunities Act that I have proposed today is offered as a framework for Congressional debate and action.

The Congress has both the Constitutional authority and a special capability to debate and define new methods for implementing Constitutional principles. And the educational, financial and social complexities of this issue are not, and are not properly, susceptible of solution by individual courts alone or even by the Supreme Court alone.

This is a moment of considerable conflict and uncertainty; but it is also a moment of great opportunity.

This is not a time for the courts to plunge ahead at full speed.

If we are to set a course that enables us to act together, and not simply to do more but to do better, then we must do all in our power to create an atmosphere that permits a calm and thoughtful assessment of the issues, choices and consequences.

I propose, therefore, that the Congress act to impose a temporary freeze on new busing orders by the Federal courts—to establish a waiting period while the Congress considers alternative means of enforcing 14th Amendment rights. I propose that this freeze be effective immediately on enactment, and that it remain in effect until July 1, 1973, or until passage of the appropriate legislation, whichever is sooner.

This freeze would not put a stop to desegregation cases; it would only bar new orders during its effective period, to the extent that they ordered new busing.

This, I recognize, is an unusual procedure. But I am persuaded that the Congress has the Constitutional power to enact such a stay, and I believe the unusual nature of the conflicts and pressures that confront both the courts and the country at this particular time requires it.

It has become abundantly clear, from the debates in the Congress and from the upwelling of sentiment throughout the country, that some action will be taken to limit the scope of busing orders. It is in the interest of everyone—black and white, children and parents, school administrators and local officials, the courts, the Congress and the executive branch, and not least in the interest of consistency in Federal policy, that while this matter is being considered by the Congress we not speed further along a course that is likely to be changed.

The legislation I have proposed would provide the courts with a new set of standards and criteria that would enable them to enforce the basic Constitutional guarantees in different ways.

A stay would relieve the pressure on the Congress to act on the long-range legislation without full and adequate consideration. By providing immediate relief from a course that increasing millions of Americans are finding intolerable, it would allow the debate on permanent solutions to proceed with less emotion and more reason.

For these reasons—and also for the sake of the additional children faced with busing now—I urge that the Congress quickly give its approval to the Student Transportation Moratorium Act.

No message to the Congress on school desegregation would be complete unless it addressed the question of a Constitutional amendment.

There are now a number of proposals before the Congress, with strong support, to amend the Constitution in ways designed to abolish busing or to bar the courts from ordering it.

These proposals should continue to receive the particularly thoughtful and careful consideration by the Congress that any proposal to amend the Constitution merits.

It is important to recognize, however, that a Constitutional amendment—even if it could secure the necessary two-thirds support in both Houses of the Congress—has a serious flaw: it would have no impact this year; it would not come into effect until after the long process of ratification by three-fourths of the State legislatures. What is needed is action now; a Constitutional amendment fails to meet this immediate need.

Legislation meets the problem now. Therefore, I recommend that as its first priority the Congress go forward immediately on the legislative route. Legislation can also treat the question with far greater precision and detail than could the necessarily generalized language of a Constitutional amendment, while making possible a balanced, comprehensive approach to equal educational opportunity.

CONCLUSION

These measures I have proposed would place firm and effective curbs on busing—and they would do so in a Constitutional way, aiding rather than challenging the courts, respecting the mandate of the 14th Amendment, and exercising the responsibility of the Congress to enforce that Amendment.

Beyond making these proposals, I am directing the Executive departments to follow policies consistent with the principles on which they are based—which will include intervention by the Justice Department in selected cases before the courts, both to implement the stay and to resolve some of those questions on which the lower courts have gone beyond the Supreme Court.

The Equal Educational Opportunities Act I have proposed reflects a serious and wide-ranging process of consultation—drawing upon the knowledge and experience of legislators, Constitutional scholars, educators and government administrators, and of men and women from all races and regions of the country who shared with us the views and feelings of their communities.

Its design is in large measure the product of that collaboration. When enacted it would, for the first time, furnish a framework for collaborative action by the various branches of Federal and local government, enabling courts and communities to shape effective educational solutions which are responsive not only to Constitutional standards but also to the physical and human reality of diverse educational situations.

It will create more local choice and more options to choose from; and it will marshal and target Federal resources more effectively in support of each particular community's effort.

Most importantly, however, these proposals undertake to address the problem that really lies at the heart of the issue at this time: the inherent inability of the courts, acting alone, to deal effectively and acceptably with the new magnitude of educational and social problems generated by the desegregation process.

If these proposals are adopted, those few who want an arbitrary racial balance to be imposed on the schools by Federal fiat will not get their way.

Those few who want a return to segregated schools will not get their way.

Those few who want a rollingback of the basic protections black and other minority Americans have won in recent years will not get their way.

This Administration means what it says about dismantling racial barriers, about opening up jobs and housing and schools and opportunity to all Americans.

It is not merely rhetoric, but our record, that demonstrates our determination.

We have achieved more school desegregation in the last 3 years than was achieved in the previous 15.

We have taken the lead in opening up high-paying jobs to minority workers.

We have taken unprecedented measures to spur business ownership by members of minorities.

We have brought more members of minorities into the middle and upper levels of the Federal service than ever before.

We have provided more support to black colleges than ever before.

We have put more money and muscle into enforcement of the equal opportunity laws than ever before.

These efforts will all go forward—with vigor and with conviction. Making up for the years of past discrimination is not simply something that white Americans owe to black Americans—it is something the entire Nation owes to itself.

I submit these proposals to the Congress mindful of the profound importance and special complexity of the issues they address. It is in that spirit that I have undertaken to weigh and respect the conflicting interests; to strike a balance which is thoughtful and just; and to search for answers that will best serve all of the Nation's children. I urge the Congress to consider them in the same spirit.

The great majority of Americans, of all races, want their Government—the Congress, the Judiciary and the Executive—to follow the course of deliberation, not confrontation. To do this we must act calmly and creatively, and we must act together.

The great majority of Americans, of all races, want schools that educate and rules that are fair. That is what these proposals attempt to provide.

RICHARD NIXON

The White House,
    March 17, 1972.

NOTE: On the same day, the White House released drafts of the two proposed bills and a fact sheet summarizing their provisions. The White House also released the transcript of a news briefing on the President's meeting with the Congressional bipartisan leadership to discuss the message. Participants in the news briefing were John D. Ehrlichman, Assistant to the President for Domestic Affairs; George P. Shultz, Director, and Paul O'Neill and Kenneth W. Dam, Assistant Directors, Office of Management and Budget; Elliot L. Richardson, Secretary, and Wilmot R. Hastings, General Counsel, Department of Health, Education, and Welfare; Richard G. Kleindienst, Acting Attorney General, and Daniel J. McAuliffe, Deputy Assistant Attorney General for Internal Security, Department of Justice; and Edward L. Morgan, Assistant Director, Domestic Council.

On April 26, 1972, the White House released the transcript of a news briefing on the President's proposed legislation on equal educational opportunities and school busing by Mr. Ehrlichman.

92 Letter to the Senate Minority Leader About the Proposed Constitutional Amendment on Equal Rights for Men and Women. *March* 18, 1972

Dear Hugh:

This is in response to your inquiry requesting my stand on the Equal Rights Amendment currently under consideration by the Senate.

As you remember, as a Senator in 1951 I cosponsored a Resolution incorporating the original Amendment; in July of 1968 I reaffirmed my support for it as a candidate for the Presidency.

Throughout twenty-one years I have not altered my belief that equal rights for women warrant a Constitutional guarantee—and I therefore continue to favor the enactment of the Constitutional Amendment to achieve this goal.

Sincerely,

RICHARD NIXON

[Honorable Hugh Scott, Minority Leader, United States Senate, Washington, D.C.]

NOTE: H. J. Res. 208, proposing an amendment to the Constitution of the United States relative to equal rights for men and women, is printed in United States Statutes at Large (86 Stat. 1523).

93 Special Message to the Congress on Minority Enterprise. *March* 19, 1972

To the Congress of the United States:

From its start, America has prided itself on being a land of opportunity.

In recent years, we have done much to press open new doors of opportunity for millions of Americans to whom those doors had previously been barred, or only half-open. In jobs, housing, education, old obstacles are being removed. But for Blacks, Mexican Americans, Puerto Ricans, Indians and other minorities who have known discrimination, economic opportunity must also increasingly be made to mean a greater chance to know the satisfactions, the rewards and the responsibilities of business ownership. Such opportunities are not only important in themselves; they also help make possible the economic and social advances that are critical to the development of stable and thriving communities on which the social and economic vitality of the Nation as a whole depend.

Despite a long history of frustration and lost potential, minority Americans want business ownership—and they should. Potential minority entrepreneurs are eager to join the mainstream of the Nation's commerce. Many need help in getting started—and increasing numbers are getting that help. A working coalition of the Government, the private sector and minority communities is moving rapidly to provide disadvantaged Americans with opportunities to own and control their own successful businesses.

The principal need of minority business today is for a greater supply of investment capital. Technical assistance, training, promotion and business opportunities are all fundamentally related to investment capital, that centripetal force which draws together the people, skills, equipment and resources necessary to operate a profitable business.

The coalition of public and private sectors and minority interests supporting disadvantaged business enterprise must be strengthened now, if we are to achieve the goal of generating the additional investment capital needed.

Today, therefore, I am turning to the Congress for its cooperation and help. I urge the approval by the Congress of the following:

—first, the Minority Enterprise Small Business Investment Act of 1972;

—second, a budget request for the Office of Minority Business Enterprise of $63.6 million for fiscal 1973;

—third, a variety of other small business legislation currently pending in Congress which will directly and collaterally aid minority enterprise.

THE PRESSING NEED

The Nation's Black, Spanish-speaking and Indian and other minorities constitute about one-sixth of the American population. Yet in 1967—the last year for which final figures are available—these American minorities accounted for well below one percent of the total business income of the Nation. Gross receipts of almost $1.5 trillion were reported in that year by all American businesses. Of this amount, minority-owned firms received only $10.6 billion, or less than one percent. In the United States today, there are more than 8 million businesses; minority Americans presently own only about 4 percent of these businesses, despite the fact that they constitute almost 17 percent of our population.

These statistics starkly summarize the gross disparity of the minority enterprise imbalance, but they do not adequately outline the broader effects on our society at large. The human cost, in terms of lost potential and lowered horizons, is immeasurable.

RESPONDING TO MINORITY NEEDS

Recognizing the need for Government incentives and leadership, I took steps in my first months in office to awaken the Federal establishment and the private sector to the potential for development of minority business. First, I established the Office of Minority Business Enterprise (OMBE) within the Department of Commerce to plan and coordinate comprehensive minority business development. Secondly, the Small Business Administration (SBA) undertook to increase minority participation in its many business programs. Thirdly, I directed all Federal departments and agencies to respond to the aspirations and needs of minority entrepreneurs, particularly by use of their procurement powers.

PROGRESS REPORT

I am pleased to report to the Congress that our efforts to stimulate the Federal Government and private sector have been highly productive. A comprehensive statement of accomplishments was published in January of this year entitled, "Progress of the Minority Business Enterprise Program." Let me summarize the highlights of that report for you and outline our current status.

Office of Minority Business Enterprise. Only the private sector working with the Government can reverse a century's discouragement of minority enterprise; the Government cannot do it alone. The Nation's established corporations, financial institutions, professional associations, foundations, and religious organizations are indispensable to meet the demand of minority businessmen for seed capital, operating funds, suppliers, markets, expert technical and management assistance and related business essentials.

Three years ago, there were no precedents, no rule books, no methods, no blueprints on how to focus the resources of these groups on a common objective. OMBE's greatest achievement during these past three years has been to forge an alliance of Government, private sector and minority business interests. The Office has succeeded in launching a carefully contoured, integrated set of programs that will work to engage minority entrepreneurs fully in our Nation's economic life.

Gains. Since the establishment of OMBE, American minorities have gained greater access to both Government and private sector contracts and concessions, business loans and loan guarantees, technical and management assistance, and other business aid. This access has been developed without reducing programs available to non-minority small businessmen. Federal assistance, channeled through these vehicles, has been enlarged from less than $200 million in 1969 to some $700 million currently, and the $1 billion threshold for fiscal 1973—five times the 1969 level—is within reach. New markets have been opened as minority suppliers and businessmen have expanded their operations and sales in unprecedented volume.

Funding OMBE and SBA. Our efforts on behalf of minority business secured substantial congressional approval, and OMBE was appropriated a supplemental budget increase of $40 million for the last six months of fiscal 1972, as I requested. I am hopeful that both the House and Senate will give favorable consideration to our present request for a fiscal 1973

OMBE budget of $63.6 million to provide urgently needed technical and management assistance to minority business. Together, these budgets will total more than $100 million. This figure offers a dramatic index of the commitment of this Administration to the purposes of an Office which was originally funded for fiscal year 1972 with less than four million dollars.

OMBE is a coordinating agency of the Federal Government, and as such does not itself engage directly in business financing. Direct loans, loan guarantees, surety bonding, lines of credit, and contract set-asides are supplied by the Small Business Administration (SBA) to small businessmen, including minority businessmen.

THE IMMEDIATE NEED: MESBIC LEGISLATION

Enactment of the Administration's proposed Minority Enterprise Small Business Investment Act of 1972 would give major impetus to the minority enterprise program, and would create a more productive mechanism to achieve its objectives.

Background. When the Congress passed the Small Business Investment Act of 1958, it recognized that small business generally lacks seed money and working capital. To give incentives for small business investment, the act empowered SBA to license "Small Business Investment Companies" (SBICs). Such companies are private investment institutions capitalized at a minimum of $150,000 from private sources. SBICs are eligible to borrow from SBA at an incentive ratio of $2 from SBA for every $1 of its private capital. Thus, a $150,000 SBIC can borrow $300,000 from SBA for investment in its own account. Also, after it raises $1 million in private capital, a SBIC is eligible to borrow $3 from SBA for every $1 of private capital.

Because of these incentives, substantial amounts of private capital have been invested in small business through SBICs. More than 40,000 small business financings have been completed by SBICs from the program's inception, totaling $1.9 billion in risk capital. *But only a small fraction of that amount has gone into minority businesses,* because usually risks and costs are even higher for minority small businesses than for small businesses generally.

MESBICs

To fill the need for minority enterprise high risk capital, the SBA evolved the *Minority Enterprise* Small Business Investment Company (MESBIC). A MESBIC is a specialized SBIC: 1) it limits its investment to minority enterprises; 2) it is supported by financially sturdy institutional sponsors; 3) it is underwritten in large part by its sponsors.

In 1969 OMBE joined with SBA in launching a national network of MESBICs with SBA licensing and regulating MESBICs and OMBE promoting them. Today, 47 MESBICs operate throughout the Nation with private funds totaling in excess of $14 million. Since MESBIC seed capital has the potential of freeing $15 for investment in minority enterprises for every one privately invested dollar, more than $210 million is currently available through this program. All this is achieved at relatively low cost to the Government.

MESBICs have the potential of becoming sophisticated investment companies, knowledgeable in the peculiar problems of minority business investment, and able to bring sound business principles and practices to their tasks. Seeking a fair return on investment, MESBICs can act effectively to raise the success prospects of portfolio companies.

MESBIC Limitations. Despite the proven values of the MESBIC mechanism, it labors under burdens which endanger further development. The cost of administering minority business investments and the risk of early loss are both very high. Moreover, the short term success pattern of minority businesses has not been sufficiently encouraging to enable them to attract equity investment in normal competitive markets. But the recent successes of minority enterprises have shown that they can compete if they are given enough equity assistance to carry them through this early period.

THE MINORITY ENTERPRISE SMALL BUSINESS INVESTMENT ACT OF 1972

The primary object of my message today is to urge that the proposed Minority Enterprise Small Business Investment Act be acted on favorably and with dispatch by the House in its upcoming small business hearings. This act will restructure SBA financing of MESBICs so that they can operate on a fiscally sound basis.

Provisions of the Act. The legislation proposes a statutory definition of a MESBIC and authority to organize it as a nonprofit corporation. This status would facilitate foundation investments and tax-deductible gifts to MESBICs.

Building on our experience with SBICs and MESBICs, the act would reduce the level of private capital required to qualify for $3 to $1 assistance from SBA, from $1

447

million to $500,000; provide increased equity to MESBICs in the form of preferred stock to be purchased by SBA in place of part of the debt instruments purchased by SBA from MESBICs under current law; and lower the interest rate on SBA loans to MESBICs to three points below the normal rate set by the Treasury during the first five years of the loan.

Restructuring Effects of the Act. The immediate impact of this legislation would be to materially restructure the MESBIC program and stimulate increased private investment and gifts to MESBICs, resulting in greatly increased capital for minority business enterprises, at startlingly small Federal cost.

The legislation would: Lower the high cost of starting the investment program of a MESBIC; allow MESBICs to take advantage of full SBA financing; enable MESBICs to invest more in equity securities and to reduce interest rates to portfolio companies; provide special incentives to existing smaller MESBICs which have pioneered the program.

In the act, I am proposing a fairer partnership between the private and public sectors—a partnership that would yield enabling capital for minority enterprise. The MESBIC program is sound, practical and necessary. It equitably extends our free enterprise system by making it work for all Americans.

CONCLUSION

Opening wider the doors of opportunity for one-sixth of our people is a social necessity, which responds to an imperative claim on our conscience. It also is an economic necessity. By stimulating minority enterprise—by permitting more of our people to be more productive, by creating new businesses and new jobs, by raising the sights and lifting the ambitions of millions who are enabled to see that others who started under handicaps like theirs are writing records of economic success—we help to stimulate the whole economy.

I therefore urge the Congress to give its swift approval to the Minority Enterprise Small Business Investment Act of 1972, to my fiscal year 1973 budget request for $63.6 million for OMBE, and to our other small business proposals currently pending in the Congress.

Hard work, private risk, initiative, and equal chance at success—these are the American way. Helping ensure for all of our people an opportunity to participate fully in the economic system that has made America the world's strongest and richest nation—this too is the American way. And this lies at the heart of our program for minority enterprise.

RICHARD NIXON

The White House,
    March 20, 1972.

NOTE: The message, released March 19, 1972, was transmitted to the Congress March 20.

On March 19, the White House released a fact sheet and the transcript of a news briefing, held on March 18, on the message. Participants in the news briefing were Peter G. Peterson, Secretary, James T. Lynn, Under Secretary, and John L. Jenkins, Director, Office of Minority Business Enterprise, Department of Commerce; and Thomas S. Kleppe, Administrator, and Anthony G. Chase, Deputy Administrator, Small Business Administration.

94   Remarks During a Visit to New York City To Review Drug Abuse Law Enforcement Activities. *March* 20, 1972

Ladies and gentlemen:

Before leaving New York, I want to say how very impressed I have been with the dedication of both the Federal officials who are working in the field of dangerous drugs, and also the State officials.

Many times when we think of a national problem, one we have not yet solved, we do not give enough credit to the hundreds of thousands of people who are working on it, some voluntarily and tens of thousands working as Government officials. I am very proud of the fact that at the Federal level we have such dedicated people, and I am impressed by all of them and I feel that they deserve our total support.

Coming out of this day, I want to emphasize these points: As I talked to the people from New York State, I realized the need for money to deal with this problem. I am glad that in this Administration we have increased the amount of money for handling the problem of dangerous drugs sevenfold. It will be $600 million this year. More money will be needed in the future.

I want to say, however, that despite our budget problems, to the extent money can help in meeting the problem of dangerous drugs, it will be available. This is one area where we cannot have budget cuts because we must wage what I have called total war against public enemy number one in the United States: the problem of dangerous drugs.

The other point I wish to emphasize is that we see here in the Kennedy Airport the supply end of our program, and it is really a four-sided program:

We have got to stop the supply by such operations as this, by checking passengers as they come through, to see that they are not smuggling drugs in.

Second, we have to reduce the demand. That is through education and through other programs where people who might otherwise become addicted would know that this was the wrong step to take.

Third, we must have law enforcement that is effective. In this particular area, it is important to differentiate between those who are users and those who are trafficking in drugs. Both, of course, are violating the laws.

But for those who are users, we need a program—and this is the fourth part of our program—a program of treatment and rehabilitation. For those who traffic in drugs, for those who, for example, make hundreds of thousands of dollars, sometimes millions of dollars if you are looking at the business generally, and thereby destroy the lives of young people throughout this country, there should be no sympathy whatever, and no limit insofar as the criminal penalty is concerned.

I will only say in conclusion that I consider this to be the number one domestic problem that concerns the American people, because they realize parents are concerned about what happens to their children, but also the American people realize that when any nation, any people, goes down the road toward addiction to drugs, that nation has something taken out of its character.

We must not let it happen in America,

and I am confident, based on the kind of people that we have working in our programs at the Federal and State level here in New York City, that we are making a major offensive effort that is going to pay off—pay off in criminal penalties for those that are guilty, pay off also on rehabilitation for those who are users, and also, here in the supply area, will pay off by stopping the source of supply, the source of supply which could destroy the character of so many of our young people, and eventually the character of this Nation.

Thank you.

NOTE: The President spoke at 1:25 p.m. at John F. Kennedy International Airport after reviewing customs inspection procedures. He spoke without referring to notes.

Earlier he had gone to the regional office of the Office for Drug Abuse Law Enforcement at the Federal Plaza in New York City for a meeting of Federal, State, and local law enforcement agencies on the Drug Abuse Law Enforcement program. He then joined Gov. Nelson A. Rockefeller in attending a meeting of State and local judges, members of the New York State Narcotics Addiction Control Commission, and city prosecutors to discuss operations of 12 new special narcotics courts in the city.

The President and Myles J. Ambrose, Special Assistant Attorney General, Office for Drug Abuse Law Enforcement, also met privately with undercover agents from the Bureau of Narcotics and Dangerous Drugs and the Bureau of Customs for a report on heroin trafficking in New York City.

On the same day, the White House released a fact sheet on the President's trip to New York City and on Administration efforts to combat drug abuse.

95   Remarks of Welcome to Prime Minister Nihat Erim of Turkey.   *March* 21, 1972

Mr. Prime Minister and our distinguished guests:

Mr. Prime Minister, it is a very great privilege to welcome you on this first day of spring to our country, and to welcome Mrs. Nihat Erim and the members of your party on this occasion.

Your visit comes at a very special time. It is halfway between the visits that I will have paid to the P.R.C. and the U.S.S.R., and it reminds us of a very profound truth. At a time that we seek better relations with those who have been our adversaries, we do not forget those who have been and are our friends.

Turkey and the United States have been allies and friends for many years. That alliance has been particularly strong in NATO, and from the standpoint of friendship, I shall never forget the warm welcome that the people of Turkey and your Government extended to Mrs. Nixon and me when we visited your country in 1956. We hope that we can make you, your wife, and the members of your party feel just as welcome as you visit Washington, our Nation's Capital today.

We are reminded, too, that our alliance and friendship goes beyond military matters. We know, for example, that in a cause that is interesting to not only people in your country, but in ours, people all over the world, that of dealing with dangerous drugs, your Government has taken strong positions of leadership and cooperation that have been most helpful in dealing with this problem, and for that we are most grateful.

As I think of your country and its great history, the motto which came from your great leader Ataturk, "Peace at home and peace in the world," is one that we in the United States can also say is our goal. That is the purpose of our meeting to-day—peace at home, peace in the world—and we know that our talks will contribute to that great goal.

NOTE: The President spoke at 10:45 a.m. on the South Lawn at the White House where Prime Minister Erim was given a formal welcome with full military honors. The President spoke without referring to notes.

See also Items 98 and 99.

The Prime Minister responded as follows:

Mr. President, Mrs. Nixon, ladies and gentlemen:

I am overwhelmed by your heartwarming words welcoming us to Washington. Mrs. Erim and I are most happy to have this opportunity to get to know you personally and to pay this official visit to your beautiful Capital City.

I am looking forward to our talks, and feel sure that I shall benefit from your vast experience as a great statesman in tireless pursuit of efforts to lay the foundations of a lasting structure of peace. I am fully aware also of your concern to improve the quality of life for all the peoples of the world so that one basic reason of discord may be eliminated.

In our part of the world, we follow a course that seeks détente while remaining alert to meet any threat. We have closely followed and greatly admired your extensive undertakings toward the initiation of an era of worldwide understanding and peace, and we ardently support you, Mr. President, in these efforts to lower tensions and establish a new order in which all peoples may prosper in security.

Almost exactly 20 years ago, Turkey joined the North Atlantic Treaty Organization, thereby formalizing and strengthening her ties with the Western community, and in particular with the United States of America. The last quarter of a century bears witness to the success of the cooperation between our countries in maintaining peace and security for our peoples.

Our peoples share many common traits. Both nations are unflinchingly dedicated to liberty and parliamentary democracy and stand ready to defend what they hold dear. Both nations pursue the same goals: establishment of a just and lasting peace in the world, where nations may determine freely their future and respect each other's territorial integrity and way of life.

I therefore feel confident that, based on these common traits and ideals, our solidarity and friendship will continue to flourish in the years ahead as we hopefully enter a new era of global understanding and stability. I firmly believe that the rapport between our two countries continues to be a vital element of security and peace. We value this happy partnership between our two countries in the same measure as we appreciate your global efforts in promoting understanding and confidence on a worldwide scope.

Mr. President, I am indeed looking forward to exchanging views with you on bilateral subjects, as well as on others that are of mutual interest. I am confident that this exchange will enhance the already close relations between our two countries.

96   Remarks on Signing the Drug Abuse Office and Treatment Act of 1972. *March 21, 1972*

I REGRET that I am a little late for this ceremony, because I know that there is a very large bipartisan representation from the House and Senate here for this particular signing of this bill, but I think it is quite significant to note that the reason that I am late has something to do with this program.

I have just completed a meeting with the Prime Minister of Turkey. As I told him I was coming over to sign this bill, he said, "You can assure the Members of the House and the Senate, and all those gathered here, and those who may be listening or hearing on television or radio, that the present Turkish Government is totally committed to stopping all growing of the opium poppy, and also totally committed to stop smuggling through Turkey in any way that will add to the drug problem in the United States of America."

This, incidentally, is a major tribute to our State Department people and our Ambassador and others who have worked on this problem. It is also certainly a major tribute to our great friends and allies in the Turkish Government who have taken this step, and who, despite the fact that this is a very profitable crop, one that has been grown for hundreds and hundreds of years by farmers in their country, despite the fact that it is a difficult political issue for them, they, on the basis of the program that we have worked out, are cooperating with us in dealing with what is a bigger problem, and that is the destruction of the lives of people who become addicts to heroin.

Now, in signing the bill, as you know, it is a rather unusual bill in one sense. There wasn't a vote against it in either the House or the Senate. There are not many that I sign that are that type, or that any President has the opportunity to sign. The fact that it is bipartisan, that it has total support, indicates the enormous interest in the country in moving forward in this field.

To give you an indication of what this bill deals with and why it is so essential, let me tell you what happened yesterday in New York. I met with eight undercover agents from the law enforcement side and with the Federal Government, who on a daily basis go out—undercover agents go out on the streets in New York and buy heroin to see what the situation is, and also to set up the necessary procedures for arrest of those who may be violating the law.

The eight agents said that in the last 4 days, when a new program has been initiated, a stronger program of law enforcement in New York City and across the country, that they noted that the price of heroin had gone up, and that the quality had gone down.

To show you that that is not simply an isolated incident, we also checked with the Washington, D.C., Police Department. The same thing has happened here: The price of heroin has gone up, and the quality has gone down.

What this means is that on the law enforcement side, stopping the source of supply through arrangements that we have like the one with the Government of Turkey, criminal penalties which will be strongly enforced, and on the law enforcement side we are having some success. But, on the other hand, we can see what can happen unless we take action in treating the addicts because as the price goes up and the quality goes down, someone who is hopelessly addicted to drugs will inevitably do what is necessary to obtain them. And that is, it must mean that he will or she will indulge in criminal activities in order to serve the habit.

This is where this Office comes in. There are so many who think of some simplistic answer to every problem, and particularly in this field. There are many who feel, rightly, that we should have strong criminal penalties against the pushers and against those who are engaged in the drug traffic. We do have such penalties, and they should be enforced.

On the other hand, a program of law enforcement alone is not enough, because, as we succeed in the law enforcement side, we may increase crime, increase crime because of the inability of those who are unable to obtain drugs to feed their habit, and so this means that on the treatment of addicts we must go parallel with the program which was strong in this field, and here is where the Jaffe Office, as we now call it, comes into play and this bill comes into play.

As we increase our efforts in law enforcement, as we reduce the supply, what we must do is to increase our efforts to treat the addicts, to treat them and also to reduce the demand, through a program of education and prevention across this country. We feel that a lot of progress has already been made in this field, but with this legislation now funding what we have been doing previously from other funds that we had to scratch to find from time to time, it means that this Office can go forward in a major program across the country where we can make some new breakthroughs in treating drug addiction.

I simply want to say in conclusion that the country owes a debt of gratitude to all the Members of the Congress, and particularly the members of the committee who have worked for this legislation and who have helped to get it to the President's desk.

Now the task goes to Dr. Jaffe.

One final thought: Why do we have him here, and why do we have this Office in the White House?

The reason is that this particular program of drug abuse, and the particular program, also, on the side of enforcing the law against those who violate it in terms of trafficking and arrest, has the direct interest in and the President assumes direct responsibility for it.

There is another reason for it. When Dr. Jaffe took over this Office, I asked him to find out how many Government agencies were involved in these programs. He said there were nine. I asked him yesterday how many Government agencies he had found were involved in it, and he said, "I was wrong. There were 13." In other words, there were 13 Government agencies, all of which had a bit or a piece of the drug prevention program.

Now this doesn't mean this was necessarily bad, because in some instances the agencies were working together. But in other instances the inevitable had happened: Petty bureaucrats seeking credit, empire building, were more interested in what they were doing in terms of building up their bureau than in dealing with the problem.

I have given Dr. Jaffe—when I made the appointment of him for this Office— the responsibility of knocking the heads together, and unless the people in this Government and all of the agencies—and all of them are represented here today— are willing to cooperate and work together, then instead of the heads being knocked together, the heads will roll. That is his responsibility.

The reason we do that is that this is a cause that is bigger than who is going to get the credit, bigger than whether this agency or that agency is going to be the more important agency. This is a cause we have all got to work on together, and under Dr. Jaffe's leadership and his coordination, I am sure that this bill will provide the means for us to do it and make a major breakthrough in this area.

Thank you.

Now, as is usually the custom, I will sign this with one pen, but in spite of the fact that this is one of the larger groups for a signing ceremony, I have pens for everybody who is here, and particularly pens for the Members of the House and the Senate who are here, just to remind them that when they support a bill, they get a pen.

Dr. Jaffe, if I could hand you your pen now.

NOTE: The President spoke at 12:45 p.m. in the East Room at the White House. He spoke without referring to notes.

As enacted, the bill (S. 2097) is Public Law 92-255 (86 Stat. 65).

Following the President's remarks, Dr. Jaffe spoke briefly as follows:

I don't think I can add very much to what the President said. I believe with this bill we have laid the groundwork for truly coordinated national effort. We have recognized over the years that law enforcement is not enough; treatment is not enough. Both sides have to work together. I am confident that under your leadership, sir, the various agencies will work together and we will make some progress in bringing this very serious problem—perhaps the most serious of our national health problems—under control.

97 Statement About the Drug Abuse Office and Treatment Act of 1972. *March 21, 1972*

TODAY I am pleased to sign into law the Drug Abuse Office and Treatment Act of 1972, a bipartisan bill designed to mount a frontal assault on our number one public enemy.

The support which this legislation received in the Congress—it passed unanimously in both Houses—not only reflects the wisdom of this measure but also attests to the determination of all our people to wipe out drug abuse in America.

The critical feature of this legislation is the statutory authority which it gives to the Special Action Office for Drug Abuse Prevention. This Office is charged with the responsibility for coordinating all Federal activities concerned with drug abuse prevention, education, treatment, rehabilitation, training, and research. Thus it will be at the cutting edge of our attack.

Among the other features of the bill are these:

—A National Drug Abuse Training Center will be established to develop, conduct, and support a full range of training programs relating to drug abuse pre-

vention functions.

—On December 31, 1974, a National Institute on Drug Abuse will be created within the National Institute of Mental Health. The new institute will administer drug abuse programs assigned to the Secretary of Health, Education, and Welfare.

—A new formula grant program is authorized to assist States in coping with drug abuse.

—Authorization is also provided for $350 million in grants and contracts to be administered by the Department of Health, Education, and Welfare between fiscal years 1972 and 1975.

—Four advisory bodies are established to provide counsel and recommendations to the President, the Secretary of Health, Education, and Welfare, and the Director of the Special Action Office on means of curbing drug abuse. They are the Drug Abuse Strategy Council, the National Advisory Council on Drug Abuse, a Federal Drug Council, and the National Advisory Council on Drug Abuse Prevention.

It was in June of 1971 that I first pro-

454

posed the creation of a Special Action Office for Drug Abuse Prevention. Because time was so critical in the fight against drug abuse, I determined that immediate steps had to be taken pending passage of the proposed legislation. As a temporary measure, I therefore established the Special Action Office for Drug Abuse Prevention by Executive order [11599] and charged it with the responsibility for overseeing all Federal programs—excluding law enforcement, international diplomacy, and intelligence gathering—related to the control of drug abuse. I appointed Dr. Jerome Jaffe to direct its activities.

A RECORD OF ACCOMPLISHMENT

Since the creation of the Special Action Office, substantial progress has been made toward controlling and reducing drug abuse in America.

—The Special Action Office is working to ensure that treatment and rehabilitation facilities will be available to all who need them, that lives will not be lost because a person who sought treatment found it unavailable. The number of federally funded drug treatment programs has increased from 78 last June, when operations began, to 166 today. I said last June that we would make available as much money as could be used effectively to fight the drug menace in America. In 1969, when I took office, Federal obligations for drug law enforcement and anti-drug abuse programs were at the $80 million level. By fiscal year 1972, they were $474 million, and I have asked for another increase of $120 million for this effort in fiscal year 1973, bringing the total to $594 million.

—The Special Action Office, working with the Office of Management and Budget, has examined the budgets and evaluated the policies of all civilian Federal agencies involved in drug abuse prevention. It has established specific goals for each of these agencies and has recommended adjustments in their budgets to match their responsibilities. A control system to oversee these efforts is presently under development.

—The Special Action Office has worked to eliminate the severe shortage of personnel trained for work in drug treatment, rehabilitation, and education programs. A National Training Center has been planned to train individuals who have responsibility for creating and operating community drug control programs. These people will be taught, in turn, to train others in their communities, and the pyramid effect of this approach will result, by the end of 1972, in an annual drug abuse training capacity of more than 16,000 men and women in federally funded programs.

—The Special Action Office is developing a program of technical assistance to help State and local governments develop their own capacities to deal with drug problems. This project involves, in part, an expanded information effort within the National Clearinghouse for Drug Abuse Information, including a computerized retrieval system providing easy access to information about on-going drug abuse activities.

—In a direct application of drug control procedures at the Federal level, the Special Action Office, working with the Department of Defense, established a massive screening, treatment, and rehabilitation program to assist armed services personnel in Vietnam and elsewhere. Rapid and appropriate action in this area has gone a long way toward arresting a

455

problem that one year ago threatened to assume massive dimensions. This program now includes all military personnel in the United States who are being discharged, sent abroad, or are returning to the United States from abroad. The programs of the Veterans Administration will have the capacity to offer treatment and rehabilitation services to some 20,000 addicts in 1972.

—Methadone is proving to be a helpful tool in the treatment and rehabilitation of drug users, but this tool is itself subject to abuse by addicts. The need for daily doses of methadone can create problems in the rehabilitation and control process. The Special Action Office, in conjunction with the Department of Defense and the National Institute for Mental Health, has initiated testing of a form of long-lasting methadone which would reduce the number of times weekly that the drug must be dispensed to the addict. If this new drug is effective, the present problems connected with methadone maintenance could be reduced considerably.

—In conjunction with the National Bureau of Standards, the Special Action Office has created a system of unique identification for use in methadone maintenance programs. This system can help to prevent diversion of methadone into illegal channels by eliminating duplication of treatment.

TOWARD A COORDINATED ATTACK

Those who are directly victimized by drug abuse often victimize others. They help to create enormous social problems through criminal activities, through an antisocial life style, and through the destruction of the fabric of the family, which is at the heart of a strong society. They deprive our country of their talents, their skills, and their energy. And, perhaps worst of all, the victims of drug abuse often help to create new victims. They bring others under the domination of narcotics.

This is why I feel so strongly that no effective approach can be made to the problem of drug abuse if it is not a balanced approach. Strong law enforcement measures are essential. But they must be coupled with a strong effort to treat those who have become dependent and to protect those who are not afflicted from falling prey to this enemy.

With the signing of the Drug Abuse Office and Treatment Act, we have written into law part of the balanced attack we need. Meanwhile, other elements of the attack are also moving forward.

On January 28, 1972, I established by Executive order [11641] the Office for Drug Abuse Law Enforcement in the Department of Justice. That Office, under the direction of Myles J. Ambrose, is giving the same coordinated and comprehensive attention to the street-level heroin pusher that the Special Action Office for Drug Abuse Prevention is giving to the pusher's victims.

Working through nine regional offices, the first of which has been established in New York City, the new enforcement program will use special grand juries to gather information on drug trafficking which can then be pooled for use by enforcement agencies at the Federal, State, and local level. The Office will draw on the Departments of Justice and the Treasury to assist State and local agencies in detecting, arresting, and prosecuting heroin traffickers.

Heroin is an import. We do not produce it in America, and yet we have the world's largest population of heroin addicts.

Clearly, the heroin problem is one that requires international cooperation. As part of our continuing effort to foster such cooperation, I established last September the Cabinet Committee on International Narcotics Control, chaired by Secretary of State Rogers. As a part of this effort, Narcotics Control Coordinators in 57 American embassies are now actively engaged with their respective host governments in the effort to stem the export of illegal drugs to America.

The bill I have signed into law today puts the full authority of the Federal Government behind a comprehensive program aimed at our most vicious and debilitating social problem. But while the Federal Government can help provide leadership in this crucial area, this is a problem which affects every one of our citizens and each of us must play a part in meeting.

The fight against drug abuse is complex and difficult, but there are signs that we are making progress. More victims are under treatment than ever before. More and better ways of treatment are becoming increasingly available. More illegal drugs are being seized—both within this country and without. More nations around the world are joining with us in a vigorous effort to stop drug trafficking. More Americans are becoming involved in the fight in their communities, their churches, their schools, and their homes.

Now we must continue to build on this progress until success is assured.

NOTE: On the same day, the White House released a fact sheet on the provisions of the act.

98   Toasts of the President and Prime Minister Erim of Turkey.   *March* 21, 1972

Mr. Prime Minister, Mrs. Erim, and our distinguished guests from Turkey and from the United States:

A few moments ago we heard the strains of "Around the World in 80 Days," and as we heard that song, I was reminded of how really small the world is and has become, and how fast events move. Exactly one month ago tonight, Mrs. Nixon, the Secretary of State, and I arrived in Peking and we were being received at a banquet in the Great Hall of the People by the Premier of the People's Republic of China.

Tonight, here in the White House, we honor the Prime Minister of Turkey.

In these two events, just one month apart, we see something which is very important for us always to remember, and that is that while a nation must always seek, as we seek, to have better relations with those who have been our adversaries, that we must never forget our friends, and tonight we honor true friends in honoring the Prime Minister, his wife, and our friends from Turkey.

Mr. Prime Minister, that friendship goes back, as you and I recalled in our discussions today, many years. I am reminded of the fact that this is also the month, 25 years ago, when, as a freshman Member of the Congress, along with one of our distinguished guests from the Congress, Senator Bentsen, he a Democrat, I a Republican, both voted for the Truman Doctrine—the Truman Doctrine for aid to Greece and Turkey. We voted for it, crossing party lines, because we knew what was involved was far more important than party; it involved the freedom that allows

457

any parties to exist. And as we think back over those 25 years, we are grateful for the friendship that we have enjoyed, the alliance that we have had with Turkey through those years.

We realize that Turkey is a nation and a people which has had a long and proud history, and we realize that you, Mr. Prime Minister, are developing the programs that will build an even greater future.

But what is important is that you are attempting to build that future, despite great pressures that might be applied upon you, in the paths of independence and freedom, rather than succumbing to the great influences of dictatorship and oppression.

As I looked over the Prime Minister's background, I find that he and I have much in common. We were born in the same year, 1913. We both studied the law and were relatively successful in that field. And as political men, we both have lost elections as well as won some.

But although we were born over 4,000 miles apart, in countries very different in background, we have something very much in common, as we knew from knowing each other's records and as we had firmly embedded in our minds by our conversations today. We are devoted to the same ideals: We are devoted to peace in the world; we are devoted to the independence of nations; we are devoted to a system of government which provides a freedom of choice, a parliamentary system in your country and the system of government which we have here in the United States.

And it is these common ideals, even more important than the common interest that we have, that bring us together and that make us the close friends that we are. We are proud of the friendship that we have had with Turkey going back over those 25 years, and we know that the visit of the Prime Minister to our country, the talks that he will have at all levels with people in our Government, will contribute to a continuing close relationship, a relationship which is not based simply on the signing of a piece of paper, a treaty, whether it is in NATO or bilateral, but a relationship which is much deeper than that—a relationship based on ideals that are immortal, ideals that we both believe in, that we both share, that we want for our own people in each country and for other people where they might have that opportunity, as well.

And so it is in that spirit that I know that everybody here, people who come from all over the United States as well as our friends from Turkey, people of both political parties in our country, of all walks of life, will want to join me in the toast that I will propose.

It will be, of course, to a continued friendship between our two peoples, to the progress and the prosperity of the people of Turkey, and particularly to the one who provides the progressive, enlightened, strong leadership in Turkey that all the world admires today, the Prime Minister of Turkey.

NOTE: The President spoke at 9:54 p.m. in the State Dining Room at the White House. He spoke without referring to notes.

See also Items 95 and 99.

The Prime Minister responded as follows:

Mr. President, Mrs. Nixon, ladies and gentlemen:

I would like, first, to thank you, Mr. President, for your most friendly remarks. Your words set the tone not only for this exquisite function but also are indicative of the spirit in which our talks were held. As this memorable day ends, I can say without hesitation that the understanding between our two countries has been invigorated immensely. Turkey and America feel closer tonight.

Mr. President, I have arrived in the United States at a time when, under your leadership, the United States is exploring the possibilities for a global understanding among all nations of the world. We, in Turkey, greatly admire and fully support your endeavors. We pray that these efforts will be crowned with the success they deserve, and that the foundations of a new era of dignity and peace for all mankind will be solidly established.

Turkey also subscribes to the policy of easing tensions in Europe, as well as in other parts of the world. Coexistence with states having different social systems is not unattainable if each state behaves with good will, refraining from causing harm to the social fabric of the other, and respecting the sanctity of the line respectively limiting their area of action.

Mr. President, I hardly need to elaborate on the excellent and close relations our two countries have been fortunate enough to enjoy. The cornerstone of Turkey's post world war foreign policy has been solidarity with the United States of America and the Western World as a whole.

The Turkish people will never forget the support and friendship extended to them by the United States during the difficult period in their history immediately after World War II. I should like to renew our homage here to President Truman for his statesmanship in laying down the principles for a long-term and happy partnership between our two nations which eventually led to our participation in the North Atlantic Treaty Organization about exactly 20 years ago. We also remember that our cooperation within NATO was enhanced and enlarged during the following years, starting with the Presidency of the great soldier and statesman, General Dwight Eisenhower.

We are proud of the democratic institutions we have been able to guard in face of many difficulties and threats. The will of the Turkish people to uphold these institutions is unshakable. The Turkish people are endeavoring to achieve full economic and social development under a democratic system.

As you know, Mr. President, the primary objective of my Government is to speed up this long-sought social and economic advancement through the eradication of conditions causing instability while introducing new reforms inspired by the guidelines set forth by Kemal Ataturk. Turkey will succeed in her new strides which will strengthen her constitutional structure, while making it possible for its people to enjoy, without hindering, their freedoms. Our main strength is the resolve of our people dedicated to the preservation of both the independence and security of their country, as well as to their personal liberties under a stable parliamentary democracy.

Mr. President, it is with this confidence that I am approaching our problems back home and those relating to the international arena. Today, as I have briefly remarked a while ago, we are hopefully on the threshold of an era of understanding and accommodation which may lead to the termination of the era of mistrust. Your tireless endeavors to open the channels of communication and pull down the walls and barriers of mistrust have undoubtedly been the major factor in bringing about this hope for a future in peace and dignity for all mankind.

We will contribute, to the best of our ability, to this praiseworthy cause. However, we continue to believe that unless we build from strength and credibility, our efforts will be fruitless and even self-destructive. Therefore, it is our firm belief that NATO should continue to be the cornerstone of any future structure for peace and security in the Western World, while sustaining the efforts for political unification for which Europe has been groping over many centuries.

We value our solidarity within NATO in the same measure that we value efforts for global détente, and we do not believe that one can be divorced from the other.

Mr. President, I appreciated your comments regarding Turkey's contribution to international efforts to eradicate the ills of drug abuse in the world. The humanitarian motive behind our plan of action, I hope, is well understood by the international community and will be matched and supported, in the same spirit, by their cooperative efforts.

Mr. President, next year, on October 29, we will be celebrating the 50th anniversary of the Turkish Republic. This has been for us an eventful half-century. The striking fact is that, dedicated to the legacy of Kemal Ataturk, the founder of the Republic, we were able to give substance to his motto, "Peace at home, and peace in the world," which you so eloquently quoted today. However, neither our peace will be complete nor our joy full, if by then Cyprus will not have ceased to be a "problem" for the Turkish Community and for Turkey itself. Let us hope that common sense will prevail and a just and peaceful solution safeguarding the contractual rights and interests of all concerned will be found.

Let me express this final thought: Next year and the years and decades to come will find the peoples of Turkey and America proceeding together on the road to peace, in mutual respect, trust, and everlasting amity.

Ladies and gentlemen, will you rise with me in a toast to the President of the United States of America.

99 Joint Statement Following Discussions With Prime Minister Erim of Turkey. *March 22, 1972*

PRESIDENT Nixon and Prime Minister Erim during their meeting on March 21, 1972, discussed the full range of Turkish-American bilateral relations as well as major international issues. The President stressed the importance that the United States attached to its relations with Turkey and to Turkey's role as an important NATO ally. In discussing the close and harmonious security relationship between the two countries, the President expressed the strong continuing support of the United States for the security, territorial integrity and independence of Turkey. Both leaders agreed to the principle of noninterference directly or indirectly in Turkey's internal affairs. Both leaders also agreed that continued close cooperation between their two nations is essential and that NATO is vital to their security as well as to the security of the other members of the Atlantic alliance.

The President and the Prime Minister also discussed the modernization of Turkey's armed forces. The Prime Minister explained the plans recently developed in the High Military Council of Turkey for the reorganization of the Turkish Armed Forces, for the strengthening of Turkey's defenses, and for the strengthening of the security of the southeastern flank of NATO. The President expressed the sup-

port of the United States for Turkey's efforts to modernize her armed forces, and said the United States would continue to assist the Turkish defense effort.

There was an exchange of views on the worldwide problem of drug abuse. The Prime Minister said the Turkish Government was proud to contribute to a humanitarian endeavor by its decision to stop opium poppy cultivation. He indicated that plans and programs had been devised to prevent loss of income to Turkish farmers, for which international participation was essential. The President expressed the appreciation of the American people for Turkey's courageous and humanitarian decision to ban opium production. He also indicated his special interest in efforts to improve the livelihood of Turkish farmers. The President said the United States attaches importance to bilateral and multilateral efforts to assist Turkish development in this field.

In addition, one of the main subjects dealt with by the President and the Prime Minister was the economic development of Turkey and the social advances made in that country. The Prime Minister expressed appreciation for past development aid and said Turkey would continue to pursue modernization within a democratic system. Both leaders agreed that the

Consortium for Aid to Turkey has provided an efficient multilateral mechanism to this end. Both agreed that this and other endeavors in multilateral institutions should continue and be further enhanced. The President also said the U.S. would continue its financial support of Turkey in its efforts to reach its declared goal of vigorous, self-sustaining economic growth.

The President described his China trip and discussed his upcoming trip to the Soviet Union. The Prime Minister indicated that Turkey has followed with admiration the efforts of the President to strengthen the peace of the world. He emphasized his belief that the visits of President Nixon to Peking and Moscow will have a special bearing on the promotion of world peace. The Prime Minister said that Turkey, on her side, encourages and supports efforts for peace in her region and is constantly improving her good relations with her neighbors.

President Nixon and Prime Minister Erim agreed that it is important that there be a just settlement of the Cyprus problem which would contribute to the wellbeing of the concerned parties and to peace in the Eastern Mediterranean. Proceeding from the binding effects of existing treaties and recognizing the beneficial peacekeeping role of the United Nations, it was agreed that such a settlement can best be reached through negotiation by the concerned parties.

NOTE: See also Items 95 and 98.

100   Special Message to the Congress on Older Americans. *March* 23, 1972

To the Congress of the United States:

When I addressed the White House Conference on Aging last December, I pledged that I would do all I could to make 1972 a year of action on behalf of older Americans. This message to the Congress represents an important step in fulfilling that promise.

Many of the actions which are outlined in this message have grown out of concerns expressed at the White House Conference and at related meetings across the country. The message also discusses a number of steps that have already been taken or that were announced at an earlier date. All of these actions are part of our comprehensive strategy for helping older Americans.

The momentum which has been generated by all these steps—old and new—will move us toward the great national objectives which the White House Conference set forth. I pledge that this momentum will be sustained as we follow through on these initiatives and as we keep other recommendations of the White House Conference at the top of our agenda, under continuing review.

This message, then, does not represent the last word I will have to say on this important subject. It does, however, identify those administrative steps which we are taking immediately to help older Americans, along with a number of legislative initiatives which should be of highest priority on this year's Congressional agenda.

We often hear these days about the "impatience of youth." But if we stop to think about the matter, it is the elderly who have the best reason to be impatient. As so many older Americans have candidly

461

told me, "We simply do not have time to wait while the Government procrastinates. For us, the future is now." I believe this same sense of urgency should characterize the Government's response to the concerns of the elderly. I hope and trust that the Congress will join me in moving forward in that spirit.

A Comprehensive Strategy for Meeting Complex Problems

The role of older people in American life has changed dramatically in recent decades. For one thing, the number of Americans 65 and over is more than six times as great today as it was in 1900—compared to less than a 3-fold increase in the population under 65. In 1900, one out of every 25 Americans was 65 or over; today one in ten has reached his 65th birthday.

While the number of older Americans has been growing so rapidly, their traditional pattern of living has been severely disrupted. In an earlier era, the typical American family was multigenerational—grandparents and even great-grandparents lived in the same household with their children and grandchildren, or at least lived nearby. In recent years, however, the ties of family and of place have been loosened—with the result that more and more of our older citizens must live apart or alone. The rapid increase in mandatory retirement provisions has compounded this trend toward isolation. Under such conditions, other problems of older persons such as ill health and low income have become even more burdensome. And all of these difficulties are intensified, of course, for members of minority groups and for those who are blind or deaf or otherwise handicapped.

The sense of separation which has characterized the lives of many older Americans represents a great tragedy for our country. In the first place, it denies many older citizens the sense of fulfillment and satisfaction they deserve for the contributions they have made throughout their lifetimes. Secondly, it denies the country the full value of the skills and insights and moral force which the older generation is uniquely capable of offering.

The major challenge which confronts us, then, as we address the problems of older Americans is the new generation gap which has emerged in this country in recent decades between those who are over 65 and those who are younger. The way to bridge this gap, in my judgment, is to stop treating older Americans as a burden and to start treating them as a resource. We must fight the many forces which can cause older persons to feel dependent or isolated and provide instead continuing opportunities for them to be self-reliant and involved.

If we can accomplish this goal, our entire Nation will reap immense benefits. As I put it in my speech to the White House Conference on Aging, ". . . any action which enhances the dignity of older Americans enhances the dignity of all Americans, for unless the American dream comes true for our older generation, it cannot be complete for any generation."

From its very beginnings, this Administration has worked diligently to achieve this central objective. To assist me in this effort, I established a special task force on aging in 1969. In that same year, I elevated the Commissioner on Aging, John Martin, to the position of Special Assistant to the President on Aging, the first such position in history. Later, I created a new Cabinet-level Committee on Aging, under the leadership of the Secretary of Health, Education, and Welfare, to ensure that the concerns of the aging were regularly and thoroughly considered by this Administration and that our policies to help older persons were effectively carried out. To provide greater opportunity for older Americans to express their own concerns and to recommend new policies, I convened the White House Conference on Aging—which met last December and which was preceded and followed by many other meetings at the grassroots level. I asked the Cabinet-level Committee on Aging to place the recommendations of the Conference at the top of its agenda. And I also asked the Chairman of the Conference, Arthur Flemming, to stay on as the first Special Consultant to the President on Aging, so that the voice of older Americans would continue to be heard at the very highest levels of the Government.

One dimension of our efforts over the last three years is evident when we look at the Federal budget. If our budget proposals are accepted, overall Federal spending for the elderly in fiscal year 1973 will be $50 billion, nearly 150 percent of what it was when this Administration took office. One particularly important example of increased concern for the elderly is the fact that overall Federal spending under the Older Americans Act alone has grown from $32 million in fiscal year 1969 to a proposed $257 million in fiscal year 1973—an eight-fold increase. This figure includes the $157 million I originally requested in my 1973 budget, plus an additional $100 million which I am requesting in this message for nutrition and related services.

How much money we spend on aging programs is only one part of the story,

however. *How* we spend it is an equally important question. It is my conviction that the complex, interwoven problems of older Americans demand, above all else, a *comprehensive* response, one which attacks on a variety of fronts and meets a variety of problems.

This message outlines the comprehensive strategy which this Administration had developed for bridging the new generation gap and enhancing the dignity and independence of older Americans. That strategy has five major elements:

1. Protecting the income position of the elderly;
2. Upgrading the quality of nursing home care;
3. Helping older persons live dignified, independent lives in their own homes or residences—by expanding and reforming service programs;
4. Expanding opportunities for older people to continue their involvement in the life of the country; and
5. Reorganizing the Federal Government to better meet the changing needs of older Americans.

A SUMMARY OF MAJOR INITIATIVES

In addition to discussing important actions which have been taken in the past or are now underway, this message focuses attention on the following major items of new and pending business.

1. *To protect the income position of older Americans,*

The Congress should:

—enact H.R. 1 as soon as possible, thus providing older Americans with $5½ billion of additional annual income. H.R. 1 would increase social security benefits by 5 percent, make social security inflation-

proof, increase widow, widower and delayed retirement benefits, liberalize earnings tests, and establish a floor under the
income of older Americans for the first
time;

—repeal the requirement that participants in part B of Medicare must pay a
monthly premium which is scheduled to
reach $5.80 this July. This step would
make available to older persons an additional $1.5 billion—the equivalent of
roughly another 4 percent increase in
social security benefits for persons 65 and
over;

—strengthen the role played by private
pension plans by providing tax deductions
to encourage their expansion, requiring
the vesting of pensions, and protecting the
investments which have been made in
these funds;

—enact revenue sharing proposals designed to provide the opportunity for significant property tax relief; and

—enact my proposed consumer protection legislation which deals with problems
which are especially acute for older
citizens.

The Administration will:

—continue its investigation of alternative methods for financing public education in such a manner as to relieve the
present heavy reliance on property taxes;

—propose major improvements in the
military retirement system, including a
one-time recomputation of retired pay;

—continue the battle against price inflation, with special emphasis in the health
care field;

—develop a program to foster greater
awareness among older citizens of their
legal rights under the Interstate Land
Sales Full Disclosure Act; and

—develop a program designed to help

each State create consumer education
programs for older citizens.

2. *To upgrade the quality of nursing
home care,*

The Congress should:

—make it possible for the Federal Government to assume the entire cost of State
inspection of homes receiving payments
under the Medicaid program; and

—approve my request for additional
funds for training nursing home personnel.

The Administration will:

—continue to strengthen and expedite
other portions of my 8-point program for
upgrading nursing homes, including my
commitment to withdraw Federal funds
from those homes that refuse to meet
standards and to make adequate alternative arrangements for those who are displaced from substandard homes; and

—develop proposals for protecting older
persons in the purchase of nursing home
services.

3. *To help older persons live dignified,
independent lives in their own homes
or residences,*

The Congress should:

—appropriate the $100 million I re-
quested for the Administration on Aging
in my 1973 budget;

—appropriate an additional $100 mil-
lion for nutritional and related purposes;

—appropriate $57 million for other
programs under the Older Americans Act,
bringing total spending under this act to
$257 million—an eight-fold increase over
fiscal year 1969;

—renew and strengthen the Older
Americans Act, which so many older persons rightly regard as landmark legislation in the field of aging—extending it for

an indefinite period rather than for a specified period of years;

—create a new, coordinated system for service delivery under this act, so that the Administration on Aging can help develop goals for such services, while State and area agencies create specific plans for achieving these goals; and

—allow States and localities to use some of the funds now in the Highway Trust Fund to finance their mass transit programs, including special programs to help the elderly.

The Administration will:

—ensure that Departments and agencies involved in the field of aging identify the portion of their total resources that are available for older persons and ensure that use of these resources is effectively coordinated all across the Government;

—strengthen the role already played by local officials of the Social Security Administration and other agencies in providing information about Federal services to older persons and in receiving their complaints;

—launch this summer a new Project FIND—a program which will enlist the services of Government workers at the grassroots level in an outreach effort to locate older persons who are not involved in Federal nutrition programs and who should be;

—step up efforts to meet the special transportation needs of older Americans, giving priority to community requests for capital grants that aid the elderly from the Urban Mass Transportation Fund;

—provide more and better housing for older Americans by issuing new guidelines for two HUD programs to make them more readily applicable to the elderly, by

extending the mortgage maturity for the FHA-insured nursing home program, by drawing upon research of the Law Enforcement Assistance Administration to reduce crime, by encouraging the provisions of more space for senior centers within housing projects for the elderly, and by developing training programs in the management of housing for older persons.

4. *To expand opportunities for older persons to continue their involvement in the life of our country,*

The Congress should:

—appropriate the funds I have requested for such action programs as Retired Senior Volunteers and Foster Grandparents;

—authorize the ACTION agency to expand person-to-person volunteer service programs, helping more older Americans to work both with children and with older persons who need their help; and

—broaden the Age Discrimination in Employment Act of 1967 to include State and local governments.

The Administration will:

—work with 130 national voluntary groups across the country in a special program to stimulate volunteer action; and

—develop a national program to expand employment opportunities for persons over 65, through programs such as Senior Aides and Green Thumb, by urging State and local governments to make job opportunities available under the Emergency Employment Act of 1971, by working through the public employment offices to open part-time job opportunities in both the public and private sector, and by reaffirming Federal policy against age discrimination in appointment to Federal jobs.

5. *To improve Federal organization for future efforts,*

The Administration will:

—strengthen the Secretary of Health, Education, and Welfare's Advisory Committee on Older Americans—providing it with permanent staff capability to support its increased responsibilities;

—arrange for the Commissioner of Aging, in his capacity as Chairman of the Advisory Committee on Aging, to report directly to the Secretary of Health, Education, and Welfare;

—create a Technical Advisory Committee on Aging Research in the Office of the Secretary of Health, Education, and Welfare to develop a comprehensive plan for economic, social, psychological, health and education research on aging.

PROTECTING THE INCOME POSITION OF OLDER AMERICANS

Perhaps the most striking change in the lives of most Americans when they turn 65 is the sudden loss of earned income which comes with retirement. The most important thing we can do to enhance the independence and self-reliance of older Americans is to help them protect their income position. I have long been convinced that the *best* way to help people in need is not by having Government provide them with a vast array of bureaucratic services but by giving them money so that they can secure needed services for themselves. This understanding is fundamental to my approach to the problems of the aging.

The success of this income-oriented strategy depends in turn on giving effective attention to two factors: first, where older Americans' money comes from and second, what it is used for.

WHERE THE MONEY COMES FROM: REFORMING AND EXPANDING GOVERNMENT INCOME PROGRAMS

The most important income source for most older Americans is social security. Accordingly, improvements in social security have been the centerpiece of this Administration's efforts to assist the elderly. Today, approximately 85 percent of all Americans over 65 receive regular cash benefits from social security, while 93 percent of those now reaching age 65 are eligible to receive such benefits when they or their spouses retire.

Since 1969, social security cash benefits have been increased twice—a fifteen percent increase in January of 1970 and another ten percent increase one year later. These increases represent a $10 billion annual increase in cash income for social security beneficiaries. As I suggested, however, in my 1969 message to the Congress concerning social security reform, *bringing* benefit payments up to date alone is not enough. We must also make sure that benefit payments *stay* up to date and that all recipients are treated fairly.

My specific proposals for achieving these ends are presently contained in the bill known as H.R. 1—legislation which is of overwhelming importance for older Americans. This bill passed the House of Representatives in the first session of the 92nd Congress and is presently pending before the Senate Finance Committee. I continue to believe firmly that H.R. 1 is the single most significant piece of social legislation to come before the Congress in many decades.

Let us consider the several ways in which this legislation would help the elderly:

1. *An Additional Increase in Social Security.* Under H.R. 1, social security benefits would be increased by an additional 5 percent effective in June of 1972. This increase would provide $2.1 billion in additional income for older Americans during the first full year that it is effective. It would mean that social security benefits would be one-third higher after this June than they were just 2½ years ago. *This represents the most rapid rate of increase in the history of the social security program.*

2. *Making Social Security "Inflation Proof."* Under H.R. 1, social security payments would, for the first time, be automatically protected against inflation. Whenever the Consumer Price Index increased by 3 percent or more, benefits would be increased by an equal amount. Payments that keep pace with the cost of living would thus become a guaranteed right for older Americans—and not something for which they have to battle again and again, year after year.

3. *Increased Widows' Benefits.* About 58 percent of the population age 65 and over are women, most of whom depend primarily on social security benefits earned by their husbands. Under the present law, however, widows are eligible for only 82½ percent of the retirement benefits which would be paid to their late husbands if they were still alive. H.R. 1 would correct this situation by increasing widows' benefits to 100 percent of the benefits payable to their late husbands. It would similarly expand the eligibility of a widower for benefits payable to his late wife. Altogether, this provision would mean that about 3.4 million widows and widowers would receive increased benefits totaling almost three quarters of a billion dollars in the first full year.

4. *Increased Benefits for Delayed Retirement.* Under present law, those who choose *not* to retire at age 65 forfeit their social security benefits for the period between the time they are 65 and the time they finally retire. H.R. 1 would allow retirees to make up a portion of these lost benefits through higher payments after retirement. Benefits would increase by one percent for each year that a person had worked between the ages of 65 and 72.

5. *Liberalized Earnings Tests.* Like the increased benefit for delayed retirement, the liberalized earnings tests contained in H.R. 1 would encourage more of our older citizens to remain active in the economic life of our country. This is a step which I promised to take in the 1968 campaign and for which I have been working ever since.

It is high time this step was taken. Those who *can* work and *want* to work should *not* be discouraged from working—as they often are under the present law. By reducing the barriers to work, we can increase the sense of participation among older citizens and at the same time tap their energies and experience more effectively.

Under H.R. 1, the amount that a beneficiary could earn without losing any social security would be increased from $1,680 a year to $2,000 a year. That ceiling, in turn, would be automatically increased each time there was a cost of living benefit increase in social security. In addition, for those who earn in excess of $2,000, the potential reduction in social security payments would also be lessened. Under the present law, benefits are reduced by $1 for each $2 of extra earnings but this rate applies only to the first $1,200 earned above the exempt amount. Additional earnings beyond that level now cause benefits to be reduced on a $1 for $1 basis. Under H.R. 1, benefits would be reduced on a $1 for $2 basis for all earnings above $2,000—no matter how much a person earned.

6. *Adult Assistance Reform.* One of the most important elements of H.R. 1—and one of the most under-publicized—is its provision to place a national floor under the income of every older American. H.R. 1 would replace the present Old Age Assistance program with a single, federally-financed program which would provide a monthly income of $150 for an individual and $200 for a couple when fully effective.

This program would assist 4.5 million elderly persons instead of the 2.1 million currently reached. It would also eliminate the practice of placing liens on homes as a condition of eligibility. Eligibility for assistance would be determined on the basis of need without regard to the income or assets of relatives. Relative-responsibility rules would not be a part of this new program.

I believe this reform is particularly important since it channels massive resources—some $2.8 billion in additional annual benefits—to those whose needs are greatest.

7. *Special Minimum Benefits.* H.R. 1 would also provide special minimum benefits for people who have worked for 15 years or more under social security. The guaranteed minimum benefit would range from $75 a month for a person who had worked 15 years under social security to $150 a month for a person with 30 years of such work experience. At maturity,

this provision would increase overall benefit payments to $600 million.

H.R. 1: THE NEED FOR PROMPT ACTION

In addition to all of these benefits for older people, H.R. 1 would have enormous benefits for many younger Americans as well. Clearly the passage of this bill is a matter of the very highest priority. I have made that statement repeatedly since I first proposed this far-reaching program in 1969. As I make that statement again today, I do so with the conviction that further delay is absolutely inexcusable. To delay these reforms by even one more year would mean a loss for older Americans alone of more than $5 billion.

It is my profound hope that the Senate will now carry forward the momentum which has been generated by the passage of H.R. 1 in the House of Representatives, thus seizing an historic opportunity—and meeting an historic obligation.

WHERE THE MONEY COMES FROM: MILITARY, VETERANS AND FEDERAL EMPLOYEE BENEFITS

We are also making significant progress toward improving the retirement income of career military personnel, veterans and Federal employees.

1. *To improve military benefits,* I will soon submit legislation to the Congress for recomputing retirement pay on the basis of January 1, 1971 pay scales, thus liberalizing annuities for current retirees. I will also submit legislation to provide—for the first time—full annuities for retired reservists at an earlier age, and to revise benefit payments so that retirees receive their full annuities when they are

most needed, at the conventional age of full retirement. I hope these proposals will receive favorable consideration.

In addition, I support legislation to provide military retirees with a less expensive survivor annuity plan—one which is similar to that now provided to retired civil servants.

2. *Benefits for veterans* are also improving. Our efforts to improve both the quality of care and the number of patients treated in Veterans Administration hospitals will have a major impact on older veterans, since more than one-fourth of all VA patients are over 65. The staff to patient ratio at VA hospitals will be increased to 1.5 to 1, an all-time high, if our budget proposals are accepted.

The fiscal year 1973 budget also provides for further increases in nursing home care with the result that the authorized number of VA-operated nursing beds will have doubled since 1969 and the number of community contract beds and State home beds built and operated with VA subsidies will have increased by one-third over the same period.

In addition, I have signed into law significant improvements in pensions for elderly veterans which relate benefits more closely to need and protect recipients from income loss because of increases in the cost of living. In January of 1971, pensions were increased by an average of 9.6 percent. One year later, they went up an additional 6.5 percent and a new formula was adopted relating benefits more closely to need for the first time.

3. *Federal Employee Benefits* are also up. Retirement benefits for Federal employees have been liberalized in several instances, and—under a more generous formula for determining cost of living in-

creases—annuities have gone up nearly 16 percent in the last 2½ years. In addition, the Government's contribution to Federal health benefit premiums of current and retired employees has been substantially increased.

WHERE THE MONEY COMES FROM: RE-FORMING THE PRIVATE PENSION SYSTEM

Only 21 percent of couples now on our social security rolls and only 8 percent of non-married beneficiaries are also receiving private pensions. While this picture will improve somewhat as workers who are now younger reach retirement, nevertheless—despite the best efforts of labor and management—only half the work force is presently covered by private pension plans. As the White House Conference on Aging pointed out, the long-range answer to adequate income for the elderly does not lie in Government programs alone; it also requires expansion and reform of our private pension system.

Late last year, I submitted to the Congress a five-point program to achieve this goal. It includes the following items:

1. *Tax deductions to encourage independent savings toward retirement.* Individual contributions to group or individual pension plans should be made tax deductible up to the level of $1500 per year or 20 percent of earned income, whichever is less. Individuals should also be able to defer taxation of investment earnings on these contributions.

2. *More generous tax deductions for pension contributions by self-employed persons.* The annual limit for deductible contributions to pension plans by the self-employed—on their own behalf and for those who work for them—should be

raised from $2,500 or 10 percent of earned income, whichever is less, to the lesser of $7,500 or 15 percent of earned income.

3. *Requiring the vesting of pensions.* Persons who have worked for an employer for a significant period should be able to retain their pension rights even if they leave or lose their jobs before retirement. Unfortunately, many workers do not now have this assurance—their pensions are not vested. To change this situation, I have proposed a new law under which all pensions would become vested as an employee's age and seniority increased. Under this law, the share of participants in private pension plans with vested pensions would rise from 31 percent to 47 percent and the overall number of employees with vested rights would increase by 3.6 million. Most importantly, among participants age 45 and older, the percentage with vested pensions would rise from 60 percent to 92 percent.

4. *The Employee Benefits Protection Act.* This legislation was first proposed to the Congress in March of 1970; it was strengthened and resubmitted in 1971. It would require that pension funds be administered under strict fiduciary standards and would provide certain Federal remedies when they are not. It would also require that plans provide full information to employees and beneficiaries concerning their rights and benefits.

5. *A study of pension plan terminations.* In my December message, I also directed the Departments of Labor and the Treasury to undertake a one-year study concerning the extent of benefit losses which result from the termination of private pension plans. This study will provide the information we need in order to make solid recommendations in this field, providing needed protection without reducing benefits because of increased costs.

WHERE THE MONEY GOES: THE BURDEN OF HEALTH COSTS

Growing old often means both declining income and declining health. And declining health, in turn, means rising expenditures for health care. Per capita health expenditures in fiscal year 1971 were $861 for persons 65 and older, but only $250 for persons under 65. In short, older Americans often find that they must pay their *highest* medical bills at the very time in their lives when they are *least* able to afford them.

Medicare, of course, is now providing significant assistance in meeting this problem for most older Americans. In fiscal year 1971, this program accounted for 62 percent of their expenditures for hospital and physicians services and 42 percent of their total health payments. In addition, an estimated 40 percent of Medicaid expenditures go to support the health costs of the elderly, while other programs provide significant additional assistance.

But serious problems still remain. Accordingly, this Administration has been working in a number of ways to provide even more help for the elderly in the health-care field. One of our most important proposals is now pending before the Congress. I refer to the recommendation I made more than a year ago that the Congress combine part B of Medicare—the supplementary medical insurance program, with part A—the hospital insurance program, thus eliminating the special monthly premium which older persons must pay to participate in part B—a premium which will reach $5.80 per month by July. I have reaffirmed my commitment to this important initiative on other occasions and today I affirm it once again. Elimination of the premium payment alone would augment the annual income of the elderly by approximately $1.5 billion, the equivalent, on the average, of almost a 4 percent increase in social security for persons 65 and over. I hope the Congress will delay no longer in approving this important proposal.

Our concern with health costs for older Americans provides additional reasons for the prompt approval of H.R. 1. Under that bill:

—Provision is made for extending Medicare to many of the disabled (about 60 percent of whom are age 55 and over) who are drawing social security benefits and who have had to give up work before reaching regular retirement age;

—Medicare beneficiaries would have the opportunity to enroll in Health Maintenance Organizations—organizations which I strongly endorsed in my special message on health policy because of my conviction that they help to prevent serious illness and also help to make the delivery of health care more efficient;

—Provision is made for removing the uncertainties relative to coverage under Medicare when a person needs to use extended care facilities after hospitalization.

In my recent message to Congress on health policy, I indicated a number of other measures which will help reduce the cost of health care. I spoke, for example, of the special attention we have been giving under Phase II of our New Economic Policy to the problem of sky-rocketing health costs, through the special Health Services Industry Committee of the Cost of Living Council. I indicated that a number of cost control features would be introduced into the Medicare and Medic-

aid reimbursement processes—with the overall effect of reducing health costs. I have also called for new research efforts in fields such as heart disease, cancer, and accident prevention—initiatives which also promise to reduce health problems—and health bills—for older persons.

WHERE THE MONEY GOES: INFLATION

Inadequate retirement incomes are strained even further when inflation forces older persons to stretch them to meet rising costs. Because older persons are uniquely dependent on relatively fixed incomes, they are uniquely victimized by the ravages of inflation. While my proposals for making social security benefits inflation-proof will provide significant help in defending the elderly against this menace, it is also important that we take on this enemy directly—that we curb inflationary pressures.

This goal has been a central one of this Administration. When I came to office this country was suffering from a massive wave of price inflation—one which had resulted in large measure from the methods chosen to finance the Vietnam War. The problem of reversing this wave by conventional methods was a more stubborn problem, frankly, than I expected it to be when I took office. By the summer of 1971, it became clear that additional tools were needed if inflation was to be quickly and responsibly controlled. Accordingly, I announced last August a New Economic Policy—one which has received the strong support of the Congress and the American people.

I have been especially gratified that older Americans—whose stake in the battle against inflation is so high—have rallied to support this new economic program. With their continued support—and that of all the American people—we can carry this battle forward and win a decisive victory.

One key element in that battle, of course, is to be sure that Government spending programs, including those which help the elderly, are responsibly financed. If they are not, then inflation will merely be reignited and Government policy will merely be robbing older Americans with one hand of the aid it gives them with the other.

WHERE THE MONEY GOES: PROPERTY TAXES

Two-thirds of all older citizens—and 78 percent of older married couples—own their own homes. For these Americans—and for many younger Americans as well—the heavy and growing burden of property taxes constitutes one of the most serious of all income-related problems. Even those who rent their homes often bear an unfair burden since property tax increases are frequently passed along in the form of higher rents. The reason these burdens are so onerous, of course, is that the income from which property taxes must be paid by the elderly is usually going *down* at the very time the taxes are going *up*.

Property taxes in the United States have more than doubled in the last ten years. The problems which this fact implies are felt by Americans of all ages. But elderly Americans have a special stake in their solution.

I am committed to doing all I can to relieve the crushing burden of property taxes. I have been proceeding toward this end in two ways. First, I am continuing to push for passage of our General and Special Revenue-Sharing proposals, legislation which would channel some $17 billion into State and local budgets and thus provide a significant opportunity for property tax relief. At the same time, as I indicated in my recent State of the Union Address, I am also moving to change the system through which we finance public education. In developing a new approach, I will draw on the recommendations of the President's Commission on School Finance, the Advisory Commission on Inter-governmental Relations, and other analyses such as those which are being performed under the direction of the Secretaries of the Treasury, and of Health, Education, and Welfare. The purpose of this intensive investigation is to develop ways of putting this Nation's educational system on a sounder financial footing while helping to relieve the enormous burden of school property taxes.

REDUCING INCOME TAX BURDENS

Recently approved and pending changes in the income tax laws also provide special help to older persons. Under these provisions, a single person age 65 or over would be able to receive up to $5,100 of income without paying any Federal income taxes, while a married couple with both husband and wife 65 or over would be able to receive up to $8,000 of such tax-free income.

WHERE THE MONEY GOES: PROTECTING ELDERLY CONSUMERS

The quality of life for older Americans depends to a large extent upon the responsiveness of the marketplace to their special needs. It is estimated that elderly persons now spend over $60 billion for goods and services every year—and they will be able to spend billions more if my proposals for increasing their income are enacted. Our economy should be responsive to the needs of older Americans; they have a high stake in advancing consumer protection.

Through organizational changes, administrative actions and legislative recommendations, this Administration has been working to provide needed protection for the American consumer in general—and for the older consumer in particular. The several pieces of consumer legislation which I have submitted to the Congress are designed to reduce dangers which are especially acute for older consumers—and I again urge their enactment.

In addition, I am asking my Special Assistant for Consumer Affairs, in cooperation with the Secretary of Housing and Urban Development, to develop a program for helping to enforce the Interstate Land Sales Full Disclosure Act by fostering greater awareness among older citizens of their legal rights under this legislation.

Recognizing that the complexity of today's marketplace demands great sophistication by the individual consumer, our primary and secondary schools have stepped up their programs for consumer education. Unfortunately, many older Americans have never had the opportunity to benefit from such programs. The Office of Consumer Affairs is therefore developing guidelines for adult consumer education programs with particular emphasis on the needs of the elderly. To carry out these guidelines, I am asking my Special Assistant for Consumer Affairs, working in cooperation with the Secretary of Health, Education, and Welfare, to develop a program of technical assistance to help the States create consumer education programs specifically designed for older citizens.

A COMPREHENSIVE EFFORT FOR IMPROVING INCOME

The key characteristic of my strategy for protecting the income position of older Americans is its *comprehensiveness*. For it would help to augment and protect the income older persons derive from social security, adult assistance, Federal military, veterans and civilian benefits, and private pensions, while at the same time curbing the cruel drain on those incomes from rising health costs, inflation, taxes and unwise consumer spending. I hope now that the Congress will respond promptly and favorably to these proposals. If it does, then the purchasing power of the elderly can be enhanced by billions of dollars a year—an achievement which could do more than anything else to transform the quality of life for Americans over 65.

UPGRADING THE QUALITY OF NURSING HOME CARE

Income related measures can help more older Americans to help themselves; they build on the strong desire for independence and self-reliance which characterizes the older generation. We must recognize, however, that some older Americans—approximately five percent by recent estimates—cannot be primarily self-reliant. These older men and women require the assistance provided by skilled nursing homes and other long-term care facilities. For them, a dignified existence depends upon the care and concern which are afforded them in such settings.

473

In June of 1971, at a regional convention of the National Retired Teachers Association and the American Association of Retired Persons, I pledged to meet the challenge of upgrading nursing home care in America. I expressed my determination that nursing homes, for those who need them, should be shining symbols of comfort and concern. I noted that many such facilities provide high quality care, but that many others fall woefully short of this standard. I observed that those who must live in such facilities are virtual prisoners in an atmosphere of neglect and degradation.

Following that speech, I directed the development of an action plan to improve nursing home care and I announced that 8-point plan in August of 1971. I am pleased to be able to report that we have made significant progress in carrying out that plan. We have delivered on all of the eight promises implied in that program. Let us look at each of them:

1. *Training State Nursing Home Inspectors*—Through February of 1972, almost 450 surveyors had been trained in federally-sponsored programs at three universities. Contract negotiations are underway to continue ongoing programs and to establish new ones at two university training centers.

2. *Complete Federal Support of State Inspections Under Medicaid*—Legislation to raise the level of financial participation by the Federal Government in this activity to 100 percent was submitted to the Congress on October 7, 1971, as an amendment to H.R. 1. This proposal is awaiting Congressional action.

3. *Consolidation of Enforcement Activities*—A new Office of Nursing Home Affairs has been established in the Office of the Secretary of Health, Education, and Welfare. This unit is directly responsible for coordinating all efforts to meet our July 1, 1972, deadline for inspections of skilled nursing homes and for certification of these facilities in accordance with proper procedures.

4. *Strengthening Federal Enforcement*—142 new positions have been allocated to the Medical Services Administration to enforce Medicaid standards and regulations. Added emphasis is being placed on the audit process as a tool for enforcement: 34 additional positions are being added in HEW's Audit Agency to perform audits of nursing home operations.

5. *Short-term Training for Professional and Paraprofessional Nursing Home Personnel*—This program is currently funded at the $2.4 million level and is scheduled to train 20,000 persons. The fiscal year 1973 budget which I submitted to the Congress contains $3 million to train an additional 21,000 persons.

6. *Assistance for State Investigative Units*—A program to develop and test investigative-ombudsman units to respond to individual complaints and to other problems in the nursing home area has also been initiated. As an interim mechanism, nearly 900 social security district and branch offices have been designated as listening posts to receive and investigate complaints and suggestions about nursing home conditions.

7. *Comprehensive Review of Long-term Care*—The Office of Nursing Home Affairs is now carrying out a comprehensive analysis of issues related to long-term care.

8. *Cracking Down on Substandard Nursing Homes*—Progress is also being made on this important front. Last December I signed legislation which, among other things, authorizes Federal quality standards for intermediate care facilities,

thus giving us additional authority to guarantee a decent environment for those who live in long-term care facilities.

Every State providing nursing home care under the Medicare and Medicaid programs has now installed systems for surveying and certifying nursing homes. In the area of fire-safety and other safety guidelines, a coordinated set of standards for homes providing care under these programs is being put into effect.

Medicaid compliance activities have also been stepped up. Onsite Federal reviews of State Medicaid certification procedures have been carried out. Deficiencies in those procedures were found in 39 States. These deficiencies were publicly announced by the Secretary of Health, Education, and Welfare on November 30, 1971, along with a timetable for correcting them. Since that time, 38 of the 39 States have made the necessary corrections. We have determined that every facility receiving Medicaid funds must have been inspected and correctly certified by July 1, 1972.

While we prefer to upgrade substandard homes rather than shut them down, we will not hesitate to cut off money when that is necessary. As of February 11, 1972, in fact, 13 extended care facilities had been decertified for participation in Medicare. In such cases, as I have often pledged before, we are firmly committed to seeing that adequate alternative arrangements are made for those who are displaced.

In fiscal year 1971, the Federal Government contributed $1.2 billion to the cost of nursing home care. We should also remember, however, that more than 40 percent of the annual expenditure for nursing homes is borne by private sources. In addition to seeing that Federal tax dollars are properly spent in this area, it is also im-

portant that private individuals are protected when they purchase nursing home services. I have asked the Secretary of Health, Education, and Welfare to develop proposals to deal with this dimension of the nursing home challenge.

SPECIAL SERVICES TO FOSTER
INDEPENDENCE

Improving the income position of older Americans and upgrading nursing homes—these are two concerns which have been of highest priority for this Administration in the past and which will continue to be central in the future. As we work to develop a truly comprehensive strategy, however, other agenda items have also been emerging as areas of special emphasis, particularly those involving public and private services which can help older persons live dignified, independent lives in their own homes for as long as possible.

INCREASED RESOURCES FOR THE
ADMINISTRATION ON AGING

Since the passage of the Older Americans Act in 1965, the Administration on Aging has had the lead Federal role in developing and coordinating such services. While that office has accomplished many significant things, the importance and urgency of its mission have outstripped its financial resources.

It was to help remedy this situation that I announced at the White House Conference on Aging last December that I would call for a five-fold increase in the budget of the Administration on Aging—from $21 million to $100 million. As I will discuss below in greater detail, I am now requesting an additional $100 million for

475

nutritional and related purposes, money which would also be spent through the Administration on Aging.

With this substantial increase in funds, we would be able to step up significantly our efforts to develop and coordinate a wide range of social and nutritional services for older Americans. Our central aim in all of these activities will be to prevent unnecessary institutionalization—and to lessen the isolation of the elderly wherever possible.

EXTENDING THE OLDER AMERICANS ACT

Since its passage in 1965, the Older Americans Act has served as an important charter for Federal service programs for the elderly. Unless the act is promptly extended, however, the grant programs it authorizes will expire on June 30th. This must not happen. I therefore urge that this landmark legislation be extended— and that the extension be indefinite, rather than limited to a specific period of time.

STRENGTHENING THE PLANNING AND
DELIVERY OF SERVICES

In addition, I am asking that the Older Americans Act be amended to strengthen our planning and delivery systems for services to the elderly. Too often in the past, these "systems" have really been "non-systems," badly fragmented, poorly planned and insufficiently coordinated. My proposed amendments are designed to remedy these deficiencies.

We should begin by helping to develop and strengthen the planning capacities of the State agencies on aging and of new area agencies on aging which would be established within each State. Up to 75 per-

cent of the administrative costs of these new area planning agencies would be funded by the Administration on Aging, which would also establish general goals to which activities at the State and local levels would be directed. One of the major priorities would be to enhance and maintain the independence of older citizens.

The State and area planning agencies would plan for the mobilization and coordination of a wide range of resources— public and private—to meet such goals. The Administration on Aging would be authorized to fund up to 90 percent of the cost of social and nutritional services provided under plans developed by the area planning agencies. In fiscal year 1973, $160 million would be allocated in formula grants for nutritional and social services. An additional $40 million would be allocated in special project assistance to develop new and innovative approaches and to strengthen particularly promising area plans.

By establishing overall objectives and by providing both money and mechanisms for a stronger planning and coordination effort, we can ensure that resources and energies which are now widely scattered and fragmented can be pulled together in ways which will notably increase their impact.

COORDINATING FEDERAL EFFORTS

Even as we strengthen coordination at grassroots levels, so we must do a better job of coordinating Federal programs. As this message makes clear, efforts are being made all across our Government to help older citizens. But if there was one clear message at the White House Conference on Aging, it was that this wide range of Federal resources must be better coordinated. To help achieve this important objective, I have directed my Special Consultant on Aging to work with all these agencies in an intense new effort to develop coordinated services.

As the first step in this effort, I have directed those agencies whose programs have a major impact on the lives of older persons to provide the Cabinet-level Committee on Aging, within sixty days, with the amounts they identify as serving the needs of the elderly. In addition, I am directing that each agency identify, within the total amount it expects to spend for its aging programs, a sum that will be available to the States and localities for purposes related to the Older Americans Act. The Administration on Aging will then provide this information to the States so that it can be utilized in the State and local planning process. State aging agencies will also be able to transmit their views on proposed Federal programs, thereby furthering the interchange of information and strengthening overall coordination.

Under these procedures, we can ensure that all resources for helping the elderly are fully marshalled and coordinated, in a way which is responsive to the special needs of every State and locality in our land.

ESTABLISHING INFORMATION AND
COMPLAINT CENTERS

We must also work to improve communications between the Federal Government and older Americans and to alert the Government to areas of special need. Because older persons often have some difficulty moving about conveniently, and because services are often fragmented and channeled through complex bureaucratic mechanisms, it is especially important that

the elderly have one place to turn where they can obtain needed information and let their views be heard.

As I have already noted, we have been moving in this direction under my program to upgrade the quality of nursing home care. Following the directive which I announced at the White House Conference on Aging, Social Security offices have also been expanding their information and referral services for the elderly. District and branch offices are now handling more than 200,000 such inquiries each month—and that number is expected to increase. A task force is now at work within the Social Security Administration to examine ways of improving this service.

As another step in this direction, I have directed the Cabinet-level Committee on Aging to examine ways in which we can use other Government offices—such as the General Services Administration's Federal Information Centers and the Agricultural Extension Service's local offices—in further expanding and improving our information and complaint services.

FIGHTING HUNGER AND MALNUTRITION

In addition to our overall funding and coordination proposals concerning Federal services, we are also moving ahead in a variety of specific service areas. One of the most important is the fight against hunger and malnutrition among the elderly.

The thought that any older citizens—after a lifetime of service to their communities and country—may suffer from hunger or malnutrition is intolerable. Happily, since I submitted my message on hunger and nutrition to the Congress in May of 1969, we have made significant strides toward eliminating this problem among all age groups in America. Our efforts to increase incomes have been central to this endeavor, of course. But our special food assistance programs have also been substantially augmented.

If my budget proposals for fiscal year 1973 are accepted, overall spending for food stamps will have increased nine-fold since 1969. In the coming fiscal year, an estimated 2 million elderly participants in the Food Stamp Program will receive benefits of $343.5 million, compared with only $45.8 million in fiscal year 1969. Virtually every county in the Nation now offers either the Food Stamp or the Food Distribution Program; in early 1969, nearly 500 counties offered neither. In all, 2.5 million older Americans benefit from at least one of these programs.

Food assistance is important to the elderly. They benefit not only from nutritious food but also from the activity of preparing meals and sharing mealtimes with others. To maximize these benefits, the Department of Agriculture in January revised its regulations to improve the nutrition program and expand participation.

But more needs to be done. Many older persons who are entitled to food stamps or to surplus commodities are still not receiving them. Why is this the case? In many instances, older Americans do not realize they are eligible for participation. The agencies which provide assistance are often unaware of older persons who need their services. Some older persons choose not to participate—out of pride or out of fear that accepting food assistance may subject them to the arbitrary treatment they associate with the present welfare system. In some cases, older persons want to participate but find that necessary transportation is unavailable.

To overcome the barriers which keep older Americans from full participation in food assistance programs, we are launching this year a major outreach campaign called Project FIND. This campaign will be conducted through a senior citizen awareness network made up of federally operated or funded field offices and out-reach workers. It is my hope that Federally-supported personnel will be augmented in this effort by volunteers from State [and] local government offices and from the private sector. For ninety days, all these workers will go out across our country to find those who should be participating in nutrition programs but who are not yet involved.

Last night, I signed into law S. 1163 [Public Law 92–258], a new national nutrition program for the elderly. This program will provide prepared meals in a group setting and delivered meals for those who are confined to their homes. I welcome this effort. Because of my strong feeling that this area should be one of priority action, I will submit to the Congress—as I suggested above—an amendment to my 1973 budget to provide an additional $100 million for nutritional and related services. My proposed amendments to the Older Americans Act would further strengthen this effort by ensuring that the Food Stamp Program is planned as part of a more comprehensive service effort.

Other steps will also be taken in this area. In some areas, for example, space at federally-assisted housing projects will be utilized for feeding older persons. The support of State and local governments, of civic and religious organizations and of the food services industry will also be solicited. Maximum use will be made of existing technical resources, including skilled personnel who have worked with the school lunch program and other special programs of the Department of Agriculture. The time has come for marshalling all of our resources in a comprehensive campaign to meet the nutrition needs of older Americans.

PROVIDING BETTER TRANSPORTATION FOR
THE ELDERLY

For many older Americans, lack of mobility means poor access to friends and relatives, to government services and to meaningful participation in the community. Unless we meet the challenge of providing better transportation for older persons, our efforts in other fields will not be as effective as they should be. This is why I told the delegates to the White House Conference on Aging that I would, by administrative action, require that Federal grants which provide services for older persons also ensure that the transportation needed to take advantage of these services is available.

In addition, the Department of Transportation is significantly increasing its program for developing new ways to meet the public transportation needs of older persons. The approaches which are being tested include special new transportation services to take elderly citizens from housing projects and other residential areas to hospitals, senior citizen centers, social service agencies, employment opportunities and the like; and demand-responsive services whereby the elderly are picked up at their doorsteps and taken to specific desired destinations.

Once new ways have been developed for meeting the transportation needs of the elderly, we must also make them generally available. One proposal which could

help significantly in this effort is the recommendation recently submitted to the Congress by the Secretary of Transportation under which some of the funds now in the Highway Trust Fund could be used by States and localities to augment resources in the mass transportation area.

I hope the Congress will give prompt approval to this important plan. The flexibility it provides would allow State and local officials—who know best the transportation needs of the elderly within their own jurisdictions—to give special consideration to meeting those needs. I am asking the Secretary of Transportation to develop specific suggestions for assisting the States and localities in these undertakings.

In addition, the Department of Transportation is ready to give priority attention to community requests for helping older Americans through capital grants from the Urban Mass Transportation Fund and is willing to commit significant resources to this end. I urge the States and localities to move immediately to take advantage of these resources.

MEETING THE HOUSING NEEDS OF
OLDER CITIZENS

This Administration has also worked hard to respond to the very special housing needs of older Americans. It is expected, for example, that an all-time record in producing subsidized and insured housing and nursing homes for the elderly will be achieved this year by the Department of Housing and Urban Development. In the current fiscal year, nearly 66,000 units of subsidized housing for the elderly will be funded under HUD's housing assistance programs—a figure which should rise to over 82,000 in fiscal year 1973. In addition, accommodations for over 14,000 people, mostly elderly, will be provided this fiscal year under HUD's nursing and intermediate care facility programs—and nearly 18,000 such accommodations will be provided next year. Finally, a large number of elderly citizens will benefit from other housing funded by this year's record number of nearly 600,000 subsidized housing unit reservations. Clearly, we are making substantial progress in this important area.

A number of other administrative steps have also been taken to ensure that this new housing is responsive to the special needs of the elderly. For example, Secretary Romney recently announced new guidelines for the Section 236 subsidized rental program for lower income elderly tenants. These guidelines will help ensure greater variety in building types, including highrise structures, and more flexibility in their locations. As a result of these guidelines, older persons will find such housing arrangements even better suited to their particular needs.

The Department of Housing and Urban Development has also issued initial guidelines for the new Section 106(a) program which will provide technical assistance to non-profit sponsors of low and moderate income housing—including housing which is specially designed for the elderly.

In addition, the Department will extend the mortgage maturity for its Federal Housing Administration insured nursing home program up to a maximum of 40 years. This decision will not only reduce monthly occupancy charges to patients, but it will also enable sponsors of residential housing to "package" residential and nursing home complexes more easily. The proximity of these facilities will permit elderly persons temporarily to

vacate their residential units for short term nursing care—and at the same time remain close to family, friends, and the environment to which they are accustomed.

I have also directed the Secretary of Housing and Urban Development to work with the Administration on Aging in developing training programs dealing with the management of housing for the elderly.

The Law Enforcement Assistance Administration has undertaken an intensive research effort to determine factors which encourage or inhibit crime in residential settings and to develop total security systems to reduce crime in housing projects. The Department of Housing and Urban Development plans to use the results of this effort in its housing programs. I have also made grant funds available through the Law Enforcement Assistance Administration for reducing crime in areas housing older persons. Already, in two cities, funds have been granted specifically for this purpose.

Crime is an especially serious problem for our older citizens. Through these and other measures, we will continue our strong effort to meet this challenge.

Two years ago my task force on aging observed that "older persons would make greater use of many of the services society intends them to receive if these services were made more accessible to them. One reason that the number of senior centers has increased so fast is because centers facilitate the packaging, marketing, and delivery of services." The task force also noted that, "although the number of senior centers has rapidly grown in recent years, centers are still too limited in number to reach more than a fraction of the older population." In my judgment, a natural location for a senior center is a housing facility occupied primarily by older persons.

The Department of Housing and Urban Development administers two housing programs under which such facilities can be made available to older persons living in the project and in the surrounding neighborhood: the Section 236 Program and the Public Housing Program. Both of these programs provide specially designed housing for lower income older persons. The law under which these programs are administered contains language which allows the financing of facilities designed primarily for use by older persons including "cafeteria or dining halls, community rooms, workshops, infirmaries, . . . and other essential service facilities."

To increase the supply of well located senior centers, I have instructed the Department of Housing and Urban Development to encourage greater provision of community space for senior centers within subsidized housing projects for the elderly. The Department will consider the community's overall need for these centers in determining the appropriate scale of centers within such housing projects.

On other fronts, the Farmers Home Administration in the Department of Agriculture is taking steps to meet the housing needs of elderly persons who live in rural areas. Under the Section 502 program, for example, thousands of elderly families have received millions of dollars in loans for home ownership and repair. The Section 515 program, which provides favorable interest loans with repayment periods of up to 50 years to stimulate the development of rental housing in rural areas, has also moved forward. Rental units financed under this program have tripled from 1969 to 1973.

EXPANDING OPPORTUNITIES FOR INVOLVEMENT

It is important that we give sufficient attention to the things our Nation should be doing for older Americans. But it is just as important that we remember how much older Americans can do for their Nation. For above all else, what our older citizens want from their country is a chance to be a part of it, a chance to be involved, a chance to contribute.

I am determined that they will have that chance. For as I told the White House Conference, "we cannot be at our best if we keep our most experienced players on the bench." This Administration is deeply committed to involving older citizens as actively as possible in the life of our Nation—by enhancing their opportunities both for voluntary service and for regular employment.

IMPROVING VOLUNTARY SERVICE PROGRAMS

Voluntary social action has long been recognized as one of the great distinguishing characteristics of America, a force which has helped to unite and focus our diverse people in the pursuit of common goals. And even as the voluntary spirit has helped our country move forward more effectively, it has also provided those who have volunteered for service with a greater sense of fulfillment.

The voluntary spirit is particularly relevant to the lives of older Americans. The White House Conference on Aging, for example, called attention to "ways in which older Americans could fulfill themselves by giving service to one another and to their communities." Delegates to the Conference called for "a national policy . . . to encourage older adults to volunteer," and urged "that existing national older adult voluntary programs should be expanded and funded at adequate levels in order to serve extensive numbers of volunteers." They urged a mobilization of public and private organizations to strengthen the volunteer movement.

I agree completely with these judgments. That is why, at the time of the White House Conference, I pledged to move successful voluntary programs from demonstration status to full operation on the national level, an expansion effort that is rapidly moving forward.

I requested, for example, that the Foster Grandparent program be doubled to $25 million, providing for 11,500 foster grandparents to serve 23,000 children each day—50,000 children in all each year—in some 450 child care institutions throughout the country. I also asked that ACTION's Retired Senior Volunteer Program (RSVP) be tripled to $15 million so that as many as 75,000 senior volunteers could be involved in community services.

When the RSVP program has developed to the full extent permitted by the new appropriations, as many as 11,000 volunteers will be serving older persons in nursing homes and other extended care facilities, bringing companionship and personal assistance to some 45,000 residents who might otherwise be lonely and isolated. At the same time, as many as 13,000 part-time RSVP volunteers will be serving as homemaker and health aides, enabling thousands of older persons to continue to live in their own homes. By using senior volunteers in a variety of programs, we can foster that human contact which brightens the lives both of those who are served and those who volunteer.

But other new steps are also needed in this area.

As one such step, the Congress should enact legislation which would enable the ACTION agency to expand person-to-person volunteer service programs for older Americans. These efforts would build on the successful experience of the Foster Grandparent program. One important characteristic of such programs is that so much good can be accomplished, so many people helped, for a relatively small dollar investment. It would indeed be tragic if we did not capitalize on this opportunity.

Measures are also needed to improve coordination among the many Federal and non-Federal volunteer activities which affect the aging. As one important step in this direction, the Administration on Aging and the National Center for Voluntary Action have enlisted the cooperation of 130 national voluntary organizations in a program to help older men and women in 300 communities live dignified lives in the familiar settings of their own homes. Too often, older Americans are displaced from such settings simply because small problems such as simple home repairs, shopping and trips to obtain health care have become too difficult. And yet, with only minimal assistance from volunteers, these problems could easily be met.

I have directed the ACTION agency to work in every possible way to help provide such assistance. Already, the RSVP program is moving forward in this area. I am confident that other ACTION program volunteers can also make a major impact in this field. It is my hope, too, that communities will consider the elderly residents of federally assisted housing projects as a source of volunteer manpower for serving other older persons.

As we move ahead with this entire program, we should take encouragement from successes of the past. One which is particularly noteworthy is the program in Mount Vernon and Edmunds, Washington, where local citizens have designed a unique bridge across the generation gap called STEP—Service To Elderly Persons. Under this program, volunteers from the local high schools have undertaken, on a regular basis, to assist elderly persons in performing small tasks, while at the same time providing them with companionship and renewed hope. Everyone gains from a program of this sort. If leaders at every level are alert to such possibilities, our progress can be enormous.

Often in quiet ways, the people of the United States have been responding to the challenges of our society with compassion and resourcefulness. Now it is for those of us who have the responsibility for national leadership to provide the Federal assistance which can help such voluntary efforts go even further and accomplish even more.

EMPLOYMENT OPPORTUNITIES FOR
OLDER CITIZENS

Discrimination based on age—what some people call "age-ism"—can be as great an evil in our society as discrimination based on race or religion or any other characteristic which ignores a person's unique status as an individual and treats him or her as a member of some arbitrarily-defined group. Especially in the employment field, discrimination based on age is cruel and self-defeating; it destroys the spirit of those who want to work and

it denies the Nation the contribution they could make if they were working.

We are responding to this problem in a number of ways. The Department of Labor, for example, has filed over 80 suits under the Age Discrimination in Employment Act of 1967—30 of which have been successfully concluded. I will soon propose to the Congress that this act be broadened to include what is perhaps the fastest growing area of employment in our economy—the State and local governments. I will also send a directive to the heads of all Federal departments and agencies reaffirming and emphasizing our policy that age shall be no bar to a Federal job which an individual is otherwise qualified to perform.

The Age Discrimination in Employment Act relates to persons between the ages of 45 and 65. I recognize that persons falling within this age group are confronted with special problems in the employment area and that we should do everything we can to resolve these problems. It is also important, however, that we help open employment opportunities for persons over 65. To this end, I have requested the Secretary of Labor to urge the States and local communities to include older persons in the opportunities provided by the Emergency Employment Act of 1971, and to work with our public employment offices so that they will be in a position to help open job opportunities for the over 65 group, including opportunities for part-time employment in both the public and private sectors.

I also asked last fall that funds be doubled for special Operation Mainstream projects for low-income older workers—such as Green Thumb and Senior Aides. This measure can mean that as many as 10,000 older persons will be employed in activities that provide useful community service.

Organizing for Future Action

One of the important concerns of the White House Conference on Aging was the way in which the Government is organized to deal with the problems of older Americans. It was because I share this concern that I established my original task force on aging, appointed the first Special Assistant to the President on Aging and the first Special Consultant to the President on Aging, set up a new Cabinet-level Committee on Aging and called the White House Conference.

In a similar manner, the Secretary of Health, Education, and Welfare has taken steps to ensure that the voice of older Americans speaks loud and clear within that Department. He has informed me that he will strengthen the Department's Advisory Committee on Older Americans and provide it with staff capability to support its increased responsibilities. The Commissioner of Aging, in his capacity as Chairman of the Advisory Committee, will report directly to the Secretary.

Another important organizational concern involves Government research activities which concern the process and problems of aging. It is important that the same scientific resources which have helped more people live longer lives now be applied to the challenge of making those lives full and rewarding for more Americans. Only through a wise investment in research now, can we be sure that our medical triumphs of the past will not lead to social tragedies in the future.

What we need is a comprehensive, coordinated research program, one which includes disciplines ranging from biomedical research to transportation systems analysis, from psychology and sociology to management science and economics. To coordinate the development of such a program, a new Technical Advisory Committee for Aging Research will be created in the office of the Secretary of Health, Education, and Welfare.

A Generation No Longer Forgotten

We all grow old; the younger generation today will be the older generation tomorrow. As we address the needs of older Americans, therefore, we are truly acting in the best interest of all Americans. The actions and proposals which have been outlined in this message are designed to address those needs and meet those interests.

When I spoke about the problems of the elderly back in 1968, I described our older citizens as "an entire generation of forgotten Americans." But since that time, as this message clearly demonstrates, that situation has sharply changed. Today, it can truly be said that at all levels of Government and in all parts of the country, "the aging have come of age." Much work still remains, to be sure, but we can conclude with assurance that the aging are forgotten no longer.

Just before the First World War, one of the brilliant young writers of that day penned a line which has since become a hallmark of the period: "It is the glory of the present age," he wrote, "that in it one can be young."

Since that time, the generation of which he wrote has come through a troubled and challenging time—through two World Wars and a Great Depression, through the difficult experiences of Korea and Vietnam. The members of that same generation have led this country through a time of social and economic change unparalleled in world history. And they have come through all of these challenges "with colors flying." Because of their success, we now have the opportunity to complete their quest for peace and justice at home and around the world.

At such a moment, one obligation should be very high on our list of priorities: our obligation to this older generation. Let us work to make ours a time of which it can be said, "the glory of the pres-ent age is that in it men and women can grow *old*"—and can do so with grace and pride and dignity, honored and useful citizens of the land they did so much to build.

RICHARD NIXON

The White House,
     March 23, 1972.

NOTE: On the same day, the White House released a fact sheet and the transcript of a news briefing on the message. Participants in the news briefing were Elliot L. Richardson, Secretary, and John B. Martin, Commissioner of the Administration on Aging, Department of Health, Education, and Welfare; and Arthur S. Flemming, Special Consultant to the President on Aging.

101   Remarks About the Resignation of George Meany From the Pay Board. *March* 23, 1972

Ladies and gentlemen:

At the conclusion of my statement, Mr. Ziegler will issue a longer, written statement, and also an Executive order [11660] that I have just signed after meeting with the Cost of Living Council.

When I announced our new economic policy on August 15 of last year, I said that fighting inflation must be everybody's job. Yesterday, George Meany walked off the job. The decision to walk out came after the ruling on the longshoremen's contract.

While other American workers are being held to a 5½ percent wage increase, the Pay Board ruled against a 20 percent wage increase for the longshoremen. Mr. Meany supported the increase. The Pay Board was right. Mr. Meany was wrong.

I respect Mr. Meany as a powerful spokesman for the Nation's largest union organization, the AFL–CIO. But only 17 percent of America's 80 million wage earners belong to the AFL–CIO. It is my responsibility to act and speak for all the people, and I shall meet that responsibility.

As President, I cannot permit any leader representing a special interest, no matter how powerful, to torpedo and sink a program which is needed to protect the public interest. Consequently, I have directed the Pay Board to continue, but as a single public unit, with those labor leaders who wisely wish to remain on it balanced by a reduced number of business leaders.

I have directed the Price Commission to proceed on course, working alongside the Pay Board to cut inflation in half by the end of the year.

All rules and regulations remain in full

force. All Americans, including particularly the 80 million wage earners in this country, have a stake in winning the fight against inflation. This is a fight to the finish, and, with the support of the American people, we shall win it.

NOTE: The President spoke at 4:05 p.m. in the Briefing Room at the White House. He spoke without referring to notes.

102   Statement About New Composition of Pay Board Membership Following Resignations of Certain Labor Members.   *March* 23, 1972

THE SPIRIT of voluntary cooperation is the key to victory in the battle against inflation. I emphasized this point when I first announced my new economic policy last August and repeated it last October outlining the price stabilization program. I described at that time some of the sacrifices which millions of Americans were making in the fight against rising prices. And I indicated that our success in this struggle would ultimately depend on the willingness of all our people to "put the public interest ahead of the special interest"—and thus to continue that good fight.

That is why the decision of three of the five representatives of organized labor to resign from the Pay Board is a disservice to the American people.

Since it was established last October—at the specific urging of organized labor—this tripartite Board has been a central part of the Phase 2 program.

There has been much strong evidence that this program is succeeding. In the 6 months from August 1971 to February 1972, the rise in the Consumer Price Index was cut to an annual rate of 3.3 percent, down from a 4.1 percent increase in the previous 6 months. Real, spendable weekly wages after taxes rose 5.4 percent in the last 6 months, compared to a 1.3 percent increase in the previous 6 months.

In the last 6 months, seasonally adjusted employment rose 1,123,000, while unemployment declined by 234,000.

Any program of controls in a free economy will have its ups and downs. But what is important is that we are moving in the right direction. The wage and price control system is working. But continued cooperation of all Americans is needed if we are to win the battle against inflation.

In these circumstances, the decision of three of the labor representatives to walk off the job of fighting inflation is totally selfish and irresponsible.

The west coast longshoremen's settlement was the only specific case referred to in yesterday's statement by the executive council of the AFL–CIO, a statement which severely criticized the general pattern of Pay Board decisions. The Pay Board disallowed a 20.6 percent compensation increase which Mr. Meany and his colleagues supported but approved a 14.9 percent increase, even though it was more than double the general limit which the Board had set.

The Pay Board was right and Mr. Meany was wrong on this issue.

The general pattern of decisions of the Pay Board is one with which the labor representatives have largely agreed. Of the 54 Pay Board decisions to date, labor has agreed in 36 of the votes—two-thirds of the total. It has disagreed with only 13 decisions—or 25 percent. In one instance labor's representatives were split and in four instances they abstained. Over half of the Pay Board's decisions have been unanimous, and of the eight major wage cases voted on by the full Board which have been the most controversial, labor has agreed with the outcome in five. When the labor representatives say that this general pattern is one of "flagrant favoritism," they must recognize that the pattern is one to which they have generally agreed.

It is true, of course, that labor's representatives have not prevailed in every instance—and that they did not succeed in their effort to uphold the full 20.6 percent longshoremen's increase. In a free society no one is right all the time and no one can have his way all the time. All participants must be ready to accept a reasonable amount of give and take.

Organized labor's views have not been ignored by the Pay Board. In fact, they have usually been accepted. But we cannot and will not allow any single group—business or labor—to be the exclusive judge of fairness in its own case. The public interest must come before any special interest.

Our economic policies will continue to require certain sacrifices of the American people. But I am convinced that these policies are also in the best interests of all the American people. I am especially confident that they serve the best interests of our working men and women. For wage earners know that wage increases which are inflated are illusionary wage increases—they are inevitably canceled out by rising prices.

Although a few labor leaders have chosen to reject their public responsibility and have sought to justify their action with standard political rhetoric, this Administration will not accept an "anti-labor" label. On the contrary—there can be no more "pro-labor," pro-workingman stand than a firm decision to protect the buying power of the wage earner's dollar.

Inflation is a dangerous and difficult enemy. We have set the course in the battle against that enemy—and our decisions have won the overwhelming approval of the Congress and the American public. I am determined to stay that course; I shall not be deterred by the disaffection of a few union leaders who represent only 17 percent of America's 80 million wage earners.

My obligation is to serve the public interest—and the public interest will be served.

I have directed the Pay Board to continue, but as a single public unit, with those labor leaders who wisely wish to remain balanced by a reduced number of business leaders. All will be public members with the special perspectives of labor and business represented in their deliberations.

I have directed the Price Commission to proceed on course, working alongside the Pay Board to cut inflation in half by the end of this year.

All rules and regulations remain in full force.

The fight against inflation will go on until the American consumer and the American worker win the fight.

NOTE: On March 22, 1972, three members of the Pay Board, George Meany, president of the AFL–CIO, I. W. Abel, president of the United Steel Workers, and Floyd E. Smith, president of the International Association of Machinists and Aerospace Workers, resigned. The next day, Leonard Woodcock, president of the United Automobile Workers, also resigned from the Board.

Before issuing the statement, the President met at the White House with members of the

Cost of Living Council to discuss his decision on the new composition of the Pay Board.

The White House also released the transcript of a news briefing by George P. Shultz, Director, Office of Management and Budget, on the President's statement and Executive Order 11660.

103   The President's News Conference of *March* 24, 1972

QUESTIONS

PARIS PEACE TALKS

[1.] THE PRESIDENT. Miss Lewine [Frances L. Lewine, Associated Press], we will take your question first.

Q. Mr. President, in view of the suspension of the Paris peace talks, can you tell us if the hopes are dimming for a negotiated peace settlement and what you assess the situation as?

THE PRESIDENT. What we are really trying to do there, Miss Lewine, and this has been done under my direction, is to break a filibuster. There has been about a 3½-year filibuster at the peace talks on the part of the North Vietnamese. They have refused to negotiate seriously. They have used the talks for the purpose of propaganda while we have been trying to seek peace. Whenever the enemy is ready to negotiate seriously, we are ready to negotiate. And I would emphasize we are ready to negotiate in public channels or in private channels.

As far as the hopes for a negotiated peace are concerned, I would say that the way the talks were going, there was no hope whatever. I am not saying that this move is going to bring a negotiation. I do say, however, that it was necessary to do something to get the talks off dead center

and to see whether the enemy continued to want to use the talks only for propaganda or whether they wanted to negotiate.

When they are ready, we are ready, but we are not going to continue to allow them to use this forum for the purpose of bullyragging the United States in a propaganda forum rather than in seriously negotiating peace, as we tried to do as exemplified by not only our private contacts in the 12 meetings that I discussed on January 25, but also in my speech of January 25, in which I made a very forthcoming offer.

MR. KLEINDIENST'S NOMINATION

[2.] Miss Thomas [Helen Thomas, United Press International].

Q. Mr. President, was there any link between the ITT antitrust settlement and the contribution to San Diego as a convention city and do you think that Mr. Kleindienst will be confirmed as the Attorney General?

THE PRESIDENT. Well, I have noted that you ladies and gentlemen of the press have been pressing on this matter, as you should, because it is a matter of very great interest in the Senate and in the Nation.

I will simply limit my remarks to these observations: First, Mr. Kleindienst is being considered for, as you have indicated, confirmation as Attorney General of the United States.[1] That is the purpose of the hearings. I had confidence when I appointed him that he was qualified for this position. I still have that confidence. I believe that he should be confirmed and I believe that he will be confirmed.

Now, as far as the hearings are concerned, there is nothing that has happened in the hearings to date that has in one way shaken my confidence in Mr. Kleindienst as an able, honest man, fully qualified to be Attorney General of the United States.

However, I am not going to comment on any aspects of the hearing, any aspects of the case, while the Senate is still conducting them and while the Senate is still trying to determine the authenticity of some of the evidence that is before it. That is a matter for the Senate committee under the chairmanship of Mr. Eastland to continue to consider. But I would point out that Mr. Kleindienst asked for these hearings. We want the whole record brought out because as far as he is concerned, he wants to go in as Attorney General with no cloud over him. He will not have any, in my opinion, once the hearings are concluded, and what we are talking about will be proof, rather than simply charges which as yet have been unsubstantiated.

ROLE OF WHITE HOUSE AIDES

[3.] Q. Mr. President, on another aspect

which I think is not directly related to the ITT case, I wondered if you could give us your view on the proper role of White House Staff members in contacts with executive departments and regulatory agencies concerning matters that are before those departments or agencies.

My specific reference, of course, is to the involvement of Mr. Flanigan[2] in some of these matters, but I wondered if you could give us, on a more general basis, what you consider the proper role and the limits of that role for a Presidential aide in dealing with regulatory and law enforcement matters.

THE PRESIDENT. A Presidential aide must listen to all of those who come to the White House, as they do in great numbers on all sides of all cases with regard to complaints that they have or causes that they wish to work for, just as they go to the Members of the House and the Senate and others in that connection.

What is improper is for a Presidential aide to use influence for personal gain, and to use influence in any way that would not be in the public interest. As far as Mr. Flanigan is concerned, Mr. Ziegler has responded to that charge at considerable length with my total authority and his views represent mine. I have nothing further to say.

WAR ON INFLATION

[4.] Q. Mr. President, how do you expect the war on inflation to succeed without the cooperation of George Meany and his friends?[3]

THE PRESIDENT. The war on inflation will succeed with their cooperation, if pos-

---

[1] On February 15, 1972, White House Press Secretary Ronald L. Ziegler announced the President's intention to nominate Richard G. Kleindienst as Attorney General of the United States. On the same day, the White House also released a biography of Mr. Kleindienst, which is printed in the Weekly Compilation of Presidential Documents (vol. 8, p. 440).

[2] Peter M. Flanigan, Assistant to the President.

[3] See Items 101 and 102.

sible, but without it, if necessary. I think the best indication of the fact that it is succeeding is that as far as that part of the Consumer Price Index which is made up of those items that are under control, as Mr. Stein pointed out in his briefings yesterday, the wage-price controls have been effective.

The only part of the Consumer Price Index or the major part of the Consumer Price Index which resulted in what we thought was a disappointing increase in prices, at least a one-month increase, was the food index.

The food index, as we know, is not controlled. Now, insofar as that food index is concerned, we discussed that at considerable length at the Cost of Living Council yesterday. What we found is that it is a mistake and totally unfair to make the farmer the scapegoat for the high meat prices and the high food prices.

Approximately a third of what the prices are that the consumer pays in the grocery store or the supermarket for food, approximately only a third of that amount is a result of what the farmer receives as farm income. The other two-thirds goes to middlemen, to retailers, and others. And our preliminary investigation of this situation shows that the spread between what the farmer receives and what the consumer pays in the grocery store and the supermarket has widened. It is too great.

That is the reason why the Price Commission is, on April 12, as you know—I think it was announced this morning—is going to conduct a hearing on this matter to determine whether or not the profit margins in this period have gone beyond the guidelines that have been laid down.

I will simply say that as far as we are concerned, we can say that on the one hand we are glad to see that, looking at a 6-month period, the rate of inflation has decelerated. On the other hand, we are disappointed at even a one-month figure in which the rate of inflation is at the level it was this time.

We are particularly disappointed that the food component was as high as it was. That is why we welcome the action of the Price Commission looking into that component as to why it is, and then in the event that those food prices do not start to move down, then other action will have to be taken. I am prepared to have such other action taken. I have directed those who have responsibility in this field to see what action can be taken. I would simply conclude by pointing out that to feel that the action that will be effective is to control or move on the one-third, that which the farmer receives as income for what he sells, is not the most effective way to do it.

One little example that I can use which I think is quite graphic—and Secretary Connally was discussing this matter in the Cost of Living Council yesterday. He said that he had been in Texas and had talked to a rancher who raised chickens. He asked him how much he got a dozen for eggs. He got 30 cents a dozen. A couple of days later he got breakfast at the Hotel Pierre in New York and he ordered a couple of eggs for breakfast. It was $5 for two. That is at the rate of $30 a dozen. Now, of course, the eggs have to be transported, processed, cooked, and served, but 30 cents a dozen to the farmer and $30 a dozen to whoever buys those eggs in a restaurant, that is just too much, and we are going to get at that middleman one way or another.

POLITICAL CONTRIBUTIONS

[5.] Q. Mr. President, will you give us your views on the general proposition of large political contributions either by corporations or individuals in terms of possibly getting something back for it?

THE PRESIDENT. Nobody gets anything back as far as the general contributions are concerned in this Administration. As a matter of fact, I think some of our major complaints have been that many of our business people have not received the consideration that perhaps they thought that an Administration that was supposed to be business-oriented would provide for it.

As far as such contributions are concerned, they should always, of course, comply with the law.

Second, as far as those who receive them are concerned, they must be accepted with no understandings, expressed or implied, that anything is to be done as a result of those contributions that would not be done in the ordinary course of events.

Let me just say on that point that looking at ITT, which, as I understand, has been a contributor to a number of political causes over the years, it is significant to note—and I would hope that the members of the press would report this; I have not seen this in many stories—it is significant to note that ITT became the great conglomerate that it was, in the two previous administrations primarily, in the Kennedy Administration and in the Johnson Administration. It grew and it grew and it grew, and nothing was done to stop it.

In this Administration we moved on ITT. We are proud of that record. We moved on it effectively. We required the greatest divestiture in the history of the antitrust law. And second, we also, as a

result of the consent decree, required that ITT not have additional acquisitions, so that it became larger.

Now, as Dean Griswold [4] pointed out, that not only was a good settlement, it was a very good settlement. I think under the circumstances that gives the lie to the suggestion that this Administration, in the handling of the ITT case, just using one example, was doing a favor for ITT. If we wanted to do a favor for ITT, we could just continue to do what the two previous administrations had done, and that is nothing, let ITT continue to grow. But we moved on it and moved effectively.

Mr. McLaren [5] is justifiably very proud of that record, and Dean Griswold is very proud of that record, and they should be.

BUSING AND EDUCATIONAL OPPORTUNITY

[6.] Q. Mr. President, could we discuss your speech the other night and your moves on the problems of the schools, particularly with the blacks in our society? There are those who feel that in the combination of the constitutional issue that has been raised, in which you have asked that the courts have a moratorium, and at the same time by putting more money into black schools, what you are doing, in effect, is going back to the old doctrine of separate but equal facilities for blacks. Could you comment on that?

THE PRESIDENT. Yes, I see that that charge has been made and I can see how that understanding, or misunderstanding, could develop. But let me explain what

---

[4] Erwin N. Griswold, Solicitor General, Department of Justice.

[5] Richard W. McLaren was Assistant Attorney General, Antitrust Division, Department of Justice, from January 1969 to February 1972.

we were trying to do and what I believe our proposals, if they are enacted by the Congress, will accomplish.

In the first place, we have to analyze what the constitutional problem is. The Constitution under the 14th Amendment provides for equal protection of the law. The Constitution does not provide, as a remedy, busing or any other device. The Constitution in the 14th Amendment expressly grants power to the Congress to set up the remedies to accomplish the right of equal protection of the law.

We turn now to busing. Let me relate this to *Brown* v. *the Board of Education. Brown* v. *the Board of Education,* as its name indicates, was about, primarily, education. *Brown* v. *the Board of Education* held, in effect, that legally segregated education was inherently inferior education. I agree with that.

On the other hand, how do we desegregate and thereby get better education? Here is where busing compounds the evil. Busing for the purpose of achieving racial balance not only does not produce superior education, it results in even more inferior education.

So what I was trying to do was to tackle the issue by saying we can and should have desegregation, but we should not compound the evil of a dual school system, of legal segregation, by using a remedy which makes it even worse.

That is why I have concluded that, first, a moratorium on busing for a year was the right move to make. I believe, incidentally, that the moratorium is constitutional. I believe it will be so held by the Supreme Court due to the fact that it deals with a remedy and not a right. That is the fundamental difference. Lawyers will disagree on that, but the Court will decide. I

think the Court will decide that the moratorium is constitutional.

That is why, also, I moved in another field. When we talk about education, we must remember that if we had busing at the maximum degree suggested by the most extreme proponents of busing, it would still leave the vast majority of black schoolchildren living in central cities, going to what are basically inferior schools, a lost generation, as I described it.

I decided that we could not allow that situation to continue without trying to move on it. How have we tried to move? We have tried to move through a program which has not yet been fully tested—I am not sure that it will work, but we have got to do something—and that is in the field of compensatory education, a program in which we, rather than doing it with a shotgun approach which has proved ineffective, that we use the "critical mass" approach, $300 as has been described per pupil, for the purpose of improving education in those schools where no plan for desegregation that anybody has suggested will ever affect. We cannot leave those people, those students, there without having some action and some attention paid to them.

One other thought with regard to this whole matter of compensatory education. I noted on one of the networks, not yours, but NBC's, a very thoughtful series to the effect that compensatory education is a failure. We looked into that. As a matter of fact, on the basis in which it has been used up to this point of a shotgun approach where you have $100, $150, $200 a student, it has not worked.

You have an example in the District of Columbia where over $300 has not helped. But on the other hand, in California and in four other States which came to our attention, we have found that there is substantial evidence to indicate that if we can get $300 a student or more into those schools, it will raise the level of education in those areas. That is why we are going down this road.

Another point I should cover, incidentally, since this subject has been raised, is the matter of new money. Let me say there is certainly a great deal of new money in this program. First, you must remember that the Congress has not yet passed and has not yet sent to my desk a request for a billion dollars in emergency school aid funds that I have asked for; that billion dollars will go into this program.

Second, we have asked not only that that billion dollars come here, but that the program be 4 years, rather than simply one year, because our proposal, as you know, was simply a one-shot proposal for a billion and a half. So that means that you have $2½ billion in new money.

I would say in conclusion, I would like to be able to assure everybody here that this program of compensatory education, concentrating money in some of these areas on students who will never be helped by any program of busing at all, no matter how extreme, I would like to say that it will succeed. I am not sure, but I do know that we cannot go on with the present situation where we leave them there growing up in inferior schools with no chance for hope.

I know Mr. Shultz believes—and others, experts that I have talked to—this "critical mass" approach will get at the problem. I just want to say, however, that as far as desegregation is concerned, this Administration has made great progress in desegregation. There are more black students that go to majority white schools in the South than in the North at the present time. The dual school system has been virtually eliminated.

What we were trying to get at is the problem of busing, busing which is a bad means because it compounds the evil which *Brown* v. *the Board of Education* was trying to get at. Also it poisons relations between the races, its creates racism, and it was time for somebody to move on it in what I thought was a responsible way.

MR. FLANIGAN

[7.] Q. To go back to the ITT case for a moment, since you have said that you see nothing improper in Mr. Flanigan's activities in the various cases that you mentioned, will you permit him to testify before the Senate Judiciary Committee if he is invited to do so?

THE PRESIDENT. Mr. Ziegler answered that question, I will not respond further.

PRE-CONVENTION POLITICAL ACTIVITIES

[8.] Q. Would you care to comment on the primaries and do you expect Congressman Ashbrook to go right down to the wire to the convention and go for the nomination?

THE PRESIDENT. I realize that a lot of you have political questions. You may remember, as, I think, the first president of the Press Club that I ever introduced at one of your meetings many, many years ago, that I stated several months ago that in Presidential press conferences I would not answer questions on partisan political matters until after the Republican Convention. That includes the Republicans. That includes the Democrats. That includes those who may leave the Republicans or leave the Democrats.

Q. And it is still your intention, Mr. President, not to campaign until after convention time?

THE PRESIDENT. It is. As a matter of fact, I will not be making any political speeches—well, you may call them political—but I will not be appearing, Mr. Warren [Lucian C. Warren, Buffalo Evening News], before any partisan political groups, making partisan political speeches, and I am not going to answer any partisan political questions one way or another in any Presidential conference or in any other forum of this kind.

Between now and the Republican Convention, I shall continue to meet the responsibility of President of the United States and I will answer all questions in that area. I will not answer political questions. I will have plenty of time to answer them after the Republican Convention.

MILITARY SITUATION IN SOUTHEAST ASIA

[9.] Q. Mr. President, how do you assess the military situation in Vietnam and Laos and Cambodia, and will you be able to follow your schedule for withdrawal of troops and perhaps tell us something more of it?

THE PRESIDENT. I will not tell you more about the withdrawal at this time because, as you know, we make these announcements at the time that they are scheduled and on the basis of the situation as it exists then. Another announcement will be made before the 1st of May.

Second, with regard to our program for withdrawal, it has gone well, as you know. The casualties again were low this week—still not zero, which is our goal, but, too, it is better than 200 or 300, which is what it was when we came in. As far as the mil-

itary situation is concerned, an ominous enemy buildup continues. The press has very well reported the threats to the Laotian base of Long Tieng. There have been some sporadic mortar attacks in Cambodia and there has been a considerable amount of action in South Vietnam. On the other hand, I have gotten a report from General Abrams just a few days ago. He says that they still expect—he doesn't guarantee it—but he says they are still prepared for some attacks in this dry season. They have not come yet. He says if they do come he is confident that the South Vietnamese will be able to contain them. He is also confident that while the South Vietnamese lines, in the event the attacks are heavy, may bend, that they will not break. If this proves to be the case it will be the final proof that Vietnamization has succeeded.

SAN DIEGO INVESTIGATION

[10.] Q. Mr. President, have you satisfied yourself, sir, that the Justice Department acted properly in quashing an investigation of campaign contributions to San Diego last year?

THE PRESIDENT. I have covered that question already.

INTEGRATION

[11.] Q. Mr. President, you spoke in terms of busing a minute ago and that the patterns of living are the root cause of it. Have you then thought of some kind of new programs to try to break up the patterns that keep the blacks in the inner city, to try to get at integration in that way?

THE PRESIDENT. It is very difficult to find any new programs because so many have been suggested and I imagine there are not any that could be classified as new. The breaking up of these patterns is something that probably is going to occur over a period of time as economic considerations and educational considerations come more into play. I am confident of this: That we cannot put—as I said, not in my statement on busing a few days ago but in my original statement on the whole educational process of last year—we cannot put the primary burden for breaking up these patterns on the educational system.

The purpose of education is to educate. Whenever a device is used to desegregate which results in inferior education, we are doing a grave disservice to the blacks who are supposed to be helped.

WORLD POWERS

[12.] Q. Mr. President, is it a pragmatic observation that the world now is divided into three parts: the United States, China, and the Soviet Union?

THE PRESIDENT. Some would perhaps describe the world that way, but I think the world is much bigger and much more complicated. I don't think that you can rule out by such a simplistic observation the future of Latin America, the potential in Africa, the potential in South Asia and the rimland of Asia, the future of Japan, which is an economic giant even though it is a mini-military power.

At the present time, it could be said that the United States and the Soviet Union are the two major super powers from a military standpoint, that the People's Republic of China is the most populous nation in the world with the potential of becoming a super power, and therefore anyone who is interested in trying to build a structure of peace must deal with the relationships between these three great power centers now.

I think that is the key to the future. But we must also, at the same time, have policies that look to the future of Japan, the future of Western Europe, because it will play a major role, and, of course, the future of Latin America and Africa.

FIDEL CASTRO

[13.] Q. Mr. President, sir, you have sort of a pattern of making peace with enemies around the world. Are you next going to see Fidel Castro?

THE PRESIDENT. No. I have not been invited.

MARIHUANA REPORT

[14.] Q. Mr. President, do you have a comment, sir, on the recommendation of your commission on drugs that the use of marihuana in the home be no longer considered a crime?

THE PRESIDENT. I met with Mr. Shafer. I have read the report.[6] It is a report which deserves consideration and it will receive it. However, as to one aspect of the report, I am in disagreement. I was before I read it, and reading it did not change my mind. I oppose the legalization of marihuana and that includes its sale, its possession, and its use. I do not believe that you can have effective criminal justice based on a philosophy that something is half legal and half illegal. That is my position, despite what the Commission has recommended.

---

[6] On March 21, 1972, former Governor Raymond P. Shafer, Chairman, Commission on Marihuana and Drug Abuse, met with the President at the White House to present the Commission's first report.

AGENDA FOR CANADIAN VISIT

[15.]   Q. Mr. President, on your trip to Canada, do you intend to try to do something about getting us in a better trade position and, also, do you intend to take up the matter of cleaning up the Great Lakes?

THE PRESIDENT. We are working out the agenda for our Canadian trip at the present time. I would have to say quite candidly that we have had very little success to date in our negotiations with our Canadian friends, which shows, incidentally, that sometimes you have more problems negotiating with your friends than with your adversaries. But that is as it should be. They have a right to their position; we have a right to ours. But we will discuss certainly trade, and we will discuss the Great Lakes and the environment. I am sure we will also discuss the world situation in which Prime Minister Trudeau has some, based on my previous visits with him, some very constructive ideas to suggest.

In addition, on my trip to Canada, I will, of course, brief Prime Minister Trudeau personally on the results of my visit to China and also brief him, prior to my going to the Soviet Union, on my visit to the Soviet Union.

I think it is a very helpful thing that at this point we are meeting with our friends from Canada, although we will find that we have some very basic disagreements, probably, after the meeting as well as before.

THE CHINA TRIP AND VIETNAM

[16.]   Q. Mr. President, when you went to China there were a lot of people in this country who sincerely hoped that your trip would be helpful in terms of settling the Vietnam war in some fashion or another. Did you find that trip helpful in that respect and, if so, can you tell us how?

THE PRESIDENT. At the time that we went to China, I indicated that the purpose of that trip was to discuss relations between the two countries, and that its purpose was not to discuss the situation with regard to other nations.

As far as the discussions that did take place, the agenda did include the whole range of problems in the world in which the People's Republic of China is interested, as we are interested.

As far as Vietnam is concerned, I don't think it would be helpful to indicate what was discussed, what was not discussed. Only time will tell what is going to happen there.

AMBASSADOR ARTHUR K. WATSON

[17.]   Q. Mr. President, there has been some question raised about Ambassador Watson's qualifications to negotiate with the Chinese in Paris.[7] Do you still have confidence in his ability to negotiate exchange agreements with the Chinese?

THE PRESIDENT. Mr. Lisagor [Peter Lisagor, Chicago Daily News], the best test of that—and I should know—is how the negotiations are going. They are going very well. Mr. Watson is conducting them with great competence and, I understand, total sobriety.

I realize that there are those who raise

---

[7] On March 10, 1972, the White House announced that the primary channel for further communication between the United States and the People's Republic of China would be the Ambassadors of the two countries in Paris. Arthur K. Watson was the United States Ambassador to France.

questions about the personal conduct of an Ambassador when he travels to his post. I see that some Members of the House and Senate are raising such questions about that. I would say that people in glass houses shouldn't throw stones. [*Laughter*]

GEORGE MEANY

[18.] Q. Do you plan to have any more breakfasts with George Meany, or do you consider that a political question?

THE PRESIDENT. Not at $30 a dozen for eggs.

Seriously, Paul Healy [New York Daily News], I do want to say that I respect Mr. Meany not only as a powerful labor union leader but as a patriotic American who, at a time that many of his weak-spined business colleagues were ready to throw in the sponge with regard to the security of the United States and what was best for this country in dealing with its adversaries abroad, stood firm.

On the other hand, in this particular area, I think Mr. Meany, I respectfully say, has overstepped. In the latter part of the 19th century this country determined that no business leader could take the attitude of "The public be damned." And in the latter part of the 20th century that applies to both business leaders and labor leaders.

Mr. Meany, in his case, I am sure, thinks he is acting in the best interest of his members, but I would respectfully suggest that I believe that a great number of his members, possibly a majority, realize that the wage increases that are eaten up by price increases are no wage increases at all. They will also remember, as they look at their income, that in the past 6 months since Phase 2 began we have had an increase in real wages, something that we have not had for 5 years before that time in any significant degree, and while we have had this one month of bad figures—and believe me, I am not satisfied with bad figures; I want these food prices down—nevertheless, our wage-price controls are working. We are going to reach our goal, in my opinion, or are going to come very close to it, cutting the rate of inflation in half.

Even though Mr. Meany is not with us, I think what we do will be in the best interest of his members, and I hope in the end that maybe he will invite me to breakfast.

VICE PRESIDENT AGNEW

[19.] Q. With respect to Mr. Agnew, do you still not feel like breaking up the winning combination?

THE PRESIDENT. I covered that question in a rather lengthy discussion with Mr. Rather [Dan Rather, CBS News], sitting right in this room, a few months ago.[8] My views are the same now as they were then.

THE MOSCOW TRIP AND SALT

[20.] Q. Mr. President, I would like to ask one question on the forthcoming Moscow trip, even though it is down the road. Are you still hopeful of having a strategic arms limitation agreement not only to discuss, but hopefully to sign?

THE PRESIDENT. Mr. Semple [Robert B. Semple, Jr., New York Times], I realize that there are many of you here, I hope, who will be able to go on that trip, who went to the P.R.C., and many who did not go to the P.R.C. can also go.

---

[8] See Item 1.

The Moscow trip, at the present time, will be very different from the P.R.C. trip in the sense that it will be primarily devoted to a number of substantive issues of very great importance. One of them may be SALT, if SALT is not completed before Moscow. It does not appear now likely that they can complete SALT before Moscow, because in my conversations with Ambassador [Gerard C.] Smith before he left, I find that while we are agreed in principle on the limitation of offensive and defensive weapons, that we are still very far apart on some fundamental issues—well, for example, whether or not SLBM's [submarine launched ballistic missiles] should be included, matters of that sort.

Mr. Smith went back to the meetings,

this time in Helsinki, with very full instructions from me, both written and oral, to do everything that he could to attempt to narrow those differences. I believe there is a good chance at this point, particularly in view of Mr. Brezhnev's quite constructive remarks in his speech the other day, that we may reach an agreement on SALT in Moscow on defensive and offensive limitations, and also agreements in a number of other areas.

This is our goal, and I would say that at this time the prospects for the success of this summit trip are very good.

NORMAN KEMPSTER (United Press International). Thank you, Mr. President.

NOTE: President Nixon's twenty-third news conference was held at 3:03 p.m. in the Oval Office at the White House on Friday, March 24, 1972. He spoke without referring to notes.

104 Statement About Signing a Bill Creating the Oregon Dunes National Recreation Area. *March* 24, 1972

I HAVE signed S. 1977, which creates a 32,000-acre Oregon Dunes National Recreation Area within the Siuslaw National Forest in Oregon.

The Oregon Dunes are one of the largest areas of active coastal dunes in the world. Sand from the natural erosion of extensive sandstone formations in the coast range to the east is carried by rivers and streams to the sea, where coastal currents distribute it along about 40 miles of beach. Prevailing westerly winds blow the sand inland where it is formed into shifting dunes as high as 300 feet through the interaction of wind, precipitation, and vegetation.

The Dunes are as beautiful as they are unique—a mix of desolate whiteness with

sparkling blue lakes and bright green foliage.

Now this beauty may be preserved for all Americans for years to come. Since they are located just a few hours drive from the major population centers of the Northwest, the Dunes will truly be a preserve of the people.

This legislation adds another page to the long story of wise use and conservation of the Oregon Dunes as it provides a careful blending of Federal, State, and private responsibilities for the public benefit. The Agriculture Department's Forest Service and the State of Oregon will work closely to manage the areas they control in a way that will benefit the greatest number. Private individuals may continue to own portions of the area so long as they, too, promote the purposes of conservation. The creative and coordinated land use made possible by this legislation will provide a good foundation for the coordinated and careful use of key environmental areas envisioned by the proposed national land use policy act.

NOTE: As enacted, S. 1977, approved March 23, 1972, is Public Law 92–260 (86 Stat. 99).

105   Statement About Signing the Equal Employment Opportunity Act of 1972.   *March* 25, 1972

I AM gratified to have signed into law H.R. 1746, the Equal Employment Opportunity Act of 1972.

By strengthening and expanding the Government's powers against discrimination in employment, this legislation is an important step toward true equality on the job front. Where promises have sometimes failed, we may now expect results.

This bill is the result of hard work and constructive debate in both branches of Congress by Members of both parties. It is an act of Congressional collaboration in the best tradition.

Under this legislation, the Equal Employment Opportunity Commission and the Justice Department will now be able to make substantial advances against employment discrimination.

The most significant aspect of this legislation is a new authority consistently advocated by this Administration since 1969—a provision arming the Equal Employment Opportunity Commission with power to bring lawsuits in the Federal district courts to enforce the rights guaranteed by title VII of the Civil Rights Act of 1964. Such actions are to be expedited by the courts whenever possible.

Everyone familiar with the operation of title VII over the past 7 years has realized that the promise of that historic legislation would remain unfulfilled until some additional, broad-based enforcement machinery was created. This bill provides that enforcement capability.

Additionally, the legislation extends the protections of title VII to millions of American citizens previously excluded from its coverage. The experiences of both the Justice Department and the EEOC under title VII have demonstrated that considerable discrimination problems have existed in State and local governments, with small employers, and in some educational institutions. Individuals employed in these areas have not heretofore been protected by title VII. This bill corrects that defect.

Also created by this legislation is the Equal Employment Opportunity Coordinating Council, a new interagency group which will coordinate, monitor, and report on the Government's enforcement drive against all remaining job discrimination.

This will support our determination to take continuing care that we are making the most effective efforts to bring about equal opportunity for all in the crucial area of employment rights.

One of the basic principles of our way of life in America has always been that individuals would be free to pursue the work of their own choice, and to advance in that work, subject only to considerations of their individual qualifications, talents, and energies.

This bill, addressing specific needs in concrete and practical ways, is bound to make a real difference in the lives of great numbers of minority Americans. It thus is another step toward writing our best principles into the day-to-day realities of our economic system.

NOTE: As enacted, H.R. 1746, approved March 24, 1972, is Public Law 92–261 (86 Stat. 103).

106   Special Message to the Congress on Welfare Reform. *March* 27, 1972

To the Congress of the United States:

The American welfare system is a national disgrace.

Thirty-one months ago, I first proposed to the Congress my plan for total reform of that system.

Since that time, the welfare situation has continued to worsen, and sweeping changes have become even more imperative.

There can be absolutely no excuse for delaying those changes any further. The present system must be reformed.

Its shocking inequities continue to drain incentive from the many poor who work but who see some families making as much or more on welfare.

Its widely varying, discriminatory benefits continue to force needy families, millions of children, and the needy aged, blind and disabled into a web of inefficient rules and economic contradictions.

Its vast costs have continued to escalate, undermining State and local governments and threatening to erode taxpayer support for a welfare system of any kind.

The present system continues to contribute to the breakup of poor families, rather than reenforcing the role of the family in our national life. The welfare life-style continues to dehumanize those who are caught in it, and threatens now to create yet another "welfare generation."

Now Is the Time for Action

This year must be the year in which we raze the ramshackle welfare system, patched up so many times in the past but still basically unchanged since it was first enacted as emergency legislation in the mid-1930s. In its place, we must build a new system, taking a new direction. We must create an environment that will draw forth and support—rather than smother—the innate ambitions and personal obligations of all needy Americans.

Last December, the Congress did pass transitional legislation which took parts of my welfare reform package—certain of the workfare provisions for job training and work requirements for all employable welfare recipients—and applied them to the present system of welfare. These actions will become effective later this year.

Acceptance of those workfare provisions by the Congress was a step in the right direction, as I said when I signed the measure. But it is still part of the patchwork approach. Now something far better than a patchwork approach is required if the needy are to receive rational assistance, if waste and inefficiency are to be abolished, and if America's work in-centive-job reward system is to be placed within reach of every citizen.

We should never forget that it is pre-cisely this system that has enabled us to develop the highest standard of living—with the most widely shared advantages—in the history of the world. We should continue to rely on it as we drive to close the final gaps between economic promise and economic reality.

On June 22 of last year the House of Representatives, for the second time, passed by a wide majority omnibus legis-lation which would implement my overall welfare reform. This legislation is now being closely scrutinized by the Senate Finance Committee, whose able Chair-man, Senator Long, has assured me that the committee will report H.R. 1 to the Senate floor as soon as possible. H.R. 1 continues to have my full support, and I hope that it will be enacted into law this year in the basic form approved by the House of Representatives.

We need reform this year so that, in-stead of pouring billions more into a sys-tem universally recognized as a failure, we can make a new start.

We must not forget that H.R. 1 contains basic reforms in social security and medi-cal benefits, as well as welfare reform.

These benefits, by themselves, are path-breaking in scope and impact—including a further 5 percent benefit increase in social security, the automatic adjustment of so-cial security benefits in the future to make them inflation proof, and a host of addi-tional reforms discussed in my recent mes-sage to the Congress on older Americans. As I said in that message, even one more year of delay in the passage of H.R. 1 would cost older Americans some $5½ billion in annual benefits.

H.R. 1 clearly lies at the heart of eco-nomic progress of millions of Americans in 1972—and into the future. It is the most important single piece of social legis-lation to come before the Congress in several decades. I strongly urge the Con-gress to pass it as soon as possible this year. No legislation should have a higher priority.

THE WELFARE MESS WORSENS

When I first presented my welfare re-form proposal to the Congress on Au-gust 11, 1969, I declared that "America's welfare system is a failure that grows worse every day."

Nine hundred and fifty eight days have passed since that message and that com-ment. The welfare landscape today is a greater fiscal and ethical wasteland than ever:

—*Injustice and inequities are wide-spread:* There are glaring differences be-tween welfare benefits paid in various parts of the country—they can range from $60 a month to $326 a month for a woman with three children, depending on in which State she happens to live. More-over, too many Americans can get more money by going on welfare than by going to work. There is no real requirement that a recipient seek, much less accept, a job.

—*The basic immorality of the system still prevails:* In most States welfare still offers a man a bounty to desert his family.

—*Incentive continues to be penalized:* A man working hard for low wages can see neighboring families on welfare that are better off than his own family.

—*Millions of children suffer:* They are forced to live in degrading and deplorable conditions because the present system pre-cludes their families from any benefits.

—Waste continues unabated: State quality control surveys indicate that as many as one in 20 welfare recipients may actually be ineligible for benefits, and that inaccurate payments are being given to as many as one case in every four—a potential total annual waste of more than $500 million.

—Administration remains a quagmire of red tape: There are 1,152 separate State and local welfare jurisdictions, with separate eligibility determinations and administrative procedures—making program integrity a virtual impossibility.

What we have in short, is a crazy quilt of injustice and contradiction that has developed in bits and pieces over the years with little serious thought of basic reform. I believe that H.R. 1 is the best and most comprehensive answer yet devised to meet this challenge.

Fiscal Crisis: Washington and the States

The present welfare system is not only morally bankrupt—but is a significant factor in driving the States toward fiscal bankruptcy.

Since I first proposed reform in 1969, the costs of maintaining the present system have mounted at an alarming rate. Each day of delay means further costs—without any offsetting benefits. For example:

—Welfare costs have skyrocketed from $6.2 billion in 1969 to an estimated $9.4 billion in 1971, *a 51 percent increase in just two years.*

—The overall welfare caseload has risen from 9.6 million people in 1969 to 13.5 million today. It has been estimated that, if no changes are made, 17.3 million

people will be on welfare in 1974, *an 80 percent rise in just five years.*

What we have on our hands is nothing less than a social and political time bomb. And, in a development of concern to all of us, the patience and support of the American public for welfare programs has been slipping dangerously. Those who are truly needy are becoming scapegoats in the eyes of taxpayers understandably angered about waste and inconsistency.

What we are seeking is an end to the need for public support for people who are essentially employable, but have not been able to work for reasons beyond their control, just will not work, or will not even make themselves available for work-related training—and this is what H.R. 1 would cure.

We also need to establish a nationally uniform system of efficient aid for totally needy families and the old and infirm—and H.R. 1 would achieve that goal, too.

Outline of Reform

My program, as embodied in H.R. 1, would place a floor beneath the income of all American families not able to adequately support themselves. Its payments would vary, according to family size and resources, from a minimum of $1,600 to a maximum of $3,600. The basic benefit for a family of four with no other income would be $2,400.

Employable adult members of such families would have to register with the Department of Labor in its Opportunities for Families Program for manpower services, work training and employment availability before *any* benefits were paid to such persons. Exceptions would include mothers of children younger than 6, and mothers whose husbands were either working or registered for work.

Families without employable adult members would not be subject to registration requirements but would receive the same basic benefits under the Department of Health, Education, and Welfare's Family Assistance Program.

For the first time in our history, national wage supplements would be paid to the working poor on a proportionate sliding scale designed to spur, rather than kill, the incentive to start working and keep on earning.

Eligible persons would be able to keep the first $720 earned during the year without reduction in their supplements. As job income rose beyond that, supplements would be reduced by two-thirds of job income until a cut-off point were reached and the recipient had attained a degree of self-sufficiency.

A family of four thus could earn $720 and receive a benefit of $2,400—for a total income of $3,120. When such a family's earnings reached $3,600, it still would be eligible for a supplement of $480 for a total income of $4,080.

When such a family reached earnings of $4,320 it would move completely out of the Federal assistance program.

Under the terms of H.R. 1, the Opportunities for Families program, the Family Assistance Plan and programs for the needy, aged, blind and disabled would be totally financed by the Federal Government—thereby providing much-needed financial relief for the States, which now share welfare costs.

In several respects, the proposed payments to the working poor constitute the basic conceptual foundation of my new approach.

These payments would encourage those who are working to keep on working, rather than sliding into welfare dependency. And they would motivate welfare recipients to start work.

We must hit head-on the cruel fallacy that any income, no matter how low, is sufficient for an American family merely because that money comes from full-time work.

We must establish the more humane and relevant principle that the total income of each American family must reach a certain minimum standard.

Another foundation of my approach is the strong work requirement and the provisions which would help implement that requirement, including child care benefits, manpower services, job training and job locating, and a program of 200,000 transitional public service jobs.

Recipients, with very few exceptions, would have to register for training and accept jobs which were offered, or benefits would be terminated for that recipient.

An entirely separate new Federal program would be established for needy aged, blind and disabled individuals and couples. While no work requirements would be included, of course, those who could work would be provided with strong incentives for doing so.

The current State payments to such individuals and couples, varying widely across the Nation, would be replaced by a Federal benefit of $130 a month for an aged, blind, or disabled individual, rising to $150 in two steps. For a couple in these categories, $195 a month would be provided, rising to $200. Such benefits now can be as low as $70 a month for an individual and $97 a month for a couple.

In all, some $2 billion in new money

would go directly into the hands of the aged, blind and disabled in the first full year.

TIGHT ADMINISTRATION AND PROGRAM INTEGRITY

Those who receive welfare, while they are the most visible victims, are not the only ones who suffer because of the myriad confusions and contradictions of the present welfare mess. The taxpayers are victims as well, for they are paying for a program that not only fails to accomplish its objectives, but is virtually impossible to administer.

Welfare administration is woefully outmoded in this country, with its 1,152 separate State and local welfare jurisdictions. Although virtually all have the same basic programs—Aid to the Blind, Aid to the Disabled, Aid to the Aged, and Aid to Families with Dependent Children—each operates with its own eligibility determination and administrative methods.

In the administrative area, especially, there is nearly an incomprehensible variety of management philosophies, operating policies and methods, and personnel arrangements. Only 20 percent of these jurisdictions have automated management techniques.

Under such conditions, it is not surprising that there are major management problems which exacerbate the skyrocketing costs and add to the growing public concern about welfare. Moreover, because of currrent open end financing arrangements, States and localities have what amounts to a blank check on the Federal treasury for this activity.

Thousands of dedicated people are doing their best to operate this ponderous machinery. But this system has been patched and repaired too many times. The frustration of current State program managers has resulted in very substantial support among Governors and State welfare administrators for Federal administration of the benefit payments function.

In recent months we have documented the failings of the current system, including the absence of cross-checks of records in adjacent areas, inadequate verification of income and benefits from a variety of benefit programs, and rapid turnover of personnel.

While decentralized management is highly desirable in many fields and is indeed central to my philosophy of government, I believe that many of these problems in welfare administration can best be solved by using a national automated payments system, which would produce economies and considerably increase both equity of treatment and tightened administration.

Such a unified system—partially modeled on the Social Security system—would reduce errors and provide greater controls for fraud and duplicate payments.

H.R. 1 would require each recipient to have a social security number for identification to prevent duplicate benefits and to facilitate the receiving of recipient income information from such sources as the Social Security Administration, the Internal Revenue Service, the Veterans Administration, and other units.

National administration and standards would also ensure equitable treatment for individuals: they would no longer be subject to conflicting rules in different areas, to delays caused by back-ups, and to the confusing tangle of red tape.

Under such a system, States and counties would be freed to concentrate on social services to recipients, making use of their closer understanding of the needs of local residents.

AN INVESTMENT IN THE FUTURE

Because we want a *better* system—not just a new one—welfare reform will cost more in the early years and cover more needy people.

Against the increased initial costs of my proposals in H.R. 1, however, we must weigh the unknown future costs—both human and fiscal—if the present chaotic system, with its present soaring growth rates, is continued. The new system contained in H.R. 1 would be far less costly in the long run—both in terms of dollars and in terms of people.

Historians of the future no doubt will focus on America's 200th birthday—and the years leading up to that significant anniversary—as one important point for measuring the progress of our Republic.

They will find, of course, that over 200 years America's mastery of the industrial revolution, its bountiful economic system, its military might and its technological triumphs helped to make it preeminent in the family of nations.

They will rightfully highlight our moon landings, our deep space probes, our satellite communications, our electronic innovations, and our extraordinary gross national product.

Penetrating observers, however, will also ask other questions:

What did all of this mean to the average American?

What was the quality of the daily life and the basic spirit of all the American people in the 1970's?

How, in particular, did our great Nation provide for those citizens who—through no fault of their own—were unable from time to time to provide for themselves and their families?

I believe that the program contained in H.R. 1 will stand us in good stead when such historical evaluations are considered, for this is a program which has grown out of a fundamental concern for our least fortunate citizens.

The enactment of H.R. 1 would demonstrate both our concern for what is responsible and our concern for what is compassionate.

RICHARD NIXON

The White House,
   March 27, 1972.

NOTE: On the same day, the White House released a fact sheet and the transcript of a news briefing on the message. Participants in the news briefing were James D. Hodgson, Secretary of Labor; and Elliot L. Richardson, Secretary, and John G. Veneman, Under Secretary, Department of Health, Education, and Welfare.

107 Special Message to the Congress on Executive Reorganization. *March* 29, 1972

To the Congress of the United States:

The sand is running in the glass, and the hour is growing late, for enactment of a critically needed reform, one that merits the very best support which you as legis-

lators for 208 Americans, and I as their Chief Executive, are able to give it.

That reform is reorganization of the executive branch of the Federal Government—the most comprehensive and carefully planned such reorganization since the executive was first constituted in George Washington's administration 183 years ago. Its purpose is to make American government a more effective servant to, and a more responsive instrument of, the American people. Its method is to organize departments around the ends which public policy seeks, rather than (as too often in the past) around the means employed in seeking them.

The broad outlines of the reorganization proposals which I presented to the Congress just over a year ago are now well known. The seven domestic departments which sprang into being under pressure of necessity one at a time since 1849 would be viewed as a single system for the first time, and their functions regrouped accordingly. *The product would be four entirely new, goal-oriented departments concerned with our communities, our earth, our economy, and our potential as individuals—plus a revitalized fifth department concerned with keeping America in food and fiber.*

A Department of Community Development, a Department of Natural Resources, a Department of Economic Affairs, and a Department of Human Resources would be created to replace the present Departments of Interior, Commerce, Labor, Health, Education, and Welfare and Housing and Urban Development, and Transportation. And the Department of Agriculture—under our plans as I ordered them revised last fall—would be streamlined to increase its ability to serve the farmer and so to serve us all. Several independent Federal agencies would be drawn into the consolidation process as appropriate. Further management reforms would be instituted *within* the new departments, to provide author-

ity commensurate with responsibility at every level and to make form follow function intelligently.

ELECTING BETTER GOVERNMENT MACHINERY

I do not speak lightly or loosely in characterizing this measure as *critically needed.* To say that we must prepare government to perform satisfactorily in the years ahead is only another way of saying that we must provide for its very survival. *This Republic, soon to begin its third century, will surely grow old unless we take wise and decisive action to keep it young.* "Adapt or die"—the Darwinian choice is ours to make.

Hard evidence of this danger abounds—dismal statistics about the low effectiveness of Federal spending, case upon case of national problems stubbornly resisting national programs. "Most Americans today," as I put it in announcing these executive reorganization proposals in my 1971 State of the Union Message, and again in transmitting the detailed legislation for them, "are simply fed up with government at all levels."

For us here and now to make a strong beginning at making government work better for the ordinary citizen would hearten the Nation immensely; and it would do so honestly, by getting at the real roots of the fed-up feeling. Yet some may question whether this political year is a time when public men can afford to meet public frustrations head on. "Mollifying gestures, yes," they may say in effect, "but fundamental reform, no—at least not in 1972." Our reply should be that this is a most appropriate year to move ahead with reorganization.

For what is it, after all, that the people

506

want and deserve from the public processes of any year, an election year especially? More effective government. One way they seek to get it is by calling the officials who run the government to account at the polls, as is being done in 1972. Another way is by regulating the Federal purse strings through their elected representatives in the Congress, as is also being done in 1972. Yet this necessary periodic scrutiny of men and money alone will not reach the heart of the problem. For it is axiomatic among those who know Washington best that, as I pointed out in my earlier message on this subject, "the major cause of the ineffectiveness of government is not a matter of men or of money (but) principally a matter of machinery." We cannot, therefore, in good conscience hold out to the people the hope that this will be a year of change for the better, if we fail to come to grips with reform of government's jerry-built mechanisms.

Institutional structure here in Washington tends to coast along all too comfortably under the protection of an inertia which does not shield elected officials and public expenditures. These last come up for renewal every one, two, four, or six years; not so the structure, which endures with little or no burden of proof for its own worthiness to continue. Now, though, the structure has been weighed in the balances and found wanting.

In less sweeping reorganizations than the one I am urging, of course, a President can institute changes through plans submitted under the Reorganization Act, whereby the burden of proof rests with defenders of the status quo. However such authority no longer extends to the creation, consolidation, or abolition of executive departments. In any event we would

have felt it wise to submit so massive a reform as this one for regular statutory enactment, so as to permit consideration of amendments and to provide time for full hearings and review. *My hope now is that the Congress will honor the best spirit of democratic change by electing now, in this election year, to modernize the executive structure and redeem the flagging public faith in our ability to order our national affairs effectively.*

AN OPPORTUNITY WE MUST NOT LOSE

Considerations of practicality, equally with those of principle, make the present time the best time to move ahead on this reform. The efforts of the past several years have amassed significant momentum toward overcoming the inertia which protects obsolete institutions. My proposals of last March 25 have behind them the weight of two years' exhaustive study and analysis by my Advisory Council on Executive Organization, and behind that the substantially similar recommendations of President Johnson's Task Forces of 1964 and 1967 on Government Organization. Since I laid those proposals before the Congress, the Administration and the Government Operations Committees in both Houses have made further headway on perfecting the reform legislation. A spirit of cooperation has been established; good faith and constructive attitudes have been demonstrated on all sides. We must not let these gains go to waste.

The pace of progress so far has not been disappointing, for no measure this broad and this complex can or should be pushed through the Congress overnight. *What would be deeply disappointing, though—to me, and far more importantly to mil-*

lions of Americans who deserve better than their government is now organized to give them—is to lose, in this rapidly passing Second Session of the 92nd Congress, our opportunity to record some solid achievement by creating at the very least one, and hopefully two or more, of the four proposed new departments.

The men and women who begin a new Presidential term and a new Congress next January should not have to start over again on reorganization. They will not have to, if we push ahead now with the realism to see what is wrong with the old structures, the vision to see what benefits new forms can bring, and the courage to take the long step from old to new.

Obsolete Structure: How It Hurts

What is wrong, and what reorganization could do to set it right, is best illustrated with two actual examples. We cannot remind ourselves often enough that this matter of government organization is no mere shuffling of abstract blocks and lines on a wall chart—that it has to do with helping real people, building real communities, husbanding real resources.

The plethora of diverse and fragmented Federal activities aimed at assisting our communities is a glaring case in point. If there is any one social concept which has clearly come of age in recent years, that concept would certainly be the idea of balanced, comprehensively planned community development. Yet where do we find this reflected in government organization? We grope toward it, as with the well-intentioned and (at the time) fairly progressive formation of a

Department of Housing and Urban Development; but even that step was premised on an unrealistic, artificial, and harmful distinction between urban and rural communities. In altogether too many instances the dollars and efforts earmarked for communities end up producing more derangement than development.

This is hardly surprising when we consider that:

—A city or town may now seek Federal grants or loans for sewer or sewage treatment facilities from three departments and one independent agency, each with different criteria, different procedures, and a separate bureaucracy.

—Responsibilities for housing assistance are also entrusted to different offices in some of the same departments, and to several other entities as well.

—Highway and mass transit programs have been isolated in a separate department with only partial consideration for what such programs do to our communities, large and small, forcing us to learn the hard way that highways and mass transit must be developed integrally with land use decisions, housing plans, and provisions for other essential community facilities.

Efforts have been made to clarify agency roles on the basis of urban/rural, type of facility, type of applicant, et cetera—but the real need is for unified authority, not artificial jurisdictional clarifications. *In sum, it has become painfully clear that effective integration of all Federal activities relating to community development can be achieved only under a vigorous new Department of Community Development created expressly for that purpose.*

The conservation and development of our rivers offers another pointed example. This important trust, where stakes are high and mistakes irretrievable, has at present so many guardians in Washington that in the crunch it sometimes seems to have none at all. The Department of the Interior, the Department of Agriculture, and the U.S. Army Corps of Engineers, together with several independent agencies, are all empowered to plan river basin development, to build dams and impound water, and to control water use. Elaborate interagency coordination efforts and all good intentions have not prevented waste and error from thriving under this crippling fragmentation of responsibility. Such costly fiascos as the reservoir built by the Bureau of Reclamation for drinking water supply but severely polluted and depleted by conflicting Soil Conservation Service projects upstream have been repeated too frequently. *The answer? A unified Department of Natural Resources, where comprehensive authority to develop and manage water resources would be concentrated under a single departmental secretary.*

Additional examples of dispersed responsibility could be cited in such areas as consumer protection, manpower and job training programs, and economic development activities. In each case, obsolete departmental structures have made it difficult to move forward effectively.

Even the newest of our domestic departments, like Housing and Urban Development and Transportation, now see the challenges of the seventies and beyond outrunning their own relatively narrow mandates. Departmental missions long circumscribed by law or historical development are suddenly outgrown; departmental preoccupations with limited constituencies no longer serve the public interest as reliably as before. Too often the ability of one department to achieve an important goal proves dependent upon the authority and resources of other departments, departments which inevitably attach only secondary importance to that goal. The new Federal commitments undertaken year by year are increasingly difficult to locate in any one department—usually several can claim partial jurisdiction, but none can show full ability to follow through and get the job done.

DECENTRALIZATION AND ACCOUNTABILITY

The solution to this rapidly worsening snarl of problems is regrouping of related programs by major purpose in a smaller number of executive departments. Besides opening the way for sharp improvements in government performance, such a consolidation would make the executive branch more sensitive to national needs and more responsive to the will of the people, in two ways.

First, it would decentralize decision-making. Far too many matters must now be handled above the department level by the Executive Office of the President or within the White House itself—not because of the inherent importance of those matters, but because no single department or agency head has broad enough authority to make and enforce decisions on them. But the four new Secretaries created by my reorganization proposal would have such breadth of authority. Their resultant ability to conduct domestic policy on the President's behalf should speed, streamline, and strengthen the whole process significantly.

Comparable decentralization could also be achieved within each department. At present, too many questions can be decided only in Washington, because of the multiplicity of field organizations and the limited authority of their regional directors. By enlarging the scope of responsibility of the departmental Secretaries and by giving them the tools they need, we could facilitate broad delegation of authority to appropriate field officials. And this in turn means that citizens across the country would receive faster and better service from their Federal Government.

Secondly, the new alignment of domestic departments would enhance the accountability of Federal officials to the people. It is easy to see how the new Secretaries, each with his or her own broad area of responsibility to discharge, would be useful to the President and the Congress in monitoring compliance with direction and accomplishment of objectives. Once scattered responsibility was concentrated, today's frequently used and often quite accurate excuse, "It was the other fellow's fault," would no longer apply.

More importantly, though, whatever slack and tangle can be taken out of the lines of control *within* the Federal establishment will then result in a tightening of those same lines *between* elected Federal officials and a democratic electorate. Notwithstanding the famous sign on President Truman's desk—"The buck stops here"—there will be no stopping of the buck, no ultimate clarification of blame and credit, and no assurance that voters will get what they contracted for in electing Presidents, Senators, and Congressmen, until the present convoluted and compartmentalized Washington bureaucracy can be formed anew and harnessed more directly to the people's purposes.

COOPERATING FOR REFORM

Where, then, does the reform effort stand today? I am pleased to note that the Congress, acting through its Committees on Government Operations, has held extensive hearings on my proposals; that testimony, most of it favorable, has been taken from a broad, bipartisan array of expert witnesses; and that committee work on the House side is nearly complete on the bill to establish a Department of Community Development.

For our part, we in the Administration have continued working to perfect the legislation and the management concepts set forth in my message of March 25, 1971. The Office of Management and Budget has taken the lead in working with Members of the Congress, adopting a flexible and forthcoming approach which has led to refinements in our legislation: one to clarify responsibility for highway safety, another to remove doubts concerning the reform's impact on the Appalachian Regional Commission and the Title V regional planning and development commissions, another to guarantee Community Development participation in airport access and siting decisions, and several more. They have also clarified that the reorganization need not entail any shift in congressional committee jurisdiction.

I am confident that this refinement and

clarification process has improved our bills. *I pledge the fullest continuing cooperation of my Administration in seeing that the Congress has what it needs to move forward.*

COMMUNITY DEVELOPMENT AND NATURAL RESOURCES: ACHIEVABLE GOALS FOR 1972

There is still much work to do. For all the excellent hearings conducted to date, action has yet to be completed on any of the departmental bills which were sent to the Congress 370 days ago. Yet their passage by this Congress is still possible— especially for the Departments of Community Development and Natural Resources.

I would call special attention to H.R. 6962, the legislation for a Department of Community Development, which has now undergone 15 days of hearings in the House Government Operations Committee. Prompt, favorable action on this bill would represent a much-needed victory for common sense and the public good. Its defeat or emasculation would serve no interest except entrenched privilege and private advantage, and would cruelly disserve the interest of literally thousands of urban and rural communities with millions of people who are tired of waiting for Washington to get itself together and help them.

I urge all those concerned with the cause of executive reorganization to redouble their efforts to bring H.R. 6962 to my desk for signature during 1972—and, further, to press ahead on enactment of H.R. 6959, the Department of Natural Resources bill, and of legislation for the other two new departments which we need to govern effectively in the seventies.

ORGANIZING TO MEET THE CHALLENGES OF PEACE

Twenty-five years ago, when the United States was realizing that World War II had marked not the end, but only the beginning, of its leadership responsibilities in the world, a reorganization of the executive machinery in the defense area was undertaken. That reform, which created the Department of Defense, marks the only major streamlining of the Cabinet and the only departmental consolidation in our history. The new structure thus established has served America and the free world well in the challenging period since.

Now the time has come to take a similar bold and visionary step on the domestic side of national affairs. The 1960s, troubled, eventful, and full of progress as they were, were only the prelude to a period of still faster change in American life. The peace which we find increasing reason to hope will prevail during the coming generation is already permitting us to turn somewhat from the formerly absorbing necessity to "provide for the common defence," the necessity which motivated the last major executive branch reorganization.

Other great purposes now move to the foreground: "to form a more perfect Union, establish Justice, insure domestic Tranquility, . . . promote the general Welfare, and secure the Blessings of Liberty to ourselves and our Posterity." To serve these purposes, let us act decisively once again, and forge new institutions to serve a new America.

RICHARD NIXON

The White House,
  March 29, 1972.

NOTE: The President's message, together with additional information on executive reorganization, is printed in "Papers Relating to the President's Departmental Reorganization Program: A Reference Compilation; Revised February 1972" (Government Printing Office, 311 pp.).

On March 29, 1972, the White House released a fact sheet and the transcript of a news briefing on the message. Participants in the news briefing were George P. Shultz, Director, and Frank C. Carlucci, Associate Director, Office of Management and Budget.

108 Statement on Receiving the First Report of the National Commission on Fire Prevention and Control. *March 31, 1972*

NINE months ago a National Commission on Fire Prevention and Control began a 2-year study of ways to reduce the number of disasters caused by fire. Today I am pleased to have received the initial findings of this study from Chairman Richard Bland and other members of the Commission.

The Commission has impressed upon me once again how much we pay for fires through loss of life, needless pain and injury, and damage to property.

The sacrifice of human life is perhaps most startling, for we continue to suffer more deaths and injuries from fire than we did from polio even in its worst years. During 1971, over 12,000 Americans were killed in fires and more than 330,000 were crippled or injured. The 2.5 million fires of that year also caused nearly $3 billion in property damage.

Our main line of defense is now made up of more than one million firemen. To my great sorrow, firefighting ranks as one of the most hazardous occupations in America. Some 210 firemen were killed in fires last year. We are indeed grateful for the splendid and heroic efforts of these men, but their valor should no longer be a substitute for finding effective ways to pre-

vent fires and to protect firemen in the hazardous environment in which they must work.

In its preliminary report, the Commission has made it clear that in addition to controlling fires, we must place far greater emphasis on prevention. Many local fire departments, for instance, are experiencing success in this endeavor by making periodic inspections of buildings, wiring, heating, and cooking equipment.

During the next several months, the Commission will hold regional hearings across the country, visiting Dallas, Los Angeles, San Francisco, Chicago, and Washington, D.C. I am hopeful that these hearings will be a subject of serious concern in each community, for the Commission has made an excellent start, and I am sure it can help us to identify new and more effective ways to reduce the terrible costs of fires.

NOTE: Members of the Commission, headed by Chairman Richard E. Bland, met with the President at the White House to present and discuss the 10-page progress report.

On the same day, the White House released the transcript of a news briefing by Mr. Bland and W. Howard McClennan, Vice Chairman of the Commission, on the report.

109   Statement About Signing the Par Value
Modification Act. *April 3, 1972*

ON AUGUST 15, 1971, I launched a major effort to restore the strength of the American economy by clamping down on inflation at home and by moving to adjust the free world's monetary and trading systems to the realities of competition in the 1970's.

By that time, the international arrangements set in the post World War II years had become outmoded, leading to recurring international monetary crises and a chronic U.S. imbalance of payments.

The Smithsonian Agreement of December 18, 1971 [1]—in which we agreed to propose a change in the par value of the dollar to the Congress as part of a realignment in which other countries increased the values of their currencies—was a significant step forward in our overall effort for a stronger and more competitive U.S. economy.

That realignment makes American products more attractive in foreign markets and at home, expands export opportunities for American industrial and agricultural products, and creates more jobs for American workers in factories, and on farms and in export-supporting businesses.

The legislation I sign today, S. 3160, the Par Value Modification Act, is necessary for fulfillment of our part of that historic agreement—an agreement that is vital to the economic future of all Americans. I am gratified that this important legislation received overwhelming support in the Congress. It authorizes and directs a change in the par value of the dollar

from $35 to $38 per ounce of gold. The change will take effect upon notification to the International Monetary Fund by the Secretary of the Treasury.

The legislation also requires that steps be taken to fulfill our obligations to maintain the gold value of U.S. subscriptions to various international financial institutions such as the International Monetary Fund.

We will soon submit a request to the Congress for the appropriations necessary to enable us to meet this legislated obligation.

This dollar adjustment is a basic point of departure in working toward a new international economic stability. This action cannot—and does not—stand alone.

The strength and competitiveness of our economy also depends on our success in dealing with inflation at home. We are making progress in that struggle, with the rise in the Consumer Price Index in the 6 months ending in February declining to a 3.3 percent annual rate—down from the 4.1 percent rate of the preceding 6 months.

We pledge a strong continuation of the efforts, also launched last summer, to assure the American workman, farmer, and businessman fair access to foreign markets—an access which was limited in the 1960's when a resurgent Europe and Japan, along with a number of other nations, offered increasingly tough competition.

A measure of success has already been achieved in this key area with the conclusion of agreements of value with Japan and with the European Commu-

---

[1] See 1971 volume, Item 401.

nity. We look forward to more comprehensive negotiations this year and next.

The eventual results of all these efforts will be to restore a healthy trade surplus and a strong financial position for the United States. This will be not only in our own interest—but in the interest of a prosperous world economy, a stable monetary system, and an equitable trading order.

International discussions have now begun, leading toward the ultimate objective of a fundamental and overdue restructuring of the entire international monetary and trading system. Conditions have changed greatly since the Bretton Woods agreement of 1945, and we must adapt the system to meet those changes. The Smithsonian Agreement—in addition to achieving immediate currency realignments—recognized the need for long-range change, established a reform agenda, and provided for continuing discussions among the nations toward these longer term improvements.

The United States is committed to work with other nations to bring about necessary reforms. However, the long-range international economic issues we face are complex and affect fundamental interests. The ultimate reforms will take, and should take, time to work out. We seek no patchwork. We seek responsible arrangements that will withstand the test of time and which will be fully equal to the magnitude of the problems and opportunities presented.

This international economic reform is not a task that we can or should do alone—it is the mutual responsibility of the entire free world.

The basic significance of the Smithsonian Agreement, and the resulting dollar legislation which I sign today, is that it provides for continued cooperation among our allies and ourselves—and thus strengthens our unity—as we work toward an "open world" based on a more balanced monetary system and a more equitable international trading environment.

NOTE: As enacted, S. 3160, approved March 31, 1972, is Public Law 92-268 (86 Stat. 116).

On April 3, the White House released the transcript of a news briefing by Paul A. Volcker, Under Secretary of the Treasury for Monetary Affairs, on the provisions of the act.

110 Message to the Congress Transmitting Annual Report on Operation of the International Coffee Agreement. *April 4, 1972*

To the Congress of the United States:

I transmit herewith my report on the operations of the International Coffee Agreement during 1971.

Last year the International Coffee Agreement proved its continuing value as an instrument of international economic cooperation. The 62 members of the International Coffee Organization worked together effectively to stabilize world coffee trade.

This stability serves the interests of the United States in two important respects.

First, it benefits the American consumer by helping to prevent the recurrence of the extremely high coffee prices recorded in the years prior to the Agreement. In 1971, for example, the International Coffee Organization successfully dealt with the supply crisis of the previous year and served to bring down the price of our imported green coffee by eight cents per pound between January and December.

Secondly, the International Coffee Organization reduces the fluctuation in the foreign exchange earnings of coffee producers. It thereby supports the development efforts of over 40 nations in Latin America, Africa, and Asia and supports our own aid objectives.

The recent passage by the Congress of enabling legislation permits us to fulfill certain of our obligations under the Agreement. Approval of this important legislation constitutes an important reaffirmation of our determination to cooperate with the developing countries.

RICHARD NIXON

The White House,
    April 4, 1972.

NOTE: The report entitled "1971 Annual Report of the President to the Congress on the International Coffee Agreement" (15 pp. plus annexes) was published by the Department of State.

---

111   Letter Accepting the Resignation of John H. Chafee as Secretary of the Navy.   *April 4, 1972*

Dear John:

It is with special regret that I accept, as you have requested, your resignation as Secretary of the Navy, effective upon a date to be determined. In doing so, I want to express my deep gratitude for your superb service to the Navy and the country for the past three years.

From the first days of this Administration, you have brought to your challenging responsibilities a rare combination of managerial skill, sound judgment, and uncommon dedication, giving the men and women of our Navy and Marine Corps the wise leadership they so richly deserve.

As Secretary of the Navy, you have contributed enormously to our national security. I have especially valued your outstanding efforts in helping to carry out our Vietnamization policy, while simultaneously taking the needed steps to modernize our Fleet. The new, bold programs developed under your guidance hold great promise for the future of our naval forces.

You have every reason to take the fulest measure of satisfaction from the splendid work you have accomplished. On behalf of all your friends here in Washington—and your fellow citizens across the nation—I welcome this opportunity to say "Well Done!" and to extend warmest good wishes for your continued success in the years ahead.

Sincerely,

RICHARD NIXON

[Honorable John H. Chafee, Secretary of the Navy, Washington, D.C. 20350]

NOTE: A White House announcement of the President's intention to nominate John W. Warner as Secretary of the Navy was released on April 7, 1972, and is printed in the Weekly Compilation of Presidential Documents (vol. 8, p. 733).

Mr. Chafee's letter of resignation was released along with the President's letter and read as follows:

Dear Mr. President:

I submit herewith my resignation as Secretary of the Navy to be effective at your pleasure at the earliest practical date which would allow for an orderly turnover of the office. It has been a tremendous pleasure and privilege to serve in this position and as a member of your Administration. I am most grateful for the trust you have placed in me.

During my tenure as Secretary of the Navy, the Navy and the Marine Corps have been in transition as a result of our winding down the war in Vietnam and our preparation for the period beyond Vietnam. We are modernizing our forces and they are ready to meet the challenges of the future.

Under your leadership and that of Secretary of Defense Laird, we in the Department of the Navy have participated in the development and implementation of the Nixon doctrine and the national security strategy of realistic deterrence. I take great pride in having been a part of so vital an enterprise.

The nation is greatly in your debt for your untiring efforts to bring a generation of peace to the world and to promote domestic tranquility. The Navy and Marine Corps appreciate your support and have benefitted from your compassion and interest in the individual Sailor and Marine.

With deep appreciation for the opportunity you have given me to be of service to our country, I wish to you and Mrs. Nixon continued good health and happiness in the coming years.

Respectfully yours,

JOHN H. CHAFEE

[The President, The White House, Washington, D.C. 20500]

112 Statement About the Death of Buford Ellington. *April 4, 1972*

MRS. NIXON and I join in mourning the death of Buford Ellington.

As Governor of Tennessee for two terms, he helped to improve the quality of life in rural areas of his State and promoted economic development throughout the region, and as Director of the Office of Emergency Planning under President Johnson, he made a significant contribution to the entire Nation.

Buford Ellington will be remembered as a fair and independent man who served his State and Nation well when they were in need of his service.

NOTE: Mr. Ellington, 64, died of a heart attack in Boca Raton, Fla., on April 3, 1972. He was Governor of Tennessee from 1959 to 1963 and from 1967 to 1971. He was Director of the Office of Emergency Planning from 1965 to 1966.

The statement was posted for the press.

113 Remarks at the Annual Convention of the National Catholic Education Association in Philadelphia, Pennsylvania. *April 6, 1972*

Your Eminence Cardinal Krol, Mayor Rizzo, all of the distinguished guests on the platform, and all of the distinguished attendees at this National Catholic Education Association conference:

I am most grateful for the very warm reception that you have provided, a reception which I realize is not for just the man

but more for the office that I represent. And I am most grateful to His Eminence Cardinal Krol, for his very generous remarks.

In turn, I can say that we have been proud that he has come to the White House to participate in one of our Sunday worship services; in addition to that,

that we have talked about other things than simply the problems of nonpublic school education and its support. I value him as one who is, in my view, a great religious leader, but also one who has a deep understanding of philosophy and of government.

I often think, after talking to him about philosophy and government, and what makes the great nations of the world go and what makes them fail, that when he chose to go into the priesthood and, of course, has become one of the princes of the church, what might have happened had he chosen a political career. He probably could have gone all the way.

Now, speaking of politics, of course, I want to say a word about my good personal friend, Mayor Rizzo. My appearance here, of course, is a nonpolitical appearance, and his presence on the platform clearly indicates that, because while he is a personal friend, the Mayor is a member of a party to which I do not happen to belong. But I do know this: That when the security of America is involved, when great principles that transcend any partisan differences are involved, he is a very great American, and that is what really counts. And also, I should add that he is rather unique in his party. He is one of the few prominent members in his party who is not a candidate for President.

I also understand, since reference has been made to the fact that school is to be out tomorrow, I hope the parents will not blame me—they are old enough to vote. And as far as the children are concerned, I understand most of them are not yet 18, so there is nothing political about letting them out of school tomorrow.

Let me begin my remarks by telling you that it is a very great privilege for me to be here in Philadelphia, in this great convention hall, and to speak before this group, because you are a group of Americans who truly hold the future of our country in your hands—you are the educators of the United States.

We meet today in a testing time for American education. We can look back over the last generation and we see that public funding for public education has never been higher in America. And yet, ironically, across the Nation we can also see serious evidence of lack of confidence in our educational systems.

Traditional means of financing public education are destined for fundamental change. Look at some of the indications of the problems that public education faces across the country. Local property taxes, which have long been the mainstay of the public school system, have become an increasingly intolerable burden against which millions of homeowners have begun to rebel, and that has shown itself in local school bond issues being rejected in significant numbers all over the country.

Inner city schools seem less and less capable of providing education for the poor and for the racial minorities who more and more make up their enrollment.

I recognize, as we consider these problems, that among educators, among those here as well as among our people of good will across the Nation, there is an honest difference of opinion with regard to the problem that has been much discussed in recent months: The use of busing to achieve racial balance in our schools. As one who is completely committed, as I know everyone in this audience is, both to school desegregation and to quality education, I would like to state my views on this issue directly and candidly, because it relates, as you will see, to the problem you have of the role of the nonpublic schools.

We have found that where we have heavy reliance on cross-city busing of schoolchildren, it has failed to meet either of its intended purposes—it has failed to promote quality education for all, it has failed to end the racial isolation which we all agree must be ended. Instead, what it has done in community after community, is disrupt and divide increasing numbers of schools and communities.

Now, let us go to the heart of the problem. Even the strongest proponents of busing recognize this fact: It would be physically impossible to transport pupils on a scale large enough to solve the most pressing problem of all, and here it is— for even the most massive busing imaginable would still leave the vast majority of black and poor children in the inferior schools of the inner city; they would not be affected, and there they would be. They would be a lost generation, deprived of the educational opportunity to which they, like all Americans, are entitled.

It is for these reasons that I have asked the Congress, 3 weeks ago, to declare a temporary national moratorium on new busing decrees, and then to enact new legislation to accomplish these things:

—One, to establish in the law of the land, for the first time, the right of every American child to equal educational opportunity more clearly and strongly than it has ever been established before.

—Two, to curb excessive busing by putting its usefulness into perspective with other more workable school desegregation remedies.

—And three, to redirect billions of dollars in effective aid into the inferior schools of this Nation, many in our central cities where such aid is so urgently needed.

The Equal Educational Opportunities Act of 1972, which we have proposed to accomplish these ends, I would not contend is the final answer to quality education for all Americans, but we believe—I believe—it points in the right direction.

You, in this audience, know all too well how limited our public and private funds for education are. That is why I believe it makes compelling sense to use those limited funds to provide better education for all of our children, rather than more transportation for just some of our children.

As we consider all of our children, let me describe the heart of this new legislation. Under the act, the old piecemeal approach to compensatory education would be replaced by a new concentration of resources which experts call the "critical mass" approach. Instead of, in effect, using the shotgun, in which not enough is given to the various areas that need it, we use the approach of the rifle, a "critical mass" approach.

Under title I, from which many of your schools already benefit, about $200 per pupil is now being applied to disadvantaged areas. Our new legislation would increase this average by over 50 percent— on the basis of encouraging experimental evidence that assistance in excess of $300 per pupil constitutes the "critical mass"— the very minimum—which begins to produce the results that smaller amounts have failed to achieve.

Now the question comes: Can I guarantee this new approach will work? If $200 didn't work, will $300 or $350 work in breaking that barrier in producing better education? We can't be sure. But the evidence in our judgment is strong enough to indicate that we ought to try it. What we are sure of is that the old ways have failed and, therefore, we must move to a new way.

Therefore, today, in this effort to redeem the promise of public education, I come to ask you, as educators, to give us your support for this purpose. I have also come for another reason, a reason alluded to by His Eminence in his introduction: If public education in America faces a severe testing time, as it does, nonpublic education confronts what can only be described as a crisis of the first magnitude.

You are familiar with the basic statistics, but let the Nation now hear what this crisis is, because this is the problem not just of those involved here but of the whole Nation. Taken together, the nonpublic schools in this country educate 5,200,000 children. That is more than the public school system of the whole State of California. That is more than the public school system of the whole State of New York. Eighty-three percent of those children are in Catholic schools.

But while that is a very significant number, 5,200,000, as you all know, the rise in nonpublic school enrollment has crested. In the past 9 years, the Catholic schools alone have lost almost a million pupils. Every day—and this is something that His Eminence Cardinal Krol, told me—every day at least one, and sometimes two, of our parochial schools are forced to close their doors forever.

It would be misleading to suggest that Catholic education and nonpublic schools in general are about to disappear altogether because of that fact. But at the same time, it would be irresponsible to pretend that all is well, because it is not. So let me, therefore, outline hypo-thetically, not just for this audience but for the whole Nation, the consequences of a total collapse of nonpublic education, since this is perhaps the best way of emphasizing the stake that every American has in preventing any such collapse from taking place.

Let us begin: The disappearance of all nonpublic schools in this country would saddle the American taxpayer with an additional $3 billion annually in school operating costs, plus as much as $10 billion in new school construction. Seventy percent of that burden would fall upon seven States: California, New York, Illinois, Ohio, New Jersey, Michigan, and Pennsylvania.

And the impact would fall most heavily upon our central cities, where in some cases as many as one-third of all children attend nonpublic schools, and where many public school systems are on the verge of bankruptcy today.

Here in Philadelphia, for example, collapse of the nonpublic schools would force 146,000 students into the public schools; in Chicago the figure would be over 200,000; in New York City over 300,000. In short, if the nonpublic schools were ever permitted to go under in the major cities of America, many public schools might very well go under with them, because they simply couldn't undertake the burden.

I have been speaking of what it would cost in terms of money. The fiscal catastrophe, however, would be far from the only consequence. For many Americans, allegiance to their nonpublic community schools is their strongest and sometimes, perhaps, their only single tie to city life. If their schools should close, many of these families would abandon the city and go to the suburbs. This, in turn, would further worsen the racial isolation of our central cities—a development we must not permit.

At a time when many other urban institutions have been crumbling or leaving the city, Catholic education has courageously stood its ground, continuing the effort to maintain good schools in these poor and racially isolated communities which need them most.

Let me quote from your NCEA charter. It outlines an educational philosophy which ". . . upholds and encourages a strong and special effort to bring the benefits of good education to all minority groups . . . to all without regard to economic status. . . ."

That is what we need in our central cities today. As we look at that philosophy, it has been borne out in the fine examples set by hundreds of schools, your schools, in urban centers across the country. These are schools that now constitute beacons of hope in many neighborhoods where hope is pretty hard to come by. That is one reason why I believe that the future of nonpublic education cannot be divorced from the future of the American city.

So that is one of the reasons I wanted to come here today—to salute you for the service to your country, to reaffirm the commitment I made last August when I said to the Knights of Columbus meeting in New York City, in your fight to save your schools, "You can count on my support."

Now, let me just spend a moment analyzing the problem. Why are the nonpublic schools closing? There have been many articles written, many speeches made. Many of you are more expert in this than I am, but we have been studying the problem.

There are shifting population patterns, changing attitudes and values, steeply rising operating costs forcing higher tuitions. All of these things seem to contribute. To understand this trend, and then to stop it, we need scientific data, we need professional studies, something that has been seriously lacking in the past.

But we finally have begun to assemble the basic tools for intelligent action. Let me tell you some of the things we have done. The President's Commission on School Finance, which I appointed in 1970, has recently made public its findings and recommendations after 2 years of pioneering investigations in this field.[1] My special panel on nonpublic education, chaired by Dr. Walton of Catholic University, will be submitting its report in about 2 weeks.[2] I intend to give the reports of both these groups the full and serious consideration and action that they deserve.

I have already requested that certain proposals and alternatives relating to the findings of the Commission on School Finance, as well as to the urgent need for property tax reform, be studied by the Advisory Commission on Intergovernmental Relations. Now this is a committee

---

[1] On March 6, 1972, members of the President's Commission on School Finance met with the President to present the Commission's final report. On the same day, the White House released the transcript of a news briefing on the report by Neil H. McElroy, Chairman, and Norman Karsh, Executive Director, of the Commission.

[2] On April 20, 1972, members of the President's Panel on Non-Public Education met with the President to present the Panel's final report. On the same day, the White House released the transcript of a news briefing on the report by Clarence Walton, Chairman, and Ivan E. Zylstra and the Most Reverend William E. McManus, members, of the Panel.

that covers the Federal Government, the State governments, the city governments, and county governments, as well as the private sector, because the solutions we seek must ultimately involve not just the Federal Government, but these other units as well.

When that Advisory Commission—and, incidentally, it is a totally bipartisan commission—has completed its study, I shall make specific legislative recommendations to the Congress that deal with three great interrelated national problems:

First, relief of property taxes—the mainstay of public school support—which have now become an intolerable burden upon millions of American homeowners.

Second, development of alternative sources of finance for public schools.

Third, specific measures designed to preserve the nonpublic school system in the United States.

This whole process that I have just described takes time. You know and I know that we do not have much time. The appointing of commissions, the launching of studies is sometimes regarded as a stall, an excuse for inaction. Let me assure you in the strongest possible terms that is not my intent.

I am irrevocably committed to these propositions: America needs her nonpublic schools. Those nonpublic schools need help. Therefore, we must and will find ways to provide that help. Yet, at the same time, I shall not make promises to you which cannot be kept nor raise hopes which will later be disappointed. You are all aware of the grave constitutional questions which have risen in the past, each time the States or the Federal Government has undertaken to provide aid to nonpublic schools.

I was talking to His Eminence and to the Mayor about a case that has just been decided yesterday dealing with one of these problems. We are all aware of the extra difficulties which tax measures encounter in Congress any time, but particularly in an election year. But with these hard realities in mind, I feel the only responsible way to proceed is to take the extra time required to guarantee that the legislative recommendations which we finally submit will be equitable, will be workable, will be constitutional and so held by the Supreme Court.

Too much is at stake for us to act in haste. We share a great obligation—to improve the public school system of this country and also to preserve the nonpublic schools—and in that obligation we shall not fail.

Let me put it now in the broader terms of the Nation at large. What we really seek in America is an educational free market.

Nonpublic schools give parents the opportunity to send their children to institutions that they choose. The reasonable preferences of parents in this matter should be respected by governmental authorities.

As we consider the nonpublic schools—whether they are Catholic or Protestant or Jewish or even nonsectarian—they often add the dimension of spiritual values in the educational process. Children who attend these schools are offered a moral code by which to live. At a time when the trend in education is too often toward impersonal materialism, I believe America needs more, rather than less, emphasis on education which emphasizes moral, religious, and spiritual values.

The American people and their government cannot remain indifferent to the accelerating disappearance of such schools. No single school system, whether public or private, must ever gain an absolute monopoly over the education of our children, because such a system, one that had a total monopoly, would never reflect the diversity and richness of our national heritage and character. It would lack altogether that essential spur of competition to innovate, to grow and reform. It would lead inevitably toward mediocrity and dull uniformity in American education—conditions which this Nation cannot tolerate.

The American public school system, which is the greatest in the world, which today educates nine of every ten children in the United States, has nothing to fear and everything to gain from the presence of a vigorous, diverse, competitive private school system, the kind of system which we still have today, but which we can preserve for tomorrow only by decisive action now.

I think we all have to recognize the fact that too often in the past an atmosphere of mutual suspicion and hostility has divided the public schools from the nonpublic schools in this country. Yet, such an atmosphere can only weaken both school systems and do a disservice to the public interest in quality education. Worst of all, it can only penalize the children whose future is our most sacred trust.

The education of our children is too important for us to be divided over it by party, by religion, by race, or by region in this country.

So I say let all Americans join together in a new recognition of the vital and positive roles which both the public and the nonpublic school systems play.

Let all America follow the example of this city of Philadelphia where the Committee of 31 made up of leaders of all religions, and made up of the nonpublic as well as the public schools, work together to meet the educational needs of a city. That is an example that the Nation can follow.

This new spirit of constructive cooperation and good will can serve our children better, and it can make our country stronger. That is why I say let us do all in our power to make this spirit the keynote of the coming era in American education.

I should like to close my remarks with, if I might, a rather timely, if personal, anecdote. A few weeks ago, on my visit to the People's Republic of China, I visited the Great Wall. Some of you perhaps saw that on television. As I stood there and looked at that Great Wall and thought of when it was built and of the great empire that had built it, I thought how well they had built it materially—it still stood. And yet the empire was gone.

I thought back to other civilizations and other peoples who have had similar experiences. I shall never forget when, as a young Congressman, I walked on the Acropolis in Athens at night and saw those magnificent columns built so well that they still stand as examples of architecture for all the world to see. But the civilization is gone.

And I thought of the Roman Forum. Walking through there one evening 25 years ago for the first time, and many times since, there again you see buildings and columns standing because they were built so well materially. But the civilization is gone.

And there is a pattern that runs through these stories, and the pattern is very simply this: When those civilizations went down, they were rich, they were strong militarily, and yet they were not able to survive.

And, also, it can be said that they went down at a time when, in terms of education, they were better educated in a material sense than they had been at any time in their history up to that time.

I know that it is fashionable in talking to a group of educators—and I have done this myself sometimes in the past—to quote H. G. Wells when he said civilization is "a race between education and catastrophe." Maybe. It depends, however, on the education.

What I am simply saying is this: A nation can be rich, a nation can be powerful, a nation can be well educated, but if its people lack character it will not stand.

So I simply say to all of you today, you, the educators—and to all of the public school educators as well—you do have the future of America and the future of our children in your hands. I hope and I know you will teach them well. I hope you will teach them with all of the new techniques, the new math, the new science, the new technologies. But I hope as those new techniques are taught so well that you will not forget to teach them also and to remind them of the old values of honor, of morality, of love of country, and remind them also that America's religious faith has always kept us strong in times of testing. Let us not lose it now in the years ahead.

NOTE: The President spoke at 12:05 p.m. in the Civic Center.

His Eminence John Cardinal Krol was Archbishop of Philadelphia. Frank L. Rizzo was the mayor of Philadelphia.

The President spoke from a prepared text. An advance text of his remarks was released on the same day.

114 Remarks About a Heroin Seizure by Miami Customs Patrol Officers. *April 8, 1972*

Ladies and gentlemen:

I have just had an opportunity to express my appreciation and the appreciation of the people of the United States to these two Customs officers for what they have accomplished in the seizure yesterday.

Mr. Cascavilla has a background of having served in the U.S. Marine Corps and for 15 years in the Customs Service, and Mr. Torres has been in the Customs Service for only 5 months. The suitcase which they picked up off of an incoming ship had in it heroin, 99 percent pure [90 percent], of a retail value of $5 million.

In checking with Mr. Ambrose,[1] the estimate is that this is enough heroin to provide what they call "fixes" for 200,000 individuals. We can see, therefore, the vital importance of what the Customs Office is doing in providing for these seizures, and this gives me an opportunity to make two points:

When I was in New York the other day, going down the line at the airport, I saw many passengers who had come in from Europe and other parts of the world. They

---

[1] Myles J. Ambrose, Special Assistant Attorney General, Office for Drug Abuse Law Enforcement, Department of Justice.

were standing in long lines, and I am sure they were very impatient. If a passenger has to wait an extra half hour in order to have his baggage searched, whereas he is an absolutely innocent person, if it means that as a result of that time that there is going to be some kind of seizure, as was the case in this instance, which could affect the lives—not just 30 minutes of a life, but the lives—of thousands of young people across this country, then it is all worthwhile. Therefore, we ask for the patience of passengers as we step up and crack down in our search, as Mr. Ambrose has been directed to do.

The other point is a very personal point. Mr. Torres said that he has dedicated his life to this work, because immediately after he became a Customs officer, his cousin, 23 years old, was found dead in the streets of New York from an overdose of heroin. This is an indication that this problem of drug abuse strikes home very close to all of our families, and that men like this, who are working out in the frontlines, who spend many tedious hours going through baggage, searching ships, searching planes, finding nothing, and then one day do have a great success like this, deserve the appreciation of the whole Nation.

I would say, finally, that it is rather significant that this occurred on the day that we announced the Hotline—the "Heroin Hotline" [2]—through which citizens all over the country can cooperate

with Mr. Ambrose and his office. The purpose of this is not to have people send in charges that may reflect on innocent people, but the purpose is to get the information, get the information which Mr. Ambrose and his officers will then use to the very best of their ability to search out the pushers, to search out those who are destroying the lives of people like Mr. Torres' cousin.

This, as I have often said, is the most reprehensible crime I can think of. I think, under the circumstances, that every American wants to cooperate—those Americans who come in, with 30 minutes of their time waiting for a Customs officer to go through their baggage, and the baggage of others, and people throughout this country—to cooperate through letting the Government officials know when they have what they believe to be fairly good proof, or very good proof that some kind of activity by law enforcement officials could be effective in leading to the arrest and eventually the conviction of anyone engaged in this illegal traffic.

Thank you.

NOTE: The President spoke at 10:10 a.m. at his residence at Key Biscayne, Fla. He spoke without referring to notes.

Customs Patrol Officers Philip J. Cascavilla and Frank Torres, Jr., were on a routine patrol of the Miami seaport when they observed a suitcase being loaded into a vehicle parked on the dock. When the car attempted to leave the dock, it was stopped, and a search of the suitcase revealed 70 plastic bags containing 22 pounds of heroin.

---

[2] On April 7, 1972, the President directed the establishment of a nationwide toll-free telephone number to be manned on a 24-hour basis, 7 days a week. The Hotline, a phase of the Drug Abuse Law Enforcement program,

was designed to provide citizens a direct line to help the national effort to eliminate heroin trafficking through the contribution of information anonymously.

115   Remarks at the Signing Ceremony of the
Biological Weapons Convention.   *April* 10, 1972

Mr. Secretary of State, Ambassador Cromer, Ambassador Dobrynin, Your Excellencies, ladies and gentlemen:

First, may I subscribe to the statements that have been made by the British Ambassador and the Soviet Ambassador.[1]

Second, may I congratulate all of those not here at this head table, but many in this room and all over the world, representatives of our various governments who for years have worked for the achievement of these agreements. The contributions that have been made by the British Government, by the Soviet Government, by the Government of the United States, and others concerned, would not have been possible except for those working for arms control in each of our countries. We congratulate all of them who have been working in these activities.

As has already been indicated, we have been here in this room before. We recall the nonproliferation agreement ceremony which occurred in 1970. We recall also the seabed ceremony, and that treaty will soon come into force, and now we have this ceremony today.

The Soviet Ambassador has referred to the negotiations with regard to the limitation of strategic arms. We are working toward that end, an end, as he has indicated, which will serve not only the interests of peace between our two countries, but, we trust, also will serve the interests of peace

---

[1] Preceding the President's remarks, the Earl of Cromer, Ambassador from Great Britain, and Anatoly F. Dobrynin, Ambassador from the Soviet Union, spoke. Their remarks are printed in the Department of State Bulletin (vol. LXVI, pp. 615 and 616).

for all the world.

But as we look at these various agreements, we must understand how much they mean, and also what they still need if we are to achieve our ultimate goal. As far as these agreements are concerned, they are basically not an end in themselves. They limit arms, but they do not mean the end of war. They are means to an end, and that end is peace.

In terms of the agreement that is being signed today, it has very great significance. It means that all the scientists of the world, certainly a universal community, whatever their language, whatever their race, whatever their background, instead of working to develop biological weapons which one nation might use against another nation, now may devote their entire energy toward working against the enemy of all mankind—disease.

For that reason, that agreement is one of enormous significance to all of those who have followed its development. But as we look at these agreements and recognize that they are only means to an end, we must recognize also what more needs to be done to achieve our goal: Not just to limiting arms, but of ending the threat of war which hangs over the world.

Insofar as that goal is concerned, we begin with one proposition, and that is that each nation of the world must renounce the use of force, the use of aggression against other nations. We must also recognize another proposition, and that is that a great responsibility particularly rests upon the great powers, that every great power must follow the principle that it should not encourage directly or indirectly any other nation to use force or armed aggression against one of its neighbors.

It is these great principles which we must eventually implement if we are truly to have a world of peace, and it is these great principles that I am confident all of us will work toward as we take this step today.

NOTE: The President spoke at 11:22 a.m. in the Main Conference Room at the Department of State. He spoke without referring to notes.

The convention was signed on behalf of the United States, the United Kingdom, the Soviet Union, and 71 other countries. Similar cere-

monies were held in London and Moscow. Signing for the United States in Washington were Secretary of State William P. Rogers and James F. Leonard, Jr., Assistant Director for International Relations, United States Arms Control and Disarmament Agency. Ambassador Cromer and Ambassador Dobrynin signed in Washington for Great Britain and the Soviet Union.

The "Convention on the Prohibition of the Development, Production, and Stockpiling of Bacteriological (Biological) and Toxin Weapons and on Their Destruction" was negotiated by the Conference of the Committee on Disarmament (CCD) in Geneva. Ambassador Leonard headed the U.S. delegation to the CCD conference.

116   Statement About the Death of James F. Byrnes. *April* 10, 1972

JAMES F. Byrnes was one of those men who ranked principles first—and that should be his legacy to all of us who seek to serve our country.

No man in American history has held so many positions of responsibility in all branches of our Government with such distinction. He was a great patriot who always put his country ahead of his party.

Governor Byrnes acted always for the best interests of the United States of America, as he saw those interests from the solitary viewpoint of his personal conscience.

He was trained as a lawyer, began his public service as a solicitor, and became an Associate Justice of the Supreme Court of the United States.

He was also a legislator, representing the people of South Carolina in the Congress for 24 years. He served the executive branch of the Federal Government with particular distinction, as "Assistant President" and Secretary of State. And he then returned to his beloved home State

of South Carolina to serve its people as Governor.

America was served exceedingly well by this distinguished South Carolinian who became one of the dominant American statesmen and political leaders in the turbulent years that bridged the new eras spawned by two world wars and the tensions and realignments resulting from each.

I, for one, was always grateful that I could seek his wise counsel. I will miss it now that I cannot.

Mrs. Nixon joins me in expressing deepest sympathy to Mrs. Byrnes.

NOTE: Governor Byrnes, 92, died at his home in Columbia, S.C., on April 9, 1972.

On April 10, the President signed Executive Order 11665 ordering the flag to be flown at half-staff as a mark of respect to the memory of Governor Byrnes.

On April 12, Mrs. Nixon represented the President at the funeral services.

On May 3, 1969, the President and Mrs. Nixon visited Governor and Mrs. Byrnes at their home. See 1969 volume, Item 182.

117 Letter to Governors Urging Citizen Participation in Environmental Programs During Earth Week. *April* 12, 1972

Dear Governor:

Recently I proclaimed the week of April 17–23 as national "Earth Week," and I would like to ask your assistance in making that period an occasion for all citizens to work together on improving and restoring our environment. Surely there could be few issues of greater moment to America.

As I observed in that proclamation, "The environmental awakening marks a new maturity in our attitudes toward the relationship of man to his surroundings. . . . We have made a beginning in this new era of environmental enlightenment. But it is only a beginning. Every American and every citizen of the world must make a conscious and sustained effort if we are to succeed in protecting this earth which we all share."

At the Federal level, we have made a strong and irreversible commitment to this cause, setting up new agencies within the government, greatly increasing our financial support, and asking for a very large package of new laws, as set forth most recently in my message to Congress of February 8, 1972. I am most anxious that we now secure passage of these 24 pieces of legislation, for we must have the proper tools if we are to succeed in this task.

As you are aware, there is also a special need to enlist our young people in this effort. Their involvement will not only serve to renew our environment but should also be an important step in developing an informed and concerned citizenry. Last October I established the Environmental Merit Awards Program so that secondary school children could fulfill their deeply felt commitments; already, more than 2,500 high schools representing all 50 States have registered in this program.

During this coming Earth Week, I hope you will impress upon the citizens of your State how important it is that they seek a better understanding of environmental needs and opportunities on a continuing basis. Certainly we will achieve the quality of life that we want only if we make each and every day a part of Earth Week.

With best personal regards,

Sincerely,

RICHARD NIXON

NOTE: The text of identical letters addressed to the Governors of the States and the Territories was dated April 11, 1972, and released April 12.

On March 24, the President signed Proclamation 4119, Earth Week, 1972.

118 Message to the Congress Transmitting Annual Report of the National Science Board. *April* 13, 1972

To the Congress of the United States:

I am pleased to submit to the Congress this Fourth Annual Report of the National Science Board, "The Role of Engineers and Scientists in a National Policy for Technology." This Report has been prepared in accordance with Section 4(g) of the National Science Foundation Act, as amended by Public Law 90–407.

Many of the key recommendations in

527

this Report are in close accord with the initiatives I have set forth this year in my address on the State of the Union, my Budget Message, and my recent message to the Congress on science and technology.

The Report stresses that in the field of research and development, a vigorous partnership between private industry, the universities, and the Government can be an important asset for strengthening our economy and spurring new technological solutions to problems of the modern world. The Report also points out that intensive research is needed to refine our understanding of the complexities of contemporary life and to develop better ways of bringing our talents to bear on domestic concerns.

As I have indicated on several occasions, I have great hope that we can realize the full potential of American technology for serving our national purposes. The commitment of this Administration to continued progress toward that goal is clearly reflected in the array of programs which I have detailed in my latest Budget Message.

I am confident that the Congress will find this Report useful.

RICHARD NIXON

The White House,
April 13, 1972.

NOTE: The report is entitled "The Role of Engineers and Scientists in a National Policy for Technology—Report of the National Science Board" (Government Printing Office, 48 pp.).

---

119   Letter to Delegates of the 1971 White House Conference on Youth Transmitting a Report of Executive Branch Review of Conference Recommendations.   *April* 13, 1972

To the delegates of the 1971 White House Conference on Youth:

Just over two years ago, we became convinced that the conditions of the seventies demanded a departure from the "children and youth" conference format followed by Presidents since Theodore Roosevelt—that the time had come to convene a separate White House Conference of, by, and for youth themselves. Since that time, I have followed your work with interest and hope.

National Chairman Stephen Hess and his young staff skillfully planned a meeting which could, as I charged them, "listen well to the voices of young America." The project represented an honest effort to improve the Nation's understanding of the concerns and ideals of our youth; thus its design and objectives were necessarily un-

usual and, to some, controversial. But the deliberations and results of the Conference underscored the fact that bonds can be found between the generations and that young people can contribute constructively to solving today's complex problems.

You will recall that Secretary Richardson, speaking at the opening session of the Conference, pledged this Administration to "look carefully at every one of the recommendations" you might direct to us, and to "render to you an accounting not only of what we have done, but of what we have not done, and why." Within a week from adjournment of the Conference, I reviewed its results with the full Cabinet; and I directed each member to set his department at work preparing the promised accounting. This volume is the result.

The many thousands of words in these

25 sections of response to over 300 recommendations defy simple summation. Some comments about the spirit of our review process are in order, however. The process was long because I insisted that it be thorough, honest, and open-minded. Aware that Federal activities are often contradictory in their effects on the young, and anxious to further the development of a comprehensive national youth policy, we have endeavored to acquire useful guidance from the work of your Conference.

The process was also critical, in the sense that it steered a middle line between the standpat and the start-over attitudes toward change. Your readings of the facts, your judgments on what to do about them, have been weighed against our own as fairly as possible.

In retrospect, the Chairman's metaphor for the Conference report—"blueprint for change for this decade"—seems apt. At Estes Park certain foundational premises were assumed, and on them a rather remarkable structure was sketched. The Administration finds many aspects of this blueprint already being followed in our own programs and policies, other aspects unacceptable for reasons of principle or practicality, still others well worth following in the future. This report indicates where we agree and differ with the Conference at the present. But it alone does not and could not offer a final answer to your concerns and recommendations. For as our Nation builds, revision of its master blueprint must go on continuously, responding to the ideas of many architects sifted through what might be thought of as a broad design competition.

Your report, then, was very right in choosing to address not only the government and other institutions, but also the people as a whole, and in specifying that it is really the people who must judge your recommendations. The responses of the Federal executive, like those later to come from other institutions, can and will be reviewed and revised in the time ahead as the people themselves assimilate the ideas you have put forward and act on them through the political process.

My own positions on most of the issues addressed at Estes Park are a matter of record and need little reiteration here. Some of your recommendations, such as the abrupt unilateral withdrawal from Vietnam, I oppose. Other recommendations, including an opening to China, a volunteer armed force, an income floor for the poor, and a recasting of the Federal budget in favor of human resources, I welcome as close kin to our initiatives of the past three years.

To me, however, the significance of the Conference report emerges much less through enumeration of the parts than through evaluation of the whole. It is threaded through with basic human values, noble ideals, and the deeply American reach for a better future. Even the preamble—emotional, hyperbolic, and combative as it may sound to older ears— has at its core a broadly appealing call for new dedication to the Declaration of Independence and the Constitution. On such common grounds and despite all our differences, we can surely reciprocate what the delegates affirmed: a sense of "kinship with persons of good will of all generations."

We can also extend the Nation's thanks to you who gave your best to this important pioneering effort. The first White House Conference on Youth has been good for the young, good for the Government, good for the country. Now quite logically the question presses, what next? While the convening of more frequent youth conferences, as your report recommends, might further useful dialogue, this would not seem to go to the heart of young people's right—and need—to participate. Conferences, after all, cannot legislate. In fact, the study-and-recommend approach can easily become what your preamble calls "a mechanism to divert the attention and energy of the people."

"This conference," you have said, "shall not be so used." I concur absolutely. We must treat last April's meetings not as a closed episode, but as an effective first step. The Administration's next step must and will be action, respecting the Conference's sincerity even where we cannot follow its prescriptions. Your next step should be to focus attention on a "mechanism" which is neither intermittent nor potentially diversionary, as the best of conferences are, but which is instead continuous, powerful, and newly accessible to the young—the American political process.

This young generation—which is already (as I said in my Inaugural Address) "better educated, more committed, more passionately driven by conscience" than any before it—now has the chance to be more effectively involved than all earlier ones as well. My hope is that you and your contemporaries by the millions—of all political preferences, all ideological persuasions, and all opinions pro and con the positions taken at Estes Park—not only will go conscientiously to the polls this year and years to come, but will remain informed and engaged at a level of citizenship equal to the demands of America's coming third century. With your energy and idealism directed to this goal, you will do your country and your own best interests a signal service.

Sincerely,

RICHARD NIXON

NOTE: The letter, dated March 15, 1972, is printed in the report entitled "Federal Executive Branch Review of the Recommendations of the 1971 White House Conference on Youth" (Government Printing Office, 414 pp.). The report was made available to the press on April 13.

Stephen Hess, who was Chairman of the Conference, and three representatives of the Youth Conference Follow-Up Executive Committee met with the President at the White House on Thursday, April 13, to receive the report.

On the same day, the White House released a fact sheet on the Conference followup program.

120 Remarks on Arrival at Ottawa, Canada. *April* 13, 1972

Mr. Governor-General, Mr. Prime Minister, Your Excellencies, and ladies and gentlemen:

I wish to express on behalf of all of the members of our party my very great appreciation for the very warm words of welcome which you have spoken. And since you have referred to the weather, I can only say that while the weather may be cool, the welcome is very warm and for this we are most grateful.

You have referred also to the fact that we are close neighbors, that we have a long border. I think it is appropriate for me to point out that the first official visitor who came to the United States after I was inaugurated as President of the United States was the Prime Minister. The first individual head of government with whom we consulted before the trip to the People's Republic of China was the Prime Minister and other members of the Government of Canada.

It is also significant to mention that the only trip outside the United States that I am taking between the visit to the People's Republic of China and the visit that we will be making to Moscow in the latter part of May is to Canada.

Now, this tells us something—something which means very much between our two countries and also, I think, means something to the world:

First, at a time that we in the United States are seeking a new relationship with our adversaries, we realize the imperative importance of having better relations with our friends and close neighbors, and that is one of the reasons we are here.

Second, in order to contrast the three visits to which I have referred, I recall that one of the great sights that we saw in the People's Republic of China was the Great Wall of China, which runs thousands of miles down through that country, a barrier between that country and others that might invade it.

As we go to the Soviet Union, we will, of course, be thinking of the term "Iron Curtain" and of another wall, the Berlin Wall, which is the symbol of the division between East and West.

And when we come to Canada, we think of a boundary 4,000 miles, one we always refer to as the longest unguarded boundary in the world.

But as we refer to the fact that in two nations which we will have visited, one before and one after our visit to Canada,

there are walls which have been barriers, and that in Canada, and between Canada and the United States, we have this unguarded boundary, let us recognize the true significance of that boundary.

As you have very well pointed out, while we have been friends and are friends, while we have a great unguarded boundary, we have differences: We have differences in forms of government, we are competitive economically in many areas, and we have our own separate identities.

As I come here to Canada, I want to say what I have said to our Canadian friends when they have come to the United States: We respect the separate identity, the right to pursue its own way that the people of Canada desire for their own destiny.

What we are really saying very simply is this: that while we do not have a wall between us, while we do have this great unguarded boundary, this does not mean that we are the same, it does not mean that we do not have differences, but it does mean that we have found a way to discuss our differences in a friendly way and without war, and this is the great lesson for all the world to see.

So as we visit Canada, halfway between the visit to the People's Republic of China and the visit to the Soviet Union, this is the hope that we have in mind, that these visits, all of them, will contribute to the goal of an open world in which there will not be walls that divide people, in which people can be different—different in their forms of government, competitive in many ways, but in which they can settle their differences by talking rather than fighting.

The Canadian-American example is an example for all the world to see, and our visit here, we trust, will contribute to the strength and the vitality of that splendid example.

Thank you.

NOTE: The President spoke at approximately 6:45 p.m. at Uplands Airport in response to the welcoming remarks of Governor-General Roland Michener. He spoke without referring to notes.

On April 11, 1972, the White House released a list of members of the U.S. official party for the President's trip to Canada.

The Governor-General's remarks were as follows:

Mr. President:

I welcome you and Mrs. Nixon and your official party with the deep feelings of warmth and esteem which one accords to good neighbors, good friends, and trusted allies.

This is not the first time that you have been in our country. You know, as we do, that the almost invisible line which has been drawn across our continent by the vagaries of history divides us as sovereign nations, but does not separate us as people with countless interrelationships of family, friendship, and personal interests.

We are all North Americans, with origins which touch at many points. Although our systems of representative government have developed somewhat differently, and our relative positions in the community of nations in terms of numbers and power are on a rather different scale, nevertheless our purposes and our goals as neighbors and in the world at large are broadly parallel.

This is not to say that we are always in agreement nor that our perspectives and approaches to problems must necessarily converge at all points. But our relationships have generally been characterized by sympathy and by efforts to understand and to respect each other's viewpoint.

As I have said, Mr. President, you have been in Canada before, but this visit has particular significance for us, for you come to us for the first time as head of state. Canadians who pride themselves on knowing about your country are well aware of the weight of responsibility and the demands of time and energy which fall upon the President of the United States of America. This responsibility and these demands are the measure of the honor which you do to us in coming to Canada, not from the necessity to resolve any critical issues of conflict or tension but, rather, to bring the message which we want most to hear—that of the friendship of Americans for Canadians, and of their desire to strengthen the partnership which we have built and maintained together over this past century and a half.

Mr. President, a Canadian welcome to be as full and wholehearted as we wish yours to be should be expressed in two languages which are ours by inheritance.

Alors, Monsieur le Président, je vous adresse, au nom de tous les Canadiens, la plus cordiale bienvenue. Votre présence nous honore, dans cette heureuse tradition des visites que nous ont faites vos illustres prédécesseurs. Je vous souhaite, ainsi qu'à Madame Nixon et aux membres de la délégation éminente qui vous entoure, un heureux séjour ici. Que votre visite, comme les autres avant elle, aide à consolider nos relations, dont l'harmonie est pour nous tous une condition préalable de notre vie en commun sur le continent que nous partageons.

We could have wished to have you longer, Mr. President, and also at a season which is more definitely one thing or the other, but we hope sincerely that your visit, although brief, will be both happy and productive.

I am happy to welcome you, Mr. President, in the name of all Canadians.

121   Toasts of the President and Governor-General Roland Michener of Canada.   *April* 13, 1972

Mr. Governor-General and Lady Michener, Mr. Prime Minister, Mrs. Trudeau, Your Excellencies, ladies and gentlemen:

The very warm words which have been spoken by His Excellency, the Governor-General, make Mrs. Nixon and me feel very much at home in this country, in which we truly have felt at home on many occasions in the past. And I can only say, in view of the political reference, that it is a very great pleasure to have at this head table at least two or three people who are not running for the office which I now hold.

This trip to Canada has been one which has been very much in our minds, and to which we have been looking forward for many months; as a matter of fact, since entering office. It has given us a chance already to see old friends like former Prime Minister Mr. Diefenbaker—we met in Washington when I was Vice President of the United States—and renew acquaintances with others whom we have worked with during the period that I have served as President of the United States. And I would say one of the real pleasures of this trip has been the opportunity to know better—I have met him once before—His Excellency, our host tonight, the Governor-General.

He speaks, of course, of the fact that he has no political power, but I would only say that when I look back on his distinguished career, his service at the bar, his service in India, and in other posts of very great importance, the Speaker of the Parliament, of the Lower House, and I think now of his service to his country in the post he presently holds, that we made only one mistake in planning this trip. It was a week too early. Next week he celebrates his birthday and his fifth anniversary as Governor-General. So in advance, we congratulate you, Mr. Governor-General.

The Prime Minister and I have had an opportunity to have chats on several occasions, and we had one particularly interesting interlude on the last occasion that I visited Canada very briefly, when we cele-

brated the tenth anniversary of the inauguration of the St. Lawrence Seaway. Governor Rockefeller [1] was our host on the American side that day. A few of you here were there; Secretary Rogers and Mrs. Rogers will remember that occasion.

Governor Rockefeller, with his great, expansive charm, was introducing the various guests. He said, "Secretary and Mrs. Rogers," and they stood up, "the President of the United States and Mrs. Nixon," "the Prime Minister and *Mrs. Trudeau.*" That was in 1969.[2]

Fortunately, I spoke after he did, and I was able to save the situation somewhat by saying that the Governor was simply meaning to be prophetic. I didn't realize what a good prophet the Governor was.

But I think that as far as the Prime Minister is concerned, and Mrs. Trudeau whom we have had the privilege and honor of meeting for the first time tonight—that the Prime Minister has proved that he is a very effective political leader. He has shown his devotion by his marriage to the great interest in beautification in Canada. And also, he is doing something about underpopulation.

Could I say just a few words now that will not be in the formal sense that I will be speaking tomorrow when I will be privileged to address the Parliament, but which will try to let those here in this company, and those who may be hearing what we say over this electronic device, provided the unions are not boycotting it— that is another thing we have in common—but in any event, may I tell you what one American and his wife, what

---

[1] Nelson A. Rockefeller was Governor of New York.

[2] Prime Minister Pierre Elliott Trudeau was not married until March 1971.

87-234—74——38

we have in common with Canada and why we feel especially close to Canadians.

My secretary, many years ago when I was a young, practicing lawyer, was then an American, but she was very proud that she had been born in Canada. And as a result, after my wife and I were married, about 30 years ago—you wouldn't know it, but it was that long ago—but in any event, the year that we were married, we, with another couple, drove on a vacation to Canada. We were in Victoria and British Columbia, and brought back many pleasant memories of our first visit to Canada. It was because my secretary recommended that we go there, and we had no regrets.

Then I recall in the year 1942, just before World War II came along, as far as our lives were concerned, and before going overseas, we had saved a little money and we had some time for a vacation, and we took the train to Quebec, and I shall never forget those 3 days that we had, and my wife will never forget, in Quebec. The Hotel Frontenac, that magnificent view from the promenade down over the river. But more, the warmth and friendship of the people that we met on that occasion.

Then there have been other occasions through the years. When we first came to Congress in 1946, and the next year, 1947, we had a few days off and we drove up the eastern part of the United States through the beauty of New England in the summertime, and we learned to know Nova Scotia and St. John, that side of Canada.

Then, during the years out of office, I, of course, had the opportunity to visit Ottawa on one occasion, Toronto on another occasion, and Montreal.

But there was one particular occasion

that I think stays in my mind more than all the others. I have been to Picton. Now, most Americans will not know what Picton is, but you Canadians will know. Or maybe you don't.

But in the year 1957, the Secretary of State and I—I was then Vice President and he was Attorney General of the United States—were invited by the publisher of the Rochester paper, Mr. Paul Miller, to sail across Lake Erie, and to go over to the Canadian side and see the beauties of Canada. It was to be a wonderful trip.

I didn't realize that even on Lake Erie one could get seasick, but finally when I saw Canadian soil, believe me, it was the most welcome soil I ever stepped on.

But the incident which I would like to leave on this occasion with our friends from Canada was what happened in Picton that day. It was a Saturday night. We had played golf earlier in the day. We were still in sports clothes—in sports jackets—and we decided to go to one of the local pubs, just as we were.

We went in and sat down. We had no Secret Service at that time with us, and the waiter looked us all over, and some way he seemed to think he recognized me, but he wasn't sure.

We noted, or Secretary Rogers at least noted—he was then Attorney General and is supposed to note such things—that the waiter was talking to the bartender after serving us. The bartender was looking over and saying, "No, it can't be, it can't be."

After we had finished—he was a very polite waiter—after we had finished and were ready to leave, the waiter came up and said, "Sir, if you don't mind, I have a bet with the bartender, and you can help me win it or I might lose it." I said, "What is the bet?" He said, "I bet him $5 that you are Vice President Nixon."

I said, "Well, call him over and we will confirm it." So the bartender came over and said, "Is it true?" I said, "Yes." He said, "I would never have believed it."

He gave him the $5, and as we started to move on, I heard him mumble to the waiter, "You know, he doesn't look near as bad in person as he does in his pictures."

Now, that little story tells us something about why this trip is important and why it is quite necessary. Maybe none of us look quite as bad in person as we may in our pictures, and we Canadians and Americans, because we are only an hour and 10 minutes apart by air, must never miss the opportunity to see each other in person, to discuss our differences, maybe to continue them but at least to discuss them, and to maintain the individual dignity, the parallel courses to which the Governor-General has referred so eloquently just a few moments ago.

I said, when I arrived at the airport, that the example that we in Canada and the United States have set is one which all the world could well look to and perhaps in years ahead might well follow: Two nations, very much alike but also very different, and very proud—proud of what we are like and proud of how we are different—but two nations living together in peace, discussing differences, not fighting about them.

And as I thought tonight of how I could relate that particular thought to this occasion, I looked at this room—in this respect I must admit I am a bit old-fashioned, I like a room like this, the high ceilings, the sense of history, all that has happened

here—and I think of other great rooms around the world where this same sense of history fills us.

I had the privilege in 1958 of speaking in Guild Hall in London, and I remembered tonight some of the great speeches that have been made there: one by President Eisenhower at the end of World War II, and many others. Perhaps the most eloquent speech, and the briefest speech, ever made in Guild Hall was one made by a British Prime Minister 150 years ago. After Nelson's victory at Trafalgar, William Pitt was toasted as the savior of Europe. He rose to respond. He answered in these words: "For the honor you have done me, I return you many thanks. But Europe will not be saved by any single man. England has saved herself by her exertions, and will, I trust, serve Europe by her example."

Tonight I think we could well say the world will not be saved by any single nation, but Canada and the United States, by their example, can contribute enormously to a new world in which nations can live together in peace, friendship, and understanding, maintaining their dignity, maintaining their individuality. This is the example which Canadian-American friendship stands for, and it is one that all of us can be very proud of.

NOTE: The President spoke at approximately 10:40 p.m. in Rideau Hall, Government House, Ottawa in response to a toast proposed by the Governor-General. He spoke without referring to notes.

The Governor-General's remarks were as follows:

Mr. President:

When such good friends as your charming wife and yourself come to dinner, and from a long distance, it would be a poor return of kindness to interrupt the pleasures of the occasion with too much speaking. That is usually the apology to a long speech. As Santayana recognized, "The language of friendship is not words, but meanings."

The delight of my wife and me to receive you as guests in our official home has its meanings, as has the presence here, in your honor, of our Canadian guests, leaders in state and church, meanings as intelligible and eloquent, I hope, as they are real.

In any event, a few hours ago at the airport I tried with words, *en français et en anglais,* to express for ourselves and for the Canadian people our great appreciation of the honor of your visit and the spirit of good will in which you have come, and that, Mr. President, in the midst of many and great responsibilities.

I ask only one favor: that you put no significance or meanings on our backward weather. Our tulips, the local equivalent of your cherry blossoms, are unintentionally late, and the snow which loiters in our fields seems to be giving point to what your poet, Walt Whitman, wrote in his "Diary in Canada," presumably as a compliment to us. He said, "I have sometimes doubted whether there could be a great race without the hardy influence of winters in due proportion." By April, we put a heavy emphasis on the "due proportion."

For many generations, your people and ours have lived side by side in harmony and understanding, while seeking, in separate but parallel ways, to develop our respective shares of this continent. Our relationship has been casual and easy, seldom requiring much articulation, and scarcely ever causing any sustained anxiety.

We look proudly on the success in your country of many of our Canadian emigrés. They are like the Scots in London. It took a little time for the Honorable Mr. Macdonald [Minister, Department of Energy, Mines, and Resources, Canada] to appreciate that one.

At the same time, we acknowledge our great debt to countless Americans who have come to settle in Canada.

I could cite my own family as an example of these exchanges. My paternal great-grandfather was a Quaker from Pennsylvania, whose fore-

bears had lived there for five generations before he moved to Ontario in 1819, for what reason I was never able to ascertain.

Today, a reverse movement gives me a sister domiciled in California, another in Florida, a daughter and grandchildren in Rhode Island, without depleting too much the Canadian stock. We all remain one family, even though our allegiance and electoral activities are different. Perhaps I should not mention the latter in this particular year, especially as I am the only one present who never engages in electoral activity and, in fact, never votes.

However, in the generation since 1945, the United States, Canada, and the entire world have undergone great changes. In the process, the relations between our two countries have become increasingly complex. With the growing interaction in almost every field of daily life, the once tacit and, one might almost say, instinctive understanding between us has perhaps become partially obscured. This should not surprise us, nor does it reflect a fading of our traditional friendship. At the same time, it does oblige us to put forward greater efforts to achieve what before seemed easily attainable.

Mr. President, for Canadians, your great office, with its power and prestige throughout the world, symbolizes the virtues and the strength of the United States and its people. Since assuming that office, you have given leadership in a long-sighted transformation of America's foreign relations and her role in the world. The full measure of your initiatives in the military, political, and economic fields is just beginning to be recognized, together with their implications for the peace and the well-being of people everywhere. In the case of Canada and the United States, I have no doubt that they will help us in defining anew the many areas where our desires and our policies converge.

At a time, Mr. President, when both our countries are adjusting to a world in transition, it is a happy omen to have you and Mrs. Nixon in our midst, an omen of enduring and advantageous new relationships to come, an omen that the sympathy, respect, and understanding which we have achieved in the past may be projected indefinitely into the future.

122   Address to a Joint Meeting of the Canadian
      Parliament. *April* 14, 1972

Monsieur l'Orateur de la Chambre des Communes, Monsieur le Président du Sénat, Monsieur le Premier Ministre, Messieurs les Membres des Chambres du Parlement Canadien, éminents hôtes et amis:

J'apprécie vivement votre aimable invitation ainsi que votre accueil chaleureux.

To all of you who have welcomed Mrs. Nixon and me so warmly on this occasion, I trust you will give me allowances for trying to speak in the language that I studied 37 years ago. When I tried it, the day before I came, on the top linguist in the American Government, General Walters,[1] he said, "Go ahead. You speak French with a Canadian accent."

I will have to admit that I am not very much at home in the French language, but as a former parliamentarian in my own country, I feel very much at home in this chamber. I am grateful for the high privilege which your invitation represents.

I am grateful for this chance to return to Canada, for the opportunity of signing here an historic agreement to restore and protect forever the quality of the Great Lakes we share together. That agreement testifies to the continuing vitality of our unique relationship, which has been described so eloquently by the Prime Minister. In discussing that relationship today, I wish to do so in a way that has not

---

[1] Lt. Gen. Vernon A. Walters, USA, frequently served as interpreter for United States officials on foreign trips. He was Defense and Army Attaché at the American Embassy in Paris from 1967 until April 1972 when he became Deputy Director of the Central Intelligence Agency.

always been customary when leaders of our two countries have met.

Through the years, our speeches on such occasions have often centered on the decades of unbroken friendship that we have enjoyed and our 4,000 miles of unfortified boundary. In focusing on our peaceful borders and our peaceful history, they have tended to gloss over the fact that there are real problems between us. They have tended to create the false impression that our countries are essentially alike.

It is time for Canadians and Americans to move beyond the sentimental rhetoric of the past. It is time for us to recognize:

—that we have very separate identities;

—that we have significant differences; and

—that nobody's interests are furthered when these realities are obscured.

Our peaceful borders and our peaceful history are important symbols, to be sure. What they symbolize, however, is the spirit of respect and restraint which allows us to cooperate, despite our differences, in ways which help us both.

American policy toward Canada is rooted in that spirit. Our policy toward Canada reflects the new approach we are taking in all of our foreign relations—an approach which has been called the Nixon Doctrine. That doctrine rests on the premise that mature partners must have autonomous, independent policies:

—each nation must define the nature of its own interests;

—each nation must decide the requirements of its own security;

—each nation must determine the path of its own progress.

What we seek is a policy which enables us to share international responsibilities in a spirit of international partnership. We believe that the spirit of partnership is strongest when partners are self-reliant. For among nations—as within nations— the soundest unity is that which respects diversity, and the strongest cohesion is that which rejects coercion.

Over the years, the people of Canada have come to understand these concepts particularly well. Within your own borders, you have been working to bring a wide variety of peoples and provinces and points of view into a great national union—a union which honors the integrity of its constituent elements.

It was Prime Minister Laurier who said of Canada's differing components: "I want the marble to remain the marble; I want the granite to remain the granite; I want the oak to remain the oak." This has been the Canadian way. As a result, Canadians have helped to teach the world, as Governor-General Massey once said, that the "toleration of differences is the measure of civilization."

Today, more than ever before, we need to apply that understanding to the whole range of world affairs. And to begin with, we must apply it to our dealings with one another.

We must realize that we are friends not because there have been no problems between us, but because we have trusted one another enough to be candid about our problems—and because our candor has nourished our cooperation.

Last December, your Prime Minister and I met in Washington, and he asked me if I thought that the United States would always want a surplus trade balance with Canada so that we could always export capital here. My answer then, and my answer now, is "no."

As I said to him at that time, we in the United States saw this same problem from the other side before World War I. We then depended on European capital for our development, and we wanted to free ourselves from that dependence. And so we fully understand that Canada is in that same position today.

Canada is the largest trading partner of the United States. It is very important that that be noted in Japan, too. [*Laughter*] Our economies have become highly interdependent. But the fact of our mutual interdependence and our mutual desire for independence need not be inconsistent traits. No self-respecting nation can or should accept the proposition that it should always be economically dependent upon any other nation. And so, let us recognize once and for all that the only basis for a sound and healthy relationship between our two proud peoples is to find a pattern of economic interaction which is beneficial to both our countries— and which respects Canada's right to chart its own economic course.

We must also build a new spirit of partnership within the Western Hemisphere that we share together.

It has been said that Canada is bounded "on the north by gold, on the west by the East, on the east by history—and on the south by friends." We hope that will always be the case and we hope it will be the case not only with respect to the United States, your immediate neighbor to the south, but with respect to all your southern neighbors—and ours—who are bound by the great forces of geography and history which are distinctive to the New World.

But geography and history alone do not make a community. A true community must be a living entity in which the individuality of each member is a source of pride to all members, in which the unity of all is a source of strength to each, and the great community of the Americas cannot be complete without the participation of Canada.

That is why we have been encouraged by the recent decisions of Canada to upgrade its participation as an observer in the Organization of American States to ambassadorial status and to apply for membership in the Inter-American Development Bank, for both of these institutions make the abstract concept of community within the Americas a living reality.

A sound concept of community is also important in another international arena that we share, the Atlantic Alliance. Just one month after my inauguration as President of the United States, I observed that a new spirit of cooperation within that Alliance was essential as we began a new search for cooperation between East and West. The recent agreements concerning Berlin—the fact, for example, that thousands of families were reunited this Easter for the first time in many years— these are among the first fruits of a new era of East-West negotiation.

But as we seek better relations with our adversaries, it becomes all the more important to strengthen the alliances with our friends. We must never forget that the strength and the unity of the West has been an indispensable element in helping to bring about the new era of negotiation with the East. And that is why we began our round of summit talks last December by meeting with the Prime Minister of Canada, and then with the leaders of other close allies. That is why our East-West conversations will always be accompanied by full and genuine consultation within the Atlantic Alliance.

That Alliance began as a way of pooling military resources. Today it is a way of pooling our intellectual and our diplomatic resources as well. Like our Federal approaches to nationhood, like our Canadian-American brotherhood, like our inter-American neighborhood, the Atlantic Alliance has achieved a creative unity in which the individuality of its members is respected and advanced.

Let us turn now to the world as a whole—for this is where the challenge of building a true community will be most difficult—and most important.

We in Canada and the United States have always been proud to live in what is called the New World. Today there is a new world coming for everyone who lives on this globe. It is our responsibility to make this new world a better world than the world we have known.

Canadians and Americans have fought and died together in two World Wars in this century. We live now in what has been called the post-war era. But mankind has known a long succession of post-war eras. And each one of them has turned out to be a pre-war era as well.

The challenge we face today is to build a permanent post-war era—an era of lasting peace.

My visit to Ottawa comes midway between visits to Peking and to Moscow.

In many respects, these journeys are very different. In the People's Republic of China we opened a new dialogue after 22 years of virtually no communication. In the Soviet Union there is an opportunity to bring a continuing dialogue to productive conclusions.

But in their central aim, these journeys

to Peking and Moscow are alike. Neither visit is directed against anyone—adversary or ally. Both are for the betterment of everyone—for the peace of all mankind.

However, we must not allow the fact of summit meetings to create any unrealistic euphoria.

The responsibility for building peace rests with special weight upon the great powers. Whether the great powers fulfill that responsibility depends not on the atmospherics of their diplomacy, but on the realities of their behavior.

Great powers must not treat a period of détente as an interlude between periods of tension. Better relations among all nations require restraint by great nations—both in dealing with each other and in dealing with the rest of the world.

We can agree to limit arms. We can declare our peaceful purposes. But neither the limitation of arms nor the declaration of peaceful purposes will bring peace if directly or indirectly the aggressive use of existing weapons is encouraged.

And great powers cannot avoid responsibility for the aggressive actions of those to whom they give the means for embarking on such actions.

The great powers must use their influence to halt aggression—and not to encourage it.

The structure of world peace cannot be built unless the great powers join together to build it, and its strength will grow only as all nations—of all political and social systems—come to accept its validity and sustain its vitality. This does not mean that the great powers must always agree.

We expect to continue to have profound philosophical and significant diplomatic differences with the Soviet Union and with the People's Republic of China in a number of areas. But, through opening new lines of communication, we hope to increase the chance that in the future we shall talk about our differences and not fight about them.

As we have prepared for both of these journeys, the experience of Canada has been most helpful. I am grateful to both the Prime Minister and to the Opposition Leader, Mr. [Robert L.] Stanfield, for sharing their insights with us as we embark on these endeavors.

As we continue toward our common quest for a better world order, let us apply the lessons we have learned so well on this continent:

—that we can walk our own road in our own way without moving further apart, that we can grow closer together without growing more alike;

—that peaceful competition can produce winners without producing losers, that success for some need not mean setbacks for others;

—that a rising tide will lift all our boats, that to go forward at all is to go forward together;

—that the enemy of peace is not independence but isolation, and that the way to peace is an open world.

And let us remember, too, these truths that we have found together:

—that variety can mean vitality;

—that diversity can be a force for progress; and

—that our ultimate destiny is indivisible.

When I spoke at the St. Lawrence Seaway ceremonies in 1969, I borrowed some words from the monument there which I had joined Queen Elizabeth in dedicating just 10 years before. That monument, as its inscription puts it, "bears witness to the common purpose of two nations whose frontiers are the frontiers of friendship,

540

whose ways are the ways of freedom, whose works are the works of peace."

The truth to which that inscription testifies is of profound importance to people everywhere in this world.

For the ability of our two nations, Canada and the United States, to preserve the frontiers of friendship, to walk in the ways of freedom, and to pursue the works of peace provides example and encouragement to all who seek those same objectives, wherever they may live.

There is nothing more exciting than a time of new beginnings. A member of this body caught that spirit when he spoke in Parliament about the beginnings of Canadian nationhood 100 years ago. Listen to him: "Blood pulsed in our veins, new hopes fired our hearts, new horizons lifted and widened, new visions came to us in the night watches."

May that same sense of excitement inspire our two nations as we help lead the world to new beginnings today.

NOTE: The President spoke at 3:19 p.m. in the House of Commons in Ottawa.

He spoke from a prepared text. An advance text of his address was released on the same day.

123   Remarks on Signing the Great Lakes Water Quality Agreement Between the United States and Canada. *April* 15, 1972

Mr. Prime Minister, Mr. Foreign Minister, Your Excellencies, ladies and gentlemen:

In responding to the remarks of the Prime Minister, I particularly wish to express at this occasion our grateful appreciation for the warm reception that we have received here. And after having been here for the first time on a state visit, I can only say that we hope that we can return, either on that kind of visit or another kind of visit. Of course, I do not have control over which kind of visit it will be.

When the first European explorers sailed the Great Lakes three centuries ago, they were deeply moved by the Lakes' striking beauty and boundless promise. And from that time to this, generation after generation of Canadians and Americans have looked upon the Great Lakes as great highways to the future for both of our countries.

But in recent years, as we know, the quality of the Great Lakes' water has been declining, with ominous implications for 30 million Americans and 7 million Canadians who live near their shores.

The signing today of the Great Lakes Water Quality Agreement represents a significant step toward reversing that decline. This agreement extends a great tradition of cooperation between the United States and Canada. Just as the St. Lawrence Seaway transformed the Great Lakes into highways of peaceful commerce among nations, so the Great Lakes Water Quality Agreement can make them great symbols of international cooperation as man makes his peace with nature.

This agreement represents an important beginning, one which has been made possible by the cooperation of our two national governments and of State and Provincial governments as well. And now we must all follow through on the beginning. Under the agreement, the International Joint Commission will provide important leadership in this effort.

But it is also essential that governments at all levels, in both of our countries, and private industry as well, work within their own constitutional frameworks to achieve the objectives the agreement defines.

It is with very great pride and pleasure that I have signed the Great Lakes Water Quality Agreement between Canada and the United States, for this agreement bears witness to all the world of great concerns which unite our two countries: our common appreciation for the natural heritage which undergirds our national strengths, our common recognition that problems which cross international boundaries require international solutions, and our common confidence that our traditional relationship can grow to meet new demands.

NOTE: The President spoke at 9:35 a.m. in the Confederation Room, West Block, Parliament Hill, Ottawa, in response to the remarks of Prime Minister Pierre Elliott Trudeau.

The President spoke from a prepared text. An advance text of his remarks was released on the same day.

The text of the Prime Minister's remarks was made available by the Embassy of Canada in Washington as follows:

President Nixon, Secretary Rogers, Premier Davis, Minister Goldbloom, distinguished guests:

The importance of what we have done this morning cannot be described or measured by conventional means, for this agreement does not fall within the normal categories of international activity. It will not contribute materially to the economies of either of our countries; it makes neither of us more secure in our relations with one another or the world beyond; it does little to diminish or remove any of the social problems which worry Americans and Canadians alike. Yet while doing none of these things it accomplishes much more. For it marks our recognition of the fragility of our planet and the delicacy of the biosphere on which all life is dependent. This agreement deals with the most vital of all issues—the process of life itself. And in doing so it contributes to the well-being of millions of North Americans, for it promises to restore to a wholesome condition an immense area which, through greed and indifference, has been permitted to deteriorate disgracefully.

[After delivering the above remarks in English, the Prime Minister continued his remarks in French. A translation follows:]

Any catalogue of the distinctive features of this continent surely includes the farflung water system we know as the Great Lakes. In them is contained the world's largest reservoir of fresh water. Out of them flows one of the world's mightiest and most important rivers. The beauty and the utility of these waters have proved attractive to men for centuries. That attractiveness has led to extraordinary changes. The birchbark canoes of the Indians and the *coureurs-de-bois* have given way to giant ocean-going vessels; the handful of explorers who earlier stood in awe at the beauty of Niagara Falls or the Thousand Islands have been replaced by millions of tourists; the first few settlements and factories have burgeoned into sprawling cities and giant industrial complexes. In the process the lakes have suffered.

[The Prime Minister then resumed speaking in English:]

We now have the opportunity and the responsibility to ease that suffering and to restore to the Great Lakes a large measure of the purity which once was theirs. That task is being shared by those Provinces and States that border the lakes and whose governments have encouraged this agreement and contributed to its success. The presence here this morning of the Premier of Ontario [William C. Davis] and the Minister of the Environment of Quebec [Victor C. Goldbloom] as well as the members of the IJC [International Joint Commission] is proof of the solid foundation of support which our acts enjoy. The tireless dedication of the Canadian Minister of the Environment, Mr. Jack Davis, is recognized in what we are doing, as is the fine level of cooperation which he enjoys with his American colleagues present this morning, Mr. Train and Mr. Ruckelshaus. This treaty is an example to the world of the interdependence of all men and women and of the advantages which flow from cooperative measures. Indeed, Mr. President, your visit to Canada this week offers an opportunity to all nations to note the high standards which Canadians and Americans have achieved in their neighborhood, of the benefits which flow from their friendly competition, of the room which exists for their individuality. In our talks yesterday each of us assured himself that he understood the other; each of us dedicated himself to the continuation of a relationship which has few parallels in history and which owes as much to the willingness of the American people to accept on their northern border an independent state, with all the differences that that entails, as it does to the desire of Canadians to pursue their own destiny. Canadians are happy that you came, Mr. President. We hope you will come again. We wish you and Mrs. Nixon a safe journey home and wisdom and stamina in the important days ahead.

On the same day, the White House also released a fact sheet and the transcript of a news briefing on the agreement. Participants in the news briefing were George Soteroff, Chief Information Officer, Fisheries Service, Hon. Jack Davis, Minister, and A. T. Davidson, Assistant Deputy Minister, Policy, Planning, and Research, Department of the Environment, Canada; W. K. Wardroper, Director General, Economic and Scientific Affairs, Department of External Affairs, Canada; Russell E. Train, Chairman, Council on Environmental Quality; and William D. Ruckelshaus, Administrator, Environmental Protection Agency.

124   Remarks at a State Dinner for Representatives of the Organization of American States.   *April* 15, 1972

President Mora, Your Excellencies, and ladies and gentlemen:

I understand that during the past week that all of you have been exposed to a great number of speeches and tonight therefore, at this very, shall we say, friendly occasion, I hesitate to impose upon you another speech. But I will speak briefly and then I would like to add a few words directly in a very personal sense to those who are members of what I call, and what I think most of you call, the American family, our family.

First, we want to welcome you here, as I have welcomed you previously. Yesterday in the Canadian Parliament, as Senator Aiken, who is Canada's Senator in the United States Senate, they told me at least, in any event, knows, I was told that unless I spoke some French I would have no success in my speech. So I went back 37 years and picked out a few words and one way or another managed some French that some probably misunderstood.

But whatever the case might be, let me say that as far as my Spanish is concerned, it is limited, but it is from the heart when I say, *"Estan ustedes en su casa,"* and we are very honored to welcome you here again.

As you know, we come from southern California and we have a strong Spanish heritage—not only where we lived, but also our honeymoon was in Mexico and we have memories that we will always carry with us of those times. So our home in San Clemente, California, is one that we named Casa Pacifica. Casa Pacifica has two meanings. If you have seen this home, it is one that has a magnificent view of the Pacific so it is "The House on the Pacific" or "of the Pacific." But also it has another sense. It also, we believe and trust, will be recorded in history as a "House of Peace." And therefore we think that that Spanish word, Casa Pacifica, and that sentiment is one that should particularly characterize our thoughts tonight.

When we think of Pan American Week, it is hard to realize that 82 years ago the First International Conference established the International Union of American Republics, which of course was the forerunner of this organization.

And we have to realize and I have noted that during the course of your discussions that we have had some differences, differences this week and differences over those 82 years, but considering what happened in those 82 years, in the Americas and in the world, it would be considered remarkable that an organization like this, which is comprised, as it is, of many diverse viewpoints, could endure at all over these eight decades of change.

So, we stand tonight, not only in existence in the OAS, but we stand poised for even more progress as partners. But let me put the term partners in a different sense: Partners in principles, but not necessarily partners in every policy. And, of course, partners in principle is what really matters.

This week has been Pan American Week, in creative deeds as well as in the generalized words of the customary proclamations and resolutions. Yesterday, on Pan American Day, I addressed the Parliament of Canada, as I referred to a moment ago, the American nation of the North. And tonight, here in Washington, we gather with the representatives of the American nations of the South, after a week of conferences that you have had.

We are, in the year 1972, in a year that world attention is focused on East-West relations, the relations for example of the great powers, great in terms of their military strength, their potential military strength—the Soviet Union and the United States, the Soviet Union and China, China and the United States. And in this year of East-West activities, it is good for the United States and for all our fellow American nations to devote this week to the vitality of the North-South relationship. Because, as I said in Canada, at a time that we in the United States, we believe in the interest of world peace, are attempting to develop a new relationship with our adversary, it is enormously important to develop better relationships with our friends and particularly our friends in the American community.

Our Western Hemisphere ties provide the basic strengths which sustain us as we move toward that goal.

And now if I could turn to my good friend Galo Plaza [Secretary General, Organization of American States]. He spoke of the "fresh winds of change" that are blowing through the OAS and through the Americas in general and he is right. And we have felt those winds of change. That is good, that we have felt them and, frankly, that they are blowing, because we live in a world in which there must be change, change for the better, progress for all people.

Our basic policy position is a new practical acknowledgment that the general term "Latin America" now means something that it didn't used to mean. It means not a uniform voice, Latin America, all those countries down there speaking with one voice, one language, in a sense, but rather a plurality of views.

If I could interpolate here, I am the first President of the United States who has visited every country in Central America and every country in South America, and I know that what the State Department tells every visitor to these parts of the world before he goes, and what they told me is true. That the greatest mistake a traveler in Central America and South America and, for that matter, the Caribbean can make, is to assume that it is just one great part of the world that is very much alike. It is alike in many ways, but very different in other ways. They are proud peoples, they are different peoples. Many speak the same language, many have the same ideals, but, on the other hand, the important thing for us in the United States to do is to recognize and respect each country in Latin America for what it is and what it stands for and to know them for what they are and what they stand for. This I know from having traveled to all of these countries.

We recognize that diversity has resulted in different kinds of government within Latin America, with varying national goals and methods, and we realize that all of this presents problems.

The United States is no stranger to policy differences and to the efforts needed to forge strengths from the fires of discord.

Consequently, we stand prepared to work as a mature and equal partner on the inevitable differences that have arisen and have continued to arise because of the developing new realities in the American hemisphere.

Let us all recognize that when we talk about differences there are some things that will not change as far as U.S. policy is concerned. We will continue to give a special priority to our unique relationships with Latin America.

I say that here; I could say it also with regard to all of the American hemisphere, to the Americas generally, to Canada, and to the American family in its largest sense. We have special relationships with many countries in the world, but priority must necessarily go to our closest friends and our closest neighbors in the American hemisphere.

We will deal realistically with governments as they are, not seeking to impose our political structure on other nations. We recognize that each nation must seek its own way and we respect the right of all people in the various countries with whom we deal in the American family to seek their own way, and we shall continue to demonstrate our deep humanitarian concern for the people of the hemisphere.

If I could interject here just a sense of the feeling that Mrs. Nixon and I have for the countries that you the Foreign Ministers, the Ambassadors, and the others represent here today.

We think of you as representatives of government and we respect you as representatives of government. But also, we think of you as representatives of people. When I think of Latin America I remember, for example, the friends I have met there. I remember a very handsome, vigorous, young man from the Foreign Office—he was young then, in 1955. He had gone to the University of California, had played football, had been a great star and was back in his country of El Salvador, his name means nothing to you. It was Quinones. But he was such a good man and strong man and spoke so fervently about his small country that I realized and sensed from him the sentiment that the people in the countries to the south have for their countries, the patriotism they feel for their countries, large or small.

I remember a ride one night, as we were going to a state dinner in Bolivia. We were riding down a mountain road. It was rather dark and we saw along the road a group of students gathered. They were young students and their teachers were there with them. I asked the driver, "Who are they?" They were waving. He said, "That is the school for the blind." We stopped the car. We got out. We shook their hands, a few of them. We talked to the Sister who was in charge of the school.

I have seen and my wife has, schools for the blind all over the world. But only as you see and feel the hand of a blind person can you realize the universality of the feelings each of us has in his heart for all the people of this world. And I shall always remember that school for the blind in La Paz, Bolivia.

And then my wife had an experience that she says was the mountain top experience of her travels in the world. She went to Peru after the 1970 earthquake, and she flew with Señora Velasco,[1] for whom we gave a dinner, a luncheon here, into the earthquake zone. She saw the great tragedy, all of the destruction, but what impressed her was the courage, the strength, the dignity of the people, young and old, those beautiful faces—in the face of adversity they are going to build a new country, and she brought back with her therefore a feeling for the people of Peru which she communicated to me, and I think also communicated to the American people.

What I am saying to my friends here in the American family—we do not think of you simply as representatives of government, but we think of you very truly as members of our family. There are blind people in our family. There are people who have suffered adversity, and Peru, of

---

[1] Consuelo Gonzalez de Velasco, wife of Gen. Juan Velasco Alvarado, President of Peru.

course, has had another earthquake. There are people who are old friends and dear friends, and it is that special relationship that we hope that all Americans can understand, because as we understand that we are a family, then we can develop a more understandable policy for the Americas.

What I am suggesting here is that an intangible force forms the basis of the solidarity among the Americas. This force was well defined over 50 years ago by another President standing in this room. Listen to his words—Woodrow Wilson: "We must prove ourselves their friends and champions upon terms of equality and honor. You cannot be friends upon any other terms than upon the terms of equality. You cannot be friends at all except upon the terms of honor. We must show ourselves friends by comprehending their interest whether it squares with our own interest or not."

I say to you tonight, we, the United States, do comprehend. The United States is and will remain your friend, your champion, no matter what difficulties present themselves, in your countries, in ours, or any place on earth.

Now comes the time for the traditional toast at this dinner. There are so many people of high rank that we would have to go around the table Chinese style, tipping every glass in order to do it adequately, but I am afraid most of us probably couldn't survive the evening in the event we did that, so we have selected one of your members, the President of this Organization, as the one who will receive the toast on behalf of all of you.

Before toasting this very distinguished statesman, President Mora, let me say a word about the profession he represents. He is one who has been in diplomacy most of his life, as most of you have been in diplomacy. Now diplomats have very difficult times in every country, including the United States, but let me tell you how very important they are. I had it brought home to me today.

I signed a very thick treaty today with the Prime Minister of Canada. They brought the treaty over, they turned the page, they said, "Sign here." And I signed. Now as a lawyer, or a former lawyer, I know better than to sign something without reading it. Why did I sign it? I will tell you why.

While the Prime Minister of Canada and I were being seen on television, while we were meeting, a meeting at the summit of our two countries, discussing these important things, the work was being done that made possible our agreements, by scores of able, dedicated people. Some were Foreign Ministers, some were Secretaries of State, others were at other levels in their Foreign Service, but all were enormously important.

I simply want to say that in this year of summitry, here is one who goes to the summit, who knows that without the help of those who make it possible for him to go, who dig out the little places on those mountains where you step before you get to the top, there could be no summitry whatever.

And for that reason, as I raise my glass with yours, to the President of this Organization, let me say, it is raised to all of those in this room who have given your lives to the service of diplomacy, to the service of peace and therefore to the service of your own country and to the American family. So I ask that you rise, raise your glasses to *la familia americana* and to President Mora.

NOTE: The President spoke at 9:58 p.m. in the State Dining Room at the White House.

José A. Mora, Minister of Foreign Affairs of Uruguay, was President of the General Assembly, Organization of American States.

President Nixon spoke from a prepared text. An advance text of his remarks was released on the same day.

On April 10, 1972, the President signed Proclamation 4122, Pan American Day and Pan American Week.

125   Remarks to Members of the Table Tennis Team From the People's Republic of China. *April 18, 1972*

Ladies and gentlemen, and members of the Chinese table tennis team:

I am delighted to have the opportunity to welcome this team to the United States.

It is hard to realize that it was just a year ago that the American table tennis team, with Mr. [Graham B.] Steenhoven and his group, were welcomed in the People's Republic of China.

Premier Chou En-lai welcomed our American players, and as the President of the United States, on behalf of all the American people, I welcome the representatives of the Chinese team.

We know that in the course of your tour of the United States you will receive a good welcome. We know, too, that in the course of your contest there will be winners and losers. But there is one big winner, and that is more important than who wins a match in table tennis. The big winner, because of this people-to-people contact that you are initiating between our two peoples, will be friendship between the people of the United States and the people of the People's Republic of China.

Friendship between our two great peoples will mean a better chance for peace for all the world. And now we thank you for making this long journey. We hope that you continue to have great success and receive a warm welcome, and at the conclusion of our remarks, we want you to have a special tour of the White House.

NOTE: The President spoke at 12:10 p.m. in the Rose Garden at the White House. He spoke without referring to notes.

Chuang Tse-tung, head of the Chinese delegation, responded in Chinese. His remarks were translated by an interpreter as follows:

Mr. President:

After our arrival in the United States, the Chinese table tennis delegation visited the industrial city of Detroit, and also Williamsburg, an old, historical town which played a progres-

sive role in the War of Independence, and on the 16th we have arrived here in Washington, the U.S. Capital.

During our visit, we have had friendly contacts with students, players, workers, faculty members, and schoolteachers, and were accorded a warm welcome by them all. We have personally felt the friendly sentiments of the American people towards the Chinese people.

This time last year the U.S. table tennis team, headed by Mr. Steenhoven, made a friendly visit to China, and today, in the warm spring season, when flowers are in full bloom, the Chinese table tennis delegation is here on a reciprocal visit.

The exchange of visits between the Chinese and American table tennis delegations is conducive to the furthering of the friendship and the mutual understanding between the peoples of our two countries, and this is in conformity with the desire of our two peoples.

In conclusion, I wish to extend our thanks to you, Mr. President, for receiving us in the name of our delegation.

126 Remarks Commending the District of Columbia Metropolitan Police Department on the Decline in the District's Crime Rate. *April* 19, 1972

I WOULD like to say a word, if I could, to the whole group.

Ladies and gentlemen, 3 years ago the rate of crime in the District of Columbia was one of the highest in the Nation. As a matter of fact, there were some who were describing Washington, D.C., as the potential crime capital of the world.

We went to work on that problem, and the statistics that have been issued just this week for the month of March show how much has been accomplished: The rate of crime in the District of Columbia has been cut in half in the past 3 years.

The credit for that goes to Chief Wilson for his leadership, and to the officers and men that I have just met, the dedicated

people that have worked on the police force of the District of Columbia, and of course, credit also to the citizens of the District who have backed up law enforcement in the best possible way.

Now Washington, D.C., instead of being an example of lawlessness, is one of the safest cities in this country for the millions of tourists who come to this city every year, particularly at this springtime of the year.

Chief, we congratulate you, and will you also congratulate the hundreds of men that I could not meet, for this marvelous achievement.

CHIEF JERRY WILSON. I certainly will, Mr. President.

It is certainly a pleasure to have these

men up here to represent the force, and it is more than just the police force that has done this though, as you well know.

There were a great deal of programs that you instituted in 1970 in terms of court reorganization, in terms of narcotics treatment, but more than anything else, I think the thing that has made the difference to the men has been that we have known unequivocally that we had your support, and also the support of the citizens. A great deal of credit belongs to the citizens—and the atmosphere, I think, that has prevailed in the last couple of years in this city has done much to bring about this crime decline—and I say that without intending to take anything away from the hard work that is done by the members of the department. But we certainly do appreciate the support we have gotten.

THE PRESIDENT. All we can do is ask you to cut it in half again by next year.

CHIEF WILSON. We will try, Mr. President.

NOTE: The President spoke at 2:50 p.m. in the Rose Garden at the White House, where Chief Wilson introduced him to the annual award winners in the Metropolitan Police Department. The President spoke without referring to notes.

On the same day, the White House released the transcript of a news briefing on domestic matters including District of Columbia crime statistics by John D. Ehrlichman, Assistant to the President for Domestic Affairs, and Egil Krogh, Jr., Deputy Assistant to the President for Domestic Affairs.

---

127   Statement About Transmittal to the Congress of a Request for Supplemental Appropriations for the Cancer Research Program.   *April* 26, 1972

I HAVE sent to the Congress a supplemental appropriation request for $40 million to expand the campaign against cancer. This brings the total amount requested in this fiscal year for the expanded attack on cancer to $378 million, a 100 percent increase over the amount requested in the 1970 budget. These additional funds would increase fellowship and training grants by $4 million and construction grants by $36 million.

This action follows the recommendation of 250 outstanding cancer scientists who are involved in the development of a total national cancer plan. As a result of numerous planning sessions, these men and women have urged that one of our first priorities in the development of the expanded cancer research program should be a rapid increase in training and construction funds.

The added training programs would assure that additional technical and professional staff are available to carry out the expanded cancer research program.

Additional funds for construction are required to strengthen the Cancer Research Centers Program. This program has been designed to promote the development of facilities throughout the Nation which would combine the fundamental research competence of the university medical schools with the long experience and special skills of the best cancer institutes. The goal is a system which will provide facilities for generating new research and development and for translating cancer research results into regular clinical and public health practices.

I urge the Congress to give these requests prompt and favorable attention so that we can continue to move forward as rapidly as possible in our campaign against cancer.

128   Statement on the Death of Arthur E. Summerfield. *April 26, 1972*

MRS. NIXON and I join with fellow citizens across the country in mourning the death of Arthur Summerfield, and in expressing our deepest sympathy to his family.

He was a loyal and good friend. He was an ardent and dedicated Republican. He was devoted to his country, and in his service to both party and country he earned the high admiration of men and women from both sides of the political aisle. He will be remembered by history as a great American whose career was symbolic of the finest aspects of our national çharacter.

NOTE: Mr. Summerfield, 73, died of pneumonia at Good Samaritan Hospital, West Palm Beach, Fla.

He served as chairman of the Republican National Committee, 1952–53, and as Postmaster General, 1953–61.

129   Address to the Nation on Vietnam. *April 26, 1972*

Good evening:

During the past 3 weeks you have been reading and hearing about the massive invasion of South Vietnam by the Communist armies of North Vietnam.

Tonight, I want to give you a firsthand report on the military situation in Vietnam, the decisions I have made with regard to the role of the United States in the conflict, and the efforts we are making to bring peace at the negotiating table.

Let me begin briefly by reviewing what the situation was when I took office and what we have done since then to end American involvement in the war and to bring peace to the long-suffering people of Southeast Asia.

On January 20, 1969, the American troop ceiling in Vietnam was 549,000. Our casualties were running as high as 300 a week. Thirty thousand young Americans were being drafted every month.

Today, 39 months later, through our program of Vietnamization—helping the South Vietnamese develop the capability of defending themselves—the number of Americans in Vietnam by Monday, May 1, will have been reduced to 69,000. Our casualties—even during the present, all-out enemy offensive—have been reduced by 95 percent. And draft calls now average fewer than 5,000 men a month, and we expect to bring them to zero next year.

As I reported in my television address to the Nation on January 25, we have offered the most generous peace terms in both public and private negotiating sessions. Our most recent proposal provided for an immediate cease-fire; the exchange of all prisoners of war; the withdrawal of all of our forces within 6 months; and new elections in Vietnam, which would be internationally supervised, with all political elements including the Communists participating in and helping to run the elections. One month before such elections, President Thieu and Vice President Huong would resign.

Now, Hanoi's answer to this offer was a refusal even to discuss our proposals and, at the same time, a huge escalation of their military activities on the battlefield. Last October, the same month when we made this peace offer to Hanoi, our intelligence reports began to indicate that the enemy was building up for a major attack. And yet we deliberately refrained from responding militarily. Instead we patiently continued with the Paris talks, because we wanted to give the enemy every chance to reach a negotiated settlement at the bargaining table rather than to seek a military victory on the battlefield—a victory they cannot be allowed to win.

Finally, 3 weeks ago, on Easter weekend, they mounted their massive invasion of South Vietnam. Three North Vietnamese divisions swept across the demilitarized zone into South Vietnam—in violation of the treaties they had signed in 1954 and in violation of the understanding they had reached with President Johnson in 1968, when he stopped the bombing of North Vietnam in return for arrangements which included their pledge not to violate the DMZ. Shortly after the invasion across the DMZ, another three North Vietnamese divisions invaded

South Vietnam further south. As the offensive progressed, the enemy indiscriminately shelled civilian population centers in clear violation of the 1968 bombing halt understanding.

So the facts are clear. More than 120,000 North Vietnamese are now fighting in South Vietnam. There are no South Vietnamese troops anywhere in North Vietnam. Twelve of North Vietnam's 13 regular combat divisions have now left their own soil in order to carry aggressive war onto the territory of their neighbors. Whatever pretext there was of a civil war in South Vietnam has now been stripped away.

What we are witnessing here—what is being brutally inflicted upon the people of South Vietnam—is a clear case of naked and unprovoked aggression across an international border. There is only one word for it—invasion.

This attack has been resisted on the ground entirely by South Vietnamese forces, and in one area by South Korean forces. There are no United States ground troops involved. None will be involved. To support this defensive effort by the South Vietnamese, I have ordered attacks on enemy military targets in both North and South Vietnam by the air and naval forces of the United States.

I have here on my desk a report. I received it this morning from General Abrams. He gives the following evaluation of the situation:

- The South Vietnamese are fighting courageously and well in their self-defense. They are inflicting very heavy casualties on the invading force, which has not gained the easy victory some predicted for it 3 weeks ago.

- Our air strikes have been essential in

protecting our own remaining forces and in assisting the South Vietnamese in their efforts to protect their homes and their country from a Communist takeover.

• General Abrams predicts in this report that there will be several more weeks of very hard fighting. Some battles will be lost, he says; others will be won by the South Vietnamese. But his conclusion is that if we continue to provide air and sea support, the enemy will fail in its desperate gamble to impose a Communist regime in South Vietnam, and the South Vietnamese will then have demonstrated their ability to defend themselves on the ground against future enemy attacks.

Based on this realistic assessment from General Abrams, and after consultation with President Thieu, Ambassador Bunker, Ambassador Porter, and my senior advisers in Washington, I have three decisions to announce tonight.

First, I have decided that Vietnamization has proved itself sufficiently that we can continue our program of withdrawing American forces without detriment to our overall goal of ensuring South Vietnam's survival as an independent country. Consequently, I am announcing tonight that over the next 2 months 20,000 more Americans will be brought home from Vietnam. This decision has the full approval of President Thieu and of General Abrams. It will bring our troop ceiling down to 49,000 by July 1—a reduction of half a million men since this Administration came into office.

Second, I have directed Ambassador Porter to return to the negotiating table

in Paris tomorrow,[1] but with one very specific purpose in mind. We are not resuming the Paris talks simply in order to hear more empty propaganda and bombast from the North Vietnamese and Vietcong delegates, but to get on with the constructive business of making peace. We are resuming the Paris talks with the firm expectation that productive talks leading to rapid progress will follow through all available channels. As far as we are concerned, the first order of business will be to get the enemy to halt his invasion of South Vietnam and to return the American prisoners of war.

Finally, I have ordered that our air and naval attacks on military installations in North Vietnam be continued until the North Vietnamese stop their offensive in South Vietnam.

I have flatly rejected the proposal that we stop the bombing of North Vietnam as a condition for returning to the negotiating table. They sold that package to the United States once before, in 1968, and we are not going to buy it again in 1972.

Now, let's look at the record. By July 1 we will have withdrawn over 90 percent of our forces that were in Vietnam in 1969. Before the enemy's invasion began, we had cut our air sorties in half. We have offered exceedingly generous terms for peace. The only thing we have refused to do is to accede to the enemy's demand to overthrow the lawfully constituted

---

[1] On April 25, 1972, Press Secretary Ronald L. Ziegler announced an agreement by the United States and the Republic of Vietnam to resume the plenary sessions of the Paris peace talks. The announcement is printed in the Weekly Compilation of Presidential Documents (vol. 8, p. 790).

Government of South Vietnam and to impose a Communist dictatorship in its place.

As you will recall, I have warned on a number of occasions over the past 3 years that if the enemy responded to our efforts to bring peace by stepping up the war, I would act to meet that attack, for these three very good reasons: first, to protect our remaining American forces; second, to permit continuation of our withdrawal program; and third, to prevent the imposition of a Communist regime on the people of South Vietnam against their will, with the inevitable bloodbath that would follow for hundreds of thousands who have dared to oppose Communist aggression.

The air and naval strikes of recent weeks have been carried out to achieve these objectives. They have been directed only against military targets which support the invasion of South Vietnam and they will not stop until the invasion stops.

The Communists have failed in their efforts to win over the people of South Vietnam politically. And General Abrams believes that they will fail in their efforts to conquer South Vietnam militarily. Their one remaining hope is to win in the Congress of the United States and among the people of the United States the victory they cannot win among the people of South Vietnam or on the battlefield in South Vietnam.

The great question then is how we, the American people, will respond to this final challenge.

Let us look at what the stakes are—not just for South Vietnam, but for the United States and for the cause of peace in the world. If one country, armed with the most modern weapons by major powers, can invade another nation and succeed in conquering it, other countries will be encouraged to do exactly the same thing—in the Mideast, in Europe, and in other international danger spots. If the Communists win militarily in Vietnam, the risk of war in other parts of the world would be enormously increased. But if, on the other hand, Communist aggression fails in Vietnam, it will be discouraged elsewhere, and the chance for peace will be increased.

We are not trying to conquer North Vietnam or any other country in this world. We want no territory. We seek no bases. We have offered the most generous peace terms—peace with honor for both sides—with South Vietnam and North Vietnam each respecting the other's independence.

But we will not be defeated, and we will never surrender our friends to Communist aggression.

We have come a long way in this conflict. The South Vietnamese have made great progress; they are now bearing the brunt of the battle. We can now see the day when no more Americans will be involved there at all.

But as we come to the end of this long and difficult struggle, we must be steadfast. And we must not falter. For all that we have risked and all that we have gained over the years now hangs in the balance during the coming weeks and months. If we now let down our friends, we shall surely be letting down ourselves and our future as well. If we now persist, future generations will thank America for her courage and her vision in this time of testing.

That is why I say to you tonight, let us bring our men home from Vietnam; let us end the war in Vietnam. But let us end it in such a way that the younger brothers

553

and the sons of the brave men who have fought in Vietnam will not have to fight again in some other Vietnam at some time in the future.

Any man who sits here in this office feels a profound sense of obligation to future generations. No man who sits here has the right to take any action which would abdicate America's great tradition of world leadership or weaken respect for the Office of President of the United States.

Earlier this year I traveled to Peking on an historic journey for peace. Next month I shall travel to Moscow on what I hope will also be a journey for peace. In the 18 countries I have visited as President I have found great respect for the Office of President of the United States. I have reason to expect, based on Dr. Kissinger's report, that I shall find that same respect for the office I hold when I visit Moscow.

I do not know who will be in this office in the years ahead. But I do know that future Presidents will travel to nations abroad as I have on journeys for peace. If the United States betrays the millions of people who have relied on us in Vietnam,

the President of the United States, whoever he is, will not deserve nor receive the respect which is essential if the United States is to continue to play the great role we are destined to play of helping to build a new structure of peace in the world. It would amount to a renunciation of our morality, an abdication of our leadership among nations, and an invitation for the mighty to prey upon the weak all around the world. It would be to deny peace the chance peace deserves to have. This we shall never do.

My fellow Americans, let us therefore unite as a nation in a firm and wise policy of real peace—not the peace of surrender, but peace with honor—not just peace in our time, but peace for generations to come.

Thank you and good night.

NOTE: The President spoke at 10 p.m. in the Oval Office at the White House. His address was broadcast live on radio and television.

The President spoke from a prepared text. An advance text of his address was released on the same day.

The White House also released the transcript of a news briefing on the President's address by Henry A. Kissinger, Assistant to the President for National Security Affairs.

130   Letters to the Chairman and Ranking Minority Member of the House Committee on Banking and Currency About Proposed Minority Enterprise Small Business Investment Legislation.   *April 27, 1972*

Dear Wright:

On March 18, 1972, when I sent a message to the Congress on the subject of Minority Business Enterprise, I urged swift approval by the Congress of the Minority Enterprise Small Business Investment Act of 1972.

At that time it was my understanding

that the MESBIC legislation was to be given early hearings before the Subcommittee on Small Business, of your Committee on Banking and Currency. I was most gratified to know that your Committee would be giving prompt attention to this vital legislation. As my message indicated, I believe the proposed MESBIC legislation will vastly expand the opportunities for minority entrepreneurs, and this expansion should not be delayed.

The Minority Enterprise Small Business Investment Act, as you know, would fall within the purview of the responsibilities of the Small Business Administration. Administrator Thomas Kleppe is prepared to testify in support of this legislation, which is urgently needed, and he awaits your invitation.

Not only will the MESBIC legislation expand available capital to give minority businessmen a greater "piece of the action," but it will in turn stimulate the employment of minority individuals and provide inroads into the unacceptably high unemployment rate for minorities.

I am most hopeful that your Committee and the Subcommittee on Small Business will schedule the MESBIC legislation for hearings in early May, so that it can be presented at an early date for consideration by the House of Representatives. I certainly hope that I can count on you to join with me to achieve the all-important goal of providing expanded, new opportunities for minority Americans.

Sincerely,

RICHARD NIXON

[Honorable Wright Patman, Chairman, Committee on Banking and Currency, House of Representatives, Washington, D.C. 20515]

Dear Bill:

I think you know that I am strongly committed to the Minority Enterprise program. My proposed MESBIC legislation would substantially increase the business opportunities for minority Americans, and would in turn help to provide jobs for minority individuals facing an unacceptably high unemployment rate.

We should avoid delay on this bill. The minority community recognizes that the opportunity for a "piece of the action" is the avenue to economic equality, and they know the time is *now*.

It is of great importance that the MESBIC legislation be given early attention by Congress. I hope you will use your good offices to influence a scheduling of early hearings, and prompt consideration of the legislation by the House of Representatives.

Sincerely,

RICHARD NIXON

[Honorable William B. Widnall, House of Representatives, Washington, D.C. 20515]

NOTE: The letters were dated April 25, 1972, and released April 27.

131   Statement Designating Russell E. Train as Special Representative to a Meeting of the International Whaling Commission.   *April* 27, 1972

I AM pleased to announce today that the Honorable Russell E. Train, Chairman of the Council on Environmental Quality, will serve as my special representative to the meeting in London this June of the International Whaling Commission.

Mr. Train's participation in this meeting demonstrates the high priority which my Administration attaches to the protection of whales. It is my hope that other governments will also take steps to strengthen the work of the International

Whaling Commission. In particular, I hope the delegations to the June meeting will include officials concerned with environmental matters.

My concern for the conservation of whales is widely shared—both throughout the Government and throughout the country. By unanimous votes, both Houses of the United States Congress have passed resolutions urging a 10-year international moratorium on commercial whaling. The Department of the Interior has placed all eight species of great whales on the endangered list. As a result, the United States no longer participates in commercial whaling and does not permit the importation of any whale products.

Our participation in the work of the International Whaling Commission allows us to pursue these same concerns at the international level. Mr. Train will take with him to London my very best wishes for the success of the Commission's endeavors.

NOTE: The statement was released at Key Biscayne, Fla.

132 Statement Following Splashdown of Apollo 16. *April 27, 1972*

THE JOURNEY of Apollo 16 has ended, but the contributions of this mission to scientific progress have only begun. Rarely if ever has so much new information been made available to science in such a brief period. As the work of evaluation and analysis goes forward, the impact of Apollo 16 will be felt for many years to come.

On behalf of all Americans, I am pleased to welcome Astronauts Young, Duke, and Mattingly back to Earth and to salute them for a job well done. Their skill, their courage, and their enthusiasm have written another proud chapter in the stirring story of mankind's struggle to unlock the mysteries of the unknown.

NOTE: The statement was released at Key Biscayne, Fla.

The President telephoned the astronauts, Capt. John W. Young, USN, Lt. Col. Charles M. Duke, Jr., USAF, and Lt. Comdr. Thomas K. Mattingly II, USN, aboard the U.S.S. *Ticonderoga* in the Pacific to express his personal congratulations on the successful completion of their mission.

133 Statement About the Status of Women Within the Administration. *April 28, 1972*

ONE year ago this month, I asked an intensification of this Administration's efforts to make better use of the talents of women in Federal Government service.

Now, one year later, I am gratified by the results. We are making real progress, not only in striking down barriers to women serving and advancing in the Government, but in affirmatively reaching out to encourage and recruit them to do so.

This Administration has appointed and promoted more women to full-time, policymaking positions in the Federal Government than ever before. The number of women we have placed in policymaking positions paying $28,000 and up has nearly tripled since April 1971—from 36 to 105. More than half of these hold positions previously held only by men.

We reached another milestone with the employment and/or advancement of more than 1,000 women in middle-management positions during the past year. This is particularly noteworthy because it occurred during a time when budget policy required a 5-percent reduction in the Federal work force.

We have made an impressive start, but now we must do even better in giving women the equal opportunity they have so long deserved.

I ask the private sector and State and local governments to follow our lead by taking a close look at employment practices which may be discriminatory, and by doing all that can be done to guarantee women equal opportunity for employment and advancement as well as equal pay for equal work.

In this era of great challenges and potentials, the Nation—in the private sector as well as in government at *all* levels—needs the capabilities and brainpower of every single American. The full and equal participation of women is crucial to the strength of our country.

NOTE: On the same day, the White House released a fact sheet and the transcript of a news briefing on the status of women in the Administration. Participants in the news briefing were Jayne B. Spain, Vice Chairman, United States Civil Service Commission, and Barbara H. Franklin, Staff Assistant to the President for Executive Manpower.

134 Remarks and a Question-and-Answer Session With Guests Following a Dinner at Secretary Connally's Ranch in Floresville, Texas. *April 30, 1972*

THE PRESIDENT. [1.] Well, I want to say first of all that we are most grateful for the welcome that you have given us to Texas, and speaking in a very personal sense, I, of course, rather than saying "Mr. Secretary," would like to say to John and Nellie Connally that we are particularly happy that we have had a chance to visit this ranch, to see a lot of old friends, and also to make some new friends, as well.

As I listened to John Connally, and as I listened to some of the things he had to say about me and my age, and as I thought back on some of those dope stories suggesting that he was no longer a potential candidate for anything, I began to wonder. [*Laughter*]

I would like to return the compliment, not simply because it is a case of when one man scratches your back, you scratch his in return—and, of course, it is much more pleasant when it is a lady—but nevertheless, whatever the case might be, I would like to say a word about the appointment that I made of John Connally as Secretary of the Treasury; how it was greeted with such surprise in many quarters, applause from some, a wonder among others, and criticism, of course, from many that you would expect.

Generally speaking, the line was, well, what does John Connally know about being Secretary of the Treasury? They recognized he was a fine lawyer, they recognized he was a very successful political leader in Texas, they recognized he had been a great Governor of this State, but what in the world did he know about

557

being Secretary of the Treasury? And the country has found out.

All that I can say is this: When I named him to this position, I named him to the position because I had had the privilege of knowing him as a man through many years, and particularly well during the years I have been President. And based on the—and it is hard to realize that it has been 18 months, almost, now that he has been in this position—based on those 18 months, I can say that John Connally, who has been a Governor and now a Cabinet officer and was a former Secretary of the Navy, is, in my view, a man who has demonstrated that he is capable of holding any job in the United States that he would like to pursue.

I am just glad he is not seeking the Democratic nomination. [*Laughter*]

If I could just add to that by saying that we remember the new economic policy of August 15. We remember the United States at long last standing up for its position in international monetary affairs, in trade matters and the rest, and the leadership that the Secretary of the Treasury provided. We remember his leadership in the fight on inflation, in all of the other areas, but I also recall those times when clearly out of his special capacity as Secretary of the Treasury, his capacity as the head of the Cost of Living Council, as an adviser, as a friend, as a counselor in all areas, I remember how much he has contributed to this Administration.

And to all those, I would add one final thing. Certainly his greatest contribution was bringing Nellie Connally to Washington, D.C. She has been a scintillating star on the Washington social scene. Don't get the idea that that is bad, necessarily,

but I can assure you that in our Cabinet family and among those who have known her, be they Democrats or Republicans, that they have all been as warmly affectionate toward her as the people of this State are. And we are so happy that here with their friends, we can share this special evening with you.

Because I know you have had a very splendid dinner tonight, and because I know this has probably never happened on this ranch before—well, at least if it has happened, it has never been done by one who held the office that I hold—I think that all of you would like to join me in raising our glasses to John and Nellie Connally.

Now, with that, let me just say a word with regard to what John has suggested. It did occur to him as we were sitting here that so many of our guests don't have the opportunity to talk with the one who happens to be the guest of honor, as those who are at only the one table at which we are seated. It doesn't mean that there are many pearls of wisdom that are passed out here that you are missing, but it does mean simply that perhaps on an occasion like this, since this is a party of close friends, since this whole great State is covered, that I know that both Pat and I would have liked to have sat at every table and talked to each one of you.

So for the next few minutes, if you like, in a totally nonpartisan, nonpolitical way, if you would like to just rather imagine that we were sitting in your living room, and you were chatting and asking questions, I will try to answer them.

I can assure you, if I don't know the answers, John will.

So with that, in that very informal way, we will be glad to take any of your questions that you have for a few minutes, and we will not keep you too long, unless the questions take too long.

QUESTIONS

VIETNAM

[2.] Q. Mr. President, do you anticipate any developments in Vietnam other than those courageous statements we heard on the television the other night, that you might tell us here?

THE PRESIDENT. Briefly I would respond by saying that the evaluation of the situation in Vietnam today is the same that I gave then.

As General Abrams reported then, and as he has updated his report as of today, the South Vietnamese on the ground are resisting very bravely a massive Communist North Vietnamese invasion of South Vietnam. That invasion will continue. The offensive will continue in its intensity, and we can expect over the next 4 to 5 weeks that there will be some battles lost by the South Vietnamese and some will be won, but it is his professional judgment— General Abrams' professional judgment— that the South Vietnamese will be able to hold and deny to the North Vietnamese their goal, which, of course, is to impose on the people of South Vietnam a Communist government.

Now to keep it all in perspective, let us understand that when we hear about this town or that one that is under attack, we must remember that as of this time, the North Vietnamese have utterly failed in their ability to rally the South Vietnamese people to their cause.

We also must remember that despite their moving in on certain territory and in certain towns, that over 90 percent of the people of South Vietnam are still under the Government of South Vietnam, and not under control of the Communists.

So keeping it in perspective, while we can expect, and should expect, as is always the case in a war of any kind, and particularly a war of this type—we can expect some days when the news may be a South Vietnamese setback, and other days when it will be otherwise. It is the view, the professional view of the man on the spot, best able to judge, that the South Vietnamese will be able to hold, provided—and this comes to what we do— provided the United States continues to furnish the air and naval support that we have been furnishing to stop this invasion.

Now, without repeating what I said last Wednesday night, but simply to underline it, I would like to make just two or three points quickly, frankly, to this group of friends here in Texas.

Questions have been raised about the decision that I have made, which is to the effect that as long as the North Vietnamese were conducting an invasion and an offensive in South Vietnam, and were killing South Vietnamese and Americans in South Vietnam, that I would, as Commander in Chief of our Armed Forces, order air and naval strikes on military targets in North Vietnam.

I realize that that decision has caused considerable controversy in this country. I understand why that would be the case. There are many people who believe that the United States has done enough in South Vietnam, that what we should do is to find a way to get out as quickly as we can, and let whatever the consequences are flow from that, which would mean, of course, a Communist takeover.

Let me tell you the reasons why I feel that it is vitally important that the United

States continue to use its air and naval power against targets in North Vietnam, as well as in South Vietnam, to prevent a Communist takeover and a Communist victory over the people of South Vietnam.

First, because there are 69,000 Americans still in Vietnam—that will be reduced to 49,000 by the first of July—and I, as Commander in Chief, have a responsibility to see to it that their lives are adequately protected, and I, of course, will meet that responsibility.

Second, because as we consider the situation in Vietnam, we must remember that if the North Vietnamese were to take over in South Vietnam, as a result of our stopping our support in the air and on the sea—we have no ground support whatever, there are no American ground forces in action in South Vietnam and none will be—but when we consider that situation, if there were such a takeover, we must consider the consequences.

There is, first, the consequence to the people of South Vietnam. We look back to what happened historically. In 1954, when the North Vietnamese took over in North Vietnam, the Catholic Bishop of Danang estimated that at least 500,000 people in North Vietnam who had opposed the Communist takeover in the North were either murdered or starved to death in slave labor camps.

I saw something of that when Mrs. Nixon and I were in there in 1956, when we visited refugee camps where over a million North Vietnamese fled from the Communist tyranny to come to the South. If, at this particular point, the Communists were to take over in South Vietnam, you can imagine what would happen to the hundreds of thousands of South Vietnamese who sided with their own Government and with the United States against

the Communists. It would be a bloodbath that would stain the hands of the United States for time immemorial.

That is bad enough. I know there are some who say we have done enough, what happens to the South Vietnamese at this particular time is something that should not be our concern. We have sacrificed enough for them. So let's put it in terms of the United States alone, and then we really see why the only decision that any man in the position of President of the United States can make is to authorize the necessary air and naval strikes that will prevent a Communist takeover.

In the event that one country like North Vietnam, massively assisted with the most modern technical weapons by two Communist super powers—in the event that that country is able to invade another country and conquer it, you can see how that pattern would be repeated in other countries throughout the world—in the Mideast, in Europe, and in others as well.

If, on the other hand, that kind of aggression is stopped in Vietnam, and fails there, then it will be discouraged in other parts of the world. Putting it quite directly then, what is on the line in Vietnam is not just peace for Vietnam, but peace in the Mideast, peace in Europe, and peace not just for the 5 or 6 or 7 years immediately ahead of us, but possibly for a long time in the future.

As I put it last Wednesday night, I want, and all America wants, to end the war in Vietnam. I want, and all Americans want, to bring our men home from Vietnam. But I want, and I believe all Americans want, to bring our men home and to end this war in a way that the younger brothers and the sons of the men who have fought and died in Vietnam won't be fighting in another Vietnam 5 or 10 years from now. That is what this is all about.

[3.] Q. May we raise our glasses and pay tribute to the courage of the President of the United States.

THE PRESIDENT. I am most grateful for that toast. Incidentally, I hope the champagne holds out for the evening.

But I do want to say that in the final analysis, what is really on the line here, of course, is the position of the United States of America as the strongest free world power, as a constructive force for peace in the world.

Let us imagine for a moment what the world would be like if the United States were not respected in the world. What would the world be like if friends of the United States throughout the non-Communist world lost confidence in the United States? It would be a world that would be much less safe. It would be a world that would be much more dangerous, not only in terms of war but in terms of the denial of freedom, because when we talk about the United States of America and all of our faults, let us remember in this country we have never used our power to break the peace, only to restore it or keep it, and we have never used our power to destroy freedom, only to defend it.

Now, I think that is a precious asset for the world. I also feel one other thing, and I will close this rather long answer on this point: John Connally has referred to the office of the Presidency of the United States. Earlier this evening I talked to President Johnson on the phone. We are of different parties. We both served in this office. While I had my political differences with him, and he with me, I am sure he would agree that each of us in his way

tries to leave that office with as much respect and with as much strength in the world as he possibly can—that is his responsibility—and to do it the best way that he possibly can.

Let me say in this respect I have noted that when we have traveled abroad to 18 countries, particularly even when we went to the People's Republic of China, the office of President, not the man, but the office of President of the United States is respected in every country we visited. I think we will find that same respect in Moscow. But if the United States at this time leaves Vietnam and allows a Communist takeover, the office of President of the United States will lose respect, and I am not going to let that happen.

[4.] Q. Mr. President, may I ask you about strategic targets in North Vietnam? I have been told for years by the pilots that there are dams up there that would be very much defeating to the North Vietnamese, who have defied what you have tried to prove in the way of peace. Is this true or false? Has this crossed your mind?

THE PRESIDENT. The question is with regard to the targets in North Vietnam, and particularly with regard to the dams and the dikes, which many of the pilots believe would be very effective strategic targets.

I would say on that score that we have, as you know, authorized strikes, and we have made them over the past 4 weeks, since the Communist offensive began, in the Hanoi-Haiphong area.

I have also indicated, as this offensive continues, if it does continue, that we will continue to make strikes on military targets throughout North Vietnam.

Now, the problem that is raised with regard to dams or dikes is that, while it is a strategic target, and indirectly a military target, it would result in an enormous number of civilian casualties. That is something that we want to avoid. It is also something we believe is not needed.

Just let me say that as far as the targets in North Vietnam are concerned, that we are prepared to use our military and naval strength against military targets throughout North Vietnam, and we believe that the North Vietnamese are taking a very great risk if they continue their offensive in the South.

I will just leave it there, and they can make their own choice.

In other words, I believe that we can limit our strikes to military targets without going to targets that involve civilian casualties. That is what we have done, and we can do that in the future, and do the job.

DOMESTIC AMERICA

[5.] Q. Mr. President, turning to domestic America. You know there are great misgivings in the press about how America feels about itself, and where we are going. I don't think there is anyone better equipped to tell us how you feel about where America is going, not today, but for its future, and about its own confidence in itself, and I would like to hear your remarks.

THE PRESIDENT. The question relates to domestic America, the feeling that many Americans have that possibly we, in America, are losing confidence in ourselves. The question asks me to evaluate how I see the mood of America, as I understand it, and what the future for America is in terms of confidence in itself.

That, of course, would allow a rather extended reply. Let me see if I can get at the heart of it. First, let me relate it to the last question.

I know there are those who say that the trouble with America's confidence, most of it, is due to the fact that we are involved in Vietnam, and that once the war in Vietnam is over that then the trouble on the campus will go away, the division in the country, the polarization and all the rest. That is just nonsense.

Let me say the American people do not want war. We did not start this war. Let me say also that when I see people carrying signs saying "Stop the War," I am tempted to say "Tell it to Hanoi; they are the ones that have started the war, not the United States of America."

Nevertheless, while peace is our goal, and peace will be achieved—not just peace in our time, but we hope peace that will live for a generation or longer—that is why we went to Peking. That is why we are going to Moscow. That is why we are trying to end the war responsibly, in a way that would discourage those who would start war, rather than encourage them.

Let us well understand, that if the United States, as a great nation, fails in Vietnam as we come to the end of this long road, and as we see the end, and as we know that it is not necessary to fail, I can think of nothing that would destroy the confidence of the American people more than that. So I would begin with that proposition, answering it on the negative side.

Now, turning to the domestic issue, what about the attitude of America toward itself? We often hear it said that we, in this country, are so divided about race issues, we are divided between labor and management, rich and poor, environmentalists, those who are against doing anything about the environment, and so forth and so on, that it is a rather hopeless future.

I would simply raise this one question in that respect. If you sit in Washington, if you limit yourself to the group that we in Washington generally talk to, and this is no reflection on them, because we all tend to be sort of victims of intellectual incest there, what happens is that you get the impression that everything is wrong with America; that the majority of the people of this country have lost faith in themselves, faith in their country; they no longer have the will to work, the will to defend the country, the will to build a great nation.

That is a point of view. That point of view tends to be fed—and I say this, incidentally, not in anger, and perhaps more in sorrow—it tends to be fed by the tendency of some in the media—not all, but some in the media—constantly to emphasize a negative. I am speaking now more of the national media, rather than those who are out across the great heartland of America. But the tendency to emphasize those negatives and to create in the minds of the American people the impression that this country, just before its 200th birthday, has reached the point where it has lost its sense of destiny; the American people no longer have the will to greatness which they once had.

I can only say that as I travel through America I find a different story. Let me point it out to you in a different way. I was talking to an ambassador recently from a country in Europe who had recently been accredited to this country. This was several months ago. This ambassador told me that he had lived in Washington for a while, and then he had taken a trip out through the country. He said,

"Mr. President, as I traveled through the country"—he had been to Illinois; he had been to California; he had also been to Texas, as a matter of fact, to Florida, to Georgia, and back to Washington—and he said, "As I go out into the country I see a different America than I see in Washington, D.C." I believe that the heart of America is still strong. I believe that the character of America is still strong. But I think now is the time when we must stand up against the trend toward permissiveness, the trend toward weakness, the trend toward something for nothing, and if we do that, this country is going to regain its self-confidence.

I believe that is going to happen.

WAR CRITICS

[6.] Q. Mr. President, I would like to ask you this question: Mr. Moncrief [1] spoke my sentiments, and I think most of the people in Texas or at least 99 percent of them are in favor of what you are doing in Vietnam, but why is it in the East you get the newspapers, the students, and Members of the Congress and the Senate are complaining about what you are doing, but they never mention what the Communists and North Vietnamese are doing by invading South Vietnam, and they are killing thousands of people. They seem to think that is right, and what we are doing is wrong. But why don't they ever mention that?

THE PRESIDENT. I think that would be a very excellent editorial for somebody to write.

Let me, in all fairness, say this: I do not question the patriotism of any critics of

---

[1] W. A. Moncrief, Sr., was an oilman and businessman from Fort Worth, Tex.

this war. Reasonable and honest and decent Americans can disagree about whether we should have gotten into Vietnam. They can disagree about how the war has been conducted, disagree about who is at fault now, and so forth, but let's just look at the record as it is at the present time.

Since I have come into office we have withdrawn half a million men from Vietnam. We have offered everything that could be offered except to impose a Communist government on the people of South Vietnam, and their answer has been a massive invasion of South Vietnam by the North.

Now, under these circumstances, instead of the critics criticizing brave Americans flying dangerous air missions, hitting military targets in North Vietnam and military targets only, instead of criticizing them trying to prevent a Communist takeover, I think they ought to direct a little criticism to the Communists that are trying to keep this war going. That is what they ought to be doing.

TRADE WITH CHINA AND RUSSIA

[7.] Q. What are the possibilities of trade with China and Russia, as you now see it?

THE PRESIDENT. Looking at both of these countries, we must realize—and I know that there are many here who have traveled certainly to Russia, and to other Communist countries, although very few perhaps have been to China, at least in recent years—and looking at both of these countries realistically, as far as China is concerned, while we have now opened the door for a new relationship insofar as trade is involved, realistically, the amount of trade that the United States will have

with the People's Republic of China will be considerably limited over a period of time.

The Japanese, for example, have found that out. They, of course, are much closer to Mainland China, and they have been trying to trade with them over a period of years, and yet they find that the amount of trade that they are able to have with the People's Republic of China is, frankly, much less than they expected when they began to open trade up.

We should not expect too much in the short range. We could expect a considerable amount further down the road.

Now, with the Soviet Union, this, of course, will be a major subject that will be discussed at the summit meeting. There will be considerable opportunities for trade with the Soviet Union.

The Secretary of Agriculture, Mr. Butz, was there discussing the possibilities of trade insofar as agricultural products are concerned—the selling of some of our grain to the Soviet Union.

We have also had some discussions between the Secretary of Commerce, Mr. Stans—and Mr. Peterson, now the new Secretary of Commerce, is discussing this with the Russian delegation, and we expect more trade opportunities to develop with the Soviet Union.

Realistically, however, we must recognize that where you have a Communist country dealing with a capitalist country, or non-Communist country, the possibilities of trade are seriously limited because of an inability to have a method for financing it.

I know I have heard some American businessmen say, wouldn't it be great if we could just sell just a few consumer items to 800 million Chinese. That is fine, but what are they going to sell us, and how are we going to finance it?

That is a problem, to a lesser extent, with the Soviet Union, but also a problem with them.

I would say then these new relationships we have developed and are developing with the People's Republic of China and with the Soviet Union will certainly lead to more trade in the years ahead— trade in nonstrategic items, of course, so long as those countries are engaged in supporting activities such as those in Vietnam.

Q. Mr. President, leave it to John. He will work it out. [*Laughter*]

TACTICS IN VIETNAM

[8.] Q. Mr. President, one thing that is bothering me is, what is the basis for the criticism of our bombing Haiphong and Hanoi? Were the United States in war, do you not think that they would immediately bomb Washington and San Francisco and New York, and isn't the quickest way to stop this war to stop the supplies that are going to North Vietnam from their friends?

THE PRESIDENT. The United States has shown restraint such as a great power has never shown in history in its handling of the war in Vietnam. At the present time, however, now that we have gone the extra mile in offering a peace settlement and peace terms, a cease-fire, an exchange of prisoners of war—and Mr. Ross Perot [2]

---

[2] H. Ross Perot, a Texas businessman, headed United We Stand, a private organization formed to call attention to the plight of American prisoners of war. In 1969, as part of efforts to improve the treatment of the POW's, he attempted unsuccessfully to deliver Christmas packages to American prisoners in North Vietnam.

can tell you about some of the things we have gone through there and the barbarism with which our prisoners of war are treated. We have offered a total withdrawal of all our forces within 6 months. President Thieu has offered to resign a month before a new election that would be internationally supervised in which the Communists would participate in the election, participate in the supervisory body.

Having offered all that, and then faced with this invasion, certainly the least the United States can do—and that is all that I have ordered—is to use our air and sea power to hit military targets in North Vietnam. That is what we have done and that is what we are going to continue to do until they stop their invasion of South Vietnam.

GOLD PRICES AND PRODUCTIVITY

[9.] Q. Mr. President, most of us who have observed the moves that you have made in freeing the gold and expecting the rest of the world to let their currencies float are pleased. At least the ones that I know.

The greatness of the country is built on the willingness of its people to work. The success of this country is built on that. When Japan can settle a strike in 2 days, a shipping strike, and we take 6 months, why can't we do this a little more efficiently and quickly? When we take people away from their jobs and do not have them produce, we are losing the productive value of these people, and if we don't do this, will we not face a further devaluation in the ensuing months ahead?

THE PRESIDENT. I think most of you could hear the question. It relates to what I think is the totally correct policy of the Secretary of the Treasury in which we sought a new alignment of currency, we raised the price of gold, as a result we improved the competitive position of American products in world markets.

But when we come to the fundamental point—and this is the one you are getting at—it is very simply this: Unless the United States is prepared to build a wall around itself, we have to compete with other nations in the world. Now in order to compete with other nations in the world, we, who pay by far the highest wages in the world, have to be more productive than other people in the world, and that means that we can't afford work stoppages that are too long.

The strike that you refer to, the longshoremen's strike, was one that was certainly not defensible and had enormously negative effects on the economy of this country.

We also, in that connection, if we are going to be competitive, have to have a tax structure which will encourage new investment in capital rather than discourage it, and we also have to have, if I may boldly suggest it, a recognition of the need to respect what I call the work ethic in this country.

Now, briefly, on all three points. With regard to strikes of the longshoremen, railroads, transportation generally, the Congress of the United States has had before it for the past 2 years a bill that would require, in effect, compulsory arbitration of such disputes and bring them to a halt, and the Congress has not acted.

I think this, of course, is a major failure on the part of the Congress, and it is time that we had Congressmen and Senators—and incidentally, this is not partisan—Democrat and Republican, that have the courage to go down to Washington and

vote for legislation in the public interest that will stop these transportation tieups as we had on the docks and other places, and I think we should get them.

Second, with regard to the competitive position of American products in the world, there has been a lot of talk lately about the need for tax reform, and a great deal of criticism of so-called tax loopholes. I am not going to go into that in any detail, when I have the major expert on tax reform right here in front of me. And it is no accident he is on my right, incidentally, in this respect. [*Laughter*]

But I simply want to say this: One of the loopholes is supposed to be depreciation. Another loophole is supposed to be depletion. Now all of you here in this State know my own position on depletion and depreciation, and you also know that this Administration has been subjected to considerable criticism on the ground that we are for big business and we are for rich oilmen and against people.

I will tell you what we are for. What we are for is for more jobs for America and for American industry to be able to compete abroad. Do you know where the most efficient steel plant in the world is? It is not in the United States. It is in Japan. Do you know where some of the most efficient new kinds of chemical plants in the world are? We have some very good ones in the United States, but the best new ones may be in Germany.

How did this happen? It didn't happen because our American businessmen are less imaginative, our scientists and engineers less capable. I believe we have got the best in the world. But in both Japan and Germany, after they had gone through the devastation of World War II, they adopted a tax policy in terms of the depreciation that encouraged investment in new plants and equipment and research on a basis unheard of in any capitalist country in the world before.

As far as I am concerned, that is why I strongly favor not only the present depreciation rates, but going even further than that, so we can get our plants and equipment more effective. That is why, in terms of depletion, rather than moving in the direction of reducing the depletion allowance, let us look at the fact that all the evidence now shows that we are going to have a major energy crisis in this country in the eighties. To avoid that energy crisis we have to provide incentive rather than disincentive for people to go out and explore for oil. That is why you have depletion, and the people have got to understand it.

Now, if I can just spend a moment on the last point, the work ethic. First, let us well understand that there are millions of fine Americans that work hard, are proud of their work, and they have made this country, they built this country, and they are going to build it bigger in the future.

But let us also understand that there has developed—and this goes back to the earlier question which I could not answer too precisely because it is difficult to answer in an effective way a question so profound in its implications—but in recent years there has grown up the idea more and more and more of something for nothing; the idea that where a job is concerned that we will take those jobs only if they happen to be jobs that we consider, as the term is used, not menial.

Let me ask any of you who have traveled to Los Angeles, to Miami, to New York, and so forth, Denver, Dallas, anyplace, pick up your papers, look at the Help Wanted ads, and you will find thousands of Help Wanted ads in those particular papers, and yet you will find unemployment, and in the city of New York alone, a million on the welfare rolls.

Now this is not always true. It may not even be true in a majority of cases, but it is sometimes true, and very simply, it is that in case after case, an individual who is able to work refuses to work because the job is not one that he feels is up to his capabilities. He feels that it is too menial a job.

Well, I must have grown up in a different time. I say that no job is menial if it provides bread on the table and shelter for a family. Rather than for a man to have to go on public welfare, he ought to take the job.

It is that spirit that we need revived in this country, and we have to revive it not only down among those who might potentially be on welfare rolls, but up and down our whole society, because let us be quite honest in our own self-evaluation: The tendency, too often, in modern education, in some of our great colleges and our great universities, is to downplay the necessity for excellence, for pride in work, and all these other great values that have made this country what it is.

I just want to say on that point, I have great confidence in the future as far as America's competitive position is concerned, but let us make no mistake about it: Simply letting the dollar float, having a realignment of currency, erecting temporary barriers, a 15-percent or a 10-percent surcharge or the rest, isn't going to do the trick. The United States will be able to compete in the world only when the United States and the people of this country are competitive in every sense of the word. We can do it, but we have to tighten our belts if we are going to meet that task.

BUSING

[10.] SECRETARY CONNALLY. Ladies and gentlemen, the President has been going for about an hour. Let's see if we can take one more question, and we won't count this: Mr. President, the people here from Dallas, Corpus Christi, Houston, Austin, and in very recent months, I suppose, perhaps, the most emotional, most critical issue in those cities has been the question of busing. Do you have any comment on it?

THE PRESIDENT. My views on the merits of busing have been expressed on many occasions. I will repeat them only briefly, and then talk about the remedy briefly.

The reason that I am against busing for the purpose of achieving racial balance in our schools is that it leads to inferior education. Let's look at the situation with regard to what the whole busing controversy is about, and there are many lawyers here tonight, and all of you are, of course, familiar with the famous, landmark case of *Brown* v. *the Board of Education* in 1954.

The very title of that case tells us something. *Brown* v. *the Board of Education,* which provided that the dual school system had to be eliminated, was about education, and correctly, in the opinion of observers at that time, and I was one of them, and certainly most observers now, a system that legally sets up a dual school system and divides people according to race is one that could lead and would inevitably lead to inferior education. So *Brown* v. *the Board of Education* dealt with that problem.

That problem has been moved on very effectively, particularly during this Administration, to the great credit of those particularly in Southern States, where some of the dual school systems had to be removed. We now find that the South has gone really further than the North insofar as meeting the goal of getting rid of a dual school system.

Let's look at busing. Where busing comes in, is when in attempting to deal with the problem a board of education or a court orders that schoolchildren be bused across town away from their neighborhood schools in order to create some artificial racial balance.

If you will read the decisions, they never use the term "racial balance," but there are over 23 that we already have identified where that is exactly what the court was ordering.

Now, why do I believe this is wrong? Because in my view, when you bus children, particularly young children, away from their neighborhood schools, into an unfamiliar neighborhood, whether they are black or white, it leads to inferior education. It also has some other disadvantages. It divides communities; it creates hostility among people that didn't exist before. I think that for that reason, we have got to find more effective ways to have equality of education opportunity for all Americans than to use busing.

So that is why I have come up with these remedies: First, a moratorium on any new busing orders for a year. We have asked the Congress to act on that.

Second, I have ordered the Attorney General of the United States to intervene in those cases where the courts have gone beyond what the Supreme Court presently has laid down as the requirement insofar as eliminating the dual school system is concerned.

And then, third, we have asked for the enactment of the Equal Educational Opportunity Act, under which we would upgrade education in inferior schools, but we specifically provide that busing would not be required at all for children sixth grade and below, and then for any other cases above that, would be used not as the first resort, but only as a last resort, and then only temporarily.

It also provides, incidentally, when this act is passed, that in those States that have had imposed upon them busing orders that went beyond what the new legislation would require, those cases could be reopened.

Now, where do you stand? At the present time, the Congress has had this request for legislation for over 2 months. It has not acted. The prospects for its acting do not appear hopeful at the present time. In my view, before the Congress goes home for its election recess, the Congress owes it to the American people to act, because unless it does act, it means that tens of thousands of students in scores of communities across this country are going to be subjected to busing orders that will provide inferior education for them, and that should be avoided. So I believe that the Congress should act to deal with the problem. If the Congress does not act, and refuses to face up to the problem, then the only resort that we have left is to proceed with the constitutional amendment.

So under these circumstances, I realize that the position that I have taken is subject to honest criticism, honest debate by people who have considered the subject just as I have tried to consider it, with the interest of better education as well as eliminating the dual school system, and providing equality of opportunity of education for all concerned.

But I simply conclude my answer to this question by saying that in this country if you were to provide for—I am talking now about the most extreme advocates of busing—if you were to provide for busing students in the major metropolitan centers like New York and Chicago and Detroit and Los Angeles, in plans that go further than even the most liberal plans have ever provided, it would still leave the great majority of black children in inferior schools in central cities who would never get the benefit of a so-called better education.

So I say that the better answer is to upgrade the education for those children who would otherwise be a lost generation, but let's do not impair the education for all other children as a result of busing orders. That is the way I think we should approach it.

FELIX McKNIGHT (managing editor, Dallas Times Herald). Mr. President, your days and nights are very long, and we are very grateful for your services. As a newspaperman, I would like to exercise my prerogative and say thank you, Mr. President.

NOTE: Secretary Connally introduced the President at 9:14 p.m. on the lawn of the Picosa Ranch as follows:

My friends, may I have your attention for a moment, please. Please go ahead with eating your food, if you wish, but time is running, and while we have you all here, there are a few things that I would like to say for myself and for Nellie.

First, I think I have known most of you, or all of you, long enough to where you will completely and fully understand when I say how perfectly delighted Nellie and I are to have you on this ranch. Under this roof are many—not all; I can't say all, because I think we have a few members of the press here—but many of the dearest friends that we have in this world. [*Laughter*]

I am always an optimistic fellow, and at times a little vain, perhaps, and I wouldn't want our distinguished guest to leave you assuming I had assembled under one roof 40' by 60' all the friends I had. But in all seriousness, everybody by the name of Connally, or married into or kin to the family, so far as I am concerned, is grateful to all of you for so much.

Years ago I said to many of you, as I traveled about this State, that I hoped that no occasion ever presented itself where I had a microphone and the opportunity to do so, when I did not express our profound thanks for the kindness, for the generosity, for the thoughtfulness, for the support, and, above all, for the confidence which all of you have so clearly shown over the years, and I am grateful for that.

But if I am grateful for the occasion for those reasons, think how doubly pleased we are that on this particular evening we have the great and rare privilege of hosting the President and the First Lady of the United States.

You rose, you applauded, you manifested your confidence and your support and your feeling about the President, his lovely wife, but before we go further, let me impose upon your time just a moment or two to say to you that I have been privileged to serve in the Cabinet of President Nixon for a number of months. During those months, I have had an opportunity to see him in moments of satisfaction, in moments of serenity, in troubled moments, and moments of decision. And I must say to you that I respect the office of the President of the United States, but I want to go much further than that and say to all of you, my dear friends, that I respect this particular President of the United States for the manner in which he conducts himself, and the First Lady—the pride and the dignity which she so obviously has in maintaining the role that is so unique in American society and culture and political life—and to the President, who is a scholar in the affairs of this Nation and the foreign affairs of this country, who is as disciplined a man as I have ever known, mentally and physically. He is trim and slender and boyish looking. You wouldn't think he was older than I, would you?

But part of it, at least, is because he is physically disciplined, but more importantly, he is mentally disciplined. He understands the role of the President of the United States. He understands the role that this Nation plays among the nations of the world in conducting its foreign affairs, the foreign policy of this country. He disciplines his time among the many duties

that he has as head of government, head of state, as head of party, and he allocates to each of those grave responsibilities and great responsibilities the time which he feels he can devote to them without sacrificing the more responsible task that the President of the United States has.

I think, above all else, he studies the difficulties that he has. He has the ability and the intelligence to perceive those problems. He has the tenacity and the perseverance to seek a solution to them, but above all else, he has the courage to do what he believes to be right in the interest of this Nation.

At this point, Nellie, would you join me here, and we are going to ask all our friends to join us in a toast to the President of the United States and Mrs. Nixon.

You know, I don't know how the press is going to particularly handle this gathering, but I am going to find out, and I trust their judgment, at times, but you know, it is a social occasion, I suppose, by any standards, and it was designed to be such, but I always try to put myself in the position of other people, on an occasion of this kind, and Nellie and I are grateful that we were hosts and got to sit at this head table up here, if this is a head table, we got to sit with President and Mrs. Nixon at any event, and the distinguished former mayor of Dallas, Mayor [J. Eric] Jonsson, and his lovely wife, Margaret, and the former mayor of San Antonio and his lovely wife, Mayor and Mrs. W. W. McAllister, and if you think this is just a party of "ex's," you couldn't be more wrong.

I never learned much in politics, but I always learned that you had to fish with live bait, and we are not without some in this gathering this evening. But be that as it may, I try to put myself in other people's positions.

We have been here, we have sat, we had an occasion to talk with Mrs. Nixon and the President. We heard him early this afternoon, on the ride, talk about some problems of this country, and some of his ideas about those problems that range all the way from foreign affairs, the war in Vietnam, the forthcoming trip to Russia, ITT, and busing, and a few other things in between. I think I know something about those views, but those of you sitting at these other tables have not been privileged to talk to them in that light or in that vein to discuss these matters, and it has been my privilege to have the opportunity to do that.

Frankly, I guess it is just an old political instinct of mine that when you have a fellow kind of at your mercy, you never let him get away without trying to prevail on him if you can. And during dinner I did mention to the President that I thought this particular gathering would be profoundly interested in some of his views about some of the problems that this country has and that this world has. And if you would be, I think we can prevail on him to frankly respond to some of your questions if you would like it.

Mr. President, they talk about the ivory towers of the White House, but I assure you that they are not so high nor the walls so thick that the call of applause cannot permeate them, and I know that a man with a political instinct such as you have is always willing to respond to such acceptance. Need I say more?

Ladies and gentlemen, for what remarks he would like to make, and what questions he would like to respond to, the President of the United States.

Will you please be seated for just a moment, because before I turn the microphone over to him, I again want to ask your indulgence to afford me another very great privilege.

I know what a wonderful woman can do to a man's life. No one knows that better than I, unless it is Richard Nixon. So I want the rare privilege—because, hopefully not, but perhaps the only time I will ever have the opportunity on this ranch and on this soil that Nellie and I love so much—to present to you a marvelous woman, a lovely lady, a real First Lady of America, Mrs. Richard Nixon.

135   Memorandum on Appointing a New Chairman of the Interdepartmental Savings Bonds Committee. *May 1, 1972*

Memorandum to the Heads of Departments and Agencies:

I have appointed the Secretary of Agriculture, Earl L. Butz, as Chairman of the Interdepartmental Savings Bond Committee, replacing Maurice H. Stans. The Secretary of Defense, Melvin Laird, will remain as Vice-Chairman.

The Savings Bond program is making a major contribution to the management of the public debt. What is equally important is that it is adding to the economic security of all individuals who take part. The success of this program owes a great deal to the participation of Federal employees in the Payroll Savings Plan. Because they are vitally involved in the operations of our government, the example they set for others means much. Savings Bonds are important to the nation, and the leadership of the Interdepartmental Savings Bond Committee will encourage all employees under your direction to save regularly through the purchase of "Shares in America."

RICHARD NIXON

NOTE: The memorandum was announced to the press by the White House.

136   Remarks on the Death of J. Edgar Hoover. *May 2, 1972*

Ladies and gentlemen:

It is with a profound sense of personal loss that I learned of the death of J. Edgar Hoover. This truly remarkable man has served his country for 48 years under eight Presidents as Director of the FBI with unparalleled devotion and ability and dedication.

For 25 years, from the time I came to Washington as a freshman Congressman, he has been one of my closest personal friends and advisers. Every American, in my opinion, owes J. Edgar Hoover a great debt for building the FBI into the finest law enforcement organization in the entire world.

I have ordered that all the flags on government buildings be flown at half-mast. But I will say that in doing so, Edgar Hoover, because of his indomitable courage against sometimes very vicious attack, has made certain that the flag of the FBI

will always fly high.

NOTE: The President spoke at 11:10 a.m. in the Briefing Room at the White House. He spoke without referring to notes.

Mr. Hoover, 77, died at his home in Washington, D.C.

On the same day, the President signed Executive Order 11669 ordering the flag to be flown at half-staff as a mark of respect to the memory of Mr. Hoover.

On May 3, 1972, the White House released the transcript of remarks by Acting Attorney General Richard G. Kleindienst and L. Patrick Gray III on Mr. Gray's designation as Acting Director of the Federal Bureau of Investigation. Their remarks are printed in the Weekly Compilation of Presidential Documents (vol. 8, p. 819).

137   Statement on the Death of J. Edgar Hoover. *May 2, 1972*

ALL Americans today mourn the death of J. Edgar Hoover. He served his Nation as Director of the FBI for 48 years under eight American Presidents with total loyalty, unparalleled ability, and supreme dedication.

It can truly be said of him that he was a legend in his own lifetime. For millions he was the symbol and embodiment of the values he cherished most: courage, patriotism, dedication to his country, and a granite-like honesty and integrity.

In times of controversy, Mr. Hoover was never a man to run from a fight. His magnificent contribution to making this a great and good Nation will be remembered by the American people long after the petty carpings and vicious criticisms of his detractors are forgotten.

The FBI he literally created and built is today universally regarded as the finest law enforcement agency in the world. The FBI is the eternal monument honoring this great American.

138   Message to the Congress Transmitting Annual Plan for United States Participation in the World Weather Program. *May 3, 1972*

To the Congress of the United States:

By monitoring and predicting weather over the globe and by assessing the impact of man's activities upon the atmosphere, the World Weather Program helps significantly to improve the quality of our life and the safety of the earth's inhabitants.

I am pleased to report that the World Weather Program is making significant strides forward:

—Through new satellites, telecommunications, and computer technology, global information for early predictions and hazardous weather warnings is being acquired, processed, and then distributed in increased volume and detail.

—Under the Global Atmospheric Research Program intensive planning activities are underway for a 1974 international experiment to be conducted in the tropical Atlantic. The experiment will attempt to discover what role tropical weather systems play in maintaining the general circulation of the atmosphere. It will also probe tropical weather systems, with a view to improving weather prediction, including hurricane forecasts. Scientific data from this experiment will also help in making weather forecasts that are longer range, and in resolving important environmental problems. Many nations will participate in this experiment with ships, aircraft, satellites and other facilities.

—Active international involvement in the program by many member nations has yielded peaceful collaboration on an impressive international scale.

The World Weather Program is essential to a total environmental monitoring system for our planet. The program can serve as a model, moreover, for other environmental systems. The atmosphere is but one part of our global ecology. Data on other aspects of our environment can be collected and exchanged through a vehicle like the World Weather Program.

In accordance with Senate Concurrent Resolution 67 of the 90th Congress, I am pleased to transmit this annual report which describes the advances of the World Weather Program made during the past year and the activities planned for the program by participating Federal agencies for the coming fiscal year.

RICHARD NIXON

The White House,
    May 3, 1972.

NOTE: The report is entitled "World Weather Program, Plan for Fiscal Year 1973" (Government Printing Office, 33 pp.).

---

139   Telegram to the Mayor of Kellogg, Idaho, About the Sunshine Silver Mine Disaster.   *May 4, 1972*

THE TRAGIC loss of life that resulted from the fire at the Sunshine Mine profoundly touched the hearts of all Americans. On their behalf, I want to extend my deepest sympathy to the families struck by this disaster.

I have directed both the Secretary of the Interior and the Office of Emergency Preparedness to keep me closely informed on the recovery work in the area, and to insure that the full spectrum of Federal assistance is made available to the people of your community. I join all those who pray that God may give your community the special strength to persevere through this difficult time.

RICHARD NIXON

[Honorable Roger Fulton, Mayor of Kellogg, Kellogg, Idaho]

NOTE: The text of the telegram was posted for the press.

A copy of the telegram was sent to the Honorable Cecil D. Andrus, Governor of Idaho.

Ninety-one miners died in a fire that swept through the Sunshine Silver Mine on May 2, 1972.

573

140 Eulogy Delivered at Funeral Services for J. Edgar Hoover. *May 4, 1972*

Dr. Elson, Mrs. Eisenhower, Your Excellencies from the diplomatic corps, my fellow Americans:

Today is a day of sadness for America, but it is also a day of pride. America's pride has always been its people, a people of good men and women by the millions, of great men and women in remarkable numbers, and, once in a long while, of giants who stand head and shoulders above their countrymen, setting a high and noble standard for us all.

J. Edgar Hoover was one of the giants. His long life brimmed over with magnificent achievement and dedicated service to this country which he loved so well. One of the tragedies of life is that, as a rule, a man's true greatness is recognized only in death. J. Edgar Hoover was one of the rare exceptions to that rule. He became a living legend while still a young man, and he lived up to his legend as the decades passed. His death only heightens the respect and admiration felt for him across this land and in every land where men cherish freedom.

The greatness of Edgar Hoover will remain inseparable from the greatness of the organization he created and gave his whole life to building, the Federal Bureau of Investigation. He made the FBI the finest law enforcement agency on the earth, the invincible and incorruptible defender of every American's precious right to be free from fear.

Yet, America has revered this man not only as the Director of an institution but as an institution in his own right. For nearly half a century, nearly one-fourth of the whole history of this Republic, J. Edgar Hoover has exerted a great influence for good in our national life. While eight Presidents came and went, while other leaders of morals and manners and opinion rose and fell, the Director stayed at his post.

I recall that President Eisenhower, a Republican, and President Johnson, a Democrat, both strongly recommended, after my election, that I keep him as Director of the FBI.

He was one of those unique individuals who, by all odds, was the best man for a vitally important job. His powerful leadership by example helped to keep steel in America's backbone, and the flame of freedom in America's soul.

He personified integrity; he personified honor; he personified principle; he personified courage; he personified discipline; he personified dedication; he personified loyalty; he personified patriotism.

These are his legacies to the Bureau he built and the Nation he served. We can pay him no higher tribute than to live these virtues ourselves, as he lived them all of his years, to love the law as he loved it, and to give fullest respect, support, and cooperation to the law enforcement profession which he did so much to advance.

When such a towering figure—a man who has dominated his field so completely for so many years—finally passes from the scene, there is sometimes a tendency to say, "Well, this is an end of an era."

There is a belief that a changing of the guard will also mean a changing of the rules. With J. Edgar Hoover this will not happen. The FBI will carry on in the future, true to its finest traditions in the past, because regardless of what the snipers and detractors would have us believe, the fact is that Director Hoover built the Bureau totally on principle, not on personality. He built well. He built to last. For that reason, the FBI will remain as a memorial to him, a living memorial, continuing to create a climate of protection, security, and impartial justice that benefits every American.

The good J. Edgar Hoover has done will not die. The profound principles associated with his name will not fade away. Rather, I would predict that in the time ahead those principles of respect for law, order, and justice will come to govern our national life more completely than ever before. Because the trend of permissiveness in this country, a trend which Edgar Hoover fought against all his life, a trend which was dangerously eroding our national heritage as a law-abiding people, is now being reversed.

The American people today are tired of disorder, disruption, and disrespect for law. America wants to come back to the law as a way of life, and as we do come back to the law, the memory of this great man, who never left the law as a way of life, will be accorded even more honor than it commands today.

In times past, in the days of the American frontier, the brave men who wore the badge and enforced the law were called by a name we do not often hear today. They were called peace officers. Today, though that term has passed out of style, the truth it expressed still endures. All the world yearns for peace, peace among nations, peace within nations. But without peace officers, we can never have peace. Edgar Hoover knew this basic truth. He shaped his life around it. He was the peace officer without peer.

The United States is a better country because this good man lived his long life among us these past 77 years. Each of us stands forever in his debt. In the years ahead, let us cherish his memory. Let us be true to his legacy. Let us honor him as he would surely want us to do, by honoring all the men and women who carry on in this noble profession of helping to keep the peace in our society.

In the Bible, the book which Edgar Hoover called his "guide to daily life," we find the words which best pronounce a benediction on his death. They are from the Psalms: "Great peace have they which love Thy law." J. Edgar Hoover loved the law of his God. He loved the law of his country. And he richly earned peace through all eternity.

NOTE: The President spoke at 11:18 a.m. at the National Presbyterian Church. The funeral services were broadcast on radio and television. The President spoke from a prepared text.

Rev. Edward L. R. Elson, S.T.D., was Chaplain of the U.S. Senate and pastor of the National Presbyterian Church, where Mr. Hoover was a member. Mamie G. (Doud) Eisenhower was the widow of former President Dwight D. Eisenhower.

On the same day, the President directed Harold S. Trimmer, Acting Administrator of General Services, to designate the FBI Building which is presently under construction as the J. Edgar Hoover Building.

141 Memorandum About Small Business Week.
May 4, 1972

Memorandum for Heads of Executive Departments and Agencies:

In keeping with tradition, I am proclaiming the week of May 14 as Small Business Week. During this period, it will be important to focus public attention on the vital role played in our economic and social life by small firms and the people who own and run them.

To insure that the activities of this Administration contribute a full measure to the small business concept, I would like to see participation by the maximum number of agencies. Specifically, I propose that you review the actions which you take that affect small business, including minority-owned business. These actions may be regulatory in nature or may be confined to purchasing, but it is important to insure that they contribute to the preservation of small concerns. In purchasing and other programs through which Federal funds are injected directly into our economic systems, I would hope that you meet or exceed established goals and adopt affirmative steps to insure that small business participants receive the largest share feasible.

It would be especially appropriate for the announcement of such actions to take place during Small Business Week.

RICHARD NIXON

NOTE: The memorandum was announced to the press by the White House.

On the same day, the President signed Proclamation 4130, Small Business Week, 1972.

142 Statement About the Report of the Commission on Population Growth and the American Future.
May 5, 1972

THE Commission on Population Growth and the American Future has formally presented its report to me today, thus completing its 2 years of work.

The men and women on this panel have performed a valuable public service in identifying and examining a wide range of problems related to population, and have contributed to an emerging debate of great significance to the future of our Nation.

I wish to thank the able and energetic Chairman of the Commission, Mr. John D. Rockefeller 3d, for his tireless efforts, not only on this Commission but in other capacities, to focus the Nation's attention on these important issues.

The extensive public discussion already generated by this report clearly indicates the need to continue research in areas touching on population growth and distribution.

While I do not plan to comment extensively on the contents and recommendations of the report, I do feel that it is important that the public know my views on some of the issues raised.

In particular, I want to reaffirm and reemphasize that I do not support unrestricted abortion policies. As I stated on April 3, 1971, when I revised abortion policies in military hospitals, I consider abortion an unacceptable form of population control. In my judgment, unrestricted abortion policies would demean human life. I also want to make it clear that I do not support the unrestricted distribution of family planning services and devices to minors. Such measures would do nothing to preserve and strengthen close family relationships.

I have a basic faith that the American people themselves will make sound judgments regarding family size and frequency of births, judgments that are conducive both to the public interest and to personal family goals—and I believe in the right of married couples to make these judgments for themselves.

While disagreeing with the general thrust of some of the Commission's recommendations, I wish to extend my thanks to the members of the Commission for their work and for having assembled much valuable information.

The findings and conclusions of the Commission should be of great value in assisting governments at all levels to formulate policy. At the Federal level,

through our recent reorganization of the Executive Office of the President, we have the means through the Domestic Council and the Office of Management and Budget to follow up on the Commission's report. The recommendations of the Commission will be taken into account as we formulate our national growth and population research policies, and our agency budgets through these processes for the years ahead.

Many of the questions raised by the report cannot be answered purely on the basis of fact, but rather involve moral judgments about which reasonable men will disagree. I hope that the discussions ahead will be informed ones, so that we all will be better able to face these questions relating to population in full knowledge of the consequences of our decisions.

NOTE: The report is entitled "Population and the American Future" (Government Printing Office, 186 pp.).

Commission Chairman John D. Rockefeller 3d and members Graciela Gil Olivares and Christian N. Ramsey, Jr., met with the President at the White House to present the report.

143　Statement About Voluntary Restraints by Foreign Steel Producers To Limit Exports to the United States. *May 6, 1972*

I AM pleased to announce that the steel producers of Japan, the European Community, and the United Kingdom have expressed their intention to restrain on a voluntary basis their exports of steel mill products to the United States during the next 3 years.

This welcome development—which will lead to the preservation of jobs in our domestic steel industry—successfully con-

cludes more than a year of discussions.

For some time, I have been deeply concerned about the serious problem that excessive imports have posed for our steelworkers and our steel industry. Consequently, I directed that efforts be made to limit the impact of steel imports.

The Deputy Under Secretary of State for Economic Affairs, Nathaniel Samuels, undertook discussions with the Japanese and European steel producers with respect to their renewal—on improved terms—of the voluntary restraints on steel exports.

After more than a year's effort, Mr. Samuels has succeeded in this important endeavor. The Secretary of State has advised me that he has received communications from the steel producers in these countries in which they pledge a 3-year restraint—with improved terms—of their voluntary limits on their steel exports to the United States.

This undertaking represents a substantial improvement over the arrangements of the last 3 years and will enable domestic steel producers to make their plans with confidence that imports will not be disruptive in the domestic market. It will help preserve the jobs of American steelworkers.

I am especially pleased that this undertaking was reached on a voluntary basis.

Such statesmanlike cooperation is vital to our mutual efforts to build a more equitable and a more progressive system of international trading arrangements.

NOTE: On the same day, the White House released the texts of letters to the Secretary of State from the Associations of the Steel Producers of the European Coal and Steel Community (ESCS) and the Association of Steel Producers of the United Kingdom, and from the Japan Iron and Steel Exporters' Association on their intention to limit exports of steel to the United States. A White House announcement of the voluntary restraints agreement was released on the same day and is printed in the Weekly Compilation of Presidential Documents (vol. 8, p. 824).

The White House also released a fact sheet and the transcript of a news briefing on the voluntary restraints agreement. Participants in the news briefing were Nathaniel D. Samuels, Deputy Under Secretary of State for Economic Affairs, and Stanley Nehmer, Deputy Assistant Secretary of Commerce for Resources.

144 Statement About Proposed Expansion of School Nutrition Programs for Needy Children. *May 6, 1972*

I SHALL propose to the Congress next week a three-part program to expand and improve Federal efforts to provide food for needy children.

First and most important, I shall submit a comprehensive school nutrition bill to revise and reform the present school lunch and school breakfast programs—so that incentives will be provided for expanding these programs and so that each dollar spent on them will do more good.

Second, I will also ask that an additional $25 million be allocated for feeding needy children in our cities this summer.

Third, I will request an additional $19.5 million to extend the school breakfast program to some 3,000 additional schools in the coming year.

In order to maintain budget discipline, I have directed the Secretary of Agriculture to offset these added expenditures by an equal amount—$44.5 million—in other areas so that the Department's outlays will not be increased by this decision.

The new school nutrition legislation which I shall send to the Congress would simplify and improve the structure for Federal funding in several ways. One of its most important provisions would substitute a performance system for the traditional apportionment system in allocating Federal funds for both the school lunch and breakfast programs. Under the performance system, the more pupils served in a State the more Federal assistance it receives. This arrangement establishes an incentive for States to insure that all needy children will be fed. This incentive has not been present in the traditional statutory apportionment system—under which funding did not readily reflect increases in participation.

The proposed legislation would also establish new minimum and maximum eligibility standards for needy children. It would require that all children from families below the poverty line—who now may be served either a free or a reduced price lunch—would receive lunches free. To account for geographical differences, the legislation would allow States flexibility to set higher eligibility standards within reasonable limits.

The additional $25 million for the summer food program would bring total funding for this program to $50 million, 2½ times as high as last summer's level. These new sums would make it possible to support all applications for this program that meet the criteria which have been spelled out in laws and regulations. At the same time, I am instructing the Secretary of Agriculture to work with States and cities to improve local program administration in order to eliminate the severe mismanagement that marred these programs in some cities last summer.

The additional $19.5 million for the school breakfast program would bring total funding for this program in the coming school year to $52.5 million, compared to $31 million in the school year now ending. This new money would make it possible to accept applications from all the schools indicated in State plans of operation as potential candidates for establishing breakfast programs.

It was just 3 years ago, on May 6, 1969, that I sent to the Congress my first message on hunger and malnutrition. I noted in that message that America has long shared its bounty with hungry peoples in all parts of the globe, but that now "the moment is at hand to put an end to hunger in America itself. For all time."

In the last 3 years, with the cooperation of the Congress, we have made immense strides toward reaching that goal. For example, the budget I proposed last January allocated nine times as much money for food stamps and seven times as much money for school lunches for needy children as was allocated in fiscal year 1969.

My new proposals would allow us to improve even further on our record of accomplishment. I urge the Congress to give early and favorable consideration to these important measures.

NOTE: On the same day, the White House released a fact sheet and the transcript of a news briefing, held on May 5, 1972, on the proposed programs for needy children. Participants in the news briefing were Earl L. Butz, Secretary, and Richard Lyng, Assistant Secretary, Marketing and Consumer Services, Department of Agriculture.

On March 7, the White House released a fact sheet and the transcript of a news briefing on the first annual report of the National Advisory Council on Child Nutrition. Participants in the news briefing were Secretary Butz and Assistant Secretary Lyng.

145 Letter to the Secretary of Labor Directing Expansion of the Jobs for Veterans Program. *May 8, 1972*

Dear Mr. Secretary:

As we near the end of the first full year of the Six-Point Jobs for Veterans Program, I am encouraged that our efforts have done a great deal to reduce the intolerably high unemployment rate for Vietnam-era veterans. This is not a time to slacken our efforts, however, for the rate of military separations is still substantial and we can not yet be satisfied with the unemployment of those who have already returned to the civilian labor force.

Therefore, I would like you to undertake a new Six-Point Jobs for Veterans Program for fiscal year 1973, building on the solid foundation of this year's program by raising our goals, further accelerating our campaign and improving the Government's ability to deliver the necessary resources. This letter provides basic guidance for such expansion.

I regard this effort as of the highest priority in Federal manpower and training programs, and with your personal leadership, I am confident that it is in good hands. Our campaign is of such importance that its goals must be achieved—even if this means diverting staff and funds from other activities. I also call upon all Government agencies to draw fully on available resources and authority.

You have my personal mandate to carry out the following actions:

(1) *Continue to draw upon the resources of the National Alliance of Businessmen.*

You should develop, with the Chairman of the Board of the National Alliance of Businessmen, a strategy to increase the participation of American business in providing additional employment opportunities for Vietnam-era veterans. NAB should increase its goals beyond the 100,000 pledged last year, through its promotion of the Job Opportunities Business Sector (JOBS) Program.

(2) *Provide the job training necessary for servicemen who lack civilian skills in occupations available in the labor market.*

Separating servicemen who have educational and civil job deficiencies should have the opportunity to receive civilian job training and related services (for up to 60 days).

Training of servicemen for civilian jobs should be concentrated in special skill centers at military installations where returning veterans who have educational and skill deficiencies will have an opportunity to receive job training and related services. The Department of Defense (DOD) should concentrate resources at selected military bases to provide high quality job training, counseling and placement services with the full support of Labor, HEW, and VA.

Employment briefings and counseling to servicemen overseas should provide job market information essential for them to enter the labor market and apply their maximum skills. Servicemen who lack skills should be provided assistance for the determination of a plan suitable for job training or education to prepare them for employment. The program already underway should be continued and improved.

(3) *Continue to augment the number of job training and educational opportunities for returning veterans, with appropriate emphasis on college, technical and high school education.*

Enrollments in classroom type manpower training programs of the Department of Labor should be increased for unemployed and underemployed Vietnam-era veterans. Efforts should also be made to increase veteran participation in GI Bill training and manpower assistance programs and to augment benefits through the coupling of MDTA and GI Bill training programs. Further, priority modifications which are necessary to assure adequate enrollment of returning veterans in MDTA and HEW education programs should be made without delay.

These actions lend themselves well to both State and local participation, and to plans for coalition among VA, Labor, OEO, HEW, HUD, and other public and private agencies and institutions.

I am particularly hopeful that participation in GI Bill programs can be increased through specific outreach into urban and rural areas, fully informing veterans of available educational and other benefits.

Apprenticeship training programs should be specially adapted and publicized to provide for maximum participation by recent veterans.

(4) *Assure that listing of job openings with the U.S. Employment Service is being accomplished by all agencies and contractors funded by the Federal Government.*

Based upon Executive Order 11598, there should be a sizeable increase in the number of jobs listed with local public employment offices and available to returning veterans. The effectiveness of the Order will be greatly increased by monitoring of Federal procurement officers.

(5) *Increase the number of appropriate job openings for Vietnam-era veterans and the placement of veterans in those jobs.*

All public employment programs should realistically aim for higher goals and accomplishments in order to infuse government at all levels with the unique capabilities of returning veterans. The Civil Service Commission should expand its programs in this area. Every agency should maximize job opportunities involving on-the-job training for veterans, particularly the Veterans Administration, the U.S. Employment Service, and the National Alliance of Businessmen. VA and USES should design "coupled on-the-job training programs" throughout the country to allow the employer to be reimbursed for training costs while the veteran trainee receives a GI Bill training allowance in addition to his regular wage. All new opportunities of this type should also be widely publicized.

(6) *Provide special Labor/VA services to Vietnam-era veterans who have been drawing unemployment compensation for three or more months.*

These veterans should be referred immediately to the U.S. Employment Service, VA, or—where serious employment handicaps are indicated—to State vocational rehabilitation agencies for special counseling, job placement and training.

Beyond these tasks, I would expect that the veterans' assistance programs already initiated by the Office of Economic Opportunity, the Civil Service Commission, and the U.S. Postal Service will be expanded in the year ahead.

I also anticipate that the Jobs for Veterans—National Committee (JFV) will continue to conduct effective promotional measures. Working closely with the Advertising Council, JFV should bring our message to the entire nation through extensive use of mass media. Employers and veterans will be brought together at Job Fairs throughout the country, while advice and assistance will be provided to the hundreds of Veterans Task Forces organized by Governors, Mayors, and communities to help veterans find suitable jobs and training.

Because of the importance of this effort, I would like you to continue to make progress reports to me and prepare a special twelve-month report on actual program accomplishments and shortfalls for Cabinet discussion. The arrangements for these reports and any other necessary assistance should be made with the Office of Man-

agement and Budget. I know that I can continue to count on your full energies and the support of all Government agencies in this vital national campaign.

Sincerely,

RICHARD NIXON

[Honorable James D. Hodgson, Secretary of Labor, Washington, D.C. 20210]

NOTE: The letter was dated May 5, 1972, and released May 8.

On May 8, the White House released a fact sheet and the transcript of a news briefing on the Six-Point Jobs for Veterans Program. Participants in the news briefing were James D. Hodgson, Secretary, and Malcolm R. Lovell, Jr., Assistant Secretary for Manpower, Department of Labor; and Donald E. Johnson, Administrator of Veterans Affairs.

146   Message to the Congress Transmitting Annual Report of the United States Civil Service Commission. *May* 8, 1972

To the Congress of the United States:

I am hereby transmitting the United States Civil Service Commission's Annual Report for fiscal year 1971.

The report encompasses a year marked with considerable progress and innovation in Federal personnel management. Among the year's highlights were significant liberalizations in retirement and health benefits; increased emphasis on employment opportunities for returning Vietnam veterans; a strengthened program in equal employment opportunity for minorities and women; considerable progress in job evaluation policy and personnel management evaluation; and preparations by the Commission to implement the Intergovernmental Personnel Act of 1970 which should bring a new partnership between Federal, State, and

local governments.

These improvements resulted from the joint action and cooperation of the Commission, the Congress, the executive agencies, employee organizations, and the President. I therefore hope you share my pride in these achievements which not only have made the Government a better employer but have also provided sharpened government responsiveness to the changing social and economic needs of the American people.

RICHARD NIXON

The White House,

May 8, 1972.

NOTE: The report is entitled "A Pace-Setting Year—for Personnel Management; 88th Annual Report, Fiscal Year Ended June 30, 1971, United States Civil Service Commission" (79 pp. plus appendixes).

147   Address to the Nation on the Situation in Southeast
      Asia.   *May 8, 1972*

Good evening:

Five weeks ago, on Easter weekend, the Communist armies of North Vietnam launched a massive invasion of South Vietnam, an invasion that was made possible by tanks, artillery, and other advanced offensive weapons supplied to Hanoi by the Soviet Union and other Communist nations.

The South Vietnamese have fought bravely to repel this brutal assault. Casualties on both sides have been very high. Most tragically, there have been over 20,000 civilian casualties, including women and children, in the cities which the North Vietnamese have shelled in wanton disregard of human life.

As I announced in my report to the Nation 12 days ago, the role of the United States in resisting this invasion has been limited to air and naval strikes on military targets in North and South Vietnam. As I also pointed out in that report, we have responded to North Vietnam's massive military offensive by undertaking wide-ranging new peace efforts aimed at ending the war through negotiation.

On April 20, I sent Dr. Kissinger to Moscow for 4 days of meetings with General Secretary Brezhnev and other Soviet leaders. I instructed him to emphasize our desire for a rapid solution to the war and our willingness to look at all possible approaches. At that time, the Soviet leaders showed an interest in bringing the war to an end on a basis just to both sides. They urged resumption of negotiations in Paris, and they indicated they would use their constructive influence.

I authorized Dr. Kissinger to meet privately with the top North Vietnamese negotiator, Le Duc Tho, on Tuesday, May 2, in Paris. Ambassador Porter, as you know, resumed the public peace negotiations in Paris on April 27 and again on May 4. At those meetings, both public and private, all we heard from the enemy was bombastic rhetoric and a replaying of their demands for surrender. For example, at the May 2 secret meeting, I authorized Dr. Kissinger to talk about every conceivable avenue toward peace. The North Vietnamese flatly refused to consider any of these approaches. They refused to offer any new approach of their own. Instead, they simply read verbatim their previous public demands.

Here is what over 3 years of public and private negotiations with Hanoi has come down to: The United States, with the full concurrence of our South Vietnamese allies, has offered the maximum of what any President of the United States could offer.

We have offered a deescalation of the fighting. We have offered a cease-fire with a deadline for withdrawal of all American forces. We have offered new elections which would be internationally supervised with the Communists participating both in the supervisory body and in the elections themselves.

President Thieu has offered to resign one month before the elections. We have offered an exchange of prisoners of war in a ratio of 10 North Vietnamese prisoners for every one American prisoner that they release. And North Vietnam has met each of these offers with insolence and insult. They have flatly and arrogantly refused to negotiate an end to the war and bring peace. Their answer to every peace offer we have made has been to escalate the war.

In the 2 weeks alone since I offered to resume negotiations, Hanoi has launched three new military offensives in South Vietnam. In those 2 weeks the risk that a Communist government may be imposed on the 17 million people of South Vietnam has increased, and the Communist offensive has now reached the point that it gravely threatens the lives of 60,000 American troops who are still in Vietnam.

There are only two issues left for us in this war. First, in the face of a massive invasion do we stand by, jeopardize the lives of 60,000 Americans, and leave the South Vietnamese to a long night of terror? This will not happen. We shall do whatever is required to safeguard American lives and American honor.

Second, in the face of complete intransigence at the conference table do we join with our enemy to install a Communist government in South Vietnam? This, too, will not happen. We will not cross the line from generosity to treachery.

We now have a clear, hard choice among three courses of action: Immediate withdrawal of all American forces, continued attempts at negotiation, or decisive military action to end the war.

I know that many Americans favor the first course of action, immediate withdrawal. They believe the way to end the war is for the United States to get out, and to remove the threat to our remaining forces by simply withdrawing them.

From a political standpoint, this would be a very easy choice for me to accept. After all, I did not send over one-half million Americans to Vietnam. I have brought 500,000 men home from Viet-

nam since I took office. But, abandoning our commitment in Vietnam here and now would mean turning 17 million South Vietnamese over to Communist tyranny and terror. It would mean leaving hundreds of American prisoners in Communist hands with no bargaining leverage to get them released.

An American defeat in Vietnam would encourage this kind of aggression all over the world, aggression in which smaller nations armed by their major allies, could be tempted to attack neighboring nations at will in the Mideast, in Europe, and other areas. World peace would be in grave jeopardy.

The second course of action is to keep on trying to negotiate a settlement. Now this is the course we have preferred from the beginning and we shall continue to pursue it. We want to negotiate, but we have made every reasonable offer and tried every possible path for ending this war at the conference table.

The problem is, as you all know, it takes two to negotiate and now, as throughout the past 4 years, the North Vietnamese arrogantly refuse to negotiate anything but an imposition, an ultimatum that the United States impose a Communist regime on 17 million people in South Vietnam who do not want a Communist government.

It is plain then that what appears to be a choice among three courses of action for the United States is really no choice at all. The killing in this tragic war must stop. By simply getting out, we would only worsen the bloodshed. By relying solely on negotiations, we would give an intransigent enemy the time he needs to press his aggression on the battlefield.

There is only one way to stop the killing.

That is to keep the weapons of war out of the hands of the international outlaws of North Vietnam.

Throughout the war in Vietnam, the United States has exercised a degree of restraint unprecedented in the annals of war. That was our responsibility as a great Nation, a Nation which is interested—and we can be proud of this as Americans—as America has always been, in peace not conquest.

However, when the enemy abandons all restraint, throws its whole army into battle in the territory of its neighbor, refuses to negotiate, we simply face a new situation.

In these circumstances, with 60,000 Americans threatened, any President who failed to act decisively would have betrayed the trust of his country and betrayed the cause of world peace.

I therefore concluded that Hanoi must be denied the weapons and supplies it needs to continue the aggression. In full coordination with the Republic of Vietnam, I have ordered the following measures which are being implemented as I am speaking to you.

All entrances to North Vietnamese ports will be mined to prevent access to these ports and North Vietnamese naval operations from these ports. United States forces have been directed to take appropriate measures within the internal and claimed territorial waters of North Vietnam to interdict the delivery of any supplies. Rail and all other communications will be cut off to the maximum extent possible. Air and naval strikes against military targets in North Vietnam will continue.

These actions are not directed against any other nation. Countries with ships presently in North Vietnamese ports have already been notified that their ships will have three daylight periods to leave in safety. After that time, the mines will become active and any ships attempting to leave or enter these ports will do so at their own risk.

These actions I have ordered will cease when the following conditions are met:

First, all American prisoners of war must be returned.

Second, there must be an internationally supervised cease-fire throughout Indochina.

Once prisoners of war are released, once the internationally supervised cease-fire has begun, we will stop all acts of force throughout Indochina, and at that time we will proceed with a complete withdrawal of all American forces from Vietnam within 4 months.

Now, these terms are generous terms. They are terms which would not require surrender and humiliation on the part of anybody. They would permit the United States to withdraw with honor. They would end the killing. They would bring our POW's home. They would allow negotiations on a political settlement between the Vietnamese themselves. They would permit all the nations which have suffered in this long war—Cambodia, Laos, North Vietnam, South Vietnam—to turn at last to the urgent works of healing and of peace. They deserve immediate acceptance by North Vietnam.

It is appropriate to conclude my remarks tonight with some comments directed individually to each of the major parties involved in the continuing tragedy of the Vietnam war.

First, to the leaders of Hanoi, your people have already suffered too much in your pursuit of conquest. Do not compound their agony with continued arrogance; choose instead the path of a peace that redeems your sacrifices, guarantees true independence for your country, and ushers in an era of reconciliation.

To the people of South Vietnam, you shall continue to have our firm support in your resistance against aggression. It is your spirit that will determine the outcome of the battle. It is your will that will shape the future of your country.

To other nations, especially those which are allied with North Vietnam, the actions I have announced tonight are not directed against you. Their sole purpose is to protect the lives of 60,000 Americans, who would be gravely endangered in the event that the Communist offensive continues to roll forward, and to prevent the imposition of a Communist government by brutal aggression upon 17 million people.

I particularly direct my comments tonight to the Soviet Union. We respect the Soviet Union as a great power. We recognize the right of the Soviet Union to defend its interests when they are threatened. The Soviet Union in turn must recognize our right to defend our interests.

No Soviet soldiers are threatened in Vietnam. Sixty thousand Americans are threatened. We expect you to help your allies, and you cannot expect us to do other than to continue to help our allies, but let us, and let all great powers, help our allies only for the purpose of their defense, not for the purpose of launching invasions against their neighbors.

Otherwise the cause of peace, the cause in which we both have so great a stake, will be seriously jeopardized.

Our two nations have made significant progress in our negotiations in recent months. We are near major agreements on nuclear arms limitation, on trade, on a host of other issues.

Let us not slide back toward the dark shadows of a previous age. We do not ask you to sacrifice your principles, or your friends, but neither should you permit Hanoi's intransigence to blot out the prospects we together have so patiently prepared.

We, the United States and the Soviet Union, are on the threshold of a new relationship that can serve not only the interests of our two countries, but the cause of world peace. We are prepared to continue to build this relationship. The responsibility is yours if we fail to do so.

And finally, may I say to the American people, I ask you for the same strong support you have always given your President in difficult moments. It is you most of all that the world will be watching.

I know how much you want to end this war. I know how much you want to bring our men home. And I think you know from all that I have said and done these past 3½ years how much I, too, want to end the war to bring our men home.

You want peace. I want peace. But, you also want honor and not defeat. You want a genuine peace, not a peace that is merely a prelude to another war.

At this moment, we must stand together in purpose and resolve. As so often in the past, we Americans did not choose to resort to war. It has been forced upon us by an enemy that has shown utter contempt toward every overture we have made for peace. And that is why, my fellow Americans, tonight I ask for your support of this decision, a decision which has only one purpose, not to expand the war, not to escalate the war, but to end this war and to win the kind of peace that will last.

With God's help, with your support, we will accomplish that great goal.

Thank you and good night.

NOTE: The President spoke at 9 p.m. in the Oval Office at the White House. His address was broadcast live on radio and television. He spoke from a prepared text.

Before delivering his address to the Nation, the President met with the bipartisan leadership of the Congress to discuss its contents.

On May 9, 1972, the White House released the transcript of a news briefing by Henry A. Kissinger, Assistant to the President for National Security Affairs, on the situation in Southeast Asia. The transcript is printed in the Weekly Compilation of Presidential Documents (vol. 8, p. 842).

148   Statement About Proposed Legislation Authorizing Continued Government Support of Radio Free Europe and Radio Liberty.   *May* 10, 1972

UNDER Public Law 92–264, which I signed on March 30, 1972, grants in support of Radio Free Europe and Radio Liberty were authorized through the end of fiscal year 1972.

The decision to continue Government support for these radios was approved by large majorities in Congress and reflects the judgment that has been expressed overwhelmingly by newspapers throughout this country and by leading citizens in all walks of life that Radio Free Europe and Radio Liberty continue to perform a unique and valuable service. As I stated in a recent letter to the chairman of the Radio Free Europe Fund:

"... we have followed closely the work of RFE and are satisfied that it continues to serve a fundamental national interest."

I also said that:

"... the free flow of information and ideas among nations is indispensable to more normal relations between East and West and to better prospects for an enduring peace."

I have therefore asked the Secretary of State to submit today a bill which would continue Government support to the radios through fiscal year 1973. As with the fiscal year 1972 authorization, this bill would make the grants to the radios through the Secretary of State under such terms and conditions he deems appropriate.

A number of different views have been expressed in Congress as to how the radios might best be funded for the future. No consensus on this important matter has emerged. The House version of the fiscal year 1972 authorization and Senate Resolution 272 make clear that majorities in both Houses believe this should be given further study before a definitive solution is adopted.

To this end, I plan to appoint a Presidential study commission [1] with in-

---

[1] A White House announcement of the establishment and membership of the Commission on International Radio Broadcasting was released on August 10, 1972, and is printed in the Weekly Compilation of Presidential Documents (vol. 8, p. 1221).

structions to render its report and recommendations by February 28, 1973, so that the Administration and Congress can take them into consideration in formulating authorizing legislation for fiscal year 1974. In making its study, the Commission will be particularly concerned to consult exhaustively with Members of Congress.

In undertaking this task, the Commission will have the benefit and will take full account of the in-depth studies of each radio that were prepared by the Congressional Research Service at the request of the Senate Foreign Relations Committee, together with companion studies recently completed by the General Accounting Office. Two subsequent studies by the Congressional Research Service—one a survey and analysis of the available options with respect to future funding methods and the other an examination of the foreign policy aspects of these broadcasting operations—will also materially assist the Commission.

It is evident that the choice of the method or mechanism for future funding of the radios must depend upon a proper perception of the relationship of those operations to the national interest and specifically to this Nation's foreign policy objectives. In my view, that relationship exists for one fundamental reason, but one reason only: Namely, that it has always been and must always be part of our national purpose to promote free, responsible communication among nations, not just at the government level but at all levels. Thus, these radios are not spokesmen for American official policy—that role belongs in broadcasting to the Voice of America. Rather, they are expressions of our profound conviction that a responsible, in-

dependent, and free press plays an indispensable part in the social and political processes that look to better understanding and more effective cooperation, not only within a nation, but also among nations.

It is this conception, I believe, that lies at the base of the article of the Universal Declaration of Human Rights which declares it to be the right of everyone "to seek, receive, and impart information and ideas through any media and regardless of frontiers." International broadcasting is of course only a part of that process; our international exchange programs are another important part.

The Commission will render a great service by undertaking a critical examination of this subject and by providing the best possible basis for determining the methods by which support for these valuable organizations can be maintained without impairment to the professional independence upon which their present effectiveness depends.

While this Commission produces its recommendations, it is essential that the authorization providing support to Radio Free Europe and Radio Liberty be extended for fiscal year 1973. While I continue to believe that the Department of State is not the appropriate channel for grants to the two radios, I believe that discussion of the alternatives should be deferred until we have the benefit of the recommendations of the Commission. I therefore strongly recommend that the bill which we are submitting to Congress for a 1973 authorization be given favorable consideration before the beginning of the new fiscal year.

149 Letter to Congressional Leaders Urging Action on the General Revenue Sharing Bill. *May* 13, 1972

THE House Ways and Means Committee, led by Chairman Mills, has developed a General Revenue Sharing bill which essentially incorporated the fundamental principles I have advocated. Recent reports, however, suggest that a logjam on appropriation bills may develop during June and July. This prospect, together with the forecast of a short session, suggests that the Senate might not have time to act upon General Revenue Sharing during this Congress.

The serious fiscal crisis facing State and local governments requires action by this Congress. I am confident that the House will pass General Revenue Sharing by a large majority, and it is essential that this be done quickly. If we are to meet the pressing needs of our nation, I urge you and other members of the House leadership to call the Committee's bill to the Floor this month.

Sincerely,

RICHARD NIXON

NOTE: This is the text of identical letters addressed to the Honorable Carl Albert, Speaker of the House of Representatives, the Honorable Hale Boggs, Majority Leader, and the Honorable Gerald R. Ford, Minority Leader. The letters were dated May 11, 1972, and released May 13.

On May 12, John D. Ehrlichman, Assistant to the President for Domestic Affairs, held a news briefing on the general revenue sharing bill, tax reform, and Government reorganization. A transcript of the news briefing was released by the White House on May 13.

150 Statement About Peace Officers Memorial Day and Police Week, 1972. *May* 15, 1972

I JOIN with millions of other grateful Americans in paying tribute to the men and women of the law enforcement profession during Police Week, May 14 to May 20, and in honoring on Peace Officers Memorial Day, May 15, the sacrifices of peace officers killed or disabled in the line of duty.

These observances focus deserved recognition on the quiet but perilous heroism of the policemen and policewomen in communities across the land. They provide an occasion for us to thank these dedicated professionals for doing an often thankless job so superbly.

An observation made shortly before his death by the late J. Edgar Hoover, for so long America's foremost peace officer, might well keynote Police Week, 1972. Despite the special challenge now posed to police pride and morale by some extreme elements which revile law enforcement, Director Hoover said we must not ignore the steady improvement in police-citizen relations over the past half century—from the 1920's when "citizens had only minimal respect" for law enforcement, until today, when "as never before, our profession is respected and supported."

This is a trend which augurs well for the future of ordered freedom in the United States. It is a trend which all Americans must work to sustain—by making sure that the enforcement process and the laws themselves are worthy of respect, and then by rendering them the full respect they deserve.

After a long, hard battle against rising crime and lawlessness in our society, we have begun to win some victories, slowing the tide overall and even reversing it in some categories. The lion's share of the credit for this important breakthrough certainly belongs to the people on the front lines: the men and women of the Nation's peace forces.

I wish it were possible for me to meet with representatives of the police forces in every American community and extend my personal thanks to them, as I was able to do recently with a group of officers from the District of Columbia Metropolitan Police Department, which has spearheaded a 50 percent reduction in major crime in the Capital over the last 3 years.[1]

---

[1] See Item 126.

What is possible is for local leaders across the land to foster similar recognition of their communities' "finest"—and I hope many of them will do so this week and in the future.

Finally, this Peace Officers Memorial Day, let us deepen our resolve to do a better job of protecting those who risk so much in protecting us. The increase in physical attacks on police officers, and the rise in police killings (up 26 percent last year to 126), must be reversed. This Administration has extended FBI assistance to local authorities in bringing police killers to justice; we have sought the establishment of Federal survivors benefits for the brave wives and families bereaved by these tragedies; and we shall continue seeking measures not only to deal with the aftermath of police killings but, most importantly of all, to deter and prevent their occurrence. I appeal once again for determined efforts by citizens and public officials everywhere to counter this vicious threat, which by menacing the safety of our peace officers menaces the safety of us all.

151 Statement About Attempt on the Life of Governor George C. Wallace of Alabama. *May* 15, 1972

I JOIN Americans everywhere in deep concern for Governor Wallace's condition. I ask all Americans to join me in praying for his speedy and full recovery, and also for that of the others who were wounded in this senseless and tragic incident.

Our Nation has suffered more than enough already from the intrusion of violence into its political processes. We must all stand together to eliminate its vicious threat from our public life; we must not permit the shadow of violence to fall over our country again.

NOTE: The statement was read to reporters by Press Secretary Ronald L. Ziegler.

On May 15, 1972, Governor Wallace was shot and seriously wounded while attending a political rally at Laurel Shopping Center, Laurel, Md.

152 Remarks at a Reception Marking the Reopening
of the Blue Room Following Its Redecoration.
May 15, 1972

Good evening, ladies and gentlemen:

It is with great regret that on this very happy occasion, one that we hoped would be a completely happy one, that we have had an incident this afternoon, only 2 hours ago, that all of you are aware of.

Governor Wallace's condition, incidentally, has been described as stable. I just talked to Mrs. Wallace on the telephone. She said his spirit was very good. An operation by the very best team of physicians in the Washington area is now taking place, and we are all very hopeful that it will be a successful one and that he will be returned to good health.

I know that all Americans, whatever their political affiliations, will not only have him in their thoughts, but in their prayers on this particular occasion.

On this occasion, too, I do want to express, on behalf of Mrs. Nixon and myself, and all Americans, a million and a half who visit this house every year, our appreciation to those in this room who make the White House what it is.

I think many of you probably wonder what our foreign visitors think of the White House when they come here, and perhaps I can give you an idea by telling you how we look at the White House, we who have traveled now to over 70 countries abroad, as compared with other houses like it abroad.

This is not the largest. I would say most of the residences of chief executives in other countries, including most of the smaller countries, are considerably larger

than the White House. This is not the grandest. I know many that, in terms of decoration and in style, and so forth, would be considered to be much more grand than the White House.

But there is something that others say when they come here that I think will please those of you who have helped to make the White House what it is, whether they are emperors or kings or prime ministers, whatever great country or small country they represent, however large the house in which they may live may be. They say, "There is something about the White House that is different. It is that it is a home. It is very personal. It is not like, really, a government house."

That is quite true. I am sure you must get this feeling as you walk through these magnificent rooms, and I am sure that as you take the tour today, not only on this floor, which you helped to make, but also on the second floor, which we have opened up so that all of you can see the very special rooms that only a very few people like this can see on occasion—the Lincoln Room, the Queen's Room, the Treaty Room, and the rest—I am sure that as you walk through this room you will see why our foreign visitors say the White House is different not because of its size, not because of its grandeur, but because it has a feeling of a home, a personal feeling that can only come from, I would say, the touch of a First Lady.

I have not known many First Ladies. I remember the first one I met was Mrs.

Herbert Hoover. I knew her when I was a member of a college board of trustees, a small Quaker college in California, and she was also a member, back in 1939.

I saw Mrs. Roosevelt once. I met Mrs. Truman once in a receiving line when I came here, along with Mrs. Nixon, when we had just come to Washington. But then, of course, during the Eisenhower years and after, we have known the First Ladies and what they have contributed to this house. Mrs. Eisenhower, Mrs. Kennedy, Mrs. Johnson, and, of course, Mrs. Nixon—each has made a contribution; each has left the house with that personal feeling and the personal touch that only a lady can give to a great house like this.

But in order for them to do it, let me say, it would not have been possible without the personal contributions that you have made. It would have been so much easier simply to go down to the Congress and to have a certain amount of money appropriated to buy all the things that we need to buy and then to see what would be the result. The result would be a house that was a government house, like the other government buildings and the other government houses around the world.

Because each of these rooms, and virtually every item in them, through the years, has come from an individual, from a person, it has meant that this house has a character and a personality which all Americans feel, which our visitors from abroad appreciate, which you have made possible.

So, on behalf of America, all of the visitors, particularly all the young people who come here and look with wonder at these rooms, thank you very, very much.

I am sure you will understand that under the circumstances I will want to return to the office to see what the situation is with regard to Governor Wallace's condition, which we all hope will be better.

We do hope, however, that those of you who have come from so far will move through this house as if it were your own, because it is, really. You helped to make it what it is. Mrs. Nixon will be here to receive you in the Blue Room, the last room to be redone, perhaps the most famous room in the house, the one where one President was married, Grover Cleveland, and the one where, incidentally—and this is a bit of historical reference—where President Rutherford Hayes received the first Chinese diplomatic representative to the United States of America.

In this year when we have attempted to open a new dialogue with the leaders of 800 million people who live in the People's Republic of China, it is significant, it seems to me, that the room where the first Chinese representative was received by an American President is the one that will be open tonight for your viewing.

Thank you very much. I hope we meet on another occasion when we will not have the kind of news that I had to report tonight.

NOTE: The President spoke at 6:22 p.m. in the East Room at the White House. He spoke without referring to notes.

Guests at the reception included sponsors, donors, and lenders to the White House collection; the trustees of libraries, museums, foundations, universities, and historical societies which have given or lent furnishings and paintings to the White House; and members of the Committee for the Preservation of the White House and the White House Historical Association.

153 Remarks Announcing Changes in the Cabinet and White House Staff. *May* 16, 1972

INTRODUCTORY REMARKS ON GOVERNOR
WALLACE'S CONDITION

I have an announcement today, but before making the announcement, I would like to refer briefly to the reports I have received in regard to Governor Wallace. I have been keeping in close touch with the hospital through Dr. Lukash, as you know, who is the specialist in this area.[1] I talked to him last night around 11:30, and then around 8 o'clock this morning again.

I have nothing to add to the bulletins that have been publicly made in this respect. I know that all of us certainly wish that Governor Wallace, in this very difficult time, will have not only the very best medical care, but that he can recover from the wounds that he has received. I can assure you the best medical care is being provided.

One point that has been raised is where the Governor would like to go for his recuperation period. At the present time he has told Dr. Tkach, the chief White House doctor, that either he would like to go to Alabama or to possibly Walter Reed here in Washington. I have instructed Dr. Tkach to inform Mrs. Wallace that if he does want to go to Walter Reed that, of course, he would be most welcome there and have all the facilities of the hospital available there, and, of course, the Presidential suite would be made available for him at Walter Reed Hospital.

If the decision is for him to go to Alabama, a decision which he, of course, and his family must make, we will provide an Air Force plane, hospital plane, which will, of course, provide the necessary facilities to transport an individual who is under medical care. That is all I have to report on Governor Wallace's situation as far as the condition is concerned.

One point I should make is that the Secret Service agent [Nicholas J. Zarvos] who was injured, I have learned from Secretary Connally today, and also from talking directly to the head of the Secret Service, as well as the doctor, his condition has substantially improved. The major concern we have is whether there is damage to his larynx, which might affect what is called the voice box.

At the present time, they think there is a better than even chance, the doctors say, that he has not suffered such damage. The wound that he received, the wound also that the officer from the State of Alabama [Capt. Eldred C. Dothard of the Alabama State Police] received, reminds us all that the security men who guard the Presidential candidates and, of course, who guard the President and other officials, and those in law enforcement generally, take very great risks and deserve our support and our sympathy at this time.

With that, ladies and gentlemen, I do have an announcement to make. It involves three people, and I will ask all of them to step up here on this rather narrow platform for the announcement.

We are sorry, we don't have room for the ladies on this occasion, but there will be another occasion when we will have all the ladies on the platform with us.

---

[1] Dr. William M. Lukash, Assistant Physician to the President, was head of the Gastroenterology Clinic and Research Branch, Internal Medicine Service, Naval Hospital, National Naval Medical Center, Bethesda, Md.

SECRETARY OF THE TREASURY

Ladies and gentlemen, you will remember the time in this room that I made the announcement with regard to my nomination of Secretary Connally, Secretary of the Treasury. It is hard to realize it was 18 months ago, on December 14. At that time, Secretary Connally had agreed to come to Washington to take this very arduous assignment, arduous for him, particularly, because he was not one who had had that kind of background, although he had enormous capability, as he later demonstrated in handling the position.

But he agreed to take that assignment for one year. When the year ended, we had a discussion. It was December 14, and the time was right in the middle of the very, very sensitive monetary negotiations that were taking place. Through, shall we say, some persuasion, I was able to get the Secretary to stay on through those negotiations, and after that time I discussed the matter again with him when we were in San Clemente for the meeting with Mr. Sato,[2] and he agreed that he would extend his 12 months to 18 months.

The 18 months now has been reached. This is now May 16 and Secretary Connally has asked that we send a new nomination for Secretary of the Treasury, which I am prepared to do.

Before doing so, and before presenting the man that I have selected for that position, I would like to say a word with regard to Secretary Connally, a word now, and I will elaborate later when he

finally does leave the position, when his successor is confirmed, because, of course, he will stay on as Secretary during the transition period and until his successor is confirmed.

I know that when he was appointed, there were those who wondered how a man who had had a great background as Secretary of the Navy, in government, a Governor, a lawyer could handle this position. I think even the most skeptical critics agree that perhaps no Secretary of the Treasury, as a matter of fact, no member of the Cabinet, in an 18-month period has contributed more to this country than has Secretary Connally.

Then I look back and think of the new economic policy of August 15—he was the architect of that policy. As Chairman of the Cost of Living Council he has led the fight against inflation, a fight which we are now winning. He has also led the Administration in the direction of our economic policy for expansion of the economy. And when we look at the first quarter results we can see there, too, our policy is proving to be successful.

The activities he has undertaken in the international field have not been as well understood by people in this country, but they are certainly understood abroad. I remember a conversation I had with the Chancellor of the Exchequer, Mr. Barber, of Great Britain, when we met in Bermuda. This was right after the Smithsonian agreement had been reached. That was a pretty rugged session for all concerned. I must say that there are people abroad who may have objections to the Secretary because he stands up so strongly for America, but they respect him. The Chancellor of the Exchequer said to me that without any question, without Secretary Connally's leadership,

---

[2] Eisaku Sato, Prime Minister of Japan, met with the President at the Western White House on January 6 and 7, 1972. See Items 4 and 5.

his forceful, dynamic, and skilled leadership, there would have been no agreement with regard to the realignment of currencies in the Smithsonian Institute on that occasion.

These are activities of the Secretary that are well known. There are others that are not as well known in which he has been a tower of strength for the President. I refer to his service in the National Security Council. I refer to the fact that whenever I have had a very difficult decision, and I have had one or two in recent weeks that have been perhaps quite difficult, I have found that when the going is the hardest, when the going is the toughest, that Secretary Connally is at his best.

Needless to say, his loss, from a personal standpoint, in terms of his counsel and advice, apart from his official responsibilities as Secretary of the Treasury, will be a very great one for me and for this country and for this Administration. Naturally, we very much regret losing Mrs. Connally, who has been such a bright star in our Cabinet family in the time she has been in Washington.

However, there are some compensations. The Secretary has agreed that after I return from Moscow he will undertake some temporary assignments. One of those will be announced after I return from Moscow. His service in any capacity is something which we most deeply appreciate.

I will only say finally that the Nation is very fortunate to have had his dedicated service over these past 18 months, and I look forward to a continued close association and for his service in any capacities that we may, on a temporary basis, work out in the future with him.

Now, for his successor. The Secretary and I had a long discussion about this several weeks ago. There was only one candidate that we thought really measured up to what was needed at this time as Secretary of the Treasury. He is superbly qualified, having been in the Cabinet, having been the Director of the Office of Budget and Management, an economist, of course, but also one who has shown great skill in management, one who has a keen understanding of the problems of taxation, one who has shown a rare ability to understand the intricacies of international finance and international economic policy.

George Shultz will return to the Cabinet—I say "return" to it in the sense that he now, after having his salary reduced when he was Secretary of Labor and went up to the Office of Management and Budget, now gets back the Cadillac and the salary.

DIRECTOR, OFFICE OF MANAGEMENT AND BUDGET

Cap Weinberger, of course, is the natural successor as the Director of the Office of Budget and Management. I had hoped that it meant an increase in salary—it doesn't, not very much. He already has a car, so there really is not much reason for him to take the new position. The office he receives as Director of the Office of Budget and Management, I find, is not nearly as nice and not nearly as commodious as the office that he presently has where he is Director of the Budget. But he is making the sacrifice and is willing to take the position of Director of the OMB.

595

Neither George Shultz nor Cap Weinberger will, of course, make any statement now or will be open to questions, because they have to be confirmed.[3] When I say "have to be confirmed," I hope they are confirmed, and soon, and I believe they will be, sooner than some others that have been nominated. Otherwise, Secretary Connally will have another 6 months. [*Laughter*]

But in any event, while they will leave with me, Secretary Connally, now that he is leaving government, will be able to

___

[3] The position of Director of the Office of Management and Budget is appointive and does not require Senate confirmation.

stay to make a brief statement and to take two or three questions, I understand, before some of you may want to file a bulletin.

NOTE: The President spoke at 11:38 a.m. in the Briefing Room at the White House. He spoke without referring to notes.

Following the President's remarks, Secretary Connally answered reporters' questions about his resignation. A transcript of the question-and-answer session was released by the White House.

Later, the President went with Secretary Connally and Director Shultz to the Department of the Treasury where he spoke informally to key Department staff members about the personnel changes.

154 Remarks to Members of the 12th Mexico-United States Interparliamentary Conference. *May* 16, 1972

Ladies and gentlemen:

Mrs. Nixon and I are delighted to welcome this interparliamentary group, our friends from Mexico. In welcoming you, I can only say that we think it is rather historic that this is the first official group to be received in this house since probably the most famous room in the house, the Blue Room, has been restored and redecorated.

It could not be better to have guests from a country which is so very close to us, not only physically but spiritually, the people of Mexico, representatives of the Parliament of Mexico.

As you know, we are looking forward to welcoming the President of Mexico for a state dinner in the middle of June, after I return from my trip abroad. I can say that we consider presidents of any country very important people, but I know from my relationships with the Congress, the Senate and the House, that Senators

and Congressmen are also very important people, and we welcome you in that spirit, because Presidents can have understandings between each other, but unless they have the support of members of their legislatures, they will not be able to carry out those understandings.

The fact that we have such a close and friendly relationship between our Senators and your Senators, and our Representatives and your Representatives, means that not only—and this is true— the President of Mexico and the President of the United States are personally and officially good friends, but the legislators that represent Mexico and the United States are also good friends. That means friendship—friendship now, friendship in the future between Mexico and the United States.

Finally, in conclusion, I would like to say to all of our friends that we will be receiving you and greeting each of you personally at the entrance to the State Dining Room. In that room, you will see there is only one portrait, the portrait of Abraham Lincoln.

It is significant, as members of your delegation, the leaders of your delegation presented a medal commemorating the Year of Juárez, and this is the Year of Juárez in Mexico, that Juárez and Lincoln were contemporaries, that they corresponded with each other. Juárez was not only a great man, a great Mexican, but a great leader of the world. Lincoln, we believe, not only was a great American, but a great leader of the world.

And may the spirit of Juárez and the spirit of Lincoln guide the relations between our two great countries in all the years ahead. And from now on, *estan ustedes en su casa.*

[At this point, Enrique Olivares Santana, President of the Mexican Senate, addressed the delegates in Spanish. A translation of his remarks is printed in the Weekly Compilation of Presidential Documents (vol. 8, p. 869). President Nixon then resumed speaking.]

Thank you very much, Senator. Now Mrs. Nixon and I will look forward to receiving all of you who can work it into your schedule, down the hall, before going into the State Dining Room for refreshments.

I, incidentally, should take note of one fact: When the Ambassador arrived he thought he was late, but he was right on time, but Ambassadors always want to be 15 minutes early. He said, "The trouble was, I was not on the list and they didn't let me come in the gate."

I want everybody in this room to know that the Ambassador from Mexico is always on our list, and from now on he always comes in this gate.

We have some mementos for the Senators and for the Members of the Congress, as well as their wives, just little things for you to take back. The aide will give them to you as you leave the dining room. Thank you.

NOTE: The President spoke at 3:12 p.m. in the East Room at the White House. He spoke without referring to notes.

155   Statement on Signing the National Sickle Cell Anemia Control Act.   *May* 16, 1972

IT IS with special pleasure that I am today signing into law the National Sickle Cell Anemia Control Act.

Sickle cell anemia is an inherited blood disorder, caused by a genetically determined change in the chemical constituents of hemoglobin, thus affecting the oxygen-carrying capacity of the blood. No cure has yet been found.

This disease is especially pernicious because it strikes only blacks and no one else.

An estimated 25,000 to 50,000 black individuals are currently afflicted with the disease. Some 1,000 infants are born yearly with sickle cell anemia, and an estimated 2 million black Americans are carriers of the sickle cell trait. Many sickle cell anemia victims are crippled long before death, and some die from it prematurely.

In February 1971, I pledged that this Administration would reverse the record

597

of neglect on this dread disease. To accomplish that end, $10 million was used to expand sickle cell programs in fiscal 1972, a tenfold budget increase over fiscal 1971. In my March 1972 health message, I proposed that we raise the funding level of sickle cell anemia activities for fiscal 1973 to $15 million. Also, at my direction, the Veterans Administration is now expanding its sickle cell program.

The National Sickle Cell Anemia Control Act, which I am today signing, follows the course that we have charted. These actions make clear, I believe, the urgency with which this country is working to alleviate and arrest the suffering from this disease.

The chief provisions of the new act are as follows:

1. *Screening and Counseling Programs.* Funds are provided for establishing and operating voluntary screening and counseling programs on sickle cell anemia.

These activities will be part of the existing public health care operations.

2. *Information and Education Activities.* The new legislation also provides funds to develop and disseminate educational materials on sickle cell anemia both for health care personnel and for the general public.

3. *Research.* The act authorizes project grants and contracts for research in the diagnosis, treatment, and control of sickle cell anemia.

The legislation closely parallels existing Federal legislative authorities and activities.

Under the programs we have already initiated, we can look forward to the day when sickle cell anemia will be conquered as a debilitating menace to many Americans.

NOTE: As enacted, the bill (S. 2676) is Public Law 92-294 (86 Stat. 136).

156 Statement on the Appointment of John S. D. Eisenhower as Chairman of the Interagency Classification Review Committee. *May 17, 1972*

FOR ALMOST 16 months this Administration has made a determined push to overhaul the security classification system within the Government, and now I am pleased to announce a major step forward in that effort.

Effective today, I have appointed John S. D. Eisenhower as Chairman of the Interagency Classification Review Committee.

This Committee will oversee the implementation and operation of the new system for classification and declassification of Government documents which I established in Executive Order 11652 of March 8, 1972. Also serving on the Committee will be senior representatives of the Departments of Defense, State, and Justice, the Central Intelligence Agency, and the Atomic Energy Commission. David R. Young of the National Security Council staff will act as Executive Director.

Concurrent with the appointment of this panel, we have also acted today to implement several important features of the new system. Under a directive issued by the National Security Council, each department originating classified information has been asked to set up a computerized data index system for classified material and to compile name lists of all persons with authority to classify documents. This application of computer technology across the board should lead to a much more manageable classification system and greatly enhance the flow of information to the public.

Overseeing our new approach to Government documents will not be an easy task, for a delicate balance must be struck between the public's right to know and the Government's obligation to protect the national security.

In obtaining the services of Ambassador Eisenhower for this assignment, the public can be certain of wise and vigorous leadership. An Army officer for many years, an Ambassador to Belgium for more than 2

years, and with considerable experience in historical writing and research, John Eisenhower has perhaps a unique understanding of the competing interests in this field.

More than that, he shares his father's abiding belief that the strength of a democracy rests heavily upon an informed and active citizenry. I have asked him to give unswerving allegiance to this belief in his new post, and I am confident he will do so.

NOTE: A White House announcement containing biographical information on Mr. Eisenhower was released on the same day and is printed in the Weekly Compilation of Presidential Documents (vol. 8, p. 871).

The White House also released the text of a National Security Council directive governing the classification, downgrading, declassification, and safeguarding of national security information, and the transcript of a news briefing by Mr. Young on the directive. The directive is published in the Federal Register of May 19, 1972.

157　Special Message to the Congress Proposing the Allied Services Act of 1972. *May* 18, 1972

To the Congress of the United States:

In responding to steady public demand over recent decades for more and more human services, the Federal Government created a host of assistance programs designed to meet a wide variety of human needs.

These many programs were established one-by-one over a considerable number of years. Each of the target problems was examined in isolation, and a program to alleviate each problem was devised separately—without regard to programs which had been, or would be, developed

for allied problems.

The result is that a compassionate government unwittingly created a bureaucratic jungle that baffles and shortchanges many citizens in need. The unintended administrative snarl wastes taxpayers' money. And it frustrates needed efforts to treat "the whole person."

The Allied Services Act of 1972, which I am proposing today, would give State and local officials authority to consolidate the planning and implementation of the many separate social service programs into streamlined, comprehensive plans—each

599

custom-designed for a particular area.

Such plans could eventually make it possible to assess the total human service needs of an entire family at a single location with a single application. Most applicants need more than one service, and now must trudge to office after office applying for assistance from one program at a time—with the result that they may not obtain all the services they need, or may be discouraged altogether from seeking help.

The Department of Health, Education, and Welfare administers some 200 different human assistance programs in about a dozen major fields—to help needy citizens with such services as mental health, vocational rehabilitation, manpower training, food and nutrition, special programs for the aged, education, juvenile counseling, alcoholism and drug abuse, housing, and public health.

Each of these programs has its own eligibility rules, application forms, management, and administrative policies. Each program usually has its own office location and its own geographical coverage area.

Federal rules and regulations, in short, now keep each social service program locked up in a little world of its own. This is not only wasteful and inefficient—it also prevents State and local efforts to close the gaps in social service delivery systems.

As I stated in my State of the Union Message this year, "We need a new approach to the delivery of social services—one which is built around people and not around programs. We need an approach which treats a person as a whole and which treats the family as a unit."

For the uninformed citizen in need, the present fragmented system can become a nightmare of confusion, inconvenience, and red tape.

The father of a family is helped by one program, his daughter by another, and his elderly parents by a third. An individual goes to one place for nutritional help, to another for health services, and to still another for educational counseling.

They are not the only victims of fragmented services—others include the taxpayers, and the public officials and government employees seeking to operate these diverse programs. Vast amounts of time, money, and energy are expended in administrative procedures which overlap and duplicate—rather than being efficiently organized to help people.

The Allied Services Act of 1972 would give State and local governments greater legal freedom and planning tools needed for the long-overdue job of modernizing the delivery of social services into consolidated programs. This process would begin at the option of elected State and local officials, and would be highly responsive to their needs.

It would permit knowledgeable State and local people to break through rigid categorical walls, to open up narrow bureaucratic compartments, to consolidate and coordinate related programs in a comprehensive approach to related social aid problems—designed to match widely-varying State and local needs.

Under the Act, the Federal Government would make dollars available for the costs of developing consolidated plans, and it would also be prepared to underwrite the administrative startup costs when the comprehensive services program went into effect.

To encourage and facilitate such unified services, the Secretary of Health,

Education, and Welfare would be empowered by the Act to approve the transfer of up to 25 percent of any existing program's funds into any other purpose or programs involved in an approved local allied service plan—a logical flexibility now hindered by Federal program regulations.

The Secretary also could provide a waiver of any existing program regulation which barred or hampered an existing program from participating in such activity.

The Allied Services Act charts a new course for the delivery of social services. It is a complex reform proposal with many major ramifications for many established groups—government and private—on the Federal, State, and local levels.

The consideration and eventual passage of this legislation by the Congress would only be a start. At the same time, human service delivery reform would have to be debated all across the country by affected governments and groups, in order to decide how they would make best use of the proposed freedoms and incentives in their particular areas.

This is one more effort by my Administration to make government more sensible, more responsive and more effective at the local level—where most citizens actually meet the practical impact of government.

In this important proposal, as in my recommendations for Revenue Sharing, we would summon forth the creative energies and the local expertise of State and local officials, rather than keeping them strapped in a straitjacket of inflexible Federal regulations.

They would be freed—and thus would be challenged—to direct the development of customized comprehensive social services plans to treat the special needs, resources and desires of their particular areas.

Such efforts should result in government built for people, geared for across-the-board performance, and designed for results rather than bureaucratic ritual.

If we bring this about, we shall not only be providing better social services—we also shall be taking a giant step toward the restoration of the people's confidence in the common sense performance of their government.

RICHARD NIXON

The White House,
    May 18, 1972.

NOTE: The proposed Allied Services Act of 1972 was introduced as H.R. 15856, H.R. 15857, and S. 3643.

On May 18, 1972, the White House released a fact sheet on the provisions of the proposed legislation and the transcript of a news briefing by Secretary of Health, Education, and Welfare Elliot L. Richardson on the President's message.

158 Statement About Increased Attention to the Arts and Design in Enhancing Federal Buildings and Publications. *May* 18, 1972

ONE YEAR ago I asked the heads of 63 Federal agencies to determine ways by which their agencies could more vigor- ously assist the arts and, in turn, how the arts might be used to enhance their programs. The response to that request has been gratifying, calling fresh attention to the importance of the arts in the daily operations of Government and leading to the development of several recommendations by the National Endowment for the Arts.

Today, based upon this first set of recommendations by the Endowment, I am pleased to announce that we shall move forward on three fronts:

—First, I am asking the Federal Council on the Arts and Humanities to sponsor an annual Design Assembly for Federal administrators and artists.

—Second, I am asking the National Endowment for the Arts to appoint a special ad hoc task force committee to review and expand the publication, "Guiding Principles for Federal Architecture"; this document was first printed in 1962 and set forth broad aesthetic recommendations of considerable value. I am also asking the National Endowment to recommend a program for including art works in new Federal buildings.

—Third, I am taking a series of actions

to improve Federal graphics and publications. The National Endowment will now be responsible for coordinating the efforts of the executive agencies to upgrade their graphics. I am also requesting Federal agency heads to make a comprehensive review of their own graphics and production, and I am asking the Civil Service Commission to review existing procedures for employing artists, architects, and designers for Federal service. The Commission is also to evaluate the need for expert rating panels to review credentials and portfolios of applicants for such jobs, as is done in other professional areas.

The people of this country are increasingly concerned—and properly so—with the physical appearance of their communities. There should be no doubt that the Federal Government has an appropriate and critical role to play in encouraging better design, and I am hopeful that the actions announced today will enable the Government to reflect new standards of excellence in all of its design endeavors.

159 Remarks to Reporters About Forthcoming Trip to Austria, the Soviet Union, Iran, and Poland. *May* 19, 1972

Ladies and gentlemen:

I understand that almost everybody here is going to leave with us tomorrow for the trip to Austria, the Soviet Union, Iran, and Poland, and to the ones who are not going we are sorry you can't go on this trip and we will report to you when we come back.

I thought it might be useful to give a little background with regard to the trip and perhaps some information that would

be helpful to you in covering it. This trip is one which has been in the process of planning going back perhaps over 3 years. You may recall the first time that I had a press conference in the East Room, I was asked about summitry.

At that point I expressed a very dim view of summitry unless it was well planned in advance. I said that because I have memories, as all of you have memories, of some of the summits of the past. I remember what term was used by ladies and gentlemen of the press in describing them. There was the "spirit of Vienna," the "spirit of Geneva," and the "spirit of Glassboro," and the "spirit of Camp David."

What they all added up to was cosmetics, a big feeling of hope in the world and in the United States in particular and then a letdown because there was all froth and very little substance.

This trip is one, and I do not want to overestimate what you may expect to have from it in the way of substance, but it is one primarily directed toward substance rather than toward cosmetics.

We are not taking the trip simply for the purpose of opening a new relationship, as was the case when we went to Peking. That, of course, was enormously important and it was important to go to Peking for that very purpose, if nothing else was served at all—and other things were served, we believe.

In this case, we have had relations with the Soviet Union, as you know, for a number of years. There have been contacts at various levels, Cabinet levels, with the Soviet Union, and we have had meetings between the top Soviet leaders and top American leaders going back over a period of time through World War II and, of course, in the postwar period.

What has happened in the last 3½ years is that we have started a long process in several areas of trying to determine on both sides—it has been mutual on both sides—as to whether a meeting of the leaders at the summit would serve a useful purpose, and that is why we did not make the decision, again a mutual decision, that it would be useful to have such a meeting

until just a few months ago.

You will recall that perhaps the single event which brought about the decision on the part of the Soviet leaders and our decision to go to the summit was the success of the understandings on Berlin. We thought if we had made progress in that very critical area for both of us that we should try with some hope of success of making progress in other areas that were also difficult.

Now, in coming to this meeting, I would suggest that it would not be useful to speculate as to what agreements or understandings will come out of it. I would touch on just the three subjects that have been very much written about in the press that will be on the agenda and three subjects, three areas, in which there is a possibility, not a certainty by any manner of means, but a possibility of agreement, provided at the highest level we can break some bottlenecks which still exist.

One, of course, is arms limitation. Considerable progress has been made in this area. There are still some very difficult problems that remain unsolved. We will discuss them directly. I will discuss them directly with Mr. Brezhnev throughout the course of the visit, and we hope that we may be able to reach agreement in this area.

However, on both sides we recognize that we have some difficult problems in which a decision at the top only can bring agreement. We are hopeful, but we do not want to leave the implication that it is certain that we can reach agreement.

The second area is the area of trade. You have all, of course, followed Secretary Butz' trip to the Soviet Union and Secretary Stans', then the trips, of course, that have been made by the Soviet Agricultural

Minister and the Soviet Minister of Trade to the United States—their meetings with Mr. Peterson and Mr. Flanigan—and of course, I have had meetings with both of them.

In this area, having just met with Congressional leaders discussing such matters as most-favored-nation and the others, the matter of credits, I would say that the chances for some positive results are good, not certain, but certainly good.

You will be wanting to follow that very closely during the course of our visit there.

A third area that is worth your watching is the area of cooperation in space. In this respect, I was looking over the speech that I made to the Soviet people on television in 1959. I had forgotten that I said it, as a matter of fact, and most things are well forgotten that you have said, but, in any event, I said at that time—those 12 who are here who went to the Soviet Union on that trip will remember—I said let us go to the Moon together.

I would not like to suggest and would not suggest that we are going to discuss, "Let us go to the Moon together, let us go to Mars together." But I do know that considerable progress has been made over the past several months with regard to cooperation in terms of the exploration of space. We are going to try to see a culmination of that progress in this area.

By mentioning these three, I do not mean that they are exclusive. I do mean that they are areas that perhaps offer considerable promise.

As far as other agenda items are concerned, both sides have submitted items for the agenda. The agenda is agreed. It will be primarily bilateral. I emphasize that all of the talks that we have will take place looking to the interests of each country vis-a-vis the other, and not at the expense of or in derogation of any country's interest toward its allies or other countries in the world.

On the other hand, there will be discussion on the agenda on such items as Vietnam and other areas of the world where the United States and the Soviet Union do have sometimes conflicting interests.

I will not go beyond that in discussing those areas because only the results of our conversations will determine whether progress is possible. We are quite far apart, as you know, in several of those areas. I can only say that there will be an open, free, and frank discussion building upon discussions that we have had previously in these areas.

Now a word about the preparation. I mentioned the preparation and I do not want to indicate that it has all been done simply at the Presidential level. I have had, as you know, both by correspondence and through other contacts, a very great volume of exchange of views directly with Mr. Brezhnev. That exchange of views, I think, even though I met him only briefly in 1959, means that both he and I will start, at least, on a basis where we understand what our differences are and therefore will be able to come to grips quickly with the problems that we, and perhaps only we, can solve at the highest level.

In addition to that, the State Department, of course, has had major responsibilities in certain areas; the Department of Commerce, the Department of Agriculture, the Science Adviser, our NASA people, a number of others, all have been working toward the time when this meeting would take place.

Having in mind the fact that if we do

not succeed—and we will not, of course—in reaching agreement in all the areas that will be discussed, we will at least continue the process of negotiation, so that following the summit, there may be not only dialogue but possibly future agreements depending upon what happens at the summit.

Now, with regard to your problems. I know that when you were in Peking it was rather difficult to cover. The reason was, of course, that we did not have diplomatic relations with the People's Republic of China. We did not have, as we have in this instance, an on-going process of negotiation in various levels on which to build. And consequently, I know that from the standpoint of substance day by day until we finally got to the communique, that it was very difficult for members of the press to get the hard news, which I know you have to get and that you must get in order to justify your going so far. [*Laughter*]

In this instance I can inform you that there will be daily briefings. I can also say that in terms of substance, without indicating what will happen in the three areas that I mentioned, or other areas, there will be two very substantive speeches made on my part.

The first night at the dinner in the Kremlin, Chairman Brezhnev, or Secretary Brezhnev I should say, the General Secretary will make a substantive speech, and I will respond with a substantive speech. That will be released in advance so that you will be able to write your stories and then enjoy your dinner.

The other will be on Sunday. On Sunday, I will be speaking on the Soviet television and radio network to the Soviet people. This, of course, brings back memories of 1959. I shall never forget the long period that I worked with Ambassador Tommy [Llewellyn] Thompson, whom you all will remember, on that speech. He said a very interesting thing as I was working on it. He said, "You must think of the fact that what you said is to two audiences—the Soviet audience, the American audience. There are things you could say to the American audience that would not be helpful to the Soviet audience because they have not yet heard a top American official speak to them in this way."

And as we worked on that speech, cut this and added this, and so forth, he gave me one admonition. He said, "This is the first time that a top American official will ever have addressed the Soviet people on radio and television." He said, "Write the speech and make the speech in a way that it will not be the last time."

I think we accomplished that, and in this instance the speech that I will make on Sunday will be directed to the Soviet people, not with any naive attitude that we are going to convince them that all of our policies are right and that everything that they have heard about us is wrong, but simply to give them some observations about what we have found in the Soviet Union and to give them as well as we can a true and accurate picture of the United States, the American people, of the desire that we have, a desire which is shared by the Russian people, a desire for peace in the world and for better relations.

It will be, in other words, a speech directed to the Russian people rather than to the American people. I think, however, most of the American people would approve because this will be the first time the President of the United States has ever spoken to the Russian people by radio and television. I don't want it to be the last time.

As far as other activities are concerned, Mrs. Nixon, as was the case in Peking, will have a very intensive schedule and I am sure you will find it most interesting to follow her on days that we may be closeted in meetings. I would also suggest one other point, that there will be, in this instance, plenary sessions, probably two plenary sessions, and then we will have parallel conversations.

My conversations will be with the General Secretary, Mr. Brezhnev, or with others that he may add from time to time from his own personal staff in addition to the plenary sessions. And Secretary Rogers will be meeting with Foreign Minister Gromyko. We will divide the work, and in some instances, we, of course, will be discussing the same problems.

This way, with the amount of work that we do have, we feel we can cover a massive amount of material that is before us.

Eight days seems a long time, and it will be a long time, I can assure you, from the standpoint of your own workload. But we could really take 8 days to consider even one of the subjects that I have mentioned—SALT, commercial relations, even space—and so we are cramming a great deal of work into a relatively brief period of time. We think that that, however, can be quite useful.

In mentioning, incidentally, our visit to the Soviet Union, I want you all not to overlook the fact we are going to Iran. I know you will enjoy our visit there. I consider it very important to go to Iran to return a visit that the Shah made here, to show America's friendship and our close association with this strong friend of the United States in that part of the world.

We will be going to Austria, stopping there for tomorrow and Sunday, and I look forward to going back there, having had the opportunity to see Austria in 1956 and being back on other occasions as well.

And then, of course, our trip will conclude with a visit to Poland.

I would advise that in all of these areas, to the extent you can—as you will in the Soviet Union—if you can find time from your work, do some sightseeing, because they are all great cities, extremely interesting, and I just wish I had the time to do a little sightseeing myself.

Now, one little personal note. On trips like this, virtually everybody who is going for the first time asks me, "Now, what would you advise that we see?"

Well, naturally you want to see the Kremlin. You ought to see the university; you ought to see certainly one of the great industrial plants in Moscow, the magnificence of the gardens and the former Czar's Palace in Leningrad, and so forth.

But one place that may not have occurred to you that I would urge, if you have the time, to get a real feel of the new Soviet Union and the old Russia, is to go to the marketplace. I have always gone there on all four of my trips. You will find the Russian people extremely friendly when they know you are from the United States, and extremely interested, asking many questions about our country, and you will get a flavor there you can't get in the GUM department store, which is also very much worth going to see, too.

I don't have stock in either one—neither do they. [*Laughter*] It is a different system.

Let me just close my remarks with one final thought. Everybody in this Government has worked extremely hard on this trip over the past months—some for years:

the SALT delegation, our State Department people, the people in the other departments that I have mentioned, the White House Staff. Dr. Kissinger, of course, has made an enormous contribution with the trip that he has made to the Soviet Union, in talking to Mr. Brezhnev and the other Soviet leaders. It is basically one where we are all going with one common purpose, and that is to attempt to establish a different relationship, one in which there will still be very significant differences—we must always remember this—in philosophy and in approach and so forth, but one in which two great powers, each looking to its interests, decides that in certain areas we should work together rather than against each other.

I think that in terms of trying to give you the flavor of what to expect, I would not raise hopes too high, because there are some knotty problems left to be solved. What will determine whether they will be solved will be the attitude of the Soviet leaders, and our attitude as well.

I can say this: That from the correspondence that I have had, the contacts I have had directly with and from Mr. Brezhnev in the last few days, his attitude is positive. Mine is positive.

Mr. Dobrynin came up to Camp David yesterday and brought me a personal message from Mr. Brezhnev, raising some questions that we had to discuss, but also indicating a positive attitude toward attempting to resolve some of these differences, so that when we do meet at the summit, it will not simply be one of those spirits that comes and goes, but there will really be some substance that remains, one which will mean that the American people and the Russian people will have a more friendly relationship as people to people, despite differences in philosophy and government, and in which, perhaps—and I would hope this beyond everything else—the cause of peace would be served.

Perhaps I can best describe it with a story that Mr. Brezhnev told Dr. Kissinger when he was there. Mr. Brezhnev was expressing his desire for making some progress at the summit—not just talking, not just agreeing to disagree, not just putting out the usual communique which papers over all differences—and he said it was important to take a step. He said, not just a little step, but a step that is significant in the relations between our two countries, because that will tell us where we are going.

And then he told what for Mr. Brezhnev is one of his favorite Russian stories. He said there was a tradesman from a town who was walking in the woods one day, and he came to a fork in the road. He saw the sign leading to a village, and decided to go toward that village. He saw a woodsman at the fork of the road, and he said, "How long will it take me to reach the village?"

The woodsman said, "I don't know." The tradesman couldn't believe him. He thought he was being just totally obnoxious, because he knew that he lived in this area; he knew he had to have been to the village.

So the tradesman started off down the road, and after he had walked a few steps, the woodsman said, "It will take you 15 minutes." He turned around, "Why didn't you tell me that in the first place?" He said, "I had to see how long your steps were."

So we are taking a step here. How long

the steps will be, you ladies and gentlemen will have to evaluate. We hope that it can be a significant step. It will not end all differences, but it could mean certainly that the United States and the Soviet Union, building on this very careful structure that we have developed over the past, could have a constructive relationship in which both great nations will use their influence, not only between each other, but in other areas of the world where we have influence, to discourage aggression, and to encourage the forces of peace.

This is our goal. We trust and hope that it will be, too, the Soviet goal, because for these two great nations to come in conflict, either directly, or to be drawn into conflict because of disputes in other parts of the world where they are indirectly affected, is a threat to the peace of the world which none of us can certainly look forward to without very great concern.

So my remarks deliberately are not with the overblown rhetoric for which you have properly criticized me in the past. [*Laughter*] This is a trip with very sober objectives. I intend to be very sober, but you don't have to be. [*Laughter*]

Thank you.

NOTE: The President spoke at 6 p.m. in the State Dining Room at the White House. He spoke without referring to notes.

Earlier in the afternoon, the President met at the White House with the bipartisan leadership of the Congress to discuss his forthcoming trip.

160   Statement About Signing the Black Lung Benefits Act of 1972. *May* 20, 1972

TODAY I have signed H.R. 9212, the Black Lung Benefits Act of 1972.

This legislation extends for 18 months the Federal responsibility for operating a transitional program enacted in 1969 to provide cash benefits for coal miners disabled by black lung disease.

Under the original law, lifetime monthly benefits have been awarded to more than 260,000 miners, widows, and dependents at a Federal cost of more than $600 million.

The Black Lung Benefits Act of 1972 will mean that tens of thousands of additional miners and their dependents will be eligible for lifetime benefits from the Federal Government, because of its extension of filing time and because it provides for generous liberalization of eligibility requirements.

I am heartened that this legislation provides benefits for orphans of black lung victims, who are excluded in the present law through legislative oversight. Other dependents are covered but not orphans. Under the new law, some 2,000 orphans of black lung victims—and all such orphans in the future—will receive the benefits to which they should be fully entitled.

Nevertheless, I sign this legislation with mixed emotions, not over whether miners, widows, and their dependents need this assistance—they do—but because of the precedent it tends to establish.

This legislation departs from the U.S. tradition that compensation for work-related accidents and diseases should be provided by State workmen's compensation laws, financed by the owners of the industries containing the hazards. Responsibility for black lung compensation clearly should lie with the owners and operators of the mines.

In this case, however, the States have not yet improved their owner-financed laws to meet the challenge posed by black lung—and there are too many victims of this dread disease for me not to have acted.

Therefore, I have moved to pick up the responsibility that others have neglected— so that disabled miners and their families will not be deserted by our society in their hour of critical and justified personal need.

The health and safety of coal miners has been a primary concern of this Administration. One of my earliest legislative recommendations was for more effective Federal laws in the area of coal mine health and safety, culminating in the enactment of the Federal Coal Mine Health

and Safety Act of 1969. Since that law was enacted, major progress has been made in improving working conditions in our Nation's coal mines and in the protection offered to those who work in them.

The 1969 act established the temporary black lung benefits program. The legislation I have signed today will extend Federal responsibility for this program from January 1, 1972, to June 30, 1973. In the latter half of 1973, the Federal Government will continue to accept applications for black lung benefits but beneficiaries enrolled during this period will be transferred to the State programs on January 1, 1974.

I urge that all mining States review their workmen's compensation programs to make certain that adequate laws exist for the black lung disease by that time.

NOTE: As enacted, H.R. 9212, approved May 19, 1972, is Public Law 92–303 (86 Stat. 150).

161   Statement on Signing Executive Order Providing for Return of Certain Lands to the Yakima Indian Reservation. *May* 20, 1972

IT IS with particular pleasure that I sign this Executive order [11670] which places 21,000 acres of land in the State of Washington under the trust jurisdiction of the Secretary of the Interior for the Yakima Indian Tribe.

This action rights a wrong going back 65 years.

The U.S. Government lost the treaty map in its own files and by the time it was found actions had been taken which had mistakenly displaced the Indians from this land.

The Indian Claims Commission has

ruled that the Yakima Tribe has a rightful claim, but rather than accept cash compensation, the tribe, with the permission of the Commission, sought to have the land itself restored.

In a comprehensive opinion, Attorney General Mitchell reviewed the unintentional but mistaken actions of 1907 and ruled that the executive order [Proclamation 725] of that time did not constitute a "taking" of the land by the Government in the legal sense and that it can be restored by executive action now.

Ordinarily, of course, Indian land

claims are being, and should be, settled by cash award, but this case has exceptional circumstances which the Attorney General has described.

I am equally pleased to note that the Yakima Tribe itself has pledged by tribal resolution to "maintain existing recreation facilities for public use" and to "recognize the dedication of that portion included in the Mt. Adams wilderness use."

162 Statement About the Cost of Living Council's Quarterly Report on the Economic Stabilization Program. *May* 20, 1972

THE LATEST quarterly report of the Cost of Living Council provides encouraging evidence that the Nation continues to make progress in the battle against inflation.

Prices did advance moderately—as expected and forecast—after the 3-month freeze ended last November. But as statistics analyzed in the report show, the anticipated "bulge" was modest in view of the actual increases in wages and other costs that went into effect after the freeze ended.

By the end of the first quarter of 1972, there was some evidence that the "bulge" was tapering off and the impact of the controls was becoming more evident. The most recent Consumer Price Index continues this pattern.

As pointed out in the report, consumer prices rose at a rate of 3.9 percent a year in the 7 months prior to the freeze, which began last August 15. In the 7 months since the freeze started, that rate of increase declined to 2.8 percent—with no monthly increase registered in March, and only a small increase experienced in April, the eighth month.

The quarterly report also contains convincing evidence that workers are beginning to score an impressive net gain in their purchasing power. Since the economic stabilization program began, real take-home pay for the typical production worker with three dependents has increased about twice as fast since August as in the corresponding period before the freeze.

The national economy is now expanding significantly. This makes the success of the stabilization program more important than ever.

Will this new economic growth result in real prosperity? Or will it be eroded by inflation and thus result only in meaningless bigger numbers?

The stabilization program can make the critical difference, and the stabilization program will succeed if the American people continue to give it their full support.

I am certain this critical public support will be forthcoming. I believe the American people share this Administration's determination to hold inflation to an acceptable rate.

NOTE: The report, covering the period January 1 through March 31, 1972, is entitled "Economic Stabilization Program Quarterly Report" (Government Printing Office, 117 pp.).

162A   Chronology of Visit to Austria, the Soviet Union, Iran, and Poland. *May 20–June 1, 1972*

Editor's Note: The following chronology of events was prepared from White House announcements and outlines public activities of the President and Mrs. Nixon during their visit to Austria, the Soviet Union, Iran, and Poland.

Saturday, May 20

The President and Mrs. Nixon boarded the Spirit of '76 at Andrews Air Force Base for the flight to Salzburg, Austria.

Arriving at Salzburg Airport at 10:30 p.m., they were greeted by Chancellor Bruno Kreisky of the Federal Republic of Austria.

Sunday, May 21

The President and Chancellor Kreisky met for discussion at Klessheim Palace.

Mrs. Nixon entertained Mrs. Kreisky at tea at Klessheim Palace.

The President and Mrs. Nixon were then guests of the Chancellor and Mrs. Kreisky at luncheon at the Kobenzl-Gaisberg Hotel.

Monday, May 22

After departure ceremonies at Salzburg Airport, the President and Mrs. Nixon flew to Moscow, where they were greeted at Vnukovo II Airport by President Podgorny, Premier Kosygin, Foreign Minister Gromyko, and Ambassador Dobrynin.

In the afternoon, the President met for more than 2 hours with General Secretary Brezhnev.

In the evening, the President and Mrs. Nixon were guests of honor at a dinner hosted by the Presidium of the Supreme Soviet of the U.S.S.R. and the Government of the U.S.S.R. in Granovit Hall in the Grand Kremlin Palace.

Tuesday, May 23

The President and members of the United States party met with Soviet officials in plenary session in Catherine Hall in the Grand Kremlin Palace.

In ceremonies in St. Vladimir Hall, the President and President Podgorny signed an agreement on environmental protection. Secretary Rogers and Soviet Health Minister Petrovsky then signed an agreement on medical science and public health.

The President and General Secretary Brezhnev met for 2 hours of discussion before the ceremony and for 3 additional hours later in the evening.

During the day, Mrs. Nixon visited a secondary school, toured the Moscow Metro, and had tea with Mrs. Brezhnev, Mrs. Podgorny, and wives of other Soviet officials in the Imperial Living Quarters in the Grand Kremlin Palace.

Wednesday, May 24

In the morning, the President went to the Aleksandrov Gardens to lay a wreath at the Tomb of the Unknown Soldier. He returned to the Grand Kremlin Palace for further discussions with Soviet leaders.

In afternoon ceremonies, the President and Premier Kosygin signed the space cooperation agreement and Secretary Rogers and Committee Chairman Kirillin signed the science and technology agreement.

The President then went to Chairman Brezhnev's country residence for additional discussions.

The First Lady visited the Moscow State University and the GUM department store. In the evening, she attended a performance at the New Circus.

Thursday, May 25

The President met for 2 hours with Soviet leaders, and a maritime agreement on the prevention of incidents at sea was signed by

Navy Secretary Warner and Admiral Gorshkov.

Mrs. Nixon visited the Bolshoi School of Choreography and the All-Union Fashion House for a showing of men's and women's clothing by Soviet designers.

In the evening, the President and the First Lady attended a performance of the "Swan Lake" ballet at the Bolshoi Theater.

Friday, May 26

After discussions on trade matters, a communique was issued on an agreement between Soviet leaders and President Nixon to establish a U.S.-U.S.S.R. Commercial Commission.

Mrs. Nixon, with Mrs. Brezhnev, Mrs. Gromyko, Mrs. Dobrynin, and Mrs. Jacob D. Beam, wife of the U.S. Ambassador, toured the Moscow Watch Factory and visited with workers there.

In the evening, the President and the First Lady hosted a dinner in honor of Soviet leaders at Spaso House, the American Ambassador's residence.

Following the dinner, the President and General Secretary Brezhnev signed a treaty and an interim agreement on the limitation of strategic arms in a televised ceremony in St. Vladimir Hall in the Grand Kremlin Palace.

Saturday, May 27

The President and Mrs. Nixon, with President Podgorny and other Soviet officials, flew in a Soviet aircraft to Leningrad. They visited the Piskaryev Cemetery, dedicated to those who died in the Leningrad siege during World War II, and the President laid a wreath at the Tomb of the Unknown Soldier.

After a luncheon hosted by the Executive Committee of the Leningrad Council of Workers Deputies in the Mariinsky Palace, the President and the First Lady visited Pavlovsk, formerly an Imperial summer palace, almost destroyed during World War II, and now completely restored as a museum.

They returned to Moscow in the early evening.

Sunday, May 28

The President and the First Lady attended services at the Baptist Church in Moscow.

Mrs. Nixon made a walking tour of the Grand Kremlin Palace, viewing exhibits of armor, royal regalia, and ceremonial carriages, and the Diamond Fund, a collection of precious stones, minerals, and jewelry work. She also visited two Kremlin churches.

At 8:30 p.m., Moscow time, the President addressed the Soviet people on radio and television.

Monday, May 29

In a ceremony in St. Vladimir Hall in the Grand Kremlin Palace, the President and General Secretary Brezhnev signed the "Basic Principles of Relations Between the United States of America and the Union of Soviet Socialist Republics." A joint communique was also issued.

The President and Mrs. Nixon were then honored at a reception given by the Presidium of the Supreme Soviet of the U.S.S.R. and the Government of the U.S.S.R. before flying to Kiev aboard a Soviet aircraft.

In Kiev, the Presidium of the Supreme Soviet and the Government of the Ukrainian Soviet Socialist Republic hosted a dinner for the President and the First Lady.

Tuesday, May 30

The President went to Kiev's Park of Eternal Glory to the Soldiers of the Great Patriotic War, where he laid a wreath at the Tomb of the Unknown Soldier.

Mrs. Nixon visited the Young Pioneers' Palace, a contemporary building with classrooms, laboratories, and other facilities for youth activities.

The President and Mrs. Nixon together then visited St. Sophia's Cathedral and Museum, before flying to Tehran.

From the airport at Tehran, the President and Mrs. Nixon went to the Shahyad Monument where the Mayor of Tehran presented a key to the city.

The President and the Shah met for discussions at the Saadabad Palace.

After a reception for the diplomatic corps at the Saadabad Palace, the President and the First Lady were guests of honor at a state dinner at the Niavaran Palace.

Wednesday, May 31

The President went to the tomb of the Shah's father, 20 miles from Tehran, to lay a wreath. He returned to the Saadabad Palace for further discussions with the Shah. A joint communique was issued.

After tea with the Empress, Mrs. Nixon visited the Pahlavi Welfare Center and a children's library.

The President and Mrs. Nixon then hosted a luncheon honoring Their Imperial Majesties at the Saadabad Palace before departing for Warsaw.

They were greeted at Okecie International Airport at Warsaw by Henryk Jablonski, Chairman of the Council of State, and Prime Minister Jaroszewicz.

Driving from the airport, the President stopped to lay a wreath at the Tomb of the Unknown Soldier.

He then met with Eduard Gierek, First Secretary, Polish United Workers' Party, at the Parliament.

Earlier, Secretary of State Rogers signed the Consular Convention between the United States and Poland.

In the evening, the President and Mrs. Nixon attended a state dinner at the Palace of the Council of Ministers.

Thursday, June 1

The President called on President Jablonski.

The President met for further talks with Mr. Gierek, and they issued a joint communique.

Mrs. Nixon went to the Lazienski Palace and a Chopin concert in the park near the Chopin Monument.

The President and Mrs. Nixon then hosted a luncheon at the Wilanow Palace in honor of Polish leaders.

Returning to the United States aboard the Spirit of '76, the President and Mrs. Nixon landed at Andrews Air Force Base, Md., then went by helicopter to the Capitol Grounds, and the President addressed a joint session of the Congress to report on his trip.

163   Remarks on Departure From Andrews Air Force Base for Austria, the Soviet Union, Iran, and Poland.   *May 20, 1972*

Mr. Vice President, members of the Cabinet, Members of the Congress, and ladies and gentlemen:

We really do appreciate your coming to the airport today on this rainy day to wish us Godspeed on this trip. In just a few minutes we will be boarding the plane, the Spirit of '76, on a trip that will take us first to Austria, then to the Soviet Union, then to Iran, and finally to Poland before returning here on the first of June.

I know that as we visit these four countries that I can say to the people of all of these countries that I bring with me the best wishes, the friendship of all the people

of the United States for the people of these countries because we Americans feel friendship for the Austrian people, for the Russian people, for the people of Iran, and for the Polish people.

As you know, the visit that we will be making to the Soviet Union is the first state visit that a President of the United States has ever made to that country. It is a visit that will be different from those that have occurred on previous occasions between American Presidents and the leaders of the Soviet Union. The others were important, but they did not deal primarily with substance. That is why we often hear them referred to as the "spirit of Camp David," or the "spirit of Vienna," or the "spirit of Geneva," or the "spirit of Glassboro."

In this case we are not going there simply for a better spirit, although that is important, and we think that may be one of the results of the trip. But we are going there for substance, very important substantive talks. We are not going there to make headlines today. We are going there in order to build what we hope will be a structure that can lead to better relations between the Soviet Union and the United States, and a better chance for peace tomorrow and in all the years ahead.

The negotiations will cover a wide range of subjects. Many of these areas are ones where we have not agreed in the past and where we will not find agreement in the period of discussions that we have on this occasion. But, on the other hand, we do expect to make some progress. And the progress that we make, we trust, will lay the foundation for more progress in the future in which two great peoples, the Russian people and the American people, can find a way despite philosophical differences that are very deep, despite competitive positions in the world that are quite different, can find ways to live in peace in the world and to use their great

influence along with other nations to avoid those situations that lead to conflict any place in the world.

This is our goal, and it is one that all of us will be working toward on this trip.

I simply want to say finally that we have been very touched that over the past week, as was the case before we took off for Peking a few months ago, we have received so many calls and letters and wires from people all over the country wishing us well. We thank you for wishing us well. We go there not in any personal sense, but we go there representing all the American people and the hopes and aspirations of all of our people, particularly the hopes of the children of America, those of generations to come. And we hope that we can conduct ourselves in a way that will be worthy of your hopes and worthy of your prayers for a better relation between the Soviet Union and the United States, between the Russian people and the American people, between the people of all the countries that we will visit and the American people, and your hopes and prayers for what all people in the world want, a world of peace, a world of progress for all.

Thank you very much.

NOTE: The President spoke at 9:10 a.m. at Andrews Air Force Base, Md. He spoke without referring to notes.

164 Exchange of Remarks With Reporters and Spectators at Klessheim Palace, Salzburg, Austria. *May 21, 1972*

THE PRESIDENT. How do you do? Nice to see you. You from here? Vienna? Oh, it is a lovely city. I have pleasant memories of Vienna. I have been there four or five times, once with my daughters in 1963.

We stayed in the Imperial Hotel, in one of the great suites of the world. But after seeing this, I am not sure. Everything here is nice. I see why the tourists all want to come here. Sometime I will come as a tourist.

I know that some of you have been to this city and some have not, but I hope you have a chance this afternoon to really get around, because it is one of the most beautiful cities in the world. One of the points that I made when I was in Vienna in 1956, I found that of the tourists that came to Europe, the American tourists, only 8 percent got to Vienna, and that, of course is a great loss to them. I think the percentage now is up.

As I remember my trips to all of the European countries—virtually all of them—Vienna and Salzburg are a must, not only because of the historical things to see, but the beauty of the countryside, and also the Austrian people are just enormously hospitable and friendly. So you can put that in and tell the Austrian Chamber of Commerce, I expect my 5 percent.

Q. Mr. President, have you had a chance to check as to whether or not those refugee camps are still in this area?

THE PRESIDENT. Remember when we went to them? I haven't had a chance. Remember when I went there just before Christmas and talked to them? All the people were so moved, those young Hungarians. They are all gone now. They must be. The Hungarians have gone all over the world. Those camps were extremely well run. The Austrians deserve great credit for the hospitality that they showed the refugees during that period. It is hard to realize that was 17 years ago.

Q. Will you get a chance to do any sightseeing, Mr. President?

THE PRESIDENT. I have just done it. No, I am going to study this afternoon. I will be in all afternoon. I have been sort of doing it on the plane. I have, of course, a great deal of work to be done. There are so many substantive conversations involved here that it requires a great deal of concentration. Over the past 3 days in Camp David, of course, I caught up considerably, but now I have to go over all the final papers to be prepared for a number of very intensive discussions on a number of pretty knotty issues. This is the way it should be.

I know that Mr. Brezhnev and his colleagues will be very well prepared on the details as well as the generalities, and I have to be well prepared, too. That is one of the reasons why we think that the possibilities of some progress—I don't want to raise hopes—but some progress here are perhaps greater than in some cases, because both sides will be well prepared, both sides know where we differ. They know where we will have to negotiate those differences. Whether we are able to resolve them remains to be seen. But where conferences of this type fail is where one side or the other is not prepared, does not know what the real heart of the problem is.

In this case that will not be the problem. We will be able to go very directly to the points of difference and the points of agreement, and then we can talk about the points of difference.

I look forward to perhaps the most intensive negotiations that I have participated in on substantive matters, and that is why I will not be doing any sightseeing.

Q. Do you remember Brezhnev from your past visits to Moscow?

THE PRESIDENT. Yes, I remember him, but we did not have any conversations at the time.

NOTE: The exchange of remarks took place during a walk which the President took in the Palace grounds.

615

165   Toasts of the President and Chancellor Bruno Kreisky
of Austria at a Luncheon in Salzburg.   *May* 21, 1972

Mr. Chancellor and Mrs. Kreisky, and our distinguished hosts and all of our guests today:

Mrs. Nixon and I are very moved by the remarks you have just made and by the reception that you have given us on our brief visit to Salzburg and to Austria.

Mr. Chancellor, you said that this is one of the most beautiful cities in your country. As we look at this view and as we look back at the mountain in back of us, this is one of the most beautiful cities in all the world.

It is not my first visit here. I recall in 1956—when the now Secretary of State was then Deputy Attorney General and I was Vice President—when we visited Austria. We were in Vienna, we were in Salzburg around Christmastime. We learned then to know the hospitality, the grace, the warmth of the Austrian people.

We learned then to know the beauty of this country and of this city and of all the country. We learned then, too, to admire the Austrian people for what they did for the refugees who came into the country from Hungary. It was a difficult time for the world, for those refugees, for this country. But the great warmth, the hospitality, as a matter of fact, the sacrifice that was made by the Austrian people in order to help those who were having very difficult times made an enormous impression upon us.

We wish to pay tribute to the Austrian people for what they did then and what they have contributed then, before then, and since then to the kind of a peaceful world that we all want to build.

You, Mr. Chancellor, have said that this is a small country. I would simply respond by saying that as we leave tomorrow on a visit that will bring us to a meeting between the two most powerful nations in the world—the Soviet Union and the United States—that one of our major purposes will be to try to make progress toward the time when all countries in the world, whatever their size, may have the right to choose their own way, the right to independence, to whatever form of government they desire—a right which we see here in Austria exemplified in the highest degree.

Finally, Mr. Chancellor, I think you should know that while our talks have been necessarily brief and informal, it has been most helpful for me to get the benefit of your thinking on the problems of Europe, the problems of the world in which you are so well versed because you have not only served in this capacity but also as Foreign Minister.

I can only say that the size of a country does not determine the quality of its leadership. And a small country has produced, in the present Chancellor of Austria, one of the top statesmen of the world who contributes greatly to the thinking which the world needs if we are to build what we all want—generations of peace in the years ahead, peace with progress for all people, and peace with independence for all nations.

NOTE: The President spoke at approximately 2:43 p.m. in the Kobenzl-Gaisberg Hotel. He spoke without referring to notes. Chancellor Kreisky's remarks were as follows:

Dear Mr. President Nixon:

It is both an honor and a profound pleasure for me to be able to welcome you in one of the most beautiful cities of our country.

I know that you are on your way to what

will undoubtedly be one of the great political events in many years. Small countries do not have sufficient power of their own to immunize themselves against the slings and arrows of outrageous fortune and so are, therefore, particularly interested that such events turn out to be fruitful.

As a representative of a small nation, I may, therefore, wish you every possible good luck for your forthcoming trip to Moscow.

Finally, I hope that you and Mrs. Nixon will leave Austria with good memories, that one day we may be able to meet you again in the capital of our country.

---

166   Message to the Congress Withdrawing Philadelphia as the Site of an International Exposition During American Revolution Bicentennial Celebrations. *May* 22, 1972

To the Congress of the United States:

In a message to the Congress on September 11, 1970, transmitting a report of the American Revolution Bicentennial Commission, I strongly endorsed the Commission's view that the primary emphasis in our commemoration of the Nation's birth should be a nation-wide celebration, involving every State, city and community.

At the same time, I agreed that we should encourage international participation in our celebration. Philadelphia seemed a natural choice as the principal site for an international exposition because it was there that the Declaration of Independence was signed and the Constitution created. Accordingly, I informed the Congress that the Secretary of State was being instructed to proceed officially with the Bureau of International Expositions in registering an international exposition in Philadelphia in 1976.

At that time, I also pointed out that this exposition was dependent upon the assurance of suitable support and a review of financial and other arrangements by appropriate parties, including high-level government officials.

The Chairman of the Bicentennial Commission, David J. Mahoney, has now informed me that on May 16, the members of his commission voted not to approve the proposal submitted by the Philadelphia 1976 Bicentennial Corporation for this international exposition. Among the reasons cited were the large costs to the Federal government, a question of whether it was still appropriate to hold such a large exposition in one city, the Commission's continuing commitment to a nation-wide celebration, and a question of whether sufficient time remained to make all necessary arrangements. The vote of the Commission was 23–4 against the exposition.

Also, I have been jointly advised by the Secretary of Commerce and the Director of the Office of Management and Budget, that we should not proceed unless certain basic conditions could be met. There is no evidence now that we can fulfill those conditions.

Under the full weight of these recommendations, I have reluctantly concluded that we cannot prudently go forward with the international exposition in Philadelphia.

I am therefore asking the Secretary of State to take action at the impending meeting of the Bureau of International Expositions to withdraw the registration of the international exposition in Philadelphia. I have also asked the Secretary to make clear to the Bureau of International Expositions that the United States, and its many State and local governments, will warmly welcome foreign participation—both public and private—in our Bicentennial. And, I am asking the American Revolution Bicentennial Commission to ensure that their plans include encouragement for such participation.

I remain firmly convinced that Philadelphia, in commemoration of its unique place in American history, will and should play a major role in the Nation's 1976 observances, and that the celebration of this birthday will reflect the vital and abundant spirit of our Nation.

RICHARD NIXON

The White House,
May 22, 1972.

167 Message to the Congress Transmitting First Annual Report on Occupational Safety and Health. *May* 22, 1972

To the Congress of the United States:

On-the-job protection of American workers continues as a high priority goal in this Administration's effort to improve the quality of life for all Americans.

The Occupational Safety and Health Act of 1970, which I signed into law on December 29, 1970, is a major step towards improving workplace conditions. As I said at that time, this legislation is one of the most important measures ever taken in behalf of those American workers who are covered by the provisions of the act.

The accompanying President's Report on Occupational Safety and Health describes what has been done to implement the act during the first year of its operation, and it also indicates the magnitude and direction of the task ahead. The report examines the responsibilities of the Department of Labor for setting safety and health standards, and for gaining compliance with those standards. Another part of the report explores the activities of the Department of Health, Education, and Welfare in research and training.

Like many problems that we face today,

the improvement of job safety and health cannot be accomplished by simply pressing a button. If we are to reduce the injuries, the illnesses, and the deaths connected with working conditions, we must take determined actions: we must increase the number of people who are trained in health and safety techniques; knowledge of the causes of accidents and illnesses must be developed; this knowledge must be translated into effective standards; employers and employees require adequate instructions; and standards must be enforced through energetic and rigorous inspection programs.

Above all else, if we are to be successful, the full collaboration of private industry, the States and the employees must be enlisted.

The Occupational Safety and Health Act of 1970 recognizes the need of reinforcing the role of the States in resolving our national problems. As a consequence, the implementation of the act has emphasized cooperative programs with State Governments. The involvement of the States in these programs has been gratifying. It is a testimonial to the flexibility and vigour of our Federal-State system that the fifty States, the District of Columbia, Puerto Rico, Guam and the Virgin Islands have all expressed a willingness to develop plans for setting and enforcing standards that are at least on a par with the Federal requirements fixed by the act.

In addition, many States are actually aiding the Federal Government by gathering superior statistical data that will provide a basis for charting the future direction of safety and health programs. Many States, too, are now assisting the Federal Government in the enforcement of standards.

In short, I feel that the essential groundwork has been laid for genuine progress in on-the-job safety and health. This report describes the structures that have been set in place, and it outlines how the building process will continue.

RICHARD NIXON

The White House,
  May 22, 1972.

NOTE: The report is entitled "The President's Report on Occupational Safety and Health— Including Reports on Occupational Safety and Health by the United States Department of Labor and by the United States Department of Health, Education, and Welfare" (Government Printing Office, 210 pp.).

168   Toasts of the President and Nikolai V. Podgorny, Chairman of the Presidium of the Supreme Soviet of the U.S.S.R., at a Dinner in Moscow.   *May 22, 1972*

Mr. President, Mr. General Secretary, Mr. Prime Minister, and all of the distinguished guests from the Soviet Union and from the United States:

I would like first to express our very grateful appreciation for the hospitality which has been extended to Mrs. Nixon and myself, and all the members of our party, on this, the first visit of an American President to Moscow.

The courage of the Russian people, who generation after generation have heroically defended this city from invaders, makes this vivid point: The only way to enter Moscow is to enter in peace.

All of us in this great room can feel the history that is here. Here, as comrades in arms, Russians and Americans met together to work out some of the key decisions of World War II, setting an example of selfless cooperation and of wartime cooperation that has taken us too long to

follow in peacetime. And now here this week, 25 years later, we meet within these walls to make decisions that could help pave the way to peace for all the world.

The Soviet Union and the United States are both great powers. Ours are both great peoples. In the long history of both of our nations, we have never fought one another in war. Let us make decisions now which will help insure that we shall never do so in the future.

The American people want peace. I know, from my travels through the Soviet Union, the people of the Soviet Union want peace. My fervent hope is that we, we who are the leaders of the people, that we can work together to insure that all the people of the earth can enjoy the blessings of peace.

We meet at what is called a summit meeting. Summit meetings of the past have been remembered for their "spirit," but we must strive to make this Moscow summit memorable for its substance.

Over 2 years of careful preparation have proven our common seriousness of purpose and brought us to this meeting prepared to make concrete agreements.

Not so long ago, our attention centered on our relative positions of strength. But in a nuclear age, when there is no such thing as security in a preponderance of strength, great powers have learned this fact of life: Agreements based on exploiting the presumed weaknesses of one party only cause it to redouble its efforts to catch up, but agreements based on mutual respect and reciprocity have a far greater chance of enduring.

Because we are both prepared to proceed on the basis of equality and mutual respect, we meet at a moment when we can make peaceful cooperation between our two countries a reality.

To make the most of this opportunity, we should recognize that while many of our differences are fundamental and profound, we have a powerful common interest in peace and security.

We should recognize that great nuclear powers have a solemn responsibility to exercise restraint in any crisis, to take positive action to avert direct confrontation.

With great power goes great responsibility. It is precisely when power is not accompanied by responsibility that the peace is threatened. Let our power—the power of our two countries—always be used to keep the peace, never to break it.

We should recognize further that it is the responsibility of great powers to influence other nations in conflict or crisis to moderate their behavior.

Let me outline briefly what I believe we both want to see take place this week.

First, we want to complete work on the matters that years of patient negotiations have brought to the decision point. These bilateral matters will serve as the point of departure: Our two nations can work together in the exploration of space, the conquest of disease, the improvement of our environment.

Progress in economic cooperation will benefit both our nations. The Soviet Union and the United States are the two largest economies in the world, and yet they live presently in relative isolation. The opportunity for a new commercial relationship opens up a strong potential for progress for both of our peoples.

The attention of the world is primarily directed to the possibility of an initial limitation of strategic arms. Here in Moscow, for the first time, major nations—the two most powerful nations in the world— would put restrictions on a range of their most significant weapons systems. An agreement in this area could begin to turn our two countries away from a wasteful and dangerous arms race and toward more production for peace.

With a positive attitude shown on these bilateral matters, fresh impetus will be given to the resolution of other issues in other areas of the world.

A few minutes after I took the oath of office as President of the United States, I told my countrymen that the time had come for us to move from a period of confrontation to an era of negotiation. This week in Moscow can prove that the era of negotiation between the two most powerful nations in the world has begun. There is hard bargaining ahead, and statesmen dealing with real differences will have their share of obstacles.

We will have our different interests, our different approaches; neither of us will be reluctant to point them out. But the

Above: At the Republican National Convention, August 23, 1972.

Photographic Portfolio of the Nixon Administration 1972

Above: Speaking with a young Chinese girl at West Lake in Hangchow, February 26, 1972.

Right: Premier Chou En-lai welcomes the President at Capital Airport in Peking, February 21, 1972.

Opposite page top: Meeting with Chairman Mao Tse-tung in Peking, February 21, 1972.

Opposite page bottom: Presidential party sightseeing on the Great Wall of China, February 24, 1972.

Above: In Moscow the President and Mrs. Nixon attend a performance of the Bolshoi Ballet, May 25, 1972.

Left: The President and General Secretary Brezhnev shake hands after the signing ceremony for the arms limitation agreements, May 26, 1972.

Opposite page: Walking in the Kremlin grounds with Presidential Adviser Henry A. Kissinger, May 29, 1972.

Above: A motorcade through Atlanta, Georgia, October 12, 1972.

Right: At a campaign rally in Uniondale, New York, October 23, 1972.

Above: Holding a news conference in the Oval Office at the White House, June 22, 1972.

Center left: A welcome on the grounds of the Western White House for Prime Minister Eisaku Sato of Japan, January 6, 1972.

Lower left: The President and the Shah of Iran driving through the streets of Tehran, May 30, 1972.

Above: Visiting the Italian
Fall Festival at the Villa Rosa
Rest Home, Mitchellville,
Maryland, September 17, 1972.

Right: Presenting the
Heart-of-the-Year Award to
Pearl Bailey, in the Oval Office
at the White House,
February 2, 1972.

Photography under the direction of Ollie Atkins,
Personal Photographer to the President of the United States

foundation of healthy competition must be a willingness to cooperate and reciprocate on matters of overriding importance.

Therefore, we do not just meet in an atmosphere of good will, which I know we shall have as we have it tonight; we do not just meet to conclude agreements, which I hope we shall conclude; we meet to begin a new age in the relationship between our two great and powerful nations.

Looking toward that future, let me reaffirm to all of you the American commitment: The United States is ready to work closely with all nations in the establishment of a peaceful world in which each nation determines its own destiny.

Our two peoples, the Soviet people and the American people, learned to admire each other when we joined together to defeat a common enemy in a time of war. We learned to respect each other as adversaries in a time of tension after that war. Let us now learn to work with each other in a time of peace.

Let us remember that if we begin to lift the burden of armed confrontation from both our peoples, we shall lift the hopes for peace of all the peoples of the world.

Never have two peoples had a greater challenge or a greater goal. Let us, the leaders of our peoples, be worthy of the hopes of the Soviet people, the hopes of the American people, the hopes of all the people on this earth as we work together toward the goal of a peaceful world.

NOTE: The President spoke at 9 p.m. in Granovit Hall at the Grand Kremlin Palace. He spoke from a prepared text.

Chairman Podgorny spoke in Russian. A translation of the advance text of his toast was made available by the TASS news service as follows:

Esteemed Mr. President, esteemed Mrs. Nixon, ladies and gentlemen, comrades:

Let me, on behalf of the Presidium of the Supreme Soviet of the U.S.S.R. and the Soviet Government, greet you, Mr. President, your wife, and all those who accompany you, on your visit to the Soviet Union. This is the first official visit by a President of the United States of America in the history of relations between our countries. This alone makes your visit and meetings between you and the Soviet leaders a momentous event. The results of the talks will predetermine in many ways prospects of relations between the Soviet Union and the United States. Their results will, apparently, have an effect on the further development of the international situation either toward a lasting peace and stronger universal security or toward greater tension.

We proceed from the fact that personal contacts and frank exchange of opinions between the leaders of states help search for mutually acceptable decisions in line with the interests of the peoples and of preserving peace, and overcome difficulties caused by factors of different origin and character.

Therefore great importance is attached in the Soviet Union to Soviet-American talks which should cover a wide range of questions. We approach these talks from realistic positions and will make every effort in accordance with the principles of our policy to achieve positive results and try to justify the hopes placed in our countries and beyond them in the Soviet-American summit meeting in Moscow.

We expect a similar approach from the American side.

Mr. President, you already had today a meeting with L. I. Brezhnev, General Secretary of the CPSU Central Committee, during which an exchange of opinions was started on the problems of Soviet-American relations and the present international situation.

The principles of our policy in international affairs and in relations with other states, the United States of America included, are well known. They were recently set forth again most definitely and clearly in the decisions of the 24th Congress of our Party and the just closed plenary meeting of the CPSU Central Committee. We have been guided and intend to be guided unswervingly by these principles in our practical activities. The Soviet Union, together with the countries of the Socialist community and all other peace forces, comes out consistently in defence of peace, for the deliverance of the present and future generations from the threat of war, from the disasters of a nuclear conflict and for the elimination of hotbeds of war.

We stand for a radical turn toward relaxation of the existing tensions in all continents of the world, for freeing the peoples from the heavy arms burden, for a peaceful political settlement of problems through negotiation and with due account taken of the aspirations and will of the peoples and their inalienable right to decide their destinies themselves without interference and pressure from outside.

As far back as in the early years of the young Soviet state, its founder V. I. Lenin substantiated the objective need for and possibility of peaceful coexistence of countries with different social systems. Today, as before, the Soviet Union is prepared to develop and deepen relations of business cooperation and mutually beneficial ties with states of a different social system.

This fully applies to the relations with the United States also in the sense that peaceful coexistence must not be limited to absence of war. When we say that there is no exception for the United States in our policy of peaceful coexistence, these words are backed by our actual striving for the improvement and development of Soviet-American relations. The Soviet Union deems it possible and desirable to establish not merely good but friendly relations between the U.S.S.R. and the United States, certainly, not at the expense of any third countries or peoples.

It stands to reason that the differences of social systems, the divergence of the positions of our states on a number of very important aspects of the world politics create serious complications in Soviet-American relations and we do not underestimate them, by any means.

But even though there exist principled differences, there are objective factors that determine similarity of interests and require that the U.S.S.R. and the U.S.A. should act in such a way as to ward off the danger of a global war, to remove the vestiges of cold war from Soviet-American relations and as far as possible to rid their relations of all that complicated them in the past and burdens them even now.

The Soviet Union and the United States are the powers that are most advanced in science and technology, have vast economic potentials and rich natural resources. Our peoples made a weighty contribution to the treasury of world culture. All this serves as a solid foundation which, given mutual agreement, makes it possible to establish Soviet-American cooperation in the most varied fields, to implement large-scale projects worthy of the level which the Soviet Union and the United States have reached in the world of today.

The peoples of our countries have traditions of mutual respect and friendship. Our joint struggle in the years of the Second World War against Hitler Germany and militarist Japan lives in the memory of the Soviet people. The fact that our countries were allies in the two World Wars is very important in itself.

Under the United Nations Charter, the Soviet Union and the United States as permanent members of the Security Council are called upon to play an important role in maintaining international peace together with other members of the Security Council. Experience confirms that whenever our countries succeeded in ensuring by joint efforts the sane balance of interests both of our two countries and other states concerned, opportunities opened for solving acute conflicts and situations and concluding important international agreements and treaties.

In other words, cooperation between the U.S.S.R. and the United States in the spirit of good will, the improvement of Soviet-American relations was always favourable for the cause of peace. We proceed from the view that Soviet-American talks will promote the solution of the urgent international problems to the benefit of the Soviet and American peoples, the peoples of all the countries, in the interests of world peace.

We believe, Mr. President, that your visit will enable you and Mrs. Nixon to see more of our country, to become aware of the scope of the great plans of Communist construction which the Soviet people are bringing into life, to feel the rhythm of their constructive work, to get convinced once more in the Soviet people's adherence to peace.

I would like to propose a toast to the success of the talks, to their serving the interests of the peoples of our countries, the interests of peace and international security.

To the health of Mr. President and Mrs. Nixon.

---

169   Message to the Ministerial Council of the Organization for Economic Cooperation and Development on the 25th Anniversary of the Marshall Plan. *May* 24, 1972

IT GIVES me great pleasure to greet the Ministerial Council of the Organization for Economic Cooperation and Development as it commemorates the twenty-fifth anniversary of the Marshall Plan. There could be no finer tribute to the continuity of European and American policy than the celebration of this event in the home of this Ministerial Council.

The Marshall Plan was a milestone in a policy which has been remarkably steadfast in its two-fold purposes of building a healthy European economy and founding our American relationship with Europe on a basis of partnership in political, economic and security fields. At the time, the United States gave generously of its resources, recognizing that its strength imposed special responsibilities.

Now, on this anniversary, we face a new world and new tasks. With restored strength in Europe and Japan comes the need to redefine those early post-war responsibilities. Together we must erect a new international monetary system and make renewed progress toward a free and fair system of trade. We must deal too with the problems of our environment and with the need to assure that continued economic growth will lead to actual improvements in the quality of life. And we must extend the spirit of international cooperation—the spirit of the Marshall Plan—by assisting the developing nations through an adequately funded aid effort and responsive trade policies.

The tasks ahead will not be easy, but surely if we could rebuild from the ashes of war, we can succeed now in rebuilding a new era of growth and prosperity in the service of peace.

RICHARD NIXON

NOTE: Under Secretary of State John N. Irwin II read the message at the Ministerial Council's meeting in Paris. The occasion marked the 25th anniversary of former Secretary of State George C. Marshall's speech of June 5, 1947, at Harvard University, in which he proposed an organized program of U.S. economic assistance to Europe.

---

170   Communique About a Joint United States-Soviet Union Commercial Commission. *May* 26, 1972

IN ORDER to promote the development of mutually beneficial commercial relations and related economic matters between the two countries, Soviet leaders and the President of the United States Richard M. Nixon have agreed to establish a U.S.-U.S.S.R. Commercial Commission.

The U.S.-U.S.S.R. Commission is to Negotiate:

—an overall trade agreement including reciprocal MFN [most-favored-nation] treatment;

—arrangements for the reciprocal availability of government credits;

—provisions for the reciprocal establishment of business facilities to promote trade;

—an agreement establishing an arbitration mechanism for settling commercial disputes.

Study possible U.S.-U.S.S.R. participation in the development of resources and the manufacture and sale of raw materials and other products.

Monitor the spectrum of U.S.-U.S.S.R. commercial relations, identifying and, when possible, resolving issues that may be of interest to both parties such as patents and licensing.

Sessions of the Commission will be held alternately in Moscow and Washington. The first session of the Commission is to take place in Moscow in July of this year.

NOTE: On the same day, the White House released a fact sheet and the transcript of a news briefing on the U.S.-U.S.S.R. Commercial Commission. Participants in the news briefing were Peter M. Flanigan, Assistant to the President for International Economic Affairs, and Ronald L. Ziegler, Press Secretary to the President.

On July 10, 1972, the White House announced the membership of the U.S. delegation to the first session of the Commission convening in Moscow on July 20. The White House also released a fact sheet on the Commission and on the membership of the U.S. delegation and the transcript of a news briefing on preparations for the first session in Moscow by Peter G. Peterson, Secretary of Commerce and head of the U.S. delegation to the Commission.

On July 17, the White House released the transcript of a news briefing by Secretary Peterson on his meeting with the President to discuss the forthcoming session of the Commission.

---

171   Toasts of the President and Aleksei N. Kosygin, Chairman of the Council of Ministers, at a Dinner in Moscow Honoring Soviet Leaders. *May 26, 1972*

Mr. General Secretary Brezhnev, Mr. Chairman of the Presidium, Mr. Chairman of the Council of Ministers, and all of our distinguished guests:

This house, which is the American Embassy, is greatly honored tonight by the presence of our Soviet guests.

I say this not only because of your rank, the leaders of the great Soviet people, but also because of the boundless hospitality you have extended to all of us on our visit to Moscow. We look forward to the time when we shall be able to welcome you in our country and in some way respond in

an effective manner to the way in which you have received us so generously in your country.

This has been described as a visit of the summit. But as we all know, there are many summits in the world. This is the first meeting. There will be others.

And now this is, of course, an evening that will always be remembered in this house for another reason: Tonight at 11 o'clock there will be signed an historic agreement between the Soviet Union and the United States.

It is an agreement which will limit

strategic arms between the two most powerful nations in the world. It is an enormously important agreement, but again it is only an indication of what can happen in the future as we work toward peace in the world. But I have great hopes on that score.

The Soviet people and the American people demonstrated over 25 years ago how they could fight together to win a war. And now in our meetings this week, and particularly culminating in the signing of this agreement tonight, we shall demonstrate to the world how these two great peoples, the Soviet people and the American people, can work together to build a peace.

Every leader of a nation wonders at times how he will be remembered in history. But, as I have met with the top Soviet leaders—with General Secretary Brezhnev, with Chairman Kosygin, with Chairman Podgorny—I am convinced of this fact: We want to be remembered by our deeds, not by the fact that we brought war to the world, but by the fact that we made the world a more peaceful one for all peoples in the world.

It is in that spirit that, here in the American Embassy, we all proudly raise our glasses to the leaders of the Soviet peoples and to the great cause of peace— peace between our two countries and peace for all peoples to which we think this visit, this meeting, has contributed and will contribute in the future.

NOTE: The President spoke at 9:25 p.m. in Spaso House. He spoke from a prepared text.

Chairman Kosygin responded in Russian. A translation of the text of his remarks was made available by the TASS news service as follows:

Mr. President, Mrs. Nixon, esteemed guests:

On behalf of the Soviet guests present here I would like to express gratitude to President Richard Nixon and his wife, the U.S. Ambassador to the U.S.S.R. and his wife who have invited us here to the Embassy to mark this memorable occasion.

Today is the end of the working week which was devoted to talks between the President of the United States and the Soviet leaders—the General Secretary of the CPSU Central Committee, L. I. Brezhnev, the President of the Presidium of the U.S.S.R. Supreme Soviet, N. V. Podgorny, the Chairman of the U.S.S.R. Council of Ministers. Like the President, we positively assess the work done. It will be continued.

The talks held made it possible to reveal more precisely both the fields in which it is possible to develop cooperation and the fields where the stands of the two states are at variance, since the U.S.S.R. and the United States objectively represent different social economic systems in the world. It seems to us that both sides realistically appraise possible prospects of cooperation.

A number of Soviet-American agreements, bound to serve peaceful aims, have been signed these days. We have agreed, specifically, on pooling the efforts of our countries in environmental protection, in peaceful exploration and mastering of outer space, in cooperation in the fields of science and technology, medicine and public health.

We are having an exchange of opinions of questions of development of trade and other economic ties between the two countries. It is obvious that realistic solutions can also be found here, solutions which would reflect mutual interest in normalization and widening of economic exchanges in keeping with the generally accepted international practice.

Today the General Secretary of the Central Committee of the CPSU, Leonid Brezhnev, and the President of the United States, Richard Nixon, are to sign in the Kremlin joint documents on the limitation of strategic arms. Agreement on these questions, we hope, will go down in history as a major achievement on the road towards curbing the arms race. It has become possible only on the basis of strict observance of the principle of equal security of the sides and the inadmissibility of any unilateral advantages. This is a great victory for the Soviet and American peoples in the matter of easing international tension, this is a victory for all peaceloving peoples, because security and peace is their common goal.

Whether peace becomes stronger as a result of our talks, concerns, of course, not the Soviet Union and the United States alone, however great their influence in the world, but will depend on all other peoples and states as well. Of little worth would be the decisions about which we have agreed or may agree, were they contrary to the legitimate interests of other states, the interests of their security and independence. It is not to decide for other peoples and countries that we are meeting with the President of the United States at the conference table.

During these talks the Soviet Union and the United States are seeking approaches to a settlement of international problems bearing directly on the two states, in the interests of the peace and security of the peoples. We are making serious steps in this direction. But in order to advance confidently towards the goal of a lasting peace, everything possible should be done to eliminate the existing hotbeds of war in Vietnam and in the Middle East on the basis of strict respect for the rights of the peoples to independent development, to noninter-

ference in their internal affairs, to the inviolability of their state territories.

We would like to express the hope that stronger peace for the people of the Soviet Union, for the people of the United States of America, for all the peoples of the world, will be the main outcome of the Soviet-American talks.

How effectively the agreements and understandings reached are translated into life and serve peace will be, of course, of great importance. Any agreement, any treaty only then leaves a trace in history when its proclaimed principles and intentions become the content of the practical activities of states. So, may the agreements we reached be just such agreements.

We would like to express our deep respect for the great people of the United States of America with whom the Soviet people want to live in cooperation and peace. We ask President R. Nixon, upon returning home, to convey that this is our sincere and earnest desire.

May I ask all those present to join me in this toast to the American people, to the President of the United States of America, to Mrs. Nixon and all those accompanying the President, to peace and cooperation among the peoples.

172 Toast at a Luncheon in Leningrad. *May 27, 1972*

Mr. Chairman of the Presidium, Mr. Mayor, and all of the distinguished guests on this very great occasion:

We first want to express our deep appreciation for the hospitality that has been extended to all of us on our visit to Leningrad.

We realize that this visit is very brief and we only regret that we don't have more time to spend here in this great city. With memories of what we saw in 1959 and then of what we have seen in our few hours here today, I would say that we all feel somewhat like the first American Ambassador to this city when, after spending

3 hours in the Hermitage,[1] he said he only wished he could spend 3 months even there in that one place.

As we leave your city later this afternoon, each of us will carry away a special memory. All will remember this splendid banquet, the delightful music, the new friendships that we have made with our Soviet friends. We will remember the spectacular beauty of this city, a city that refused to die and came back after destruction more beautiful than ever before.

---

[1] A museum of fine arts which was once part of the winter palace of the tsars.

We will remember grand buildings like this. We will remember the dynamism and the strength of the people of Leningrad.

I would like to share with you one memory I will take with me for the rest of my life. It will be the memory of a little girl, 12 years old. At the cemetery today I saw her picture and a few pages from her diary. She was a beautiful child—brown eyes, a pretty face. The pages of her diary were there for all to see.

She recorded how first her mother died, her father died, her brothers and her sister, and then finally only she was left.

As I think of Tanya, that 12-year-old girl in Leningrad, I think of all the Tanyas in the world—in the Soviet Union, in the United States, in Asia, in Africa and Latin America, wherever they may be. I only hope that the visit that we have had at the highest level with the Soviet leaders will have contributed to that kind of world

in which the little Tanyas and their brothers and their sisters will be able to grow up in a world of peace and friendship among people—all people in the world.

My glass today will be raised with yours not only to our distinguished Chairman of the Presidium, not only to your mayor and to the other distinguished officials, but to Tanya, who stands for the heroism of a great city.

If I could try to say it in your language, may I also ask that we raise our glasses to this thought: *Vechnaya slava geroiskomu Leningradu.* [Eternal glory to heroic Leningrad.]

NOTE: The President spoke at 3:32 p.m. in Mariinsky Palace, St. Isaac's Square, at a luncheon hosted by the Executive Committee of the Leningrad Council of Workers Deputies. He spoke from a prepared text.

Sizov A. Aleksandrovi was the mayor of Leningrad.

173 Statement About Signing the Second Supplemental Appropriations Act, 1972. *May* 28, 1972

I HAVE signed H.R. 14582, the Second Supplemental Appropriations Act, 1972. This act contains appropriations of more than $4.4 billion, largely for increased pay costs and for other requirements which are mandatory under existing law.

I must comment briefly on one provision in the bill which I am advised by the Attorney General is an unconstitutional "coming into agreement" clause, infringing on the fundamental principle of the separation of legislative and executive powers.

This provision is in the appropriation for "Construction, Public Buildings Projects" of the General Services Administration. The bill appropriates definite sums

for three public buildings projects but conditions the availability of the appropriation on the approval by the committees on public works of revised prospectuses for these buildings.

Under the Public Buildings Act of 1959, no appropriations may be made for public buildings projects until the public works committees have approved GSA's prospectuses for such buildings. The Congress regards this "no appropriation may be made" provision, I understand, as internal Congressional rulemaking not affecting the executive branch, and this Administration has acquiesced in that construction.

On the other hand, H.R. 14582 makes

an appropriation to the General Services Administration but then conditions its use by GSA on that agency's getting the approval of the public works committees on revised prospectuses. This reversal of the normal Public Buildings Act procedure is found by the Attorney General to be an unconstitutional "coming into agreement" provision.

I have no objection to the review and approval of revised prospectuses for the three buildings in question under the procedures of the Public Buildings Act, but I cannot act under a "coming into agreement" requirement. Accordingly, I will submit a budget amendment to the Congress to eliminate the unconstitutional problem.

NOTE: As enacted, H.R. 14582, approved May 27, 1972, is Public Law 92–306 (86 Stat. 163).

174 Memorial Day Statement. *May 28, 1972*

AS ALL America pauses today to pay tribute to the brave men and women who have given their lives in our country's defense over the past two centuries, and to pray for a lasting peace, Mrs. Nixon and I join in that homage and in those prayers.

Though we observe Memorial Day in a far country, our hearts are very much with our own countrymen, the honored dead and the hopeful living alike. Our purpose in the Soviet Union is to open a new era of negotiation and cooperation between our two great powers. We seek a world where no more men need die for peace, but where instead all men may live in peace.

Each American in his way has much to contribute, through thought and action, to the building of such a world. We can make no more fitting resolve on this day, than a resolve to press forward to that goal.

NOTE: The statement was released at Moscow, U.S.S.R.

175 Statement on the Death of the Duke of Windsor. *May 28, 1972*

MRS. NIXON and I are both deeply saddened by the death of the Duke of Windsor. He was a man of noble spirit and high ideals, for whom millions of Americans felt a deep respect and affection. We join in extending our profound sympathy to the Duchess, and to the many others who will mourn his passing.

NOTE: The Duke of Windsor, 77, died at his home in Paris, France, following a prolonged illness. He became King Edward VIII of England in January 1936 after the death of his father, George V, and then abdicated the throne in December 1936 in order to marry Mrs. Wallis Warfield Simpson.

The statement was released at Moscow, U.S.S.R.

176　Radio and Television Address to the People of the Soviet Union.　*May 28, 1972*

Dobryy vecher [Good evening]:

I deeply appreciate this opportunity your Government has given me to speak directly with the people of the Soviet Union, to bring you a message of friendship from all the people of the United States and to share with you some of my thoughts about the relations between our two countries and about the way to peace and progress in the world.

This is my fourth visit to the Soviet Union. On these visits I have gained a great respect for the peoples of the Soviet Union, for your strength, your generosity, your determination, for the diversity and richness of your cultural heritage, for your many achievements.

In the 3 years I have been in office, one of my principal aims has been to establish a better relationship between the United States and the Soviet Union. Our two countries have much in common. Most important of all, we have never fought one another in war. On the contrary, the memory of your soldiers and ours embracing at the Elbe, as allies, in 1945, remains strong in millions of hearts in both of our countries. It is my hope that that memory can serve as an inspiration for the renewal of Soviet-American cooperation in the 1970's.

As great powers, we shall sometimes be competitors, but we need never be enemies.

Thirteen years ago, when I visited your country as Vice President, I addressed the people of the Soviet Union on radio and television, as I am addressing you tonight. I said then: "Let us have peaceful competition not only in producing the best factories but in producing better lives for our people.

"Let us cooperate in our exploration of outer space. . . . Let our aim be not victory over other peoples but the victory of all mankind over hunger, want, misery, and disease, wherever it exists in the world."

In our meetings this week, we have begun to bring some of those hopes to fruition. Shortly after we arrived here on Monday afternoon, a brief rain fell on Moscow, of a kind that I am told is called a mushroom rain, a warm rain, with sunshine breaking through, that makes the mushrooms grow and is therefore considered a good omen. The month of May is early for mushrooms, but as our talks progressed this week, what did grow was even better: a far-reaching set of agreements that can lead to a better life for both of our peoples, to a better chance for peace in the world.

We have agreed on joint ventures in space. We have agreed on ways of working together to protect the environment, to advance health, to cooperate in science and technology. We have agreed on means of preventing incidents at sea. We have established a commission to expand trade between our two nations.

Most important, we have taken an historic first step in the limitation of nuclear strategic arms. This arms control agreement is not for the purpose of giving either side an advantage over the other. Both of our nations are strong, each respects the strength of the other, each will maintain the strength necessary to defend its independence.

629

But in an unchecked arms race between two great nations, there would be no winners, only losers. By setting this limitation together, the people of both of our nations, and of all nations, can be winners. If we continue in the spirit of serious purpose that has marked our discussions this week, these agreements can start us on a new road of cooperation for the benefit of our people, for the benefit of all peoples.

There is an old proverb that says, "Make peace with man and quarrel with your sins." The hardships and evils that beset all men and all nations, these and these alone are what we should make war upon.

As we look at the prospects for peace, we see that we have made significant progress at reducing the possible sources of direct conflict between us. But history tells us that great nations have often been dragged into war without intending it, by conflicts between smaller nations. As great powers, we can and should use our influence to prevent this from happening. Our goal should be to discourage aggression in other parts of the world and particularly among those smaller nations that look to us for leadership and example.

With great power goes great responsibility. When a man walks with a giant tread, he must be careful where he sets his feet. There can be true peace only when the weak are as safe as the strong. The wealthier and more powerful our own nations become, the more we have to lose from war and the threat of war, anywhere in the world.

Speaking for the United States, I can say this: We covet no one else's territory, we seek no dominion over any other people, we seek the right to live in peace, not only for ourselves but for all the peoples of this earth. Our power will only be used to keep the peace, never to break it, only

to defend freedom, never to destroy it. No nation that does not threaten its neighbors has anything to fear from the United States.

Soviet citizens have often asked me, "Does America truly want peace?"

I believe that our actions answer that question far better than any words could do. If we did not want peace, we would not have reduced the size of our armed forces by a million men, by almost one-third, during the past 3 years. If we did not want peace, we would not have worked so hard at reaching an agreement on the limitation of nuclear arms, at achieving a settlement of Berlin, at maintaining peace in the Middle East, at establishing better relations with the Soviet Union, with the People's Republic of China, with other nations of the world.

Mrs. Nixon and I feel very fortunate to have had the opportunity to visit the Soviet Union, to get to know the people of the Soviet Union, friendly and hospitable, courageous and strong. Most Americans will never have a chance to visit the Soviet Union, and most Soviet citizens will never have a chance to visit America. Most of you know our country only through what you read in your newspapers and what you hear and see on radio and television and motion pictures. This is only a part of the real America.

I would like to take this opportunity to try to convey to you something of what America is really like, not in terms of its scenic beauties, its great cities, its factories, its farms, or its highways, but in terms of its people.

In many ways, the people of our two countries are very much alike. Like the Soviet Union, ours is a large and diverse nation. Our people, like yours, are hard working. Like you, we Americans have a strong spirit of competition, but we also have a great love of music and poetry, of sports, and of humor. Above all, we, like you, are an open, natural, and friendly people. We love our country. We love our children. And we want for you and for your children the same peace and abundance that we want for ourselves and for our children.

We Americans are idealists. We believe deeply in our system of government. We cherish our personal liberty. We would fight to defend it, if necessary, as we have done before. But we also believe deeply in the right of each nation to choose its own system. Therefore, however much we like our own system for ourselves, we have no desire to impose it on anyone else.

As we conclude this week of talks, there are certain fundamental premises of the American point of view which I believe deserve emphasis. In conducting these talks, it has not been our aim to divide up the world into spheres of influence, to establish a condominium, or in any way to conspire together against the interests of any other nation. Rather we have sought to construct a better framework of understanding between our two nations, to make progress in our bilateral relationships, to find ways of insuring that future frictions between us would never embroil our two nations, and therefore the world, in war.

While ours are both great and powerful nations, the world is no longer dominated by two super powers. The world is a better and safer place because its power and resources are more widely distributed.

Beyond this, since World War II, more than 70 new nations have come into being. We cannot have true peace unless they, and all nations, can feel that they share it.

America seeks better relations, not only with the Soviet Union but with all nations. The only sound basis for a peaceful and progressive international order is sovereign equality and mutual respect. We believe in the right of each nation to chart its own course, to choose its own system, to go its own way, without interference from other nations.

As we look to the longer term, peace depends also on continued progress in the developing nations. Together with other advanced industrial countries, the United States and the Soviet Union share a twofold responsibility in this regard: on the one hand, to practice restraint in those activities, such as the supply of arms, that might endanger the peace of developing nations; and second, to assist them in their orderly economic and social development, without political interference.

Some of you may have heard an old story told in Russia of a traveler who was walking to another village. He knew the way, but not the distance. Finally he came upon a woodsman chopping wood by the side of the road and he asked the woodsman, "How long will it take to reach the village?"

The woodsman replied, "I don't know."

The traveler was angry, because he was sure the woodsman was from the village and therefore knew how far it was. And so he started off down the road again. After he had gone a few steps, the woodsman called out, "Stop. It will take you about 15 minutes."

The traveler turned and demanded, "Why didn't you tell me that in the first place?"

The woodsman replied, "Because then I didn't know the length of your stride."

In our talks this week with the leaders of the Soviet Union, both sides have had a chance to measure the length of our strides toward peace and security. I believe that those strides have been substantial and that now we have well begun the long journey which will lead us to a new age in the relations between our two countries. It is important to both of our peoples that we continue those strides.

As our two countries learn to work together, our people will be able to get to know one another better. Greater cooperation can also mean a great deal in our daily lives. As we learn to cooperate in space, in health and the environment, in science and technology, our cooperation can help sick people get well. It can help industries produce more consumer goods. It can help all of us enjoy cleaner air and water. It can increase our knowledge of the world around us.

As we expand our trade, each of our countries can buy more of the other's goods and market more of our own. As we gain experience with arms control, we can bring closer the day when further agreements can lessen the arms burden of our two nations and lessen the threat of war in the world.

Through all the pages of history, through all the centuries, the world's people have struggled to be free from fear, whether fear of the elements or fear of hunger or fear of their own rulers or fear of their neighbors in other countries. And yet, time and again, people have vanquished the source of one fear only to fall prey to another.

Let our goal now be a world free of fear—a world in which nation will no longer prey upon nation, in which human energies will be turned away from production for war and toward more production for peace, away from conquest and toward invention, development, creation; a world in which together we can establish that peace which is more than the absence of war, which enables man to pursue those higher goals that the spirit yearns for.

Yesterday, I laid a wreath at the cemetery which commemorates the brave people who died during the siege of Leningrad in World War II. At the cemetery, I saw the picture of a 12-year-old girl. She was a beautiful child. Her name was Tanya. The pages of her diary tell the terrible story of war. In the simple words of a child, she wrote of the deaths of the members of her family: Zhenya in December. Grannie in January. Leka then next. Then Uncle Vasya. Then Uncle Lyosha. Then Mama. And then the Savichevs. And then finally, these words, the last words in her diary: "All are dead. Only Tanya is left."

As we work toward a more peaceful world, let us think of Tanya and of the other Tanyas and their brothers and sisters everywhere. Let us do all that we can to insure that no other children will have to endure what Tanya did and that your children and ours, all the children of the world can live their full lives together in friendship and in peace.

Spasibo y do svidaniye. [Thank you and goodby.]

NOTE: The President spoke at 8:30 p.m. in the Green Room at the Grand Kremlin Palace, Moscow. His address was broadcast live on radio and television in the Soviet Union and simultaneously, via satellite, in the United States.

The President spoke from a prepared text. An advance text of his address was released on the same day.

177   Text of the "Basic Principles of Relations Between the United States of America and the Union of Soviet Socialist Republics." *May 29, 1972*

THE UNITED States of America and the Union of Soviet Socialist Republics,

Guided by their obligations under the Charter of the United Nations and by a desire to strengthen peaceful relations with each other and to place these relations on the firmest possible basis,

Aware of the need to make every effort to remove the threat of war and to create conditions which promote the reduction of tensions in the world and the strengthening of universal security and international cooperation,

Believing that the improvement of US-Soviet relations and their mutually advantageous development in such areas as economics, science and culture, will meet these objectives and contribute to better mutual understanding and business-like cooperation, without in any way prejudicing the interests of third countries,

Conscious that these objectives reflect the interests of the peoples of both countries,

Have agreed as follows:

First. They will proceed from the common determination that in the nuclear age there is no alternative to conducting their mutual relations on the basis of peaceful coexistence. Differences in ideology and in the social systems of the USA and the USSR are not obstacles to the bilateral development of normal relations based on the principles of sovereignty, equality, non-interference in internal affairs and mutual advantage.

Second. The USA and the USSR attach major importance to preventing the development of situations capable of causing a dangerous exacerbation of their relations. Therefore, they will do their utmost to avoid military confrontations and to prevent the outbreak of nuclear war. They will always exercise restraint in their mutual relations, and will be prepared to negotiate and settle differences by peaceful means. Discussions and negotiations on outstanding issues will be conducted in a spirit of reciprocity, mutual accommodation and mutual benefit.

Both sides recognize that efforts to obtain unilateral advantage at the expense of the other, directly or indirectly, are inconsistent with these objectives. The prerequisites for maintaining and strengthening peaceful relations between the USA and the USSR are the recognition of the security interests of the Parties based on the principle of equality and the renunciation of the use or threat of force.

Third. The USA and the USSR have a special responsibility, as do other countries which are permanent members of the United Nations Security Council, to do everything in their power so that conflicts or situations will not arise which would serve to increase international tensions. Accordingly, they will seek to promote conditions in which all countries will live in peace and security and will not be subject to outside interference in their internal affairs.

Fourth. The USA and the USSR intend to widen the juridical basis of their mutual relations and to exert the necessary efforts so that bilateral agreements which they have concluded and multilateral treaties and agreements to which they are jointly parties are faithfully implemented.

Fifth. The USA and the USSR reaffirm their readiness to continue the practice of exchanging views on problems of mutual interest and, when necessary, to conduct such exchanges at the highest level, including meetings between leaders of the two countries.

The two governments welcome and will facilitate an increase in productive contacts between representatives of the legislative bodies of the two countries.

Sixth. The Parties will continue their efforts to limit armaments on a bilateral as well as on a multilateral basis. They will continue to make special efforts to limit strategic armaments. Whenever possible, they will conclude concrete agreements aimed at achieving these purposes.

The USA and the USSR regard as the ultimate objective of their efforts the achievement of general and complete disarmament and the establishment of an effective system of international security in accordance with the purposes and principles of the United Nations.

Seventh. The USA and the USSR regard commercial and economic ties as an important and necessary element in the strengthening of their bilateral relations and thus will actively promote the growth of such ties. They will facilitate cooperation between the relevant organizations and enterprises of the two countries and the conclusion of appropriate

agreements and contracts, including long-term ones.

The two countries will contribute to the improvement of maritime and air communications between them.

Eighth. The two sides consider it timely and useful to develop mutual contacts and cooperation in the fields of science and technology. Where suitable, the USA and the USSR will conclude appropriate agreements dealing with concrete cooperation in these fields.

Ninth. The two sides reaffirm their intention to deepen cultural ties with one another and to encourage fuller familiarization with each other's cultural values. They will promote improved conditions for cultural exchanges and tourism.

Tenth. The USA and the USSR will seek to ensure that their ties and cooperation in all the above-mentioned fields and in any others in their mutual interest are built on a firm and long-term basis. To give a permanent character to these efforts, they will establish in all fields where this is feasible joint commissions or other joint bodies.

Eleventh. The USA and the USSR make no claim for themselves and would not recognize the claims of anyone else to any special rights or advantages in world affairs. They recognize the sovereign equality of all states.

The development of U.S.-Soviet relations is not directed against third countries and their interests.

Twelfth. The basic principles set forth in this document do not affect any obligations with respect to other countries earlier assumed by the USA and the USSR.

Moscow, May 29, 1972

FOR THE UNITED STATES OF AMERICA
RICHARD NIXON
   President of the United States of
   America
FOR THE UNION OF SOVIET SOCIALIST
   REPUBLICS
LEONID I. BREZHNEV
   General Secretary of the Central
   Committee, CPSU

NOTE: On the same day, the White House released the transcripts of two news briefings on the statement of basic principles and the joint communique following the discussions (Item 178): the first, by Henry A. Kissinger, Assistant to the President for National Security Affairs; the second, by Ronald L. Ziegler, Press Secretary to the President, and Leonid M. Zamyatin, Director General, TASS. The transcript of Dr. Kissinger's briefing is printed in the Weekly Compilation of Presidential Documents (vol. 8, p. 951).

178   Joint Communique Following Discussions With Soviet Leaders. *May* 29, 1972

BY MUTUAL agreement between the United States of America and the Union of Soviet Socialist Republics, the President of the United States and Mrs. Richard Nixon paid an official visit to the Soviet Union from May 22 to May 30, 1972. The President was accompanied by Secretary of State William P. Rogers, Assistant to the President Dr. Henry A. Kissinger, and other American officials. During his stay in the USSR President Nixon visited, in addition to Moscow, the cities of Leningrad and Kiev.

President Nixon and L. I. Brezhnev, General Secretary of the Central Committee of the Communist Party of the Soviet Union, N. V. Podgorny, Chairman of the Presidium of the Supreme Soviet of the USSR, and A. N. Kosygin, Chairman of the Council of Ministers of the USSR conducted talks on fundamental problems of American-Soviet relations and the current international situation.

Also taking part in the conversations were:

On the American side: William P. Rogers, Secretary of State; Jacob D. Beam, American Ambassador to the USSR; Dr. Henry A. Kissinger, Assistant

to the President for National Security Affairs; Peter M. Flanigan, Assistant to the President; and Martin J. Hillenbrand, Assistant Secretary of State for European Affairs.

On the Soviet side: A. A. Gromyko, Minister of Foreign Affairs of the USSR; N. S. Patolichev, Minister of Foreign Trade; V. V. Kuznetsov, Deputy Minister of Foreign Affairs of the USSR; A. F. Dobrynin, Soviet Ambassador to the USA; A. M. Aleksandrov, Assistant to the General Secretary of the Central Committee, CPSU; G. M. Korniyenko, Member of the Collegium of the Ministry of Foreign Affairs of the USSR.

The discussions covered a wide range of questions of mutual interest and were frank and thorough. They defined more precisely those areas where there are prospects for developing greater cooperation between the two countries, as well as those areas where the positions of the two Sides are different.

I. BILATERAL RELATIONS

Guided by the desire to place US-Soviet relations on a more stable and construc-

635

tive foundation, and mindful of their responsibilities for maintaining world peace and for facilitating the relaxation of international tension, the two Sides adopted a document entitled: "Basic Principles of Mutual Relations between the United States of America and the Union of Soviet Socialist Republics," signed on behalf of the US by President Nixon and on behalf of the USSR by General Secretary Brezhnev.

Both Sides are convinced that the provisions of that document open new possibilities for the development of peaceful relations and mutually beneficial cooperation between the USA and the USSR.

Having considered various areas of bilateral US-Soviet relations, the two Sides agreed that an improvement of relations is possible and desirable. They expressed their firm intention to act in accordance with the provisions set forth in the above-mentioned document.

As a result of progress made in negotiations which preceded the summit meeting, and in the course of the meeting itself, a number of significant agreements were reached. This will intensify bilateral cooperation in areas of common concern as well as in areas relevant to the cause of peace and international cooperation.

LIMITATION OF STRATEGIC ARMAMENTS

The two Sides gave primary attention to the problem of reducing the danger of nuclear war. They believe that curbing the competition in strategic arms will make a significant and tangible contribution to this cause.

The two Sides attach great importance to the Treaty on the Limitation of Anti-Ballistic Missile Systems and the Interim Agreement on Certain Measures with Respect to the Limitation of Strategic Offensive Arms concluded between them.[1]

These agreements, which were concluded as a result of the negotiations in Moscow, constitute a major step towards curbing and ultimately ending the arms race.

They are a concrete expression of the intention of the two Sides to contribute to the relaxation of international tension and the strengthening of confidence between states, as well as to carry out the obligations assumed by them in the Treaty on the Non-Proliferation of Nuclear Weapons (Article VI). Both Sides are convinced that the achievement of the above agreements is a practical step towards saving mankind from the threat of the outbreak of nuclear war. Accordingly, it corresponds to the vital interests of the American and Soviet peoples as well as to the vital interests of all other peoples.

The two Sides intend to continue active negotiations for the limitation of strategic offensive arms and to conduct them in a

---

[1] The texts of the treaty and the interim agreement and protocol are printed in United States Treaties and Other International Agreements (23 UST 3435 and 3462). On May 26, 1972, the White House also released a fact sheet, a statement by Press Secretary Ziegler, and the transcripts of two news briefings on the treaty and the interim agreement. One of the news briefings was held by Dr. Kissinger and Ambassador Gerard C. Smith, Director, United States Arms Control and Disarmament Agency; and the other by Press Secretary Ziegler and Leonid M. Zamyatin, Director General, TASS. Mr. Ziegler's statement and Dr. Kissinger's news briefing are printed in the Weekly Compilation of Presidential Documents (vol. 8, p. 929). On May 27, the White House released the transcript of a news briefing by Dr. Kissinger on the same subjects. It is printed in the Weekly Compilation of Presidential Documents (vol. 8, p. 932).

spirit of goodwill, respect for each other's legitimate interests and observance of the principle of equal security.

Both Sides are also convinced that the agreement on Measures to Reduce the Risk of Outbreak of Nuclear War Between the USA and the USSR, signed in Washington on September 30, 1971, serves the interests not only of the Soviet and American peoples, but of all mankind.

COMMERCIAL AND ECONOMIC RELATIONS

Both Sides agreed on measures designed to establish more favorable conditions for developing commercial and other economic ties between the USA and the USSR. The two Sides agree that realistic conditions exist for increasing economic ties. These ties should develop on the basis of mutual benefit and in accordance with generally accepted international practice.

Believing that these aims would be served by conclusion of a trade agreement between the USA and the USSR, the two Sides decided to complete in the near future the work necessary to conclude such an agreement. They agreed on the desirability of credit arrangements to develop mutual trade and of early efforts to resolve other financial and economic issues. It was agreed that a lend-lease settlement will be negotiated concurrently with a trade agreement.

In the interests of broadening and facilitating commercial ties between the two countries, and to work out specific arrangements, the two Sides decided to create a US-Soviet Joint Commercial Commission. Its first meeting will be held in Moscow in the summer of 1972.

Each Side will help promote the establishment of effective working arrangements between organizations and firms of both countries and encouraging the conclusion of long-term contracts.

MARITIME MATTERS—INCIDENTS AT SEA

The two Sides agreed to continue the negotiations aimed at reaching an agreement on maritime and related matters. They believe that such an agreement would mark a positive step in facilitating the expansion of commerce between the United States and the Soviet Union.

An Agreement was concluded between the two Sides on measures to prevent incidents at sea and in air space over it between vessels and aircraft of the US and Soviet Navies.[2] By providing agreed procedures for ships and aircraft of the two navies operating in close proximity, this agreement will diminish the chances of dangerous accidents.

COOPERATION IN SCIENCE AND
TECHNOLOGY

It was recognized that the cooperation now underway in areas such as atomic energy research, space research, health and other fields benefits both nations and has contributed positively to their over-all relations. It was agreed that increased scientific and technical cooperation on the basis of mutual benefit and shared effort for common goals is in the interest of both nations and would contribute to a further improvement in their bilateral relations.

---

[2] The text of the agreement is printed in the Weekly Compilation of Presidential Documents (vol. 8, p. 922). On May 25, 1972, the White House also released a fact sheet and the transcript of a news briefing on the agreement. Participants in the news briefing were John W. Warner, Secretary of the Navy, and Herbert S. Okun, Deputy Country Director (USSR), Department of State.

For these purposes the two Sides signed an agreement for cooperation in the fields of science and technology.[3] A US-Soviet Joint Commission on Scientific and Technical Cooperation will be created for identifying and establishing cooperative programs.

COOPERATION IN SPACE

Having in mind the role played by the US and the USSR in the peaceful exploration of outer space, both Sides emphasized the importance of further bilateral cooperation in this sphere. In order to increase the safety of man's flights in outer space and the future prospects of joint scientific experiments, the two Sides agreed to make suitable arrangements to permit the docking of American and Soviet spacecraft and stations.[4] The first joint docking experiment of the two countries' piloted spacecraft, with visits by astronauts and cosmonauts to each other's spacecraft, is contemplated for 1975. The planning and implementation of this flight will be carried out by the US National Aeronautics and Space Administra-

tion and the USSR Academy of Sciences, according to principles and procedures developed through mutual consultations.

COOPERATION IN THE FIELD OF HEALTH

The two Sides concluded an agreement on health cooperation which marks a fruitful beginning of sharing knowledge about, and collaborative attacks on, the common enemies, disease and disability.[5] The initial research efforts of the program will concentrate on health problems important to the whole world—cancer, heart diseases, and the environmental health sciences. This cooperation subsequently will be broadened to include other health problems of mutual interest. The two Sides pledged their full support for the health cooperation program and agreed to continue the active participation of the two governments in the work of international organizations in the health field.

ENVIRONMENTAL COOPERATION

The two Sides agreed to initiate a program of cooperation in the protection and

---

[3] The text of the agreement on science and technology is printed in the Weekly Compilation of Presidential Documents (vol. 8, p. 921). On May 24, the White House released fact sheets and the transcript of a news briefing on the science and technology agreement, as well as the agreement on cooperation in space. Participants in the news briefing were Vladimir Kirillin, Soviet Chairman, Committee for Science and Technology, and Soviet Academician Boris Petrov.

[4] The text of the agreement on cooperation in space is printed in the Weekly Compilation of Presidential Documents (vol. 8, p. 920).

[5] The text of the agreement is printed in the Weekly Compilation of Presidential Documents (vol. 8, p. 919). On May 23, the White House released a fact sheet and the transcripts of two news briefings on the agreement. Participants in the first news briefing were Elliot L. Richardson, Secretary, Dr. Merlin K. DuVal, Jr., Assistant Secretary for Health and Scientific Affairs, Department of Health, Education, and Welfare; and Dr. Roger O. Egeberg, Special Consultant to the President; and, in the second, were Boris V. Petrovsky, Soviet Minister of Health, and Dgermen Gvishiany, Soviet Deputy Chief, Committee for Science and Technology.

enhancement of man's environment.[6] Through joint research and joint measures, the United States and the USSR hope to contribute to the preservation of a healthful environment in their countries and throughout the world. Under the new agreement on environmental cooperation there will be consultations in the near future in Moscow on specific cooperative projects.

EXCHANGES IN THE FIELDS OF SCIENCE, TECHNOLOGY, EDUCATION AND CULTURE

Both Sides note the importance of the Agreement on Exchanges and Cooperation in Scientific, Technical, Educational, Cultural, and Other Fields in 1972–1973, signed in Moscow on April 11, 1972. Continuation and expansion of bilateral exchanges in these fields will lead to better understanding and help improve the general state of relations between the two countries. Within the broad framework provided by this Agreement the two Sides have agreed to expand the areas of cooperation, as reflected in new agreements concerning space, health, the environment and science and technology.

---

[6] The text of the agreement is printed in the Weekly Compilation of Presidential Documents (vol. 8, p. 917). On May 23, the White House released a fact sheet and the transcripts of two news briefings on the agreement. Participants in the first news briefing were Russell E. Train, Chairman, and Gordon J. F. MacDonald, member, Council on Environmental Quality; and, in the second, were Mr. Petrovsky and Mr. Gvishiany. On September 11, the White House released a fact sheet on the agreement and the transcript of a news briefing on a meeting with the President to discuss upcoming meetings in Moscow of the U.S.–U.S.S.R. joint committee on implementation of the agreement. The news briefing was held by Chairman Train, head of the United States delegation to the U.S.–U.S.S.R. joint committee.

The US side, noting the existence of an extensive program of English language instruction in the Soviet Union, indicated its intention to encourage Russian language programs in the United States.

II. INTERNATIONAL ISSUES

EUROPE

In the course of the discussions on the international situation, both Sides took note of favorable developments in the relaxation of tensions in Europe.

Recognizing the importance to world peace of developments in Europe, where both World Wars originated, and mindful of the responsibilities and commitments which they share with other powers under appropriate agreements, the USA and the USSR intend to make further efforts to ensure a peaceful future for Europe, free of tensions, crises and conflicts.

They agree that the territorial integrity of all states in Europe should be respected.

Both Sides view the September 3, 1971 Quadripartite Agreement relating to the Western Sectors of Berlin as a good example of fruitful cooperation between the states concerned, including the USA and the USSR. The two Sides believe that the implementation of that agreement in the near future, along with other steps, will further improve the European situation and contribute to the necessary trust among states.

Both Sides welcomed the treaty between the USSR and the Federal Republic of Germany signed on August 12, 1970. They noted the significance of the provisions of this treaty as well as of other recent agreements in contributing to confidence and cooperation among the European states.

The USA and the USSR are prepared

to make appropriate contributions to the positive trends on the European continent toward a genuine detente and the development of relations of peaceful cooperation among states in Europe on the basis of the principles of territorial integrity and inviolability of frontiers, non-interference in internal affairs, sovereign equality, independence and renunciation of the use or threat of force.

The US and the USSR are in accord that multilateral consultations looking toward a Conference on Security and Cooperation in Europe could begin after the signature of the Final Quadripartite Protocol of the Agreement of September 3, 1971. The two governments agree that the conference should be carefully prepared in order that it may concretely consider specific problems of security and cooperation and thus contribute to the progressive reduction of the underlying causes of tension in Europe. This conference should be convened at a time to be agreed by the countries concerned, but without undue delay.

Both Sides believe that the goal of ensuring stability and security in Europe would be served by a reciprocal reduction of armed forces and armaments, first of all in Central Europe. Any agreement on this question should not diminish the security of any of the Sides. Appropriate agreement should be reached as soon as practicable between the states concerned on the procedures for negotiations on this subject in a special forum.

THE MIDDLE EAST

The two Sides set out their positions on this question. They reaffirm their support for a peaceful settlement in the Middle East in accordance with Security Council Resolution 242.

Noting the significance of constructive cooperation of the parties concerned with the Special Representative of the UN Secretary General, Ambassador Jarring, the US and the USSR confirm their desire to contribute to his mission's success and also declare their readiness to play their part in bringing about a peaceful settlement in the Middle East. In the view of the US and the USSR, the achievement of such a settlement would open prospects for the normalization of the Middle East situation and would permit, in particular, consideration of further steps to bring about a military relaxation in that area.

INDOCHINA

Each side set forth its respective standpoint with regard to the continuing war in Vietnam and the situation in the area of Indochina as a whole.

The US side emphasized the need to bring an end to the military conflict as soon as possible and reaffirmed its commitment to the principle that the political future of South Vietnam should be left for the South Vietnamese people to decide for themselves, free from outside interference.

The US side explained its view that the quickest and most effective way to attain the above-mentioned objectives is through negotiations leading to the return of all Americans held captive in the region, the implementation of an internationally supervised Indochina-wide ceasefire and the subsequent withdrawal of all American forces stationed in South Vietnam within four months, leaving the political questions to be resolved by the Indochinese peoples themselves.

The United States reiterated its willingness to enter into serious negotiations with the North Vietnamese Side to settle the war in Indochina on a basis just to all.

The Soviet Side stressed its solidarity with the just struggle of the peoples of Vietnam, Laos and Cambodia for their freedom, independence and social progress. Firmly supporting the proposals of the DRV and the Republic of South Vietnam, which provide a realistic and constructive basis for settling the Vietnam problem, the Soviet Union stands for a cessation of bombings of the DRV, for a complete and unequivocal withdrawal of the troops of the USA and its allies from South Vietnam, so that the peoples of Indochina would have the possibility to determine for themselves their fate without any outside interference.

DISARMAMENT ISSUES

The two Sides expressed their positions on arms limitation and disarmament issues.

The two Sides note that in recent years their joint and parallel actions have facilitated the working out and conclusion of treaties which curb the arms race or ban some of the most dangerous types of weapons. They note further that these treaties were welcomed by a large majority of the states in the world, which became parties to them.

Both Sides regard the Convention on the Prohibition of the Development, Production and Stockpiling of Bacteriological (Biological) and Toxic Weapons and on their Destruction, as an essential disarmament measure. Along with Great Britain, they are the depositories for the Convention which was recently opened for signature by all states. The USA and the USSR will continue their efforts to reach an international agreement regarding chemical weapons.

The USA and the USSR, proceeding from the need to take into account the security interests of both countries on the basis of the principle of equality, and without prejudice to the security interests of third countries, will actively participate in negotiations aimed at working out new measures designed to curb and end the arms race. The ultimate purpose is general and complete disarmament, including nuclear disarmament, under strict international control. A world disarmament conference could play a role in this process at an appropriate time.

STRENGTHENING THE UNITED NATIONS

Both Sides will strive to strengthen the effectiveness of the United Nations on the basis of strict observance of the UN Charter. They regard the United Nations as an instrument for maintaining world peace and security, discouraging conflicts, and developing international cooperation. Accordingly, they will do their best to support United Nations efforts in the interests of international peace.

Both Sides emphasized that agreements and understandings reached in the negotiations in Moscow, as well as the contents and nature of these negotiations, are not in any way directed against any other country. Both Sides proceed from the recognition of the role, the responsibility and the prerogatives of other interested states, existing international obligations and agreements, and the principles and purposes of the UN Charter.

Both Sides believe that positive results were accomplished in the course of the talks at the highest level. These results indicate that despite the differences between the USA and the USSR in social systems, ideologies, and policy principles, it is possible to develop mutually advantageous cooperation between the peoples of both countries, in the interests of strengthening peace and international security.

Both Sides expressed the desire to continue close contact on a number of issues that were under discussion. They agreed that regular consultations on questions of mutual interest, including meetings at the highest level, would be useful.

In expressing his appreciation for the hospitality accorded him in the Soviet Union, President Nixon invited General Secretary L. I. Brezhnev, Chairman N. V. Podgorny, and Chairman A. N. Kosygin to visit the United States at a mutually convenient time. This invitation was accepted.

NOTE: On the same day, the White House re-leased the transcripts of two news briefings on the joint communique and the statement of basic principles (Item 177): the first, by Dr. Kissinger; the second, by Press Secretary Ziegler and Leonid M. Zamyatin, Director General, TASS. Dr. Kissinger's news briefing is printed in the Weekly Compilation of Presidential Documents (vol. 8, p. 951).

During the President's visit to Moscow Press Secretary Ziegler and Director General Zamyatin held daily news briefings on discussions between United States and Soviet officials. Transcripts of the news briefings were released as follows: one on May 22, two on May 23, and two on May 24.

On May 29, the White House released the transcript of a news briefing by Dr. Kissinger on discussions held during the visit. The transcript is printed in the Weekly Compilation of Presidential Documents (vol. 8, p. 956).

On May 30, the White House released the transcript of a news briefing by John D. Ehrlichman, Assistant to the President for Domestic Affairs, and Peter G. Peterson, Secretary of Commerce, on the domestic impact of the agreements reached with the Soviet Union.

179 Toast at a Dinner in Kiev. *May* 29, 1972

Mr. Chairman of the Presidium and all of the distinguished guests here this evening:

I first express appreciation for the eloquent remarks of the Chairman and I will respond to those remarks somewhat briefly because I had the opportunity to speak at some length on television last night.

But tonight I would like to address my remarks particularly to this city and particularly to the Ukraine—a city and a republic that has meant so much to the Soviet Union and so much to the world.

We had a very difficult time selecting the cities we would visit on this trip to the Soviet Union. In consulting with Ambassador Dobrynin, he, of course, said that we must spend most of our time in Moscow for our official talks; and then, logically, it was necessary, too, and we welcomed the opportunity, to return to Leningrad, the second city of the Soviet Union.

Then we said to Ambassador Dobrynin, "What should be the third city?" And he answered, "The mother of all Russian cities, Kiev." And so we come here for the first time and we are glad that we came.

We are glad to have enjoyed this wonderful dinner, these fine wines that are the product of this very rich country. We are glad, too, to have the opportunity to know some of the people of the Ukraine— a people who are world famous for their warmth, for their strength, for their courage.

As I think of a way to describe our feelings on this occasion, I noted that in history—and this city is so full of history—in the 11th century a golden gate was erected in the Ukraine, in Kiev. So, in a way, we can say that Kiev is the City of the Golden Gate.

In America we have a city, San Francisco, that is called the City of the Golden Gate. Many of our friends who have visited America believe that San Francisco is our most beautiful city. But at the turn of the century it suffered a great tragedy, a tragedy not of war but of what is next to war—an earthquake followed by fire which virtually destroyed the city.

And the pessimists said this city would never come back. They were wrong, because they failed to recognize the spirit of the people of the City of the Golden Gate on the western coast of California.

Then we think of this city—a city with a much older golden gate. We think of the enormous tragedy that was visited upon it during the war, the destruction of buildings and, of course, even more tragic, the destruction of human life on an unprecedented scale.

I am sure that there were people then who said that the city of Kiev would never come back because of the destruction that was wrought upon it by war.

My friend on my right, who is an engineer, said there were some who said it would take 50 years to rebuild this city.

But, again, the pessimists were wrong, because they did not reckon with the spirit, the strength, the courage, the determination of the people of the Ukraine and the people of Kiev.

So, not in 50 years, but in 7 years, the city was rebuilt and the Republic of the Ukraine continues to grow and to prosper.

So, for that reason, on this particular evening, which is the last occasion that we will be having dinner on Soviet soil, we think it is very appropriate that it should be here in this mother of all Russian cities, here in the Ukraine among a people who are so strong and who represent such a great spirit.

So in responding to the toast, the very eloquent toast of the Chairman, I would simply say we should drink tonight to the heroes who fought in war and the heroes who have rebuilt this city in peace and, we trust, to the new leadership to which our two countries, the Soviet Union and the United States, may contribute, by which the world may have a period in which the tragedy of war will never again be visited upon this city or any other city like it in the world.

I would ask you to raise your glasses, then, to the heroes of the Ukraine in war and in peace.

NOTE: The President spoke at 10:35 p.m. in Mariinsky Palace at a dinner hosted by the Presidium of the Supreme Soviet and the Government of the Ukrainian Soviet Socialist Republic. He spoke from a prepared text.

180   Remarks at the Shahyad Monument in Tehran, Iran. *May 30, 1972*

Your Imperial Majesties, Mr. Mayor, ladies and gentlemen:

Nineteen years ago, Mrs. Nixon and I were welcomed to this great city after a long trip around the world. Now we come again to Tehran, and we see the progress that has occurred in those 19 years under the enlightened leadership of Your Majesty.

As we have come thus far from the airport, we have seen thousands of schoolchildren, and as we see them we think they are the future of Iran; they are the future of the world. We hope that the talks we have had this past week will contribute to a peaceful future for them, and we know, Your Majesty, that the talks I shall be privileged to have with you will

provide counsel and wisdom also for the cause of peace and progress for all people, to which you have dedicated your life, and a cause in which we, all the people of the United States, are honored to cooperate with you.

Thank you.

NOTE: The President spoke at 4:43 p.m. at the Shahyad (Memory of the Shah) Monument commemorating the 2,500th anniversary of the Persian Empire. He spoke without referring to notes.

181   Toasts of the President and Mohammad Reza Pahlavi, Shah of Iran, at a State Dinner in Tehran.   *May 30, 1972*

Your Imperial Majesty and all of your distinguished guests:

Let me first thank you on behalf of Mrs. Nixon and all the members of our party for the very generous remarks that you have made and for the magnificent hospitality which you have extended to us on this occasion, and in speaking of that hospitality, may we particularly thank you for the welcome that we received as we came into the capital city of your country today. It will leave a memory in our hearts that will last for all of our lives, and we are most grateful for the welcome we received from the people of Iran on this historic occasion.

Since ancient times, this country has been one that has been known for its splendid hospitality, and we, of course, tonight have had a good chance to see why that reputation has become worldwide.

It is always a very great privilege to visit here, but I feel especially privileged to be here in this period in which you are celebrating what you have referred to, the 2,500th year of your country's history. I think of the fact that the United States of

America in just 4 years will be celebrating its 200th anniversary, and then I compare that 200 years with 25 centuries of history, and I realize that as we compare our two countries, we owe so much to you. As you have spoken so generously of what you may owe to us, we owe so much to you, not only for 2,500 years, but for a history that goes back even 6,000 years.

In this room, and in this company, speaking from what was once known and perhaps still is known as the New World, it is only appropriate that we pay our respects to and express our thanks to the magnificent heritage of the Old World that is now, through your efforts, a bridge to the new.

On this particular occasion, as all of you know, this is the first stop that we have made since the trip that we have taken to the Soviet Union. Your Majesty has referred to that trip, and I think it is only appropriate on this occasion for me to speak of that trip, the visit we had there, what it means to the world, and what it means to all nations in the world.

Before doing so, I wish to say that I

have had the opportunity during the period that I have served in office—8 years as Vice President, when Mrs. Nixon and I first had the opportunity of visiting Tehran, and then over 3 years as President of the United States—and even some years out of office, the opportunity of visiting over 70 nations. I have met the heads of state and the heads of government of most of those nations, and I think that all of this company should know that in evaluating those that I have met, heads of state and heads of government, His Imperial Majesty is one who has an understanding not only of the bilateral problems that our two countries sometimes have—fortunately relatively small ones— but beyond that, an understanding of the area in which he lives and of the international problems.

His advice and counsel have been invaluable through the years, and it was for that reason that, after my visit to the Soviet Union, I was glad that the opportunity was provided, through Your Majesty's invitation, to come here, to consult with you, and to get the benefit of your wisdom in terms of the future policies of the United States of America.

Speaking now of what these visits mean, and what the future is, I think it is important for us to bear in mind that while we have been at what is called the summit, that there has been no intention on the part of the two governments represented at that summit conference—no intention to divide the world into two spheres of influence, no intention to set up a condominium. Certainly on our part—and I express here the policy of the United States in the past and the present, and I know what will be the policy in the future—we consider it important and vital that as a great nation and a powerful

nation, that we seek good relations with all nations in the world.

But we also recognize that as we begin a dialogue with some nations with which we have had no dialogue at all— I refer to the visit that we paid earlier this year to the People's Republic of China—and when we begin conversations that can, and we trust will, develop a better relationship with a nation that from time to time since the great World War II has been an adversary on occasion—that as we do both of these things, we have not overlooked a very fundamental fact of international life, and that is that it is vital that we build our policy on the alliances and the friendships that we have had in the past, that we have now, and that we hope to have in the future.

That is one of the things that this visit symbolizes. We are proud that Iran is a friend of the United States, that the United States is a friend of Iran.

We are proud of the fact that we have some bonds between us—bonds that have been formalized by treaty. But I would point out to this audience, those who are here, that bonds that are formalized by treaty can be one thing; what is more important are those bonds that are further underscored by a personal relationship, a personal respect, a personal esteem, between the leaders of the countries involved.

I value the friendship that it has been my privilege to have with His Majesty over these years. I believe that all American Presidents have valued the friendship that they have had on their part with the leaders of this country.

What I am saying, very simply, is this: We are proud to have the official relationships with the Government of Iran, which have been set down on pieces of paper sometimes called treaties, sometimes called agreements. But what is more important is that we are proud of the fact that the relationship goes beyond simply the piece of paper, that it goes to the personal relationship which we see exemplified in this magnificent dinner tonight and which we trust will always be the hallmark of the relations between our two countries.

I should like to bring my remarks to a conclusion tonight by informally referring to an impression I had as we came into the city today. It was a glorious day, as all of you will remember. The sky was blue, we could see the mountains in the distance, the weather was just right, as if it had been ordered for the occasion. And then, as the motorcade moved from the airport out through the suburbs and then finally into the city, we saw the people on the streets. We could tell from the expressions on their faces they had not been ordered to come because, while you can order people to get out on the streets, you cannot order them to smile. You cannot order them to wave, and particularly, you cannot do that with the children. It must come from their hearts, and it had come from their hearts.

We saw them there, not hundreds, not thousands, but tens of thousands of girls and boys, smiling, waving, with their American flags and the Iranian flags side by side.

I am sure that through His Majesty's mind ran the same thoughts that ran through mine: Our obligation is to them; our obligation is to their future.

What we have done in the meetings that we have had in this past week is only a beginning. It possibly builds a foundation for a better future between two great nations and a foundation, possibly, for a better chance for peace for all nations in the world.

Our meetings here helped to build that foundation, a foundation of good relations that already exists between our two great countries, but a foundation for more progress in the future—progress which will benefit not just our generation, but that generation, one that will make us, as the leaders of our countries, proud of that leadership, proud of our people, proud of our heritage—yours 2,500 years old, ours so much younger.

But proud as we are of that heritage and proud as we are of that country, recognizing that our responsibility is to keep what is best from the past but also to build for the future.

As I look at Your Majesty's record, what you have done for this country in terms of the progressive actions in everything from land reform to education, so many other areas, I realize that your thoughts are, of course, about the proud past of this great nation and this great people.

But overriding that are your hopes for the future—the future of those children we saw on the streets of Tehran today.

So tonight I would simply conclude my remarks by saying that there will be many in the days ahead who will try to evaluate the so-called summits—the one in Peking in which the most populous nation of the world and the most prosperous nation of the world met for the first time in 20 years, the one in Moscow where the two most powerful nations in the world met and made some very important agreements which could contribute not only to better relations between those two but to peace for all the world.

As the experts evaluate those summits,

let them keep the one thought in mind that I think is so close to the heart of His Majesty and so close to my heart: We as leaders of our countries do our best. We sometimes make mistakes, but our thoughts, our hopes, our dreams are for our children—not just our family's children but for the children of our countries, the children of all the world, that they may have the opportunity to grow up in a more peaceful world, a more prosperous world, a more friendly world. And if, in the brief span of time that each of us spends in the office he holds, we could have contributed to that goal, all of the efforts, all of the time, everything that we have done would have been worth it.

It is in that spirit that I would like to propose tonight that our glasses be raised, of course, to the continued friendship of the two great peoples—the Iranian people and the American people—whose friendship goes back so far, as His Majesty has pointed out, and also to the leadership which His Majesty has provided for his country and, of course, to his partner in that leadership, his Empress.

I would close, if I could, on one informal note. In 1953, right after General Eisenhower, who was a great friend of Iran and who was the last American President to be honored at a state dinner like this in Iran, right after he had become President he was talking to me in his office—and he often used to say that he didn't know much about politics. That, of course, is the understatement of the century for one who won such great political victories. That day we had had a meeting with the leaders of the Congress, Democrats and Republicans, and General Eisenhower, who was a great judge of men and of women in a leadership capacity, made this rather interesting comment:

He said, "I am puzzled about political leaders. You can't generalize about them." He said, "Some of those fellows in there are very intelligent, and others seem to be a little slow. Some spoke very, very well, and others were a bit inarticulate." He said, "About the only thing that I can think of that political leaders seem to have in common, successful political leaders, is the ability to marry above themselves."

What I am simply saying tonight is that on this particular occasion we propose a toast, of course, to His Imperial Majesty the Shahanshah, to his lovely Empress, who has been by his side, as my wife has been by my side, through adversity and also through periods of very great satisfaction.

So, ladies and gentlemen, if you would rise and raise your glasses.

NOTE: The President spoke at 11:06 p.m. in the Niavaran Palace in response to a toast proposed by the Shah. He spoke from a prepared text.

The Shah's remarks were as follows:

Mr. President:

It is a great pleasure for the Shahbanou and myself to welcome you Mr. President and Mrs. Nixon in our country. Your visit is symbolic of the friendship and deep understanding which have always marked the relationship between our two countries and which with the passage of time have gone from strength to strength.

We Iranians were acquainted with the great American nation even before the opening of diplomatic relations between our two countries through fruitful cultural and educational cooperation. It is for this reason that our relationship was from the beginning based on a truly sincere and spiritual understanding. It was almost a century and half ago when the first American school was established in Oroumieh of Azerbaijan, which is called Rezaiyeh today. In subsequent years similar schools were founded in Hamadan, Rasht, Meshed, and in several other cities of Iran. But the most important of all these schools was the American College of Tehran, founded almost 100 years ago. Many distinguished Iranian personalities had graduated from this school in the past. The management of this college was for many years entrusted to that noble American, Mr. Samuel Jordan, who is remembered very much by our people. It is for this very reason that one of our largest streets in Tehran has been named after him in order to keep his memory alive.

Our people have also unforgettable memories of another American friend, Mr. Morgan Shuster, who came to Iran at the invitation of the Iranian Government in the year 1911 in order to reorganize our customs and financial affairs which were at that time disorderly and confused. Although his tour of duty, due to the prevailing diplomatic conditions at that time which were really no concern of the Iranian Government, did not last more than 9 months, yet his memory as a noble, humanitarian, and an honest individual has been recorded in the contemporary history of Iran and will never be forgotten.

I deem it necessary to stress the fact here that the relationship between our two countries from the very beginning has never been impaired due to ill intentions, greed, grudge, revenge, and so forth, but from the time we can remember the policy of your country towards ours was respectful, liberal, and based on the principles of justice and human welfare and fellowship. I can cite as the best example of this fact the proclamation issued in the year 1919 by the Government of the United States, defending the sovereign rights of Iran.

After the Second World War, the financial assistance granted by the United States of America to my country was effective in the resurrection of the national life of Iran, and we shall not forget this assistance. During all these years the ties between Iran and the United States of America in the various political, economic, cultural, and artistic fields have always continued to expand, and actually serve as an outstanding example of relations between two countries.

On numerous occasions, during these past years, I have had the pleasure of hosting leaders and other high ranking American personalities, including yourself, **Mr. President**, and also on numerous occasions I have personally traveled to your country, either as an official guest or for participation in various university ceremonies. Presently in these universities and other cultural centers of the United States thousands of Iranian students are studying in order to gain the latest and most progressive scientific experiences and technical knowledge of the present day to bring back to their homeland.

Mr. President, you, who have come from your great land to visit our country, have charge of the leadership of the United States of America in one of the most grave periods of its history. It has very rarely happened in the history of the world that the decisions of a head of a state has such far-reaching effects on the destiny of the whole of mankind. Naturally, under these conditions the enormity of the responsibilities you shoulder as the head of such a country, vis-a-vis your nation, the other nations of the world, and history, is commensurate with the immense abilities and powers at your disposal.

A real leader under these circumstances and under such conditions before anything else needs to have a realistic spirit and foresight, and we have always admired these qualities which you possess to the greatest extent.

We have always been and are witnessing, during your term of office, that in facing all problems and the grave difficulties, you have placed the interests of your country over and above your personal interests, and this is what history demands from real leaders. We sincerely wish you every success in performing your important duties, because your efforts are related with the destiny of all mankind.

In this regard, within the recent few months we have witnessed your two historic visits to China and the U.S.S.R. Certainly these two visits have had immeasurable bearing on the international evolution of the world today. Your visit to China, before anything else, assisted the universal aspect of our present day world. Your unprecedented visit to the U.S.S.R., apart from the bilateral aspects of it, from the point of view of agreements reached in regard to health, environment, outer space, science and technology the agreement to set up a trade commission, and especially the agreement reached on strategic arms limitation controls, is of the utmost importance. I hope the latter is the first stage in the materialization of world disarmament under close international control, and will prepare the ground for the creation of an atmosphere and system which will eliminate the dangers of war altogether. In this respect we all have high hopes and interests, and obviously, until such time that these wishes come true, we cannot neglect the maintenance of our defenses even for a moment.

Our country is governed by an independent national policy and the maintenance of the true interests of the people. We are following this path with due attention to our national and world responsibilities. Thus repaying friendship with friendship and for this very reason we highly value the friendly policy of your country towards ours.

We are proud that we have more than 2,500 years of recorded history which started with one of the most honored and humanitarian documents of the world history, namely the Freedom Proclamation of Cyrus the Great. Your country last year, like many other countries alongside us, celebrated this as one of the greatest events of the history of mankind. At this opportunity I would like to commend the American Committee for Cyrus the Great Celebrations, which arranged detailed artistic, scientific, and university programs throughout the United States. I would like to thank especially Mrs. Nixon for accepting the honorary chairmanship of this committee in your country.

Depending upon at least 25 centuries of national heritage and sovereignty, we today have started a new period of renewing our past glories, based on the eternal values of our culture and civilization, and hope that the pages of our future history will also be thumbed through with the same national pride based on honor, righteousness, peace, and justice.

We have based our independent national policy on international understanding in the path of national reconstruction and the strengthening of world peace, coexistence, and, above all, cooperation. It is to be noted that we shall not tolerate any inequality from any quarter in our relations with other countries. Certainly under no circumstances will we allow any violation of our land or our rights.

Your visit to Iran, Mr. President and Mrs. Nixon, certainly represents a further step in the expansion and strengthening of our longstanding friendship and cooperation. And we are sure that this visit will also be fruitful from the point of view of international peace and understanding.

Mr. President, allow me to raise my glass to your personal health and happiness and that of Mrs. Nixon, and to wish increasing progress and welfare for the noble American people and the further strengthening of the friendship between our two countries.

182   Toasts of the President and the Shah of Iran at a Luncheon in Tehran Honoring Their Imperial Majesties. *May* 31, 1972

I WOULD just like, informally, to say a word to His Majesty and our guests—very informally, because we spoke last night.

First, we were very glad to come here after our visit to the Soviet Union, which was important, and which we will always remember because of what we saw and what may have been accomplished.

It was good to come to a country where we saw so many friends and people who have been longtime friends, and where we felt not only the fresh air blowing off the mountains but the freshness of the people

and their attitudes as we went through the streets.

We will always be grateful for that little respite after our 8 days in the Kremlin. And while the Kremlin is a great palace, to be there for 8 days is a long time.

The other thing that I would say is that we are grateful for the fact that all of our party has been received so hospitably and that His Majesty has made available this beautiful summer palace, as it is called, I understand, for our use and for this luncheon.

It is very unusual for me to stand up in a house that is not my own, or one which the Government allows me to live in for 4 years at a time, and be able to act as the host.

But this, of course, is typical of the hospitality which is legendary here, which we have learned to know over almost 20 years, and which is enriched each time we come.

Perhaps the best way it can be said— and I am not a language expert, unfortunately, and most everybody here is, being from a world of diplomacy and the rest— but the way I feel now in this position of being able to offer the informal toast to Their Imperial Majesties is the way the Spanish say it. In our country whenever we invite anybody into our house, when somebody comes in, we say, "Make yourself at home." That is the phrase. But the Spanish say it in two different ways. They will say, *"Estan en su casa,"* or *"Mi casa es su casa,"* which means, "My house is your house," or, "You are in your own house."

So because His Imperial Majesty and Her Majesty have been so kind to say *"Mi casa es su casa,"* we have had a memorable 24 hours here.

We aren't able to pay the rent, but on the other hand we hope that we can show our appreciation in a very easy way for us—through that continued, deep friendship which has characterized our relations for so many years and that, perhaps, is worth more than the rent.

So I suggest we all raise our glasses to Their Imperial Majesties.

NOTE: The President spoke at 1:08 p.m. in the Saadabad Palace. He spoke from a prepared text.

The Shah responded as follows:

It was a long time since we were expecting you, Mr. President and Mrs. Nixon, to come to this country—although you have been here before—but in your present capacity as President of the United States. And this is for many reasons.

But the first one, and foremost, because we have established friendship with you and your country at one of the greatest moments of our history. It was almost a question of touch-and-go. And at that time we found you and your country right at our side. And, obviously, we cannot forget these things.

So I personally followed the career of the man who in those hours came to see us also in an important capacity as Vice President of the United States.

And I could not hide it from you that I was personally very happy to see this man be elected as the President of his country.

And since his election, standing to all the highest standards that anybody could show during his tenure of office, which was heartening for us because it came from a friend, but also the head and the President of a country whose friendship we value so high and also we need so much. And I don't think that we are the only people who need that friendship and those high standards of conduct and model; many others do. Some say it openly; some others just profit by it without saying something. Some others profit by it by even kicking you.

But be sure that we are not one of those. By sticking to our principles, we are sticking to our friends also at the same time.

In first of all congratulating you on what you have achieved internally in the United States and what you have achieved in these two historic trips abroad, I say that we fully agree with everything you have done and you have said. We wish you Godspeed, happy return to your country, very happy and successful future. And we regard your success very much also as our own success, because we know that this success represents something on which we can count and something with which we are familiar and that we can trust.

So thanking you once again for having accepted this heartfelt invitation, we wish you, on behalf of my wife, of our people that you saw yesterday in the streets, the actual generation,

650

and especially and fortunately on behalf of the future generation, all the best in the world for yourself, Mrs. Nixon, and the very good people of America, which I am sure the tremendous majority are sound, reasonable, good-hearted, humanitarian people. God be with you.

Would you please raise your glass with me to drink to the health of the President of the United States and Mrs. Nixon.

183   Joint Communique Following Discussions With the Shah of Iran.   *May* 31, 1972

AT THE invitation of His Imperial Majesty the Shahanshah Arya Mehr and Her Imperial Majesty the Shahbanou of Iran, the President of the United States of America and Mrs. Richard Nixon paid an official visit to Iran from May 30 to May 31, 1972. The President and Mrs. Nixon were received with exceptional friendliness and warmth by Their Imperial Majesties and by the Government and people of Iran.

During his visit the President held discussions with His Imperial Majesty the Shahanshah in a warm and cordial atmosphere, reflecting the close and friendly relations that exist between the two countries.

The President and His Imperial Majesty discussed recent developments on the international scene. The President told His Imperial Majesty of his visits to Moscow and Peking and of his efforts to reduce East-West tensions and restore peace and stability to Southeast Asia. They held the view that the conflict in Indochina should be settled through negotiations and that the Geneva agreements could serve as a basis for resolving problems among the states in the area and for guaranteeing their right of self-determination without any outside interference.

The President and His Imperial Majesty also discussed developments in the Middle East. They were gratified that a cease-fire continues to be observed but expressed their concern over the serious situation existing in the Middle East and reaffirmed their support for a peaceful settlement in accordance with Security Council Resolution 242.

The President and His Imperial Majesty agreed that the security and stability of the Persian Gulf is of vital importance to the littoral States. Both were of the view that the littoral States bore the primary responsibility for the security of the Persian Gulf.

His Imperial Majesty reaffirmed Iran's determination to bear its share of this responsibility.

The President and His Imperial Majesty also agreed that the economic development and welfare of the bordering States of the Persian Gulf are of importance to the stability of the region. Iran declared itself ready and willing to cooperate with its neighbors in fostering an atmosphere in which stability and progress can flourish.

The President and His Imperial Majesty voiced the hope that Pakistan and India would find ways to reach a just and honorable settlement of the existing issues. They noted with satisfaction the initiative taken by both countries for meetings which hold the promise through further talks of progress toward a peaceful settlement in South Asia built on lasting relationships of friendship and mutual respect.

The President expressed his admiration

for Iran's impressive record in the development of a strong economy and the successful implementation of His Imperial Majesty's "White Revolution." His Imperial Majesty outlined the main features of Iran's new five year plan with particular emphasis on agro-industry and socio-economic projects. The President reiterated the readiness of the United States to cooperate with Iran as appropriate in this extensive program and important enterprise.

The President and His Imperial Majesty also discussed the worldwide narcotics problem. They noted that Iran and the United States were taking vigorous action against the illicit international narcotics traffic. Both took satisfaction in Iran's effective measures to control domestic opium production. The President expressed understanding of Iran's declared policy to cease internal cultivation of the opium poppy when Iran's neighbors also cease internal cultivation of the opium poppy. They agreed that the two governments should continue their close cooperation in international forums dealing with narcotic matters. The President noted with appreciation the active support provided by Iran at the recent United Nations conference which adopted a protocol amending the 1961 single convention on narcotic drugs. The President reaffirmed United States' support for regional cooperation in solving international narcotics problems.

Both sides expressed deep satisfaction over the excellence of relations between their two countries and the expectation that they would continue in the future. His Imperial Majesty stressed once again Iran's determination to strengthen its defensive capability to ensure the nation's security. The President confirmed that the United States would, as in the past, continue to cooperate with Iran in strengthening its defenses. They reaffirmed their respect for the sovereign right of every nation to choose its own destiny in its own way without any outside interference.

In expressing appreciation for the warm hospitality shown him and Mrs. Nixon, the President invited Their Imperial Majesties to visit the United States at a mutually convenient time. The invitation was accepted with deep appreciation.

NOTE: The joint communique was released in Tehran, Iran.

184 Remarks on Arrival at Warsaw, Poland. *May 31, 1972*

Mr. Chairman of the Council of Ministers and all of our distinguished guests:

We express our very deep appreciation to you for your generous words of welcome.

This, for me, is a very special moment. While I was here 13 years ago with Mrs. Nixon, I was here then in my capacity as Vice President of the United States. And now, at this very moment, for the first time in the long history and friendly history between our two countries, a President of the United States stands on Polish soil.

It is fitting that this should be so, first, because I bring greetings of friendship from all of the American people to all of the Polish people. And particularly as you, Mr. Chairman, referred to them, I bring you specially warm greetings from millions of Americans who are so proud of their Polish background.

Americans of Polish background have added enormously to the strength and the vitality and the culture of the United States.

But there is also an even more significant reason why the last stop on this journey that I have taken is here in Warsaw, and in Poland. Perhaps no people in all the world, no country in all the world, has suffered more from war than have the Polish people and the Polish nation.

President Eisenhower told me that when he visited Poland as General of the Armies in 1945, that 85 percent of Warsaw had been destroyed. I know that the strong Polish people have rebuilt your great capital city of which you are so justly proud.

But I can assure you that the major purpose of my visit here, and to the other countries that I have visited over the years that I have served in my present office, is to build a new structure of peace in the world. Poland has suffered too much from war and Poland, along with other peoples in the world, wants peace, and that is our goal: to achieve a world of peace for all nations.

I am confident that the talks that I will have with you, Mr. Chairman, and with the other representatives of the Polish Government, will contribute to our common goal of friendship between the American people and the Polish people and of peace for all the world.

Niech zyje Polska. [Long live Poland.]

NOTE: The President spoke at 4:50 p.m. at Okecie International Airport in response to the welcoming remarks of Piotr Jaroszewicz, Chairman of the Council of Ministers of the Polish People's Republic. He spoke from a prepared text.

185   Toasts of the President and Piotr Jaroszewicz, Chairman of the Council of Ministers of the Polish People's Republic, at a Dinner in Warsaw.   *May 31, 1972*

Mr. Prime Minister, Mr. Gierek, Mr. President, and all of the distinguished guests:

On behalf of all the Americans present, we express our appreciation for this beautiful dinner and for the hospitality which you have extended to us on our visit to Warsaw.

I recall that it was 13 years ago that Mrs. Nixon and I had the privilege of visiting this beautiful city. Each time we have come, the schedule has permitted us only 24 hours. All that I can say is that is an insult to our intelligence, because having visited most of the great capitals of the world, I can truthfully say that we only wish we could spend days—as a matter of fact, weeks—in this capital city of Poland.

I say that for two reasons: One, because of the traditional hospitality for which the Polish people, wherever they are in the world, are famous; and second, because the people of Poland and the Polish Government had the good sense, after their city suffered so terribly during the war, not to erect horrible monstrosities of modern buildings, but to rebuild Warsaw with the grace that it had been known for through the centuries, and if anyone claims after that remark that I do not like

653

modern architecture, he is absolutely right. I prefer the beautiful buildings of Warsaw.

As we are here tonight in Warsaw, we cannot help thinking that this city, and this country, has been often the subject of very difficult conflicts in the past, from which it has suffered. The partitions of Poland through the centuries are well known, but vivid in our memories is that Poland was the victim of aggression in 1939, that it was cruelly occupied for many long years. But now I believe we can look ahead with some assurance that the history of war and suffering which has been inflicted upon this city and this country will not repeat itself.

Last week in Moscow, major steps were taken to slow and eventually, we trust, halt the arms race. This week, treaties vital to the peace and security of Europe, and of Poland, are nearing their moment of completion. And in the months ahead, we can look forward to new progress in the building of a broad structure of friendship and cooperation throughout Europe. Already, Polish-American relations, based on a long history of friendship and of ties between our peoples, are marked by extensive programs of contact and cooperation.

After a very long discussion with Mr. Gierek today, I believe I can confidently say that this trend of cooperation between Poland and the United States will continue and be developed even further in the future.

As we move toward broader negotiations in Europe, we recognize the efforts which Poland has long made in this field. Our two countries have not always agreed on specific proposals, but we do not question the desire that we both have to live in peace and dignity. We know that Poland's

contributions to the coming negotiations will be major contributions.

In our view, the European Conference, when it meets, should have real promise of achievement. That is why we believe it should be carefully prepared.

We see particular importance in measures that will reduce the division of Europe, that will open new avenues for contact among its peoples and ideas, new opportunities for exchanging experience and knowledge.

We hope that a European Conference could elaborate realistic principles by which the states involved will conduct their relations in the decade to come. And we particularly hope that the multilateral consultations in which Poland will participate, as well as the United States— that are to take place later this year— can prepare the ground for progress in these and other areas.

Also, we should like to see early talks on the reduction of the ground forces facing each other in Europe. We recognize that this is a complex subject and we have done much intensive study of this subject within our Government and with our allies.

One objective is a reciprocal reduction of forces that will leave both sides more secure, or at least not less secure. And we hope the preparatory talks among the countries involved can get under way soon; preferably paralleling the multilateral consultations on the European Conference.

And here it is important to point out the major role that Poland, in the heart of Europe, has played in the past and will continue to play in the future in reducing the tensions that divide Europe today.

The journey that we are concluding tonight and tomorrow has been described as a "journey for peace." And to our Polish friends here tonight, I would say that to have Warsaw as the last stop of that journey is altogether appropriate.

America knows, the world knows, the fortitude, the character, the courage of the Polish people. And America knows and the world knows that no country in the world has suffered more from war than has Poland.

And so, in a very real sense, peace in the world means peace for Poland and, therefore, it is fitting that we should end in this capital what we hope will be recorded in history as a Journey for Peace.

Niech zyje przyjazn Polsko-Amerykanska. [Long live Polish-American friendship.]

To the health of all our Polish friends.

NOTE: The President spoke at 10:27 p.m. in the Palace of the Council of Ministers. He spoke from a prepared text.

Eduard Gierek was First Secretary of the Central Committee of the Polish United Workers' Party and Henryk Jablonski was President of the Council of State of the Polish People's Republic.

Chairman Jaroszewicz spoke in Polish. A translation of his toast was made available by the White House Press Office as follows:

Mr. President, Madame Nixon, ladies and gentlemen:

I am very glad to have the honor to welcome you Mr. President, Madame Nixon, and members of your party.

We hope that the first visit of a United States President in Poland's history will exert a profound influence on the development of our bilateral relations, and at the same time will make it possible to discuss a number of important international issues of interest to Poland and the United States.

Mr. President, the ties between our two nations have behind them agelong, fine traditions. Many eminent Poles had fought for independence of the United States. Millions of Polish hands and minds have participated in building the American statehood, American society, and American economy.

Neither will we ever forget that in a lifespan of a single generation we have fought twice on the same side in two World Wars. This imposes on us an obligation to cooperate in the building of peace, too.

People's Poland which has bound her fate to socialism and which is an unflinching, important unit in the community of socialist countries, has been lifted by a selfless effort from war ravages and has now considerable achievements in peaceful construction. At present, in liberating the creative energies of the Polish people, she finds herself at a stage of dynamic economic, social, scientific, and cultural development. This permits Poland to look into the future with confidence, and to assign herself new ambitious tasks on her way to modernity, mindful of the people, their prosperity and personal advancement. In carrying out our program we assign an important place—over and above our own capabilities—to development of cooperation with foreign countries. A crucial part in this cooperation is being played by socialist countries, especially our tested friend—the Soviet Union. Simultaneously we are actively advancing our relations with all countries willing to do so. We see great opportunities for substantially expanding Polish-American bilateral relations.

We welcome with satisfaction the United States interest in developing these relations. We are convinced that great possibilities exist for substantially developing Polish-American economic, scientific, and technical cooperation which has, incidentally, a good, long past record. We believe that development of economic cooperation between our countries may bring about in the near future mutual benefits in the form of multiplying our trade turnover.

May I be allowed to express the hope, Mr. President, that your visit here and our talks will greatly contribute to mutual knowledge of our standpoints and to major progress in our bilateral relations.

Mr. President, Poland's development and future are inseparably bound to world peace. From this results our activity aimed at strengthening peace and security in Europe, at holding a European Security and Cooperation Conference.

We think that the United States may bring an important, positive contribution to the cause of the European Security and Cooperation Conference. We welcome with satisfaction the United States expressed readiness to participate in the many-sided, practical preparations for this conference.

We have always held that recognition of political and territorial realities resulting from the victory over Nazi Third Reich and from postwar developments are of crucial significance for Europe's lasting peace and security, for progress, détente, and mutual trust in international relations. At present, when the treaties which Poland and the Soviet Union have concluded with the Federal Republic of Germany are becoming effective, this requirement is being met. This is particularly important because it closes the postwar chapter in European history, and opens a new one. To our people it also means that our national frontiers are universally recognized as final and are no longer disputed by anyone. The accord on West Berlin, furnishing conditions for eliminating a major source of tension, will be put into effect parallel with the treaties referred to.

General recognition of the German Democratic Republic and the Federal Republic of Germany, admission of both German states to the United Nations should be—we believe— the next, important step along the newly entered way toward a peaceful Europe.

Speaking of European affairs, dear to our heart, we remember however, that world peace is indivisible. We consider it indispensable to extinguish all hotbeds of war and tension which are a threat to world peace. In asserting this we are backed by the tragic historical experience our nation has lived through—as probably no other nation has—of the bitterness of being partitioned and of the cruel horrors of destructive wars.

Mr. President, before coming here you have had meetings and important talks with Secretary General of CPSU CC Leonid Brezhnev and other Soviet leaders. Poland welcomes with gratification the historic outcome of these talks and lends them her full support. We consider that the treaties and agreements concluded in Moscow are of fundamental importance to international détente, to consolidation of peace in the interest of all nations.

We congratulate you, Mr. President, and the leaders of the Soviet Union on this success.

We see in the results of Soviet-American talks a practical confirmation of the principle of peaceful coexistence and an indication of transition from an era of confrontation to an era of negotiations.

In this spirit, too, we welcome your arrival in Warsaw.

Ladies and gentlemen. Allow me to raise a toast:

—your health, Mr. President, and that of Madame Nixon;
—to successful progress of your visit here;
—to the health of all American guests;
—to prosperity of the American people;
—to friendship between the Polish and American peoples.

186   Toast at a Luncheon in Warsaw Honoring Polish Leaders.   *June 1, 1972*

Mr. Prime Minister, Mr. Chairman of the Council of Ministers, all of our distinguished guests:

We feel somewhat embarrassed to be the hosts in this great palace which is not ours, but yours. But this is an indication of the great hospitality which our friends from Poland have extended to us on this visit.

We shall take away many memories of this visit: the memories of the warm reception of the people of Warsaw, the memories of our very constructive talks, of the agreements which we reached. But most important, we shall take away the memories of the people at this table, the leaders of this country whom we have had the privilege to talk to face to face, man to man, and learn to know, because an agreement can be made at any time by any group of leaders, but what really matters is the continuity; what really matters is the followthrough.

Now that we know each other so well, we have the opportunity, through direct contact, to follow through on some of the great objectives we talked about in our discussions. But unless the leaders get, perhaps, too confident of their abilities, let me say that Mrs. Nixon and I agree that just as great a privilege was to meet the wives of the leaders and to have them here on this occasion.

I will only say in conclusion that tonight, while you are asleep, but when it is only 9:30 in the United States, I will be addressing the United States Congress in joint session. I will report on many things—the results of our trips to Austria, to Iran, to the Soviet Union, and, of course, to Poland. I can assure you that one of the greatest impressions that will be made upon the 500 Members of the House and Senate who will be there will

be my report that there is still that strong bond of friendship between the Polish people and the American people, because Poland has always had a special place in the hearts of Americans—from the time of our revolution, in which Poles were so helpful, through the period when we have fought side by side as allies against common enemies.

In conclusion, I can only say that we appreciate the opportunity to receive you in this magnificent room, but we also look forward to the opportunity, based on the communique that we announced today, of receiving the leaders of Poland in the White House. Now, that makes no predictions as to whether I shall be there, but you can be sure whoever is there will receive the representatives of the great Polish people with a warm heart. So, if we can raise our glasses to Polish-American friendship in the past, in the present, and for all the years to come.

NOTE: The President spoke at 1:30 p.m. in Wilanow Palace. He spoke from a prepared text.

187　Joint Communique Following Discussions With Polish Leaders. *June 1, 1972*

I.

At the invitation of the President of the Council of State of the Polish People's Republic, Mr. Henryk Jablonski, and the Chairman of the Council of Ministers, Mr. Piotr Jaroszewicz—the President of the United States, Mr. Richard Nixon, and Mrs. Nixon paid an official visit to Poland on May 31 and June 1.

On the first day of the visit, the First Secretary of the Central Committee of

the Polish United Workers' Party, Eduard Gierek, conducted talks with President Nixon.

On June 1, President Nixon called on the President of the Council of State Henryk Jablonski and had talks with him.

On the second day of the visit talks were held between First Secretary of the Central Committee of the Polish United Workers' Party Eduard Gierek, Chairman of the Council of Ministers Piotr Jaroszewicz, and President Nixon.

The following participated in the talks:

on the American side:

Secretary of State William P. Rogers

Ambassador of the United States Walter J. Stoessel, Jr.

Assistant to the President for National Security Affairs Dr. Henry Kissinger

Assistant Secretary of State for European Affairs Martin J. Hillenbrand

on the Polish side:

Vice Premier and Chairman of the Planning Commission Mieczyslaw Jagielski

Foreign Minister Stefan Olszowski

Secretary of the Central Committee of the PUWP Franciszek Szlachcic

Secretary of the Central Committee of the PUWP Jan Szydlak

Ambassador of Poland Witold Trampczynski

Minister of Science, Higher Education and Technology Jan Kaczmarek

Minister of Foreign Trade Tadeusz Olechowski

Deputy Chairman of the Planning Commission Henryk Kisiel

Vice Minister of Foreign Affairs Romuald Spasowski

Government Spokesman Undersecretary of State Wlodzimierz Janiurek

Talks were also held between Secretary of State William P. Rogers and Minister of Foreign Affairs Stefan Olszowski

During the talks, the two sides had a useful exchange of views on international questions of particular interest to them and discussed the most important subjects in the field of bilateral relations.

The talks were frank, businesslike and constructive. They were conducted in an atmosphere marked by a desire to better understand each other's position, and to expand and deepen mutual relations.

President and Mrs. Nixon expressed their warm appreciation for the hospitality they enjoyed in Poland. The President of the United States invited the First Secretary of the Central Committee of the Polish United Workers' Party, Mr. Eduard Gierek, the President of the Council of State, Mr. Henryk Jablonski, and the Prime Minister, Mr. Piotr Jaroszewicz, to visit the United States at a time convenient to both sides. The invitation was accepted with pleasure.

II.

1. Both sides agreed that the development of peaceful cooperation among states must be based on the principles of territorial integrity and inviolability of frontiers, non-interference in internal affairs, sovereign equality, independence and renunciation of the use or threat of use of force.

2. Both sides presented their views on the situation in Europe. They affirmed that the broadening of relations between all states interested in European security is of outstanding importance for world peace. Both sides welcomed the expansion of cooperation in Europe in all fields and expressed their belief that true security is indivisible and can be attained only if Europe is considered as a whole. The relations between the United States and Poland, based on sovereign equality and mutual respect, contribute to peace and stability in Europe and to the favorable development of the overall international situation.

3. Both sides welcomed the treaty between Poland and the Federal Republic of Germany signed on December 7, 1970, including its border provisions. They noted the significance of the provisions of

this treaty as well as of other recent agreements in contributing to confidence and cooperation among the European states.

4. Both sides agreed that a reciprocal reduction of armed forces and armaments, first of all in Central Europe, would contribute to the goal of ensuring security and stability in Europe. Any agreement reached on this matter should not diminish the security of any of the sides. The two sides agreed that the states concerned should reach appropriate agreement as soon as practicable on procedures for negotiations on this question in a special forum. Reduction of armed forces and armaments in Central Europe would be an important step toward attaining the objective of general and complete disarmament.

5. Both sides expressed the belief that a European Conference on Security and Cooperation may constitute an important step forward in the extensive and long-range process of the normalization of relations and detente in Europe. They agreed that the Conference should be carefully prepared, and that multilateral consultations in that regard should begin without undue delay. The two sides declared their readiness to cooperate to achieve this aim.

6. Both sides presented their known positions on the war in Vietnam and the situation in Indochina. Essential views of the two sides in this question remained divergent.

III.

1. Both sides noted with satisfaction the increasing commercial and other economic ties between the two countries and concluded that there are considerable possibilities for their further expansion. With this in mind the two sides discussed issues related to commercial exchange and financial and credit matters.

The Polish side indicated an interest in increased purchases of capital goods, licenses and technology in the United States.

The U.S. side undertook to consider in a constructive manner further steps leading to increased bilateral trade and economic cooperation.

2. The two sides will exchange information leading to expanded trade relations. In the interest of broadening and facilitating trade relations between the two countries and working out concrete steps towards that end the two sides decided to create a joint Polish-American Trade Commission.

3. The two sides will encourage and support contacts and cooperation between economic organizations and enterprises of both countries.

4. The two sides expressed their satisfaction with the expanding program of scientific and technical cooperation and appraised positively its mutually advantageous results. Last year's exchange of visits at the cabinet level, which gave attention to the development of scientific and technical cooperation, confirmed the desirability of continuing cooperation in this field.

The two sides expressed their interest in the conclusion of an intergovernmental agreement on comprehensive cooperation in science, technology and culture. Appropriate institutional arrangements will be established to promote work in these fields.

5. The two sides agreed that the increase of mutual economic and personal contacts, including tourism, justifies further development of transportation links between Poland and the United States by sea as well as by air. The two sides expect to sign in the near future an air transport

659

agreement and to establish mutual and regular air connections.

6. The two sides expressed their interest in commemorating the five hundredth anniversary of the birth of Nicholas Copernicus and discussed ways of celebrating it.

7. Both sides welcomed the signing of the Consular Convention by Secretary of State William P. Rogers and Minister of Foreign Affairs Stefan Olszowski and the conclusion of an agreement on the simultaneous establishment on December 1, 1972 of new Consulates—in New York and Krakow, respectively. Both parties welcome these steps as concrete evidence of expanding relations between the two states.

8. The two sides emphasized the positive influence exerted on their mutual relations by the traditions of history, sentiment and friendship between the Polish and American peoples. A prominent part is played in this respect by many United States citizens of Polish extraction who maintain an interest in the country of their ancestors. The two sides recognize that this interest and contacts resulting from it constitute a valuable contribution to the development of bilateral relations.

Signed in Warsaw, June 1, 1972.

NOTE: The joint communique was released at Warsaw, Poland.

On the same day, the White House released the transcript of a news briefing by Ronald L. Ziegler, Press Secretary to the President, and Wlodzimierz Janiurek, Polish Undersecretary of State for Information, on the joint communique.

On May 31, 1972, the White House released the text of a statement by Secretary of State William P. Rogers on signing the U.S.-Polish Consular Convention and a fact sheet outlining the terms of the convention. Secretary Rogers' statement is printed in the Weekly Compilation of Presidential Documents (vol. 8, p. 970).

188   Address to a Joint Session of the Congress on Return From Austria, the Soviet Union, Iran, and Poland.
June 1, 1972

Mr. Speaker, Mr. President, Members of the Congress, our distinguished guests, my fellow Americans:

Your welcome in this great Chamber tonight has a very special meaning to Mrs. Nixon and to me. We feel very fortunate to have traveled abroad so often representing the United States of America. But we both agree after each journey that the best part of any trip abroad is coming home to America again.

During the past 13 days we have flown more than 16,000 miles and we visited four countries. Everywhere we went—to Austria, the Soviet Union, Iran, Poland—

we could feel the quickening pace of change in old international relationships and the peoples' genuine desire for friendship for the American people. Everywhere new hopes are rising for a world no longer shadowed by fear and want and war, and as Americans we can be proud that we now have an historic opportunity to play a great role in helping to achieve man's oldest dream—a world in which all nations can enjoy the blessings of peace.

On this journey we saw many memorable sights, but one picture will always remain indelible in our memory—the flag of the United States of America flying high in the spring breeze above Moscow's ancient Kremlin fortress.

To millions of Americans for the past quarter century the Kremlin has stood for implacable hostility toward all that we cherish, and to millions of Russians the American flag has long been held up as a symbol of evil. No one would have believed, even a short time ago, that these two apparently irreconcilable symbols would be seen together as we saw them for those few days.

But this does not mean that we bring back from Moscow the promise of instant peace, but we do bring the beginning of a process that can lead to a lasting peace. And that is why I have taken the extraordinary action of requesting this special joint session of the Congress because we have before us an extraordinary opportunity.

I have not come here this evening to make new announcements in a dramatic setting. This summit has already made its news. It has barely begun, however, to make its mark on our world, and I ask you to join me tonight—while events are fresh, while the iron is hot—in starting to consider how we can help to make that mark what we want it to be.

The foundation has been laid for a new relationship between the two most powerful nations in the world. Now it is up to us—to all of us here in this Chamber, to all of us across America—to join with other nations in building a new house upon that foundation, one that can be a home for the hopes of mankind and a shelter against the storms of conflict.

As a preliminary, therefore, to requesting your concurrence in some of the agreements we reached and your approval of funds to carry out others, and also as a keynote for the unity in which this Government and this Nation must go forward from here, I am rendering this immediate report to the Congress on the results of the Moscow summit.

The pattern of U.S.-Soviet summit diplomacy in the cold war era is well known to all those in this Chamber. One meeting after another produced a brief euphoric mood—the spirit of Geneva, the spirit of Camp David, the spirit of Vienna, the spirit of Glassboro—but without producing significant progress on the really difficult issues.

And so early in this Administration I stated that the prospect of concrete results, not atmospherics, would be our criterion for meetings at the highest level. I also announced our intention to pursue negotiations with the Soviet Union across a broad front of related issues, with the purpose of creating a momentum of achievement in which progress in one area could contribute to progress in others.

This is the basis on which we prepared for and conducted last week's talks. This was a working summit. We sought to establish not a superficial spirit of Moscow, but a solid record of progress on solving the difficult issues which for so long have divided our two nations and also have divided the world. Reviewing the number and the scope of agreements that emerged, I think we have accomplished that goal.

Recognizing the responsibility of the advanced industrial nations to set an example in combatting mankind's common enemies, the United States and the Soviet Union have agreed to cooperate in efforts to reduce pollution and enhance environmental quality. We have agreed to work together in the field of medical science and public health, particularly in the conquest of cancer and heart disease.

661

Recognizing that the quest for useful knowledge transcends differences between ideologies and social systems, we have agreed to expand United States and Soviet cooperation in many areas of science and technology.

We have joined in plans for an exciting new adventure, a new adventure in the cooperative exploration of space, which will begin—subject to Congressional approval of funding—with a joint orbital mission of an Apollo vehicle and a Soviet spacecraft in 1975.

By forming habits of cooperation and strengthening institutional ties in areas of peaceful enterprise, these four agreements, to which I have referred, will create on both sides a steadily growing vested interest in the maintenance of good relations between our two countries.

Expanded United States-Soviet trade will also yield advantages to both of our nations. When the two largest economies in the world start trading with each other on a much larger scale, living standards in both nations will rise, and the stake which both have in peace will increase.

Progress in this area is proceeding on schedule. At the summit, we established a Joint Commercial Commission which will complete the negotiations for a comprehensive trade agreement between the United States and the U.S.S.R. And we expect the final terms of this agreement to be settled later this year.

Two further accords which were reached last week have a much more direct bearing on the search for peace and security in the world.

One is the agreement between the American and Soviet navies aimed at significantly reducing the chances of dangerous incidents between our ships and aircraft at sea.

And second, and most important, there is the treaty and the related executive agreement which will limit, for the first time, both offensive and defensive strategic nuclear weapons in the arsenals of the United States and the Soviet Union.

Three-fifths of all the people alive in the world today have spent their whole lifetimes under the shadow of a nuclear war which could be touched off by the arms race among the great powers. Last Friday in Moscow we witnessed the beginning of the end of that era which began in 1945. We took the first step toward a new era of mutually agreed restraint and arms limitation between the two principal nuclear powers.

With this step we have enhanced the security of both nations. We have begun to check the wasteful and dangerous spiral of nuclear arms which has dominated relations between our two countries for a generation. We have begun to reduce the level of fear by reducing the causes of fear, for our two peoples and for all peoples in the world.

The ABM Treaty will be submitted promptly for the Senate's advice and consent to ratification and the interim agreement limiting certain offensive weapons will be submitted to both Houses for concurrence, because we can undertake agreements as important as these only on a basis of full partnership between the executive and legislative branches of our Government.

I ask from this Congress and I ask from the Nation the fullest scrutiny of these accords. I am confident such examination will underscore the truth of what I told the Soviet people on television just a few nights ago—that this is an agreement in the interest of both nations. From the standpoint of the United States, when we

662

consider what the strategic balance would have looked like later in the seventies, if there had been no arms limitation, it is clear that the agreements forestall a major spiraling of the arms race—one which would have worked to our disadvantage, since we have no current building programs for the categories of weapons which have been frozen, and since no new building program could have produced any new weapons in those categories during the period of the freeze.

My colleagues in the Congress, I have studied the strategic balance in great detail with my senior advisers for more than 3 years. I can assure you, the Members of the Congress, and the American people tonight that the present and planned strategic forces of the United States are without question sufficient for the maintenance of our security and the protection of our vital interests.

No power on earth is stronger than the United States of America today. And none will be stronger than the United States of America in the future.

This is the only national defense posture which can ever be acceptable to the United States. This is the posture I ask the Senate and the Congress to protect by approving the arms limitation agreements to which I have referred. This is the posture which, with the responsible cooperation of the Congress, I will take all necessary steps to maintain in our future defense programs.

In addition to the talks which led to the specific agreements I have listed, I also had full, very frank, and extensive discussions with General Secretary Brezhnev and his colleagues about several parts of the world where American and Soviet interests have come in conflict.

With regard to the reduction of tensions in Europe, we recorded our intention of proceeding later this year with multilateral consultations looking toward a conference on security and cooperation in all of Europe. We have also jointly agreed to move forward with negotiations on mutual and balanced force reductions in central Europe.

The problem of ending the Vietnam war, which engages the hopes of all Americans, was one of the most extensively discussed subjects on our agenda. It would only jeopardize the search for peace if I were to review here all that was said on that subject. I will simply say this: Each side obviously has its own point of view and its own approach to this very difficult issue. But at the same time, both the United States and the Soviet Union share an overriding desire to achieve a more stable peace in the world. I emphasize to you once again that this Administration has no higher goal, a goal that I know all of you share, than bringing the Vietnam war to an early and honorable end. We are ending the war in Vietnam, but we shall end it in a way which will not betray our friends, risk the lives of the courageous Americans still serving in Vietnam, break faith with those held prisoners by the enemy, or stain the honor of the United States of America.

Another area where we had very full, frank, and extensive discussions was the Middle East. I reiterated the American people's commitment to the survival of the state of Israel and to a settlement just to all the countries in the area. Both sides stated in the communique their intention to support the Jarring peace mission and other appropriate efforts to achieve this objective.

The final achievement of the Moscow conference was the signing of a landmark declaration entitled "Basic Principles of Mutual Relations Between the United States and the U.S.S.R." As these 12 basic principles are put into practice, they can provide a solid framework for the future development of better American-Soviet relations.

They begin with the recognition that two nuclear nations, each of which has the power to destroy humanity, have no alternative but to coexist peacefully, because in a nuclear war there would be no winners, only losers.

The basic principles commit both sides to avoid direct military confrontation and to exercise constructive leadership and restraint with respect to smaller conflicts in other parts of the world which could drag the major powers into war.

They disavow any intention to create spheres of influence or to conspire against the interests of any other nation—a point I would underscore by saying once again tonight that America values its ties with all nations, from our oldest allies in Europe and Asia, as I emphasized by my visit to Iran, to our good friends in the third world, and to our new relationship with the People's Republic of China.

The improvement of relations depends not only, of course, on words, but far more on actions. The principles to which we agreed in Moscow are like a road map. Now that the map has been laid out, it is up to each country to follow it. The United States intends to adhere to these principles. The leaders of the Soviet Union have indicated a similar intention.

However, we must remember that Soviet ideology still proclaims hostility to some of America's most basic values. The Soviet leaders remain committed to that ideology. Like the nation they lead, they are and they will continue to be totally dedicated competitors of the United States of America.

As we shape our policies for the period ahead, therefore, we must maintain our defenses at an adequate level until there is mutual agreement to limit forces. The time-tested policies of vigilance and firmness which have brought us to this summit are the only ones that can safely carry us forward to further progress in reaching agreements to reduce the danger of war.

Our successes in the strategic arms talks and in the Berlin negotiations, which opened the road to Moscow, came about because over the past 3 years we have consistently refused proposals for unilaterally abandoning the ABM, unilaterally pulling back our forces from Europe, and drastically cutting the defense budget. The Congress deserves the appreciation of the American people for having the courage to vote such proposals down and to maintain the strength America needs to protect its interests.

As we continue the strategic arms talks, seeking a permanent offensive weapons treaty, we must bear the lessons of the earlier talks well in mind.

By the same token, we must stand steadfastly with our NATO partners if negotiations leading to a new détente and a mutual reduction of forces in Europe are to be productive. Maintaining the strength, integrity, and steadfastness of our free world alliances is the foundation on which all of our other initiatives for peace and security in the world must rest. As we seek better relations with those who have been our adversaries, we will not let down our friends and allies around the world.

And in this period we must keep our economy vigorous and competitive if the opening for greater East-West trade is to mean anything at all, and if we do not wish to be shouldered aside in world markets by the growing potential of the economies of Japan, Western Europe, the Soviet Union, the People's Republic of China. For America to continue its role of helping to build a more peaceful world, we must keep America number one economically in the world.

We must maintain our own momentum of domestic innovation, growth, and reform if the opportunities for joint action with the Soviets are to fulfill their promise. As we seek agreements to build peace abroad, we must keep America moving forward at home.

Most importantly, if the new age we seek is ever to become a reality, we must keep America strong in spirit—a nation proud of its greatness as a free society, confident of its mission in the world. Let us be committed to our way of life as wholeheartedly as the Communist leaders with whom we seek a new relationship are committed to their system. Let us always be proud to show in our words and actions what we know in our hearts—that we believe in America.

These are just some of the challenges of peace. They are in some ways even more difficult than the challenges of war. But we are equal to them. As we meet them, we will be able to go forward and explore the sweeping possibilities for peace which this season of summits has now opened up for the world.

For decades, America has been locked in hostile confrontation with the two great Communist powers, the Soviet Union and the People's Republic of China. We were engaged with the one at many points and almost totally isolated from the other, but our relationships with both had reached a deadly impasse. All three countries were

victims of the kind of bondage about which George Washington long ago warned in these words: The nation which indulges toward another an habitual hatred . . . is a slave to its own animosity.

But now in the brief space of 4 months, these journeys to Peking and to Moscow have begun to free us from perpetual confrontation. We have moved toward better understanding, mutual respect, point-by-point settlement of differences with both the major Communist powers.

This one series of meetings has not rendered an imperfect world suddenly perfect. There still are deep philosophical differences; there still are parts of the world in which age-old hatreds persist. The threat of war has not been eliminated—it has been reduced. We are making progress toward a world in which leaders of nations will settle their differences by negotiation, not by force, and in which they learn to live with their differences so that their sons will not have to die for those differences.

It was particularly fitting that this trip, aimed at building such a world, should have concluded in Poland.

No country in the world has suffered more from war than Poland—and no country has more to gain from peace. The faces of the people who gave us such a heartwarming welcome in Warsaw yesterday, and then again this morning and this afternoon, told an eloquent story of suffering from war in the past and of hope for peace in the future. One could see it in their faces. It made me more determined than ever that America must do all in its power to help that hope for peace come true for all people in the world.

As we continue that effort, our unity of purpose and action will be all-important.

665

For the summits of 1972 have not belonged just to one person or to one party or to one branch of our Government alone. Rather they are part of a great national journey for peace. Every American can claim a share in the credit for the success of that journey so far, and every American has a major stake in its success for the future.

An unparalleled opportunity has been placed in America's hands. Never has there been a time when hope was more justified or when complacency was more dangerous. We have made a good beginning. And because we have begun, history now lays upon us a special obligation to see it through. We can seize this moment or we can lose it; we can make good this opportunity to build a new structure of peace in the world or we can let it slip away. Together, therefore, let us seize the moment so that our children and the world's children can live free of the fears and free of the hatreds that have been the lot of mankind through the centuries.

Then the historians of some future age will write of the year 1972, not that this was the year America went up to the summit and then down to the depths of the valley again, but that this was the year when America helped to lead the world up out of the lowlands of constant war, and onto the high plateau of lasting peace.

NOTE: The President spoke at 9:40 p.m. in the House Chamber at the Capitol, after being introduced by Carl Albert, Speaker of the House of Representatives. The address was broadcast live on radio and television.

The President spoke from a prepared text. An advance text of his address was released on the same day.

On June 2, 1972, the bipartisan leaders of the Congress met with the President at the White House for a review of his trip and the agreements reached.

189 Telegram to the National Governors' Conference Meeting in Houston, Texas, Urging State Action on No-Fault Automobile Insurance. *June 7, 1972*

IT IS a pleasure to send my greetings and my high regards to the Governors of our States. Each of you is a full and vital partner in our common effort to provide better, more effective and more responsive government for all our people.

I know the Governors share my abiding interest in preserving and strengthening a truly federal system in the United States in which all levels of government—Federal, State and local—share in their proper responsibilities.

This results in problems being solved on the level of government which can be most effective on each particular issue. Some problems clearly require Federal remedies, and we have moved to provide them. Many other matters, however, can be handled most effectively by State and local governments, with Washington acting in a supporting role.

On one such important matter, I believe that the States—and not the Federal Government—can best respond to one of the most pressing consumer needs in the Nation today: the urgent question of reform for the present system of automobile insurance. I oppose involving the Federal Government in this insurance reform, and I urge the States to act.

Despite ever-increasing premiums for automobile insurance, the victims of accidents frequently receive inadequate compensation and usually experience harmful delays in the courts.

The best-known alternative to this inefficient and inequitable reparations system is the "no-fault" automobile insurance concept—which provides, in general, that an accident victim's losses are covered by his own insuring company no matter who caused the accident.

I have endorsed this system because I consider it to be a vast improvement and a genuine reform for the benefit of the consuming public.

No-fault insurance is an idea whose time has come. The concept has been gaining wide acceptance, despite the fact that some powerful groups—with a special interest in maintaining the present system— have arrayed themselves against reform.

The achievement of real automobile insurance reform through adoption of the no-fault principles would be a particularly effective way of demonstrating the responsiveness and farsightedness of State governments. I commend those States which already have moved on this important question. I urge that the other States, building on the experience gained so far, make the enactment of no-fault automobile insurance a matter of top consumer priority.

RICHARD NIXON

NOTE: The telegram, dated June 6, 1972, was addressed to Gov. Arch A. Moore, Jr., of West Virginia, Chairman of the National Governors' Conference. The text was released June 7.

190   White House Statement on the Death of John Paul Vann.   *June* 9, 1972

IT IS with a profound sense of sorrow that the President learned today of the tragic death of John Paul Vann.

The President feels John Vann was one of America's finest citizens—and a truly extraordinary public servant. For more than a decade, he worked tirelessly in the forefront of our efforts to achieve an honorable peace in Southeast Asia and to bind up the wounds of its ravaged peoples. After his initial service as a military officer in Vietnam, he returned to that country to continue his devoted work as a civilian. There he has now given "the last full measure of devotion."

The President wants to say that, as honest and outspoken as he was committed, John Paul Vann did nothing in a half-hearted manner. For him, any work that was worth his undertaking was worth his very best—and that always meant a truly exceptional effort.

John Paul Vann will be deeply missed, by the people of Vietnam who came to know and love him, and also by his fellow Americans who have taken such pride in his contributions. His fervent dedication to peace and freedom will be a continuing inspiration to all of us.

On behalf of all Americans, the President and Mrs. Nixon extend to Mr. Vann's family and friends their deepest sympathy.

NOTE: Press Secretary Ronald L. Ziegler read the statement at his regular news briefing at the White House on June 9, 1972.

Mr. Vann, 47, died in a helicopter crash near Kontum in the Central Highlands of South Vietnam. He served in the military from 1942 to 1963, attaining the rank of lieutenant colonel, and was senior adviser for the Army to

667

the 7th Vietnamese Division from 1962 to 1963. He was an adviser for the Agency for International Development in South Vietnam from 1965 and was Senior U.S. Adviser of the Second Regional Command, Civil Operations and Rural Development Support, from May 1971.

Secretary of State William P. Rogers represented the President at the burial services at Arlington National Cemetery.

On June 16, the President met with members of the Vann family at the White House where he awarded the Presidential Medal of Freedom posthumously to Mr. Vann. John Allen Vann, Mr. Vann's son, received the medal on behalf of his family. On the same day, the White House released the text of the citation accompanying the medal, which read as follows:

Soldier of peace and patriot of two nations, the name of John Paul Vann will be honored as long as free men remember the struggle to preserve the independence of South Vietnam. His military and civilian service in Vietnam spanned a decade, marked throughout by resourcefulness, professional excellence and unsurpassed courage; by supreme dedication and personal sacrifice. A truly noble American, a superb leader, he stands with Lafayette in that gallery of heroes who have made another brave people's cause their own.

191   Telegram to President Georges Pompidou of France Commending the French Government's Contribution of Facilities at Lyons to the International Agency for Research on Cancer. *June 9, 1972*

Dear Mr. President:

Because of my own deep personal interest in ensuring that everything possible is being done to expedite the campaign against cancer, I take this opportunity to warmly commend the Government of France for its generous contribution of new modern facilities to the International Agency for Research on Cancer. This action on the part of the French Government is impressive evidence of its dedication to a cause in which all nations can join—the search for effective cures to the dread disease of cancer.

The work of the International Agency for Research on Cancer during its relatively brief existence since 1965 has received wide recognition among the world leaders in cancer research. Intensive international efforts such as this are urgently needed to contribute vital new knowledge in this critical field.

Our own National Cancer Act of 1971 emphasizes the importance of supporting international programs as an essential component of the Cancer Study Program of the United States. Success in this endeavor depends on a universal sharing of knowledge and collaborative attacks on cancer without regard to national boundaries or political divisions.

The United States is proud to be a charter member of the International Agency for Research on Cancer. I pledge the strong and continuing support of my country to its important work. We are grateful to the Government of France for making it possible for the staff to have excellent physical facilities in which to conduct their urgently needed studies.

Sincerely,

RICHARD NIXON

NOTE: The text of the telegram was posted for the press.

668

192   Letter to Senate Leaders About the Foreign Assistance Authorization Bill.   *June* 10, 1972

IN MY special report to the joint session of the Congress on June 1, the evening of my return from the summit discussions in Moscow, I said that the door to the agreements that we reached there had been opened because the United States had maintained the strength it needed to protect its interests. A vital and indispensable element of that strength has been our continuing security assistance program.

The Foreign Assistance Authorization bill for fiscal year 1973, a significant portion of which is devoted to security assistance, is of direct and fundamental importance to the continued maintenance of our strength and the protection of our interests. As you know, the Senate will soon begin consideration of this bill, S. 3390.

At Guam in 1969, I made clear that the United States would look increasingly to its friends and allies to play a greater role in providing for their own defense. Since that time we have moved forward steadily toward that objective with full recognition that our own security depends importantly upon the independence, the progress and the stability of our friends. But if we are to reach that goal, we must help others to develop the ability to defend themselves. My Foreign Assistance program requests for fiscal year 1973 are based on these imperatives.

The severe cuts in my fiscal year 1972 requests, and the restrictive amendments which were imposed, significantly limited our ability to move toward the basic objectives of the program—the maintenance of the strength necessary to secure a lasting peace.

When I forwarded my fiscal year 1973 requests on March 10 [14], 1972, I reported that the foreign assistance appropriations for fiscal year 1972 were below the minimum level required to attain our foreign policy and national security goals. Such reductions and restrictions, if imposed by the Congress again in 1973, will call into serious question the firmness of our commitments abroad. Such Congressional action could have a destabilizing effect at a time when confidence in our support and perseverance will be critically needed.

In recent months we have taken bold and decisive steps in our continuing search for peace. I believe that through these efforts we have done much to enhance America's security and that of the entire world, primarily by diminishing the likelihood of direct confrontation with the Soviet Union and the People's Republic of China. Though we are making every effort to expand on these initial and significant steps, the process of building the structure of lasting peace will be long and arduous.

I share with you the desire to withdraw our remaining forces from Indochina in a timely and honorable manner. But Congressional amendments which can be misconstrued by our adversaries to be hostile to my peace proposals of May 8 do not serve this objective. As I have reported to you and to the people of the United States, we are continuing to pursue every possible avenue toward peace in Southeast Asia. I have made clear to the North Vietnamese that we are fully prepared to participate in meaningful negotiations to achieve a settlement and I am hopeful that they will be convinced that such negotiations are in the best interests of all parties.

I am firmly convinced that the achievement of our purposes—in Vietnam and elsewhere—will be far more likely if this bill is passed in substantially the form in which I submitted it. As brought to the floor, however, the bill is incompatible with these objectives.

I have always appreciated the assistance you have given me in formulating programs to ensure this nation's welfare and security. We seek the same ends—the maintenance of our strength and will, a lessening of tensions and an amelioration of the plight of the less privileged. I am confident that I can count on your firm support in the further pursuit of the goals.

Sincerely,

RICHARD NIXON

NOTE: Identical letters, dated June 9, 1972, were addressed to the Honorable Mike Mansfield, Majority Leader, United States Senate, and the Honorable Hugh Scott, Minority Leader, United States Senate. The text of the letters was released by the White House on June 10.

193   White House Statement About Floods in Rapid City, South Dakota. *June* 10, 1972

THE PRESIDENT has been following closely the reports from Rapid City, and is deeply distressed at the loss of life and the widespread destruction. He has directed General Lincoln, the Director of the Office of Emergency Preparedness, to keep personally in touch with the situation and to ensure that all appropriate help is given. The President feels that the hearts of Americans everywhere will go out to the families of those who have been lost, to those who have been left homeless, and to the many others who have suffered from this sudden and terrible disaster.

NOTE: Press Secretary Ronald L. Ziegler made the statement available to the press on June 10, 1972.

On the same day, the White House released an announcement of disaster declaration and Federal assistance for South Dakota following heavy rains and flooding. The announcement is printed in the Weekly Compilation of Presidential Documents (vol. 8, p. 1007).

On June 12, Robert H. Finch, Counsellor to the President, visited Rapid City to confer with the mayor on disaster assistance following the floods. The White House also announced a series of activities of Federal and private agencies engaged in assistance efforts.

On June 18, Mrs. Nixon attended memorial services for flood victims in Rapid City.

194   Remarks at the Swearing In of New Cabinet Officials. *June* 12, 1972

Mr. Vice President, members of the Cabinet, Members of the Congress, and all of our distinguished guests:

We, of course, are delighted to have all of you here today, but we are particularly delighted and proud to have the Chief Justice of the United States. We have a number of swearings in from time to time, but we seldom impose on him. Since this is one of those occasions when three members of the President's Cabinet are going to be sworn in, the Chief Justice was able to work it into his schedule, and we are very happy that he will be the presiding officer for this occasion.

We will swear in the new members of the Cabinet in the order that they were appointed. The first will be the Attorney General of the United States. I will make brief remarks about each, and after I have made my remarks, if the appointee, or the man who has been confirmed, will please step up with his wife, who will hold the Bible for the ceremony, then the Chief Justice will swear them in.

As far as the Attorney General is concerned, everybody is aware that I appointed him several months ago. [*Laughter*] When I called him the day of his confirmation, he said it seemed like several years ago.

But in any event, he has been, as all of you know, one of my very close friends over many, many years. But beyond that, he has been one of the very able men in this Administration, serving as Deputy Attorney General. I had great confidence in his intellectual capacity, in his honesty and his integrity, in his devotion to the law of this land, when I appointed him as Attorney General.

The long ordeal to which he was submitted when he went to the Senate for confirmation in no way reduced that confidence. As a matter of fact, it increased it, because, as many of you have heard me say on occasion, a great ship is not tested by smooth sailing, only by rough seas. Only when a man has been through adversity do you find out how really strong he is.

Richard Kleindienst, I always knew, was intellectually capable. I always knew that he had total loyalty and devotion to this country, but now there is no question that here is a man who is strong in character and who is at his best when the going is roughest. He will be a great At-

torney General. And now, to be sworn in as the 68th Attorney General of the United States of America, Richard Kleindienst.

[At this point, Warren E. Burger, Chief Justice of the United States, administered the oath of office to Attorney General Kleindienst. The President then resumed speaking.]

The next member of the Cabinet to be sworn in did not have quite the ordeal that Mr. Kleindienst has. As a matter of fact, when I called him the day that the Senate confirmed him, I congratulated him on winning with such a close vote. [*Laughter*]

I do want you to know that the Senate's confirmation of him unanimously, however, only underlined the fact that when we tried to find the man to succeed Secretary John Connally, the decision was also a unanimous one. I remembered having a long discussion with Secretary Connally at the time that the decision was made that he would have to leave the Cabinet, and independently we both reached the conclusion, unanimously between the two of us—[*laughter*]— that the man best qualified, the first choice for the next Secretary of the Treasury would be George Shultz.

You all know his years of Government service as Secretary of Labor, as Director of the Office of Budget and Management. You also, of course, are aware of the fact that he has an unusual combination of qualities which qualify him for this position. He is a fiscal expert. He is a very respected economist. In addition to that, he has demonstrated ability in the field of organization in running a huge department, a very important department, and has, of course, particular competence in the field of international economics, which is one of the special responsibilities of the Secretary of the Treasury.

671

We are very proud to have him here to be sworn in as the 62d Secretary of the Treasury of the United States, Mr. George Shultz.

[At this point, Chief Justice Burger administered the oath of office to Secretary of the Treasury Shultz. The President then resumed speaking.]

Just for the Secretary of the Treasury's, at least, protection from any attack that might be made upon him, I think the record must show that when he assumed this position he took a $20,000 salary cut, when he left the Cabinet, the position of Secretary of Labor, to take the other Cabinet position of Director of the new Office of Budget and Management. He now gets a $20,000 salary increase, but that is not in violation of the law. [*Laughter*]

I have known, of course, both of the two outstanding members of the Cabinet, the Secretary of the Treasury and the Attorney General, for a number of years, but the new Director of the Office of Budget and Management is a man I have known longer than either of those two. Going back to the early days in California when I first met him, in the year 1949, I have respected him as an outstanding lawyer, as an outstanding State legislator, as an outstanding servant of the State of California as its director of the budget, and then as the director of the budget under George Shultz here in Washington after serving a very splendid term as Chairman of the Federal Trade Commission.

To add any adjectives with regard to his record would be certainly gilding the lily a bit. I will simply say this: He is a man who has demonstrated extraordinary intellectual capacity. He has, certainly, managerial ability, and beyond that, he has that total integrity and fearlessness in carrying out the duties of an office that we need in a public servant. We are very proud to have Caspar Weinberger as the new Director of the Office of Budget and Management.

[At this point, Chief Justice Burger administered the oath of office to Director of the Office of Management and Budget Weinberger. The President then resumed speaking.]

Ladies and gentlemen, if you will bear with us for just a moment, for purposes of a photograph, we would like all of the three new members of the Cabinet and their wives, and Mrs. Nixon, please, to step up for a photograph that all of you might enjoy having.

I understand that many Members of Congress have to get back up to the Hill, and that others may have to leave, but for all of those who have the time, we would like very much now to receive you in the Blue Room so that you can congratulate the new appointees, and also for coffee and tea and, I understand, some cakes that are available in the State Dining Room.

Incidentally, the cakes were baked freshly this morning. I wanted to make sure, because I realize that this is the first anniversary of the Rose Garden wedding. This is not the wedding cake from last year. [*Laughter*]

Thank you.

NOTE: The President spoke at 11:23 a.m. in the East Room at the White House. He spoke without referring to notes.

195 Message to the Congress Transmitting Annual Reports of Five River Basin Commissions. *June* 12, 1972

To the Congress of the United States:

I am pleased to transmit herewith the annual reports of the five river basin commissions established under the Water Resources Planning Act of 1965. These reports are from commissions that have been set up in the Pacific Northwest River Basins, the Souris-Red-Rainy River Basins, the Great Lakes Basin, the New England River Basins, and the Ohio River Basin and reflect the accomplishments of each commission during Fiscal Year 1971.

The primary responsibility of each commission is to develop plans for the best use of its water and related land resources, and to recommend priorities for implementing its plans. These commissions, though comprised of State and Federal members, are established at the initiation of the Governors of the States involved within the commission areas. They are unique in that they are neither wholly Federal nor State, but rather jointly financed partnerships working to develop the resources of their respective regions.

The commissions provide an opportunity for all interested persons, especially the residents of the river basins, to contribute to water resource planning. This has become particularly important in recent years because the wise use of our natural heritage is a critical public concern.

The substantial number of programs which these commissions have already begun will help to meet both existing and emerging problems of water and land use within their regions. They are also making studies that will promote effective solutions, with full recognition of the need both to preserve and to enhance the environment.

RICHARD NIXON

The White House,
June 12, 1972.

NOTE: The five reports are entitled:
Pacific Northwest River Basins Commission: Annual Report for Fiscal Year Ending June 30, 1971 (44 pp.).
Souris-Red-Rainy River Basins Commission: Annual Report—Fiscal Year 1971 (45 pp.).
Great Lakes Basin Commission: Annual Report—Fiscal Year Ending June 30, 1971 (21 pp.).
New England River Basins Commission: Annual Report—Fiscal Year 1971 (51 pp.).
Ohio River Basin Commission: Annual Report—Fiscal Year Ending June 30, 1971 (8 pp.).

196 Remarks on Transmitting to the Congress the Antiballistic Missile Treaty and the Interim Agreement on Strategic Offensive Arms. *June* 13, 1972

I AM sending to the Congress today the nuclear arms limitation agreements that I negotiated with the Soviet leaders in Moscow.

I am convinced that these agreements are in the security interest of the United States. They will enable the United States to maintain defenses second to none, defenses that will protect the interests of the United States at home and abroad.

I believe that prompt approval by the Senate of the treaty limiting defensive weapons and prompt approval by the Congress of the agreement limiting certain classes of offensive weapons will contribute to the goal that I know all Americans share—a goal of ending the arms race and building a more peaceful world.

NOTE: The President's remarks were filmed in the Family Theater at the White House for later broadcast on radio and television.

On the same day, the White House released a letter from Secretary of State William P. Rogers transmitting to the President the ABM Treaty and the Interim Agreement on Strategic Offensive Arms, with agreed interpretations and unilateral statements. The letter, dated June 10, 1972, is printed in the Weekly Compilation of Presidential Documents (vol. 8, p. 1027).

197   Message to the Senate Transmitting the Antiballistic Missile Treaty and the Interim Agreement on Strategic Offensive Arms.   *June 13, 1972*

To the Senate of the United States:

I transmit herewith the Treaty on the Limitation of Anti-Ballistic Missile Systems and the Interim Agreement on Certain Measures with respect to the Limitation of Strategic Offensive Arms signed in Moscow on May 26, 1972. Copies of these agreements are also being forwarded to the Speaker of the House of Representatives. I ask the Senate's advice and consent to ratification of the Treaty, and an expression of support from both Houses of the Congress for the Interim Agreement on Strategic Offensive Arms.

These agreements, the product of a major effort of this administration, are a significant step into a new era of mutually agreed restraint and arms limitation between the two principal nuclear powers.

The provisions of the agreements are explained in detail in the Report of the Secretary of State, which I attach. Their main effect is this: The ABM Treaty limits the deployment of anti-ballistic missile systems to two designated areas, and at a low level. The Interim Agreement limits the overall level of strategic offensive missile forces. Together the two agreements

provide for a more stable strategic balance in the next several years than would be possible if strategic arms competition continued unchecked. This benefits not only the United States and the Soviet Union, but all the nations of the world.

The agreements are an important first step in checking the arms race, but only a first step; they do not close off all avenues of strategic competition. Just as the maintenance of a strong strategic posture was an essential element in the success of these negotiations, it is now equally essential that we carry forward a sound strategic modernization program to maintain our security and to ensure that more permanent and comprehensive arms limitation agreements can be reached.

The defense capabilities of the United States are second to none in the world today. I am determined that they shall remain so. The terms of the ABM Treaty and Interim Agreement will permit the United States to take the steps we deem necessary to maintain a strategic posture which protects our vital interests and guarantees our continued security.

Besides enhancing our national security, these agreements open the opportunity for a new and more constructive U.S.-Soviet relationship, characterized by negotiated settlement of differences, rather than by the hostility and confrontation of decades past.

These accords offer tangible evidence that mankind need not live forever in the dark shadow of nuclear war. They provide renewed hope that men and nations working together can succeed in building a lasting peace.

Because these agreements effectively serve one of this Nation's most cherished purposes—a more secure and peaceful world in which America's security is fully protected—I strongly recommend that the Senate support them, and that its deliberations be conducted without delay.

RICHARD NIXON

The White House,
    June 13, 1972.

198   Letter to the Speaker of the House Transmitting the Antiballistic Missile Treaty and the Interim Agreement on Strategic Offensive Arms.   *June* 13, 1972

Dear Mr. Speaker:

I transmit herewith copies of the Treaty on the Limitation of Anti-Ballistic Missile Systems and the Interim Agreement on Certain Measures with respect to the Limitation of Strategic Offensive Arms signed in Moscow on May 26, 1972. Copies of these agreements are also being forwarded to the President of the Senate. I am asking the Senate's advice and consent to ratification of the Treaty, and an expression of support from both Houses of the Congress for the Interim Agreement on Strategic Offensive Arms.

These agreements, the product of a major effort of this administration, are a significant step into a new era of mutually agreed restraint and arms limitation between the two principal nuclear powers.

The provisions of the agreements are explained in detail in the Report of the Secretary of State, which I attach. Their main effect is this: The ABM Treaty limits the deployment of anti-ballistic missile systems to two designated areas, and at a low level. The Interim Agree-

ment limits the overall level of strategic offensive missile forces. Together the two agreements provide for a more stable strategic balance in the next several years than would be possible if strategic arms competition continued unchecked. This benefits not only the United States and the Soviet Union, but all the nations of the world.

The agreements are an important first step in checking the arms race, but only a first step; they do not close off all avenues of strategic competition. Just as the maintenance of a strong strategic posture was an essential element in the success of these negotiations, it is now equally essential that we carry forward a sound strategic modernization program to maintain our security and to ensure that more permanent and comprehensive arms limitation agreements can be reached.

The defense capabilities of the United States are second to none in the world today. I am determined that they shall remain so. The terms of the ABM Treaty and Interim Agreement will permit the

675

United States to take the steps we deem necessary to maintain a strategic posture which protects our vital interests and guarantees our continued security.

Besides enhancing our national security, these agreements open the opportunity for a new and more constructive U.S.-Soviet relationship, characterized by negotiated settlement of differences, rather than by the hostility and confrontation of decades past.

These accords offer tangible evidence that mankind need not live forever in the dark shadow of nuclear war. They provide renewed hope that men and nations work-ing together can succeed in building a lasting peace.

Because these agreements effectively serve one of this Nation's most cherished purposes—a more secure and peaceful world in which America's security is fully protected—I strongly recommend that the House of Representatives support The Interim Agreement on Strategic Offensive Arms, and that its deliberations be conducted without delay.

Sincerely,

RICHARD NIXON

[Honorable Carl B. Albert, Speaker of the House of Representatives, Washington, D.C. 20515]

199   Remarks at a Briefing for Five Congressional Committees on the Antiballistic Missile Treaty and the Interim Agreement on Strategic Offensive Arms.   *June* 15, 1972

Ladies and gentlemen:

We are beginning a little late because I understand traffic is quite heavy around the White House this morning due to the arrival of the President of Mexico. We, however, must go forward with the schedule, because there is a joint session, as you know, today, and we do want the members of the committees present here to be able to attend that session. We will have to adjourn this meeting at approximately 12 o'clock, or at best, 5 minutes after 12, and we want to give you plenty of time for questions.

A word about the format of this meeting. I will make a statement, and then I will have to depart in order to prepare for the arrival of the President of Mexico. Dr. Kissinger will then make a statement, and then will be open to questions to the members of the committees that are present here.

In order to get some recognition factor developed by someone who knows all of the members who are here, Clark MacGregor will moderate the question-and-answer period, but we will try to be just as fair as possible among the members of the committees and between the House and the Senate, and Clark, of course, will be responsible in the event that it isn't fair.

In any event, let me come directly now to my own remarks, which will not be too extended, because Dr. Kissinger today will be presenting the Presidential views. He will be telling you what the President's participation has been in these negotiations. The views he will express I have gone over with him in great detail, and I will stand by them.

I noted in the press that it was suggested that I was calling down the members of these committees for the purpose of giving you a pep talk on these two agreements. Let me lay that to rest right at the outset. This is not a pep talk, and Dr. Kissinger is not going to make you a pep talk either.

When I came back from the Soviet Union, you will recall in the joint session I said that we wanted a very searching inquiry of these agreements. I want to leave no doubt about my own attitude.

I have studied this situation of arms control over the past 3½ years. I am totally convinced that both of these agreements are in the interest of the security of the United States and in the interest of arms control and world peace. I am convinced of that, based on my study. However, I want the Members of the House and the Members of the Senate also to be convinced of that. I want the Nation to be convinced of that.

I think that the hearings that you will conduct must be searching because only in that way will you be able to be convincing to yourselves and only in that way will the Nation also be convinced.

In other words, this is not one of those cases where the President of the United States is asking the Congress and the Nation to take on blind faith a decision that he has made and in which he deeply believes.

I believe in the decision, but your questions should be directed to Dr. Kissinger and others in the Administration for the purpose of finding any weaknesses that you think in the negotiations or in the final agreements that we have made.

As far as the procedures are concerned, as you know, you will be hearing the Secretary of State, the Secretary of Defense, the head of the CIA, and, of course, Ambassador [Gerard C.] Smith in your sessions of the various committees.

I know that a number have suggested that Dr. Kissinger should appear before the committees as a witness. I have had to decline that particular invitation on his part, due to the fact that executive privilege, I felt, had to prevail.

On the other hand, since this is really an unprecedented situation, it seemed to me that it was important that he appear before the members of the committees in this format. This is on the record.

All of you will be given total transcripts of what he says. All of you will have the opportunity to ask these questions, and in the event that all of the questions are not asked on this occasion, he, of course, will be available to answer other questions in his office from members of the committees as time goes on, during the course of the hearings.

What we are asking for here, in other words, is cooperation with, and not just rubber-stamping by, the House and the Senate. That is essential because there must be follow-through on this and the Members of the House and Senate, it seems to me, must be convinced that they played a role, as they have up to this point, and will continue to play a role in this very, very important field of arms control.

Now, let me go to the agreements themselves and express briefly some of my own views that I think are probably quite familiar to you, but which I think need to be underlined.

I have noted a great deal of speculation about who won and who lost in these negotiations. I have said that neither side won and neither side lost. As a matter of fact, if we were to really look at it very, very fairly, both sides won, and the whole world won.

Let me tell you why I think that is important. Where negotiations between great powers are involved, if one side wins and the other loses, clearly then you have a built-in tendency or incentive for the side that loses to break the agreement and to do everything that it can to regain the advantage.

This is an agreement which was very toughly negotiated on both sides. There are advantages in it for both sides. For that reason, each side has a vested interest, we believe, in keeping the agreement rather than breaking it.

I would like for you to examine Dr. Kissinger and our other witnesses before the committees on that point. I think you also will be convinced that this was one of those cases where it is to the mutual advantage of each side, each looking to its national security.

Another point that I would like to make is Presidential intervention in this particular matter—Presidential coordination—due to the fact that what we have here is not one of those cases where one department could take a lead role. This cut across the functions of the Department of State, the Department of Defense, it cut across, also, the AEC, and, of course, the Arms Control [and Disarmament] Agency.

Under these circumstances, there is only one place where it could be brought together, and that was in the White House, in the National Security Council, in which all of these various groups participated.

There is another reason, which has to do with the system of government in the Soviet Union. We have found that in dealing with the system of government in the Soviet Union, that where decisions are made that affect the vital security, in fact, the very survival of a nation, decisions and discussions in those cases are made only at the highest level. Conse-

quently, it is necessary for us to have discussions and decisions at the highest level if we are going to have the break-throughs that we have had to make in order to come to this point of a successful negotiation.

The other point that I would make has to do with what follows on. The agreement that we have here, as you know, is in two stages: one, the treaty with regard to ABM defensive weapons, and second, the offensive limitation, the executive agreement, which is indicated as being, as you know, not a permanent agreement—it is for 5 years—and not total. It covers only certain categories of weapons.

Now we are hoping to go forward with the second round of negotiations. That second round will begin, we trust, in October. That means that we can begin in October, provided action is taken on the treaty and on the offensive agreement that we have before you at this time, sometime in the summer months; we would trust before the 1st of September. I don't mean that it should take that long, but I would hope you can finish by the 1st of September so we can go forward with the negotiation in October.

The other point that should be made with regard to the follow-on agreements is not related to your approval of these agreements. It is related to the actions of the Congress on defense. I know there is disagreement among various Members of the Congress with regard to what our defense levels ought to be. I think, however, I owe it to you and to the Nation to say that Mr. Brezhnev and his colleagues made it absolutely clear that they are going forward with defense programs in the offensive area which are not limited by these agreements.

Under those circumstances, since they

will be going forward with their programs, for the United States not to go forward with its programs—and I am not suggesting which ones at this point, you can go into that later—but for the United States not to go forward with its offensive programs, or worse, for the United States unilaterally to reduce its offensive programs would mean that any incentive that the Soviets had to negotiate the follow-on agreement would be removed.

It is for that reason, without getting into the specifics as to what the level of defense spending should be, as to what the offensive programs should be, I am simply saying that if we want a follow-on agreement, we have to have two steps: We need first, of course, to approve these agreements, and second, we need a credible defensive position so that the Soviet Union will have an incentive to negotiate a permanent offensive freeze. That is what we all want.

These are just some random thoughts that I had on this matter. I will simply close by saying that as one stands in this room and in this house, one always has a tendency to think of some of the tragedies of history of the past. As many of you know, I have always been, and am, a great admirer of Woodrow Wilson. As all of you know, the great tragedy of his life was that after he came back with the Treaty of Versailles and the League of Nations, due to ineffective consultation, the Senate rejected the treaty and rejected the League.

We, of course, do not want that to happen. We do not think that it will happen, because we have appreciated the consultation we have had up to this point, and we are now going forward with this meeting at this time.

I will only say that in looking at what Wilson said during that debate, when he was traveling the country, he made a very, it seemed to me, moving and eloquent statement. He said: "My clients are the children. My clients are the future generation."

This is an election year, and I realize that in an election year it is difficult to move as objectively as we ordinarily would move on any issue. But I would respectfully request the Members of the House and Senate, Republican and Democratic, to approach this in the spirit that Wilson explained in that period when they were debating whether they should go forward with the League of Nations, remembering that our clients are the next generation, that approval of these agreements, the treaty limiting defensive weapons, the agreement limiting offensive weapons in certain categories, and also the continuation of a credible defense posture, will mean that we will have done our duty by our clients, which are the next generation.

Thank you.

NOTE: The President spoke at 9:18 a.m. in the State Dining Room at the White House. He spoke without referring to notes.

Invited to the briefing were 122 members of the five Congressional committees having jurisdiction over the details of the agreements: the Joint Committee on Atomic Energy, the Senate Committee on Foreign Relations, the House Committee on Foreign Affairs, the Senate Committee on Armed Services, and the House Committee on Armed Services.

On the same day, the White House released the transcripts of remarks on the agreements by Henry A. Kissinger, Assistant to the President for National Security Affairs, and the question-and-answer session which followed. Dr. Kissinger's remarks are printed in the Weekly Compilation of Presidential Documents (vol. 8, p. 1045).

200   Remarks of Welcome to President Luis Echeverría Alvarez of Mexico.   *June* 15, 1972

Mr. President, Señora Echeverría, all of our distinguished guests:

Mr. President, we welcome you very warmly on your first official visit to Washington. We welcome you as the head of state of a great nation, our great and friendly neighbor to the South. And we welcome you also as a world leader of the first rank.

During the course of our discussions we will have the opportunity to talk about bilateral issues between our two countries. I will be extremely interested in getting your views on hemispheric problems, particularly in view of your very eloquent comments in which you enunciated the Echeverría Doctrine in Santiago a short time ago.

And since you are the first head of government or head of state to visit Washington since my visit to Moscow, I shall look forward to the opportunity to talk with you about international problems of mutual interest. We shall discuss these problems with great frankness and great candor. But what is even more important, we will discuss them as friends.

Mr. President, the people of the United States of America have a very warm place in their hearts for the people of Mexico. I personally, and my wife, have a warm place in our hearts for your country and we feel that as we meet you today, we meet not only as official friends but also as personal friends. We believe that Mexican-American friendship is an indispensable cornerstone to our foreign policy and we believe that our talks will contribute to that friendship and to the cause of peace and progress for all people in the world.

NOTE: President Nixon spoke at 10:14 a.m. on the South Lawn at the White House where President Echeverría was given a formal welcome with full military honors. President Nixon spoke without referring to notes.

See also Items 201 and 203.

President Echeverría spoke in Spanish. His remarks were translated by an interpreter as follows:

President Nixon, Mrs. Nixon:

A few yards away from us we can turn and see young mothers holding children in their arms and as we see them we must think of young mothers all over the world holding children in their arms, the children that are the new generation, the new hope for the world.

These mothers look towards the future with either uncertainty or with hope. They want to see how the present leaders of this changing world are going to act and thus affect the future of these new generations.

The great powers will be working and making decisions that will affect the future of these mothers and these children, and they will want to know what the future is.

This is what we must think of, all the leaders of the world today, that we have the fate of the world in our hands and that we are changing the world, that we will affect the course of history, and let us hope our contributions will be towards a world of peace, of security, and prosperity.

Mr. President, we should never forget—and as we look around we are reminded by these young mothers and their children—how we are responsible for the conditions facing this new generation and we will be the ones responsible for deciding whether this will be a world for them of anguish or a world for peace.

Mr. President, the people of Mexico bring to you and to the people of the United States, this great and friendly neighbor, our best and most cordial greetings from all of us, and I am certain that out of our conversations will come agreements that will be positive and will contribute toward the further progress of peace and prosperity in this changing world.

We hope that we will be able to do this so

that no matter what our ideologies, the young of the small and great countries of the world will work together with a hope to contributing to peace in a better world today that we may have an international order that will enable us to face the future with greater hope so that we will benefit these new generations that are the essence and the heart of our preoccupations, of our concern, and of our work.

My warmest thanks to you, Mr. President, and to the great people of our friendly neighboring country, the United States, and in closing I express the hope, and I have no doubt, that out of our conversations will come agreements that will be mutually beneficial for both peoples.

[At this point, President Echeverría called to the platform where he was speaking two mothers and their daughters who had been viewing the ceremony. They were Countess Logan Lessana of Rome, now living in Washington, D.C., with her 4-year-old daughter Barbara, and Mrs. Julie Robinson of McLean, Va., a member of Mrs. Nixon's staff, with her 4-year-old daughter Tegan. They remained on the platform during his closing remarks.]

Mr. President, in the whole world you can see beautiful scenes like this, children held in the arms of the mothers, and these young generations should be always on our minds, and I like to think, I wonder, what will be the world—what will be the world that we will leave to them, what will conditions be like in the year 2000 when these two beautiful young girls are grown up, what will be the world for their children and their grandchildren?

Will there be years of danger because of man's technological progress or will we turn this technological progress into a better world and into better living conditions for all people?

This is a thought, Mr. President, we should also bear with us—the thought of these young mothers with children in arms, of this new generation that we are working for.

201   Toasts of the President and President Echeverría of Mexico.   *June* 15, 1972

Mr. President, Señora Echeverría, our very distinguished guests:

As all of you know, Mrs. Nixon and I during this year, along with the Secretary of State, have traveled a great deal. We traveled halfway around the world to Peking. And then we traveled almost halfway around the world the other way to Moscow.

And on this occasion in this house, we want all of you, our guests tonight, to know that it is very good to be home in the United States and to welcome our very good and dear friends from our great neighbor to the south, the President of Mexico and his wife.

I would like to tell a little story as to how we feel about the President and his wife. This is not their first visit to this house. When he was President-elect, we had the honor of receiving them in the family dining room upstairs. And that was appropriate, because whenever the President of Mexico visits the President of the United States, we feel that they are part of our family. We are all part of the American family in this hemisphere.

But the story that I want to tell you relates to a very unfortunate experience. Just before I went to Moscow, when we entertained in this room the parliamentarians from Mexico, on that occasion the distinguished Ambassador to the United States from Mexico was held up at the gate. He was not a parliamentarian. He was not a Senator. He had no invitation.

When he told me why he was delayed, I said to him, "The Ambassador from Mexico is always welcome in this house. He needs no invitation."

And I say to the President of Mexico, to his wife and all of our friends from Mexico, you need no invitation. I will say to you, *"Está usted en su casa."*

And now returning to a more serious vein, I noted this morning in my remarks welcoming the President that we expected to discuss many things, bilateral problems, hemispheric problems, and international problems. We have had very good talks and we will continue them tomorrow.

But as I talked to the President of Mexico, I thought of what kind of man he was and what I could say about him in presenting him to our guests tonight. And I thought of another man whom it would be appropriate to mention, particularly in this room, as I stand below the only portrait that hangs in this room, the portrait of Abraham Lincoln.

Lincoln was the great American President of the 19th century, and a contemporary of Lincoln was Benito Juárez. They did not know each other, but they respected each other. And each in his way kept his country together at a time that it would otherwise have been torn apart. Both became revered national heroes. And we are receiving the President of Mexico on the occasion of the 100th anniversary of the death of Benito Juárez, whose statue is just a few blocks from here in Washington, D.C.

He said many interesting and very profound things during his life. But one very simple thing he said remains in my memory. He said, "Peace is respect for the rights of others."

As I talked to the President of Mexico today, 100 years after the death of Juárez, I heard that theme expressed: Peace is respect by great nations for the rights of smaller nations. Peace is respect of the strong for the weak. Peace is respect of the rich for the poor.

Never have I heard a more eloquent expression on the part of a world statesman for the smaller nations, for the weaker nations, and the proud nations who are moving upward toward progress and prosperity, hopefully in a world of peace.

It has been my privilege in 25 years in government service, and as a private citizen, to meet and know personally over 100 heads of state and heads of government in the world. And I can say to my friends here from America, the United States of America, and to our good friends and guests from Mexico, that in your President you have a man who, because of his intelligence, his enormous energy, his humanity, and his understanding of the problems not only of his own country, but of the world, is in the first rank of the statesmen of the world that I have met in this last quarter of a century.

That would be a high compliment to any man, but in proposing my toast tonight, I propose an even higher compliment. One hundred years after the death of Benito Juárez, we are fortunate to have in the great nation to the south of us, a President who is in the great tradition of Juárez, who expounds eloquently the philosophy of Juárez, a man who has been and will be one of the great leaders not only of his own country but of this whole hemisphere.

And so to the man who proudly and justifiably today wears the mantle of Juárez, President Echeverría of Mexico, I propose that we raise our glasses.

NOTE: President Nixon spoke at 10:01 p.m. in the State Dining Room at the White House. He spoke without referring to notes.

See also Items 200 and 203.

President Echeverría spoke in Spanish. His remarks were translated by an interpreter as follows:

Mr. President, Mrs. Nixon:

We Mexicans cannot help but remember with great pleasure the fact that a few years ago—a little over 30 years ago—a young California lawyer who had just married a delicate and attractive schoolteacher, picked our country for his honeymoon. They took a long journey, made careful observations throughout their journey, without knowing that destiny would enable him some day to apply those observations more directly and more carefully in this new relationship of ours that we are working at perfecting.

We appreciate even more, however, the fact that 25 years after that wedding trip, the Nixons went back, with their children this time, went back over the trail of their honeymoon to show the children the various places where they had traveled on that occasion.

And we believe, Mr. President, and Mrs. Nixon, that especially on this second journey when you went back with your daughters that this was a testimony of your affection, of a cordial expression of your sentiments that has nothing at all to do with politics but is just your personal opinion and sentiments towards this country.

Mr. President, you have recalled the figures of Lincoln and Juárez. Both men emerged victorious from a very divisive civil war in their own countries, a war that had rendered deep divisions among their people.

Both of them in practice led their peoples to the victory of the cause of what is right and both of them consolidated the unity of their people.

And what better than to recall them now when the world is trying to emerge from an era of deep divisions, is trying to find a path under law, so that with justice we, as we especially aspire to in the Americas, are trying to solve the problems that affect us.

And so daily, as we seek to find solutions to some of these terribly complex problems, some of them so complex as to seem insoluble, I think it is positive, therefore, to find our inspiration in the best men produced by our history. And it is right then that we should look back upon these heroes of our past who with justice, recognizing how—through their very efforts, their arduous struggles, their daily sacrifices—how they won victory for their countries and served their people through that cause. Their best reward for them was to achieve a victory for the good cause that they espoused.

You had invited us in December of 1970 to a small friendly dining room on the second floor of the White House. On that occasion, Mr. President, you told me that after I took office that you would invite me and my wife to come to Washington on a full state visit, which is what we are in the process of engaging ourselves in now, and that on this occasion we would talk about a number of subjects that you have just mentioned which then, as President-elect, I was not in a position to discuss.

Some might think that we have come to speak on behalf of Mexico with frankness, perhaps with excessive frankness, about some of our common problems. But your various journeys, Mr. President, to these two great world powers of recent months have shown that we are living new days indeed, and days in which problems must be faced, and when we say face problems it means show our face and face up to the problems that do exist.

And so I ask—and I will answer in the affirmative before I even finish the question—is this a new style that is being introduced into international political life? Is this a new diplomatic style that we are using that is coming from the Americas that will have effects on the entire world? And the answer, as I said, is in the affirmative.

Because this is a process of renewal, this new style, this new approach that we are showing in this hemisphere that will affect the entire world. This is a very special style, a very effective style because it has a very great sense of realism.

So we are in a sense rediscovering contemporary realism and facing up to our problems close up and I think this will permit us to overcome the crisis of our days.

Mr. President, in thinking of your temperament as a fighter, and your will to fight and to win, we really could not find a full explanation of these virtues without looking at the moral strength that you derive from this delightful lady who is your wife.

And so, ladies and gentlemen—and this is not a mere formula of courtesy and affection—but please, if you would, rise and join me in a toast to the President and to this distinguished lady, with all of her high virtues, who has been a great companion to this great fighter, and as Mexicans we invite you to reiterate this expression of our deep affection for President and Mrs. Nixon and our great appreciation for their warm hospitality.

202   Statement About the Dedication of the Veterans Administration Hospital in Columbia, Missouri.   *June* 16, 1972

TODAY the Veterans Administration is dedicating a new hospital in Columbia, Mo. This brings the nationwide system of veterans hospitals to a total of 167, with more under construction and in the planning stage.

This latest addition will provide health care services primarily to the veterans of central Missouri. But its opening also symbolizes the strong and continuing commitment of this Administration to making the best possible medical care available to every eligible veteran.

Fulfilling the Nation's obligation to its veterans is a matter of justice and national honor. Meeting their medical needs is one of our highest national priorities. To insure that they are met, I intend to maintain and reinforce the independent system of Veterans Administration health care facilities when and as required.

203   Joint Communique Following Discussions With President Echeverría of Mexico.   *June* 17, 1972

PRESIDENT Richard Nixon and President Luis Echeverría Alvarez welcomed this opportunity to renew their personal friendship and the cordial dialogue which began at their first meeting here in 1970. They regarded this visit as particularly appropriate at a time when the eyes of the world have been focused on President Nixon's recent visits to Peking and Moscow. The visit of the Mexican President to the United States serves to direct broad attention to the equally important tasks of advancing new approaches to Latin America and the less developed nations of the world.

They also agreed that their meetings had contributed to the establishment of a new era, an opening characterized by a spirit of frankness, with Mexico and which they hoped would characterize intra-Hemispheric relations.

The two Presidents exchanged impressions on world and Western Hemisphere affairs in considerable detail. President Nixon described his talks with the Chinese and Soviet leaders. President Echeverría recounted his experiences on recent visits to Japan, Chile and Peru. They found this review informative, useful as well as stimulating. They were firmly united in the view that world peace with social justice is essential to the well-being of all mankind.

The Presidents discussed overall relations between their two countries—political and economic affairs, and cooperation in the scientific, technical, cultural and other fields.

The President of the United States recognized the important role developing countries could and should play in erecting a new international monetary system and in progressing toward a free and fair trading system. In endorsing trade policies more responsive to the problems of both developed and developing countries, he reaffirmed his intention to seek congressional authorization at the appropriate time for the United States to participate with other industrialized countries in a system of Generalized Tariff Preferences for imports from developing countries.

Regarding the problem of the salinity of the Colorado River, President Echeverría told President Nixon that Mexico reiterates its position as regards receiving its assignment of original waters from the Colorado River, to which the Treaty of February 3, 1944 refers, and therefore, with the same quality as those derived from the Imperial Dam.

To this, President Nixon replied that this was a highly complex problem that needed careful examination of all aspects. He was impressed by the presentation made by President Echeverría and would study it closely. It was his sincere desire to find a definitive, equitable and just solution to this problem at the earliest possible time because of the importance both nations attach to this matter.

As a demonstration of this intent and of the goodwill of the United States in this connection, he was prepared to:

(a) undertake certain actions immediately to improve the quality of water going to Mexico;

(b) designate a special representative to begin work immediately to find a permanent, definitive and just solution of this problem;

(c) instruct the special representative to submit a report to him by the end of this year;

(d) submit this proposal, once it has the approval of this Government to President Echeverría for his consideration and approval.

President Echeverría said that he recognized the goodwill of President Nixon and his interest in finding a definitive solution to this problem at the earliest possible time. He added that based on two recent trips to the Mexicali Valley and his talks with farmers there, his Government, while reserving its legal rights, had decided to stop using waters from the Wellton-Mohawk project for irrigation purposes while waiting for receipt of the US proposal for a definitive solution.

Both Presidents agreed to instruct their Water and Border Commissioners to prepare and sign a Minute containing the above program and commitments as soon as possible.

The Presidents discussed the many areas of ongoing cooperation between Mexico and the United States, and their conviction that such cooperation serves to bind our people even closer together in mutual effort and understanding. They took note of the agreements concluded during the visit by their respective Secretaries for Foreign Relations: a bilateral agreement with regard to the exchange of information, training and research in the fields of science and technology; a subsidiary agreement which contemplates

87-234—74——47

the exchange of young technicians and scientists (including the training of some 100 young Mexican technicians and scientists through US Government agencies); renewal of the agreement on Cultural Relations.

President Nixon and President Echeverría discussed the serious nature of the illicit international traffic in narcotic drugs. They reviewed the joint enforcement measures which their countries have successfully undertaken over the past two years. President Nixon informed President Echeverría of recent measures taken to combat the drug problem in the United States. They agreed to acquire and employ additional equipment in the antinarcotics campaign and to make available increased training of personnel for this purpose.

With regard to the question of migratory Mexican workers, the two Presidents discussed the economic, social and political factors that produce this problem and agreed it was desirable for each government to undertake immediately a study of this question with a view to finding a mutually satisfactory solution.

Recognizing the communality of many environmental problems and the need to seek cooperative solutions through the exchange of research and experience, the two Presidents have agreed that appropriate policy level officials from Mexico and the US will meet on a regular basis for discussion and consultation concerning current and future environmental problems of mutual concern and the methods for dealing with them in a more systematic way.

The conversations between Presidents Nixon and Echeverría were at all times cordial and marked by the spirit of good neighborliness which exists between Mexico and the US. At the same time problems were discussed frankly and openly as between true friends in an atmosphere of mutual respect and trust. President Echeverría particularly wished to convey on behalf of Mrs. Echeverría, his party and himself, his deep appreciation for the warm hospitality which was extended to them by President and Mrs. Nixon.

President Nixon expressed his great pleasure that President and Mrs. Echeverría will now have an opportunity to visit other areas and cities of the United States and assured them they will receive a warm and friendly welcome from the American people.

NOTE: The joint communique was released at Key Biscayne, Fla.

See also Items 200 and 201.

On June 15, 1972, the White House released an announcement of the exchange of diplomatic notes by Secretary of State William P. Rogers and Secretary of Foreign Relations for Mexico Emilio O. Rabasa on bilateral agreements in the scientific, technological, and cultural fields. The announcement is printed in the Weekly Compilation of Presidential Documents (vol. 8, p. 1054).

204 Statement About Signing the Public Buildings Amendments of 1972. *June 17, 1972*

I HAVE signed S. 1736, the Public Buildings Amendments of 1972, the major features of which were proposed by the Administration.

S. 1736 established a public building fund to finance construction, maintenance, and operation of Federal buildings from user charges collected from those

Federal agencies which are furnished space or services by the General Services Administration. It provides 3-year authority for construction of public buildings by purchase contracts with terms of up to 30 years. It also authorizes the National Park Service to provide maintenance, security, and information services for the John F. Kennedy Center for the Performing Arts.

The requirement that agencies budget for their own space and pay user charges approximating commercial rental rates should provide an incentive for more efficient space utilization and will move agency budgets one step nearer to the goal of reflecting total program costs.

It is regrettable that S. 1736 contains two provisions which I am advised by the Attorney General are unconstitutional "coming into agreement" clauses, infringing upon the fundamental principle of the separation of legislative and executive powers.

These provisions appear in section 7(d) of the Public Buildings Act of 1959, as amended by section 2(4) of the bill, and in section 5(f) of the bill.

The amended section 7(d) provides that no emergency lease authorized by that section shall be for a period of more than 180 days without approval of a prospectus for such lease by the Committees on Public Works.

Section 5(f) provides that, except for previously approved prospectuses, no purchase contract shall be entered into until a prospectus has been submitted and approved by the Committees on Public Works.

Under section 7(a) of the Public Buildings Act of 1959, as it would be amended by this bill, no appropriations may be made to construct, alter, purchase, or acquire a public building, or to lease any space at an average annual rental in excess of $500,000, until the Public Works Committees have approved GSA's prospectuses for such projects. I understand that Congress regards this "no appropriation may be made" provision as internal Congressional rulemaking which does not affect the executive branch. This Administration has acquiesced in that construction.

However, the two sections of this bill previously referred to give the General Services Administration the authority to enter into leases and purchase contracts and then condition the use of that authority on that agency's getting the approval of the Public Works Committees on prospectuses. This conditioning of the authority of the executive branch upon an action by committees of the Congress is found by the Attorney General to be an unconstitutional "coming into agreement" provision.

In signing the Second Supplemental Appropriations Act on May 27, 1972,[1] I commented on the unconstitutionality of a similar clause contained in that act. I wish to emphasize, as my predecessors have done, my firm opposition to any "coming into agreement" provisions and also to indicate that I cannot act under such a provision.

Therefore, I am directing GSA to cooperate with the Committees on Public Works in assuring full compliance with the acceptable procedures contained in section 7(a) of the Public Buildings Act, without regard to the unconstitutional provisions I have previously referred to.

---

[1] See Item 173.

Further, I am directing that agency to submit appropriate legislation to the Congress to eliminate the unconstitutional language in S. 1736.

NOTE: The statement was released at Key Biscayne, Fla.

As enacted, S. 1736, approved June 16, 1972, is Public Law 92-313 (86 Stat. 216).

205 Message to the United States Conference of Mayors Meeting in New Orleans, Louisiana. *June* 19, 1972

MY warmest greetings, today, to the United States Conference of Mayors as you meet in New Orleans. Yours is one of the most experienced, most able, most valuable organizations in our struggle to find new sources of hope, security, dignity—and revenue—for our cities.

For decades in America, of course, our efforts in this regard seemed to run counter to tradition. When President Jefferson completed the Louisiana Purchase in 1803, he said it was necessary for us to think continentally. But he sometimes thought of the cities, as he had written to a friend, as "pestilential to the morals, the health, and the liberties of man."

But I would like all of you to share with me the beginning of hope that we are reversing things. In the revenue-sharing proposals we have sent to the Congress—and no organization has been more helpful in shaping and shepherding these than the Conference of Mayors—we are in fact setting a new course for America.

For example, I have asked Congress to approve general revenue sharing legislation which would provide $3.5 billion to urban areas this year.

I have also asked Congress to enact urban special revenue sharing legislation which would consolidate $2.3 billion of grants for local development needs, enabling local general-purpose governments to set their own priorities and use these funds to meet their own development needs without interference from Washington.

I have also proposed a sweeping reform of our discredited welfare system, and we have secured passage of a 12-year, $10 billion urban mass transit improvement program.

Let me summarize just a few other advances:

Since 1969, our Administration has increased housing production for low and moderate income families fourfold—by 400 percent.

We have increased the budget authority for municipal waste treatment projects from $214 million in 1969 to $2 billion in 1973.

We have increased Federal anti-crime aid since 1969 by 253 percent in affirmative action for law, order and justice for all.

Your past support of these initiatives, individually as well as through the Conference, has been most welcome. It has also been a profound public service. However, the task has only just begun, and I urge your continued efforts in behalf of these long-needed reforms.

Together, we can rebuild and maintain our cities as desirable, pleasant places in which to live.

I pledge you my continued personal commitment to this objective.

I thank you very much indeed, and my best wishes to you for a successful meeting in New Orleans.

RICHARD NIXON

NOTE: The text of the message, dated June 17, 1972, was released June 19 at Key Biscayne, Fla.

206   Statement About the United Nations Conference on the Human Environment in Stockholm, Sweden. *June* 20, 1972

I HAVE just received a report on the United Nations Conference on the Human Environment concluded last Friday at Stockholm from Chairman Train who headed the large and distinguished U.S. delegation.

The United States has worked long and hard over the past 18 months to help make the Conference a success. Representatives of 113 nations met together for 2 weeks to produce an impressive number of agreements on environmental principles and recommendations for further national and international action in this important field.

The United States achieved practically all of its objectives at Stockholm.

(1) The Conference approved establishment of a new United Nations unit to provide continued leadership and coordination of environmental action, an important step which had our full support.

(2) The Conference approved forming a $100 million United Nations environmental fund which I personally proposed last February.

(3) The Conference overwhelmingly approved the U.S. proposal for a moratorium on commercial killing of whales.

(4) The Conference endorsed our proposal for an international convention to regulate ocean dumping.

(5) The Conference endorsed the U.S. proposal for the establishment of a World Heritage Trust to help preserve wilderness areas and other scenic natural landmarks.

However, even more than in the specific agreements reached, I believe that the deepest significance of the Conference lies in the fact that for the first time in history, the nations of the world sat down together to seek better understanding of each other's environmental problems and to explore opportunities for positive action, individually and collectively.

The strong concern of the United States over the fate of our environment has also been demonstrated in our direct dealings with individual nations. The Great Lakes Water Quality Agreement which I signed in Ottawa this April with Prime Minister Trudeau was evidence of the high priority this Administration places on protecting the environment. The Environmental Agreement which I signed in Moscow on May 23 is proof of the desire of our Nation to work together with the others on the common tasks of peace.

I am proud that the United States is taking a leading role in international environmental cooperation, and I congratulate our U.S. delegation on its success at Stockholm. The governments and people of the world must now work together to make the objectives of the Stockholm Conference a reality.

NOTE: The Conference was held June 5–16, 1972, in Stockholm.

On June 20, the White House released a fact sheet and the transcript of a news briefing on the Conference. Participants in the news briefing were Russell E. Train, Chairman, Council on Environmental Quality, and Chairman, U.S. delegation to the Conference; Senator Howard H. Baker, Jr., Chairman, Secretary of State's Advisory Committee on the United Nations Conference on the Human Environment; and Robert M. White, Administrator, National Oceanic and Atmospheric Administration, Department of Commerce.

207   The President's News Conference of *June* 22, 1972

THE PRESIDENT. *Ladies and gentlemen:*

Next week before the Congress recesses, I am planning to have a general news conference. Prior to that time, in talking to Mr. Ziegler, I found that a number of members of the press, looking back at previous news conferences, have indicated that there is a tendency for foreign policy and defense policy questions to dominate the conferences so much that questions on domestic policy do not adequately get covered.

As a matter of fact, I have noted several of you in your commentaries, after some news conferences, have indicated that we have not given enough attention to the domestic issues.

So, subsequently, after discussing the matter with Mr. Ziegler, I thought it would be useful this week, on this occasion, to have you here in the office for the purpose of covering domestic issues only. The session next week will be open to both foreign policy-defense policy and domestic issues.

So, today we will take all questions on domestic issues, and next week you can cover all three areas to the extent you wish to.

QUESTIONS

BUGGING OF DEMOCRATIC HEADQUARTERS

[1.] Q. Mr. O'Brien [1] has said that the people who bugged his headquarters [2] had a direct link to the White House. Have you had any sort of investigation made to determine whether this is true?

THE PRESIDENT. Mr. Ziegler and also Mr. Mitchell,[3] speaking for the campaign committee, have responded to questions on this in great detail. They have stated my position and have also stated the facts accurately.

---

[1] Lawrence F. O'Brien was chairman of the Democratic National Committee.

[2] On June 17, 1972, five men were arrested for illegally entering the Democratic National Committee headquarters in an office building at the Watergate complex in Washington, D.C. On September 15, they were indicted by a Federal grand jury on charges which included conspiracy to use illegal means to obtain information from the Democratic headquarters, intent to steal property of another, and intent to intercept willfully, knowingly, and unlawfully oral and wire communications.

[3] Former Attorney General John N. Mitchell was campaign director of the Committee for the Re-Election of the President.

This kind of activity, as Mr. Ziegler has indicated, has no place whatever in our electoral process, or in our governmental process. And, as Mr. Ziegler has stated, the White House has had no involvement whatever in this particular incident.

As far as the matter now is concerned, it is under investigation, as it should be, by the proper legal authorities, by the District of Columbia police, and by the FBI. I will not comment on those matters, particularly since possible criminal charges are involved.

FOOD PRICES

[2.] Q. Mr. President, wholesale food prices have led to increases in the cost of living in the last few weeks. Are you considering any kind of controls over the price of food?

THE PRESIDENT. In the whole area of inflation we have had a period of pretty good news generally. As you know, in 1969 and early 1970 the rate of inflation, the CPI, peaked out at 6 percent. Since that time it has been moving down and particularly since the August 15 new policy with the control system was announced, it has now been cut approximately in half, running at around the rate of 3 percent. The most troublesome area however is the one you have referred to—food prices.

We cannot take too much comfort from the figures that came out yesterday because, as you know, they actually reflected a slight drop in food prices. I met yesterday, however, with the Quadriad, and Mr. Stein reported that the weekly reports that we get, which, of course, were not reflected in yesterday's numbers, indicate that meat prices particularly are beginning to rise again and rising very fast.

For that reason, I have directed that the Cost of Living Council, which will be meeting this afternoon, look into this matter to see what further action can be taken to deal specifically with food prices, but particularly with meat prices.

Now with regard to meat prices, to give you an indication of the direction of my thinking, you can move on the control side. But as we all remember in that period immediately after World War II, when we had controls but too much demand and too little supply and all the black markets, controls alone will not work unless you also move on the supply side.

At the present time, we have apparently a world shortage of meat, and particularly a shortage of meat in the United States, where the demand is constantly going up as the income of our people goes up.

We have to get, therefore, at the problem of supply. Consequently, one of the areas that I am exploring is the quota system. I have directed our staff to check into the advisability of a temporary lifting of quotas on imported meat which will move on the supply side. It will not affect the problem immediately, but at least it would affect it over the next few months.

That does not rule out, also, the possibility of moving on the control side, and the control side is a matter where the Cost of Living Council is presently, or will be at 4 o'clock this afternoon, considering a number of options which I will consider as the matter develops.

DEFENSE BUDGET AND SALT
AGREEMENTS

[3.] Q. Mr. President, this may be a borderline question in the domestic field, but I believe it may fall there since the issues are before Congress. Could you tell us your view of the relationship between the development of offensive weapons, as proposed in your defense budget, and the SALT agreements?

THE PRESIDENT. I have noted the progress of the debate in the committee, and particularly the controversy, or alleged controversy and contradiction which seems in some quarters to have been developed between the views of the Secretary of Defense and the views that I have expressed and the views that have been expressed by Dr. Kissinger and Secretary Rogers.

I think that I can put the thing in context best by first pointing out the Secretary of Defense's position, and then relating that position to the overall position of the United States in attempting to develop policy that will adequately protect the security of the United States and also move forward on the arms limitation front.

The Secretary of Defense has a responsibility, as I have a responsibility, to recommend to the Congress action that will adequately protect the security of the United States. Moving on that responsibility, he has indicated that if the SALT agreement is approved and then if the Congress rejects the programs for offensive weapons not controlled by the SALT agreement, that this would seriously jeopardize the security of the United States. On that point he is correct.

What I would suggest to the Congress and would recommend to individual Congressmen and Senators, who will have the responsibility of voting on this matter, is the following course: First, the arms limitation agreements should be approved on their merits. I would not have signed those agreements unless I had believed that, standing alone, they were in the interest

of the United States. As a matter of fact, the offensive limitation is one that is particularly in our interest because it covers arms where the Soviet Union has ongoing programs which will be limited in this 5-year period, and in which we have no ongoing programs.

So, consequently, I would recommend and strongly urge that the Congress approve the ABM treaty, and also the limited, temporary, offensive limitations curb. However, after the Congress moves in that field, all Congressmen and Senators—and this would, of course, include them all—who are concerned about the security of the United States should then vote for those programs that will provide adequate offensive weapons in the areas that have been recommended by the Secretary of Defense and by the Administration.

Now the reason for that is twofold: First, because if we have a SALT agreement and then do not go forward with these programs, the Soviet Union will, within a matter of a very limited time, be substantially ahead of the United States overall, particularly in the latter part of the seventies.

If the United States falls into what is a definitely second position, inferior position to the Soviet Union overall in its defense programs, this will be an open invitation for more instability in the world and an open invitation, in my opinion, for more potential aggression in the world, particularly in such potentially explosive areas as the Mideast.

Therefore, it is important from the standpoint of the United States being able to play its role of maintaining peace and security in the world—a role that the United States, of all the non-Communist nations, is the only one capable of playing—it is essential that the United States not fall into an inferior position.

Therefore, the offensive weapons programs—which incidentally were not conceived after the SALT agreements, they were recommended prior to the SALT agreements—stand on their own because the Soviet Union has programs in which they are moving forward. As I pointed out to the leaders, and you ladies and gentlemen were present there, or some of you were and the rest of you, of course, covered it through the broadcasting system, the Soviet Union is moving forward.

Mr. Brezhnev made it absolutely clear to me that in those areas that were not controlled by our offensive agreement that they were going ahead with their programs. For us not to would seriously jeopardize the security of the United States and jeopardize the cause of world peace, in my opinion.

Now, the second reason why those who vote for the arms limitation agreement should vote for an ongoing program in those areas not covered by it, is that this arms control agreement, while very important, is only the first step and not the biggest step.

The biggest step remains. The biggest step is a permanent limitation on offensive weapons, covering other categories of weapons and, we trust, eventually all categories of weapons. This would be as dramatic as the one step that we have already taken—this would be an even more dramatic step in limiting arms overall between the two super powers.

In the event that the United States does not have ongoing programs, however, there will be no chance that the Soviet Union will negotiate phase two of an arms limitation agreement. I can say to the members of the press here that had we not had an ABM program in being there would be no SALT agreement today, because there would have been no incentive for the Soviet Union to stop us from doing something that we were doing and, thereby, agree to stop something they were doing.

Now in the event that we do not therefore have any new offensive systems underway or planned, the Soviet Union has no incentive to limit theirs. And so consequently—and I have studied this very, very carefully, I can assure you that there is nothing I would like better than to be able to limit these expenses—I am convinced that to achieve our goal, which is the goal, I think, of all Americans, to achieve our goal of an offensive limitations curb, covering all types of nuclear weapons, that it is essential for the United States to have an ongoing, offensive program. For that reason, I think that the position of the Secretary of Defense, speaking for the security of the United States, is a sound one.

I would hope that Members of the House and Senate, on reflection, would recognize that the SALT agreement, important as it is by itself, does not deal with the total defense posture of the United States. By itself it is in the interest of the United States and it stands on its own, but by itself, without a continuing offensive program, we can be sure that the security interests of the United States would be very seriously jeopardized and the chances for a permanent offensive agreement would, in my opinion, be totally destroyed.

NEWS CONFERENCE QUESTIONS

[4.] Q. Mr. President, is Mr. Ehrlichman correct when he says that you sometimes get irritated with us for our dumb and flabby questions so-called?

THE PRESIDENT. You are not dumb and flabby. [*Laughter*] No, I noted that comment and expected a question on it. I am afraid if I begin to characterize the questions, you will begin to characterize my answers, but you probably will anyway. In any event, as far as questions are concerned, I think what Mr. Ehrlichman was referring to was the tendency in the big East Room conferences for questions to come in from all over the place and no followup, as there can be in a conference like this.

Sometimes the questions may appear somewhat less relevant. I have found, for example—although we do not rule out the big conference where everybody gets to come—I have found that these smaller sessions do provide an opportunity for members of the regular White House press, who study these issues day by day and who know what is relevant and what is not relevant and who can follow up, I think that the possibility of dumb and flabby questions is much less and I don't, frankly, complain about it.

The other point that I should make is this: In looking over the transcripts of various press conferences, I have not seen many softballs, and I don't want any because it is only the hardball that you can hit or strike out on.

WELFARE BILL

[5.] Q. Mr. President, how badly do you want a welfare bill to pass Congress and how much are you willing to compromise either on the principles or the price tag of H.R. 1?

THE PRESIDENT. Well, as you know, I have been having a number of meetings on this matter over the past week and I will expect to have more during the next week and after the Congress returns from its vacation in Miami.

But, whatever the case may be, looking at the welfare program, I believe that the position that we have taken, a position that has been overwhelmingly approved by the House, is the right position.

It provides for welfare for those who need it. It provides also for those incentives that will move people from welfare rolls to jobs, and it does so at a cost we can afford. And all of those matters, I think, have to be taken into consideration in any program that we recommend.

Now, the tactical situation is that Mr. Ribicoff [Senator Abraham Ribicoff] and several Republicans have indicated that unless the Administration moves toward their position, that we have no chance to get a bill.

First, I question their analysis on that point.

Second, I believe that, on the merits, moving in that direction is the wrong step because it would substantially increase the cost of welfare and move in the direction that I think the country does not want, and that, I believe, would not be in the interest of the welfare recipients themselves.

On the other side of the coin, when it was known that I had had, as I did have, long conversations with those who were advocating the movement toward the Ribicoff positions, the members of the Senate Finance Committee have requested equal time. I intend to give them equal time, of course, to hear their arguments, after the bill is written in its final form. As you know, it has not yet been finalized.

My own present intention, however,

is to stay by our middle position. I think it is the right position and I believe that it is a position that can get through this Congress.

Now on that score, I would just point out that we can all go back and look at speeches that have been made and maybe a few columns that have been written, indicating that the Administration's failing to move from the position that we had taken on revenue sharing meant that we would never get revenue sharing.

Well, we got it today in the House because our position was sound and I think we are going to follow the same tactics, the same position now. I will watch it, of course, day by day, because I want welfare reform, the country wants welfare reform. But we cannot have welfare reform that moves in the direction of enormously increasing the cost and, frankly, putting more people on welfare rather than getting people off of it.

ALIENS AND UNEMPLOYMENT

[6.] Q. Sir, I have seen a letter from a high official in the immigration department of the State Department saying that we had 4,800,000 people in this country on temporary visas who were employed. I wonder, in view of the large number who come in illegally, if you don't think these two groups together have a great impact on our high rate of unemployment?

THE PRESIDENT. The President of Mexico spoke to me about that problem, the problem of illegal aliens, and, of course you know, it is a problem in which many of our labor organizations are very vitally interested. It does certainly contribute to the unemployment problem. It is one which administration after admin-

istration has wrestled with without too much success.

It is one, however, after my consultation with the President of Mexico, that I have asked the Department of Labor to examine to see what steps could be taken to see that illegal aliens and particularly those—the Mexican problem is the biggest one, as you know—those from our friends and neighbors to the south, where that could come under better control.

COURT DECISIONS ON WIRETAPPING AND ORGANIZED BASEBALL

[7.] Q. Mr. President, two questions about recent Supreme Court decisions, if I may ask them as two questions, because I am asking in both cases if you have any plans for meeting the situation.

In the first case, the Supreme Court ruled your wiretapping program unconstitutional, saying that in cases of domestic security, wires could not be tapped without a court order. So my first question is whether you have any plans to ask Congress for legislation to restore that authority in the form of an amendment to the Safe Streets Act or other legislation?

In the second case, the Supreme Court left it up to Congress whether organized baseball came under the antitrust laws. This being a matter of some national interest, I think, I wonder if you have any plans to ask for legislation to clarify the status of organized baseball?

THE PRESIDENT. On the first question, I think it is appropriate to point out that the wiretapping in cases of civilian activity, domestic civilian activity, is not, as you have described it, just this Administration's policy. As you know, this type of activity of surveillance has been undertaken, to my knowledge, going back to World War II. It reached its high point in 1963 when there were over 100 cases, as Mr. Hoover testified, in which there were taps used in cases involving domestic security.

Since that time the number of taps has gone down. It went down during the Johnson Administration, and it has sharply been decreased during the 3½ years that this Administration has been in office.

Now, as far as the Supreme Court's decision is concerned, I see no need to ask for legislation to obtain the authority, because the Supreme Court's decision allows the Government, in a case that it believes necessary, to go to a court and get a court order for wiretapping. It simply prohibits wiretapping unless there is a court order. So we will abide by that.

I should also point out that the Supreme Court's decision does not rule out wiretapping in the United States in domestic matters where there is a clear connection between the activity that is under surveillance and a foreign government. That, of course, allows us to move in the internal security area where there is a clear connection between the two. So we will, of course, abide by the Supreme Court's decision in this instance, and I see no need to ask for additional authority from the Congress.

On the baseball matter, I must say I cannot even tell you who is in first place at the present time because I have not had a chance to check it lately.

Yes, I can. I called the mayor of Houston and congratulated him on the fact that he had just been elected to be head of the Conference of Mayors, Mr. Louie Welch. He thought I was calling to congratulate him on the Astros being in

first place. So they must be in first place. [*Laughter*]

In any event, as an old baseball fan, and the rest, I have no present thoughts on that. I would like, perhaps, to talk to Bowie Kuhn [Commissioner of Baseball], who is a good lawyer and also interested in baseball.

CAMPAIGN DEBATES

[8.]   Q. Mr. President, can you give us some of your reasons, sir, for deciding against debating your Democratic opponent this fall?

THE PRESIDENT. He asked if I had any good reasons for deciding against debating my Democratic opponent this fall. As you ladies and gentlemen have often heard me say, and I will continue to hold to this position, questions that deal with the campaign, questions that deal with matters that involve candidacy, are ones that I will respectfully not comment upon until after the Republican Convention. At that time I will be glad to take that question and I will give an answer then.

I have not made a decision on it yet. That is my point.

EDUCATION BILL

[9.]   Q. Mr. President, can you tell us what your plans are for the higher education bill? Do you intend to sign it?

THE PRESIDENT. I have to make the decision tomorrow. I will be very candid with you to tell you that it is one of the closest calls that I have had since being in this office. Some of the members of my staff and Members of the Congress are enthusiastic for signing it, and others are just as enthusiastic for vetoing it.

I have mixed emotions about it. First,

as far as many of the education provisions, strictly education provisions, they are recommendations of this Administration. I think they are very much in the public interest. If they could be separated from the rest of the bill, and stand on their own, there would not be any question about signing the bill. On the other hand, the Congress, as you know, did add a provision, section 803, with regard to busing. It was certainly a well-intentioned position, but from a legal standpoint it is so vague and so ambiguous that it totally fails to deal with this highly volatile issue.

What brought that home to me was when I asked the Attorney General for an opinion as to whether or not it could deal with the problem of the busing order that has been handed down in Detroit. The answer is that it is highly doubtful that section 803 of the higher education act, in the event that it is signed into law, will deal with that problem, because of its vagueness, because of its ambiguity.

The Detroit case is perhaps the most flagrant example that we have of all of the busing decisions, moving against all the principles that I, at least, believe should be applied in this area. It completely rejects the neighborhood school concept. It requires massive busing among 53 different school districts, including the busing of kindergarten children, up to an hour and a half a day, and it puts the objective of some kind of racial balance or attempting to achieve some kind of racial balance above that of superior education, of quality education for all.

I believe that the fact that this section 803 would not deal with the Detroit case means that we are going to have other cases of that type, possibly in other cities before school begins this fall, and the responsibility, if we have them, and if we are unable to stop those orders from going into effect, falls squarely on the Congress because a very simple moratorium bill that I have presented to the Congress and asked for enactment would stop this. And then the Congress moving forward and I am glad to see that there has been some movement in committee at least with the equal educational opportunities act, this action on the part of the Congress would deal with problems like the one in Detroit.

My own view is that in this whole area we face very serious problems this fall unless the Congress moves on the moratorium legislation, clear-cut and soon and before the school year begins.

I have digressed a bit from the bill. It is a close call. I will make the decision tonight and will announce it tomorrow. But that gives you an idea of some of the things that have been going through my mind.

Q. Just to follow that up, if you were to veto it, sir, what are the prospects do you think of getting a separate busing bill and a higher education bill without the busing?

THE PRESIDENT. As a matter of fact, that is one of the matters that I have been discussing with the Congressional leaders—for example, Senator Griffin, who is, as you know, somewhat interested in this issue because he comes from Michigan—and the prospects of getting the higher education bill here on the President's desk as it should be, in the proper form, and then getting an adequate, straight-out moratorium on new school busing orders, the prospects are, frankly, somewhat doubtful.

That is the reason why, in determining whether I sign this bill or veto it, it is a very close call, but I think my statement tomorrow will address that question.

I have an idea which way I am going to go but I promised to talk to one more Senator before I make the final step and I will not tell you today until I talk to him.

Q. Will that be the Senator from Tennessee?

THE PRESIDENT. As a matter of fact, Miss McClendon [Sarah McClendon, Sarah McClendon News Service], you have touched upon a rather raw nerve there, because Nashville is a case which 803 might cover. I say "might." We can't even be sure it would.

So consequently, the Senators from Tennessee strongly advocate signing this, even though it won't handle Detroit, because they say, "We are interested in Detroit, but we are a lot more interested in Tennessee." But I have to be interested in the whole country.

CAMPAIGN CONTRIBUTIONS

[10.] Miss Angelo [Bonnie Angelo, Time-Life].

Q. Mr. Mitchell has declined to make public the source of about $10 million of contributions to your reelection fund. I know that this is in the letter of the law, but I wonder in the spirit of the law, of more openness, what you think about that and might you make them public?

THE PRESIDENT. Mr. Ziegler has, I think, responded to that, and Mr. Mitchell and Mr. Stans.[4] I think it is Mr. Stans who has declined to do that. I support the position that Mr. Stans has taken.

When we talk about the spirit of the

---

[4] Maurice H. Stans was chairman of the Finance Committee to Re-Elect the President.

law and the letter of the law, my evaluation is that it is the responsibility of all individuals, a high moral responsibility to obey the law and to obey it totally.

Now, if the Congress wanted this law to apply to contributions before the date in April that it said the law should take effect, it could have made it apply. The Congress did not apply it before that date and under the circumstances Mr. Stans has said we will comply with the law as the Congress has written it, and I support his decision.

FEDERAL TROOPS AT MIAMI CONVENTIONS

[11.] Q. Mr. President, it has been decided that Federal troops will be deployed to the Miami Beach area for both Presidential conventions. First, were you a part of that decision, and secondly, what is your reaction to this?

THE PRESIDENT. Well, I was not a part of the decision, actually. I think that was probably done consistent with our policy of accepting, when requests are made, the advice of the local officials as to the need for Federal troops. I would hope they would not be needed, but apparently the city of Miami Beach, the State officials in Florida, felt that they might not have adequate personnel to handle what might be conduct that would be quite explosive.

I will just make a guess at this point. I don't think that—at least speaking as to what goes on outside the convention halls is concerned—I don't think that we are going to have those great demonstrations and the violence and so forth that everybody has been predicting. I don't believe we are going to have another Chicago situation such as we had in 1968.

I believe that many of the younger people who have engaged in such activities in the past are rather turned off by it now. I think they will try their best to, of course, affect the outcome of the conventions, both inside the hall and outside, but I think when it comes to violence, the kind of thing that we saw in Chicago, I think that fortunately, while we are not through with it as we saw in the tragic incident involving Governor Wallace, I think that we are not going to have that great a problem. But the Federal troops will be there if they are requested, but only if necessary.

SCHOOL FINANCING AND TAX REFORM

[12.] Q. Mr. President, would you tell us what progress you are making toward keeping your promise about finding a way to relieve property taxes and provide fair and adequate financing for public schools and save the private schools?

THE PRESIDENT. First, with regard to the general problem of tax reform, I would like to commend Chairman Mills for the position that he has taken. I had breakfast with him and Congressman Byrnes and with Secretary Connally before I went off to the Soviet Union.

We discussed the problem of tax reform. He is very interested in tax reform. I am interested in tax reform and, of course, I have noticed several candidates that have expressed themselves on this point.

The problem is that tax reform, or tax legislation, in an election year, as Mr. Mills, as one of the most experienced men in this field, and Mr. Byrnes both agree, is simply not a wise course of action. It is hard enough to get a responsible tax law in a nonelection year. In an election year it will be totally impossible.

Consequently, I think Chairman Mills'

announcement that he will begin hearings on tax reform legislation early in the next session of the Congress shows high statesmanship. Now we will be ready for those hearings.

Secretary Connally instituted, at my request, an intensive study within the Treasury Department of how we could reform the tax system to make it more equitable and to make it more simple and also to deal with problems like property tax which fall upon 65 million people and therefore are, in my view, unfair.

These studies have gone forward. Considerable progress has been made. Secretary Shultz is continuing these studies, and I will make a decision on it prior to submitting the budget and will present recommendations to the next Congress dealing with these issues.

I will not at this time prejudge the various proposals that have been presented before me. Certainly included in that decision will be relief for nonpublic schools. I am committed to that, and the approach of tax credits in this area will be included in that proposal.

Just so that somebody won't say I was trying to duck a hard one here, I know the question of value-added [tax] will come up. There has been a lot of speculation about that. Value-added—I have instructed or directed the Secretary of the Treasury, along with my Council of Economic Advisers—can be considered as a possible approach but only if we can find a nonretrogressive formula.

Tax reform should not be used as a cover for a tax increase. Value-added has to be evaluated then under those circumstances.

One final point I will make is that as we move in this area we have to realize that we have had considerable tax reform over the past 3 years. Nine million poor people have been totally removed from the Federal tax rolls. The lower-income taxpayers have had reductions of 83 percent in their taxes since 1969 and middle-income taxpayers have had reductions of 13 percent.

But there are still inequities. One point I particularly emphasize: At a time that we have made some necessary reforms, some of which I have referred to, we have moved in the wrong direction in another way. The tax system, particularly the Federal income tax system, is hopelessly complex. I majored in law school in tax law. As a lawyer I used to do quite a bit of tax work. I naturally don't take the time to make up my own income tax returns now. But when Manolo [5] came in recently and asked me to help him figure out the forms, I had to send him to a lawyer, and when that is the case with a man who is in basically not a high income bracket, then it is time to do something to make the system not only more equitable but make it more simple. It will put some lawyers and accountants out of business, but there are other things they can do.

Q. Are you saying all these proposals won't come until after the first of the year?

THE PRESIDENT. We will make the proposals before the first of the year, but they will not be considered by the Congress until after the first of the year.

It would not be fair to the American people, it would not be fair to those, for example, interested in the nonpublic school relief, to suggest that the Congress, in this sort of sputtering, start-and-stop period—I mean, they are stopping next week and they come back for 6 weeks and maybe come back after the Republican Convention and the rest—that it could enact tax reform. It is not going to happen, and I am aware of that.

ANTI-BUSING AMENDMENT

[13.] Q. Mr. President, back on the subject of busing, are you moving at all toward the position of favoring an anti-busing constitutional amendment?

THE PRESIDENT. A constitutional amendment is a step that should be taken only if the legislative route proves to be inadequate or impossible—impossible due to the fact that the Congress will not enact it. As far as I am concerned, we do need action here. I prefer the legislative route. I think it is the most responsible route, but if the Congress does not act, then the only recourse left is for a constitutional amendment, and I will move in that direction. We must deal with the problem.

GENERAL LAVELLE

[14.] Q. Mr. President, do you think that there should be a court-martial in the case of General Lavelle [6] to bring out all the facts there, and what is your opinion about that?

THE PRESIDENT. First, that does deal with the foreign policy-defense area, Vietnam and so forth. But since it does involve a current case, I will comment upon it.

The Secretary of Defense has stated his

---

[5] Manolo Sanchez, the President's valet.

[6] Gen. John D. Lavelle had been accused of carrying out unauthorized air strikes against North Vietnam between November 1971 and March 1972. In April 1972, after an investigation by the Air Force, he was demoted and retired from active service.

view on that, has made a decision on it. I think it was an appropriate decision. I will not go beyond that.

FRANK CORMIER (Associated Press). Thank you, Mr. President.

NOTE: President Nixon's twenty-fourth news conference was held at 3:01 p.m. in the Oval Office at the White House on Thursday, June 22, 1972. He spoke without referring to notes.

208   Statement on Signing the Education Amendments of 1972.   *June* 23, 1972

TODAY I am signing into law the Education Amendments of 1972. This legislation includes comprehensive higher education provisions, authority for a new effort to revitalize our educational research effort, and authority to provide financial assistance to school districts to meet special problems incident to desegregation.

It also contains provisions supposedly directed at limiting court decisions dealing with busing. These provisions, however, are inadequate, misleading, and entirely unsatisfactory.

In March of 1970, I asked that aid to students enrolled in postsecondary institutions be expanded and redirected to assure every qualified student that he would be eligible for a combination of Federal grants and subsidized loans sufficient to make up the difference between his college costs and what his family is able to contribute. Congress has provided that opportunity, to an extent, through a program of grants for eligible students and aid from the existing Educational Opportunity Grant, College Work-Study, and National Defense and Guaranteed Student Loan programs.

Unfortunately, certain restrictions placed in the law by the Congress mean that we will not be able to realize fully our principles of equity. But as confidence develops in the new programs, we look forward in the near future to having a set of Federal student assistance programs devoted to the goal of equalizing opportunities for all.

The Congress has also recognized the need for a new Federal role in encouraging and facilitating reform and innovation throughout postsecondary education. To this end, I had proposed a National Foundation for Higher Education. While the Congress did not create a new agency to deal with institutional innovation, it has provided the Secretary of Health, Education, and Welfare with the authority to carry out—on a modest scale—the purposes I had intended for the Foundation. In future years, we may wish to reconsider the need for a statutory foundation for postsecondary education.

One of the act's most constructive features is its establishment—as I had requested—of a National Institute of Education. In proposing the NIE, I expressed the expectation that when fully developed, it would be an important element in the Nation's educational system.

The NIE will be a new research institution within the Department of Health, Education, and Welfare, with a Presidentially appointed Director and a distinguished national advisory council. A primary purpose of the Institute is the initiation of a serious, systematic national effort to find ways to make educational opportunity truly equal—the study of what is needed, both inside and outside the school, to ensure that our compensatory education efforts will be successful.

In the amendments dealing with the busing of public school children, however, this measure is most obviously deficient. Had these disappointing measures alone come to this office—detached from the higher education reforms—they would have been the subject of an immediate veto.

Some months ago, Congress was called upon to make a joint commitment with the Executive, to resolve the spreading social crisis that has arisen in this Nation as a result of massive court-ordered busing of public school children for the purpose of racial integration. One city after another—South, North, East, and West—has been confronted with court orders requiring an enormous price, not simply in the well-being of the children involved but in educational funds, community tensions, and community division. Because, by and large, these orders have been handed down by *Federal* courts, the American people looked to the *Federal* Government for clarification, for guidance, for relief. Congress has provided virtually none.

We asked the Congress to draw up new uniform national desegregation standards for all school districts—South, North, East, and West. The Congress determined to allow the existing inequities and injustices to remain.

We asked the Congress to provide uniform guidance to Federal judges so that court-ordered busing to integrate public school systems would be used only as a last—never a first—resort. The Congress apparently declines to provide such guidance.

We asked the Congress to put a limit on any future court-orderd busing of schoolchildren from kindergarten through the sixth grade. Congress refused to act. As a result future court decisions may treat the kindergarten children in the same fashion as they treat seniors in high school. That is wrong, but the Congress has thus far refused to correct the situation.

We asked the Congress for legislation granting relief for those many school districts already operating under court orders that require busing far in excess of reasonable standards. Congress has thus far provided those dozens of districts with no hope, and no relief.

We asked the Congress for a moratorium—no more Federal court-ordered school busing until such new standards were set up and applied equally to cities South and North. Congress refused—providing instead only a temporary stay, pending appeal, and applied only to a very limited type of court order, and only so long as litigants can manage to keep an appeal alive. It applies only to certain kinds of court orders. An adroit order-drafter may be able to prevent any effective application of this law. This action by the Congress can be construed, not unfairly, as a breathing spell designed less for the harassed school districts of this country than for Congressmen themselves.

Congress has not given us the answer we requested; it has given us rhetoric. It has not provided a solution to the problem of court-ordered busing; it has provided a clever political evasion. The moratorium it offers is temporary; the relief it provides is illusory.

Confronted with one of the burning social issues of the past decade, and an unequivocal call for action from the vast majority of the American people, the 92d Congress has apparently determined that the better part of valor is to dump the matter into the lap of the 93d. Not in the course of this Administration has there been a more manifest Congressional retreat from an urgent call for responsibility.

NOTE: As enacted, the bill (S. 659) is Public Law 92–318 (86 Stat. 235).

On the same day, the White House released the transcript of a news briefing on the act by Elliot L. Richardson, Secretary of Health, Education, and Welfare, and John D. Ehrlichman, Assistant to the President for Domestic Affairs.

209   Remarks on School Busing in Connection With the Education Amendments of 1972.   *June 23, 1972*

THIS bill contains a wholesale retreat by the Congress from responsibility on school busing. Congress has refused to put a limit to court orders busing small children under 11 out of their neighborhoods. Congress has granted no relief whatsoever to school districts which have been ordered by the courts to institute massive busing programs. This is not good enough.

Cross-city and cross-county busing is wrong; it is harmful to education; it does not unite races and communities; it divides them. If Congress continues to refuse to act on the proposal I have made to solve this problem—a moratorium on all busing orders—we will have no choice but to seek a constitutional amendment which will put the goals of better education for all of our children above the objective of massive busing for some children.

NOTE: The President's remarks were filmed in the Family Theater at the White House for later broadcast on radio and television.

210   Letter to the Secretary of State Directing Suspension of Restrictions on Meat Imports.   *June 26, 1972*

Dear Mr. Secretary:

After careful study of the changed conditions in the U.S. and world markets in beef, I have determined that we should now take action to increase the importation of meat into the United States for the remainder of this year.

I request that you take steps immediately with our foreign suppliers to remove restraints established under present arrangements with these suppliers. I ask that you indicate to them that since we have now moved toward a freer market in meat for the remainder of this year, it is my hope that the effect of this action will be to increase the amount of imports entering the United States.

I further request that you collaborate as closely as possible with the Secretary of Agriculture to insure that the steps I have taken are implemented with all possible speed.

Sincerely,

RICHARD NIXON

[Honorable William P. Rogers, Secretary of State, Washington, D.C.]

NOTE: The text of the letter was made available to the press.

211 Remarks on Suspending Restrictions on Meat Imports.
     June 26, 1972

TO COUNTER recent rises in the cost of meat, I have today directed removal of all restrictions on meat imports for the balance of 1972.

Prices of meat have been rising because increased demands have not been matched by increased supplies. This action is designed to increase the supply of meat.

Increased supplies from abroad will not have an immediate effect in reducing prices in the supermarkets, but this action will definitely help in the future.

In the meantime, I intend to take whatever further measures are necessary to prevent increases in the cost of food.

NOTE: The President's remarks were filmed in the Family Theater at the White House for later broadcast on radio and television.

On the same day, the White House released a fact sheet and the transcript of a news briefing on suspension of restrictions on meat imports. Participants in the news briefing were George P. Shultz, Secretary of the Treasury, Raymond A. Ioanes, Administrator, For-

eign Agricultural Service, Department of Agriculture, and Julius L. Katz, Deputy Assistant Secretary, International Resources and Food Policy, Department of State.

On June 29, 1972, the President signed Executive Order 11674 extending economic stabilization controls to unprocessed agricultural products after the first sale. On the same day, the White House released the following related material: a fact sheet, the text of a Cost of Living Council regulation, and a statement and the transcript of a news briefing by Donald Rumsfeld, Counsellor to the President and Director, Cost of Living Council. Mr. Rumsfeld's statement is printed in the Weekly Compilation of Presidential Documents (vol. 8, p. 1110).

On June 30, the White House released the transcript of a news briefing by Secretary Shultz and Mr. Rumsfeld on the President's meeting with the Cost of Living Council to discuss meat imports and stabilization of food prices.

On July 7, the White House released the transcript of a news briefing by Secretary Shultz and Herbert Stein, Chairman, Council of Economic Advisers, on a meeting with food industry representatives to discuss further actions to stabilize food prices.

212 Statement About Suspension of Restrictions on Meat
     Imports. *June 26, 1972*

TO COUNTER recent rises in the cost of meat, I have today directed the Secretary of State to remove all quota restrictions on meat imported into the United States for the balance of 1972. Nations which export meat to the United States until today have been observing voluntary quotas.

The recent rise in the price of meat is in part due to an improving economy here at home causing increased demands for meat which have not been matched by

increased supplies. This action is intended to encourage more meat imports into the United States, thereby increasing the supply available here.

This action alone may not fully solve the problem. Further measures will be taken as necessary and appropriate.

I intend to monitor this situation closely, and I want to assure every American housewife that this Administration is firmly determined to prevent unjustified increases in the cost of food.

We have made significant progress in our battle against rising prices. We are going to do whatever is necessary to see that that battle is won.

Earlier this year, we announced an import program to increase meat imports 11 percent over meat imports during 1971.[1] Since that time, however, the continuing shift in demand and supplies has become

---

[1] By Proclamation 4114 of March 9, 1972.

much more pronounced.

All meat imports, of course, will be subject to the same high standards of sanitation that apply to domestically produced meat.

This action is not aimed at the American farmer; his income has only begun to approach reasonable levels. It is intended to remedy a short-term shortage which is beyond the ability of our farmers to fill.

---

213 Letter to the Secretary of Agriculture About Suspension of Restrictions on Meat Imports. *June 26, 1972*

Dear Mr. Secretary:

I have taken action today to liberalize the imports of beef. The action is being taken to help us meet the exploding demand for beef in this country.

As I have discussed with you, I am satisfied that in taking this action we are not endangering the economic position of our livestock producers.

Over the years they have made a sustained and essential contribution to meeting our growing demand for beef. I recognize fully that their continued economic

health is essential so that they can play their full part in meeting our future demands. I know you are confident that they will continue to make this contribution and that you will call on me for any assistance you may need.

Sincerely,

RICHARD NIXON

[Honorable Earl L. Butz, Secretary of Agriculture, Washington, D.C.]

NOTE: The text of the letter was made available to the press.

---

214 The President's News Conference of *June 29, 1972*

QUESTIONS

THE PRESIDENT. [1.] Mr. Cormier [Frank Cormier, Associated Press] has the first question tonight.

Q. Mr. President, I don't want to ask a soft or flabby question because, as you know, your associate John Ehrlichman has suggested that news conferences really are not all that important because we tend

to ask that type of question too often.

So I want to submit one for the Ehrlichman Award this evening.

THE PRESIDENT. As long as it is not soft and flabby.

ENDING THE WAR IN VIETNAM

Q. Mindful that ending the war was one of your major campaign themes in

1968, mindful that our bombings in Indo-china now are at a 5-year high, according to the Pentagon, mindful that troops are still coming out but even more are going into Thailand and the 7th Fleet, I wonder if you can say with any confidence that you can end the war by January 20 of next year?

THE PRESIDENT. Mr. Cormier, we have made great progress in ending the war and particularly in ending American involvement in the war.

Since you have recounted the record to an extent, let me recount it also from the positive side.

When we came into office, there were 540,000 Americans in Vietnam. Our casualties were running as high as 300 a week, the cost was $22 billion a year. We have taken out 500,000 men since that time.[1] Our casualties have been reduced 95 percent, down to 2, that is too many, but from 300 to 2. As far as the cost is concerned, instead of $22 billion a year, it is down to $7 billion a year.

As far as the situation on the negotiating front is concerned, instead of being in a position where we did not have a positive offer on the table, we have made what Mr. Brinkley of NBC characterized last night as being a very constructive offer, one in which in return for an all-Indochina cease-fire and the return of POW's and an accounting for all of our missing in action, that we would stop all military activities in Indochina and we would withdraw all Americans, all those that remain, within 4 months.

---

[1] On June 28, 1972, Press Secretary Ronald L. Ziegler announced the President's decision to withdraw additional United States troops from Vietnam. Mr. Ziegler's statement is printed in the Weekly Compilation of Presidential Documents (vol. 8, p. 1110).

Now, having reached this position at this time, we believe that that is an excellent record. The only thing that we have not done is to do what the Communists have asked and that is to impose a Communist government on the people of South Vietnam against their will. This we will not do because that would reward aggression, it would encourage that kind of aggression and reduce the chances of peace all over the world in the years to come, and it would dishonor the United States of America.

RESUMPTION OF PARIS TALKS

[2.] On the negotiating front, we have informed the North Vietnamese, after consultation with the Government of Vietnam, that we will return to the negotiating table in Paris on April [July] 13, Thursday; we have been informed by the North Vietnamese and the Vietcong, that they, too, will return on that date. We have returned to the negotiating table, or will return to it on the assumption that the North Vietnamese are prepared to negotiate in a constructive and serious way. We will be prepared to negotiate in that way. If those negotiations go forward in a constructive and serious way, this war can be ended, and it can be ended well before January 20. If they do not go forward on that basis, the United States will continue to meet its commitments. Our bombing, as far as that is concerned, our mining, is for the purpose only of preventing Communist aggression from succeeding, to protect the remaining Americans, 40,000 or so, that are still in Vietnam, and to have some bargaining position in getting our POW's back.

One last point with regard to the POW's: I know that every American is concerned about these men. I have been somewhat concerned about them. I will only say that I have had some experience, and a great deal of experience as a matter of fact in this past year, in dealing with Communist leaders. I find that making a bargain with them is not easy, and you get something from them only when you have something they want to get from you. The only way we are going to get our POW's back is to be doing something to them, and that means hitting military targets in North Vietnam, retaining a residual force in South Vietnam, and continuing the mining of the harbors of North Vietnam.

Only by having that kind of activity go forward will they have any incentive to return our POW's rather than not to account for them as was the case when the French got out of Vietnam in 1954 and 15,000 French were never accounted for after that.[2]

I shall never have that happen to the brave men who are POW's.

GENERAL LAVELLE'S ACTIVITIES

[3.] Q. Mr. President, before you ordered a resumption of the bombing of North Vietnam, General Lavelle authorized or initiated some unauthorized strikes there. In your view, did this affect any diplomatic negotiations going on at that time, and are you concerned that

---

[2] The number referred to by the President is an estimate of French Union forces unaccounted for in Indochina after the cessation of hostilities in 1954. The French Union forces included French Metropolitan, French Foreign Legion, French colonial, and Vietnamese troops. All French Metropolitan prisoners of war were accounted for.

you apparently didn't know about it for several months?

THE PRESIDENT. It did not affect the diplomatic negotiations. As a matter of fact, a meeting took place, a private meeting, between Dr. Kissinger and the negotiators in Paris on May 2, during the period that General Lavelle's activities were being undertaken,[3] and you can be very sure that had the North Vietnamese wanted any pretext to complain about, they would have complained about that particular matter.

As far as this is concerned, as Admiral Moorer testified today, it wasn't authorized. It was directed against only those military targets which were the areas that were being used for firing on American planes, but since it did exceed authorization, it was proper for him to be relieved and retired. And I think that it was the proper action to take. And I believe that will assure that that kind of activity may not occur in the future.

EFFECT OF MINING AND BOMBING

[4.] Q. Mr. President, on May 8, at the time of the mining of the harbors in North Vietnam, your assistant, Dr. Kissinger, predicted the mining would result in the drying up of supplies and the major offensive should be over around July 1. Is that estimate still valid, and if so, do you have a timetable for the withdrawal of the support troops who have gone into

---

[3] The bombing raids carried out by forces under the command of Gen. John D. Lavelle were ended March 8, 1972.

The White House later stated that the President was referring to the private arrangements leading up to the May 2 meeting rather than events of that particular day.

the naval and into the air bases around Vietnam to support the South Vietnamese during this offensive?

THE PRESIDENT. Mr. Jarriel [Tom Jarriel, ABC News], to date the effect of the mining and also the bombing of the military targets in North Vietnam—particularly the railroads and the oil supplies—the situation in Vietnam has been completely turned around. I was looking at some news magazines that came out the week before the mining was ordered, and I noted that each one of them has as its heading, "The specter of defeat in Vietnam." That was the situation when we started it.

It has been turned around. The South Vietnamese are now on the offensive. It is not over. We expect, perhaps, some more North Vietnamese offensive, but I believe that now the ability of the South Vietnamese to defend themselves on the ground, with the support that we give them in the air, has been demonstrated. Their ability to defend themselves in Anloc and Kontum, and now in the area of Hué, is an indication that Vietnamization, as far as their ground activity is concerned, has proved to be a successful action. Now, as far as the future is concerned, I have already indicated that we will be returning to negotiations in July. That is the important area to watch at this time, as well as the battlefield. And as far as any future announcements are concerned, that will depend upon progress at the negotiating table and on the battlefront.

DIKES AND DAMS AS TARGETS

[5.] Q. Mr. President——

THE PRESIDENT. Mr. Rather [Dan Rather, CBS News]. I remember your name. [*Laughter*]

Q. Thank you, Mr. President. I remember yours, too. [*Laughter*]

The background of this question is your own statements made down in Texas, among other places, saying that you had not sanctioned and would not sanction the bombing of the dikes and dams in North Vietnam, because you considered it an inhumane act because of what it would do to civilians.

Within the past week there have been reports of eyewitnesses—one of these reports came from the French Press Agency, and another, I think, was the Swedish Ambassador in Hanoi—eyewitnesses claiming to have seen American planes hit dikes and dams.

The question is, has such bombing occurred? If so, what steps are you taking to see that it doesn't happen again?

THE PRESIDENT. Mr. Rather, we have checked those reports. They have proved to be inaccurate. The bombing of dikes is something, as you will recall from the gentleman who asked the question in Texas,[4] was something that some people have advocated. The United States has used great restraint in its bombing policy and, I think, properly so. We have tried to hit only military targets and we have been hitting military targets. We have had orders out not to hit dikes because the result in terms of civilian casualties would be extraordinary.

As far as any future activities are concerned, those orders still are in force. I do not intend to allow any orders to go out

---

[4] See Item 134 [4.].

which would involve civilian casualties if they can be avoided. Military targets only will be allowed.

SOUTH VIETNAMESE EFFECTIVENESS

[6.] Q. Mr. President, last year, or at least early this year, General Abrams relayed to you his belief that the South Vietnamese could now hack it on the battlefield. The invasion from the North occurred, and we responded with bombing.

When do you realistically think the South Vietnamese can do it alone without massive firepower from us?

THE PRESIDENT. Mr. Semple [Robert B. Semple, Jr., New York Times], I think that is being determined and also demonstrated at this time.

First, as far as the ground activities are concerned, they are being entirely undertaken by the South Vietnamese. American ground combat action has totally been finished in Vietnam. As far as Americans in Vietnam are concerned, this war is over in the future for any future draftees. No more draftees will be sent to Vietnam.

As far as air action is concerned, as General Abrams or any military man will tell you, as they have told me, air action alone, without adequate fighting on the ground, cannot stop a determined enemy.

What happened in this case was that the North Vietnamese launched a massive offensive with huge tanks, bigger than those against which they were arrayed, with new and modern weapons. In order to provide an equalizer, and it was needed, we provided air support.

But I should also point this out, something that has been little noticed, 40 percent of all the tactical air sorties being flown over the battlefields of South Viet-

nam are now being flown not by Americans, but by South Vietnamese.

So we see the South Vietnamese not only doing all the ground fighting, but increasing their ability to do the fighting in the air.

Finally, the success of our airstrikes on the North and on the battlefield, the success in turning this battle around hastens the day when the South Vietnamese will be able to undertake the total activity themselves.

I am not going to put a date on it. I can only say the outcome of the present battle, how badly the North Vietnamese are hurt, will determine it, but I am very optimistic on this point.

VICE PRESIDENT AGNEW

[7.] Q. To change the subject and not to be flabby, sir.

THE PRESIDENT. You would never be flabby.

Q. Thank you, sir.

Isn't it time you told us, will Agnew be on the ticket?

THE PRESIDENT. I know that that is a question that is very much on the minds of the delegates who will be coming to Miami in August. I will announce a decision on that, my views on it, well before the convention so that the delegates will know my views.

As far as the Vice President is concerned, my views with regard to his performance are the same that I reflected rather generously in my interview with Mr. Rather in January of this year.[5] I think he has done a fine job as Vice President. I have very high confidence in him.

But the decision with regard to the Vice

---

[5] See Item 1 [4.].

Presidency will not be announced until before the Republican Convention, in good time for them to make their own decision.

JOHN CONNALLY'S ROLE

[8.] Mr. Horner [Garnett D. Horner, Washington Evening Star].

Q. Mr. President, what role do you foresee in the future months after he returns from his present trip and after the election, for John Connally?

THE PRESIDENT. Mr. Horner, first the reports that we have had on Mr. Connally's trip have been excellent. I think that his trip to Latin America—and incidentally also the trip that Dr. Arthur Burns has made to Latin America—came at a good time and allowed the Latin American heads of state to express their views just as vigorously as did Mr. Echeverría [6] when he was here in this country. That is what we want, candid, vigorous talk between the heads of state in the American hemisphere.

Also, the discussions he is presently having in Australia, in New Zealand, in Southeast Asia, India, Pakistan, and so forth, and later in Iran, I know will be helpful. When he returns he will not undertake a permanent Government assignment, but he has agreed to undertake special Government assignments at that time. I have one in mind, a very important one, but I cannot announce it at this time. I will announce it when he returns and when he reports to me in San Clemente.

---

[6] President Luis Echeverría Alvarez of Mexico paid a state visit to the United States on June 15 and 16, 1972. See Items 200, 201, and 203.

PEACE NEGOTIATIONS

[9.] Ms. Cornell. [*Laughter*]

HELEN THOMAS (Mrs. Douglas B. Cornell, United Press International). Mr. President.

THE PRESIDENT. I said Ms.

Q. Thank you.

Can you tell us what took you back to the Paris peace table and would you support a coalition government, formation of a coalition government, or would you discuss it in Paris?

THE PRESIDENT. It would not be useful to indicate the discussions that took place in various places with regard to returning to the Paris peace table.

Let it suffice to say that both sides considered it in their interests to return to the Paris peace table. We would not have returned unless we thought there was a chance for more serious discussions and more constructive discussions than we have had in the past, although I must be quite candid and say that we have been disappointed in the past with regard to these discussions. We have had 149 plenary sessions and no significant results. I do not believe it would be particularly helpful, in a news conference, to negotiate with regard to what we are going to talk about at the conference. That is a matter that we will negotiate with the enemy.

As far as a coalition government is concerned, no. We will not negotiate with the enemy for accomplishing what they cannot accomplish themselves and that is to impose against their will on the people of South Vietnam a coalition government with the Communists.

However, we will be constructive, we will be forthcoming. An internationally supervised cease-fire, a total withdrawal of all Americans within 4 months, a total cessation of all bombing—these, we think, are very reasonable offers, and we believe the enemy should seriously consider them.

ARMS CONTROL AND WEAPONS
DEVELOPMENT

[10.] Q. Mr. President, hardly had you signed the arms control agreements in Moscow than your Administration asked for new money for new strategic weapons. Some of your critics are saying that this is almost a deception giving the Pentagon what it wants, namely concentration on developing quality weapons. Will you try to dispel this contradiction?

THE PRESIDENT. Mr. Morgan [Edward P. Morgan, ABC News], the problem with regard to arms control is that we do not deal with it in a vacuum. We have to deal with the problem as it affects the security of the United States. Now, first, let me say that if we had not had an arms control agreement, a limitation of ABM's and a temporary limitation for 5 years on certain classifications of offensive weapons, I would—and I am saying this conservatively—have had to ask the Congress of the United States to approve an increase in the defense budget for nuclear strategic weapons of at least $15 billion a year on a crash program. Reason: Had there been no arms control agreement, the Soviet Union's plans called for an increase of their ABM's to 1,000 over the next 5 years. The arms control agreement limits them to 200 as it does us. Had there been no arms control agreement, the Soviet Union had a program underway in the field of submarines which would have brought them up to over 90. The agreement limits them to 62.

Had there been no arms control agreement—and this is the most important point—in the terms of offensive strategic weapons, the Soviet Union that has now passed us in offensive strategic weapons—they have 1,600, we have roughly 1,000—they would have built 1,000 more over the next 5 years. Now, under those circumstances, any President of the United States could see that in 5 years the United States would be hopelessly behind; our security would be threatened, our allies would be terrified, particularly in those areas—and our friends like the Mideast—where the possibility of Soviet adventurism is considered to be rather great.

Therefore, the arms control agreement at least put a brake on new weapons. Now, with regard to the new weapons that you refer to, however, let me point out they are not for the next 5-year period. We are really talking about the period after that. And they are absolutely essential for the security of the United States for another reason: Because looking at this not in a vacuum but in terms of what the other side is doing, Mr. Brezhnev made it very clear that he intended to go forward in those categories that were not limited.

Now, in fairness to him, he also said, and made it very clear—he made it perfectly clear, I should say—he said that he expected that we would go forward. Now, under these circumstances, then, for the United States not to go forward in those areas that were not controlled would mean that at the end of the seventies we would be in an inferior position, and no President of the United States can take the responsibility of allowing the United States to be the second most powerful nation in the world, not because of any jingoistic idea, but because if we are in that position, our foreign policy, our commitments around the world would be very, very seriously jeopardized.

Now the most important point I have saved for the last and that is this: I think these agreements are in the interest of the United States. I think that they are very much in the interest of arms control and therefore in the interest of world peace. But, they are only a beginning; they are only the foundation. Now, what we have to do is to really go forward with the second step. That is why the phase two of the arms control limitation, which we hope will begin in October provided the Congress approves the ones that we have before them at the present time—phase two, which will be a permanent arms control agreement on all offensive nuclear weapons—this is the one that we think can have far greater significance even than phase one.

Phase one is the break-through, and phase two is the culmination. And phase two, if we can reach agreement with the Soviets—and it will take long and hard bargaining—but if we can reach it, it will mean, then, that we not only hold our arms budgets where they are, but that in these new programs instead of going forward with them on the basis presently projected we will be able to cut them back.

That is our goal, and I think we can achieve it provided we approve phase one and provided we continue a credible arms program because, believe me, the Soviets are not going to agree to limit their future programs unless they have something to get from us.

B–1 BOMBER

[11.]   Q. Mr. President, in consideration of your argument on our need for offensive weapons, why then do you insist on development of the costly B–1 bomber when in fact the Soviet Union has shown little interest in the bomber force in recent years and as far as we know has no new bomber force on the drawing boards at this time?

THE PRESIDENT. Each power, the Soviet Union and the United States, must have those forces that are needed for its own security. We basically are not only a land power but a land and sea power. The Soviet Union is primarily a land power with certain definite requirements. Having that in mind, we believe that the B–1 bomber is, for our security interest, necessary.

As far as the Soviet Union is concerned, the fact that they are not developing bombers does not mean that they do not respect ours. And I would say, too, that had we not had our present advantage in bombers we could not then stand by and allow the Soviets to have a 1,600 to 1,000 advantage in terms of missiles that are land based. So, our bomber is an offset for that.

SOCIAL SECURITY

[12.]   Q. It was made perfectly clear to us this week that you would be less than overjoyed if the Senate should attach a 20-percent social security increase to the debt ceiling extension bill which expires tomorrow night. It looks like that might happen tomorrow. I wonder what you see as the consequences, and what you could do about it?

THE PRESIDENT. Well, there should be an increase in social security. There has been an increase in the cost of living, and I have favored an increase in the social security. The problem with the 20-percent increase which the Senate will consider is what it does to the Social Security System, and also what it does to the cost of living and to future taxes in this country.

We must realize that if a 20-percent social security [increase] is passed by the Senate and by the Congress, that the increased payroll tax to pay for it will completely wipe out the tax reduction that was given to middle-income and lower-middle-income wage earners in 1969. That is a question that the Congress has got to address itself to.

If, on the other hand, the Congress passes the 20-percent increase in social security and does not finance it adequately, it will seriously jeopardize the integrity of the social security trust fund, and it could be highly inflationary which, of course, will hurt most the social security people, the retired people.

So these are considerations that have motivated me in expressing concern. It is not that we do not want an increase in social security. It isn't that we do not want as high an increase as possible. But the increase must be a responsible one. It should be funded. And the Congress, if it does not fund it, would be doing something that would not be in the interest of retired people, who would be faced with an increase in the cost of living.

THE VICE PRESIDENT

[13.] Q. Sir, I know you have said that you don't care to discuss politics until after the Republican Convention, which has to make you kind of an unusual man in Washington, but in your answer a while ago regarding Vice President Agnew, I gained the impression that he may be a one-term Vice President. Am I correct in that?

THE PRESIDENT. Certainly not, no. As

I said to Mr. Rather—I cannot reconstruct it exactly, he probably can—but in any event, as I said to him in that program, Mr. Agnew had conducted himself, I thought, with great dignity, with great courage, some controversy—which is inevitable when you have courage—and that under these circumstances, since he was a member of a winning team, I did not believe breaking up a winning team was a good idea.

That was my view then, that is my view now. However, the final decision, as I indicated in my answer a few moments ago, will be deferred until before the Republican Convention, and I will make it in time for the delegates to know what my views are.

UNEMPLOYMENT

[14.] Mr. Theis [J. William Theis, Hearst Newspapers and Hearst Headline Service].

Q. Mr. President, with all the shifts in the economy, unemployment seems to be stalled at just under 6 percent. What plans do you have to do something about that?

THE PRESIDENT. We have been making great strides on the employment side, as you know, Mr. Theis: 2,300,000 new jobs since the new economic policy was announced on August 15. We expect that the rapid expansion of the economy, which most economists agree is taking place, is going to reflect itself in reducing unemployment rolls, not as fast as we would like, but in reducing them, through the fall and winter months.

As far as additional actions are concerned, we do not contemplate any at this time, except that we are going to continue those policies that have resulted in the economy growing at a rate of 5½ percent in real growth, and that have resulted—

and this is perhaps the most important number to those who are employed, the 80 million or so—have resulted in the wage earners of this country getting off the treadmill.

For 5 years before we arrived here in 1969, wages had gone up but the wage increases had been almost entirely eaten up by price increases. The most significant thing that has happened since the new economic policy is that we have cut the rate of inflation down so that it is half of what it was in 1970, from 6 to 3 percent. Wages have continued to go up, even though at a lower rate, but real, spendable earnings of 80 million wage earners have gone up 5 percent. That is as compared with going up at the rate of only one percent a year in the sixties. It is this kind of progress that is good.

On the other hand, I am not a bit satisfied with the fact that unemployment is at 5.9 percent, and we are continuing to explore other means of trying to bring it down faster.

BOMBING AND THE PARIS PEACE TALKS

[15.] Mr. Lisagor [Peter Lisagor, Chicago Daily News].

Q. Mr. President, a clarifying question on the bombing, please. You have said that the sole purpose of your bombing and your mining, in your May 8 speech, was to protect the 60,000 American troops there. Did I understand you to say, in answer to an earlier question, that that bombing is now contingent upon the release of the prisoners? And I would like to ask an additional question that is slightly related: Were there any conditions attached by each side to the return to the Paris peace talks?

THE PRESIDENT. No, there are no conditions attached to either side. We are going back to the talks prepared to negotiate without conditions, which we think is the most constructive way to obtain results. For example, the condition—I assume this is the implication of your question—there was no condition that if we would go back to the talks we would stop the bombing. We do not intend to. We will stop the bombing when the conditions are met that I laid out in my May 8 speech.

In my May 8 speech, Mr. Lisagor, as you recall, I laid down three conditions. I said that we were bombing military targets in the North, that we were mining the harbor, and that we were doing so for three purposes: to prevent the imposition of a Communist government in South Vietnam, to protect our remaining forces in South Vietnam, which were then 60,000, and, in addition, for the purpose of obtaining the release of our POW's.

Those are the three conditions that we have as far as the bombing is concerned.

But we are prepared to negotiate on those points with the enemy. We have no desire to continue the bombing for one moment longer than necessary to accomplish what we consider to be these very minimal objectives.

CAPITAL PUNISHMENT DECISION

[16.] Q. Mr. President, do you regard capital punishment as cruel and unusual, and do you think steps should be taken to reinstate it?

THE PRESIDENT. I was expecting that question tonight, but as you know, the Court just handed down its decision,[7] and

---

[7] *William Henry Furman v. Georgia* (408 U.S. 238).

I immediately got hold of Mr. Dean, Counsel to the President, and I said, "Send it over to me." He said, "There are nine opinions."

Now I try to read fast, but I couldn't get through all nine opinions. But I did get through the Chief Justice's.

As I understand it, the holding of the Court must not be taken at this time to rule out capital punishment in all kinds of crimes. This has dealt apparently with crimes at the State level and will apply to 35 States in which we do have the situation where capital punishment does apply.

It is my view that as far as cruel and inhuman punishment is concerned, any punishment is cruel and inhuman which takes the life of a man, or woman, for that matter.

On the other hand, the point that I wish to emphasize is this: In the case of kidnaping and in the case of hijacking, Federal crimes, what we are trying to do is to prevent the loss of life.

I recall the situation at the time of the Lindbergh kidnaping. I recall that kidnapings were sort of par for the course then. Any wealthy family was a possible subject for kidnaping.

Kidnaping has been substantially reduced. Now some experts will say that the deterrent of the Lindbergh law was not what did it. Something had to have that effect. Therefore, I have said in the past and I do not retreat from that now, I believe that capital punishment is a necessary deterrent for capital crimes of that type as far as the Federal jurisdiction is concerned—kidnaping and hijacking.

As far as the Court's decision is concerned, except for three of the judges who based their decision on the Eighth Amend-ment, which rules out cruel and inhumane punishment and as far as the Court's decision is concerned, I do not understand it necessarily to apply to these Federal crimes. I would hope that it would not.

I have expressed my views and I will also say, of course, that we will carry out whatever the Court finally determines to be the law of the land. But I would hope that the Court's decision does not go so far as to rule out capital punishment for kidnaping and hijacking.

GUN CONTROL

[17.] Q. Mr. President, in light of the attempted assassination of Governor Wallace, have you changed your thinking at all on the need for Federal laws controlling the sale of handguns?

THE PRESIDENT. Well, my thinking has not changed. I have always felt there should be a Federal law for the control of handguns. As you will note, Mr. Klein-dienst testified to that effect earlier today and he did testify to that effect after checking my own position on it.

The problem there is to write the law, the legislation, in such a way that it is precise and deals with that kind of hand-gun which ought to be controlled. And I am referring now to the Saturday night specials. These are ones where you would have Federal jurisdiction because many of them come in from abroad and, being imported from abroad, it would be particularly a matter for Federal control.

I believe, however, that the legislation, if it is therefore precisely written—and we have been cooperating with the Senate committee, particularly with Senator Hruska, in attempting to work out the proper language—that the Congress should pass such a law, and I will sign it, ruling out Saturday night specials, which I think is the major source of this kind of crime you speak about.

THE SUPREME COURT

[18.] Q. Mr. President, do you consider the Supreme Court now to be in balance or do you think it needs another dose of strict constructionism if that occasion should arise?

THE PRESIDENT. I have expressed myself with regard to the Court on previous occasions, but I feel at the present time, that the Court is as balanced as I have had an opportunity to make it. [*Laughter*]

I have been interested to note that there have been several five-to-four decisions, but let me also say—and the Chief Justice was in to see me the other day and we talked about a number of things—let me also say that of the people I have appointed to that Court, and each one of them will bear this out, I have never talked to them directly or indirectly about a matter before the Court.

I had a pretty good idea before they went on how I thought they might think, but sometimes they have ruled differently, because lawyers never agree.

FUTURE GOALS

[19.] Q. Mr. President, sir, since you have taken care of many of the problems with Peking and Moscow and had some agreements and now you seem to have made great progress with the war, I wonder what areas of the world you would like to work on next?

THE PRESIDENT. Well, I don't want to go to the Moon. [*Laughter*]

EVALUATION OF BOMBING

[20.] Q. Mr. President, the history of American bombing of North Vietnam indicates that it has served to hinder negotiations rather than stimulate negotiations. Why do you think it is going to work now in view of that history?

THE PRESIDENT. I am not sure that my evaluation of the history is the same as yours. My own view is that we have tried every device possible over the past 3 years to get negotiations going. We have withdrawn forces, we have made very forthcoming offers, we have wound down combat activities on our part, and the result has been simply an ever increasing intransigence on the part of the enemy.

Believe me, it was only as a last resort that I made the very difficult decision of May 8, knowing how much rode on that decision, but having made that decision, I think it was the right decision. And I think the fact that our summit meetings went ahead despite that decision, the fact that we are going back to the negotiating table despite that decision, indicates that it may be that those who feel that a strong hand at the negotiating table is one that results in no negotiation may be wrong.

It has always been my theory that in dealing with these very pragmatic men—and we must respect them for their strength and their pragmatism—who lead the Communist nations, that they respect strength, not belligerence but strength, and at least that is the way I am always going to approach it, and I think it is going to be successful in the end.

THE VICE PRESIDENTIAL NOMINATION

[21.] Q. Mr. President, in the middle of May, Vice President Agnew told a number of reporters that he thought it was totally unrealistic for anyone to imagine a Republican convention nominating a Democrat like John Connally.

Can you tell us if you discussed that statement with him and if you knew he was going to make it?

Finally, if the answer to that question is no, can you give us your reaction to it?

THE PRESIDENT. I did not discuss it with Vice President Agnew. I almost said "Vice President Connally." But I did not discuss it with the Vice President. I would say in terms of political evaluation, he, of course, is correct. A Republican convention or a Democratic convention tends to nominate members of their own party to their high offices.

Now, as far as Secretary Connally is concerned, however, I think we can only say that he is a man who has served his country extremely well in national office, as Governor of his State, and then as Secretary of the Treasury. I certainly hope that in the future he will serve this country in some capacity.

I am not going to go further, though, on the Vice Presidency. I have expressed my views with regard to Vice President Agnew and I will at the proper time inform the delegates of my views.

PRESIDENTIAL PRESS CONFERENCES

[22.] Q. Mr. President, this is kind of an in-house question, but I think it is of interest.

THE PRESIDENT. You would not ask an "out-house" question, would you? [*Laughter*]

Q. I am not sure what an out-house question is.

THE PRESIDENT. I know.

Q. Nevertheless, I think this is of inter-est to our viewers and listeners and readers, and that is that you seem to have done very well tonight, you are certainly in command of this situation, and yet this is the first time in a year that you have been willing to meet with us in this kind of forum.

What is your feeling about these types of press conferences?

THE PRESIDENT. It is not that I am afraid to do it. I have to determine the best way of communication and also, and this will sound self-serving and is intended to be, I have to use the press conference—I don't mean use the reporters, but use the press conference—when I believe that is the best way to communicate or inform the people.

Now, for example, I had to make a decision—it may have been wrong—but I concluded that in the very sensitive period leading up to the Peking trip and the period thereafter and in the even more sensitive period, as it turned out to be, leading up to the Moscow trip and the period immediately thereafter, that the press conference, even "no-commenting" questions, was not a useful thing for the President of the United States to engage in.

I felt I was, of course, on television enough in that period anyway, if that was the problem. As you know, I have met the press, not perhaps as often as some members of the press would like, or maybe as often as I would like, but I have met them in other formats than the televised conference.

The other point that I should make is this: I know that many members of the press have been discussing the press conference and they feel that perhaps the President, this President, is tempted to downgrade the press or downgrade the press conference. I am not trying to do that. It is useful, it is important. It requires hard work in preparing for it, I can assure you. But I think I can best put it this way: Every President has to make a decision when he enters the office about his relations with the press and about his job. I mean, I am as human as anybody else, I like to get a good press. But on the other hand I had to determine, and I did determine, as I am sure most Presidents do, that what was most important at this time was for me to do a good job because the stakes were so high, particularly in foreign policy, and also in some areas of domestic policy.

Now, if I do a good job, the fact I get bad press isn't going to matter; if I do a bad job, a good press isn't going to help. When November comes, the people will decide whether I have done a good job or not and whether I have had so many press conferences is probably not going to make a lot of difference.

I trust I can do both because it is essential for a President to communicate with the people, to inform the press who, of course, do talk to the people, either on television, radio, or through what they write.

I hope perhaps in the future we can avoid the feeling on the part of the press that the President is antagonistic to them. I can't say whether the President thinks the press is antagonistic to him, but that is another matter.

MR. CORMIER. Thank you, Mr. President.

NOTE: President Nixon's twenty-fifth news conference was held at 9 p.m. in the East Room at the White House on Thursday, June 29, 1972. It was broadcast live on radio and television. The President spoke without referring to notes.

215 Veto of Public Broadcasting Bill. *June 30, 1972*

To the House of Representatives:

I find it necessary to return without my approval H.R. 13918 which is intended to provide increased financing for the Corporation for Public Broadcasting and to modify the Public Broadcasting Act of 1967 by making various changes in the structure of the non-commercial, educational broadcasting system.

Public broadcasting can and does make important contributions to our Nation's life by presenting educational and cultural programs of diversity and excellence. Programs such as "Sesame Street" and "The Electric Company" already have begun to repay the far-sighted decision the Nation made in the 1950s when channels were reserved for educational purposes. Public broadcasting deserves to be continued, and to be strengthened.

The legislation before me, however, offers a poor approach to public broadcast financing. It ignores some serious questions which must be resolved before any long-range public broadcasting financing can be soundly devised, and before the statutory framework for public broadcasting is changed.

There are many fundamental disagreements concerning the directions which public broadcasting has taken and should pursue in the future. Perhaps the most important one is the serious and widespread concern—expressed in Congress and within public broadcasting itself—that an organization, originally intended only to serve the local stations, is becoming instead the center of power and the focal point of control for the entire public broadcasting system.

The Public Broadcasting Act of 1967 made localism a primary means of achieving the goals of the educational broadcasting system. Localism places the principal public interest responsibility on the individual educational radio and television stations, licensed to serve the needs and interests of their own communities. By not placing adequate emphasis on localism, H.R. 13918 threatens to erode substantially public broadcasting's impressive potential for promoting innovative and diverse cultural and educational programming.

The public and legislative debate regarding passage of H.R. 13918 has convinced me that the problems posed by Government financing of a public broadcast system are much greater than originally thought. They cannot be resolved until the structure of public broadcasting has been more firmly established, and we have a more extensive record of experience on which to evaluate its role in our national life.

This Administration has demonstrated its dedication to the principle of public broadcasting by increasing appropriations to the Corporation sevenfold in the past three years, from $5 million in FY 69 to $35 million in FY 72. On top of this, I have requested an additional 30 percent increase for next year to $45 million. The funding proposed in H.R. 13918, which almost doubles next year's appropriation, and more than doubles the following year's appropriation over FY 1972, is unwarranted in light of the serious questions yet unanswered by our brief experience with public broadcasting.

I urge the continuation of carefully measured annual funding for the Corporation, under the existing statutory framework, subject to regular budgetary oversight and review. Specifically, I ask the Congress to follow my budget recommendation by enacting a one-year extension of the Corporation's authorization and providing it $45 million. Since interim funds for the Corporation are included in a continuing resolution currently before the Congress, there should be no interruption of the Corporation's activities.

RICHARD NIXON

The White House,
June 30, 1972.

NOTE: The House of Representatives referred the veto message to committee, and no further action was taken.

216   Statement Announcing Award of Contracts for the Construction of 16 Merchant Ships.   *July 1, 1972*

I AM PLEASED to announce today the award of nearly $660 million in contracts for the construction of 16 new, advanced-design merchant ships in five U.S. shipyards. This action makes an important contribution to my continuing program to revitalize the American merchant marine.

In addition to adding 16 new ships to our merchant fleet, these five contracts will bring more than 18,000 man-years of work to the five shipyards—at Baltimore, Md., San Diego and San Pedro, Calif., Brooklyn, N.Y., and Bath, Maine—plus an additional 18,000 man-years of work in supporting industries supplying steel and machinery.

My new program for a new American merchant marine—embodied in the Merchant Marine Act of 1970—is designed to restore our merchant fleet to a vigorous, competitive position on the high seas, and to restore employment and profit in our shipping and shipbuilding industries at home.

Today's awards, plus the other contracts which have been signed for other new or remodeled ships under my program, will bring us measurably closer to those two important economic goals.

The United States, as the leading Nation engaged in world trade, must in its own self-interest have a merchant marine commensurate with its large stake in international commerce. This Administration has a firm commitment, which we are fulfilling, to restore the United States to the rank of a first-class maritime power.

Today's awards, when added to the previous contracts under my program, make a grand total so far of $1.1 billion in new or modernized merchant ships. In keeping with Federal policy of assisting the American shipbuilding industry to compete effectively against lower cost competitors abroad, the Government is bearing $479 million of the overall total cost.

I am pleased to note, however, that the percentage of subsidy is dropping, as I urged in announcing my new program. These new contracts, for example, will require 43 percent subsidy as compared with the 55 percent which was permitted prior to my program.

This is clear and heartening evidence that the U.S. shipbuilding industry will meet the challenge I offered: To rebuild our merchant fleet at reasonable cost, which is a vital necessity in these years of close attention to Federal budget demands.

While paring costs and subsidies, however, we are getting the best. One of today's contracts involves the construction of three van-type freighters which will be the largest of their type ever built in this country. Another calls for construction of three modern tankers which are the largest ships ever ordered in the United States.

The American merchant marine and the industries and workers which support it clearly are on their way to a promising new era of modern and competitive American merchant shipping.

NOTE: On the same day, the President met at the White House with maritime union officials, shipowners, and shipbuilders to discuss progress in the U.S. maritime program.

The White House also released a fact sheet and the transcript of a news briefing on merchant ship construction contracts. Participants in the news briefing were Peter G. Peterson, Secretary, Andrew E. Gibson, Assistant Secretary, and Robert J. Blackwell, Acting Assistant Secretary for Maritime Affairs, Department of Commerce.

217   Statement About Signing a Bill Extending the Emergency Unemployment Compensation Act of 1971.   *July 1, 1972*

I AM pleased to have signed H.R. 15587 which extends for an additional 6 months the Emergency Unemployment Compensation Act of 1971.

This bill provides up to 13 extra weeks of unemployment compensation for workers who have exhausted their benefits in States where unemployment remains high.

Despite dramatic increases in employment nationally—from 78.8 million jobs in May 1971 to 81.4 million jobs in May 1972—some areas of stubborn unemployment continue to persist, largely because of a continuing shift of expenditures from defense and defense-related industries to domestic needs.

I am deeply concerned with the economic well-being of all American workers. While the economy is showing encouraging signs of growth, the anticipated reduction in unemployment is taking more time in some areas and, therefore, a temporary continuation of emergency unemployment compensation benefits is needed. When I signed the Emergency Unem-

ployment Compensation Act of 1971 last December, I called attention to the serious deficiency in the financing of that bill.[1] I pointed out that it was a departure from the usual principle under which our unemployment insurance programs have operated since the 1930's.

I am gratified that the Congress, in responding to my request for extending this legislation, accepted my suggestions that it should be properly financed.

I am pleased that we can provide this extended eligibility to our unemployed American workers.

NOTE: As enacted, H.R. 15587, approved June 30, 1972, is Public Law 92–329 (86 Stat. 398).

―――――――――――

[1] See 1971 volume, Item 419.

218   Statement About Signing the Veterans' Compensation and Relief Act of 1972.   *July 1, 1972*

I AM pleased to have signed into law S. 3338, the Veterans' Compensation and Relief Act of 1972.

At my request the Veterans Administration proposed legislation to increase veterans disability compensation benefits in order to meet rises in the cost of living, and I am gratified that the Congress has responded to my request with this act.

I would also like to express my appreciation to the Congress for their cooperation with my efforts to have this act delivered to me so that I can sign it into law before midnight tonight [June 30]. As a result, the increased compensation benefits will now be delivered to disabled veterans beginning August 1, 1972, rather

than a month later.

Among other things, this act provides for a 10-percent increase in the monthly payment for disabled veterans and a similar increase in allowances for those more seriously disabled veterans with dependents.

This is the second opportunity I have had during my Administration to sign into effect an increase in disabled veterans compensation benefits. I am pleased that these benefit increases will soon be helping over 2 million of our most deserving men and women.

NOTE: As enacted, S. 3338, approved June 30, 1972, is Public Law 92–328 (86 Stat. 393).

219   Statement About Signing a Bill Establishing the
       San Francisco Bay National Wildlife Refuge.
       July 1, 1972

THE PATTERN of urbanization and growth in our great Nation, while beneficial in many respects, has not been accomplished without a certain amount of environmental degradation and the despoliation of important wildlife habitat. The large metropolitan complex surrounding San Francisco Bay is no exception to this pattern. At one time the Bay covered about 700 square miles. Today only 400 square miles remain.

As a result, important wildlife habitat in San Francisco Bay has been reduced by 75 percent. In all of California, dredge and fill activity destroyed two-thirds of the estuarine wildlife habitat between 1947 and 1967.

The bill I have signed will not reclaim those wetlands which have been lost. It will, however, provide some assurance that a very important wetland complex in south San Francisco Bay will remain. By establishing the San Francisco Bay National Wildlife Refuge, this legislation will protect the natural habitat for thousands of migratory birds, for three wildlife species threatened with extinction (California clapper rail, California least tern, and the salt marsh harvest mouse), and for other wildlife species.

In addition to preserving an important wildlife habitat, this legislation will also establish a wildlife-oriented public use area providing opportunities for fishing, animal and bird observation, wildlife interpretation, research, and environmental education.

The establishment of this refuge would not have occurred without the deep concern and commitment of many dedicated citizens toward this end for some time. Their efforts have resulted not only in this Federal action, but in numerous other favorable and complementary steps at other governmental levels. The "San Francisco Bay Plan," developed by the San Francisco Bay Conservation and Development Commission, is a particularly fine example of local environmental initiatives.

The new San Francisco Bay National Wildlife Refuge will be administered by the Bureau of Sport Fisheries and Wildlife within the Department of the Interior. The Nation's leading wildlife resource management agency, this Bureau will now develop the San Francisco Bay Refuge into one of the most appreciated and beneficial units of the National Wildlife Refuge System. Located within a major metropolitan area, the refuge will become a wildlife showcase and study center where many Americans will be able to gain a first-hand exposure to some of nature's fundamental handiwork.

NOTE: As enacted, the bill (H.R. 12143), approved June 30, 1972, is Public Law 92–330 (86 Stat. 399).

220   Statement on Signing a Bill Extending Temporary Ceiling on National Debt and Increasing Social Security Benefits.   *July 1, 1972*

I HAVE today signed H.R. 15390, which extends the temporary ceiling on the national debt, and which, among other measures, provides for an across-the-board increase of 20 percent in social security benefits.

One important feature of this legislation which I greet with special favor is the automatic increase provision which will allow social security benefits to keep pace with the cost of living. This provision is one which I have long urged, and I am pleased that the Congress has at last fulfilled a request which I have been making since the first months of my Administration. This action constitutes a major break-through for older Americans, for it says at last that inflation-proof social security benefits are theirs as a matter of right, and not as something which must be temporarily won over and over again from each succeeding Congress.

Another important section of H.R. 15390 provides for accelerated tax refunds for disaster losses. This provision, the passage of which this Administration also urged on the Congress, extends from 3½ months to 6 months the period after the end of the tax year in which a person can claim a deduction for disaster losses. This means, for example, that a person suffering disaster losses between April 15 and June 30 of this year can recompute his or her 1971 taxes and receive a refund check now, while the money is needed most, rather than waiting until next April to claim the same amount. This is particularly timely in the wake of the extensive damage caused by the recent floods.

As I have indicated on other occasions, however, H.R. 15390 includes some serious shortcomings.

It fails the test of fiscal responsibility by failing fully to finance its increase in social security benefits. As a result of this failure, it would add an additional $3.7 billion to the more than $3 billion by which earlier actions and inactions by the Congress have already thrown the full employment budget for fiscal year 1973 into deficit—thus threatening dangerously to escalate the rate of inflation at a time when this Administration's economic policies are succeeding in turning it back.

I am determined that we shall win the battle against inflation—and that fiscally irresponsible policies shall not again penalize all Americans, and especially the older citizens whom these benefit increases are designed to help, by taking away in higher prices what they have gained in higher wages and higher benefits.

Therefore, it will be necessary for the Congress and the Administration to offset the additional $3.7 billion deficit created by this measure through cuts in other Federal programs.

An additional fault with H.R. 15390 is that it jeopardizes the integrity of the Social Security Trust Fund by substantially reducing the necessary coverage of trust fund reserves to ensure annual benefit payments. I shall request the next Congress to restore this full 100-percent protection.

My belief that offsetting cuts in other programs can be made—although they may be painful—together with my belief that older Americans need and deserve increased benefits, permits me to sign this measure. However, I note that the Congress has extended the debt ceiling only until October 31, thus setting the stage for what could become a frantic, election-eve scramble to attach a whole collection of seemingly attractive, politically popular, but fiscally irresponsible, riders to the debt ceiling bill at that time. Debt ceiling bills are a tempting target for such maneuvers, because the Government quickly becomes unable to function if the ceiling falls back below the actual level of Government debt. I place the Congress on notice now that if this occurs—if fiscally irresponsible riders are then attached to that debt ceiling bill, for which it is not possible to find offsetting cuts in other programs—then I will not hesitate to exercise my right and responsibility to veto.

Beyond the shortcomings I have noted in this measure, it should be noted that the added benefits will not come without cost. Even though it is not fully funded, the measure still imposes considerable additional tax burdens on all wage earners. However, the overriding and finally determining factor in my decision to give my approval to this act is my deep concern for the well-being of our older Americans. They both need and deserve a significant increase in social security benefits.

With the signing of H.R. 15390, social security benefits since this Administration took office will have increased by a compound total of 51 percent. It is now our responsibility to see that these needed increases in income for our senior citizens are not eaten up by increases in the cost of living. The Congress has a solemn responsibility to join me in fighting inflation, adopting an unbreakable rule—that there shall be no future increases in spending above my budget without providing for tax increases to pay for such spending increases. Our older Americans deserve full and fair consideration at the hands of their Government, and I have made every effort to see that they receive it. It is in consideration of their just requirements, and in spite of the fiscal irresponsibility that the Congress has demonstrated in its deficit funding of this legislation, that I have signed H.R. 15390.

NOTE: As enacted, H.R. 15390 is Public Law 92–336 (86 Stat. 406).

---

221 Message to the Congress Transmitting Annual Report of the National Endowment for the Arts and National Council on the Arts. *July 1, 1972*

To the Congress of the United States:

It is with profound pleasure and pride that I transmit to the Congress the Annual Report of the National Council on the Arts and the National Endowment for the Arts for the Fiscal Year 1971.

The report mirrors the vitality of musicians, actors, dancers, painters, sculptors, architects, writers, poets—extending our cultural renaissance into all of our communities. It reports and reflects the dedicated work of the producers and planners, the budgeters and the backstage hands, even the special grace of such as the museum guides who turn routine tours into lifetime experiences with their flashes of expertise and insight.

I invite the members of the Congress to share my pleasure and pride in the truly remarkable work of the National Council on the Arts and the National Endowment for the Arts. This work has been possible because you have recognized the importance of the arts, and because you have joined in voting across party lines to approve dramatic increases in our appropriations for the arts.

You have seen that individual, creative effort is an essential element of the American character. You have understood that the enrichment of the human spirit, and the sudden lifting of the soul, are legitimate objectives of government in the finest sense.

Just as 18th century America was dedicated in large part to the achievement of political liberty, and 19th century America to the attainment of economic opportunity, historians of the future may cite 20th century America for its dedication to the definition of the quality and justice of life. In all of these things our national point of view about the arts is fundamental. And right now, we are becoming increasingly a nation of *participants* in the arts.

There now are 44 million amateur musicians in the United States, more than one in five of our population. To take a

second example, there are more than 5,000 amateur theatrical companies. And these are more than mere statistics: I am saying that the arts are *not* for a privileged few, but for everybody. And the arts are not merely sights and sounds: I believe the arts can teach us to hear when we listen, to understand when we see, to enjoy when we perform.

Individual, corporate, foundation, State and local support for the arts remains central to the national *interaction* that gives our culture its unique vitality. But I do believe that, as I said in September 1969, "the Federal Government has a vital role as catalyst, innovator and supporter of public and private efforts for cultural development." And I am sure that in the National Council on the Arts and the National Endowment for the Arts we have a national asset of worth and luster.

I take a very special satisfaction in this annual report. I hope you will enjoy reading it. And I urge you to make it possible for this good and bountiful work to go on.

RICHARD NIXON

The White House,
  June 30, 1972.

NOTE: The message was delivered to the Congress June 30, 1972, and the text was released by the White House July 1.

The 129-page report is entitled "National Endowment for the Arts and National Council on the Arts: Annual Report—Fiscal Year 1971."

222   Independence Day Statement.
July 1, 1972

INDEPENDENCE DAY marks more than the birth date of America. It marks the beginning of one of history's greatest

and most noble adventures. Today, it continues to unfold, 196 years after that small, brave beginning in Philadelphia where a handful of inspired men pledged their lives, their fortunes and their sacred honor to a new nation.

For nearly two centuries, through good times and bad, the ideals of individual rights and opportunity that inspired men like Washington, Jefferson and Adams have survived and flourished. More than any other nation of any area, America has truly been the home of the free and the haven of the weak and oppressed from other parts of the world. And the catalyst of American values has transformed the weak and the oppressed into part of a strong and a just people.

Great trials and greater triumphs still lie ahead for us as a people. There are still wrongs to be righted, and new goals of peace, prosperity, justice and a better environment to be met. But as long as we remain true to the ideals of America, as long as our energy does not flag and our faith does not fail, no problem is too great and no evil is too strong to be overcome by a united American people.

RICHARD NIXON

NOTE: The statement was made available to the press.

223 Letter of Sympathy About the Death of Mormon Leader Joseph Fielding Smith. *July 3, 1972*

Dear President Lee:

Mrs. Nixon and I were deeply saddened to learn of the death of Joseph Fielding Smith, and on behalf of all Americans, we send our sincere sympathy to the members of the Church and to President Smith's family.

For over 70 years—from his first days as a missionary, then as a leading religious scholar, and finally as the tenth President of the Church of Jesus Christ of Latter-day Saints—Joseph Fielding Smith gave enormously to others, helping them to find greater fulfillment in their relationship to God. As son of another president of the Church and grandnephew of its first president, he received a rich heritage from the past; perhaps his greatest accomplishment was the way he carried forward and enriched that legacy for the future.

I had the privilege of enjoying the friendship of Joseph Fielding Smith in the closing years of his life. This was a pro-

found experience for me, and I know that men and women everywhere have lost a devoted and inspirational leader.

To you and others who will now guide the Church, Mrs. Nixon and I send our prayers and warmest best wishes.

Sincerely,

RICHARD NIXON

[President Harold B. Lee, The Council of the Twelve, The Church of Jesus Christ of Latter-day Saints, 47 East South Temple Street, Salt Lake City, Utah]

NOTE: Mr. Smith, 95, died in Salt Lake City, Utah, on July 2, 1972. He was named to the Council of the Twelve of the Church of Jesus Christ of Latter-day Saints in 1910 and became president of the Council in 1951. He was president and prophet of the Church from 1970.

Secretary of Housing and Urban Development George W. Romney and Senator Wallace F. Bennett of Utah represented President Nixon at the funeral services in Salt Lake City.

The text of the letter was made available to the press at San Clemente, Calif.

224   Address to the Nation Announcing Plans for America's Bicentennial Celebration.   *July 4, 1972*

Good morning:

This Fourth of July holiday is an appropriate time for every American to reflect on the deeper meaning of the momentous events at Philadelphia 196 years ago today.

John Adams, later to be our second President, summed up that meaning in a letter to his wife on the night of July 3, 1776. The Continental Congress, to which Adams was a delegate, was to complete its work on the Declaration of Independence the following day. About that event he wrote:

"I am well aware of the toil and blood and treasure that it will cost us to maintain this Declaration. . . . Yet, through all the gloom, I can see the rays of ravishing light and glory. I can see that the end is more than worth all the means. And that posterity will triumph in that day's transaction. . . ."

You and I, and all of the 209 million Americans living today, are the posterity of which he spoke, and we have triumphed, in ways the Founding Fathers scarcely dreamed of.

Over the past two centuries our revolutionary heritage of self-government has helped to make the United States the freest and strongest nation history has ever seen. It has enabled us to bear with unfailing honor the responsibility of world leadership in the cause of peace.

As we look back to America's beginnings, therefore, we are surely entitled to a feeling of pride and gratitude. At the same time, as we look forward to America's Bicentennial, just 4 years from today, we also have a feeling of healthy impatience for change—a determination to make this good land even better.

It is in this traditionally American spirit of pride in our past and present, and purpose for our future, that I would like to talk today about some of our preparations for the year 1976.

In 1966, 10 years ago, the Congress established an American Revolution Bicentennial Commission. I have worked closely with this Commission and its Chairman, David Mahoney. At our urging, its membership has recently been expanded to make it more broadly representative of all the American people.

The Commission's excellent plans call for truly national participation in our Bicentennial observance. Thousands of communities in all 50 States will contribute to a celebration as wide as America's land and as richly diverse as its people, within a framework of three interrelated programs.

One is called Heritage '76. This will focus on the unfolding panorama of our Nation's history over the course of two centuries.

Another is called Horizons '76. This will involve looking ahead into our third century, selecting goals to help make America the "more perfect Union" we all want it to become, and working together to achieve those goals.

The third major program, the one I especially want to talk about this morning, will be known as Festival USA. Its concern will be travel, discovery, and hospitality—hospitality by Americans to Americans, and hospitality by Americans to millions upon millions of visitors from nearly every other country of the globe.

In the near future, I will be sending, in

727

the name of all the people of the United States, formal and official invitations to the governments of nations around the globe, extending a welcome to the people of those nations to visit the United States, as laws and circumstances permit, during the Bicentennial Era—and especially during the year 1976.

This unprecedented invitation to the world is particularly appropriate for two reasons:

First, because America is and always has been a nation of nations. Patriots from France and Prussia and Poland helped us win our Revolution. Strong men and women of every color and creed from every continent helped to build our farms, our industry, our cities.

The blood of all peoples runs in our veins, the cultures of all peoples contribute to our culture, and, to a certain extent, the hopes of all peoples are bound up with our own hopes for the continuing success of the American experiment.

Our Bicentennial Era is a time for America to say to the nations of the world: "You helped to make us what we are. Come and see what wonders your countrymen have worked in this new country of ours. Come and let us say thank you. Come and join in our celebration of a proud past. Come and share our dreams of a brighter future."

A second compelling reason for this invitation to the world relates to our hopes for a genuine and lasting peace among nations.

Of course, we are all aware that a real structure of peace cannot be built on good will alone. Its foundation must be the resolution of those basic national differences which can lead to war.

The United States is doing everything in its power to lay down that kind of foundation for peace. It is in this cause that I have traveled to Peking and Moscow, worked for a just peace in Vietnam, acted to check the nuclear arms race, moved to revitalize our alliances.

As we succeed in reducing the danger of war, however, we must also work at enhancing the quality of peace. One of the best ways of doing this is through people-to-people contacts—contacts aimed at reducing the fear and the ignorance which have divided mankind down through the ages, and at fostering habits of trust and patterns of cooperation. That was one of the major purposes of the visits Mrs. Nixon and I made to the People's Republic of China and to the Soviet Union.

Some of you have heard the story which Woodrow Wilson liked to tell about the English writer Charles Lamb. "I hate that fellow," Lamb said of another one day; to which a friend replied, "I didn't think you knew him." Then Lamb admitted, "Oh, I don't—I can't hate a man I know."

The point is that nations, like individuals, stand a better chance of working constructively together if people on both sides can learn to respect one another as fellow human beings. Our invitation to the world can contribute significantly to that crucial process.

As we move toward 1976, the American Revolution Bicentennial Commission will follow up on this invitation with a vigorous action program. I urge every American to join in support of that program. Here are some ways we can all help:

Business and industry can expand their present efforts to bring the costs of travel, lodging, and meals within the reach of millions of additional visitors.

Air carriers and shipping lines can con-

728

tinue exploring new ways of offering inexpensive transportation to and from this country.

Corporations with interests abroad, private organizations with foreign ties can encourage the participation of their foreign colleagues in the Bicentennial.

Cities which have sister communities in other countries can intensify contacts with them.

Families which have relatives abroad or which speak a second language, or any family that wishes to do so, can make special hospitality plans for foreign visitors.

And volunteers young and old can serve as guides, as interpreters, as hosts and hostesses, to help greet a flood of Bicentennial guests which may be double the nearly 14 million people who visited the United States last year.

State and local governments, the Congress, and the Federal executive branch can assist the national and State bicentennial commissions in every way possible.

In issuing this invitation to the world, the American people will also be issuing a challenge to themselves.

This is the time to open our hearts and our homes and our communities to those who come to America for the first time. This is the time not only for reaching outward, but for reaching inward, for discovering and appreciating parts of our own land and people and heritage which we

may not have known before.

This is the time to put our best foot forward in every aspect of our national life—to prove what America is and can be.

My deepest hope for the Bicentennial Era is this: that all America and all the world can earn the name which Mrs. Nixon and I have chosen for our house here at San Clemente—"La Casa Pacifica," the House of Peace—and that the American people can open their arms to the people of the world with the traditional Latin welcome, *"Estan ustedes en su casa,"* you are in your own house. Let America be known throughout the world as the "Land of the Open Door."

Reaching out in this way, we can prove once again that the Spirit of '76 is a spirit of openness, of brotherhood, and of peace.

We can share with all mankind the eternal message of the Fourth of July— the message of liberty, of opportunity, and of human dignity.

I hope that each one of you will join me in extending, and in wholeheartedly supporting, America's Bicentennial invitation to the world.

NOTE: The President spoke at 9:06 a.m. from the Western White House, San Clemente, Calif. His address was broadcast live on nationwide radio.

The President spoke from a prepared text. An advance text of his address was released on the same day.

225   Statement on Signing the Ports and Waterways Safety Act of 1972.   *July 10, 1972*

IN MANY respects, petroleum is the lifeblood of modern-day America. However, the increasing use of waterways for transporting oil poses grave environmental hazards, setting the scene for ecological

tragedies like the tanker collision which dumped over a half million gallons of oil into San Francisco Bay early last year. We must—and can—prevent such incidents from recurring.

It is for this reason that I especially welcome the action of the Congress in passing H.R. 8140, the Ports and Waterways Safety Act of 1972, which I first proposed almost 26 months ago as part of a 10-point action program to prevent marine pollution from oil spills, and which I am today signing into law.

Under this act, the Coast Guard gains much-needed new authority to protect against oil spills—by controlling vessel traffic in our inland waters and territorial seas, by regulating the handling and storage of dangerous cargoes on the waterfront, by establishing safety requirements for waterfront equipment and facilities, and by setting standards for design, construction, maintenance, and operation of tank vessels. The legislation provides a firm basis for the safeguards we will need to handle increased tanker traffic with minimum environmental risk.

Passage of the Ports and Waterways Safety Act is also significant in that this is the first of my major environmental proposals to receive final action in the 92d Congress. In a special message on the environment last February, I asked the Congress to make 1972 a year of action on the numerous measures I have put before it in this field—a field where the costs of legislative delay can be so terribly high.

My hope is that the enactment of H.R. 8140 is the beginning of a sustained response to this appeal, and that I shall soon have the opportunity to sign others of the more than 20 environmental bills now pending in the Senate and House. Among this backlog are bills which would:

—update our water quality laws,
—improve pesticide regulation,
—control the disposal of toxic substances,
—combat noise pollution,
—curb ocean dumping,
—establish a national land use policy,
—coordinate powerplant siting,
—regulate strip mining,
—strengthen wildlife protection, and
—expand recreational areas and wilderness preserves.

Time is not on our side on any of these fronts. The trends and forces which contribute to environmental degradation continue apace, even in a political season.

With determined action when the Congress goes back to work later this month, however, there is still time to write a fine record of environmental achievement this year.

Once again, I appeal most urgently to the leaders, the committee chairmen, and the individual members of both parties in both Houses to meet their responsibility to the American people and to America's share of the earth by writing such a record.

NOTE: The statement was released at San Clemente, Calif.

As enacted, H.R. 8140 is Public Law 92–340 (86 Stat. 424).

226   Remarks Proposing Additional Emergency Disaster Relief Following Tropical Storm Agnes.   *July* 12, 1972

NO ONE who has ever witnessed a natural disaster can forget the terrible devastation it leaves behind—or can fail to be moved by the heroism and the heartache of those who live through it.

Millions of Americans today are struggling to rebuild their lives in the wake of Tropical Storm Agnes. More than 80 persons perished in the floods that it brought. More than 128,000 homes and businesses have been damaged or destroyed. In terms of the property damage and of the sweeping extent of the territory affected, this has been the worst natural disaster in the whole of America's history.

Confronted with so massive a disaster emergency, our response as a Nation must also be massive. Conscience commands it; humanity impels it.

From the earliest days of our Nation, whenever a disaster or hardship struck, Americans have pulled together, neighbors helping neighbors. That spirit enabled countless thousands to overcome seemingly hopeless obstacles in the past—and it is still a source of strength for America today.

I know, because I saw repeated evidence of that same spirit of neighborliness and sharing when I visited the disaster area in Pennsylvania to inspect the damage firsthand. The destruction and loss were immense, almost overpowering. But even more moving were the spirit, the optimism, the determination of the disaster victims themselves, and that of the government and volunteer workers who were striving side by side with them to undo the damage nature had wrought.

The progress that has been made to date is impressive. Temporary shelter, feeding, and medical treatment have been provided to more than 350,000 people.

Debris removal and restoration of public facilities are underway.

An estimated 70,000 workers who are unemployed as a result of the disaster will be receiving temporary unemployment insurance benefits under regular and disaster assistance programs, and direct Federal payments will create over 50,000 man-years of jobs for workers in affected areas.

All of this is impressive, in the best tradition of American disaster relief work. But, when so extraordinary a disaster strikes, only extraordinary measures—something beyond the normal effort—will suffice.

That is why I am today announcing massive new measures to supplement those which have already been taken. When a friend or relative is stricken hard by an accident or illness, we rally to him. When this large a part of the Nation is stricken by disaster, it is a family affair for all of us, for every American. So, when the Congress reconvenes, I will submit a special request for additional emergency funds totaling more than one billion seven hundred million dollars—the largest single amount ever allocated to recovery efforts in this country.

If the Congress approves these funds, they will be channeled into every aspect of long- and short-term disaster assistance. They will help clear away existing damage. They will help communities begin to build anew. They will restore regular services and facilities in the affected States of New York, Pennsylvania, Maryland, West Virginia, Virginia, and Florida.

Never before has so thorough and so all-embracing a recovery effort been launched and never was it more uniquely necessary.

But when we talk about the suffering of States, counties, and communities, we are really talking about the suffering of individual people. Almost invariably, the hardest hit victims of any natural disaster are individual homeowners and small businessmen.

Again, because of the special nature of this disaster, their needs also require special attention. We must not permit the nightmare of destruction which has wrecked so many of their homes and places of business to be followed by the equally grim specter of bankruptcy or ruin.

With this in mind, I shall also propose to the Congress vital legislative action that would authorize special disaster loans to affected homeowners and businessmen at only one percent interest—and with no repayment required on the first $5,000 of the loan. There is no quicker, more effective way of helping the people of these stricken communities to get back on their feet and resume their normal, productive lives than to provide them with this source of low-interest credit for rebuilding their homes and businesses.

Finally, knowing as we do that no amount of effort can be truly effective without cooperation and understanding at all levels of government, I have invited 500 mayors, county executives, and other leaders from disaster-struck communities to attend a special conference with Federal officials to be held in Washington this Friday. Presiding over that confer-

ence will be the Vice President [1] and the Deputy Director of the Office of Management and Budget, Frank Carlucci. He is a native of one of the hardest hit communities in Pennsylvania—Wilkes-Barre.

The purpose of the meeting will be to speed up relief efforts, to explain our proposed new measures, to improve communications between Federal, local, and civic leaders who share the responsibility for directing this massive disaster relief effort.

The challenge we face is not an easy one. But I have faith that, working together, we can overcome the terrible devastation that the floods have left behind. And we can do more than that. We can give the world a shining new example of the kind of proud, vibrant communities Americans can build, even in adversity, when they put their heads and their hearts into the effort.

NOTE: The President spoke at 9:25 a.m. from his office at the Western White House, San Clemente, Calif. His remarks were broadcast live on radio. He spoke from a prepared text.

On the same day, the White House released a fact sheet on the President's proposals for additional emergency disaster relief.

---

[1] On July 14, 1972, the White House released a transcript of remarks by Vice President Spiro T. Agnew at the conference.

227   Statement About National Crime Statistics for the First Quarter of 1972.   *July 12, 1972*

THE Attorney General reported today that serious crime in the first quarter of this year showed the lowest percentage gain in 11 years—a rise of only one percent over the same period last year—and that in 80 of the largest cities the number of serious crimes was actually reduced.

This represents truly significant progress in this Administration's determination to roll back the wave of crime which swept our Nation in the 1960's. It is the best news yet on the crime front.

The right of all citizens to feel safe on the streets and secure in their homes is fundamental to individual liberty and national progress.

It is a right on which this Administration has placed a new and major emphasis. We have dramatically increased Federal assistance for State and local authorities. Where the Federal Government has direct enforcement authority, such as in organized crime, drug trafficking, and in the District of Columbia, we have both strengthened the laws and poured more men and money into enforcement. Through court appointments, conferences on the judiciary and on corrections, and other Administration actions, law enforcement has been given additional vigor.

Another key ingredient in the crime fight has been the development of a new, less permissive public attitude toward crime and criminals. The American public now is fully awake to the social menace of crime, and fully determined that criminals must be defeated if America is to make continued social progress.

This one-percent rise for the first quarter of this year compares with a 6-percent increase for the same period in 1971, 13 percent in 1970, and 10 percent in 1969. The increase from 1960 to 1968 totaled an alarming 122 percent. It is clear from this that we at last are making real headway against the forces of crime.

This can mean that we are ending the first phase of our battle to turn back crime in America: the phase in which we had to stop it from going up in order to start it going down.

These first quarter figures bring us to the one-yard line in that effort—so let us join together to make 1972 the year in which we score that first goal. Let us make this the year of victory in our battle to stop the rise in crime, so that from this year on we at last can begin measuring not the decrease in the rate of increase, but the rate of decrease, period. What was achieved in those 80 cities where crime was reduced must now be our goal for the Nation.

Together, we can do this. Therefore, I call on all of our law enforcement officers—Federal, State, and local—to keep up their valiant battle against crime in our communities. I call on all citizens to give them their full support, and I pledge the total support of the Federal Government. Together, let us show that the day of the criminal is past in America, and the day of the citizen is here.

NOTE: The statement was released at San Clemente, Calif.

228   Telegram About the Reduction of Serious Crime.
July 12, 1972

THE Attorney General has just told me that 80 of America's largest cities have actually reduced the number of serious crimes during the first quarter of 1972. Chicago was among those leaders, and I want to extend to you and to all members of your department my heartiest congratulations for this great achievement.

The first quarter statistics also show that the overall increase in crime across the nation was down to 1%—by far the lowest rate in more than a decade. At long last we are pushing back the criminal forces, and now that we are on the one-yard line, I am determined that 1972 be the year we score a victory against the crime rate in America.

With the unstinting efforts of law enforcement officials at all levels of government, this can be the year in which crime stops going up and starts going down. On behalf of all Federal authorities, let me assure you that we feel privileged to work with you in this cause and stand ready to assist you to the greatest extent possible.

Once again, congratulations and continued best wishes.

RICHARD NIXON

[James B. Conlisk, Jr., Superintendent, Chicago Police Department, Chicago, Ill. 60605]

NOTE: The text of the telegram was made available to the press at San Clemente, Calif.

Similar telegrams were addressed to the chiefs of police in the following 79 cities:

Akron, Ohio	Cleveland, Ohio
Albany, N.Y.	Columbus, Ohio
Allentown, Pa.	Corpus Christi, Tex.
Amarillo, Tex.	Dallas, Tex.
Atlanta, Ga.	Dearborn, Mich.
Baltimore, Md.	Des Moines, Iowa
Birmingham, Ala.	Detroit, Mich.
Boston, Mass.	Elizabeth, N.J.
Bridgeport, Conn.	Evansville, Ind.
Cambridge, Mass.	Flint, Mich.
Charlotte, N.C.	Ft. Lauderdale, Fla.

Ft. Wayne, Ind.	Oakland, Calif.
Ft. Worth, Tex.	Oklahoma City,
Hartford, Conn.	Okla.
Hialeah, Fla.	Parma, Ohio
Hollywood, Fla.	Peoria, Ill.
Honolulu, Hawaii	Pittsburgh, Pa.
Huntington Beach,	Portsmouth, Va.
Calif.	Providence, R.I.
Huntsville, Ala.	Raleigh, N.C.
Indianapolis, Ind.	Richmond, Va.
Jacksonville, Fla.	Rochester, N.Y.
Kansas City, Mo.	Sacramento, Calif.
Knoxville, Tenn.	St. Louis, Mo.
Lexington, Ky.	Salt Lake City,
Little Rock, Ark.	Utah
Los Angeles, Calif.	San Francisco, Calif.
Louisville, Ky.	Savannah, Ga.
Lubbock, Tex.	Scranton, Pa.
Macon, Ga.	Seattle, Wash.
Miami, Fla.	Springfield, Mo.
Milwaukee, Wis.	Stamford, Conn.
Mobile, Ala.	Syracuse, N.Y.
Montgomery, Ala.	Tacoma, Wash.
Nashville, Tenn.	Topeka, Kans.
Newark, N.J.	Torrance, Calif.
New Haven, Conn.	Warren, Mich.
New Orleans, La.	Washington, D.C.
Newport News, Va.	Worcester, Mass.
New York, N.Y.	Yonkers, N.Y.
Norfolk, Va.	Youngstown, Ohio

229   Statement About Signing the National Capital Transportation Act of 1972.   *July 14, 1972*

IT IS with special pleasure that I have signed H.R. 15507, the National Capital Transportation Act of 1972. I join with my fellow residents of the Washington metropolitan area, and with millions of other Americans across this country who want the best in urban services for their Nation's Capital, in thanking the bipartisan Congressional majority which worked for passage of this important legislation.

METRO—the areawide rapid rail transit system which figures so centrally in our vision of a new Washington for the Bicen-

tennial and beyond—moves a long step toward successful completion with this new law. Responding to a proposal I put forward in April 1971, the act provides a Federal guarantee for METRO revenue bonds, greatly enhancing the hitherto dubious marketability of these securities. It authorizes an increase of nearly 25 percent in the District of Columbia's contribution to METRO funding. It approves needed amendments broadening the interstate compact under which the system is to operate. It orders a special study looking to possible additional Federal funding to insure adequate METRO service for the elderly and the handicapped.

Late last year, when it appeared that METRO might die altogether because of a complex legislative and judicial tangle, I appealed to the Congress for responsible action to cut the Gordian knot. The metropolitan Washington community was enormously heartened when such action was forthcoming. At that time I also asked that there be no further derailments of METRO progress—and enactment of this bond guarantee proposal now offers encouraging evidence that the Congress means to follow through and prevent such delays.

The role of municipal legislature for Washington, D.C., which the House and Senate must often of necessity play, is not an easy one—either for the city or for the Congress. But as METRO construction now moves forward at a quickening pace with solid Congressional support, there is reason to hope that the lessons learned en route to completion of the world's most modern subway for our National Capital area may also mark the beginning of a new and more effective Federal-local partnership in District of Columbia government. This Administration is committed, and I am committed personally, to furthering that result by every means available to us.

NOTE: The statement was released at San Clemente, Calif.

As enacted, H.R. 15507, approved July 13, 1972, is Public Law 92–349 (86 Stat. 464).

---

230   Message to the Congress Proposing Additional Disaster Relief Measures Following Tropical Storm Agnes. *July* 17, 1972

To the Congress of the United States:

Tropical Storm Agnes has caused unparalleled destruction in many areas of the eastern United States. More than 128,000 homes and businesses have been damaged or destroyed, and whole communities have been dealt a heavy blow. The losses to so many individuals cannot be measured only in terms of destruction of property and belongings; they must also be counted in terms of loss of jobs, disruption of families, personal privation, and anxiety about the future. In the whole history of our Nation, we have not before encountered such massive destruction over so wide-spread an area as a result of natural disaster.

Individuals, private groups and governments have responded magnificently to this calamity in the finest tradition of neighbor helping neighbors. The stamina, the courage and the spirit to fight back and recover are already evident throughout the devastated areas. My statement of July 12, 1972 summarized these impressive efforts. I also pointed out at that time, however, that an unparalleled disaster requires extraordinary measures to help in recovery. I announced my intention to recommend to the Congress supplementary and massive measures aimed at short and long-term recovery. I herewith transmit those recommendations, and the proposed legislation to carry them out.

My proposals are in three parts.

First, I propose the Agnes Recovery Act of 1972. This measure deals with disaster loans for homeowners, farmers and businessmen. Because of the unprecedented scope of the destruction, unprecedented measures to deal with it are required. Under the provisions of this proposal, disaster loans for Agnes victims would be changed from present law in the following ways:

—The maximum amount of principal which can be cancelled or forgiven would be increased from $2,500 to $5,000 on loans made by the Small Business Administration or the Farmers Home Administration.

—The forgiveness feature would be applicable to the first dollar of a loan rather than after the repayment of the first $500 of principal as is now the case.

—The interest rate on the loans would be dropped to 1 percent instead of its current rate of 5⅛ percent.

This liberalized assistance to individual homeowners and small businessmen can mean the difference between recovery and bankruptcy or ruin. The situation is urgent. Individual people are now making decisions on whether to rebuild or not. While my proposal would apply retroactively to all victims of Agnes, it is important to them to know now the terms of assistance which will be available to them.

Therefore, I call on the Congress to respond to this emergency by acting on the Agnes Recovery Act so that it can become law within one week.

Second, I recommend supplemental appropriations totaling $1,569,800,000 for this emergency, the largest single request of its kind in our history. The vast majority of these funds would be used for disaster loans, with $1.3 billion for the Small Business Administration and $1.8 million for the Farmers Home Administration. The SBA funds would be used to provide loans for homeowners and small

businessmen in disaster areas whose property has been damaged or destroyed. The FHA funds would provide sufficient personnel to process expeditiously loan requests in rural areas, for which adequate loan funds now exist. Also included in my supplemental request are:

—An additional $200 million for the President's Disaster Relief Fund, to speed repair and reconstruction of public facilities and to provide temporary housing, food and unemployment compensation.

—$40 million for the Economic Development Administration, $16 million for the Appalachian Regional Commission and $12 million for the Corps of Engineers, all to assist in the recovery of damaged communities. The funds for the Corps of Engineers would go toward flood control projects in the Susquehanna River Basin.

Third, I recommend that the existing authorization for appropriations for highway emergency relief be increased by $200 million. Current authority limits amounts to $50 million per year, which is clearly not adequate to cope with a disaster of this magnitude.

I urge that the Congress also act promptly on these second and third proposals.

The Federal Government must act quickly and decisively to do its part in providing relief and aiding recovery in a cooperative effort with the States and communities struck by Agnes. We can do no less. I am confident that the Congress will share this view.

RICHARD NIXON

The White House,

July 17, 1972.

NOTE: The text of the message was released at San Clemente, Calif.

The text and a section-by-section analysis of the proposed legislation were made available with the message.

In announcing the message, Press Secretary Ronald L. Ziegler stated: "The President has also instructed members of his staff to work with Congress to effect legislation which would give coverage benefits to victims of the Rapid City [South Dakota] disaster equal to those of the victims of Hurricane Agnes."

On July 19, 1972, the White House released an announcement of disaster assistance for Ohio following Tropical Storm Agnes. The announcement is printed in the Weekly Compilation of Presidential Documents (vol. 8, p. 1162).

---

231   Letter to the Speaker of the House Recommending Supplemental Appropriations for Disaster Assistance Following Tropical Storm Agnes.   *July* 17, 1972

Sir:

I ask the Congress to consider proposed supplemental appropriations for fiscal year 1973 in the amounts of $1,569,800,000 in budget authority and $20,000,000 in proposals not increasing budget authority.

These appropriations, together with a $200,000,000 Federal highway emergency relief authorization request, which will be sought separately, will provide over $1.8 billion in Federal funds to help repair the damage caused by Tropical Storm Agnes.

These funds will help the hundreds of thousands of Americans who are struggling to rebuild their lives after the destruction wrought by Tropical Storm Agnes. From the earliest days of our Nation, whenever a disaster or hardship struck, Americans have pulled together, neighbors helping neighbors. It is fitting that we carry on this tradition now, in the wake of the worst natural disaster in American history, in terms of property damage and the extent of territory affected.

The details of these proposals are set forth in the enclosed letter from the Director of the Office of Management and Budget with whose comments I concur.

Respectfully,

RICHARD NIXON

NOTE: Director Weinberger's letter is printed in House Document 92–325.

---

232   Statement on the Death of Under Secretary of the Interior William T. Pecora.   *July* 19, 1972

DR. WILLIAM T. Pecora, Under Secretary of the Interior, was a remarkable civil servant and an internationally respected figure in the scientific community. His death today is a sad occasion for everyone who has had the pleasure of working with him and benefiting from his enormous contributions to our Government.

Dr. Pecora's expertise as a leading authority in the field of geology proved invaluable to our country from the day he joined the Interior Department in 1939. He built a shining record for 6 years as Director of the U.S. Geological Survey, and then for 2 years as Under Secretary of the Department of the Interior.

Mrs. Nixon and I extend our heartfelt

condolences to his family in their bereavement for this fine American.

NOTE: Dr. Pecora, 59, died at George Washington University Hospital following surgery

for diverticulitis. He was Director, Geological Survey, Department of the Interior, from 1965 to 1971 and Under Secretary of the Interior from 1971.

233   Letter About the Death of the Metropolitan Opera's General Manager, Goeran Gentele. *July* 19, 1972

Dear George:

The untimely and tragic death of Goeran Gentele came as a shock to me personally and to countless fellow Americans.

His tenure at the Metropolitan Opera Association revealed an able man who had a clear perception of his enormous responsibilities to maintain the Metropolitan Opera's prestigious role as a great international opera house, and one who possessed the vision to set new patterns for opera programming in the near future.

Mrs. Gentele and her daughter are in our thoughts and prayers at this difficult time, and Mrs. Nixon and I hope that you will convey to them our deepest sympathy as well as our heartfelt wishes for their

recovery.

Sincerely,

RICHARD NIXON

[Mr. George S. Moore, Chairman of the Board, Metropolitan Opera Association, Lincoln Center Plaza, New York, New York 10023]

NOTE: Mr. Gentele, 54, died in an automobile accident on July 18, 1972, while vacationing on the Italian island of Sardinia in the Mediterranean. His daughters, Anne and Beatrice, were killed, and Mrs. Gentele and her daughter Janette were injured in the accident.

Mr. Gentele was director of the Royal Opera House in Stockholm, Sweden, from 1963 through 1971. His appointment as general manager of the Metropolitan Opera for the 1972–73 season was announced in 1970, but he officially assumed the position July 1972.

The text of the letter was made available to the press.

234   Message to the Senate Transmitting Amendments to the International Convention for the Safety of Life at Sea, 1960. *July* 24, 1972

To the Senate of the United States:

I herewith transmit for the advice and consent of the Senate eleven amendments to the Convention for the Safety of Life at Sea, 1960.

Three of these amendments were adopted on November 26, 1968 by the Assembly of the Intergovernmental Maritime Consultative Organization (IMCO) at its fourth extraordinary session held in London November 26–28, 1968 and are

annexed to the enclosed certified copy of Resolution A. 146(ES. IV). The other eight amendments were adopted on October 15–29, 1969 and are annexed to the enclosed certified copy of Resolution A. 174(VI).

The three amendments adopted in 1968 are the outcome of studies undertaken by IMCO in 1967 following the Torrey Canyon tragedy. They are preventive measures designed to avoid the repetition of such disasters by requiring that specified navigational equipment be carried aboard certain vessels, specifying conditions of operation that must be met by vessels using automatic pilot, and requiring that all ships subject to the Convention carry adequate and up-to-date nautical publications.

The 1969 amendments are designed to improve requirements for firemen's outfits and personal equipment in cargo ships as well as requirements for lifebuoys, lifejackets, radio installations and shipborne navigational equipment.

For the information of the Senate, I am also transmitting the report of the Department of State with respect to the amendments.

I recommend that the Senate give swift and favorable consideration to all of these amendments.

RICHARD NIXON

The White House,
July 24, 1972.

NOTE: The text of the amendments and the report of the Secretary of State are printed in Senate Executive O (92d Cong., 2d sess.).

---

235   Statement About a Report of the Property Review Board. *July 25, 1972*

MEMBERS of the Property Review Board reported to me today on major new initiatives that are underway to improve the management of Federal real property. I am especially pleased to note the progress under the Legacy of Parks program which has now reached 39 States, leading to the creation of 144 new parks.

The Federal public lands belong to all Americans and are part of the heritage and birthright of every citizen. They are the breathing space of the Nation, and it is essential that they be preserved for future generations.

Government must work as the trustee for the future to ensure that the environmental, ecological, and recreational values of these lands will be safeguarded. Our goal, the goal of the Property Review Board—to manage our public lands wisely and well to best serve the greatest number—has resulted in more parks and recreational opportunities for all Americans.

By returning federally owned land to States and localities to fill locally determined needs, the Property Management Program administered by the Board is reversing the trend of the past decade towards government so big it loses touch with its citizens.

The program is a creative avenue for Federal, State, and local cooperation in achieving two of this Administration's principal domestic aims—bringing government closer to the people and improving our environment.

NOTE: Members of the Property Review Board met with the President at the White House to present their report entitled "New Directions in Federal Real Property Management: A Progress Report by the President's Property Review Board" (31 pp. plus annexes).

On the same day, the White House released a fact sheet and the transcript of a news briefing on the report. Participants in the news briefing were Donald Rumsfeld, Counsellor to the President and Chairman, Property Review Board, and Darrell M. Trent, Executive Secretary of the Board.

236 Telephone Conversation With Prime Minister Golda Meir of Israel. *July* 26, 1972

THE PRESIDENT. Hello, Madam Prime Minister.

THE PRIME MINISTER. Mr. President, *shalom.*

THE PRESIDENT. Thank you very much. I want you to know that as I speak here from the Oval Office, where you and I have met so many times, that I extend the very best wishes of all of the people of the United States to all of the people of Israel.

I think this program, as I saw the countries you were talking to, instead of being called "Around the World in 80 Days," could be called "Around the World in 60 Minutes."

THE PRIME MINISTER. That is right. Mr. President, it is extremely kind of you to take time off and speak to us. I can only tell you that the best wishes of all the people of Israel, appreciation, and all the friendship that we can express goes out to you and the people of the United States.

I remember the Oval Room very well, always with a great feeling of satisfaction and appreciation and joy and thankfulness that you have always taken so much of your time to listen to my long stories of troubles and wishes and so on.

But I must say I always came out with the right answers.

THE PRESIDENT. Madam Prime Minister, I want you to know that you, needless to say, are always welcome here. I only regret that while I have visited Israel on other occasions, I have never been able to do so as President, but you can be sure that we will continue to work together for

what you are interested in, what we are interested in, and that is a just peace in the Mideast which will protect the integrity of Israel, for which your people have suffered so much and sacrificed so much.

THE PRIME MINISTER. Thank you very, very much. It is easier to face difficulties when you speak as you do, and I know what you have done, so thank you very much.

There is a large group here. They are all smiling, and they are all happy to hear your voice.

THE PRESIDENT. I want to say just one last thing. I think the fact that we do have this new television communication will mean that the programs that will be carried from Israel to the United States, and from the United States to Israel, will mean that more of our people here will have an opportunity not only to see Israel by television, but perhaps to go there as tourists and we hope that more people from Israel can come here. We hope that will be one of the dividends of this new program.

THE PRIME MINISTER. This is a commercial that will work both ways.

THE PRESIDENT. That's right. That's right. I know that I have enjoyed my visits, and we want you and any of your friends to know they are always welcome here in our country.

THE PRIME MINISTER. Thank you very, very much.

THE PRESIDENT. Thank you. We will look forward to seeing you. Goodby.

THE PRIME MINISTER. Goodby.

NOTE: The telephone call began at 11:52 a.m. The President spoke from the Oval Office at the White House.

His conversation with the Prime Minister

inaugurated communications satellite service for Israel via its first ground station at Emeq Ha'ela.

237   Letter to Prime Minister Golda Meir on the Inauguration of Communications Satellite Service for Israel. *July 26, 1972*

Dear Madame Prime Minister:

As your nation inaugurates its station connecting Israel with the Intelsat system, you have the best wishes of the American people.

Clear and effective communication is basic to building the generation of peace we so earnestly seek, and to ensuring the kind of sound relationships among nations which will enable that peace to endure.

We are delighted that Israel is joining the family of nations linked by this new system, and happy to convey through our

representative, Mr. Dean Burch, our warmest greetings and hopes that this important step may benefit your fellow citizens and all mankind.

Sincerely,

RICHARD NIXON

[Her Excellency Golda Meir, Prime Minister of Israel]

NOTE: The letter, dated July 20, 1972, was delivered to the Prime Minister on July 26 by Dean Burch, Chairman, Federal Communications Commission. The text of the letter was made available to the press.

238   Special Message to the Congress on Federal Government Spending. *July 26, 1972*

To the Congress of the United States:

This is an urgent appeal for the Congress to join with me to avoid higher taxes, higher prices and a cut in purchasing power for everyone in the Nation.

Just when we have succeeded in cutting the rate of inflation in half, and just when we have succeeded in making it possible for America's workers to score their largest real spendable income gains in eight years, this tangible, pocketbook progress may be wiped out by proposed excessive spending.

Specifically, Federal spending for the fiscal year 1973 (which began on July 1,

1972) already is estimated to be almost $7 billion higher than was planned in my budget.

That figure by itself is bad enough. But even more spending beyond the budget—and beyond emergency flood relief funds—appears to be on the way.

The inevitable result would be higher taxes and more income-eating inflation in the form of higher prices.

I am convinced the American people do not want their family budgets wrecked by higher taxes and higher prices, and I will not stand by and permit such irresponsible action to undermine the clear progress we have made in getting America's workers off the inflation treadmill of the 1960's.

While specific Federal programs are important to many people and constituent groups, none is more important to all the American taxpayers than a concerted program to hold down the rate of taxes and the cost of living.

In view of this serious threat I again urge the Congress—in the economic interest of all American citizens—to enact a spending ceiling of $250 billion. I urgently recommended a spending ceiling when I submitted the fiscal 1973 budget earlier this year.

Our concern with sustaining the increasing purchasing power of all the people requires and demands such responsible action. Our concern with the cost of living requires and demands such responsible action. Our determination to avoid higher taxes requires and demands such action. The basic fiscal integrity of the Nation requires and demands such action.

At fault is the hoary and traditional procedure of the Congress, which now permits action on the various spending programs as if they were unrelated and independent actions. What we should have—and what I again seek today—is that an annual spending ceiling be set first, and that individual program allocations then be tailored to that ceiling. This is the anti-inflationary method I use in designing the Federal budget.

The present Congressional system of independent, unrelated actions on various spending programs means that the Congress arrives at total Federal spending in an accidental, haphazard manner. That is no longer good enough procedure for the American people, who now realize that their hard-won economic gains against inflation are threatened by every deficit spending bill—no matter how attractive the subject matter of that bill might be. And there are impressive gains which I am committed to help guard:

—We have achieved a substantial success in our battle against the inflation we inherited in 1969. Instead of the more than 6 percent of 1969, we are now down to a rate of 2.9 percent per year. Inflation has been cut in half.

—We have cut the personal income tax so that a family of four with an income of $5,000 has had its individual income taxes reduced by 66 percent since 1969, and a family of four with an income of $10,000 has had its income tax reduced by 26 percent since that date.

—We have thus brought about conditions in which real, spendable weekly earnings have risen four percent in the last year, the largest such gain since 1964.

If we permit unbridled increases in Federal spending to go on month after month, however, we are in real danger of losing the advantages of the tax cuts and our victories in the battle against inflation.

These are the compelling reasons which require me to ask again in the most urgent and explicit language I can frame that the Congress enact at the earliest possible opportunity a spending ceiling—without loopholes or exceptions—to force Government spending back to the $250 billion level in fiscal year 1973.

I again remind the Congress of the situation I cited last January, when I submitted the fiscal year 1973 budget:

"It will be a job-creating budget and a non-inflationary budget only if spending is limited to the amount the tax system would produce if the economy were operating at full employment."

"Those who increase spending beyond that amount will be responsible for causing more inflation."

Since that time, various Congressional actions and inactions have heavily underscored all of the reasons I then made for speedy passage of a spending ceiling.

Such a ceiling cannot be completely effective unless the Congress enacts it as I have requested—without exceptions and without loopholes. But if the Congress fails to do this, I do not propose to sit by and silently watch individual family budgets destroyed by rising prices and rising taxes—the inevitable end to spending of this magnitude.

With or without the cooperation of the Congress, I am going to do everything within my power to prevent such a fiscal crisis for millions of our people.

Let there be no misunderstanding: If bills come to my desk calling for excessive spending which threatens the Federal budget, I will veto them.

It is now generally recognized that the national economy is in a period of vigorous expansion. The Gross National Product soared at an annual growth rate of 8.9 percent in the second quarter of the year—the best such increase since 1965. About 2½ million additional civilian jobs have been added in the last year.

We do not plan to reduce or restrict the very substantial fiscal stimulation we have already provided. But *further* massive Federal stimulation of the economy at this time—whatever its superficial political attractiveness—is certain to lead to the kind of inflation that even wage-price control machinery would find impossible to restrain.

In other words, the American people will have to pay, and pay quickly, for excessive Federal spending—either by higher taxes or by higher consumer prices, or both. Such an intolerable burden would shortly cause an end to the period of economic growth on which we are embarked.

There are desirable features in some of the individual bills now pending in the Congress, but to them have been attached some very excessive spending proposals.

The Federal Government cannot do everything that might be desirable. Hard choices must be made by the Congress in the national interest, just as a family must decide what it will buy with the money it has. Moreover, the experience of the past decade proved that merely throwing money at problems does not automatically or necessarily solve the problems.

I have every confidence that the American people, in this era of wide public awareness of inflation and wide public opposition to its clear causes, understand these realities about Federal spending.

I believe that all of us, the President and the Congress, have a clear duty to protect the national interest in general prosperity—and therefore to resist temptations to overspend for desirable special programs, or to spend for partisan political advantage.

I favor and have submitted to the Congress responsible and effective programs designed to cleanse the air, to purify the water, to develop and preserve rural America, to improve education, and for many other worthy purposes. No individual and no political party has a monopoly on its concern for the people, individually and in groups. But I am required always to ask:

What is best for *all* the people? What are the hard choices that must be made so that the general welfare is secured?

Of what use is it for us to pass these measures, and more, if they are going to destroy the family budget by higher prices and more taxes?

No matter what the political pressures, no matter how frequently I may be told that in an election year a President cannot veto a spending measure, I will simply not let reckless spending of this kind destroy the tax reductions we have secured and the hard-won successes we have earned in the battle against inflation. I intend to continue to do my utmost to preserve the American family budget and to protect it from the ravages of higher taxes and inflation.

The time for fiscal discipline has long since come. The threat demands bold and difficult decisions. Let the Congress make them now.

RICHARD NIXON

The White House,
    July 26, 1972.

NOTE: On the same day, the White House released the transcript of a news briefing on the message by John D. Ehrlichman, Assistant to the President for Domestic Affairs.

239   The President's News Conference of *July 27, 1972*

THE PRESIDENT. Now we will go forward with some questions if you like, please.

QUESTIONS

BOMBING TARGETS IN NORTH VIETNAM

[1.] Q. Mr. President, you have said that it is against U.S. policy to bomb the dikes and dams in North Vietnam. Yesterday, the State Department acknowledged there had been incidental and inadvertent damage from the bombing nearby.

My question is this: Is it worth the risk of possible flooding or of having world opinion turn against us to bomb military targets near the dikes and dams?

THE PRESIDENT. I think your question perhaps could be better answered by my discussing the policy toward bombing of civilian installations in North Vietnam generally, and then coming down to the specifics of your question, in giving the general answer.

Some of you who were in Texas with me will recall that that question was raised at the Connally Ranch,[1] and it was raised, actually, by an advocate of bombing dikes as to why we did not bomb dikes. And I said it had not been U.S. policy even before the bombing halt of 1968 to bomb the dikes, that it was not our policy now, that it would not be in the future, because it is the policy of the United States in all of its activities against North Vietnam to direct its attacks against military targets only.

That was the policy in the sixties, and it is now the policy since we have had to resume the bombing for the purposes that I mentioned in my speech of May 8.

Now with regard to the situation on the dikes, let us understand what we are confronted with here. This is approximately a 2,700-mile chain of installations, including perhaps a half-dozen major dams which are the heart of the system and then

_____
[1] See Item 134 [4.].

peripheral areas getting down to mounds, which have, of course, the purpose of controlling the floodwaters in that particular area.

If it were the policy of the United States to bomb the dikes, we could take them out, the significant part of them out, in a week. We don't do so for the reasons that I have mentioned, because we are trying to avoid civilian casualties, not cause them.

Now, with regard to the reports, reports that have come from Hanoi that there had been some damage to some parts of the dike system, I think it is important to note two things: One, there has been no report of any flooding; second, there has been no report of any strikes on the major dike areas.

What I am referring to is the big dams which are the heart of the system. There have been reports of incidental damage to some of the peripheral installations in this 2,700-mile system which covers the country of North Vietnam.

Now, under these circumstances, I think that it is well to keep in context, first, what our policy is, and second, what its effect has been. Our policy is not to bomb civilian installations, and second, our restraint, it seems to me, rather than being subject to criticisms should be subject to objective analysis and, it seems to me, a considerable amount of support.

As far as this matter is concerned, I think, too, it is time to strip away the double standard. I noted with interest that the Secretary General of the U.N., just like his predecessor, seized upon this enemy-inspired propaganda, which has taken in many well-intentioned and naive people, to attack what he called the American bombing of civilian installa-tions and risking civilian lives, and yet not raising one word against deliberate bombing of civilian installations in South Vietnam.

Now just so the record will be kept straight—and it should be stated at this point—all of you ladies and gentlemen, of course, are aware of it, and you have printed it, and perhaps you will see fit to again in this context:

I just got a cable from Ambassador Bunker. I had asked him what had happened to civilians in the new offensive. You recall in my speech of May 8, I said that 20,000 civilian casualties, including women and children, had resulted because of the deliberate shelling of the cities and the slaughtering of refugees indiscriminately by the North Vietnamese.

The number is now 45,000, including women and children, of which 15,000 are dead.

I asked him for the number of refugees. It is higher than I had thought. There have been 860,000 made homeless by the North Vietnamese invasion of South Vietnam, this newest invasion to date; 600,000 of them are still in refugee camps, away from their homes.

Looking back over the period of this very difficult war, we find that since 1965 there have been 600,000 civilian casualties in South Vietnam as a result of deliberate policy of the North Vietnamese Communists, not accidental, but deliber-ate.

And in North Vietnam, in the period from 1954 to 1956, in their so-called land reform program, a minimum of 50,000 were murdered, assassinated, and—according to the Catholic Bishop of Danang, whom I talked to when I was there in 1956 in South Vietnam—in addition to the 800,000 refugees who came south, there were at least a half million who died in slave labor camps in North Vietnam.

Now, I do not relate this series of incidents for the purpose of saying, because they did something bad, we can do something bad.

What I am simply saying is, let's not have a hypocritical double standard. The United States has been restrained—greater restraint than any great power has ever shown—in handling this war. We will continue to be restrained. We have to do what is necessary against military targets in order to accomplish the objectives that I have described in my goal in my speech of May 8.

But on the other hand, as far as this particular matter is concerned, I can only say that if damage did occur that we are making every possible effort to see that it will not occur again, which gets to your question. Military commanders, aircraft commanders, and so forth, in terms of where military targets are, are instructed to avoid civilian damage where they can.

That is why some targets in the heart of Hanoi—for example, major power installations, fuel installations, in the heart of Hanoi—have not been hit, because I have not wanted to have civilian casualties if we could possibly avoid it.

I will simply close by saying that this is a major propaganda campaign; it is one that does concern us. But let us keep the record straight. In the event that the United States followed the course of action recommended by some of those who have voted for the so-called End the War Resolution in the Senate of the United States, it would mean that there would be visited upon South Vietnam the same atrocities that were visited upon North Vietnam, with perhaps at least a million

marked for assassination because they had fought against the North Vietnamese attempt to conquer South Vietnam.

I will add one other thing. As far as the negotiations are concerned, we are negotiating. We have negotiated in public. We have had one private conference a week ago, lasting approximately 6 hours. We hope to continue to negotiate.

We have made fair offers on withdrawal, on cease-fire, on political settlement. We have not made them on a take-it-or-leave-it basis.

We made fair offers on exchange of prisoners of war and accounting for missing in action every place in Southeast Asia.

But having done this, there is one thing that we have not offered—and this is the one hangup in the settlement today—and that is the demand of the enemy indirectly or directly to do what they cannot accomplish themselves: impose a Communist government in South Vietnam. That would be the height of immorality, to impose on the 17 million people of South Vietnam a Communist government with the bloodbath that would follow.

POLITICAL SETTLEMENT IN VIETNAM

[2.] Q. Mr. President, you mentioned a political settlement. What do you foresee as a possibility without necessarily elections—do you see the two factions in South Vietnam coming together in some kind of an agreement without an election as one possible solution in the Paris talks?

THE PRESIDENT. That is a very perceptive question, but it is one that I think any of you here would agree that I should not comment upon for the reason that negotiations are now underway. I have read these long negotiating sessions—the public ones, of course, and even more important, the private ones—in great detail. At a time that matters are being discussed, it is not well for me to state anything with regard to what is happening in the negotiations.

I will only say that we are negotiating with the desire of ending this war as soon as possible. The fastest way to end the war and the best way to end it is through negotiation. We would hope that public figures in their comments will not do anything to undercut the negotiations, that Congress, in its actions, will not in effect give a message to the enemy, "Don't negotiate with the present Administration; wait for us; we will give you what you want—South Vietnam."

SAM SITES ON DIKES AND DAMS

[3.] Q. Mr. President, to follow up the first question, if I may, there had been reports that SAM sites have been put on top of some of those dikes or dams. Does your policy rule out the bombing of that particular area where there are SAM sites?

THE PRESIDENT. I have seen those reports, Mr. Lisagor [Peter Lisagor, Chicago Daily News]. As you know, the Secretary of Defense has made some indirect comment about it. The situation there is one that we would lean against the taking out of SAM sites on targets that would result in civilian casualties of a substantial amount.

However, I have not seen in recent days any reports indicating that any such SAM sites have been hit, and in view of the present debate, I think we are going to be very careful with regard to hitting them. We would do so only if we had to do so in order to protect American fliers who otherwise would be hit down by the SAM's.

CANDIDATES' HEALTH HISTORY

[4.] Q. Mr. President, do you think that anyone with a history of mental illness should run for high office?

THE PRESIDENT. Well, Miss Thomas [Helen Thomas, United Press International], the question that you ask, of course, is related to some of the conjecture with regard to the ticket on the other side. Mr. Ziegler has correctly reported to all of you ladies and gentlemen of the press that I have given the strictest instructions that there are to be no comments directly, or, in the case of your question, indirectly, on this subject. This is a personal matter.

The question of the selection of a Vice Presidential candidate is one which is a matter for the Presidential candidate to decide, with, of course, the advice and consent of his convention. I am not going to interject myself in that problem except to say that since it is a personal matter, it does give me an opportunity to say that not now on this matter, nor in this campaign in the future, are we going to campaign on personalities or on party labels.

The issues that divide the opposite side and this Administration are so wide—in fact, it is the clearest choice in this century—that we must campaign on issues. There is an honest difference of opinion on foreign policy, an honest difference of opinion on domestic policy, and an honest difference of opinion on most major defense issues.

Under these circumstances, this is a campaign which I think should be waged—I would think all would, but this one particularly should be waged—on the issues so that the American people can make their choice between two: the present President and the challenger, who honestly so basically disagree on fundamental ends and goals for the American people.

CRITICS OF U.S. BOMBING POLICY

[5.] Q. Mr. President, are we to understand perhaps that now that "Stop Bombing the Dikes" has been made a political slogan this year, that perhaps those who have gotten behind it have not thoroughly checked the background of those accusations?

THE PRESIDENT. I did not use the word "naive" unintentionally. The North Vietnamese are very skillful at propaganda. They have, of course, brought those who have been invited into the country to the areas where they have found bomb damage. They have not gone to any great pains to fill those holes, which they would naturally want to do before the possibility of rain and flood again comes to the North.

In my view, this is a deliberate attempt on the part of the North Vietnamese to create an extraneous issue, to divert attention from one of the most barbaric invasions in history, compounded by a violation of all concepts of international law in handling the prisoners of war. For them, with their policy of deliberate murder and assassination and otherwise attacks on civilians for the purpose of killing civilians, for them to try to seize on this and divert attention from them, first, to me it is a patent propaganda effort, and it is one that I think needs to be answered.

We have to, of course, be responsible for what we do. But it is time that in this terribly difficult war some Americans, or

that most of us, should perhaps realize that when we talk about morality, that it is never an easy question.

If I can digress for a moment, then I will come to your followup question on the other matter. I remember one of the first conversations I had with President Eisenhower about war. We were riding back from Quantico. You may remember it. Charlie Wilson [2] used to have those meetings in Quantico of the Defense Establishment people. He asked me to ride back with him. It was very early in the Administration, in the first year.

He was talking a little about the decisions he had to make in World War II. One of the questions I raised with him was: Here, on our part, the deliberate bombing of German cities, the tragedy of Dresden, of Essen, of Hamburg, not to mention Berlin. General Eisenhower said that was a terribly difficult decision for us, the strategic bombing of civilians in Germany. But he said, "On the moral question, we had to answer to ourselves this fundamental problem." He said, "The height of immorality would be to allow Hitler to rule Europe."

Now, in our case we have not gone that far. We are not going to bomb civilian targets in the North. We are not using the great power that could finish off North Vietnam in an afternoon, and we will not. But it would be the height of immorality for the United States at this point to leave Vietnam, and in leaving, to turn over to the North Vietnamese the fate of 17 million South Vietnamese who do not want a Communist government, to turn it over to them.

That is what this is about. That is the

---

[2] Charles E. Wilson was Secretary of Defense 1953–57.

only issue that is left. Those who say "End the war" really should name their resolution "Prolong the war." They should name it "Prolong the war" not because they deliberately want to. They want to end the war just as I do, but we have to face this fact: We have only one President at a time, as I said in 1968. At that time, as you may recall, I was pressed quite often by you ladies and gentlemen, "What do you think we ought to do about negotiations?" I didn't think there was much chance for successful negotiations then.

But I said, I thought quite correctly, we have only one President, and I didn't want to destroy any chance he might have to end this war. At this point, the chance for a negotiated settlement is better now than it has ever been. Oh, it is not sure, and I am not going to raise any false hopes, but the enemy is failing in its military offensive, although there is still some hard fighting to take place in the Quang-tri-Hué area, but the enemy also is, of course, suffering the consequences of our mining action and in cutting the roads and the other systems that would bring in supplies to North Vietnam.

Under these circumstances, the enemy—because also we have made a very fair offer—has every incentive to negotiate. But when you put yourself in the position of the enemy, and then they hear that the Congress of the United States says, in effect, "We will give you what you want regardless of what the President has offered," why not wait? This is the problem, and I would hope that as Senators and Congressmen consult their consciences, they would realize that we have just 3 months left before the election. In those 3 months we hope to do everything we can to bring this war to an end, and they

should take no action which would jeopardize those negotiations. I can only say that the resolutions to this point cannot help. They can only confuse the enemy at best, and at the worst, they will prolong the war.

SELECTION OF VICE PRESIDENTIAL NOMINEES

[6.] Q. The Vice Presidential nominee often is chosen under great pressure. This means often that the Vice President eventually is under great pressure of time and circumstance. Sometimes this turns out all right and sometimes it doesn't. Do you think that that method could be improved?

THE PRESIDENT. I was a Vice President once, too. [*Laughter*]

I will answer. I can only give my own experience, and I know that this was the experience of President Eisenhower. When an individual feels that he is quite—shall we say, has a better than even chance or an even chance to be President, he does a lot of thinking about who should be the Vice Presidential candidate, both because of his potentialities as a candidate and in terms of could he fill the office of Vice President and, in the case of an accident to the President, the President.

I can assure you that naturally I went through that process in making my own decision and I would think that any candidate would do that. I don't think it is quite as, shall we say, off the top of your head as you would indicate, because most of us, when we are seeking the Presidency, long before the convention, have a pretty good idea as to whether we have a good shot at it and we do a lot of thinking about the Vice Presidential nomination.

749

CANDIDATES' FINANCIAL AND MEDICAL
RECORDS

[7.] Q. Mr. President, given the continuing demand for revealing the financial
backgrounds of candidates and officeholders, what is your reaction to the suggestion that medical records of candidates
and officeholders be revealed and, as a
corollary to that, which you will understand, have you ever felt yourself in more
danger of being overconfident? [*Laughter*]

THE PRESIDENT. Is that something to
do with medical records?

Q. There is a bridge, but it is not direct.

THE PRESIDENT. Well, let me say that
for me to answer that question is really
so self-serving that I hesitate to do so. My
medical records, of course, like my financial records, are now already on the books,
open to the press.

You will recall in 1968, the question
was raised about my medical history, and
Mr. Ziegler, at that time, put out the
medical history, including the examinations, some of the examinations, what the
yearly examinations that we all have were,
going back to the time that I came to
Washington in 1946.

So, as far as my financial records are
concerned, they also have been made public, and then every year my medical record is made public by Dr. Tkach [3] in
briefings which seem to create some interest among the press. I don't know why.

I would also suggest that in my case,
too, it was somewhat of a self-serving record, because Dr. Tkach was pointing out
to me a few days ago that according to his
computation, and I will not vouch for
these figures, that probably I have set a
record: I have been in this office now 3½

_____
[3] Maj. Gen. Walter R. Tkach, USAF, Physician to the President.

years and have never missed an appointment because of health.

Considering what I have been through,
I mean some fairly stern crises I would
say and rather extensive travel, I don't
think anybody would question the state
of my health.

I think that in answer to your question,
that that is a matter that will inevitably
be a subject that will be raised and in
which the candidates will have, each of
them, to make his own determination. I
made mine. I don't suggest that others
should do likewise.

Now as far as overconfident—about
what, my health?

ELECTION PREDICTIONS

[8.] Q. No, sir, in terms of the circumstances and the situation, given your position today as an incumbent President
running for reelection, you are the favorite. Events in the past 2 or 3 weeks, let
alone the last 2 or 3 days, have enhanced
that. That is what I was talking about.

THE PRESIDENT. Well, I recall historically an incident, and you were covering us at that time. We both go back 25
years I remember. I recall in 1952 when
another Vice Presidential candidate was
urged to get off the ticket, and there were
many who thought that the fact that he
was urged to get off it, whether he stayed
on or got off, that it was going to sink
the Presidential candidate. It did not.

So, I would say that that incident certainly would not enter into my predictions
at this time. As far as making a prediction
is concerned, I will give it more thought
and will be glad to respond to it when I
have what I call a political press conference, which I will have immediately after
the Republican Convention, at the West-

ern White House in San Clemente.

As far as what the situation is now, though, looking at the fact that the Democratic Party has a much higher registration than the Republican Party, looking at the volatile mix of the American voting public, it is my belief—and I have told all of my associates this—that regardless of what the polls show, whether we are ahead or behind, this will be a close, hard-fought election right down to the wire.

People who make predictions now could look very, very bad later. We are going to assume throughout this election that we have a very hard fight on our hands. We think that it is a good thing that it is going to be a fight on the issues, a good, hard, clean fight on the issues before the American people. We think it will be close, and we hope to win.

THE MIDDLE EAST

[9.] Q. What impact on American policy in the Middle East is the withdrawal of Soviet personnel from Egypt likely to have?

THE PRESIDENT. This question I noticed has been reflected on by some lower level officials in the Government, but not—because Secretary Rogers and I have talked about this matter, and Dr. Kissinger and I—not by us. For this reason: Our goal, as you know, is a just settlement in the Midde East. The situation there is still one that is not clear and any comment upon it, first, might possibly be erroneous, and second, could very well be harmful to our goal of a just settlement.

So I am not trying to dodge your question, but I just do not think it would be helpful to our goal of a just settlement in the Middle East. It might exacerbate the problem by trying to evaluate what happened between Sadat [4] and the Soviet leaders.

REPUBLICAN VICE PRESIDENTIAL CANDIDATE

[10.] Q. Mr. President, on the subject of the Vice President, of your selection of Mr. Agnew,[5] could you tell us if you considered anybody else for the job and who they were?

THE PRESIDENT. No. My thoughts with regard to Vice President Agnew were expressed at rather great length in this very room in an interview with one of the other networks.[6] I think it was CBS.

On that occasion, I expressed my confidence in the Vice President. I won't go over those matters that I covered at considerable length then now, except to say that I reaffirm that confidence as expressed then.

Under the circumstances, I believe that the choice I made 4 years ago is one that should now be reaffirmed by asking him to run for the office again.

Now, there has been speculation, I would hasten to say, about other people for the Vice Presidency. That is inevitable. The Vice President could get sick or the Vice President might decide not to run,

---

[4] Anwar al Sadat was President of the Arab Republic of Egypt.

[5] On July 22, 1972, the President informed Vice President Spiro T. Agnew, Republican National Chairman Robert Dole, Campaign Director Clark MacGregor, Convention Floor Leader Hugh Scott, Permanent Chairman of the Convention Gerald R. Ford, and Campaign Chairman Frank Dale of his intention to recommend to the Republican National Convention the nomination of Vice President Agnew for a second term.

[6] See Item 1 [4.].

all of these things. I don't think he is going to get sick. He is also in excellent health, better than I. He plays tennis. But, in any event, there has been a lot of speculation. Secretary Connally's name comes to mind.

I should point out that a really great injustice was done to Secretary Connally in the suggestion, I think, on one of the news reports to the effect that I gave Secretary Connally the "bad news" that he was not going to be the Vice Presidential candidate when I saw him Friday night.

This was not bad news to him. As a matter of fact, it was not news at all. He and I had discussed this problem when he came to California after his world trip. At that time, I discussed the Vice Presidency. After all, not only from the standpoint of ability to hold the office of Vice President but from the standpoint of ability to win the election, Secretary Connally, whose political judgment I respect very much, strongly urged that Vice President Agnew be continued on the ticket.

THE MILITARY AND BOMBING POLICY

[11.] Q. Mr. President, on the bombing of the dikes and dams, would you say that you have been resisting pressure from the military to bomb such installations?

THE PRESIDENT. No. The pressure does not come from the military. I have talked this over with Admiral Moorer and naturally General Abrams. As a matter of fact, let me just say one thing about our military, because somebody ought to speak up for it now and then.

We get the idea they are a bunch of savage flyboys, and they love to get down and machinegun innocent little civilians and all the rest.

We can be very proud of our military, not only the men that are flying, they are brave and courageous, but the men on the ground. We can be very proud of the Marines, all of them have gone now, for what they have done—the Marines, the Army, the ground soldiers—for the civilians and refugees there. It is a story of generosity in a country that has never been equaled by American fighting men or anybody else.

As far as our military commanders are concerned, while they do give me their judgment as to what will affect the military outcome in Vietnam, they have never recommended, for example, bombing Hanoi. You have seen some of those signs "Bomb Hanoi," in fact, they were around in '68 even, a few, as well as '64.

Our military don't want to do that. They believe it would be counterproductive, and second, they believe it is not necessary. It might shorten the war, but it would leave a legacy of hatred throughout that part of the world from which we might never recover. So our military have not advocated bombing the dikes; they have not advocated bombing civilian centers. They are doing their best to carry out the policy we want of hitting military targets only.

When, as a result of what will often happen, a bomb is dropped, if it is in an area of injury to civilians, it is not by intent, and there is a very great difference.

THE VICE PRESIDENT AND POLICY
DECISIONS

[12.] Q. Sir, a similar question was asked another President in your experience.[7] Would you please tell us what

---

[7] The reporter was referring to a question asked in a news conference held by President Eisenhower on August 24, 1960. See "Public Papers of the Presidents, Dwight D. Eisenhower, 1960–61," Item 268.

policy decisions Vice President Agnew has contributed to in your Administration?

THE PRESIDENT. Well, I only need a couple of minutes. [*Laughter*]

Miss McClendon [Sarah McClendon, Sarah McClendon News Service], as a matter of fact, one of the considerations that motivates a President when he selects a Vice President for running again is: How does he handle himself with the tough decisions? Now, the Vice President does not make decisions. I learned that, and Vice President Agnew knows that. Decisions with regard to his schedule, yes, advice, et cetera, but not decisions. The President only makes them.

But in the Cabinet Room, and sometimes in this office, we have had some pretty hard ones—the May 8 decision was a very tough decision; the Cambodian decision was not easy; the November 3 decision, the speech that I made on that occasion; the decision with regard to the SALT agreements, which involved a fight between the hawks and doves, was not an easy one.

I don't mean to indicate that Vice President Agnew just sat there as a "yes man." He is very outspoken—very quiet but very outspoken—and articulate. But what has impressed me about him in those meetings is that he is a man of poise, calm, and judgment. When it gets down to the final tough decision, he, from my evaluation, is always cool and poised and is one who therefore could be expected to make decisions in the future in a calm, cool, judicial way.

Now, that does not mean that all of his decisions will be good because calm, cool, judicial men make bad decisions just as emotional men sometimes make good decisions. But my point is that in his case, in all of the mini-crises and major crises

we have had in the Administration, he has been strong, courageous, and loyal. Those are attributes that are interesting to come by.

Let me say one other thing since you are talking about the Vice Presidency. I think we who have been Vice Presidents ought to form a little club. It is the most maligned office, you know. The reason is that we tend not to look at the records of Vice Presidents who have become President. Now that did not happen to me so this is not a self-serving statement in this case. I mean, became President as a result of being Vice President.

But look at this century: two striking examples. Around the turn of the century, Theodore Roosevelt—and some of you remember Mark Hanna, a great McKinley man. McKinley was in marvelous health and he was shot. Theodore Roosevelt came into the Presidency, and Mark Hanna, who did not care much for Theodore Roosevelt, said, "Now we have this fanatic in the White House," and yet Theodore Roosevelt became a great President.

Perhaps that is not the best analogy because Theodore Roosevelt added, they thought, a great deal to the ticket.

Let's look at Harry Truman a moment—and I must say I was in the group at that time, being in the other party— but here is Harry Truman succeeding the towering figure of his time, Franklin Roosevelt. I remember the editorials: "Harry Truman, the man from Independence"—the very question somebody asked here a few moments ago, "Shouldn't we have a better method of selecting Vice Presidents?" They said, "How in the world? Now we have this little man from Missouri in the Presidency." Well let me say, you all know that Harry Truman and

I have had our differences. You will also remember that on public occasions I have praised him for three very tough decisions he made.

I was reading Winston Churchill the other night, his first meeting with Truman at Potsdam when Truman took him over in a corner and told him about the bomb, the use of the bomb. This was a terribly difficult decision. But he thought, probably correctly—and President Eisenhower agreed with this—that it would save a million American lives, as probably it did, and that is why he used the bomb in ending the war with Japan.

The second decision, which I had the opportunity to support, was the Greek-Turkish aid program. That was a tough one. It split his party. It split it into the Henry Wallace wing and his wing. Byrnes and Wallace, remember, had their fight. But it was a good decision, and I supported it in the Congress of the United States.

Incidentally, I still support aid to Greece and Turkey. It is just as necessary today as it was then, for most of the same reasons, now particularly added because of the fact that without aid to Greece and aid to Turkey you have no viable

policy to save Israel.

Finally, there, of course, were decisions that Mr. Truman made on the Korean war. I criticized the conduct of the war as did many of us who were out. But his decision to go into Korea was right, it was necessary, it was tough.

Just before Dean Acheson died he was in this office. We talked about how Truman had made that decision. I have talked too long on that; what I am simply saying is this: Here was the little man from Missouri. He was the Vice President. People said, "Gee, why didn't Roosevelt pick so many others of the towering figures from his Cabinet or the Senate or the rest, rather than the little man from Missouri?"

But the little man from Missouri had that indefinable quality, as did the big man from New York, Theodore Roosevelt, a character, that made him a man capable of making tough decisions, and that is the most important thing a Vice President needs.

MISS THOMAS. Thank you.

NOTE: President Nixon's twenty-sixth news conference was held at 3:02 p.m., in the Oval Office at the White House on Thursday, July 27, 1972. He spoke without referring to notes.

240   Statement on the Death of Senator Allen J. Ellender of Louisiana.   *July 27, 1972*

SENATOR Ellender was a good friend, a fine Senator, and a splendid American. His elevation to the chairmanship of the Appropriations Committee and the presidency pro tem of the Senate capped a long and distinguished career. In the course of his 35 years of service in the Senate, he left a deep imprint on the legislative history of this century—and he proved himself a

representative not only of Louisiana but of the Nation, determined to do what he considered was right for America.

I often had the benefit of his counsel, and I valued the opportunity to talk with him before my recent visit to the Soviet Union about his own travels in that country.

Mrs. Nixon joins with me and with his

many other official and unofficial friends in expressing our profound sorrow at his death and our sympathy to his family.

NOTE: Senator Ellender, 81, died of a heart attack at Bethesda Naval Hospital.

He served in the Louisiana State House of Representatives 1924–36, in the United States Senate from 1936, and as chairman of the Committee on Appropriations and president pro tempore of the Senate from 1971.

The President and Mrs. Nixon attended funeral services for the Senator in Houma, La., on July 31.

241   Remarks on Signing a Bill Amending the Federal Crop Insurance Act. *July* 28, 1972

I JUST want to say to the Future Farmers of America—and this is your meeting—that on several occasions during the time I have been in office over the past 3 years, I have welcomed delegations from the Future Farmers at the White House, usually your leaders, either in my Oval Office or in the Cabinet Room. This is a larger group. I did meet one of the larger groups, a group about this size, I think it was in 1971.

Each time I have had the occasion to extend greetings to you, say the things that we usually say to young Americans and particularly to young Americans who are leaders, as you are, in your communities across this country. But today, I told my staff that I thought we ought to try to do something different.

Now, when you ask for something different, of course, you just can't make it up, but we found there was something that could be done today that was very significant, very significant that tied in directly to the Future Farmers of America, and this brings me to the occasion that you will now witness, an occasion of some historical importance, but an occasion which is very important to you and your future.

Generally, when bills are signed, they are signed by the President in his office.

Often, however, a bill is considered to be so important to the national interest that it is signed in public before the television cameras and the newspapermen and the others, with Members of the House and the Senate who have been instrumental in getting the legislation through, in this case, of course, Senator Dole and Congressman Mathias and Congressman Poage, who is the chairman of the Agriculture Committee in the House of Representatives.

Now the Federal Crop Insurance Act is one that would not normally be a bill that would be signed in the presence of television cameras, because it is one that has almost unanimous support in the House and the Senate. It is a very important piece of legislation, but not being controversial, it isn't one that really makes news. But this year something different happened, and that brings me to you.

When this bill was up for consideration on the floor of the Senate, Senator Dole, reflecting on a letter he had received from one of his constituents, told this story.

An application had been made for Federal crop insurance by a Kansas farmer [Gary Atkinson]. The Kansas farmer completely complied with every requirement of the law. He was a good risk, he was entitled to the insurance, but he was turned down. He was turned down for only one reason. He was only 19 years of age.

And Senator Dole pointed out that this was unfair, that if an individual completely complied with all the requirements to get crop insurance he should not be turned down simply because of his age and particularly in view of the fact that we had had the historic action taken last year of reducing the voting age to 18.

So, Senator Dole, responding to the letter he had received from Gary Atkinson, who is standing on my right—and his fiance on the right of Senator Dole, who is separating the two at the moment—but in any event, Senator Dole introduced an amendment in the Senate and that amendment was passed.

As a result of that amendment being passed, it is now in this bill that I am going to sign.

Now that story, it seems to me, tells us three things that are very important to you and important to the country. First, it shows you that your Government is responsive. It doesn't mean that every time you write a Senator or Congressman you are going to get what you want, but it does mean if you have got a good case, you write to your Senator or your Congressman and he can get it into law. It happened. Gary Atkinson knows and all of you know, being below 21 years of age, that now if you are farmers that you and other young people in the future can apply for crop insurance.

The second thing that it tells us is that there is really a future, a great future for young people in farming. I had not realized, except for meeting with groups like this, how important that future was. But I can certainly say that having met you, having realized that here was a young farmer who could apply for and receive crop insurance, that this indicates that that future is indeed a bright one.

When we hear that only the old people are in farming, that no young people are coming in, all they have to do is to look at this group of young people and you know that farming has a future in America.

The point, of course, is that this shows, finally, that your Government has faith in young people. We believe you are a good risk. We believe you can help to build a better America—not just a better farming community, but a better America for all of us.

That is what this signing ceremony is going to indicate and that is why in this very historic room, the State Dining Room of the White House, we are glad to welcome you, representing the leadership of the Future Farmers of America. Because on this day, by the action that we take, we are demonstrating your Government is responsive, we are demonstrating your Government has confidence and faith in young Americans, and we are demonstrating that farming has a future, a great future.

It is in that spirit that I now will sign the bill and after signing it, I will give the two signing pens, one to Senator Dole and the other to Gary Atkinson, but since there are so many here, and also several other distinguished Members of the Congress, I found that we just have enough pens to go around to every one of you when I finish the signing.

[At this point, the President signed the bill. He then turned to Gary Atkinson and his finance, Dianne Ryff, and resumed speaking.]

Is there a minister in the house? I just thought you might as well get married now.

Well in any event, we congratulate you in advance and we want all of you to know that you are always welcome in this house, because this house belongs to all the American people and particularly to the young people of America, because in this house is your future.

Thank you.

NOTE: The President spoke at 12:14 p.m. in the State Dining Room at the White House. He spoke without referring to notes.

As enacted, the bill (S. 1139) is Public Law 92–357 (86 Stat. 501).

A summary of the highlights of the bill, released the same day by the White House, is printed in the Weekly Compilation of Presidential Documents (vol. 8, p. 1186).

242 Message to the Congress Transmitting Annual Report on Comparability of Federal and Private Enterprise Salaries. *August 1, 1972*

To the Congress of the United States:

I am forwarding herewith the annual comparison of Federal salaries in the statutory pay systems to the salaries paid in private enterprise, as required by section 5305 of title 5, United States Code.

The report, prepared by the Director of the Office of Management and Budget and the Chairman of the Civil Service Commission, compares the General Schedule pay rates to the rates paid in private enterprise for the same levels of work, as published in the Bureau of Labor Statistics Bulletin No. 1742, *National Survey of Professional, Administrative,*

Technical and Clerical Pay, June 1971.

No adjustment based upon the comparison was made in Federal pay rates because of the substitute measure enacted as a part of the Economic Stabilization Act Amendments of 1971 (Public Law 92–210, approved December 22, 1971).

In addition, the Advisory Committee on Federal Pay reviewed the report and its comments are enclosed.

RICHARD NIXON

The White House,

August 1, 1972.

NOTE: The report (3 pp. plus appendixes) is printed in House Document 92–332.

243 Message to the Congress Transmitting a Proposed Amendment to the Disaster Recovery Bill. *August 2, 1972*

To the Congress of the United States:

Tropical Storm Agnes caused the most widespread destruction and devastation of any natural disaster in the history of the United States. On July 17, 1972, I sent to the Congress a proposal authorizing special disaster recovery measures which would aid victims of Agnes and also

of the flood in Rapid City, South Dakota during June 1972.

As I stated in my transmittal message, the need for prompt enactment of these aid proposals, aimed at short and long-term recovery, is extreme and urgent. I asked the Congress then to consider and enact them within seven days. Sixteen days have passed without final Congressional action on the Disaster Recovery Act of 1972. I again urge the Congress to act immediately, because the victims of these disasters desperately need the help these measures would provide. And they need it now.

Today, I am transmitting an amendment which would make private, non-profit educational institutions eligible for disaster relief grants under the Act. I urge that the Congress consider and enact promptly this amendment, which would authorize reconstruction relief for these institutions comparable to the disaster reconstruction relief already available to public educational institutions.

The Office of Emergency Preparedness estimates that property loss and damage at private non-profit educational institutions in the storm affected areas has exceeded $19 million. Many of these institutions have undergone damage so extensive that they would be unable to rebuild facilities or reopen without extraordinary assistance. For example, at one alone, Wilkes College in Wilkes-Barre, Pennsylvania, which is not a large or wealthy institution, the storm caused havoc and destruction estimated at several millions of dollars.

The proposal I am transmitting today would provide financial assistance to restore, reconstruct or replace disaster-damaged education facilities, supplies and equipment used primarily for nonsectarian educational purposes. I believe this temporary authority is required if we are to meet our public responsibilities equitably and in a just manner.

Again, I cannot stress too strongly that it is essential that the Congress immediately enact the pending disaster relief legislation I have proposed. It is imperative that this massive recovery program begin at once. Millions of Americans—individual homeowners, farmers and city dwellers, small businessmen—are struggling to rebuild their lives in the wake of these natural disasters. They need their Government's help. And they need it now.

RICHARD NIXON

The White House,
August 2, 1972.

NOTE: On the same day, the White House released a fact sheet and the transcript of a news briefing on the proposed amendment. Participants in the news briefing were Frank C. Carlucci, Deputy Director, Office of Management and Budget, and George A. Lincoln, Director, Office of Emergency Preparedness.

244 Statement on Launching Project FIND To Provide Food Assistance for Older Americans. *August 2, 1972*

THE THOUGHT that any older citizens—after a lifetime of service to their communities and country—may suffer from hunger or malnutrition is intolerable.

The White House Conference on Aging last December underlined the particular nutritional problems of the elderly—the

problems of living on a fixed income and problems arising from isolation. The delegates called for action programs to help the malnourished aged.

In response to this call, I am today launching Project FIND, a program to seek out the elderly who are not receiving the assistance which could be theirs. I first described this program in my special message to the Congress on older Americans on March 23, 1972.

The Federal Government has increased significantly the resources available annually from food stamp and food distribution programs. Outlays for food stamps alone have increased from $248 million 4 years ago to $1.9 billion in fiscal year 1972—more than an eightfold increase. Virtually every county in the Nation now offers one program or the other. Some 15 million persons now receive assistance from Federal family food programs. These efforts can do much to help stretch the fixed incomes of the elderly.

Unfortunately, however, many older persons who are eligible for assistance are not enrolled in these programs. Tens of thousands, perhaps hundreds of thousands, of older persons are unaware of these and other resources, private and public, which could do so much to improve the quality of their lives.

It is the objective of Project FIND to discover these older persons—and to build a bridge between them and the society which stands ready to help them in time of need. As a part of this effort, a leaflet describing these programs and how to apply for them will be available to all persons receiving social security checks. For those who feel they need additional help in establishing their eligibility, personal contacts will be made by tens of thousands of volunteers recruited and trained by the American Red Cross.

Project FIND is a cooperative effort on the part of the public and private sectors to replace despair with hope in the lives of many older persons. It represents one more way in which all our people can honor a generation of Americans which has given so much to all of us.

NOTE: On the same day, the White House released the transcript of a news briefing on Project FIND by Arthur S. Flemming, Special Consultant to the President on Aging and Cochairman of Project FIND, and Vicki L. Keller, Staff Assistant to the President.

Mrs. Nixon will serve as Cochairman with Dr. Flemming.

245   Letter Congratulating the Board of Foreign Scholarships on its 25th Anniversary.   *August 2, 1972*

Dear Professor Billington:

As the Board of Foreign Scholarships marks the close of its 25th year, I congratulate you and your fellow Board members, past and present, for your diligence and resourcefulness in promoting scholarly exchanges between the United States and other countries of the world.

The educational exchange program has a proud record of achievement in its first quarter century. In all, more than 100,000 students, teachers and scholars from 110 countries have participated in this program, including over 36,000 Americans. Its contribution to mutual understanding, and ultimately to world peace, is incalculable.

Looking ahead, I would like to commend the Board for the forward-looking initiatives in its program for the Seventies and especially for the Lincoln Lectureships, which are being inaugurated today. Please convey my deep appreciation to the four distinguished scholars who will launch this significant new lecture series—Professors Franklin, Samuelson and Townes, and Mr. Updike. The Lincoln Lectureships typify this country's willingness to share with the rest of the world the finest in American scholarship and intellectual achievement. And I am pleased to know that eminent foreign lecturers, in turn, will give Americans the benefit of their talents and thought.

I also take this opportunity to commend the wisdom and foresight of the exchange program's many Congressional founders and supporters. Their backing, over the years, has enabled this program to play an increasingly significant role in our relations with other countries and cultures.

The Board and the program it supervises have my very best wishes for every success in meeting the new challenges of the next quarter century.

Sincerely,

RICHARD NIXON

[James H. Billington, D. Phil., Professor of History, Woodrow Wilson School of Public and International Affairs, Princeton University, Princeton, N.J. 08540]

NOTE: The letter was dated August 1, 1972, and released August 2.

Dr. Billington was Chairman of the Board of Foreign Scholarships.

The four scholars chosen to lecture abroad in the Lincoln Lectureships series were John Hope Franklin, professor of history, University of Chicago; Paul A. Samuelson, Nobel prize-winning professor of economics, Massachusetts Institute of Technology; Charles H. Townes, Nobel prize-winning professor of physics, University of California at Berkeley; and John H. Updike, novelist and poet, Ipswich, Mass.

246 Message to the Congress Transmitting Annual Report of the National Advisory Council on Extension and Continuing Education. *August 3, 1972*

To the Congress of the United States:

The Sixth Annual Report of the National Advisory Council on Extension and Continuing Education is submitted herewith. The Council is authorized by Public Law 89–329.

I congratulate the Council on its comprehensive study of the Federal role in community service, extension and continuing education for adults through the resources of colleges and universities. The study points up the need for increased coordination of the support the Federal government lends to these efforts.

Several of the Council's proposals are receiving thorough consideration by the Department of Health, Education, and Welfare, including those relating to improved coordination of Federal assistance to extension, community service, and continuing education programs.

The Council also recommends that additional funds be provided for the program authorized by Title I of the Higher Education Act of 1965. I continue to hold as a basic principle that greater emphasis should be placed on broad funding approaches for Federal grant-in-aid programs, and that narrow categorical grant programs such as Title I should be relied on less as a means of channeling Federal funds to individual institutions.

RICHARD NIXON

The White House,
August 3, 1972.

NOTE: The 112-page report is entitled "A Question of Stewardship: A Study of the Federal Role in Higher Continuing Education."

247   Letter to the Secretary of Health, Education, and Welfare on Pending Revenue Sharing and Welfare Reform Legislation.   *August 3, 1972*

Dear Elliot:

As you know, George Shultz is leading the Administration's effort to obtain a clean general revenue sharing bill.

I have been advised that the revenue sharing proposal will probably be considered by the Senate prior to consideration of H.R. 1. There is speculation that some selected elements of H.R. 1 might be amended to the revenue sharing bill. I would strongly oppose such a move, because it could doom the possibility of real welfare reform in this Congress and could seriously jeopardize the revenue sharing bill. As we proceed on general revenue sharing, I would like you to make known to the Senate leadership my reasons for this position.

The H.R. 1 bill is likely to follow revenue sharing to the Senate floor. After a three year struggle, during which welfare reform has twice been passed by the House of Representatives, I am certain that the Senate will carry out its public obligation to consider and vote upon H.R. 1.

I remain firmly committed to welfare reform and to revenue sharing, but they should be passed and signed as separate bills. The House-passed version of welfare reform contains the major elements of our original proposal:

—Strong work incentives and requirements;

—National eligibility standards and minimum benefit standards;

—Coverage of the working poor;

—Fiscal relief for the States.

This legislation, by eventually bringing under control the exploding costs of our current wasteful welfare programs, is a strong step forward toward the fiscal integrity we are determined to achieve.

Sincerely,

RICHARD NIXON

[Honorable Elliot L. Richardson, Secretary of Health, Education, and Welfare, Washington, D.C. 20201]

NOTE: The text of the letter, dated August 2, 1972, was made available to the press on August 3.

248   Statement About Signing a Bill Providing Emergency Highway Repairs Following Tropical Storm Agnes and the South Dakota Flood.   *August 4, 1972*

I AM gratified to have signed H.R. 15950, the first of the emergency measures I have recommended to the Congress for relief in those areas devastated by Tropical Storm Agnes and the flood in Rapid City, S. Dak.

This measure, which will add $150 million to the normal $50 million program for emergency highway repairs, is a most welcome and vitally needed aid program— but it should be regarded only as a down payment on the total disaster relief program of $1.8 billion I proposed to the Congress on July 17, 1972.

H.R. 15950 will give us a total of $200 million in this fiscal year and $100 million in future years to repair and reconstruct Federal-aid highways and Federal roads and trails damaged by natural disasters.

The highway repair money, however, will not provide any direct, personal assistance to the many individuals struggling to repair or rebuild homes, farms, and small businesses.

I am pleased, therefore, that the Senate today has scheduled consideration of a major element of my relief program, one which would substantially improve the terms of loans made to homeowners, farmers, and small businessmen. Speedy action is urgently needed on this part of my program, and I urge the House of Represent-

atives to follow up quickly.

Another pending element of my recommendations is for supplemental appropriations to provide the necessary funds for the Federal Government's relief and recovery measures.

Again, I urge that the Congress place the highest possible priority on approving my entire package of disaster relief legislation, so that tangible help can start flowing at the earliest possible time to the tens of thousands still in dire need weeks after the disasters.

NOTE: As enacted, H.R. 15950, approved August 3, 1972, is Public Law 92–361 (86 Stat. 503).

249 Statement on Signing a Bill To Facilitate the Preservation of Historic Structures Donated to State and Local Governments. *August 4, 1972*

ALTHOUGH Jefferson reminded us that "the earth belongs to the living, not to the dead," the value of historical preservation can no longer seriously be challenged. We need to know where we have been if we are to understand where we are—and who we are.

Although it is true that historical preservation of buildings may seem to many to have a low priority, we should not turn our backs upon these quiet, stately, authentic reminders of our heritage. As we look upon these structures we hear the voices of past heroes—strengthening our resolve to create a future that will be worthy of them.

And although the GSA surplus property bill I am about to sign may appear to some not to be significant, I do sign it with a sense of deep significance. This is, in fact, one of the key initiatives for historic

preservation that I presented to the Congress in my 1971 message on the environment. The bill will give us the tools we need to permit States and localities to receive title to surplus Federal structures of historic and architectural interest.

Until today, law has prevented the free transfer of Federal surplus buildings to the States or localities unless they were to be used as museums or for other nonrevenue producing activities. Many States and cities simply could not afford to take title and maintain these buildings under such terms.

Under the new law, the States and localities will be able to use the Federal surplus buildings as centers for urban commerce and tourism. They will be able to preserve the historic buildings, to cherish them, and to use them as active facilities which will raise sufficient revenue to keep them well maintained. The buildings themselves can be living parts of the community, preserving their historic past not as a thing apart but as a vital presence. Any excess revenues will be used for parks, recreation, and other local historic preservation projects.

There remain before the Congress a number of additional measures I have proposed to aid historic preservation. Among these are the National Land Use Policy Act, which will help States to exercise protective controls over historic buildings and districts, proposed changes in the Internal Revenue Code to provide

tax benefits for the restoration and tax penalties for the destruction of historic structures, and a new program of loan guarantees through the Department of Housing and Urban Development for the restoration and rehabilitation of historic structures for residential purposes.

I urge the Congress to enact all these measures for the benefit of our American architectural and historic values—and I sign the GSA surplus property bill with pride and satisfaction.

NOTE: As enacted, the bill (S. 1152) is Public Law 92–362 (86 Stat. 503).

250   Message to the Congress Transmitting Annual Report of the Council on Environmental Quality. *August 7, 1972*

To the Congress of the United States:

At the dawn of the twentieth century, almost as a voice in the wilderness he loved, President Theodore Roosevelt proclaimed an environmental ethic for America. He said:

I recognize the right and duty of this generation to develop and use our natural resources; but I do not recognize the right to waste them, or to rob by wasteful use, the generations that come after us.

At the dawn of the 1970's there was still no more significant challenge facing Americans than the task of wisely conserving our natural resources and leaving the Nation a cleaner and healthier place for our children and grandchildren.

In my 1970 State of the Union Message I asked our people:

Shall we surrender to our surroundings or shall we make our peace with nature and begin to make reparations for the damage we have done to our air, to our land, and to our water?

This year's report of the Council on Environmental Quality examines the environmental conditions of a dynamic and mature society. The report addresses some very complex issues—the need for indices of environmental quality and forecasting, the costs and impact on the economy of pollution control requirements, and the effects of environmental standards on international trade—and puts these issues in sharper perspective. The increasing sophistication which we are bringing to our perception of environmental problems is itself an encouraging indication of progress.

This Annual Report on Environmental Quality also offers an assessment of how we are faring. I am pleased that the data presented in the Council's report indicate that the quality of the air in many of our cities is improving. Across the nation, emissions from automobiles—a significant portion of total emissions—are declining. We can expect these welcome trends to accelerate as the new standards and compliance schedules called for by the Clean Air Act of 1970 become fully effective.

Although the Report shows that we still have a major battle ahead to restore the quality of our waters, and urgently need effective new legislation which I submitted to the Congress over a year and a half ago, impressive strides have been made under present authorities. These include a four-fold increase in enforcement actions under the Refuse Act of 1899 since 1968.

The private sector is performing far more effectively in environmental protection. Throughout the country, industry is developing and using new technology to reduce pollution. Surveys indicate that business has increased its spending on pollution controls by about 50 percent in each of the last two years.

The future will bring new challenges to both the private and the public sectors in arresting environmental decay. The Council's report estimates that in order to meet current environmental protection requirements, both the public and private sectors together will need to spend an annual amount of $33 billion in 1980. Cumulative expenditures of more than $287 billion are estimated over the 10 years from 1971 to 1980.

So—we have only just begun to face up to the environmental question, even though we may have awakened just in time for us to stave off catastrophe.

The encouraging news in this report by the Council—as well as the hope we have for mastering the many difficult problems that still persist—is the rapid step-by-step progress in institutionalizing and reorganizing the Federal environmental structure, the dramatic funding, the wide range of administrative actions that have been taken, the strict enforcement of pollution control laws, the new international agreements which have been forged, and the broad array of major new legislation which has been submitted to the Congress for action.

YEARS OF PROGRESS

With the creation of the Council on Environmental Quality and the Environmental Protection Agency, we have brought about a major institutional reform within the Federal Government and a far more effective organization for environmental policy-making and enforcement. This reform has produced major progress—evidenced, for example, by the broad legislative proposals for environmental improvement which I have submitted to the Congress and by the vigorous enforcement of our pollution laws. The establishment of the National Oceanic and Atmospheric Administration gives us a focus on the marine environment. I have proposed a Department of Natural Resources, for coordinated resource management, and a Department of Community Development, for a systematic approach to both urban and rural growth. The Congress has yet to act on these two crucial reorganization proposals.

Under the National Environmental Policy Act (NEPA), we have undertaken a fundamental reform in the requirement that Federal agencies give careful analysis to the potential environmental impacts of proposed Federal actions. Already this changed emphasis has led to reconsideration of some projects, improvements of many others, and, overall, a far more thoughtful and comprehensive planning process. Our requirement that this whole process of environmental analysis must be open to the public for examination and comments—well before proposed actions are taken—is providing a new and more open dimension to Government. We can be proud of this record of improved citizen participation in the vital process of public decision-making.

The level of Federal funding for environmental protection has never been higher. In the four years since fiscal year 1969, Federal outlays for environmental protection have increased fivefold. Funding for cleanup of pollution at Federal facilities has increased from a $52 million annual level at the outset of my Administration to my 1973 budget of $315 million.

Regulatory and enforcement actions have accelerated dramatically over the past four years. The number of criminal actions taken by the Justice Department against water polluters was increased four fold—from 46 to 191—between 1968 and 1971. EPA has taken action to halt harmful discharges into Lake Superior and shut down major industries during an air pollution crisis in Birmingham, Alabama.

In our long-term determination to provide tangible benefits for our children and grandchildren, we have created the Legacy of Parks program. Over 140 Federal properties have already been made available for park and recreation use, covering more than 20,000 acres in thirty-nine states and Puerto Rico. Most of these natural retreats are located in and near cities

where the need for open space is greatest. The estimated fair market value of these properties is almost $100 million. In addition, we proposed major urban parks at gateways to both of our coasts—New York City and San Francisco. These two parks would comprise almost 50,000 acres, including valuable cultural, historic, and recreation assets accessible to millions of people.

My Administration has tackled a host of controversial issues of environmental protection. We have limited oil drilling in the Santa Barbara Channel off the California coast. We helped protect the Everglades in Florida by stopping a proposed jetport. In addition, I proposed legislation to acquire interests in the Big Cypress Swamp to protect the Everglades' water supply. We halted the Cross-Florida Barge Canal and are considering the inclusion of the Oklawaha River in the system of scenic and wild rivers. And we have restricted use of DDT almost solely to public health purposes. We stopped the use of poisons on public lands. And we stopped all commercial whaling by the United States as well as all imports of whale products into this country. These are examples of the rigorous executive action taken by my Administration to protect the environment.

New Laws We Need

New legislation is still badly needed in a number of areas, and in a series of environmental messages to Congress I have set forth a comprehensive legislative program designed to clean up the inherited problems of the past and to deal with emerging problems before they become critical. Many of these problem areas are defined in this Annual Report. To date, much of the proposed legislation has been the subject of congressional hearings, where it has attracted heartening interest and support. However, the record of final congressional action is entirely inadequate, with more than 20 major environmental proposals still pending.

Last month, I signed an important Port and Waterways Safety Act into law. This new law, which I proposed in May 1970, will help protect our inland waters from oil and other hazardous pollutant spills. This is a welcome beginning, but passage of my other major proposals to give us effective tools to deal with the environmental challenge—together with creation of a new Department of Natural Resources—will be essential, in my judgment, if we are to have an adequate base for improving environmental quality. I urge the Congress to complete final action on responsible legislation to give us authority to upgrade water quality and to control the dumping of wastes at sea. We urgently need the new controls I have proposed over the use of toxic substances such as mercury, over the increasing problem of excessive noise, and over the misuse of chemical pesticides.

I have proposed a Toxic Wastes Disposal Control Act under which the Environmental Protection Agency would establish Federal Guidelines and requirements for State programs to regulate disposal on or under the land of those toxic wastes which pose a hazard to health. The Act would provide for Federal enforcement action if a State should fail to establish its own program.

Legislation which I have proposed is urgently needed to protect the land from the potential ravages of mining, by imposing adequate standards of reclamation.

Strip mining alone now disturbs almost 4,650 acres a week. My proposed Power Plant Siting Act, for which the need is more evident with each passing month, would allow us effectively to reconcile environmental protection and energy needs.

I have proposed new legislation calling upon the States to assume control over land-use planning and regulation in areas of critical environmental concern and to regulate land use around major growth-industry facilities such as highways and airports. I have asked the Congress for authority to initiate at the State level regulatory programs to control sediment affecting water quality from earth-moving activities such as building and road construction. Federal enforcement would be imposed in situations in which a State failed to implement such a program.

I proposed a new type of law for pollution control purposes—a charge on harmful sulfur oxides emissions. This proposal embodies the principle that the price of goods should be made to include the costs of producing and disposing of them without harm to the environment. I also proposed a law that would employ our tax structure to discourage potentially harmful development in our precious coastal wetlands.

I have asked for a new and more effective Federal law to protect endangered species of wildlife—by covering species likely to become endangered as well as those more immediately threatened, and by imposing Federal penalties for taking of such species.

These proposals, and others I have put forward, are vital to all Americans in the years to come. But the critical final steps have yet to be taken. The Nation needs these laws, and they should be enacted this year. The Congress has a splendid opportunity to leave an historic record of environmental achievement, an opportunity which it must seize. The time for deliberation has passed. It is now time for action.

NATIONS ACTING TOGETHER

While our most immediate concern must be for the quality of our national environment, it is clear that we are part of a global environment whose long-range protection must be achieved by a mix of national and international efforts. This past year witnessed three historic milestones in the field of international environmental activity.

On April 15, in Ottawa, Prime Minister Trudeau and I signed the Great Lakes Water Quality Agreement providing a common commitment to work together to clean up these important, shared resources.

On May 23, in Moscow, President Podgorny and I signed a Co-operative Agreement on Environmental Protection which opens a new area of U.S.-Soviet cooperation and permits our two peoples to work together on the solution of environmental problems in eleven broad areas.

Between June 5–16, in Stockholm, the United Nations Conference on the Human Environment brought together the representatives of 113 nations representing nine-tenths of the world's people to explore together the opportunities for national and international action on common environmental problems. The Conference achieved nearly all of the goals which the United States had urged in advance. Specifically, the nations:

—Reached agreement on the establish-

ment of a permanent new organization within the United Nations to coordinate international environmental activities.

—Agreed to the establishment of a United Nations environmental fund to be financed by voluntary contributions from U.N. member governments. I shall ask Congress to authorize and appropriate $40 million as our Nation's share of a five-year, $100 million fund.

—Endorsed completion of a convention proposed by the United States to control ocean dumping of shore-generated waste. The favorable prospect for international action heightens the urgency of passing the domestic legislation. I have proposed to curtail ocean dumping from our shores.

—Approved an "earthwatch" program for worldwide environmental monitoring.

—Endorsed in principle a convention on endangered species, designed to protect species of plants and animals threatened with extinction by imposing control in international shipment, import and export.

—Endorsed our recommendation for a ten-year moratorium on commercial whaling. (Despite vigorous U.S. efforts, this moratorium was not agreed to by the International Whaling Commission at its recent meeting, although we were successful in achieving substantially reduced quotas and other protective measures.)

In addition, a proposal which I made in 1971 for a World Heritage Trust—to give uniquely important historic, cultural and natural areas of the world special

767

international recognition and protection—was strongly supported at Stockholm. When established, the Trust will provide vital new international dimension to the national park concept.

Environmental problems do not distinguish between national boundaries or differing social and economic systems. Environmental cooperation offers nations an opportunity for dealing constructively with each other and for responding to the growing aspirations of ordinary people around the globe to live decently and well in healthful surroundings.

I am hopeful about the prospects of international cooperation in the environmental field. The U.S. will continue to provide leadership in developing such cooperation. I am encouraged—even more profoundly—that the common search for a better environment can be one of those activities which serves to unify nations.

The Environment and Our People

In October 1971, I initiated the Environmental Merit Awards Program. Administered by the Environmental Protection Agency in cooperation with the Office of Education, this program gives national recognition to successful student projects leading to environmental understanding or improvement. Qualifications for the awards are determined by local boards. Each board consists of secondary school students, faculty, and representatives of the local community. Already thousands of high schools and summer camps from all fifty states are registered in the program. This Fall the program will be expanded to include junior high schools as well.

As I said in my 1972 Environmental Message to Congress:

The starting point of environmental quality is in the hearts and minds of the people. Unless the people have a deep commitment to new values and a clear understanding of the new problems, all our laws and programs and spending will avail little. The young, quick to commit and used to learning, are gaining the changed outlook fastest of all. Their enthusiasm about the environment spreads with a healthy contagion. Their energy in its behalf can be an impressive force for good.

As we reflect upon the characteristics and problems of the dynamic and mature society that this Annual Report of the Council on Environmental Quality describes, there should be a sober realization that we have not done as well as we must, that changes in laws and values come slowly, and that reordering our priorities is difficult and complicated. But there is ample room for encouragement in the growing capacity of a people able to assess their problems, take stock of their situation and get on with the unfinished business of shaping the United States as a model of a satisfying and healthful environment.

I welcome and salute the lead that our young people are taking in this great endeavor.

Long before America was powerful or wealthy, we were already looked to for leadership in demonstrating the possibilities of a vigorous, free society. By the time of the Constitutional Convention this country had captured the world's imagination and stood high in international esteem, not for its material wealth, but for its ideals.

Today as nations around the globe strive to enhance the lives of their citizens, the effort directed toward a cleaner and healthier environment is a vital measure of a country's stature.

This is a hopeful sign that the productive pursuits of peace are coming gradually to command increasing attention in the discourse and competition among nations. In the 197th year of American Independence, the quality of life enjoyed by our citizens has become a new sign to the world of our progress as a people.

I am reminded of Benjamin Franklin's remark at the Constitutional Convention in Philadelphia, when he pointed to the golden half-sun engraved on the back of General Washington's chair: "Now at length I have the happiness to know that it is a rising and not a setting sun."

RICHARD NIXON

The White House,
    August 7, 1972.

NOTE: The message is printed in the report entitled "Environmental Quality: The Third Annual Report of the Council on Environmental Quality—August 1972" (Government Printing Office, 450 pp.).

On the same day, the White House released a fact sheet and the transcript of a news briefing on the report. Participants in the news briefing were Russell E. Train, Chairman, and Robert Cahn and Gordon J. F. MacDonald, members, Council on Environmental Quality.

---

251 Statement About Signing a Bill Permitting Presidential Appointment of Sons of Prisoners of War and Missing in Action to the Military Academies. *August 8, 1972*

I HAVE signed into law S. 2945, a bill which makes it easier for sons of our POW's and MIA's to attend our military service academies if they so choose. Without lowering admission or rating standards, this measure assigns the highest priority to those qualified candidates whose fathers have proven their devotion to their country to the fullest measure.

I am particularly pleased to sign this measure because it reaffirms our country's appreciation of the tremendous service and sacrifice of our prisoners of war and missing in action in Southeast Asia.

This measure is one more reminder that, as a government and as a people, we are determined to do everything we can to help the families of these men who have sacrificed so much in our behalf. Fathers and sons, they both deserve no less from us.

NOTE: As enacted, S. 2945, approved August 7, 1972, is Public Law 92–365 (86 Stat. 505).

---

252 Statement About Signing a Bill Providing for a National Safety Inspection Program for Dams. *August 9, 1972*

I HAVE signed into law H.R. 15951, a bill which requires the Secretary of the Army, through the Corps of Engineers, to initiate a program of safety inspections for dams throughout the United States.

Under this legislation, the Secretary of

the Army is to report to the Congress on his progress on or before July 1, 1974. The report is to include an inventory of all dams, a description of inspection activities undertaken, and recommendations for a national program of dam inspections and for the proper allocation of responsibilities between Federal, State, and local governments as well as public and private interests.

The objective of this bill—to reduce the risk of dam failures—is highly desirable, as we have learned from painful experience. I think the particulars of this bill are most unfortunate, however, for they depart from the sound principle that the safety of non-Federal dams should primarily rest with the States.

This bill is also marred because it was enacted hastily, without benefit of committee hearings, advice from the concerned agencies of the executive branch, or comments by the affected States. As a result, the bill ignores the fact that some States are already conducting effective safety programs. More than 28,000 dams may be involved, but the bill fails to establish any inspection priorities. And the cost of the program may run as high as $100 million.

Nevertheless, I have approved the recommendation of the Secretary of the Army that the Corps of Engineers begin the activities specified in the bill. His recommended program contemplates an inventory of all non-Federal dams along with inspections necessary to define the scope of the problem and to identify those dams which may pose a serious threat to life and property. Under such a program, "the Congress would have an opportunity to reexamine the entire situation based on the first 2 years of reliable experience," to use the words of the House Public Works Committee.

Finally, I have directed the Secretary to seek the greatest possible degree of State participation under this legislation. This will have the particular advantage of utilizing the experience of those States which have effective dam safety programs.

NOTE: As enacted, H.R. 15951, approved August 7, 1972, is Public Law 92-367 (86 Stat. 506).

253   Message to the Senate Transmitting Biological Weapons Convention.   *August* 10, 1972

To the Senate of the United States:

I am transmitting herewith, for the advice and consent of the Senate to ratification, the Convention on the Prohibition of the Development, Production, and Stockpiling of Bacteriological (Biological) and Toxin Weapons, and on their Destruction, opened for signature at Washington, London and Moscow on April 10, 1972.

The text of this Convention is the result of some three years of intensive debate and negotiation at the Conference of the Committee on Disarmament at Geneva and at the United Nations. It provides that the Parties undertake not to develop, produce, stockpile, acquire or retain biological agents or toxins, of types and in quantities that have no justification for peaceful purposes, as well as weapons, equipment and means of delivery designed to use such agents or toxins for hostile purposes or in armed conflict. The provisions of the Convention are described in detail in the accompanying report of the Secretary of State.

It was about two years ago that this Government renounced, unilaterally and unconditionally, the use of all biological and toxin weapons and affirmed that we would destroy our existing stocks and confine our programs to strictly defined defensive purposes. These initiatives reflected a deep national conviction and contributed in a very substantial way to the ultimate success of the negotiations leading to this Convention.

At that same time, we looked to the day when the community of nations would act together to prohibit biological warfare and weaponry. We accompanied our renunciation of these weapons with support for the principles and objectives of the United Kingdom's 1968 draft convention in this field. On December 16, 1971, the Convention transmitted herewith, which would provide a binding international prohibition on the weapons we have renounced, was overwhelmingly commended by the General Assembly of the United Nations.

This Convention is the first international agreement since World War II to provide for the actual elimination of an entire class of weapons from the arsenals of nations. The safe destruction of biological and toxin stocks in this country is expected to be completed by the end of this year. All the stocks at Pine Bluff Arsenal in Arkansas have already been destroyed, and the former biological warfare facility there is now a new national center for research on the adverse effects of chemical substances in man's environment. The former military biological research facility at Fort Detrick, Maryland, is becoming a center for cancer research. Other nations are being invited to share in the humanitarian work at these centers.

I believe this Convention will enhance the security of the United States and the world community. It will help ensure that scientific achievements in the field of biology will be devoted not to destruction but to the service of mankind. It represents a significant advance in the field of arms control and disarmament and I recommend that the Senate give it prompt and favorable attention.

RICHARD NIXON

The White House,
August 10, 1972.

NOTE: The text of the convention and the report of the Secretary of State are printed in Senate Executive Q (92d Cong., 2d sess.).

254   Introduction to a Report by the Council of Economic Advisers on the New Economic Policy.
August 12, 1972

IT IS now almost exactly a year since the New Economic Policy was launched on August 15, 1971. What has happened since then adds up to solid economic gains which are a tribute to the public spirit of the people, as well as tangible pocketbook progress for the people.

The actions of last August 15 were designed to intensify previous measures that had reduced the rate of inflation and had started economic resurgence. They included a freeze on wages and prices to help reduce the inflation further, tax reductions to speed up the expansion and get unemployment down, and steps in international finance and trade to lay the basis for increasing the competitiveness of the United States in the world economy.

The August 15 policy consisted of actions the Government would take. But, as I said in my speech that night, the key to success would be in the hands of the American people.

I asked for public cooperation on the ground of patriotism—for the sake of America's economic health. But I also asked for cooperation on the ground of intelligent self-interest. Only by acting together could we get off the inflationary treadmill which for years had been keeping all of us from enjoying the rising prosperity the American economy was capable of producing.

This report by the Council of Economic Advisers describes what has happened since the New Economic Policy was adopted. The performance has been impressive:

- The rate of increase in the cost of living, which had been cut by one-third before the freeze, has now been cut in half.
- There are 2.5 million more civilian jobs than there were one year ago.
- The unemployment rate has declined from about 6 percent to 5½ percent.
- Our economy is growing at a rate of almost 9 percent a year, the highest since 1965.
- Workers' real weekly spendable earnings have risen 4 percent in the last year, three times the average rate from 1960 to 1968.
- We have led the world on the path to international financial and trade reform which will substantially help us

to improve our international competitive position as well as help other countries strengthen their economies.

I want to emphasize that the success of the New Economic Policy has been due to the cooperation of the American people. This cooperation has taken many forms:

- Voluntary compliance by workers, businesses, landlords, consumers and tenants with the price-wage freeze and then with Phase II has been remarkable.
- During the period when the Phase II program was being developed, leaders of business, labor, agriculture, and State and local governments were most helpful in consulting with the Federal officials involved. In the following months, many outstanding citizens have participated in running the program.
- Productivity—output per man-hour —rose 4.3 percent in the past year, the biggest year-to-year gain since early 1966. Such an increase of productivity is impossible without the positive mutual contributions of labor and management.
- The fraction of working time lost from strikes has been at an exceptionally low level.

The American people can congratulate themselves on their performance in the past year and are increasingly enjoying the tangible benefits of what they and their Government have done together.

We still have economic problems to solve, however, and again the key to success lies in the hands of the people. We must firmly establish a lower rate of inflation—both in fact and in the public expectations which help shape the economic future. While we have cut the rate of inflation in half the price of food remains a major concern. We have to get the unemployment rate down much further. We have to continue to improve U.S. competitiveness to strengthen our international economic position.

To accomplish all these things will require continued efforts by everyone—including the Government—to comply with the letter and the spirit of the price-wage control system and to raise productivity even higher.

The critical point at which the help and understanding of the American people is now needed is the Federal budget. If we allow Federal expenditures to soar again, to a point far exceeding the revenues even under conditions of full employment—as they did between 1965 and 1968—we will risk destroying the hard-won gains we have already made. The result would be big increases in the cost of living, or big new taxes—or the first followed by the second.

This Administration is determined to do its best to resist this course by keeping the budget under control, and I have urgently called upon the Congress for help.

But the outcome will depend most of all on the wishes of the American people: If the people insist on spending beyond the $250 billion ceiling I have urged, such spending will be done. But if the people join me in insisting that Federal spending be held down, to avoid reviving inflation now and paying higher taxes soon, the Government will act responsibly.

This critical situation poses a great test of our mature determination to manage our economic affairs soundly. I am confident that we will meet it, and that our national economy—which includes all of us—will continue to rise to new heights of prosperous greatness.

RICHARD NIXON

NOTE: The introduction is printed in the report entitled "The Economy at Mid-1972" (Government Printing Office, 109 pp.).

255   Message to the Congress on Plans for an International Exposition on the Environment To Be Held in Spokane, Washington.   *August* 15, 1972

To the Congress of the United States:

In accordance with Public Law 91–269, I wish to inform the Congress today of current plans for the six-month International Exposition on the Environment to be held in Spokane, Washington in 1974.

This exposition will be a particularly welcomed event in America. The Spokane exposition and the 1976 Winter Olympics are now the only internationally recognized events scheduled for this country during our Bicentennial Era. In addition

to stimulating trade and cultural exchanges, the exposition through its theme—"How Man Can Live, Work and Play in Harmony with His Environment"—will also focus fresh attention on one of the most pressing concerns of our time.

In November 1970, Expo '74, the non-profit corporation which is sponsoring the exposition and is responsible for its planning and operation, applied for Federal recognition of the exposition under the provisions of Public Law 91–269. After reviewing the plans of the sponsor, the Secretary of Commerce submitted to me the detailed report required under Section 2(a)(1) of Public Law 91–269 and recommended Federal recognition. A copy of the Secretary's report is transmitted herewith. In this report the Secretary indicated that the sponsor had fulfilled all of the requirements of that law and the regulations issued thereunder (15 CFR § 667).

The Secretary concluded that the environmental theme of the exposition was relevant to current national concerns and was appropriate to the exposition site. He also determined that the sponsors had obtained from the State of Washington, the local governments involved, business and civic leaders of the region and others the financial and other support necessary to assure the successful development of the exposition.

The Secretary of State also reported under Section 2(a)(2) of Public Law 91–269 that the event qualified for registration by the Bureau of International Expositions as a Special Category event.

Based on these favorable reports, I advised the Secretaries of State and Commerce on October 15, 1971, that the exposition warranted Federal recognition as provided by statute. I also indicated that it was my intention to extend this Administration's fullest possible support to foster a successful event.

On November 24, 1971, upon request of the United States, the Bureau of International Expositions in Paris officially recognized the event as a Special Category exposition and approved its General Rules and Regulations by unanimous vote. At its meeting on May 16, 1972 the Bureau also established procedures for sanctioning the special rules and regulations for the exposition.

On January 31, 1972, I issued a proclamation [4103] directing the Secretary of State to invite such foreign countries as he may consider appropriate to participate in this event. The Secretary issued those invitations through diplomatic channels on February 15, 1972. Thus far, Canada, the USSR, and Iran have accepted—and many other countries are now expected to accept. In that proclamation, I also indicated that I planned to appoint a United States Commissioner General to exercise the responsibility of the United States Government for fulfillment of the Convention Relating to International Expositions of November 22, 1928, as modified. Pending this appointment, I am designating the Secretary of Commerce to serve in that capacity on an acting basis. In addition, the Secretary is currently preparing a plan for Federal participation under Section 3 of Public Law 91–269, which I will transmit to the Congress at some later date.

RICHARD NIXON

The White House,
    August 15, 1972.

NOTE: On September 22, 1972, the President transmitted to the Congress a proposal for participation by the United States Government in the exposition.

256   Statement on Signing a Disaster Recovery Bill.
       August 16, 1972

FOUR weeks ago I proposed to the Congress three extraordinary measures to relieve the record damage inflicted by Tropical Storm Agnes and the flooding of Rapid City, S. Dak.

The immensity of these disasters is measurable not in destruction of property alone, but also in terms of loss of jobs, disruption of families, personal privation, and anxieties about the future.

The scale and scope of these disasters demanded special action by a compassionate Government, and it was this kind of action I called for.

One of my three proposed measures, H.R. 15950, concerned with the reconstruction of highways, became law on August 3, 1972. Today, I am gratified to sign into law the second of my proposals, H.R. 15692.

This measure contains highly significant changes in the terms of Government disaster loans. Interest rates are reduced to one percent, and up to $5,000 of loan principal does not have to be repaid. This bill will help victims who were homeowners to rebuild their homes. It also makes special assistance available to the disabled and retired. It will make loans available to stricken farmers and will encourage damaged businesses to rebuild and to remain in their communities by providing working capital loans as well as loans for restoration of existing plants.

In addition, this legislation provides emergency assistance for nonprofit private educational institutions comparable to assistance already provided for public educational institutions.

This legislation is evidence that when the country is faced with a serious disaster, the Government can respond quickly and effectively. The stamina, courage, and spirit of the disaster victims evidenced throughout the stricken areas have earned them nothing less than the unprecedented response.

I am pleased that the Congress has acted to provide this essential and immediately needed relief for the victims of the Agnes disaster, but I am also concerned about the future. The Congress has reflected a similar concern by including a provision in the bill calling for this Administration's review of and recommendations for a comprehensive revision of the Disaster Relief Act of 1970 by next January.

It is my intention to comply with this request, but I believe that, in addition to disaster relief, equal emphasis must be placed on strengthening our efforts in preventive measures. Consequently, I have instructed the appropriate agencies to provide me with recommendations to strengthen the Federal flood insurance program.

NOTE: As enacted, H.R. 15692 is Public Law 92–385 (86 Stat. 554).

On the same day, the President signed Executive Order 11678 providing for the repair and restoration of nonprofit private educational institutions damaged by Tropical Storm Agnes.

257 Message to the Congress Requesting Emergency Legislation for Continuation of the Guaranteed Student Loan Program. *August 16, 1972*

To the Congress of the United States:

In recent years, a major source of aid to students attending post-secondary schools has been the Guaranteed Student Loan Program. During the year ending this past June 30, over 1,000,000 students were able to borrow $1.3 billion to finance their education. Over 8,000 schools and 20,000 financial institutions are currently participating.

Support of this program has been bipartisan. It was created under the Administration of President Johnson, and it has been expanded and improved by the present Administration.

However, some provisions of the "Education Amendments of 1972," because of ambiguities in the language of the legislation, have had an unintended effect of raising the possibility that many thousands of students who have benefitted under the subsidized loan portion of the program in the past may not be able to obtain the loans they are counting on to return to school this fall.

We are doing everything possible in the regulations implementing the law to avoid this result, which was intended neither by the Administration nor by the Congress. But uncertainty remains. Because we are at the peak of the borrowing season under this program, I request that the Congress enact emergency legislation that would delay the implementation of the troublesome section of the law—specifically that it amend Section 132C(1), so that the lenders could continue to provide loans on the same basis as they did last year.

This would make it possible for students, parents, schools, and lenders to use a system with which they are all familiar, and which has served the students well. It would make it possible for students to obtain loans in time to go to school—which after all is the purpose of the program.

RICHARD NIXON

The White House,
August 16, 1972.

258 Veto of the Departments of Labor, and Health, Education, and Welfare Appropriation Act, 1973. *August 16, 1972*

To the House of Representatives:

Today, I must return without my approval H.R. 15417, the appropriations bill for the Department of Labor, the Department of Health, Education and Welfare and certain related agencies. Exceeding my budget recommendations by $1.8 bil-

lion, this bill is a perfect example of that kind of reckless Federal spending that just cannot be done without more taxes or more inflation, both of which I am determined to avoid.

Moreover, the bill fails to include a limitation on Federal matching payments for social services for public assistance recipients, although such a limitation was passed by the Senate. Because this is currently an open-ended program, this Congressional *inaction* could require a later supplemental reaching as high as $3.5 billion. By increasing the face amount of the bill on the one hand and failing to place a limitation on payments for social services on the other, the Congress has produced a budget overrun that could exceed *$5 billion.*

Inherent in this kind of spending, but not publicly specified by its sponsors, is a cut in purchasing power for every American family. *No program has a higher priority than continued expansion of the purchasing power of all the people.*

As I said in my special message of July 26: "I do not propose to sit by and silently watch individual family budgets destroyed by rising prices and rising taxes—the inevitable end to spending of this magnitude." Our mounting economic resurgence is at stake and I mean to protect it.

We have cut inflation in half, but spending such as this bill would require would clearly undermine that progress.

We have reduced Federal income taxes by 26 percent for a family of four making $10,000 a year but spending such as this would undermine that progress.

We have achieved conditions in which the purchasing power of the average production worker with three dependents has gained four percent in one year, the best increase since 1964, but spending such as this would undermine that progress.

What the Congress has done is to take my ample and carefully considered 1973 budget proposals and balloon them to fiscally dangerous dimensions.

This Administration is second to none in its concern for America's health, education and manpower program needs. From the very beginning we have consistently proposed and supported desirable programs in both the health research and health service areas, and we will continue to do so. For example, we proposed—and in November of 1971 I signed into law— the most comprehensive health manpower legislation in the Nation's history. This Administration launched the first separate Federal effort to combat sickle cell anemia. We have nearly doubled the Federal commitment to finding a cure for cancer. We have also proposed fundamental reform of education and manpower training programs coupled with recommendations for major fund allocations for education revenue sharing, emergency school assistance and public service jobs.

The failure of the Congress to use balance and restraint in the framing of H.R. 15417 has turned it into a big-spending measure that impairs the Nation's economic health.

The budget request that I submitted to the Congress proposed an increase of $2.1 billion for the HEW programs contained in this bill. That addition permits substantial expansion over the fiscal year 1972 level while recognizing competing priorities in other areas and the necessary discipline of keeping total Federal spending within the limit of full employment revenues.

The Congress would add to my proposals $1.8 billion in new spending authority. Increases of this magnitude are clearly excessive and must be revised.

Aside from increasing the face amount of this bill to unacceptable levels, the Congress, as I have previously noted, threatens to bring on a separate fiscal crisis of a dimension involving billions of dollars by its continuing inaction with regard to the social services program of HEW. Under this program the Federal Government provides matching funds, on a three-to-one basis, for social services provided by the States for past, current and potential public assistance recipients.

As I have previously proposed on several occasions, the Congress should place a ceiling on spending for this program which is now open-ended and not subject to any effective control by the Federal Government. But H.R. 15417 does not contain such a cutoff.

We now provide matching money for whatever amounts of services the States choose to provide. Since the authorizing legislation for the social services programs is vaguely written, the States have been able to include services far beyond what the Congress must have originally intended.

The result amounts to opening up a trap-door in the Federal Treasury through which billions are now flowing and through which more billions will pour unless the Congress enacts a specific limitation.

The rate of increase has been quickening. From 1970 to 1971, expenditures rose 37 percent. In 1972, they more than doubled—shooting up to more than $1.9 billion. In 1973, they threaten to more than double again as State claims approach $5 billion.

Elementary fiscal responsibility demands that this loophole for unlimited Federal funds for undefined services must be closed now. The Congress must harness this multi-billion-dollar runaway program by enacting a social services spending ceiling.

I also urge that the Congress, in drawing up a new measure, provide that the line items in the bill should not, in the aggregate, exceed my budget request. This could be accomplished either by revising the recommendations for each of the items, or by including a general provision in the bill which would limit spending to this overall aggregate amount.

I know the usual practice is to repass such a bill with a slight reduction and assume that the second bill will have to be signed.

Such action would obviously not satisfy the objections to this measure I have set forth here.

In returning this measure without my approval, I again urge the Congress to join with me to avoid higher taxes, higher prices and a resulting cut in purchasing power for the American people by enacting a general spending ceiling of $250 billion. That action would get us away from this Congressional credit-card approach to Government finances—an approach that will add up to bad news for everybody when the eventual and inevitable bills must be paid.

RICHARD NIXON

The White House,
   August 16, 1972.

NOTE: The House of Representatives sustained the President's veto on August 16, 1972.

259   Message to the Senate Transmitting a United
      States-Japanese Convention on Migratory Birds.
      August 18, 1972

To the Senate of the United States:

With a view to receiving the advice and consent of the Senate to ratification, I transmit herewith the Convention Between the Government of the United States of America and the Government of Japan for the Protection of Migratory Birds and Birds in Danger of Extinction, and their Environment, signed at Tokyo on March 4, 1972. I transmit also, for the information of the Senate, the report from the Department of State regarding the Convention.

This Convention, which marks the culmination of several years of intensive study and consultations between experts of both countries, is designed to provide for the protection of species of birds which are common to both countries or which migrate between them. Recognizing the importance of the preservation of the environment of birds and recognizing that island environments are particularly susceptible to disturbance, the Convention provides that each country will develop programs to preserve and enhance the environment of the birds which are protected under the Convention.

I believe that the Convention establishes an effective basis for cooperation in taking measures for the management and protection of the birds included under the Convention. I recommend that the Senate give early and favorable consideration to the Convention and give its advice and consent to ratification.

RICHARD NIXON

The White House,
   August 18, 1972.

NOTE: The text of the convention and the report of the Secretary of State are printed in Senate Executive R (92d Cong., 2d sess.).

260   Statement Announcing Continuation of the Planned
      Variations Program.   *August 18, 1972*

I AM pleased to announce that the Planned Variations demonstration of revenue sharing principles, inaugurated one year ago in 20 cities, has received a very favorable response from participating cities and that it will be continued for a second year.

This test project indicates what local communities can do to plan and implement local improvements when freed from heavyhanded Federal regulation and second-guessing.

In the past—and at present under most existing Federal grant programs—local governments have been given sums of Federal money, told what specifically to do with it, checked by Uncle Sam at every step along the way, and sometimes scolded if things on the local scene do not turn out as bureaucrats in Washington have imagined they would.

Instead of focusing these decisions in Washington, one fundamental thrust of my Administration has been to develop power-to-the-local-people programs under which local officials—who know the local scene the best—are given funds and the freedom to allocate those funds as local conditions suggest, with a minimum of Federal redtape and regulations.

The Planned Variations demonstration has given local general purpose governments some of the tools they need in order to serve their citizens better, and its extension for another year will give the participating 20 cities an opportunity to follow through on the important local-reliance initiatives begun in the past 12 months. Some of these tools include:

—freedom to designate their own priorities,

—greater influence over Federal funds flowing into their communities,

—substantial simplification of Federal rules and regulations.

Bringing about changes in patterns of behavior that have developed over many years is a difficult undertaking. The past year's experience in Planned Variations has highlighted many of the difficulties in transferring decisionmaking authority from Federal to local hands. New working relationships must be established among local officials and between local and Federal officials.

But these cities *have begun to solve these problems and in doing so they have verified my conviction* that local government, given the resources and the authority, is best qualified to identify and satisfy the needs of urban America, because it is the level of government that is in most direct touch with the people.

In a letter to me dated August 2, 1972, from all of the mayors of the 20 participating cities, they stated clearly their support for these principles. Their letter declared:

"We appreciate our good fortune in having been selected in this effort and we believe that Planned Variations has amply demonstrated that the kinds of capacity building which it embodies are critical to all cities if they are to make maximum use of the community development legislation."

Local elected officials have far too long been held accountable for actions over which they have little or no authority. This Administration is dedicated to giving local officials the authority so that they can get on with the job.

Therefore, I again call upon the Congress to redouble its efforts to enact the general revenue sharing legislation now under consideration. This Nation needs such legislation now.

The experience of these 20 cities will be of great value to all local communities which must accept new responsibilities under revenue sharing. To further strengthen the value of this demonstration during its second year, I am hereby directing each Federal department and agency to take the following actions as it works with Planned Variations cities:

1. Provide units of general purpose government in the immediate area of each Planned Variations city with the opportunity to review and comment on all applications for Federal funds which have a direct major impact on their residents.

2. Intensify efforts to eliminate administratively imposed Federal regulations which restrict local government efforts to meet local priorities.

3. Encourage negotiations between the cities, represented by their chief executives, and Federal departments, through the Federal Regional Council, to develop annual funding strategies which are responsive to locally established priorities.

The new federalism is more than a

change in procedures—it is a basic change in philosophy which requires a change in attitudes on the part of the Federal Government. I am convinced such a change is essential. In that sense the Planned Variations demonstration is a testing ground—and a successful one—for some of the new initiatives of this Administration and an essential part of the underpinning for our revenue sharing programs.

As I said when I announced the program last year, it is designed to demonstrate "the validity of the principle that when local governments are given the opportunity and the resources, they can and will manage their affairs effectively and in a way which is responsive to the needs of all of their citizens."

NOTE: On the same day, the White House released a fact sheet on the Planned Variations program.

261 Statement on Signing a Bill Permitting Continuation of the Guaranteed Student Loan Program. *August* 19, 1972

I HAVE today signed S.J. Res. 260, which amends the Higher Education Act amendments of 1972. In signing S.J. Res. 260, I want to express my thanks to the Congress for responding so promptly to an urgent problem. If the Congress had not responded promptly—enacting this legislation 48 hours after I requested it—thousands of deserving young people, ready to return to college or other post-secondary schools, might have been denied the loans they need for the coming school year.

The effect of this new legislation will be to delay the implementation of new regulations until March 1, 1973. This delay will permit lending and educational institutions to conduct the program this fall under ground rules they all understand—regulations that were in effect prior to June 30, 1972. The task now is to make certain that the continuing promise of a truly fine program is fulfilled.

Since its inception in 1965, this program has been an overwhelming success—more of a success than even the creators of the program foresaw. Since that time, some 5 million loans totaling more than $4.6 billion have been made to more than 3 million young men and women seeking to further their education. In fiscal year 1972 alone, more than a million applicants borrowed $1.3 billion.

Those educational and financial institutions which made this record possible deserve the gratitude of the American people for their past achievements. I call upon all concerned to bend every effort to make up for lost time during this lending season—time lost as a result of unintended ambiguities in the 1972 amendments to the law. I especially urge everyone involved in the program to reestablish contact with student applicants who have been turned down because of the uncertainty which has unfortunately arisen and to process pending applications as rapidly as possible.

NOTE: As enacted, S.J. Res. 260 is Public Law 92–391 (86 Stat. 563).

262 Letter to Representative Peter A. Peyser Supporting Legislation To Prevent Heroin Maintenance Programs. *August 20, 1972*

Dear Pete:

I was greatly heartened to learn of the measure you just introduced in the House to prevent the implementation of heroin maintenance programs in the United States. Your bill reflects the very significant study and service you are giving the nation in our fight against drug abuse.

The concept of heroin maintenance represents a concession to weakness and defeat in the drug abuse struggle, a concession which would surely lead to the erosion of our most cherished values for the dignity of man. Heroin maintenance would condemn an undetermined number of our citizens, desperately in need of help, to a lifetime of degradation and addiction at the very time when other, more positive methods of treatment and rehabilitation are rapidly becoming available throughout the country.

As we know, the Federal Government has initiated a series of bold programs to combat drug abuse, designed to help bring about a *lasting* solution to the drug problem in America. Our vastly expanded enforcement and diplomatic efforts are beginning to take effect. Federal resources are being focused on the expansion and improvement of established systems to meet the growing demands for voluntary treatment, and significant research is now underway to develop non-addictive drugs for such treatment. Heroin maintenance would not only undermine these substantial programs but, perhaps even more importantly, would not offer any prospect for a lasting solution to the addiction problem.

The bill you have introduced to prevent implementation of heroin maintenance programs has my full support. I hope that you, as Chairman of the Congressional Ad Hoc Committee Against Heroin Maintenance, will take all possible steps to ensure its prompt enactment by the Congress and that you will keep me apprised of what actions we might jointly take to expedite consideration and passage of this vital legislation.

As I have often stated, drug abuse—especially the terrible scourge of heroin addiction—is this nation's Public Enemy Number One. We have a solemn obligation to ourselves and to our children to rid drug addiction from America, and I am confident that with measures such as you have proposed, we will be victorious in this all-important battle.

With every good wish,

Sincerely,

RICHARD NIXON

[Honorable Peter A. Peyser, House of Representatives, Washington, D.C. 20515]

NOTE: The letter, dated August 18, 1972, was made available to the press August 20.

Representative Peyser's bill was introduced as H.R. 16458.

263   Statement on Signing a Disaster Assistance Supplemental
      Appropriations Bill.   *August 20, 1972*

IT GIVES me special satisfaction today to sign H.R. 16254, the last of the three emergency measures I recommended to the Congress in mid-July for relief and recovery in areas devastated by Tropical Storm Agnes and by the flooding of Rapid City, S. Dak.

On August 3 I signed H.R. 15950 covering reconstruction of highways. On August 16 I signed H.R. 15692 providing major changes in the disaster loan terms and assistance to private nonprofit educational institutions. These measures, together with existing laws, provided the needed authorities to cope with the massive effort of relief and recovery that is now underway.

H.R. 16254 adds the necessary additional funds to go with those already being used to give financial substance to the programs now authorized. This supplemental appropriation totals almost $1.6 billion, the largest single appropriation for a disaster relief in our history. The lion's share of the funds—some $1.3 billion— are for disaster loans to help the victims rebuild their homes, restore their farms, and reopen their businesses. Some $200 million is added to almost $300 million already available in my Disaster Relief Fund to rebuild and restore public facilities, to provide temporary housing, and for other authorized relief programs. Smaller but also important amounts are provided for repair and accelerated flood prevention work by the Corps of Engineers and for recovery projects through the Economic Development Administration and the Appalachian Regional Commission.

The needed authorities are in place, and the added financial resources are now available. We have in hand the necessary Federal tools to continue the enormous undertaking of recovery in concert with the people and the local and State governments. We must also continue the hard work of all to use these tools wisely, quickly, and well.

The job yet ahead requires persistence, courage, and cooperation. I know the citizens of the badly damaged communities have all of these. I am determined that the Federal officials responsible for implementing the Federal relief and recovery programs will match them. I have and will continue to keep in close touch with these efforts. My personal representative to the Pennsylvania disaster area—Frank Carlucci, Deputy Director of the Office of Management and Budget— reports to me that the Federal programs have gained momentum and progress is evident on all fronts. With everyone working together—with the determined spirit of the people, leadership from State and local government, and effective use of Federal programs now provided by the Congress—I am convinced that the hard-hit communities can be brought back better than ever.

NOTE: As enacted, H.R. 16254 is Public Law 92–393 (86 Stat. 576).

On August 12, 1972, the President had directed Frank C. Carlucci to go to Wilkes-Barre, Pa., to take personal charge of Federal disaster relief activities.

On July 1, the White House released an announcement of the signing of H.J. Res. 1238 (Public Law 92–337), providing an additional $200 million for the President's Disaster Relief Fund. Funds were included for areas damaged by Tropical Storm Agnes. The announcement is printed in the Weekly Compilation of Presidential Documents (vol. 8, p. 1123).

264 Remarks on Arrival at Miami, Florida.
August 22, 1972

Mayor Kennedy, Mrs. Kennedy, all of the distinguished guests who have come here to welcome us:

I was under some illusion that the convention was downtown. I thank you so much for bringing the convention here to this airport. This brings back some memories to me because 4 years ago I arrived in Miami to attend another convention—and we won in November.

[*Crowd chanting: "Four More Years"*]

Well, I don't know anybody who has a better idea.

I do want you to know that as we stand here, while I have not attended the convention because that is, of course, the custom, that candidates do not attend the convention until they are nominated, and I really should not be here now—but I think I am going to be nominated tonight, I think so; and so is Vice President Agnew, he is going to be nominated, too—but we do not attend until then. I want you to know that I have had the opportunity to see much of the convention on television.

I want to thank you first for the tribute you paid to my wife Pat. I know that out here are so many young people who probably are thinking that one day they are going to be standing in the place that I am standing. I will just give you a little free advice: The first thing you have got to do is marry above yourself. Then you will do pretty well in politics.

I wrote a book after the 1960 campaign. It was about some of the problems I had had during my political career. I had to dedicate it to somebody, and I dedicated it "To Pat. She Also Ran." And I know that the tribute you paid to her

she appreciated—Tricia and Julie and Ed and David, all of us. But I appreciated it very much because she is a great campaigner and she is representative of the role that women have played in this Administration. Let me say in that connection, I am very proud of the fact that we have more women in places of responsibility never before held by women, than in any administration in history.[1]

[*Crowd chanting: "We Want Pat"*]

You can't have her. I've got to keep her.

Now, could I add one other word? I know that you are going to have to be exposed to my speech tomorrow night, and I do not want to impose it on you now, but I do want you to know that I see that there are a great number of young people here. I hope to address some of you when you are in the hall tomorrow night. But I would like to say a word to you just now: Based on what I have seen on television at this convention, based on the reception that I see and feel here today, those who have predicted that the other side is going to win the young voters are simply wrong. We are going to win them.

If I could put that in the proper context, I want you to know that as young people, as new voters, for the first time in history you are going to play a role in electing the next President of the United States. You, as young voters, I know, find this exciting.

I know, too, that when the election is over, particularly when we win the election, as we hope we will win it, you will

---

[1] On August 26, 1972, the White House released a fact sheet on employment of women in the Federal Government.

feel very, very cheered up by that and you will want to go on in political life. But I want you to know what your participation in this campaign, what your enthusiasm, what your hard work means to me. I will tell you what it means:

Of course we want your votes. We want them very much because your votes could make the difference. And we are going to work for them; we are going to talk to you; we are going to work with you. But we also want something else. We want an Administration after the election, in the next 4 years, in which we can be worthy of the enthusiasm and the trust and the hopes and the ideals of young Americans.

As I look at your faces, I know what you want. I know that you are filled with the desire to find America at peace in the world, not just a temporary but a lasting peace. And you want this country to be one of great opportunity for yourselves, for your children, for all Americans. All of these things you want, and you want to work for that. You want to participate. You don't want to be put off and shunted off on the sideline. In a campaign you just don't want to just blow up the balloons and carry the banners. You want to participate, and you are going to.

So I will simply say to all of you, young and old, who are here today: The welcome you have given us is one that we will always remember, and I also assure you that we will try to be worthy of your hopes, your ideals, the very best that is in you in those next 4 years that you are going to make possible.

Thank you.

NOTE: The President spoke at 4:10 p.m. at Miami International Airport. He spoke without referring to notes.

David T. Kennedy was mayor of Miami.

265   Remarks to a Young Voters Rally in Miami, Florida. *August 22, 1972*

Pam Powell, Sammy Davis, all of those who have entertained here so splendidly at this program, I understand, earlier, and to all of you who are attending this Young Voters rally:

As I was driving over here from my home in Key Biscayne—as you know it is the custom that anyone who is nominated for the Presidency does not appear at the convention until after the nomination, and consequently I have not been there except to see it on television—but as I was driving over, the thought occurred to me that this was one of those moments in history that has never happened before and that will never happen again.

I do not mean by that that I have not been nominated before. As a matter of fact, I was nominated in 1952 and '56, for Vice President, and I have twice had the honor of being nominated for President and tonight makes it the third time.

Now, to put this all in the historical context, all of you know that this is the first time in the 195-year proud history of America that young voters 18 to 21 are going to participate in the election decision. And I believe that it is particularly appropriate that the first appearance of the President of the United States, after his nomination, be made before first voters who are voting as you are.

Now as I was coming in, I was stopped by one of the fine television commentators, a commentator for the ABC network, and he asked me—as we were trying to talk over the rather, shall we say, quiet audience at the moment—he asked me what was going to happen to the youth vote.

He said he was beginning to wonder whether I had concluded that perhaps the estimates that the youth vote was just automatically going to go to our opponents might be a little high. I can say this, and I want to give you an answer that I want you to think about a bit. I don't think the youth vote is in anybody's pocket. I don't think it ever will be. I think young people are not likely to vote party label. I think they are going to vote what they believe in. They are going to be independent. I think the young people of America are going to listen to both candidates. They are casting their first vote, they want it to be a good vote.

We have just as good a shot at it as the other side, and we are going to get it—with your help.

Now, I want to express appreciation to all of the celebrities—that is the word we use for them, for Sammy Davis, Jr., and the marvelous groups that you have been hearing here, to Pam Powell—and I want to ask all of you to realize what it means for them to be here.

Now, my business is the business of politics. It is a very honored business. I hope lots of you get into it, maybe full time. But I want you to know that when you are in politics you assume—you have to under our system—that what you are trying to do is to get somewhat over half the vote and the other man, or woman, as the case might be, is going to get somewhat less than half.

Now, in show business, which is Sammy Davis, Jr.'s business, and the business of others who are here, they are not trying to get half; they are trying to please everybody. So you see, when somebody in show business comes and participates in a political rally, he or she is doing something that is a very great personal sacrifice and even a personal risk.

I heard on Monday night one of the television commentators question Sammy Davis, Jr., when he was sitting there with Mrs. Nixon in the Presidential box. He pointed out what I have known and what Sammy Davis, of course, quickly agreed with, that he had been a very enthusiastic supporter of President Kennedy when we ran against each other in 1960. He said he was still a very good friend of the Kennedy family. Then the commentator said, "What is your reaction, Sammy, to the fact that many people who have been your friends and your supporters, perhaps many who think you are great in show business, think maybe that you have turned against them and that you have done so"—as he put it—"you have sort of sold out because you were invited to the White House to see the President?"

Well, just let me give you the answer. You aren't going to buy Sammy Davis, Jr., by inviting him to the White House. You are going to buy him by doing something for America, and that is what we are doing.

When Sammy and I and his wife were chatting there that day, I want you to know it was one of the most moving experiences for me and I hope it was for him. We talked about our backgrounds. We both came from rather poor families. We both have done rather well. [*Laughter*]

I know Sammy is a member of the other party. I didn't know, when I talked to him, what he would be doing in this election campaign. But I do know this. I want to make this pledge to Sammy. I want to make it to everybody here, whether you happen to be black or white, or young or old, and all of those who are listening. I believe in the American dream. Sammy Davis believes in it. We believe in it because we have seen it come true in our own lives.

But I can assure you, my friends, that the American dream can't be fully realized until every person in this country has an equal chance to see it come true in his life.

Today I pledge to you we have worked toward that goal over the past 4 years, we are going to work toward it over the next 4 years. And I want you to know that we are grateful for the celebrities who have stuck their necks out—stuck their necks out, taken the chance, as they have, that they might lose some support, because they realize it is important to get into a campaign that affects their future and the future of their country and the future of their children.

Now, I would like to just close on one note about you. This is your first election campaign. It will not be your last. I know that many of you will go into public service. I hope all of you will continue to participate in politics.

As you go along, some of you will go into business. Some of you may go into show business. Some of you may go into some other kind of activity where somebody is going to come up to you one election year and say, "Stay out of the campaign because you might risk some money, you might risk some customers or clients or whatever the case might be."

And I just want to urge you, don't ever do that, because what you do for America is more important than anything you do for yourself. That is what really counts.

I want all of you, the young voters of America listening here and those who might be listening on television now, simply to know this: I have been trying to work for your future. We have had some disappointments, but we have had some successes, and I am going to talk about both tomorrow as I make the acceptance speech.

But should the opportunity come to serve 4 more years, I am not going to be resting on what we have done in the past. I am going to be thinking of these wonderful young faces I see out here, your enthusiasm, your idealism, your hard work. This is your first vote, and years from now I just hope you can all look back and say it was one of your best votes.

Thank you.

NOTE: The President spoke at 11:23 p.m. in the Miami Marine Stadium. He spoke without referring to notes.

Pam Powell was national chairman of Young Voters for the President, and Sammy Davis, Jr., was master of ceremonies for the entertainment portion of the rally.

266   Remarks on Accepting the Presidential Nomination of the Republican National Convention. *August 23, 1972*

Mr. Chairman, delegates to this convention, my fellow Americans:

Four years ago, standing in this very place, I proudly accepted your nomination for President of the United States.

With your help and with the votes of

millions of Americans, we won a great victory in 1968.

Tonight, I again proudly accept your nomination for President of the United States.

Let us pledge ourselves to win an even greater victory this November, in 1972.

I congratulate Chairman Ford. I congratulate Chairman Dole, Anne Armstrong[1] and the hundreds of others who have laid the foundation for that victory by their work at this great convention.

Our platform is a dynamic program for progress for America and for peace in the world.

Speaking in a very personal sense, I express my deep gratitude to this convention for the tribute you have paid to the best campaigner in the Nixon family— my wife Pat. In honoring her, you have honored millions of women in America who have contributed in the past and will contribute in the future so very much to better government in this country.

Again, as I did last night when I was not at the convention, I express the appreciation of all of the delegates and of all America for letting us see young America at its best at our convention. As I express my appreciation to you, I want to say that you have inspired us with your enthusiasm, with your intelligence, with your dedication at this convention. You have made us realize that this is a year when we can prove the experts' predictions wrong, because we can set as our goal winning a majority of the new voters for *our* ticket this November.

------

[1] Representative Gerald R. Ford was permanent chairman of the 1972 Republican National Convention; Senator Robert Dole was chairman of the Republican National Committee; and Anne Armstrong was secretary of the convention.

I pledge to you, all of the new voters in America who are listening on television and listening here in this convention hall, that I will do everything that I can over these next 4 years to make your support be one that you can be proud of, because as I said to you last night, and I feel it very deeply in my heart: Years from now I want you to look back and be able to say that your first vote was one of the best votes you ever cast in your life.

Mr. Chairman, I congratulate the delegates to this convention for renominating as my running mate the man who has just so eloquently and graciously introduced me, Vice President Ted Agnew.

I thought he was the best man for the job 4 years ago.

I think he is the best man for the job today.

And I am not going to change my mind tomorrow.

Finally, as the Vice President has indicated, you have demonstrated to the Nation that we can have an open convention without dividing Americans into quotas.

Let us commit ourselves to rule out every vestige of discrimination in this country of ours. But my fellow Americans, the way to end discrimination against some is not to begin discrimination against others.

Dividing Americans into quotas is totally alien to the American tradition.

Americans don't want to be part of a quota. They want to be part of America. This Nation proudly calls itself the United States of America. Let us reject any philosophy that would make us the divided people of America.

In that spirit, I address you tonight, my fellow Americans, not as a partisan of party, which would divide us, but as a partisan of principles, which can unite us.

Six weeks ago our opponents at their convention rejected many of the great principles of the Democratic Party. To those millions who have been driven out of their home in the Democratic Party, we say come home. We say come home not to another party, but we say come home to the great principles we Americans believe in together.

And I ask you, my fellow Americans, tonight to join us not in a coalition held together only by a desire to gain power. I ask you to join us as members of a new American majority bound together by our common ideals.

I ask everyone listening to me tonight— Democrats, Republicans, independents, to join our new majority—not on the basis of the party label you wear in your lapel, but on the basis of what you believe in your hearts.

In asking for your support I shall not dwell on the record of our Administration which has been praised perhaps too generously by others at this convention.

We have made great progress in these past 4 years.

It can truly be said that we have changed America and that America has changed the world. As a result of what we have done, America today is a better place and the world is a safer place to live in than was the case 4 years ago.

We can be proud of that record, but we shall never be satisfied. A record is not something to stand on; it is something to build on.

Tonight I do not ask you to join our new majority because of what we have done in the past. I ask your support of the principles I believe should determine America's future.

The choice in this election is not between radical change and no change. The choice in this election is between change that works and change that won't work.

I begin with an article of faith.

It has become fashionable in recent years to point up what is wrong with what is called the American system. The critics contend it is so unfair, so corrupt, so unjust, that we should tear it down and substitute something else in its place.

I totally disagree. I believe in the American system.

I have traveled to 80 countries in the past 25 years, and I have seen Communist systems, I have seen Socialist systems, I have seen systems that are half Socialist and half free.

Every time I come home to America, I realize how fortunate we are to live in this great and good country.

Every time I am reminded that we have more freedom, more opportunity, more prosperity than any people in the world, that we have the highest rate of growth of any industrial nation, that Americans have more jobs at higher wages than in any country in the world; that our rate of inflation is less than that of any industrial nation, that the incomparable productivity of America's farmers has made it possible for us to launch a winning war against hunger in the United States, and that the productivity of our farmers also makes us the best fed people in the world with the lowest percentage of the family budget going to food of any country in the world.

We can be very grateful in this country that the people on welfare in America would be rich in most of the nations of the world today.

Now, my fellow Americans, in pointing up those things, we do not overlook the fact that our system has its problems.

Our Administration, as you know, has

87–234—74——54

provided the biggest tax cut in history, but taxes are still too high.

That is why one of the goals of our next Administration is to reduce the property tax which is such an unfair and heavy burden on the poor, the elderly, the wage earner, the farmer, and those on fixed incomes.

As all of you know, we have cut inflation in half in this Administration, but we have got to cut it further. We must cut it further so that we can continue to expand on the greatest accomplishment of our new economic policy: For the first time in 5 years wage increases in America are not being eaten up by price increases.

As a result of the millions of new jobs created by our new economic policies, unemployment today in America is less than the peacetime average of the sixties, but we must continue the unparalleled increase in new jobs so that we can achieve the great goal of our new prosperity—a job for every American who wants to work, without war and without inflation. The way to reach this goal is to stay on the new road we have charted to move America forward and not to take a sharp detour to the left, which would lead to a dead end for the hopes of the American people.

This points up one of the clearest choices in this campaign. Our opponents believe in a different philosophy.

Theirs is the politics of paternalism, where master planners in Washington make decisions for people.

Ours is the politics of people—where people make decisions for themselves.

The proposal that they have made to pay $1,000 to every person in America insults the intelligence of the American voters.

Because you know that every politician's promise has a price—the taxpayer pays the bill.

The American people are not going to be taken in by any scheme where Government gives money with one hand and then takes it away with the other.

Their platform promises everything to everybody, but at an increased net in the budget of $144 billion, but listen to what it means to you, the taxpayers of the country. That would mean an increase of 50 percent in what the taxpayers of America pay. I oppose any new spending programs which will increase the tax burden on the already overburdened American taxpayer.

And they have proposed legislation which would add 82 million people to the welfare rolls.

I say that instead of providing incentives for millions of more Americans to go on welfare, we need a program which will provide incentives for people to get off of welfare and to get to work.

We believe that it is wrong for anyone to receive more on welfare than for someone who works. Let us be generous to those who can't work without increasing the tax burden of those who do work.

And while we are talking about welfare, let us quit treating our senior citizens in this country like welfare recipients. They have worked hard all of their lives to build America. And as the builders of America, they have not asked for a handout. What they ask for is what they have earned—and that is retirement in dignity and self-respect. Let's give that to our senior citizens.

Now, when you add up the cost of all of the programs our opponents have proposed, you reach only one conclusion: They would destroy the system which has made America number one in the world economically.

Listen to these facts: Americans today pay one-third of all of their income in taxes. If their programs were adopted, Americans would pay over one-half of what they earn in taxes. This means that if their programs are adopted, American wage earners would be working more for the Government than they would for themselves.

Once we cross this line, we cannot turn back because the incentive which makes the American economic system the most productive in the world would be destroyed.

Theirs is not a new approach. It has been tried before in countries abroad, and I can tell you that those who have tried it have lived to regret it.

We cannot and we will not let them do this to America.

Let us always be true to the principle that has made America the world's most prosperous nation—that here in America a person should get what he works for and work for what he gets.

Let me illustrate the difference in our philosophies. Because of our free economic system, what we have done is to build a great building of economic wealth and money in America. It is by far the tallest building in the world, and we are still adding to it. Now because some of the windows are broken, they say tear it down and start again. We say, replace the windows and keep building. That is the difference.

Let me turn now to a second area where my beliefs are totally different from those of our opponents.

Four years ago crime was rising all over America at an unprecedented rate. Even our Nation's Capital was called the crime capital of the world. I pledged to stop the rise in crime. In order to keep that pledge, I promised in the election campaign that I would appoint judges to the Federal courts, and particularly to the Supreme Court, who would recognize that the first civil right of every American is to be free from domestic violence.

I have kept that promise. I am proud of the appointments I have made to the courts, and particularly proud of those I have made to the Supreme Court of the United States. And I pledge again tonight, as I did 4 years ago, that whenever I have the opportunity to make more appointments to the courts, I shall continue to appoint judges who share my philosophy that we must strengthen the peace forces as against the criminal forces in the United States.

We have launched an all-out offensive against crime, against narcotics, against permissiveness in our country.

I want the peace officers across America to know that they have the total backing of their President in their fight against crime.

My fellow Americans, as we move toward peace abroad, I ask you to support our programs which will keep the peace at home.

Now, I turn to an issue of overriding importance not only to this election, but for generations to come—the progress we have made in building a new structure of peace in the world.

Peace is too important for partisanship. There have been five Presidents in my political lifetime—Franklin D. Roosevelt, Harry Truman, Dwight Eisenhower, John F. Kennedy, and Lyndon Johnson.

They had differences on some issues, but they were united in their belief that where the security of America or the peace of the world is involved we are not Republicans, we are not Democrats. We are Americans, first, last, and always.

These five Presidents were united in their total opposition to isolation for America and in their belief that the interests of the United States and the interests of world peace require that America be strong enough and intelligent enough to assume the responsibilities of leadership in the world.

They were united in the conviction that the United States should have a defense second to none in the world.

They were all men who hated war and were dedicated to peace.

But not one of these five men, and no President in our history, believed that America should ask an enemy for peace on terms that would betray our allies and destroy respect for the United States all over the world.

As your President, I pledge that I shall always uphold that proud bipartisan tradition. Standing in this Convention Hall 4 years ago, I pledged to seek an honorable end to the war in Vietnam. We have made great progress toward that end. We have brought over half a million men home, and more will be coming home. We have ended America's ground combat role. No draftees are being sent to Vietnam. We have reduced our casualties by 98 percent. We have gone the extra mile, in fact we have gone tens of thousands of miles trying to seek a negotiated settlement of the war. We have offered a ceasefire, a total withdrawal of all American forces, an exchange of all prisoners of war, internationally supervised free elections with the Communists participating in the elections and in the supervision.

There are three things, however, that we have not and that we will not offer.

We will never abandon our prisoners of war.

Second, we will not join our enemies in imposing a Communist government on our allies—the 17 million people of South Vietnam.

And we will never stain the honor of the United States of America.

Now I realize that many, particularly in this political year, wonder why we insist on an honorable peace in Vietnam. From a political standpoint they suggest that since I was not in office when over a half million American men were sent there, that I should end the war by agreeing to impose a Communist government on the people of South Vietnam and just blame the whole catastrophe on my predecessors.

This might be good politics, but it would be disastrous to the cause of peace in the world. If, at this time, we betray our allies, it will discourage our friends abroad and it will encourage our enemies to engage in aggression.

In areas like the Mideast, which are danger areas, small nations who rely on the friendship and support of the United States would be in deadly jeopardy.

To our friends and allies in Europe, Asia, the Mideast, and Latin America, I say the United States will continue its great bipartisan tradition—to stand by our friends and never to desert them.

Now in discussing Vietnam, I have noted that in this election year there has been a great deal of talk about providing amnesty for those few hundred Americans who chose to desert their country rather than to serve it in Vietnam. I think it is time that we put the emphasis where it belongs. The real heroes are 2½ million young Americans who chose to serve their country rather than desert it. I say to you tonight, in these times when there is so much of a tendency to run down those who have served America in the past and who serve it today, let us give those who serve in our Armed Forces and those who have served in Vietnam the honor and the respect that they deserve and that they have earned.

Finally, in this connection, let one thing be clearly understood in this election campaign: The American people will not tolerate any attempt by our enemies to interfere in the cherished right of the American voter to make his own decision with regard to what is best for America without outside intervention.

Now it is understandable that Vietnam has been a major concern in foreign policy. But we have not allowed the war in Vietnam to paralyze our capacity to initiate historic new policies to construct a lasting and just peace in the world.

When the history of this period is written, I believe it will be recorded that our most significant contributions to peace resulted from our trips to Peking and to Moscow.

The dialogue that we have begun with the People's Republic of China has reduced the danger of war and has increased the chance for peaceful cooperation between two great peoples.

Within the space of 4 years in our relations with the Soviet Union, we have moved from confrontation to negotiation, and then to cooperation in the interest of peace.

We have taken the first step in limiting the nuclear arms race.

We have laid the foundation for further limitations on nuclear weapons and eventually of reducing the armaments in the nuclear area.

We can thereby not only reduce the enormous cost of arms for both our countries, but we can increase the chances for peace.

More than on any other single issue, I ask you, my fellow Americans, to give us the chance to continue these great initiatives that can contribute so much to the future of peace in the world.

It can truly be said that as a result of our initiatives, the danger of war is less today than it was; the chances for peace are greater.

But a note of warning needs to be sounded. We cannot be complacent. Our opponents have proposed massive cuts in our defense budget which would have the inevitable effect of making the United States the second strongest nation in the world.

For the United States unilaterally to reduce its strength with the naive hope that other nations would do likewise would increase the danger of war in the world.

It would completely remove any incentive of other nations to agree to a mutual limitation or reduction of arms.

The promising initiatives we have undertaken to limit arms would be destroyed.

The security of the United States and all the nations in the world who depend upon our friendship and support would be threatened.

Let's look at the record on defense expenditures. We have cut spending in our Administration. It now takes the lowest percentage of our national product in 20 years. We should not spend more on defense than we need. But we must never spend less than we need.

What we must understand is, spending what we need on defense will cost us money. Spending less than we need could cost us our lives or our freedom.

So tonight, my fellow Americans, I say,

let us take risks for peace, but let us never risk the security of the United States of America.

It is for that reason that I pledge that we will continue to seek peace and the mutual reduction of arms. The United States, during this period, however, will always have a defense second to none.

There are those who believe that we can entrust the security of America to the good will of our adversaries.

Those who hold this view do not know the real world. We can negotiate limitation of arms, and we have done so. We can make agreements to reduce the danger of war, and we have done so.

But one unchangeable rule of international diplomacy that I have learned over many, many years is that, in negotiations between great powers, you can only get something if you have something to give in return.

That is why I say tonight: Let us always be sure that when the President of the United States goes to the conference table, he never has to negotiate from weakness.

There is no such thing as a retreat to peace.

My fellow Americans, we stand today on the threshold of one of the most exciting and challenging eras in the history of relations between nations.

We have the opportunity in our time to be the peacemakers of the world, because the world trusts and respects us and because the world knows that we shall only use our power to defend freedom, never to destroy it; to keep the peace, never to break it.

A strong America is not the enemy of peace; it is the guardian of peace.

The initiatives that we have begun can result in reducing the danger of arms, as well as the danger of war which hangs over the world today.

Even more important, it means that the enormous creative energies of the Russian people and the Chinese people and the American people and all the great peoples of the world can be turned away from production of war and turned toward production for peace.

In America it means that we can undertake programs for progress at home that will be just as exciting as the great initiatives we have undertaken in building a new structure of peace abroad.

My fellow Americans, the peace dividend that we hear so much about has too often been described solely in monetary terms—how much money we could take out of the arms budget and apply to our domestic needs. By far the biggest dividend, however, is that achieving our goal of a lasting peace in the world would reflect the deepest hopes and ideals of all of the American people.

Speaking on behalf of the American people, I was proud to be able to say in my television address to the Russian people in May: We covet no one else's territory. We seek no dominion over any other nation. We seek peace not only for ourselves, but for all the people of the world.

This dedication to idealism runs through America's history.

During the tragic War Between the States, Abraham Lincoln was asked whether God was on his side. He replied, "My concern is not whether God is on our side, but whether we are on God's side."

May that always be our prayer for America.

We hold the future of peace in the world and our own future in our hands. Let us reject therefore the policies of those who whine and whimper about our frustrations and call on us to turn inward.

Let us not turn away from greatness.

The chance America now has to lead the way to a lasting peace in the world may never come again.

With faith in God and faith in ourselves and faith in our country, let us have the vision and the courage to seize the moment and meet the challenge before it slips away.

On your television screen last night, you saw the cemetery in Leningrad I visited on my trip to the Soviet Union—where 300,000 people died in the siege of that city during World War II.

At the cemetery I saw the picture of a 12-year-old girl. She was a beautiful child. Her name was Tanya.

I read her diary. It tells the terrible story of war. In the simple words of a child she wrote of the deaths of the members of her family. Zhenya in December. Grannie in January. Then Leka. Then

Uncle Vasya. Then Uncle Lyosha. Then Mama in May. And finally—these were the last words in her diary: "All are dead. Only Tanya is left."

Let us think of Tanya and of the other Tanyas and their brothers and sisters everywhere in Russia, in China, in America, as we proudly meet our responsibilities for leadership in the world in a way worthy of a great people.

I ask you, my fellow Americans, to join our new majority not just in the cause of winning an election, but in achieving a hope that mankind has had since the beginning of civilization. Let us build a peace that our children and all the children of the world can enjoy for generations to come.

NOTE: The President spoke at 10:27 p.m. in Convention Hall, Miami Beach, Fla. His remarks were broadcast live on radio and television.

The President spoke from a prepared text. An advance text of his remarks was released on the same day.

267   Remarks at the American Legion's Annual National Convention in Chicago, Illinois. *August 24, 1972*

Commander Geiger, my comrades in the American Legion, those who are here from the Legion Auxiliary, all of our very distinguished guests, and all of the past commanders and others who are distinguished guests here on the platform:

It is indeed a very great honor for me to appear before this convention. It seems that this is my week to appear before conventions. But having first addressed a Legion convention when I was a junior Senator from the State of California back in the year 1951, I know that we do not discuss partisan politics, so I won't tell you which party nominated me.

What I would like to say today is that, first, I am aware of the magnificent tradition of the Legion, the fact that we think in terms of our country; we recognize that partisan differences really don't matter where the national defense is involved and where the peace and security of America is involved. We are not Republicans, we are not Democrats, we are Americans. And that is what the Legion feels.

My friend Don Johnson—I was saying to Commander Geiger that he was the tallest man who had been commander of the Legion since Johnson, and they are both from Iowa. That is where the corn grows tall. But in 1965, when he was the commander and I had the privilege of addressing the convention—incidentally, I appreciated your invitation to come today when I am serving as President. I appreciated it even more when I didn't hold any office in 1965.

On that occasion, Don Johnson, as commander, introduced me. He later, as you know, has become the head of the Veterans Administration. Something has happened that is very important that may not have come to your notice, that we have appointed him as a member of the Cabinet Domestic Council which raises, for the first time in this country, the status of the man in this country with responsibility for veterans affairs to the position of Cabinet status. That is where it ought to be because we have to have those matters discussed in the Cabinet.

Now I could stand here and tell you all of the great things that Don Johnson has stood for and what this Administration has done, and immediately we could write that into a partisan context.

I don't do that because, first, it is not true, and that is a good reason. I could say that perhaps the best way to describe the attitude we have on veterans affairs in the House, in the Senate, in the Administration, whether it is a Republican administration or Democrat administration, is: We must do the right thing for our veterans, for those who have served.

And on that score, it is very significant to note that when we look at the House Veterans' Affairs Committee, that we have, of course, a Democrat who is chairman of the committee and a Republican who is the minority leader. Both of them, however, have the name of Teague, but I can tell you that if I call Tiger [Olin]

Teague or Charlie Teague, I get the same answer on veterans affairs, because they agree all the time.

We are proud of our record in this area. We appreciate your advice and I know, commander, that you have a number of resolutions that have been passed. I want you to, of course, submit them to us for our consideration, and we hope that, in all the years ahead, whoever serves in the office of President will remember that it is so easy to forget those who have served. Let's never do it in the United States of America.

Now I have selected for my subject to address this great convention of the American Legion here in Chicago— national defense.

When I use the subject of national defense before a Legion convention, I am sure that many would say that is like the preacher talking to the choir, because after all, you are already converted. I hope all members of the choir are converted, but in any event, you are people who believe in national defense.

You pass resolutions for strong national defense year after year. And whenever issues come up, whoever is President of the United States, he can be sure that the commander of the American Legion as he comes to the White House, as your commander here now and others through the years have been there, will be there, always supporting strong national defense.

I tell you why I talk about it today. I talk about it because it is an issue. It happens to be an issue in an election campaign. But even if there were not an election, it would be an issue, because the American people naturally would like to spend more of their money on domestic needs. They would like to spend enough to defend the country, but they don't want to spend more than they need to.

And so naturally there is honest difference of opinion as to how much we ought to spend in order to have an adequate national defense. I want to talk to you about it now with those thoughts in mind.

How much is enough? What do we really need?

Let me begin by saying something that is quite obvious, and that is that when we speak before a group like the American Legion, you know from personal experience the importance of keeping America strong.

I think perhaps the most eloquent statement in recent times in that respect was by General MacArthur in his very famous speech on the plain at West Point, "Duty, Honor, Country." If you haven't read it, read it again. It is one of the greatest speeches perhaps ever made on national defense, and also on what is great about America. About the soldier, he told them, those young men on the plain, "above all other people," he said, the soldier "prays for peace, for he must suffer and bear the deepest wounds and scars of war."

That is something we forget sometimes. We think that a veterans organization is primarily interested in the problems of war. I have found that veterans organizations have the strongest commitment to peace, because you know what war is, and you are for strength because you want to avoid more war.

Others may talk of the dream of peace and the horrors of war, but no one understands them better than you, you who have to pay the toll. It is the military man, as much as the poet or the politician, who is the guardian of peace when it comes, and is the restorer of peace when it is challenged.

History is strewn with the ruins of countries that sometimes, for the most idealistic of reasons, lost the will to defend themselves and ultimately lost the will to survive at all.

George Washington stated it also very well, perhaps it has not been surpassed, when he said, "To be prepared for war is one of the most effectual means of preserving peace." Let us not forget that warning of his, because the stakes now for us and for the rest of the world are infinitely greater than it was in that early period when the United States was a very strong country in terms of its own spirit, but very weak militarily, and not a great factor in the world.

Washington was not alone in his conviction that it takes a strong America to keep a free America. Lincoln, Wilson, Theodore Roosevelt, Franklin Roosevelt, Harry Truman, Dwight Eisenhower, John Kennedy, Lyndon Johnson—each time we have found that they have spoken on this subject—always reflected in eloquent terms the need for a strong national defense.

I am convinced those are the views of a majority of Americans, whatever their partisan affiliations. I feel, of course, that there are naturally some small antimilitary activists who totally disagree. They have rights to their opinions.

As I will point out, I believe that when we consider what the goal is—and the goal is peace—that it is certainly irrefutable that we need the strong national defense if we are going to reach the goal.

That is why my principle, like yours, is that the United States must never have a defense which is second to that of any other nation in the world.

I say that for a number of reasons which, I suppose, might be open to question, but one of them is not that it is a matter of jingoistic pride, although we should be proud of our country; it is not a matter of national ego, although we should not be ashamed of our country. But, you see, I have sat across the bargaining table with representatives of other great powers. I know what they stand for. I know that the only way that we can get a reduction of arms, the only way that we can get agreements that will limit the danger of war, is to be sure that the President of the United States, whoever he is, is never negotiating from weakness. That is what we have to have.

Now the question is, "What is enough?" because I realize that others have spoken to this convention and others will speak to Legion conventions in the future and say, "We have enough; we can cut." You should consider that, but I ask you now to consider, very calmly, very quietly, what I have to say about what is enough. I have studied this a great deal. I have had the opportunity not only to negotiate, where I found out what the other side had and I knew what we had, but I also have had an opportunity, as we have wound down the war in Vietnam, to do something that we all want to do—to cut on defense where it is not needed.

We have economized. We will continue to economize on military spending whenever it is safe to do so. But I have never gambled, and I never will gamble, with the safety of the American people under the false banner of economy.

Lasting peace is built on strength. Economy always, but weakness never.

Now, look at the record. Let's see what we have done.

We have been able to reduce defense spending to a safe minimum without betraying our security or dishonoring our treaty commitments.

We have successfully reduced our overall military manpower by nearly one-third. This is all over the past 3½ years.

We have closed overseas bases which were no longer needed for our national security, and we have done that without undermining the confidence of our allies.

We have successfully persuaded our allies to take up a greater share of the free world defense burden than they have in the past, under the Nixon Doctrine.

Separate the facts from the campaign rhetoric and you will find that the 1973 defense budget, which has been subject to so much criticism, accounts for only 6.4 percent of our GNP, and that imposes the smallest economic burden on our country of any defense budget in more than 20 years. Now, that is real progress.

Now we come to the key point.

We have cut our defense budget in terms of its burden on our American economy. Can we go further? In my belief, it would be a mistake to go further, and I am supported in that belief by a bipartisan majority in the House and the Senate. And to their great credit, let me say, speaking as one who is a member of the minority party as reflected in those two bodies, Democrats and Republicans who put their country above their party voted down big defense cuts because they knew it would cut into the muscle of American defense, and that we must never do.

Now that, of course, is a conclusion. Let me give you the facts to back it up. Let me give you the reasons why I think that Democrats join with Republicans in voting overwhelmingly in both the House and the Senate against these big cuts in defense that were supported by other people who believed that we could cut and still be strong enough, still be, as some have said, the strongest nation or at least with a defense second to none.

When we talk about who is going to be first, who is going to be second, let's put it in terms of what is sufficient for both countries. In that connection, what we find as we look at the Soviet Union and the United States, taking the two strongest powers in the world, we find that today they are relatively equal when we balance it all out in terms of their defenses. We are ahead in some areas; they are ahead in others. We are ahead in the areas we believe are necessary for our defense; they are ahead in the areas that they believe are necessary for their defense.

At the present time, for example, the Soviet Union has a much greater army than we have because they are a land power. They need more. On the other hand, in other areas we are ahead. But now let's look at these various cuts.

If we want to keep the United States from having the second best defense, we must recognize that if we should take the Minuteman III program, the Poseidon missile program, and if we should halt the development of those programs, it would mean that the United States would be the second strongest country in the world in missiles. We would be number two, not number one.

So now we start. We are second in manpower already. Now we are second in missiles. If we were to cut 60 percent of our strategic bomber force, which is the second recommendation made by some of the others, and if we cancel development of the B–1 bomber, it would mean that the United States would become the second strongest nation in the world in airpower. There are no other conclusions you can reach.

If we cut back on our naval strength, as some have recommended, and they have recommended that we can cut carrier forces from 16 to 6, if we do that at a time when the Soviet Union is actively engaged in the greatest naval buildup in history, the United States would become the second strongest nation in the world in naval power.

What this adds up to, my friends, very simply is this: We would be second on the ground; we would be second in airpower; we would be second in terms of missiles; and we would be second as far as the Navy is concerned. That means we would be hopelessly behind. We cannot let that happen to America. We have to see that America always has enough.

So the issue of whether we cut or don't cut is very simply this: The cuts that I have mentioned make the United States the second strongest nation in the world. That is why I have had to oppose them. That is why a majority of the Members of the House and Senate oppose them, and that is why I ask the American Legion to oppose them in the interest of strong national defense for this country.

Let's turn to a couple of other areas.

Many of the Legionnaires here have served in Europe, either in World War II or, after that, in our peacetime forces in NATO. If we would have a major, unilateral reduction of our forces in NATO, what it would do would be to undercut the confidence of our friends, but more important, it would destroy an initiative that we are now undertaking with the Soviet Union and with the Warsaw Pact forces mutually to reduce our forces.

Let's look at another point, looking to the future. If we were to cut back the money going into research and development for a more modern national defense, we risk the safety of the next generation of Americans, because this I know: The Soviet Union is not cutting back on its research and development.

Let us remember: We have made a significant step forward in our talks with the Soviets, but it was hard-headed bargaining. We expected them to bargain hard. We bargained hard. We have had the first step taken to limit nuclear arms. We have had a treaty to limit, of course, nuclear arms as far as defensive arms are concerned. We have an offensive limitation as an understanding. We are going to go on with further negotiations, we trust, later in this year.

But, my friends, the only way, in any kind of a negotiation, you can get something in dealing with a major power like the Soviet Union, or any other major power—the only way you can get something is if you have something to give. If the United States unilaterally cuts back on what we have, you have destroyed their incentive to come to the conference table, because they will already have what they want.

That is another reason why we have to keep these defenses up. That is the responsible position. We are going to continue to be responsible. If we do, putting it on the positive side, we stand today on the brink of a more peaceful, more secure era for all mankind, because from a positive standpoint, we can negotiate in these areas— negotiating not from weakness.

Now, none of this could have been achieved without the strong moral support of groups like the American Legion, of individual Americans of both political parties, as I have indicated. If there is one thing that can sustain a President in trying times, it is the support and faith of the

people themselves. More than any other American, the President has the opportunity to witness this faith in a thousand big and little ways.

People write letters. They say they are praying for you. A commander of the American Legion or the VFW or another veterans organization comes in or he calls on the phone. These things mean a great deal, particularly when we have difficult times. I am grateful for the support that you have given, not to me as an individual, not to my party, but to the President of the United States, who is Commander in Chief of our Armed Forces. You have stood behind your Government during the difficult but successful policy of winding down the war in Vietnam and settling it in an honorable way.

That is why we have been able to bring home half a million American fighting men from Vietnam. But what is more important, we have done it without selling out our allies, without surrendering to our enemies, and without abandoning our prisoners of war or our missing in action. That we will never do.

Now, I would like to say something, if I could, about the men who have served and are serving our country in Vietnam and other parts of the world. I know that it has become rather fashionable in recent times, perhaps in the last 4 or 5 years as we have gone through the terribly difficult war in Vietnam, to find everything that is wrong about the men who serve in our Armed Forces: They are drug addicts; they are dangerous people; they are savage; they are people that are really the inferior people, the ones who, from a moral standpoint, agreed to serve rather than not to serve, and so on and so forth.

Let me tell you that I have been to Vietnam a number of times. Since our involvement there began, I have been there in '64, '65—six times, as a matter of fact, before I became President, and once since. I have gone out in the field. I have been to Danang with the Marines. I have been up in the highlands with the Army. I have been down in the Delta, also with Army forces. I have seen some of the Naval forces, too.

Let me tell you, yes, there are, as there always are in every war, as there always are in any American community of young men, there are men who don't live up to the standards that we would like. But I can tell you that as I have seen the young men who have served in Vietnam, I am proud of them. They are fine young men, and we should stand up for them.

I am very proud, for example, of Marine and Army groups who, in the year 1967—and it has happened every year since then, that was the last time I was there and had a chance to look at it though in this particular matter—contributed $1 million out of their very small pay for the purpose of helping to build schools and community centers and roads for the people of South Vietnam.

I have seen Marines, I have seen young men, enlisted men, not officers necessarily—oh, they were there, too—but I have seen them out there teaching language, working, taking their time, helping these people in a peaceful way. Let me say, instead of making moral heroes of a few hundred who have deserted their country, let's honor the real heroes who have served their country in Vietnam.

They are gallant men. They are not ashamed of their country. They are brave men who did not desert their Nation. They are heroes who will stand just as tall as those who fought at Normandy and Iwo Jima. America is not going to turn her back on them. We are not going to make a mockery of their sacrifice and devotion by talking of amnesty for deserters while some of their comrades are held captive in brutal North Vietnamese prisons.

What they fought for and what we seek today is a true generation of peace, not a short and humiliating truce that will encourage aggression and have the effect of rewarding the foes of freedom. I know that many say that the journey to such a peace is long, and of course it is. But it is a journey that we have begun. We have begun it in opening a new relationship with the world's most populous country, the People's Republic of China. We have begun it in our negotiations with the Soviet Union. I have gone to the four corners of the earth, including even other countries that a President never visited before.

I don't mean that trips alone do it, but I do mean that because the United States is strong, because the United States is respected, the United States can be and should be the leader in the world for peace.

That is why we must keep our strength, because if we were not strong we would not be respected. Let's never have a President in that position as he goes abroad. I found a desire for peace in Peking and Moscow. Many of you will find that hard to believe, but it is not desired for the same reason or the same terms in each of these world centers. But it is desired, so that if America does not falter or weaken we have a basis to build on.

We can have a hope that the next generation of Americans will not have to face the same specter of war in their time that we have had in ours. This is a noble hope, a hope we all should work to build into reality. It will not become a reality if we heed the honest but misguided voices of those who say we should weaken America today and naively hope for peace tomorrow.

But it can become a reality if we continue to follow a responsible, rational foreign policy, if we keep America strong enough to make that policy credible.

Therefore, I say, let us join together—join together to keep America strong. If we do this, a strong America can continue to lead the world toward a just and lasting peace.

I should like to close my remarks, if I could, Commander Geiger and my comrades in the American Legion, with these rather personal notes: Having been a member of the Legion since 1947, spoken to local posts, then State groups, and then national conventions, I think I know my comrades and I know what you want for your country.

These parting words are what I think the role of the Legion can be in these years as we move from war to peace:

First, it is vitally important to keep America strong; I know you will support that proposition. Second, it is vitally important to honor the men who have served, because, remember, we are now moving to a volunteer armed force. In order for that volunteer armed force to be adequately served, it is going to have to be something more than money. We are going to have to give respect to those that guard the United States in times of peace.

Finally, my third request to my comrades in the American Legion is this—in addition to keeping our country strong and honoring those who serve, continue the wonderful work you are doing with young Americans. I was tremendously excited to see the young voters that I saw in Miami over this last week. The fact that for the first time the 18- to 21-year-olds are voting means that we have a new element in American politics. It will be good for the country and good for both parties because they bring idealism and enthusiasm that we need.

But let me say that I have also been tremendously moved when I have seen the representatives of Boys Nation and Girls Nation, and Mrs. Nixon has met with them, too, when they have come to Washington. You wonder whether that kind of work is worthwhile. I will tell you, it certainly is, because the important thing for our young Americans to realize—and a great majority of them, I believe, do realize that—is that they should not give up on the system, which was the fashionable thing 3, 4, 5 years ago, is that they should remember that this American system is one that you can change peacefully by working within the system. Here is the message to give them: Tell them that the answer to throwing a rock is to cast a vote. That is the answer.

Finally, let us also tell them and tell all of our fellow Americans that we have nothing to be ashamed of in terms of what we seek in the world. Oh, we have made our mistakes in foreign policy. I know that we look back to World War I—and there are not so many of those veterans still here, but some fortunately are still with us—World War II, Korea, Vietnam. Do you realize we have sent millions of Americans abroad in four wars in this century? But never for the purpose of destroying freedom, only to defend it; never for the purpose of breaking the peace, only to keep it.

The United States has had, in terms of

its foreign policy, an idealistic thrust which has been very unusual in the history of great nations. That is why strength in the hands of the United States means safety for the world. Keep America strong. Be proud of what America has done in fighting its wars and how it is now fighting to bring about generations of peace for the years ahead.

NOTE: The President spoke at 12:01 p.m. in the McCormick Place convention center.

The President spoke from a prepared text. An advance text of his remarks was released on the same day.

268 Remarks at the Dedication of the Dwight David Eisenhower High School in Utica, Michigan. *August* 24, 1972

THANK you very much, Suzanne,[1] and thank all of you for this wonderfully warm welcome. I thought I left the warm weather in Florida, but I am not so sure. Outside, incidentally, I think, listening on the public address system are even more than are inside.

My wife and I are very, very flattered that so many of you would welcome us on this occasion, an occasion which we want to share with you because it is a memorable one in terms of the dedication of this school to General Eisenhower. Participating in that dedication ceremony, we would like to have the president of the senior class, and it is Bill—we will get his name here—Bill Hellebuyck.

Before we show you this plaque, I am aware of the fact that we now have the 18-year-old vote, and I think of Bill and Suzanne, these wonderfully attractive young people—and I just want to say to Congressman O'Hara and to my good friend, Senator Griffin, they better watch out, they will be running some day.

WILLIAM C. HELLEBUYCK. On behalf of the entire student body of Dwight D. Eisenhower, it gives me great honor being able to say thank you, Mr. President.

THE PRESIDENT. And thank you, Bill Hellebuyck.

Now I have just a few remarks that I would like to make to everybody here, but particularly to the students, those that are going to be attending this school in the years ahead and those who will be attending it in this next year.

Occasions like this are ones in which it is quite difficult to find the right words, particularly when a school is named for one of the very great men of our time. Now, the usual thing that you do, of course, is to talk about the man, but everybody here knows about General Eisenhower: that he was the man who led the forces of freedom to victory in World War II, and then was President of the United States who ended one war and kept the peace for 8 years.

We know of that. We know of his background and also of his great service to the country after he left the Presidency. I am not going to go into that for another reason. I would like to tell you a little story about General Eisenhower.

As I was trying to think, coming over

---

[1] Suzanne M. Jaroszynski, chosen for her citizenship and scholarship as a student representative of the high school, introduced the President.

here in the plane, what he would have liked for me to say, I remember a conversation I had with him very early in his Presidency.

We were riding by automobile from Quantico, the Marine Corps base, back up to Washington, D.C., and he was reminiscing about World War II and the generals who had served under him— Patton and Bradley and the rest, Simpson—all of them, of course, having a different talent, and Eisenhower having the genius to know how to put each general in that area where he could do the best.

As we were riding, I asked General Eisenhower, in the selection of men for leadership, what was the one quality that he looked for the most.

You know, how would you answer that question? I was thinking how I might answer it.

You say maybe intelligence or maybe hard work or maybe brilliance or genius or something like that. But his answer was something different. He said, "Based on all of the time that I have worked with men through the years, and women, I have found that the quality that is most important is selflessness."

In other words, not thinking of self, but thinking of duty, duty to country, duty to whatever particular assignment that one happens to have.

Consequently, I think that General Eisenhower today would rather have me talk not about him, but really about you, about your school, and perhaps we could begin with your teachers.

When he returned from Europe, as you know, he ran for President of the United States. Politics was rather difficult for him and particularly his first speech he made in Abilene, Kansas, where he had grown up. He went back to the little high school

that he had attended, and his first words were, "I thank you humbly for your teachings." He was referring, of course, to that small town, which like this— perhaps this is a bigger town than Abilene. There was a high school. There was a community. There was a strong feeling of community pride. There was a church, which of course he had attended—many churches, of course, were there—but there was a very great loyalty to church and devotion, and also to school and community.

But General Eisenhower said, probably speaking to teachers by that time long dead, "I thank you for your teachings."

Now, if I could personally reflect for one moment about your teachers, could I tell you something of the effect that they have? Mention has been made of the fact that one of my daughters is a teacher and that Mrs. Nixon was a teacher until I married her. I had to have somebody support me when I was practicing law on occasion.

In any event, just running back over a lifetime and quickly sketching it, see if you don't remember some of your teachers this way. I remember a wonderful teacher I had in the fifth grade. Those were the days when you only had one teacher for the whole room and all the subjects. Her name was Miss Burum, and her specialty was geography. She loved geography. She loved the world. Because of her love of geography and all the nations of the world she inspired everybody in that classroom to want to travel, to see the world, to be interested in the world. It made an impression on me. I wanted to travel. I wanted to see the world. That is why I ran for President— I have seen so many countries as a result. [*Laughter*]

But it was part of the educational process far beyond that. The interest that was developed by a young student so many years ago came at that time. Then I remember another teacher in high school. Her name was Miss Ernstberger. She was tough, really hard. In fact, I found that my best teachers, looking back, were the ones who were the toughest. I mean by that they graded the hardest. I didn't like the grades, but I have to say the teachers were pretty good because they made me work hard.

I would like to say to all the parents, back up the teachers. They are usually right whenever they are handling problems. Miss Ernstberger I had when I was a sophomore in high school. I hated math. Math was hard for me. In fact, it was hard for me all my life.

I could never tell you how embarrassed I was, you know, when our children were growing up and going to grade schools. Now and then, of course, my wife, Mrs. Nixon, having been a teacher, could help them a lot with their homework, but they sometimes would ask me to help too, and I would try and they would ask me to help them with their math. So, I looked at the math book. It was that new math. I couldn't even learn the old math, let alone the new math. [*Laughter*]

Let me tell you what I learned from Miss Ernstberger. I didn't learn much math. The subject was geometry, a very, very difficult subject, and at the end of the year, I recall she gave an assignment of a problem. She said whatever members of the class could bring back the solution to that problem in the morning would get an A in the course. I recall that I stayed up all night long working on that problem. I finally got the answer.

It isn't the point that I got it, because I still hated geometry, even though I got the problem and the A. Incidentally, when I got the chance to elect subjects in college I didn't take any more math.

But the point I make is that from Miss Ernstberger I learned something that is terribly important—stick to it. And particularly the test of a person, of a boy or a girl, are those subjects that are hardest for you, not the ones that are the easiest. The teachers that can inspire you and make you put your nose to the grindstone and get it done, those are the ones you want to be thankful for.

Then I remember another teacher. This was a man, this teacher, and I was a freshman in college. He taught history. He loved history and he loved books. I remember him getting before the class and lecturing. He would have a book in his hand, some new book that we had not read, and he would fondle that book so affectionately. He would say, "This is a wonderful book. This is a beautiful book. You have just got to read it."

And what happened out of all that? He inspired some of us—I know he inspired me—with a love for history and for biography. So, I carried that throughout my life, and it helped me in years later in developing the background that I had to have for the law and eventually for politics and all the rest.

Since I am speaking in a school gymnasium, I don't want to leave out my coach. Now, let me say, being in this school gymnasium, on the floor, is something new for me. I was usually in the bleachers or on the bench. I was never out here. But I remember my coach very well. He was an American Indian. We called him "Chief," Chief Newman. He was an all-American football star for the University of Southern California back in 1923 or

1924. He was a great, great builder of men. He could take men who were not too talented in football and make stars out of them, except he couldn't do it with me. I never made the team.

But I learned a lot sitting on the bench talking to the coach. Believe me, that is the way to learn something about it. I was going to say I remember Chief Newman. I went out for 4 years, went out on the practice field, so I got into a few games after they were hopelessly won or hopelessly lost, you know, when they put the substitutes in, and finally the water boy, and then me. That is the way it worked.

I remember one year, the last year, I came up to the Chief and I said probably I shouldn't go out that year, because I really couldn't contribute too much, and he needed somebody to be on the taxi squad to run the other teams' plays, and he said, "Look, you really have to come out." Then he said something very interesting. He was a man who used to talk about winning and losing. His definition of being a good loser is something that affected me for the rest of my life.

You have all heard the traditional definition about being a good loser. "Oh, well, it is just a game; forget it. Be a good loser. Smile about it and try something else." Not the Chief. He hated to lose, and he told all of us on the team, he said, "You have got to hate to lose." He said, "The way to be a good loser is to commit yourself that you are going to try again and try harder." And when I told him, I said, "Chief, I really think I oughtn't to come out for the team this year," he said, "No, you ought to come out." He said, "Really, what is wrong is not losing. What is wrong is not not making the team. What is wrong is not trying. What is wrong is not playing the game. What is

wrong is when you lose, not getting up off that floor and coming back and fighting again."

Now, out here in this audience there are a lot of young people—grade school, junior high, high school. You are going to win some battles and you are going to lose some. You all aren't going to get into politics, some will, but it is very hard to lose and it is a lot of fun to win. I know. I have done both. [*Laughter*] But I can assure you, however, that in life it will be that way. Sometimes you will apply for a job and you won't get it and you will think it is the greatest setback, but just remember it isn't losing that is wrong; it is quitting. Don't quit. Don't ever quit. Keep trying, because this country needs the very best that you, the young generation of America, can give to it.

Now I want to relate all of that to present day, shall we say, politics. As you know, there is an election this year. It will be very exciting, as all elections are. It is going to be particularly significant because for the first time in the 195-year history of this country, men and women 18 to 21 years of age will have the chance to vote.

The important thing, let me say to all of you who may be voting for the first time—naturally, I have an interest; I have an idea of how you ought to vote [*laughter*]—and I am sure others would tell you something else [*laughter*]—but the main point is getting in and playing that game. Be for the candidate of your choice. Don't sit on the sidelines. Don't fail to participate, because the more that we have your participation, the participation of all of our people in our voting procedure, the better this country is going to be.

It has often been said that politics is too important to leave to the politicians. Now, that means, of course, that "politicians" may be a bad word, and I don't agree with that, because politics is an honorable profession. But, on the other hand, what it does mean is that citizens ought to get in, too, and whatever you do in your life— and the majority of you will not get into politics, you will get into business, you will work at a job, some of you may teach, some of you may be heads of families, whatever the case may be—but whatever you do, take some time out of your life to work in the field of making this country a better country, of making our government a better government.

Be a Republican. Be a Democrat. Pick the party of your choice. But the main thing is, play that game, because it is the most important game in life and we need the best, and young America has so much to give. You see, you have enthusiasm, you have vitality, you have idealism, and a nation needs your enthusiasm, your vitality, and your idealism.

Here is what I think: I think when we look at the 18- to 21-year-old vote—for the first time they vote in 1972—that you are going to be good for America because I believe in America's young people. I believe in you. I know your idealism. I know your enthusiasm. And I know that this country, which is going to be 200 years old in just 4 years—and that is pretty old—at that time will need an infusion of youth. We don't want to become old. We want to stay young, and the only way you stay young is to have young people participating in politics.

So we want you. Get in there and fight for the candidate of your choice. Will you do that?

Now I think General Eisenhower would have wanted me to say one other thing to this group, since I have referred to politics,

and I know that all of you will understand when I say what I am just about to say.

America at this time in our history is in an enormously significant position. We think of the young America, 3 million people, weak, poor, but it excited the imagination of the world because it stood for something other than military strength or economic power. We think of the America today, a strong nation, a rich nation, the richest in the world, and America still means something more than military strength and economic wealth.

It is a spirit, a spirit that is ours. It is what we stand for. It is what we do. It is how we treat each other. America has a meaning in the world.

I know General Eisenhower would want me to say, "Love your country." Don't love it because it is always right, because it isn't. Love it because we have a system that allows you to change those things that are wrong. Love it because there is more right about America than in any country in the world, and believe me that is the case.

And in that connection, I know that General Eisenhower would want me to mention peace, peace in terms of not just bringing an end to a war which has long been a very difficult problem for the United States, but more in terms of the long term. How can we have a peace that is not just an interlude between wars, but one that would last?

That is why Mrs. Nixon and I went to the People's Republic of China. We cannot have lasting peace in the world, peace that you young people can enjoy, if 800 million people, one-fourth of all the people in the world—and incidentally one-fourth of the ablest people in the world— are isolated from the rest of the world.

We have to communicate with those people.

Our systems of government are different. Our philosophies are different. But what we have to build is a world in which differences between governments do not lead to a situation where people cannot be friends, and that is what we have done, and that is why we have opened the communication. It reduces the possibility, for example, of war in the Pacific involving perhaps the People's Republic, or others.

That is why we have gone to the Soviet Union. We have gone there and we have negotiated. We have very great differences. Our philosophies are totally different. Theirs is Communist; ours is free. But we realize that we either have to learn to live with our differences or our children are going to have to die for them. We don't want that to happen. So that is why we have negotiated a limitation on nuclear arms. We have begun to negotiate it, and more, we trust, will come.

That is why we have negotiated agreements that will peacefully settle some problems, and that is why we also have moved toward cooperation.

Let me tell you one interesting thing about cooperation. We have a wonderful program in our country which has been supported by Senator Griffin, of course. I remember the leadership meeting, in which he participated as one of the leaders of the Senate, in which we made the decision to go forward with the program on cancer.

Congressman O'Hara, of course, supported it in the House of Representatives. It is bipartisan. Everybody is for it. We are spending $100 million to try to find an answer to cancer in the United States.

Let me tell you something. When I was in the People's Republic of China and when I was in Russia, I found leaders of those countries asking me about our program on cancer, "Had we found something? Would we share it?" And my answer was, we were making progress. Whatever we found we would share.

But more important, and this is what developed out of our Russian trip, we have now worked it out so that Russian doctors and American doctors, instead of exchanging information and then working separately from each other to try to find cures for diseases, will work together in the same room to try to find them.

Let me ask you this question: You have all studied the history of nations. Where is the genius, that wonderful genius that will find the answer to cancer? It may be a woman. It may be a man. It may be a black person. It may be a white person. It might be an American, but it might be a Russian and it might be a Chinese.

What we have got to do is to build a world in which, in fighting the great plagues of disease and hunger, we work together with people in the world and not against them. That is what we are trying to do.

You sometimes wonder, I know, what people abroad think of us. Let me say, Mrs. Nixon and I have traveled to 80 countries, countries with many different political systems. They don't all agree with us on many things, but you can be sure of one thing. They respect the United States of America and in many of those countries they love America. As I said, not because we are rich and not because we are strong, but because we stand for something which is in their eyes very good.

I noted—and I asked Suzanne about this—that she was of Polish background. I remembered, as she was introducing me, my visit to Warsaw, right after I had been to the Soviet Union. Mrs. Nixon and I laid a wreath at the Polish War Memorial, and then we got into our car and started to move through the huge crowds over to the residence, and there were such big crowds and they were cheering and we stopped the car. We got out for a minute to talk to the people.

Now look at Poland. Here is a country that for 25 years has had a Communist government, a government different from ours in its philosophy. Here is a country that for 25 years has not heard too much that is favorable to the United States of America. But when we got out of that car the people swarmed around. They shook hands. Some of them cried. And they said, *"Niech zyje Ameryka."* It means "Long live America." They then said, *"Sto lat, sto lat."* That means, may you live 100 years.

They didn't do that for me or for Mrs. Nixon. They did it because they love America. And let me say, let you in the Eisenhower High School set as your goal participating in your government to make it a government worth loving, worth respect in the world. Let you participate in your government so that America can play a role in building a peaceful world, peace for you and your children in the years to come, because, let us always be worthy of the faith, the confidence, the hope, of our own people and the people of the world.

I dedicate this high school, then, to the teachers whom I hope you will learn from, who devote so much to you. I dedicate it also to the memory of a man and of the country he loved, and I hope you will always honor and love your country. And I dedicate it finally to your parents. Remember, they have sacrificed a great deal for you to be here.

My father only finished the fifth grade. He wanted to go on to school but his mother died. They were very poor, and he had to go to work. His greatest desire for his children was for them to get a college education because he only finished the fifth grade.

I remember, sometimes people would remark he didn't have very good grammar. That didn't matter. What mattered to me was not the words but the heart and the character.

Be proud of your parents. Be proud of your school and love your country.

Thank you.

NOTE: The President spoke at 2:45 p.m. in the gymnasium of the high school. He spoke in part from a prepared text.

269   Statement About Pending Legislation on School Busing.   *August 24, 1972*

IN CONNECTION with this visit to the Detroit area, I should call attention to a recent court decision which emphasizes the need for speedy Congressional action.

In March, I proposed to Congress two bills to stop excessive busing.

I proposed these bills because education, not transportation, is the name of the game. Busing forced by a court to achieve an arbitrary racial balance is wrong. It adds nothing whatever to the children's learning. An hour and a half a day on a bus will, if anything, impair the education process, whatever a child's race or color.

Shuffling our youngsters about in this way weakens the neighborhood school. I believe in the neighborhood school. It is important to the youngsters of a community and it strengthens the neighborhood as well. It is important to the child and it is important to the family.

My first proposal to the Congress is a moratorium on all new and additional busing of schoolchildren. That would stop any further busing now.

Second, I proposed that Congress set uniform national standards for school desegregation, in which busing would be a remedy of last resort. That bill also provided means to aid and improve poor quality schools.

Although the House of Representatives passed an equal educational opportunities act this month, which restricts busing, there has been no action in the Senate. Neither House has acted on the moratorium.

Earlier this summer the Congress included an amendment to another bill, the Higher Education Act, which was intended to stay the implementation of court-ordered busing until all court appeals had been exhausted. When I signed that bill, I expressed concern that different lower courts might construe that amendment in different ways, and I continued to urge immediate passage of the moratorium.

On Monday of this week we had the first example of the very thing I feared: The Ninth Circuit Court of Appeals held that the amendment did not provide relief from busing in a California case.

Now school is about to open, and the Congress so far has failed to take the needed action. They must act promptly when they return into session. If children begin the new term under court-ordered busing plans, the present law apparently will be ineffective in terms of providing stays to parents who wish to appeal.

I am sure the citizens of Michigan join me in urging the Congress, and particularly the Senate, to give vigorous and diligent attention to this needed legislation at once.

NOTE: The statement was released at Utica, Mich.

270 Remarks on Arrival at San Diego, California. *August 24, 1972*

WE WANT to express our very, very great appreciation to you for the wonderful welcome that you have given us as we return home to California.

Incidentally, some people have suggested if you would put your signs down, they could see a little better. I like the signs, but you put them down for them.

I think you probably are aware that we were attending a convention yesterday across the country, and at that convention there were some very distinguished people. I didn't bring them with me on the plane, but they haven't been introduced, and before I say a few words, I would just like to present some of these people to you.

First, the Governor of our State, Governor Reagan, who was the temporary chairman.

GOV. RONALD REAGAN OF CALIFORNIA. This is once when we can say "fellow Californians" not only to all of you, but to our guests, and we are so happy to have them here. As the President explained to you, there were 3 days of preliminaries, but finally, for the climax of the convention, on the fourth day, here we are in San Diego.

Mr. President and Pat—because she is the First Lady of our land, but I think in the hearts of all of us she is "Pat," and we are just going to take advantage of it and keep it that way—we are also very proud, proud to have you here, proud that you are one of us. And, of course, those people who tried to pretend that what was taking place the last few days in Miami Beach was unexciting because we knew how it was going to turn out, well, I have never seen a John Wayne movie that was unexciting because you knew he was going to get the bad guy in the end. [*Laughter*]

[*Crowd chanting: "Four More Years."*]

You are right. It is going to be four more years.

It is a great pleasure to welcome you here, and now I think you would rather present these other people that are here. Bless you. Thank you.

THE PRESIDENT. And then, of course, somebody who—nobody here, of course, needs introduction. Everybody is a celebrity. You know, for somebody from Whittier to see all of these celebrities, it is really something, believe me. But I do want you to know we have Bob Wilson. We brought him back. I asked for a new majority in the country, and Bob is trying to get a new majority in the House of Representatives. Come on up.

REPRESENTATIVE BOB WILSON OF CALIFORNIA. Thank you, Mr. President. I can assure you we are going to give you the conventional Nixon landside in the election this year in San Diego. Thank you very much.

THE PRESIDENT. And the Lieutenant Governor of our State, Ed Reinecke. Ed, come up here.

LT. GOV. ED REINECKE OF CALIFORNIA. Thank you, Mr. President, and Mrs. Nixon.

I would like to introduce you to a whole lot of delegates that helped to win that vote you just won the other night, Mr. President. These are the delegates that have just come back from—San Diego was it,[1] or was it that other city, or wherever we were? These are the people who helped put you across, and we are going to put you across in November, just like I am sure thousands, hundreds, millions of people are going to do. God bless you.

THE PRESIDENT. And the Mayor, Pete Wilson.

MAYOR PETE WILSON OF SAN DIEGO. Thank you, Mr. President, Mrs. Nixon. These folks came here to listen to you, so all I am going to say is that America's finest city welcomes America's finest citizens, and we are going to be happy to see you back in the White House.

THE PRESIDENT. Now, I understand you have been here a long time and you have had a wonderful show. I will not talk long, because what I have to say I think you will understand very clearly, and we would like the chance to shake hands with a few more of you before we go on to San Clemente.

First, I would like to express appreciation not only to all of you, but to this wonderful group of celebrities that I have referred to, and they are celebrities, believe me. We couldn't possibly afford them, but they are here as volunteers.

I said the other night—some of you may have heard—when I spoke to the youth rally in Miami Beach, I was talking about

---

[1] San Diego was the site first scheduled for the 1972 Republican National Convention.

the fact that when people in show business come out into a political rally, this is really a risk for them, because we in politics, when we go to a rally, of course, we know that the game is winning over 50 percent. You always expect the other fellow to get perhaps a little less than 50.

But in show business you are trying to please everybody. So somebody in show business who tries to be nice to everybody, when he gets into politics, he has got to be convinced that the country's needs come before even show business, and these people feel that way. Let's give them a hand.

We appreciate their sticking their necks out for us, and we just hope that as a result of what happens that their business will be better, and that the country's business will be better. We know that we are most grateful for what they have done.

I should also like to say a word, too, about Governor Reagan. I saw him in Camp David when he reported to me on his trip to Europe where he represented the United States so successfully in talking to our friends after a period, of course, when we had necessarily been having conversations with some of those who had been our adversaries.[2]

Then in Miami Beach, he, of course, presided the first day. He made one of the finest speeches of the convention, and at that time he said that when he didn't expect to be in the position of making the speech of the temporary chairman, that

---

[2] On August 18, 1972, Governor Reagan met with the President to report on his 3-week trip to Europe as the President's special representative for the purpose of underlining the importance the Administration attaches to our ties with Europe, to our NATO commitment, and to mutually beneficial relations with the enlarged European Community.

he expected to be making the welcoming speech.

Well, he has made it here in San Diego. This is the welcoming speech as we all know.

Now, I want to turn, if I can, for a moment, to San Diego, what this city means, what this county means. It is a very special place in my heart for a number of reasons.

A moment ago Mayor Wilson said that he had proclaimed that San Diego for this week would be America's finest city. Now, I have just been today in Miami—that is Florida. [*Laughter*] And I have been in Chicago, and that means Illinois. I have been in Detroit and that means Michigan. Now, as I come to San Diego, which, of course, is enormously important in California, I might lose Illinois, I might lose Michigan, and we might lose Florida. You wouldn't want us to do that.

So I am going to say this: I think the Mayor has made a declaration that is a fine one. This is certainly a wonderful city. I won't say it is the finest city. I can't say that. I can't pick and choose right now. But I will say this: This is the finest reception we are ever going to have in this whole campaign, and we thank you for that.

And I will also say, it is, as far as I am concerned, my luckiest city. You know, I have run for office—I hadn't realized it until I jotted it down coming out on the plane, how many times I had been on the ballot in this city and county of San Diego. Nineteen hundred fifty was the first time. Some of you are old enough here to have been around for that one. Nineteen hundred fifty, 1952, 1956, 1960, 1962, 1968— six times I have been on the ballot in the State of California, and in the city of San Diego. I haven't lost it once. I have lost some elections, but I have never lost San Diego, and I am not going to start now.

Now, if I could turn to one other thing that San Diego means to me. It has a special place in my heart, because after I served overseas in World War II, I came home to San Diego, and there is where I met Pat after having been overseas. So I will always have that memory of when we met after that period of time.

San Diego is a very special place to us. It is special for another reason. In 1968 after having been nominated in Miami, we came to San Diego first off, and so it was lucky then, because after coming to San Diego right after Miami, we won in November.

Now there is one difference. This crowd is twice as large as we had in 1968. We are going to win twice as big in 1972.

I don't mean by that that we are going to be complacent about it. We are going to work hard and we are going to work hard for reasons that I will describe very briefly, reasons that are terribly important to all of you, and terribly important to the future of America.

Let me describe my day very briefly to you. As I left Miami, I was at Homestead Air Force Base and there were 500 GI's out there. They had come down from Fort Bragg. They were fine young Americans. They had come down there to handle some of the problems that might arise. They weren't all that difficult. We really didn't even need them.

But I went over and shook hands with some of them and I could see that they were proud to wear the uniform of the United States. Oh, they were like all GI's; they were counting their days to when they are going to get out—some of them. Some of them are going to stay in, in the volunteer army.

But it made me feel that whoever is President of this country has got to be proud of the young men who instead of deserting their country, serve their country. And let us remember that.

Then, after that, I flew to Chicago and I talked to a crowd of 5,000, a packed house in Chicago, of Legionnaires, the American Legion. There were a few from World War I, a number from World War II, some from Korea, and the Legion now has 500,000 members from Vietnam. And the thought that ran through my mind as I talked to the American Legion was this: That is four wars in this century. Every generation has had a war. We have never had a generation of young Americans who have grown up without a war. That is why I have been talking about a generation of peace.

We want not only to end the war in which we are involved, and end it in a way that will discourage other wars, in an honorable way, but we want to build a lasting peace. And we have got to build that not simply by being for peace, but doing something about it, doing something not simply by negotiating, but negotiating in a way that we are respected. And that comes down to the very significant point that I wish to make with regard to the other stop that I made.

It was in Detroit, Michigan. Not really in Detroit, in one of the suburbs, a little town called Utica. Well, it is not so small. It is a little bigger than Whittier, I think, as a matter of fact. I dedicated the Dwight Eisenhower High School.

There were 2,500 inside and about 8,000 or so outside. Most of them were young people. Oh, there were junior high school students and high school students and their parents and, of course, many of their teachers, as well.

It was a wonderfully exciting crowd, and as I looked at their faces, I thought of their future, all of those young people, just as I thought of the future of America when I saw those young volunteers down in Miami Beach, and just as I think of the future of America when I see all of the younger people here.

I don't mean that we don't think of our future, too, but I simply want you to know that as I put all of those things together, as I remember returning from war in the Pacific to San Diego, as I remember seeing those wonderful GI's in Miami Beach this morning, as I remember speaking to the American Legion—a fine group of Americans—as I recall those young people, those boys and girls so idealistic, so enthusiastic, with so much to give to their country, so much to live for, I became even more dedicated than ever before to the proposition that it is the job of whoever is President of this country to do everything that he can to bring peace, but to do everything that he can to be worthy of the people of this country and particularly of that new generation, who for the first time, are going to have a chance to vote.

Oh, worthy of the older generation, too, but let's now talk about the new generation for just a moment—18 to 21. Here they are all voting. You know a lot of people said, "Oh, we don't know whether we ought to give them the vote. Are they responsible enough? Are they going to vote in a way that is going to consider the issues? Are they really old enough?"

The answer is: They are bright enough and they are patriotic enough. And we can count on young America. I believe in young America—and we are going to do very well among them.

Now, as I crossed the country, and as I came back to San Diego, one final thought went through my mind: How much times have changed in the last 4 years—and they have changed for the better. Everything isn't all right. It never will be in any country in this imperfect world. Ours is still, of course, the best country. We know that and we are so lucky to be here. But as we look at it we see that our cities are safer. We see that what was happening on some of our campuses isn't happening as much today. People are there for an education.

We see, too, that we have been able to cut the rate of inflation in this country which was nagging so many. We have made progress in dealing with the problems of the environment. We have moved forward on many programs in health and education for the interest of the American people.

This country is really a better place than it was 4 years ago. But looking also abroad, I was thinking this morning—I looked out on the Atlantic and today I am going to look out on the Pacific—how different it is in both of those areas. In the Pacific we find that the war that we are in has had the effect in these past 4 years—we have been able to move it down in terms of the American involvement. We have been bringing men home and we have reached the point where we can certainly say that we in the United States of America are seeing to a conclusion a war that has been terribly difficult, but we are seeing it to a conclusion in the right way rather than in the wrong way.

We have not heeded in the past and we will not heed in the future those who say that the United States, which has an honorable history throughout its history in terms of those wars in which it has been involved—that we will end this war as we have ended the others, without, of course, abandoning our POW's, without turning over the country that we are allied with to Communists, and also without staining the honor of the United States. It is a goal that we can achieve.

But beyond that, we have had the opening to the People's Republic of China. This doesn't mean that the Communist government of that country and the free government of the United States don't have enormous differences. We do, and we always will as long as they are Communist and as long as we are free. But it means that 800 million of potentially the most able people in the world are no longer shut off from the United States. It means that we have laid the groundwork for Americans and Chinese who live in the People's Republic of China, as well as Chinese in other parts of the world who have contributed so much to this world to work together rather than to be driven apart. That is a great thing for the world. It means that our young people, looking ahead, as they look at this wonderful world we live in, and it is a good world with all of its problems, that they will be able to go there and see the wonders that we saw, the Great Wall, and see those people, despite the differences in government. We did that. That is a good thing.

We want to try to continue that kind of thing for the United States and for the world.

Looking out across the Atlantic, we saw the Soviet Union, and here again we had very great differences between the United States and the Soviet Union as far as philosophy is concerned. But now we have started the limitation of arms. We are starting cooperation in so many fields. We are finding that the Russian people, as we have always known, are a great people. And we have started that communication between the Russian people and the American people that is needed, while recognizing still that there is no time for complacency, while recognizing that the United States, as the guardian of freedom in the world and as the guardian of peace in the world, must always negotiate any reduction of arms—and please don't ever send a President to the negotiating table as the head of the second strongest nation in the world. Don't do that.

That brings me to a point that I would like to particularly make in San Diego. I covered this in part at the Legion. I emphasize it here.

The Soviet Union is a great land power. They have an armed force, as far as the numbers in their Army is concerned, much larger than ours, because they need it as a land power. We are a great sea power. We have the largest Navy in the world, and we need it as a great nation. The United States cannot have a viable foreign policy—Dave Packard, I think, will agree with this as a former Under Secretary of Defense—we cannot have a viable foreign policy unless the United States, without question, not only now but in the future, continues to have the strongest Navy in the world, because we have two great coasts. We have the Atlantic. We have the Pacific. We have the Mediterranean. We need that Navy.

Now we do have, I can assure you, my fellow Californians, my fellow Americans, the strongest Navy in the world. We must keep it that way, and that is why even though we would like to cut our expenses in any area so that we could put more into other problems—education, health, the rest—let me say the most important thing to remember is that you can have the best health program and the best school system and the best welfare system in the world, and it isn't going to mean anything unless you are around to enjoy it. So let's be sure we have enough to strengthen the United States and to maintain it.

And that is why—and this is the only political note I will make in these remarks—we will have to do everything we can to see to it that those who would cut the strength of the United States Navy by reducing our carriers, for example, from 16 to 6, those who would do that would inevitably make the United States Navy the second strongest Navy because the Soviet Union is on a navy-building program, which we are all aware of, which will make it first.

So, therefore, looking to the years ahead, if we really want peace, let me say, here are the ingredients: First, we must negotiate with those who might be our adversaries—the People's Republic of China, the Soviet Union—so that we can negotiate differences rather than fight about them.

But second, in order to be able to negotiate, the United States must be strong, we must be respected in the world, we must never reduce our strength unless they do, too, and that means let's don't go to the negotiating table unless, in the areas where we are supposed to be strong, we are strong enough, and the Navy is indispensable.

San Diego. Whenever we hear that, it is the Navy's town. It is a great city, and as San Diegans, let me say, I pledge to you, we are going to keep our naval strength and we are going to stop those, however well intentioned they may be, who would cut the strength of the Navy and make it the second strongest in the world. We are going to be number one in

our Navy so that America can continue to be a peaceful nation.

I have delayed you too long. I know you have been here a long time. I just close with this final note: I have traveled a great deal, of course, since going to Washington as a Congressman 25 years ago. I have been to 80 countries, and it has been a wonderful experience. But the best part of going away is coming home. To come home, to see you, all of you who have worked with us over the years, and to see all of you younger people who will be working with us and with other candidates of your choice in the future, gives us certainly a very great feeling of pride in being Californians and adopted San Diegans.

We thank you very much for this welcome. We are going on now to a campaign over the next 2 months which will be long, which will be hard. It will be very vigorous. We go into it with no complacency, but we go into it with confidence. We go into it with confidence because we are going after all the American people. We are not going to concede anybody to the other side, and particularly we are not going to concede America's young people to the other side because they are part of our new majority.

You know, I have a real treat here. I didn't realize when I saw Art Linkletter here that he hadn't just arrived when we did, because he had been there in Miami Beach doing a wonderful job of emceeing, and to have Art Linkletter here and not to have him on this program—Art, won't you say something?

Incidentally, don't you ever believe, when you look at him, that you look at this young fellow. He is as old as I am.

ART LINKLETTER. You know, I always get these lovely spots right after the President talks. When I was in Washington a few weeks ago, they introduced me right after Billy Graham prayed, and I had to do that. But actually, I was in Miami to do the opening gala there, and I was so excited about being there that my opening remarks were: "Good evening, ladies and gentlemen. Welcome to San Diego." Then I realized we had moved. But it was a wonderful evening and it was a great breakfast the next morning.

You know, I had dinner with your wife Sunday night, and breakfast with your wife Monday morning, and I hope that both you and Lois [Mrs. Linkletter] will be understanding. It was a marvelous convention. I flew down to introduce Ronnie Reagan, who was going to introduce the President, and all of a sudden here you were. You didn't need any introduction. They knew who you were. Isn't this re-markable? But we have been friends for 30 years. This is no new alliance for me. Breakfast Club and programs back when the President was running for Congress, and I have seen his family grow up, and the finest, not just the First Family, the best American family, and they will be there another 4 years.

THE PRESIDENT. Incidentally, when Art talks about all that business of breakfast and dinner with Pat, I just want to keep the record straight. He has also slept in the White House. He slept in the Queen's Room. When Pat's room is being painted or anything, she sleeps there, so we can say that Art Linkletter has slept in Pat's bed. [*Laughter*]

ART LINKLETTER. Well, you have my vote.

NOTE: The President spoke at 6:04 p.m. at San Diego International-Lindbergh Field. He spoke without referring to notes.

271   Remarks on Arrival in San Clemente, California. *August 24, 1972*

WE WANT to express our very great appreciation to all of you for this very wonderful welcome. When we were flying in here by the helicopter I was told, that after we had had a crowd of about 15,000 down at San Diego, that a few friends were going to visit us here at San Clemente. I am glad we have so many friends right at home. We thank you very much for coming.

Also you have seen Pat, my wife, and here is Tricia, born in Whittier, and Ed Cox.

I know that the hour is late. I know, too, as I saw all those cars parked, how hard it was for you to get here and how long you have been here. I want to say to everybody here that, as you know, I have done a lot of traveling over the past few years. I was just thinking of today. I started this morning in Miami at the Homestead Air Force Base where I saw about 500 GI's who were from Fort Bragg and shook hands with a lot of them before they went back to duty up there.

Then we flew to Chicago where we had a great crowd with the American Legion, 5,000 at McCormick Place. Then we flew over to Detroit. Then by helicopter, another 20 minutes, to a city about the size of Whittier where I dedicated a new high school, the Dwight Eisenhower High School. We had an opportunity to see there 2,500 inside, 10,000 outside. Then on to San Diego where we had a marvelous crowd at the airport. Then home again.

All of these places are wonderful places. I know that I can't select one from the other, but to come back here and find the mayor of Whittier, the mayor of Yorba Linda, the mayor of Fullerton, and the mayor of San Clemente and all of our friends from this area means the most of all. We thank you for that, too.

I want you to know that each brings back a memory: Yorba Linda, the town I was born in. I was there until I was through the fifth grade. Then we moved over to Whittier, I went to the East Whittier Grammar School from the fifth to the eighth grade. It was the one, you remember, in the Long Beach earthquake that was knocked down and they had to rebuild it. It is still a fine school. Then I went to Fullerton High School my first 2 years. That is when I met Arky Vaughan, whom I put on my all-star team for baseball. He was a great football player in Fullerton in those days, and became a star for the Pittsburgh Pirates. Then I went to Whittier High School for the next 2, and then to Whittier College for 4 years, and then after that to law school at Duke, and back to Whittier where Pat and I met. We were married, Tricia was born. Then came the war, and in 1947 back to Congress.

Since then in those past 25 years we have been all across this country, every one of the 50 States. We have been to 80 countries around the world. We have been to countries that no President of the United States has ever seen before or visited before. We have been to the People's Republic of China, to Peking, of course, as you know. We were in Moscow, the first President ever to go to Moscow.

We were in Romania—Bucharest—the first President ever to visit there. We were also in Warsaw in Poland, the first President to go there.

These travels were extremely interesting. They, of course, had one very great purpose. What they really were about, they were about all of you, and particularly this younger generation. Oh, I don't mean that we in the older generation don't matter, too, because all of us vote and all of us care, but what we are trying to build—and I saw the sign as we came in here, "House of Peace," that is the name of our house, Casa Pacifica—what we are trying to build in the world today is a world of peace. That is not easy because there are many differences in the world between governments.

The Communist governments see the world very differently from us, and they always will as long as they are Communists and as long as we are free.

But at a time when we have nuclear weapons in the world we just have to find a way where there can be differences between governments without having people have to fight wars about them. Because if the great powers engage in a war there won't be any more wars, because that is going to be the last one—there are not going to be people to fight a war.

Now, to talk in such melodramatic terms, of course, points up the issue. Let me put it in a more hopeful note.

As we have gone to these countries, I have had very, very hard negotiating sessions with the Russians, of course, on the limitation of nuclear arms and on more positive things: exchange in the field of science and cooperation in the field of health, in space, and other things. The same is true with regard to an historic visit to the People's Republic of China.

But the reason that I could take this trip as the President of the United States was that the United States was respected, respected for what it stood for and respected because it was strong. Now, as long as the world does have in it, as it does now and as it will for the foreseeable future, governments that do disagree, as we disagree, and many others in the free world, with the Communist governments, it is essential that the United States, as the only nation in the free world with the power to keep the peace, it is essential that the United States be strong.

The only way that you can negotiate is to be sure that the President of the United States is respected and that he does not represent a country that is weaker than whoever is on the other side of that negotiating table.

Let me just say one thing: I have great respect for the Chinese people. I have great respect for the Russian people. I have respect for their leaders. I don't agree with their leaders, and they don't agree with me. But I don't want to have the President of the United States, whoever he is, to sit down across the table from the leaders of those countries representing— as the President of the United States—I don't want to see him ever representing the second strongest nation in the world.

So, you see, that is why I told the American Legion, and that is why I told those young GI's who were from Fort Bragg that I was proud of them. I think we have had enough of running down our men who have served their country rather than deserting it and running off to Canada. I think we ought to stand up for those who have served.

I can tell you we are going to do everything we can in the cause of peace. We have traveled hundreds of thousands of miles, and we will travel more, in the cause of peace. We have already made this a safer world. It means these young people right here—I see one here is about the age I was when I finished the fifth grade in Yorba Linda. I want them to be able to go to the mainland of China, as I did. That could not have happened when I was a youngster, but you are going to be able to do it.

The world is going to be more open. You are going to know people, wonderful people all over the world. That is one of the things we have been able to do.

I have heard a lot of you say something about "Four More Years," I simply want to say why. Why do we want four more years? So that we can continue to make this breakthrough for peace. I think I have learned how to negotiate. I think I know what we want and what they want. I think I know the next steps that can be taken. I know that we have to be strong, and yet I know that we have to negotiate.

With that experience, I want to have the chance to continue the work that we have done so that the world can be safer, so that we can reduce the burden of arms, so that we can have a real peace in the world that will last longer than a generation.

This is what the goal is all about: so that we can have here in America an America in which we can have jobs without inflation, without war, in which we can have an attack on all the problems of the environment and health and education that we want to work on, make this a better country, a freer country, and one primarily of opportunity.

That allows me to conclude with a little personal note. We have many wonderful people who come to the White House to entertain—incidentally, before I mention them, let's give a hand to those wonderful bands that have entertained us here tonight. Haven't they been great? We had one group, it was a black group, a singing and dancing group that came from Los Angeles. They made a big hit. After the entertainment, which was in the famous East Room in the White House, I walked up to the stage and I shook hands with the leader of the band. I said, "Thank you very much. We are honored to have you in the White House." He got up to the microphone and he said that he and his group were honored to play in the White House.

Then he went on to say, "You know, I never thought it would happen." He said, "It's a long way from Watts to the White House." You know, he was right. But then I got up and I said, "You know you are right. It is a long way from Watts to the White House, but it is also a long way from Whittier to the White House."

I just want to say, let's build a country in which our young people can grow up in peace. Let's build a country in which any young person, a boy or a girl, if he is an American, an American citizen, whatever his background, has a chance to go to the top. That is what America is all about. The American dream can never come true unless it has a possibility to come true in the lives of anyone who is an American citizen. That is what we believe in. That is what we want you to vote for. That is what that "Four More Years" is all about.

Thank you very much.

NOTE: The President spoke at 7:17 p.m. in front of the Western White House. He spoke without referring to notes.

272   Memorandums About the Combined Federal Campaign. *August 25,* 1972

Memorandum for Heads of Executive Departments and Agencies:

I am very pleased to announce that Honorable James D. Hodgson, Secretary of Labor, has agreed to serve as Chairman of the Combined Federal Campaign for the National Capital Area this fall.

This campaign, to begin in the fall, will combine into one single drive the campaigns of the United Givers Fund, the American Red Cross, the National Health Agencies, and the International Service Agencies. In this one drive we will be seeking to do our share to meet the needs of more than 150 local, national, and international health, welfare, and social service agencies.

Because these organizations perform a vital function in our society, they need our support. Each of us wants to do as much as possible to help a neighbor or a friend who has a special need. While alone we can do little, together we can do much.

The Combined Federal Campaign offers us this opportunity to work together to help persons in our community, in our nation and in overseas lands. We can help by making only this one gift—by wholly voluntary payroll deduction if preferred—and by making it only this one time in the year. I am sure that Secretary Hodgson will have your wholehearted support and the support of those who work in your departments and agencies. And I am certain you will commend the good purposes of their campaign and its payroll deduction feature to Federal employees and military personnel in your organization.

I request that you serve personally as Chairman of the combined campaign in your organization and appoint a top assistant as your Vice Chairman. Please advise Secretary Hodgson of the person you designate as your Vice Chairman.

RICHARD NIXON

Memorandum for All Federal Employees and Military Personnel:

This year, Federal personnel in approximately 500 communities across our nation will have an opportunity to participate in a Combined Federal Campaign, which combines in one annual on-the-job drive the campaigns of the local United Givers Fund, the American Red Cross, the National Health Agencies, and the International Service Agencies.

The spirit of voluntarism, of willingness to reach out to help another, is an important part of the American way of life. This spirit abounds in our people, and Federal employees and military personnel have amply demonstrated this in the past by their support of voluntary causes.

While we cannot each personally provide help to all those who need it, we can combine together and support the volun-tary charitable organizations who can provide that help on our behalf. In this way we can best carry out the spirit of voluntarism. While alone we can do little, together we can do much.

Charitable organizations hold out the helping hand of the volunteer in providing services to older people, to youths, to those who are ill, and they help all of us through programs of medical research as well as provide assistance to our friends in overseas lands. These splendid organizations need our support. I am sure they will get our support.

I commend to you, therefore, the Combined Federal Campaign which permits all of us together by our gifts to strengthen the services of the voluntary charitable organizations, gifts made easier by the availability of payroll deductions. Generosity and concern for others have always been the tradition of those who serve in the United States Government. I am proud of the Federal family and feel confident you will continue this great tradition which is the hallmark of the Federal service.

My best wishes go to each of you during this year's Combined Federal Campaign.

RICHARD NIXON

NOTE: Both memorandums, dated August 22, 1972, were made available to the press August 25 at San Clemente, Calif.

273 Remarks at a Reception for Celebrities of the Entertainment Industry, San Clemente, California. *August 27, 1972*

Mr. Vice President, Governor and Mrs. Reagan, and all of our very distinguished guests tonight:

I am not going to impose on you an-other speech after what many of you had to endure last week in terms of so many speeches, but I did not want this opportunity to go by without expressing, on

821

behalf of Mrs. Nixon, my wife Pat, and myself, our appreciation to all of you. I would like to do it in three really different ways.

First, as I met all of you coming through the line tonight, I thought back over the years, and it has been a long time. Many of you here won't even remember, but some of you were here then, and I recall 1946, 1950, '52, '56, '60, '62 '68, and here it is '72 and you are still with us. We thank you very much.

I remember, too, that I wanted this opportunity to express special appreciation to those who have entertained at the White House. We know that it is a great, certainly a burden to have to pick up everything and come to the White House and entertain, and then not even be able to deduct it from your taxes. [*Laughter*]

But nevertheless, on the other hand, we have been most grateful. Many of you have been there, and this is the only campaign promise I am going to make tonight: Anybody who hasn't been invited to the White House to entertain, in the next 4 years you will be there, too.

Second, I wanted to express appreciation for those who participated in our convention, for those who have participated in the various rallies and so forth that we have had, over and over again. I know that sometimes we arrive, you think we aren't even aware of what you have done, but I know those audiences really wouldn't be up to have to listen to what I have to say unless you had been there before. In other words, you warm them up, and that is certainly most appreciated.

But beyond that, those that have entertained at the White House, those that have participated in conventions, I simply wanted to say that, speaking to all of you, and to everybody in this whole community

that we call Hollywood, I would like to express appreciation as an individual, and also speaking as the President of the United States, for what you, the people of Hollywood, have done for America and have done for the world.

I can speak with some feeling on this point. Let me begin by saying that my wife and I like movies. We like them on television. We fortunately now have our own projection set in the White House. [*Laughter*] That is one of the reasons I ran again. I just can't stand those commercials on the Late Show. [*Laughter*]

But we have seen many movies. We haven't yet shown an X-rated movie in the White House. We had an "R" one night, and I said, "That is as far as you can go."

Be that as it may, we have seen some of the old ones and some of the new ones, and we like them. Now, I am going to say something that Charlton Heston,[1] I know, will appreciate, and also his successor, and all of those who are interested in seeing that this great industry stays alive and remains strong. Any of you who may be reporting this will consider this to be a little bit jingoistic and pro-American. If so, make the most of it.

But I like my movies made in Hollywood, made in America, and I don't mean that I can't appreciate a good foreign movie, or a foreign movie star or starlet, or whatever the case may be. But I think that the motion picture industry—it started here, it has grown up here—this is something that is typically American and it is something that means a lot in presenting America to the world.

Oh, I know, we hear a lot of talk about

---

[1] Charlton Heston, actor and president of the Screen Actors Guild 1966–71.

bad movies being shown in various places, and so forth, but in all the countries that my wife and I have visited, about 80, I can assure you that Hollywood, in most of them, has been there before. We go along streets in the cities of Africa and Asia and Latin America, everyplace, and on that marquee you will see the Hollywood names that we are so familiar with. It makes us feel at home as we see those names.

Just to give you an idea of how what Hollywood produces has such a great effect abroad—we have a wonderful couple working for us, a Spanish couple, Manolo and Fina Sanchez. The other day at Camp David we were looking over the movie list, and there wasn't anything that had been made recently that particularly appealed, so we wanted to get something that could be shown to younger people safely, and consequently, we ended up by selecting a John Wayne movie. I asked Manolo, my very wonderful aide, I said, "Manolo, do you think this would be a good movie?" He said, "Oh, yes, sir. I saw it 30 years ago in Spain." Now, that dates either John Wayne or me or Manolo.

But what I am going to suggest is that he said that movie played for 2 months— I mean in La Coruña, the town in Spain in which he lived—and he had seen it on that occasion. So here we have Hollywood projecting America to the world.

Let me say a word, too, about what Hollywood says in the United States. We talk about the influence of politicians on America, and we do have influence on America, and we must always remember it. We talk about the influence of ministers on America, and a man like Billy Graham, and the priests, the rabbis, the ministers, do have a great influence on America, an influence for good.

We talk about the influence of teachers, and we all remember great teachers that we have had and how much they have meant to us. We have to realize that today, because of the advent of television, you in motion pictures and television have perhaps more time of the children of America than the preacher, the teacher, the politician, or even the parents.

That shows you how very important what you do is to the future of America. They see you. They look up to you. They want to be like you. I am not suggesting that every movie, therefore, must be educational. I am not suggesting that every television production must be educational or have a lesson. As a matter of fact, on the contrary, I think when we see a movie or when we see a television program, that sometimes we need to laugh, maybe sometimes we need to cry. Sometimes we need to be taken out of the humdrum life that we live. Sometimes we need to dream.

So make the movies, and as you do make them, or the television shows, that do give us that lift, that little extra dimension in our lives, that also serves the future of this country in a very, very great way. But what I am suggesting is this: That you who make and produce the motion pictures and the television shows, do have an enormous influence on America, and I think it has been, I think it will continue to be in the future with your help, an influence for good.

Now, if I can turn, in conclusion, very briefly, to the field of politics. I have often said that I wonder why people who are enormously successful in motion pictures or television will take time for politics. I think I know why. It is because you have show business. It is because you are interested in that, but you realize that the bigger business is the business of America.

You realize that the future of show business, the future of your personal lives, the future of America and the world will depend upon the leadership that we have in America, and you are willing, therefore, to go out and speak up for America, each in your own way.

In that connection, incidentally, I know that there are those who will not do that, and I understand and I do not criticize them, but let me just suggest this to you: I said a moment ago that when those of us who are not in show business have the opportunity to see a good movie or a good television show, and when it takes us away from all of our problems, that is good for us.

Putting it in terms of yourselves, when you move out of your business, when you do something in the field of politics, you are engaging in an activity that is bigger than yourselves, and that is good for you, it is good for any of us.

I think that President de Gaulle said it best of all in terms of a nation when he said that "France is never her true self unless she is engaged in a great enterprise." That is true of a nation; it is true of an individual. We are never our true selves unless we are engaged in an enterprise bigger than ourselves.

And I think we all are—you, those of us who are working in this campaign, and for that matter, those working on the other side. What we are doing is engaging in an enterprise as big as America, and as big as the world, because what happens in America will determine the future of the world over these next 25 years.

That is what this election is about. That is why I am so very proud that we have such a magnificent group of Americans, from Hollywood, our own State, our own town, supporting us.

Just to show you why I now welcome the opportunity, as Pat will, to talk with you, and meet each of you personally for a little while longer, I end with a true story about what happened at the White House just a few months ago.

We had a meeting on narcotics with a group of Congressmen from the New York area, and Congressman Rangel, a Democratic Congressman, a very able man, from Harlem, spoke to me very movingly about the necessity of doing something about heroin. He said, "Everybody talks about welfare and everybody talks about all the other things that can be done for the people of my district, but," he said, "the most important thing you can do is to stop that heroin that is destroying the lives of so many of my people, so many of my constituents." And he said, "For one thing, can't you do something to stop the production of and the export of the heroin poppy from Turkey into the United States?" I said, "We will do what we can, Mr. Congressman."

As a result of what we were able to do after that occasion, we worked with the Government of Turkey, we got an agreement worked out whereby all the heroin poppy production in Turkey will be stopped within a year.

I called the Congressman on the phone because I was rather pleased, and I thought he would be. I said, "Mr. Congressman, I think you will be interested to know that we have reached an agreement with the Turkish Government which will be announced later today to the effect that they will stop all heroin poppy production within the next year." The Congressman was somewhat overwhelmed by the call, and we talked a bit, and he said he appreciated it—the followup.

Then he said, "You know, Mr. President, when I was growing up in Harlem, if I had told my old man that some day I would be talking to the President of the United States, he would have told me I was crazy." And I said, "Well, Mr. Congressman, if when I was growing up in Yorba Linda, had I told my old man that some day I would be talking to a Congressman on the phone, he would have thought I was crazy."

I will simply close my remarks tonight by saying if I had told my old man—and this will date us both, my old man and the man I am going to mention and me, too—if I had told my old man when I was growing up in Yorba Linda that some day I would be talking to Jack Benny, he would have said that I was crazy.

Thank you.

NOTE: The President spoke at 6:18 p.m. in his California residence. He spoke without referring to notes.

274   Statement About Progress Toward Establishment of an All-Volunteer Armed Force.   *August 28, 1972*

BASED on the report submitted to me this morning by Secretary Laird, and provided the Congress enacts pending legislation I have recommended, we will be able, as planned, to eliminate entirely by July 1973 any need for peacetime conscription into the armed forces.

Four years ago I pledged that if elected I would work toward ending the military draft and establishing in its place an all-volunteer armed force—and that during such time, as the need for a draft continued, I would seek to make its working more equitable and less capricious in its effect on the lives of young Americans.

Immediately on taking office, my Administration began its fulfillment of that pledge—and I take deep and special satisfaction in the progress that has been made.

Within 18 months, the old, outmoded draftee selection process, with its inequitable system of deferments, was replaced by an even-handed lottery system based on random selection. The uncertainty created by the draft was further minimized

by reducing the period of draft vulnerability from 7 years to one. As a result of these and other reforms, confidence in the fairness of the Selective Service System has been restored.

Meanwhile, we have also been working toward the all-volunteer force.

Secretary Laird today delivered to me an encouraging report detailing the substantial progress we have made in reducing dependence on the draft to meet military manpower needs. The experience of the past 3 years, as indicated in this report, seems to show that sufficient numbers of volunteers can be attracted to the armed forces to meet peacetime manpower needs, and that ending all dependence on the draft will be consistent with maintaining the force level and degree of readiness necessary to meet our vital long-term national security needs.

This remarkable record of progress in reducing our dependence on the draft is a direct result of the strong support given by Secretary Laird, by the Service Secretaries, by the Service Chiefs, and by the entire Defense Department. They can all be justifiably proud of the record:

—Draft calls have been reduced from 299,000 in 1968 to 50,000 in 1972— one-sixth of the previous level.

—The proportion of enlistees who are "true volunteers"—that is, who enlist out of their own free will and not because of pressure from the draft— has increased from 59 percent to 75 percent in the last year alone.

—The quality of enlistees has remained high, even improving slightly, while the economic and racial profile of the enlistees has not been significantly changed.

—Our military readiness has not suffered.

Some problems, however, remain to be overcome, and doing so will require the full support of the Department of Defense, the Congress, and the public. These problems include:

—Avoiding potential manpower shortages which will occur unless legislation currently pending before the Congress is passed, so as to bolster vigorous Service efforts already underway to improve manpower utilization enlistments and retention;

—Providing sufficient numbers of doctors and other highly trained specialists in critical skills;

—Maintaining Guard and Reserve force manning, which will remain below congressionally mandated strength unless pending legislation is passed.

I am confident that these problems can and will be overcome—assuming prompt action by the Congress on the necessary pending legislation and assuming continued public and Service support. In particular:

—The benefit and worth of a military career must be more effectively communicated to the American people, while all four Services continue to improve their personnel management and manpower utilization procedures. Military careerists deserve the respect and the gratitude of the public they serve.

—The Congress must assist through timely passage of pending legislation—particularly the Uniformed Services Special Pay Act of 1972, which will provide needed bonus authority to help fill projected shortages in critical skills and other possible shortages in the number of enlistees available under a zero draft.

Given this kind of support, we will no longer need conscription to fill manpower requirements after July 1973. This means that it will not be necessary to require from the Congress an extension of induction authority of the Selective Service Act past July of 1973; further authority to conscript thereafter would rest with the Congress.

In reaching this goal, we will finally— 28 years after the end of World War II— have done what I said in 1968 that we should do: that we should "show our commitment to freedom by preparing to assure our young people theirs."

NOTE: The statement was released at San Clemente, Calif.

On the same day, the President met at the Western White House with Secretary of Defense Melvin R. Laird and members of the Youth Advisory Board of the Selective Service System to discuss Secretary Laird's report on progress being made toward an all-volunteer armed force.

The White House released the transcript of a news briefing by Secretary Laird on the meeting and the report.

275   Memorandum of Disapproval of a Bill To Restore
        Seniority Rights to a Postal Service Employee.
        August 29, 1972

I HAVE withheld my approval from S. 889, a bill "To restore the postal service seniority of Elmer Erickson."

Under this bill, Mr. Erickson would receive special benefits denied other postal employees who lost seniority rights under similar circumstances or who made decisions and choices based on then existing rules. Such action by Congress would be discriminatory and without justification.

The seniority rules in question here represent the result of bargaining between the postal unions and postal management. They are not a matter on which Congress has legislated in the past. The seniority involved has to do with preferred assignments, eligibility for promotions, and similar matters covered by agreements between the Postal Service and the postal unions. Employees displaced on the seniority list by Mr. Erickson certainly would have good cause to complain if this bill were to become law.

In my opinion, if seniority rights are to be retroactively restored to postal employees, it is for postal management and the postal unions to negotiate an equitable solution which covers all employees similarly situated.

RICHARD NIXON

The White House,
    August 29, 1972.

NOTE: The memorandum was released at San Clemente, Calif.

276   The President's News Conference of
        August 29, 1972

THE PRESIDENT. We will go right ahead with your questions, because I know you want to cover perhaps some international as well as domestic matters, including, I understand, for the first time, political matters.

QUESTIONS

HANDLING OF CAMPAIGN FUNDS

[1.] Q. Mr. President, are you personally investigating the mishandling of some of your campaign funds, and do you agree with former Secretary Connally that these charges are harmful to your re-election?

THE PRESIDENT. Well, I commented upon this on other occasions, and I will repeat my position now.

With regard to the matter of the handling of campaign funds, we have a new law here in which technical violations have occurred and are occurring, apparently, on both sides. As far as we are concerned, we have in charge, in Secretary Stans, a man who is an honest man and one who is very meticulous—as I have learned from having him as my treasurer and finance chairman in two previous campaigns—in the handling of matters of this sort.

Whatever technical violations have occurred, certainly he will correct them and will thoroughly comply with the law. He is conducting any investigation on this matter, and conducting it very, very thoroughly, because he doesn't want any evidence at all to be outstanding, indicating that we have not complied with the law.

INVESTIGATIONS OF POLITICAL CONTRIBU-
TIONS AND WATERGATE CASE

[2.] Q. Mr. President, wouldn't it be a good idea for a special prosecutor, even from your standpoint, to be appointed to investigate the contribution situation and also the Watergate case?

THE PRESIDENT. With regard to who is investigating it now, I think it would be well to notice that the FBI is conducting a full field investigation. The Department of Justice, of course, is in charge of the prosecution and presenting the matter to the grand jury. The Senate Banking and Currency Committee is conducting an investigation. The Government Accounting Office, an independent agency, is conducting an investigation of those aspects which involve the campaign spending law. Now, with all of these investigations that are being conducted, I don't believe that adding another special prosecutor would serve any useful purpose.

The other point that I should make is that these investigations, the investigation by the GAO, the investigation by the FBI, by the Department of Justice, have, at my direction, had the total cooperation of the—not only the White House—but also of all agencies of the Government. In addition to that, within our own staff, under my direction, Counsel to the President, Mr. Dean, has conducted a complete investigation of all leads which might involve any present members of the White House Staff or anybody in the Government. I can say categorically that his investigation indicates that no one in the White House Staff, no one in this Administration, presently employed, was involved in this very bizarre incident.

At the same time, the committee itself is conducting its own investigation, independent of the rest, because the committee desires to clear the air and to be sure that as far as any people who have responsibility for this campaign are concerned, that there is nothing that hangs over them. Before Mr. Mitchell left as campaign chairman he had employed a very good law firm with investigatory experience to look into the matter. Mr. MacGregor [1] has continued that investigation and is continuing it now. I will say in that respect that anyone on the campaign committee, Mr. MacGregor has assured me, who does not cooperate with the investigation or anyone against whom charges are leveled where there is a prima facie case that those charges might indicate involvement will be discharged immediately. That, of course, will be true also of anybody in the Government. I think under these circumstances we are doing everything we can to take this incident and to investigate it and not to cover it up. What really hurts in matters of this sort is not the fact that they occur, because overzealous people in campaigns do things that are wrong. What really hurts is if you try to cover it up. I would say that here we are, with control of the agencies of the Government and presumably with control of the investigatory

---

[1] Clark MacGregor was campaign director, Committee for the Re-Election of the President, from July to November 1972.

agencies of the Government, with the exception of the GAO which is independent. We have cooperated completely. We have indicated that we want all the facts brought out and that as far as any people who are guilty are concerned, they should be prosecuted.

، This kind of activity, as I have often indicated, has no place whatever in our political process. We want the air cleared. We want it cleared as soon as possible.

VIETNAM SETTLEMENT PROSPECTS

[3.] Q. Mr. President, in your last news conference, on July 27, you said the chances for a settlement have never been better. Mr. Rogers in late August forecast early settlement, and you were quoted by Stewart Alsop as having told him the war won't be hanging over us the second term.[2] I want to know whether this is just politics or is there substance to it—any movement in negotiations or any other track toward peace?

THE PRESIDENT. Mr. Potter [Philip Potter, Baltimore Sun], as I also told Mr. Alsop, as you noted, in that interview, I did not indicate to him that any breakthrough had occurred in the negotiations that have been taking place between Dr. Kissinger and Mr. Le Duc Tho at this point. Now, let me divide the answer into its component parts, if I may.

First, with regard to negotiations, I will not comment on past negotiations. I will not comment upon any negotiations that may take place in the future. By agreement of both sides, we are not going to

comment, either the other side or we on our part, on the substance of negotiations or whether or when or what will happen in the future. All that we will do is to announce, after negotiations do take place, if they do—and I do not suggest that more will occur—we will announce the fact that they have taken place.

Second, with regard to what the prospects are, I think what we are all referring to is that this long and difficult war—long and difficult and costly for both sides—has reached a point where it should be brought to an end. We have made every reasonable negotiating proposal that we can. We are being very reasonable in the proposals that we have made in our various discussions with the other side. Also, with regard to the battlefront, it is significant to note that the South Vietnamese, by heroic efforts, have stopped the invasion from the North on the ground, and they have done that without our assistance on the ground.

It is also significant to note that the enemy at this point, while it is able to launch a spurt here and there, does not have the capability or has not demonstrated the capability to overrun South Vietnam.

Now, under these circumstances, we believe that this is the time for a negotiated settlement. If the enemy does not feel that way, then we are prepared to go on as we have indicated, to continue the training of the South Vietnamese—we have completed virtually the ground training because they are undertaking the ground fighting entirely by themselves—but to continue the training in the air and on the sea so that they, by themselves, can defend their country against the Communist invaders from the North.

---

[2] Mr. Alsop interviewed the President aboard the Spirit of '76 en route to Miami, August 22, 1972. The interview appeared in the September 4 issue of Newsweek.

VIETNAM TROOP LEVELS

[4.] Q. Mr. President, you announced today another reduction in the force levels in Vietnam,[3] and it was unclear from the announcement whether this is your last announcement. Do you see this as the residual force in Vietnam necessary as bargaining leverage?

THE PRESIDENT. I can't imagine that Mr. Ziegler didn't make everything perfectly clear. [*Laughter*] But I shall try to, under those circumstances. The announcement of 27,500 [27,000] does not indicate that 27,500 [27,000] is the force that is going to remain in South Vietnam indefinitely. We are going to look at the situation again before the first of December, after the election, incidentally, because we are not going to play election politics with this next withdrawal—or this next announcement, I should say, because I am not suggesting that there will be another withdrawal.

We will look at the situation, and the three principles that I have always applied with regard to withdrawals will in this case control it: the status of our POW and MIA situation, the status with regard to negotiations, and the status of enemy activity. At that time we will determine what the American force level should be. It should be noted that the present force level of 39,000, and the level that we will reach of 27,500 [27,000] involves no ground combat personnel. It involves only advisory and training personnel and, of

---

[3] A statement announcing the withdrawal of additional U.S. troops from Vietnam was read by Press Secretary Ronald L. Ziegler at a news briefing at the Western White House in San Clemente, Calif., on August 29, 1972. The statement is printed in the Weekly Compilation of Presidential Documents (vol. 8, p. 1306).

course, air support personnel. It is entirely a volunteer force.

I will add something that perhaps everyone here is quite aware of: that as far as any so-called residual force is concerned, our offer is for a total withdrawal. We want to withdraw all American forces, but that offer is conditioned on what I laid down on May 8, and one of those conditions is the situation with regard to our POW's and MIA's. As long as there is one POW in North Vietnam, or one missing in action, not accounted for, there will be an American volunteer force in South Vietnam.

1968 CAMPAIGN STATEMENTS AND
ACTIONS IN VIETNAM

[5.] Q. Mr. President, how do you reconcile your 1968 campaign promise to end the war with the massive bombing of North Vietnam that is now going on?

THE PRESIDENT. Well, in terms of what I said in 1968, all you who were following me will remember that I said that we would seek an honorable end to the war. We have come a long way in reaching that. We have reduced our casualties by 98 percent; we have withdrawn over half a million men from the forces that we found that were there; we have completely finished the American ground combat role.

Only volunteers will be serving in Vietnam in the future. What is left now simply is to complete the long-term involvement of the United States in a way that does not destroy respect, trust, and, if I may use the term, honor for the United States around the world. I think that we have come—it seems to me made very significant progress in this respect, and we expect to make more.

On the negotiating front, we have gone very far, as far as any reasonable person, I think, would suggest, and under the circumstances I believe the record is good.

As far as what can happen in the future, I know that there are those who believe— I noted some report out of the Air Force to the effect that we probably would be bombing in North Vietnam 2 or 3 years from now. That, of course, is quite ridiculous. As far as the future is concerned, we believe that our training program for the South Vietnamese, not only on the ground but in the air, has gone forward so successfully that if the enemy still refuses to negotiate, as we have asked them to negotiate, then the South Vietnamese will be able to undertake the total defense of their country.

At the present time, let the record show that while we hear a lot about what the Americans are doing in terms of undertaking bombing activities, that now approximately 50 percent of all ground support air sorties are being made by the South Vietnamese air force, which is a good air force and which is growing in strength.

Q. Is there a possibility that you would call off the bombing or slacken it even if there is no all-inclusive agreement on Indochina?

THE PRESIDENT. Absolutely not. I have noted some press speculation to the effect that since 1968, the bombing halt seemed to have a rather dramatic effect on the election chances of Senator Humphrey— Vice President Humphrey, now a Senator—that people have suggested that as a gimmick, or more or less as an election-eve tactic, that we would call a bombing halt even though our prisoners of war are not accounted for. No progress has been made there, and even though the enemy continued its activities and was still stonewalling us in the negotiations, unless there is progress on the negotiating front which is substantial, there will be no reduction of the bombing of North Vietnam and there will be no lifting of the mining.

Q. Mr. President, I would like to ask about a 1968 statement you made and find out whether you still agree with it. It is: "Those who have had a chance for 4 years and could not produce peace should not be given another chance."

THE PRESIDENT. I think that the answer I gave to the other question is as responsive as I can make it. We always, of course, set our goals high. We do our very best to reach those goals. I think there are those who have faulted this Administration on its efforts to seek peace, but those who fault it, I would respectfully suggest, are ones that would have the United States seek peace at the cost of surrender, dishonor, and the destruction of the ability of the United States to conduct foreign policy in a responsible way.

That I did not pledge in 1968. I do not pledge it now. We will seek peace. We will seek better relations with our adversaries, but we are going to keep the United States strong. We are going to resist the efforts of those who would cut our defense budget to make us second to any power in the world, and second particularly to the Soviet Union, and in order to do that, it means that we have to continue the responsible policy that we have carried out.

Q. Mr. President, if it is, as you say, "quite ridiculous" that we will be bombing 2 or 3 years from now—by the way, I don't know if you mean North Vietnam or all of Vietnam—then how about a year from now? Is it likely that bombing would no longer be necessary in your present plan or thinking?

THE PRESIDENT. No, I would not comment on what the situation will be a year from now because, with the fact that we have had negotiation proposals made—I am not indicating progress, I am simply indicating they have been made—and with also the progress that is being made by the South Vietnamese, very outstanding progress in their ability to defend themselves and also to undertake the air effort as well as the ground effort, I am not going to put any limitation on when the U.S. activities in the air would stop.

Also, I am not going to indicate they are going to continue for any length of time. We are going to continue to watch the situation month by month. We will do what is necessary to protect our interests. We will do what is necessary to assure the return of our POW's and accounting for our missing in action. We will do what is necessary to prevent the imposition, against their will, of a Communist government on the people of South Vietnam.

All this we will do, but on the other hand, we are not there for the purpose of staying any moment that is longer than is necessary.

CAMPAIGN CONDUCT AND GOALS

[6.] Q. Mr. President, the confidence expressed at the Republican Convention suggested that many Republicans, perhaps yourself included, consider the election a mere formality. Yet you have said, at your last press conference, that you expected this election to be a close one that goes right down to the wire. Do you still feel that way?

THE PRESIDENT. Yes, I do. That has always been my theory. I recall the year that I ran for the first time for Congress in 1946. I was somewhat of a neophyte, never having run for public office before.

I talked to someone who had had great experience in running for office. He gave me very good advice that has been my guiding principle in campaigns since. He said, "Pay no attention to the polls. Pay no attention to what your friends say about your chances, or your opponents." He said, "Always run as if you are one million votes behind, and then you might win by one vote."

In 1960 I learned what he meant, because elections can be very, very close in this country.

I am conducting this campaign, and I have urged on my colleagues in the campaign to conduct it, without regard to the polls. I am not going to comment on polls one way or the other, when they are good or when they are bad. We are running on the basis of the great issues before the country. We are presenting, we think, a very clear choice before the country. We are seeking in this election something that no President has had since 1956, with the exception of President Johnson in '64 after his landslide, and that is a majority, because there was not a majority even in 1960 and of course there was not in 1968 because of third-party candidates. I think what we need now is a clear majority, a clear majority of the American people. That means a clear mandate, a mandate for what I have described as change that works, for progress. Because, when I see what has happened to, for example, revenue sharing, government reorganization, our health plan, our welfare reform, and all of our programs—there are 12 different bills on the environment that are still stuck in the mud of Senate and House controversy—when I see that, I think that the country needs to speak out.

I would also suggest, Mr. Lisagor [Peter Lisagor, Chicago Daily News], because I know that you, like myself, have sort of followed campaigns over the years, and we go back this far, at least I do— I believe that if we can get a clear majority, if we can get a new majority at the Presidential level in this campaign, which we are going to seek by crossing the country and crossing all the lines of various age groups and religious groups and ethnic groups, et cetera, that we could have a legislative record in the first 6 months of the next Congress which could equal in excitement, in reform, the 100 days of 1933. It will be very different from the 100 days but we have it all there, and my State of the Union Message summed it up early this year.

What we are seeking here is not only a majority for the President, but we are seeking a new majority, of course, in the House and the Senate which will support the President in terms of his domestic policies, and we trust continue to support us on national defense and foreign policy.

CAMPAIGN TRAVEL AND DEBATES

[7.] Q. Mr. President, how are you going to conduct the campaign personally in terms of your travel plans, and would you be willing to debate with Senator McGovern over national television?

THE PRESIDENT. Mr. Schecter [Jerrold L. Schecter, Time-Life], let me turn to the debate question first, because it is one which I know many of you have speculated about, and we might as well set the speculation to rest.

Mr. MacGregor, and before him Mr.

Mitchell, both indicated it would be not in the national interest for the President to debate. I did not share that view in 1964. Quite candidly, you may remember that when Senator Goldwater was a candidate I said that having been a Vice President and having debated and knowing all of the information that the President debated, I saw no reason why the President shouldn't debate.

Frankly, I think I was wrong. I was wrong, in that President Johnson was right, Senator Mansfield was right, and even Senator Pastore, who supported the amendment to 315[4] but who said that even in supporting the 315 amendment, he said he had serious doubts about whether a President of the United States should debate.

Now just to say why. The reason does not have so much to do with confidential information that a President has, because such information can be made available to the other candidate, if he desires to obtain it. What really is involved is that when a President speaks, as distinguished from a Vice President even, he makes policy every time he opens his mouth. For example, just as I spoke a moment ago with regard to our plans in Vietnam, what is going to happen, that is policy.

Now, when we are involved—even though it is the concluding phases—but

---

[4] The requirements of section 315 of the Communications Act of 1934, as amended, which provide equal broadcasting opportunity to any legally qualified candidate for public office, were suspended for the period of the 1960 campaign with respect to the Presidential and Vice Presidential nominees (Public Law 86–677, 74 Stat. 554).

In 1963 a bill (H.J. Res. 247) was introduced to suspend the requirements of section 315 for the period of the 1964 Presidential campaign, but it was never enacted into law.

when we are involved in a war, for a President in the heat of partisan debate to make policy would not be in the national interest. So I have decided that there will be no debates between the President and the challenger in this year 1972.

Now, with regard to my own plans. You have often heard me describe that a President wears two hats. Well, he wears three actually, but we put the Commander in Chief off here. We have already discussed those questions. The other two hats he wears are that as President of the United States and as leader of his party, and as candidate after the nomination.

Now, I am a candidate in the one sense and the President in the other. What comes first? Putting priorities where they belong, I shall always have to put my responsibilities to conduct the Presidency first. I had hoped that the Congress would be out of here with a record, which they have not yet made. Incidentally, this Congress, in order to avoid being called a very inept Congress, one that never talked as much and did less, to avoid that, is going to have to do 4 months work in 4 weeks, and it will be a real issue in this campaign, the fact that the Congress has not acted on revenue sharing and on government reorganization and on health and on welfare.

But, since the Congress is going to be in, I understand, until October 10, or the 15th, or maybe the 1st, or whatever it is, as long as the Congress is there, my responsibilities as President will require that I stay in Washington except for perhaps an occasional trip to the country, but only for a day. I could perhaps over a weekend, I haven't figured it out yet, but we will, of course, inform you so that you can pack your bags. None of those will be overnight trips, you will be glad to know.

After the Congress adjourns, then I, of course, still have my responsibilities as President, and I cannot go out and spend 6 to 7 days a week. I realize that some Presidents have done that. Harry Truman did in 1948. But the problems that we had then, great as they were, are not as great as those we have now. It will be necessary for me to continue to spend a great deal of time in Washington, but I don't want to leave the impression that the one-day trips that I will make between now and the time Congress adjourns, and then the time I will be able to devote to campaigning in the last 3 weeks, means that it will be a leisurely, complacent, take-it-easy campaign.

As I have indicated in my answer to Mr. Lisagor, I consider this campaign enormously important. It provides the clearest choice that certainly I have seen in my political lifetime. I believe we have to hit hard on the issues; in other words, hit hard on the problems, and not on the personalities. And we are going to do that, and I would assume that the other side would do likewise. In order to do that, we are going to cover the whole country. We are not going to take any State for granted. We are not going to concede any State, and more than that, we are going to cover all groups.

One thing I should mention when I speak of the new majority, I reject the idea of a new coalition. A coalition is not a healthy thing in a free society. Coalition automatically adds up the young against the old, the black against the white, the Catholics against the Protestants, the city people against the country people, et cetera, et cetera.

What we are doing is to make our appeal across the board and try to build a new majority on the basis of people from all groups supporting us on the basis of what we believe.

Q. Mr. President, you have objected and given your reasons for not entering a debate with your opponent. Would you entertain the possibility of a debate on a lower level, between the Vice Presidential candidates?

THE PRESIDENT. I would be very confident as to the result on that, because I think Vice President Agnew's 4 years of experience, his coolness, his lawyer's background, would serve him in good stead in a debate. I do not believe, however, that a debate at the Vice Presidential level would serve any useful purpose, but I don't rule it out. I don't think it would serve any useful purpose.

MEETING WITH THE PRIME MINISTER
OF JAPAN

[8.] Q. Mr. President, may I ask a question concerning your meeting with Mr. Tanaka?

THE PRESIDENT. Sure.

Q. Mr. Tanaka has made his intention clear, that he would like to discuss further with you China and discuss less economic problems. But I am also told that the United States wants to discuss the economic problems as widely and deeply as the other issues, and it can be said that it is an open secret that the United States is asking Japan for another revaluation of the yen in the near future. Could you tell me to what extent are you going to discuss with Tanaka the economic issues?

THE PRESIDENT. Our meeting with Mr. Tanaka is, first, very important because it is the first chance that I will have to

meet him as Prime Minister, although I did meet him here, you recall, when he came with Premier Sato, and I have known him for many years and have great respect for him as one of the new leaders of Japan. So it will first provide an opportunity for establishing a dialogue between these two countries, both of whom are economic super powers.

Second, we will naturally cover the whole range of problems of the Pacific. Both Japan and the United States are tremendously interested in peace in the Pacific. On the economic side, I think both sides will be prepared to discuss the fact that there is now an unfavorable balance of trade between Japan and the United States of $3.4 billion a year. Naturally, that is not healthy for the United States, but responsible Japanese leaders do not believe it is healthy for Japan because what will happen if that kind of an imbalance continues? It will inevitably feed the fire of those in this country who would want to set up quotas and other restrictions, and the interests of Japan and the United States will better be served by freer trade rather than more restrictive trade.

I believe that out of this meeting will come some progress in trying to reduce that unfavorable balance between Japan and the United States.

Now, with regard to the devaluation of the yen, and that sort of thing, I won't comment on that. I have no expectation that that kind of technical international monetary matter will be one that we will discuss. I say that for the reason that saying anything else is likely to have the stock markets in Tokyo and New York go up and down, so I will categorically say that revaluation of the yen is not on the agenda, but the other matters of how we can adjust this trade balance so that it is less favorable to the United States is, of course, in order.

One final thing that I would say from a symbolic standpoint: Since World War II, Presidents of the United States have welcomed Prime Ministers of Japan to Washington on several occasions. I welcomed, as you know, the Emperor in the United States, in Anchorage, and we have met here with Prime Minister Sato.

It seems to me that we could have no better proof of the fact that the war is over, not only the shooting but also the enmity, than the fact that we are having this meeting between the leader of Japan and the leader of the United States in Hawaii, where the war began. And I am very glad that the Prime Minister and I mutually agreed that we should have it in Hawaii because we talk about the initiatives towards the People's Republic of China and towards the Soviet Union and the rest. As I have often said, and I repeat again, Japan being an economic giant with great potentials for political and other leadership in the Pacific plays an indispensable role if we are going to have peace in the Pacific.

As I have said, Japanese-American friendship and cooperation is the linchpin of peace in the Pacific, and we are going to try to strengthen that linchpin in these meetings.

CAMPAIGN FINANCING

[9.] Q. Mr. President, back to the campaign financing. You said that there had been technical violations of the law on both sides. I was just wondering what Democratic violations you had in mind.

THE PRESIDENT. I think that will come out in the balance of this week. I will let the political people talk about that, but I understand there have been on both sides.

VIEWS ON AMNESTY

[10.] Q. Mr. President, you have touched on the question of amnesty before, but since it is obviously a campaign issue, I wonder if you could spell out what you perceive to be the differences between your thoughts on amnesty and those of your opponent.

THE PRESIDENT. Mr. Semple [Robert B. Semple, Jr., New York Times], the Vice President made a very responsible statement on that, and I read it before he made it. That statement totally reflects my views and I back it, in other words—the speech that he made just a few days ago. Insofar as my own views are concerned, without going into that statement, because as you know it involves legal matters and a lot of other things, it is my view, and I hold it very strongly, that those who chose to desert the United States or to break the law by dodging the draft have to pay the penalty for breaking the law and deserting the United States before they can obtain amnesty or pardon or whatever you want to call it.

Now, where we disagree, apparently, is that the other side does not share that view. I say: Pay a penalty; others paid with their lives.

THE NEW MAJORITY

[11.] Q. Mr. President, the majority you talked about a minute ago, what kind of majority will it be, a Nixon majority or a Republican majority, and will it bring a Congress along with it?

THE PRESIDENT. First, with regard to the majority, the thrust of our campaign,

I have tried to emphasize to our campaign people, should be to make it a positive majority rather than a negative majority. There has been a great deal of talk with regard to why people should be against the challenger in this respect, mainly because his views, as I pointed out in the acceptance speech, departed from the bipartisan policy of his predecessors and departed from their economic philosophy and some of their basic views.

Now, what we want, however, is a positive mandate, in other words, what we are for, not simply what we might be against or what the country is against. Now that means that this majority will be one that we would hope would send us in with a clear mandate to keep the United States strong and not to go along with a $30 billion defense cut which would make the United States second in the air, the second strongest Navy, the second strongest in missiles, as well as the second on the ground, which we already are with the Soviet Union, and would completely destroy the chance for arms limitation and completely, in my view, destroy the ability of the United States to be the peacemaker of the world as the major free world power.

At home—and here are the areas that we don't often get into in these conferences—that we could have at home the kind of a mandate where the country would say we want change, but we want change that works. It is not a question of whether it is radical or not. My trip to China was radical, it was bold, radical, different. What really matters is: Does it work? Has it been thought through, or is it a half-baked scheme where you have one today and one tomorrow and then you check the PM's to see whether or not there is a new one?

As far as this thing is concerned, what we are saying is that we need a mandate for revenue sharing, we need a mandate for welfare reform, we need a mandate for our programs in the environment, for our new health programs, a mandate to continue progress without raising taxes, a mandate to continue to help those who are poor without having an enormous increase in the welfare rolls.

Finally, we believe that we need support in this country—and this is something that is rather hard to put your finger on, it is an intangible attitude. There has been a subtle shift over the last 4 years. Some may not have seen it. I think I have. Four years ago the country was torn apart, torn apart physically and torn apart inside. It has changed very subtly, but very definitely. What we need in this country is a new sense of mission, a new sense of confidence, a new sense of purpose as to where we are going.

The fact that abroad this country does not follow Hitlerite policies, that the President of the United States is not the number one warmaker of the world, but that as a matter of fact, the United States, with its great power, is using it well, and that the world is fortunate to have the United States as the most powerful of the free world nations—and at home, that the United States is not a country where we are repressive to the poor and play always to the rich, pointing out the fact, for example, that when we look at our tax laws that we provided the biggest individual tax reduction in history in 1969 and at the same time increased the burden for corporations by $4 billion, that we moved against the auto companies, for example, to have them roll back a price increase, that we moved against other companies that have been polluting.

In other words, this is not a pro-business or pro-labor Administration. It is an Administration that calls it right down the middle. When labor is wrong we say so, as I did when I was in Miami with Mr. Meany. When business is wrong we say so.

Now, I have digressed a bit, but let me come back to the point. We need a mandate, therefore, in which the President receives a clear majority. We are going to work for a clear majority and as big a one as we can get. Although as I say, we don't assume that it is going to be big, but it will be clear because there is not a third party candidate of significance.

Second, we need a new Congress. Now, on the Congress, I am sophisticated enough, as all of you are, because I have read some of your columns here, to know that in both the House and the Senate it is tough for us to elect a Republican majority. Also, I am honest enough to say

that there are several Democrats in the House and several Senators without whose support I could not have conducted the foreign policy of the United States over these past 4 years.

When I speak of a new Congress, I mean of a Congress I would hope that would be a Republican Congress because then we at least could have responsibility for leadership, but if it is not, I hope there is a new majority in Congress made up of Republicans and Democrats who support what the President believes in. Then we can get action on some of these things rather than being stuck in the mud as we have been these past 3 years, particularly since we have offered our new initiatives.

FRANK CORMIER (Associated Press). Thank you, Mr. President.

NOTE: President Nixon's twenty-seventh news conference was held at 11:03 a.m. on the grounds of his residence in San Clemente, Calif., on Tuesday, August 29, 1972. The President spoke without referring to notes.

277   Letter Accepting the Resignation of Arthur K. Watson as United States Ambassador to France. *August 29, 1972*

Dear Dick:

Your gracious letter has just come to my attention, and I was saddened to learn your doctor has recommended that you leave your post. I will, of course, abide by your wish and accept your resignation as Ambassador to France effective upon a date to be determined.

In doing so, I want you to know how greatly I have valued your distinguished service in Paris. You have been a superb representative to our oldest ally and friend, bringing to your position an uncommon understanding and profound appreciation

for the importance of ties between our two countries. On a broad range of issues vital to our national interest—from drug abuse to a new relationship with the People's Republic of China—you have played a key role. The prospects for a more stable era of peace have been significantly strengthened by your outstanding efforts.

As Nancy and you prepare to leave the Embassy you both served so well, you may be certain you take with you not only the admiration of your American colleagues and many French friends, but also my lasting gratitude and thanks. Pat joins me in hoping that the period of rest you now begin will help bring back the full measure of good health you so richly deserve.

With warm personal regards,

Sincerely,

RICHARD NIXON

NOTE: Ambassador Watson's letter, dated August 16, 1972, and released with the President's letter at San Clemente, Calif., read as follows:

Dear Mr. President:

For the last 6 months I have been very troubled by asthma. Having had a physical checkup, my doctor advises me that I must resign from my post in France.

This has been the most difficult decision I have ever made. You are doing such a superb job as our President, and I have been honored to serve under you. Yet the climate in Paris has aggravated my condition and I am told I must take 6 months off.

My plans, if you agree, Sir, would be to return to Paris after Labor Day to say our farewells. Then we shall return to private life— always in your corner.

Again, I repeat, what a great privilege it has been to have worked for you.

All our best wishes and warmest regards and appreciation.

Respectfully,

DICK

278   Statement on Signing the Rural Development Act of 1972.   *August 30, 1972*

DURING the last year and one-half I have on three separate occasions sent to Congress proposals designed to marshal more effectively the energies of the private sector and of government at all levels in a cooperative program of rural development. The most important of those proposals are:

—Rural community development special revenue sharing to provide additional financial resources to State and local government without counterproductive Federal strings attached.

—The creation of a Department of Community Development to coordinate and focus all Federal programs for rural and urban community development.

—New loan authority for commercial, industrial, and community development under a credit-sharing system which would allow the States themselves to select most of the loan recipients. And strengthening certain of the Department of Agriculture's conservation and environmental programs.

The Rural Development Act of 1972 which has finally been enacted by the Congress — H.R. 12931 — incorporates some of the important provisions which I originally proposed:

—It authorizes new loans for commercial and industrial development in communities whose population is under 50,000, as well as for various local facilities in communities whose population is under 10,000. These new loans represent a major potential for increasing employment opportunities and modernizing our communities in rural areas.

—The new loans which it authorizes would be insured and guaranteed, rather than direct, Federal loans. This means that the private sector can play a major role in rural development and that the inflationary impact on the Federal budget will be reduced.

—It authorizes new cost-sharing provisions including those related to improving water quality and conserving natural resources which I proposed on February 1 of this year in my message to the Congress on rural development.

—And, it includes various improvements in the administrative machinery of the Farmers Home Administration which would facilitate more effective program administration.

The most disconcerting feature of this act is that it does not include one of my most important proposals for rural development, the substitution of special revenue sharing for categorical grants, and instead creates a number of new categorical grant programs. That means more decisionmaking in Washington instead of decentralized decisionmaking at the State and local level where the pressing needs actually exist. While this act is praiseworthy in providing additional Federal funds for community development, it unfortunately will also bring Federal decisionmakers into fields of community activity that were previously free from such outside involvement. In addition, this act—if fully funded—would add $400 to $500 million in expenditures to the Federal budget at a time when it has already been overloaded with large spending increases by the Congress this year.

In short, while I would have much preferred that this act contain the provisions which I proposed and reiterated last February, I believe that it probably represents the best compromise which could be enacted by this Congress. Even with the shortcomings I have noted in this act, it is a significant first step in our determination to strengthen economic opportunity and community life through rural America. I do strongly urge, however, that the Congress act quickly and affirmatively on my government reorganization and special revenue sharing proposals related to rural development. They hold substantially greater promise than this act does for community development in rural and urban areas. Because this act represents an important step—but only the first of several essential steps—I take pleasure in signing it today. But I look forward to early Congressional action on my other proposals which would provide our communities with the tools so desperately needed to attain this Nation's objective of balanced and beneficial growth.

NOTE: The statement was released at San Clemente, Calif.

As enacted, H.R. 12931 is Public Law 92–419 (86 Stat. 657).

On the same day, the White House released a fact sheet on the provisions of the act.

279   Remarks on Arrival at Honolulu. *August 30, 1972*

Governor and Mrs. Burns, Senator and Mrs. Fong, Congressman Matsunaga and Mayor Fasi, Admiral McCain, and all of our very distinguished and fine guests here in Hawaii:

Over the past 25 years, my wife and I have received welcomes in 80 countries and 50 States, but every time we come to Hawaii we say there is nothing like a welcome in Hawaii, and we are most grateful for the warm reception we have received.

I appreciate your signs. I see *"Nixon No Ka Oi."* [Nixon is the best.] I know what it means.

Governor Burns has very eloquently described the purpose of our visit. Because the rain is coming down a bit, I will not take much of your time. I would like very simply to tell you what this State means to America and what this visit can mean to America and to the world.

We go back to the year 1969, which was the first year that I had the privilege of coming to Hawaii after being elected to the Presidency. That was the time that we went on to Midway and began the reduction of forces in Vietnam which has brought 500,000 Americans home and which has moved toward the peace with honor that all Americans want, there and throughout the world.

Then we were here again at the time of the Apollo 13 flight, when we welcomed back brave men who hadn't succeeded but who came back, and it was one of those epics in American bravery which all of us wanted to pay tribute to.

Then, as Governor Burns has indicated, it was February of this year that we stopped in Hawaii. We were here 2 days planning the trip to the People's Republic of China, which opened a dialogue between the most populous nation in the world and the United States of America, a dialogue that is essential if all of these wonderful young people we see here—the real young ones—are going to grow up in a world of peace. We cannot have a world of peace and have a fourth of the world's people outside of any communication with the United States and other nations.

And now, we come for another purpose. We come not to meet with those who have been our adversaries in recent times. We come to meet with those who have been very close friends of the United States going back over the past 20 years, and I refer to the Prime Minister of Japan and his official party.

This is a working visit. We shall discuss many problems, particularly problems of trade, and problems of cooperation. But what this visit signifies more than anything else, coming as it does in Hawaii, is how much the world has changed—and changed for the better—not only over the last 4 years to which I referred, but over the last 25 years. It was here just 26 [31] years ago that war in the Pacific began, and now here in Hawaii the Prime Minister of Japan, the President of the United States meet for the purpose of building a structure of peace in the Pacific. Because without peace and cooperation and friendship between the people of Japan and the people of the United States, there cannot be peace in the Pacific and there cannot be peace in the world.

We value that friendship, and we know that these meetings will contribute to it.

Let me say that you here in Hawaii have set a magnificent example of what that friendship can mean. Governor Burns has referred to the fact that so many people of Japanese background live here, and other backgrounds as well.

Let me say in that connection what you have demonstrated here as to how people of different backgrounds can work together, can create together, can live together, that is what we need to demonstrate in the world so that we can have that world of peace that we want not only for ourselves, but for all the children of the world.

We are delighted to be here and meeting here in Hawaii. I think with this nice rain falling this means a good omen for this trip. It will produce certainly good news for the United States, good news, we trust, also for Japan, but more important, good news for all the people of the world interested in peace.

Thank you.

NOTE: The President spoke at 4:37 p.m. at Hickam Air Force Base, Hawaii. He spoke without referring to notes.

John A. Burns was Governor of Hawaii, Hiram L. Fong was United States Senator, and Spark M. Matsunaga was United States Representative. Frank F. Fasi was mayor of Honolulu. Adm. John S. McCain, Jr., USN, was Commander in Chief, Pacific.

280   Remarks of Welcome to Prime Minister Kakuei Tanaka of Japan at Honolulu.   *August 30, 1972*

Mr. Prime Minister, and all of our distinguished guests from Japan:

In the word of welcome which is so famous not only here in Hawaii, but throughout the world, I say *Aloha*.

And, Mr. Prime Minister, I am very honored to welcome you not only in your official capacity for the first time, as Prime Minister, but also to welcome you again as a personal friend. This is as it should be, because the alliance between our two countries is one not only of necessity, but it is one that is strengthened also by the bonds of friendship. And the fact that the relationships between Presidents of the United States and Prime Ministers of Japan over the years have been not only official but personal has meant that that alliance has been thereby strengthened.

It is particularly appropriate that your first official visit, as Prime Minister, to the United States should be in this State of Hawaii, because here 30 percent of the population of this State is proud of its Japanese background. And we are reminded, as we meet in Hawaii, of how much Americans who have Japanese background have contributed to the strength, the diversity of our country.

As we see what has happened in Hawaii, and as we see what has happened in other parts of our country where people of Japanese background and the other diverse backgrounds of America have worked together, we realize how much the Japanese people of your country and the American people can do together in the cause of building a structure of peace in the world.

I know that this meeting that we will have will contribute to the desire of both of our peoples to strengthen the structure of peace so that we can continue on the road to progress which we fortunately both are moving on together today.

Mr. Prime Minister, I can say only that I extend this welcome not only personally, but from all the American people to you and to the people of Japan. May we always meet as we meet today, working for the great goals of peace in the Pacific and peace in the world.

NOTE: The President spoke at 8:35 p.m. at Hickam Air Force Base, Hawaii, where Prime Minister Tanaka received a formal welcome with full military honors. The President spoke without referring to notes.

See also Item 282.

The Prime Minister spoke in Japanese. A translation of his remarks was made available by Japanese officials as follows:

Mr. President, Mrs. Nixon, Mr. Secretary of State, ladies and gentlemen:

I wish to thank you most sincerely, Mr. President, for your very kind words and for this extremely cordial and warm reception accorded to us today.

Since I assumed the post of Prime Minister, it has been my strong wish to meet and have discussions with President Nixon and other leaders of the United States Government at the earliest possible opportunity. It is indeed a great pleasure for me that the opportunity is now realized.

I feel that it is most appropriate and significant that the meeting is taking place here in Hawaii, where peoples of diverse races with diverse traditions and cultures in the Pacific area have come and toiled together under the American flag to build a paradise in the Pacific.

All of you are aware that Japan and the United States, as partners situated across the Pacific, have maintained close cooperative relations in a variety of fields for many years. Today we are living in an increasingly multi-polarized world where Japan has come to assume greater responsibilities in the international community commensurate with her increased national strength. With this in mind, we wish to strengthen further the already solid foundation of friendship and mutual trust between Japan and the United States and to promote even more wide-ranging cooperative relations in the coming years. I earnestly hope that my meeting with President Nixon will mark the beginning of a new era of constant dialogue between our two countries.

Let me lastly convey, on behalf of the people of Japan, their very sincere greetings to the people of the United States.

281 Special Message to the Congress Recommending Delay in Pay Increases for Federal Employees. *August* 31, 1972

To the Congress of the United States:

As we approach the October date on which pay rates for Federal employees under the statutory pay systems would normally be adjusted, I wish to advise the Congress that I will recommend a pay increase for Federal employees effective January 1, 1973. I believe it is appropriate to point out that section 3 of Public Law 92-210, the Economic Stabilization Act Amendments of 1971, requires that this adjustment this year be delayed until January 1973.

The pay raise required by section 3 of the Economic Stabilization Act Amendments was limited by the terms of the law to the guideline that the Pay Board has established for pay increases throughout the economy, 5.5 percent a year. Clearly it was the intent of this law to see that Federal employees would be treated in a comparable manner with private enterprise employees under the Economic Stabilization Program. In recognition of this intent, on January 11, 1972, I directed that Federal wage employees should also have their pay increase limited by the Pay Board guidelines.

The necessary comparability studies have been completed and, under the Federal Pay Comparability Act of 1970, I will recommend that the increase necessary to achieve comparability, be paid, starting January 1, 1973, the first date our employees will be eligible to receive an increase under the Economic Stabilization Act. Our employees received their full 5.5 percent annual increase last January, and therefore their next increase cannot be effective until January 1, 1973. The provisions of Public Law 92-210 preclude submission of an alternative plan under section 5305(c)(1) of title 5, United States Code.

I believe it is important to express once again my strong personal support for the principle that our Nation's public servants should receive pay that is comparable with pay in private industry. For our Government to operate efficiently in these increasingly complex and demanding times, we must have a civil service of the highest caliber, and to recruit and retain these necessary employees, we must offer them a fair and just wage. Nevertheless, in our efforts to stabilize and revitalize our Nation's economy, it is also appropriate that they be treated the same as employees in the private sector, who are also able to receive such an increase no more frequently than once every 12 months.

RICHARD NIXON

The White House,
   August 31, 1972.

282   Joint Statement Following Meetings With Prime Minister Tanaka of Japan in Hawaii.   *September 1, 1972*

1. PRIME MINISTER Tanaka and President Nixon met in Hawaii August 31–September 1 for wide ranging discussions on a number of topics of mutual interest. The talks were held in an atmosphere of warmth and mutual trust reflecting the long history of friendship between Japan and the United States. Both leaders expressed the hope that their meeting would mark the beginning of a new chapter in the course of developing ever closer bonds between the two countries.

2. The Prime Minister and the President reviewed the current international situation and the prospects for the relaxation of tension and peaceful solutions to current problems in the world, with particular reference to Asia. It was stressed that the maintenance and strengthening of the close ties of friendship and cooperation between the two countries would continue to be an important factor for peace and stability in the evolving world situation. Both leaders reaffirmed the intention of the two governments to maintain the Treaty of Mutual Cooperation and Security between the two countries, and agreed that the two governments would continue to cooperate through close consultations with a view to ensuring smooth and effective implementation of the Treaty.

3. In discussing the increasing indications for peace and stability in Asia, the Prime Minister and the President welcomed the recent opening of dialogue in the Korean Peninsula, and the increasingly active efforts of Asian countries for self-reliance and regional cooperation, and shared the hope for an early realization of peace in Indochina. The Prime Minister and the President recognized that the President's recent visits to the People's Republic of China and the USSR were a significant step forward. In this context, they shared the hope that the forthcoming visit of the Prime Minister to the People's Republic of China would also serve to further the trend for the relaxation of tension in Asia.

4. The Prime Minister and the President discussed the recent agreements reached by the United States and the USSR on the limitation of ballistic missile defenses and the interim arrangement on the limitation of strategic offensive missiles, and they agreed that such measures represented an important step forward in limiting strategic arms and contributing to world peace. They agreed to consult

on the need for further steps to control strategic arms.

5. The Prime Minister and the President exchanged views in a broad perspective on issues related to economic, trade and financial matters. The Prime Minister and the President emphasized the great importance of economic relations between Japan and the United States. Both leaders expressed their conviction that their talks would contribute to closer cooperation between the two countries in dealing with economic issues of a bilateral and global nature.

6. The Prime Minister and the President shared the view that fundamental reform of the international monetary system is essential. They committed their governments to work rapidly to achieve such reform. In trade, they reaffirmed the February 1972 commitments of both countries to initiate and actively support multilateral trade negotiations covering both industry and agriculture in 1973. In this connection they noted the need in the forthcoming trade negotiations to lay the basis for further trade expansion through reduction of tariff and nontariff barriers as well as formulations of a multilateral non-discriminatory safeguard mechanism.

7. The Prime Minister and the President agreed that both countries would endeavor to move towards a better equilibrium in their balance of payments and trade positions. In this regard, the President explained the measures undertaken by the United States to improve its trade and payments position and stated that the Government of the United States was urging U.S. firms to expand the volume of exports through increased productivity and improved market research, particularly to Japan. The Prime Minister indicated that the Government of

Japan would also try to promote imports from the United States and that it was the intention of the Government of Japan to reduce the imbalance to a more manageable size within a reasonable period of time. The Prime Minister and the President agreed that it would be most valuable to hold future meetings at a high level to review evolving economic relationships, and that they intend to hold a meeting of the Joint United States-Japan Committee on Trade and Economic Affairs as early in 1973 as feasible.

8. The Prime Minister and the President noted the endeavors of the two countries, in cooperation with other developed countries, to help bring stability and prosperity to the developing countries in Asia and other regions of the world. They acknowledged the need for adequate levels of official development assistance on appropriate terms. They also reaffirmed that the two governments intend to continue to help strengthen the international financial institutions for the purpose of economic development of the developing countries.

9. The Prime Minister and the President reaffirmed the need to promote efforts to improve the mutual understanding of the cultural, social and other backgrounds between the peoples of the two countries. They agreed further that new and improved programs of cultural and educational exchange are an important means to this end. In this connection the President underlined his high hopes for the successful activities of the Japan Foundation to be inaugurated in October this year.

10. The Prime Minister and the President noted with satisfaction the growing momentum of cooperation between the two countries in increasingly diverse fields

under the common aims of maintaining and promoting peace and prosperity of the world and the well-being of their countrymen. They agreed to strengthen and expand the already close cooperation between the two countries in controlling the illegal traffic in narcotics and other dangerous drugs, and they also agreed on the need for further bilateral and multilateral cooperation concerning the development and better utilization of energy and mineral resources and on the pressing problems of environmental protection and pollution control. They pledged to continue appropriate assistance through the UN and its specialized agencies for the solution of problems caused by too rapid population growth.

11. The Prime Minister and the President discussed cooperation in space exploration including Japan's goal of launching geo-stationary communications and other applications satellites. The President welcomed Japan's active interest in and study on the launching of a meteorological satellite in support of the global atmospheric research program.

12. The Prime Minister and the President expressed satisfaction with their talks and agreed to continue to maintain close personal contact.

NOTE: The joint statement was released at Kahuku, Hawaii.

See also Item 280.

On August 31, 1972, Prime Minister Tanaka was the President's guest at a working dinner at the Kuilima Hotel, Oahu, Hawaii.

On September 1, the White House released an announcement on the results of talks between Robert S. Ingersoll, U.S. Ambassador to Japan, and Kiyohiko Tsurumi, Japanese Deputy Vice Minister for Foreign Affairs, on U.S.-Japanese economic and trade matters. The White House also released the transcript of a news briefing by U. Alexis Johnson, Under Secretary of State for Political Affairs, and Ambassador Ingersoll on the joint statement and the announcement. The announcement and the news briefing are printed in the Weekly Compilation of Presidential Documents (vol. 8, p. 1335).

283   Remarks at a Ceremony Marking the Retirement of Admiral John S. McCain, Jr., as Commander in Chief, Pacific. *September 1, 1972*

Mr. Secretary of State, Governor Burns, Senator Fong, Congressman Matsunaga, Admiral Moorer, Admiral McCain, Admiral Gayler, all of the distinguished guests, and all of you who are here on this memorable occasion:

It is for me a very great honor to be here, to be here in my capacity as Commander in Chief of the Armed Forces, but also representing all of the American people, to pay respects to one of the great families of a proud Navy tradition, the McCains: John McCain, Commander of the Second Carrier Task Force and Task Force 38; Admiral McCain, Jr., who has just received his second Distinguished Service Citation and has completed 4 years of outstanding service as Commander in Chief of our Pacific Forces, one who has served in World War II, in Korea, and in Vietnam; and his son, John McCain III, a splendid Naval aviator who has been a prisoner of war in Vietnam for the past 5 years.

In the story of the McCains we see the greatness of America. We see service to this country. We see men who have devoted their lives to this country to keep it strong so that America could be free and so that America could play its role of being the guardian of peace in the world.

When we think of America's role in this century, the wars in which we have fought, it is a record which no American need be ashamed of, and which every American ought to be proud of: World War I, World War II, Korea, and Vietnam. We have not asked for anything in the way of conquest. We have gone to defend freedom, not to destroy it. We have tried to keep the peace rather than to break it. And when the war is concluded, we have been generous to those who have been our enemies.

We had a striking example of this in the meetings that have just been concluded—Japan, an enemy of the United States 26 years ago, now our ally and friend. And the United States has returned to Japan Okinawa. We stand with Japan today, helping Japan economically, first to get on its feet and then to become one of our major competitors, and also helping to maintain the strength without which Japan could not be an independent, free country in the world.

The same can be said of every one of these conflicts in which we have been engaged, including the war in Vietnam. Here, whatever differences of opinion that may exist, we can be proud of the fact that our goal is not conquest; it is defense of the right of people to be independent of foreign domination.

We seek an end to a war, but it must be an honorable end. We have offered the most generous terms for peace, but there are some things we cannot and will not offer. We will never abandon our prisoners of war. We will never impose on the 17 million people of South Vietnam a Communist government against their will. And we will not stain the honor of the United States of America.

We take this position because the United States is respected in the world because we stand by our friends, and once the United States departs from that great policy which has characterized us from the beginning of our period as a nation, then we will lose respect and the friends who count on us, and allies around the world would lose confidence in their ability to remain free.

Honoring the McCains also gives us an opportunity to point up the necessity for the United States to remain strong, to remain strong because we know that we will always use our strength in the interest of preserving peace, in the interest of defending freedom—and power in the hands of the United States is in the interest of peace and freedom in the world.

We must also remember that around the world there are other nations, large and small, who depend on the United States for their freedom, their independence, and the peace that they enjoy. Once the United States does not have the strength, the power to defend those areas of the world according to our treaty and other commitments, then those nations would be in deadly jeopardy.

That is why, on such an occasion as this, when we honor this great Navy family, we commit ourselves to this proposition: We shall never take steps that will make the United States the second strongest nation in the world. We must always have a strength second to none in the world. And to maintain that strength we need, of course, the weapons of war—guns and ships, all the other instruments that we are quite aware of—but above all, we need men and women, men and women like this magnificent group that we see before us here in Hawaii.

All of you know that we are moving

847

toward an all-volunteer force, hoping to reach that goal in June of next year. Too much emphasis has been put on the fact that if only we would pay those in the Armed Forces the same amount of money that they could get in comparable positions in civilian life, that that would solve the problem of getting the volunteers that we need to maintain the strength that America must maintain.

That is important, and certainly we should have adequate pay, comparable pay, for those who choose the profession so proudly represented here today. But even more important—and I say this to all of the American people today—more important than the money that we pay to those who defend America and peace around the world is the respect which is due those who wear the uniform of the United States of America. Let's honor and respect them.

Every American, every man, every woman in the armed services of the United States, can be proud of the record of this country over this past century, and every American in the armed service of the United States, as we move toward a period of peace, can be proud of the fact that he is serving the cause of peace, because the United States, a strong United States, let us never forget, is not the enemy of peace; it is the guardian of peace.

So, finally, I say that in honoring this magnificent family, John McCain, John McCain, Jr., John McCain III, we honor three magnificent men, but I know that each of them would want it said that not just these men, but that all the men and women who serve in the Armed Forces, are honored today by this ceremony. Let us always respect the men and women who maintain the strength that keeps us free.

NOTE: The President spoke at 12:55 p.m. at Hickam Air Force Base, Honolulu, Hawaii. He spoke without referring to notes.

Adm. Noel A. M. Gayler, USN, succeeded Admiral McCain as Commander of the Pacific forces.

The President presented the Distinguished Service Medal to Admiral McCain at the ceremony. The citation which accompanied the award read as follows:

The President of the United States takes pleasure in presenting the DISTINGUISHED SERVICE MEDAL (Gold Star in lieu of the Second Award) to

ADMIRAL JOHN S. MC CAIN, JR.
UNITED STATES NAVY

for service as set forth in the following

Citation:

For exceptionally meritorious service to the Government of the United States in a position of great responsibility as Commander in Chief Pacific from July 1968 through August 1972.

Admiral McCain's inspiring personal leadership and consummate strategic direction of military forces in the Pacific Command have contributed substantially toward reducing the conflict in Southeast Asia to a level at which peace and stability are attainable. His rapport with Asian leaders forged a unity of purpose and regional cooperation essential to achieving this goal.

Admiral McCain's perception of national objectives and strategy has been instrumental to implementing the Nixon Doctrine in Pacific-Asia. Further, his foresight and leadership in implementing the significant military adjustments resulting from the application of the Nixon Doctrine, the reversion of Okinawa and the rapidly-changing situation in Southeast Asia have helped perpetuate the United States as the bulwark of peace.

By his historic contribution to American interests in a most difficult period and his unswerving dedication to the ideals and aspirations of his country, Admiral McCain has upheld the highest traditions of the military profession and the United States Naval Service.

RICHARD NIXON

284   Labor Day Message.
September 3, 1972

My fellow Americans:

On this Labor Day, 1972, America's working men and women can be confident that the Nation is on the road to the kind of real prosperity that will last.

For 5 long years—from 1965 to 1970—the American worker was on a treadmill. His paycheck kept going up, but he was no better off. Year after year, wage increases bargained for him by his union or provided by his employer were eaten away by taxes and inflation, the result of too much Government spending in the sixties.

In the past 2 years, however, that picture has changed dramatically for the better.

The real income of the average worker, after all Federal taxes and after inflation, is up a total of 6 percent. The days of the treadmill are over—the average workingman is now making real progress.

More Americans have jobs now than ever before, 2½ million more than a year ago, with new jobs being created at the fastest rate in more than 20 years. As a result, the unemployment rate is lower now than it was last Labor Day. We are not going to be satisfied, however, until we reach our goal—full employment without inflation and without war.

We will reach that goal for two reasons:

First, when it comes to cracking down on prices, this Administration means business. We've already cut inflation in half, and we're not about to let up now. Moreover, we're going to continue to squeeze down on excessive Government spending, which is a root cause of inflation. When Congress passes bills calling for new spending which would lead to higher taxes or higher prices, I shall veto them.

The second reason we're going to achieve a peacetime prosperity is due to the American worker's cooperation in new and better production methods. His productivity has consequently risen strongly in the past year, after years of standing still, and I am convinced it will continue to rise in the years ahead.

With higher productivity, the worker's paycheck will buy more. Our ability to compete more successfully in the world will mean more and better jobs.

There is a way that Government can help keep our "productivity momentum" rolling to the benefit of the worker.

We all know how work stoppages cut into both paychecks and productivity, how strikes often harm both the worker and the economy. Today, we have achieved an era of relative calm on the labor-management front, with work stoppages at a 6-year low. This is the best time for labor, management, and Government to get together and see how we can make an even more regular habit of industrial peace.

I want to see the American worker get all that he deserves. I want to see him get it through the healthy process of free collective bargaining. And I want to see him get it without long and costly strikes that interrupt the workingman's income and sometimes are harmful to all Americans.

I am today announcing the formation of the National Commission for Industrial Peace.

The purpose of this Commission will be to explore ways that labor and management can harmonize their differences at the bargaining table, freely and constructively.

849

I will look to the Commission on Industrial Peace for recommendations in these areas:

— how to improve the process of collective bargaining by the men and women at the bargaining table,

— how Government can be more helpful to the parties in the bargaining process,

— how the interest of the public can be reflected in the outcome as well as in the process of collective bargaining.

It is vital that partisan politics play no role in the work of this Commission. For that reason, I shall wait until after election day before asking leaders of labor and business to serve. In the meantime, I am directing the Secretary of Labor and the Director of the Federal Mediation and Conciliation Service to begin preliminary staff work and consultations immediately.

On this Labor Day, I would like to discuss with you some of the decisions you will be facing this year—decisions that will affect your job, your paycheck, and your future.

Today, this Nation is operating under a system that is rooted in the values that built America:

— We believe that an able-bodied person should earn what he gets and keep most of what he earns. We must stop increases in taxes before they reach the point that the American wage earner is working more for the Government than he is for himself.

— We believe it is wrong for someone on welfare to receive more than someone who works.

— We believe that a person's ability and ambition should determine his income, and that his income should not be redistributed by Government or restricted by some quota system.

— We believe that when Government tampers too much with the lives of individuals, when it unnecessarily butts into the free collective bargaining process, it cripples the private enterprise system on which the welfare of the worker depends.

Because we have held fast to those values, the American worker has a higher standard of living and more freedom than any worker in the world today.

Because we have held fast to those values, the American people have been able to be more compassionate and more generous to the dependent and helpless than any other people in the world.

Now, despite that record of success, and despite the evidence all around us that the new prosperity is reaching into more homes than ever before, those traditional values have come under challenge.

That challenge to our values is serious, and it cannot be ignored. The person whose values are most directly threatened is the American worker, and it is up to the American worker to understand the nature of the challenge and to move strongly to turn it back.

We are faced this year with the choice between the "work ethic" that built this Nation's character and the new "welfare ethic" that could cause that American character to weaken.

Let's compare the two:

The work ethic tells us that there is really no such thing as "something for nothing," and that everything valuable in life requires some striving and some sacrifice. The work ethic holds that it is wrong to expect instant gratification of all our desires, and it is right to expect hard work to earn a just reward. Above all, the work ethic puts responsibility in the hands of the individual, in the belief that self-reliance and willingness to work make a person a better human being.

The welfare ethic, on the other hand, suggests that there is an easier way. It says that the good life can be made available to everyone right now, and that this can be done by the Government. The welfare ethic goes far beyond our proper concern to help people in need. It sees the Government, not the person, as the best judge of what people should do, where they should live, where they should go to school, what kind of jobs they should have, how much income they should be allowed to keep.

The choice before the American worker is clear: The work ethic builds character and self-reliance, the welfare ethic destroys character and leads to a vicious cycle of dependency.

The work ethic builds strong people. The welfare ethic breeds weak people.

This year, you are not only going to choose the kind of leadership you want, you are going to decide what kind of people Americans will be.

Let me give you three specific examples of the difference between the work ethic and the welfare ethic, and how the choice directly affects your life.

The believers in the welfare ethic think it is unfair for some people to have much more income than others. They say we should begin right away to redistribute income, so that we can reduce the number of poor and bring about that day when everybody has much closer to the same income.

I believe that a policy of income redistribution would result in many more Americans becoming poor, because it ignores a human value essential to every worker's success—the incentive of reward.

It's human nature for a person who works hard for a living to want to keep most of what he earns, and to spend what he earns in the way he wants. Now, some may call this work ethic selfish or materialistic, but I think it is natural for a worker to resent seeing a large chunk of his hard-earned wage taken by Government to give to someone else who may even refuse to work.

The people who advocate the welfare ethic spend their time discussing how to cut up the pie we have, but those who believe in the work ethic want to bake a bigger pie, and I'm for baking that bigger pie. That's the kind of people Americans are, and that's the best way to take care of those who cannot care for themselves. Putting a ceiling on the opportunity of those who work is not the way to provide a floor for the support of those who do not work.

Let me give you a second example of the challenge to our traditional values that is being made today.

It shows how well-intentioned people, who believe that a paternal government in Washington can solve everything, can defeat their own good purposes by refusing to recognize the realities of human nature.

I am talking about the involuntary busing of schoolchildren away from their neighborhoods for the purpose of achieving racial balance.

We have come a long way in the past 4 years in ending segregation in this country. Just as important, we have done it without the riots, without the bitterness, without the hatred that plagued this Nation during the sixties. We're getting where we want to go in a way that permits understanding and friendship to grow instead of prejudice and fear.

But that steady progress does not satisfy everyone. The master planners who want more power in a central government believe they know what is best for the welfare of every locality. They fail to see how their zeal sets back the cause of good race relations, of orderly desegregation, and of quality education.

Busing for racial balance is a mistake because it runs counter to a basic American value—the interest of parents in sending their children to a neighborhood school. When an American family thinks of moving to a different home, when they think of buying a house, the first question parents ask is "What are the schools like in this neighborhood?"

And they ask that question because they want the best quality education possible for their children. That's a bedrock interest. You don't run roughshod over that interest in a country that values personal freedom and close family ties.

Our children are America's most priceless national asset. We must not allow them to be used as pawns in the hands of social planners in Washington, many of whom basically believe that children should be raised by the Government rather than by their parents.

That is why I have spoken out so strongly against involuntary busing, and why I am making every effort in the Congress and in the courts to put an end to it.

The ruling of Supreme Court Justice Powell this week clearly demonstrated that the action Congress has taken to limit busing is totally inadequate.[1]

I call on the Congress as a matter of the highest priority, to approve, before it adjourns, the busing moratorium legislation I have proposed.

The Powell decision leaves no doubt whatever that only the anti-busing legislation I have proposed will do the job.

We can make the most progress in race relations not by attacking our basic values, but by supporting them—not by treating people as masses, but as individuals.

A third traditional value that is coming under attack today by the welfare ethic has to do with ability, the great American idea that a person should be able to get ahead in life not on the basis of how he looks or who he knows, but rather on what he can do.

In employment and in politics, we are confronted with the rise of the fixed quota system—as artificial and unfair a yardstick as has ever been used to deny opportunity to anyone.

Again, as in many attacks on basic values, the reasons are often well-intentioned. Quotas are intended to be a shortcut to equal opportunity, but in reality they are a dangerous detour away from the traditional value of measuring a person on the basis of ability.

You cannot have it both ways: You cannot be for quotas in limiting political opportunity and against quotas in limiting economic opportunity.

The basic idea of quotas is anti-ability wherever it is applied. It is just as bad for the voter as it is for the worker.

And so, which way shall it be for America? Shall we become a people who place our individual welfare in the hands of Government bureaucrats, limiting each other's opportunity by race, religion, sex, age, national origin? Or shall we continue to try to erase false restrictions, judging

---

[1] On September 1, 1972, Associate Justice Lewis F. Powell, Jr., in *Ann Gunter Drummond et al.* v. *Robert L. Acree et al.,* denied an application for a stay on a busing order for the Richmond County (Augusta), Ga., school district.

each person by the quality of his work and the reach of his mind?

I say that America, to be true to her highest ideals, must remain on the road that makes way for individual ability.

In every case I have discussed with you today, the difference in approach is not a matter of degree, but a matter of principle. It makes no sense to gloss over the fundamental difference in approach between those who believe in the "good life" under the work ethic, and those who vainly seek the "easy life" under the welfare ethic.

Does the American workingman want to turn over a large part of his economic freedom, including much of his freedom to bargain collectively, to economic theorists who think they can permanently manage the economy with a system all their own?

Does the American workingman want to turn over his power of decision on how he lives his life and spends his earnings to a powerful central government? Does he want to trade away opportunity for the false promise of government security?

Does the American workingman want

his country to become militarily weak and morally soft? That is certainly not in the tradition of American labor.

But the choices must be made. If the workingman does not see the danger, if he decides to sit out this election, the choices will be made without him.

That is why I call upon working men and women across the Nation to make this Labor Day commitment: to understand all that is at stake for them and their families and to make their decision out of a conviction of what is best for themselves and best for all the people of America.

I call upon American labor to speak out and to turn out as it never has before:

—to defend the economic progress it has fought for over the years,

—to move this Nation along the path to full employment without inflation, in a generation of peace, and

—to pass on to our children the respect for the dignity of work that makes a person strong and makes a people great.

NOTE: The message was recorded for use on radio. The President spoke from a prepared text, and a copy of the text was released at San Clemente, Calif.

285 Remarks Following a Meeting With the Citizens' Advisory Committee on Environmental Quality in San Francisco, California. *September 5, 1972*

Ladies and gentlemen:

I will make a brief statement with regard to the meeting in which we have just participated. Then Secretary Morton and Mr. Rumsfeld will brief the members of the press and answer questions on this project which we have been discussing today.

With regard to the Gateway West proj-

ect, it is the companion project for the two that we have been working on over the past 2 years—Gateway East and Gateway West. Between the two of them, 25 million people will have the opportunity to visit park areas. This is part of the program of bringing parks to people, of not having parks just for the sake of parks, but having parks for the sake of people, a major objective of the Legacy of Parks program.

It is interesting to note, too, how this idea was conceived. In the 19th century, the man who conceived the idea of Central Park in the heart of New York City, Frederick Law Olmsted, saw San Francisco, and he envisaged the day when San Francisco would have a great park, of course much larger in size and much more spectacular than Central Park, a man-made park in the heart of the city. And now we have the chance to see this come to fruition.

The committee on environmental concerns, chaired by Mr. Rockefeller—the one who is not the Governor, Laurance Rockefeller—and a distinguished group of people from all over the country, have recommended that we go forward with the Gateway West project. We have moved along as fast as we possibly can. We have had very strong support from Congressman Mailliard, who has been prodding the Congress to act. Fortunately, his House, the House of Representatives, has begun to act. We are stalled in the Senate at the present time, but hope that Senator Jackson, the chairman of the committee who is very interested in this project, will proceed to push it in the Senate.

We would like to get action before the end of this session. We would like to get action also before the end of this session on a number of other environmental legislation proposals that are before the Congress which are totally bipartisan and which, like this one, would get virtually unanimous votes in the Congress if the leadership of the House and the Senate would simply bring them to the floor and let the Congressmen and Senators express their will.

Since these are totally nonpartisan, since they are ones in which people are generally interested, there is simply no excuse for any further Congressional delay either on Gateway East, Gateway West, or the scores of other programs that have to do with the environment that have been before the Congress for, in some cases, 3 years, in some cases, 2 years.

Another point that I would like to make that I think indicates the interest in this particular matter is that on this committee, the committee on the environment, the citizens' committee, we have a number of distinguished people. We have Mr. Lindbergh, who was the man, as we all remember, who symbolizes man's conquest of the air. We have Mr. Borman, who is the man, we all remember, who symbolizes man's conquest of space, the first man, along with his crew, to circle the Moon. And here these two men, one who is known for the conquest of space and another who is known for the conquest of the air, their primary concern at this time in their lives is the quality of life on earth.

It is the fact that people like this, with this type of background, are so dedicated to dealing with this problem gives us high hopes that we can get the Congress to go along with what we believe is the feeling of the majority of the people in this country to improve our natural environment and to make it possible for people in all walks of life, people living in the great cities who can't get, for example, to the great national parks of the West because of lack of financial ability, but to make it possible for them to enjoy the beauties of nature which are here right next to us, here in this area, and in so many other parts of this country.

I will say finally that I have appreciated the opportunity to stop briefly in San Francisco to see again the beauties of this area, and in looking to the future, as to what can be left as a legacy, I would say there is nothing of which we would be more proud in this Administration than to see Gateway West come into reality so that future generations could enjoy the natural beauties of this magnificent area.

Thank you.

NOTE: The President spoke at 1:25 p.m. on board the harbor ferry *Golden Gate* where the meeting with the Committee had been held. He spoke without referring to notes. Following his remarks, the President toured the proposed national recreation area, Gateway West, aboard the *Golden Gate*.

The White House also released a fact sheet on the President's visit to the San Francisco Bay Area and on the Committee.

286 Statement About the Environmental Legislative Program. *September* 5, 1972

THE GOLDEN Gate National Recreation Area—Gateway West—when approved by the Congress, will provide recreational facilities serving an estimated 4.5 million people a year. It will be a key element in our program to provide a Legacy of Parks for the next and future generations.

However, like so much of our needed environmental legislation, Gateway West still awaits Congressional action.

This points up the fact that success in our efforts to restore and renew the American environment depends on cooperation in the partnership between the executive and the legislative branches of the Government. Therefore, let us review the record of how well each branch has performed in this partnership.

Looking first at the executive branch, during this Administration we have increased budget requests for pollution control programs by 400 percent.

While awaiting new legislation from the Congress, we have made use of the Refuse Act of 1899 to provide authority now to crack down on flagrant polluters— and we have increased enforcement actions by 600 percent.

We have named the first Council on Environmental Quality and created the Environmental Protection Agency, to provide strong institutional leadership both in formulating environmental policies and in enforcing environmental standards. I have proposed—but the Congress has not yet approved—creation of a Department of Natural Resources which would complete the needed reorganization for environmental and natural resources programs.

Most important, I have proposed the most comprehensive legislative program in the Nation's history not only to solve the environmental problems of today but also to prevent environmental damage in the future.

In 1970—2½ years ago—I sent a sweeping, 37-point environmental message to the Congress, proposing a wide range of pioneering new legislation to control air and water pollution and to provide more parks and open spaces within reach of urban areas. In 1971 I sent a second major environmental message, again proposing comprehensive water pollution control legislation, which would allow the Nation to achieve clean water without causing inflationary pressures. I also recommended new initiatives to control ocean dumping, pesticides, toxic substances, noise, strip mining, and powerplant siting. In a third major environmental message in 1972 I urged a number of additional measures, including a tax on harmful emissions of sulfur oxides, controls over underground disposal of toxic pollutants and sediment from construction, and a measure to protect endangered species.

These many proposals I have made, if enacted, would provide the authority to protect and preserve our natural environment for decades. But the Congress has failed to perform its part of the partnership. Legislation needed now languishes in the Congress, mired in inaction and jurisdictional squabbles.

Most of my clean water and other environmental proposals have now been before the Congress for over a year and a half, and more than 20 of them are still pending. Every day of inaction sees more of our land despoiled, our water further polluted, noise levels mounting, and harmful substances spreading throughout the environment. The members of the Senate and House are simply not keeping pace with the concern of citizens throughout the Nation for positive action. In some cases, the quality of the environment is taking second place to Senators' concerns over which Senatorial committee has jurisdiction over a particular problem.

Last week, I referred to the wide range of measures that have been "stuck in the mud" of the 92d Congress. This metaphor, unfortunately, is particularly applicable to action on my environmental proposals.

The Congress still has an opportunity to rid itself of this label and to write an historic record of environmental achievement. In the short time left in this Congress, most of these bills can be enacted.

We cannot afford to allow our priceless natural heritage to become a hostage to partisanship. Restoring and protecting the environment is not a Democratic or Republican issue. All Americans recognize the importance of this endeavor.

To the American people, I pledge that the pressures of this political season will in no way diminish my Administration's sense of urgency in environmental action. But the Congress must also fulfill its part of the partnership. I again urge the Congress to act without further delay on these critically needed proposals to protect and restore the American environment.

NOTE: The statement was released at San Francisco, Calif.

On the same day, the White House released a fact sheet on the environmental legislative program.

A White House announcement of the transfer of certain lands to State and local governments for park and recreational use under the Legacy of Parks program and a fact sheet on the property review program were also released. The announcement is printed in the Weekly Compilation of Presidential Documents (vol. 8, p. 1346).

287   Remarks to Reporters About the Assault on Israeli
Athletes at the Olympic Games in Munich,
Germany.   *September* 5, 1972

GENTLEMEN, I had the opportunity this morning before I left San Clemente to call Prime Minister Meir on the phone. I reached her just before we left. I talked with her about 7 or 8 minutes.

I expressed sympathy on behalf of all of the American people for the victims of this murderous action that occurred in the Olympic village in Munich. I also told her that she could expect total cooperation from the Government of the United States in any way that would be helpful in obtaining the release of the hostages.

In addition to that, I raised with her the problem of what we could do in the future in this respect. I asked her whether or not Israeli intelligence had any information with regard to the possibility of this happening. They did not have any information.

Incidentally, Israeli intelligence, we have found, is one of the best in the world. She said that, perhaps, the reason was that while the Olympic Games were being held there in Munich, there just weren't any expectations that this kind of a group would be able to get in and engage in the kind of activities that they have engaged in. However, we are dealing here with international outlaws of the worst sort who will stoop to anything in order to accomplish their goals, and who are totally unpredictable.

Under the circumstances, I said to the Prime Minister that I thought that, looking to the future, we had to anticipate that Israeli citizens traveling abroad would be subjected to such activities in the future. Naturally, we cannot do anything with regard to what happens in other countries—that is their responsibility primarily—except to indicate our interest from the diplomatic standpoint. But I said in the United States that we would try to do everything we could with regard to groups of Israeli citizens traveling in the United States to see that where there is any information at all with regard to a possible attempt of this sort, that adequate security measures are taken.

Finally, as you know, the games, as I understand, are being postponed until the hostages are released and the people who are guilty are apprehended, or those charged with the guilt. There is very little that words can say to indicate the concern we have for the families of the victims. But to have this happen in an international event that has an unblemished record—this being the 20th Olympiad going back over 80 years—an unblemished record of no incidents of this sort, this is indeed a great tragedy, and I know the whole world shares the views that I have expressed to Mrs. Meir.

Q. Are you satisfied about the security of American athletes, particularly American Jewish athletes at the Olympic Games?

THE PRESIDENT. I am never satisfied with security when you see incidents like this, but I believe that we have adequate security measures and, as I have indicated, or at least implied by my remarks here, since we are dealing with international outlaws who are unpredictable, we have to take extra security measures, extra security measures to protect those who might be the targets of this kind of activity in the future. That might include Americans of Israeli background, American citizens. It is more likely to be directed, however, against Israeli citizens, because what they want to do is get leverage with the Israeli Government with regard to people that are held by the Israeli Government. However, we are not taking any chances. We will do everything we can to protect our own citizens, whatever their background.

NOTE: The President spoke at approximately 1 p.m. at the Golden Gate Pier, San Francisco, Calif.

Early in the morning on September 5, 1972,

eight Arab terrorists, members of the Black September group, entered the dormitory which housed the Israeli Olympic athletes, killed two Israelis, and took nine others hostage. After hours of negotiation with German officials, the terrorists and their hostages were flown in three helicopters to nearby Furstenfeldbruck airport where, shortly before midnight, five of the terrorists, all of the hostages, and a German policeman were killed during an exchange of gunfire.

On September 6, the President asked Secretary of State William P. Rogers to meet with Israeli Ambassador Yitzhak Rabin concerning the assault on Israeli Olympic athletes, and also to consult with other governments on an urgent basis to determine what collective measures by the international community could be brought to bear on the problem of terrorism.

288   Message to Prime Minister Golda Meir of Israel About the Deaths of Israeli Athletes at the Olympic Games in Munich, Germany.   *September 6, 1972*

Dear Madame Prime Minister:

The heart of America goes out to you, to the bereaved families and to the Israeli people in the tragedy that has struck your Olympic athletes. This tragic and senseless act is a perversion of all the hopes and aspirations of mankind which the Olympic games symbolize. In a larger sense, it is a tragedy for all the peoples and nations of the world. We mourn with you the deaths of your innocent and brave athletes, and we share with you the determination that the spirit of brotherhood and peace they represented shall in the end persevere.

Sincerely,

RICHARD NIXON

289   Message to the Congress Transmitting Annual Report on Location of New Federal Facilities in Rural Areas.   *September 7, 1972*

To the Congress of the United States:

I am transmitting today the second annual report on the location of new Federal facilities in areas of low population density.

This report describes the second year efforts of all executive departments and agencies with respect to the location of new offices and other facilities in low population density areas as required by the Agricultural Act of 1970. This Administration is committed to both the revitalization of rural America and the maintenance of a sound balance between rural and urban America. This commitment is reflected by the data in this report showing that during the last year more than half of all newly located offices and other facilities have been placed in areas of lower population density.

The philosophy of this administration concerning the location of Federal facilities was expressed in Executive Order 11512 in February of 1970:

> Consideration shall be given in the selection of sites for Federal facilities to the need for development and redevelopment of areas and the development of new communities, and the impact a selection will have on improv-

ing social and economic conditions in that area. . . .

We have since moved to carry out this philosophy through a wide variety of actions. The Agricultural Act of 1970 serves as a further stimulus in the same direction. I am confident that our choice of locations for new offices and facilities is strengthening the balance between rural and urban America.

RICHARD NIXON

The White House,
  September 7, 1972.

NOTE: The 157-page report, entitled "The Second Annual Report on the Location of New Federal Offices and Other Facilities," was prepared within the executive departments and agencies and compiled by the Department of Agriculture for transmittal to the Congress by the President.

290   Memorandum on the 10th Anniversary of the Federal Labor Relations Program. *September 7, 1972*

Memorandum to Heads of Departments and Agencies:

This year the Federal Government marked the tenth anniversary of its labor relations program, which now covers more than one million Federal employees.

I support collective bargaining for Federal workers, and I have demonstrated that support during the past three years by strengthening the program with the issuance of two Executive Orders [11491 and 11616] broadening the scope of bargaining.

Now, at the end of the first decade of this, the largest organized labor relations program in the Nation, I am calling on you to make this program even more ef-

fective. At my request, the Chairman of the U.S. Civil Service Commission and the Director of the Office of Management and Budget have drawn up a set of guidelines for Federal agencies under the Federal labor-management relations program. These guidelines are a solid step forward and should be implemented as quickly as possible.

If we can make this program work better, we can make Government work better.

I cannot urge you too strongly to take a personal interest in the labor relations activities in your agency and to make your managers aware of your interest. You should impress on your top managers that good labor-management relations has a high priority in my Administration. It is as much a part of their overall managerial responsibility as is the accomplishment of their basic mission, whether it be in the defense of our country or in the effective delivery of services to the public.

RICHARD NIXON

NOTE: The memorandum, dated September 6, 1972, was made available to the press September 7.

291 Message to the Congress Transmitting Annual Report on United States Participation in the United Nations. *September 8, 1972*

To the Congress of the United States:

It is a pleasure to transmit to the Congress the 26th annual report on United States participation in the work of the United Nations. This report covers the calendar year 1971.

During the period under review there were many developments within the UN framework of importance to the United States and to other member states. Some of these events were favorable; others were not. Among the former:

—The General Assembly decided to seat the representatives of the People's Republic of China, and this was followed by corresponding action in the Security Council.

—The United Nations established a Fund for Drug Abuse Control that will finance a concerted worldwide action program to assist member states in reducing both the demand for and the supply of dangerous drugs.

—At a plenipotentiary conference in Vienna sponsored by the United Nations, a Convention on Psychotropic Substances was adopted, designed to curb the misuse of such substances as the hallucinogens, amphetamines, barbiturates, and tranquilizers.

—The 26th General Assembly endorsed two treaties, both sponsored by the United States, and expressed its hope for the widest possible adherence to them. The first was the Convention on International Liability for Damage Caused by Space Objects; the second was the Convention on the Prohibition of Development, Production and Stockpiling of Bacteriological (Biological) and Toxin Weapons and on Their Destruction.

—In December the United Nations elected a new Secretary General, Ambassador Kurt Waldheim of Austria.

—At an international conference in Montreal sponsored by the International Civil Aviation Organization, a Convention for the Suppression of Unlawful Acts Against the Safety of Civil Aviation was adopted.

—The UN Economic and Social Council was strengthened by the Assembly's decision to adopt and submit to member states for ratification an amendment to the Charter that will double the Council's membership to 54, thereby making it a more representative body. In addition the Council created two new standing committees, one concerned with review and appraisal of the progress toward the goals of the Second UN Development Decade, and the other concerned with problems of science and technology.

—The United Nations created the position of Disaster Relief Coordinator within the UN Secretariat to assist countries stricken by disasters.

In addition to these favorable developments there were others that were disappointing.

—The Republic of China, a member in good standing for many years, was deprived of representation by the same resolution that gave representation to the People's Republic of China. This action was extremely regrettable and was strongly opposed by the United States.

—Despite determined efforts by the United States and others, the war between India and Pakistan demonstrated again the severe limitations on the organization's ability to carry out its primary function, the maintenance of international peace and security.

—No progress was made toward resolving the differences among UN members on the organization and conduct of peace-keeping missions.

—The General Assembly's effort to rationalize its organization and procedures fell far short of our hopes.

—The United Nations made no great progress toward resolving its difficult financial problems.

During 1971 the United States Government announced its intention to negotiate a reduction in the rate of its UN assessment to a level no higher than 25 percent. This decision is in line with a recommendation by the Commission for the Observance of the 25th Anniversary of the United Nations, chaired by Ambassador Henry Cabot Lodge, and is consonant with our belief that an organization of almost universal membership should not be overly dependent upon a single member for its financial support.

This proposed reduction in our rate of assessment does not affect our voluntary contributions to various UN programs. Indeed, the Lodge Commission recommended increases of at least corresponding size in voluntary contributions whose size depends on each nation's judgment of its own interests and capabilities.

These and many other topics are covered in the report. I commend to the Congress this record of our participation in the United Nations during 1971.

RICHARD NIXON

The White House,
September 8, 1972.

NOTE: The message is printed in the report entitled "U.S. Participation in the UN, Report by the President to the Congress for the Year 1971" (Government Printing Office, 238 pp.).

292 Statement for the Jewish High Holy Days. *September 8, 1972*

THE SPIRIT of self-examination and moral rededication in which fellow citizens of the Jewish Faith across the country observe the High Holy Days is one from which all of us can draw courage and inspiration. It is the spirit on which the greatness of the Jewish people has been built. And it is also the spirit in which America's greatness has flourished.

So as we send greetings to our Jewish friends on the coming of a New Year in their calendar, it is well that we reaffirm the ethical principles and traditional values we so proudly share. As we ponder the message of these solemn religious days, we are reminded of the dynamic leadership which Jews have always displayed in man's struggle for freedom,

human dignity and justice. And we find sustenance and strength not only in the significance of their beliefs, but in the substance of their deeds.

May the New Year bring our fellow Americans of the Jewish Faith nearer to the fulfillment of their individual hopes, and may it bring the world a just and lasting peace.

RICHARD NIXON

NOTE: The statement was made available to the press.

293   Remarks on Presenting Federal Funds to Wilkes College for Repair of Damage Caused by Tropical Storm Agnes.   *September 9, 1972*

Dr. Michelini, Mr. Carlucci, ladies and gentlemen:

I am very happy that the first opportunity to say anything in Wilkes-Barre is at this small college. If I can speak in personal terms, I took my law at Duke University, one of the larger universities in the country, a very fine one. I took my undergraduate work at a small college, Whittier College, about the size of Wilkes College. Both were great experiences. Both the large universities and the smaller colleges serve a very, very important purpose in our educational system.

The point is that we need both. So often people think only of, and they make contributions and the rest to, the large universities who naturally have lots more publicity and consequently attract much more funds.

I have found in studying the situation within the past 4 years that small colleges across this country are having an increasingly difficult time, apart from any floods, apart from anything else, because costs are going up and contributions many

times are not coming in to the extent that they should. This action here, this check, I should make clear, is not from the President of the United States or Frank Carlucci; it is from all the people of the United States to this small college. But it indicates our feelings that the small college in America contributes something that is very much worth preserving, that we need. It contributes a spirit where the faculty and the students work together to build a better institution and a better community.

So, we say we know the money will be well spent. The dollars that come to this small college will probably go further than the dollars that would go to a large university. You need it more. You know what it means. You are going to spend it well, and the beneficiaries will be all these wonderful young people I have seen as I have traveled through the streets of Wilkes-Barre here today.

We wish you well. We wish your college well in all the years ahead, and we will continue to do everything that we can to keep the interests of the small college up front as well as, of course, the interests of the large universities, both of which deserve our support.

NOTE: The President spoke at approximately

1:15 p.m. at Wilkes College, Wilkes-Barre, Pa. He spoke without referring to notes.

Francis J. Michelini was president of the college. Frank C. Carlucci, Deputy Director, Office of Management and Budget, coordinated Federal disaster relief activities in Pennsylvania.

294   Remarks in Kingston, Pennsylvania, Following Inspection of Damage Caused by Tropical Storm Agnes. *September* 9, 1972

I APPRECIATE the opportunity to meet so many of you on this visit to Wilkes-Barre, and also to express appreciation to those in government who are working here and particularly to Frank Carlucci, who symbolizes the Government effort.

He came, of course, from Wilkes-Barre. He is a strong man. He is a very intelligent man and he cares about people. I think what I like about his effort most of all is that he has personalized the Government.

You know, you usually think of the Government and all that money that it has and all the agencies—there is HUD, and then there is HEW, and all those initials. But in Frank Carlucci you see a man who cares. He talks to every individual person. That is what we want your Government to be, one that cares about each of you individually.

Now, I also realize that as we look at this effort here that a lot remains to be done. This has been a devastating flood. I saw what happened in Harrisburg when I visited right after the floods. I have had an opportunity to see what the situation is here, months after the floods have occurred. I know that as I drove through the business district and through the residential district that so many places of business, so many houses, still remain to

be rebuilt. And as a result many are living in these Government facilities, the trailers, the mobile homes that we have just looked at.

Let me just give one thought to the people here, perhaps from a bigger viewpoint. Sometimes when something terrible happens in your life, your home is washed away or something like that, you tend to just think about your own problems and you lose sight of the bigger picture. You lose your spirit and you lose your hope. The most important thing as far as Wilkes-Barre, Kingston, all these areas are concerned, is what you feel in your hearts about your future and the future of your town and the future of your State and the future of your country.

I have seen a lot of devastation in my travels around the world. For example, we all have heard of San Francisco as being one of the most beautiful cities in the world. In fact, foreign diplomats, they all want to go to San Francisco, the most beautiful city. Yet, it was only 60 years ago that San Francisco was almost totally destroyed by an earthquake and a fire. Then they rebuilt it and they rebuilt it until it was more beautiful than ever. Today everybody goes to San Francisco to see that beautiful city.

It isn't just in America that you see

that. Rotterdam, for example, was a city that was almost totally destroyed by bombs, and there was only one building in the center of the town where the few that were left on the council of the city got together and talked not about the destruction, but how they were going to rebuild the city. Today it is one of the most beautiful cities in Europe, but rebuilt from the ground up. All of the old that should probably have been replaced now has been replaced with something new, something better.

I was in Kiev, Russia, down in the Ukraine. You watched the Olympics. You know some of the great runners, the athletes, came from the Ukraine. They are very proud there that after that city was almost totally destroyed in World War II they rebuilt it better than ever.

I wondered when I came up to Wilkes-Barre—I wondered, of course, whether Carlucci was doing a good job—I know he is. I wondered whether or not we were providing the money that we should and I know we are providing a great deal, and of course we will provide what is necessary, what we can. I wondered, too, whether the Federal agencies were working together rather than against each other. Due to Carlucci they are working together and they are not fighting each other; they are fighting the problem. That is what government is supposed to do.

But the thing that I wondered about the most was whether the people of Wilkes-Barre had the spirit of the people of San Francisco, the spirit of the people of Rotterdam, the people of Kiev. And I think I saw it.

This is something that I want to leave with all of you. What impressed me as I drove through—I saw the people, I have met you, I see the smiles on your faces,

I see the courage of the young and the old—but what really impressed me was to see a house almost totally destroyed and a flag on it, an American flag flying there high in the breeze. That tells us something about America.

You wonder, of course, about this kind of a visit. I know that many of the people were very kind. They said, "Thank you for coming, you have made us feel better." I want you to know that you have made me feel better. I have never been so proud of America and of the American people as I am today. You are great people. We appreciate what you have done for the spirit of Wilkes-Barre, the spirit of this country.

In that connection, I would simply close by saying that as I went by the Paramount Theatre I saw a sign on it, a wonderful sign. It says, "We will be opening soon with a brand new look." That is going to be Wilkes-Barre. Wilkes-Barre is going to be cleaned up. It is going to be opened up. It is going to have a brand new look. It is going to be better than ever. But it is going to be better than ever not because of what government did—we can help—but it is going to be better than ever because of what you did, what you believe in, your faith, your spirit. You are going to make it better than ever, and we are going to help you.

Thank you very much.

NOTE: The President spoke at approximately 2:15 p.m. at Scanlon Field Mobile Home Park. He spoke without referring to notes.

Prior to the President's departure for Wilkes-Barre, Frank C. Carlucci, Deputy Director, Office of Management and Budget, met with him at Camp David, Md., to report on Federal disaster assistance in Wilkes-Barre and other areas of Pennsylvania following Tropical Storm Agnes.

On the same day, the White House released

the text of a memorandum to the President from Mr. Carlucci on disaster recovery efforts in Wyoming Valley, Pa. The memorandum is printed in the Weekly Compilation of Presi-

dential Documents (vol. 8, p. 1353). The White House also released a fact sheet on Tropical Storm Agnes recovery efforts.

295   Message to the Congress Transmitting Annual Report on the Federal Ocean Program.
September 11, 1972

To the Congress of the United States:

It is with pleasure that I transmit today the report of the Federal Ocean Program. It has been a year of significant accomplishments and continued evolution of new directions to know, conserve, and use the sea.

A most important characteristic of our maturing ocean program is that we are increasingly viewing our efforts in the marine environment from the fresh perspectives illuminated by our need for its abundant resources and by the necessity to search carefully into the consequences of our actions in its development. We must insure the proper balance of these through measures which are compatible with the long-term maintenance of a healthy marine environment.

During 1971, strong emphasis was placed on improvements in the management of our marine living and nonliving resources, on easing pressures which threaten certain species with extinction, and on enforcement of measures to prevent environmental pollution and degradation. We have stepped up our studies of the ways in which we must manage our coastal zones to protect our fisheries, to make them available for marine transportation, to minimize pollution, and to enhance their recreational values. I have recommended legislation to establish national land use policy programs which include priority provisions for coastal zone management.

Further, in view of our increasing concern with energy supplies to sustain the Nation's economic growth and the health and well-being of our people, the Federal Ocean Program moved to explore the geophysical and geological character of our continental shelves. It should be recorded that 1971 was the year in which the Federal Government began to move vigorously to map and chart these promising submerged lands and their resource potential.

A major share of the Federal Ocean Program continued to support vital national defense objectives related to operations in the marine environment. Nevertheless, the major program increases of the past few years and those for the coming year are in the civil sector. Among the important accomplishments have been the increasing momentum to provide the operational capability for man to do useful work beneath the sea through application of research submersibles and laboratory habitats; the development of a system for the asesssment of the abundance and distribution of harvestable living marine resources; and the designation of the first four Sea Grant Colleges.

Our efforts to explore the marine environment have been increasingly characterized by the trend toward major

865

large-scale studies conducted by Federal agencies in national programs such as the Marine Ecosystems Analysis study of the New York Bight, and with other nations in international programs, such as the International Field Year for the Great Lakes and the International Decade of Ocean Exploration. In these, we are moving out to the ocean "laboratories" with arrays of ships, specially designed buoys, aircraft, earth-orbiting satellites, and submersibles to apply collective efforts to solve special problems and to advance knowledge and understanding.

I am pleased to report, also, the continued strengthening of Federal ties, both in scope and level of activity, with industry, state and local governments, and universities. I consider this a most essential aspect underlying our marine programs. As I have stated in the past, private industry, state and local governments,

scientific and other institutions must increase their own efforts if we are to continue our headway toward solving the myriad of marine problems.

My budget request for the Fiscal Year 1973 provides $672 million in support of our programs in marine science, engineering, and services, an increase of more than $60 million over last year's request. This budget will enable us to continue our advances in all areas of importance to our vital and increasing national interest in the seas.

RICHARD NIXON

The White House,
September 11, 1972.

NOTE: The message is printed in the report entitled "The Federal Ocean Program: The Annual Report of the President to the Congress on the Nation's Efforts to Comprehend, Conserve, and Use the Sea—April 1972" (Government Printing Office, 121 pp.).

296   Message to the Senate Transmitting the Patent Cooperation Treaty.   *September* 12, 1972

To the Senate of the United States:

With a view to receiving the advice and consent of the Senate to ratification, I transmit herewith a copy of the Patent Cooperation Treaty, signed at Washington on June 19, 1970, together with the Regulations under the Patent Cooperation Treaty annexed thereto. I transmit also, for the information of the Senate, the report from the Department of State with respect to the Treaty.

The Patent Cooperation Treaty offers several major advantages. One is to simplify the filing of patent applications on the same invention in different countries by providing, among other things,

centralized filing procedures and a standardized application format.

Another advantage offered by the Treaty is the longer period of time available to an applicant before he must commit himself by undertaking the expenses of translation, national filing fees and prosecution in each country. Today, a twelve month priority period is provided by the Paris Convention for the Protection of Industrial Property, while under the Patent Cooperation Treaty an applicant will have generally twenty months or more. This advantage should permit the applicant to be more selective of the countries in which he ultimately decides to file, by giving him more time and information to evaluate the strength of his potential patent and to determine his marketing plans. Thus, this Treaty would serve to expand established programs of industry to file foreign patent applications as well as to encourage smaller businesses and individual inventors to become more actively engaged in seeking patent protection abroad.

A third advantage is to facilitate the examining process in those member countries which examine applications for patents.

In order to carry out the provisions of the Treaty, proposed implementing legislation will be forwarded to the Congress in the near future.

I recommend that the Senate give early and favorable consideration to the Treaty submitted herewith and give its advice and consent to ratification subject to three of the declarations for which provision is made in the Convention under Article 64, paragraphs (1)(a), (3)(a), and (4)(a), respectively, as explained in the report from the Department of State.

RICHARD NIXON

The White House,
  September 12, 1972.

NOTE: The text of the treaty and the report of the Secretary of State are printed in Senate Executive S (92d Cong., 2d sess.).

297   Message to the Congress Transmitting Annual Reports on Highway, Traffic, and Motor Vehicle Safety Programs. *September* 13, 1972

To the Congress of the United States:

This Administration has serious and growing concerns about the tragic number of traffic accidents that each year exact a heavy toll in human life and suffering and economic loss in our society.

Nearly half of the 115,000 annual accidental deaths in America are due to transportation accidents, and regrettably most of the transportation accidents occur on our streets and highways.

To these 55,000 annual traffic deaths must be added the nearly four million injured each year in traffic accidents. Many of the injured suffer permanent disabilities.

The traffic death and injury toll is alarming enough. But when we add to this the $46 billion annual drain on our economy from lost wages, medical expenses, legal fees, insurance payments, home and family care, and other expenses, we realize that we must do more to cut our human and economic losses.

The Federal Government is providing leadership and some financial assistance to reduce the losses. And much has been done by States, communities, industry and private organizations. But we must all resolve to do even more to cut this tragic waste of human life and economic drain.

The Reports of the National Highway Traffic Safety Administration transmitted with this letter have been prepared in accordance with the Highway Safety Act of 1966, as amended, and with the National Traffic and Motor Vehicle Safety Act of 1966, as amended. They describe basic causes and effects of this problem and efforts of Federal, State and local governments to alleviate it.

Much progress has been made in recent years. For example, the rate of death per 100 million vehicle miles driven has declined from 5.5 in 1967 to 4.7 in 1971. This is an annual decrease of 3.85 percent and a five-year decrease of 14.55 percent. Had the old rate continued, 65,000 persons would have died in traffic accidents in 1971, 10,000 more than the actual number. We can also take some comfort that traffic deaths have decreased in spite of the fact that we now have more cars, more drivers, more cyclists and more pedestrians on our roads.

But progress is no cause for complacency. We must work even harder to make our highways and cars safer, to educate drivers and pedestrians and to clear our roads of drunken drivers, who are the cause of approximately half the traffic deaths each year.

The three volumes of these reports taken together map our progress in this important area, and I hope they will be read closely by Members of the Congress. Your continued support will be required to back up our national commitment to make our highways and vehicles safer for all Americans.

RICHARD NIXON

The White House,
   September 13, 1972.

NOTE: The reports are entitled:

"Safety '71, A Report on Activities of the National Highway Traffic Safety Administration and the Federal Highway Administration Under the Highway Safety Act of 1966 and the National Traffic and Motor Vehicle Safety Act of 1966" (Government Printing Office, 72 pp.).

"Safety '71, A Report on Activities Under the Highway Safety Act" (Government Printing Office, 77 pp. plus appendixes).

"Safety '71, A Report on Activities Under the National Traffic and Motor Vehicle Safety Act" (Government Printing Office, 83 pp. plus appendixes).

298   Memorandum About Age Discrimination in Federal Employment.   *September 13, 1972*

Memorandum for Heads of Departments and Agencies:

For many years, the Federal Government has been fighting against discrimination in employment. On the basis of age, creed, ethnic origin, sex or skin color, discrimination is an intolerable wrong. As discrimination is an affront to our society, it cannot be countenanced in our government.

In my message to the Congress earlier this year transmitting this Administration's recommendations for action on behalf of older Americans, I stressed the importance of giving serious attention to the problems of our older citizens. One such problem is age discrimination. As the largest employer in the Nation, the Government has a special responsibility to take the lead in eradicating age discrimination from the world of employment.

It is appropriate, at this time, to reaffirm our commitment to the long-standing policy of the Federal Government that age, by itself, shall be no bar to a Federal job which an individual is otherwise qualified to perform. In doing so, I want to emphasize that our older Americans possess talents, experience, and skills which the Government needs and which our older citizens deserve the chance to contribute.

I call upon each of you to review your agency's programs to make sure that the skills and experience of our older citizens are being effectively utilized. I also ask that you review your agency's employment practices and take immediate steps to eliminate any which may directly or indirectly stand as a barrier to equal opportunity for older persons. We must not tolerate any practice that denies older citizens fair and full consideration for employment and advancement in the Federal service.

RICHARD NIXON

NOTE: The memorandum was posted for the press.

299   Message to the Congress Transmitting the Cost of Living Council's Quarterly Report on the Economic Stabilization Program. *September* 13, 1972

To the Congress of the United States:

In accordance with Section 216 of the Economic Stabilization Act Amendments of 1971, I am transmitting with this the Cost of Living Council's third quarterly report on the Economic Stabilization Program covering the period April 1 through June 30, 1972.

The report reflects the significant progress which the country is continuing to make toward the joint goals of reducing the rate of inflation and restoring vigorous health to the economy:

1. In the battle against inflation, the annual rate of increase in consumer prices has been cut to 2.9 percent since I announced the New Economic Policy on August 15, 1971. During the same period, real spendable weekly earnings have increased at an annual rate of 3.8 percent.

2. The recovery which the economy is experiencing is evidenced by nearly all of the key economic indicators. Last quarter's real GNP grew at an annual rate of 9.4 percent, the greatest increase in seven years. Productivity increased at a 6 percent annual rate in the second quarter of 1972, with an accompanying decline in unit labor costs. Employment has increased by 2.6 million workers since the program began, and the rate of unemployment has declined moderately.

While this encouraging progress has resulted from the interaction of many economic factors, the temporary wage and price controls of the Economic Stabilization Program have played an important role in maintaining price stability during a period of rapid expansion. The disciplines of the controls program, together with responsible fiscal and monetary policies and the continued support and cooperation of the private sector, can enable us to move into a new era of unprecedented prosperity for all Americans.

RICHARD NIXON

The White House,
    September 13, 1972.

NOTE: The report, covering the period April 1 through June 30, 1972, is entitled "Economic Stabilization Program Quarterly Report—Cost of Living Council" (Government Printing Office, 49 pp.).

300 Message to the Senate Transmitting Convention for the Suppression of Unlawful Acts Against the Safety of Civil Aviation. *September 15, 1972*

To the Senate of the United States:

With a view to receiving the advice and consent of the Senate to ratification, I transmit herewith a copy of the Convention for the Suppression of Unlawful Acts Against the Safety of Civil Aviation, signed at Montreal on September 23, 1971. The report of the Department of State with respect to the Convention is also transmitted for the information of the Senate.

The problem of sabotage, armed terrorist attacks, and other criminal acts against aircraft and air travelers poses an increasingly grave threat to civil aviation around the world. Events have shown that no country or area is exempt from the human tragedy and immense costs which result from such criminal acts.

At the International Conference on Air Law at The Hague in December of 1970, the Hijacking Convention was adopted. It contains provisions to ensure that all hijackers, wherever found, would be subject to severe punishment. The United States and 39 other countries have now ratified that Convention. It is hoped that all States will join in this major step to deter the peril of air piracy.

The work of applying similar provisions to other acts directed against the safety of civil aviation was completed by the Diplomatic Conference at Montreal in September 1971. The Convention which that Conference produced and which I am transmitting today covers sabotage and other criminal acts. Like the Hijacking Convention, it requires States to extradite offenders or prosecute them where they are found. It is designed to ensure the prosecution of saboteurs and other terrorists who attack aircraft, and it can help serve to quell this increasingly serious problem for civil aviation worldwide.

This Convention and the Hijacking Convention are vitally important to achieve safe and orderly air transportation for all people of the world. I hope all States will become Parties to these Conventions, and that they will be applied universally. I recommend, therefore, that the Senate give early and favorable consideration to this Convention.

RICHARD NIXON

The White House,
    September 15, 1972.

NOTE: The text of the convention and the report of the Secretary of State are printed in Senate Executive T (92d Cong., 2d sess.).

301 Remarks in Mitchellville, Maryland. *September 17, 1972*

Father Donanzan and all of those who are attending this wonderful picnic here so very close to Washington and so very close to the heart of America:

I want to say that it is a very great privilege for me to have the opportunity on this Sunday afternoon to come to an event which tells us so much about the strength of our country. I know you are having a wonderful time. I went by some of the food shops. I just had lunch. I'll have to take some home to eat tonight at the White House.

I know, too, that you realize that this serves a very good cause, this home for some of our senior citizens and also the church in Washington which supports it.

But I would like to speak very briefly to you about what you and those of Italian background have meant to America and what you make it possible for America to mean to the world.

Just a moment ago I met the leader of this band. He told me a very interesting thing. He said that almost all the members of this orchestra are from the Army and the Marines and the Navy—they generally are in the Army and the Marines and the Navy, but here, they are joining in this band at this Italian event.

Now, that tells us something, of course, about Italians generally, their great sense of music and love of music. Anybody who has been to Italy, as I have been so many times, knows this. Anybody who has been to an Italian affair knows it. But perhaps you did not know that the President's official band, or orchestra, in the White House, is the Marine Band. The way it was set up, the way it was gotten together, was in the very early days of this country when Thomas Jefferson was trying to find a suitable orchestra, or band, for the White House. He couldn't find it among those in the Colonies at that time, and so he sent off to Italy and got some Italians to come over and they formed the nucleus of the band. But you all know the contribution in the field of music.

You have had an opportunity today to see something in the field of government.

I am very proud that one of the most outstanding members of our Cabinet is John Volpe, the former Governor of Massachusetts. And with the record of Italians in discovering this country, as travelers, naturally he is in charge of transportation, and he is taking us a long way, I can assure you.

I, too, want to pay my respects to John Scali. As a matter of fact, he was the one that delivered the invitation. John Scali is a member of our White House Staff. And he has traveled with me all over the world, when he was a reporter for one of the television networks. You wonder how anybody in a television network got to work for the White House Staff. Well, I can assure you that he is one of the very best, and he does a fine job representing the great profession of the news media and also for the President of the United States.

And then, too, on such an occasion as this, I would like to refer to a lot of others. I was trying to think if I could claim any Italian background. All I can say is this: Every time I have been in Italy and every time I attend an Italian picnic, I think I have some Italian blood, I can assure you of that.

And Larry Hogan, the Congressman from this district, told me the same thing as we were walking up here.

Let me just put this in one very nonpolitical sense, which I know all of you will appreciate. Many years ago—it was 1956, as a matter of fact—I went to the border of Hungary to help receive the Hungarians, the young Hungarians who were fleeing from the Communist Government, crossing into Austria. It was Christmastime. It was a very desperate time. And about 150,000, you will remember, came across that border, and many of them were received in the United States. And at that time, many people in the United States, shortsighted people, said, "This is a bad thing, because all of these new immigrants are going to make it harder for us to get jobs, it is going to make it more difficult for us to build the kind of a country we want."

The man who, at the very late years of his life, was put in charge of that program was Herbert Hoover—Herbert Hoover, who went back many, many years, who had handled refugees for many years. I asked him about that charge that had been made, and this is what he said. He said: "I have studied the whole history of America and of all of those people that have made America. And every new group of people who come from a country abroad to the United States make America richer, because they help build America, they bring a more diverse culture to America, they bring music, they bring culture, they bring religion, they bring strength." I think that we can say that about every group, but I can certainly say it about those who are proud of their Italian-American background.

Let me tell you what I know about you and what you have contributed, some things that are so characteristic of your homes, your communities, your families. First, when you run into an Italian-American community you will find that there is a strong sense of patriotism. Oh, they are proud of their Italian background, but they are proud first to be Americans all the way.

And in our armed services there is no group in this country that has a finer record of volunteering and serving courageously than those of Italian back-

ground. And we are proud of that.

Second, those of Italian background are builders. I don't say that just because John Volpe is a builder and a contractor, but I say it because all over this land they have a marvelous record of working hard, they believe in hard work, they believe in earning what they get. And that is something that builds America.

And there is something else they add—the people of Italian background—as this event here today demonstrates, they have a deep religious sense, they have a loyalty to their church and to their community, which helps their church and their community and their Nation as well.

And then finally—and this is the last point and it tells us a lot about this event—they love their families, their children, and also their parents and the older people, like the people who are living in this home. And that is the final message I would leave with all of you today.

This is a time when we naturally are thinking of the future, of our young people. We want them to have a better life than we have had, but let's always remember that what we have today wouldn't be here if a lot of people hadn't come to America, hadn't worked hard and built America. Let's give our older people, our mothers and our fathers and our grandparents, the respect that they deserve and the honor that they deserve.

And now with all that, I have been trying to think of something that I could say in conclusion. I know a few Spanish words. I know even a few Russian words. Whenever I travel in Italy I pick up a few Italian words, but if the pronunciation is wrong, you blame John Volpe, not me. *Grazie à tutti.* [Thank you all.]

NOTE: The President spoke at 3:20 p.m. at the Villa Rosa Rest Home, where the 12th annual Italian Fall Festival was being held to benefit the home and Holy Rosary Church in Washington, D.C. He spoke without referring to notes.

Rev. Caesar Donanzan was pastor of the church.

302   Remarks to the Washington Conference on International Narcotics Control.
September 18, 1972

Mr. Secretary, and ladies and gentlemen:

As I look over the guest list for this Conference, I realize that most of you have been attending conferences all of your official lives and I suppose that when you come to another conference you wonder how this one is different, whether this one is any more important than all the others.

I simply want to say at the outset that I consider this Conference to be as important as any that any one of you has ever attended. I consider it certainly as important as any I have ever attended since the period I have been in public life, because winning the battle against drug abuse is one of the most important, the most urgent national priorities confronting the United States today.

As President of the United States, I feel that I bear no more solemn trust than to help to win this battle, and as public officials, everybody in this room, people who represent America in this country and all over the world, you could not be engaged in a finer humanitarian cause than in winning this battle against drug abuse.

As we all know, the global drug problem is enormously difficult. It doesn't lend itself to immediate or simplistic solutions. Nevertheless, looking back over the 3 years since I declared total war on drug abuse and labeled it America's public enemy number one, I think the depth of our national commitment is clear. Our total Federal funding for this effort has increased 11 times over what it was in 1969. It is up to almost three-quarters of a billion dollars of the budget currently pending in the Congress.

From an organizational standpoint, we have mobilized to meet this problem on all fronts. We have set up a Special Action Office for Drug Abuse Prevention to direct the treatment and rehabilitation work under Dr. [Jerome H.] Jaffe. We have also set up in the Department of Justice a new Office for Drug Abuse Law Enforcement to attack domestic distribution and pushers. And I have named a Cabinet Committee on International Narcotics Control which coordinates our worldwide campaign to cut off the sources of supply.

Here we are attacking the problem therefore on all fronts in the most effective way that we can through our various Government agencies.

I also have assumed some personal responsibilities. I have been deliberately cracking the whip, as many of you in this room know, in my personal supervision of this program, and I will have to admit that we have knocked some bureaucratic heads together because of my directive, which I gave in the East Room 2 years ago, that Government agencies should quit fighting each other about this problem and start fighting the problem.

I wanted to see some solid results coming through in terms of saving the lives of thousands of young people who otherwise would have become hopeless drug addicts. And now we can look at some of the results. We can view them not with complacency, but with some pride and also with the determination to go forward to get even better results in the future.

Dr. Jaffe, in his field, reports that we have created more federally funded drug treatment capacity in the past year than in the 50 years before that. We now have the capability to treat over 100,000 drug addicts in these programs.

If the Congress approves the pending drug funding request, we should have the capacity, if needed, to treat a quarter of a million heroin addicts in America by this time next year.

Now that, of course, is a sobering number—the fact that we might need the capacity to treat a quarter of a million indicates the enormity of the problem and the need to work on it, not only on the treatment area but also particularly in the source of the supply and in the enforcement area.

Turning to the law enforcement area, the number of arrests of drug traffickers in this last fiscal year was double the number in 1969. The seizures of heroin and other illicit drugs are at an alltime high. But as I have told those who have reported to me just within the last month on this, this isn't good enough. We have to double the number, triple the number, and go from there to a complete victory over those who are engaged in this illicit trade.

Very sharp recent increases in the prices of heroin throughout the eastern United States indicate that the supply is drying up and that the pressure is on the criminal drug trade. And I can assure all of you, and I can assure those who may be the subject of those who might be prosecuted, that we are going to keep the heat on until the despicable profiteers in human misery are driven out of their hiding places and are put in prison where they belong. Nor will this effort stop at our own borders.

The men and women who operate the global heroin trade are a menace not to Americans alone, but to all mankind. These people are literally the slave traders of our time. They are traffickers in living death. They must be hunted to the end of the earth. They must be left no base in any nation for their operations. They must be permitted not a single hiding place or refuge from justice anywhere in the world, and that is why we have established an aggressive international narcotics control program in cooperation with the governments of more than 50 countries around the world. That is why I have ordered the Central Intelligence Agency, early in this Administration, to mobilize its full resources to fight the international drug trade, a task, incidentally, in which it has performed superbly.

Let me interject here a word for that much maligned agency. As I have often said, in the field of intelligence we always find that the failures are those that are publicized. Its successes, by definition, must always be secret, and in this area there are many successes and particularly ones for which this agency can be very proud.

The key priority here is to target on the traffickers wherever they are, to immobilize and destroy them through our law enforcement and intelligence efforts. And I commend all of you on the fine initial progress which has been made in these programs.

France, Paraguay, Laos, Thailand,

Turkey are just a few examples of the many countries where the work of American officials, from the ambassadors down, throughout the embassies abroad, in partnership with local officials, has produced important breakthroughs—huge heroin seizures, key arrests, and, in the case of Turkey, the courageous decision to eradicate the opium poppy itself. And that action, incidentally, is a great tribute not only to that Government but to our own Government and particularly to those in the State Department and in the Embassy in Turkey who worked on this problem.

The people of the United States, especially the young people, are profoundly indebted to you, all of you in this room, most of whom I will not have a chance to meet personally, to thank personally for what you have worked on and what you have done. And yet, we have to do a lot more, as you all know, to win this war, and we must do it with even more of a sense of urgency than in the past.

In working on narcotics control around the world, I want you to convey this personal message from me to the foreign officials with whom you may be meeting. Any government whose leaders participate in or protect the activities of those who contribute to our drug problem should know that the President of the United States is required by statute to suspend all American economic and military assistance to such a regime, and I shall not hesitate to comply with that law where there are any violations.

I consider keeping dangerous drugs out of the United States just as important as keeping armed enemy forces from landing in the United States. Dangerous drugs which come into the United States can endanger the lives of young Americans just as much as would an invading army landing in the United States. Every government which wants to move against narcotics should know that it can count on this country for our wholehearted support and assistance in doing so.

Three years ago, the global heroin plague was raging almost completely out of control all over the world; time was running out for an entire generation of our children, the potential drug victims of the next few years.

But then we launched our crusade to save our children and now we can see that crusade moving off the defensive on to the offensive, and beginning to roll up some victories in country after country around the world and in the United States as well.

And what is our goal now? We are living in an age, as we all know, in the era of diplomacy, when there are times that a great nation must engage in what is called a limited war. I have rejected that principle in declaring total war against dangerous drugs.

Our goal is the unconditional surrender of the merchants of death who traffic in heroin. Our goal is the total banishment of drug abuse from American life. Our children's lives are what we are fighting for. Our children's future is the reason we must succeed.

We are going to fight this evil with every weapon at our command, and, with your help and the support of millions of concerned Americans, we are going to win.

NOTE: The President spoke at 9:58 a.m. in the West Auditorium at the Department of State. The President spoke from a prepared text.

An advance text of his remarks was released on the same day.

The 3-day Conference, convened by Secretary of State William P. Rogers, Chairman, Cabinet Committee on International Narcotics Control, was attended by some 60 senior U.S. narcotics control officials from U.S. embassies abroad, and Federal officials in Washington, D.C., with responsibility for narcotics control.

303   Message to the Congress Transmitting Annual Report on the Foreign Assistance Program. *September* 19, 1972

To the Congress of the United States:

The fiscal 1971 Annual Report on the Foreign Assistance Program, which I transmit herewith, contains much hopeful news.

—The continuing success of the Green Revolution was evident in record crops of food grains, moving such countries as India, Pakistan, Turkey, and Indonesia steadily closer to a goal of self-sufficiency in basic foodstuffs and giving hope to others that this goal, considered inconceivable a few short years ago, can now be attained.

—Modern technologies in education are being explored with a view toward reducing the heavy cost of education, expanding its availability and improving its quality.

—Pilot projects for improving the delivery of health services in remote rural areas offer great promise.

—Support provided by the Agency for International Development for population-related efforts rose to a record $95.9 million, as developing countries, recognizing the heavy burden of high population growth rates, intensified their programs to achieve effective family planning.

—Developing nations showed increasing awareness of the environmental impact of proposed projects in their national planning process.

During the past fiscal year, the United States Government provided $3.4 billion in economic assistance to the less developed world. This aid took a variety of forms—technical assistance, development loans, financial grants, concessional sales of agricultural products, emergency relief, and contributions to international lending institutions as well as to the United Nations Development Program, and other UN-related activities. Just over half the total—$1.9 billion—was authorized by the Foreign Assistance Act and administered by the Agency for International Development. This report is essentially concerned with these programs.

Viewed in the perspective of the past decade, the less developed nations have made excellent progress. Their annual rate of economic expansion—averaging about 5.6 percent—exceeded even the five percent target projected by the United Nations for the Decade of Development that ended in 1970, reaching a level of more than six percent per year in the last years of the decade. This pace is more rapid than the growth rate of the United

States at comparable stages of its development.

A major factor contributing to this record growth has been the increasing availability to lower income countries of external assistance from many sources. The United States can take pride in its role as an innovator and sustainer of this pattern of cooperation.

During the same ten years, the lower income countries also amassed a variety of other important resources for growth. Their technical and managerial experts have grown in number and experience, acquiring greater confidence in their ability to perceive national needs and to design and execute national development strategy. As the lower income nations have gained greater perspective and greater understanding of their own problems, they have been formulating more of their own development plans and organizing more of their own resources.

Other developments that must be taken into account in planning United States aid programs include the growth of new centers of economic and political power, the rapid pace of social and political change, and the increasing emphasis on man's relationship with his environment. Perhaps most significantly, there has been a substantial increase in the aid contributions of other nations and in the role of international lending institutions. Whereas a decade or so ago the United States was the predominant source of development resources and guidance, other industrialized nations and international lending institutions have since expanded both their contributions and their administrative capabilities. Today the United States is the foremost of donor nations in absolute terms, but the other industrialized nations have increased their participation to the extent that in many cases they are contributing a greater percentage of their total resources to development assistance than is the United States.

We have been working to adjust our aid programs to all these new conditions. A number of important reforms were embodied in two pieces of draft legislation submitted to the Congress in April 1971. We hope that those proposals will provide a basis for a discussion with the Congress of ways in which we can structure our programs to increase their effectiveness.

While the Congress has been considering these proposed reforms, the Agency for International Development has moved ahead with steps to increase the effectiveness and efficiency of its operations within the constraints of existing legislation. These initiatives have included:

—Separation of economic supporting assistance activities from development programs within the AID structure;

—Reduction of AID's American staff, by an additional six percent, reflecting a total reduction of nearly one-quarter over the past three years and bringing total AID personnel to the lowest level in the Agency's history;

—Substantial simplification of AID procurement policies and procedures;

—Substantial progress in concentrating technical assistance programs in priority sectors of agriculture, education, population, and health;

—Steps toward centralizing overseas lending operations in Washington.

877

While we look back with satisfaction at our accomplishments in the past and while we plan for further changes to help meet new challenges, we remain aware that the problems of development are stubbornly complex and that the solutions to some of them are still beyond our grasp. Yet each year's experience gives us new insights and firmer hope. And each year's experience also confirms two fundamental facts of development: (1) what the recipient country does to stimulate and accelerate its own growth is ultimately of greater value than anything we do or are able to do; and (2) a measure of help from the United States can be the vital factor in assuring steady progress toward development.

I believe most earnestly that the developed nations of the world cannot long prosper in a world dominated by poverty and that improvement in the quality of life for all peoples enhances the prospects of peace for all people.

RICHARD NIXON

The White House,
    September 19, 1972.

NOTE: The message is printed in the report entitled "The Foreign Assistance Program, Annual Report to the Congress, Fiscal Year 1971" (Government Printing Office, 85 pp.).

304   Message to the Senate Transmitting the United States-Polish Consular Convention. *September* 19, 1972

To the Senate of the United States:

I am pleased to transmit for the Senate's advice and consent to ratification the Consular Convention between the Government of the United States of America and the Government of the Polish People's Republic, with Protocols, signed at Warsaw on May 31, 1972, on the occasion of my recent visit there. The Convention was accompanied by two related exchanges of notes, which are transmitted for the information of the Senate.

The signing of this treaty is a significant step in the gradual process of improving and broadening the relationship between the United States and Poland. Consular relations between the two countries have not previously been subject to formal agreement. This Convention will establish firm obligations on such important matters as free communication between a citizen and his consul, notification to consular offices of the arrest and detention of their citizens, and permission for visits by consuls to citizens who are under detention.

The people of the United States and Poland enjoy a long tradition of friendship. I welcome the opportunity through this Consular Convention to strengthen the ties between our two nations. I urge the Senate to give the Convention its prompt and favorable consideration.

RICHARD NIXON

The White House,
    September 19, 1972.

NOTE: The text of the convention and the report of the Secretary of State are printed in Senate Executive U (92d Cong., 2d sess.).

305   Message to the Senate Transmitting the United
States-Romanian Consular Convention.
September 19, 1972

To the Senate of the United States:

I transmit herewith, for Senate advice and consent to ratification, the Consular Convention between the United States of America and the Socialist Republic of Romania, signed at Bucharest on July 5, 1972.

The Convention was signed by Secretary of State William P. Rogers, who was paying an official visit to Romania, and by Foreign Minister Corneliu Manescu. It is evidence of the continued improvement and expansion of United States-Romanian relations.

This new Convention, replacing one concluded in 1881, will make possible improved consular services in both countries. It will ensure unhindered communication between a citizen and his consul and prompt visit by consuls to citizens who are detained. Under the Convention, American citizens in Romania will have a fuller degree of consular assistance and protection than ever before.

I hope that the Senate will act favorably on the Consular Convention with Romania at an early date.

RICHARD NIXON

The White House,
September 19, 1972.

NOTE: The text of the convention and the report of the Secretary of State are printed in Senate Executive V (92d Cong., 2d sess.).

306   Message to the Senate Transmitting the United
States-Hungarian Consular Convention.
September 19, 1972

To the Senate of the United States:

I am transmitting for the Senate's advice and consent to ratification the Consular Convention between the United States of America and the Hungarian People's Republic, signed at Budapest on July 7, 1972.

Secretary of State William P. Rogers signed the Convention for the United States during his official visit to Hungary. It is the first bilateral treaty concluded between the Governments of the United States and Hungary since World War II and reflects the increasingly warm contacts developing between Americans and Hungarians as well as between their Governments.

The Consular Convention, like others recently negotiated with Poland and Romania, will make possible improved consular services, including guaranteed communication between a citizen and his consul and prompt notification in case of detention.

I believe that this Convention will provide a cornerstone for the development and maintenance of friendly relations with Hungary, and I recommend that the Senate advise and consent to its ratification.

RICHARD NIXON

The White House,
  September 19, 1972.

NOTE: The text of the convention and the report of the Secretary of State are printed in Senate Executive W (92d Cong., 2d sess.).

307   Statement About Signing the National Heart, Blood Vessel, Lung, and Blood Act of 1972. *September 20, 1972*

DISEASES of the heart, blood vessels, blood, and lungs are among the major causes of death and disability in America. They are among the most feared diseases in our country. Their cost in human suffering is intolerable, and they also result in extensive economic losses—in terms both of medical care costs and of lost wages.

In my State of the Union Message this year, I indicated that this Administration would give increased attention to the fight against diseases of the heart, blood vessels, and lungs. I also stated my intention, which I reaffirmed in my message to the Congress on health care of March 2, to form a panel of distinguished experts to help determine how best to combat these diseases. I have appointed a group of distinguished citizens to serve on this panel, and, in addition, I have made a budget request of more than $250 million for 1973 to support the fight against these diseases.

Today I welcome the opportunity to strengthen the attack on heart, blood vessel, and lung diseases by signing S. 3323, the National Heart, Blood Vessel, Lung, and Blood Act of 1972.

Substantial progress has already been achieved in our battle against this enemy, much of it under the auspices of the National Heart and Lung Institute, which has been charged with the responsibility for developing an intensified program. I am confident that with the added impetus of this new legislation, our Nation's scientists will continue that progress and hasten the day when the threat of this devastating health menace will be significantly diminished.

NOTE: As enacted, S. 3323, approved September 19, 1972, is Public Law 92–423 (86 Stat. 679).

308   Statement About Establishment of an Advisory Committee on the Economic Role of Women. *September 21, 1972*

WOMEN are playing an increasingly important role in the economy of our Nation. We in this Administration believe that women must have full equality of opportunity and freedom of choice to pursue their careers, whether they be in the home or outside of the home.

We have taken many strong steps to promote equality and that freedom, but we must recognize clearly that much more needs to be done, especially in the subtle areas of changing attitudes.

Accordingly, I am asking the Chairman of the Council of Economic Advisers to organize an Advisory Committee on the Economic Role of Women. The Committee will be composed of women and men in both the private and public sectors, who are concerned with the changing role of women in our Nation's economy.

The Committee will meet periodically with the CEA Chairman to appraise prog-

ress and problems in this crucial area. I am confident that it will also fulfill a significant role in the vital areas of education and communication to ensure that progress and change in this important area of human rights will be constructive.

NOTE: On the same day, the White House released a fact sheet and the transcript of a news conference on the Committee. Participants in the news conference were Marina von Neumann Whitman, member, Council of Economic Advisers, and Barbara H. Franklin, Staff Assistant to the President for Executive Management.

309   Message to the Congress Proposing Establishment of New National Wilderness Areas.   *September* 21, 1972

To the Congress of the United States:

Everywhere in America, we seek the horizons where escape is free and where despair can never catch up. We sense that our wilderness, more than a concept, is an experience, where we may find something of ourselves and of our world that we might never have known to exist.

Wide-winged birds soaring over remote treetops can set our dreams in new directions. Serrated cliffs can tell us about our geological past. Mountain flowers beside woodland trails can teach us vital lessons about our ecological relationships. Sea winds blowing across lonely beaches can refresh us for new accomplishments.

It is a prime objective of government to balance the use of land sensibly to ensure that the world of nature is preserved along with the world of man.

"A wilderness . . ." according to the epochal Wilderness Act of 1964, "is hereby recognized as an area where the earth and its community of life are untrammeled by man, where man himself is a visitor who does not remain." Within the National

Wilderness Preservation System established by this act, the first 9.1 million acres of our country were set aside, to be conserved, unimpaired, in their natural state.

Today, I am proposing to the Congress 16 new wilderness areas which, if approved, would add 3.5 million acres to our wilderness system. This is the largest single incremental increase in the system since passage of the act.

Five would be located in our National Wildlife Refuge Areas. They are the Brigantine National Wildlife Refuge in New Jersey, the Blackbeard Island National Wildlife Refuge in Georgia, the Chassahowitzka National Wildlife Refuge in Florida, and the Lostwood National Wildlife Refuge and the Chase Lake National Wildlife Refuge in North Dakota. A sixth area, administered by the National Park Service, would be within the Cumberland Gap National Historical Park on the borders of Tennessee, Virginia, and Kentucky. These six additions would add 40,257 acres to the Wilderness Preservation System.

In the Western States, in units administered by the National Park Service, my proposals today would designate as wilderness 2,016,181 acres in Yellowstone National Park, 512,870 in the Grand Canyon complex, 646,700 acres in Yosemite National Park, and 115,807 acres in Grand Teton National Park.

I further propose for inclusion in our National Wilderness Preservation System an additional 216,519 acres in some of the most beautiful regions of our country. These would include designated areas in the Great Sand Dunes National Monument in Colorado, the Theodore Roosevelt National Memorial Park in North Dakota, the Badlands National Monument in South Dakota, the Guadalupe Mountains National Park in Texas, the Carlsbad Caverns National Park in New Mexico and the Haleakala National Park in Hawaii.

The 1964 Wilderness Act further directed the Secretaries of Agriculture and of the Interior to review federally owned lands which they administer and to report to the President, who transmits to the Congress their and his recommendations for those areas which qualify as wilderness as defined by the act. This wilderness review process, to be conducted in three phases, was to be completed by 1974.

Beginning in 1969, I accelerated this program, and on April 28, 1971, I forwarded to the Congress 14 new wilderness proposals which, when enacted, would substantially increase the acreage added since passage of the Wilderness Act. I warned that we would need a redoubled effort by the Departments of Agriculture and the Interior in completing the review process and prompt action on these proposals by the Congress.

On February 8, 1972, I transmitted a second package of 18 new wilderness proposals to the Congress, which, if enacted, would designate 1.3 million additional acres as wilderness. At that time I reported that the September, 1974 statutory deadline for reviews could and would be met. I also pointed out that the majority of the wilderness areas recommended to date had involved western lands. Therefore, I directed the Secretaries of Agriculture and Interior to accelerate the identification of areas in the Eastern United States having wilderness potential.

The Congress has now received 78 wilderness proposals which would add 5.8 million acres to the original 9.1 million acres designated by the Congress.

To date, however, the Congress has acted on only 35 proposals, approving 1.7 million acres for inclusion in the system. This leaves pending 43 wilderness proposals encompassing 4.1 million acres.

I now urge the Congress—in this centennial year of our National Park System—to act quickly in favor of these new proposals as well as the ones already pending.

I am aware of the commercial opportunities in potential wilderness areas such as mining, lumbering, and recreational development. I believe we must achieve a sensible land use balance—America can have economic growth *and* the unspoiled nature of the wilderness.

Increasingly, in fact, the preservation of these areas has become a major goal of all Americans. The process of developing wilderness proposals is now exemplifying public participation and cooperation with the governmental process. Commercial and conservation groups—and individuals from all over the country—have, through public hearings and direct contact with government agencies, done much more than is generally realized to contribute to the wilderness program.

I believe the value of this cooperative effort between the public and their government officials is reflected in the wilderness proposals I am proud to submit today. This is an excellent example of the responsive way in which our government is meant to work.

The first man on earth, according to the scriptures was placed in a natural garden, and he was charged "to dress it and keep it." Our own great naturalist John Muir said that our "whole continent was a garden and . . . seemed to be favored above all the other wild parks and gardens of the globe."

The addition of these new areas to our national wilderness system will help to keep it that way.

RICHARD NIXON

The White House,
  September 21, 1972.

NOTE: On the same day, the White House released a fact sheet and the transcript of a news briefing on the President's message. The news briefing was held by Secretary of the Interior Rogers C. B. Morton.

310 Remarks on Signing a Bill Providing Better Survivor Benefits for Dependents of Military Retirees.
September 21, 1972

I WANTED to say to you gentlemen that on occasions of bill signings, we usually have a statement made briefly by the President. I noted the great number who are here for this bill signing. It allows me to make a point that many times we sign bills that have an enormous effect on groups of people, but very few people in the Nation are aware of it, very few people, really, would seem to care.

This happens to be one of those bills that would go unnoticed, except for the fact that there are Members of the House and Members of the Senate, who have felt strongly for many, many years that an inequity ought to be corrected. The bill came to my desk. When I saw it, I suggested that we invite down Members of the House and the Senate, Republicans and Democrats, who had supported this legislation.

In order that the Nation will know that a government can be responsive to an inequity, an inequity involving men and women who have served in our Armed Forces and their survivors, I thought the Secretary of Defense could take a few minutes to explain the details of the bill, and then I will sign it. Mr. Secretary.

SECRETARY LAIRD. *Mr. President, ladies and gentlemen:*

This bill is a very significant bill. It is significant in the lives of the families of 900,000 military people who have already retired. They have an opportunity to qualify for the survivors benefits under the terms of this bill.

In addition to that, it affects the families and the lives of the men and women of the military service that are currently serving in our Armed Forces. They have an opportunity to be treated as other civilian workers in Government have been treated, as members of the Foreign Service have been treated, for many years.

For 25 years, the House and Senate Armed Services Committees have been

883

considering legislation along this line. It was through the efforts of the House and the Senate committees, and the bipartisan support on the floor of the House and the Senate, that this legislation is a reality today. I would like to express the appreciation not only of our Commander in Chief but of those of us in the Defense Department who are working for an all-volunteer force for our Army, our Air Force, our Navy, and our Marine Corps, that these military men are involved in a very real sense in a different way, because of their separation from their families during their careers in military service. And this means a great deal to them because it is the support of their families that makes it possible for them to do the kind of job that is so necessary in the defense of freedom in the world and in making possible our efforts and our objective of peace throughout the world.

And so on behalf of all of us in the Department of Defense, I would like to express to all of you from the Congress our appreciation for making this opportunity available not only to the 900,000 that have already retired from military service but to all those men and women that are currently taking part in the defense of our country and serving in the Armed Forces. Thank you.

THE PRESIDENT. Ladies and gentlemen, I would only add to that by saying that we have taken action on the pay front with regard to military personnel. We are now taking action on the survivors front for benefits that should be provided for those who serve in our Armed Forces.

But most important of all, we have to remember that what the men and women who serve in our Armed Forces really need more than anything else is respect. Whatever we pay them, whatever survivor benefits we provide, certainly should be equivalent to what they could do in civilian life, but the respect must come from all of the American people for those who serve in our Armed Forces. The fact that so many of you have come down from the House and the Senate today not only indicates your interest in this legislation, but it indicates that on a bipartisan front we respect the men and women who serve America all over the world, in war and peace.

NOTE: The President spoke at 12:05 p.m. in the Cabinet Room at the White House. He spoke without referring to notes.

As enacted, the bill (H.R. 10670) is Public Law 92–425 (86 Stat. 706).

---

311   Statement About a Bill Providing Better Survivor Benefits for Dependents of Military Retirees.
September 21, 1972

IT IS too often overlooked that America's military families serve our country in as real a way as do the men and women in uniform—they share the sacrifices and the hardships of duty, as well as its satisfactions and glory. The Nation's true and just obligation to those who bear arms in its defense remains as Lincoln defined it: "to care for him who shall have borne the battle and for his widow and his orphan."

H.R. 10670, which I have signed, will enable us to meet this standard more fully by establishing a much improved system of survivors benefits for the **wives and** children of military **retirees.**

Flowing from the recommendation of an interagency committee I established in 1971, this new law will permit military retirees—at a reasonable cost shared by the Federal Government—to provide better benefits for their survivors. The benefits will range up to 55 percent of the member's retired pay to a surviving spouse and will include benefits for dependent children. The payments will be adjusted according to the Consumer Price Index so that their purchasing power will be steadily maintained.

This will replace a present survivors benefit system offering lesser benefits at a cost which must be borne entirely by each individual retiree.

Many times in the past, men who have devoted their lifetimes to careers in the uniformed services have died soon after their retirement, without having either enjoyed their earned retirement themselves or being able to pass a significant portion of that earned right on to their surviving families.

To help remedy the hardships caused in the past by this deficiency in the retirement system, this legislation also permits those who have already retired from the service to elect to participate in this program and provide coverage for their survivors.

Nine hundred thousand persons now retired—as well as all those who retire from armed services careers from now on—will be eligible to participate in this program. The extra security and peace of mind which it will afford them and their loyal, self-sacrificing families, at the end of a job well done, are richly earned. I am most gratified to be able to approve this legislation.

312   Remarks to Customs Agents and Inspectors After a Tour of the Laredo, Texas, Customs Facility. *September 22, 1972*

Ladies and gentlemen:

I want to take this opportunity while I am on the border here at Laredo to express the appreciation of the American people and the appreciation, too, of the people of Mexico for the work that our people in the Customs group are doing.

As I have walked among you, I haven't had the chance to shake hands with you and to thank each of you, but when I see men who have served 30 years, 32 years— in fact, one was here when I came across this border on our honeymoon in 1940, 32 years ago—I think of how devoted your service has been to this country, and you have the gratitude of all.

Right at the present time, of course, the primary emphasis, as far as the American public is concerned, is the drive against narcotics, and particularly heroin, and I know all the work that you are doing in this particular field. Let me say that in that respect you have the total backing of the Federal Government and you also have the total backing of the American people.

Now, I realize that when you see a movie or one of those television specials about how exciting it is to be a Customs official and how somebody is a hero and he is consequently rewarded by his city or by his country, or the rest, I realize that most of you know that that is the way it is in the movies or on the TV. But you know that for the most part in your work it is long hours, sometimes it is very dull, sometimes it is very routine. You go through car after car and there doesn't seem to be any reason for doing it—and then one time something happens. Very few of you are really recognized for the work that you are doing, but all of you are vitally important, and we are grateful for that.

When I speak of backing you up, let me emphasize one thing. I met with a group of 40 young lawyers from all over the United States who have the responsibility for conducting prosecutions by the Federal Government in this field. They told me that one of their problems was that when they found a heroin pusher and when they brought him to trial and when he was convicted, that in many cases a lenient judge or a lenient probation officer would let him out, and then he went right back to what he had been doing before.

Now let us clearly understand: We naturally want to have concern for those that are found guilty of this kind of activity. But the primary responsibility we all have is concern for the victims of those who are the pushers of heroin, this deadly drug. And in that connection, let me say that I have issued orders to the entire Administration to do everything we can at the national level to back up our law enforcement people.

If you go out, if you risk your lives in order to bring one of these people to justice, then it is the responsibility of the courts to see to it that justice is done to them so that they cannot be let off too soon to practice their nefarious traffic again.

Let me just close with one thought that may be of interest to you. Sometimes this is very impersonal. I mean, we see it in terms of statistics. You were telling me how many pounds of heroin had been picked up and how much marihuana, and so forth and so on, how many cars you go through. And I know that when you make out those reports, it must be very, very tiring and very boring at times.

If you think of it in terms of statistics, it really isn't worthwhile; you really ought to have some other job. But I would like for each one of you to think of it in terms of one individual boy or girl in this country who, as a result of what you have done, does not become a heroin addict. And if what you have done has helped make that come true, it is all worthwhile.

In 1968, when I was a candidate for President, I received a letter from my home State of California. It was unsigned. It was from a girl 19 years old, who lived in San Diego. She said she was from a very good family. She had become addicted to heroin, and then the deterioration that occurs inevitably in those cases had happened to her.

The closing paragraph of her letter I want to read to you so that we can all understand what your job means, not in statistics, but in human, personal terms. She says, "Mr. Nixon, I think you are going to be elected. If you are, as President, will you try to do something to see that what happened to me does not happen to other young people across this country."

That is your job. That is my job. Let's think of those young people, let's see that what happened to this 19-year-old does not happen to other young people across this country.

Finally, one other thought that is not perhaps related to what I have said, but in a way it is. The great majority of the people that cross this border, whether they are Mexicans coming to visit the United States or Americans returning from Mexico, are good, law-abiding citizens. Be courteous to them. Be kind to them.

I remember, when I crossed the border in 1940, how very kind the Mexican officials were to us, a newlywed couple from California on our honeymoon. And I also remember that when we came back across the border at Laredo, first, naturally, after all we had seen, we were still very glad to get back home, but I remember how very kind and thoughtful the Customs officials were. They went through our car, as they should have. They didn't find anything. But they didn't make us feel unwelcome.

And I simply want to say that in your long hours and your long days, do your job, go after those that are guilty, but, also, make the good people—and that is the great majority, whether they are Mexicans or Americans—make them feel welcome, make them feel that it is good to be in the United States of America.

Thank you.

NOTE: The President spoke at 12:43 p.m. at the United States Customs border station in Laredo. He spoke without referring to notes.

On the same day, the White House released a fact sheet on the Laredo Customs facility.

313   Statement About Drug Abuse Law Enforcement. *September 22, 1972*

THE U.S. Customs agents with whom I met today at the International Bridge between Texas and Mexico are representative of the many thousands of dedicated Federal, State, and local law enforcement officials engaged in our total war against drug abuse all across this country—men and women to whom every American owes a debt of gratitude for their efforts to defeat the menace which is truly "public enemy number one."

Keeping heroin and all dangerous drugs out of the United States is every bit as crucial as keeping out armed enemy invaders. In this effort, the Bureau of Customs is one of our first lines of defense. Its agents on all our coasts and borders do an important job comprised of equal parts of vigilance, exacting detail, tedium, and constant danger. Here in Laredo these men put their lives on the line daily, as do their Mexican counterparts across the border in Nuevo Laredo, in order to help save countless other lives from drug addiction.

My firsthand inspections of our drug abuse enforcement efforts, together with the continuous reports I am receiving on the subject, have convinced me that those responsible for making the arrests, the seizures, and the investigations are doing their part and more. But others farther up the chain of our criminal justice system must also do their part. For the sake of America's children and our young people, we simply cannot tolerate a weak link anywhere in that chain—and this is why I am so distressed by some indications that some judges may now have become such a weak link.

Sources ranging from news reports to

887

letters from outraged citizens to personal appeals from the 40 young lawyers from the Office for Drug Abuse Law Enforcement with whom I recently met have called my attention to shocking instances of convicted heroin pushers who have been released onto the streets again rather than sentenced to the long prison terms they deserve. The rationale sometimes advanced for such action on a judge's part—that prison can warp a first offender's life forever, whereas probation or a very light sentence may rehabilitate him—is well intentioned. But I believe it is very mistaken. Above all else, society must be protected from these despicable narcotics profiteers who spread the drug plague for personal gain. Far too many heroin victims never get a second chance at life—and we must see to it that heroin pushers do not get an immediate second chance at dealing, either. Rather, they must get the punishment they deserve.

I have asked the Attorney General to launch a full and immediate investigation into this phase of the war on drugs. As soon as he presents his findings, I shall do whatever is necessary to halt this dangerous permissive trend.

NOTE: The statement was released in connection with the President's tour of the Laredo, Tex., Customs facility.

314 Remarks to the Student Body of Rio Grande High School, Rio Grande City, Texas. *September 22, 1972*

Principal Saenz, President Gebhart,[1] *Senator Tower, Senator Bentsen, Congressman—and this is his birthday—shall we call him "Kika"? [Laughter]*

I learned on the plane coming over that "Kika" [Congressman Eligio] de la Garza has his 45th birthday today, and as I came into the hall I asked anybody if there was a piano here, and they said, "No, there was a band." But somebody just handed me a note that there is a piano in the back of the room.

It seems to me that when you have a distinguished Congressman from your district, one who has proved that you can go clear to the top if you have the will—and he certainly has that—that the President of the United States ought to play "Happy Birthday" for him, and I am going to do it right now.

[At this point, the President went to the piano and accompanied the student body in singing "Happy Birthday."]

Now that we have the Congressman launched on his 46th year, I want to tell you what a very great privilege it is for me to keep that promise that I made in the Rose Garden just a little over a year ago on April 16, when this wonderful group of students from the Rio Grande High School came there and when I learned from Senator Tower and his office that they were there, and Congressman de la Garza, and I walked out into the Rose Garden and met them and talked to them.

I am very happy that some of those students who were there, most of whom have graduated now, unless some of them failed—I don't know—but I am sure that

[1] Ruben Saenz was the principal of Rio Grande High School, and Donald Gebhart was president of the student body.

most of them graduated, and I understand Patsy Ramirez is actually going to school in Manhattanville in New York—and I am happy that they could be here, because while your principal has paid a tribute to them, I would like to say a word about them, and in talking about them to say a word about you, about what you mean to the President of the United States, but also about what you mean to this country—how much we count on you, how much what you do, in whatever occupation you go into, will mean to the future of America.

The principal pointed out that this was a rather unusual group. It is unusual. Let me say that there are not hundreds, but thousands of groups, high school groups, grammar school groups, who come to Washington in the spring of every year. And, of course, the President has many responsibilities, whoever he is—he can't see them all. He can only see very few.

I was glad that on that beautiful spring day in April I could come out and meet this group, glad because they were so proud of what they had done, and rightfully so, glad because what they did told me that this was a strong, young generation, that we could have hope in the future of America because we can believe in the young people of America. That is what they told me when they came there.

Afterwards, when I was talking to one of the members of the White House Staff and told him how these young people had made their way to Washington by doing a lot of things—they had washed cars, they had done babysitting, they had done all sorts of chores. As a matter of fact, they got into some businesses. They, I remember, made some tamales and sold them at 50 cents apiece from door to door. Believe me, that is a real bargain, I can assure you.

But after doing all that, and then getting to Washington, they weren't able to take a plane. They came in a bus. And they probably didn't stay in the best hotel in town, although in an adequate one.

My friend on the staff said, "You know, wasn't it really a shame to think of many of those young people, and some of them not from very wealthy families, some from poor families, that they had to come that way? Wouldn't it have been possible to find some wealthy man in Texas or some foundation that would have put up the money so they wouldn't have had to work, so they could have come, for example, in a plane? Wouldn't it have been much better?"

And I said, "Not at all." Not at all, for a reason. Not because we don't want to help anybody who can't help himself, but because the great American tradition is—and that is what the students of this school proved—the American tradition is that we help ourselves when we can, and we only ask somebody else to help us when we can't help ourselves. That is what made this country great.

Now the visit of this school—or at least the representatives of this school—to Washington told me something else about America, something I have known all my life from the time I grew up in southern California, where we have a great many students and young people, Americans of Mexican background and other backgrounds as well, something about the strength of this country.

I knew from what I had heard about this group—they always give me a little sheet, the background of the group—that probably a majority of those who attend this school are proud of the fact that they are Americans of Mexican background.

When I met this group in the Rose Garden, I thought of all the groups that make up America. I thought of all the countries I have visited, and it is a very great privilege to have visited them all. My wife and I together have been to over 80 countries in this world—North America, South America, Africa, Asia, the first time to visit the People's Republic of China, Peking, and then, of course, to Moscow, as you know.

We met many wonderful people. We have been impressed by the countries that we have seen. But you know, when you come home to America, what you realize [is] that America is a very unique country, America is all the world in one nation. It is all here.

Right here in Texas, within 50 miles of where we are, there is a Polish community, there is a German community, there is a Czechoslovakian community, there are Mexican communities, there are other various religious groups. There is one that was founded by people of the Jewish faith, of course Catholics, Protestants, and the like.

In other words, you don't have to go out of America to see the world. It is here. That is why we are a rich country. We are rich because all the cultures of the world are here. We are proud of those of Mexican background who have added their wonderful warmth and all of their talent and all of their spirit and all of their hard work to make this a great country.

We are proud of those of Italian background, of Polish background, Irish, you name it, whatever it is. The important thing is this: I often hear people say, when they are speaking of this person or that person, he is an Italian or he is a German or he is a Mexican. What I say is, he is an American. That's what he is.

That brings me now to how very much you can contribute to your country, this country, our country—it belongs to all of us. What a wonderful time to be growing up in America. What a wonderful time to be in high school. To think that you are the first generation of young Americans to be able to vote at 18 years of age. You seniors, most of you, will be voting, if not this year, next year. To think that you are going to have a part in determining the future of your country.

I am not going to talk to you in terms of whether you should be Democrats or Republicans. The future of this country is much more important than what our party label is. I am simply talking about your responsibilities and your opportunities as American citizens with the right and the power to vote.

In that respect, I think the new generation of American voters is going to be good for this country. You are going to bring enthusiasm to our elective process, that is for sure. You are going to bring idealism to it. You are going to bring a lot of impatience, I am sure of that.

I remember when I was in high school and in college, too, I used to be so impatient with the way things were. I used to think, "Why can't we change things, why can't we make them better?" My mother and father would say, "You have to wait a little while. It will change. This country does progress."

But the wonderful thing about young people is that you are impatient with what is wrong. You want to change it. And it is good that you constantly infuse your communities, your State, your Nation with that spirit of progress, that spirit of making this country and this world a better place in which to live.

So, I urge all of you, as you are here

in high school, let your minds become as open as they possibly can to the wonderful world around you. Learn about your country. Learn about this political process. Participate in it. Oh, I don't mean by that that all of you are going to run for office. After all, the Congressman doesn't have any opposition this year. He wouldn't want all of you running against him. [*Laughter*]

I am simply suggesting this though: Some of you will run for office, and some of you will win and some of you will lose.

I was saying to President Gebhart a few moments ago, I said, "Who ran against you?"

He said, "Nobody."

I have never been so lucky. [*Laughter*] Let me tell you an interesting thing. In all the biographies that have been written— you know, once they write biographies of people who become President, they forget all the times that they may have lost and they only write about the times they have won. You think, oh, it was easy sledding going to the top.

It is never that way. When I was in high school in my junior year, or early in the senior, I ran for student body president and I lost. So you see, you win some, you lose some. The important thing is to try. The important thing, of course, is not to run for every office, but the important thing is—whether you are going after a job or whether you are going after an office or whether you are trying to make some project in which you are interested succeed—when you do have a failure, when you do have a setback, don't give up, keep trying.

That is what has made America the great country it is. We are a people that is impatient wherever we find anything that is inequitable in our country, and we want to change it. We are also a people that is very ambitious. And that is a good thing. We are competitive. We want to win.

As I was coming in here, for example, I suppose somebody knows that I am from Washington, that I sort of pull for the Redskins. This fellow reached over and he grabbed me and he said, "The Cowboys are going to win it. The Cowboys are going to win it." [*Laughter*]

You know, I kind of liked that. I mean, I like his saying it. I have to be for my team. But the point that I make is: I urge you, be for your school, be for your team, be for your State, but above all, be for your country, for America. That is what we need, that kind of spirit.

Now, just a few words perhaps reminiscing into background. You know, when I remember when I was in high school and college, we would get these older people up and we would sit there and wonder, "When are they going to finish?" [*Laughter*] Because they try to give us advice and we wonder about it. And sometimes we got a little impatient with our parents—"Oh, ma, I know all about that. You haven't read the latest books," and all that and so on.

Well, it is a pretty good thing that you haven't. [*Laughter*] But whatever the case may be, could I just, without being perhaps a bit presumptuous, leave you with some thoughts that made a very great impression upon me when I was your age.

First, respect your teachers. I met so many of them as I came in.

Incidentally, there are thousands of people outside and there is one thing this school needs, it needs a great big new building that will take care of all the people—and they are going to get it, I hear.

People often ask me to measure what is success and what is failure. On the

25th anniversary of my graduation from college, I was Vice President of the United States. That was 1959. I remember a member of my class. He had not become Vice President of the United States. He was a teacher, a teacher in a little school down in southern California in the Imperial Valley. But he was such a good teacher and he was so loved by his students and their parents—he was a teacher in high school—that in that 25th year after our graduation, they took up a collection in that town and sent him and his wife to Washington, D.C., so that they could see the Capital.

And as he came there—my friend, Byron Netzley—and I talked to him and his wife, I thought, who is to judge who contributes the most to his country. When I thought of all the lives he had changed, how much he had meant to the students that he had taught, I thought that was a worthwhile life.

Just down on the border a few moments ago, I met a lot of border guards. It is a tough job, boring many times, going through all that luggage and people saying, "Oh, gee, please leave me alone." You know it is pretty hard.

I met one man very proud. He stood there. His name was [Willie] Peña. For 30 years he has been a border guard. For 30 years he has had a magnificent record. As a result of what he has done, there are probably hundreds of boys and girls in this country who didn't become addicted to heroin because of what he did. He isn't a man that is going to be known as a hero when his life is ended, but he is one who, in his way, has rendered a service that is invaluable to his country and to his fellow man.

I think of others in my high school class—some of them became workers, some became wealthy, some did not. The important thing is that in this country, remember, as your principal has just said, have respect for the dignity of hard work, have respect for any person, whatever work he undertakes. Remember, he is contributing to the greatness of America. Some will be workers, some will be laborers, some will be teachers, some will be government employees, some will be like some of the servicemen I saw at the base at Laredo, serving their country in the peacetime forces so that America can live at peace with the world and so that freedom will be able to survive in the world—and each one of these occupations is important and worthwhile.

One final thought I would leave with you, something I said to another high school group when I spoke in Michigan a few weeks ago. A few of your parents are here. Always respect them. Always remember what they did. I mentioned the tamales a moment ago. I didn't realize at the time, but when I was in high school and in college, I had an older brother who was sick with tuberculosis, and consequently it took a lot of money from our little grocery store that we had.

Nevertheless, we did well, at least we thought we did all right. But I knew that in 5 years—I learned later, one of my mother's sisters, one of my aunts, told me—in 5 years she never had a new dress, and we never knew it. She always looked nice. And the reason was she had to be sure my brother was taken care of and that she was taking care of the other boys in the family, and see that they got an education.

I remember her getting up at 4:00 in the morning, baking pies to sell in that store.

I remember my father. He wasn't very

well educated, because he came from a very poor family, quit school in the fifth grade, but he worked hard. And he earned the respect of his sons and he saw to it that every one of his sons had a chance to have what he did not have, to go to college and get an education.

I simply want to say to everyone here in this class, it is wonderful to be alive in America and to be 14, 15, 16, 17, 18. You are going to see your country live at peace with all the nations of the world in the years ahead. There are more jobs, more opportunity, more freedom in America than in any country in the world.

You will travel abroad, I hope, and every time you come back you are going to say how fortunate we are to live in America. But as you do that, as you come home to America, remember, if you will, what I have told you. Remember that your teachers, your fathers, your mothers, your minister, your priest, all of them have made a contribution to your life which you can never repay. Respect them. Respect them and love your country, and you, this wonderful young, new generation, will make America the greatest country in the world, which it is now, but the best country, a good country, respected in the world—respected because the people of the world will know that here in this country that any boy or girl, whatever his background, has a chance to go to the top in whatever occupation he chooses.

That isn't true in most of the world. It is true here. And as I look back to that day in the Rose Garden in 1971, as I see the faces of the boys and girls of the class of 1971, I again say what I said then: I have never been so proud of America and proud of our young people as I was on that day and as I am today as I see you here.

Thank you.

NOTE: The President spoke at 2:08 p.m. in the multipurpose center of the high school. He spoke without referring to notes.

315   Remarks at a Buffet Dinner at the Texas Ranch of John B. Connally.   *September 22, 1972*

ALONG WITH a few of the others who are guests here tonight, my wife and I have had the honor and the privilege of having been guests before at this ranch, or affairs like this, where John and Nellie Connally were our hosts. We have enjoyed them. We have enjoyed the hospitality, the good fellowship, meeting their friends.

But I must say that there is one thing I have a complaint about, and that is that John Connally is awful hard to follow. [*Laughter*]

In following him, I first want to say something on a purely personal basis that may be of interest to you. We were trying to think of something to give you that you could take back in your luggage without having it searched at the airport, and so this is small enough you can carry it in a purse. But in any event, I hope the men aren't carrying purses [*laughter*]—at least not over your shoulders. [*Laughter*] A few of you have these, but we have had developed by a very good friend of ours, some new Presidential cuff links. They are completely nonpartisan. They don't have my name on them, and there is no party label. [*Laughter*] All it has is the seal of the President of the United States; it is in living color. And so for the men you have the Presidential cuff links, and, since ladies do not wear cuffs—although I have seen that some of them now are wearing them—but since you do not have them, we have for the ladies a seal in a pin. We have cuff links and a pin for all of you here tonight, for those who are here with your wives. And for those whose wives could not come, we will give you one of these to take home to prove where you were. [*Laughter*]

Now, if I could say a word about John Connally before speaking just briefly with regard to my appreciation of your support and your friendship.

I was thinking tonight as I read the morning news summary of how much this country and this Administration owes to John Connally. A year ago, on August 15, as you know, we initiated a new economic policy.[1] He was the architect of that policy. If you picked up your newspapers today you found that in that year since August 15 we have seen this economy take off, take off in the right direction, and we have seen also inflation go down, inflation cut in half, real spendable earnings—and that is what really counts for 80 million American wage earners—finally going up for the first time significantly in 5 years.

We have seen our gross national product move up. We have seen income for all Americans move up. We have seen this economy strong and vibrant and moving in the direction of becoming less affected by inflation than it has ever been in recent years.

If you want to put it comparatively, when we look at all the great industrial nations of the world—and I have seen them all, visited them all, and know

them all—whether it is Japan and the Far East or whether it is any of the countries of Western Europe, of all the free nations in the world, the United States today has the lowest rate of inflation. We have the most jobs at the highest real wages. We have more opportunity, more freedom than in any country in the world, and we have the fastest rate of growth. And John Connally deserves a great deal of the credit for that.

Of course, he was the Secretary of the Treasury, but as the Secretary of the Treasury he also sat on the National Security Council. He spoke of decisions. He was there. He helped in giving his advice when those decisions were made.

Some of you may have noted another piece of good news yesterday. For the first time since 1965, since the long and very difficult war in Vietnam began, no American was killed in action in Vietnam. But what is more important is that that has been accomplished—the withdrawal of over half a million Americans and the reduction of our casualties—it has been accomplished without staining the honor of the United States of America.

And over this year—it was more than a year that John Connally was in the position as Secretary of the Treasury and served on the National Security Council—we had some hard decisions. I will never forget, however, his participation in one of the most difficult ones—May 8 this year, just before the Soviet summit.

In order to stop the Communist invasion of South Vietnam, it was necessary to do something and do it effectively. I decided that we had to mine the harbors of Haiphong and bomb military installations in North Vietnam. There was much disagreement within the Administration, honest disagreement. Some

[1] See 1971 volume, Item 264.

wavered. But John Connally was like a rock. He is the kind of man that you really wanted in such a crisis.

So after all that you know about him, just let me say that this country has been fortunate to have had him in its service in many capacities. I have been fortunate to have had him as an adviser in this Administration, and, certainly, as we look to the future, this is a man who is destined for great service to his Nation in the years ahead.

I come now to this organization. It is called Democrats for Nixon. I think it should have another name. Tonight I would like to talk to you in terms of not "Democrats for Nixon," which puts it in highly personal terms, but I would like to talk to you in terms of "Democrats for America," which really puts it where it belongs.

What I say now will deal therefore not with partisanship and not with personal matters—those really do not belong in a great Presidential campaign. In this particular instance, the only matters that we should consider are what is best for America, because when an individual, be he a man or a woman, has been proud to be a member of one of the two great political parties for many, many years, when, as has been the case with most of the people here, of individuals who have always supported the candidates of their party for local office, for State office, for national office, and for the Presidency, when individuals then decide in a critical election year that they are going to support a candidate of the other party, it cannot be simply on personal terms, it cannot be simply on selfish terms, it must be on terms of whether America's interest requires it.

That is the basis on which I speak to you, you my friends, the Democrats for

Nixon. I would like to call you "Democrats for America" tonight.

As I see America in these next few years, I see a time of enormous challenge and of enormous opportunity. John Connally has spoken of what has happened around the world. One of the great difficulties an individual has when he lives through great events is that he really doesn't realize how much is happening, how much the world is changing. And only when the history books are written, 10 years, 15 years, 20 years later, does he look back and realize, "I was there. I helped to make it happen."

Tonight I say to all of you here gathered in Texas that we have witnessed in these past few months, and particularly over this past year, and we are witnessing and are going to witness over these next 3 to 4 years, very great changes in the world and changes in America.

What is important for us is to help to make those changes move in the right direction, make them move in the direction of peace for America, make them move in the direction of freedom for America and peace and freedom for all peoples in the world, wherever they can have it. That is our responsibility.

You are all aware—several of you as you came through the receiving line mentioned that you were aware—of the trips that had occurred this past year to Peking and to Moscow. I should point out that they are only a beginning. I should point out that we have begun a new relationship with the People's Republic of China, which controls one-fourth of all the people in this world.

But having begun it, now the real challenge begins. How does it develop? How does it develop in a way that it will be to the advantage of the United States and to the advantage of the Chinese people? This is the question. How does it develop in a way that it will contribute to peace in the Pacific, rather than unrest in the Pacific? This is the question.

And so we look at the Soviet Union and we see some striking things that have happened. We see an arms control agreement. We see agreements developing in the field of trade and the environment and health and many, many other areas—in cooperation in space, for example. But again I point out, they are simply a beginning, because in the field of arms control, for example, all that we have done is simply to provide for the limitation of arms in certain areas, defensive nuclear weapons and certain classes of offensive weapons.

In the future, in the next few months, over the next few years, we will move on to new negotiations with the Soviet Union, between these two great super powers. Those negotiations will not be easy. They will not depend simply on personal friendship, although there will be and might be personal friendship between the leaders of the two great powers. They will not depend on simply good will, although we hope there may be good will, but they will depend upon how each of the great nations consults its own interests and defends those interests in such negotiations.

I know, because I have been through it. And as I look at that challenge in the future, I realize, and I want all of you to realize, all of the American people to realize, that what we must do is, of course, to negotiate with those who might be our adversaries, but to negotiate in a way that builds a lasting peace, negotiate in a way that does not weaken the United States of America in its role of being the major free world country that can keep the peace and defend freedom around the world.

Let me put it quite bluntly. The mili-

tary strength of the United States, the economic strength of the United States, and, even more important, the moral strength, the unity, the character of the United States will determine whether peace and freedom survive in this last part of this century. And it is the responsibility of all Americans, whether they be Democrats or Republicans, to see to it that the United States remains strong in all these areas, strong not for the purpose of being simply stronger than somebody else— there is no jingoism in this—but strong because in the whole free world today there is no one else, no one else that can do the job.

In the Pacific there is no other power that has the strength or the potential. In Europe there is no other free world power that has that potential. And that is why one of the planks in my campaign program, one of the things I have fought for in the past, that I will fight for in the future is this:

I believe, of course, that we should always do everything that we can to see that the burden of expenditures for the American people is as low as possible. I believe, of course, that we should see to it that in the field of military expenditures that we should not spend more than is necessary. But I also believe that it is vital and essential to the survival of the United States, to the survival of peace and freedom in the world, that we reject the arguments of those who say that we should cut our defenses so that we become the second strongest nation in the world.

So a strong national defense is the beginning. We will negotiate reduction in arms, but you cannot negotiate from a position of weakness. It is very simple, and this is a point, of course, that we are all quite aware of.

We come now to the question of our economic strength. Without that we couldn't, of course, have the military strength that we need. And as far as our economic strength is concerned, we have to realize where it comes from. What has made America the economic wonder of the world is not what government did for people, but what people did for themselves, and that is the way we have to build this country in the future.

And that is why, even though it might be politically, shall we say, somewhat appealing in some quarters to call for a redistribution of income, to see that those who do not work are rewarded more than those who do, I say that it is vital for us to remember that in this country, what brought us where we are is the fact that we have always recognized that an individual who works will receive what he is entitled to, that his government will not take more than is necessary. But above everything else, we must always remember that once any government goes to the point that its taxes become so high that an individual is working more for the government than he is working for himself, then we have gone too far. We must not go that far in the United States.

I spoke about character. I am going to use an example, perhaps an example right here from this State of Texas to prove it.

As some of you know, I stopped in Laredo earlier today, and then we paid a visit to a little high school, the Rio Grande High School, in the valley between here and Laredo. Many of those from the national press who were following us probably wondered, why Rio Grande High School?

It is a very small high school, only a thousand students. It is in a district which is so hopelessly Democratic that they don't even have a Republican running for Congress this year. [*Laughter*] It is a district, incidentally, in which 80 percent of those who live in it are of Mexican background, and generally speaking Republican candidates, except for John Connally, have not done very well in that particular district. [*Laughter*]

So the question is, why? Why stop at Rio Grande? Let me tell you why. Because Rio Grande, that little high school and its students, had a message for me and a message for America in April of 1971.

There are literally thousands of classes from high schools who come to Washington in the spring. It is a wonderful thing to do. And they see the cherry blossoms and they go to the Capitol and they have tours of the White House and they call on their Congressmen and the Senators and the rest.

Of course, the President of the United States can see very, very few of them, because his schedule will not permit. One day I got a call from Senator Tower. He told me about a group from Rio Grande High School. He said they were going to be down there and he understood they might even have an opportunity to visit the Rose Garden.

I said, "Well, John, how can I make an exception and see this group and not some others?" Then he told me about it. This is the story.

This is a poor district. As a matter of fact, some describe it in terms of income as the poorest district in Texas. It may not be. It is irrelevant. It at least is not a rich district. But as far as the students from that district are concerned, they were the greatest. Let me tell you what happened:

They wanted to come to Washington.

They didn't run around to the rich businessmen and say, "Look, will you pay our way?" They didn't go to some foundation and say, "Look, will you put up the money for us?" They decided to earn their way, and for a year they washed cars, they did babysitting, they did all sorts of what are called menial chores in order to earn the money so that they could come to Washington. As a matter of fact, they even went into business. They made tamales and then they went house to house and sold those good Texas tamales for 50 cents apiece and they kept building up the kitty so that they could go.

Then, finally, on April 21, 1971, they stood in the Rose Garden on a beautiful spring day, proud because they had earned their way, and I stepped out and talked to them for a few minutes, and as I talked to them and I looked at them— young, idealistic, from working families for the most part—I realized they had the stuff that made this country great from several different standpoints.

I mentioned the fact that most of them were of Mexican background. You know, I often hear people say, "That fellow is a Mexican or this one is an Italian or this one may be a Jew or this one may be a Catholic or this one may be a Pole or this one may be a German." Let me tell you my attitude. They may have that kind of background, but to me every one of them is an American first, last, and always.

As I came back into the White House that day, one of the members of my staff said, "Isn't it a shame that those poor kids had to work all year in order to make that trip? Why couldn't one of those rich Texas oilmen put up the money so that they could come? Why didn't some foundation do it so that they could have had an easier time? Wouldn't it have been

better?" And my answer was, "Not at all." Because they told us something about the strength of America. They wanted to earn their way. They didn't want something for nothing, and that is the kind of spirit we need in America if we are going to meet the challenges that face America today.

When we think of Texas, we think of a State that is primarily Protestant, with a rather heavy Mexican population. Did you know that within 50 miles of where you sit tonight there is a German settlement, there is a Polish settlement, there is one that was founded by a Jewish group, there is another that is Czechoslovakian? Of course, there are some that are Mexican and some of other groups. In fact, 26 different nationalities are represented within 100 miles of where we sit. That is Texas.

What is America? I have traveled, along with my wife, to most of the countries of the world, over 80, and when you really think of America, America is a great country because all of the nations of the world are right here, and we have taken the diversity, the qualifications, the character, the richness of all and have molded them into a great people.

What we must remember as we build America for the future is how we became what we did. And what we must remember is that those who came to these shores, and then those who, after they came to the eastern shore, moved across these prairies into Texas and then across the mountains into California, they were strong people, they were good people, they had character. Let's not destroy the character of the American people today. Let's keep it strong.

I said to you at the outset that instead of calling this organization "Democrats for Nixon," call it "Democrats for America." In 1947, I recall one of the first votes I cast as a freshman Congressman. At that time, as you remember, the Republicans had won the Congress in the elections of 1946. President Truman was in the White House. There was a threat to Greece and Turkey from the Communists. President Truman came before the Congress and asked for the enactment of the Greek-Turkish aid program.

It seems so long ago, but anyone who writes the history of those times will realize how tremendously important drawing that line at that time was, not simply in saving Greece and Turkey, but in also saving the rest of free Europe from what could have been an eventual Communist envelopment.

It was a hard vote for those of us who were Republicans. There was a Democratic President. We had just won the House of Representatives. There were great partisan appeals to us to vote the party and not vote the country. I looked at the vote as it occurred and—it is recorded in the Congressional Record—just a few days ago. I saw the names of those who voted in the affirmative, voted with President Truman. There was a young Congressman from Texas who later became President of the United States, Lyndon Johnson. He was 40 years of age then. There was a young Congressman, a freshman Congressman from Massachusetts who later became President of the United States, John Kennedy. He was 31 years of age. And I am proud to say there was a young Congressman from California, who was 34 years of age, who later became President of the United States—but all put America above their party.

And I simply want to say to you tonight,

speaking not in partisan terms, not in personal terms, but speaking of this country that we all love so much, that I am very proud to have the support of leaders of the Democratic Party from across this country. I know the risk that you have taken. I know the heat that you are taking. But I can only assure you that if we prevail in this election, I am going to do everything I possibly can to make your votes and your support look good for America.

Thank you.

NOTE: The President spoke at 9:42 p.m. at a dinner sponsored by the Democrats for Nixon and hosted by former Secretary of the Treasury and Mrs. Connally at their home, the Picosa Ranch, Floresville, Tex. The President spoke without referring to notes.

Mr. Connally introduced the President as follows:

May I first say to all of you here how delighted Nellie and I are to welcome you to this home of ours. You came from many States, many miles to be here. We know you didn't come to see us. [*Laughter*] But we are thrilled to host you anyway. I want you to know that.

I can't tell you how honored we are to host the President and the First Lady in your behalf. Nearly everyone here is a Democrat, but you are here in support of the President of the United States. And by your presence here and by your actions in your home States and your home cities and your home communities, you have proven beyond any doubt that you are going to put your country above your party in this election year, 1972.

I wish that each of you had been privileged to have had the great pleasure and privilege that has been mine, to serve a President of the United States, who also so clearly puts his country above his party. I wish that each of you could know the President of the United States as I know him to be, a man who is concerned about this country, about its people, a man who has great respect for its past and yet who has such unbounded faith and hope for its future.

I wish that each of you could have seen him

899

as I have been privileged to see him, in moments of trial, in moments of great decision, display a compassion and a courage that would warm the heart of any person in this world and, most particularly, any American.

Because we are all Democrats, most of us, I think, have known the President of the United States only by reputation, and I must say in all candor that some of the things we have heard about him over the years have not necessarily endeared him to us. [*Laughter*] But I must say to you also, in all candor and in all frankness, that he, like all of us who are in public life, and he more than any of us here, has been misinterpreted a bit at times throughout his political life.

And I have seen the sympathy, the concern, the compassion, the interest, the dedication that is so much a part of him. And I can't help but think as we sit here on this grass tonight, and as Mayor [Charles S.] Stenvig of Minneapolis said a little bit ago, that this is indeed a wonderful country, and he said to think that a man who is a policeman in Minneapolis can be here and rub shoulders with all of the wonderful people who are here tonight. He said this indeed is a great country.

And I responded that, yes, I knew that it was indeed a wonderful country when a country boy from Floresville, Texas, who grew up in these sandy fields, raising peanuts, could host, in behalf of the Democrats of this country, the President and the First Lady of this Nation.

And as I look around this assemblage tonight, there are a great many of you whom I have met just tonight for the first time, but there are a great many others who I have known for a long, long time. And many of you weren't policemen in Minneapolis or peanut farmers in Floresville, but you had just as humble a beginning as we did, I assure you, because I know. And I know that the President of the United States had a beginning that was as humble as any one of us here, and he never lost those lessons that he learned, those lessons of humility, of care, of consideration, of kindness, and of thoughtfulness. It has been a part of his life.

It doesn't make any difference to him whether you are Democrat or Republican, or black or brown or white or yellow, or what you do, what your social status is, or what your bank account shows. He is a man who concerns himself with the problems of this country, and I suppose in one way it is perhaps not appropriate to describe the President of the United States as a professional, but President Nixon is a professional.

He is a professional scholar about this world and its problems and the role that this Nation plays in the scheme of things. He is a professional when it comes to caring for those who really can't care for themselves. He is a professional when it comes to studying and understanding the temper of this Nation and the needs of this country. He is a professional when it comes to looking into the future and not being satisfied with what is past or even present, but planning instead for the future of those who are going to follow us.

He is a professional in the discipline that he manifests in his personal life. He is a professional in the honesty that he displays in his personal, as well as his political, life. He is a professional in every sense that that word can be used to describe a great statesman of this world who understands the role of leadership that this Nation must play and the role that the President of the United States must be in seeing that this country lives up to its duties, to its responsibilities, and even to its manifest destiny.

And I must say to all of you that I, like you, have no doubt about what we are doing. I have no regrets whatsoever about what we are doing. I, as a lifelong Democrat, am proud to say to each of you here tonight, as I have said to you before and as I will say to all Americans who will listen to me, that this year we have a choice. The conventions are over, the election process is well on its way. It is 6 weeks off. And we have a choice of whom we shall select to be our next President. There are only two men that we can choose—Mr. Schmitz [2] wouldn't agree with that, he would probably say there would be three—but I think for all practical purposes, there are two men that really we can choose, and, so far as I am concerned, the interest of this country leaves no choice.

The interest of this country clearly dictates that whatever you are, whatever your political

---

[2] Representative John G. Schmitz of California was the American Party's candidate for President in the 1972 election.

affiliation, that you don't have a choice, that you only have one course to follow, and that is the message that we ought to preach to all of the precincts of this Nation, and that is: The President of the United States should be reelected.

And ladies and gentlemen, before I present the distinguished President, may I also have the privilege of asking my wife, Nellie, to come up here and stand, because she has labored harder and longer to put on this party than anyone.

And now it is my great privilege and high honor to present to you a lady who is a lady in

every sense of the word, who has been a magnificent helpmate, who has been as fine a mother as any woman could be, who has a steady hand, a calm hand, a reasoning hand, always in the support of her President, in victory and in defeat, a lady who can walk the streets of Moscow or the schoolrooms of China and be at home and reflect nothing but great dignity, great poise, and great credit on the United States. Mrs. Nixon.

Ladies and gentlemen, it is a signal honor for me, under these circumstances, to present to you the President of the United States.

316   Statement About the Latest Economic Statistics.   *September* 23, 1972

THE LATEST economic statistics, issued yesterday in Washington, confirm the steady expansion in the purchasing power of the Nation's workers—and Texans are sharing fully in this healthy prosperity trend.

This is greatly pleasing to me—it shows we definitely are on the right track with our economic policies.

In the year our new economic policy has been in effect, the real spendable weekly earnings of the average production worker have increased by more than 4 percent—even after price increases and Federal taxes have been accounted for.

For such a worker, that means his purchasing power has gained more than $200 in the past year—the equivalent of two extra weekly paychecks.

The plain fact is that American workers have scored greater increases in spendable income in the past year than at any time in the past 8 years.

The price statistics kept for Dallas, for example, as part of the nationwide cost of living calculation, indicate that Texans are sharing fully in this mounting purchas-

ing power prosperity.

In Dallas, as in the Nation, the latest consumer price statistics show that the 1969 rate of inflation has been cut by more than half.

Inflation was running at a cruel 6.4 percent in Dallas in 1969, while the nationwide rate was 6.1 percent. The rise in prices has been reduced in the past year to 2.3 percent in Dallas and to 2.9 percent nationally.

These statistics remind us what it was like when this Administration first took office. It then was necessary for the average U.S. worker to get a raise of more than 6 percent just to stay even in purchasing power—any smaller increase meant his family actually fell behind on the inflation treadmill of the late 1960's.

We have made solid progress in the battle against inflation, but that battle is not yet won. We are determined to cut the rate of inflation even more than we have, in Texas and in the Nation.

NOTE: The statement was released at San Antonio, Tex.

317 Remarks to Members of Young Labor for Nixon. *September 23, 1972*

Ladies and gentlemen:

I am very delighted to welcome you here in the East Room of the White House. I want you to know that after I speak to you briefly that some refreshments are available. It is a little early, but they will be very nice. A little coffee and the best hors d'oeuvres you can possibly imagine, and all of you are young, so eat them up so that we won't have to eat them tomorrow.

I was under the impression that this was "Young Labor for the President," or "Young Labor for Nixon," and as I went along, you know, people were reaching out handing me things. This is an interesting thing. I guess that is the hardhat vote, so I will put that in there. [*Laughter*] And some fellow gave me a cigar and since it said "Young Labor for the President," I said, "Your daughter?" He said, "No, my granddaughter." So we have one that is a little older.

Then one little boy—here he is right here in front—shook hands with me, and I said, "Well, you are not old enough, are you?" And he said, "Oh, not to vote, but old enough to work." [*Laughter*] There is a little girl over there.

Let me say in speaking to you, I know that you have had a very heart-warming announcement today. I am most grateful for that support. I know, too, that you have come from most of the States in this eastern seaboard. I know, too, that giving up a Saturday, when you have been doing a lot of work all week, is somewhat of a sacrifice to come here, and we want you to feel very much at home. I want you to remember this visit as one that was worth coming to, worth coming here.

I would like to speak to you in terms of what this election is about, not in partisan terms of Democrats versus Republicans, or one individual against another, but in terms that I was trying to describe last night in speaking to a group in Texas. There were leaders from all over the country of an organization called Democrats for Nixon. And when I addressed them, I said, of course, in a personal sense I liked the name of the organization, but I said, on the other hand, in a larger sense I would prefer another name. Rather than saying "Democrats for Nixon," why not "Democrats for America." That is what it is really all about.

I would like for you to think in those terms. You have the wonderful asset of being young. You have all those great years ahead of you, and they will be good years I am sure, better years than any generation in our history. We are all working for that.

But being young, and looking ahead, you think of your country and America, and whatever your party, whatever your background, whatever you are doing, whatever job you have, you want this country to be better, you want it to play the role that it should play in making a better world, and that is what I have been trying to work for. That is what every President tries to work for, be he a Democrat or Republican.

So, in telling you why I think many of you are here, let me say that I believe one of the reasons is that you believe that America needs to be strong, strong not simply in the sense of being bigger than somebody else and wanting to put somebody else down, but strong because we know that a strong America is the world's best guarantee of peace and freedom. That is why we have to be for a strong America.

During the past 4 years I have had to make some rather difficult decisions with regard to national defense, decisions with regard to whether we went through with this weapon system or that one that I thought was necessary in order for the United States not to become the second strongest nation in the world. Some of those votes were very close, and always, of course, I sought support from all areas of our country, from businessmen, from people in organized labor and people in unorganized labor, working men and women, others throughout the country.

Also, I have made some very hard decisions in the conduct of foreign policy. One of the hardest was the one I made on May 8, when a massive Communist invasion took place of South Vietnam, where the Communists moved into the South, and where, in order to protect the 50,000 Americans that were there and in order to prevent the Communist imposition of a government on the people of South Vietnam, I ordered the mining of the harbors of Haiphong and the bombing of military targets in North Vietnam.

Many thought that was not the thing to do. That was their opinion. They had a right to it. I was criticized quite roundly for it. Many thought that it would jeopardize the summit that was scheduled in just 3 weeks with the Soviet Union, but I had to do what I felt was right for America, right for the cause of peace, right for our servicemen.

Under the circumstances, I made that decision. I think you should know this:

Polls were taken at that time of all segments of our society. Polls were also taken at the time we had some of those close decisions with regard to whether America would remain strong enough militarily to keep its position of being second to none in the world, or whether we should become weak.

You will be interested to know that the strongest support of the President in those two areas came from the working men and women of America. That is where the strength was.

That isn't because working men and women are for war, it is because they are for peace. It is because they are for freedom. It is because also they are very practical. They know that the only way that we are going to keep peace and we are going to keep freedom is for the United States of America—that has no designs on any other country, that doesn't want to conquer any other country, that has fought four wars in this century without asking for an acre of territory or any concession from any other country, fought to defend freedom and not to destroy it— they know that for the United States to have that strength is the world's best guarantee in the future for peace.

If we don't have it, we leave a vacuum. Because, as we look at the free nations of Europe, as we look at the only nation in Asia that could develop that strength, Japan, not one of them now can do it. And so, it is all right here. If the United States backs down, if we turn inward, if we turn away from responsibility, if we allow this country to become second to any country in the world in terms of arms strength, it means that the chances for this 9-year-old to grow up in a period of peace and freedom are much less than they would otherwise be.

I simply want you to know that I am grateful for the support that I have had from you, from 80 million wage earners in this country, who saw that and saw it more clearly than some people in business, some people in the professions, some people in the media, some people in the universities—not all, but some. You saw it because you helped to build America. You believed deeply in America and you know that strength in the hand of America is not a bad thing. It is a good thing. It is a necessary thing.

The other point I want to make with regard to what I would call "Young Labor for America" is this: You want good jobs, good jobs for yourselves and better jobs for your children. You want good jobs and opportunity for yourselves, a chance to go up as far as your talents will take you, an opportunity for everybody in this country, whatever his background, whatever his color, whatever his religion, whatever his national origin. We all want that.

You also want your country to be one that can be generous, generous to those who can't help themselves, generous to the poor, generous to the old, generous to others who, because of some physical disability, cannot work as you are able to work, and let me say sometimes we are bored with our jobs and sometimes I am sure we think, gee, why do I have to work. Just let me say, to be able to work, to be able to take care of yourself, the dignity of work is something we all ought to appreciate in this country of ours. And every job is a good job if it puts bread on the table and provides housing and clothing for a man's children, or for a woman's, for that matter. We all must remember that this is something that we must respect.

Some of us do one thing, some do another, but all help to build America. And

it is because you represent that strength that has built America from the time of its beginning that you are here, I believe, today.

We believe in helping those who can't help themselves. But just let me make one thing very, very clear. It seems to me that a man or a woman should work for what he gets and get what he works for. It seems to me, too, that it is wrong for anyone who works to get less than someone who may be on welfare.

That does not mean that we do not want to help those who have to be on welfare. We should, and we can be thankful that in this country we do take care of those who cannot help themselves. But do you realize—I am sure all of you do—that those who cannot help themselves, those who have to have government assistance, could only get it if other people worked. That is where you get the taxes. That is where this government gets the money. They talk about what the government is going to do. We have no money. You produce it, and I say that we in government owe an obligation to the working men and women in America to see that your money is not wasted, to see to it that it goes for good causes and not for wasteful causes.

There is one last point that I would like to leave with you, without going into any detail with regard to the future, as far as our foreign policy and the rest is concerned. We are coming to the end of a very long and very difficult war. It has been one that has divided Americans. It is one, however, which we are ending and ending in a way without staining the honor of the United States of America. It is one in which 17 million people of South Vietnam will not have a Communist government imposed upon them against their will, in which they have developed the strength to defend themselves with our help as they have been defending themselves, particularly on the ground, in these past months.

And sometimes when we hear about good news and bad news, I think one of the best pieces of news that I have seen in the almost 4 years I have been here was that for the first time since 1965, not one American was killed in action this last week.

So, I want that war to end, just as President Johnson wanted to end it before me. I want it to end. I want it to end in a way that it will discourage others who might engage in that kind of aggression, but beyond that, I want America to help to build a new world.

That is what my trip to the People's Republic of China is about. You can't have peace in the world and have one-fourth of all the people of the world—and one-fourth of the people of the world live on the mainland of China—you can't have them without any communication with the United States of America.

So, we have opened that line of communication. Oh, our philosophies are very different, and we are going to have our differences, but there is now a better chance that they will be settled peacefully, without war.

That is why we have started these historic communications with the Soviet Union in arms control, in the environment, cooperating in programs in health, space, and others, not because we don't recognize that they have a very different philosophy than we have, but because we realize that if we are going to have a world of peace, it is essential that the United States and the Soviet Union negotiate rather than confront and eventually break

out into a war that could well be the last one.

That is why, looking to the future—because all we have had is a beginning—what I am really asking for in this election campaign is a chance to continue, a chance to continue to build a structure of peace in the world, so that this young man and that little girl that was sitting on her father's shoulders a moment ago—so that they can grow up in an open world where they can go to China, they can go to Russia, where they can learn to know the Chinese people and the Russian people and all the peoples of the world, Africa and Asia, where at last in this last fourth of the 20th century, there will be no war any place in the world.

That is what I want. That is what I want for the world, that is what I want for America, that is what you want. And I want an America in which we continue to have, as we have today, the best jobs, at the highest real wages, with the greatest opportunity and the most freedom of any country in the world.

Oh, there is lots more to be done. There are inequities in our system. But what is great about America is that we can change what is wrong and change it peacefully. And that is another reason you are here, because you believe in our system, you are working through it, rather than attempting to destroy it from the outside.

In that connection, I mentioned a moment ago that this had been a long and a very difficult war. I know that one of the subjects that has been discussed in your group, as well as in many others in this country, is that of the question of amnesty for those who chose to desert America rather than to serve it.

When you think of it in solely human terms, in personal terms, I know that there might be a tendency to say, "Why not? Once the war is over, why not? From a personal standpoint, let's forget it, let them come back."

Let me tell you my view. Let me tell you in terms of another President, Abraham Lincoln—he was a strong President. He was a very great President. He was a very kind man. But he was a man who knew that you had to have discipline. He was a man who knew that if the United States was going to be able to be first, be unified, and then to continue to have people that would serve in the armed forces, there had to be penalties for those who refused to serve.

And there is a story told in Sandburg's Lincoln. One day in 1863, Abraham Lincoln was in the upstairs office—the office was then there, they didn't have the East Wing or the West Wing at that point— and a messenger brought in a note from a man who was standing outside at the gate. He was one who had deserted and gone to Canada. He had stayed there for a year or so, and the message came in and he asked the President for amnesty, for the right to come back.

And President Lincoln, who was a very kind man, but also a very strong man, and one who knew what was right and what was just, wrote on that little note these words, as I recall it. He said, "He may return, but there are hundreds of thousands of others who served. Some of them lost their lives, and this man who went to Canada and who has come back, he shall stay in prison until he has served the number of days he was out of this country before we give him amnesty."

At first blush that would seem harsh, but on the other hand, what we must realize, that as we think of the hundreds of thousands—yes, 2½ million Americans

who served their country in Vietnam—I am sure most of them didn't want to go, didn't want to leave their families, didn't want to take all that risk, and some of them did lose their lives, but they chose to serve. A few didn't, and under the circumstances, under the rules, it is essential that those who serve get the respect that they deserve and those who chose to desert must pay the penalty that they have earned. That, very simply, is the position that I take on this issue.

Now, one last point. When I was your age, or perhaps a little younger—let's see. 1932 to 1939—in those years, I was in high school, later went on to college, then to law school, finished law school, and incidentally, worked all the way through. But in any event, during those periods this country was in a great depression. Many people had lost confidence in the country and I remember sometimes in our bull sessions we used to say, "Gee, maybe there is a better place to go. I wonder how it is in Latin America. I wonder how it is in Europe, or some place else."

Of course none of us then could afford to go and find out. We just had to keep working, because there weren't that many jobs. Fortunately, the situation has changed considerably. But let me tell you this: You are young. You have most of your lives ahead. And you hear many things that are wrong about this country, and there are some. But let me tell you, I have been to over 80 countries in this world. I have been to Communist countries. I have been to socialist countries. I have been to the great free countries of Europe and of Asia and of Latin America and of Africa. I have enjoyed every visit. I have respected all of the people of the countries that I have met. But every time I come back to America, this is what I know: Anybody who lives in America, who is young in America at this time, is the most fortunate young man or woman in the world. This is the place.

So let's help make this a better country, a country of better jobs, of more opportunity, of better retirement for all of us when we do retire, more generosity for those who cannot help themselves, but above all, let's remember, Americans can be proud of the fact that their country, as we near our 200th birthday, is the strongest nation of the world. We can be proud of the fact that our strength according to all of the leaders of the world that I have met, when you talk to them, really face to face, know that that strength will never be used for the purpose of destroying their freedom or their peace.

Let us remember that the strength of America, its military strength, its economic strength, its moral strength which you represent here today, that that is not only good for us, but it is good for the world. Let's be proud to be Americans and let me say, I am mighty proud to have "Young Labor for America" here today.

Just let me say, when anybody asks you what it is all about, when they ask you what politics is about, whether you are in it as a vocation or whether you are in it as an avocation, working for the candidate of your choice, here it is: It is their future, let's make it the best.

NOTE: The President spoke at 2:25 p.m. in the East Room at the White House. He spoke without referring to notes.

318 Remarks at the Annual Meeting of Boards of Governors of the International Monetary Fund and the International Bank for Reconstruction and Development. *September 25, 1972*

Mr. Secretary, distinguished guests, Governors, ladies and gentlemen:

I have had the privilege of visiting most of the 124 countries represented here in this distinguished audience, and on this occasion I would like to extend my welcome to you, my best wishes to the heads of government that I have also had the privilege to meet, and particularly the best wishes of the American people to all of the people of the many countries represented at this gathering.

It is customary in addressing such a significant international gathering to say that we are participating in a great moment of history. Great moments in history are easy to perceive. The headlines

blaze and the world is riveted at television screens as world leaders meet. But great movements in history are much harder to perceive, and particularly while we are living through them. The action is slower, it is less dramatic, it is infinitely more complex as changing circumstances and the new needs of people alter the behavior of nations.

I am convinced, on the basis of the evidence of the past year, that we are not only participating today in a great moment in history, but that we are witnessing and helping to create a profound movement in history.

That movement is away from the resolution of potential conflict by war, and toward its resolution through peaceful means. The experienced people gathered in this room are not so naive as to expect the smoothing out of all differences between peoples and between nations. We anticipate that the potential for conflict will exist as long as men and nations have different interests, different approaches, different ideals.

Therefore, we must come to grips with the paradoxes of peace. As the danger of armed conflict between major powers is reduced, the potential for economic conflict increases. As the possibility of peace grows stronger, some of the original ties that first bound our postwar alliances together grow weaker. As nations around the world gain new economic strength, the points of commercial contact multiply along with the possibilities of disagreements.

There is another irony that we should recognize on this occasion. With one exception, the nations gathered here whose domestic economies are growing so strongly today can trace much of their postwar growth to the expansion of international trade. The one exception is the United States—the industrial nation with by far the smallest percentage of its gross national product in world trade.

Why, then, is the United States—seemingly with the least at stake—in the forefront of those working for prompt and thoroughgoing reform of the international monetary system, with all that will mean for the expansion of trade now and in the future?

One reason, of course, is our national self-interest. We want our working men and women, our business men and women, to have a fair chance to compete for their share of the expanding trade between nations. A generation ago, at the end of World War II, we deliberately set out to help our former enemies as well as our weakened allies, so that they would inevitably gain the economic strength which would enable them to compete with us in world markets. And now we expect our trading partners to help bring about equal and fair competition.

There is another reason, more far-reaching and fundamental, that motivates the United States in pressing for economic and monetary reform.

Working together, we must set in place an economic structure that will help and not hinder the world's historic movement toward peace.

We must make certain that international commerce becomes a source of stability and harmony, rather than a cause of friction and animosity.

Potential conflict must be channeled into cooperative competition. That is why the structure of the international monetary system and the future system of world trade are so central to our concerns today. The time has come for action across the entire front of international economic problems. Recurring monetary crises such as we have experienced all too often in the past decade, unfair currency alignments and trading agreements which put the workers of one nation at a disadvantage with workers of another nation, great disparities in development that breed resentment, a monetary system that makes no provision for the realities of the present and the needs of the future—all these not only injure our economies, they also create political tensions that subvert the cause of peace.

There must be a thoroughgoing reform of the world monetary system to clear the path for the healthy economic competition of the future.

We must see monetary reform as one part of a total reform of international economic affairs encompassing trade and investment opportunity for all.

We must create a realistic code of economic conduct to guide our mutual relations—a code which allows governments freedom to pursue legitimate domestic objectives, but which also gives them good reason to abide by agreed principles of international behavior.

Each nation must exercise the power of its example in the realistic and orderly conduct of internal economic affairs so that each nation exports its products and not its problems.

We can all agree that the health of the world economy and the stability of the international economic system rests largely on the successful management of domestic economies. The United States recognizes the importance of a strong, noninflationary domestic economy, both in meeting the needs of our own citizens and in contributing to a healthy world economy. We are firmly committed to reaching our goals in this country of strong growth, full employment, price stability.

We are encouraged by the record of our current economic performance. We are now experiencing one of the lowest rates of inflation, one of the highest rates of real economic growth, of any industrial nation.

Recent gains in the productivity and the real income of American workers have been heartening. We intend to continue the policies that have produced those gains.

We also recognize that, over the longer term, domestic policies alone cannot solve international problems. Even if all countries achieved a very large measure of success in managing their own economies, strains and tensions could arise at points of contact with other economies.

We cannot afford a system that almost every year presents a new invitation to a monetary crisis in the world. And that is why we face the need to develop procedures for prompt and orderly adjustment.

It is very easy for me to use the term "prompt and orderly adjustment." And many would say that that is a term that only concerns bankers and finance ministers and economists. But that phrase "prompt and orderly adjustment" in international monetary matters encompasses the real problems of working men and women, the fears and hopes of investors and managers of large and small businesses, and, consequently, it is the concern of the political leadership of every nation represented in this group today. No nation should be denied the opportunity to adjust, nor relieved of the obligation to adjust.

In the negotiations ahead, there will be differences of opinion and approaches. You saw some of those differences at the Smithsonian not a year ago, even. I had the opportunity to see them at another level in meetings with President Pompidou in the Azores, with Prime Minister Heath at Bermuda, with Chancellor Brandt in Florida, with Prime Minister Sato in California, and I know how intricate, how difficult the problems are that you will be considering at these meetings. Immediate interests inevitably will seem to be in conflict, and there will be times when impasses develop that may seem impossible to resolve.

But the world has had some experience recently with long, hard negotiations, and I refer in another field to a long, hard negotiation—the strategic arms limitation agreements signed by the Soviet Union and the United States early this summer.

Now, that was bilateral negotiation. It involved just two nations, not 124. But its complexity, when those negotiations began 3 years or so ago, seemed almost infinite; the obstacles had been hardening for over 25 years; the issue of national security for each nation was as sensitive a matter as can exist in negotiations between two powers.

We came to an agreement in Moscow, nevertheless, because the issue that united us—seeking an end to the wasteful and dangerous arms race—was greater than the issues that divided us.

We reached agreement because we realized that it was impossible for either side to negotiate an advantage over the other that would prevail. The only agreement worth making was one in which each side had a stake in keeping.

Now, these two principles can guide us in building the monetary system of the future.

We recognize that the issues that divide us are many and they are very serious and infinitely complex and difficult. But the impetus that will make this negotiation successful is the force that unites us all, all the 124 nations represented here today: that is a common need to establish a sound and abiding foundation for commerce, leading to a better way of life for all the citizens of all the nations here and all the citizens of the world.

That common need, let us call it the world interest, demands a new freedom of world trade, a new fairness in international economic conduct.

It is a mark of our maturity that we now see that an unfair advantage gained in an agreement today only sabotages that agreement tomorrow.

I well remember when I was a first-year law student, 32 years ago, what the professor of contracts said as he opened the course. He said, "A contract is only as good as the will of the parties to keep it."

The only system that can work is one that each nation has an active interest in making work. The need is self-evident. The will to reform the monetary system is here in this room, and, in a proverb that has its counterpart in almost every language here, where there is a will there is a way.

We are gathered to create a responsible monetary system, responsive to the need for stability and openness, and responsive to the need of each country to reflect its unique character.

In this way we bring to bear one of the great lessons of federalism: that often the best way to enforce an agreed-upon discipline is to let each member take action to adhere to it in the way that is best suited to its local character, its stage of development, its economic structure.

For its part, I can assure you, the United States will continue to rise to its world responsibilities, joining with other nations to create and participate in a modern world economic order.

We are secure enough in our independence to freely assert our interdependence.

These are the principles that I profoundly believe should and will guide the

United States in its international economic conduct now and in the years ahead.

We shall press for a more equitable and a more open world of trade. We shall meet competition rather than run away from it.

We shall be a stimulating trading partner, a straightforward bargainer.

We shall not turn inward and isolationist.

In turn we shall look to our friends for evidence of similar rejection of isolationism in economic and political affairs.

Let us all resolve to look at the ledgers of international commerce today with new eyes—to see that there is no heroism in a temporary surplus nor villainy in a temporary deficit, but to see that progress is possible only in the framework of long-term equilibrium. In this regard we must take bold action toward a more equitable and a more open world trading order.

Like every leader of the nations represented here, I want to see new jobs created all over the world, but I cannot condone the export of jobs out of the United States caused by any unfairness built into the world's trading system.

Let all nations in the more advanced stages of industrial development share the responsibility of helping those countries whose major development lies ahead, and let the great industrial nations, in offering that help, in providing it, forgo the temptation to use that help as an instrument of domination, discrimination, or rivalry.

Far more is at stake here than the mechanics of commerce and finance. At stake is the chance to add genuine opportunity to the lives of people, hundreds of millions of people in all nations, the chance to add stability and security to the savings and earnings of hundreds of millions of people in all of our nations, the chance to add economic muscle to the sinews of peace.

I have spoken this morning in general terms about how we can advance our economic interdependence. Later this week, Secretary Shultz will outline a number of proposals which represent the best thinking of my top economic advisers. I commend those proposals to you for your careful consideration.

The word "economics," traced to its Greek root, means "the law of the house."

This house we live in—this community of nations—needs far better laws to guide our future economic conduct. Every nation can prosper and benefit working within a modern world economic order that it has a stake in preserving.

Now, very little of what is done in these negotiations will be widely understood in this country or in any of your countries as well. And very little of it will be generally appreciated.

But history will record the vital nature of the challenge before us. I am confident that the men and the nations gathered here will seize the opportunity to create a monetary and trading system that will work for the coming generation—and will help to shape the years ahead into a generation of peace for all nations in the world.

NOTE: The President spoke at 11:18 a.m. in the Ballroom of the Sheraton Park Hotel at the opening session of the annual joint meeting of the Fund and Bank Boards of Governors.

Secretary of the Treasury George P. Shultz, who was the United States Governor on the Boards, introduced the President.

The President spoke from a prepared text. An advance text of his remarks was released on the same day.

319   Memorandum Establishing a Cabinet Committee To Combat Terrorism.   *September 25, 1972*

Memorandum for the Secretary of State:

SUBJECT: Action to Combat Terrorism

Your report to me on the measures that are being taken to combat terrorism indicates that we are moving effectively against the problem of thwartng acts of terrorism both here and abroad. The two committees you have set up to cope with this major problem are making commendable progress toward this end.

Because of the great importance and urgency I attach to dealing with the worldwide problem of terrorism, which encompasses diplomatic, intelligence, and law enforcement functions, I am hereby establishing a Cabinet Committee to Combat Terrorism.

The Cabinet Committee will be chaired by the Secretary of State and will comprise

The Secretary of State
The Secretary of the Treasury
The Secretary of Defense
The Attorney General
The Secretary of Transportation
The United States Ambassador to the United Nations
The Director of Central Intelligence
The Assistant to the President for National Security Affairs
The Assistant to the President for Domestic Affairs
The Acting Director of the Federal Bureau of Investigation

and such others as the Chairman may consider necessary.

The Cabinet Committee will be supported by a Working Group comprised of personally designated senior representatives of the members of the Committee, chaired by the designee of the Secretary of State.

The Committee will consider the most effective means by which to prevent terrorism here and abroad, and it will also take the lead in establishing procedures to ensure that our government can take appropriate action in response to acts of terrorism swiftly and effectively. The Secretary of State will be in touch with other governments and international organizations toward this goal.

Federal officers and Federal departments and agencies are to cooperate fully with the Cabinet Committee in carrying out its functions under this directive, and they shall comply with the policies, guidelines, standards, and procedures prescribed by the Cabinet Committee.

More specifically, the Cabinet Committee shall:

(1) Coordinate, among the government agencies, ongoing activity for the prevention of terrorism. This will include such activities as the collection of intelligence worldwide and the physical protection of U.S. personnel and installations abroad and foreign diplomats, and diplomatic installations in the United States.

(2) Evaluate all such programs and activities and where necessary recommend methods for their effective implementation.

(3) Devise procedures for reacting swiftly and effectively to acts of terrorism that occur.

(4) Make recommendations to the Director of the Office of Management and

Budget concerning proposed funding of such programs; and

(5) Report to the President, from time to time, concerning the foregoing.

RICHARD NIXON

NOTE: The memorandum was made available to the press.

On the same day, the White House released an announcement of the establishment of the Cabinet Committee.

320   Message to the Congress Transmitting Annual Report on the Coal Mine Health Program. *September 26, 1972*

To the Congress of the United States:

I am pleased to submit to you the second annual report on health matters covered by the Federal Coal Mine Health and Safety Act of 1969, Public Law 91–173.

The report covers the implementation of the health program carried out by the National Institute for Occupational Safety and Health of the Department of Health, Education, and Welfare. The report provides a compendium of coal mine health research, medical examinations of coal miners, and other activities of 1971.

It is encouraging to note that, in 1971, the Department of Health, Education, and Welfare completed the first round of medical examinations of coal workers required in the act. Many of the X-rays taken in the examination have been completely processed and those miners with

abnormal chest conditions have been notified of these conditions and of their rights under the act.

A comprehensive research program, which has as its basic objective the determination of the development and progression of coal workers' pneumoconiosis, continued in 1971 along the lines established in 1970. Significant progress was made in 1971 toward the attainment of this goal.

I commend this report to your attention.

RICHARD NIXON

The White House,
September 26, 1972.

NOTE: The 155-page report, entitled "Health Program of the Federal Coal Mine Health and Safety Act of 1969; 1971 Annual Report," was prepared by the Department of Health, Education, and Welfare.

321   Remarks at the Dedication of the American Museum of Immigration on Liberty Island in New York Harbor. *September 26, 1972*

Secretary Morton, Governor Rockefeller, Governor Cahill, Congressman Peyser, all of the distinguished people who are here:

I appreciate this opportunity to participate in the dedication of this museum.

In dedicating this museum, I wish particularly to pay tribute to all of those who have helped to make this country what it is.

[At this point, members of the audience chanted "Four More Years" in response to several demonstrators who were attempting to interrupt

913

the President. The President then resumed speaking.]

Thank you. Ladies and gentlemen, I would only suggest that on your television screens tonight, in addition to showing the six there, let's show the thousands that are over here.

Secretary Morton has referred to this memorial building which we have just dedicated. I simply want to say that as far as this memorial is concerned, that those who came to these shores, the shores of the United States of America—they have built their own memorial, because they built America and we are proud of those who built America.

A few moments ago, as we got off the helicopter, four little girls were there in native costumes to greet us. One of my aides pointed out the helicopter window and said, "That one is Italian and this one is Polish and this one is Ukrainian and this one is German." Let me say that every one of us is proud of his national background, but I say that instead of referring to someone, "He is an Italian, he is a German, he is a Pole, he is a Ukrainian," let's say, first of all, "He or she is an American," because those who came to this shore, if you go through this museum, have contributed so much to America.

One thing they have contributed is something that we see in America more than in any other country, and that is the diversity. My wife and I have had the privilege of visiting over 80 countries in the world—Asia, Africa, Latin America—but you don't have to go abroad, you don't have to cross the Atlantic or the Pacific, to see the world. All the world is right here in America. That is the greatness of America.

And so in America, whether it is in the field of music, whether it is in the field of art, whether it is in the field of architecture, in any area, we come from all of the world, and we have built a nation which carries out that great saying that "The hallmark of freedom is diversity," and the diversity of America is what makes us an interesting country.

So while we are all Americans, let us always be proud of our background, whatever that is, because that makes America a greater country.

I could speak of many ways in which those who came to these shores have enriched America, but let me point out one way in particular: They believed in hard work. They didn't come here for a handout. They came here for an opportunity, and they built America.

There is one other thing that I have found about those who have come from other countries, or their children. I have found that when it comes to love of country, when it comes to patriotism, those who came to America from other lands are very first in their hearts as far as love of America is concerned.

One of the great privileges a President of the United States has is to participate in citizenship ceremonies and to greet and shake hands with people from all the continents of the world and all the nations of the world. And, my friends—and particularly you boys and girls that are down here in front—let me just simply say to you that there is nothing that makes you appreciate this country more than to see somebody that has just become an American citizen with tears in his or her eyes because they are so proud to be an

American.

On our part, therefore, as we dedicate this memorial, let us dedicate ourselves also to a great proposition that brought people to these shores—and that is to make the American dream come true.

By the "American Dream" let us recognize that the American dream cannot be realized fully until every American has a chance to realize it in his own life. Let's give that opportunity to every American, whatever his background.

Then finally, if I could bring you just one message from other countries around the world. On my recent visit to the Soviet Union we stopped at Warsaw on the way back to the United States. I remember thousands of Poles in the heart of Warsaw welcoming the President of the United States and his wife with these words, *"Niech zyje Ameryka,"* which means "Long live America."

To all of our friends here today, let us pledge ourselves that we not only will work for better opportunity for all Americans, whatever their national background, but let us work for the chance that all Americans can see all the world freely. And let us work for the chance that people who live in the countries from which we came, whether it is Poland or Italy or the Orient or wherever they may be, so that all of those people, and particularly the children of those lands, can grow up in a world of peace. That is what we want for all the world.

Finally, today, we thank you for welcoming us on this occasion. I urge all of you to spend the time that we did not have to see this museum and as you see it, you will realize that a very strong people came across those waters to America. Let's always be worthy of their strength, of their patriotism, of their love of America, and of their love of peace.

Thank you.

NOTE: The President spoke at 3:14 p.m. outside the American Museum of Immigration, which is located in the base of the Statue of Liberty. He spoke without referring to notes.

On the same day, the White House released a fact sheet on the museum.

322   Statement About the Dedication of the American Museum of Immigration.   *September 26, 1972*

SPEAKING about the nature of our country, President Eisenhower once said that America "is best described by one word, freedom."

It is especially appropriate that we recall that description as we dedicate the American Museum of Immigration, at the base of this great national monument.

The idea for this museum was born in 1954, when a group of citizens met with President Eisenhower to suggest a permanent memorial to the millions of immigrants who came to these shores in search of freedom.

Now, 18 years later, the museum is a reality. And for one who served with President Eisenhower, as I did, this occasion has a double meaning. We are witnessing today the completion of something that meant a great deal to a great American, President Eisenhower. And we are also paying tribute to millions of other

American heroes—many of whose names may be forgotten but whose vision and sacrifice have added so much to our American heritage.

In dedicating this museum, we mark the fact that ours is a nation of many nations, that, uniquely among all the nations of the world, ours draws its people from every continent, from every corner of the world, and what we have and what we are today is the result of what they brought to these shores.

So we dedicate this museum, not to a dead chapter of our history, but to a living ideal. The displays inside this building will remind us and our descendants of where many of our people came from. Every facet of American life today is filled with examples of what they did when they got here, of what they added to America, and of how they strengthened and enriched all of our lives, and continue to do so today.

The skyscrapers that dot the skyline of New York City, the railroads that connect the continent, the industrial might of modern America—all of these are the work of immigrants and of the descendants of immigrants. All of these are monuments to the strong hearts and hands of men and women from all nations, all races, and all religions who came here and became proud Americans. The walls of this museum, even if they were a hundred times this size, could not begin to house the full story of their contributions—yet it is a story that must and shall be told, especially now, as we complete our second century as a nation and prepare to celebrate our Bicentennial.

America has often been called a melting pot, perhaps because it has forged the cultures and traditions of many lands into a strong new alloy—an American alloy. But let us never forget that one of the finest things about our country is that it does not force its people into a narrow mold of conformity. America is a rich mosaic of many cultures and traditions, strong in its diversity. Each new immigrant has added another piece to the mosaic of American life—a fresh perspective and a fresh appreciation of what it means to be an American.

Edouard de Laboulaye, the French patriot who inspired the idea for the Statue of Liberty and who persuaded the sculptor Bartholdi to create it, looked upon the monument not only as a symbol of the love for freedom shared by the French and American people but as a monument to the spirit of freedom itself—a spirit that beats in the hearts of people everywhere.

The words he used to describe the Statue of Liberty should also serve to describe this museum we dedicate today: ". . . a symbol that braves the storms of time. It will stand unshaken in the midst of the winds that roar about its head and the waves that shatter at its feet."

The American ideal has also braved the storms of time. And it always will, as long as we keep alive the spark of freedom, ambition, opportunity, and self-respect, as long as we keep alive the faith and the commitment that transformed the poor, the oppressed, and the downtrodden of the earth into proud, free citizens of the United States.

NOTE: The statement was released at Liberty Island, N.Y.

323 Remarks at a "Victory '72" Dinner in New York City. September 26, 1972

Mr. Vice President and Mrs. Agnew, and all of the distinguished guests at this dinner in New York and at the other 26 dinners across this country:

It is hard to realize that 4 years have passed since September 19 when we were last in New York for a dinner of this kind.

As I look back on that dinner, and as I remember the funds that were contributed on that occasion, I realize how very important they were to the victory that we won 4 years ago. We thank you for what you did then.

On behalf of the Vice President, who has been so generous in his introductory remarks tonight, speaking from Chicago, let me express my appreciation and his for the thousands across this country attending these dinners who, by your help, are making it possible for us to win an even greater victory, a more important victory, in this year 1972.

I would like to describe that victory for you in perhaps different terms than we usually hear such victories described. It will be, I would trust, not simply the victory of a man and his running mate, not simply the victory of a party, but in the very deepest and most profound sense I would hope that we could make it a victory for America. That is what we are working for.

I believe one of the reasons why our campaign this year has support across the party lines, across the regional lines, across all parts of this great country, across the so-called generation gap—I think one of the reasons that is the case is that we are representing in our campaign what people believe is best for America. Let me explain it to you in three or four of the great issues that you have heard discussed earlier this evening, and perhaps that I can elaborate on briefly in my own remarks.

First, the subject that the Vice President has addressed in his remarks from Chicago. He has spoken of the record we have made in the field of foreign policy. We are proud of that record. But let me speak quite candidly with you. We have only begun, and there is so much left to do.

We have had a dialogue, a beginning of a dialogue with the leaders of one-fourth of all of the people in this world, and as a result, the world will be safer in the years ahead; not certainly, but it can be. If we had not had the dialogue, it would have been a very dangerous world just a few years from now, and that is an achievement.

We have begun negotiations, as the Vice President has pointed out, in a number of fields with the Soviet Union, fields that were not even anticipated 4 years ago, anticipated insofar as success was concerned. But particularly, as was indicated in the vote that was completed in the House yesterday, now we have passed the first phase of the limitation of nuclear arms. But note, I use the words "first phase" because in opening these negotiations with the Soviet Union, we still have a long way to go.

What we must recognize is that whether it is continuing our dialogue with the People's Republic of China, whether it is continuing our negotiations in the second phase of arms limitation with the Soviet Union, whether it is building our friendship with our allies in Europe, in the Mideast, and other parts of the world,

Latin America and Africa, whatever the case might be—we have begun.

I think it is not an overstatement to say that over these past 4 years we have been part of a great movement. We have changed the world, and the world will be better for it. But it will be better for it only if we can follow through. And what we ask tonight from you is not just your contributions, but your work, so that we can finish the job, so that we can continue the work that we have begun.

To say "finish the job" is really an overstatement because the job will never be finished. Whoever is President of the United States of America in the next 4 years, or the next 4 years after that, will have to continue to do as well as he possibly can in the field in which he has responsibility, primary responsibility, as the Vice President has pointed out—the field of foreign policy—to provide the kind of leadership that will make the world a more peaceful world and that will preserve freedom in the world.

That is why one of the major issues of this campaign, one in which we want a mandate from the American people, involves the position not only of the next President but of Presidents after him. One of the reasons we have been able to lead the world in a more peaceful direction over the past 4 years is because the United States was strong. And I simply say to all of you, let us never send the President of the United States to the conference table with anybody as the head of the second strongest nation in the world.

I make this statement in no belligerent sense, because I know the American people. I know we have made mistakes in foreign policy, as all peoples have. But I say it is time that we be proud of the fact that in four wars in this century we have always fought to preserve freedom, not to destroy it; to defend the peace, not to break it. Let us remember that the power of the United States is not a threat to the peace of the world; it is the guardian of peace in the world.

So let's keep America strong, and reject the advice of those that would make us weak.

At home we have similar goals, goals that in a way may not appear quite as exciting as these great global issues that we talk about, but goals that affect the lives of every American family.

I refer, for example, to the new prosperity, the new prosperity which we believe received enormous impetus from the programs that we announced on August 15 of last year. Just 2 days ago, or, as a matter of fact, just yesterday morning, speaking in Washington, D.C., before 124 nations in the world, I was proud to be able to say that the United States of America today has the lowest rate of inflation, the highest rate of growth, the highest real income for its workers of any industrial nation in the world. That is what we have.

But here, again, we say "That is not enough." We are never satisfied because we have a goal out there, one that we must achieve. I will tell you what it is: We want full prosperity, without war and without inflation, and that is something we have not had in this country since the days of President Eisenhower in 1955 and '56.

We can get it, and we will have it again. But in order to build that kind of prosperity, we must continue the sound policies in the economic field. We must reject that kind of philosophy that would penalize those who produce the jobs that make

America the best fed, the best clothed, the best housed people in the world. And we certainly must reject the philosophy that someone on welfare should receive more than someone who works in the United States of America.

There is a third area where we have made some progress in the past 4 years— not nearly as much as we would have liked. Some of you perhaps find it hard to remember what America was like in 1968. You remember what was happening on the campuses and in the cities. You remember the escalating rate of crime, of dangerous drugs and narcotics across this country. You remember that we declared that we would launch a massive offensive across this Nation on the forces of crime, narcotics, and the like.

We have not accomplished as much as we would like, but under the leadership of Attorney General John Mitchell and his successor, Attorney General Kleindienst, and due to the fact that we have appointed to the Supreme Court judges who have recognized that their primary responsibility is to protect the first civil right of every American, the right to be free from domestic violence, we have finally turned the corner on the fight against crime, but we need to go on. Let us not turn back to the era of permissiveness that got us where we were in 1968.

Then there is another area in which all of us, as Americans, have an enormous interest. I was talking earlier with Governor Rockefeller, at a reception of the New York Committee to Re-Elect the President, about the difference in the problems a President faces in the field of foreign policy and domestic policy. Let me confide, in this rather select group and those who are listening in the other 26 cities, the problem that a President faces when he was elected, as I was in 1968 along with Vice President Agnew, but does not have a majority mandate due to the fact that there was that year, you recall, a third party candidate.

In the field of foreign policy, a President can act and he should act and he should lead and, generally speaking, he can carry the country with him, even though the Congress may be carried in this instance by a majority of the other party. I found that when I first came to the Congress, for example. The Republicans were a majority in the 80th Congress, but when it came to the Greek-Turkish aid program, when it came to the Marshall Plan, President Truman was able to carry the Congress with him, and I, as a Republican, joined with Democrats in supporting those programs because we put the country first when the security of America was involved.

But in the field of domestic policy, it is a very, very different matter. Here a President can propose, and then the Congress does what it pleases, and sometimes it does not go along.

For example, we have proposed, as you know, much needed reforms in this Government of ours, reforms in the field of welfare, reforms in the field of health programs, in the field of education, in the field of Government reorganization. And in area after area where the Congress should have acted, the Congress has not acted.

One of the reasons for that is that the Congress quite rightfully could claim that the President did not have a majority mandate. But let me say this: In one area we have succeeded and that one success, as not only Governor Rockefeller will tell you but all the other Governors who are listening here tonight—Governor Cahill,

Governor Meskill, Governor Ogilvie in Chicago [1]—that one success, revenue sharing, is a great victory for the American people.

But now let me come to the point. What we need and what you can help provide through giving us a clear majority, a new American majority this year: You can give us the opportunity to carry forward exciting, new programs on the domestic front that are just as important as those that we have been able to carry forward on the international front.

That is why this election is so terribly important to the American people. What I am saying to you tonight is that whether it is in the field of foreign policy, whether it is in the field of domestic policy, that what we need and what we ask for is not simply the support of a party, but the support of a clear majority of the American people so that we can do those things that America needs to have done for it.

We have a program. We have submitted it to the Congress. We will have more to submit. But we need the majority, and you can help provide that majority. That is what you have done by your contributions here.

Now, in very personal terms, may I tell you what this election is really about? What does a man think, what does Vice President Agnew think, what do I think as we crisscross the country, as much as the duties of our office will permit, in campaigning for reelection? Of course, we think of winning. Of course, we think of what we can do when we get in. But above all, we think of our obligation to the generations that have made this country

in the past, to the older citizens, for example, who have contributed so much and who deserve so much in respect as well as in care from those that they have served in this country.

And we think, too, of the younger people in this country. This year, more than in any election in our history, the candidates for the Presidency and the Vice Presidency are thinking of younger people as well as older people.

One of the reasons, of course, is quite a selfish one. They can vote, and being able to vote, they can affect this election very much. But it is good that we are reminded of that. It is rather significant that this is Student Government Day [2] all over the United States. It is significant right here in this room, that at this great dinner where it costs, I understand, a great deal to sit down and eat, that the young people were able to come in and at least enjoy the speeches.

Could I tell all of the people listening here, all the young Americans and their parents and all of those who think of this country and what we want it to mean, what I want for you, for this new generation?

I want you to grow up in a world with peace. We have had a war in every generation in this century. That is too many and that is too long, and it doesn't need to be the case. I want you to grow up in an open world. I want you to be able to take the trips that Mrs. Nixon and I have taken, to the People's Republic of China, to the Soviet Union, to nations that up to this time have been relatively closed to young people or any people,

---

[1] Gov. William T. Cahill of New Jersey, Gov. Thomas J. Meskill of Connecticut, and Gov. Richard B. Ogilvie of Illinois.

[2] On June 26, 1972, the President signed Proclamation 4140 designating September 26, 1972, as National Student Government Day.

for that matter, who might want to visit them from the United States of America.

I want you to know all the people of the world. Even though we may have differences in government, let's not let the differences between governments keep people, and particularly young people, from being friends.

I want every young person in this country to have real prosperity. That means full employment without war and without inflation. It means also opportunity, opportunity for every American, regardless of his background, but opportunity that is not limited by putting you in a quota so that you can't go as high as your talents are going to take you. And there is something else that I want for this younger generation as you vote for the first time. I tried to say it in Miami when I said that I hoped that this first vote of yours you might look back upon as being one of your best.

In another way I would like to say this: It has been very distressing to me from time to time as I have talked to audiences across this country to find that some of our young people had lost confidence in America. Some of them have felt that this was not a good country to be living in, that this

was a poor time to be alive and particularly a poor time to be alive in America.

Above everything else in this campaign and in those next 4 years you have talked about so well, I want you to be proud of America and proud of our role in the world. This is a great country, and let's always remember that.

It is news when a few young Americans try to obstruct or disrupt some meeting that is being held, like this. It is bigger news, in my opinion, when millions of young Americans are doing what they are doing this year, peacefully supporting the candidate of their choice in a Presidential election.

I say, let's make it the biggest news of all by having a majority of young Americans join a majority of older Americans in winning a great victory for America this November.

NOTE: The President spoke at 10:21 p.m. in the Imperial Ballroom of the Americana Hotel. He spoke without referring to notes. His remarks were broadcast live on closed-circuit television to similar Republican fundraising dinners in 28 cities.

Vice President Spiro T. Agnew was the principal speaker at the dinner in Chicago and introduced the President from there.

324   Statement About Action To Combat Terrorism.
      September 27, 1972

MONDAY, here in New York, Secretary of State Rogers urged prompt action by the United Nations on three measures to combat the inhuman wave of terrorism that has been loosed on the world. I am gratified that the United Nations has agreed to take up the urgent matter of terrorism, and—in the strongest possible terms—I endorse the plea which the Secretary made on behalf of the United States and of human decency.

Also Monday, in Washington, I directed the establishment of a Cabinet Committee to Combat Terrorism—to be chaired by Secretary Rogers—aimed at bringing the full resources of all appropriate United States agencies to bear effectively on the task of eliminating terrorism wherever it occurs. I have charged it to move vigorously and immediately toward this end.

The use of terror is indefensible. It eliminates in one stroke those safeguards of civilization which mankind has painstakingly erected over the centuries.

But terror threatens more than the lives of the innocent. It threatens the very principles upon which nations are founded. In this sense, every nation in the United Nations, whatever its ideological assumptions, whoever its adversaries, wherever its sympathies, is united with every other nation by the common danger to the sovereignty of each. If the world cannot unite in opposition to terror, if we cannot establish some simple ground rules to hold back the perimeters of lawlessness, if, in short, we cannot act to defend the basic principles of national sovereignty in our own individual interests, then upon what foundations can we hope to establish international comity?

There are those who would tell us that terror is the last resort of the weak and the oppressed, a product of despair in an age of indifference, and that it seeks only political justice. This is nonsense. The way to seek justice is through negotiation. We have sought in our own relations to turn from confrontation to negotiation. We believe that this is the only way for grievances to be resolved in a way that will contribute to peace and stability.

In recent months we have seen nations moving to achieve accommodation and the resolution of differences, and we have seen terrorists acting to destroy those efforts. The time has come for civilized people to act in concert to remove the threat of terrorism from the world.

The world is reaching out for peace. The way may be hard and treacherous, but men of reason and decency are determined today, as perhaps never before, to make the effort. Let us not be disrupted or turned away by those who would loose anarchy upon the world; let us seek no accommodations with savagery, but rather act to eliminate it.

NOTE: The statement was released at New York City.

325   Statement About the San Francisco Bay Area Rapid Transit System.   *September 27, 1972*

THOUGH the Bay Area Rapid Transit system has been in operation only a matter of days, it already appears that the San Francisco Bay area may become as widely renowned in the future for the space-age efficiency of BART as it has been in the past for the romance of the cable car. I congratulate all the Bay Area communities that have taken part in this trailblazing achievement in modern metropolitan transportation. The people of this area are setting an example for the Nation.

The foresight, initiative, and constructive partnership demonstrated by the cities and counties which have joined in planning and building BART over the past two decades prove that workable new answers can be found for urban problems. Government support from the State and

Federal levels, under administrations of both political parties, has also been important; so has private sector participation, particularly that of California's own industrial community, with contractors like the Rohr Corporation applying aerospace technology to the work of meeting human needs here on earth.

The Federal role in BART underscores the commitment I made in 1969 to treat public transportation as one of the chief domestic priorities of this Administration. Through 1972, Federal funds for BART have totaled $181 million—about 13 percent of overall costs. I am pleased to be able to announce today a further Federal capital grant of an additional $38.1 million to BART from the Urban Mass Transportation Administration, to help complete the remaining 47 miles of the basic BART system.

Not only here in California but all across the Nation, the urban transportation picture is brightening as we move into the 1970's. Not only are some cities, such as Washington, following San Francisco in the installation of fixed rail systems, but others are meeting their transportation needs through innovations such as exclusive-use rights-of-way for buses.

I have sought to speed these developments by pushing for passage of the $10 billion Urban Mass Transportation Assistance Act of 1970 and by increasing the Federal budget for mass transit from the previous high of $175 million in one year to $1 billion this year. The better transportation balance which we are striving for is indicated by the fact that in fiscal year 1973, for the first time, Federal funds for urban mass transit will surpass spending on urban highways.

My general revenue sharing program, which I hope soon to sign into law, would further increase the ability of cities and States to deal with their own transportation problems in their own way. And one other piece of legislation now nearing passage would address this need even more specifically: the Federal Aid Highway Act of 1972, which recently passed the Senate and is now under consideration by the House.

I was most gratified—as were city officials across the country, and the millions of citizens they serve—when in passing this bill the Senate accepted my Administration's proposal that the Highway Trust Fund be opened up to permit urban areas to use monies from the fund for public transportation if they so choose. This provision would not in itself take a cent away from highway needs—in fact, it scrupulously plays no favorites among the various alternative answers to urban transportation problems. What it would do is to give the people at the local level— the people who know best—a freer hand than they have had before in choosing that combination of answers which best suits their own particular needs.

I hope that this sensible provision, together with the Administration's proposal to provide funds directly to metropolitan transportation agencies for the first time, will remain in the bill which both Houses finally approve. Certain other features of the present Senate and House bills are much less desirable, but I hope that these can be eliminated, the strong features retained, and a sound bill sent to my desk for signature before the Congress adjourns.

Now that BART is demonstrating how pleasant and convenient movement within our urban centers can be, we should be less disposed than ever to be patient with how congested and difficult it all too often is. The speedy resolution of America's chronic and worsening traffic jams is far too urgent a matter to be stalled any longer by legislative or bureaucratic logjams, and I will continue my own determined efforts to keep it moving ahead.

NOTE: The statement was released at San Leandro, Calif.

The President and Mrs. Nixon boarded a BART train at the San Leandro Station and rode to the Lake Merritt Station where they visited the BART Control Center and met with employees.

On the same day, the White House released a fact sheet on BART.

326   Statement About the Election Campaign and National Security.   *September* 27, 1972

IT HAS been suggested by some that I ought to take off from the White House and campaign virtually full time between now and election day.

I want to win this election. I particularly want to win California. I would welcome the opportunity to take the case for this Administration directly to the American people. But my first responsibility is to do my job as President of the United States. I intend to meet that responsibility. I shall campaign only when I conclude it will not interfere with doing the job the people elected me to do.

Vice President Agnew made the right decision when he left the campaign to come back to Washington yesterday so that he could be ready, if necessary, to break a tie on a critically important foreign policy vote.

Proposals that would put the United States in the position of having the second strongest Navy, the second strongest Air Force, the second strongest Army in the world would massively increase the danger of aggression around the world. It would be a move toward war, not a move toward peace.

If we reduce our Army, Navy, and Air Force to the point that the only option open to us, when a friend or ally of the United States is threatened, is to launch a nuclear war and bring massive nuclear attack on the United States, our commitments to small nations whose survival did not directly affect the security of the United States would not be worth the paper they were written on.

The policy of massive nuclear retaliation during the Eisenhower years, when we had a 15- to 20-to-1 superiority over the Soviet Union, was a credible policy. A policy which would leave the United States with only a nuclear option at a time when the Soviet Union and the United States are approximately equal in their nuclear capability would have no credibility whatever where the survival of small nations was involved.

NOTE: The statement was released in connection with the President's visit to San Francisco to attend a "Victory '72" luncheon.

327 Remarks at a "Victory '72" Luncheon in San Francisco, California. *September 27, 1972*

Governor Reagan, Chairman Miller, Chairman Packard, all of the distinguished guests at the head table, and all of the distinguished guests in the audience:

I am sure you can see now how far the Governor and I will go to win the vote of women's lib, but let me say that as I stand here, after having flown across the country today from New York City, in our home State of California, that it is really a very, very great privilege to be received so warmly in the world's favorite city, San Francisco.

I can assure you, when I talk about the world's favorite city, as Governor Reagan will agree, whenever you travel to the countries of the world you will find leaders disagreeing about many things, but it is virtually unanimous—San Francisco is their favorite city. One of the reasons is that all the world is here. The world has made this city, and it is one of the reasons that today I have selected as the primary subject the problems of the world.

Let me say that in discussing that subject, I first want to say a word with regard to what has been termed the limited campaigning that I have been doing in this election year. I am quite aware of the fact, from long experience, that we have only 6 weeks, less than 6 weeks, before election day. Also, I want very much to win this election. I want very much to carry California. And there is nothing I welcome more than the opportunity to take the case for this Administration, for the last 4 years and for the next 4 years, to the American people.

But I believe my first obligation is to do my job as President of the United States of America, and that is the reason why, whenever it is necessary, when I feel it is necessary to stay in Washington to do the job that the people elected me to do, I will be there. When I can, I will be campaigning. That is why I ask you not only to contribute, as you have by attending this luncheon, but to work—do the work, perhaps, that we won't be able to do, by being out on the campaign trail.

Let me say, too, that in that same vein, I feel that Vice President Agnew certainly made the right decision when he broke off his campaign to fly back to Washington to be there when a very close tie vote involving national security was occurring in the United States Senate. That is the attitude, in other words, that we are approaching this campaign in. We want to win, but we recognize that our first responsibility is to this country. Our first responsibility is to carry on the great programs that we have begun, and in that connection, I want to direct my remarks to that area of greatest interest, I think, to this audience.

I say to this audience—perhaps because San Francisco is an international city in every sense of the word, because San Franciscans generally are international in their attitudes toward problems and not parochial, perhaps because Dave Packard, our chairman in northern California, has contributed so much to this Administration's defense policy and also to its successful foreign policy—for these and other reasons, I want to talk to this audience today about our foreign policy and our defense policy.

I do not want to talk to you in partisan

political terms. I want to talk to you, in terms that are far more important, about this Nation: Where it is going, where it has been, and what the next 4 years can mean, because this is what is important.

I know these luncheons and dinners that we are having across the country are called Victory 1972, and that sounds real good; that is fine. But the question is: Victory for what? I say to you today, not victory for a man, or a man and his running mate, and not just victory for a party, but victory for America. I want this to be a victory for all the people of America. I want this to be a victory for what is best in America, and, particularly in this field of foreign policy, it is important that we recognize what the stakes are, how important it is, in our view, that the policies that we have begun be continued for 4 more years.

Let me go back, if I can, to the time that we came into office. It is rather hard to realize what some of the problems were that we faced in the United States and in the world at that time. But you will recall there were 550,000 men in Vietnam; there were 300 killed in action every week, on an average. You will recall, too, that there were no negotiations going on that had, certainly, any indication of progress or movement, and certainly at that point there was no American peace plan on the negotiating table.

You will also recall that, looking at the world scene, the world seemed to be frozen into hostile confrontation. Here in the Pacific, in which you in San Francisco, we in California, have such an enormous interest, we looked across this broad Pacific; we realized that three times in this century war has come to America from the Pacific. World War II for the United States started in the Pacific. Korea started in the Pacific. Vietnam came in the Pacific. Therefore, we know that the policies of the United States that are developed toward the Pacific are going to have an enormous effect in determining whether we have war or peace in the years ahead—not just ending the war in which we presently are involved, but preventing such wars in the future.

As I looked at that problem, I saw that for over 20 years the United States and the leaders of the Government, over one-fourth of all the people in this world, the People's Republic of China, had been without communication. I knew, of course, that the philosophies, as far as we were concerned and they were concerned, were totally different. That was the case then. That is the case now.

But I also realized that if we did not do something to thaw that out, something to establish some communication with the leaders of one-fourth of the most able people in all the world, that we were going down the road to an inevitable confrontation which might bring a war not only in the Pacific, but a war which could be destructive to all of civilization.

We look across to the other side of the world, as far as our relations with the Soviet Union were concerned, we find that 4 years ago negotiation was really at a standstill in all areas. There was no progress in arms control. There was no progress in the field of trade. No one thought of a possible cooperation in the field of space or environment or health or in the other areas that we have heard so much about in recent weeks and recent months. That was the world we found 4 years ago.

And here, again, we found an interesting situation. Dave Packard will remember, as he attended the meetings of the

National Security Council, we found that in terms of the balance of power between the United States and the Soviet Union, that that enormous lead that the United States had had at the end of the Eisenhower era had evaporated, and that now, in terms of nuclear capability, the two great super powers were virtually even.

The world had changed, and unless something was done to exchange a period of confrontation and move from that to one of negotiation, and then possibly to cooperation, we were certainly going down the road to an inevitable clash which could lead again to a world disaster. That was the world that we found.

We worked on those problems. We have worked on them long and hard. We have not had total success, but we have had significant success. You all know that as far as the war in Vietnam is concerned that we not only have brought home over a half-million, we have not only reduced our casualties, but we have also now ended the American ground combat role. We have prepared the South Vietnamese so that they have demonstrated the ability to stop a major invasion of the Communists from the North, and we have done this without staining the honor of the United States of America. We have maintained the respect for the United States of America.

It would have been very easy to have moved in another direction, very easy simply at the beginning of the term in January of 1969 to have said: We didn't send these men there, the two previous administrations sent them there, get them home, blame it on the previous administrations and be a big hero. But we also knew that if the United States of America at that particular time had taken that step, that it might have ended that war,

but it would have planted the seeds for others, because it would encourage that kind of aggression not only there but in the area of Indonesia, the other areas that are so important to freedom and so important to peace and progress in the Pacific and that part of the world.

So we made those decisions and we have had that degree of success, and we will continue until we achieve our goal, which will be ending the war, but ending it in a way that the United States maintains the respect of its friends around the world and, for that matter, of its adversaries.

But looking beyond that, it would have been very easy at the beginning of this term simply to look at the war we inherited, to realize that if we could deal with that, that would be an accomplishment in itself which the American people would appreciate.

But we did not stop there. We saw these other problems. We realized that we were living in a period—and this is the point that all of us must realize—we were living in a period when the time when the United States might be able to exert an influence for lasting peace in the world might never come again. It could pass us by. And so we moved. We made the initiative toward the People's Republic of China. We made the initiative toward the Soviet Union.

Let me emphasize again, our philosophies with both governments are totally different. As far as the leaders are concerned, we have not proceeded on the basis of any mushy sentimentality that friendship between leaders is going to bring friendship among people with different philosophies and governments with different philosophies. But we did proceed on this assumption: that we live in the world together. We did proceed on the assumption that in the event there was a nuclear war, that all of us would suffer together, and we, therefore, said that we had to find a way for governments with different philosophies to live together, to negotiate their differences rather than fight about them.

We had to find a way, for example—and thinking of all of these young people who have honored our luncheon today—a way in which the leaders of governments might disagree, but where the people, and particularly the younger people of the world, might still be friends. So we have proceeded on these assumptions.

We have made some progress, but don't let us overestimate it—and here is where I come to the job that lies ahead. As far as the People's Republic of China is concerned, we have begun a dialogue. We must now continue it, but it must be continued with no illusions that simply because we are talking that all the problems will evaporate. They are strong people. I am speaking now of the leaders as well as the people that they lead. They are determined. Their interests are different from ours in many cases; in some cases they are the same.

And only as each of us consult our interests and find that they are compatible will we get along. But the important thing is to continue, and we believe we have the experience, the know-how, to continue this dialogue so that it can develop into perhaps cooperation in the future.

Looking at the Soviet Union and our relations there, look at some of the things that have happened—they are significant. A cooperative venture in space is on the way, cooperation in the field of science, in the field of the environment, in the field of health, to which I will refer a little later,

cooperation also in the field of trade, in which there will be significant announcements at a later date as these various agreements are reached, and cooperation, perhaps most important of all, in the field of arms control.

But let me take the last, which has captured the imagination of the American people the most, and put it in the context of what this election is about.

Arms control is important. We have agreed to a total ban, or agreement with regard to the limitation I should say, of defensive nuclear weapons. We have agreed to a partial limitation on offensive nuclear weapons. But the really hard negotiations lie ahead. Those negotiations will involve going forward on offensive nuclear weapons, limiting them, in Phase 2, and then, eventually, we trust, reducing them so that these two great powers can reduce the burden of arms which now rests upon their peoples and thereby also potentially reduce the danger of war.

It will not be easy. It was not easy to get where we did. But in order to continue from where we are, it is essential again that we do it in a realistic, pragmatic, nonsentimental way, because that is the kind of men we are dealing with, and we must be exactly that way in dealing with them.

Now I come to the point, then, of why the next 4 years are important. I am proud of this record of the last 4 years. I wish we could have done more. But we have changed the world. A thaw has occurred in the relations between the People's Republic of China and the United States. An even greater thaw has occurred in relations between the United States and the Soviet Union.

But you all know that the time of thaw is one of either very great promise or one

of very great danger. And now the leadership that is important is to go forward in
these areas that we have made these
breakthroughs [in] and to continue them.

That is why we are asking the American
people, that is why I am asking our friends
here in California, in this San Francisco
area, who have so much understanding of
the world and so much interest in the
problems of the world, to give us the
chance to go forward.

We believe that we have demonstrated
that we know how to make progress toward real peace in the world. But in order
to, it seems to me, reach the inevitable
result that we all want, of a world that is
not totally peaceful—it will never be that
because people will always have differences—but one where we can have differences without resorting to war, in order to
reach that, we must continue on the path
which has proved to be so successful up to
this point.

Let me be very specific with regard to
what we need to do in a couple of areas
that have been discussed considerably in
the press, and I understand also in some
public forums. First, if we are to be successful in our continued negotiations with
our friends and with our potential adversaries, and particularly in our negotiations
with the Soviet Union, it is essential that
the United States maintain a strong national defense.

I know there is a great deal of argument to the effect that it is not necessary for the United States to have a defense, as some have said, that is second to
none. There are some who believe that we
should make cuts in our defense budget,
that we can safely make those cuts, that
it doesn't really make any difference
whether the United States has the second
strongest Navy, the second strongest

Army, the second strongest Air Force in
the world.

As a matter of fact, we find that proposals have been made that would do
exactly that. Let me say that as far as
this particular proposal is concerned, it is
one of the clearest issues of this campaign.
Because I can assure you, based on the
experience of the last 4 years, and based
on looking back over 25 years of examining the world scene and traveling all over
the world, the day the United States of
America becomes the second strongest
nation in the world, the danger of war will
be enormously increased and the prospect
of peace will be harmed. Let's not let that
happen any time.

Because this audience is one that I know
understands some of the intricacies of this
problem, let me be somewhat more specific—the argument is sometimes made
that it really doesn't make any difference
whether the United States has a strong
Navy, or a strong Air Force, or a strong
Army compared with that of the Soviet
Union, provided we have a sufficient nuclear deterrent.

Let me show you the fallacy of that
argument. During the Eisenhower years,
when the United States had a 15 to 20
times advantage over the Soviet Union in
terms of nuclear capacity, a policy based
on massive retaliation all around the world
was a credible policy because when you
are that far ahead of any potential opponent no potential opponent is going to test
you. It was even true at the time of the
Cuban missile crisis when our advantage
was in the neighborhood of 8 to 10 times
as great.

But the world has changed since then.
Today we live in a situation when, in
terms of nuclear capability, the Soviet
Union and the United States are roughly

equal—in some areas they are ahead and in some areas we are ahead, but we are roughly equal.

Consequently, whenever it is suggested that the policy of the United States, its foreign policy, should be based on the proposition that whenever a friend or an ally of the United States is threatened our only option will be a nuclear strike, this is not credible. It is not credible particularly where small nations are concerned whose survival does not affect directly the security of the United States of America, because every leader in the world will know that if a President of the United States is faced with a decision involving a small ally of the United States or a small nation with which we have a commitment, faced with a decision when that nation is threatened that requires him and allows him only to launch a nuclear war which would lead to nuclear devastation of the United States, he knows, and our potential adversaries know, that we would not do it. That is why we have to have a Navy which is the strongest in the world, that is why we cannot be second best in the field of the Air Force. That is why the United States of America, if it is to maintain a credible foreign policy, if our friends and allies, particularly among those small nations of the world whose survival does not directly affect us, if we are to have with those nations a credible foreign policy, it is essential that the United States maintain a strength overall in the nonnuclear area which is adequate and second to none.

That is why, even though I and Dave Packard—when he served in that enormously important position of Under Secretary of Defense, where he had to make these decisions and recommendations to the President—have had to oppose, much as we would have wanted the money for other purposes, we have had to oppose cuts in the defense budget which would result in making the United States second.

Let me just put it very bluntly this way: We don't want to spend one dollar more on defense than we need, because we need it for domestic purposes. But let us remember that spending more than we need in defense may cost us money, but spending less than we need could cost us our lives. Let's put the security of America first.

Now, let me put this in a much more positive context. I have spoken, I think quite properly and soberly, of the pragmatic situation that the leaders of the United States will face in dealing with the leaders of the Soviet Union and the People's Republic of China and other nations in the years ahead. Let us also look at the promise. Let us see how the world has changed and how it can change even more for the better.

I think of our trip to Peking. I think of 800 million people who live in the People's Republic of China. I think of Chinese people that I have known in America—in San Francisco, in New York, in Los Angeles. I think of people I have known all over the world, the Chinese people, how able they are, in Singapore, in Saigon, Bangkok, Taiwan. And I think of those 800 million people. I think then of our own young people. I want the young people of America to live in an open world.

I don't mean that their government will be one that we will like, but I want the young people of America, our children and their children, not to be cut off from one-fourth of all of the people in the world. That is one of the things that this policy is about.

And I think of something else. I think of how much we can do working together. Here in San Francisco you see it all. When you think of the heritage from Asia, from Europe, from Latin America, from Africa, all the world is here. But working together, you have built a great city, a great area, and it is becoming greater and more beautiful all the time.

Let's put it in terms of the relations between nations. I am not referring now to those political areas where we will be in conflict and where we will have debates and where necessarily we may not agree. I recall a conversation I had a few weeks ago with the Russian Minister of Health. He, I found, was one of the major open heart surgery men in the world. He had just been down talking to Dr. DeBakey whom many of you know, the great surgeon in Texas, one of the best in the United States. We talked about how American doctors and Russian doctors might be able to develop methods to work together on finding cures for various diseases, in the field of heart, in the field of cancer, and all the rest.

When I saw Mr. Chou En-lai one evening, I talked to him about the work that doctors in China were doing and doctors in our own country were doing and whether it might not be possible at some time in the future where we could share our knowledge and possibly even work together.

Then I think that tomorrow in Los Angeles I will be addressing a national cancer conference. I think of the fact that we in this country have launched a massive campaign to find a cure for cancer, because each year cancer takes more lives than were lost in all of World War II—right here in America it takes more lives.

Now, our campaign is a good one; it is a big one. But the genius that may find a cure or the cures, because there may be many approaches for cancer or any other

disease, may not be in America. It might be a Chinese. It might be a Russian. It might be a woman. It might be a man. It might be a young doctor. It might be an old one. It might be one from a small country in Latin America or Africa.

What we who are the leaders in the world community must do is to find ways that, where the common enemies of mankind are concerned, like disease and misery, we work together to fight those enemies. That is what this colloquy is about.

I would like to tell all of this audience today, and particularly our younger visitors, that with these next 4 years, that we will accomplish all these great goals. We will make progress toward them, and I think we will make considerable progress. The world is going to be safer. Your lives are going to be better, I trust, because of what we have done. But in order to do so we need the chance. We need a mandate. We need to go before the American electorate and then have the support of the American electorate, so that in meeting with leaders of the world, in dealing with the Congress, they will know that the American people back what this Administration has done.

That is why we say, give us a chance and we will do the job. That is what we are asking from the American people and from you today.

In that connection, may I simply add one final note with regard to what I said a few moments ago, to San Francisco, New York, what has made this country great. I helped to participate in the dedication of a museum for the immigrants who have come to the United States through Ellis Island, 34 million over about 90 years. As I went through that museum I thought of all the people that came, how strong they must have been. We saw replicas of the ships in which they moved. They were Poles and Italians and Germans. They were people from other continents.

Then as I come to San Francisco I think of the people that have come to this shore, not only come to this shore from across the Pacific, but have come here from across the continent, the strong people that they were. But the greatness of it all is that America, and particularly San Francisco, is all the world in one place. That has brought a rich diversity to our country and particularly to this city. It has brought hard work and determination, but it has also brought something else, something else that is enormously important if we are going to be able to carry forward with the kind of responsible leadership in the world that America must have in the years ahead.

I find that those who have come to America from other countries, or second generation or even third, have a deep appreciation of this country that sometimes those of us who live here have not had. I think of the time at the Bohemian Grove 5 years ago when a man celebrated what he said was his 45th birthday.[1]

Now, George Mardikian, 5 years ago, was much older than 45, but he called it

_____

[1] The Bohemian Grove was a redwood grove in northern California owned by the Bohemian Club of San Francisco and site of the club's annual encampment. The club's members are nationally known artists in music, theater, and all the arts, as well as distinguished civic, business, and professional leaders in California and other parts of the United States. George Mardikian, author and restaurateur, was a member of the club.

his 45th birthday because that was the year that he became a citizen of the United States. I remember the tears in his eyes as he spoke of America. And there were tears in our eyes, too.

As I have participated in citizenship ceremonies over these last years as President of the United States, in Chicago, in New York, have welcomed new citizens, I see the pride in their faces, how proud they are to be American citizens.

Let me say to our young people today: Sure, there are some things wrong with this country, but there is so very much right about it. One of the great things that is right about it is that you are participating in this process in a peaceful way. Oh, there are other ways. You can get out and try to shout down a speaker, but the way to do it is the way that you are doing it, participating, listening to the candidates, and supporting the candidates of your choice.

But the most important thing that I want to tell you is this: I have spoken of the world. Along with Mrs. Nixon, we have visited most of the countries of the world, in fact, over 80. And every time you come back to the United States you know that the people fortunate enough to live here are the most fortunate people in the world. This is a great country. Let's never forget that.

NOTE: The President spoke at 1:40 p.m. at a Republican fundraising luncheon in the Garden Court Restaurant of the Sheraton Palace Hotel. He spoke without referring to notes.

Otto N. Miller was chairman of the "Victory '72" luncheon. David Packard, Deputy Secretary of Defense 1969–71, was chairman of the Committee for the Re-Election of the President in northern California.

328 Statement About Congressional Spending and the Nation's Welfare. *September 27, 1972*

AT THE present time there are pending in Congress a number of huge spending proposals which, if enacted into law, would lead inevitably to a tax increase. The best way I can serve the American people is to stay in Washington, when I consider it necessary, to fight those proposals—to veto them if they are passed, and to enlist enough support in the Congress to sustain my vetoes.

What we must recognize is that a veto of a spending proposal which substantially exceeds the budget that I have submitted to Congress is, in effect, a veto of a tax increase. A vote for such a proposal is a vote for a tax increase.

It is considered to be good politics in a campaign to promise huge new spending programs for good causes like the environment, health, education, and welfare. But I believe it is known that I have recommended programs in these fields to the Congress which we can afford without increasing taxes.

I shall make no promises in this campaign for any spending programs—no matter how popular—if such programs would lead to a tax increase.

_____

Those who call for a redistribution of income and a confiscation of wealth are not speaking for the interests of people; they are speaking against the interests of people.

We can be proud of the fact that the United States has the most generous program for aid to the poor, the elderly, and others who need assistance, of any country in the world. We can afford these programs only because the 82 million Americans who work for a living and the businesses of this country produce the taxable income which can finance them.

Let us reject any program which makes it more profitable for a person to go on welfare than to go to work.

Let us reject any program which would discourage business from providing the new jobs that America needs if we were to have full employment without war and without inflation.

Massive redistribution of income is not the way to make the poor rich. It is a way to make everybody poor.

Many nations abroad have gone down the road to the welfare state and have lived to regret it. Let's not make the same mistake in the United States.

NOTE: The statement was released in connection with the President's visit to Los Angeles to attend a "Victory '72" dinner.

329 Remarks at a "Victory '72" Dinner in Los Angeles, California. *September 27, 1972*

Governor and Mrs. Reagan, Chairman and Mrs. Carter, all of the distinguished guests at the head table, in the audience, and our very special guests who have added such excitement, enthusiasm, and idealism to our campaign, the Young Voters for Nixon-Agnew:

May I also express appreciation to all of those who have participated in the program up to this point, the very generous remarks of Governor Reagan—we had also met earlier in San Francisco, and he flew down with us to this dinner tonight—the superlative performance, and it is always superlative, of Bob Hope. I have often thought that he is without question the most generous man in giving his time to good causes, and the most ungenerous man, as an opponent on the golf course, of any man I know. I am just going to have my daughter play him from now on, though.

But I do know that so many people, people I have never had a chance to meet—tonight I have met some of you, only a few—but so many people have helped to make this dinner a success, have worked in order to make it the enormous success that Ed Carter has just announced. You can imagine how I feel representing our ticket.

I spoke in New York, which at that time was the biggest dinner ever held in New York or in the country, just last night. I spoke in San Francisco at noon today. It was the biggest dinner ever held in the Bay Area. And now tonight, here in really our home area of southern California, we have the biggest dinner in the whole history of American politics.

I would like to tell you what I think this dinner is about. I would like to tell you what I think this victory is about that we talk about, Victory 1972. It is more than simply victory for a man or a party; it is victory, in my view, for this Nation, for what we want it to stand for.

I have heard, as you have heard so often, starting at the convention in Miami, and here tonight before we came in, and now right here in this auditorium, those words "Four More Years." I think all of us for a moment would like to think about, "What does 'Four More Years' mean?"

Oh, it could simply mean winning an election, and, of course, we want to win, or it could simply mean 4 more years of what we have been doing, and that wouldn't be bad because we have a record we are very proud of.

But I want to tell you that what I think about this "Four More Years"—what you have contributed to, what you are working for and will be working for between now and the election day, November 7, all of you here, all of the young people, all the others across this country who are working in our cause, Republicans and Democrats and independents—is not just 4 more years of standing on a record, not just 4 more years of what we have done, but what I would hope would be four of the best years in the whole history of the United States of America.

That is a very high goal. This country has had many good 4-year periods, more than sometimes we realize, because in these days when we find so much fault with America, we overlook some of the greatness of our country, not only in the past but also in the present.

But as I look over these next 4 years and what we want it to be, let me outline briefly for you tonight, in three areas, how I think we can achieve that great goal: four of the best years in the history of America.

We have to start, of course, with peace. We start with that because that affects every American, his family, his hopes, his future. Here we look to our record. It is a record we are proud of. We have not accomplished everything we would have desired as fast as we might, but as we look at that terribly difficult war in Vietnam, we have brought home 500,000 men. We have cut our casualties, as you are quite aware. We have ended the American combat role. We have ended the sending of any draftees to Vietnam. We have prepared the South Vietnamese so that it is now very clear that they will be able soon to undertake their complete defense without our assistance.

All of this has been accomplished without staining the honor of the United States of America. We have not played politics with the issue, as we might. We have not blamed the difficulties that we have had on the previous administrations, as we might, and then have done something that would have been very wrong for America: simply get out and blame it on the other people and hope that the American people would not regret what would have been a highly immoral act.

Let me say we are not going to play politics with it now. We are going to end our involvement. We will end the war. But we are going to end it without betraying our allies, and we are not going to abandon our prisoners of war or play politics with our prisoners of war.

But as we think of peace, we in this country too often have spoken of peace and thought of peace only in terms of ending the war. We ended World War I. We ended World War II. We ended the Korean war. And then every generation another one comes along. I think this Administration will be remembered not so much for what we have done in ending the war which we inherited, but will be remembered for the actions that we have taken in changing the world and in reducing the possibility of other wars in the future.

Oh, I do not mean that because we have an opening of a dialogue with the People's Republic of China, whose government leads one-fourth of all of the people that live on this globe, that opening that

dialogue means that we will have no more difficulties with them and that government, because our differences are still there, the philosophical differences. They have not changed.

I do not mean that because we have negotiated with the Soviet Union an unprecedented series of agreements in the area of trade, in the area of the environment, cooperation in space, and most important of all, a beginning in the limitation of nuclear arms, that that means that we will not continue to have difficulties with the Soviet Union because of our differences of interests, our differences in philosophies. They are there, and they will remain.

But I do suggest this: that we could have left it as it was. We could have been left frozen, as we were, in confrontation with the Soviet Union, not negotiating those differences, and going down the road to an inevitable collision with all the destruction that would bring to America, to the Soviet Union, and all the people in the world.

We could have left the People's Republic of China isolated from us and from the rest of the world, with the inevitable result 15, 20 years from now, that 800 million, or probably a billion, of the most capable people in the world might be lined up against us in an inevitable confrontation.

So we have begun, and I emphasize tonight that despite the progress we have made in this field of foreign policy toward a world of peace, it is only a beginning, and for 4 more years, the reason we want it is that we need 4 more years to build on this beginning. We think we know how to do it. We think we have demonstrated that we do know how.

I will not go into detail as to what we

will do, except I will tell you one thing that we must not do. I know that the reason we were able to open the dialogue with the People's Republic of China, the reason that we were able to begin negotiations with the Soviet Union, was that they respected the United States of America as a strong nation, standing for its principles.

I can tell you that the day that the President of the United States represents the second strongest nation in the world, they won't be interested in talking to us. And we will never let that happen. We must remember that even though we did not want this responsibility, that we are the only nation in the free world that has the potential, the power to save the cause of peace and freedom in the world, and it is for that reason that we must retain our strength so that we may be able to continue to build on these initiatives, initiatives in limiting arms, and then perhaps later in the future reducing them, but always on the basis of mutuality, never on the basis of unilateral disarmament as far as the United States is concerned.

Turning to the domestic front, when we speak of making this one of the best 4 years in this Nation's history, we think first of something that is called that pocketbook issue. Putting it more bluntly—jobs. I was proud to be able to say, in addressing 124 nations at the International Monetary Fund meeting in Washington on Monday of this week, that the United States of America, at this time, had the lowest rate of inflation, the highest rate of growth, the highest real income of any industrial nation in the world.

That is what our economic policy has done. And that, just like our leadership in the field of foreign policy, is a good record. But we are not satisfied with it,

because there is more to do. What do we want to do in those Four More Years?

What we want to do is to continue to have this economy grow, to continue to provide the incentives that will mean more jobs for the American people, until we achieve a goal that we have not had in this country since President Eisenhower was President in the years 1955 and '56, and that means full employment without war and without significant inflation.

We can do that, and that goal we can achieve. But in order to achieve that goal, we must remember that we cannot take those steps that would inevitably destroy the incentives that produce the jobs, that produce the income that makes it possible for us to do good things in the world and good things for the American people. That is why, even while this present Congress is still in session, I am going to find it necessary to veto some huge spending bills for what are really good causes, but where the choice is: Do we spend money for a good cause if it means that increasing the spending by that amount will raise the taxes of the American people?

I say to this audience here tonight, as I have said previously on many other occasions, that whether it is a bill passed by the Congress which exceeds the budget and would lead to a tax increase or whether it is making a promise in a political campaign, which many think is good politics, which would lead inevitably to a tax increase because of exceeding the budget, that I intend to make no promises and I intend certainly to approve no bills that would lead to a tax increase for the American people.

This is not said because this happens to be a dinner of people of, shall we say, considerably better than average means. It is said because the great majority of the American people work for a living, the great majority of the American people pay taxes, and taxes are high enough. That is why we must limit our spending for whatever that cause may be, good as it is, limit it to what we can afford. This is the way we can build that new prosperity that we want, looking to the years ahead.

Then, if we are going to have these next 4 years one of the best 4-year periods of America's history, we not only have to have peace abroad, we have to have peace at home. Many people have forgotten the situation that this country was in 4 years ago. You will remember, some of you, the conditions in our cities, the conditions on some of the campuses of our universities and colleges. It has taken time to change it. It has also taken time to change an attitude of permissiveness that had grown up in our courts, that had grown up in some of our law enforcement agencies across this country.

I pledged in the 1968 campaign that we would change that. I said over and over again it was necessary to appoint judges to the highest courts of this land and all the courts of this land who would recognize that it was essential to strengthen the peace forces as against the criminal forces in this country. We have done that, and, as a result of doing that, we have seen progress finally being made in dealing with the criminal forces in this country. Progress is being made in dealing with the forces of narcotics and dangerous drugs.

But 4 years isn't enough. We need more. And in order, in the next 4 years, to accomplish the goal that we need to accomplish, we must continue to appoint to the courts of this land and in the positions of enforcement of the law, men and women who recognize that the first civil right of every American, whatever his background,

is the right to be free of domestic violence, and we are going to see that that right becomes a real one for every American.

Let me put all of this, if I may, in terms of the hopes and the dreams of the young Americans, Republicans, Democrats, independents, who are supporting our ticket this year. We want them to grow up in a world of peace. We want them to have what no generation in this century has had in America: a full generation of peace.

We think we have helped to begin to build that possibility. Certainly, while we do not want to overstate the case, the chance that this generation can have a full generation of peace as a result of what we have done, as a result of these great initiatives, if we can continue them with the same pragmatic, realistic approach, the chance is greater than it has ever been, certainly in my lifetime. It is this, then, that we want for them.

Putting it also in positive terms, I want this new generation of Americans to grow up to the greatest extent possible in an open world. There will always be differences between governments. There will be differences in philosophies. But I would hope that we could have a world in which, despite differences between governments, the peoples of the world could be friends. I think that is possible.

I would like for the young people of this generation to be able to take the trip that my wife and I took to the People's Republic of China, to know those people. I am not referring to their government, with which I do not agree insofar as its philosophy is concerned, but the Chinese people, as a people, are an able people. The Soviet people are an able people.

What we must do is to recognize that differences between governments must not be allowed to keep people apart where they can work together. Let me give you an example. As I was meeting a few of the vice chairmen of this dinner tonight, one of them told me that his wife was unable to come because she had had an operation for cancer. Fortunately, it was successful. I was thinking of the fact that early in the morning I am addressing a group, right here at the Century Plaza, of doctors engaged in the fight against cancer. I was thinking also, in terms of that battle, with the great wars that this country has fought, and that each year more people die with cancer in the United States than were killed in all of World War II.

As I thought of that, I realized how important our initiative was, which we began, to put more funds into research for cancer. Then I thought of my trip to the Soviet Union and my trip to China where Chou En-lai discussed the problem of how we might cooperate in that field of finding answers to the dread diseases that afflict mankind, whatever their color or background or political philosophy.

I remember a meeting just a few days ago with the Russian Minister of Health. He is a famous heart surgeon. He does two open-heart surgery operations a week. He works regularly and corresponds with Dr. DeBakey, who is one of the leaders in our field here. We talked about this problem. Then I thought in terms of how we could find the answer, the answer to cancer, to the other diseases on which we are attempting to develop programs. It may not be found by an American. We have to search the world. It may be a Russian. It may be a Chinese. It may be somebody from Africa or Latin America, a small country, a large country. It may be a woman. It may be a man. The main point

is that in attacking this kind of a problem where we find that the whole of mankind is affected, let's get all of the people of the world working together to deal with that problem.

I want this new generation, voting for the first time in America this year, not only to live in a peaceful world, not only to live in an open world, but to have here the jobs without war and without inflation to which they are entitled, an opportunity to go to the top, without being limited by a quota, on the basis of their abilities, and finally, I want them, and this is one, certainly, of the strongest motivations I think all of us should have tonight, I want them to feel about this country the way I feel about it, the way you feel about it.

I think one of the tragedies of our time, one of the tragedies of the sixties, was that so many young people seemingly gave up on America. Part of the reason was they could see everything wrong, and they allowed what was wrong to blind them to what was right; not all, of course, but many did.

And now we have seen the situation begin to turn. I think one of the good things, one of the helpful things about this new generation and its participation in this campaign is that with that responsibility they are looking at their country through new eyes. Oh, that means they are not uncritical. Because young people, to their great credit, are idealistic. They are impatient. They want change. They want progress. And may it always be that way.

But on the other hand, they know they can work peacefully within the system in America. Just let me say: They know, too, if they have had the opportunity to travel abroad, as I have and my wife has, to over 80 countries, that every time you come back to the United States of America you realize how fortunate it is to be alive and to live in the United States of America.

To put it very simply, I want the record of these next 4 years in the field of foreign policy leading toward peace, in the field of domestic policy leading toward opportunity and jobs and progress for all Americans, I want those next 4 years to be ones that will convince this new generation of voters that this is a great and a good and, yes, a beautiful country. We must believe that because it is the truth.

A few months ago a very splendid musical group entertained in the famous East Room of the White House where Bob Hope and Art Linkletter and others have also entertained. It was a black group from the Los Angeles area. They got an immense ovation when they finished. I walked up, as was the custom, afterwards to shake hands with the leader and congratulate him. He spoke briefly, very movingly, to that very fine audience that was there. He said, "Mr. President, it has been a very great honor for us to be invited to appear in the White House." He said,

"You know, it's a long way from Watts to the White House."

Then I responded to him, and I said, "Yes, I know, and it's a long way from Whittier to the White House."

Here, before this great audience of my oldest friends, you know how long that road has been. It has had its ups and downs, its twisting and turning, its defeats and its victories. But what I want for every American, whatever his background, whatever his beginnings, however humble, I want him to have the same opportunity that I could have had and did have, a boy born in Yorba Linda, growing up in Whittier, and going to the White House.

That is the ideal that made America great and that is what these next 4 years are going to be about.

Thank you.

NOTE: The President spoke at 10:33 p.m. at a Republican fundraising dinner in the Grand Ballroom of the Century Plaza Hotel. He spoke without referring to notes.

Edward W. Carter was chairman of the "Victory '72" dinner.

330   Statement About the Nation's Economy.
September 28, 1972

NOWHERE in the United States does the goal of a new prosperity—full employment without inflation and without war—mean more than here in California, America's largest State and one whose economy, as a State, actually ranks ahead of all but a few of the nations of the world. Californians can take satisfaction in our steady progress toward the new prosperity—progress in which they share fully.

One of the best measures of our robust national economic health is the fact that

the growth rate of our total goods and services produced (gross national product)—9.4 percent per annum in the second quarter of this year—leads the world today. Employment is at an alltime high, with 82 million workers now on the job, 2.6 million more than a year ago. The rate of inflation has been cut from 4.4 percent a year ago to only 2.9 percent today.

Most important, as a result of these gains, the real wage of the average American worker has finally climbed off the inflationary treadmill of the 1960's, registering a gain of more than 4 percent in the past year alone. This means $200 in new purchasing power for the average wage earner—the equivalent of two extra weekly paychecks in a year.

Since 1969, we have succeeded in moving the U.S. economy from a wartime to a peacetime basis with a minimum of disruption. The rate of unemployment, while still too high, continues to move downward.

In California, for example, unemployment has declined statewide from 7.1 percent in August 1971, to 5.8 percent in August 1972. Here in Los Angeles, the progress against unemployment has been even more marked—from 6.9 percent in August 1971, to 5.5 percent in August 1972. This has meant an increase of 63,000 jobs in Los Angeles alone in one year. And the job situation in Los Angeles should continue to grow stronger, provided that the Nation continues on the path of sound economic policies, with our defense maintained at realistic and effective levels.

California has become one of the world's great research centers. Future economic growth in this country, with more and better jobs, requires that the United States strengthen its research and technological capacities. This is one reason why this Administration's budgets in the past 3 years have greatly increased the allocation of Federal funds to research and development. My budget for fiscal year 1973, for example, recommended an increase of more than $1 billion for research and development in the Department of Defense budget alone. The National Aeronautics and Space Administration and the Atomic Energy Commission have intensified their efforts to utilize the technological advancements developed under their programs. Overall, there has been a 65-percent increase since 1969 in R & D investment for all purposes other than defense and space. These obligations amount to $5.4 billion in 1973.

The new economic policy which I initiated in August 1971 has played a role in the achievement of America's heartening economic resurgence.

But the real driving force has been the talents and the energies of America's workers—the millions who seek nothing more from their Government than a favorable economic climate for their job skills, unmatched now or at any other time by any other society.

These are the people who know that the economic greatness of America was built by the incentives and rewards of work, and who believe that it is a continued dedication to work and earnings that will keep America great.

The goal of my Administration is not more welfare, but more work—more dignity, more self-respect, more opportunity. We have fought for 3 years to reform the welfare mess without help from those who now seem to point to it with confused criticism.

We say the Government should set policies which tax the working man and woman at a minimum, protect their purchasing power at a maximum, and ensure job access for everyone. Only then can every American raise his family's living standard to the highest point his skills and dedication will permit.

NOTE: The statement was released at Los Angeles, Calif.

331   Remarks to a National Cancer Conference in Los Angeles, California. *September 28, 1972*

Dr. Rauscher, Dr. Letton, Dr. Clark, all the distinguished ladies and gentlemen attending this conference:

I very much, of course, appreciate the award that has just been presented, but I think it should be presented to you, each of you, who have been in the forefront in this battle for so many years. You are, after all, the frontline soldiers in the fight against cancer.

The Government, which I represent in this particular capacity, can help to provide the resources, but you are the ones who do the work. I know that biomedical research and treatment is a notoriously uncertain enterprise. I know that when we talk about a cure for cancer, that it is not some simplistic answer that you find, that there are many, many approaches that are being tried at different times and many areas in which movement may occur.

No one can control or even predict how fast this program is going to go. But we can control—and this is the reason that I am here—we can control our own contribution to the progress of the program. We can be sure this progress is not delayed because of too few resources or too much redtape, for we know this: Cancer is a scourge we must fight. That fight deserves, from all of us, all the money, all the resources, and all the ingenuity that are required to win it.

That is why, in my State of the Union Address, January 1971, I called for a total national commitment to the anti-cancer crusade. That is why we followed up on that call for action. As you know, in the last 2 years we have more than doubled the Federal budget for cancer, to over $450 million. We have converted the facilities at Fort Detrick from research on biological weapons to cancer research, and the National Cancer Institute has been strengthened and streamlined, made directly accountable to the President. We have established the new National Cancer Advisory Board, the President's Cancer Panel, to help us coordinate our resources in the Government, and to the extent we possibly can, to strip away that inevitable redtape.

But all the money and all the organization in the world—and we have the money and we have lots of organization in Government—but all of it, by themselves, will not win this fight. I know that and all of you know that. Whether we win it or not, and when we win it, depends on you, the doctors, the scientists, the volunteers who support them all across America and all around the world.

What governments can do is to help mobilize not only this Nation's but the world's best brains wherever they exist, and to insure that they have the chance to make their full contribution to this cause, because it often occurs to me, as I travel to various countries around the world—to Africa and Asia and Latin America, to the People's Republic of China, to the Soviet Union—that no one knows where we are going to find that one individual who may make a breakthrough in this field. It might be a woman out studying in a great university in Europe. It might be a young boy who sits in a schoolroom in Asia, or perhaps in the People's Republic of China. It could be an American doctor, a Russian biologist, a Chinese chemist, or maybe the breakthrough will come through from an African or Latin American scientist, or it might come from someone sitting in this room.

But perhaps more likely, from what I have learned in my rather brief acquaintance with the intricacy of this problem, there will not be any single cure, it will not come suddenly. It may be that many people will each contribute partial cures—progress for various forms of this dread disease. But whenever and wherever the answers come, what they are going to represent is the final steps of a long journey, a journey that many of you in this room have been on for many, many years. And those who took all the other steps, the first very difficult early steps when government did not provide as much support, when it was harder to get the volunteers to put up the money that was necessary, those of you who took those steps, who carried the fight then, when it was difficult, you are going to deserve the credit when the victory finally comes.

It is somewhat like the relays that we watched in the Olympics. One runner would break the tape. He was the winner, but all four stood there to receive the victory gold medal. Scientific progress is like a vast relay race in which thousands of men and women in every part of the world carry the baton for a distance before they pass it on, pass it on from one to another, from one generation to another, until finally they break the tape; the race is won.

That is why the agreement we signed in Moscow last May to cooperate with the Soviet Union in medical research can be so important. When most people think of the Moscow summit and the many agreements that were signed there in the field of cooperation in space and trade, medical research, et cetera, there is a tendency naturally to put first on the list of importance, and naturally this should be the case, the agreement to limit strategic nuclear arms.

I sincerely hope that what is called the SALT agreement will be remembered as a great turning point in the control and limitation of nuclear arms, and perhaps eventually in their reduction and thereby in reducing the risk of war in the world. But it may well be 20, 40, maybe 100 years from now that another moment in Moscow will be remembered with that moment when Mr. Brezhnev and I signed the nuclear arms control agreement, for our agreement to cooperate in the field of medicine could mark another great turning point in the struggle against disease.

It is like drug abuse, or hijacking, terrorism. Cancer is not just a national, it is an international menace, and we must confront it with an international alliance. The barriers between nations are very great. They are very great, for example, from a philosophical standpoint, despite the visits that we have taken between the People's Republic of China and the United States, between the Soviet Union and the United States.

The fact that the leaders of the two nations meet, that we have days of conversations, and that we reach agreement, does not mean that those deep philosophical differences have basically changed. They have not. They probably will not.

What we have tried to do, of course, is to find a way to have disagreements without fighting about those disagreements, and what we have tried to do also is to find areas where we can agree and where we can cooperate.

In fighting disease, I have found that

both in my conversations with Premier Chou En-lai and my conversations with Mr. Brezhnev, Kosygin, Podgorny, and their colleagues, that this was one area where there was no question of the desire to work together, to cooperate. It, of course, will not be easy.

Many in this room have gone to the Soviet Union. You know the differences in language and the differences in background and so forth that are involved. Very few of you have had the opportunity to go to the People's Republic of China. But we do know that both there and in the Soviet Union there are people of ability. There are Russian scientists and Russian doctors who are able people. There are Chinese scientists and Chinese doctors— one-fourth of the people of the world, after all, live there—they are able people. The ability of those people there to cooperate with doctors here and in other free nations, this, of course, can have an enormous effect.

Perhaps this fight against cancer, against disease, can help to teach the world that despite immense differences between cultures and values and political systems, nations must work together and can work together to meet their common needs and fight their common enemies.

Those who join hands against disease help advance the day when nations may no longer raise their hands against each other.

I mentioned the laboratories at Fort Detrick. It seems to me that this is one of the great symbols of our progress toward the use of our resources for peaceful purposes. I am sure some of you have been there. But as I think of it here this morning, I think of the past, the present, and then what could take place in the future.

For years some of the most sophisticated scientific facilities on the face of our planet were there. They employed the best minds that we could find in the scientific community, and they were used for research on biological warfare, perfecting the instruments of death. It was a top secret installation, totally isolated. As a matter of fact, even though I had been a Congressman and Senator, Vice President of the United States, I had never seen it until I went there after it had changed its character.

Now it has been converted, as you know, into a laboratory for research on cancer, dedicated to the preservation, not the destruction, of life.

I remember my visit. It was just one year ago.[1] I remember saying on that day that Fort Detrick should now be thrown open, not only to scientists and doctors from the United States but from all over the world. Last month, as a part of our new cooperation in medicine, the Russian Minister of Health, a great heart surgeon incidentally, came to the United States. One of the places he visited was Fort Detrick. That shows how the world has changed in this last year. It shows it most, it seems to me, effectively, because no one could even think of the possibility of anyone from the Soviet Union going to this top secret installation in past years. But there he stood, in a place that just a few years earlier had been the symbol of a closed world, a world of suspicion and confrontation and a place where some of the best minds of our Nation had prepared for a possible war against his nation or some other nation.

Now he stood there, this man from the Soviet Union. This place has become a symbol of an open world, a world of co-

---

[1] See 1971 volume, Item 334.

operation and trust, at least in this particular area. It had become a meeting ground where the best minds from every nation can work together to save life anywhere on earth.

We have a long way to go, but our goal is clear. For me its symbol is Fort Detrick, Maryland, welcoming the Soviet Minister of Health. This is the kind of world we want to leave to our children. We want it to be a better world. We want it to be a more peaceful world. Let us hope that it may be a world in which the genius that split the atom, the genius that took men to the moon, is turned not to the conquest of other peoples, but to cooperation in the conquest of cancer and the other common diseases which afflict mankind.

I would not want to leave an impression from the remarks that I have made that in this very intricate field of foreign policy that we are going to expect instant cooperation in all areas. As I emphasized a few moments ago, the philosophical differences, the fact that nations have different interests, are there now, and they will last for years to come.

But I do suggest here this morning that a beginning is occurring. We now have a dialogue with the leaders of one-fourth of the people of this earth where we had nothing but angry isolation on both sides for over 20 years. From confrontation we have moved to negotiation and then cooperation with the leaders of the Soviet Union, and particularly with some of them in their scientific endeavors where previously we have not had that opportunity. This indicates the kind of a world we can build. It also indicates how much counts on you.

I would simply conclude with this final thought. When we think of arms control, when we think of wars and the lives that they take, one statistic brings home how important your battle is, how important you are as the frontline soldiers in this battle. I understand that each year in the United States more people die of cancer than were killed in action in all of World War II.

So, as you begin this conference, as you work in this conference, as you have in years past when you have met, let me say it may not get the headlines of a great international conference which deals with the problems of resolving differences in arms control, et cetera. But I know and you know that there is no battle that is more important than the one you are waging, and our best wishes go with you as well as the resources that the Government can provide.

Thank you.

———————

Ladies and gentlemen, before we fly back to Washington, I just want to say one thing with regard to the Nixon family and its contribution to this particular cause. This is the first chance I have had since I signed this legislation—except for the meeting that we had in the signing ceremony in the White House which some of you attended—this is the first chance I have had to attend a meeting of this sort where the National Cancer Institute and other organizations are joined together.

I am very proud to say that as far as the members of our family are concerned, that my wife, Mrs. Nixon, my daughter Julie, my daughter Tricia, in the past 3 months—I have not looked back beyond that, but I had the record checked—

across the country have appeared at various times before 12 different meetings and dinners and so forth, in the field of cancer. This shows that our family is with you, as well as the President in his official capacity.

Thank you.

NOTE: The President spoke at 10:28 a.m. in the Biltmore Bowl of the Biltmore Hotel where he was presented with a distinguished service award by the American Cancer Society.

The conference, jointly sponsored by the American Cancer Society and the National Cancer Institute, was attended by more than 1,500 physicians, including cancer specialists and general practitioners.

Frank J. Rauscher was Director of the National Cancer Institute; Dr. A. Hamblin Letton was president of the American Cancer Society; and Dr. R. Lee Clark, president and professor of surgery of the University of Texas M.D. Anderson Hospital and Tumor Institute in Houston, was chairman of the program committee for the conference.

The President spoke from a prepared text. On the same day, the White House released an advance text of his remarks and a fact sheet on the "Conquest of Cancer" program.

332   Remarks on Signing a Joint Resolution Approving the Interim Agreement With the Soviet Union on Limitation of Strategic Offensive Arms. *September 30, 1972*

Gentlemen:

We are gathered here, as you know, for the signing of the executive agreement, and I would like to repeat something that I said in the White House to this group of leaders when I returned from the trip to Moscow.

I pointed out both in my statement to the Congress and also to the Members of the Congress, both House and Senate, who had to consider these agreements, that we considered this a cooperative venture and we wanted the Congress to examine the agreements and to reach a conclusion, independently of the Executive, that they were in the interest of the United States.

The Congress has now so acted. Its debate has, in both the Senate and the House, served to inform the American people of the contents of the agreement, and also what its implications are.

I think what is particularly pleasing— pleasing in the sense of how our system works—is that this agreement has had bipartisan support in the fullest sense. Democrats and Republicans have joined together in debating it and criticizing where they felt there was room to criticize, and finally in voting for it in the form that it has now reached the desk here, and as I will sign it.

We have asked you to come to this room because we do feel this agreement is one that has a very special significance. All of you who have been here many times before know that it was the Cabinet Room from the period of Abraham Lincoln up until 1902, when the West Wing was completed. But it is now known as the Treaty Room because the war between Spain and the United States, as you know, was ended by a treaty signed in this room.

I would simply say in that connection, this is not a treaty which ends a war. This is not an agreement which guarantees that there will be no war. But what this is is the beginning of a process that is enormously important that will limit now, and, we hope, later reduce the burden of arms, and thereby reduce the danger of war. We think, therefore, it deserves this kind of attendance by the leaders of the Congress, the Administration, the Armed Forces, and it deserves also being signed in this room.

NOTE: The President spoke at 10:05 a.m. in the Treaty Room at the White House. He spoke without referring to notes.

As enacted, the joint resolution (H.J. Res. 1227) is Public Law 92–448 (86 Stat. 746). The text of the interim agreement is printed in United States Treaties and Other International Agreements (23 UST 3462).

On the same day, the White House released a fact sheet on previous actions concerning the interim agreement and on the history of the Treaty Room.

333 Proclamation 4160, National Heritage Day. *September 30, 1972*

By the President of the United States of America a Proclamation

The special quality of the United States is the interaction of many peoples from many lands, each asserting the freedom to be different, each respecting and honoring his own ethnic heritage, while contributing to a nation in which all are Americans together.

The shining guarantee of our national future is precisely the repeated rebirth, the reinvigoration, the gift of renewal, implicit in this constant meeting of the world's peoples here in our own land.

The unusual virtue of the United States is that all men and women are accepted for what they are, with friendship and respect founded upon knowledge and understanding of all races, creeds, and national origins.

The "melting pot" is one of unity, but never of uniformity.

The national pride of the United States is, in this sense, pride of our people in the heritage we draw from all nations.

In order that we may pause for a moment to express our appreciation of America's heritage, the Congress, by House Joint Resolution 1304, has requested the President to issue a proclamation designating Sunday, October 1, 1972, as National Heritage Day.

Now, THEREFORE, I, RICHARD NIXON, President of the United States of America, do hereby proclaim Sunday, October 1, 1972, as National Heritage Day. I call upon all Americans to reflect upon the composite vitality, enthusiasm and tenacity of the many separate peoples who have built our beloved country, and to celebrate, with appropriate ceremonies, the fact that our one nation is many nations, and our many nations are one nation, dedicated to freeeedom, under God.

IN WITNESS WHEREOF, I have hereunto set my hand this thirtieth day of September, in the year of our Lord nineteen hundred seventy-two, and of the Independence of the United States of America the one hundred ninety-seventh.

RICHARD NIXON

NOTE: The full text of this proclamation is included as an example of the proclamations the President issues. All the proclamations issued by the President in 1972 are listed in Appendix C.

334   Remarks at a Ceremony Marking Entry Into Force
of the Treaty on the Limitation of Anti-Ballistic
Missile Systems and the Interim Agreement on the
Limitation of Strategic Offensive Arms.
October 3, 1972

Mr. Vice President, Mr. Foreign Minister, Mr. Secretary of State, members of the Cabinet, Members of the Congress, and all of our distinguished guests:

As has already been indicated, the documents we have signed today place into force the first limitation on offensive and defensive nuclear arms ever entered into, and particularly it is important that this limitation is entered into between the Soviet Union and the United States of America.

On this particular occasion, I would like to pay a personal tribute to and express the thanks of the Nation to the Members of the House and the Senate who, in a bipartisan manner, gave approval and support to these historic agreements.

Also, I would like to pay tribute to and express personal appreciation to the scores of people in both governments who are not seated here at the table, but who worked with those at the table in working out the details of these agreements and their substance over almost 3 years.

It would not be fair to mention the names of all of them, or even a few, but I am sure that everyone would appreciate the fact that I would say that one name particularly comes to mind today, a former Ambassador from the United States to the Soviet Union, who also served with Ambassador [Gerard C.] Smith on the delegation to SALT from the United States—Ambassador Llewellyn Thompson.

It can truly be said of him, as it can be said of so many others who have worked in this field, that he gave his life to the cause of peace.

On this occasion, we recognize that these agreements mean the first step in limiting the burden of nuclear arms as far as our two nations are concerned. Also, these agreements mean a first step in reducing the danger of war in the world and increasing the chances of peace.

I have used the term "first step" quite deliberately, because—while these agreements have enormous significance in the ban on defensive nuclear weapons beyond the points that are covered in the agreement and in the treaty, an enormous significance in terms of the limitation of certain offensive categories—there remains a significant number of categories in the nuclear field that are not covered. And that is why I share the views that have been expressed by Foreign Minister Gromyko that we must now move from this first step to the vitally important next step in which we consider the whole range of offensive nuclear weapons and try to find agreement between our two nations in that field.

And then beyond, after that step is taken, we can look to the possibility of reducing the burden of nuclear arms and eventually to the possibility of limitations and restrictions on the use of such arms.

What we are in effect witnessing today,

then, is, we believe, the beginning of a great historical process in which we have learned by working out these agreements, following, as they do, the Non-Proliferation Treaty and the Test Ban Treaty, that we have found the way to make progress in other fields which can eventually lead to the goal that we all want, a world that is much safer and particularly a world that may possibly be free from the enormous danger of a nuclear disaster.

I think all of us are quite aware of the fact that the signing of these documents today, the signing of the documents that occurred earlier this year in the Kremlin, raise the hopes of all the people of the world for a dream of mankind from the beginning of civilization, a world of peace, a world in which peoples with different governments and different philosophies could live in peace together.

We believe that we have contributed to that cause and to the realization of that dream. And as we take this first step, we look forward to working together in taking the next steps, we look forward particularly in being worthy of the hopes of the people of the world. And we can be worthy of those hopes if our two great nations can move together, not only to limit the burden of arms on ourselves but to lift the burden of fear of war from all of the people of the world.

NOTE: The President spoke at approximately 10:15 a.m. in the East Room at the White House following the remarks of Andrei A. Gromyko, Soviet Minister of Foreign Affairs. The President spoke without referring to notes.

Foreign Minister Gromyko spoke in Russian. His remarks were translated by an interpreter as follows:

Mr. President, Mr. Secretary of State, ladies and gentlemen:

The treaty and the interim agreement on questions of strategic arms limitation, which were signed in Moscow by you, Mr. President, and by the General Secretary of the Central Committee of the Communist Party of the Soviet Union, Leonid Brezhnev, and which are today coming into force, will go down in history as a significant achievement in restraining the arms race.

This is how the significance of this event is evaluated by world public opinion. The Soviet Union attaches great importance to these accords which are a continuation of the process initiated by the conclusion of the Moscow Test Ban Treaty, the Treaty on the Non-Proliferation of Nuclear Weapons, and other important agreements limiting the arms race in the world.

The Soviet people firmly intend to go on implementing the peace program approved by the 24th Congress of the Communist Party of the Soviet Union. We are confident that the question on the nonuse of force in international relations and on the permanent prohibition of the use of nuclear weapons, which we have submitted for consideration by the current session of the United Nations General Assembly, is also of signal importance for the cause of peace.

The treaty and the interim agreement entering into force today are based on recognition of the principle of the equal security of the parties, and they offer no one any unilateral military advantages. At the same time, these accords meet not only the interests of our two nations but also the interests of international security as a whole and the interests of all nations because security and peace are their common goal.

Practical steps to limit rocket nuclear armaments rightfully hold an important place among the very real political changes taking place in relations between our two countries, and this signifies a success for the policy of peaceful coexistence and it has a positive effect on the entire international situation as a whole.

For the first time since the Second World War, agreements are coming into force aimed at slowing down the race in the most destructive types of armaments, but any treaty and any agreement can have a genuine historic significance only when the principles and the intentions proclaimed in them become the content of the practical activity of states and lead to further important achievements in that direction.

The Soviet Union is fully resolved, for its part, to do all that is necessary to that end.

Today when these important documents are entering into force, it should be noted that in accordance with the understanding achieved between our two countries, negotiations will be continued with a view to deepening and broadening agreements to limit strategic arms.

As is evidenced by the treaty and the interim agreement entering into force today, vigorous efforts aimed at removing the threat of war and at disarmament do yield their concrete positive results.

We are convinced that the interests of the Soviet and American peoples and the interests of the peoples of all the countries of the world demand that efforts to limit the arms race should continue unabated.

Thank you.

The texts of the treaty and the interim agreement are printed in United States Treaties and Other International Agreements (23 UST 3435 and 3462).

On October 2, 1972, the White House released a fact sheet on the treaty and the interim agreement.

On October 3, the White House released the texts of the instrument of ratification of the treaty, the proclamation of the treaty, and the protocol of exchange of instruments of ratification of the treaty and notices of acceptance of the interim agreement.

335   Letter to Chairman Nikolai V. Podgorny of the Soviet Union Accepting for the United States the Interim Agreement on the Limitation of Strategic Offensive Arms.   *October 3, 1972*

Dear Mr. Chairman:

I am pleased to inform you that the United States of America accepts the Interim Agreement Between the United States of America and the Union of Soviet Socialist Republics on Certain Measures with Respect to the Limitation of Strategic Offensive Arms, and the Protocol thereto, signed at Moscow on

May 26, 1972.

Sincerely,

RICHARD NIXON

[His Excellency Nikolai V. Podgorny, Chairman of the Presidium of the Supreme Soviet of the Union of Soviet Socialist Republics, Moscow]

NOTE: The letter was dated October 2, 1972, and released October 3.

336   Statement About Signing a Bill Providing for Relief of Certain Prewar Japanese Bank Claimants.   *October 4, 1972*

I HAVE great pleasure in signing into law H.R. 8215, for the relief of certain prewar Japanese bank claimants. This act will permit Japanese-Americans who were interned or paroled during the Second World War under the Alien Enemy Act to file claims, and to be re-imbursed, for funds deposited by them in certain branches of the Yokohama Specie Bank Ltd., Japan.

The signing of this act, in a very much larger sense, symbolized how far we have finally come in our human relationships in this country since World War II. After

87–234—74——64

Pearl Harbor, more than 100,000 Japanese-Americans were uprooted from their homes and moved into evacuation centers, whether they were citizens or aliens. Even during the war, there was considerable sentiment that we had over-reacted. President Franklin D. Roosevelt said, "Americanism is a matter of mind and heart; Americanism is not, and never was, a matter of race or ancestry."

Japanese-Americans were recruited for the United States Armed Forces, and their 442d Regimental Combat Team became famous as the "Go For Broke" outfit that was one of the most highly decorated units in the United States Army in World War II.

Not until the enactment of the Immigration and Nationality Act in 1952, however, were lawfully admitted alien Japanese permitted to become naturalized citizens of the United States. And not for many years were the Congress and the courts able to redress one particularly unfair aspect of the treatment of the Japanese-Americans. Only gradually were more than 15,000 Japanese-Americans who had been evacuated, but not interned or paroled, permitted to recover their money which had been deposited in United States branches of Japanese banks. The assets of these banks had been seized along with all other Japanese assets under the Trading with the Enemy Act during the war.

Now, this act finally permits between 1,000 and 2,000 Japanese-American depositors who were interned or paroled during the war, or their heirs, to file claim for their assets—31 years after Pearl Harbor.

The House Interstate and Foreign Commerce Committee has stated: ". . . It is the opinion of the committee that the predominant legal and moral right to these funds belongs to the Americans of Japanese ancestry who are the beneficiaries of this legislation."

I agree—and I now take this opportunity to express my gratitude for the contributions Japanese-Americans have made, and make today, to our country of which we say, *E Pluribus Unum,* one out of many.

NOTE: As enacted, H.R. 8215, approved October 3, 1972, is Public Law 92–458 (86 Stat. 763).

337   Veto of Railroad Retirement Benefits Bill. *October 4, 1972*

To the House of Representatives:

I today am returning without my approval H.R. 15927, a bill which would jeopardize the fiscal integrity of the railroad retirement system and hasten its bankruptcy.

This bill would provide a "temporary" increase of 20 percent in railroad retirement benefits, matching the recent increase in social security benefits—but without any provision for financing the new benefits.

It would be the third railroad retirement benefit increase in three years—totaling 51.8 percent in all—to be made without an accompanying increase in taxes to finance the benefits.

I am in favor of increased railroad retirement benefits. I would sign a measure which was adequately financed. But H.R.

15927 does not meet this test and thus it would threaten the very existence of the railroad retirement fund which already is on shaky financial ground. In addition, the bill in its present form would contribute to inflation which harms all the people, including the railroad retirees themselves.

I have often stated my strong belief that the millions of older men and women who did so much to build this Nation should share equitably in the fruits of that labor, and that inflation should not be allowed to rob them of the full value of their pensions. By providing a 20 percent benefit increase without adequate financing, however, this bill goes far beyond reasonable equity.

In passing this bill, the Congress has mistakenly assumed that railroad retirement benefits should be increased by the same percentage as social security benefits. In fact, the two systems are entirely different. Railroad benefits are much higher than social security benefits—for full-career workers the benefits may be twice as high.

The railroad retirement system payments are a combination of social security benefits augmented by the equivalent of a private pension. There is no valid reason why the private pension equivalent necessarily should be increased whenever social security benefits are raised. Other industries have not raised their pension benefits by 20 percent as a result of social security increases, even though most of them provide less adequate benefits.

The argument that these "temporary" benefits do not require a tax increase is, in my judgment, a delusion. I cannot imagine that the Congress would find it possible or desirable to slash railroad retirement benefits next year or in any year.

The imprudence of H.R. 15927 is underscored by the recent report of the Commission on Railroad Retirement. That Commission was created by the Congress in 1970 to study the troubled railroad retirement system and recommend measures necessary to place it on a sound actuarial basis. Yet the Congress acted on H.R. 15927 before it had an opportunity to consider and act on the recommendations of its own Commission for basic changes in the railroad retirement system.

The Commission's findings do not support H.R. 15927 and a majority of the Commissioners recommended against such legislation.

The Commission found that existing railroad retirement benefits are adequate, particularly for workers retiring after a full career. Retired railroad couples receive higher benefits than 9 out of every 10 retired couples in the country. The Commission also reached the sobering conclusion that the enactment of an across-the-board 20 percent increase, without adequate financing, would bankrupt the system in 13 years.

I believe that railroad beneficiaries should now receive the same dollar increases in benefits as social security recipients with similar earnings. A 20 percent increase in the social security portion of railroad retirement benefits can be financed without worsening the financial position of the Railroad Retirement Trust Fund. The Congress followed this sound approach when it increased railroad retirement benefits in 1968.

Therefore, I propose that the Congress enact a bill which again applies this principle, instead of H.R. 15927. The 1972 increase under my proposal would average $28 per month for single retired railroad workers and would be about $47 a month for married couples. It would not deepen the presently-projected deficits of the Railroad Retirement Trust Fund.

I urge the Congress to adopt this prudent alternative, which would give these deserving pensioners an equitable benefit increase on a timely basis and which would still preserve the flexibility for basic readjustments that will be needed later in the railroad retirement system.

Working together, I hope that we can constructively reform this system so it can continue to serve the needs of railroad workers and their families for decades ahead.

RICHARD NIXON

The White House,
    October 4, 1972.

NOTE: On the same day, H.R. 15927 was enacted over the President's veto as Public Law 92–460 (86 Stat. 765).

338 The President's News Conference of October 5, 1972

QUESTIONS

CHARGES OF CORRUPTION

[1.] Q. Mr. President, what are you planning to do to defend yourself against the charges of corruption in your Administration?

THE PRESIDENT. Well, I have noted such charges. As a matter of fact, I have noted that this Administration has been charged with being the most corrupt in history, and I have been charged with being the most deceitful President in history.

The President of the United States has been compared in his policies with Adolf Hitler. The policies of the U.S. Government to prevent a Communist takeover by force in South Vietnam have been called the worst crime since the Nazi extermination of the Jews in Germany. And the President who went to China and to Moscow, and who has brought 500,000 home from Vietnam, has been called the number one warmaker in the world.

Needless to say, some of my more partisan advisers feel that I should respond in kind. I shall not do so—not now,

not throughout this campaign. I am not going to dignify such comments.

In view of the fact that one of the very few Members of the Congress [1] who is publicly and actively supporting the opposition ticket in this campaign has very vigorously, yesterday, criticized this kind of tactics, it seems to me it makes it not necessary for me to respond.

I think the responsible members of the Democratic Party will be turned off by this kind of campaigning, and I would suggest that responsible members of the press, following the single standard to which they are deeply devoted, will also be turned off by it.

SENATOR MC GOVERN'S CAMPAIGN

[2.] Q. Mr. President, do you feel, as Vice President Agnew said the other day, that Senator McGovern is waging a smear campaign against you? Would you characterize it as that?

THE PRESIDENT. I am not going to

---

[1] Representative Jerome R. Waldie of California.

characterize the Senator's campaign. As a matter of fact, I don't question his motives. I think he deeply believes in a number of actions that he believes that this Government should take that I think would be very disastrous for this Nation, as I pointed out in my acceptance speech. Consequently, as far as I am concerned, I will discuss those issues, but I am not going to raise any doubts about his motives. Incidentally, I have no complaint when he raises doubts about mine. That is his choice.

A VIETNAM SETTLEMENT

[3.] Q. Mr. President, in Vietnam, do you see any possibility of a negotiated settlement before the election?

THE PRESIDENT. The settlement will come just as soon as we can possibly get a settlement which is right—right for the South Vietnamese, the North Vietnamese, and for us—one that will have in mind our goals of preventing the imposition by force of a Communist government on South Vietnam and, of course, a goal that is particularly close to our hearts in a humanitarian sense, the return of our prisoners of war.

I should emphasize, however, that under no circumstances will the timing of a settlement, for example, the possible negotiation of a cease-fire, the possible negotiation of, or unilateral action with regard to, a bombing halt—under no circumstances will such action be affected by the fact that there is going to be an election November 7.

If we can make the right kind of a settlement before the election, we will make it. If we cannot, we are not going to make the wrong kind of a settlement before the election. We were around that

track in 1968 when well-intentioned men made a very, very great mistake in stopping the bombing without adequate agreements from the other side.

I do not criticize them for that, of course, as far as their motives are concerned. I simply say, having seen what happened then, we are not going to make that mistake now.

The election, I repeat, will not in any way influence what we do at the negotiating table.

Second, because I know this subject has been discussed by a number of you, as it should be, in your commentary and in your reports, the negotiations at this time, as you know, have been, in the private channel, very extensive. We have agreed that neither side will discuss the content of those negotiations. I will not discuss them one way or another.

I will only say that the negotiations are in a sensitive stage. I cannot predict and will not predict that they will or will not succeed. I cannot and will not predict when they will succeed.

But I will say that any comment on my part with regard to how the negotiations are going could only have a detrimental effect on the goal that we are seeking, and that is, as early as possible a negotiated settlement of this long and difficult war.

Q. Mr. President, it has been said that Hanoi may be waiting until after the election to make a final settlement on the theory that if they got a Democrat elected they would get better terms for them. How do you answer that?

THE PRESIDENT. They could be motivated by that. There are those who believe that they were motivated to an extent in 1968 by political considerations in agreeing to a bombing halt before the election with the thought that defeating me was more in their interest than electing my opponent.

I do not claim that that was the case. I must say that both Senator Humphrey and I, I think, were quite responsible in that election campaign in refusing to comment on what were then only preliminary negotiations, recognizing that any comment by one who might be President might jeopardize the success of negotiations.

Now, as far as Hanoi's putting their eggs in that basket, that only indicates that the American political scene is one that no one can predict. Despite what the polls say and despite some indications on our side that we believe we have a good chance to win, there are many in this country and many abroad who think that there is a chance the other side might win.

Under those circumstances, they obviously could conclude, with some justification, that my insistence that we will never agree to a settlement which would impose a Communist government directly or indirectly on the people of South Vietnam, as compared with the statements of our opponents to the contrary on this particular point, might be influencing them.

On the other hand, we are talking. If we have the opportunity, we will continue to talk before this election and we will try to convince them that waiting until after the election is not good strategy.

THE BOMBING OF NORTH VIETNAM

[4.] Q. Mr. President, there are those of your critics who say that the bombing is really serving no useful purpose and it is needless. What purpose is the bombing now serving in view of the fact that the

negotiations have not resulted in a settlement and in view of the fact that there still seems to be a good deal of military activity in the South?

THE PRESIDENT. Well, I think, Mr. Lisagor [Peter Lisagor, Chicago Daily News], you could really go further. There are those who say that the bombing and the mining have served no useful purpose and are serving no useful purpose. Those same critics, however, as I pointed out in San Clemente, and have since had an opportunity to review, on May 1, that weekend, all had reached the conclusion that South Vietnam was down the tube. Time, Newsweek, the New York Times, the Washington Post, the three television network commentators—I am not referring, of course, to you ladies and gentlemen who are reporters—all in varying degrees wrote and spoke of the specter of defeat and the hopelessness of the South Vietnamese cause.

On May 8, I acted to prevent that Communist takeover, which all of these same critics then predicted. After I took that action of mining and bombing, the same critics predicted that the summit was torpedoed. Some even went so far as to say we were risking World War III.

Those predictions proved to be wrong. Now these same critics say that the bombing and mining was not necessary, it has accomplished no purpose, and is not necessary for the future. Well, I would say, based on their track record, I would not give much credence to what the critics have said in this respect.

I will only say the bombing and mining was essential to turn around what was a potentially disastrous situation in South Vietnam. The back of the enemy offensive has been broken. They hold no provincial capitals now at all.

This could not have been accomplished without the mining and the bombing, and the mining and the bombing will continue, of course, until we get some agreements on the negotiating front.

GRAIN SALES TO SOVIET UNION [2]

[5.] Q. Mr. President, what is your reply to critics who charge there is scandal involved in your Russian wheat agreement?

THE PRESIDENT. My reply is to have such allegations investigated—incidentally, with the thorough agreement and complete agreement of Secretary Butz. Secretary Butz and the House Committee on Agriculture both looked into these charges that some of the big grain dealers, the so-called Big Six, got advance information and made a lot of money, and that particularly some of the wheat growers in the Southwestern part of the country who sell their wheat early, usually, in order to get a premium, were left holding the bag when, if they had the advance information that there was going to be a deal, they could have made some more money.

Now, if there was any impropriety, if there was any illegality, we want to know it. The way to find out is to put the best investigative agency in the world to work in finding out. As soon as their investi-

[2] On July 8, 1972, the White House released a fact sheet and the transcripts of two news briefings on the U.S.-Soviet grain purchase agreement. The first news briefing was held by Henry A. Kissinger, Assistant to the President for National Security Affairs, and the second by Secretary of Commerce Peter G. Peterson and Secretary of Agriculture Earl L. Butz. The transcript of Dr. Kissinger's news briefing is printed in the Weekly Compilation of Presidential Documents (vol. 8, p. 1142).

gation is completed—and we want it just as quickly as we can—it will be made available to the Secretary, and he will take whatever action is needed if there is illegality or impropriety.

Let me turn, if I could, on the wheat deal, however, to another side of it that has also come to my attention. I have been rather amused by some of the comments to the effect that the wheat deal was really a bad one for the United States, that we got snookered by the Russians. When I used that term with Mr. Gromyko he asked for a translation, but in any event—and I said, "Well, you acted like capitalists"—but in any event—"because you didn't tell us that your grain failure was as great as it was."

Of course, his response was, "Well, what would you have done?" He said, "We knew we had to buy a lot of wheat, and we didn't want to push the price up as fast."

But in any event, let me take very briefly a moment of your time to point out what was in it for us and what was in it for them. First, the wheat deal cost us $120 million in, as you know, payments, farm payments. But this is what we got from it: The farmers got $1 billion in more farm income. There were thousands of jobs created, including jobs in the American merchant marine as well as on the farm and in the processing areas, as a result of the wheat deal.

The taxpayers were saved $200 million in farm payments that otherwise would have had to be made if we had kept the wheat in storage and not sold it.

Now, in addition, the wheat deal, this one, the one we have made with the Chinese, the one we have made with the Japanese for grain, and so forth and so on, have had a very significant effect in improving our balance of trade and balance of payments position.

As far as the terms were concerned, when we went in—I negotiated this directly after a lot of preliminary work had been done, and very good preliminary work, by Secretary Peterson and, of course, Secretary Butz—they wanted 10 years at 2-percent credit, and they finally took 3 years at over 6 percent.

Now they got something they needed. They have a short wheat crop and they needed this wheat in order to feed their people, but it was also good for us. Despite that, however, we certainly want no one to have gotten any inside information to make a profit out of it which was illegal or improper. If that did happen, we are going to find out, and we will take action against it.

Q. Mr. President, do you agree with Secretary Butz that if he had known that one of his aides was going to join a grain dealer that he would not have taken him along in negotiating the Russian deal?

THE PRESIDENT. Well, I have very great respect for Secretary Butz's judgment in this matter. The only addition I would make to it is that when we announced the grain deal on July 8 in San Clemente, as you recall, it was only then that we were sure—and incidentally many, of course, are now wondering what is going to happen to the trade agreement.

I can't tell you whether there will be one, or when. I think there will be one, but my point is that when we negotiate in this economic field, as is the case when we negotiate in the field of arms control, it is tough bargaining up and down the line, and until we get it nailed down we are not sure that we are going to get it. In this instance, while Mr. Butz's assistant did take a trip to the Soviet Union, he

certainly, I think, would have been very unwise to rely on the possibility there was going to be a deal until one was made.

If he did rely on it, he probably, in this instance, came out well. He could have come out the other way.

PROPERTY TAX RELIEF

[6.] Q. Mr. President, on the question of property taxes, Mr. Ehrlichman has said that the Administration's long-term goal is to reduce property taxes by 50 percent, which would mean about $16 billion from the Federal Government presumably to States to make up for the property tax loss. How will you find that $16 billion without having to increase Federal taxes?

THE PRESIDENT. We can't do it all in one bite. We have to begin with that. As Mr. Ehrlichman has indicated, that is why we have set as a goal a 50-percent reduction.

Now, let me indicate to you the priorities that I see developing with regard to property tax relief. We have to start first with the elderly. When I met with Mr. Merriam,[3] who, as you know, is the professional working with the advisory committee on intergovernmental relations, he gave me some statistics which to me were terribly depressing. There are one million retired people in this country who have incomes of less than $2,000 a year, and, who, on the average, pay a property tax of 33⅓ percent of that income.[4]

---

[3] Robert E. Merriam, Chairman of the Advisory Commission on Intergovernmental Relations.

[4] The 33⅓-percent figure refers to low-income retired persons in the Northeast. Nationwide, the average is about 16 percent of retiree's income.

Now that is fiscally wrong, morally wrong, and certainly tax wrong. We must begin by lifting that burden from those people who have worked all their lives, are now retired on what is basically an inadequate amount, and are paying a third of their taxes [incomes] for property taxes to send, basically, children to school.

I have discussed this matter not only with Mr. Merriam, but Mr. Shultz and I have had, as you have noted, a number of meetings on this in the past few weeks. We hope to have a plan which we can present at an early date. I cannot indicate to you what that date will be, but I will say this: One, we are going to propose to the next Congress a plan that will relieve—that will start down the road of reducing the burden of property taxes.

The first priority will be to reduce the burden of property taxes on the elderly; and second, whatever step we take, one condition is, it must not require any increase in other taxes. We think we have found a formula to do that.

THE WATERGATE CASE

[7.]   Q. Mr. President, don't you think that your Administration and the public would be served considerably and that the men under indictment would be treated better, if you people would come through and make a clean breast about what you were trying to get done at the Watergate?

THE PRESIDENT. One thing that has always puzzled me about it is why anybody would have tried to get anything out of the Watergate. But be that as it may, that decision having been made at lower levels, with which I had no knowledge, and, as I pointed out——

Q. But, surely you know now, sir.

THE PRESIDENT. Just a minute. I certainly feel that under the circumstances that we have got to look at what has happened and to put the matter into perspective.

Now when we talk about a clean breast, let's look at what has happened. The FBI assigned 133 agents to this investigation. It followed out 1,800 leads. It conducted 1,500 interviews.

Incidentally, I conducted the investigation of the Hiss case. I know that is a very unpopular subject to raise in some quarters, but I conducted it. It was successful. The FBI did a magnificent job, but that investigation, involving the security of this country, was basically a Sunday school exercise compared to the amount of effort that was put into this.

I agreed with the amount of effort that was put into it. I wanted every lead carried out to the end because I wanted to be sure that no member of the White House Staff and no man or woman in a position of major responsibility in the Committee for the Re-Election had anything to do with this kind of reprehensible activity.

Now, the grand jury has handed down indictments. It has indicted incidentally two who were with the Committee for the Re-Election and one who refused to cooperate and another who was apprehended. Under these circumstances, the grand jury now having acted, it is now time to have the judicial process go forward and for the evidence to be presented.

I would say finally with regard to commenting on any of those who have been indicted, with regard to saying anything about the judicial process, I am going to follow the good advice, which I appreciate, of the members of the press corps,

957

my constant, and I trust will always continue to be, very responsible critics.

I stepped into one on that when you recall I made, inadvertently, a comment in Denver about an individual who had been indicted in California, the Manson case. I was vigorously criticized for making any comment about the case, and so, of course, I know you would want me to follow the same single standard by not commenting on this case.

CAMPAIGN PLANS

[8.] Q. Mr. President, when are you going to begin intensive campaigning, and are you going to begin intensive campaigning?

THE PRESIDENT. I repeat, Mr. Warren [Lucien C. Warren, Buffalo Evening News], what I have said previously in San Clemente and at San Francisco. Until the Congress adjourns, my primary responsibility is to stay here, and particularly to stay here to fight the battle against bigger spending that would lead to bigger taxes.

I have made a commitment, and I make it here again today. There will be no tax increase in 1973. However, there is one problem with that commitment. There will be no Presidential tax increase. But, we need the cooperation of the Congress, and there could be a Congressional tax increase. If the Congress, for example, does not approve the $250 billion ceiling that we have requested, that is going to make the chances of avoiding a tax increase more difficult.

It does not make it impossible, however, because we have a second line of defense. If the Congress, as appears likely, continues to pass bills that substantially exceed the budget, which already is at

the highest limits that our tax income will pay for, if the Congress continues to pass bills and send them to the President's desk that exceed that budget, the Congress will have voted for a tax increase. However, I still have one weapon left, that is the veto.

My own prediction is that after talking to our own leaders and after hearing from some responsible Democrats in the House and Senate, that even though the Congress will probably send to my desk in the next 2 or 3 weeks a number of bills that will substantially exceed the budget and that would result in a Congressional tax increase, I think my vetoes of those bills will be sustained and that that will make it possible for me to keep my commitment for no tax increase.

That shows one of the reasons why it is important for me to stay on the job here in Washington until the Congress adjourns and until that very great danger of a tax increase caused by Congressional overspending is met and defeated.

Now, once the Congress leaves, or once I see that danger passing, then I can make plans to go into various parts of the country. In the meantime, I am going to have to limit my travel, as I have indicated, to perhaps once a week, on a day that I see no significant problems that I need to attend to here, but I will not do more than that.

If I have to choose between engaging in all of the spectaculars of a campaign, which I have been doing virtually all my life every 2 years for 25 years—if I have to choose between that and staying on the job and doing something that would result in avoiding a tax increase for the American people, I am going to stay right here on the job.

ELECTION PREDICTIONS

[9.] Q. Mr. President, to follow that up, if you can be a prognosticator—in 1968 you received 301 electoral votes—what do you see for yourself in 1972?

THE PRESIDENT. Three hundred and one was enough, wasn't it?

Q. True.

THE PRESIDENT. Our goal is to get as many as we can, electoral votes, and as many popular votes as we can. I know that the political questions have been discussed very broadly. I would take a moment on that and might refer to your question, too, but then you follow up if I don't answer.

The problem with a candidate who is ahead in the polls—of course, I like this kind of a problem better than being behind—but the problem of a candidate that is ahead in the polls, and his organization, is a very significant one in this respect: It is the problem of getting his vote out. What we need above everything else is a big vote. In order to get a big vote, it means that people have to be stimulated to vote. That is one of the reasons that going to the country and participating will help get that big vote out, and when the time permits, I will go to the country in order to get the vote out, among other things.

With the candidate who is behind substantially in the polls, he doesn't have that problem. With all the pollsters—and the pollsters always remember when they predicted right, but never when they predicted wrong—this doesn't prove anything necessarily, because when the margins are up in the 60-40 range, on the fringes it is always quite soft either way.

But in 1964 I was interested to find that Gallup never had Goldwater as more than 32 percent as against Johnson. In fact, Gallup's poll, taken one week before the election, showed Goldwater at 32 percent. He got 39 percent. Why? The Goldwater people voted, and many of the Johnson people thought they had it made.

We, of course, have the same problem. Of course, Johnson still won. Maybe we will. What I am simply suggesting is that as far as predictions are concerned, I have told all of our people: "Don't rely on the polls. Remember that the candidate who is behind will tend to get his vote out. Ours will tend not to get out. Get our vote out and try to win as big a popular vote as we can and as big an electoral vote as we can."

The purpose: Not to make the other candidate look bad, but the purpose is to get what I have described as the new American majority in which Republicans, Democrats, and independents join together in supporting not a party, or not an individual, but supporting the record of the past 4 years, the positions which are very clear-cut that I have taken on the great issues, and thereby giving us the opportunity to continue in the next 4 years.

THE PRESIDENT'S AVAILABILITY TO THE PUBLIC AND THE PRESS

[10.] Q. Mr. President, as election day comes closer, you have also been criticized for isolating yourself, not making yourself available for questioning.

THE PRESIDENT. Hiding [*laughter*]— isolating is a great big word.

Q. Hiding. Apart from going out and hitting the hustings, do you plan to have more press conferences between now and election day?

THE PRESIDENT. Well, I would plan to try to find ways to be as available for purposes of presenting my position as I can. For example, on the matter of taxes, how we avoid a tax increase, I know that Mr. Ehrlichman has represented my views and Mr. Shultz has and a number of others. I have tried to cover it here briefly this morning.

But at Camp David yesterday, I completed a speech that I had made on the subject, and while I cannot get away this weekend, I am going to deliver it by nationwide radio—we'll buy the time, incidentally, nationwide radio—on Saturday night. So for the writing press, you will have it in time for the Sunday papers. That is only coincidental, of course.

Q. In light of the fact that because Congress has not adjourned, you cannot get out, why can't you accept us as a surrogate for the people you can't see and have more press conferences between now and November 7?

THE PRESIDENT. If you would like to be surrogates, we have plenty——

Q. We can ask the questions the public is asking.

THE PRESIDENT. Well, Mr. Potter [Philip Potter, Baltimore Sun], the press conference, to me, is not basically a chore. When I say "a chore," it is always a challenge, and it is one that requires hard work. I recall, incidentally, in that connection, speaking of the press conference, I think I have told you once when we were riding in the back of the plane—it was not as good as the one we have got now, but you remember those days, we had very few good planes, a DC–3. But I recall that we were talking about speechwriting and how I hated to write speeches and I talked to Foster Dulles about it after

he returned from one of his many trips abroad and he always made a speech, and I said, "Don't you hate to write speeches?"

He said, "Yes, I used to. But," he said, "now I do it. I consider it necessary to go through the torture, because the writing of the speech disciplines my mind, it makes me think through the issue."

I must say the preparation for the press conference helps to discipline the mind to talk about the issues. To come precisely now to your question, I think that the format of questions and answers, for members of the press, can be useful. Certainly I will consider the possibility of using that format. Maybe not just here, maybe in other places as well. But we won't stack the questions.

WELFARE REFORM

[11.] Q. Mr. President, now that welfare reform appears to be dead, or at least going, on Capitol Hill, I am wondering, if after all this, whether you still support the principle implicit in H.R. 1 of minimum income assistance for poor families and whether you would push for that principle in a second term?

THE PRESIDENT. The answer is yes to both questions. As far as welfare reform generally is concerned, the Senate yet has not completed its actions, its consideration. The problem with the Roth amendment,[5] of the test, is that it lacks the trigger device and it means you would start all over again.

The one point, however, that I want

---

[5] Senator William V. Roth, Jr., of Delaware sponsored an amendment to H.R. 1 proposing a 2-year pilot test of the major proposals for welfare reform.

to emphasize with regard to welfare re-form, the program that we have presented for welfare reform, with its strong work requirements and with its assistance to the working poor, with the purpose of pro-viding a bridge for them to get, and an incentive to get, off of welfare and into work, from a fiscal standpoint, stretches the budget as far as it can be stretched. We can't add anything to it.

And, from the standpoint of the amount to be provided, it goes as far as it should go, and I would oppose any program that would add more people to the welfare rolls, millions more, as would all three of the programs advocated by our opponents, whichever one you want to pick. I would oppose any program that would add more to the welfare rolls than H.R. 1.

What we need are programs that will move toward moving people off of wel-fare and not raising the ante so that people are encouraged to go on it.

So, I would take H.R. 1. I would very greatly strengthen the work require-ments in it. If the Senate and the House, as appears possible now, not certain, I hope not certain, fail to act, we will grapple with it in the new term and try to get the support for it.

SCHOOL BUSING

[12.] Q. Mr. President, there is an anti-busing bill on the Senate calendar that I believe you support. Its passage is problematical, as I understand it. If it is not passed, I wonder if you would sup-port a constitutional amendment?

THE PRESIDENT. I have indicated that, first, I am against busing. This is, of course, one of those clear-cut issues in this campaign. When people wonder what they are: I am against amnesty. I am against busing. I am against massive in-creases in spending that would require a tax increase. I am against cutting our de-fenses by $30 billion, which would make us second to the Soviet Union.

I am for the domestic proposals that I set forth in such great detail in the '72 State of the Union, and that, incidentally, Mr. Semple [Robert B. Semple, Jr., New York Times], you recall, was in it. I en-dorsed all of those. Those are part of the program for the future—health, govern-ment reorganization, welfare reform, and the rest—and we hope to have a Congress that will be more responsive in getting them through.

Now, the question of what to do about busing is now right in the Congress' lap. If the Congress fails to act in a way that pro-vides some relief from these excessive bus-ing orders that have caused racial strife, and primarily in Northern cities as distin-guished from Southern cities, then I in-tend to find another way.

There are two ways we can go: With a new Congress, which might be very much more responsive on this issue after they have found out what people think on the hustings, with a new Congress we might get very quick action on the legislative front. That I would prefer.

If we cannot get Congress to act on the legislative front, then we would have to move on the constitutional amendment front.

I would point out that, however, the legislative front is preferable, and also easier and quicker, because it requires only a majority and not a two-thirds and also can move quickly on the issue.

So, if we don't get it now, we will go for it as a matter of the highest priority in the first session of the next Congress.

FRANK CORMIER (Associated Press). Thank you, sir.

NOTE: President Nixon's twenty-eighth news conference was held at 11:04 a.m. in the Oval Office at the White House on Thursday, October 5, 1972. The President spoke without referring to notes.

339   Memorandum About Employment of Vietnam Veterans.   *October* 5, 1972

Memorandum to the Heads of Executive Departments and Agencies:

As we continue to wind down this Nation's participation in the Vietnam conflict, increasing numbers of our veterans are returning home and entering the labor market. They have done their part and now need our help in making the transition back into the civilian economy.

Education and employment are their most immediate priorities. As a responsible employer, the Government must continue to use every means available to meet the needs of those who have served their country.

I am resolved that no returning veteran will be turned away from lack of zeal on our part. Many Federal officials have done an exemplary job in employing veterans whenever possible, even though employment opportunities have diminished. I want you to ensure that all managers, supervisors, and personnel officials in your organization accept, as a personal challenge and obligation, the responsibility for extending maximum job opportunities to returning veterans.

Veterans preference granted by law provides opportunities for hiring returning veterans. The Veterans Readjustment Appointment which I authorized in March, 1970,[1] provides an excellent additional avenue. But we must pursue with skill and determination every conceivable approach including the splitting of full-time jobs.

The Chairman of the Civil Service Commission will continue to provide leadership and guidance on employment of the returning veterans within the Federal Government and the Secretary of Labor will continue to direct our efforts on their behalf. Those who have given so much of themselves will not be forgotten.

RICHARD NIXON

_____

[1] By Executive Order 11521 of March 26, 1970.

340   Letter to Four Members of the Advisory Panel on South Asian Relief Assistance.   *October* 6, 1972

I DEEPLY appreciate the time and thought that you and the other members of the Advisory Panel on South Asian Relief Assistance have devoted over the past year to our emergency economic assistance programs in South Asia. The perspective and insight which all of you have brought to your continuing review of these programs have been of great value to us.

Your reflections concerning your first-hand observations in Bangladesh are most gratifying. It has been my objective throughout this difficult period in South Asia to assure that, at a minimum, the absence of the essentials of life would not further heighten the tension that already existed there. I recognized in 1971 and I recognize now that making available the economic necessities cannot by itself assure peace or peaceful development. These objectives can ultimately be achieved only in a stable political environment and only when neighbors have enough confidence in one another so that normal relationships can be established across their borders.

At the same time, the United States could not and cannot ignore the needs and the aspirations of the more than 700 million South Asians. Our effort to join other nations in meeting the most urgent needs of those who live in this area has reflected not only our compassion for them in their distress but also our recognition that an orderly society depends on the capacity of governments to "promote the general welfare."

Again, my warmest thanks for your help.

Sincerely,

RICHARD NIXON

NOTE: The letter, dated October 5, 1972, and released October 6, was sent to each of the four members of the Panel who had made the visit to Bangladesh. They reported to the President in a joint letter dated September 8, which was released with the President's letter and read as follows:

Dear Mr. President:

The undersigned members of your Advisory Panel on South Asian Relief Assistance have recently completed an intensive visit to Bangladesh. We hereby submit our views and conclusions derived from many visits and con-versations. We have met with Ministers, officials and private citizens of Bangladesh, with United Nations officials, with representatives of American voluntary agencies and with members of the U.S. Mission. These conversations were supplemented by field trips.

The emergency aid to Bangladesh since its independence struck us forcefully as a truly superb example of the traditional American response to the need of people in deep distress. The American people, in giving through the Government, the United Nations and voluntary agencies, one-third of a total world-wide relief effort of approximately $800 million to rescue a new country half way around the world—more than any other country—have once again been true to their inheritance.

This humanitarian effort has contributed significantly toward helping this new, war-torn country and its Government under Prime Minister Sheikh Mujibur Rahman to make the painful transition to independence. We believe that the Prime Minister and his colleagues are aware of that fact.

We should like to record our conviction that the mobilized efforts and resources of the world have forestalled a major famine. The United Nations, through the Secretary General's appeals last year and this and through its operations in the field, has played a major role in this achievement. The performance of the UN has justified the United States in deciding, after we had seen the danger, that the UN could play such a role and our determination to help it do so effectively.

The newly emerging nation of Bangladesh is facing an extremely complex range of human problems. Certainly the potential for catastropic suffering is unparalleled in modern history. But the end of the present crisis appears to be approaching. Unless another natural disaster should strike, Bangladesh should, by the spring of 1973, be emerging from the relief stage and launched upon a period of reconstruction and development. The United Nations coordinating organization, UNROD (United National Relief Operation, Dacca), is expecting to turn over its major responsibilities to the Government of Bangladesh next spring and to leave to the regular UN agencies tasks such as they have traditionally undertaken in this and other developing countries.

Bangladesh is now turning to a new task in a new set of circumstances. Serious problems will unquestionably arise and there will be many hard decisions to make. We believe that the United States can contribute to this difficult—even dangerous—transition in a number of useful ways. We shall spell out our suggestions in some detail in a report to Mr. Maurice J. Williams, your Coordinator for U.S. Humanitarian Assistance for South Asia.

Our visit has underlined for us the importance of your request for $100 million of grant aid for Bangladesh for the current fiscal year and the necessity that the Congress act favorably upon that request. We urge that, in addition, appropriate amounts of PL–480 foodstuffs be earmarked for Bangladesh.

From the observation of the performance of the remarkably vigorous staff—all in their early thirties—of the A.I.D. office in Dacca, we are confident that these funds will be imaginatively and effectively used.

We believe on the basis of preliminary projections we have seen that the proposals for fiscal 1974 will set forth the basis for an effective development program for Bangladesh.

We wish to express our appreciation of the opportunity you have given us to serve you in an endeavor that reflects great credit on our country and its humanitarian traditions.

Faithfully yours,

JEANNE R. FERST
GLEN HAYDON
JOSEPH E. JOHNSON
MAXWELL RABB

341 Radio Address on Federal Spending. *October 7, 1972*

Good afternoon:

I want to talk with you today about an issue that strikes directly at every pocketbook and every savings account in America, the clear and present danger that excessive spending by the Congress might cause a Congressional tax increase in 1973.

When the Congress votes to increase spending above the Federal budget, there are only two alternatives: either taxes will go up or a new surge of inflation will begin and prices will go up.

I am totally opposed to either of these bad choices. I oppose higher taxes, and I oppose higher prices. My budget will not require higher taxes. It will not cause higher prices.

I shall fight every attempt by the Congress to bust that budget, because a big spending spree by the Congress will have only one result: a hangover of higher taxes or higher prices for every working family in America.

No goal and no program has any higher priority with me than protecting our people's growing purchasing power, and when taxes or prices go up, purchasing power goes down.

In order to clamp a lid on Congressional spending, I have proposed a 1973 spending ceiling of $250 billion, a proposal that will be voted on by the Congress next week.

Let me lay it on the line in clear and unmistakable terms. A vote against the spending ceiling could prove to be a vote for higher taxes. A vote for the spending ceiling will clearly be a vote against higher taxes.

This spending ceiling should get the active support of every American concerned with avoiding higher taxes or higher prices. It should be approved.

But if the spending ceiling is not passed, I still have one weapon left, the Presidential veto. And I will not hesitate to use that weapon on behalf of the

American taxpayer. I will veto even bills whose purposes I agree with, if I conclude that the price tags of those bills are so high that they will lead to tax increases.

I consider the battle against higher prices and higher taxes to be the major domestic issue of this Presidential campaign. The issue is clear. I am holding spending in a range not requiring a tax increase now or over the next 4 years. I will not make any promises in this campaign that would require a tax increase now or in the future.

Our opponents in their platform, in their campaign promises, are committed to huge new spending programs that would add $100 billion to the budget and would require the largest tax increase in America's history. The major burden of those increased taxes would fall on America's 82 million wage earners.

My goal is not only no tax increase in 1973 but no tax increase in the next 4 years.

To achieve this, we must put a tax-proof ceiling on spending now and we must be sure there are no holes in that ceiling. To buy now and pay later would be the sure road to higher taxes or higher prices, or both.

Another reason this spending ceiling is needed is to enable us to fulfill our firm commitment to provide relief from property taxes. When property tax relief comes, and it will come if the Congress cooperates with me now on harnessing runaway spending, the first to receive relief will be those who most need it.

Today there are more than one million retired Americans over 65. They live in their own homes with an income of less than $2,000 a year. They pay an average

from $300 to $700 of that $2,000 in property taxes. To allow that to happen to Americans who have worked all their lives to build this great country and to earn their retirement is a national disgrace.

Relief for those Americans is going to be a first order of business in our next Federal budget. It has been charged by some prominent economists that a tax increase in 1973 is unavoidable.

I disagree. There is nothing desirable and nothing inevitable about a tax increase in 1973 or beyond. But while a President can promise there will be no tax increase, as I have, he can keep that promise only if the Congress cooperates with him in holding down spending.

I do not point the finger of blame at the Members of Congress as individuals. As one who once proudly served in both the House and Senate, I know how hard it is for the Congress to join with the President in achieving a goal which is so much in the interest of every American family.

But, let's face it, the Congress suffers from institutional faults when it comes to Federal spending. In our economy, the President is required by law to operate within the discipline of his budget, just as most American families must operate within the discipline of their budget.

Both the President and a family must consider total income and total outgo when they take a look at some new item which would involve spending additional money. They must take into account their total financial situation as they make each and every spending decision.

In the Congress, however, it is vastly different. Congress not only does not consider the total financial picture when it votes on a particular spending bill, it does not even contain a mechanism to do so if it wished.

This is why the spending ceiling vote next week will be so critical to every family in America. The spending ceiling will give the Congress what it needs to bring order to its spending decisions and for the Congress to become a partner, rather than an opponent, in the fight against higher taxes and against higher prices.

Congress works largely through committees and subcommittees. There are more than 300 of these committees and subcommittees. Each is an independent world of its own, specializing in one or more fields of activity. For example, one committee handles urban matters, another farm programs, still another public works programs. These 300 committees and subcommittees authorize spending for their favorite programs without direct regard for what the others are doing. Other committees appropriate the actual money for these programs, and still other committees have the responsibility of raising the taxes to pay for the programs.

Since most programs have some attractive features, it is easy for the committees and the Congress itself to approve them one at a time simply because the one program then up for decision would advance a worthy goal. But no one individual or committee in the Congress is officially charged with keeping track of the totals involved in all of this.

The Congress, thus, has no sure way of knowing whether or when its many separate decisions are contributing to inflation and higher prices, or possibly to higher taxes.

The Congress operates the way a family would if all of the individual family members went out on their own, spent what they wanted or signed up for long-term payments for things they desired, without regard to what other members of the family were spending and without regard to the total income of the family and the total of the bills all of the members of the family were running up on their own.

And that is why I am calling for a rigid spending ceiling for fiscal year 1973, so that we can make certain that Federal spending does not exceed $250 billion and thus does not contribute to higher prices or generate an urgent need for higher taxes.

People of good will can disagree over spending priorities, but if the Congress wishes to increase spending in one area, then it must be prepared either to reduce it in another area or to include higher taxes if we are to escape more inflation.

But the Congress is not meeting this responsibility. I do not make this statement in any partisan sense. Both of our major parties have their share of big spenders, and there are responsible Democrats as well as responsible Republicans serving on the Appropriations Committees of the Congress, the Ways and Means Committee of the House, the Finance Committee of the Senate, who are as deeply concerned as I am about the trend toward higher spending and higher taxes.

The problem is the inherent weakness in the present structure of the Congress as a whole to deal with this danger. This has been confirmed by the House Ways and Means Committee, which is composed of some of the most experienced men in the Congress and which has a majority of 15 Democrats to 10 Republicans.

In reporting the spending ceiling legislation to the House, 21 members of this committee, 11 Democrats and 10 Republicans, included a frank discussion of the problem the Congress has with spending control. Here is a direct quote from the committee's report:

"The need for an expenditure ceiling of this type arises from the difficulty Congress has experienced in establishing overall program priorities. Even when it is generally recognized that expenditures need to be limited, the total expenditures actually occurring seem to keep rising because, in a period of strong, competing concepts of program priorities, all are accepted rather than choices being made among them."

Now that is what the Congress said, the Ways and Means Committee, by this overwhelming majority.

As things now stand, most observers predict that Congress will vote billions of dollars more than my January budget asked. Almost without exception the programs being considered are for good purposes, but when you take them all together, they add up to an inflationary catastrophe or a higher tax nightmare, and I do not intend to let this happen.

An example is the debate in the Congress and in this campaign over welfare. Our opponents have proposed in Congress, in their platform, and in their campaign speeches, programs that would add millions to the welfare rolls and billions to the tax burden of working Americans.

I have refused to compromise my welfare reform program to meet the demands of those who favor higher welfare payments. I want this Nation to be as generous as possible in helping those who cannot help themselves, but I shall always be guided by this principle: I shall oppose any program which increases payments to those who do not work if it requires an increase in taxes for those who do work. If necessary, as I announced last July, I will continue to veto bills which call for significantly larger expenditures than my no-tax-increase budget. If those vetoes are sustained by the Congress, we can hold the line against higher taxes.

But the spending ceiling would be better. It would be foolproof. A spending ceiling would be absolute insurance that no new taxes will be required and that no Federal spending excesses will destroy our successful anti-inflation program in which in this year we have cut the rate of inflation in half in this country and which we now have in the United States the lowest rate of inflation of any major industrial country in the world.

Beyond this, the new budget I am preparing for next year will be a no-new-tax budget. Further, to enable me to keep that promise, I shall make no promises in this campaign which would require an increase in taxes. Federal spending can be held down, and, in my budgets this year and for the next 4 years, spending will be held down.

But a President, any President, must have a partner in controlling spending, and that partner must be the Congress.

My fellow Americans, this Government does not need any more of your income, and it should not be allowed to take any more of your salary and your wages in taxes.

America needs not a tax increase, but tax relief. The spending ceiling will get us started toward that goal. One quarter of a trillion dollars for 1973 is enough.

Thank you and good afternoon.

NOTE: The President spoke at 12:06 p.m. from Camp David, Md. He spoke from a prepared text.

The address was broadcast live on nationwide radio. Time for the broadcast was purchased by the Committee for the Re-Election of the President.

On October 2, 1972, the White House released the transcript of a news briefing on the proposed ceiling on Federal spending by John D. Ehrlichman, Assistant to the President for Domestic Affairs, and Caspar W. Weinberger, Director, Office of Management and Budget.

342   Remarks at a Columbus Day Dinner. *October 8, 1972*

Mr. Secretary, all of the distinguished guests at the head table, and all of the distinguished guests on this occasion here in Washington:

I consider it a very great privilege to come in to your dinner right at the dessert course and to participate in it in a way that I think not only honors the man we are going to honor, but honors the office of the President of the United States.

An award is being made tonight, I understand, for the first time by this organization. It is Amerito's Outstanding Citizen Award. All of you know to whom that award is going to be made. He is sitting here at this head table, along with his wife, and so, consequently, it will be no surprise when I read the citation. I will speak briefly about him. He will respond as he receives the award, and then I will have the opportunity to speak to you briefly about the general subject that brings you all here together on this occasion, and annually.

But first about Peter Fosco. You can honor him tonight as one of the great leaders of American labor—500,000 men and women are members of his organization. You can honor him tonight as one of the great civic leaders of this country. He is one who participates in the Knights of Columbus and all of its civic activities, as Mr. McDevitt [1] will tell you. He is one also who is active in all kinds of youth

work—in the Boy Scouts of America, in the Catholic Youth Organization, and I think perhaps even more than this award, he will be proud all of his life that he has done so much for youth that a park for youth has been named for him in Chicago, Fosco Park.

Tonight you honor him because he is one of the millions of Americans of Italian background who have succeeded—succeeded here in this country in his chosen profession. Let me say that I could refer to him tonight as an Italian, but taking a cue from the name of this organization, all of you in this room are rightly proud of your Italian background, but all of you in this room are also very proud that you are Americans.

So now I read the words from the award:

"This award is proudly presented to an outstanding American who has brought honor to his Italian heritage, to Peter Fosco, the General President of the Laborers International Union of North America, in recognition of his many years of devotion to the interests and advancement of the members of his organization and the working men and women of America.

This plaque is tendered with deep appreciation and gratitude for his many years of silent, unselfish and untiring service.

From Antonio M. Martinelli, the President of Amerito."

---

[1] John W. McDevitt was Supreme Knight of the Knights of Columbus.

[Following the presentation of the award and Mr. Fosco's response, the President resumed speaking.]

Now, ladies and gentlemen, if I may take just a little of your time to pay my own special tribute to the organizations that are represented here, and also to the day that will be celebrated all day tomorrow, Columbus Day. May I speak of what that day means to America. May I speak also of what the Italian heritage means to America.

In speaking to you on this occasion, I, of course, could mention a number of areas in which people of Italian background have contributed to the greatness of this country. For example, in the field of government, the man on my right, Secretary Volpe. There are others. We have honored one of the top labor leaders of America, he, of course, of Italian background.

But whatever area you pick, whether in the area of business or politics or labor, you will find that those of Italian background have made their way to the top, and they are justly honored. It seemed to me quite appropriate that your program last year was at the Kennedy Center and that opera stars from all over the world were brought there, because everyone knows not only of the Italian contribution to America but to the world, in the field of music.

John Volpe suggested that perhaps some of you in this great audience might not know that that band that you have heard tonight is also one that we owe to our Italian background. When Thomas Jefferson was first trying to get an appropriate band for the White House, he found that there were not enough good musicians in the then new Capital of the United States, and so he, who had traveled much in the world, sent people to Italy. They recruited Italians to come to join the Marines, and the Marine Band came from Italy. Now, if any of you think that that story is apocryphal just for this occasion, I can tell you something that I know has been checked historically, as has that story, and that is that over one-half of all of the leaders of this distinguished band, which is called the President's Band—it is the one that always plays in the White House—over one-half of them, over 180 years, have been men of Italian background. So it is the President's Band.

While I will not have the opportunity to hear Connie Francis [2] tonight, she has been honored and has honored the White House by singing there.

But when we describe professions, the profession of politics, labor leaders, business, music, and the like, we could, of course, describe various groups who have contributed to the greatness of America. Let me indicate to you some other factors that I think more closely touch the subject in which we are all interested tonight, what those of Italian background have contributed to this country over the years.

When we honor Peter Fosco, we see one of those factors very clearly, and that is, putting it quite bluntly, hard work. Italian immigrants came to this country by the hundreds of thousands, and then by the millions. They came here not asking for something, asking only for the opportunity to work. They have worked and they have built.

I think it can truly be said that they, along with many other groups who have come from all over the world to America,

_____

[2] Popular recording artist who presented a program of songs later in the evening.

have helped to build this country. They are the builders of America, and, consequently, we owe a debt to this group for what they have done in building America, for what they have done in teaching us all that the dignity of work is what made this country what it is and that we must always respect the dignity of work and the dignity of those who lead the workers of America, as does Peter Fosco so well.

There is a second feature which is represented by this head table tonight. Those of Italian background bring with them a very deep religious faith. We in America have varying religious backgrounds, but the day when America loses its religious faith, this will cease to be a great country. Those of Italian background, with their deep religious faith, have helped to sustain the strength of America, the moral strength, which is more important than all the military strength and the economic strength in the world. For that religious faith which is represented here in so many different ways—by the Knights of Columbus and by other organizations—we are, of course, in the debt of those of Italian background as well as other groups who have come to this country.

There is another factor that this evening reminds us of. Those of Italian background have a deep love of family. I think tonight that Peter Fosco, as we honor him, would want us all to honor his wife, Mrs. Fosco. But most important of all is the fact that those of Italian background, along with so many other immigrant groups who have come to this country, are proud of where they came from, where their parents or grandparents came from, but they are prouder still to be Americans.

As we think of that particular fact, I would like to put it in terms of what we really owe to so many groups who have come to America from abroad and have added character and strength and fiber to this country's idealism, to the love of country which sustains us through difficult times and other times as well.

Speaking of American labor, for example, of which Mr. Fosco is proud to be one of the major leaders, I recall a time in 1947 which Ambassador Ortona [3] will recall, and some of the rest of you here may recall. I was a freshman Congressman then. I was visiting Italy immediately after the war, studying, along with other Congressmen, a bipartisan group, what we could do to assist that country to get back on its feet.

An election was coming up. It was an election in which many felt that the Communist Party in Italy might succeed. But they did not reckon first with the Italian people and their love of freedom and their antagonism toward any kind of government that would impose a dictatorship upon them, but they also did not reckon with another factor.

Naturally, the Government of the United States cannot and did not interfere in an election in another country, but the people of the United States of Italian background wrote letters by the hundreds of thousands to their relatives in Italy, and that may have made the difference in that election.

I should also say that I know what American labor did not only then but in supporting free labor in Europe and Latin America and all over the world. We know

---

[3] Egidio Ortona was Italian Ambassador to the United States.

of what American labor does in this country. Very few are aware of the fact that throughout the world, members of American labor make it possible for support to be given to free trade union movements in other nations in the world.

They helped in that period immediately after the war in helping to build a free trade union movement in Western Europe, where it could have gone one way or the other except for that influence which was exerted at that time.

And so a tribute should be paid to Peter Fosco, to George Meany,[4] and the others who represent America's labor, who not only do a job for American workers here at home, but who stand up for America abroad and stand up for a free trade union movement all over the world.

I come now to a personal point. Any President of the United States, whatever his party may be, has problems, has crises that he confronts during his term of office. When he faces a difficult problem, he asks for help from the American people, not on a partisan basis, particularly when the problem involved is one involving the foreign policy of this country or its national defense.

Over these past 4 years, I have confronted some problems that have been rather difficult. I have noted that whenever the problem involved the defense of the United States of America, and whenever there needed to be public support for a policy that we determined was in the best interests of the United States so that the United States would have a defense second to none, it was not necessary for me to call the leaders, for example, like Peter Fosco, of American labor. They

---

[4] George Meany was president of the AFL–CIO.

called me and said, "We give you support."

Also, I recall in May of this year when I had to make a very hard decision, one that I felt was essential, essential to protect American fighting men, essential also to help to bring to an end the long and difficult war in Vietnam in an honorable way, when I had to order the mining of the harbors of Haiphong and order the bombing of military installations in North Vietnam. When I did that, let me say again, that in attempting to enlist support for that very hard decision, it was not necessary for me to call these men. They called and offered their support. For this I am most grateful.

But most of all tonight, on this special occasion, let me leave this thought with this distinguished audience: You come from all over the United States. You represent 12 different organizations. You are proud, justly proud, of your national background, as every American is proud of his national background, whatever it may be.

But you know, as I know, that what America needs and what it will always have when we have men like Peter Fosco, who came here 50 years ago with nothing and worked his way to the top, what we need is a country in which a man or a woman has an equal chance at that starting line and an equal chance to go to the top.

Let me say, as one who came not from an Italian background, but from a not very affluent background, that I always feel very grateful that I was born in America. But also, I always recall that in the term I have been President the moments that perhaps have touched me the most have been those when I have attended citizenship ceremonies—one in Chicago, one in New York, one in Washington—

and new citizens have come by, just getting their American citizenship for the first time. Whether they happened to be from Poland or Italy or Germany or the Orient or wherever they were, more often than not tears would be in their eyes when they said, "I am so proud now to be an American citizen."

Let us be proud to be Americans tonight.

NOTE: The President spoke at 9:11 p.m. in the Ballroom of the Sheraton Park Hotel. He spoke without referring to notes.

The dinner was sponsored by Amerito, a federation of American/Italian organizations of the metropolitan Washington area, in cooperation with the Knights of Columbus.

343 Statement About House Action on Proposed Federal Spending Ceiling. *October* 10, 1972

I AM grateful for the responsible action by the House of Representatives tonight in passing the debt limit with my recommended $250 billion spending ceiling.

The Nation's taxpayers are the real winners in this action to provide insurance against any need for a tax increase.

This by no means is a bare-cupboard approach to Federal financing. A quarter of a trillion dollars is enough to provide generously for the Nation's needs—including the need to draw the line against higher prices and against higher taxes.

I urge the Senate now to take quick and positive action on the House-passed bill—without creating any loopholes—so that excessive spending and inflation can be held in check and higher taxes can be avoided.

344 Message to the Congress Transmitting Annual Report on the International Educational and Cultural Exchange Program. *October* 11, 1972

To the Congress of the United States:

I transmit herewith the Annual Report on the International Educational and Cultural Exchange Program conducted during Fiscal Year 1971 by the Department of State under the Mutual Educational and Cultural Exchange Act of 1961 (Public Law 87–256, the Fulbright-Hays Act).

Mutual understanding between our own people and the people of other countries is an essential ingredient of the peace we seek. The exchange program is directed at increasing world understanding at the most basic, people-to-people level. It likewise aims to develop and strengthen enduring unofficial relationships between institutions, organizations, private businesses and professional societies here and abroad.

One measure of this program's impact is that, in 25 years, more than 142,000 people have taken part in exchanges, including over 36,000 Americans. During 1971 more than 5,000 scholars and leaders in various fields took part in exchange visits.

In this manner, the exchange program

has created in the United States and abroad reservoirs of mutual understanding and empathy among a cross-section of leaders in many professions. These vital reservoirs are drawn upon more and more frequently as the number of people who influence foreign policy decisions increases both in this country and abroad.

This report presents a brief summary of the exchange program over its first 25 years. Limited at first to scholarly exchanges, the program now includes observation-study visits by outstanding foreign leaders and professionals. This aspect of the program has progressed to the point that the chief of state or prime minister of one out of every 10 countries of the world has visited the United States before assuming office. The present-day program also encompasses presentation abroad of some of the country's top performing artists, with special emphasis on reaching important areas ordinarily missed by regular commercial performing arts tours, such as the Soviet Union and Eastern Europe.

The program also includes exchanges of outstanding young people with leadership potential, as well as special projects designed to enrich the experience of foreign students coming to the United States under private sponsorship, many of whom return home to rise to positions of leadership.

In particular, this report pays tribute to the hundreds of private agencies, business corporations, and other organizations as well as to the thousands of individuals who, from the very beginning, have voluntarily contributed funds, time and effort to make this exchange program not only truly representative of the people of the United States, but a unique example of citizens' diplomacy in action.

I commend this report to the thoughtful attention of the Congress.

RICHARD NIXON

The White House,
    October 11, 1972.

NOTE: The report, entitled "Educational and Cultural Exchange: People's Diplomacy in Action" (31 pp. plus addenda), was published by the Bureau of Educational and Cultural Affairs, Department of State.

345   Statement About the Proposed Federal Spending Ceiling and the Economy.   *October* 12, 1972

THE TAXPAYERS of the Nation won a significant victory this week when the House of Representatives approved my $250 billion spending ceiling. The financial fate of the taxpayers now rests with the United States Senate, which should approve the ceiling—without adding loopholes—as a guarantee against excessive Federal spending that could generate economic pressure for a tax hike.

It should be emphasized that my tax-proof ceiling on spending would not be a pinchpenny approach to government. A quarter of a trillion dollars is a lot of dollars, a sum that would permit continued generous Federal financing of all worthy programs—such as Atlanta's rapid transit system, for which the Federal Government recently committed additional design funds.

The $250 billion, huge as it is, would not be inflationary—that is the real significance of the figure. We know from our experience with the impact of Federal

973

spending that $250 billion can be expended in fiscal year 1973 without putting inflationary pressure on prices and without developing a need for higher taxes to relieve such price pressure.

The spending ceiling thus would be a key requirement in my effort to protect and enhance the remarkable economic progress we have achieved since 1969—progress which has been fully shared by Atlanta and by the South in general.

When my Administration took office, inflation was running at an annual rate of more than 6 percent, primarily because of excessive Federal spending prior to 1969.

That meant that the average worker had to get a pay increase of 6 percent just to stay even in purchasing power—any less and his family's buying power actually fell behind on the inflation treadmill.

Now we have cut that rate of inflation by half—to the lowest rate of any major industrial country in the world.

And, in just the past year, the real purchasing power of the average production worker has advanced by more than 4 percent—the equivalent of two extra weekly paychecks.

Here in Atlanta, and in the South generally, that overall progress is fully reflected.

In Atlanta, the latest available Consumer Price Index put the annual rate of inflation here at just 2 percent, significantly lower than the national rate. The unemployment rate of 4.2 percent in Atlanta also is substantially better than the national average. And a recent report showed personal income in the State of Georgia has jumped more than 10 percent in the past year.

Clearly, Atlanta and the South are joining the rest of the Nation in a surging return to real prosperity.

What we must do to continue this dynamic economic tempo is to make certain that we ourselves do not place any barriers in our own way—such as permitting excessive Federal spending to start up the inflation treadmill again or to bring about the need for a Congressional tax increase.

This is why my spending ceiling is so important, and that is why the vote in the U.S. Senate is so vital to the pocketbook of every family here in Atlanta, in the South, and in the Nation.

NOTE: The statement was released at Atlanta, Ga.

On the same day, prior to his departure for Atlanta, the President met with a group of Republican Senators at the White House to discuss Federal spending ceiling legislation. The White House released the transcript of a news briefing on the meeting by Senator Hugh Scott, John D. Ehrlichman, Assistant to the President for Domestic Affairs, and Caspar W. Weinberger, Director, Office of Management and Budget.

---

346   Informal Exchange With Reporters After Motorcade Through Atlanta, Georgia.   *October 12, 1972*

WELL, I have seen some pretty big crowds before, but this was the biggest one we have had. It was very warm, very friendly, as Atlanta crowds always are, and I will have more to say in a few minutes upstairs and you are welcome to cover it.

Q. Does this make you want to go back on the trail more?

THE PRESIDENT. This thing, of course,

is enjoyable, the opportunity to see the people in the rest of the country, and I will do as much as I can between now and the election, but I have to be President first.

Q. Will this be your only trip to the South or have you decided yet?

THE PRESIDENT. No, but we are coming to the South because we consider it part of the country. The idea of dividing the North and the South, as I will say later, is now, as this election will demonstrate, over forever.

Q. Mr. President, how many more days do you think you will be campaigning?

THE PRESIDENT. It will have to depend on how much business we have in the Congress. We will determine that in the next week.

NOTE: The exchange took place shortly after 1 p.m. in front of the Regency Hyatt House.

347   Remarks at a Campaign Reception for Southern Supporters in Atlanta, Georgia.   *October* 12, 1972

Ladies and gentlemen:

As I am sure all of you know who are here from the various States represented, this is a meeting which covers the entire South, and, consequently, the remarks I will make at the outset, before having the opportunity, with Mrs. Nixon, to meet each of you, will be directed not just to this State but to the whole South and, as a matter of fact, to the whole Nation, as you will soon see.

Before, however, referring to the South in general, I would like to say a word about the reception we have had in Atlanta today.

It is a very great privilege, of course, to represent this country as Mrs. Nixon and I have in various capacities, as Vice President for 8 years and then as President. We have seen many very big crowds. We have seen some that are bigger. However, I have never seen a bigger crowd in Atlanta. I understand it is the biggest crowd in Atlanta's history.

While there are some cities that are larger than Atlanta, and that would only account for a larger crowd in some places, I have never seen a crowd that had what I call a higher "E.Q." We all hear about "I.Q." That is very important. But "E.Q." sometimes is even more important. That means "Enthusiasm Quotient," and there was enthusiasm in that crowd.

Now, to all of you ladies and gentlemen, and to the ladies and gentlemen of the press who are here from the Washington press corps and from all over the South, let me direct my remarks to this campaign—what it means to the South, what it means to the Nation.

This election marks the beginning of a new era in the political alignment of the South and of the Nation. For 100 years, one party took the South for granted, and the other party, as a matter of fact, wrote it off. Now that is entirely changed. Neither party is going to take the South for granted, and neither party can afford to write it off.

This is going to be good for the South. It is going to be good for the Nation. I have seen this develop. This is not the first time that we have had a motorcade in Atlanta; the first was in 1960. It was one of the most exciting motorcades of the entire campaign. It was a huge crowd, an enthusiastic crowd, not as big as today, but big.

Afterwards, some members of the press said, "Why did you go; you know you are not going to carry Georgia?" I said, "I am quite aware of that." But I went to all 50 States in 1960, and then in 1968 I visited almost all of the States, and many, many States in the South. As President of the United States, I have visited every one of the 50 States. And in the next 4 years I am planning, to the extent that my schedule will permit, to visit every one of the 50 States.

There is a reason for that. I do not believe in dividing this Nation—region against region, young versus old, black versus white, race versus race, religion versus religion. I believe this is one country. I believe this is one Nation. And I believe that while we are all proud of our backgrounds—some are westerners, some are southerners, some are northerners, some are black, some are white, some are of Italian background, some are of American stock, as they call it—but whatever we may be and whatever our backgrounds may be, we are Americans first, and that is what we must always remember.

Now, it has been suggested that my campaigning the South in 1960, and then again in 1968, and now again in 1972, means that we have, I have, a so-called Southern strategy. It is not a Southern strategy; it is an American strategy. That is what it is, and that is what the South believes in and that is what America believes in.

I must admit, more than many recent American Presidents I perhaps have a closer affinity to the South because of my education. I took my law at Duke University. It was a fine law school. I learned a lot of law. I also met a lot of fine young men and women who came from the South. I learned a lot about law and I learned also a lot about this Nation's background, and the differences, and I learned some of the things I had thought were right when I got there might not be right.

I remember, since I was somewhat of a student of history, that when I went to Duke University in 1934, after a very good college education at Whittier in California, I was utterly convinced that Ulysses S. Grant was the best general produced on either side in the Civil War. After rooming for 2 years with Bill Perdue of Macon, Georgia, I found, and was almost convinced by Bill Perdue's constant hammering on it, that Ulysses S. Grant would be lucky to be about fourth behind Robert E. Lee, Joseph Johnston, and Stonewall Jackson.

Who was the better general or the best general in the Civil War, fortunately, is something that is not important now. What is more important now is that we find a way to make this one Nation, that we find a way to work together, that we find the way in this campaign and in this election to be guided by our hopes and by our ideals, and not by our fears and our hates.

That is why I am campaigning in all regions, among all races, among all religions, among all age groups. People don't have to be for me for me to talk to them. What I am trying to do is to appeal to all.

That is why we seek what I call a new American majority. Let me talk about that majority, if I can, in terms of the South. Many southerners will be part of that majority. They will be part of it for reasons that their fathers and grandfathers could never have accepted.

There was a time in the South—and this is still true among some, as it is in some Northern States with regard to Republicans—but there was a time in the South when any southerner would vote for any Democrat and never vote for a Republican.

What this new political development is that we see in this election, and I think will be reflected in this election in Georgia and throughout the Southern States, is that that is no longer going to be true. Candidates of either party are going to have to seek support not on the basis of the party label, but on the basis of what they believe, and people of the South are going to vote for the man or the woman, rather than the party.

Now let me come right down to the issues. What are the so-called Southern issues? This answer is going to surprise you. They are the same here as they are in America. Let me take the one that everybody assumes is a Southern issue—I say everybody, everybody who takes a superficial view of politics and thinks of the old politics and the old South, rather than the new politics and the new South—it is said that the major issue in the South is race.

Let me tell you something. I was looking at some polls recently. I know, too, that the issue of busing is one that is a very hot one right here in this State. But as I was looking at some polls of various issues in the State of Michigan and the State of Alabama, did you know that busing is a much hotter issue in Michigan today than it is in Alabama?

Now, what does that mean? It does not mean that the majority of the people in Michigan are racist, any more than the majority of the people of Alabama, because they happen to be opposed to busing. It simply means this: It means parents in Michigan, like parents in Alabama and parents in Georgia and parents all over this country, want better education for their children, and that better education is going to come in the schools that are closer to home and not those clear across town.

That is why our approach is better education, better education for all and equal opportunity for all, but not inviting into this particular matter the kind of an approach that might, in the name of so-called racial balance, produce inferior education and racial strife.

We need better education for white children, for black children, for all children. And the way we can get it, I think, is through the approach that I have suggested.

Now, getting that issue out of the way, let me tell you what the number one issues, based on the polls that we have seen, national polls—Gallup, Harris, all the rest, they all come out the same—the number one issues in the South are, and the number one issues in the Nation. These are the issues that make most southerners potential members of what we call the new American majority.

First, they want this country to be strong, not because they want the United States to be strong for jingoistic reasons, although southerners have a great deal of national pride, but because they know that a strong United States is the guardian of peace in the world and the guardian of freedom.

Southerners know, as do other Americans, that the day the United States becomes the second strongest nation in the world, freedom and peace will be in deadly danger around the world, and we are not going to let that happen.

The second issue, and this is true of the South and it is true of the Nation, is that you want peace, you want

977

it now, you want it in the future, but you want peace with honor. Not simply because honor is something that you have to be for because this Nation got committed, but because you realize that if we do not have peace with honor we really are planting the seeds for war in the future. We are really inviting the aggression that none of us want in the future.

And that is why the peace with honor we seek in Vietnam and that peace that we have made so much progress in obtaining over these past 4 years, that peace with honor is supported by most southerners and that is why the peace with honor that we seek is one that rejects betraying our allies, abandoning our POW's, or providing amnesty for draft dodgers and deserters who leave this country.

The third issue: It is a Southern issue, it is a national issue—the people of the South want an opportunity for good jobs, high wages, and cost of living kept under control so that you are not on a treadmill.

High prices are an issue in the South. Taxes are an issue in the South. Jobs are an issue in the South. That is why most southerners I have found approve of this Administration's policies that have cut the rate of inflation in half and that will cut it even more if we are given the chance. And second, they approve this Administration's policies that have made it possible for us to have the highest rate of growth of any major industrial nation in the world and why they approve of an Administration's policies that will go forward until we achieve a goal we haven't had in this country since President Eisenhower was President in 1955 and '56, and that means full employment

without inflation, without war. That is what we are for, and that is what southerners are for.

Issue number four: Most southerners and most Americans, East, West, North, and South, want respect for law, respect for order, and they want justice, justice to all people. And in wanting respect for law and order and justice, they realize that in 1968 we were on an escalating trend toward massive crime in this country, drugs, narcotics, going up and up and up. They realize that we have launched an all-out offensive in this Administration against the forces of crime, against the forces of drugs, and we are beginning to win.

The rate of crime increase in 1968, in the last 6 months, was 28 percent. We brought that almost to a standstill. In the first 6 months of this year it was only one percent. If we get the chance, we can turn it around, and one way we can turn it around that I want to mention right here today is this: I have made some appointments to the Supreme Court. I have made appointments to other courts. I have selected men and women that I consider to be good lawyers.

But one thing that I insist upon for all appointees is this: They must recognize that the first civil right of every American, whatever he may be, what he wants is to be free from domestic violence, and that it is necessary in our decisions in this country that we strengthen the peace forces against the criminal forces. We have appointed judges like that, and I want to say that if we have the opportunity in the next 4 years, I am going to appoint more judges like that so that we can strengthen the peace forces in this country.

Issue number five: The people of the

South are just like the rest of the country in wanting progress. They don't want to stand still. It is a myth. It was a myth in 1934 to '37 when I was in law school, when I talked to these young law students and they spoke with such idealism of the future of the South and how they wanted to get up with the rest of the country. They were proud of it, but they wanted to come up.

You look at this great skyline of the city of Atlanta. Look at New Orleans, look at Texas, look across this whole area, Florida, for example, North Carolina, Tennessee, and you can see that the progress in this part of the country, along with the West, is probably the greatest of all in the Nation.

They want more of that progress, and, in order to have that progress, they know that we need the kind of a government that will avoid confiscatory taxes. That is one of the reasons why they support the proposals I have made to put a spending ceiling on spending in Washington, so that we don't raise taxes for the American people.

That is why also they support the historic movement—and of course we sometimes perhaps overuse that word, but in this instance it is historic, because it is a great change in the approach to our constitutional responsibilities in this country—which provides for revenue sharing.

Let me tell you what it means. Sure—as I told the mayor of Atlanta today—it is going to mean money for the city of Atlanta. It is going to be money for the counties and cities of this State and all States of the Nation. It is going to be money for the State governments that they can use to deal with local problems. But

what is involved that is far more significant is this:

It means that after 180 years of power flowing from the people and the States and the cities to Washington, we have finally turned it around, and the money and the power is going to go back to the States and back to the cities so that the people can decide what they want for themselves rather than having it done in Washington, D.C.

Think what this means: This means better education. It means an opportunity in the future to lower the burden of property taxes. It means better opportunity. It means the kind of progress that the people of this part of the country want just like the people in all parts of the country.

One other point that I would make before concluding is that sometimes there is a tendency to speak of the South as being sort of the Bible belt, and that is said by some in a complimentary way and some in, shall we say, a rather derogatory way.

I would only suggest I would put it in a broader sense. There is, in this part of the country, a deep religious faith. There is a great respect for moral values. There is a great devotion to what we call character. But let me say that in that religious faith and in that devotion to moral values and in that respect for character, while it exists in the South, it exists throughout this Nation.

My Indiana mother and my Ohio father—they put it in me just as your mothers and fathers put it in you. And I see it, for example, when I visit an Italian picnic and I see new people, first generation Americans, who are proud of their national backgrounds, with deep religious ties, who have faith in this country, faith in their God, and who believe in moral virtues.

Oh, you can call them old-fashioned, but the day America loses its moral values, its dedication to idealism and religion, this will cease to be a great country. We are not going to let that happen.

Ladies and gentlemen, related to that point is the final one, and this is something that is somewhat at times derided as patriotism, as if patriotism were a bad thing. Let me quote two southerners, one known to the people of Georgia and the people of the South as a southerner, and one, of course, who was born in Virginia and, therefore, was the last President of the United States really to have a Southern background, Woodrow Wilson.

I remember when I first became President, Dick Russell [1] and I had a talk about the Vietnam war. He hated war as much as I did. He wanted to find a way to end this war honorably as much as I did. But when there were demonstrators by the hundreds of thousands marching around the White House, he came down to see me and he said, "When my flag is committed, I am committed." That was his attitude.

And Woodrow Wilson put it all in context and at a different level when he spoke at Constitution Hall in Philadelphia in 1912, on the Fourth of July, and he said: A patriotic American is never so proud of the flag under which he lives as when it comes to mean to others, as well as to himself, a symbol of hope and liberty and freedom.

---

[1] The late Richard Brevard Russell was United States Senator from Georgia 1933–71.

That is the message I would leave with you finally today. I would only say we are proud of our record. We are proud not only of what we have done in moving toward a more peaceful world, in moving toward a new prosperity without inflation, without war, in moving toward progress and toward opportunity for all, but there is much left to be done.

I want you to know that as I saw the thousands of young people on the street today—high school, grade school, some college students, some were white, some were black, all were American—I thought my obligation and yours is to them and to future generations.

As I see it, what I want is a world in which the United States leads the way toward peace and, remember, if we don't, no other nation has the power to do so. That is why I went to Peking. That is why I went to Moscow. That is why I ask the chance to continue on those great initiatives, so that we can build a world in which young men will not have to fight in another Vietnam or another Korea or something like that.

And at home it means that we need to continue, to continue to build a nation in which the hatreds that divide us are put aside, in which we have our differences but we discuss them in an intelligent, rational way, and in which we can be lifted by our dreams and by our hopes rather than divided by our fears and our hatreds. That is the legacy we want to leave.

I want to say to all of you, from all over the South, some of you are Democrats, some of you are Republicans, all of you are Americans, all that I ask, as you go back to your States, is take this message: Join the new American majority. Join it not as region against region or party against party or class against class, but join it in order to build a better, freer America for every person in this country.

Thank you.

NOTE: The President spoke at 2:25 p.m. in the Hanover Room of the Regency Hyatt House. He spoke without referring to notes.

The reception was attended by Southern representatives of the Republican Party, State Committees for the Re-Election of the President, and Democrats for Nixon.

348   Message to the Congress Transmitting the Cost of Living Council's Quarterly Report on the Economic Stabilization Program.   *October* 13, 1972

To the Congress of the United States:

Through the Economic Stabilization Program, which was introduced as part of the New Economic Policy of August 15, 1971, we have taken forceful steps to curb the spiraling inflation that was eroding the buying power of the American wage earner—and that program is working. This fourth quarterly report of the Economic Stabilization Program describes the solid gains which have been made in revitalizing our economy and stemming the erosion of the value of the dollar.

I invite your special attention to the rise of more than 4 percent in real weekly spendable earnings which the American worker has enjoyed over the past year. This is three times the average rate of increase from 1960 to 1968.

To the average production worker, this gain represents an annual growth in purchasing power of more than $200—the equivalent of two extra weekly paychecks. Clearly, the treadmill of inflation is being transformed into wheels of economic progress.

Each American can take pride in the encouraging achievements which we have realized in the past year, for they have been made possible only through the determined efforts and the voluntary cooperation of all our people.

As this report points out, problems remain—but if our stabilization program continues to receive the wide public support it has received over its first year, and which it enjoys today, they will be solved.

This Administration will continue to exercise strong leadership in furthering that progress—we are determined to control inflation. Ultimately, however, it will be only through the determination, resourcefulness and patriotic cooperation of the American people that the victory of a full new prosperity will be won.

RICHARD NIXON

The White House,

October 13, 1972.

NOTE: The message is printed in the report entitled "Economic Stabilization Program Quarterly Report, Covering the Period July 1 Through September 30, 1972" (Government Printing Office, 74 pp.).

349 Statement Announcing Transfer of the 200th Federal Property Under the Legacy of Parks Program. *October 13, 1972*

I AM pleased to announce the transfer of the 200th Federal property to the people of this Nation through the Legacy of Parks program. Under this program, 43 States and the Commonwealth of Puerto Rico have received underutilized Federal lands for park use in the last 19 months.

As a result, 180 communities in this country can now provide their citizens with parks and recreation areas they could not enjoy 4 years ago.

My appreciation goes to the officials of States, cities, and other municipalities who have worked with our Federal officials to develop these parks for local use.

The goal of this Administration is to make available an increasing number of parks and recreation areas to provide for both the physical and spiritual enrichment of all Americans. Through this program we are also insuring that the most sensible use is made of our natural resources.

The establishment of 200 new parks is an accomplishment of which we can be proud. But we will not stop here. The Property Review Board will continue to work closely with Federal agencies as we carry forward our efforts to identify Federal property which can be converted to recreational uses. This Administration is determined that more Americans should be able to share more fully in the natural wealth of our Nation.

NOTE: A White House announcement of the transfer of additional lands for park and recreational use under the Legacy of Parks program was released the same day and is printed in the Weekly Compilation of Presidential Documents (vol. 8, p. 1516).

350 Radio Address on Crime and Drug Abuse. *October 15, 1972*

Good afternoon:

Four years ago, at the close of a turbulent decade which had seen our Nation engulfed by a rising tide of disorder and permissiveness, I campaigned for President with a pledge to restore respect for law, order, and justice in America. I am pleased to be able to report to you today that we have made significant progress in that effort.

During the 8 years from the end of the Eisenhower Administration until we took office in 1969, serious crime in the United States had skyrocketed by 122 percent, and there were predictions that it would double once again during the following 4 years.

Those predictions have not come true. Instead, we have fought the frightening trend of crime and anarchy to a standstill. The campuses which erupted in riots so often in the late 1960's have become serious centers of learning once again. The cities which we saw in flames summer after summer a few years ago are now pursuing constructive change.

The FBI crime index showed an increase of only one percent during the first half of this year. That is the closest we have come to registering an actual decrease since these quarterly statistics began 12 years ago. And in 72 of our largest cities, we have already begun to see a decrease in crime this year as compared to last.

We have moved off the defensive and onto the offensive in our all-out battle against the criminal forces in America. We are going to stay on the offensive until we put every category of crime on a downward trend in every American community.

To reach this goal we must continue to fight the battle on all fronts.

In our courts, we need judges who will help to strengthen the peace forces as against the criminal forces in this country. I have applied this principle in making appointments to the Supreme Court and to other Federal courts. As a result, our Constitution today is more secure; our freedoms are better protected.

The two men who have served me as Attorney General, John Mitchell and Richard Kleindienst, have brought real backbone to our national law enforcement effort. Each has demonstrated his determination to see justice done to the overwhelming majority of law-abiding citizens, as well as to those who break the law. Neither has fallen for the naive theory that society is to blame for an individual's wrongdoing.

Tomorrow, Attorney General Kleindienst will make public the first comprehensive report ever compiled on Federal law enforcement and criminal justice assistance activities.[1] I commend this report to the attention of every American who is concerned with the rule of law. It docu-

---

[1] The report is entitled "Attorney General's First Annual Report—Federal Law Enforcement and Criminal Justice Assistance Activities" (Government Printing Office, 542 pp.).

ments the truly massive Federal commitment to crime reduction.

The Federal role, however, is only a supportive one. As J. Edgar Hoover often used to tell me, it is our local police forces who are the real frontline soldiers in the war against crime. As President over the past 4 years, I have given all-out backing to our peace officers in their dedicated efforts to make all of us safer on the streets and more secure in our homes, and I shall continue to do so.

In 3 years we have provided States and localities with law enforcement assistance grants totaling $1.5 billion. That compares with only $22 million in grants during the final 3 years of the previous Administration.

In a single year, 1970, the Congress passed four landmark anticrime bills which this Administration had recommended and fought for—an omnibus crime bill, a bill providing new tools to fight organized crime, a comprehensive reform of the drug abuse statutes, and a new charter for courts and criminal procedures in the Nation's Capital.

The city of Washington had become the crime capital of the United States during the 1960's, but during our term of office we have cut the D.C. crime rate in half.

Let me turn now to the subject of drug abuse—America's public enemy number one.

The period 1965 to 1969, when drugs were widely glamorized and when government was responding only feebly to this menace, brought America's narcotics problem to the epidemic stage. In that 4-year period alone, the number of drug addicts doubled nationwide.

To turn this situation around, I declared total war against heroin and other illicit drugs. I personally shook up the bureaucracy and took steps to create two new Federal agencies to deal with narcotics-related crime and with addict treatment. The antidrug funding which I have requested in the current budget is 11 times as great as the 1969 level.

We are winning this war. The raging heroin epidemic of the late 1960's has been stemmed.

Our domestic law enforcement operation has arrested twice as many pushers and has seized illicit drugs at four times the rate of the previous Administration. Our rehabilitation and treatment programs have created more federally funded drug treatment capacity in the last 12 months than in the 50 years before that.

Our international narcotics control work in 59 countries has achieved a doubling of global heroin and morphine base seizures in 1972 alone.

But the job is far from finished. A short time before Christmas last year, I received a heart-rending letter from a teenage boy in the Midwest. He told me in his letter how his brother, a college student of exceptional promise, after slipping deeper and deeper into drug experimentation, had gone off into the woods with a gun one day, completely without warning, and taken his own life.

Listen to the boy's letter: "If we can stop just one boy from doing what my brother did, his whole life will have been worthwhile. . . . You can beat that drug, Mr. Nixon; you can destroy it before it destroys any more lives."

This is my answer to this letter: I cannot beat this problem by myself, but if all of us work together, we can and we will beat it.

To do so, we will need more clinics to treat addicts who need help. That is why

I asked the Congress for speedy approval of funds to support additional drug treatment facilities.

We will need better cooperation abroad in apprehending the criminals who produce and smuggle heroin. That is why I shall insist on the strictest compliance with the statute which requires a suspension of United States military and economic aid to countries which protect or participate in the movement of illegal drugs to this country.

We will need absolute assurance that convicted drug peddlers will go to jail and not back to the streets. The dangerous trend of light or suspended sentences meted out to convicted pushers by permissive judges must be halted. That is why I shall ask the next Congress to require stiff mandatory sentences for heroin traffickers, and to amend other Federal statutes so as to keep these peddlers of death off our streets after their arrest.

Wherever more money, more manpower, or more teeth in the law are needed to maintain our momentum in the war against drugs and crime, I will do everything in my power to provide them.

My intention for 1973 and beyond is to continue and to expand our massive Federal funding for helping to improve our local law enforcement.

I will propose to the new Congress a thorough-going revision of the entire Federal criminal code, aimed at better protection of life and property, human rights, and the domestic peace.

I will move ahead with my comprehensive 10-year reform program for the Federal prison system, which we launched in 1969.

I will continue to apply the criteria of strict constructionism and regard for the public safety in making appointments to the Supreme Court and other Federal courts.

I will ask the new Congress to move swiftly in enacting my proposals for law enforcement special revenue sharing, to give States and cities greater decision-making power in meeting their own needs.

And I will work unceasingly to halt the erosion of moral fiber in American life, and the denial of individual accountability for individual actions.

The increasingly urbanized, technological, crowded, pluralistic, affluent, leisure-oriented society which America has become in these final decades of the 20th century poses complex new dangers to our traditional concepts of personal safety, human dignity, moral values.

Questions which were once the sole concern of novelists now intrude upon public policy. The endlessly drugged "Brave New World" which Huxley described could conceivably become our world a few years in the future.

Remote as such possibilities may seem, we cannot ignore them. We must shape our own vision for the seventies and the years ahead, a vision bright and clear and sharp, or one of the darker visions may begin to impose itself by default.

Government alone cannot determine the legal and moral tone of America's third century. Much depends on the character we build in our homes, our schools, and our churches. Much depends on the values we exalt in our art, our literature, our culture.

Yet government has an essential role, a role it must never abdicate. Government must never become so preoccupied with catering to the way-out wants of those who reject all respect for moral and legal values that it forgets the citizen's first civil

right: the right to be free from domestic violence.

Government must never mistake license for liberty, amorality for tolerance, indulgence for charity, or weakness for compassion.

Above all, government must maintain that structure of ordered freedom within which alone the human spirit can thrive and flourish.

The work of keeping the structure of freedom strong in the years ahead will not be easy, and the price may sometimes be terribly high. It was terribly high for a young Federal narcotics agent in New York named Frank Tummillo.

I met Frank Tummillo last February when he and other agents came to the White House along with a group of professional athletes who have joined the fight against drugs. He was a fine young man—alert, dedicated, selfless. Just 3 nights ago—last Thursday—he was murdered by two hoodlums in the line of his duty, trying to break up a huge cocaine transaction.

He was only 25. He lived at home with his parents. The invitations recently went out for his wedding next month. Instead of that wedding, his funeral will be held tomorrow.

We cannot bring Frank Tummillo back again, any more than we can bring back the American soldiers who have given their lives in Vietnam. But in our war against crime and drugs, as in our war against aggression in Southeast Asia, we can resolve to redeem with honor the ultimate sacrifice which these brave men have made.

Together, and in their name, let us work to end the violence and the lawlessness against which they fought. Let us make the next 4 years a period of new respect for law, order, and justice in America, a time of new hope in a land free of fear and a world at peace.

Thank you and good afternoon.

NOTE: The President spoke at 5:07 p.m. from

Camp David, Md. The address was broadcast live on nationwide radio. Time for the broadcast was purchased by the Committee for the Re-Election of the President.

The President spoke from a prepared text. An advance text of his address was released on the same day.

351 Remarks to a Meeting of the National League of Families of American Prisoners and Missing in Southeast Asia. *October 16, 1972*

Mrs. Hanson, and ladies and gentlemen:

I learned that Dr. Kissinger was scheduled to be your speaker this morning; I found that I had some time in my schedule and I decided to substitute for two very important reasons: One, of all the many groups I speak to and that I have spoken to, big or small, across America, there isn't one that inspires me more than you do. Two, I am here to thank you for your support and to urge you for your continued support.

I am not speaking of an election campaign, but I am speaking of support for a cause bigger than an election, a cause of an honorable peace, one that will contribute to peace in the world. And an honorable peace in this terribly difficult war in Vietnam will contribute to that kind of a peace that we all seek.

Since we last met—it is hard to realize it was a year ago—some very intensive negotiations have been underway. I shall not and cannot comment on those negotiations. One, I would not want to raise false hopes, and two, any comment when negotiations are taking place could jeopardize their success, and I know that none of you would want any chance for successful negotiations to be jeopardized.

However, I do want to tell this group

some conditions that I have laid down that we will insist upon in those negotiations in seeking an honorable peace in Vietnam.

First, we shall not agree to any settlement which imposes a Communist government upon the people of South Vietnam.

And second, we shall, under no circumstances, abandon our POW's and our MIA's, wherever they are.

When I use the word "abandon," I speak quite deliberately. That means that we cannot leave their fate to the good will of the enemy. We must have some strength in ourselves. And in addition to that, we shall not betray our allies; we shall not stain the honor of the United States.

These are the conditions that we have laid down. They are reasonable conditions because we seek an honorable and reasonable peace, and we shall continue to negotiate to achieve those objectives.

Now, one other point I wish to make with regard to this terribly long war which has been a subject for discussion over recent weeks and months, and that is the attitude that I have taken with regard to amnesty for those who were draft dodgers or deserters.

My position is clear. It is criticized by

some as being lacking in compassion. Let me tell you why I have taken the position that I have.

Two and a half million young Americans, when faced with the necessity of serving their country in Vietnam in war, which no one really wants—no one wants to go to war, wants to risk his life if he doesn't have to—but two and a half million young Americans, when faced with that responsibility to choose, chose to serve their country. Thousands of them died for their choice. Hundreds of them, your loved ones, are missing in action or are POW's.

And I say that when thousands of Americans died for their choice and hundreds are now POW's or missing in action for their choice, it would be the most immoral thing I could think of to give amnesty to draft dodgers and those who deserted the United States.

Your loved ones have and are paying a price for their choice, and those who deserted America will pay a price for their choice.

And now I am here also to thank you. The hardest decision I have made since becoming President of the United States was made on May 8 of this year. You will recall the circumstances. A Moscow summit was upcoming after having finished the Chinese summit. There were great hopes for an arms control agreement and other agreements that would perhaps reduce the danger of war in the world.

At that time, a massive Communist invasion took place of South Vietnam from North Vietnam. We were faced with the specter of defeat. And I had to make a choice, a choice of accepting that defeat and going to Moscow hat in hand, or of acting to prevent it. I acted.

As you recall, I made the decision to mine the harbors, to bomb military targets in North Vietnam. That decision was the right decision militarily. It has been effective. And those who predicted that it would lead to the dissolution of the summit and its failure proved to be wrong.

But let me tell you what happened immediately after that decision. It is often said that when a President makes a hard decision, the so-called opinion leaders of this country can be counted upon to stand beside him, regardless of party.

Who are the opinion leaders? Well, they are supposed to be the leaders of the media, the great editors and publishers and television commentators and the rest. They are supposed to be the presidents of our universities and the professors and the rest, those who have the educational background to understand the importance of great decisions and the necessity to stand by the President of the United States when he makes a terribly difficult and potentially unpopular decision. They are supposed to be some of our top businessmen who also have this kind of background.

Let me tell you that when that decision was made there was precious little support from any of the so-called opinion leaders of this country that I have just described.

But what was the most heartwarming thing to me was that those who had so much at stake, those who had suffered so much, the great majority of those whose husbands and loved ones are POW's or MIA's, stood by that decision, and I thank you very much for that support.

As I am sure you know, I would not have made that decision unless I thought it would contribute to our goal of achieving an honorable peace in Vietnam. I would not have made it unless I thought it would contribute to the goal that I have dedicated myself to, that I have spoken to many of you about, including to this group last year, of securing the release of our POW's and the return of our MIA's.

I know that it has been a long, long vigil for you. I know how much you have suffered. And I know how much your children have suffered, and others who are not represented here. And I know that it is difficult at such a time as this to put your trust in any person.

But at this point let me just say in conclusion, you have never been away from my thoughts and you have never been away from my prayers, and there is nothing that I want more than to bring your loved ones home and I will never let you down.

Thank you.

NOTE: The President spoke at 11:06 a.m. in the Presidential Ballroom of the Statler-Hilton Hotel. He spoke without referring to notes.

Carole Hanson was chairman of the board of directors of the League.

On May 15, 1972, the President met with representatives of the League at the White House. The transcript of a news briefing on the meeting by Maureen A. Dunn, Sybil E. Stockdale, and Phyllis E. Galanti, of the League, was released by the White House.

352   Remarks at a Reception for Foreign Labor Leaders.   *October* 17, 1972

Mr. Secretary, Mr. Kirkland, ladies and gentlemen:

I am delighted to welcome all of you to the White House on the occasion of your tour of the United States. I understand that most of those who come from the 24 countries represented here speak English. I understand that there are a number from the countries to the south who speak Spanish. My Spanish is very poor, but let me give you all a welcome in Spanish, which I think is better than the words we would use in English. In English we say, "Make yourself at home," which is a nice way of welcoming somebody. But the Spanish welcome is much warmer. They say, *"Estan ustedes en su casa,"* which means "This is your own home," and that is the way I want you all to feel here.

I want to congratulate the AFL–CIO and thank the AFL–CIO for participating in this program and sponsoring it around the world. As I read the list of countries that were represented here, I realized that many are young countries, relatively new countries. Some are very old, with a long tradition in labor-management relations.

Therefore, I thought that my remarks should be directed to what a free trade union movement means to any country, but particularly to a new country.

Now, the United States of America, by most standards, even though it is part of the New World, is like most of the countries in Latin America—it has a long and old tradition. In fact, we will celebrate our 200th birthday just 4 years from now. We have a very strong labor movement in this country, a free labor movement. And if someone were to come on the scene today, he would think that that labor movement had been part of the American tradition from the beginning.

You have all heard of the American Revolution, of Washington and Jefferson and Lincoln, and many get the impression that it sprang full blown with a free trade union movement and all the other institutions that we now have in this country.

However, any student of American history knows that is not the case. There was no free trade union movement of any strength in the young America, not even in Lincoln's America, not even in the late part of the 19th century. There were labor unions, but they had to fight all the way for recognition, recognition not only in their bargaining with management, but recognition in terms of their relations with government.

As a matter of fact, as far as the labor union movement in the United States was concerned, it wasn't until the 1930's when the Wagner Act was passed and at the highest level in our government collective bargaining was recognized in the United States.

Now having said that, I am suggesting to the labor union leaders here, who come from relatively new countries or who represent union movements that are young, that are trying to gain recognition, that you have, in looking at the American experience, an indication of what lies ahead for you. It is inevitable that you will develop a strong labor union movement in your country. It is inevitable also that that movement will be recognized by government in your country.

And also, another point I want to make is this: The AFL–CIO, from the dues of its members in this country, helps free labor unions around the world. They have groups in Africa, in Latin America, in Asia, and in Europe. They do that for two reasons: One, because they feel that they have a bond of brotherhood with working people all over the world, but second, they do it for another reason, because the leaders of our free trade union movement are devoted to the survival of

freedom and to the growth of freedom all over the world.

And one very important point should be made: I have visited most of your countries, in Asia, Africa, and Latin America. And on occasions when I was able to have more freedom and more time, I have met with many labor union leaders in the various countries represented here.

I am going to make a statement now that is tremendously important, that I trust all of you will remember and that will be recorded by those here from the press.

When we think of dictatorship and when we think of a free trade union movement, the two cannot exist together. There is no country in the world today in which there is a dictator and in which there is also a free trade union movement. And there is no country in the world today which has a free trade union movement in which there is a dictator. And so we see that a strong, vigorous, free trade union movement is essential if we are going to have free governments in this country or in this world.

That is the American experience. It will be, if it has not been already, the experience in your country.

So I feel as I speak to you that I am speaking to men and women who are devoted to the cause of freedom as well as to the cause of working for the interests of working men and women in your countries, and for that reason you have a bond of brotherhood with the workers in America, where the free trade union movement is proud of the fact that it stands for freedom here and for freedom around the world.

Let me say also that I know you are here to examine an American political campaign. That will be very interesting. The last 3 weeks are always the most important weeks of a campaign. The British have a much better system, incidentally, speaking as one who has campaigned, going back 25 years, virtually every 2 years.

Our campaigns seem to go on all the time, and traditionally they last 8 weeks, 12 weeks, even 3 or 4 months. By the time the campaigns reach this stage, the candidates are tired and the people also are a bit tired.

The British, as you know—and many of you come from the parliamentary systems—have rules whereby they call an election and the campaign is only 3 weeks.

But in reality let me tell you, in observing the American political scene, the last 3 weeks are the most important, because that is when the people are listening, that is when the people are going to make up their minds.

So as you travel around the country, as you observe the candidates of the various parties for the House, for the Senate, for Governor, and, of course, for the Presidency and the Vice Presidency, you are here at the time when many important decisions, as far as voters are concerned, will be made.

In looking at our political scene, I do not suggest that each of you in your country should have the same system, because the hallmark of freedom is diversity. We have different backgrounds. We have different governments. A parliamentary system is different from the kind of system that we have in the United States. The kind of system you have in France is different from that in the United States. And yet, freedom flourishes in Britain, in France, in the United States, and in countries that have our kinds of systems of those free countries all over the world.

I will simply conclude by saying that we welcome you here very warmly, because we are always glad to have visitors from abroad. Particularly, I am glad to have visitors from countries where I have been so warmly received, along with my wife, going back over 25 years.

And second, we wish you well in your work for the men and women, the working men and women of your countries. And third, we hope that as you travel the United States over these next 3 weeks you will enjoy it, you will go back, that you will enter politics, and that all of you will win all of your elections in all the years ahead.

Thank you.

NOTE: The President spoke at 10:22 a.m. in the State Dining Room at the White House. He spoke without referring to notes. The labor leaders from 24 countries were in the United States to study the national elections in an exchange program sponsored by the Department of State and the AFL–CIO.

George P. Shultz was Secretary of the Treasury, and Lane Kirkland was secretary-treasurer of the AFL–CIO.

353   Veto of the Federal Water Pollution Control Act Amendments of 1972.   *October* 17, 1972

To the Senate of the United States:

The pollution of our rivers, lakes and streams degrades the quality of American life. Cleaning up the Nation's waterways is a matter of urgent concern to me, as evidenced by the nearly tenfold increase in my budget for this purpose during the past four years.

I am also concerned, however, that we attack pollution in a way that does not ignore other very real threats to the quality of life, such as spiraling prices and increasingly onerous taxes. Legislation which would continue our efforts to raise water quality, but which would do so through extreme and needless overspending, does not serve the public interest. There is a much better way to get this job done.

For this reason, I am compelled to withhold my approval from S. 2770, the Federal Water Pollution Control Act Amendments of 1972—a bill whose laudable intent is outweighed by its unconscionable $24 billion price tag. My proposed legislation, as reflected in my budget, provided sufficient funds to fulfill that same intent in a fiscally responsible manner. Unfortunately the Congress ignored our other vital national concerns and broke the budget with this legislation.

Environmental protection has been one of my highest priorities as President. The record speaks for itself. With the Council on Environmental Quality and the Environmental Protection Agency, we have established a strong new framework for developing and administering forceful programs in this problem area. I have proposed more than 25 far-reaching laws to deal with threats to the environment; most still await final action in the Congress. Pending enactment of new legislation, our enforcement agencies have cracked down on polluters under old laws seldom enforced by previous administrations.

The budget authority which I have requested for pollution control and abatement in fiscal year 1973 is more than four times the amount requested in 1969. Federal grants for local sewage treatment plant construction have increased almost tenfold, from an annual rate of $214 million appropriated up to the time I took office, to $2 billion in my budget for 1973. This dramatic growth in the share of Federal Government resources being devoted to the environment exceeds, many times over, the rate of increase for funds in most other major government programs.

Every environmental spending increase that I have proposed, however, has been within the strict discipline of a responsible fiscal policy—*a policy which recognizes as the highest national priority the need to protect the working men and women of America against tax increases and renewed inflation.* Specifically, the water pollution control bill which I originally sent to the Congress last year was fully consistent with the concept of a balanced, full-employment budget. It would have committed $6 billion in Federal funds over a three-year period, enough to continue and accelerate the momentum toward that high standard of cleanliness which all of us want in America's waters.

By contrast, the bill which has now come to my desk would provide for the commitment of a staggering, budget-wrecking $24 billion. Every extra dollar which S. 2770 contemplates spending beyond the level of my budget proposals would exact a price from the consumer in the form of inflated living costs, or from the taxpayer in the form of a new Federal tax bite, or both.

Ironically, however, only a portion of the $18 billion by which my bill was fattened on Capitol Hill would actually go to buy more pollution control than the Administration bill would have done. One backward-looking provision, for example, would provide $750 million to reimburse State and local governments for work already completed on sewage treatment plants *between 1956 and 1966.* The precedent this would set for retroactive reimbursement in other matching grant programs is an invitation to fiscal chaos. Another provision would raise the Federal share of the cost of future facilities from 55 percent to 75 percent. Neither of these costly actions would, in any real sense, make our waters any cleaner: they would simply increase the burden on the Federal taxpayer.

There is a well-worn political axiom which says that any election year spending bill, no matter how ill-advised, defies veto by the President. But I say that any spending bill this year which would lead to higher prices and higher taxes defies signature by this President. I have nailed my colors to the mast on this issue; the political winds can blow where they may.

I am prepared for the possibility that my action on this bill will be overridden. The defeat of my proposal for a spending ceiling showed that many Senators and Congressmen are simply AWOL in our fight against higher taxes. And some have been lured to the wrong side of the fight by the false glitter of public works money for their districts or states. They seem to forget that it is their constituents' pockets from which the higher taxes must come as a result of their votes this week. Others, to their great credit, voted for the spending limit to try to hold taxes down. Taxpayers must be sad to learn that a majority are charge account Congressmen.

If this veto is not sustained, however, let the issue be clearly drawn. As with the spending ceiling, so with this bill, a vote to sustain the veto is a vote against

a tax increase. A vote to override the veto is a vote to increase the likelihood of higher taxes.

Even if this bill is rammed into law over the better judgment of the Executive—even if the Congress defaults its obligation to the taxpayers—I shall not default mine. Certain provisions of S. 2770 confer a measure of spending discretion and flexibility upon the President, and if forced to administer this legislation I mean to use those provisions to put the brakes on budget-wrecking expenditures as much as possible.

But the law would still exact an unfair and unnecessary price from the public. For I am convinced, on the basis of 26 years' experience with the political realities here in Washington, that the pressure for full funding under this bill would be so intense that funds approaching the maximum authorized amount could ultimately be claimed and paid out, no matter what technical controls the bill appears to grant the Executive.

I still hope, with millions of taxpayers, that at least one third plus one of the members in one House will be responsible enough to vote for the public interest and sustain this veto. It should be noted that doing so would by no means terminate the existing Federal water quality programs, because the Environmental Protection Agency will continue to operate those programs until the merits of a new water bill can be dealt with as a first order of business in the new Congress.

I look forward to cooperating with the next Congress on a prudent bill, to achieve ends on which we are mutually agreed, and by means which I trust will take better account than S. 2770 did of the working men and women who must ultimately pay the bill for environmental quality.

RICHARD NIXON

The White House,
    October 17, 1972.

NOTE: On the same day, the White House re-

leased the transcript of a news briefing on the veto message by John D. Ehrlichman, Assistant to the President for Domestic Affairs, and Caspar W. Weinberger, Director, Office of Management and Budget.

S. 2770 was enacted over the President's veto on October 18, 1972, as Public Law 92–500 (86 Stat. 816).

354   Remarks on Signing the General Revenue Sharing Bill.   *October* 20, 1972

Mr. Vice President, Mayor Rizzo, and all of our distinguished guests:

We stand today on ground in which more history has been made than any place in America. As we stand here we all realize that the American system of government was born here. We realize, too, that as we stand here that the Declaration of Independence, the Constitution, the Bill of Rights—those three great documents created the federal system. And now by the bill I will soon sign, we have the privilege to renew the federal system that was created 190 years ago.

The Constitution of the United States begins with the words, "We the People," and the bill I shall sign is a demonstration of a principle that we have faith in people, we believe in people, and we believe that government closest to the people should have the greatest support.

And on behalf of the people, all of the American people, I express appreciation today to the Members of the House and the Senate, the members of the various organizations, civic organizations, that have worked for this cause, to the Governors of the States, to the mayors, to the county officials, and all others who have supported this cause.

You will note from the program today it is a bipartisan group. Reference has al-

ready been made to the fact that when this proposal was made at the Federal level, 3½ years ago, there were some who were quite pessimistic that it would ever come into being. And at the first of this year, an election year, there were some who thought it had very little chance for success.

But as I sign this bill, we will all be reminded of another great truth, and that is: When a great national purpose is to be solved, we act—not as Republicans, not as Democrats, not as partisans, but as Americans.

And now as I sign the bill, there will be, of course, a tendency to say it is done. But it will not be done.

Perhaps the most famous painting, at least my favorite painting of the signing of the Constitution, hangs just outside the Oval Office in Washington. It is an unfinished painting. As you look at it, you will note that the faces of some are not painted in, and that painting tells us the genius of the American system.

The Constitution was a great document, but a constitution made to govern 3 million people in 13 States, 190 years ago, would have been inadequate unless it had within it what is really the genius of the American system: a process by which, through peaceful change, we can

993

take new initiatives to meet the new needs of the country. And so, today, where there are 200 million Americans, there are 50 States, there are great cities and counties and other governments that the Founding Fathers could not possibly have visualized as coming into being, and we have acted. The American Revolution, in other words, is never finished; it must always be renewed, and we are helping to renew it today.

If, as we sign this bill, we proceed on the assumption that it is finished, we will not have met the challenge which is ours. Because, if the 30 or so billion dollars which will be distributed over the years to the States and the cities and the counties will simply mean that more money will go for the same old programs and the same governments and that the people will not benefit, then we will have failed in our task.

What America wants today, at the State level and at the city level and at the county level, and, I believe, at the Federal level, is not bigger government, but better government—and that is what this is about.

And so I would hope that each mayor, each Governor, each county official, would go back to his community or his State or hers, with this dedication in mind: that these funds will be used for the needs of people; that they will mean better schools and better hospitals and better police forces; that they will mean, I would certainly hope, that we will stop the alarming escalation in local and State property taxes, income taxes, and sales taxes.

You will recall those famous words of Winston Churchill before the United States entered World War II, when Britain was holding the fort almost alone against the Nazi aggressors. He said: Give us the tools and we will do the job.

Today, through this revenue sharing bill, we are giving to the distinguished people here—the mayors, the Governors, the county officials, and your colleagues all across this country—we are giving you the tools, now you do the job.

Ladies and gentlemen, I will sign this historic bill with one of the Presidential signing pens. It is the custom when we sign bills in the White House to give souvenir pens to all of the sponsors of the bill.

In this case, because the Congress is out of session, the sponsors of course are not here, and the suggestion has been made that we might provide souvenir pens for all of the Governors and the mayors, the county officials, and the other distinguished guests, including the members of the press that are here.

When that suggestion was made, I found that it would be about 800 pens. [*Laughter*] I thought that was a little much, but in the spirit of revenue sharing, we have 800 pens for everybody who is here.

NOTE: The President spoke at 1:06 p.m. in Independence Square, Philadelphia, Pa. He spoke without referring to notes.

Frank L. Rizzo was mayor of Philadelphia.

As enacted, the bill (H.R. 14370) is Public Law 92–512 (86 Stat. 919).

On the same day, the White House released a fact sheet on general revenue sharing and a fact sheet on Independence Hall.

355 Statement About the General Revenue Sharing
     Bill. *October* 20, 1972

IN MY State of the Union Address nearly 2 years ago, I outlined a program which I described as "a new American revolution—a peaceful revolution in which power [is] turned back to the people . . . a revolution as profound, as far-reaching, as exciting as that first revolution almost 200 years ago."

The signing today of the State and Local Fiscal Assistance Act of 1972—the legislation known as general revenue sharing—means that this new American revolution is truly underway. And it is appropriate that we launch this new American revolution in the same place where the first American Revolution was launched by our Founding Fathers 196 years ago—Independence Square in Philadelphia. It is appropriate that we meet in this historic place to help enunciate a new declaration of independence for our State and local governments.

Just outside the Oval Office of the President at the White House hangs a picture of the signing of the Declaration of Independence. It is an unfinished picture. The artist has sketched in some of the figures only lightly and left many spaces blank.

I have always believed there was an important moral in that picture. For the American Revolution is also an unfinished enterprise. Each generation must do its part to carry on the work which began in Philadelphia.

As we sign this historic document today, we are carrying on the work which started here in Independence Square—where independence was declared, where the Constitution was written, and where the Bill of Rights was formally added to the Constitution.

Even as we return today to the place where our Nation was founded, we are also returning to the principles of the Founding Fathers.

They came here in the 18th century to establish the federal system. We return here in the 20th century to renew the federal system.

They came here to create a balance between the various levels of government. We come here to restore that balance.

They came here "to form a more perfect Union." We come here to make it more perfect still.

After many years in which power has been flowing away from those levels of government which are closest to the people, power will now begin to flow back to the people again—a development which can have an enormous impact on their daily existence.

—In many States and localities, it will mean lower property taxes or lower sales taxes or lower income taxes than would otherwise have been the case. Revenue sharing can provide desperately needed tax relief for millions of Americans.

—In other places, revenue sharing will mean better schools or better hospitals.

—In some communities, this money will be used to put more policemen on the beat or to start new drug control programs.

—In still other instances, it will be devoted to job training or to recreational facilities or to public transportation.

But the most important point is this: In each case it will be local officials responding to local conditions and local constituencies who will decide what should happen, and not some distant bureaucrat in Washington, D.C.

The American people are fed up with government that doesn't deliver. Revenue sharing can help State and local government deliver again, closing the gap between promise and performance.

Revenue sharing will give these hard-pressed governments the dollars they need so badly. But just as importantly, it will give them the freedom they need to use those dollars as effectively as possible.

Under this program, instead of spending so much time trying to please distant bureaucrats in Washington—so the money will keep coming in—State and local officials can concentrate on pleasing the people—so the money can do more good.

This is why I am determined to keep redtape out of this program. States and cities will not have to worry about filing complicated plans, filling out endless forms, meeting lots of administrative regulations, or submitting to all sorts of bureaucratic controls. When we say no strings, we mean no strings. This program will mean both a new source of revenue for State and local governments and a new sense of responsibility.

As State and local governments are revitalized, I believe that our people will begin to feel once again that they are in control, that they can shape events rather than being shaped by events, that they can make things happen rather than always having things happen to them.

Thomas Jefferson believed in local government because he believed every person needed to feel that he is a participant in the affairs of government. By revitaliz-

ing grassroots government, revenue sharing can make it possible for more people to be participants in events that make a difference.

Under revenue sharing, more decisions will be made at the scene of the action—and this means that more people can have a piece of the action. By multiplying the centers of effective power in our country we will be multiplying the opportunities for involvement and influence by individual citizens.

The enactment of general revenue sharing would have been impossible without the strong support of hundreds of State and local officials—from both political parties—and I extend to them my profound thanks. The Vice President has also played a leading role in the battle for revenue sharing—and I salute him for all that he has done. And, of course, the Members and leaders of the Congress have my deep appreciation—and that of all Americans—for the constructive way in which they pursued their deliberations on this matter and for the favorable action which they have taken.

We expect great things from this program—and we are going to be watching for them. I am asking the Advisory Commission on Intergovernmental Relations to monitor and evaluate the results of revenue sharing so that we can all know its full impact as we follow up on this initiative. And follow up we shall. For the enactment of general revenue sharing represents only the first part of our comprehensive design to reform the institutions of government so they can respond to the needs of the people.

It is my earnest hope that the next Congress will move on to enact other crucial parts of this design—including our six special revenue sharing programs, our proposals for streamlining the Federal Government, and our recommendations for welfare reform.

On the last day of the Constitutional Convention at Independence Hall in 1787, Dr. Benjamin Franklin looked at the President's chair—which still can be seen in the Assembly Room—and observed that he had wondered throughout the long, hot summer whether the sun which was painted on that chair was rising or setting. "But now at length," he concluded, "I have the happiness to know that it is a rising and not a setting sun."

Many people have suggested in recent years that America's sun was setting, that our glory was behind us. One reason was the government was not responding well to people's needs. But today as we come back to Independence Hall we do so with confidence that we are giving our government back to the people again. And like Franklin, we can be confident, as we approach our 200th anniversary, that the sun is rising for America.

NOTE: The statement was released at Philadelphia, Pa.

356 Radio Address on the Philosophy of Government. *October* 21, 1972

Good afternoon:

In election campaigns, it is customary to talk only about programs and differences of opinion on current issues. But even more important than what a man advocates is what he believes, because what he believes will determine how he will act when issues arise in the future which are not currently before the Nation.

That is why I want to talk today about my philosophy of government, so that the American people will know the principles which will guide me in making decisions over the next 4 years.

The central question, which goes to the heart of American government and is sure to affect every person in this land, is this: Do we want to turn more power over to bureaucrats in Washington in the hope that they will do what is best for all the people? Or do we want to return more power to the people and to their State and local governments, so that people can decide what is best for themselves?

Now, people of good conscience differ on this issue. Certainly in the past generation there were cases in which power concentrated in Washington did much to help our people live in greater fairness and security and to enable our Nation to speak and act strongly in world affairs.

When the will of the people is best expressed by the Nation acting as one people, I strongly support the use of effective Federal action. But the concentration of power can get to be a dangerous habit. Government officials who get power over others tend to want to keep it. And the more power they get, the more they want.

We all remember the waste and the resentment of the sixties, the growing alienation of people who felt that they no longer counted, the feeling of frustration in dealing with a faceless machine called the Federal bureaucracy.

In a family, when a father tells the rest of the family what to do, that's called paternalism. In a business, when an employer tells workers he knows what is best for their future, that is called paternalism. And in government, when a central authority in Washington tells people across the country how they should conduct their lives, that, too, is paternalism.

In each of those cases, the motive of the man in charge may be to do what he sincerely thinks is best for the people under his control. But the trouble is this: Most Americans don't like to be under anybody's control, no matter how benevolent that control may be. It is one thing to be well taken care of, but for those able to take care of themselves, it is far more important to be free.

At the root of all of our rights is an idea of justice and genius, the idea that government derives its power from "the consent of the governed."

Of course, every politician since Jefferson's time pays lip service to the consent of the governed, along with "majority rule" and "the will of the people."

But the truth is that a great many people in politics and elsewhere believe that the people just do not know what's good for them. Putting it bluntly, they have more faith in government than they have in people. They believe that the only way to achieve what they consider social justice is to place power in the hands of a strong central government which will do what they think has to be done, no matter what the majority thinks.

To them, the will of the people is the "prejudice of the masses." They deride anyone who wants to respond to that will of the people as "pandering to the crowd." A decent respect for the practice of majority rule is automatically denounced as "political expediency." I totally reject this philosophy.

When a man sees more and more of the money he earns taken away by government taxation, and objects to that, I don't think it is right to charge him with selfishness, with not caring about the poor and the dependent.

When a mother sees her child taken away from a neighborhood school and transported miles away, and she objects to that, I don't think it is right to charge her with bigotry.

When young people apply for jobs—in politics or in industry—and find the door closed because they don't fit into some numerical quota, despite their ability, and they object, I do not think it is right to condemn those young people as insensitive or racist.

Of course, some people oppose income redistribution and busing for the wrong reasons. But they are by no means the majority of Americans, who oppose them for the right reasons.

It is time that good, decent people stopped letting themselves be bulldozed by anybody who presumes to be the self-righteous moral judge of our society.

There is no reason to feel guilty about wanting to enjoy what you get and get what you earn, about wanting your children in good schools close to home, or about wanting to be judged fairly on your ability. Those are not values to be ashamed of; those are values to be proud of. Those are values that I shall always stand up for when they come under attack.

We will change America for the better by attacking our real problems, and not by attacking our basic values. We will improve the quality of our public dialogue by respecting, not impugning, the motives of the people that the winning candidate will ultimately represent.

998

The rights of each minority must be vigorously defended—and each minority must be protected in the opportunity to have its opinion become accepted as the majority view.

But on these basic concerns, the majority view must prevail, and leadership in a democracy is required to respond to that view. That is what "majority rule" and "the consent of the governed" really means—and we would all do well to take these ideas seriously.

We have achieved a high level of leadership throughout our history because we have put aside the notion of a "leadership class." The advantage of a superior education should result in a deep respect for—and never contempt for—the value judgments of the average person.

Does this mean that a President should read all the public opinion polls before he acts, and then follow the opinion of the majority down the line? Of course not.

A leader must be willing to take unpopular stands when they are necessary. But a leader who insists on imposing on the people his own ideas of how they should live their lives—when those ideas go directly contrary to the values of the people themselves—does not understand the role of a leader in a democracy. And when he does find it necessary to take an unpopular stand, he has an obligation to explain it to the people, solicit their support, and win their approval.

Let me cite an example: In every Presidency there are moments when success or failure seems to hang in the balance, when an expression of confidence by the American people is vitally important.

One of those moments came toward the end of my first year in office. I had declared that we were going to end our involvement in the war in Vietnam with honor. I had made it plain that we fully understood the difference between settlement and surrender. As you may recall, the organized wrath of thousands of vocal demonstrators who opposed that policy descended on Washington. Commentators and columnists wondered whether we would witness what they referred to as "the breaking of the President."

On November 3, 1969, I came before my fellow Americans on radio and television to review our responsibilities and to summon up the strength of our national character.

The great silent majority of Americans—good people with good judgment who stand ready to do what they believe to be right—immediately responded. The response was powerful, nonpartisan, and unmistakable. The majority gave its consent, and the expressed will of the people made it possible for the Government to govern successfully.

I have seen the will of the majority in action, responding to a call to responsibility, to honor, and to sacrifice. That is why I cannot ally myself with those who habitually scorn the will of the majority, who treat a mature people as children to be ordered about, who treat the popular will as something only to be courted at election time and forgotten between elections.

That is also why I speak with pride of the "new majority" that is forming not around a man or a party, but around a set of principles that is deep in the American spirit.

The new American majority believes that each person should have more of a

999

say in how he lives his own life, how he spends his paycheck, how he brings up his children.

The new American majority believes in taking better care of those who truly cannot care for themselves, so that they can lead lives of dignity and self-respect.

The new American majority believes in taking whatever action is needed to hold down the cost of living so that everyone's standard of living can go up.

And the new American majority believes in a national defense second to none, so that America can help bring about a generation of peace.

These are not the beliefs of selfish people. On the contrary, they are the beliefs of a generous and self-reliant people, a people of intellect and character, whose values deserve respect in every segment of our population.

A few weeks ago, one of the Nation's most perceptive journalists asked me what I thought it would be like to be a second-term President—free to govern with no thought of another election. Actually, he was asking one of the deepest questions of all: Would I do what I thought was best for the people, or would I do what the people thought was best for themselves?

Fortunately, what the new majority wants for America and what I want for this Nation basically are the same.

But a profound question deserves a thoughtful answer.

In the years to come, if I am returned to office, I shall not hesitate to take the action I think necessary to protect and defend this Nation's best interests, whether or not those actions meet with wide popular approval. I will not begin at this stage of my life to shy away from making hard decisions which I believe are right.

At the same time, you can be certain of this: On matters affecting basic human values—on the way Americans live their lives and bring up their children—I am going to respect and reflect the opinion of the people themselves. That is what democracy is all about.

In the next 4 years, as in the past 4, I will continue to direct the flow of power away from Washington and back to the people. In meeting our material needs, we must never overlook every American's spiritual need for personal freedom. When freedom is taken away from the individual, in the name of the people, the people lose their freedom.

This is the land of opportunity, not the land of quotas and restrictions.

This is the land that holds all men to be created equal, not the land that demands that all citizens become the same.

Above all, this is the land where an alien paternalism has no place at all—because we deeply believe in a system that derives its power from the consent of the governed.

All of my life I have had faith in the ultimate wisdom of the people and in the values of fairness and respect and compassion that spring from within the American spirit. As President, I shall never break that faith.

Thank you, and good afternoon.

NOTE: The President spoke at 12:07 p.m. from Camp David, Md. The address was broadcast live on nationwide radio. Time for the broadcast was purchased by the Committee for the Re-Election of the President.

The President spoke from a prepared text. An advance text of his address was released on the same day.

357   Statement About Signing the Motor Vehicle
       Information and Cost Savings Act.
       October 21, 1972

IT GIVES me great pleasure to have signed into law S. 976, the Motor Vehicle Information and Cost Savings Act. This legislation represents another significant victory for the American consumer, this time in the effort to roll back the soaring costs of automobile repair.

It is estimated that last year Americans spent some $25–$30 billion for automobile maintenance and damage repairs. While most of this work was necessary and legitimate, it is undeniably true that some of it was improper or unnecessary.

To help end this injustice, to promote competition between automobile manufacturers in designing safe and damage-resistant cars, and to help reduce personal injuries, this Administration proposed a Federal program to provide consumers with accurate information about the comparative safety and damageability of passenger cars. It is my belief that in a free marketplace, a well-informed consumer is the best insurance we have of obtaining quality merchandise.

I am particularly gratified that this act adopts this philosophy. Under title II of the act, the Secretary of Transportation is directed to conduct a study of the damage susceptibility, crashworthiness, and ease of diagnosis and repair among the various car makes and models. The Secretary shall develop procedures whereby auto dealers shall distribute information from this study to prospective purchasers so that they will have a better understanding of the differences between various models.

The act also authorizes the Secretary of Transportation to establish cost-effective bumper performance standards for new cars manufactured in, or imported into, the United States. Since effective bumpers are a key to preventing most automobile damage caused by low-speed collisions, these standards should help to insure substantial resistance to collision damage and significant reduction in repair cost without compromising driver safety.

An additional consumer cost-saving provision authorizes the Secretary of Transportation to assist the States in developing demonstration projects to explore and develop improved methods of diagnosing both mechanical problems and collision damage.

Finally, the act establishes a national prohibition against tampering with motor vehicle odometers. This unscrupulous practice, which has been used by interstate traffickers in used vehicles to cheat consumers out of millions of dollars, will now be brought under the authority of a single, comprehensive Federal law that will supplement existing State laws.

This act is an important and overdue initiative to aid the American consumer in the fight against the high cost of automobile repairs—and against faulty or unnecessary repairs. It reflects this Administration's commitment that our free market system shall work for the benefit of the American consumer, and I am pleased to sign it into law.

NOTE: As enacted, S. 976, approved October 20, 1972, is Public Law 92–513 (86 Stat. 947).

358 Statement About Six Bills Affecting the District of Columbia. *October 21, 1972*

IN THE first days after I became a resident of Washington again in January 1969, I stated my conviction that for the Federal Government "responsibility begins at home." Accordingly, I pledged an effort in partnership with the Congress and the local community to make the Capital a city once again "cherished by every American as part of his heritage and cherished by those who live here as a place of beauty, neighborliness, and decency."

With this commitment in mind, it is most gratifying to me to be able to sign into law six pieces of legislation which will contribute, each in its way, to making the National Capital region a better place to live and work and visit.

I am especially pleased to approve the National Capital Area Transit Act of 1972. Nothing is more essential in making a city livable than a regional transportation system which enables people to move easily among their homes, their places of employment, their leisure time pursuits and tourist attractions. During the last 4 years, Washington has taken long strides toward the development of such a system. Construction of METRO rapid rail transit system is progressing well, as is the improvement of the regional highway system. The transit act signed today is a necessary complement to these steps. It opens the way for acquisition of the area's four major bus companies by the Washington Metropolitan Area Transit Authority, and thus for the efficient coordination of bus and subway services when METRO begins operation in 1974.

I also join with the local community in welcoming the Dwight D. Eisenhower Memorial Bicentennial Civic Center Act. This new center and the activities it will host can serve as a catalyst for the revitalization of the downtown heart of the National Capital region. Thanks to the prompt action of the Congress on this bill, it should be possible to have the center open and operating by the 1976 Bicentennial year—a fitting memorial to the late President Eisenhower.

Another important measure which I have long supported and will happily sign is the Pennsylvania Avenue Development Corporation Act of 1972. This legislation will be of great assistance in the planning and development of the avenue, blending governmental and private uses to create an impressive and active main street for the Federal City.

While the civic center and Pennsylvania Avenue bills contain provisions which raise constitutional issues, I believe that those issues can be worked out satisfactorily with the Congress as we proceed to implement this legislation.

The three other measures which I have signed today are also important to the citizens of Washington. Under the District of Columbia Implied Consent Act, the city obtains a long-needed mechanism, already held by every other jurisdiction in the Nation, for dealing more effectively with the serious public safety hazards caused by drinking drivers. The District of Columbia Teachers' Salary Act Amendments of 1972 recognizes the need of adequately compensating public servants for the demanding and important work they do. The equal rights for blind and physically disabled act raises the standard of justice and opportunity for handicapped persons in the District of Columbia.

Sometimes it is difficult to know at close range whether the city's tribulations with excavated streets, barricaded construction sites, community disputes, and the like indicate progress or merely confusion. But a major legislative achievement like that represented by these six bills offers heartening proof that the system does work and that a better day is coming for all the people of the National Capital region. I commend the bipartisan effort in the Congress, and the constructive cooperation of Federal and local officials and concerned citizens, which made this possible and which points to more progress in the future.

NOTE: Five of the six bills were approved by the President on October 21, 1972:

S. 4062, National Capital Area Transit Act of 1972—Public Law 92–517 (86 Stat. 999)

S. 3943, Dwight D. Eisenhower Memorial Bicentennial Civic Center Act—Public Law 92–520 (86 Stat. 1019)

S. 4059, District of Columbia Implied Consent Act—Public Law 92–519 (86 Stat. 1016)

H.R. 15965, concerning salaries and retirement benefits for teachers in the District of Columbia—Public Law 92–518 (86 Stat. 1005)

H.R. 11032, concerning equal rights for the blind and physically disabled in the District of Columbia—Public Law 92–515 (86 Stat. 970).

The sixth bill was approved by the President on October 27, 1972:

H.R. 10751, Pennsylvania Avenue Development Corporation Act of 1972—Public Law 92–578 (86 Stat. 1266).

On October 21, the White House released a fact sheet on the provisions of the six bills.

359   Memorandum of Disapproval of the National Environmental Data System and Environmental Centers Act of 1972.   *October 21, 1972*

I AM withholding my approval from H.R. 56.

My objections to this bill are centered upon two of its titles which would establish a National Environmental Data System and create environmental centers in each State. While both of these titles sound desirable in theory, they would in reality lead to the duplication of information or would produce results unrelated to real needs and wasteful of talent, resources, and the taxpayers' money.

A third portion of H.R. 56 would direct the Federal Government to purchase the Klamath Indian Forest lands in Oregon. After studying this proposal carefully, I

believe this purchase would be sound public policy, and if the next Congress provides the necessary funds, I shall happily approve the acquisition of these unique lands.

In the form now before me, Title I of this legislation calls for the establishment of an independent, centralized environmental data system for the acquisition, storage and dissemination of information relating to the environment. Data for the system would come from governmental, international and private sources. A Director, who would be under the guidance of the Council on Environmental Quality, would   determine   what   data   would actually be placed in the system and who would have access to the data.

I believe there are serious drawbacks to such a data system which would outweigh potential benefits. The collection of data and statistics on the supposition that some day they may be useful is in itself a highly dubious exercise. Data, taken out of the context of the questions they were specifically designed to answer, can even contribute to confusion or be misleading.

With this in mind, I believe the centralized collection of environmental data should be related to specific policies and programs. H.R. 56 fails to provide such a relationship and the question of whether this basic deficiency can be overcome, and a useful centralized system designed, is now under study by the Administration. In the meantime, the Environmental Protection Agency and other agencies have consistently worked to strengthen the acquisition and exchange of such data and this effort will continue.

Title II of this legislation authorizes the establishment of environmental centers in every State to conduct research in pollution, natural resource management, and other local, State or regional problems. The centers would also train environmental professionals and carry out a comprehensive education program.

Research is a vital part of our effort to come to grips with the environmental problems we face. This Administration is currently spending literally hundreds of millions of dollars through directed research efforts sponsored by the Environmental Protection Agency, the Department of the Interior, the National Oceanic and Atmospheric Administration, the Department of Agriculture, and

the Department of Health, Education, and Welfare—to name but a few. We will continue these programs and institute others where they are needed.

Academic talent and resources have a vital role to play in the success of our environmental research programs. As members of the academic community know, grants for research are awarded on the basis of not only the merits of the project, but also the capabilities of the institution to carry out its responsibilities. By creating research centers on a rigid State-by-State basis, and requiring that each be funded, the Congress is asking us to throw away our priorities and to fund programs regardless of their merits and in spite of the limited capabilities of some institutions. Equally important, this approach also ignores the competence and available capacity of already existing institutions and laboratories to carry out this vital research.

Further, I share the view of the Administrator of the Environmental Protection Agency that environmental problems are essentially national in scope, and that most problems, even though they may appear to be local in nature, really affect many other States and localities as well. To the extent there may be local problems, our present project-by-project approach in research can be used to marshal the best scientific talents, wherever they are located, to deal with such problems. Thus, there is clearly no justification for establishing up to 51 new environmental centers specifically charged with investigation of State and local environmental problems.

Titles III and IV of the bill direct the Secretary of Agriculture to purchase a tract of 113,000 acres in the Klamath Indian Forest in Oregon. I believe that acquisition of this forest area would mark a significant and worthwhile addition to our National Forest System while, at the same time, assuring full environmental protection to this scenic part of Oregon.

RICHARD NIXON

The White House,
October 21, 1972.

360   Statement on Signing the Federal Environmental Pesticide Control Act of 1972.   *October* 21, 1972

WHILE pesticides have been regulated by Federal law since 1910, it was not until after World War II that they began to be used in large volumes for a great variety of purposes. Since that time, the use of pesticides has become one of the major reasons for the tremendous growth of American agriculture, helping our farmers to provide sufficient food and fiber for this Nation and for much of the world.

But even though pesticides have greatly aided our agricultural productivity, they can also present serious problems. For if they are not used properly and prudently, they can be damaging to the natural environment and harmful to human beings.

As part of my environmental message of February 1971, I proposed that the Congress—for the first time—give the Federal Government authority to regulate effectively the use of all pesticides in the United States. I am pleased that this recommendation has received the diligent, conscientious consideration of the Congress and especially of the House and Senate agriculture committees and the Senate Commerce Committee. The legislation which has emerged after this consideration is as strong and workable as my original proposal. I take great pleasure in signing it into law today.

The act I sign today represents the most significant legislation in this field since the Federal Insecticide, Fungicide, and Rodenticide Act was passed in 1947. That law required the registration of pesticides, but it did not address the problem of misusing properly registered pesticides and it did not control pesticides which moved solely in intrastate commerce. The new law remedies these defects. It prohibits the use of any pesticide inconsistent with its labeling, it extends Federal regulation to all pesticides including those distributed or used within a single State, and it takes a number of additional important steps to improve and strengthen the regulatory process.

As a result of this new law, the Federal Government, for the first time, will be able to exercise adequate control over the use of pesticides. We will now be able to ensure that we can continue to reap the benefits which these substances can contribute to the well-being of America, in terms of maximized agricultural production, without risking unwanted hazards to our environment and our health.

NOTE: As enacted, the bill (H.R. 10729) is Public Law 92–516 (86 Stat. 973).

361 Radio Address on the American Veteran. *October 22, 1972*

Good morning, my fellow Americans:

Veterans Day this year takes on an added meaning as American troops return from another distant conflict, because of the progress we have made this past year toward our goal of a full generation of peace.

No group has sacrificed more for this goal than the men and women who have proudly worn the American uniform. In serving their country, they have sought not glory for themselves, but peace, honor, and freedom for us all. Today, I ask all of my fellow citizens to join with me in honoring them.

The American veteran has expressed in his service much of what is finest in our Nation. Courage, selflessness, discipline, and devotion—these are qualities we will need as much to build a future at peace as we have needed in the past in time of war.

At a time when a small minority has tried to glorify the few who have refused to serve, it is more important than ever that we honor the millions who have loyally stood by their country when the challenge to freedom called for service.

Speaking for the American people, I say today that the vast majority of us have never been prouder of our country's nearly 29 million living veterans, whatever their service, whether they are the survivors of World War I or the young Americans who have served in Vietnam. To all of them I say that our respect has never been stronger, nor our gratitude greater, than on this Veterans Day, 1972.

As President I have done everything I can to see to it that this gratitude and respect is reflected by the Government's treatment of American veterans. Dollars, health care, educational opportunities can never fully repay the sacrifices our veterans have made, but they can at least serve as a beginning.

I am happy to be able to report that America is doing more for its veterans today than ever before. Since January 1969:

—We have raised veterans average compensation benefits by over 20 percent and pensions by 16 percent.

—We have increased the individual veteran's education and training benefits by 34 percent. And when I sign into law the new GI bill benefits just enacted by the Congress, they will have risen by nearly 70 percent, and our total outlays for veterans education and training benefits will have quadrupled.

—We have brought hospital and extended care treatment to over 80,000 more veterans than ever before; VA clinic-outpatient treatments have increased by 4 million.

—We have doubled the number of GI bill trainees, from 900,000 in 1969 to over 2 million expected by 1973.

—We have increased the number of guaranteed housing loans to veterans by 64 percent over the 1969 level.

Each of these achievements is important; each has brought a better life and a more promising future for millions of American veterans and their families.

But as we approach the end of our long and difficult military involvement in Vietnam, we have also had to recognize the need for special measures to meet special problems, and one of these is the problem of drug abuse. It is a social problem not a military problem, but it has made itself felt in our Armed Forces just as it has in our civilian society.

To meet it, we have mounted an unprecedented new effort to treat those veterans who have drug problems. In 1971, we increased the number of specialized Veterans Administration treatment centers for drug abuse sixfold. This year another 12 centers have been opened, and many existing facilities have been expanded.

More importantly, we have launched a massive educational and training effort to prevent drug abuse before the damage is done. It is helping the Armed Forces combat successfully a problem not of their own making. Just as we are determined to stamp out drug abuse in civilian society, we are also pledged to provide whatever is needed to stamp it out in our Armed Forces.

But in facing the drug problem, we must do so with perspective. We must never lose sight of the fact that the vast majority of Vietnam veterans have come out of this war with a clean slate and a record of honor.

As a private citizen and as President, I have been to Vietnam seven times.

I have been to Danang with the Marines; I have been up in the highlands with the Army; I have seen the Navy and the Air Force playing their part in the war effort.

And I can tell you from personal observation that we can all be proud of those Americans who have served in Vietnam.

I have seen young officers and enlisted men who have contributed hundreds of thousands of dollars out of their own pockets to build schools and community centers, roads, orphanages for the people of South Vietnam.

I have seen them spend hours of their free time teaching and helping the people of Vietnam, and particularly the children of Vietnam.

It is fitting that at this time we honor the 6 million young men and women who stood by the flag and served their country during the period of the Vietnam war.

They deserve the opportunities which we are providing, but, even more, they deserve the respect which only you can give.

They deserve it because they have earned it.

And they stand today just as tall as their fathers who fought at Normandy, Iwo Jima, and Inchon.

To them, and to their parents, wives, and loved ones, I promise that as long as I am President, America will not turn her back on those who served. We are not going to make a mockery of their sacrifice by surrendering to the enemy or by offering amnesty to draft dodgers and deserters. The 2½ million who chose to serve America in Vietnam have paid a price for their choice. The few hundred who chose to desert America must pay a price for their choice.

There is something else that we owe to the veterans of Vietnam. With America's combat role ending, with the reductions we have been able to make in our Armed Forces elsewhere, thousands of young veterans are coming home to begin civilian life again.

These young men deserve not only a welcome, they deserve a job. I am glad to be able to report that as the economy continues to expand, the job picture for American veterans is also improving. And part of the reason is the concentrated special effort being made by the Federal Government.

On June 11, 1971, I announced the Jobs for Veterans program with a target of providing one million Vietnam-era veterans with jobs and training placements by June 30, 1972.[1] We have not only met that goal; we have surpassed it. We were able to place 1.3 million veterans by the June 30 target date, and we are now working to provide jobs and training placements for another 1.3 million by next June for a 2-year total of 2.6 million.

In this connection, I would like to point out that hiring veterans is one of the best investments an employer can make. Veterans have proved their ability to work and to work hard. They know the importance of discipline. Their experience in the service has taught them the meaning of responsibility. Hiring veterans isn't just patriotic—it makes plain good business sense.

So I am confident that, with the wholehearted support of the private sector and of individual citizens, we can achieve our goal of jobs for veterans.

Most of the challenges that we face as a nation are bigger than party politics.

No challenge is greater than that of keeping the peace in a dangerous world in which nations have conflicting interests.

During the past 4 years, we have begun moving out of an era of great peril and entering an era of great promise. But if we are to continue to make progress for peace, we must keep America strong.

We must keep America strong, not out of some misguided pride or national vanity, but because, in the whole free world today, no other nation can take America's place.

That is why one of the things I have

worked hardest for as President has been to keep America strong.

There is no such thing as a retreat to peace. There is no such thing as peace without order. And if America were suddenly to slash away her defensive strength and abdicate her responsibilities as the major power of the free world, we would be retreating.

We would be leaving behind us a global vacuum that could only be filled with chaos and turmoil—a vacuum in which peace and order could not survive.

Some of the voices we hear today calling for a weak America, for an isolationist America, are little more than echoes of past blunders. The same misguided thinking they espouse today led an unprepared America into two World Wars in this century because it encouraged others to believe that their aggressions would go unpunished.

Today America is strong. Today America is prepared. And because we are strong and prepared, we have been able to make dramatic progress toward arms reductions, toward better relations with the Soviet Union and the People's Republic of China, toward the first full generation of peace our country will have known in this century.

That is something we all should think about on this Veterans Day, as we honor the Americans who have given so much in past wars. We can all be encouraged— both those who have already served to keep America free, and their children and younger brothers and sisters who, for the first time, have a realistic hope for a future in which all of our people can enjoy both peace and freedom.

Peace is not built by the weak of heart or by the weak of spirit. It is built by

---

[1] See 1971 volume, Item 200.

nations that have character, courage, and the strength to make their good intentions credible to others.

That is the kind of country America must remain. I promise that I will work to keep America that kind of country.

I can think of no better occasion than Veterans Day to renew this pledge to the American people.

Thank you, and good morning.

NOTE: The President spoke at 10:36 a.m. from Camp David, Md. The address was broadcast live on nationwide radio. Time for the broadcast was purchased by the Committee for the Re-Election of the President.

The President spoke from a prepared text. An advance text of his address was released on the same day.

362   Veterans Day Message.
October 23, 1972

AS AMERICAN troops return home with honor from another distant conflict, the hope is strong for a full generation of peace. No group has sacrificed more to achieve this goal than the men and women who have proudly worn the American uniform.

In serving God and country, they have sought not glory for themselves, but peace and freedom for us all. They have expressed in their service much of what is finest in our Nation. Courage, selflessness, discipline, and devotion—these are qualities we will need as much to build a future of peace as we have needed them in the past in time of war.

Each year we set aside a special day to salute our veterans—to pay our tribute to the millions of quiet, undemanding heroes who have served so that other generations might be spared war's anguish and destruction. At a time when a small minority has tried to make heroes of the few who have refused to serve, it is more important than ever that we honor the example of the millions of men and women who have loyally stood by their country.

Speaking for the American people, I say today that the vast majority of us have never been prouder of our country's nearly 29 million veterans, whether they are the survivors of World War I or the outstanding young men who have served in Vietnam. To all of them I say that our respect has never been stronger, nor our gratitude greater, than on this Veterans Day, 1972.

NOTE: The President's recorded message was played at ceremonies marking the observance of Veterans Day at Arlington National Cemetery.

363   Campaign Statement About Federal Spending.
October 23, 1972

THE ABJECT failure of the 92d Congress to hold to a responsible level of spending casts a long shadow over the glow of a resurging American economy.

Our economy is expanding at a very healthy rate, and it now looks as if our projection of a 6-percent production gain this year will be surpassed.

We have also cut the rate of inflation in half. Here in the New York area, the

1970 inflation increase of 7.4 percent per annum has been trimmed to 4.4 percent. The rate is still too high, but we are making progress here as well as other regions of the country.

We are also creating more new jobs than at any time in more than 16 years. Because so many people are entering the labor market, unemployment is not going down as fast as we would like, but we are confident that it can be brought down to a decent level. Here in the New York area, I am pleased to note, the unemployment rate is already below the national average.

In short, we are on the road to a new prosperity without war and without inflation—something this country has not enjoyed for more than 15 years.

All of this clear pocketbook progress is threatened, however, by the recent Congressional spending spree in which the Federal budget was ballooned dangerously by big spenders oblivious to higher prices and higher taxes.

Today I have some news for the big spenders, bad news for them but good news for the taxpayers and consumers.

I am going to use every weapon at my command to hold spending in this fiscal year as close as possible to $250 billion—so that we will not have a new wave of crippling inflation and there will be no need for higher taxes.

Back on my desk in Washington, there are more than 100 pieces of public legislation which the Congress jammed through at the same time it was rejecting my spending ceiling. While at Camp David this past weekend, I studied all of these bills carefully. I found that many of them will serve the public interest, but I am also persuaded that some of them call for spending far in excess of what we

can afford. These budget-breakers could only be financed by higher prices or by higher taxes, or both.

In the name of the taxpayers and the consumers of America, I say the time has come to stand up to the big spenders. During the coming week there will be a number of vetoes. If there are big spending bills which I must sign for policy reasons, I also promise to exercise my full legal powers to hold down these appropriations, or reduce others to make room for the new programs.

By themselves, many of these legislative measures are attractive. But we must seek a reasonable balance between dreams and reality. And in striking that balance, there is no higher priority with me than protecting our people against higher prices and higher taxes.

As I pointed out in my national radio speech of October 7, the Congress looks at these programs one at a time. It does not have any means of calculating their overall impact on the pocketbooks of our people.

As President, however, I must continually look at the total impact of Congressional action. And the total impact of the 92d Congress, if left to stand, would be higher prices or higher taxes, or both.

Revenue sharing, which I launched at a bill signing ceremony at Independence Hall in Philadelphia last Friday, soon will be putting money into States and local communities, so that the burden of property, sales, or income taxes can be relieved—or needed new schools, hospitals, recreation and transportation facilities can be built without additional local taxation—or additional police, drug control, or job training programs can be started without raising local taxes.

If there were no revenue sharing, New York City would have to increase its sales taxes from their present level of 3 percent to 4.3 percent in order to raise the same amount of revenue.

But, on the other hand, the excessive deficit spending by the Congress at the Federal level would push prices up or require new Federal taxes. Either way, it would cancel the progress that revenue sharing was providing.

I am not going to permit that to happen. I oppose higher taxes and higher prices. There will be neither if the next Congress will join me in acting responsibly on fiscal affairs.

NOTE: The statement was released in connection with the President's brief stop in White Plains, N.Y., during a motorcade through 13 communities in Westchester County.

364   Remarks on Accepting the Key to the Village of Tuckahoe, New York.   *October* 23, 1972

Ladies and gentlemen, Mr. Mayor:

I wish to express my very grateful appreciation to you for presenting this key to me. In the many years that I have traveled to 80 countries abroad and every one of the 50 States and literally thousands of towns and cities, I must say that I have perhaps over a thousand keys to cities in America and around the world.

But I want you to know this: Because of the warmth of the welcome we had today, from young and old, from people all over this village, this key from the village of Tuckahoe will mean more than, I think, almost any of them.

I just want to say that several people have said "Good luck in the election," and in return, I want to say good luck to the Tuckahoe Tigers in their next game.

MAYOR ROBERT D'AGOSTINO. Mr. President, one more thing before you go. In this corner is Tuckahoe's urban renewal project. With your help these last 5 years, we are rebuilding our small but adequate village, thanks to you.

THE PRESIDENT. With revenue sharing, you can do even more. Thank you.

NOTE: The President spoke at 3:55 p.m. in the Village Square. He spoke without referring to notes.

365   Remarks at a Campaign Reception for Northeastern Supporters, in New York State.   *October* 23, 1972

Governor and Mrs. Rockefeller—Nelson and Happy, as most of us, I think, are privileged to know them—and all of our very distinguished guests:

I was thinking, as the Governor was introducing me so generously, of the many meetings that I have attended, going back over 25 years. I ran for the House, and believe me, when I saw Peter Peyser

introduced, and thought of his race, and Carl Vergari and his race,[1] just let me say one thing at this point: There is nothing

---

[1] Representative Peter A. Peyser was the Republican candidate for Congress from the 23d District of New York; Carl A. Vergari, district attorney for Westchester County, was the Republican candidate for Congress from the 24th District of New York.

more lonely in a Presidential campaign than to be running for any other office.

Believe me, support our candidates for the House, for the State legislature, up and down the line, because they really deserve it in a Presidential year.

I was thinking, too, of all of the 50 States we had visited, of all the places that I have had the opportunity of speaking in, and I must say that coming here today to this magnificent residence to be received so generously and so warmly by Nelson and Happy Rockefeller, is certainly one of the highlights of all of our political traveling. I think they deserve a hand.

I am going to be speaking a little later over in Nassau—is this Nassau? I am going to speak at Nassau and Suffolk, in Nassau. So we are now in Westchester. I, too, was impressed by that splendid motorcade today, by the reception that we had. I must say, we had an awfully good advance man, though, because riding in the car ahead was Nelson and Happy Rockefeller, so they cleared the way for us all the way.

As you ride in a motorcade, you can get rather a feeling of how an election is going. Naturally, you see some of the opposition out, that is always the case. And you also see some of your own supporters out, usually quite a few more than they have, and that is the usual case. But the real thing that determines it is the enthusiasm of your supporters, our supporters.

What impressed me, incidentally, was the fact that there were not a lot of signs that were all made and distributed in advance. There were, on the other hand, it seemed to me—and I think, Nelson, you will agree—there was really a warm, friendly, holiday crowd, very proud to be Americans, receiving the President of the United States. They may not all vote for us, but let me say that as I drove through those towns in Westchester County, I thought what a really good country this is and what really good people we have in it and how privileged we are to be able to represent them in any form of government.

The campaigning that I can do this year is somewhat limited, due to the rather extraordinary requirements of the office of the Presidency at this time. I had, therefore, scheduled, as you know already, a regional meeting in Atlanta where all of the Southern States were gathered together, just as you are gathered here. And here in New York State, the leaders of the Eastern and Middle Atlantic States are gathered here.

This is a very important and vital group. Let me put it in terms that all of you will understand, comparing it with the past elections on which I have been a candidate at the top of the ticket.

In 1960, when we lost a very close election, in 1968 when we won an election not quite as close but still close, it was significant to note that in neither of those years did we carry the State of New York or the State of Pennsylvania or the State of Connecticut or the State of Rhode Island or the State of Maryland. Now, when you think of that, it makes you realize that what really is at stake in this room are the States that can make all the difference in this election.

I know that I don't need to tell a group of people who are what we call proudly "political professionals"—and that means whether you are doing it full time or part time you consider it so important that you will give up anything in order to participate in the campaign, and that is correct—I don't need to tell you that you never take anything for granted. I do tell you today that the area where we can have the greatest turnover compared with '68 and '60 is in the area of the East, because this year we want to win those States. I will mention another one, incidentally, that was not on the "win" list—Massachusetts.

I don't mean that we are predicting that we will win them all, but we do have a chance to win in each one of them. We are not going to take any one of them for granted. We are not going to concede any one of them. But let me say that when election night comes, there is nothing that would mean more, certainly, to all of us than to see a State like New York, Pennsylvania, Rhode Island, the ones I have mentioned, in our column this year, and you have it in your hands to do it.

Now, just a word of confiding in you with regard to the relationship that we have to each of these States. Anyone who has been a candidate for public office, or anyone who has heard candidates, knows that the candidate always tries to find some way to relate himself to the State in which he happens to be campaigning. It is interesting to note that my wife Pat and I have something in common with each of these States. We have lived, for example, in the State of New York. We have lived there for 5 years. We have lived, also—and this was long before we were in political life—in the State of Maryland for 2 months, toward the end of the war when we were settling terminated war contracts at Middle River, Maryland, and in the State of Pennsylvania where we lived in Philadelphia for about 6 weeks. So much for States we have lived in.

In addition, we have these things to relate to this area: My wife's father was born in Connecticut. Now, while we have not lived in the States I am now going to mention, it happens that we have taken vacations in each one of the following States.

We have vacationed at Kennebunk and Ogunquit in Maine. We have taken vacations also in the State of New Jersey, at Mantoloking, all that marvelous beach area there.

We have also taken vacations in the State of Delaware, at Rehoboth.

When you come down the line, that only leaves two that I have not mentioned. One is Vermont. Now, we have never vacationed in Vermont, and we haven't lived there. But I was thinking, "What do we have in common with Vermont, except that it has never done anything but vote Republican?" And we have this: Our two girls went to camp in Vermont.

I have missed Rhode Island. I was in Rhode Island for 2 months taking a course so that I could get into the Navy as an officer in World War II. So there, we have covered them all.

What I am really trying to say here at this point is very simply that as we look at this great belt of States in the eastern seaboard, with so much history, with so much character, with so much to offer America, we feel very close to each of you, to each one of these States. We visited each one of them many, many times.

Oh, I have left one State out, and I have done it quite deliberately. We have never vacationed in New Hampshire. We have never lived in New Hampshire. But believe me, as one who has been in primary after primary, I have spent more time in New Hampshire than almost any State in this country. So, there it is.

Just a couple of final words: I men-

1013

tioned the importance of your local candidates and of the candidates for the House and, in those States that are here who have candidates for the United States Senate, for the United States Senate. We have tried in every way possible where the national candidates were concerned to see them, to provide endorsements for them, and the like. You can be sure that as far as the whole ticket up and down the line is concerned, that we are very proud of our candidates for the State legislature and for local office throughout all of the States that are represented here.

The other point that I would make is one that I know all of you will totally understand. The election is only 2 weeks away. As far as what will happen on issues is concerned, no one can predict how many voters will change. Some theories are that voters change a great deal in the last 2 weeks, and others are that they really don't change that much, it is only that the pollsters don't poll late enough and find out that a change has already started. But that doesn't make any difference. What I am saying to you here now is: The vital importance is to get out the vote, to get it out up and down the line. The vital importance also is not to get out just the Republican vote, which of course, we must do, but get out the votes among independent voters and among Democrats and, here in the State of New York, among those who are conservatives, to get them out up and down the line.

Because what you are going to find, what we are finding all over the country this year, is that people are not just thinking in terms of voting party. We do find, as a matter of fact, less defection from the Republican line than in any election in recent history. But on the other hand,

we find that more Democrats at the present time will cross over and vote at the top of the ticket for us than ever before. That can help everybody.

The point that I make is: Let us keep as our goal, of course, getting out our own vote. Let us also recognize the vital importance of having a big vote, because we must remember that when there are indications that one candidate is ahead of another, the candidate who is behind tends to have his vote come out in greater numbers than the one who is ahead.

I will just say finally this last thing. We are going to meet all of you personally, the Governor and Happy and Pat and myself. But in the brief time that you go through the receiving line, while we have met many of you before, I cannot say adequately what I want to say now.

I have done, as you all know, a lot of campaigning. If I haven't been in your town it is because probably only that it was not there in 1952 or '56 or '60, not only in those years but in '54, '58, '66. We covered a lot of them, too. I can tell you that I know as a candidate, sure the speeches are important, and the television we do is important, and how we handle the issues is important. But what is really important is you, the party workers, the people who come from the ranks of labor, the people who come, who participate in politics, from any other group, but who get behind the candidate.

You are the ones who are going to make the difference. You are the ones who are going to steam up the workers. You are the ones who are going to get out the vote. On election eve, when the vote comes in, if we do have this enormous turnaround which we can have in this great eastern seaboard—understand, it can be the biggest turnaround of any section of the country—if we do have it, while I will not be able to call each of you individually, I am just telling you right now, I know who did it. You did it, and thank you very much.

NOTE: The President spoke at 6:02 p.m. at the Rockefeller estate at Pocantico Hills, Westchester County. He spoke without referring to notes. The reception was attended by Northeastern representatives of the Republican Party, State Committees for the Re-Election of the President, and Democrats for Nixon.

366   Statement About the Designation of Nassau and Suffolk Counties, New York, as a Standard Metropolitan Statistical Area.   *October 23, 1972*

ONE of the basic strengths of America is our people's concern with the identity and quality of their local communities. While we are truly one Nation, we have forged our unity from local diversity. The unique characteristics of our States and local communities rightfully remain sources of local pride and fame.

This Administration believes deeply in the strengths and wisdoms which are found on the local levels of America. Many of our programs—such as the historic revenue sharing law which I signed last week—are aimed at promoting a greater reliance on the judgment and energy of people at the State and local levels to help solve their own problems and capitalize on their own strengths.

One way in which the Federal Government helps local communities is through the official designation of statistical reporting units called Standard Metropolitan Statistical Areas. These make up nearly 300 population groupings which are given a high priority in the preparation of consolidated Federal reports on their economic trends, population, and other statistics.

Nassau and Suffolk Counties are now part of the New York City SMSA. But, when you examine their statistics, you find that together these two great counties have a combined population of more than 2½ million people. If they were a city, they would be the fourth largest in the Nation. About 750,000 persons are employed in nonagricultural pursuits in the two counties. And they have an obvious community spirit.

While these two counties have close economic and social ties to the city of New York, they also have an independent economic and social base which is larger than that of all but a handful of the Nation's largest metropolitan areas. Moreover, there is no county even close to either Nassau or Suffolk in size which is not a central county of an SMSA.

In view of these circumstances, I am pleased to announce that my Office of Management and Budget will declare Nassau and Suffolk Counties an SMSA of their own—separate and independent for statistical purposes from the New York City SMSA.

Beginning next year, Federal statistics on the Nassau-Suffolk metropolitan area will begin to be pubished, and the Federal recognition of this dynamic two-county area as a unique population and economic center will become official.

NOTE: The statement was released at Uniondale, N.Y.

367 Remarks in Uniondale, New York. *October 23, 1972*

Governor Rockefeller, all of the distinguished guests here on the platform, and all of you here in this great audience here in Nassau:

Four years ago I had the privilege of attending the windup rally in the State of New York in the new Madison Square Garden. I thought then that I would never see a bigger or a better crowd. I want to say tonight that here in Nassau, in this new stadium, this is the biggest and best rally, Joe Margiotta,[1] that I have ever seen.

And there is something else that is new here. There is this great, enormous number of people in front of me. I see you and I know that you are young people. Four years ago, at your age, you could not vote. But predictions were made that the young voters will be on the other side. Let me say a majority of America's young voters are going to be on our side this year.

Governor Rockefeller, you have introduced me very generously. I want to say this to the great audience here in the State of New York that we had a ceremony on Friday in Philadelphia where an historic bill providing for revenue sharing was signed. Credit was given on that occasion to mayors and Governors and Congressmen and Senators. I want you to know that Governor Rockefeller deserves the major credit. Without him, we would not have revenue sharing today, and my hat is off to him for it.

Now, tonight, as we are just 2 weeks away from the election, I want to talk to

you about something that perhaps at this stage in a campaign you seldom hear. You know that there are great differences between those who are seeking the office for the Presidency today. You know that those differences are honestly held by both men. You know, too, that the choice that is to be made is one that is bigger than party. It is one that is as big as America itself.

That is the reason why this year not only Republicans but millions of Democrats and independents are joining us, because they are voting for what is best for America.

Tonight I want to talk to you about what those Four More Years can mean to America. I do not want to talk about those fears and hates that divide America. I want you, all of us in this country and this great rally, to address ourselves to the hopes and to the dreams that unite America, that unite us, whatever our party, whatever our background. Let us, as Americans, look at the future of this country, and let us work for and vote for what we think is best for this country.

Let me begin, if I may, with, I know, a subject that is much in the minds, as it should be, of particularly the young people here. That is the situation with regard to the chance to have something we have not had in this country in this whole century—a full generation of peace.

In speaking to that subject, you will remember the situation when we came into office. You will recall that we had had no negotiation whatever of significance with the country or the government that had the biggest number of people in the world, the People's Republic of China. You will recall that we were in constant

---

[1] Joseph M. Margiotta was New York State Assemblyman and chairman of the Nassau County Republican Committee.

confrontation, rather than negotiation, with the Soviet Union, the other great super power.

I do not contend tonight that in these past 4 years we have accomplished the millennium, but I do say this, and I think history will record that this is the case: Because of the progress we have made, progress in ending the war in Vietnam with honor and not surrender, because of the trips that I was able to take early in the year to Peking and later in the spring to Moscow, the year 1972 will go down as the year in which more progress was made toward real peace in the world than any year since World War II.

I do not stand on that record, because it is something to build on. Let us see what kind of a world we can build looking to the future.

Let me tell you why, for example, the arms control agreement that we have reached with the Soviet Union, important as it was, is only a beginning. It was a limited agreement. We announced just a few days ago that we are going to have more negotiations in November with the Soviet Union for the limitation on all offensive nuclear weapons, as well as defensive weapons. These will be difficult negotiations, but you can be sure that we have laid the foundation for pursuing them, and we believe that we have some experience for knowing how to bring them about in a successful way.

You also know from having followed your papers and your television and your radio that an historic trade agreement has been reached between the Soviet Union and the United States. That does not mean instantly that there is going to be an enormous increase in trade between two countries with entirely different economic systems, but it does mean that these two great peoples, the Russian people and the American people, can turn more to the works of peace and less to the works of war, and that is what we want.

It means, above everything else, that as we have trade with the Soviet Union now, trade in the years ahead with the People's Republic of China, as well as trade with other nations in the world, the chance for you, all of you wonderful young people today throughout America to have a better life, and the chance for other people in the world to have a better life, is greatly increased.

Let me put it in another context. You may have seen in the papers pictures in the Oval Office at the White House that no one even a year ago would have dreamed would have been possible. Fifteen doctors from the People's Republic of China were there. Two were women, 12 were men. Another was a specialist in a certain area of science related to medicine. We discussed what they had come to America for. I do not suggest that because 15 Chinese doctors from the Communist People's Republic of China have visited the United States that this means we are going to have instant peace and no disagreement between two countries with entirely different philosophies and with many differences in interests. But let me tell you what I think it does mean.

I remember talking on a long car ride one day with one of the three top leaders of the People's Republic of China. He told me about one of his closest friends who had just died with cancer. He said he had read in the papers of the new initiative we had in this country for finding a cure for cancer. We know it is not easy, but I have determined that whatever money is required will be spent for this, and we are working on it. And he said, "Wouldn't it be a very fine thing for both countries if our doctors could work together, not separately, to try to find the cure for this disease?"

Then I pointed out to him something that may be even surprising to you, unless you have suffered from this dread disease in your own family. More people died of cancer in the United States last year than the United States lost in killed in action in all of World War II. Now what I am saying is this: I say that an initiative that will have Russian doctors and Chinese doctors and American doctors working together is good, because the genius that will find the answer to that dread disease and other diseases, it may not be in America, it may be in Russia, it may be in China, it may be in Latin America. But you can be sure we now have started on the road to get the doctors of the world, regardless of philosophy, working together on this dread disease, rather than against each other.

Now, in order to continue to make progress in making this a safer world, a safer world when the two super powers, the Soviet Union and the United States, will negotiate rather than confront each other, will limit their arms rather than engage in an arms race, in order also to make this a safer world so that the people, one-fourth of all the people of the world who live in the People's Republic of China can cooperate in some areas with the United States, let me just tell you my philosophy.

I know what the great danger is that hangs over the world: the danger of nuclear war. I know the great differences in philosophies between the Communist systems and ours, and I say that it is time

that we develop, between governments, the United States and other governments, some understandings. Because this is my desire for you, all of the people of this country, but particularly this new, young generation: Let us build a world in which, despite differences of philosophy between governments, despite differences between governments, the people of the world can be friends wherever they may be.

Now, to accomplish this goal, if we want to play the role that we want to, to lead to this generation of peace, the United States must continue to maintain the kind of defense that will command respect throughout the world. That is why I oppose such programs as would make the United States have the second strongest Navy, the second strongest Air Force, because let me tell you something: There is no other nation in the free world that can deter aggression around the world.

Let me tell you something else: The small nations in the world, like those in the Mideast and in other parts of the world, that depend on the United States for their survival, those small nations, if the United States is ever the second strongest power in the world, would be living in deadly danger. I pledge to you, we shall keep the United States in a position second to none in its national defense, because we know we will use it for peace.

If, also, the United States is to be able to play this role, a role in which we are building peace for all the world, which I know all Americans want us to do, it is also essential that we develop within our Armed Forces the kind of spirit, the kind of volunteerism which we will need, because, as you know, one of the great accomplishments of this Administration which has been little noticed, except among those who might be of draft age, is that in June of next year we move away from the draft to the all-volunteer army.

I also want to tell you here in this heart of America—because this is the heart of America, as has already been indicated by Joe Margiotta and Governor Rockefeller—I want to tell you that if we are to have an all-volunteer army, it is not going to be enough to do what we are going to do, pay them equally what they can get in civilian life, because anybody who serves in our Armed Forces in peacetime or in wartime, but particularly even in peacetime, above everything else, deserves respect. I believe in respecting the uniform of those who defend the United States.

This is Veterans Day. I have just motorcaded all through Westchester. I have seen the great bands that are here. I have heard the patriotic songs. At Eastchester I laid the first wreath at the new War Memorial that had been erected there. As I laid the wreath and stood back for the moment of silence, this thought crossed my mind as I thought of that volunteer army: The thought was that instead of having all of this talk about providing amnesty for those that desert America, let's honor those who served America, the millions.

So I can say to you, looking to the future, the road will not be easy, but I see the best chance that we have had in this century for young Americans to have a generation of peace, and I dedicate myself to do everything we can to bring that about.

There is a second great goal. That means that with peace you want jobs. What we want is something we have not had since President Eisenhower was President in '55 and '56. That means full prosperity, full employment without war and without inflation, and we are going to have that.

At the present time, you can have confidence in the fact that the United States today has the fastest rate of growth, the lowest rate of inflation, of any major industrial power in the world.

But that isn't good enough. We must continue to hold the line on prices. If we are going to continue to have growth in our economy, we must stop that kind of spending that would lead to a tax increase in this country, because taxes are already too high and we are going to keep those taxes from going up.

If we are going to continue to have progress, progress that will mean more jobs for more Americans than ever before in history, we must provide, of course, every kind of assistance that we possibly can to those that cannot help themselves, but there must be no ceiling on opportunity in America, no ceiling by quota or any other way. Let a man or woman, regardless of his background, go as high as he can. That is the way to build a great economy in America.

And while I am talking on that subject, if we are going to continue to have this economy grow and expand, to provide the new jobs that we want, let's understand that there is no real conflict when we talk about welfare versus work. Let us understand: Every American wants to provide welfare to the greatest extent possible to those who cannot help themselves. But let us also understand: Except for the taxes paid by 82 million Americans who work, there would be no welfare in the United States, so we must not penalize those who work.

I would suggest tonight an Eleventh Commandment: No one who is able to work shall find it more profitable to go on welfare than to go to work. That is the kind that we should have.

Looking to that future too, we are going to continue to make progress in the field that I discussed on national radio last week, and that means in restoring respect for law and order and justice. That means in continuing a massive drive on dangerous drugs and narcotics we need your help, and in that respect may I suggest something tonight? As I have gone through Westchester and now tonight, I have seen many men in blue, the uniforms of the police. Give them the backing and the respect they deserve for the job that they do.

On my part, I will say to you that any appointments that I have the opportunity to make to the courts of this land or to the law enforcement officials of this land, as has been the case in the last 4 years, you can be sure that the age of permissiveness is gone. We are not going to have room for more permissive judges.

In addition, and I particularly address this to those of you who have all of your future ahead, how fortunate you are to live in this country, in this place, to be here. It is not just enough to have peace. It is not just enough to have a job. You must have a goal. That means you want this country to be better. You want it to progress. Let me tell you that in the field of health, in the field of education, in the field of welfare, in the field of environment, we laid before the Congress in 1970, again in 1971, and early this year, 1972, as Governor Rockefeller will agree, historic new programs of reform. They are needed. The Congress has not acted. But I can assure you, give us your vote on

November 7, and we will get the Congress to act next year.

When the next 4 years end, as all of you know, America will celebrate its 200th birthday. It will be the oldest democracy in the world. It will have lived longer than any other one. The question is: What will we be then? What will we have done and what will we mean to the world? I believe that we can be and should be certainly the strongest nation in the world. I believe that without question we will be the richest nation in the world. But we would still possibly not be a great people unless we had something else.

Let me take you back 196 years. There in Independence Hall the thought ran through my mind, what a wonderful country it was so many years ago, and yet it was weak and it was poor, only 3 million people and 13 States. But America had something then. Its people loved this country. It had an ideal and because its people so loved this country, that ideal caught the imagination of the world, and America, from the time of its beginning, has been the hope of the world.

I just want to say to you, I have been to 80 countries. I have been to all of the 50 States. You hear what is wrong with America. Let me say, you and all the world can be thankful that it is America that has the power that we have because we do not threaten the peace of any other nation and we will never do so.

Let me say to you, too, I see here a sign, "Croatia." I was in Zagreb. I saw on a rainy day 500,000 people cheering— what?—not me as an individual, because there in Yugoslavia, in Croatia, they did not know me as an individual. But to them the United States meant something more than military power and economic strength. It meant a great ideal.

I want to say to all of this great audience, and particularly to the young ones who are here: Be proud of your country. If you ever go abroad and travel as I have and as Mrs. Nixon and I have together, when you come back you will say, we are the most fortunate people in the world to live in the United States of America.

I do not contend that the United States is perfect. The American revolution will never end. It is a continuing revolution, and the glory of it is that peacefully we can change the things we do not like, but stay to the good values. Remember that it

was not just military and material might that built America. It was our spiritual and moral strength, and never let this Nation lose that spiritual and moral strength that has made us what we are.

To all of this great audience—and as I look at this audience, let me say, I have never had so many people behind me— my friends, here in the State of New York, in the county of Nassau, may I leave this final thought with you? I know what you want for the next 4 years. I will tell you what I want. I want the next 4 years to be the best 4 years of your lives.

Thank you.

NOTE: The President spoke at 9:10 p.m. at a rally in the Nassau Veterans Memorial Coliseum. He spoke without referring to notes.

368   Remarks at Islip, New York.
October 23, 1972

Thank you very much:

Governor Rockefeller, Congressman [James R.] Grover, my wife and I want to express our very grateful appreciation to our wonderful friends here from Suffolk County who are completing one of the finest campaign days we have had in 25 years. We thank you very much.

As I went along the fence greeting a few of you, I was thinking back to an appearance in Suffolk in the year 1960. Some of you may remember. But I recall there was a heavy rain that day, and it was a marvelous rally nevertheless.

There was something about this county that struck me then. It had a special spirit. The people would come out, rain or snow for that matter, and, even more important, they voted.

I am aware of the fact that in the year

1968 the county with the biggest majority for our ticket, 90,000, was Suffolk County, New York. Now, at the present time I live in Orange County, California. Orange County is trying to have a majority of 100,000, and I have been promised by the county chairman here that you are going to beat them, beat Orange County, and I wish you well.

May I say, too, that I am proud to be here with the two Congressmen—I mean one present Congressman and one to be, my friend Jim Grover and Joe Boyd,[1] who belongs in the United States Congress. Come up here and take a bow so they can see you. Come on. Here he is. Jim, you are a cinch, but take a bow too. We need

---

[1] Joseph H. Boyd, Jr., was the Republican candidate for Congress from the First District of New York.

you. Can I say that to do the job that we need to do in Washington we need their help. I also have a special reason about Joe Boyd, particularly. I would like to say that I lived in this county and I have some special connections with it. I wrote my 1968 acceptance speech at Montauk Point, so I have a special feeling for it. Also, my daughter, my daughter Tricia, now Tricia Cox, and her husband, have as their voting residence Suffolk County, and they would like to have this fine young man, Joe Boyd, as their Congressman. So, how about voting—giving him one in this respect?

Let me say one final thing: At the great rally we had in Nassau and along the streets of Westchester County we heard many people shouting "Four More Years." I want to tell you in a word what I want for those next 4 years. We have made great progress, great progress particularly in this last year toward a goal that all Americans want, and that is peace in the whole world.

Our trips to Peking and Moscow, the winding down of the war in Vietnam, mean that we can look forward in the next 4 years to, it seems to me, achieving a goal that we have not had in this whole century, the basis for that goal at least—a full generation of peace for all Americans. It will not be easy, but we are dedicated to that goal. We realize that this is a dangerous world because there are differences between governments. The Communist Government of the People's Republic of China, the Communist Government of the Soviet Union, and the Government of the United States have very great differences in interests and differences in philosophies. But with the nuclear danger that

hangs over the world, I am determined that we must build a world order in which differences between governments do not make it impossible for people to be friends.

We must continue to have a strong United States to do that. That is why I will oppose any rash cuts in our budget which would make the United States the second strongest nation in the world. I am for that not out of any sense of simply false pride or national ego, because I know that the United States and its people are dedicated to peace and not to conquest, and power in our hands means power for peace.

We also want prosperity, something we have not had since 1955 when President Eisenhower was President, without war and without inflation, and we can have it with your help. We want an era of progress, progress for all Americans, opportunity unlimited by quotas or any other device of that sort, and opportunity for everybody, regardless of his background. Above all, let me tell you something else. This is a year which is an exciting one. For the first time young people between 18 and 21 will have the chance to vote. It will be their first vote. I want them to be able to look back and think that it was one of their best.

In that connection, let me say, when I hear "Four More Years" this is my goal and I hope it is yours: Let's make the next 4 years the best 4 years in America's history.

NOTE: The President spoke at 10:13 p.m. at a rally at MacArthur Field, Long Island, at the conclusion of his visit to Westchester, Nassau, and Suffolk Counties. He spoke without referring to notes.

369 Statement on the Death of Jackie Robinson.
October 24, 1972

I AM deeply saddened by the death of Jackie Robinson. His courage, his sense of brotherhood, and his brilliance on the playing field brought a new human dimension not only to the game of baseball but to every area of American life where black and white people work side by side. This Nation to which he gave so much in his lifetime will miss Jackie Robinson, but his example will continue to inspire us for years to come.

Mrs. Nixon joins me in sending our deepest sympathies and condolences to the Robinson family.

NOTE: Mr. Robinson, 53, died of a heart attack at Stamford Hospital, Stamford, Conn.

He was an infielder with the Brooklyn Dodgers professional baseball team 1947–56, and the first black baseball player in the major leagues.

Robert H. Finch, Counsellor to the President, represented the President at the funeral services in New York City on October 27, 1972.

370 Remarks on Signing Veterans Benefits Legislation.
October 24, 1972

Ladies and gentlemen:

Won't all of you be seated, at least those who have places to sit?

We are gathered here today for the purpose of signing two veterans benefit bills. These bills deal with Vietnam veterans primarily—one, of course, exclusively with Vietnam veterans because it provides for an increase in the amounts for educational benefits for Vietnam veterans.

I was looking over some of the statistics and found that in 1969 there were only 900,000 Vietnam veterans who had taken advantage of the educational opportunities of the GI bill as it applied to Vietnam veterans. Now there are 2 million. We hope there will be more, because this is an opportunity that those who were veterans of World War II and Korea found was enormously important to the young men and the young women in our armed services.

The increase in benefits is one that is due. It is one that will allow any veteran who desires to take training or education—it allows him to take that training and education, not with affluence, particularly, because with the way costs are, I know that you are still going to have to watch your budgets pretty closely, but it will allow you to get that education and that training so essential to get the jobs that you will later want.

The other bill deals with VA hospitals, and will provide for better care for our veterans and their dependents who may use those hospital facilities in the future.

In signing these two bills, I want to say just a word, too, to the representatives of the veterans organizations who are here and to the Vietnam veterans who surround me on either side. Incidentally, two of the Vietnam veterans are women, the rest, of course, are men—which is an indication of how both women and men have played a part in this very long and very difficult struggle for the United States.

I have referred to education. I also want to refer to jobs. As you know, we have had an all-out program in which we have had splendid cooperation from the Government agencies, from private enterprise, and from the media in working on jobs for veterans.

I am glad to report that we have made very great progress in that respect. We are not satisfied. We want to make more. We don't want to provide just an education, training, and whatever you may do in the way of school, and then find that once you have had the training and the schooling, there is no job.

I can assure you that we are going to continue to be dedicated to the proposition that our economy grows so that there is a job for every veteran who takes the training, who wants a job.

As I pointed out in my Veterans Day remarks, a radio talk, I want to emphasize again here today that I do not consider that employers are simply employing veterans as a matter of patriotism. They do have an obligation in that respect, every American has that, to see that our veterans have that chance when they come back after what they have given to their country; but as I pointed out, a veteran has some special qualities that make him particularly qualified for a job.

It is good business to hire veterans, and particularly those who have taken the advantage of education. I trust that when you finish your education that those jobs will be there. We want them to be there. We are going to work toward that end.

Another point that I want to make is that in addition to education, in addition

to jobs, that one of the things that every American can do, one of the things that all of us can be dedicated to, has nothing to do with material benefits. It has to do with what I would call idealistic or spiritual qualities. It is very simply this: This has been a long war. It is a difficult one. It is very controversial. People in the United States have disagreed about it, whether we should have gotten in, how it is being conducted, and what we should now do.

But there is one thing I am sure of. The millions of Americans—and we want to remember that there are 6 million Vietnam-era veterans of which over 2½ million have served in Vietnam—the millions who have chosen to serve our country should be honored for their service.

I think that it is time for us to think, not just on Veterans Day, but on every day of the year, that this country owes a debt of gratitude to 29 million living American veterans who fought for this country in World War I, in World War II, in Korea and Vietnam, not for glory, not for conquest, but fought for the survival of freedom and fought against aggression. Of this we can all be proud, and we can give them the honor they are due.

The other point that I wish to make, in conclusion, is that in honoring our veterans today and particularly our Vietnam veterans, that we want you to know that the best way we can repay you for what you have given to your country— we have taken time out of your lives, and some of you have paid a very high price, I see several in wheelchairs here—the best way we can honor you, the best way we can honor your comrades, many of whom have not returned, is to build a lasting peace in the world. We are all dedicated to that, Republicans, Democrats, without regard to party.

We have made great progress in that direction, particularly in the last year as we have moved, as you know, in new initiatives toward those who might have been potential enemies of the United States.

No one can be sure what will happen in the future. But I want to make this pledge to you. You can be sure that every hour that I can possibly devote to this cause will be devoted to it because I feel a deep sense of personal gratitude to the men and women that have served this country, to those that have sacrificed so much.

I can no longer serve. I think I am physically fit, but they say I am too old. But I can serve along with the Members of the House and Senate that are here, Democrats and Republicans, in another way, and that is to work unceasingly toward the goal that we have not had in this century in America: a generation with-

out war for all Americans, a world at peace. This is our goal. This is what you have fought for, and we trust that we will be able to achieve that goal for which you have sacrificed so much.

Thank you.

I shall now sign the bills. As you will note, I am using the traditional Presidential signing pen. When we sign bills we give souvenir pens to the Members of the House and Senate, of which there are several present here today, who have been supporting this legislation. We also have extra pens for all of those attending the ceremony. I trust that you can endorse the first check with that increased benefit with it!

NOTE: The President spoke at 12:41 p.m. in the State Dining Room at the White House. He spoke without referring to notes.

As enacted, the Vietnam Era Veterans' Readjustment Assistance Act of 1972 (H.R. 12828) is Public Law 92–540 (86 Stat. 1074), and the Veterans' Administration Medical School Assistance and Health Manpower Training Act of 1972 (H.J. Res. 748) is Public Law 92–541 (86 Stat. 1100).

371   Statement About Veterans Benefits Legislation. *October* 24, 1972

THIS Nation has a profound commitment to our 29 million veterans, and I pledge that we shall serve them as well as they have served us.

Today I am especially pleased to sign into law two measures which will advance us a long way toward that goal:

—H.R. 12828, the Vietnam Era Veterans' Readjustment Assistance Act of 1972, and

—H.J. Res. 748, the Veterans' Administration Medical School Assistance and

Health Manpower Training Act of 1972.

Our commitment to veterans was well demonstrated on March 26, 1970, when I signed Public Law 91–219, which substantially increased monthly GI bill educational allowances—raising those for a single veteran with no dependents from $130 to $175.

Today, with the signing of H.R. 12828, the $175 monthly figure is increased to a new alltime high of $220.

This important measure actually increases GI bill education allowance rates by 25.7 percent for able and disabled veterans and dependents. It also increases by 48 percent the rates paid to GI bill trainees taking on-the-job or apprenticeship training, and, for the first time, permits the advance payment of allowances to trainees.

The second of the two bills which I am signing addresses a separate but related concern of our veterans. It authorizes Federal grants for the purpose of founding new medical schools and training facilities as well as the expansion of existing schools affiliated with Veterans Administration hospitals.

Not only will this bill assist the VA medical care system to stay in the forefront of medical research, but it will also permit the expansion of training for much-needed health manpower.

No group is more deserving of fair treatment than the gallant men who serve their Nation in time of conflict. No measures are more deserving of the full support of the American people than this legislation which pays a small part of the debt we owe to them.

As our involvement in Southeast Asia has wound down, as the overall troop strength of our Armed Forces has been reduced, and as we shift to an all-volunteer army, increasing numbers of GI's are returning to civilian life. They must not come home to indifference; they must not come home to an America that ignores the sacrifices they have made.

They deserve the respect of us all, and they deserve every opportunity we can offer them to develop promising civilian careers. For many of them, the amended

GI bill is a special key to that opportunity.

The significant increases in benefits included in H.R. 12828 will make it easier for more returning veterans to take full advantage of the GI bill, but the wholehearted cooperation of the private sector is also needed to develop the fullest potential of this measure.

The time to act is now. There are college openings—veterans should be filling them. The economy is expanding—veterans should get first crack at the new jobs. And, for veterans enrolled in school under the GI bill, employers should consider splitting some jobs to provide part-time employment for two or more veterans, as is being done by the Federal Government. If the Government and the private sector both do their share, every GI bill veteran who needs a part-time job can soon have one.

By giving our veterans the gratitude and the opportunity they deserve, we are not only doing the right thing for them— we are also doing the right thing for all of us. Each returning veteran is a human resource, a mature, highly motivated young citizen who has proven his capacity to serve and to achieve. These young men and women form one of our strongest hopes for the future.

We can never fully repay, in dollars, in training, and in medical service, the patriotic sacrifices of the American veteran. But we can, and we shall, use this means of reaffirming our respect and gratitude towards them, and it is in this spirit that I am delighted to sign these two bills into law.

372   Radio Address on the Federal Responsibility to Education. *October* 25, 1972

Good afternoon:

I want to talk to you today about an issue that has tremendous impact on present-day America and that will play a decisive role in shaping the America of the future—education.

Americans today are the freest, best educated people in the world. We must keep it that way, and one of the surest means is to keep our educational system strong and free.

Money, of course, is part of the answer. Under this Administration the Federal Government has increased its contribution to education by over 70 percent, from $9 billion in fiscal year 1969 to $15.7 billion in the budget for fiscal year 1973.

But money is only part of the answer. Too often over the years, the American taxpayer has seen millions of tax dollars poured into education programs that did not work because not enough thought and planning went into them. Much of the resistance to the imposition of more taxes today is the result of rightful dissatisfaction at the way present tax revenues are being spent.

The roots of the taxpayer revolt lie not in selfishness, but in a sensible refusal to pay more for Government programs that have failed to meet the needs and wishes of the people in an effective way.

It is very easy for politicians to call for new millions of dollars to be allocated for every new education spending proposal that spins out of an ivory tower. The myth that all problems can be solved by throwing money at them is not easily dispelled. But the President of the United States must carefully weigh the cost of new proposals against their merits.

And there are times when he must have the strength to say "no" for the sake of the American taxpayer. Three times I have said "no" to excessive education spending legislation. In each case I did so because I believe the added tax burden would have far outweighed the benefits to be derived by the program.

In each case, the question was not whether to increase worthwhile spending on education, but how much to increase it. I believe that in those three cases the amounts proposed by the Congress were more than the public could afford to pay, and the amounts I proposed were in balance with both our educational needs and the economic well-being of the American taxpayer.

Now, here are some of the important achievements which have resulted during this Administration, following the philosophy I have just outlined:

For younger children:

—We have increased funding for early childhood education projects to over a half billion dollars.

—We have more than doubled aid to elementary and secondary schools.

—We have improved the education of disadvantaged preschool children in their first 5 years of life through the efforts of the new Office of Child Development and a twentyfold increase in food assistance program funding.

—And we have given greater support and encouragement to successful educational innovation, including television programs like "Sesame Street" and "The Electric Company."

For high school students:

—In addition to increasing Federal aid,

we have given top priority to the development of career education, vocational education, so that students leaving school have a choice of entering the job market with a salable skill or continuing their education, if they prefer, at a higher level.

For college students:

—We have more than doubled loan and grant amounts, so that today $4 billion in Federal student assistance is available.

And for all Americans:

—We have launched a Right to Read program that should soon make illiteracy a thing of the past in the United States. Thanks to this effort, we can reasonably hope that by the end of this decade nearly every American reaching young adulthood will have basic reading skills.

Under this Administration the Federal Government is also attempting to fulfill its responsibility to the Nation's black colleges. I have requested over $200 million in assistance to these institutions for fiscal year 1973. That is more than double the funding level of fiscal year 1969 when I came into office.

As a result of our initiatives, a good education is no longer a remote dream for millions of young Americans who would not have had this chance a few short years ago. The ceiling on opportunity and achievement in America today is almost unlimited.

One part of the educational community that has contributed to America from the very beginnings of our history faces special needs today, and they are urgent. I refer to our nonpublic schools.

Were these nonpublic schools to fail, the loss of diversity, the elimination of freedom of choice for millions of parents, and the new burden on the already crowded public school system would be but part of the cost.

Lost, as well, would be an irreplaceable and precious national asset—schools that have provided millions of American children with a moral code and religious principles by which to live. Nonpublic schools have served this Nation and people faithfully and well by maintaining and continuing the religious traditions and beliefs that are so integral a part of our American heritage. I believe that parents of school-age children should be provided the freedom to choose a religious-centered education for their children, if they desire—and I am determined to help guarantee that freedom of choice.

Therefore, just as in the last Congress this Administration supported a tax credit for parents of children attending nonpublic schools, so I am irrevocably committed to seeking tax credit legislation in the next Congress, since the last Congress did not act.

In my judgment, the Constitution does not prohibit tax inducements to encourage and maintain diversity in American education—and I am prepared to fight to guarantee that that diversity remains in America.

Another fundamental element of American education which goes back to our beginnings is the neighborhood school. The neighborhood school is the focal point of community involvement. It binds together students, parents, and school administrators. It brings out the best in all of them.

No one profits by the confusion and resentment that is generated when whole school systems are disrupted by the forced busing of schoolchildren away from their neighborhoods. The answer to inequities in our educational system is to spend more money on learning and less money on forced busing.

Quality education for all and an end to racial discrimination are goals that we seek, and we seek them both. The way to achieve them is to eliminate unlawful discrimination, and to make a special effort to improve the quality of education in the disadvantaged areas.

That is the policy that I am committed to as President. The emergency school aid act, recently enacted, authorizes $2 billion of new money to help meet the special problems of desegregating the Nation's schools.

This Administration's equal educational opportunities act of 1972, had the Congress approved it, would have concentrated funds for the improvement of education for underprivileged children, and would have legislated an end to arbitrary, court-ordered busing of children out of their neighborhoods. However, as you know, after passing the House of Representatives, this measure was filibustered to death in the Senate by pro-busing Senators. I will once again press the next Congress for the passage of this legislation.

The question of neighborhood schools is part of a greater issue—that of where the real decisionmaking power in the field of education should lie; whether it should lie in the hands of appointed judges or officials in Washington or in the hands of people themselves. I believe that the people themselves deserve the greatest voice in our educational system.

That is one reason why I have proposed an education special revenue sharing program to be spent on education in the way the local people and their locally elected leaders deem best, without Federal controls or Federal domination.

This is the best way I know to get American education back on the track, to relate it to the needs of our people instead of the whims of Federal bureaucrats. I will keep on working for this program until it is enacted.

Looking further ahead, the whole education process needs to be reexamined. We need to put American know-how to work analyzing the learning process itself.

The Government should never dictate to the people what kind of education is best, but it has an obligation to provide the people with the research and the information they need to decide these matters for themselves. In a changing age, education must keep pace. It must not fall behind.

To meet this challenge, we have created a National Institute of Education— not to turn out Federal regulations and quotas, but to put some of the best minds in this country to work learning more about the learning process itself. Their findings will help parents and local educators to provide our children with more effective, more useful teaching in the years ahead.

Each of these achievements and goals that I have outlined this afternoon is important. Each can help to make our education system even better than it is, and can extend the American dream to more of our people. But there is another crucial ingredient which no President, no administration, no Congress can supply. That is respect for education and for teaching, respect that must lie in the hearts of the people.

Most of us can probably think back to a teacher who opened up our minds to learning and helped plant the seeds of hope and enthusiasm in our hearts. I think, for example, of a wonderful teacher I had in the fifth grade. In those days you had only one teacher for the whole class—she had to handle all subjects. Miss Burum did that, and she did it very well, but her favorite subject was geography. I can still remember how she communicated her enthusiasm, her love of learning, her fascination with geography and with the different countries of the world to her pupils. And although she will probably never appear in the history books, you might say that in a way Miss Burum was one of the people responsible for my trips to Russia and to the People's Republic of China and for the new beginnings for peace that those trips have helped to usher in.

I mention this because I think it illustrates an important point about education today. We can spend all of the money we want. We can buy all the books, build all the classrooms, fancy new schools. We can do all that, but at the heart of any good school system, we must have talented, dedicated teachers. They are the indispensable ingredient that brings the whole combination to life. To have teachers like that, parents and students must give teachers the respect that is their due, and the standing in the community they deserve.

It was Henry Adams who wrote, "A teacher affects eternity; he can never tell where his influence stops."

The same thing is true of our education system in general. The kind of schooling we provide for our young people today will play a major role in determining the kind of country we will have well into the next century.

And so I pledge to you this afternoon that I will continue to work to make the Federal Government's role in education a positive, productive one, and to give to the people and their locally elected representatives the means with which they can play a larger role in improving education.

By seeking this basic goal together, we can build a system that brings a quality education and full opportunity to all Americans.

Thank you, and good afternoon.

NOTE: The President spoke at 12:07 p.m. from the Library at the White House. The address was broadcast live on nationwide radio. Time for the broadcast was purchased by the Committee for the Re-Election of the President.

The President spoke from a prepared text. An advance text of his address was released on the same day.

373 Remarks at Huntington, West Virginia. *October* 26, 1972

THANK YOU very much. Mrs. Nixon and I want to tell you how very much we appreciate your wonderful welcome. I was just talking to Governor Moore and he was telling me that you only learned at 12 o'clock that we were going to be able to stop here before going over to Ashland, and what a marvelous crowd you have—I understand from West Virginia, Ohio, and Kentucky. Right. Three States.

There isn't room on these steps, incidentally, for everybody, but I am going to have a word to say in a moment about that. But I want you to be sure to see everybody who is here. First, Mrs. Nixon. Pat, will you step up here so they can see you?

And now Mrs. Moore, the First Lady of West Virginia.

And next, Arch Moore, the Governor of West Virginia. Just stay right here, Arch, because I am going to have something to say about you.

One thing I said to Arch Moore when we were moving down the line here was that I thought this airstrip was a little bit short. That is why we had to bring this Convair in. He said you were taking care of that. I just want you to know that as soon as you get a long enough strip, I hope to bring the Spirit of '76, that big plane, right into this airport.

Also, I think you should know that we are very proud that this is the second visit we have been able to make to West Virginia since assuming office as President. We remember the wonderful day at the Elkins Forest Festival in 1971, in the fall. I remember, too, that on that occasion I paid my respects to a great West Virginian who since that time has traveled a great number of miles, and we have traveled with him.

Since that time in '71, as you may know, and, of course, you all do from having followed the papers and the television, we have traveled to Peking, to Moscow, to Warsaw—in fact, the first President of the United States ever to visit these three capitals of Communist countries.

Let me say the man who flew us—and I would say this is no overstatement— probably one of the greatest pilots of all time, is, of course, a West Virginian, Colonel [Ralph] Albertazzie. Wherever we went, whether it was to Peking, half-way around the world, or Moscow, a third of the way around the world, or Warsaw,

about a fourth of the way around the world, he was always on time, just as he was here tonight in West Virginia, his own State.

Come over here. Come on, so they can see you. Here he is—Colonel Albertazzie.

Now, if I could just say a few words to you about the campaign which now is drawing to a close, I would like to speak to you not as a partisan, but as all of you are and all of us try to be, as an American, speaking about your State and our country.

First about your State. I have known Arch Moore for a great number of years. I knew him when he was in the House of Representatives, and in the last 4 years I have had the privilege of working very closely with him when he has been the Governor of the State and I have been in the White House. I am here to ask the people of West Virginia, whatever your politics may be, whether you are Democrats or Republicans or independents—I am asking you to give us the chance— Arch Moore and me the chance—to work for 4 more years for the good of West Virginia and the good of this country.

Now, I was going to go down the list of things that Arch Moore has talked to me in these past 4 years about West Virginia, but it is too long and I wouldn't get over to Ashland for the speech I am supposed to make there in a few minutes. Let me tell you one thing, however: I had a decision to make about the black lung bill. I know that doesn't affect many of the people in this audience. However, it affects many of the people in West Virginia, Kentucky, all over this part of the country. It was a difficult decision because of some technical factors about the bill. I will never forget, however, the day that Arch Moore came to the White House.

He sat there in the Oval Office. You know, he doesn't pound the table. He doesn't shout. But, boy, does he come across. So I signed the bill, and, Arch Moore, we thank you for coming in for that.

Could I now say a word—and this is something I could say in West Virginia, Ohio, Kentucky, California, Maine, New Hampshire, anyplace in this country—a word about this election and what it means in terms of the younger generation particularly, and all of us, whatever our age may be. I know that in our hearts tonight, above everything else we want a world of peace. As all of you have read or heard on your television tonight, there has been a significant breakthrough in the negotiations with regard to Vietnam.[1]

Tonight I can say to you with confidence that because of the progress that has been made, I am confident that we shall succeed in achieving our objective, which is peace with honor, and not peace with surrender, in Vietnam.

There are still differences to be worked out. I believe that they can and will be worked out. But let me go on beyond that.

America has been in wars and has ended wars before in this century, but the great tragedy is that we end one war and then, before a generation is over, we are in another one. And the goal that I have sought, the goal that all of you want, that all Americans want, is not just a peace

---

[1] Earlier the same day, Henry A. Kissinger, Assistant to the President for National Security Affairs, held a news briefing on progress in the Vietnam peace negotiations. The transcript of the news briefing was released by the White House and is printed in the Weekly Compilation of Presidential Documents (vol. 8, p. 1565).

that is simply a period of rest between wars but real peace that will last.

Did you know that in this whole century we have never had a full generation, young people growing up for a full generation without war? We had World War I, and then World War II, and then Korea, and then Vietnam. I think that is enough. What I want is a generation of peace, and beyond that, another generation of peace. And that is why not only are we ending the war in Vietnam in a way that will promote the interest of lasting peace, but that is why we went to Peking, that is why we went to Moscow.

The differences between the Government of the United States and the philosophy that we hold to, and the Government of the People's Republic of China and the Government of the Soviet Union are very great. The Communist and our systems will always be different. But in the world in which we live it is essential that we build a system in which we can have differences between governments, but in which the people of those nations can be friends.

It is important that the Russian people and the American people not be enemies. It is important that the Chinese people—and that is one-fourth of all the people in this world—not be enemies of the United States. I am not suggesting tonight that in this past year in which these historic journeys have taken place that we have achieved the millennium. There is much more to be done. What I am telling you is that if you give me the chance in the next 4 years, we are going to make more progress building that generation of peace that everybody wants for all Americans and all the world.

And beyond that, we want to do something else. We want something that we haven't had since President Eisenhower was President in 1955 and '56, and that means prosperity, full employment without war and without inflation. We are working toward that goal; we are moving toward it. We are not there yet, but we are going to continue to fight inflation. We are going to continue to work for policies that will have growth for our economy, because we want every boy and girl, young man, young woman in this country, to have an opportunity for a job if he is willing to work and able to work. We think we can achieve that goal. We ask for the opportunity to continue the policies that have come so far in achieving it already.

The third point I wish to make is this: As we move into a period of peace in the years ahead, I want it to be, and all of you want it to be, a period of progress. I think of West Virginia. You, of course, live here. I have visited here quite often.

This is a beautiful State. It has so much to see, and you, the people of West Virginia, are a good people. You are a strong people. You are a patriotic people. You are builders of America. You love this country. I want the people of West Virginia to go forward with all of the American people toward an era of progress and opportunity and prosperity without war, such as we have never seen.

What I am simply saying to you at the last of my remarks tonight is this: I do not speak to you as a partisan. I speak to you with no bitterness about this campaign, but I speak with you, as we should as we begin the closing days of the campaign, about our hopes and about our ideals. And I will say to you simply, what I want for the next 4 years is that the next 4 years will be the best 4 years in this Nation's history. Give us the chance; let us do the job.

NOTE: The President spoke at 7:14 p.m. at a rally at Tri-State Airport. He spoke without referring to notes.

374   Statement About the Black Lung Benefits Program.   *October 26, 1972*

IT IS especially gratifying to me to be able to report that 13,000 additional persons have been certified for black lung benefits since I signed a major expansion of this humanitarian program 5 months ago. This means that some 273,000 individuals are now receiving these generous and justified benefits.

To make certain that this program is utilized to the fullest, and to guarantee that no undue delays are involved, I have directed the Department of Health, Education, and Welfare to cut all possible redtape so that all eligible miners and

dependents start receiving their benefits as soon as possible.

The health and safety of coal miners, and the security of their dependents, have been primary concerns of my Administration from its very first year, when the first black lung program was launched.

On May 20 of this year, I signed into law the Black Lung Benefits Act of 1972,[1] which made benefits available to tens of thousands of additional miners and their dependents because it extended filing

---

[1] See Item 160.

time and because it greatly broadened eligibility requirements. The 1972 act also provided benefits for the orphans of black lung victims—a vital category of need which had been overlooked in the original law. It is heartening that such orphans are now receiving their benefits.

As we have produced this record of progress in matters affecting coal miners, I have been guided in all my major decisions by Senators and Governors who represent mining areas.

I refer particularly to my host tonight, Governor Moore; former Governor Louie Nunn of Kentucky; and Kentucky's two great Senators, John Sherman Cooper and Marlow Cook; and Senator Robert Byrd of West Virginia.

These are men I have known over the years, men whose word I trust and men whose understanding of programs affecting coal miners is without parallel.

They not only share credit for the progress we have made in the black lung benefits program—in a very real sense they are responsible for it, because I relied heavily on their counsel in approving the legislation from which the benefits are now flowing.

When the 1972 black lung bill was before me, I received conflicting advice. Some advisers said I should not sign the bill, for various technical reasons. Louie Nunn and Arch Moore and Senators Cooper, Cook, and Byrd, however, strongly urged me to approve the legislation, arguing that the clear human needs outweighed any technical objections.

As you know, I followed their advice.

These men have served their constituents well, and I urge their constituents to support Governor Moore and Louie Nunn on November 7. They are part of my team, and I need them in office over the next 4 years as we strive for even greater progress for coal miners and their families.

We are also moving forward in mine safety.

One of my earliest recommendations was for more effective Federal laws in the area of coal mine health and safety. We achieved this in the Federal Coal Mine Health and Safety Act of 1969.

Since that law went onto the books, major progress has been made in improving working conditions in the Nation's coal mines and in the protection provided to those who work in them.

In the first 9 months of this year, for example, the coal mine fatality rate dropped by approximately 25 percent from the rate for the same period of 1971. That rate is still too high—even a single mine death is one too many—but it demonstrates clearly that we have succeeded in improving things and that we are making progress.

NOTE: The statement was released at Huntington, W. Va.

375 Remarks in Ashland, Kentucky. *October 26, 1972*

THANK YOU very much. I want all of you to know what a very great experience it is for my wife Pat and for me to return to Kentucky. I want you to know that when I think of those six visits, and others, too, in which I have come to this State, I never fail to marvel at the wonderfully warm reception that we have received.

And having noticed many of the new buildings as we came along the road, and having noticed that there are 10 times as many outside this hall as there are inside, I think we need a bigger armory right here.

To those outside—I understand they may be able to hear on the public address system—we are sorry that you couldn't get in. We are sorry we didn't have the chance to stop and greet many of you, although we did make a couple of stops on the way in, and we can only say that your devotion and your dedication to be there with your welcomes, your smiles, your flags, your signs, really touched our hearts.

Let me say, too, that the signs here are very interesting. I see one down here. It says "Sandy Says Roses Are Red, Violets Are Blue. If You Kiss Me, I'll Vote For You." [*Laughter*] She must mean Louie Nunn. [*Laughter*] Are you 18? [*Laughter*]

Could I begin first with some personal remarks. One, we owe a great deal to this State, the support we have had through the years, the friendships that we have in this State. We owe also the fact that over the last 4 years we have had a very gracious and lovely lady from Kentucky as the Social Secretary at the White House, Lucy Winchester. We are very proud of Lucy, and we are very glad that she could be there.

While this is, of course, a very happy occasion for us, this magnificent rally and all this enthusiasm with just a few days before the election, it is also for us a rather sad day in a way, as I am sure it is for you, because we realize that John Sherman Cooper is not going to be a candidate this year, and we realize, as we think of that, his service to the Nation and to his State over the years, how splen-

did it has been and how much we will miss him.

I simply want to say that I have known him, of course, through all the years. I have campaigned this State up through these mountains with him on many occasions, almost 20 years ago. Sometimes he has won; sometimes he has lost. Sometimes I have won; sometimes I have lost, although, let me say, I have never lost Kentucky and I am not going to start now.

John Cooper, not only as a Senator but as a distinguished Ambassador to India, has served his Nation in a magnificent way. I know that he will serve it in the future, I trust, in some capacity, because men of this quality, of this dedication, of this character are rare, and we are fortunate to have had him in government and to have him in the future.

Let me say, too, that as I think of him, I think of the tradition of Kentucky and Senators. You stop to think, of course, of Henry Clay. We all read about him and you read about him. Four times a candidate for President. He never made it. But he was one of the great, great Senators, and to follow in his footsteps there have been other great Senators of both parties down through the years. We think, for example, of Alben Barkley, a Senator from Kentucky. We think, too, in more recent years, of John Sherman Cooper and Thruston Morton.

We think of that tradition. I could mention others. Just let me say this: With that kind of tradition in times past, what we need now is to continue that tradition. I don't know of a better team that could represent Kentucky or any State in the United States Senate than Marlow Cook and Louie Nunn. We need them both.

I, of course, have known Louie Nunn when he managed my campaign not only in Kentucky but throughout these States in the year 1968 in this Mideastern region. I have known him as Governor of this State when he has worked so hard with us in Washington, and he has always found that door of the Oval Office open then, and he will in the future, just as any from Kentucky will.

Also, in mentioning him may I say, too, that I would not want to overlook the splendid representation in the House of Representatives—Tim Lee Carter, your Congressman, who is here.

Having spoken of that tradition, it seems to me tonight that before this splendid audience here in the heartland of Kentucky, in the heartland of America, you would appreciate my talking about the future of America. I could talk about our record. I am proud of it. We haven't accomplished everything that we would have wanted. I don't suppose any President ever can or will. All we do is to try to do the best we can, but we have made great progress in many fields.

I could talk about the past. I could talk also simply of the differences that I have with those of the opposition. But as we enter the closing days of the campaign, I think what the American people really want to hear from anyone who aspires to the office of the Presidency is what his vision is of the future.

What about those next 4 years? What do we plan? What will it mean to all of us—to the older people, to the younger people? And speaking of the younger people, let me just say an interesting thing. I noted that in Kentucky 18-year-olds have had the vote since the year 1954. In 1956, 1960, 1968, as you know, I have been on the ticket, on the ballot in Kentucky. I have always come in, or at least carried it.

And I remember when the 18-year-old vote was passed in the Congress of the United States there were those that said that was going to be a very great blow to us in the year 1972.

Well, one thing this election demonstrates, when the 18-year-olds had the vote in Kentucky, we won it. When the 18-year-olds have the vote in the Nation, we are going to win the Nation.

Now, let me turn, if I may, quickly, to that future, their future, our future, the future of this Nation, what the next 4 years can mean on the great issues that cut across State lines and regional lines and racial lines and religious lines, on the great issues that are American, not partisan.

Let us think for a few moments not about our partisan affiliation, our backgrounds, but simply that we are all very proud to be Americans tonight, and as we think of being Americans, what are the hopes of America in these next 4 years?

Let me first address myself to the subject that Louie Nunn so eloquently has touched upon, the subject of peace. When we speak of peace, I know the immediate thought that comes through our minds, and it is one that has been coming through our minds for many years, through the years that America has been engaged in the longest war in its history. It is a war that began long before I came into office in 1969. It is one that we have wound down. It is one which, as you know from reading your newspapers this afternoon and listening to the television and radio, in which there has been a significant breakthrough in the peace negotiations.

Let me say to you tonight that on May 8, when I made the difficult decision of mining the harbors of North Vietnam and bombing military targets, I laid out three goals for peace. I thought they were reasonable goals, and they were these: First, there should be a cease-fire, stop the killing. Second, all of America's POW's should be returned and all of our missing in action should be accounted for. And third, the people of South Vietnam, the 17 million people who live in South Vietnam, should have the right to determine their own future without having a Communist government imposed upon them against their will by force. Those were the three goals.

Now, based on the progress that has been made in the negotiations to date, I can say with confidence tonight that I believe that we can succeed in achieving those goals. I believe that we will succeed in achieving the goal that I have heard from those young people sitting behind us, peace with honor, and not surrender, for America. The day has not yet come. There are still some differences that must be resolved. I believe that they will be resolved.

However, let us look back for a moment about other times in this century. If you are old enough to have lived through them, as I was, or if you are old enough, certainly as all of you are, to have read about them, you remember the relief—1918, Armistice Day. I remember at that time I was only 5 years old, but I can recall the celebration in our little town at Yorba Linda, California. What a relief. The war was over.

But it was only an interlude; it was not peace that lasted. Because before the next generation grew up, the sons of those who had fought in World War I were fighting in World War II.

You remember V-J Day and V-E Day. I recall that on V-J Day I was in New York City, in Times Square, with my wife, and the wonderful elation that we all felt about the war—it was over. And then came the United Nations and all the hope for a new world order, and we thought, now we are going to have real peace.

And then the sons and the younger brothers of those who had fought, and many had died—350,000 in World War II—were fighting again in Korea.

Then during President Eisenhower's first year in office, you remember the headline—the war was over. And all of us had a sigh of relief because the young men that had died there, certainly their sacrifice had not been in vain, because South Korea retained its independence and its freedom from the North Korean invading forces.

And yet within a few years the younger brothers of those who had fought in Korea and the sons of the older ones who had fought in Korea were fighting in Vietnam. And now a day will come, one day, when the war will be over.

Let me tell you, that, of course, is a great accomplishment. I can assure you that anyone who sits in that Oval Office, as I do, and writes the letters to the mothers, to the wives, to the next of kin of those who have died, anyone who sees the wounded, the others, the ones who have served so magnificently, anyone who has talked, as I have, to the brave wives of POW's—what you want more than anything else is to get the war over.

But also, what you want is to get it over with honor, not simply because of some national ego. You want to get it over with honor because by ending it in an honorable way, by ending it in the right way,

1037

you may lay the foundation for not having another war in that same generation.

That is why we have insisted on these conditions that I have laid down, and that is why, as this war does come to a conclusion, it will be concluded in a way, we believe, that will discourage aggression in the future rather than encourage it.

That is just the beginning. Let me take you a little further, however, on this whole prospect for peace in the world.

It would have been somewhat easy, as a matter of fact somewhat tempting, during these past 4 years to work as we did only on trying to bring the war in Vietnam to an end. And it would have been some satisfaction to have brought home 500,000, as we did, to reduce the casualties 98 percent, as we did, to get into peace negotiations that now have a good chance for success, but we did not stop there. And the reason we did not stop there is that, as I looked at the world, I saw that once the war was over in this small part of the world, there still hung over the world a greater danger potentially in the future.

There was another super power, the Soviet Union. At the beginning of our term in office, we were in confrontation with that super power. And then there was the huge People's Republic of China, where one-fourth of all the people in the world were living, and with which the people of the United States and their Government had had no communication for a period of over 20 years.

As I studied that situation at the beginning of my term in office, long before it began, I determined that it was essential that we build a world order in which governments could have their differences, in which governments could be built on different philosophies, but in which the peoples of nations with different philosophies and different governments need not necessarily be enemies.

I felt this was essential, essential particularly when what was involved was not a conventional but a nuclear war which no one would win, where there would be only losers. And so we began in January 1969 not only to bring an end to the war in Vietnam but to establish a new relationship with the Soviet Union and a beginning of a relationship with the People's Republic of China. The year 1972, this year, has perhaps seen, historians will record, more progress toward true peace in the world than any year since the end of World War II.

I don't mean it is here. I don't mean simply because we went to Peking and established a dialogue that we are not going to have differences with the People's Republic of China. We will have. And I don't mean that because we have had an arms control agreement and trade agreements and exchange agreements and health agreements and environmental agreements with the Soviet Union that we are not going to continue to have differences with the Soviet Union. We will.

Theirs are Communist governments; ours is a free government. And sometimes our interests will come in contradiction to each other. But what we have done, you see, what we have done is now to have replaced what was a hopeless situation, hopeless, with the great powers moving down the road to an inevitable collision at some time in the future, with now a hopeful situation in which the United States and the Soviet Union are negotiating their differences at the conference table—we negotiate hard, but we negotiate, and we settle them—in which the

United States and the People's Republic of China talk about their differences—we negotiate hard, but we have now developed at least a dialogue.

Let me say in that connection then, I would not hold out to this audience, and particularly to these younger people behind me, the certainty that there will not be conflict in the world, the certainty that there will not be small wars in the world. But I do say this: The chance for this new generation of Americans to grow up in a world without war for a whole generation is better than it has been, in my opinion, any time in this century, and we want to keep it that way.

When we speak of these next 4 years, what we ask for is the opportunity to continue, to continue to develop these initiatives. We think we have learned somehow, some of the methods with which to deal with these problems, and in dealing with these problems, we think that over the next 4 years we can make more progress in reducing the tensions in the world, in cooling the trouble spots like the Middle East and others that might explode into war.

This is the challenge we face, and this is what we ask from the American people: the opportunity to continue the progress that we have made in that direction.

Let me relate it now to what we need if we are going to be able to accomplish that.

Louie Nunn very properly mentioned national defense. I know Kentucky's interest in national defense, and it isn't simply the interest that you have in jobs. It is more the interest you have in this country and the fact that it must maintain its strength.

I noticed, for example, that the football team—I think they are the Tom Cats, aren't they? I knew I had the name right when Happy Chandler [1] smiled right there.

I noticed that they were number two, with the possibility of being number one. Now football is a great game, and everybody wants to be number one. But there is certainly nothing wrong about being number two.

But let me tell you, in the kind of world in which we live, let the United States of America never be number two. Let's always be sure of that.

Now why? It is different from the football game. Here you like your town or your team, whatever the case might be, to be number one, and you are kind of proud, and I like to be for my school or for my town or my team, whoever they happen to be, and my country, as all of you.

But it isn't just that. The reason that the United States cannot have the second strongest navy or the second strongest air force and be the second strongest power in the world is that if we are in that position, or allow ourselves because of misguided people recommending programs that would put us in that position, it means that the danger of war in the world would be tremendously increased, and let me tell you why.

The day we become number two, there is no other nation in the world, in the free world, that can deter aggression. You see, before World War I, before World War II, there were the British and there were the French, there were other great

---

[1] Albert B. "Happy" Chandler was Governor of Kentucky 1935–39 and 1955–59, United States Senator from Kentucky 1939–45, and commissioner of baseball 1945–51.

nations with the power, but now only the United States is left. We need it for that reason.

And there is another reason, because I say today we can be proud of what U.S. foreign policy has tried to do in this century. We have fought four wars. For what? World War I, World War II, Korea, Vietnam—we didn't go for conquest, we didn't go for glory, not an acre of territory or anything else. We went to help others defend their freedom. We went to fight against aggression. The United States, in other words—when the United States has power, the people of the United States are a peaceful people. We are not going to use that power to destroy freedom or break the peace, and that is why I say that I am committed to—I know that Louie Nunn is and Marlow Cook will be and Tim Lee Carter will be—let's keep the United States in the position where our power is second to none so that we can help keep the peace in the world. That is why I am so strong on national defense.

Let me relate now this whole area of peace to what it means in other fields. We not only want peace. Obviously we want a good living. We need jobs, employment, homes, security, all of these that mean the good life in this country with which the people of our country enjoy the best life of any nation in the world.

Did you realize that you have to go clear back to President Eisenhower's Administration in the years 1955 and 1956 to find any years in which the United States has had full employment—that means prosperity with full employment—without war and without inflation?

Now I think that we can do it again. That is our goal over these next 4 years.

What we want is full employment for the people of this country without war and without inflation.

Now let me tell you what we can do and what we have done. First, in 4 years we have cut the rate of inflation in half. Also, we have moved the growth of this economy up until we have the highest rate of growth of any industrial nation in the world. We must continue to move it up so that we can produce more peacetime jobs, so that Americans can have full employment without war and without inflation. I think we can achieve that goal.

Let's see also what this new world of peace can mean to a State like Kentucky, to this entire region. Mention has been made of the farm programs. I am going to make a major farm speech on radio at 12:05 tomorrow on all the major networks, if you would like to listen, in the middle of the day.

I won't go into the details now, but let me say that when you see the sales that we have made, a billion dollar sale to Japan this year, a 3-year sale to the Soviet Union, unprecedented, in feed grains, and the beginnings of sales to the People's Republic of China, where, note again, one-fourth of all the people in the world live, you can see the future for American agriculture.

Our exports are the highest in history. They are going to be higher because the markets of the world are opening up. That is what our peace initiatives mean to the farmers, and I think the farmers of Kentucky like that kind of an initiative, too.

There is another area that hits the bread-and-butter issue. As our economy grows, we are going to have an enormous energy crisis in this country, and that means we have to produce coal, we have to produce oil. We have to have the means of meeting that crisis, and that is why a State like this has so much to offer.

What I am simply saying is that as we move from this period of war to a period of peace, it means enormous opportunities, it means prosperity without war and without inflation, it means developing the new markets in a period of peace that could not develop in a period of war, and it means also the opportunity to turn the enormous energies of this country and the people of this country to the progress that we all want, with opportunity for every American to go as high as his talents will take him—better schools, better housing, all of those things that we want and that we have laid forth in such great detail before the Congress over these past 4 years.

What I am saying to you very simply is this: I could talk tonight—and it usually is customary in the closing days of a campaign—about "we have a great record over the past 4 years" and "send us back." But let us not look back, and let us not be angry at those who oppose us.

Let us look to the future. The future is a good future. The future can be a future of peace. The future can be one in which the United States can play the role this Nation was destined to play in building a world of peace and continuing to raise the standard of living of all of our people and increasing the opportunity for all of our people.

One final note: I have mentioned what Kentucky has meant to me personally, and to my wife—your hospitality, your friendship, your energy, your coal, your agriculture, your industry. But most important, what has impressed me as I went along that street, I must say, I saw those young people and older people in the dark. They could only see the light of the car as we went by. They had their flags out.

What impressed me was not simply patriotism. It went further than that. It was something I call character. I looked back to the beginning of this country. I remember then, and Louie Nunn referred to the fact that the bicentennial of Kentucky is in 2 years, and the Bicentennial of the United States is in 4 years, as you know—look at that young country 196 years ago, 13 States, weak, poor, but the hope of the world. Why? Because we stood for something other than power, something other than wealth. We stood for an ideal, for a moral and spiritual strength that caught the imagination of the world, and here in this State of Kentucky I sense it. I sense it across our country, but I sense it in this audience tonight. I sensed it as I went around.

Let me say, as much as your hard work—and I know you work hard—and as much as what you produce in your mines and as much as what you produce on your farm, what we are most grateful for is the character and the moral and spiritual strength of the people of this State. You have it, and that means a great deal.

And so I have heard them say "Four More Years." Let me tell you what my hope is for these next 4 years. It is a very simple statement. I want the next 4 years to be the best 4 years of your lives and the best 4 years America has ever had.

Thank you.

NOTE: The President spoke at 9:02 p.m. at a rally in the gymnasium of the Paul G. Blazer High School. He spoke without referring to notes.

376 Memorandum of Disapproval of Nine Bills.
October 27, 1972

I HAVE promised the American people that I will do everything in my power to avoid the need for a tax increase next year. Today, I take another important step in the fulfillment of that sincere pledge.

This effort really began last January, when I submitted the Federal Budget for fiscal year 1973 to the Congress. As I explained at the time, that budget was carefully prepared so that all justified Federal programs could be provided without any need for higher taxes—and without causing higher prices.

When it became clear that the Congress was exceeding the budget in many bills, I proposed that a spending ceiling of $250 billion be adopted as insurance against a 1973 tax increase.

The Congress rejected that spending ceiling. Instead, it approved spending far in excess of my no-new-taxes budget.

Some of these bills have presented very difficult decisions about whether to sign or to veto. A number of them have attractive features, or would serve very worthwhile purposes—and of course I have received strong advice that to veto them just a few days before the Presidential election would be politically very damaging.

However, in this memorandum are nine measures which I cannot sign without breaking my promise to the American people that I will do all in my power to avoid the necessity of a tax increase next year.

I made that promise in good faith, and I believe in keeping the promises I make—and in making only those promises that I am confident I can keep.

If I were to sign these measures into law, I would, in effect, be making promises that could not be kept—since the funds required to finance the promised services are not available, and would not be available without the higher taxes I have promised to resist.

I believe that political leaders must lay the facts on the line, to talk straight to the people and to deliver on the promises they make to the people.

Although the choices are not easy, I am withholding my approval from 9 Congressional spending programs that would breach the budget by $750 million in fiscal year 1973 and by nearly $2 billion in fiscal year 1974.

Each of these measures by itself might seem justifiable, or even highly desirable. But the hard fact is that they cannot be considered by themselves; each has to be considered in the broader context of the total budget—in terms of how that total weighs on the taxpayers, and how it affects the struggle to curb rising prices.

I am withholding my approval from the following bills:

Labor–HEW and Related Agencies Appropriation Act (H.R. 16654)—

This is the second time I have vetoed inflated appropriations this year for the Department of Health, Education, and Welfare. This amounts to a textbook example of the seeming inability or unwillingness of the Congress to follow a prudent and responsible spending policy. In my budget for fiscal year 1973, I requested that the Congress provide an increase of $2.1 billion over fiscal 1972 funds for the HEW programs contained in this bill. On top of that generous increase—

which would have provided substantial expansion while recognizing competing priorities in other program areas—the Congress amassed a budget-breaking additional increase of $1.8 billion. I vetoed this in August because it was clearly excessive and unwarranted.

The bill now before me contains the same face amount as the measure I previously vetoed. In a partial concession to that veto, however, H.R. 16654 contains authority for the over-spending to be held to $535 million—a result that would still amount to pressure for higher taxes.

This Administration is second to none in its demonstrated concern and clear accomplishments in health, education and manpower matters. My budget represented a balanced and rational approach to the funding of many high priority domestic programs in a time of tight budget resources, while continuing this Administration's shift of priorities and funds toward the human resources activities of the Government.

H.R. 16654 is as unwarranted as the version I vetoed last August.

Public Works and Economic Development Act Amendments of 1972 (H.R. 16071)—

This bill would unnecessarily add vast new authorizations for Federal programs which have been shown to be ineffective in creating jobs or stimulating timely economic development. Public works projects have notoriously long lead times—so by the time this spending became fully effective, the need for such stimulation would be passed and the stimulation would be inflationary.

The bill would stimulate increased bureaucracy in the regional commissions by using them as a funding rather than a planning and coordinating level of Government.

It would also provide assistance to workers and firms affected by Federal environmental actions. These provisions would be highly inequitable and almost impossible to administer. The unemployment benefits provision would fragment and undermine our basic Federal-State unemployment insurance system and its costs would be essentially uncontrollable. The proposed pollution control facilities loan program has only vague and unspecified objectives.

Amendments to the Mining and Mineral Policy Act (S. 635)—

This bill would authorize the Secretary of the Interior to provide matching categorical grants to establish and support a mineral research and training institute in each of the 50 States and Puerto Rico, as well as grants for related research and demonstration projects. It would fragment our research effort and destroy its priorities. Such an inflexible program would preclude us from taking advantage of the best research talents of the Nation—wherever they may be. The Federal Government's ongoing programs of similar and related kinds of research, currently funded at about $40 million annually, have provided a flexible and efficient means of meeting minerals problems of the highest national priority and can readily be adapted to continue to do so.

Airport Development Acceleration Act (S. 3755)—

This bill would increase Federal expenditures and raise percentage participation in categorical grant programs with specific and limited purposes. I believe this would be inconsistent with sound fiscal policy. Airport development funds have been almost quadrupled since 1970 under this Administration.

Flood Control Act of 1972 (S. 4018)—

This measure would authorize federal projects which would ultimately cost hundreds of millions of dollars. It contains projects never approved or recommended by the executive branch. In addition, it contains a number of objectionable features such as authorizing ill-defined and potentially costly new programs, and limiting my authority to establish criteria and standards to measure the feasibility of water resources projects in determining which ones to recommend for Congressional authorization. However, a number of projects in this bill are in my judgment justified and I will recommend legislation to authorize their construction early in the next Congress.

Upgrading of Deputy U.S. Marshals (H.R. 13895)—

This would raise the pay of some 1,500 deputy marshals by as much as 38 percent, through wholesale across-the-board upgrading. There is no justification for this highly preferential treatment, which discriminates against all other Government employees who perform work of comparable difficulty and responsibility and whose pay is now the same as that of deputy marshals.

National Cemeteries Act of 1972 (H.R. 12674)—

This bill would block the orderly system of surplus land disposal established by general law and Executive order, by requiring an unusual Congressional approval procedure before any VA land holdings larger than 100 acres could be sold.

These property transfer restrictions would undermine the executive branch's Government-wide system of property management and surplus property disposal which is designed to assure the best and fullest use of Federal property. It would impede the Legacy of Parks program and the procedures for disposing of surplus Federal property under the Federal Property and Administrative Services Act and Executive Order 11508.

Also, the bill deals inconsistently with the serious problem of burial benefits for the Nation's veterans and war dead. It commissions a study of this problem at the same time it preempts the results of such a study by authorizing new burial benefits which would annually add $55 million to the Federal budget beginning next year. The Administrator of Veterans Affairs already is at work on such a study, which will identify the alternatives for improving burial and cemetery benefits. In the interim, it would be unwise to commit additional Federal resources as proposed by this bill.

Veterans Health Care Expansion Act of 1972 (H.R. 10880)—

The liberalizing features of this bill would unnecessarily add hundreds of millions of dollars to the Federal budget. It would open the VA hospital system to nonveterans and would expand the type of direct medical services available from VA. By providing direct medical services to veterans' dependents, the bill runs counter to this Administration's national health strategy which would provide national financing mechanisms for health care and sharply reduce the Federal Government's role in the direct provision of services.

The bill also purports to set mandatory minimums on the number of patients treated in VA hospitals. In testimony on this bill, the Veterans Administration strongly objected to this provision on the grounds that it was totally unnecessary and could result in inefficient medical treatment and wasteful administrative practices. The tragic result would be a lower quality of medical care to all patients.

While I strongly support the VA health care system and will continue to encourage its improvement in the future, I cannot approve a bad bill.

Rehabilitation Act of 1972 (H.R. 8395)—

This measure would seriously jeopardize the goals of the vocational rehabilitation program and is another example of Congressional fiscal irresponsibility. Its provisions would divert this program from its basic vocational objectives into activities that have no vocational element whatsoever or are essentially medical in character. In addition, it would proliferate a host of narrow categorical programs which duplicate and overlap existing authorities and programs. Such provisions serve only to dilute the resources of the vocational rehabilitation program and

impair its continued valuable achievements in restoring deserving American citizens to meaningful employment.

H.R. 8395 also would create organizational rigidities in the vocational rehabilitation program which would undermine the ability of the Secretary of HEW to manage the program effectively. The bill also would establish numerous committees and independent commissions which are unnecessary, would waste the taxpayers' dollars, and would complicate and confuse the direction of this program. Finally, the bill would authorize funding far in excess of the budget request and far beyond what can be made available and used effectively.

RICHARD NIXON

The White House,

October 27, 1972.

NOTE: On the same day, the White House released the transcript of a news briefing on the President's pocket vetoes. Participants in the news briefing were John D. Ehrlichman, Assistant to the President for Domestic Affairs; and William A. Morrill and Paul O'Neill, Assistant Directors, Office of Management and Budget.

377 Radio Address on the American Farmer. *October* 27, 1972

Good afternoon:

In every American home, there is special respect and gratitude for the breadwinner—the one who provides the rest of the family with food to eat and clothes to wear.

The breadwinners of our national family are this country's nearly 3 million farmers.

American agriculture leads our own economy and the world in productivity. Because of the remarkable productivity

of our farms and ranches, the people of the United States have more and better food to eat, at lower cost, than any other people anywhere. A smaller percentage of the family budget goes for food in America than in any other country in the world.

Because of that productivity, we are able to export vast quantities of our farm products to help feed the world.

Because of that productivity, we have been able in the last 4 years to more than triple the Federal effort to eliminate hunger in America, as well as maintaining generous food assistance programs abroad.

All of us owe a great debt of gratitude to those Americans for whom agriculture is a proud way of life.

Sometimes there is a tendency to think of farmers as an isolated special interest group. For example, it was suggested that I should address this talk today exclusively to farm people, and that it should be broadcast very early in the morning when most of the radio audience would be farmers.

But I wanted instead to talk with all Americans on this subject and to make the point that in this election campaign the farm issues and the national issues are one and the same, because farm people want what is best for America.

They want to keep our country strong, for they know that America's power is the guardian of peace in the world.

They want to end our involvement in Vietnam through peace with honor, not through surrender.

They want responsible government spending that can lead to tax relief and prevent renewed inflation—because inflation hits farmers doubly hard. It raises their costs on the one hand, and it erodes their buying power on the other.

Farm people want to preserve the moral and spiritual values, the religious faith, the patriotism which have always been so unshakeably strong on the farms and in the rural communities of America's heartland.

I am committed to achieving all these things. But I want to dwell now on one additional commitment—something which farmers, like the rest of us, want and deserve, but which for too many years

they have not been receiving—and that is a full, fair share in our Nation's prosperity.

When city people shop at the supermarket or sit down to a good meal, it is easy for them to take their food for granted and to forget the men and women whose hard work and sacrifice produced it.

But when you realize that the farmer's workweek runs almost double what most Americans are used to, when you realize that high risks and heavy production costs keep his profit margins paper thin, when you realize that he must often go deep into debt to maintain the $100,000 worth of capital assets required for family farming, then it is clear that farm people deserve a better reward than an average income which today is only 80 percent of the average for nonfarm people.

Helping farmers to do better has been one of the major commitments of my Administration.

When we took office, farm prices were stagnating, farm exports were down, inflation was eating heavily into farm income, family farms were disappearing at a rapid rate, and, worst of all, it seemed that Federal farm policy under the previous Administration had been part of the problem rather than part of the solution.

We set out immediately to turn that situation around. Four harvests have come in since then, and with each harvest has come evidence of solid progress for the American farmer.

Net farm income—what is left after the bills are paid—will average 24 percent higher for the 4 years of this Administration than the average for the last Administration. Net farm income this year will finally break the alltime record set 25 years ago.

During the period 1961 to 1968, farm people's per capita income after taxes averaged about one-third lower than what nonfarm people were making. But now that gap has narrowed to one-fifth, and we are going to keep working until there is no gap at all.

We have also made progress in checking the rapid decline in numbers of American farms. Farm units were disappearing at the rate of 106,000 every year during the 8 years before we took office. Since then we have cut this annual loss by more than half. This means more hope for the future in rural America, with more people able to keep on working their land as they have a right to do.

A big share of the reason for this progress is the character of farm people themselves. These are people of courage, self-reliance, and independent spirit. They just don't know the word "quit." Today, as in years past, they are the backbone of America.

But another reason things are better is that farm policies of this Administration have responded to farmers' own desires for change.

Four years ago, everyone was fed up with rigid government farm programs that kept farmers in a straitjacket. So we looked for a way to give farmers more freedom. We sought an expanding agriculture rather than a shrinking agriculture, a voluntary farm program rather than compulsory controls, a market-oriented agriculture rather than a government-dominated agriculture.

The Agriculture Act of 1970, which passed with broad bipartisan support in the Congress, has moved strongly in this direction. The new program allows a farmer to set aside a certain number of acres to keep from creating price-depressing surpluses, and then the farmer is free to plant what he wants on his remaining acres for his own best market advantage. More farmers are in these programs today than ever before.

An expanding agriculture requires expanded international markets for our farm products. When we took office, agricultural exports were stagnating. And now they are setting new records year after year.

From the annual level of $5.7 billion under the last Administration, farm exports in 1972 will pass $8 billion for the first time. And we are going to keep them growing toward our goal of $10 billion of exports every year.

We have gained our first billion dollar annual customer of farm products—Japan.

We have opened new markets in Communist countries by lifting the restrictive ocean shipping regulations of the last Administration. It was this action that led to last winter's $150 million sale of feed grains to the Soviet Union, and then to the 3-year grain sales agreement which we signed with the Soviets in July—the biggest peacetime transaction of its kind in history.

This sale holds enormous benefits for all Americans. It will raise crop value for American farmers by a billion dollars in 1972 alone. It will improve our Nation's balance of payments by a billion dollars. It will create at least 30,000 new American jobs. And it will save the taxpayers some $200 million.

Equally important, it is a striking example of the way our farm policy and our foreign policy are working hand in hand to strengthen the peaceful ties between great powers which were adversaries only a few years ago.

The new relationship between the United States and the People's Republic of China, which began when I visited Peking earlier this year, is another situation in which our farmers are both contributing to peace and profiting from peace. The grain sales which we have made to the People's Republic of China only scratch the surface of an immense trade potential between our two countries.

And today I am happy to announce that an additional contract for the sale of 300,000 tons of American corn to the People's Republic of China was signed within the last few days.

Leading the way in our efforts to bring U.S. farm products to the world, and to bring a better day for America's farmers and rural people, have been the two able and energetic men who have served in my Cabinet as Secretary of Agriculture—Cliff Hardin and Earl Butz.

It has been said of the present Secretary of Agriculture that "Nobody bullies Earl Butz." The people in Washington have learned how true that is, so have the Nation's farmers, and we can be proud to have Secretary Butz on our team.

This autumn of 1972 is a season of harvest not only for the farmers across America's countryside but for our Nation as a whole.

At home, we are beginning to reap the results of a long battle to launch a new prosperity in America, a time of full employment without inflation and without war. We are moving toward greater domestic peace, stability, and national unity. Around the world, the chances seem better and better that our children will be able to grow up in a full generation of peace.

Now the great question is: How shall we use that peace once it is achieved? We

must use it as an opportunity to better the human condition, to lift up the hearts and the hopes of all mankind. Here the American farmer has a great role to play.

It is significant, I think, that the last American to win the Nobel Peace Prize was not a statesman, not a social activist, but a man of the soil—Dr. Norman Borlaug, the man whose research with high-yield wheat has launched the "Green Revolution" which is helping to feed hungry millions around the globe today.

I wish it were possible to present a peace prize to every farmer and every farm family in America in recognition of what they have done in years past to help keep our country strong and free, and in recognition also of what they can do in years ahead to help unite all peoples in a new alliance against the common enemies of mankind—hunger and poverty and misery in the world.

But farm people do not ask for prizes. What they do ask is a fair chance to succeed, a fair share in America. That is what I am determined to help them achieve.

I will not be satisfied until farmers have the rewards, the satisfaction, and the income they so richly have earned.

I will not be satisfied until we are assured that rural America will continue to be a place of promise—a good place to live.

I pledge that during the next 4 years we will do everything in our power to justify the confidence which the strong people of America's rural heartland place in the future of agriculture, the future of America, and the future of peace in the world.

Thank you, and good afternoon.

NOTE: The President spoke at 12:07 p.m. from the Library at the White House. The address was broadcast live on nationwide radio. Time for the broadcast was purchased by the Committee for the Re-Election of the President.

The President spoke from a prepared text. An advance text of his address was released on the same day.

378 Statement About United States Cooperation With the European Community. *October 27, 1972*

I HAVE read with great interest the communique issued by the leaders of the nine countries of the enlarged European Community, demonstrating once again their commitment to greater European unity. At this important meeting, the members of the Community have set an objective of "transforming the whole complex of their relations into a European Union by the end of the present decade." The United States strongly supports that objective. It is, and has always been, my own deeply held view that progress toward a unified Europe enhances world peace, security, and prosperity.

It is also of the highest importance that the United States and Europe work closely together. For this reason I particularly welcome the Community's declared intent to maintain a constructive, forthcoming dialogue with us and its commitment to a progressive liberalization of tariff and nontariff barriers to trade on a comprehensive basis during the major multilateral negotiations to begin next year.

On behalf of the United States, I wish to reaffirm our commitment to work with the members of the European Community for reform of the international economic system in a way which will bring about a new freedom of world trade, new equity in international economic conduct, and effective solutions to the problems of the developing world.

These are the objectives with which the United States will approach forthcoming negotiations on monetary and trade reform. We will be prepared to take bold action with our European partners for a more equitable and open world economic order. The October 21 Summit declaration is evidence that our European partners are equally dedicated to the success of these efforts. In the meantime, we look to them for continued help in fostering a climate of mutual cooperation and confidence, and for a demonstration— through positive action on pressing and immediate problems—that these efforts will be crowned with success.

379 Statement About Decision To Sign 37 Bills. *October 28, 1972*

IN THE final weeks of its second session, the 92d Congress enacted several dozen separate pieces of legislation. I have given a good part of my time during the last 10 days to a careful review of these bills.

Yesterday I announced my decision to withhold my approval from nine of these bills. Released with this statement today will be a list of certain bills which I have decided to sign.

A number of these measures warrant special comment.

THE CONSUMER PRODUCT SAFETY ACT

I am pleased to sign into law S. 3419, the Consumer Product Safety Act. This legislation is the outgrowth of a proposal which I submitted to Congress in February of 1971. It is the most significant consumer protection legislation passed by the 92d Congress.

S. 3419 creates a new independent Consumer Product Safety Commission to develop consumer product safety standards and to enforce these standards, in court if necessary. In addition, the Commission will have authority to ban outright the sale of hazardous products which cannot be adequately regulated.

As beneficial as this legislation is for the consumer, the act contains certain language which will tend to weaken budget control—and a coordinated, unified budget is the consumer's ally in keeping inflation and taxes down. These provisions are unfortunate and should not be regarded as precedent for future legislation.

The most important thing about this bill, however, is its recognition that a defective lawnmower or electric heater can be just as dangerous to the consumer and his family as contaminated food or improperly packaged drugs. It is high time that the Government provided for comprehensive regulation of the many potentially dangerous products commonly used in and around American households. While the Consumer Product Safety Act differs in several ways from the legislation I proposed, it answers a long-felt need, and I am happy to give it my approval.

CONTROLLING OCEAN DUMPING

Several of the most significant of the bills which I am signing carry forward our campaign to restore and protect the quality of the environment.

H.R. 9727, the Marine Protection, Research, and Sanctuaries Act of 1972, will provide the controls over ocean dumping which have long been a matter of high priority concern for this Administration. This law is closely modeled on the recommendations I submitted to the Congress in February of 1971, recommendations which grew out of a report forwarded to me by the then newly established Council on Environmental Quality the previous October. The bill is thus one of the first fruits of our new emphasis on careful advance analysis of environmental challenges.

The practice of dumping waste into the oceans has been steadily increasing in recent years, endangering marine life, reducing the population of fish, jeopardizing marine ecosystems, and impairing esthetic values. H.R. 9727 will meet this growing problem by banning the dumping of certain hazardous materials entirely and by subjecting other substances to careful regulation through a new permit system. It also provides for further monitoring and research programs.

It is significant that this new act will be implemented by the two newest environmental agencies—both created by this Administration—the Environmental Protection Agency and the National Oceanic and Atmospheric Administration. I am directing the Administrators of these two agencies to work in close consultation to ensure that duplication can be avoided and information can be fully shared between them as they confront this vital challenge. This bill will also give strong support to the delegation we will be sending to London at the end of this month to seek a much needed international convention on this important matter.

PROTECTING MARINE MAMMALS

Even as I commend the Congress for responding to the concern over ocean dumping, I am also grateful for the opportunity to sign a second piece of legislation concerning the oceanic environment, the Marine Mammal Protection Act, H.R. 10420. This legislation will give us the important powers we need to ensure that the world's whales, porpoises, seals, polar bears, walruses, sea otters, and manatees do not become depleted or endangered species. H.R. 10420 requires a specific permit before such animals may be taken or imported and provides strong encouragements for other countries to develop similar protections.

In this area, as in the case of ocean dumping, we are ensuring that our own regulation programs are up-to-date, and we are also taking a strong position of international leadership. We share the oceans with all who live on this planet. Our actions are part of what we hope and trust will be a global commitment to protect the glory and majesty and life of the "shining" seas.

MANAGING COASTAL ZONES

S. 3507, the Coastal Zone Management Act of 1972, is also an outgrowth of earlier efforts by this Administration to provide for rational management of a unique national resource.

More than 75 percent of our population now lives in States bordering the At-lantic and Pacific Oceans, the Gulf of Mexico, and the Great Lakes. The number of people who use our coastal zones is rapidly increasing—and so are the purposes for which these areas are utilized. Commercial fisheries, ports, beaches and other recreation areas, the extraction of minerals, the siting of powerplants, the building of homes and factories, the development of transportation systems—these are among the competing functions which our coastal zones are being called upon to serve. Yet these same areas, it must be remembered, are the irreplaceable breeding ground for most aquatic life.

S. 3507 recognizes the need for carefully planned, comprehensive management programs to ensure the most rational and beneficial use of the coastal zones. This bill also recognizes that the States can usually be the most effective regulators of such a planning process. I will instruct the Secretary of Commerce to carry out this statute in a way which focuses Federal efforts on the adequacy of State processes rather than to become involved in the merits of particular land use decisions.

But the coastal zones are not the only areas which need this sort of long-range attention. This is why I proposed to the Congress in February of 1971 the national land use policy act—a bill which would help the States establish management programs for a wide range of areas which are of critical environmental concern. It is my strong hope that the next Congress will expand on the coastal zone bill which was passed this fall by approving my national land use policy act. I signed S. 3507, then, as an important first step toward a more comprehensive program.

S. 3507 locates administrative responsibility for this program in the Department of Commerce rather than in the Department of the Interior as I would have preferred—and as I called for in my proposed land use policy act. This action is not sufficient reason in my judgment for vetoing the bill, but it does underscore once again the importance of creating a new Department of Natural Resources, as I have recommended, so that we can reverse the trend toward the fragmentation and fractionalization of Federal programs and begin to coordinate our environmental efforts more effectively.

CONTROLLING NOISE

Still another important piece of environmental legislation which has grown out of an Administration proposal is H.R. 11021, the Noise Control Act of 1972. While a number of municipal governments have moved to control the rising levels of noise in our country—particularly in major urban centers—many of the most significant sources of noise move in interstate commerce and can be effectively regulated only at the Federal level. The new act will enable the Environmental Protection Agency to set limits on the amount of noise permitted both from trucks, buses, and railroad trains operating in interstate commerce and from a variety of newly manufactured products such as jackhammers and compressors, automobiles, motorcycles, snowmobiles, motors and engines. It will also permit the EPA to require the labeling of noise emission levels on products such as household appliances. It calls for a 9-month study of aircraft and airport noise leading to a procedure for regulating aircraft noise in a way which is consistent with maintaining aircraft safety.

GATEWAY RECREATION AREAS—EAST AND WEST

Two environmental projects in which I have taken a particular personal interest are the Gateway National Recreation Area [S. 1852] in and around New York City and the Golden Gate National Recreation Area [H.R. 16444] in and around San Francisco Bay. I have recently visited the sites of these recreation areas, and it is with particular pleasure that I sign the legislation which officially authorizes their establishment.

The need for open space and recreational opportunities is especially pressing in our great metropolitan centers. These two bills represent major advances in meeting this need. It is estimated that the Gateway National Recreation Area in New York and New Jersey, a 26,172-acre project, will serve some 9.5 million people in the first year of operation and some 19 million people by the 10th year. The Golden Gate National Recreation Area will contain over 34,200 acres and will serve an estimated 2 million people in the first year and 16 million by the 10th year.

Nineteen hundred seventy-two marks the beginning of the second century of national parks in America. It is fitting that we launch that second century by creating two great new recreation areas which will directly benefit so many Americans. I plan to continue my emphasis on bringing "parks to the people" through the donation of Federal lands to State and local authorities for the development of parks and recreation areas near population centers.

Other Environmental Actions

Another significant environmental bill which I am signing into law is S. 2454, which will extend authority for the Youth Conservation Corps. This program was set up on a temporary basis in 1970 to provide summer employment for young men and women in our national parks, forests, and other Federal lands and waters. S. 2454 will also establish a new pilot program of Federal grants to help the States set up similar projects.

I am also pleased to sign H.R. 10384, which will remove certain restrictions on the acquisition of lands for recreational development and on the protection of natural resources in fish and wildlife areas. Other notable forward steps will result from H.R. 11091, increasing the Federal aid to wildlife restoration fund by extending existing firearms taxes to cover archery equipment used in hunting; H.R. 12186, substantially increasing the penalties for violations of the Bald Eagle Protection Act; and H.R. 15280, doubling the spending authorization for the National Advisory Committee on Oceans and Atmosphere from $200,000 to $400,000.

Among the other bills which will help protect our environmental resources for the enjoyment of all Americans are: S. 27, establishing Glen Canyon National Recreation Area in Arizona and Utah; S. 141, establishing Fossil Butte National Monument in Wyoming; S. 493, classifying the Eagle Cap Area in Oregon as a wilderness area; S. 1198, authorizing review of the Indian Peaks Area in Colorado as to its suitability for preservation as wilderness; S. 1928, designating a segment of the Saint Croix River in Minnesota and Wisconsin as a component of the national wild and scenic rivers system; S. 1973, establishing the Thaddeus Kosciuszko Home National Historic Site in Pennsylvania; S. 2411, establishing the Cumberland Island National Seashore in Georgia; S. 3959, authorizing feasibility investigations for nine potential water resource development projects; S. 4022, authorizing the President to provide for United States participation in the International Exposition on the Environment in Spokane, Washington, in 1974; H.R. 8756, establishing the Hohokam Pima National Monument in Arizona; H.R. 13067, providing for the administration of the Mar-A-Lago National Historic Site in Florida; H.R. 13396, increasing land acquisition funds for the Delaware Water Gap National Recreation Area; and H.R. 15597, increasing land acquisition funds for Piscataway Park in Maryland.

Protecting Foreign Officials in the United States

The menace of international terrorism has become particularly vivid in recent months—and our Government has been playing a leading role in the international effort to combat it. It is with particular satisfaction, therefore, that I sign H.R. 15883, a bill which makes it a Federal offense for anyone to harass, assault, kidnap, or murder a foreign official, a member of his family, or an official guest of the United States while that person is in our country. This law will strengthen significantly the protection we can provide for such persons. And it will also strengthen our position as we work within the United Nations and the International Civil Aviation Organization for further actions to fight the scourge of terrorism.

AUTHORIZATIONS AND APPROPRIATIONS

I have also signed a number of other bills which authorize or appropriate budgeted funds for programs which have already been established, including:

H.J. Res. 1331, continuing appropriations for fiscal year 1973 until February 28, 1973, or the date of enactment of pending appropriations bills; H.R. 5066, authorizing appropriations to carry out the Flammable Fabrics Act; H.R. 13694, authorizing appropriations for the American Revolution Bicentennial Commission; H.R. 14989, making appropriations for the Departments of State, Justice and Commerce, for the Judiciary, the Small Business Administration, the United States Information Agency, and certain other related agencies; H.R. 15375, authorizing appropriations to carry out the National Traffic and Motor Vehicle Safety Act, and amending that act to enhance its effectiveness; H.R. 15641 and H.R. 16754, the military construction authorization and appropriation acts for fiscal year 1973; H.R. 16593, the Department of Defense Appropriation Act for fiscal year 1973; H.R. 16675, extending assistance to State and local programs concerning alcohol abuse and alcoholism; and H.R. 16987, authorizing certain supplemental appropriations for the maritime construction subsidy program. I am also signing H.R. 16810 which raises the public debt limit for fiscal year 1973 from $400 billion to $465 billion.

NOTE: On the same day, the White House released the transcript of a news briefing by Paul O'Neill, Assistant Director, Office of Management and Budget, and Lewis A. Engman, Assistant Director, Domestic Council, on the President's approval of the 37 bills listed in the statement and the following 7 additional bills:

H.J. Res. 984, amending joint resolution providing for United States participation in the International Bureau for the Protection of Industrial Property

H.R. 7117, amending the Fishermen's Protective Act of 1967

H.R. 9554, redesignating the Perry's Victory and International Peace Memorial National Monument as the Perry's Victory and International Peace Memorial

H.R. 14128, providing for the relief of Jorge Ortuzar-Varas and Maria Pabla de Ortuzar

S.J. Res. 247, extending the duration of copyright protection in certain cases

S. 2674, removing a cloud on the title to certain lands located in the State of New Mexico

S. 3358, prohibiting the use of certain small vessels in United States fisheries

380   Radio Address: "One America."
October 28, 1972

Good morning:

A national election campaign can unify the people, or it can divide them.

One of the most encouraging things about this election is the way in which the voters are reacting as a united people, as One America.

Too often in past years, politicians of both parties have made their appeal not to what was good for America, but to the divided and sometimes conflicting interest of various groups and blocs within America.

At times, too, politicians have tried to run campaigns on style and charisma, instead of on the facts and the issues.

This year, the election is being decided on the fundamental issues. Because it is, we are seeing the birth of a new American majority.

It is not a new partisan majority. It is not a realignment of the old political coalitions of different interest groups and blocs.

The new majority is a majority of Americans from all parts of the country who agree on certain fundamental values and principles that are basic to America's ideals and its experience.

I remember reading once about a sign outside a church in Greenville, South Carolina. Its message was simple. It said: "If God were permissive, he would have given us Ten Suggestions."

The point, of course, was that at the base of every great faith or idea, there are certain fundamental, abiding truths that must not be destroyed or distorted.

I realize that in this sophisticated age we hear a lot of scoffing at old-fashioned faith, morality, and character. But I also know that the day America loses its moral character, or the day we forget our religious heritage, we will cease to be a great Nation.

For America is more than just a plot of land—it is an ideal. And that ideal is what built 13 tiny, struggling colonies into the freest, mightiest Nation on earth today.

What is the ideal? George Washington once called it "the sacred fire of liberty"— a devotion to freedom and opportunity, a respect for the rights and dignity of the individual.

Almost two centuries later, another great soldier and statesman, President Dwight D. Eisenhower, gave us a remarkably similar definition. "America," he said, "is best described by one word, freedom."

Let us never forget that we won that freedom, and we have kept and expanded it over the years, because we have remained a single, united people—One America.

Last month I had the privilege of dedicating a new museum. It was a very special occasion for me, because this was no ordinary museum—it was the American Museum of Immigration on Liberty Island in New York Harbor.

There, at the foot of the Statue of Liberty, a museum had been created to commemorate the trials, the tribulations, and the magnificent accomplishments of millions of men and women who came to these shores to build a new life and to become part of a united American people.

Perhaps more than anywhere else, you can feel the meaning of America there on Liberty Island, in the shadow of that great national monument. During the peak years of immigration, as many as 5,000 immigrants entered New York Harbor each day, and the first thing they saw, their first glimpse of America, was that magnificent statue with its torch held high.

The world's hopes poured into America, along with its people. The people were from every nation on earth. But the hope was always the same—the burning desire for freedom and opportunity, the same hope that motivated the Founding Fathers in 1776, the same hope that has motivated generation after generation of new Americans ever since.

Today there are some who say that that spirit is dead—that we no longer have the strength of character, idealism, and faith we once had.

They say that we have become a sick society, a corrupt society. Some have even gone so far as to compare us with Hitler's Germany.

Well, those who say these things are wrong.

Those who say these things do not know the real America.

In my 4 years as President, I have visited every State in the Union.

Increasingly, everywhere I have gone I have found new evidence, not of disunity, but of unity. I have found the people of the North, the South, the East, the West, united in their basic concerns and beliefs. I have found hard evidence of something I always believed—that, despite our vast diversity of races, of ethnic origins, and of faiths, when you get down to the basics, we are still One America.

And the basics are the same in every part of the country. They are the same for the Polish-American, the Italian-American, the Mexican-American, the steelworker, the farmer.

I find that most Americans still want a strong country, not out of national vanity or jingoism, but because they know that a strong United States is the guardian of peace and freedom in the world. They reject the philosophy that we should unilaterally weaken America.

I have found that the vast majority of Americans want peace, but are convinced that it must be a lasting peace with honor. They know that only a peace built on honor and integrity can long survive. They know that retreat and surrender lead not to security, but to new provocations and confrontations and to greater risk of war.

That is why, in the difficult job of seeking an honorable negotiated settlement in Vietnam, I have been able to count on the support of a majority of Americans. That is why America has been able to preserve its pledge that we shall not betray our allies, or abandon our men held prisoner or missing in action, as we work for a full generation of peace.

I have found that most Americans everywhere agree that we should hold the line on taxes and spending. The days of the Congressional blank check for spending are gone. The people are rightly demanding an end to the government extravagance that has driven up taxes and prices. They are determined to put the brakes on the cost-of-living treadmill. I am equally determined to hold those brakes and hold them in place. They have supported this Administration's policies that have now given us the lowest rate of inflation and one of the highest rates of growth of any major industrial nation in the world, policies that are moving us toward our goal of full employment without war and without inflation—and that is a goal that we have not met since President Eisenhower was in the White House.

Most Americans are united in demanding respect for the law. They know that without law there can be no justice, without order there can be no progress. They support this Administration's all-out offensive against organized crime, against violence, against dangerous drugs and narcotics, and we are beginning to win the war against crime because of the united support of Americans.

We will not be satisfied until all our city streets are safe, until we have a system of courts that is once more capable of dispensing swift, fair justice to criminal and victim alike. That is my philosophy in appointing judges to the bench, from the Supreme Court on down. They must be qualified jurists, but they must be jurists who recognize that the first civil right of all Americans is the right to be free from domestic violence.

The new American majority knows that government ought to spring from the people. It should not be a distant alien force that dictates their everyday lives from afar. For far too long power has flowed from the people into the hands of Federal bureaucrats in Washington. And the new American majority has agreed that the time has come to reverse that flow away from Washington, back to the States, the counties, the cities, and to the people.

And together we have begun to succeed. The historic passage of revenue sharing, which this Administration has fought for for so long, means that more power and more tax dollars are now heading back where they belong, to local people and their locally elected leaders. The decision-making power, the means to carry out those decisions, are flowing back to the grassroots. This means better education, better setting of local priorities, more hope for our troubled State, city, and county governments, and an opportunity in the future for lower property taxes for the overburdened American homeowner.

Finally, I find that the American people today are united in their continued belief in honest hard work, love of country, spiritual faith.

What has made America the economic wonder of the world is not what government has done for people, but what people have done for themselves. That is why, while some politicians are calling for redistribution of income—seeking to reward those who do not work more than those who do—this Administration has stood with the new American majority. We know that it was the sacrifice and efforts of hard-working people that built America. We oppose those who would discour-age work and reward idleness.

America is a land of opportunity, not a land of handouts. Each of us deserves a fair chance to get ahead. But none of us has the right to expect a free ride—to remain idle, to take advantage of other men's labor.

Each of these basic points I have mentioned has played a part in creating the new American majority. Each of them reminds us that there is more that binds us together as a people than there is separating us.

My greatest hope for the coming elections is that we emerge from them a stronger, not a weaker, people—that when we look back at the 1972 elections we can point to them as a mandate for peace, for progress, and, above all, unity for Americans.

"This flag which we honor and under which we serve," said Woodrow Wilson, "is the emblem of the unity of our power, our thought and purpose as a nation. It has no other character than that which we give it from generation to generation. The choices are ours."

Once again this November, the choice is ours. And I urge each of you—whether you are a Democrat, a Republican, or an independent—to become a part of the new American majority, to help us keep on building a strong America, a just America—One America embodying the hopes and faith of all Americans.

Thank you, and good morning.

NOTE: The President spoke at 10:30 a.m. from the Library at the White House. The address was broadcast live on nationwide radio. Time for the broadcast was purchased by the Committee for the Re-Election of the President.

The President spoke from a prepared text. An advance text of his address was released on the same day.

381   Campaign Statement About Crime and Drug Abuse.
October 28, 1972

FROM the day we took office, this Administration has made the battle against crime and drug abuse one of our highest domestic priorities.

During the two preceding Administrations, serious crime in America had increased by 122 percent. Drug addiction had mushroomed into a national scandal during those permissive years, with the number of heroin addicts in this country more than doubling from 1965 to 1969.

Now, through the outstanding efforts of our local police forces and with massive Federal support, we have succeeded in stopping the spiraling growth in criminal activity. The FBI crime index showed an increase of only one percent for the first half of this year—the closest the Nation has come to an actual decrease since the index began 12 years ago. In nearly half of our Nation's largest cities—including Cleveland, Columbus, Youngstown, Akron, and Parma, Ohio—crime has already begun to decrease.

As a result of our total war on drug abuse, the rate of growth in new heroin addiction has declined dramatically since 1969. By next June, we will have created the capacity to treat up to 250,000 heroin addicts annually—a thirtyfold increase over the amount of federally funded drug treatment which existed when I took office.

A key to our successes against the drug menace has been the all-out attack on drug pushers. The pusher's crime is one of the most reprehensible known to man— the enslavement of other human beings to a life of degradation, dependence, and suffering. The punishment for this crime must be strict, and it must be certain.

We can be encouraged that Federal narcotics law enforcement officials are arresting pushers at twice the rate of the previous Administration, that illicit drug seizures have quadrupled in the past 4 years, and that more narcotics traffickers are being brought to justice than ever before.

Here in Ohio, the Federal Government has already put almost $6 million of treatment funds into communities across the State, with further grants nearing completion. The U.S. Office for Drug Abuse Law Enforcement, which I created last January, is currently working with State and local enforcement officials in Cleveland, Columbus, and Cincinnati to root out the heroin traffickers and bring them to justice.

Similar efforts are being pressed in other cities throughout the country, but much still remains to be done. To keep the pressure on, I intend to take the following steps:

—I will urge the Congress to appropriate whatever funds are needed for Federal drug law enforcement and to build the clinics needed to treat those addicts who seek help.

—I will expand our present massive funding for local law enforcement assistance, and will again ask the Congress to enact my proposal for law enforcement special revenue sharing.

—I will appoint judges who will help to strengthen the peace forces as against the criminal forces in our country, and who will oppose without equivocation the permissive trend toward light or suspended sentences for convicted drug pushers.

—I will ask the Congress to amend the Federal drug statutes so as to require tough, mandatory sentences for heroin traffickers.

—I will not hesitate to suspend all military and economic assistance to any country which condones or protects the international drug traffic.

—I will continue to carry out my 10-year reform program for the Federal prison system.

My goal for the next 4 years is for every American city to begin realizing the kind of victories in the war on crime which we have already achieved in the Nation's Capital—where the crime rate has been cut in half since my Administration took office, and where heroin overdose deaths have almost disappeared.

This kind of progress can and must be made all across America. By winning the war on crime and drugs, we can restore the social climate of order and justice which will assure our society of the freedom it must have to build and grow.

NOTE: The statement was released at Cleveland, Ohio, prior to an 85-mile Presidential motorcade through eastern Ohio communities between Cleveland and Youngstown.

382   Campaign Statement About the Nation's Economy. *October* 28, 1972

A DYNAMIC economic expansion is surging all across America. Today, more people are at work earning more real spendable income than ever before in our history. This record of economic success is particularly evident here in Ohio.

Across the entire State, more people are working than in 1971. And the rate of unemployment in Ohio—4.1 percent in the latest available measurement—is well below the 1971 Ohio rate.

In every major city in Ohio except one, in fact, the current unemployment is less than the national average and substantially below the Ohio rate of 1971. In Cleveland, the largest city, the rate was 4.0 percent according to the latest statistics.

Cleveland also is doing remarkably well at holding back the cost of living. In the latest available reports, prices were up only 2.4 percent over a year ago. That amounted to a reduction of more than half in the former 6.1-percent rate of price increase that was hitting the people of Cleveland 3 years ago.

Nationally, the evidence proves that our current economic policies are working to enable our people to produce a better material life for themselves and their families:

—In the past year, we have added $105 billion to our gross national product. That is a healthy 7-percent expansion rate.

—There are now 82 million Americans at work, an alltime record, and in the past year jobs increased by a near-record 2½ million.

—Real spendable earnings for the average production worker are rising at a rate of over 4 percent a year—the equivalent of two extra weekly paychecks.

—Continued strong economic activity in the future is assured by all advance indicators of job-building action. In August, for example, new orders for non-defense capital goods were 22 percent above the previous August. New plant and equipment expenditures are expected to rise about 10 percent this year, as compared with 2 percent in 1971. And all the indexes of business and consumer confidence are high.

All this heartening economic growth should be sending us this clear policy message: Continue on course. This is not a time to experiment with chancy economic theories or to add vast expenditures to the Federal budget and thereby force a tax increase. Either of these paths would upset the progress we are making and risk reversing our economic resurgence.

In Ohio, as in the Nation, we intend to keep pressing forward toward achieving what America has not had since President Eisenhower was in office—full employment without war and without significant inflation.

NOTE: The statement was released at Cleveland, Ohio, prior to an 85-mile Presidential motorcade through eastern Ohio communities between Cleveland and Youngstown.

383   Informal Remarks in North Royalton, Ohio. *October* 28, 1972

COULD I have your attention for just a moment please.

I wish that time would permit our stopping a little longer in each one of these wonderful towns that we have been traveling through today, but we have 4 hours of motorcading and each town is waiting.

I wanted to stop here for two reasons: one, to express my appreciation to you, to the mayor, to this marvelous band, and to all of the people that have come out and welcomed us so graciously.

Another reason—and I say this from having talked to my good friend and great supporter Bill Minshall, your Congressman, before, as we drove through Parma, Ohio—I saw that the flags were at half-mast. When I saw those flags at half-mast I asked one of our Secret Service men, a man who has given 30 years of his life to Government service and has risked his life many times, why the flags were at half-mast.

He told me that what had happened is that just 2 days ago a policeman, in the line of duty, trying to apprehend a criminal—who proved to be a criminal, certainly, by his actions in killing the policeman—was murdered. As a result, the town, of course, was paying its respects to that man of the law.

I just want to say this as I stand here in the presence of the United States Secret Service, people from the Sheriff's Department, and people in the Police Department: I just talked to a couple of the men in your Police Department, the Sheriff's Department. I said, "How do you like your job?" They said, "We like it fine."

Let me tell you, you can't pay these men what it is really worth. You can't pay a man enough who risks his life to help you keep your life. One thing you can do is this: Respect them, honor them. I have seen on occasion over these years sometimes some scroungy-looking people that are spitting on policemen and calling them pigs and the rest. It makes my blood boil.

When I think of that fine young man that was killed in Parma, Ohio, I say I am proud that in our Administration we have stood up for the men of law and order, and we are going to for the next 4 years.

NOTE: The President spoke at 1:30 p.m. in North Royalton where he made a brief stop during his motorcade through eastern Ohio.

384   Informal Exchange of Remarks in Mantua Corners, Ohio.   *October* 28, 1972

THE PRESIDENT. How are you? Your son lost in Vietnam? What year was he lost?

MRS. FRANK LORENCE. Nineteen sixty-nine.

THE PRESIDENT. Was he with the Army?

MRS. LORENCE. Yes. The Infantry.

THE PRESIDENT. The Infantry. Where did he serve?

MRS. LORENCE. The 25th. He was near Trang Bang.

THE PRESIDENT. Oh, I know Trang Bang. I have been there. I have been to that place, yes. I have been there quite often. I went up to see where the Army was. I have seen the Marines at Danang and all the rest, and they are wonderful men, all of them.

You know, we owe a great debt to your son and to all of them like him.

You are his father? Do you have other children? Did you serve, too? Where are your children? Isn't it wonderful that you have these other children and your grandchildren. You can be mighty proud of that fellow. He makes it possible for all others to grow up in a world that is going to be a little safer and perhaps more free from this kind of aggression. That is what it is all about. We wish we could bring him back. We are going to do everything we can to see that it doesn't happen to these boys, and no other boys. Right? That is what we are going to do.

Don't worry about that amnesty. Never. After all——

MRS. LORENCE. I don't want to feel like he went for nothing.

THE PRESIDENT. That's right. Some boys, you know, a lot of them hadn't made a choice, nobody really wants to go. They give up their lives, but they do it to serve their country, and the few hundred that deserted this country, the draft dodgers, are never going to get amnesty when boys like yours died, never. They are going to have to pay a penalty for what they did. That's the way I feel.

So we thank you for being such wonderful Americans. We thank your son for what he did for this country.

NOTE: The exchange of remarks took place at 4 p.m. when the President stopped his motorcade to talk with Mr. and Mrs. Lorence after seeing a sign they had prepared indicating that they had lost a son in Vietnam.

385   Informal Remarks in Warren, Ohio.
October 28, 1972

Mr. Mayor, and Congressman Stanton, Mrs. Stanton, Senator Taft:

I want you to know that as we complete our motorcade of the State of Ohio that it is a very great privilege for us to be here in Warren again.

I just told the mayor that I remember being in Warren in 1952, 1956, 1960. In all of those years we won. We are here in '72, and we think Warren is our lucky city in Ohio.

Also, I just gave the mayor a pen, one of the White House pens, and the revenue sharing bill that Bill Stanton, your Congressman, worked so hard for in the House, that we just signed, will soon be here in Warren, and he is going to use it to hire back some police and firemen they had to lay off. So Warren is going to be a greater city because of revenue sharing.

Most important of all, we want you to know that as we go through this campaign that we are glad we are here at a time that we have made a very significant breakthrough in bringing peace in Vietnam and building peace in the world.

And so, to all of you, we wish you the best next week. And vote on election day.

Thank you.

NOTE: The President spoke at 5:30 p.m. in Warren where he made a brief stop during his motorcade through eastern Ohio.

Arthur Richards was the mayor of Warren.

386   Campaign Statement About Federal Spending.
October 28, 1972

THE NUMBER ONE domestic issue of this election is the right of the working men and women of America to keep most of what they earn to spend as they choose, rather than seeing half of their earnings or more taxed away and given to someone else by bureaucrats in Washington.

A few politicians have called for huge new spending programs which would add as much as $150 billion to the Federal budget and would require the biggest tax increase in American history.

I have pledged to hold the line on taxes in 1973 and throughout my second term as President, assuming cooperation from the Congress.

I am committed to resisting with all the powers at my command any Federal spending which would confront us with the unacceptable choice between higher taxes, which would take more of the worker's paycheck, and renewed inflation, which would erode the buying power of that paycheck.

That is why I asked the Congress to place a $250 billion ceiling on Federal spending in the current fiscal year—which it refused to do. That is why I vetoed a number of budget-breaking money bills yesterday.

If we can succeed in keeping taxes from going any higher, and if we can continue gaining ground in the fight against rising prices—a fight which has cut the rate of inflation almost in half since 1969—then we can have the kind of vibrant, prosperous economic growth which generates real jobs and provides higher living standards for all Americans.

I believe that this country needs 4 more years of the solid pocketbook progress we have achieved this year, when real spendable earnings of the average wage earner have made their first major gains since 1965—a buying power increase equivalent to two extra weekly paychecks in a year.

I believe that Michigan needs more of the economic policies which have brought the gross weekly earnings of manufacturing workers here in Saginaw up more than 11 percent this August over last August, and which have cut inflation in the Detroit area from a rate of 6.1 percent during 1970 to 3.9 percent so far this year.

But I am far from satisfied with our record on combating inflation and on finding jobs for everyone who wants to work. We must do still better, and we shall.

In this effort, I hope to have the invaluable assistance of Senator Bob Griffin in the future as I have had it in the past.

From his key position on the Senate Finance Committee, Senator Griffin has supported my new economic policy; he has supported my efforts to clamp a tax-proof lid on the Federal budget; and he has fought for passage of general revenue sharing, the major new law I signed in Philadelphia last week, which can help to provide local tax relief and give the people of every city and State greater control over their own lives.

I consider him an exceptionally able advocate for the workingman and for Michigan, and a staunch ally in our battle against higher prices and higher taxes.

NOTE: The statement was released at Saginaw, Mich.

387   Remarks at Saginaw, Michigan.
October 28, 1972

THANK YOU. Could I have your attention for just a moment.

First I want to tell you that we are very sorry we were over an hour late, but there is a good reason. We were in Ohio. The crowds were so big that we couldn't get here until just now, and all that means is that we are going to have a big win in Ohio and a big win in Michigan.

Now I would like to say a word about all of those that are here today with us, to pay my respects, of course, to Governor Milliken, to pay my respects and express my appreciation to the Members of the Congress who are represented here, to Garry Brown, Al Cederberg, Mrs. Jim Harvey, who is here although her husband could not be here because he is a little under the weather, but boy, he is really there when it counts on the votes in the United States Congress.

But particularly I am here in Michigan to ask for your support not only of our ticket, but also for your support of these Members of the House of Representatives to whom I have referred, and particularly for a Member of the United States Senate. I want to say a word about the United States Senate because I know it well. I was a Member of the Senate before the people in that band, that marvelous band over there, were born. I remember the years 1950, '51. The Senate is a great body. I presided over it for 8 years as Vice

President. In the past 4 years, of course, I have worked with the Senate and with the House of Representatives for what I have thought and what they have thought were the interests of the Nation.

Let me tell you a thing about the Senate. It is considered to be the most exclusive club in the world. Now Members of the House won't agree with that, but at least the Senate is smaller. There are 100 Members of the Senate, two from each State, as you know. I can tell you that of those 100 Members there are five Members of the Senate who are the big men. They are the ones that will determine the future of this country, and one of those five is Michigan's Bob Griffin. I need him in the Senate, Michigan needs him in the Senate, America needs him in the Senate.

Let me tell you just a word about what Bob Griffin has worked for, what these Members of the Congress have worked for, and what we are going to work for in these next 4 years. First, I have noted the interest that everybody here and interest that I have seen all over Ohio today in what every American wants, and that means peace, just not now, but for a generation to come. As you know, we have made a very significant breakthrough in the negotiations. As you know, we now can look forward with confidence to winning the kind of peace in Vietnam that all Americans want, and that is the kind of a peace Bob Griffin has worked for and supported—peace with honor and not peace with surrender.

But beyond that, Vietnam being over, we are proud of the fact that our trips to Peking and to Moscow have paved the way not just for ending this war, but for a generation of peace so that those young people that we see over here can have something that we have not had in this century in America: a full generation without war. We have a beginning, but we need to continue, and we ask for your help to continue to work for a generation of peace over these next 4 years. I pledge you, that is what we are going to work for.

If we are going to have it, we need a strong America. Don't listen to the voices of those that would have America have the second strongest army, the second strongest navy, the second strongest air force in the world.

Let me tell you, that when it comes to football we, of course, can take a little pride in whether we are number one or number two, but let's make sure that the United States is never number two in the world so that the United States can continue to lead the world to peace.

Then here at home, could I say a word about Bob Griffin and his leadership in the Senate? Everybody in this great tri-city area, in this State of Michigan, that contributes so much to the economy of this country, is interested in jobs. But you want peacetime jobs. Our goal is full employment without war and without inflation, something we have not had in America since Dwight Eisenhower was President. We can have it again, but we need your help. We need Bob Griffin's help in the United States Senate and these men that I have mentioned for the Congress of the United States.

But jobs, as good as they are—and I know they are very good in this State—let me tell you they don't mean anything if your income is eaten up by higher prices or higher taxes.

I think that government in Washington has grown too big. Bob Griffin agrees. I believe that the Government in Washington is taking too much money out of your pocket. He agrees. He has been a strong man in voting against more spending in Washington so that you can spend more here in Michigan. We are for that, and I hope that you will send him back so he can continue to work for that cause.

Finally, let me say a word on another subject that is of great interest to everybody here in this State—I know that it is not one of particular concern in this area—and it is that of education, to which I addressed myself just a few days ago on radio. The best education is the education you get in the school that is closest to your home. The Senate needs Bob Griffin standing against any kind of program that would bus children away from their homes across town. We need him in the United States Senate for that kind of leadership. We also need him because we can have peace abroad, we can have good jobs, and it isn't going to mean anything if our cities are ridden over with crime and drugs and all the other things which are part of modern life.

Let me tell you, there is no man in this country today who, with his legal background, gives us better leadership, as he does in the United States Senate, than Bob Griffin, in developing that kind of support we need for strong judges that will strengthen the peace forces as against the criminal forces in this country. We need him in the Senate for that.

If he would step up here for one moment—let me just close with one word. In speaking of him, I speak of all of those who support these principles that I have spoken of. These are not partisan principles. Democrats as well as Republicans want peace in the world. Democrats as well as Republicans want jobs and prosperity, without war and without inflation. Democrats as well as Republicans want good education, education close to home and not clear across town. Democrats as well as Republicans want progress, progress for their children and their children's children in the years to come.

One of the things that impresses anyone who runs for any office, and particularly for President, is to see the wonderful young people that we have seen by the hundreds of thousands today, and the thousands here today, let me tell you what I feel at a moment like this. I know many of you have been here for almost 4 hours. I know that you didn't even know that we were going to have a meeting here until yesterday. Thank you for coming. Thank you for coming.

Let me tell you, I realize that for many who are here, who are 18, 19, and 20, this is the first time you will have had an opportunity to vote. I want your first vote to be remembered as one of your best votes. I want the next 4 years and Bob Griffin wants the next 4 years to be the best 4 years in this country's history.

Thank you.

NOTE: The President spoke at 6:30 p.m. at a rally at the Tri-City Airport which serves Saginaw, Bay City, and Midland. He spoke without referring to notes.

388   Radio Address on Defense Policy. *October* 29, 1972

Good afternoon:

I want to talk to you this afternoon about national defense. Defense policy is the most important single issue in this election. It represents a choice which must be made not on the basis of name-calling or appeals to emotion, but on the basis of thoughtful analysis of the alternatives. That is the purpose of my talk this afternoon.

When a President thinks of his responsibilities to the American people, he must think first of all about the need to keep this country strong, about the need to maintain a national defense second to none in the world.

A President also has an obligation to spend no more of the Nation's limited resources on defense than is absolutely required, because he knows there are other urgent human needs to be met.

Today, no nation on earth is more powerful than the United States. Not only are our nuclear deterrent forces fully sufficient for their role in keeping the peace, our conventional forces also are modern, strong, prepared, and credible to any adversary.

During the past 4 years, however, because of the progress we have made in bringing the Vietnam war to an honorable conclusion and in reducing tensions among the great powers, we have also been able to reduce substantially the size of our military establishment.

We have reduced our total military manpower by nearly one-third from the 1968 level. We have closed large numbers of unneeded military bases and installations. Under the Nixon Doctrine, we have successfully persuaded our allies to take up a greater share of the free world defense burden than they have in the past.

Before we took office, less than a third of every dollar the Federal Government spent was devoted to human resources, while close to half of every budget dollar was spent for defense. Today those proportions are reversed, with the military

down to a third and human resources getting nearly a half.

Most important, all of this has been achieved without jeopardizing our security and without betraying our allies.

But now in this campaign our opponents have proposed massive new cuts in military spending—cuts which would drastically slash away not just the fat but the very muscle of our defense.

These are the specific proposals they have made: America's strategic bomber force would be cut by 60 percent, our tactical air wings by 30 percent, development of the new B–1 bomber would be canceled.

The number of Navy warships would be cut almost in half. Our aircraft carrier fleet would be cut from 16 to 6. They would cut the Marine Corps by almost one-third. The 7th Fleet in the Far East and the 6th Fleet in the Mediterranean would be sharply reduced and weakened.

Missile modernization programs like the Minuteman III and the Poseidon would be halted.

The result would be to leave America with the second strongest army, the second strongest navy, the second strongest air force in the world.

Now some might ask, what is wrong with being second? Isn't it jingoistic and nationalistic for the United States always to have to be number one?

The answer to that question is that the day the United States becomes the second strongest nation in the world, peace and freedom will be in deadly jeopardy everywhere in the world.

We do not seek power for its own sake. What we seek is the assurance that our survival and that of other free nations will never be threatened by some other nation whose intentions are less peaceful than ours, and whose military forces are more powerful than those of the United States.

History has taught us again and again that war is caused not by the strength of one nation alone, but by the weakness of one nation in relation to another.

Last spring in Moscow I signed an agreement for the limitation of offensive and defensive nuclear weapons on the part of the United States and the Soviet Union. We would never have reached that agreement if the United States had unilaterally given up the ABM as some had recommended, or if we had begun stripping away our offensive missile forces.

If we were to take such action now, we would destroy any chance for further arms limitations in the second round of strategic nuclear arms limitation talks which are to begin with the Sovet Union next month. If we unilaterally reduced the forces now supporting our NATO allies in Western Europe, as has also been proposed by our opponents, we would throw away the prospect of mutual and balanced reductions of Soviet forces in Eastern Europe.

Strength and resolution command respect. They are an incentive for negotiation leading to peace. But weakness and naive sentimentality breed contempt. They are an open invitation to pressure tactics and aggression leading to war.

That is why I say let us never send the President of the United States to the conference table as the head of the second strongest nation in the world.

It may be argued that as long as we have our nuclear weapons we have nothing to worry about. Because the United States relied heavily on a deterrent policy of massive nuclear retaliation during the 1950's, this theory says, we can safely gut our conventional forces today and go back

to the policy of massive nuclear retaliation in the 1970's.

The flaw in that argument is that during the Eisenhower years the United States held a 15 to 1 or even a 20 to 1 ratio of nuclear superiority over the Soviet Union. Massive retaliation was credible then, in the 1950's, and it was credible during the Cuban missile crisis of 1962, when our nuclear advantage was about 8 to 1. No enemy would dare to test such overwhelming odds.

However, when I came into office in January 1969, I found that this massive nuclear superiority no longer existed. For 6 years the Soviet Union had moved forward with a massive buildup of their nuclear forces, while the United States was standing still. As a result, today the United States and the Soviet Union are equal in nuclear capability.

It has, therefore, become totally unrealistic to believe that we could any longer deter aggression against a small nation, particularly one whose survival did not directly affect our own survival, if our only option were a nuclear retaliation which would lead to nuclear suicide for the United States.

The mutual destruction would be too great, and both sides would know it. No potential aggressor would respect America's security commitments to our friends and allies under those conditions.

The Middle East is an example. In the fall of 1970, when Syrian tanks poured into Jordan, what might have become a grave world crisis was quietly defused by the movement of the United States 6th Fleet into the eastern Mediterranean. The possibility of a war which could have threatened the existence of Israel and dragged in the great powers was averted.

American naval superiority kept the

peace in that situation, where nuclear threats would have been powerless to do so. That is why, for the sake of Israel and other small nations we are committed to defend, as well as for our own sake, we must never give up our superiority on the sea and in the air in the name of false economy.

The time has come to stand up and answer those of our own countrymen who complain that American power is an evil force in the world, those who say that our foreign policy is selfish and bad.

We can be proud of the fact that in four wars in this century the United States has fought only to defend freedom, never to destroy it; only to keep the peace, never to break it.

The men and women who have fought in those wars deserve the highest respect this Nation can pay them, as do those who serve in our peace forces today and those who will serve in years to come as we end the draft next summer and move to a volunteer armed force. They are the real heroes of our time.

Rather than talking about amnesty for a few hundred who chose to desert America, let us honor the millions who chose to serve America in Vietnam. As this long and difficult war draws to an end, it is time to draw the line on this issue once and for all. There will be no amnesty for draft dodgers and deserters after the war.

Millions of Americans chose to serve their country in Vietnam. Many gave their lives for their choice. The few hundred who refused to serve, or who deserted their country, must pay a penalty for their choice.

A few days before I left for Peking last February, I had as a guest at the White House the brilliant French thinker and statesman André Malraux. Let me share with you a comment which he made to me that night.

"The United States," he said, "is the only nation ever to become the most powerful in the world without seeking to."

Think for a moment of how true this statement is and what it means. This country did not push its way to the position of world leadership which we have occupied for a generation. That position came to us unsought, but we have borne it nobly and well, guided not by ambition or greed or ideology, but only by the high ideals of human liberty and lasting peace.

Uniquely among the great powers of the world in our own time or in any previous time, the United States is trusted with power by all the peoples of the earth. No nation which refrains from aggression against its neighbors has anything to fear from America, and all nations know that is true.

For the United States to abdicate its leadership role in the world, or to attempt to meet its responsibilities through good intentions alone, without the backing of a strong defense, would be one of the greatest tragedies of history.

Let us never go down that road. That is the road which led an unprepared America into two world wars earlier in this century.

Let us remain instead on the high road of peace through strength, the road mapped out by five successive Presidents in our time, Democrats and Republicans alike—by Franklin D. Roosevelt, Harry Truman, Dwight Eisenhower, John Kennedy, Lyndon Johnson.

As long as I am your President, I shall keep America on that road. I shall keep this country strong militarily, strong economically, and strong in the moral values and the trust in God which is our ultimate defense.

Only in this way can we make certain that the 1970's will not be the twilight of America's greatness, but the dawn of a new age; not a time of tension and turmoil, but the beginning of a full generation of peace for us and for all mankind.

Thank you, and good afternoon.

NOTE: The President spoke at 12:07 p.m. from the Library at the White House. The address was broadcast live on nationwide radio. Time for the broadcast was purchased by the Committee for the Re-Election of the President.

The President spoke from a prepared text. An advance text of his address was released on the same day.

389   Statement on Signing the Social Security Amendments of 1972.   *October* 30, 1972

IT GIVES me very great pleasure to sign H.R. 1, landmark legislation that will end many old inequities and will provide a new uniform system of well-earned benefits for older Americans, the blind, and the disabled. This bill contains many improvements and expansions of the social security, Medicare, and Medicaid programs which this Administration recommended and is proud to bring into reality today.

But this legislation aims at goals which are larger than the sum of all of its various program improvements:

—It represents another step in my effort to end the gap that separates far too many older Americans from the mainstream of American life.

—It furthers my concept that, rather than being viewed as a problem, older Americans should be recognized and utilized as a priceless American resource whose energy, ideals, and commitment the Nation needs. But first they have to be protected against both the realities and the fears of income and health problems—and this bill will do much to advance such protections.

—It reaffirms and reinforces America's traditional efforts to assist those of our citizens who, through no fault of their own, are unable to help themselves. America has always cared for its aged poor, the blind, and the disabled—and this bill will move that concern to higher ground by providing better and more equitable benefits.

—Finally, it supports my conviction that the best way to help people in need is not with a vast array of bureaucratic services, but by providing them money and insurance so that they can secure needed services themselves.

H.R. 1's cost has always been a part of my budget estimates for fiscal year 1973. Due to its late enactment, the bill will actually provide a $900 million surplus over the additional outlays in fiscal year 1973.

Therefore, I am able to sign this bill without violating my promise to hold down Federal spending in order to avoid a general tax increase.

The social security taxes imposed by this bill, to pay for these benefits, also were included in my fiscal year 1973 budget estimates.

H.R. 1, as enacted, does not contain my proposals for reforming the welfare system for families with dependent children. This is a deep disappointment to all—including the taxpayers—who are the victims of the existing welfare mess.

In the next Congress, I will renew my efforts to achieve a work-oriented welfare program that will help all deserving people on a fair and equitable basis—but which will contain firm work requirements, and will not encourage idleness by making it more profitable to go on welfare than to work.

Despite this major omission, H.R. 1 does give life to many of my recommendations to improve the quality of life for older Americans, the blind, and the disabled.

Social Security—It provides increased benefits for 3.8 million widows and widowers; it liberalizes the retirement earnings test by increasing from $1,680 to $2,100 the amount a beneficiary can earn without having benefits reduced, a provision that will aid 1.6 million persons; it establishes a special minimum benefit of $170 per month for 150,000 persons who have worked for long years at low wages; and it improves benefits for men retiring at age 62 and for those who work beyond 65.

Medicare/Medicaid—It extends Medicare to cover 1.5 million social security disability beneficiaries; it limits the monthly premium under Part B of Medicare, an expense I had urged be eliminated; it permits optional Medicare coverage through health maintenance organizations; and it extends Medicare coverage for kidney transplants and renal dialysis—the cost of which is beyond most individuals—to workers under social security, and their dependents.

I am especially pleased that this legislation embodies my recommendation that the Federal Government bear the full cost

of skilled nursing home inspectors to ensure that all such institutions meet the standards that a dignified and humane existence—and the law—require.

Many of our nursing homes are of good quality. But many others fall woefully short of standards, and many patients are forced to live their later years in institutions which are unsanitary and unsafe, overcrowded and understaffed. This intensified inspection program will help clean up such neglect and degradation.

H.R. 1 also contains an important provision, sponsored by Senator Wallace Bennett of Utah, for the mandatory establishment of Professional Standards Review Organizations which will review the medical necessity, appropriateness, and quality of services covered under Medicare and Medicaid. This will assure that patients are getting exactly what they need—and nothing which they do not need—with the highest possible quality of care all along the line.

The Needy Aged, Blind, and Disabled—H.R. 1 will establish, beginning January 1, 1974, a nationally uniform system of benefits for people in these groups. As delegates to the White House Conference on Aging pointed out, these people now are subject to great inequities and considerable redtape inherent in the present system of varying State programs with different benefits, eligibility standards, and rules. The cost of this measure for calendar year 1974 is estimated to be $1.5 billion over what is being spent under the current law.

The new national plan—one I have long urged upon the Congress—will provide a minimum monthly benefit of $130 for an individual and $195 for a couple. States currently paying higher benefits would be encouraged to continue to do so by Federal assumption of any new costs involved.

This entire program will be fully financed by the Federal Government and efficiently executed with a minimum of paperwork by the Social Security Administration.

This legislation once again provides dramatic and heart-warming evidence that America is the country that cares— and translates that humanitarian care into a better life for those who need, and de-serve, the support of their fellow citizens. The American way of life is the high achievement of our era and the envy of the world, and responsive and responsible legislation such as this is one major reason why.

I am highly gratified to be able, at long last, to put my signature on H.R. 1—thus lifting these long-sought benefits out of debate and placing them into the laws of our generous and compassionate land.

NOTE: As enacted, H.R. 1 is Public Law 92–603 (86 Stat. 1329).

---

390   Statement About Decision To Sign Additional Bills Passed by the Congress.   *October 30, 1972*

LAST Saturday, I commented on several of the bills which passed the Congress during its closing days and which I decided to approve. Today I am announcing a number of additional decisions concerning bills which have come to me for signature.

A list of the additional legislation which I am signing will be released with this statement.

I am taking this opportunity to comment on some of the most significant bills which are included on that list.

HELPING MINORITY ENTERPRISES AND OTHER SMALL BUSINESSES

In messages to the Congress in late 1971 and early 1972, I requested that our program to help minority enterprise be strengthened by giving four new authorities to Minority Enterprise Small Business Investment Companies. S. 3337, the Small Business Investment Act Amendments of 1972, adopts all four of these recommendations—lowering requirements for Fed-eral assistance, providing increased equity by enabling the Small Business Administration to purchase preferred stock in such a company, lowering interest rates on SBA loans to such companies, and allowing them to organize as nonprofit corporations so as to qualify for more favorable tax treatment. It also strengthens regular Small Business Investment Companies, permitting maximum utilization of the SBIC guarantee authority which this Administration had earlier sought, and which was enacted last year. As a result of this bill, more Americans—especially disadvantaged Americans—will be able to gain a piece of the economic action in our country, and we will be closer to our goal of providing an equal opportunity for every citizen to share fully in the great American adventure.

MEETING HEALTH NEEDS

The Emergency Health Personnel Act Amendments of 1972, S. 3858, will strengthen and extend the life of the

National Health Service Corps which has been working for the last 2 years to meet the needs of areas with critical health manpower shortages. In order to improve recruitment for this program, the bill also authorizes a program of scholarships for students in the health professions. This legislation addresses a need which has concerned me for a long time, and I am pleased to sign it into law.

Another important initiative in the health field is H.R. 15475, a bill which establishes a National Advisory Commission on Multiple Sclerosis to help determine the most effective means for finding the causes and cures for this disease. It represents a promising step in our battle against a terrible and elusive enemy, and I am happy to give it my approval.

OTHER FORWARD STEPS

Among the many other bills receiving my approval are S. 2318, which will update and expand compensation benefits for longshoremen and harbor workers; S. 3843, which helps restore and replace essential railway facilities and equipment which were damaged during Hurricane Agnes and other natural disasters this past June; H.R. 8273, which liberalizes the Immigration and Nationality Act; and H.R. 15461, which implements the boundary treaty which our Government signed with Mexico in 1970. Another significant forward step is the creation, by H.R. 10751, of the Pennsylvania Avenue Development Corporation, a measure which I discussed in a separate statement last week.

One of the purposes of another of these bills, H.R. 4678, is to prohibit the importation into the United States of precious pre-Columbian art treasures illegally re-

moved from their countries of origin— our close friends and neighbors of Central America. It is with special pleasure that I sign this legislation.

I am also very happy to sign H.R. 14911, which will allow prisoners of war and those who are missing in action to accumulate military leave time at the normal rate without limitation, so that they or their survivors can be more generously reimbursed when they are returned from prisoner-of-war or missing status. This same bill also carries out another Administration recommendation by authorizing a second Deputy Secretary of Defense to be appointed by the President.

NOTE: The list of bills referred to in the statement also included the following:

H.J. Res. 733, granting the consent of Congress to certain boundary agreements between the States of Maryland and Virginia

H.J. Res. 912, granting the consent of Congress to an agreement between the States of North Carolina and Virginia establishing their lateral seaward boundary

H.R. 1467, amending the Internal Revenue Code of 1954 with respect to personal exemptions for American Samoans

H.R. 3786, providing for the free entry of a four octave carillon for the use of Marquette University in Wisconsin

H.R. 7093, providing for the disposition of judgment funds of the Osage Tribe of Indians of Oklahoma

H.R. 10556, authorizing the Secretary of the Interior to sell reserved mineral interests of the United States in certain land in Georgia to Thomas A. Buiso

H.R. 10638, providing for the relief of John P. Woodson, his heirs, successors in interest or assigns

H.R. 11563, waiving employee deductions for Federal Employees' Group Life Insurance purposes during a period of erroneous removal or suspension

H.R. 11773, relating to exclusion of D.C. Metropolitan Police Department personnel records from public inspection

H.R. 12807, establishing Federal policy for

selection of firms and individuals to perform architectural, engineering, and related services for the Federal Government

H.R. 13158, naming a bridge across the Oakland tidal canal the George P. Miller-Leland W. Sweeney Bridge

H.R. 14542, extending period for increase in the authorized numbers of certain grades of Air Force officers

H.R. 14628, amending the Internal Revenue Code of 1954 with respect to the tax laws applicable to Guam

H.R. 15735, authorizing the transfer of a vessel by the Secretary of Commerce to the New York City Board of Education for educational purposes

H.R. 15763, providing for additional members of the National Historical Publications Commission

H.R. 16074, authorizing appropriations for jellyfish control programs

H.R. 16804, renaming the Mineola Dam and Lake as the Carl L. Estes Dam and Lake

H.R. 16883, relating to compensation of members of the National Commission on the Financing of Postsecondary Education

H.R. 16925, extending authority for special pay for nuclear-qualified naval personnel

H.R. 17034, Supplemental Appropriations Act, 1973

H.R. 17038, designating the Oakley Reservoir on the Sangamon River, Decatur, Ill., as the William L. Springer Lake

S. 216, permitting suits to adjudicate certain real property quiet title actions

S. 655, providing for the relief of certain postal employees at the Elmhurst, Ill., Post Office

S. 909, providing for the relief of John C. Rogers

S. 1462, providing for the disposition of funds appropriated to pay judgment in favor of the Mississippi Sioux Indians

S. 1524, providing a limitation of actions for actions arising out of death or injury caused by a defective or unsafe improvement to real property

S. 1971, declaring a portion of the Delaware River in Philadelphia County, Pa., nonnavigable

S. 2147, providing for the relief of Marie M. Ridgely

S. 2270, providing for the relief of Magnus David Forrester

S. 2275, providing for the relief of Wolfgang Kutter

S. 2469, providing for the relief of Kenneth J. Wolff

S. 2714, providing for the relief of M. Sgt. William C. Harpold, USMC (retired)

S. 2741, expanding the program authorizing aircraft loan guarantees

S. 2753, providing for the relief of John C. Mayoros

S. 2822, providing for the relief of Alberto Rodriguez

S. 3055, providing for the relief of Maurice Marchbanks

S. 3230, providing for the division and disposition of funds appropriated to pay a judgment in favor of the Assiniboine Tribes of the Fort Peck and Fort Belknap Reservations, Mont.

S. 3240, Transportation Payment Act of 1972

S. 3257, providing for the relief of Gary Wentworth

S. 3310, establishing the authorized strength of Naval Reserve officers in the Judge Advocate General's Corps in the grade of rear admiral

S. 3326, providing for the relief of the Appalachian Regional Hospitals, Incorporated

S. 3483, providing for the relief of Cass County, N. Dak.

S. 3524, extending the provisions of the Commercial Fisheries Research and Development Act of 1964

S. 3545, amending the Fishermen's Protective Act of 1967

S. 3583, providing for the relief of Gerald Vincent Bull

S. 3671, amending the provisions of law relating to the Administrative Conference of the United States

S. 3822, authorizing the City of Clinton Bridge Commission to convey its bridge structures and other assets to the State of Iowa and to provide for the completion of interstate bridge facilities across the Mississippi River near Clinton, Iowa

S.J. Res. 204, authorizing the preparation of a history of public works in the United States

S.J. Res. 221, designating Benjamin Franklin Memorial Hall in Philadelphia as the Benjamin Franklin National Memorial

On October 30, 1972, the White House released the transcript of a news briefing on the President's decision to approve the bills by John D. Ehrlichman, Assistant to the President for Domestic Affairs, and Elliot L. Richardson, Secretary of Health, Education, and Welfare.

391 Memorandum of Disapproval of Two Bills Concerned With Programs for the Elderly. *October 30, 1972*

I HAVE announced today the signing of H.R. 1—a bill which represents a tremendous forward step in improving the income position and health services for older Americans. Two other bills concerning the elderly have also come to me for signature—the Older Americans Comprehensive Service Amendments of 1972 (H.R. 15657) and the Research on Aging Act of 1972 (H.R. 14424). Although I support some of the goals of these two bills, careful review has persuaded me that neither bill provides the best means of achieving these goals. Both authorize unbudgeted and excessive expenditures and would also require duplications or fragmentations of effort which would actually impair our efforts to serve older Americans more effectively. I have decided therefore to withhold my approval from these two pieces of legislation

to broaden the highly successful Foster Grandparents Program. The Administration will continue its vigorous pursuit of both these objectives.

However, the Congress added to the bill containing these provisions a range of narrow, categorical service programs which would seriously interfere with our effort to develop coordinated services for older persons. This is particularly the case with two categorical manpower programs which were added on the floor of the Senate and were considered without regard to manpower programs already serving older persons. Furthermore, this bill would authorize new funding of more than $2 billion between now and fiscal year 1975—far beyond what can be used effectively and responsibly.

I cannot responsibly approve H.R. 15657.

OLDER AMERICANS COMPREHENSIVE SERVICE AMENDMENTS OF 1972 (H.R. 15657)

Last March, I submitted to the Congress a plan for strengthening and expanding service delivery programs under the Older Americans Act. This program would begin the development of more comprehensive and better coordinated systems for delivering services at the local level. In addition, I submitted a proposal

RESEARCH ON AGING ACT OF 1972 (H.R. 14424)

In my Special Message to the Congress on Older Americans last March, I also emphasized the need to develop a comprehensive, coordinated program of aging research—one which includes disciplines ranging from biomedical research to transportation systems analysis, from psychology and sociology to management science and economics. The Secretary of

Health, Education and Welfare has since appointed a new Technical Advisory Committee for Aging Research to develop a plan for bringing together all the resources available to the Federal Government in the aging research field.

H.R. 14424, however, would set up an entirely separate aging research institute that would duplicate these activities. This bill would create additional administrative costs without enhancing the conduct of biomedical research for the aging. In fact, it could even fragment existing research efforts. This bill also contains a new grant program for mental health facilities for the aging which duplicates the more general and flexible authorities contained in the Community Mental Health Centers Act.

In sum, I feel that both research and mental health programs for the aging should be carried out in the broader context of research on life-span processes and comprehensive mental health treatment programs now underway.

H.R. 14424 would not enhance and could inhibit Federal efforts to respond to the needs of the elderly, and I cannot give it my approval.

RICHARD NIXON

The White House,
      October 30, 1972.

392   Statement About the Commuter Train Wreck in Chicago.   *October* 30, 1972

I WANT to express my deepest sympathy and concern over the tragic accident in Chicago this morning which has cost so many lives and inflicted so much suffering. The heart of the Nation goes out to the victims of this tragedy and to the people of Chicago.

NOTE: The statement was read by Press Secretary Ronald L. Ziegler during his regular news briefing at the White House on October 30, 1972.

An Illinois Central commuter train traveling toward the downtown area crashed into the rear of another train at Chicago's 27th Street Station, killing at least 44 persons and injuring over 300.

Mr. Ziegler announced that the President, shortly after the accident, dispatched Secretary of Transportation John A. Volpe to Chicago to survey the damage firsthand. In addition, Mr. Ziegler said that because of the tragedy, the President had canceled plans to visit Chicago on Tuesday, October 31. The visit was later rescheduled for Friday, November 3.

393   Radio Address on Older Americans.   *October* 30, 1972

Good afternoon:

A President signs many bills, but one that I signed today gave me special satisfaction because of the enormous impact it can have on the lives of millions of individual Americans.

I refer to the legislation known as H.R. 1—and especially to its provisions for helping older Americans.[1] Many of these provisions grew out of recommenda-

---

[1] See Item 389.

tions which I have been urging the Congress to act on for several years.

Let's look at some of the things H.R. 1 will do:

First, nearly 4 million widows and widowers will get larger social security benefits—the full 100 percent of what was payable to the individual's late husband or wife. This will mean more than $1 billion in additional income for these deserving people in the next fiscal year.

Second, over a million and a half older Americans who are now working can earn more income without having their benefits reduced.

Until today, if you were receiving social security, every dollar you earned above $1,680 cost you 50 cents in benefits—and every dollar you earned above $2,880 cost you a full dollar. But under the new provision—which I have advocated for years—you can earn up to $2,100 without losing a cent of social security, and every dollar you earn above that $2,100—no matter how many—will cost you only 50 cents in benefits. This will encourage more older Americans to work—helping them and helping the country.

Third, millions of older Americans who live in poverty, along with the blind and the disabled, will be helped by a new Federal floor under their income—a monthly minimum of $130 for an individual and $195 for a couple. Free of the inequities and redtape which plague the present system, this program will channel an estimated $1 billion in the next fiscal year to those whose needs are greatest. For millions of older people, it can mean a big step out of poverty and toward a life of dignity and independence.

In addition, H.R. 1 will pay a special minimum benefit of $170 per month to 150,000 older persons who worked for long years at low wages. Men who retire at 62 will also be helped. Medicare coverage will be extended to cover 100 percent and not just 80 percent of home health services, and to cover more of the cost of nursing home care, to pay for kidney transplants, chiropractors, and other services formerly not covered at all, and to cover disabled Americans of all ages. The patient's fees for Part B of Medicare will be limited. And steps will be taken to increase the quality and the appropriateness of services which are paid for by Medicare and Medicaid.

Altogether, H.R. 1 will improve the income position of millions of older Americans. That, in my judgment, is the best way to help older people—by providing them with more money so they can do more things for themselves.

H.R. 1 is only the latest in a series of steps we have taken to improve the incomes of older people. In the last 4 years, for example, social security benefits have gone up 51 percent. That is the largest and most rapid increase in history. But the important thing is not just that benefits have been brought up to date. The important thing is that they now can be kept up to date. That is a result of the automatic increase provisions which I have been pushing for many years and which finally became law this summer.

Social security, in short, is now "inflation proof." Payments that keep pace with the cost of living are no longer something the elderly have to battle for in the Congress year after year. They have at last become a guaranteed right for older Americans.

There have been other forward steps as well—proposals to make private pension programs more comprehensive and more reliable, for example, and to let older people receive more tax-free income.

Inflation is a special menace to the income of older Americans. Since 1969, we have cut the rate of inflation almost in half. In the area of medical care prices, we have cut inflation by nearly two-thirds—an achievement which is particularly important to older people because they spend more than three times as much per capita on health care as do younger people.

And we are also moving to relieve the property tax burden which falls so heavily on older citizens. Two-thirds of older Americans own their own homes. Yet, even when their income has gone down because of retirement, their property taxes have kept going up—by more than 100 percent in the last 10 years. The result: The home which was once a symbol of financial independence too often becomes a cause of financial hardship.

There are over 6 million American homeowners who are more than 65 years old. More than one million of these retired Americans live in their own homes on an income of less than $2,000 a year. In the Northeast, to take one example, these elderly citizens are paying an average of 30 percent of their income in property taxes.

This is wrong. We must stop it. One of my highest priority proposals to the new Congress will be property tax relief for older Americans.

Another problem which is of critical concern for older Americans—and for this Administration—is the quality of our nursing homes. Many of them are doing a good job, but too many have been below recent and decent standards. In 1971, I

launched a new eight-point action plan to change this.[2] Under that plan, we have already cut off Federal funding to hundreds of hopelessly inferior homes. H.R. 1 will permit the hiring and training of 2,000 inspectors to enforce strict regulations. And we have substantially expanded Federal efforts to make all nursing homes brighter and better places.

We also want to help more older Americans live decent, dignified lives in the familiar settings of their own homes. This is why we have increased budgeting under the Older Americans Act eightfold in the last 4 years, expanding a wide range of services in fields such as health, education, homemaking, counseling, and nutrition.

While the Older Americans bill is being perfected in the months ahead, these programs will all move forward under a continuing resolution. We have also taken special steps to fight crime in areas where older people are living, to provide more housing and transportation for older people, to fight job discrimination based on age, and to expand opportunities for older people to find self-fulfillment in useful voluntary action. We have doubled the budget for the Foster Grandparent Program. We have tripled the budget for the Retired Senior Volunteer Program.

---

[2] See 1971 volume, Items 259 and 260.

On July 19, 1972, the White House released a fact sheet on progress on the eight-point improvement program for nursing homes and the transcript of a news briefing on a meeting with the President to report on the program. Participants in the news briefing were John G. Veneman, Under Secretary, Dr. Merlin K. DuVal, Jr., Assistant Secretary for Health and Scientific Affairs, and Dr. Marie Callender, Special Assistant for Nursing Home Affairs, Department of Health, Education, and Welfare; and Arthur S. Flemming, Special Consultant to the President on Aging.

This summer I launched a new program called Project FIND.[3] Its purposes were expressed in its name—to "find" older people who are so isolated that they are not receiving the help which should be theirs.

The results have been remarkable. One and a half million names have already come in to us. And now, with the help of the American Red Cross, we are mobilizing an army of 20,000 volunteers to make personal contact with each one of these elderly persons.

Already over 300,000 contacts have been made. In Des Moines, for example, a group of high school students has been giving many hours a week to visiting older people. One girl, Carol Clayton, discovered a 79-year-old man a few weeks ago who spoke only Spanish. He lived on very little income, and he had never heard about food stamps. And now, as a result of Project FIND, Trinidad Medina has made contact with the Polk County Department of Social Services. Just as importantly, he has made a friend, Carol Clayton. He can't communicate with her in English, but with the help of his Spanish guitar, he has no trouble communicating friendship.

This, in the final analysis, is what our programs to help older people are all about: not lines on an organization chart, or numbers in a budget, but helping individual men and women live fuller, richer lives.

In less than 4 weeks, we will celebrate another Thanksgiving. Our family will think back to our first Thanksgiving in

the White House 3 years ago. Our guests that day were over 200 older Americans. When I talked with them, I found that many were particularly excited about the Moon walks that they had recently watched on television. And it occurred to me on that day that most of our guests could also remember the first airplane flight by the Wright Brothers at Kitty Hawk, over a half century ago.

Our older generation has lived through the greatest period of change in human history. They have brought our Nation through all that change with colors flying. We owe them more than we can ever repay.

But when we think of older Americans, we must not think only about what they have already given. We must also think about what they still can give. They are our seasoned veterans, and America can never be at its best if we keep them on the bench.

We hear a lot about generation gaps these days. We cannot afford a generation gap which shuts out the young in this country. But neither can we afford a generation gap that shuts out the old.

And so we must develop a new attitude toward aging in America, one that stops regarding older Americans as a burden and starts regarding them as a resource.

Senior power can be a tremendous source of energy for our country. Churchill was a great leader at 81. Holmes was a great jurist at 91. Clara Barton led the Red Cross at 83, and Connie Mack led the Athletics at 88. Michelangelo was painting at 89; Toscanini was conducting at 87. And for every celebrated name like

---

[3] See Item 244.

these, there are millions of ordinary citizens in their seventies and eighties who are making extraordinary contributions to their communities.

Senator Green of Rhode Island used to contend: "Most people say that as you get old you have to give up things. I think you get old because you give up things."

I believe that millions of older Americans can make great contributions to our Nation's progress if only they have the chance. This really is the point of our Government programs and policies—to help older Americans play a full, continuing role in the great adventures of America.

Thank you and good afternoon.

NOTE: The President spoke at 4:45 p.m. from Camp David, Md. The address was broadcast live on nationwide radio. Time for the broadcast was purchased by the Committee for the Re-Election of the President.

The President spoke from a prepared text. An advance text of his address was released on the same day.

394   Statement Announcing Transfer of 18 Parcels of Land Under the Legacy of Parks Program. *October 31, 1972*

TODAY I am pleased to announce that under our rapidly expanding Legacy of Parks program, the Federal Government will soon transfer 18 parcels of land to State and local governments for park and recreational use.

These transfers mark a significant milestone in the Legacy of Parks program, for when they are completed, we will have created new parklands in all 50 States, the District of Columbia, and Puerto Rico.

These 18 properties total just over 8,000 acres and are located in 14 States and the District of Columbia. They will bring the grand totals for the Legacy of Parks program to 218 transfers to local governments covering over 34,000 acres of land.

The Legacy of Parks program was inaugurated 19 months ago by my Executive Order 11508. In that order, I established a Property Review Board and directed it to identify property which was under-utilized and could be converted to higher and better use.

The success of this program has been extremely gratifying to me. It proves that with sound and thoughtful programs, we can make major improvements in our natural environment. I am particularly pleased that many of the new parks and recreational areas created by this program are located near urban areas, for this means that just as we are bringing government closer to the people, we are also bringing a better quality of life closer to our people.

NOTE: A White House announcement containing additional information on the transfer of the 18 parcels of land under the Legacy of Parks program was released on the same day and is printed in the Weekly Compilation of Presidential Documents (vol. 8, p. 1607).

395 Statement on Signing the Instrument of Ratification of the Convention for the Suppression of Unlawful Acts Against the Safety of Civil Aviation. *November 1, 1972*

IN RECENT weeks I have emphasized the commitment of this Nation to taking every step necessary to end the vicious threat of terror both here and abroad, a trend not limited to any one area of the world or to any one complex of problems. On September 25, Secretary of State Rogers also expressed to the United Nations the profound concern of the American people over the growing menace of international terrorism. On that same day, I further emphasized our deep feelings about this matter by establishing a Cabinet Committee to Combat Terrorism.

I am particularly pleased therefore to be able to sign the instrument of ratification of an international convention today which will help combat the menace of terrorism around the world: the Montreal Sabotage Convention. This convention requires the extradition or prosecution of any persons who perpetrate attacks of sabotage and violence against international civil aviation.

A civilized society cannot tolerate terrorism. Any action which makes a diplomat, a government official, or an innocent citizen a pawn in a politically motivated dispute undermines the safety of every other person. A peaceful, stable world requires that all nations vigorously join in condemning and prosecuting such acts and in preventing their further occurrence.

This convention and the bill I signed last Tuesday, H.R. 15883, making it a Federal crime for any person to harass, assault, kidnap, or murder a foreign official in the United States, are a part of our on-going efforts to combat terrorism.

In this connection the Cabinet Committee to Combat Terrorism has already taken steps to insure that stricter controls are placed on visa applications and visa extensions of possible terrorists. It has suspended the regulations which allowed one to transit the United States without a visa. And it has set up a series of working groups to insure government-wide cooperation in the sharing of intelligence and to provide for a coordinated response to any terrorist attack.

The United Nations and the International Civil Aviation Organization now have before them three additional proposals which, if adopted, would further strengthen the hands of all nations in dealing with the scourge of terrorism. In my view these measures should be acted upon promptly.

First, a draft convention providing for the prosecution or extradition of persons who attack or kidnap foreign officials.

Second, a convention providing for the suspension of air service to countries which fail to punish or extradite hijackers or saboteurs of civil aircraft.

Third, a new convention proposed by the United States which would require the prosecution or extradition of any person who seriously injures, kidnaps, or kills innocent civilians in a foreign state for the purpose of blackmailing any state or international organization.

The Montreal Sabotage Convention is

an important step in the continuing battle against terrorism. But the other measures that we are supporting in the United Nations and in the International Civil Aviation Organization are also essential if we are to establish a world in which men and nations can deal with one another without fear of these irrational and despicable acts of terrorism.

NOTE: The text of the convention is printed in Treaties and Other International Acts Series (TIAS 7570).

396 Radio Address on Urban Affairs. *November 1, 1972*

Good afternoon:

Today I would like to talk with you about a challenge which many describe as the "urban crisis." I prefer to think of it, however, as the "urban opportunity."

When we talk about "the city," we are not talking about an impersonal abstraction, but about the needs of real people—who happen to live more closely together and in larger concentrations than elsewhere. Our goal must be to improve the quality of urban life for individual human beings—to make each city a vibrant and vital place for people to live in.

In the 1960's, Federal programs for the cities grew bigger and bigger, but the problems of the cities only grew worse. Government spending increased at a record pace, but so did crime and pollution and inflation and unrest.

That is why, in addressing our urban needs, I have insisted that we concentrate not merely on how much we spend, but on how we spend it; that we measure our progress not merely by the money we put into urban programs, but by the results we get out of them; that we improve not only the quality of our resources but the quality of our thinking.

That is why we have developed an entirely new strategy for urban America in this Administration. This strategy is designed to do two things:

—First, to end the fragmented "bits and pieces" approach to urban problems, to recognize their interrelationships, to tackle them in a comprehensive, coordinated manner. This means focusing responsibility, so that public servants can do effective, long-range planning and pull together sufficient resources.

—Second, I was determined to end the logjam of power in an ever-centralizing Washington bureaucracy and to strengthen government at the grassroots.

As a result of our new strategy, our programs for the cities have not only grown in size in the last 4 years—they have also improved in effectiveness.

Let me cite a few examples.

Our average expenditures for community development and housing have been $1 billion a year higher in this Administration than in the previous 4 years. But in addition, we have worked to cut redtape and decentralize administration. We have worked to curb runaway housing costs, to find more efficient methods of finance and construction.

Now let's look at the result: Housing starts last year reached an alltime record high of 2.1 million units—and are now more than 65 percent above the 1960 to

1968 level. Federally assisted housing for low and moderate income families has increased more than fourfold since 1969.

Let's take another example—crime. We have spent more than 2½ times as much on fighting crimes this year as 4 years ago, and 11 times as much on fighting drug abuse. But what makes life better for people is not larger numbers in the crime budget, but smaller numbers in the crime rates.

At last, those numbers have begun to get smaller. Nearly half of our major cities had fewer crimes in the first 6 months of this year than a year ago. Nationwide, the rate of increase in crime was only one percent in the first half of 1972, compared to 122 percent from 1960 through 1968. Riots no longer ravage our cities as they did in the 1960's. And we made this progress by arming our crime fighters not just with more money but, even more importantly, with better, stronger laws, by backing them up and by helping to restore respect for the law and for those who enforce it.

A third example is the environment. For every $1 spent to fight pollution 4 years ago, we have budgeted $3.50 this year. But in addition, we have completely overhauled the Federal machinery and the Federal strategy for making our peace with nature.

As a result, today, for the first time, the air in our cities is getting cleaner and not dirtier. We are beginning to win the battle to clean up our lakes and rivers. We have turned 34,000 acres of unused Federal property into local parklands under our Legacy of Parks program—most of them near large population centers. That is why we describe our program as parks for the people.

In each of these areas I have mentioned,

as in others, our primary goal and concern has been how well we spend—and not just how much we are spending. Our goal has been better government—not just bigger government.

One important way of getting better government is to place more emphasis on local control.

Just last month I signed into law the first phase of revenue sharing, allocating 30 billion Federal dollars over the next 5 years for the State and local governments to use as they see fit.[1]

I signed this bill at Independence Hall in Philadelphia. That was a most appropriate site. For general revenue sharing is the first step in a comprehensive program which I have described as "a new American revolution." It represents a new Declaration of Independence for State and local government. Now, instead of power moving from the people to Washington, power will flow back from Washington to the people again.

Revenue sharing can be used for a number of purposes. It can help, for example, to hold down property taxes. It can pay for more policemen to keep city streets safe. It can build new schools, new hospitals.

But whatever it does, it will be local officials responding to local conditions and to their own local citizens, who will decide what should be done, what should have priority, rather than having those decisions made by some impersonal Federal bureaucrat.

Let me use another example to illustrate the advantages of local control.

Nothing could do more to lift the face of our cities—and the spirit of our city dwellers—than truly adequate systems of

---

[1] See Item 354.

modern transportation. The quality of urban life suffers incalculably when it takes longer to cross a city by horseless carriage today than to cross it by horse-drawn carriage a century ago. A nation that can move three persons across 240,000 miles of space to the Moon should be able to move 240,000 persons across 3 miles of a city to get to work.

To improve transportation we needed, first, more money—and we provided it. Before we came into office, the most the Federal Government made available for mass transit in any one year was $175 million. We raised this figure to $400 million in 1971 and to a full $1 billion this year. We proposed, and the Congress enacted, the Urban Mass Transportation Assistance Act of 1970, which is a 12-year, $10 billion program. We have also launched new programs for air and rail and water transportation.

But our goal has not merely been more expensive programs. We have worked to design more effective programs. And that means more local decisionmaking.

Each city, after all, has its own unique transportation needs. The highest priority for one city might be a better subway, as it was in Washington, D.C.; for another, it may be buslines; for a third, a new airport; for a fourth, a new bridge or a better highway. Good transportation must be balanced transportation—and the balance must be struck differently in each local setting.

Now, who can strike this balance best? Not some Federal bureaucrat hundreds or thousands of miles away. How can he know what each city needs? He has many cities to worry about. Often he is hopelessly bogged down in redtape. And there is really no way for local residents to keep

in touch with him or hold him accountable for his decisions.

More than that, the Federal bureaucrat is likely to specialize in a single program. His main worry may be highways, for example; his main job may be to get more highways built. And thus, he simply is often not in the best position to plan a balanced approach.

But the local official is different. He is right there—at the scene of the action. He has only one community to worry about. It is his job to understand that community inside out. If he doesn't, the local citizens can complain to him directly, or they can vote him out of office. Best of all, local officials can plan an overall transportation strategy which takes into account a wide range of transportation needs—and fits in with other urban programs.

The key point about our urban strategy, then, is not only that it gives our communities the dollars they need, but also that it gives them the freedom and the responsibility they need to use those dollars effectively.

It tells local officials to spend less time trying to please grant reviewers in Washington—so that the money will keep coming in—and spend more time pleasing the people who live in their communities—so the money will do more good.

General revenue sharing is only the first step in this new strategy. I have already charted a number of additional steps: Among those proposals that I have made that were left unenacted by the Congress were six special revenue sharing bills, including one in the transportation field, a major program of welfare reform, and sweeping plans for streamlining and decentralizing the Federal bureaucracy.

The goal of all these proposals is to make government responsive again to the voice of the average citizen.

Under this approach, people can feel that they are in control again, that they can shape events, that they can make things happen in their own lives and in their own communities.

Under this approach, more decisions will be made at the scene of the action—and this means that more people can have a piece of the action.

Thomas Jefferson said he believed in local government not only because it was a more effective government but also because it could give the individual that feeling without which life is incomplete— a sense of participation in events that really count.

If this was true in Jefferson's time— when the average Congressman represented only about 30,000 people—how much more true it is in our time, when the average Congressman represents nearly half a million people.

Several years ago a poll of the American public revealed that only 27 percent of those who lived in our cities said they did so by choice. One lesson of that poll was that the urban crisis—so often regarded merely as a crisis of money—

has also been a crisis of morale.

This Administration has addressed both of these crises. We have doubled Federal assistance to States and localities—to meet the crisis of money. But we have also increased the sense of freedom and control in our communities—to meet the crisis of the spirit.

The result, as we approach our Nation's 200th anniversary, is a growing sense that the graph of urban history is climbing again and the pendulum is swinging in a new, more hopeful direction.

This renewal of the spirit in the cities of our Nation means that they have a chance again to become in reality what they have always been in our dreams: shining centers of commerce and culture, providing a fuller, richer life for all who share in them.

This is the urban challenge—and this is our urban opportunity.

Thank you, and good afternoon.

NOTE: The President spoke at 12:07 p.m. from the Library at the White House. The address was broadcast live on nationwide radio. Time for the broadcast was purchased by the Committee for the Re-Election of the President.

The President spoke from a prepared text. An advance text of his address was released on the same day.

397 Address to the Nation: "Look to the Future." *November 2, 1972*

Good evening:

I am speaking to you tonight from the Library of the White House. This room, like all the rooms in this great house, is rich in history.

Often late at night I sit here thinking of the crises other Presidents have known—and of the trials that other gener-

ations of Americans have come through.

I think, too, of the Presidents who will be sitting here a generation from now, and how they will look back on these years. And I think of what I want to accomplish in these years. I would like to share some of those thoughts with you this evening.

Above all, I want to complete the foundations for a world at peace—so that the next generation can be the first in this century to live without war and without the fear of war.

Beyond this, I want Americans—all Americans—to see more clearly and to feel more deeply what it is that makes this Nation of ours unique in history, unique in the world, a nation in which the soul and spirit are free, in which each person is respected, in which the individual human being, each precious, each different, can dare to dream and can live his dreams.

I want progress toward a better life for all Americans—not only in terms of better schools, greater abundance, a cleaner environment, better homes, more attractive communities, but also in a spiritual sense, in terms of greater satisfaction, more kindness in our relations with each other, more fulfillment.

I want each American—all Americans—to find a new zest in the pursuit of excellence, in striving to do their best and to be their best, in learning the supreme satisfaction of setting a seemingly impossible goal, and meeting or surpassing that goal, of finding in themselves that extra reserve of energy or talent or creativity that they had not known was there.

These are goals of a free people, in a free nation, a nation that lives not by handout, not by dependence on others or in hostage to the whims of others, but proud and independent—a nation of individuals with self-respect and with the right and capacity to make their own choices, to chart their own lives.

That is why I want us to turn away from a demeaning, demoralizing dependence on someone else to make our decisions and to guide the course of our lives.

That is why I want us to turn toward a renaissance of the individual spirit, toward a new vitality of those governments closest to the people, toward a new pride of place for the family and the community, toward a new sense of responsibility in all that we do, responsibility for ourselves and to ourselves, for our communities and to our communities, knowing that each of us, in every act of his daily life, determines what kind of community and what kind of a country we all will live in.

If, together, we can restore this spirit, then 4 years from now America can enter its third century buoyant and vital and young, with all the purpose that marked its beginning two centuries ago.

In these past 4 years, we have moved America significantly toward this goal. We have restored peace at home, and we are restoring peace abroad.

As you know, we have now made a major breakthrough toward achieving our goal of peace with honor in Vietnam. We have reached substantial agreement on most of the terms of a settlement. The settlement we are ready to conclude would accomplish the basic objectives that I laid down in my television speech to the Nation on May 8 of this year:

—the return of all of our prisoners of war, and an accounting for all of those missing in action;

—a cease-fire throughout Indochina; and

—for the 17 million people of South Vietnam, the right to determine their own future without having a Communist government or a coalition government imposed upon them against their will.

However, there are still some issues to be resolved. There are still some provisions of the agreement which must be clarified so that all ambiguities will be removed. I have insisted that these be settled before we sign the final agreement. That is why we refused to be stampeded into meeting the arbitrary deadline of October 31.

Now, there are some who say: "Why worry about the details? Just get the war over!"

Well, my answer is this: My study of history convinces me that the details can make the difference between an agreement that collapses and an agreement that lasts—and equally crucial is a clear understanding by all of the parties of what those details are.

We are not going to repeat the mistake of 1968, when the bombing halt agreement was rushed into just before an election without pinning down the details.

We want peace—peace with honor—a peace fair to all and a peace that will last. That is why I am insisting that the central points be clearly settled, so that there will be no misunderstandings which could lead to a breakdown of the settlement and a resumption of the war.

I am confident that we will soon achieve that goal.

But we are not going to allow an election deadline or any other kind of deadline to force us into an agreement which would be only a temporary truce and not a lasting peace. We are going to sign the agreement when the agreement is right, not one day before. And when the agreement is right, we are going to sign, without one day's delay.

Not only in America, but all around the world, people will be watching the results of our election. The leaders in Hanoi will be watching. They will be watching for the answer of the American people—for your answer—to this question: Shall

we have peace with honor or peace with surrender?

Always in the past you have answered "Peace with honor." By giving that same answer once again on November 7 you can help make certain that peace with honor can now be achieved.

In these past 4 years, we have also been moving toward lasting peace in the world at large.

We have signed more agreements with the Soviet Union than were negotiated in all the previous years since World War II. We have established the basis for a new relationship with the People's Republic of China, where one-fourth of all the people in this world live. Our vigorous diplomacy has advanced the prospects for a stable peace in the Middle East. All around the world, we are opening doors to peace, doors that were previously closed. We are developing areas of common interest where there have been previously only antagonisms. All this is a beginning. It can be the beginning of a generation of peace—of a world in which our children can be the first generation in this century to escape the scourge of war.

These next 4 years will set the course on which we begin our third century as a nation. What will that course be? Will it have us turning inward, retreating from the responsibilities not only of a great power but of a great people—of a nation that embodies the ideals man has dreamed of and fought for through the centuries?

We cannot retreat from those responsibilities. If we did America would cease to be a great nation, and peace and freedom would be in deadly jeopardy throughout the world.

Ours is a great and a free nation today because past generations of Americans met their responsibilities. And we shall meet ours.

We have made progress toward peace in the world, toward a new relationship with the Soviet Union and the People's Republic of China, not through naive sentimental assumptions that good will is all that matters, or that we can reduce our military strength because we have no intention of making war and we therefore assume other nations would have no such intention. We have achieved progress through peace for precisely the opposite reasons: because we demonstrated that we would not let ourselves be surpassed in military strength and because we bargained with other nations on the basis of their national interest and ours.

As we look at the real world, it is clear that we will not in our lifetimes have a world free of danger. Anyone who reads history knows that danger has always been part of the common lot of mankind. Anyone who knows the world today knows that nations have not all been suddenly overtaken by some new and unprecedented wave of pure good will and benign intentions. But we can lessen the danger. We can contain it. We can forge a network of relationships and of interdependencies that restrain aggression and that take the profit out of war.

We cannot make all nations the same, and it would be wrong to try. We cannot make all of the world's people love each other. But we can establish conditions in which they will be more likely to live in peace with one another. Tonight I ask for your support as we continue to work toward that great goal.

Here at home, as we look at the progress we have made, we find that we are reaching new levels of prosperity.

We have cut inflation almost in half.

The average worker has scored his best gains in 8 years in real spendable earnings. We are creating record numbers of new jobs. We are well on the way to achieving what America has not had since President Eisenhower lived here in the White House: prosperity with full employment, without inflation and without war.

We have lowered the level of violence, and we are finally turning the tide against crime.

I could go on with what we have done—for the environment, for the consumer, for the aging, for the farmer, for the worker, for all Americans—but now we must not look backward to what we have done in the past, but forward to what we will do in the future.

It is traditional for a candidate for election to make all sorts of promises about bold new programs he intends to introduce if elected. This year's Presidential campaign has probably established an all-time record for promises of huge new spending programs for just about anything and everything for everybody imaginable. I have not made such promises in this campaign. And I am not going to do so tonight. Let me tell you why.

In the first place, the sort of bold new programs traditionally promised by candidates are all programs that you—the taxpayer—pay for. The programs proposed by our opponents in this campaign would require a 50-percent increase in Federal taxes, in your taxes. I think your taxes are already too high. That is why I oppose any new program which would add to your tax burden.

In the second place, too many campaign promises are just that—campaign promises. I believe in keeping the promises I make, and making only those promises I am confident I can keep. I have promised that I will do all in my power to avoid the need for new taxes. I am not going to promise anything else in the way of new programs that would violate that pledge.

In the third place, my own philosophy of government is not one that looks to new Federal dollars—your dollars—as the solution of every social problem.

I have often said that America became great not because of what government did for people, but because of what people did for themselves. I believe government should free the energies of people to build for themselves and their communities. It should open opportunities, provide incentives, encourage initiative—not stifle initiative by trying to direct everything from Washington.

This does not mean that the Federal Government will abdicate its responsibilities where only it can solve a problem.

It does mean that after 40 years of unprecedented expansion of the Federal Government, the time has come to redress the balance—to shift more people and more responsibility and power back to the States and localities and, most important, to the people, all across America.

In the past 40 years, the size of the Federal budget has grown from $4.6 billion to $250 billion. In that same period, the number of civilian employees of the Federal Government has increased from 600,000 to 2,800,000. And in just the past 10 years, the number of Federal grant-in-aid programs has increased from 160 to more than 1,000.

If this kind of growth were projected indefinitely into the future, the result would be catastrophic. We would have an America topheavy with bureaucratic meddling, weighted down by big government, suffocated by taxes, robbed of its soul.

We must not and we will not let this happen to America. That is why I oppose the unrestrained growth of big government in Washington. That is why one of my first priorities in the next 4 years will be to encourage a rebirth and renewal of State and local government. That is why I believe in giving the people in every community a greater say in those decisions that most directly affect the course of their daily lives.

Now, there will be those who will call this negative, who call it a retreat from Federal responsibilities.

I call it affirmative—an affirmation of faith in the people, faith in the individual, faith in each person's ability to choose wisely for himself and for his community.

I call it an affirmation of faith in those principles that made America great, that tamed a continent, that transformed a wilderness into the greatest and strongest and freest nation in the world.

We have not changed. The American people have not grown weak. What has grown weak is government's faith in people. I am determined to see that faith restored.

I am also determined to see another kind of faith restored and strengthened in America. I speak of the religious faith, the moral and spiritual values that have been so basically a part of our American experience. Man does not live for himself alone, and the strength of our character, the strength of our faith, and the strength of our ideals—these have been the strength of America.

When I think of what America means, I think of all the hope that lies in a vast continent—of great cities and small towns, of factories and farms, of a greater abundance, more widely shared, than the world has ever known, of a constant striving to set right the wrongs that still persist—and I think of 210 million people, of all ages, all persuasions, all races, all stations in life.

More particularly, I think of one person, one child—any child. That child may be black or brown or white, rich or poor, a boy whose family came here in steerage in 1920, or a girl whose ancestors came on the Mayflower in 1620. That one child is America, with a life still ahead, with his eyes filled with dreams, and with the birthright of every American child to a full and equal opportunity to pursue those dreams.

It is for that one child that I want a world of peace and a chance to achieve all that peace makes possible. It is for that one child that I want opportunity, and freedom, and abundance. It is for that one child that I want a land of justice, and order, and a decent respect for the rights and the feelings of others.

It is for that one child that I want it said, a generation from now, a century from now, that America in the 1970's had the courage and the vision to meet its responsibilities and to face up to its challenges—to build peace, not merely for our generation but for the next generation; to restore the land, to marshal our resources, not merely for our generation

but for the next generation; to guard our values and renew our spirit, not merely for our generation but for the next generation.

It is for that one child that I want these next 4 years to be the best 4 years in the whole history of America.

The glory of this time in our history is that we can do more than ever before— we have the means, we have the skills, we have an increasing understanding of how the great goals that we seek can be achieved.

These are not partisan goals. They are America's goals. That is why I ask you tonight, regardless of party, to join the new American majority next Tuesday in voting for candidates who stand for these goals. That is why I ask for your support—after the election—in helping to move forward toward these goals over the next 4 years.

If we succeed in this task, then that one child—all of our children—can look forward to a life more full of hope, promise, than any generation, in any land, in the whole history of mankind.

Thank you, and good evening.

NOTE: The President spoke from a prepared text. His address was recorded for broadcast on nationwide radio and television at 7:30 p.m. in the eastern, mountain, and Pacific time zones and at 6:30 p.m. in the central time zone. Time for the broadcast was purchased by the Committee for the Re-Election of the President.

398   Radio Address on Health Policy. *November 3, 1972*

Good afternoon:

Whenever people start talking about how exciting life would have been a century or two ago, a friend of mine likes

to respond, "But what if you had broken your leg?"

He has a good point. Nothing has done more to improve the quality of life in recent years than the progress of medical science.

I believe the best way to continue this progress in the future is to build on the system that produced our progress in the past.

We have done a lot of building in the last 4 years.

We have increased Federal spending on health more than 50 percent, from $16 billion to $25 billion.

I proposed—and the Congress enacted—the most comprehensive program in history to train more doctors and nurses and dentists, to train them faster and more effectively, to attract them to small towns and inner cities and other places where they are now in short supply.

In the last 2 years we have more than doubled Federal support for cancer research. We have stripped away the red-tape from our cancer programs. We have made them directly accountable to the President.

We have taken new steps to fight heart disease. We have launched a new campaign against sickle cell anemia, a cruel threat to black Americans. Our program to prevent occupational accidents and illnesses has been enacted.

We have taken major steps to expand Medicare and Medicaid, to improve veterans hospitals, nursing homes, and emergency medical services, to protect consumers against unsafe food and drugs and dangerous household products.

Our campaign against drug abuse is 11 times bigger than it was 4 years ago. We are spending more than three times as much to fight hunger and malnutrition. We have established a national goal to cut the incidence of mental retardation in half by the year 2000.

One of the greatest problems we faced in the 1960's was the skyrocketing cost of health care. In that 10 years, medical prices went up twice as fast as the cost of living.

Just last week [October 27] I met with the Committee on the Health Services Industry of our Cost of Living Council. They reported that under our new economic policy we have cut the rise in medical care prices by more than two-thirds, from 6.4 percent a year ago to only 2.1 percent in the last year. The health care industry, once one of the most inflationary sectors of our economy, has become one of the least inflationary. Now to keep it that way we must balance the growing demand for health care with a growing supply of health services.

As I look back at the record of the past 4 years, I think of the comment which Dr. Jonas Salk made when he received a gold medal from President Eisenhower for developing the vaccine against polio. "I feel," he said, "that the greatest reward for doing is the opportunity to do more."

Well, I feel the same way today.

As we look to the future, one of our great goals is to make our health system more efficient—so that each doctor, each hospital, and each health dollar can do more good. The Federal Government is already taking the lead in demonstrating the effectiveness of medical assistants who help doctors with routine tasks. We also want to encourage programs which will help doctors organize their services more conveniently and more efficiently, with greater emphasis on keeping people healthy rather than treating them only after they get sick.

No American family should be denied access to adequate medical care because of inability to pay. The most important health proposal not acted on by the 92d Congress was my program for helping people pay for care.

This program would fill the gaps in many current health insurance programs.

For example, most working poor families—who do not qualify for welfare—cannot afford adequate health insurance coverage. Our plan would make adequate insurance available at no cost—or at a very low cost—for these families, families who work rather than who go on welfare.

Second, present plans often fail to protect families in all income levels against the catastrophic cost of major illnesses and accidents. They often have very restrictive upper limits, which means that the insurance often runs out while the expenses are still running up. Our program would provide broad catastrophic coverage.

Third, present plans often fail to cover services in doctors' offices. As a result, many hospitals are crowded with people who are there because that's the only way their insurance will pay their expenses. Our plan would change that, too.

Under our programs, every employer would have to provide all of his workers with a health insurance policy, just as he helps pay for workmen's compensation and social security today. The employer would pay at least 65 percent of the premium cost for the first few years and 75 percent thereafter. And our proposal would see that every policy provided good, sound, adequate protection.

One of the clearest choices in the 1972 Presidential election is the choice between the comprehensive health insurance plan, which is a private health insurance plan

that I have just described, and our opponents' plan for a medical system which is paid for by the taxpayers and controlled by the Federal Government.

Let's take a look at the opposition program. According to a report prepared for the House Ways and Means Committee, its total cost to the taxpayers each year would be a staggering $91 billion. This means that health alone would take up more than one-third of the entire Federal budget. Look at this figure. The average family's Federal tax bill for health would go from $457 a year today to $1,305 a year, nearly triple, under their program.

There is another point worth noting: our opponents' claim that all their new spending programs can be financed by sweeping cuts in defense and only a few new taxes. But somehow they managed to omit this $91 billion item from that painless version of their budget. A New York Times editorial was right 2 weeks ago when it described this as a "major omission." When that $91 billion is added in, their budget is nowhere near so painless. It would require a Federal tax increase of 50 percent.

Our opponents' federalized, tax-supported system would be very costly in terms of dollars and cents. But it would also be very costly in terms of the quality of American medicine. Not only would our pocketbooks be much poorer, our health care would be much poorer, too.

If the Government pays all the medical bills, then only the Government has a stake in holding down medical costs. This means that Government officials would have to approve hospital budgets and set fee schedules and take other steps that would eventually lead to the complete Federal domination of American medicine. I think this is the wrong road for America. It is the road that has been taken by so many countries abroad to their regret.

Rather than freeing the doctor so that he can do more for his patients, our opponents' plan would burden him with the dead weight of more bureaucracy, more forms, more redtape.

Rather than expanding the range of choice for doctors and patients, it would severely narrow their range of choice. It would concentrate more responsibility in Washington. It would dull the incentive to experiment and innovate.

Some people automatically assume that the plan that costs the most will help the most. But we cannot simply buy our way to better medicine. In this case the plan that costs the most is the plan that would actually do the most to hurt the quality of our health care.

Our plan would build on the strengths of our present health insurance industry. Our opponents' plan would eliminate that industry entirely.

Our plan would reform and improve our present health care system. Our opponents' plan would tear that system apart. This is one of the clearest choices in this campaign.

Building on the strengths of our present system, we can make tremendous progress in the years ahead. One development which will speed our progress is a new spirit of international cooperation.

When I was in Moscow last May, I signed several historic agreements. Perhaps the one that most people think of first is the agreement to limit strategic weapons. But it may well be, 20 or 40 or 100 years from now, that another achievement in Moscow will be remembered with it—our agreement to cooperate in the field of medicine. Let me give one example.

Take cancer. More people died of cancer in the United States last year than were killed in action in all of World War II as far as the United States was concerned.

Disease is an international menace. We must fight it with an international alliance.

Who knows who will discover the cure for cancer? It may be a woman now studying at a university in Europe or a boy who now sits in a South American school. It could be an American or a Russian or a Chinese. Or there may be many partial cures from many sources. But this we know: The cure for cancer—or any other disease—will come faster if we all work together to find it.

The barriers between nations may be great. But when it comes to improving health, our common interests are even greater.

Several weeks after the Moscow summit, the Russian Minister of Health came to the United States. One of the places he visited was Fort Detrick, Maryland. For years, Fort Detrick was one of the most secret places in our country, dedicated to research on biological warfare—perfecting the instruments of death. But last year we decided to convert it into a laboratory for research on cancer—dedicated to the preservation of life.

I visited Fort Detrick last year, on the day I announced its conversion. I directed that it now should be thrown open to scientists from all over the world. It was in that spirit that Fort Detrick welcomed the Russian Minister of Health almost one year later.

There he stood, in a place which once

had been the symbol of a closed world, a world of suspicion and confrontation, a place where some of the best minds of our nation had prepared for a possible war against this nation.

Now this same place had become the symbol of an open world, a world of cooperation and trust. It had become a meeting ground where the best minds from every nation could work together to save life everywhere on earth.

We still have a long way to go—but our goal is clear. And for me its symbol is Fort Detrick, Maryland, welcoming the Soviet Minister of Health.

This is the kind of world we must leave for our children, a world in which the genius that split the atom and took us to the Moon is turned not to conquering one another but to conquering pain and disease, making our world a healthier, happier place—for our people and for all people.

Thank you, and good afternoon.

NOTE: The address was recorded at the White House for broadcast at 12:07 p.m. on nationwide radio. Time for the broadcast was purchased by the Committee for the Re-Election of the President.

The President spoke from a prepared text. An advance text of his address was released on the same day.

399   Campaign Statement in Illinois. *November 3*, 1972

MORE than any other city, Chicago has come to symbolize the strength and resourcefulness of the American worker.

Throughout the 20th century, Chicago has been a showplace for the growth, diversity, and progress that this dedication has made possible. The spirit of Chicago is the true spirit of America. Chicagoans, drawn from so many different ethnic backgrounds, have earned a reputation for patriotism and competitiveness.

This spirit is reflected in Chicago's economy. At a time when some politicians are constantly harping on what is wrong with America, let us consider the progress that Chicagoans have made, and continue to make.

In manufacturing, for instance, Chicagoans enjoy higher average weekly earnings (over $175 per week) than the national average ($154 per week). During the past year, when the cost of living increased by 2.9 percent in Chicago, the average weekly earnings of Chicagoans in manufacturing increased by 9.6 percent, a real increase of 6½ percent—the equivalent of three extra weekly paychecks.

Chicagoans today are working hard. They are making an enormous contribution to our free enterprise system, and they are benefiting from the results as never before.

In addressing the domestic concerns of this Nation, we have tried to apply the Chicago spirit nationally. The willingness to work has been the cornerstone of America's great economic strength.

We want to keep it that way. Therefore, the record of this Administration has been one of creating real jobs—not artificial government make-work jobs or handouts—while fighting inflation and converting our economy from war to peace.

When this Administration took office, civilian employment stood at 77 million, but approximately 3⅓ million were employed in defense-related industries and civilian Defense Department jobs. And another 3⅓ million were in the Armed Forces.

By contrast, in October of 1972, 82.5 million persons were employed, 5½ million more than when I took office and the highest number in our history. And this important progress has been achieved at the same time that defense-related employment has been scaled down. Between October of 1971 and October of 1972 alone, total employment increased by an amazing 2.3 million people. All of this has occurred while we have successfully brought back more than half a million men and women from Southeast Asia, while the size of the Armed Forces has been cut by almost a third and the number of defense-related jobs has dropped nearly 1½ million.

Yet we have picked up these people in other jobs, we have retrained many of them, and through such programs as the technology mobilization and reemployment program, we have assisted scientists and engineers in relocating and finding new jobs.

This is progress, real progress. It is based not on more handouts paid out of the taxpayer's pocket, but on the revitalization of our dynamic free economy. Much, of course, remains to be done. I am not satisfied with the current rate of unemployment at the national level. Everyone who wants to work should be able to work. That is the American way. But let us not lose sight of the impressive gains we have made already. Of all over-25 males in the labor force, only 3 percent were unemployed as of September, a lower rate than in the prosperous years of 1955, 1956, and 1957, and clearly better than the 3.3 percent rate in 1964, just before the esca-

lation of our Vietnam involvement triggered a wartime boom.

Just as we are now near achievement of this Administration's goal of peace with honor in Vietnam, so we are closer than ever to our goal of prosperity without war and without inflation in America. With your continued support, we can achieve them both.

The people of Chicago have helped us enormously in achieving many of our goals in the past. Now you can help us once again by electing the entire Republican ticket in Illinois.

The two gentlemen at the head of that ticket, Dick Ogilvie and Chuck Percy,[1] are men I have known and trusted over the years. They can give great leadership to Illinois and to the Nation.

I look forward to working with them not only on the problems of the cities— and they have been especially helpful in securing the passage of general revenue sharing—but also on the needs of the rural areas. Dick Ogilvie and Chuck Percy are the type of men we need to continue our farm policies. Net farm income this year is the highest in our history, finally breaking the alltime record set 25 years ago. In fact, net farm income—what is left after the bills are paid—has been 24 percent higher for the last 4 years than it was during the last Administration. We can continue that progress with your help.

And there is something else that the people of Chicago can help us to achieve. The strong work ethic of Chicagoans is rooted in an even deeper value—this deep cultural and spiritual heritage which is as strong today as ever. For example,

---

[1] Gov. Richard B. Ogilvie and Senator Charles H. Percy were Republican candidates for reelection.

Chicago has one of the largest nonpublic school systems in our Nation, a network of education centers that keep alive in our children the religious and moral values on which a full life must be based.

Today that nonpublic school system is threatened by the growing financial pressures which it must overcome to survive. So I ask the people of Chicago to join with me in working for the passage of legislation that will allow the parents of children attending nonpublic schools tax credits to offset a part of their tuition costs. I have actively worked for the passage of this kind of legislation in the past. I am pledged to continue working for it, so that we can achieve passage of this much needed measure to maintain diversity and to keep a strong spiritual and moral element in the American education system.

The opportunity for diverse, quality education, the chance to work hard at a meaningful job, the perpetuation of the values and beliefs that made this country great—each of these things is an important part of the "Spirit of Chicago," and of the spirit of America itself.

NOTE: The statement was released at Chicago, Ill.

400   Remarks at Chicago, Illinois. *November 3, 1972*

Governor Ogilvie, Senator Percy, Congressman Arends, all of the distinguished candidates and other guests here on the platform, and all of you who have been so kind to, on such very short notice, come here to the airport to welcome Mrs. Nixon and me here:

I want to say to you that, first, to come to Illinois is always a very great pleasure for me. I want you to know, too, that to come here at a time that I know the city of Chicago is grieving for those who were the victims of the terrible accident[1] last Tuesday, is one that is a very sad time. But in a way it, too, is a time for hope for all of us.

I want to thank and express my appreciation to all of those who, during that tragedy, handled themselves so magnificently—the people in the hospitals, the firemen, the policemen. Let's give them the hand they deserve.

---

[1] See Item 392.

I want to express also my admiration for the people of Chicago, for the way they have reacted with great compassion and great sincerity and great heart. You know, this part of the country is known as the heartland of America. Chicago is known as the capital of the heartland of America, and the way the people of Chicago responded to this tragedy proves that Chicago truly has a big heart. We thank you for that big heart.

I am very proud, too, today to be here on the platform with others who are candidates for office, as I am. I would like to mention them all by name, but time will not permit it. May I say, first, that on the national scene all of them have my support: Chuck Percy, who is one of the top men in the United States Senate, one of the leaders of the United States Senate; the entire delegation from the State of Illinois. There is only one thing wrong with it. We would like to have a few more just like them back there in Washington.

And we support the candidates, as well.

But when, out of this one State, you have two men in the leadership—Les Arends, of course, the Whip of the House; John Anderson, who is the chairman of the [House Republican] Conference—it is truly a great delegation, and I express my appreciation in their home State for what they have done for Illinois, what they have done for their districts, and what they are doing for the Nation.

Now, at the State level I have so many old friends—Bill Scott, for example; Bernie Carey,[2] all the rest. They have my support. But could I say a very personal word about the man that I stood by 4 years ago and by whom I am proud to stand again, your Governor, Governor Dick Ogilvie.

As you know, at Independence Hall just a few days ago I signed an historic act, one which changes the flow of money and power to Washington back to the people, to the States and the cities of this country. Thirty billion dollars is going to go back into State government, into city government, and local government over the next 5 years.

Now, it isn't just enough to have that money go back. What is needed is to have leaders in the States, leaders in local governments, who will spend that money well for the people of this country, who will use it, for example, to reduce the burden of taxes rather than to increase it, which they could not have done until they received this revenue sharing.

I can tell you, I know every one of the 50 Governors in this Nation, Democrat and Republican. Without regard to

partisanship, there are many who are very able men, but in the very top ranks of those that I would want to entrust my money to, to spend it well, to use it well for the people of a State, Dick Ogilvie ranks high. He deserves your support.

Now, having mentioned the other candidates, I would like to say a word for myself, if you don't mind, too.

I have been before the voters of Illinois now on five occasions: in 1952 and 1956, as a candidate for Vice President, and then in 1960 and 1968, and now in 1972, as a candidate for President.

I want to speak to you today about why I need your support. I am not going to ask for it in terms of Republicans versus Democrats, because this year we have an election, and what is important is not our party label, but what is important is what is going to happen to America.

I ask you as Democrats, as independents, and as Republicans to consider what you want for America. That is why we need a new American majority, to give us an overwhelming vote on November 7, and we would like to have it here in Illinois as well as in other States.

I could discuss at length many of the issues, the fact that we have moved toward prosperity without war and without inflation, a goal that we have not had in this country since President Eisenhower occupied the White House. I could speak to you of the progress that we have made in the fields like revenue sharing, in which power is returning from Washington to the people and to the States.

I could speak to you of what we have done in the field of the environment and health and education and all the many other areas in which we have worked. And I am very proud that during these past 4 years instead of running down the

---

[2] William J. Scott was the Republican candidate for attorney general, and Bernard C. Carey was the Republican candidate for State's attorney for Cook County, Ill.

peace officers of this country, the President of the United States has stood back of them, and I stand back of them today, against those who would run them down.

That is why we have begun to turn the tide against crime and against dangerous drugs, because we need to respect those who are peace officers and those who have to carry out the law. Laws, of course, if they are to be respected, must deserve it. And we are going to have continually that kind of law, to have the increasing justice and opportunity that every American has as his due.

Today I would like particularly to discuss with you the issue that I know is uppermost in the minds of many of you because of recent developments. As you know, the major goal that I have had over these past 4 years is to build a structure of peace in the world, a peace not just for the next election, but peace for the next generation.

We have made very significant progress in that direction. I refer to the journey we took to Peking, where, after a quarter of a century of hardly any contact, finally the world's most prosperous nation and the world's most populous nation, with over one-fourth of the people of the world living there, now are communicating with each other.

Think what that means, not to this generation—ours—but to all of these wonderful young people here, because 20 years from now instead of being engaged in ugly and dangerous confrontation with a billion Chinese, they will be communicating with them. They have a chance for peace that we did not have.

We have made progress, too, in attempting to bring peace to the Mideast, in standing by our commitments to Israel, and we will continue to stand by those

commitments, because that is the way to peace in that troubled area.

We have made progress, too, in many other areas in the world, particularly in dealing with the Soviet Union, where, as you know, we have had an historic arms control agreement, agreements in the field of trade and the environment and health and science and in many other areas.

I could stop here and talk about those agreements and also the progress that we have made in bringing the war in Vietnam to an honorable conclusion.

But my purpose in coming to Chicago is to ask your votes, not because of what we have done over the past 4 years, but to give me the chance that I need to complete the job and to build a structure of peace in the next 4 years.

Before coming to Chicago today I met for an hour in the Oval Office with Ambassador Dobrynin of the Soviet Union and the science minister from the Soviet Union [Dr. Mistislav V. Keldysh]. We spoke about the recent summit in Moscow, but we spoke about the future, how we could cooperate more in the future, and we also spoke about the new agreements with regard to the limitation of nuclear weapons, in which the negotiations will start at the end of November.

We spoke of the other negotiations which we have already begun, but which we must continue in the next Administration. I realized, as I talked to him, that it was important to go to the country and get the people of this country to give to the President of the United States the backing that he needs, to give to the President of the United States and to give a message to all the leaders of the world that when the President of the United States goes abroad, he speaks not from weakness, but from strength. Let's not have the President ever represent the second strongest nation in this world.

Let us also be sure that when the President of the United States goes abroad over these next 4 years, he speaks on the basis of pragmatism and reality and not on naive sentimentality that has always led us into war, or worse, in times past.

And let us also remember this thing: When we speak of peace, we want it; when we speak of ending a war, we want it; but let us remember we have ended wars before. The important thing is to end a war in a way that will build a lasting peace, and that is why I say, rather than peace with surrender, let's have peace with honor for the United States of America.

As I reported last night on television, we have made a very significant breakthrough in achieving that goal in our negotiations with the North Vietnamese. We have already reached basic agreement on the three major conditions that I laid down in the speech that I made to the Nation on May 8 when I ordered the bombing and the mining of Haiphong and North Vietnam, and those three agreements that we have already reached basic agreement on are these:

One, a return of all of our prisoners of war and an accounting for the MIA's; two, a cease-fire throughout not just Vietnam, but throughout all of Indochina, Cambodia, and Laos; and three, the right of the people of South Vietnam to determine their own future without having a Communist government or a coalition government imposed upon them against their will.

There are some details of the agreement that are still to be negotiated. I am confident they will be negotiated. I am confident that we will make an agreement. Let me address myself, however, to a question that one member of my staff raised this morning, to the effect that, "Why are details important? Why not just make an agreement and sign it, because that would be really great just before the election?"

Let me tell you something. Rather than having simply an agreement before an election, we want to have a peace for the next generation, and that is what we are working for. I can assure you that as far as an election is concerned, it will not delay an agreement. I can assure you, however, it will not hasten it. The main thing is, we are going to have one, and it is going to be the right kind. I think the American people want the right kind of an agreement—peace with honor and not surrender. That is what we are standing for and that is what we will achieve.

Looking far to the future, we think of the younger people here and the older people, people who are black and who are white, people who are rich and poor, people who are employers and employees. We think of those that are respectful when they come to a meeting and all those that are disrespectful. All of them have their right to be heard, and so have I. But in that respect, I would simply say this word to all of you who are here: These next 4 years are years in which America has an opportunity such as I have not seen in my lifetime or that America has not witnessed in this century.

We can build a world of peace, real peace; something we have not had in a generation, and for a generation in this whole century. We can have prosperity without war and without inflation. We can have increased opportunities for all

Americans to go as high as their abilities will take them without being limited in any respect.

We can have also a new period in this country of respect for the rights of others, of civility in our dealings with others, of decency, of carrying on our campaigns in a way in which we present the issues, in which we listen to what somebody else has to say, and then speak what we have to say.

Let me say finally to this great crowd in Chicago, it has been very proud, in terms of an experience for me, my wife, my family, to live in that great house that you saw on television last night. It has been a very proud experience to travel to all the 50 States over these last 4 years.

It has been a very proud experience to travel to 22 countries abroad, including four capitals that no President has ever been to before—to Peking, to Moscow, to Bucharest, to Warsaw. But I want you to know, in terms of that pride, what is even greater is the pride that I would feel if we can move forward on the beginning that we have made.

We are proud of our record. But we have so much more to do. We want to build a real peace. We want to build that real prosperity, and we need your support.

Let me say finally in that respect, I have noted that some have said—well, they look at the polls and they wonder really if their vote really matters.

You bet it does. First, the only poll that counts is the one that they do on November 7. Second, this is a great decision for the American people. It is the clearest choice this country has had in this century.

I say to the people of Illinois, Democrats, independents, Republicans alike, don't sit on the sidelines, don't have this great choice made by simply a minority that manage or bother to go out to vote.

Everybody vote, and as far as I am concerned, let me tell you this—and this has always been my attitude in politics—I have won some elections, I have lost some. When I have won them, I have tried to do the best I could. When I have lost them, I have pledged my support to this country and I will continue to do so in all the years ahead.

The important thing for you: Let us make this vote on November 7 a vote of a majority of the American people, and let the new majority in America speak out—speak out for peace with honor, speak out for a strong United States, speak out for prosperity without war, speak out for progress that means not bigger government in Washington, but better government, and government that belongs to you.

Let's make these next 4 years the best 4 years in America's history.

Thank you.

NOTE: The President spoke at 12:49 p.m. at a rally at O'Hare Field. He spoke without referring to notes.

401   Campaign Statement in Oklahoma.
November 3, 1972

WHETHER the product is oil, wheat, aerospace hardware, or football players, Oklahoma plays a vigorous role in keeping America moving forward.

Yesterday, Agriculture Secretary Earl Butz announced that we can now expect a 25-percent increase in the value of U.S. farm exports in the current fiscal year. This $2 billion increase in farm exports, when added to last year's record of $8.1 billion, will push U.S. agricultural exports over the $10 billion mark for the first time in history.

Earlier in this Administration we announced that our farm export goal was $10 billion. Those who thought this goal was years in the future failed to understand that by expanding our traditional markets and opening new markets in the Soviet Union and the People's Republic of China, we can dramatically increase the potential for peaceful trade among nations. They also failed to reckon with the capacity of States like Oklahoma and other major producing areas to meet the trade potential.

Oklahoma, with its vast agricultural output, is making its contribution to a new era of international trade—it is helping to make such an era possible, and it is going to profit from this new era.

But Oklahoma is more than fields of waving wheat and cattle (which recently have been selling for the highest prices in years). Tulsa is a hub of the aerospace industry in America. Construction of the space shuttle alone will mean that more than $20 million will be passing into the Tulsa economy over the next 2 years.

There are those who speak of the commercial benefits of war, but nobody profits from war at all. The profits are in peace, and Oklahoma will share the profits of peace just as she has shared in the effort to build a structure of peace in the world. The petroleum resources, the manufacturing output, the military and civilian support at the great military bases like Tinker Air Force Base and Fort Sill, and most of all the patriotism of Oklahomans,

have all played a vital role in the pursuit of peace.

We are moving toward peace in Vietnam and around the world. But in order to do this we must have a strong America with a vigorous economy. When we came into office nearly 4 years ago, we were confronted with a dangerously overheated economy. Inflation fueled by wartime spending had shot above 6 percent. Today it has been cut almost in half, and we are doing a better job of controlling inflation than any other industrialized country in the free world.

But if we are to have prosperity in peacetime, it will not be enough just to cut inflation. We must stop wages from being eroded by constantly increasing taxes. The only way you can keep taxes in line is by keeping Government spending in line. Since the Congress has refused to meet its responsibility in this matter, I have been forced to exercise the veto on frequent occasions to get rid of budget-busting and inflationary spending bills. But the long range answer is not the veto; it is a Congress that won't try to spend itself back into office every time an election rolls around.

Dewey Bartlett [1] has a proven record of sound fiscal management in Oklahoma, and he is the kind of man who understands the need for fiscal responsibility at the national level. We both need him in the U.S. Senate; Oklahoma needs him and I need him.

At the same time, State and local governments have to do their share in holding the line against increased taxes. In the last 10 years, property taxes in Oklahoma have increased over 60 per-

[1] Dewey F. Bartlett, Governor of Oklahoma 1967–71, was the Republican candidate for the United States Senate.

cent. The purpose of the revenue sharing legislation just passed is to give the tax dollar back to the States and local communities where they know best how it should be spent.

The simple fact is that one of the reasons we have high taxes is because we have such an imbalanced tax distribution system, and revenue sharing is part of an effort to change that. It was because of the property tax increases here in Oklahoma that I was so surprised to see Dewey Bartlett's opponent oppose revenue sharing as he did.

I think we are going to have the kind of Congress we need this year to enact the legislation and to accomplish the goals of the new American majority. As we achieve peace, we need men who understand how to keep the peace, men who understand that the prudent use of power

is the surest guarantee of peace. Prosperity, too, is within our reach. But we need people who understand how to bring it about. We need people who know that a nation's wealth isn't measured in how much its government spends but in how much its people have left to spend.

Oklahoma plays a great role in America. From the heart of its good land, from all its industrial and extractive output, and from the hearts of its good people, Oklahoma gives much to America. Now we ask Oklahoma to give us a vote for peace and prosperity, and give us men in the Congress and in the Senate who know how to win both peace and prosperity, and who know how to keep them both.

NOTE: The statement was released at Tulsa, Okla.

402   Remarks at Tulsa, Oklahoma. *November 3, 1972*

THANK YOU very much. To all of you who are gathered here inside the hangar, and to the thousands more outside the hangar, thank you very much for a wonderful welcome to the Sooner State.

When I scheduled this stop in Oklahoma, there were those who said "Why?" I am going to give you the reasons why. I remember saying at the time of the nomination in Miami that we weren't going to take any State for granted, and that we were not going to concede any States to the opposition. Oklahoma is one State that I have always carried, and we are not going to start losing it now.

Every time I come here to Oklahoma, believe me—I remember in '52 as a candidate for Vice President, '56, '60, '68—

you just give me a wonderful lift. Thank you for that wonderful lift that you give me.

Now, there is another reason that I am here, and that is to express appreciation not only for your support in the past, but also to ask for your help in the future. Naturally, I am going to talk about what I hope for the future for those 4 years you are talking about, but I also want to tell you that one man, the President of the United States, cannot do that job alone. He needs help. He needs it in the Senate and he needs it in the House of Representatives. I want you to know that in Henry Bellmon you have one of the strongest, best, most loyal Senators in the whole United States of America.

I know, too, that Oklahoma is a team State. You produce great teams. You believe in teamwork. You don't like to have one man cancel out another man's vote. Let me say that during the years that I have been President, I have had the opportunity to work with many Governors. Of all the 50 Governors, in this State one of my closest friends, but more important, one of the ablest men that I have met in terms of knowing the problems of his State, of knowing the problems of this Nation, is Dewey Bartlett, and I think that Bartlett and Bellmon would just make a great team in the United States Senate.

You know, another thought occurs to me. When they call that roll in the Senate, they do it alphabetically, and when you have those two "B's" high up on the roll it might affect a few more votes right down that way, so we want them both.

Over in the House of Representatives, you, of course, have had fine representation from this State. I would not want to come here, even though he is not a candidate this year, without paying the appreciation of the Nation to Page Belcher for the great service he has rendered as a Congressman, and to tell you that I, of course, support all of our splendid candidates for Congress. I will not have the time to mention them all individually, but particularly here in Tulsa the man who was your former mayor, the man who has all of the qualifications to step into those big shoes of Page Belcher, Jim Hewgley for the United States Congress.

Now, with that, if you would permit me, I would like to say a few words for myself, not really in that sense, and not just for a party. What I want to say to you now is that next Tuesday we have an election which is very different from most elections in this country. Usually an election is just a contest between two men, each of whom aspires to a high office, with somewhat different views, but some of the same views. Usually a contest for an election involves a contest between two parties; one party nominates one man and the other party nominates another man.

Let me tell you, this year what counts is not the man, and not the personality and not the party; what we need is what is best for America; Democrats, Republicans all joining together for what is best for America.

I think, for example, of those next 4 years, and naturally I think of the last 4 years and what I want and what you want for those 4 years. I was so delighted to see all these wonderful young people, most of them will not remember what I said here. They will only remember, perhaps, that they were here. But what we say here and what we do in these next 4 years will determine their futures and your future. That is what this is all about.

In that connection, for example, as I said on television last night, I want them to have the opportunity and to have something we haven't had since President Eisenhower was President, and that means prosperity without war and without inflation. I want them to have opportunity—opportunity to go as high as their abilities will take them, and we have moved in that direction in fields of education and health and environment over these past 4 years.

I want them also, all of our younger generation and the older generation, to really have a deep feeling of love and respect for this country. Let me say, I have noted that some of those who are campaigning across this country are constantly running America down. Let's speak up for America and speak up for her on November 7.

But above all, everybody here in Oklahoma, like everybody in Illinois where I was a few hours ago, and everybody in Rhode Island, where I will be about 3 hours from now, wants the same thing for their children, and that is a world of peace. Let me speak to that subject for just a moment so that you can see what is really at stake in this campaign, so that you can see the great difference between the candidates and what your votes will do for that great goal of peace in the United States.

In the first place, we have made great progress toward our goal of peace with honor over the last 4 years, I refer, for example, to the trips that I took to Peking and to Moscow which mean that those great nations, instead of being in confrontation with the United States, while we will still have differences, we will have the opportunities to have a peaceful relationship with them.

I speak also of the progress we have made toward peace in Vietnam. I speak of the fact that we have brought over 500,000 home. I also speak of what you have all read about, of the fact that we have finally made a breakthrough in the negotiations to bring about a peace with honor. We have already agreed on major provisions. Listen to these provisions because they are the ones that I laid down in my speech of May 8 when, as you remember, I ordered the mining of Haiphong and the bombing of North Vietnam: First, we have agreed, have an agreement, that all of our prisoners of war

will be returned and all of our missing in action will be accounted for. Second, we have an agreement that we will have a cease-fire throughout Indochina, in Vietnam, Cambodia, and Laos. Third, and this is a very important part of what we have agreed to, we have agreed that the 17 million people of South Vietnam shall have the right to choose their own government without having a Communist government or a coalition government imposed upon them against their will.

We have not yet signed the final agreement and the reason that we have not is that some of the details, some of the issues, are still to be finally worked out. I am confident that they will soon be worked out. Let me tell you what the election has to do with this. As far as the election is concerned, it will not have any effect in hastening us to sign an agreement that would be wrong and it will have no effect in delaying us from signing an agreement that is right.

Let me tell you, what is far more important than this next election is peace for the next generation, and we are going to have the right kind of an agreement.

You remember in 1968 when a bombing halt agreement was made just before an election. It was made with the best of intentions, I am sure, by the previous Administration. But because it wasn't nailed down in its details the war went on.

We are not going to make that mistake. We are nailing down the details. We are getting an agreement which will not simply be an interlude between wars, but which will lay the foundation for peace in the years ahead. I know that peace with honor rather than peace with surrender is what all of the people of this State want.

Now, may I come to a fundamental proposition that the people of Oklahoma have always understood in great numbers and that we in this Nation must understand if we are going to be able to build that era of peace that we want to build in the years ahead. There are those who believe that as we now negotiate with the Soviet Union and the People's Republic of China, and as we bring the war in Vietnam to an end, that the United States should drastically cut its national defense and then hope that the others do, too. Let me say this: I want all of you to know, I have sat for long days, day on day, in negotiations at the highest level in Peking and Moscow. They have been important negotiations. They have been successful negotiations. But they could not have been successful unless I was able to negotiate recognizing that I represented a nation that was strong and that was respected.

Let us now resolve that we shall never send the President of the United States to the negotiating table as the head of the second strongest nation—the United States of America. And so the issue is clear. The issue that you, the voters of this country—Democrats, Republicans, and independents—will all answer is this: Shall it be peace with surrender or peace with honor? I say peace with honor for America. That is what we stand for.

Shall it be a weak America or shall it be a strong America? I say a strong America.

Shall it be an America that withdraws from its responsibilities in the world, or an America that leads the way to peace in the world so that we can have peace at home? I say let us meet our responsibilities in the world. And also, as we look to the future of this country, let us remember that not only do we want peace for our younger generation and for ourselves, prosperity without war and without inflation, progress, but let us have in these next 4 years, as we come to the 200th birthday of this country, a restoration of something that Americans had in their youth and which we need now.

Do you remember when America was only 3 million people and 13 States, weak militarily and also poor economically? And yet that young America, 195 years ago, was respected all over the world. It was the hope of the world. Why? Because America then stood for spiritual and moral strength that could not be represented by military strength and that was stronger than any economic wealth and power.

Today America's military strength is unquestioned. America's economic strength is unquestioned. We are the richest nation in the world. Let us also remember that this is the time to strengthen that moral and religious heritage and principle in America that has made us the great nation that we are.

My friends in Oklahoma, as I said at the beginning, it is always a very great privilege to come here, to be received so warmly. It is also very heartening to know that out here in the middle of this country there are a people—a people who are strong, a people who have backbone, a people who will stand up for America, a people who believe in the religious and moral values that made this country great. Every time that I make a great decision, I know that I can count on the people of Oklahoma.

Thank you very much.

NOTE: The President spoke at 3:30 p.m. at a rally at Tulsa International Airport. He spoke without referring to notes.

403   Campaign Statement in Rhode Island. *November 3, 1972*

PRESIDENT Franklin Roosevelt once startled a convention of the Daughters of the American Revolution by telling them that we are all "descended from immigrants." Indeed, more than any other nation on earth, America is a land of immigrants.

Being so has not been a handicap. It has been an asset. It has strengthened the courage and the idealism of the American people and driven us on to even greater endeavors.

No State better typified this great American tradition than Rhode Island. Small in size but great in spirit, it has absorbed immigrants for over three centuries, from the first small group of religious refugees fleeing persecution to the massive influx of Italians, Irish, Poles, and other peoples seeking a new life on these shores in our own century.

And Rhode Island teaches us all the important lesson that while we are a diverse people, drawn from many sources, there is far more that unites us than divides us. All of us want the same basic rights and opportunities; all of us want the same kind of future for America.

We want a future in which our sons will not have to go off to another war because America was weak, or misled, or unprepared.

We want a future in which we can all live at peace with the world and with one another, free to enjoy the fruits of our own labor.

And we want to achieve something that this country has not enjoyed since Dwight Eisenhower served in the White House more than a decade ago—we want an era of prosperity without war and without inflation.

I believe we can do it. I believe we can do it because I am convinced that, when it comes down to these vital fundamentals, we are one Nation, one people—one America.

The people of Rhode Island have a crucial role to play in that future. In your plants and in your commerce, you are helping to keep the sinews of American industry strong and vibrant. In your work at the Newport Naval Base, the Quonset Point Air Station, and the Davisville Construction Center, you are keeping our national defenses first in the world. And in your patriotism and dedication to hard work, you are keeping the Nation's spirit aflame for generations yet to come.

I urge you to continue in that role by sending a man to Washington who shares your belief in a strong America—a man who served with distinction as Secretary of the Navy, and who has proven his skill as a vigorous, effective leader who knows how to get things done—John Chafee.[1]

---

[1] John H. Chafee, Governor of Rhode Island 1963–69 and Secretary of the Navy 1969–72, was the Republican candidate for the United States Senate.

John Chafee has a keen, independent mind of his own, but he stands together with the rest of us in his commitment to keep America strong and to keep Rhode Island playing an important part in sustaining our naval strength. He knows too that we are committed to achieving more than peace alone. We are determined to build not only a peaceful America, but a prosperous America as well.

There is an economic resurgence across America today, and I am confident we can keep it up with your help.

On the job front, more than 2.3 million new civilian jobs have been created in the last year. This is the highest rate of increase since 1956. Unemployment nationally and here in Rhode Island is coming down, and we are going to keep it coming down. Rhode Islanders know that John Chafee created 50,000 jobs while serving as Governor; that's the kind of progress we want in the future.

For 5 years, the average American's purchasing power stagnated because of inflation. We have changed that situation here in Rhode Island and across the Nation. We have cut the rate of inflation almost in half, and, in the last year, we have driven up real wages—the real purchasing power of the average working American by 4.5 percent—the equivalent of more than two extra weekly paychecks.

Higher taxes, the other threat to the average family's pocketbook, has been another of our prime targets. That is why I have vetoed a long line of excessive spending measures passed by the Congress. They all added up to breaking the budget and driving up taxes. That is something I am determined to prevent with every means at my disposal.

As a result of tax reform already achieved under this Administration, the average family of four making $10,000 a year has had its Federal income taxes drop by 26 percent since 1969.

A further major stride has been the enactment of general revenue sharing. The revenue sharing bill which I signed 2 weeks ago in Philadelphia will allow many State and local governments to hold the line on property taxes, a benefit that should not be lost on Rhode Islanders whose property taxes have soared more than 60 percent over the past 10 years. This legislation will make it easier for the next Governor of Rhode Island to govern wisely and well, without the constant threat of increased taxes.

From personal acquaintance, I believe that Herbert DeSimone would be the best man for the Governor's job in Rhode Island over the next 2 years. I have had the opportunity to see him at work firsthand as an excellent Assistant Secretary of Transportation, where he served as the strong right hand of another outstanding New Englander, John Volpe. I know that Herb DeSimone has the administrative skill, the leadership ability, and the strong character it takes to make a successful Governor.

Leadership that can set serious, attainable goals—leadership that knows how to get things done—that is what America needs today on every level of government, from the White House to the Governor's office to the county courthouse. That is the kind of leadership I pledge to give the Nation as we work together toward an era of peace and progress.

NOTE: The statement was released at Providence, R.I.

404   Remarks at Providence, Rhode Island.
November 3, 1972

Ladies and gentlemen:

Thank you very much, first, to those marvelous bands, let's give them a hand for entertaining while we were here.

Second, I want you to know that when I come to Rhode Island, I feel somewhat like coming home, because it was 30 years ago that I spent 2 months in Quonset Point, and from here went into the service and then overseas into the Pacific. I always remember when I, at Quonset Point, used to come in to Providence, how very warm and generous and hospitable were the people of Rhode Island and of Providence to those of us in the Navy at that time. Thank you very much for what you did 30 years ago.

Now, on this visit, I would like to mention all of the fine candidates who are running on our ticket. Time will not permit it, but there are two here that I want to mention in particular. I mention them because they have been such splendid members of our Administration during these past 4 years. I am going to start with a man who was the Assistant Secretary of Transportation. I know that in that position that he was a dedicated public servant, but what was more, he was dynamic, he was strong, he was intelligent. He was a good organizer. We didn't want to give him up, but I think the State of Rhode Island needs him as Governor of this State, Herb DeSimone.

Herb, with you standing here by me, just let me say that in these next 4 years I look forward to working with you as Governor of Rhode Island, and that door will always be open for Governor DeSimone of the State of Rhode Island.

[At this point, Herbert F. DeSimone spoke briefly. The President then resumed speaking.]

Now, turning to the national scene, I speak about a man that I know, and that you have known for many years. I remember when he was the Governor of this State and rated by all of the objective journalists as one of the top Governors in the Nation. I remember him, too, as the Secretary of the Navy in our Administration for 3 years. John Chafee, without question, is a man who was born to be in public service. He is a man that the Nation needs in public service. Let me just put it quite directly to you: Rhode Island needs him in the Senate, America needs him in the Senate, I need him in the Senate, and you are going to put him in the Senate. John Chafee.

[At this point, John H. Chafee spoke briefly. The President then resumed speaking.]

Now, I would like to say a word for another candidate, for myself. I would like to say in that respect that I have had the great honor of being a candidate for the highest office in this land on three occasions, in 1960, in 1968, and again this year, in 1972. I lost the first time in a narrow election. I won the second time, and now comes the third.

As I stand here in Rhode Island, it just occurred to me that while in those elections to which I referred, in '60 and '68, I have at one time or the other carried most of the States, Rhode Island is a State that I have never carried. Let me say, the third time will be the charm. This is the year when we take Rhode Island.

I want to tell you why I believe this is a year when the people of Rhode Island are going to vote for the national ticket, for John Chafee, for your next Governor, Governor DeSimone. I want to tell you why.

This is not going to be a contest in which the people of Rhode Island are going to divide on partisan terms, Republican versus Democrat. It is going to be a contest in which the people of Rhode Island, like the people of this Nation, realize that this is one of those elections when what is best for America must come first, and the new American majority, Democrats and independents and Republicans together, are going to give America the leadership that we need in these next 4 years.

John Chafee has mentioned the subject which is closest to my heart and closest to the heart of all the people here. From the time that I was at Quonset and came out of Quonset as a naval officer, from the time that I finished my service in World War II, I have felt, as everyone in this audience feels, a deep dedication to the cause of peace.

I have realized that in this century this great Nation has been involved in war in every generation, and every time the war ends, we think, now we can have peace. But it has not been that way. The generation that fought in World War I saw their sons fighting in World War II. The generations that fought in World War II saw their younger brothers and some of their sons fighting in Korea. The ones who fought in Korea found their younger brothers and some of their sons fighting in Vietnam.

Let me say that is why we seek peace in the world, but we seek peace with honor, the kind of a peace that will lead to a lasting peace and not peace with surrender.

We have made a breakthrough in the negotiations which will lead to peace. I have referred to that breakthrough. I want to summarize briefly where it stands and to tell you why I am confident we are going to reach the agreement which will end this war and end it with honor and without surrender.

First, we have reached agreement on the three major principles that I laid down in my speech of May 8. First, that we are going to have a cease-fire throughout Indochina, not just in Vietnam but in Cambodia and Laos. We have agreed on that.

Second, we have an agreement that all of the American POW's will be returned and our MIA's will be accounted for wherever they are in Indochina.

Third, we have reached agreement on the principle that the people of South Vietnam shall determine their future without having a Communist government or a coalition government imposed upon them against their will.

What is left to be done is to work out some details on which there are still differences. Details, however, are important. They must be worked out in the right way, because we are not going to have a repetition of what we had in 1968, when, with the best of intentions, the United States agreed to a bombing halt and when there was misunderstanding because the details were not worked out.

We are working out those details; we will work them out. We will succeed. But the most important thing is we are going to end this war and end it in a way that will lay the foundation for real peace in the years to come. That is what all Americans want.

Now, may I say a word about the role that you can play and the role that John

Chafee can especially play in the United States Senate.

I met this morning, before I took off on a trip that took me to Chicago and then Oklahoma and finally here in Rhode Island, with a very distinguished scientist, the Russian minister of science. We discussed some of the negotiations we had had in Moscow in May when we made, as you recall, an historic and very important agreement limiting nuclear arms between these great powers.

We discussed also the fact that other negotiations are going to take place, very important ones, late in November, in which we will continue to try to limit nuclear arms between our two nations and thereby reduce the burden of arms and also increase the chances for peace.

As I talked to him I thought of this visit. As I talked to him I realized, and I want you to realize, that if we are going to be successful in negotiating with the Soviet Union and if we are going to have the kind of success that will have that limitation of arms that we all want, and progress toward peace, it is vitally important that the President of the United States not be sent to the conference table as the head of the second strongest nation in this world.

Let me tell you why that is important. Not for any jingoistic reason—because when the United States has the second strongest navy, as our opponents advocate, when the United States has the second strongest air force, as they advocate, and the second strongest army, it means that any incentive that the Soviets or any other nation would have to negotiate with us would not be there.

What we must do is to reduce our arms only when it is mutual. That is the way

to build a real peace and not a temporary peace. John Chafee knows how to keep America strong. He knows that the most important element of America's peacetime strength is to have the strongest navy in the world. He built that kind of navy when he was Secretary of the Navy. We need his votes in the United States Senate and his leadership to continue to have that strong navy that John Chafee has contributed so much to as Secretary of the Navy and will, also, in the years ahead.

I want to tell you, my friends, too, that as I look at this crowd, and particularly as I had the opportunity to meet so many of the young people as we walked along the fence here, I realized that all of your hopes lie in what happens in these next 4 years and thereafter. As far as those years are concerned, let me simply summarize by saying my hopes, I think, are yours. They are these:

I want a world of peace. I want a peace that will last; not one just for an election but one that will last for a generation or more. I want something, too, that we have not had since President Eisenhower was President—that is real prosperity, full employment without inflation and without war. We can have it and we will have it, with your help.

I want progress for America, for all Americans; opportunity for Americans; opportunity in which any American, regardless of his background, can go to the very top, where there will be ceiling unlimited.

And I want respect for America. I want the people of this country, and particularly our young people, to realize that we are very fortunate at this period in our history that we, the United States of

America, have it within our power, that we have it within our leadership capability, to lead the way, the whole world, to a peaceful world. That is why the trip to Peking took place. That is why one-fourth of the world's people now, who had had no communication with the United States for 20 years, now have communication.

That is why we have negotiated with the Soviet Union. That is why we are working for peace in the Mideast. That is why in all of these areas I say, keep America strong, be sure that we see that the United States remains respected in the world. And we can do that by electing to the Congress, to the Senate of the United States, men like John Chafee, who understand peace through strength, and that is the message I leave with you today.

One final thought: On this last appearance that I will be able to make in this New England area, as somebody was saying as I went along the fence there, I asked a 13-year-old what he was going to do. He said, "I am going to go into politics." I said, "What are you going to run for?" He said, "President." I said, "Fine. You should shoot high." But then I gave him another bit of advice. "The main thing," I said, "to remember is, you don't win them all. I know. You win some; you lose some. But the important thing to remember is that particularly where the Presidency is concerned, Amer-

ica is bigger than any man and it is bigger than any party."

I want to tell you, if I receive your votes and the votes of this Nation, I will serve as well as I can. If on the other hand, my friends, if on the other hand, the verdict of the people of this Nation should go to our opponents, then I will support what is best for America and not take the position that only if I win are we going to support whoever is President of the United States of America. The President comes first in the policies that he will be advocating.

This does not mean we will not have differences, but it does mean that in our system we debate those differences intelligently. We listen when others speak. We try to do everything that we possibly can to do the best job that we can in campaigning, and then in serving in office.

But once the campaign is over, let us have the statesmanship, let us have the ability to pull this country together and to work together for a cause that is bigger than any party and bigger than any man, and that is to make the next 4 years the best 4 years in America's history.

Thank you.

NOTE: The President spoke at 8 p.m. at a rally at Theodore Francis Green State Airport. He spoke without referring to notes.

The remarks of Mr. DeSimone and Mr. Chafee are printed in the Weekly Compilation of Presidential Documents (vol. 8, p. 1638).

405   Radio Address on Foreign Policy.
November 4, 1972

Good afternoon:

Through the long years of America's involvement in Vietnam, our people's yearning for peace has largely been

focused on winning an end to that difficult war. As a result, there has often been a tendency to lose sight of the larger prospects for peace in the rest of the world.

As peace in Vietnam comes closer, we can look to the larger world and the long-term future with hope and satisfaction.

Four years ago I promised that we would move from an era of confrontation to an era of negotiation. I also said that we would maintain our own strength and work to restore that of our alliances, because the way to make real progress toward peace is to negotiate from strength and not from weakness. Because we have done so, the world today is more peaceful by far than it was 4 years ago. The prospects for a full generation of peace are brighter than at any time since the end of World War II.

In the past 4 years, we have concluded more—and more significant—agreements with the Soviets than in all the previous years since World War II. We have ended nearly a quarter century of mutual isolation between the United States and the People's Republic of China. All over the world, the tide toward negotiation is moving. North and South Korea are negotiating with one another. East and West Germany are negotiating with one another. A cease-fire has been in effect for more than 2 years in the Middle East. The leaders of India and Pakistan are talking with one another. The nations of Europe, of NATO, and of the Warsaw Pact are preparing to meet next year in a European Security Conference, and preparations are underway for negotiations on mutual and balanced reduction of armed forces in Central Europe.

All this is evidence of solid progress toward a world in which we can talk about our differences rather than fight about them.

Nineteen hundred seventy-two has been a year of more achievement for peace than any year since the end of World War II.

This progress did not just happen by itself.

In my Inaugural Address nearly 4 years ago, I said that the greatest honor history can bestow is the title of peacemaker, but I also pointed out that peace does not come through wishing for it, that there is no substitute for days and even years of patient and prolonged diplomacy.

For the past 4 years this Nation has engaged in patient and prolonged diplomacy in every corner of the world, and we have also maintained the strength that has made our diplomacy credible and peace possible. As a result, we are well on the way toward erecting what I have often referred to as a structure of peace, a structure that rests on the hard concrete of common interests and mutual agreements, and not on the shifting sands of naive sentimentality.

That term, "a structure of peace," speaks an important truth about the nature of peace in today's world. Peace cannot be wished into being. It has to be carefully and painstakingly built in many ways and on many fronts, through networks of alliances, through respect for commitments, through patient negotiations, through balancing military forces and expanding economic interdependence, through reaching one agreement that opens the way to others, through developing patterns of international behavior that will be accepted by other powers. Most important of all, the structure of peace has to be built in such a way that all those who might be tempted to destroy it will instead have a stake in preserving it.

In the past 4 years, my efforts to build that structure of peace have taken me to 22 countries, including four world capitals never visited by an American President before—Peking, Moscow, Warsaw, and Bucharest. Everywhere I have traveled I have seen evidence that the times are on the side of peace, if America maintains its strength and continues on course. For example, ever since World War II, the world's people and its statesmen have dreamed of putting the nuclear genie back in the bottle, of controlling the dreaded nuclear arms race, but always that race remained unchecked until this year.

In Moscow last May, we and the Soviet Union reached the first agreement ever for limiting strategic nuclear arms. We signed that agreement last month in Washington. This was an historic beginning. It moved back the frontiers of fear. It helped check the dangerous spiral of nuclear weapons. It opened the way to further negotiations on further limitations on nuclear arsenals which will soon begin.

As we pursue these negotiations, however, let us remember that no country will pay a price for something that another country will give up for nothing. If we had scrapped the ABM missile system, as many advocated, we would never have achieved the first arms agreement with the Soviets. If we unilaterally slashed our defenses now as our opponents in this election advocate, the Soviets would have no incentive to negotiate further arms limitations.

Or take another example. After 10 years of recurring international monetary crises, we took bold actions a year ago to strengthen the dollar and to bring about a reformed international monetary system that would be fair to the United States and fair to the world. The result of these actions has been a solid and substantial beginning on just such a system, and the stage is now set for an international effort to achieve some of the most important monetary and trade reforms in history. As

we complete these reforms in the years ahead, we can usher in a new age of world prosperity, a prosperity made even greater by the rapid expansion of peaceful trade that is now taking place, not only with our traditional trading partners but also with nations that have been our adversaries.

I cite these simply as examples of the broad, unfinished agenda of peace that now lies before us, the agenda of new starts made, of negotiations begun, of new relationships established, which now we must build on with the same initiative and imagination that achieved the initial breakthroughs. As we move forward on this agenda, we can see vast areas of peaceful cooperation to be explored.

We agreed in Peking to pursue cultural, journalistic, educational, and other exchanges, so that the world's most prosperous nation and its most populous nation can get to know one another again.

We agreed in Moscow to cooperate in protecting the environment, explore in space, fight disease. This means the day is fast approaching when a Russian cosmonaut and an American astronaut will shake hands in space, when a Russian chemist and an American biologist will work side by side to find a cure for cancer. And each time our nations join hands in the works of peace, we advance the day when nations will no longer raise their hands in warfare.

Throughout the world today America is respected. This is partly because we have entered a new era of initiative in American foreign policy, and the world's leaders and its people have seen the results. But it is also because the world has come to know America. It knows we are a nation of peaceful intentions, of honorable purposes, true to our commitments. We are respected because for a third of a century under six Presidents we have met the responsibilities of a great and free nation. We have not retreated from the world. We have not betrayed our allies. We have not fallen into the foolish illusion that we could somehow build a wall around America, here to enjoy our comforts, oblivious to the cries or the threats of others. We have maintained our strength.

There are those today who condemn as a relic of a cold war mentality the idea that peace requires strength. There are those who ridicule military expenditures as wasteful and immoral. Our opponents in this campaign have even described the great bipartisan tradition of negotiating from strength as one of the most damaging and costly cliches in the American vocabulary. If the day ever comes when the President of the United States has to negotiate from weakness, that will be a dangerous day, not only for America but for the whole world.

Those who scoff at balance of power diplomacy should recognize that the only alternative to a balance of power is an imbalance of power, and history shows that nothing so drastically escalates the danger of war as such an imbalance. It is precisely the fact that the elements of balance now exist that gives us a rare opportunity to create a system of stability that can maintain the peace, not just for a decade but for a generation and more.

The years ahead will not be easy. The choices will not be simple. They will require an extra measure of care in distinguishing between rhetoric and reality, between the easy temptation and the hard necessity. We will be told that all the things we want to do at home could be painlessly financed if we slashed our military spending. We will be told that we can have peace merely by asking for it, that if we simply demonstrate good will and good faith, our adversaries will do likewise, and that we need do no more. This is dangerous nonsense.

A heavy responsibility lies on the shoulders of those who hold or seek power in today's world, a responsibility not to court the public favor by fostering illusions that peace can be either achieved or kept without maintaining our strength and meeting our responsibilities.

As we approach the end of the war in Vietnam, the great question is whether the end of that war will be only an interlude between wars or the beginning of a generation of peace for the world.

Five months ago, I delivered the first television address to the Soviet people ever made by an American President. I tried to tell them something about America, about the people of America, about our hopes, our desire for peace and progress, not only for ourselves but for all the people of the world. In that talk, I repeated an old story told in Russia about a traveler who was walking to another village, who stopped and asked a woodsman how long it would take him to get there. The woodsman replied he did not know. The traveler was angry, because he was sure the woodsman lived in the village and knew how far it was. But then as soon as he had gone a few steps further down the road, the woodsman called out to him to stop. "It will take you 15 minutes," the woodsman said. "Why didn't you tell me that in the first place?" the traveler demanded. And the woodsman answered, "Because then I didn't know the length of your stride."

In these past 4 years, we and the other nations of the world have had a chance to measure the length of our strides. At last we are traveling in the same direction toward a world of peace, toward an era of negotiation, and of expanding cooperation. In the next 4 years, the President of the United States, whoever he is, will negotiate with the leaders of many nations on a broad range of issues vital to America, vital to the world. As we cast our ballots next Tuesday, the world will see whether we have changed the length of our stride.

If you approve the beginnings we have made, then your vote on election day to support those policies will be a message to the leaders of all other nations that the American people are not going to retreat, are not going to surrender. It will strengthen the President's hand immensely as we continue to move from confrontation to negotiation to cooperation all around the world as we build toward a generation of peace.

Thank you, and good afternoon.

NOTE: The President spoke from a prepared text. His address was recorded at the White House for broadcast at 12:07 p.m. on nationwide radio. Time for the broadcast was purchased by the Committee for the Re-Election of the President.

406   Campaign Statement in North Carolina. *November 4, 1972*

AS WE approach the end of this year's campaign, two questions stand out:

—Are we going to continue the policies that have made 1972 the year of the greatest achievements for peace since the end of World War II?

—Are we going to continue our advance toward what America has not known since President Eisenhower was in office—prosperity with full employment, without inflation and without war?

Whether we succeed in building a lasting peace in the world depends on the strength of America's resolve. There can be no retreat to peace. We cannot disarm unilaterally, and still expect others to negotiate a mutual limitation of arms; we cannot betray our allies and abandon our commitments, and still expect others to believe our word or respect our commitments.

We have made progress toward peace because we strengthened our alliances and maintained our military forces—because we refused to allow America to become the second strongest nation in the world.

As long as I am President, I will never let America become the second strongest nation in the world. That is why we are not going to do as our opponents advocate, and slash our defense budget by $32 billion, cut our Marines by almost one-third, our tactical air wings by 30 percent, and our aircraft carriers from 16 to 6. We are not going to scrap our conventional weapons, leaving us with little more than the nuclear option.

By remaining strong, by retaining the respect we have won in the world, we can continue building what we have begun in these past 4 years: a structure of peace that will last, so that the next generation can be the first generation in this century to live without war and the fear of war.

Here at home, we have been making sure and steady progress toward a new prosperity—and North Carolina is among the leaders in that progress. The economy of this forward-looking State is booming. Total personal income in North Carolina was up 7.8 percent from 1970 to 1971, which was nearly one percent better than the national increase.

North Carolina has succeeded in reducing statewide unemployment to 2.6 percent, well under the national average. Unemployment in the Greensboro-Winston-Salem-High Point area is down to 2.2 percent.

In North Carolina right now, we are close to our national goal—that anyone who wants to work will be able to work.

Nationwide, we are also making encouraging and often overlooked progress against higher prices. With our new economic policies, we have cut the rate of inflation almost in half. And just this week, the Labor Department reported that wholesale prices had remained stable all month. The total index for wholesale prices declined by 0.2 percent in October in absolute terms and rose by only 0.1 percent on a seasonally adjusted basis.

We are making these gains for peace and prosperity because the American spirit is strong—because Americans are not going to yield to the easy temptations of surrender abroad or handout at home. As one who has lived in North Carolina, I know that that American spirit is strong in this State.

With the support of the voters of North Carolina, with the help of Jesse Helms in the United States Senate, and with Jim Holshouser in the Governor's office, we can continue our progress and so make the next 4 years the best 4 years in the history of this Nation.

NOTE: The statement was released at Greensboro, N.C.

407   Remarks at Greensboro, North Carolina. *November 4, 1972*

ON BEHALF of Mrs. Nixon and myself, I want to express to all of you our really grateful appreciation for what is without question the greatest welcome we have ever received in North Carolina, and we have had some great ones.

We have appreciated the support we have had in the past. We remember how critical North Carolina was to our success in 1968. Based upon what I see today, we are going to repeat in North Carolina in '72, and even more.

May I say, too, that I am particularly interested to note what a beautiful day this is. Two or three days ago I was talking to Billy Graham on the phone, and he said, "If the weather is good, give me the credit." So, in any event, this is a magnificent day, and you have helped, of course, to make it even a better day because of your presence here.

On this occasion, I want to pay my respects, if I could, first to a man who is retiring from the Congress of the United States, a great servant of this State and of this Nation and a very close, personal friend of mine, Charlie Jonas. In paying my respects to him, I also want to indicate my complete support for all of those running for the Congress of the United States who have already been introduced. It is a great team. We would like them there in the Congress of the United States, and we will appreciate your support for them.

I also want to thank Roy Acuff [1] for entertaining you before we got here. He said to me as I came on the stage, he said, "I think you are going to do all right in North Carolina," and he says, "I can promise you Tennessee." So there are two States we have, in any event.

Now to your candidate, our candidate for Governor, Jim Holshouser. He is a man I have known personally, have worked with over many, many years. He is one of those very well organized, dedicated men who has all of the attributes which would make him a fine chief executive of this State. I look forward to the opportunity of working with him in those next 4 years, when he is the Governor, and when, I trust, I am still in Washington, D.C.

On this occasion, too, I want to speak of another old friend. As a matter of fact, the friendship goes back even further than the one with Jim Holshouser, because at the time that we met, Jim Holshouser was perhaps too young to be in politics. I remember 21 years ago when I was a junior Senator from the State of California, and some way or other, when they allocated the office space, they put my office between two Senators from North Carolina. Clyde Hoey was on the one side and Willis Smith was on the other. They were fine men. They were great Democrats. But I found that I voted as they did because we were putting America above party, those two Senators from North Carolina.

A very young man—he was young to

me at that time—Jesse Helms, came in one day to see me. He was the administrative assistant for Willis Smith. He brought with him a young man in a wheelchair, a very promising athlete who had been struck down by the polio epidemic of that year, as you remember, 1951.

I met him. We had our picture taken. I understand that Bucky Branham is still in that wheelchair, but he still is one who, with Jesse Helms, has that zest for life and has not given up because of adversity.

Ever since that time I have watched Jesse Helms. I have known his intelligence, his compassion, his dedication. I will simply state my position in a word: I know your interest, of course, always in the top of the ticket, but remember, to do the job we need Members of the Senate, Members of the House, who will support what we are trying to do at the top of the ticket.

In that connection, North Carolina needs Jesse Helms in the United States Senate. The United States—the Nation needs Jesse Helms in the United States Senate. I need him and I will deeply appreciate your support for this fine man in the United States Senate.

I have been quite interested, too, in some of the signs around here. I see one over there, "Spiro Is Our Hero." As we enter the closing days of this campaign, I would like to say a word about my running mate. I have often indicated my admiration for him and my respect, but I have noted that in recent days that the organized attempts to make him blow his cool, perhaps attempts to disrupt meetings on a scale unprecedented in American politics, have even gotten more, but let me say the test of a man is not when things go easy, but when they are trying to make it hard for you.

---

[1] Country and western entertainer and recording artist.

I simply want to say that I think all Americans are very proud that in spite of the disruption, in spite of the organized heckling, the Vice President of the United States has kept his cool, his dignity, and has come through it as the splendid man that he is.

Now I am going to suggest, so that we can give equal time here at this meeting, that our friends in the three television networks over here, ABC, CBS, NBC, who will have this on the program tonight, that they now turn their cameras to the few hundred that are over here. Let them see the kind of people that are supporting our opponents over here.

Now in the name of equal time and in the objectivity which I know all fair newsmen in North Carolina stand for, turn to the thousands over here and let's hear and see the kind of people that are supporting us.

As you know, I was very proud to have lived 3 years among you here in the Tar Heel State. It seems hard to realize that it was 35 years ago. Many of my friends, the best friends that I have, are from North Carolina. I learned to know them when I was at Duke University at law school.

Incidentally, when I was at Duke, I learned to respect all the fine schools in this country, North Carolina, North Carolina State, Wake Forest, Davidson—all of them.

But when I was in law school, having come from California and never been in the South before, I saw the South as it was then. I saw that the South was divided from the North. I saw, too, that the State of North Carolina was a heavily Democratic State where Republicans had no chance, usually, to win. It was a one-party State.

I was thinking as the airplane came up today and I saw this enormous crowd, how things have changed. They have changed for the better. They have changed not in a partisan sense, but now we find—and this is the significant thing that I wish to emphasize to this great audience—that this country is no longer, on the great issues, divided in a regional sense.

On the great issues, it is not divided in a partisan sense. When it comes to keeping America strong, when it comes to peace with honor, we are not Democrats or Republicans or Southerners or Northerners—we are Americans. That is the way the people of North Carolina feel.

That is why in this State which, according to registration, is far more Democratic than Republican, we have support that crosses the party line. Because whether it is here in North Carolina or whether it was in Rhode Island where we were last night or whether it was in Oklahoma City where we were at 2 o'clock yesterday afternoon or whether it was in Illinois where we were at noon yesterday, you can go to the East, to the North, to the South, or the Far West where we will be this afternoon in California, and you will find that Americans are joining together in a new American majority standing for issues that are above party and above regional differences.

One of the issues that joins us together is the desire, a desire that is heartfelt throughout all of this country, for peace with honor for America and the world.

As you know, we have made a major breakthrough in the negotiations which can lead to that peace with honor. In making that breakthrough I want to point out that we have reached agreement on the three fundamental principles that I laid down on May 8 when, as you recall, I ordered the bombing of North Vietnam and the mining of Haiphong.

Those three conditions on which we have reached agreement are these: one, all of our prisoners of war and those who are missing in action, all of our prisoners of war will be returned, those missing in action will be accounted for; two, we have reached agreement that there should be a cease-fire, not only in South Vietnam but in Cambodia and Laos, all over Southeast Asia; and third, we have reached agreement on the fundamental point that the people of South Vietnam should have the right to determine their own future without having a Communist government or a coalition government imposed upon them against their will.

There are some details that are still to be negotiated. We are going to negotiate them. I want to tell you why. Because in reaching an agreement like this we want to be sure that it is not just a case of peace now but peace in the years ahead. We want peace that will last and we want to be sure that as far as the details are concerned, all of the misunderstandings are removed now.

Let me take you back 4 years. You remember the bombing halt in 1968. You remember it was entered into with the very best of intentions by those who made it. But you remember also that it did not lead to peace; it simply led to a continuation of the war. There was a misunderstanding. What we are doing is insisting on continuing the negotiation on which we have basic agreement on the major principles that I have mentioned, but continue it until the details are worked out.

We are confident we can achieve that goal, but it will be a goal that we then can be proud to say is peace with honor, not peace with surrender, a peace that will last for the United States and for the world.

In that connection, the day before yesterday the mayor of Erie, Pennsylvania, a Democrat, came in to see me. He indicated his support of our ticket in his State. His wife was with him. His wife's brother had been killed in Vietnam 4 days after the bombing halt. She showed me his picture, a fine young man, a major in the United States Army. She told me about him. She said that she had received a letter from him just before his death. That letter indicated at that point support for what I was trying to advocate at that time in the campaign.

Then she said to me, "Mr. President, we all want peace, but above everything else, we want a real peace. We want a peace that will last. We want peace with honor. We want to be sure that he died, and others died, for a cause that will serve this country and serve it well."

Let me tell you: We are keeping that pledge to those who gave their lives so that America could survive as a country of peace. There is one other thought that occurred to me as she was talking to me. I think of the fact that during this very long and difficult war, a war which began 5 years before I ever came to office, but during the whole course of this long and difficult war, over 2½ million young Americans, when they had to make a decision, chose to serve their country in Vietnam, and they deserve our respect and our honor for having made that choice.

Some of those 2½ million, many of them, gave their lives for their choice, as did the brother of the wife of the mayor of Erie, Pennsylvania. A few hundred chose to desert America. I say they must pay the penalty for their choice. When this war is over, there will be no amnesty for draft dodgers or deserters. So I say to you, I gave you three of the major issues in this campaign: We stand for peace with honor versus peace with surrender. We stand for a strong America versus a weak America. We stand for no amnesty for draft dodgers and deserters. This is what we believe Americans stand for across this Nation.

But beyond this, we must also realize that what we are trying to build is not simply the end of a war, but a new kind of life here in the United States. I see all of the wonderful young people that are here, the Grimsley High School Band and the others. I think of your future. We want you to grow up in a world of peace, but we also want it to be a world in which we can have what we have not had since President Eisenhower was President, and that means progress with full employment but without war and without inflation. We are moving toward that, and we ask for your help to give us the chance to continue to find that kind of prosperity for America.

We also want progress. That means better schools, better housing, opportunity, opportunity for every young American, whatever his background, to go to the top with the ceiling unlimited. All of these things we stand for. All of these things we have made great progress in. And we believe in justice, and when we speak of justice, I say that I am proud of the men I have appointed to the Supreme Court of the United States, and we are going to appoint other men who will stand for the forces of law and order and justice, because it is time that we strengthened the peace forces as against the criminal forces in the United States of America.

Now, if I could take you a bit further beyond simply these material things I have been talking about, beyond ending a war and bringing the peace that we all want, beyond the prosperity without war and without inflation, the progress in all these other areas which we, as Americans want, let me tell you that the future is bright for America. It is bright because the world is different. We, you, all of us, have helped to change it in these last 4 years, and particularly in this last year.

The People's Republic of China, where one-fourth of all the people in the world live, is now no longer isolated from us. That means that 20 years from now, when a billion people will be living there, they will not have to be our enemies. They can be our friends. That means a good and better life for young people in America.

We have negotiated with the Soviet Union to limit arms in the nuclear field and in many other fields. That means that despite the differences we have and will continue to have in philosophy, that we will talk about differences rather than fight about them.

Finally, it means that having opened up this great world, that the young people here—young as I was, and younger, when I was here in North Carolina as a student 35 years ago—can look forward to an open world where there can be communications between people even though there are differences between governments, where there can be peace in the world and progress such as we have never had in the whole history of mankind.

But it all depends, my friends, on you, because we must continue. We have started the negotiations with the Soviet Union. They must continue. We have started the opening to the PRC. We must continue. We are moving toward the prosperity that we all want, but we need to continue.

What we need from you and what we ask from you is your consideration of what we have presented here today. It is the clearest choice that we have had in this century. On that choice, I believe that the people of North Carolina, whether they are Republicans or Democrats, will say that America wants peace with honor, not surrender; America wants a strong defense, not a second-rate defense; and America will continue on a course, a course which will lead us into a new situation in the world, in which the people of the world, and particularly the younger generations, can grow up without the fear of war hanging over them.

I say to you finally, as I speak here, I feel very close to you, to the people in this State, for the reasons that I have mentioned. I feel, for that reason, a particular responsibility to you. I just want to say that in these next 4 years, I will dedicate myself to doing the things that I have talked about, but above all, I will never forget the faces that I have seen here, the wonderful people of North Carolina. We won't let you down.

NOTE: The President spoke at 2:55 p.m. at a rally at the Greensboro–High Point–Winston-Salem Regional Airport. He spoke without referring to notes.

408 Campaign Statement in New Mexico.
November 4, 1972

THERE is probably no other place in America whose history seems so old and yet so fresh as New Mexico's. Its lands were explored even before the first European settlers came to Plymouth Rock or Jamestown. Its Palace of the Governors in Santa Fe is the oldest public building in the United States. Its Church of San Felipe de Neri in Albuquerque stands witness to nearly two and three-quarters centuries of American history.

Yet New Mexico's vast human and natural potential is only now being unlocked for the benefit of the State and its people. Indeed, the years ahead can and will become the greatest years in New Mexico's and America's history.

All Americans are united in wanting certain basic things. We want to live in peace and to know that our sons will not be sent off to war. We want jobs and expanding opportunities for ourselves and our children. We want to work and keep the fruits of our labors. That is why I believe it is so important that we achieve in the next 4 years something we have not experienced as a Nation since President Eisenhower's time in the White House—prosperity with full employment, without war and without inflation.

Here in New Mexico thousands of people are playing a large part in building that kind of peace by working in occupations dedicated to maintaining a strong defense for America. In the years ahead that could mean the crucial difference between peace and war.

And the people of New Mexico can help to maintain America's strength in the years ahead in another way, as well— by electing Pete Domenici to the United States Senate and reelecting Manuel Lujan to the United States House of Representatives. They know the importance of a strong defense—for New Mexico and for the Nation.

These two men also understand that true prosperity can only be achieved if we can keep a lid on prices and taxes. Manuel Lujan stood up in the Congress for that principle this fall when he voted in favor of a $250 billion ceiling on Federal spending. He knows, as do the people of New Mexico, that the Federal Government does not really need any more of the taxpayers' hard-earned money.

In the coming years, we will face many difficult questions in Washington, questions directly affecting the lives and prosperity of everyone in New Mexico. For your own well-being and for the sake of the Nation, I urge the people of New Mexico to send Pete Domenici and Manuel Lujan to Washington to help make those tough decisions.

NOTE: The statement was released at Albuquerque, N. Mex.

409   Remarks at Albuquerque, New Mexico. *November 4, 1972*

THANK YOU very much for being here and introducing us as you have to this wonderful crowd in Albuquerque. As you know, we started this morning from Washington, D.C. We were first in North Carolina for one of the record crowds of the campaign, and then arriving here this day in Albuquerque. I saw in advance that it was the opening day of hunting season and the homecoming game for the university, and I wondered if anybody would be here. Thank you for coming.

And although the Lobos [1] lost today, speaking as one who knows how it is to lose and win, they will come back. They will win next time.

Also, may I say to you that it is a very great privilege to be here on this platform with the other candidates who stood here a moment ago, because this is truly a team effort. We often think of the President of the United States sitting in the Oval Office making the great decisions that affect the Nation and the world. But as you all know, he can only do

the job that needs to be done with your help, the help of millions of Americans and also with the help of Members of the House and Senate.

For that reason, I am stopping here, because we are interested in what you, of course, will do, and how you will vote on election day, at the top of the ticket, but also, in asking for your support for the men we need in the House and in the Senate, so that we can do what America wants done over these next 4 years that you have been talking about.

If I could say a word, now, about Manny Lujan; Manny was one who seconded my nomination. I was not there, because, you know, the tradition is that the candidate is not supposed to go to a convention until after he is nominated, and I had to wait to make sure, but I remember seeing it on television. As I think of all the seconding speeches, the one that gave me the biggest charge was Manny's. I think it is the first time that a seconding speech has been given in both English and Spanish, and I understood the Spanish as well as the English.

---

[1] University of New Mexico football team.

As we went down the line and shook hands with the wonderful young people in the band and the other people, and received the welcome that we did, I must say that you made us feel very much at home. But I would like to put it in another way. We, I know in this State just like in my home State of California, have a great tradition, a background of Spanish-speaking Americans, as well as people of all other backgrounds, and so, consequently, we pick up a little language here and there, even though we may not be of that particular background ourselves.

I remember, however, that when we, in English, say we want to welcome somebody someplace, we say, "Make yourself at home." But those who speak Spanish have a much warmer way of saying it. They say, *"Estan ustedes en su casa"*—you are in your own home—and that's the way we feel today.

That allows me to say something that in all the years I have been in the Oval Office has meant more to me than almost anything else in terms of telling me what America really is. I remember one day Manny was in and we were talking about people of various backgrounds. Manny, of course, is, as he should be, very proud of his Spanish-speaking background. But he said, "You know, Mr. President, we shouldn't talk about hyphenated Americans," and he is absolutely right.

So often, I know, we go around, you hear people say "He is Italian," or "He is a Pole," or "He is a Mexican," or "He is black," or whatever the case might be. Let me say every one of us is proud of our background, whatever it is, but most of all, we are proud to be Americans. That is what we are, and I speak to you in that vein today.

There were many reasons for coming to New Mexico today—the sentiment, the feeling, the fact that we have always had such a wonderful welcome here. But I wanted the opportunity as President of the United States to pay a bipartisan tribute to one of the great Americans of our time.

My daughter was here just a few weeks ago to participate in that tribute. I was unable to come. He is unable to be with us today, but Senator Clinton Anderson was our neighbor when we were in Washington and when I served in the Senate and later as Vice President. He was a Democrat. I was a Republican. But Clinton Anderson, during the years that I knew him in the Senate, was an American first and a partisan second—and a great American he was.

He was also like so many from this great State of New Mexico, these great Western States—independent. That is a tradition of Senators from this part of the country—independent. A team player, but whenever he felt the interests of his State or the interests of his Nation required him to take a different position than the other people in the party did, he would take it. And he was known for that.

As I think of Clinton Anderson, he was a very big man, and it is going to take a very big man to fill his shoes. I have been thinking of whether there is a man who can fill those shoes—and there is one. It is Pete Domenici. He is the big man who can fill those shoes. I have known him, of course, when he has campaigned before. One time he lost. But again, having lost then, this time he is going to win, I know. I know that is what is going to happen.

But let's look at Pete for a moment. He is a Republican. But he is an American first. Second, speaking of that independent tradition, I have talked to him quite often about the problems of this State, the problems that he is interested in and he is a man who makes up his own mind. When he comes to Washington he is going to speak up for the people of New Mexico. He is going to speak up as he thinks the interests of the people of this State require, and that is the kind of a man you want, one who is independent, but one who above all, when the chips are down, when the great issues are involved, is going to speak up for America, and that is what Pete Domenici will do.

That brings me to the theme of what I would like to touch upon today, the fact that this is not one of those campaigns where it is party against party or one individual against another on a personality basis. This is one of those campaigns where there are great overriding issues that affect the future of this country and the future of the world, in which there is a great gulf between the two candidates for the highest position in this land, in which there is complete disagreement between the two as to what America ought to do, as to where we ought to go.

I want to state my position today. I want to say it not in terms of being against—let's understand what we are for. I want to start right out with the issue that I know is closest to your hearts as it is to that of every American, the issue of bringing peace to the world and for the United States to lead the way to peace in the world.

I begin, of course, with the progress that we have made in bringing to an end the war in Vietnam. It has been very significant. Most important, as you know, we have made a major breakthrough in the negotiations. We have already agreed, in the settlement, to the principles that I laid down in my speech of May 8, which

you may recall was made at the time that I ordered the bombing of North Vietnam and the mining of Haiphong, at the time that the Communists were invading from the North. I said then that these were the three principles that we would have to have to have a negotiated settlement: First, that there should be a cease-fire. Second, that there should be a return of all of our prisoners of war and accounting for our missing in action. Third, that the people of South Vietnam should determine their own future without having a Communist government or a coalition government imposed upon them against their will.

Those three principles are agreed upon, and that is a major breakthrough in these negotiations. There are some details, as I pointed out on television 2 nights ago, in terms of the agreement, that are still in the process of negotiation. Those details, in my belief, I am confident will be worked out. We will have a negotiated settlement and a negotiated end to this war.

But let me tell you why details are important. They are important because what we want is not just peace now. Peace now is important. What we want is peace now and for the generations ahead, and we must have the right kind of peace. You may recall back in 1968 when, with the very best of intentions, the previous Administration entered into a bombing halt of North Vietnam and everybody thought we were going to have peace now. But we didn't have it down. We didn't have it understood. We are not going to make that mistake again.

We are going to have the kind of agreement which will end this war and build the foundation for a lasting peace that we can enjoy in that part of the world and all over the world. And that kind of peace, my friends—and let us understand what the issue is, and this is the basic difference between the two candidates—I say it shall be peace with honor and not peace with surrender for the United States of America.

Beyond that, when we speak of peace, let us remember that is one small part of the world. Our eyes have been upon it because of the long and difficult war that we have been engaged in, a war that started 5 years before I became President of the United States, and that we are now bringing to an end. But there is much more of the world, and you have seen that world, all of you, on television, more than you have ever seen it before, in this year 1972.

Why the trip to Peking? Why the trip to Moscow? The first time that a President of the United States has ever been in those two capitals. I will tell you why. It has to do certainly with my generation and all of you who can say you are in my generation. But it has even more to do with their generation and their generation over there.

Let me tell you what the world would be like if I had not taken the trip to Peking. One-fourth of all the people of the world live in the People's Republic of China, one-fourth of all the people. They are among the ablest people in the world. Their government is a Communist government. I do not agree with their philosophy. We will continue to have differences with their government. We will have disagreements with their philosophy. But if a billion people in the world, 10, 15, 20 years from now, were lined up in confrontation against the United States of America it would be a dangerous world.

I had to take the steps now to reduce that danger. We have done it so we have a better chance for a generation of peace for our young Americans.

The trip to Moscow was taken for similar reasons. The Soviet Union is also a nation that has a government that is different from ours. Their interests are different. Their philosophy is different. But they are a fact of life and a very important fact of life. They are, in nuclear terms, as strong as the United States of America. They are basically one of the super powers in the world. We were going down a track, a track in which we would inevitably confront each other at some time in the future and war might be the result. We couldn't let that happen.

So, on both sides—and it was on both sides—the leaders of the Soviet Union and the leaders of the United States met in Moscow. We didn't settle all of our differences, but we made agreements with regard to trade, we made agreements with regard to the environment, we made agreements with regard to cooperation in space, we made agreements—this one will not seem important perhaps when we think of the last one I am going to mention, the one with regard to the control of nuclear weapons—we made agreements, for example, with regard to exchange and cooperation in the field of health.

Let me tell you just what that means to this younger generation. We consider, for example, the dread diseases that afflict mankind. They don't just afflict Americans. They afflict all people, wherever they are. One of them is cancer. Did you know that last year more people died of cancer in the United States than were killed in action from America in all of World War II? So we are out to find an answer to that. There may be many answers, but my point is where it is going to come from. It may come from an American. It may come from a man or a woman. But it might come from a Russian or it might come from a Chinese. It may come from somebody in Africa or Latin America. What we must do, whatever our differences may be between governments, is to work together with other people in working against common diseases that afflict mankind, and that is why we have taken this giant step in both the Soviet Union and the United States to work together on that particular problem.

But perhaps most important, and most remembered by all of you, is the agreement that we entered with regard to the control and particularly the limitation of nuclear weapons. It was a first step and a very important one.

But now comes the second step. It is to get your approval and get your support for that second step that I come here today, for that second step and the second step we will take in so many other directions.

For example, we are now going to have negotiations beginning in late November with the Soviet Union to further limit nuclear weapons and reduce the danger of war. They will make this first agreement seem important, but they will not make it look nearly as important as it was, because it will cover more weapons than previously had been the case. It will be another great step forward toward reducing the burden of arms on America and on the Soviet Union, but, more important, in reducing the threat of war that hangs over us all.

I want you to know that in these next 4 years, whether it is in dealing with the Soviet Union or the People's Republic of China, or in bringing peace to the Mideast, a real peace, or in building better relations with our friends in Latin America or in Africa or wherever the case might be, we have made a good beginning. The chances for real and lasting peace in the world are better today than they have ever been at any time since the end of World War II. We ask for a chance to continue that job and to build that lasting peace, a generation of peace for all Americans.

Now, to build that, there are some things we are going to need. We are going to need a strong America, and here, again, we have a basic difference between the two men who seek the Presidency. I will tell you where I stand. I have sat across the conference table from the men in Moscow and Peking. I simply want to say to you, never send the President of the United States to negotiate with any power in the world as the head of the second strongest nation in the world. Let's keep America, in that respect, with the power that it has.

That is why I have to oppose, I have to oppose those who would make us have the second strongest navy, the second strongest air force, the second strongest army in the world, because when that day comes, it means that the threat of war in the world would be infinitely greater because the United States is the only nation in the free world that can deter aggression in the world.

It also means that any chance for reduction of arms or limitation of arms in the future is gone, because if you have already given it away unilaterally, they have no reason to give anything to you in return.

So let us be strong, let us be for peace, but let us be for peace through strength and not peace through weakness. That is what we stand for, and what Pete Domenici and Manny Lujan and all the rest stand for.

One other point that is related to this: We are moving, fortunately, to something that has been an ideal of mine, and I know of Manny Lujan's and Pete Domenici's and all of us here for many years, and that is, we are going to have a volunteer armed force starting in the middle of next year. In order to make that volunteer armed force work, however, it is necessary not only that they be paid enough, and they will be; it is necessary that those men and women in uniform in peacetime have the respect of their fellow countrymen.

In that respect, I simply want to say that as the long war in Vietnam comes to a conclusion, I, of course, think of those 2½ million Americans who served there. It was a hard choice for them, as it is for any who have to go to war. But they chose to serve their country when they had to make that choice. Many gave their lives for that choice. A few hundred, when they were faced with that choice, chose to desert their country, and they have to pay a penalty for their choice.

And so that there will be no misunderstanding on the differences between the two candidates in this respect, when the war in Vietnam is over, there will be no amnesty for draft dodgers or deserters, because it would not be fair to those who have served, and it is not the basis on which we could develop the new volunteer armed force, with the respect that we want, for developing the strength that America needs.

I have talked about this problem particularly because I know it is so close to all of your minds. Let me say, having reached the era of peace that we want, we want to have also with it what we have not had since President Eisenhower was President, and that is prosperity without war, without inflation. We are moving toward it. We need your help to continue in that direction. We want progress, but we want the kind of progress—programs for progress—that can be undertaken without increasing the tax burden on the American people. Your taxes are already too high, and that is why you are not hearing promises that are going to raise your taxes from me on this occasion.

And above everything else, we want opportunity for Americans, opportunity for every American—those first Americans that I had the opportunity to meet over here a few minutes ago, those who have come from other countries, those who are proud Americans who are more recently citizens—we want every American, whatever his background, every child, to have a chance to go to the top, ceiling unlimited. That is our ideal. We are working toward it. We can and will achieve it.

These are some of the goals we have in mind and today I come here to our friends in New Mexico and ask your support of those goals. It is on that basis, then, that I present the case. Not Republican versus Democrat, not one individual against another, but I say to you that when we talk about peace with honor, when we talk about strength for America, when we talk about opportunity for all, when we talk about prosperity without war, without inflation, when we talk about holding the line on taxes, those are issues that transcend partisan politics.

That is what America needs and that is what you are going to help us give America by your support in this campaign.

This morning I made a call to a distinguished Senator from Maine, Margaret Chase Smith. I wished her well in her campaign for reelection. As I spoke to her, I thought of the fact that it used to be said in politics that as Maine goes, so goes the Nation. However in 1936 that proved to be untrue. As you remember, in that year Mr. Roosevelt carried all the States except Maine and Vermont. So Maine did not go the way the Nation went.

I did a little studying before getting off the plane today. I found that since the time New Mexico became a State of the Union in 1912 that New Mexico has never voted for a loser. Let me say, you are not going to vote for one this time.

Thank you.

NOTE: The President spoke at 5:03 p.m. at a rally at the Albuquerque International Airport. He spoke without referring to notes.

410   Statement on Concluding Campaign for Reelection. *November 4, 1972*

THIS election eve visit to California is not only the last rally in a long campaign, it is also my last such campaign appearance as a candidate for public office. It is fitting that it should be here, in California. This is my native State, and the State in which I began my political career 26 years ago.

This moment calls forth many memories. But what is most important to me is the fact that this campaign road is ending on a positive note—a note of hope and optimism for America. With election day fast approaching, Americans can stand united in the knowledge that, more than at any time in this century, the hope for a full generation of peace burns bright.

The world is a calmer, more rational place today than it was 4 years ago. After so much sacrifice, patience, and endurance, the American people can finally rejoice in the confidence that a fair and honorable peace in Vietnam can soon be achieved. In the world at large, 1972 has been a year of greater achievement for peace than any since the end of World War II.

I am proud that my Administration was able to make such great progress for peace, and I am determined that just as we have worked resolutely to achieve a peace with honor and without surrender, we will also achieve peace with prosperity.

And that prosperity must be real prosperity—a prosperity free of rampant inflation and ever-higher taxes. To this goal my Administration and I are pledged.

The signs are hopeful. The new economic figures announced this week give us fresh evidence that a strong tide of real prosperity is rising across the Nation. The latest employment statistics reveal that 82,500,000 Americans were at work in the month of October, nearly 300,000 more than a month earlier and more than 5 million more than when this Administration took office.

Jobs are still increasing at the fastest

rate since 1956—at a rate twice as fast as the rate of growth of the population. While unemployment remains a serious concern, the strength and thrust of this progress promises to make strong inroads into this problem in the near future.

As for the cost of living, adjusted wholesale prices rose only one-tenth of one percent in October, the lowest increase since March. And our overall rate of inflation is now the lowest of any major industrial nation in the free world.

As citizens of the number one agricultural State of the Union, Californians will also be glad to know that we have some good news for the American farmer this week. Secretary of Agriculture Earl Butz has announced that farm exports will reach our $10 billion goal during this fiscal year—a goal once scoffed at by our opponents. This high level of farm sales was made possible, in part, by our improved relations with the People's Republic of China and the Soviet Union.

All of these indicators tell us that we have been on the right course, that the support the people have consistently expressed for this Administration's policies to keep inflation, taxes, and prices down, and the American economy growing and expanding, have been right on target.

The political voices of gloom who were so quick to give up, the political prophets of doom who said that American society was falling apart, and the American economy along with it—these misguided pessimists have been proven wrong.

We are a strong country, militarily and economically. The fibers of our social fabric are strong. Our spirit is strong. It is because we are strong that we have been able to work successfully for peace in the world and prosperity at home.

As I conclude the last campaign visit of my last campaign for public office, I see a strong, respected America, and a proud, united American people. None of this could have been achieved merely by government; it was done by the people.

When it comes down to the important things, Americans still stand together—that we are one America in conscience, in purpose, and in inspiration.

This campaign—my last campaign—will be over in a few short days. But the work of building a better America goes on. The work of building an honorable peace and a real prosperity goes on. And much remains to be done. We must continue to move justly and firmly in the second round of SALT disarmament talks, in our efforts to achieve balanced, mutual troop reductions in Europe, in our efforts to keep the peace in the volatile Mideast.

We must continue the transition of the American economy from a wartime to a peacetime footing by effective means such as this Administration's technical mobilization and reemployment program, which has already relocated more than 17,000 displaced aerospace engineers and is part of our overall strategy that has successfully provided workers with 2.3 million real jobs—not government make-work jobs—in the past year alone.

I promise that in the next 4 years I will continue to use every resource at my disposal to keep us building, to keep us leading the way, and to keep America strong, decent, and united.

NOTE: The statement was released at Ontario, Calif.

411   Remarks at Ontario, California.
      November 4, 1972

Governor Reagan, all of these very distinguished celebrities on the platform, and all of you very distinguished people in our home State of California:

Earlier today we visited the State of North Carolina and, of course, in California there is probably somebody from every State in the Union, but in North Carolina, as we were there, where we had a very great airport rally, I thought of a book that had been written by one of the great American novelists, Thomas Wolfe. Many of you have read it. You remember the title, certainly, "You Can't Go Home Again."

When we landed here today, knowing that it has been a little misty earlier in the day, knowing that the traffic has been backed up for miles, and when we look back on all of the appearances in this campaign, and when we see this magnificent crowd, we know you can go home again—to California.

Tonight I want to express appreciation first to Governor Reagan for not only his very gracious introduction but for the remarks that he made before we arrived, and for the work he has done in this campaign in California and across the Nation.

I want to express, of course, my support for all of our candidates for the House, for the Assembly, many of whom I know have been introduced. I think you should know when the mayor, Mayor Snider, presented me with a plaque, that was because it was 12 years ago we finished the campaign here in Ontario at one o'clock in the morning, and we wish him well in his contest particularly here in this area.

I want to express appreciation, too, on this occasion, and I have waited now to do it because they have traveled all over this land, to this group of—well, we call them celebrities, but they are from California. They are some of the greatest names in show business; that is one thing. But they have also the greatest hearts and the greatest courage in show business, and we are glad to have them on our side. I think we should give them a hand.

Could I also express the appreciation that we all must feel for what, to me, is the greatest, and I have seen all kinds, of course, at rallies, bands and massed bands. Isn't that a marvelous sight, those massed bands behind us? How about a hand for them?

And now could I take you back 12 years and relate what happened then to what can happen now? Twelve years ago, we finished a very long day of campaigning here in California. It was the last appearance of the campaign, as is this one.

I recall there was an enormous crowd here, not as big as this one, but it was late at night, at one o'clock, and it was quite cold. We were very heartened by it.

That year, in what was the closest election in this country, we lost the Nation but we won California. This year, based on the crowd I see here, we are going to win California and the Nation.

Could I tell you just a word about that Nation as I have seen it in just 2 days? As President, of course, I have had the opportunity, with Mrs. Nixon, to travel to 50 States, all the 50 States, the first President to have had such a privilege. But in the last 2 days we have really seen all parts of the Nation.

Yesterday we were in Chicago, Illinois, in Tulsa, Oklahoma, and in Providence, Rhode Island. And today we were at Winston-Salem, North Carolina, and we were in Albuquerque, New Mexico, and now here in Ontario, California.

As you will note, we have covered the Northeast of the Nation in Rhode Island. We have been to the center of the Nation in Chicago. We have been down to the Southwest in Oklahoma. We have been in the South in North Carolina, and now we are in the capital of the West, California.

I want to tell you something about this country, and I particularly want all of you, the many wonderful young people here who—some are not old enough to vote, but you all will be—let me tell you something about this country: There was a time, and it was not too long ago, when if you traveled through the country you would see it deeply divided—the West against the East, the North against the South, and so on and so on, the cities against the farms, and so forth. But let me tell you, wherever you go, across America, this Nation is getting together.

I can tell you that whether it is in Illinois, or whether it is in Oklahoma, or whether it is in North Carolina or Rhode Island or in California, that across this Nation we find a phenomenon happening which is going to change the situation insofar as this country is concerned, and which is going to make this a better world for us as well, and it is this: An unprecedented number of people in this country are not thinking in regional terms, they are not thinking in partisan terms, but they are thinking in one term only: This year they are voting for what they think is best for America. That is what they are doing all across this Nation.

Everywhere I go, I find that people are united in what they believe is best for America. I want to speak about why they are united, and I want to ask you, my fellow citizens of California, to join people throughout this Nation—Democrats, Republicans, and independents—in giving us the support that we need to continue the work that we have begun. We have begun, but we have much more to do.

I want to begin with that subject which, of course, is on the minds of everybody everyplace in this Nation. Governor Reagan has referred to the work that we have done to try to bring peace to this world.

We have approached this subject on a world scale in our trips to Peking and Moscow, and we have also worked on this subject in that area that has been nagging this country for so many years. When I came into office, we had been in a war in Vietnam for 5 years. There was no end in sight. There were 550,000 Americans there; 300 were being killed every week.

You know what has happened, the number that we have brought home, the casualties are down. But most important, finally we have had a breakthrough in the negotiations, and I can tell you today that the significant point of that breakthrough is that the three principles that I laid down when, on May 8, I ordered the bombing of North Vietnam and the mining of Haiphong for the purpose of stopping the Communist invasion of the South, those three principles have now been agreed to, and they are these:

First, all of our POW's will be returned and our missing in action will be accounted for; second, it has been agreed that there will be a cease-fire; and third, it has been agreed that the people of South Vietnam shall determine their own future without having a Communist government or a coalition government imposed upon them against their will.

Now we have a situation in which, having made this progress, we now must negotiate the final details. Those details must however be completed and be completed in a proper way. I want to tell you why. While the general principles have been agreed upon, we have often found in the history of settlements that unless you nail down the understandings and clear away the ambiguities you may get peace now, but not peace for the years ahead. We want peace that will last, not peace that will be simply for a little while.

You remember, for example, just before the election in 1968, when, with the very best of intentions, our Government agreed to a bombing halt in North Vietnam and we thought we were going to have peace or negotiations for peace. We thought so, but the understandings were not nailed down and as a result the war continued.

We are not making that mistake this time. I can simply say this: We have agreement on the general principles and I am confident we will negotiate the settlement which will end the war and bring us what we all want—peace with honor and not peace with surrender for the United States of America.

Now moving from that part of the world, which, although it is terribly important to the people that live there and to us because we have been involved there for so long, is only one small part of the world, let me tell you now what we have at stake in this election in terms of the other parts of the world.

I mentioned the trip to Peking and

the trip to Moscow. I am going to tell you what they mean and to whom they mean so much. The trip to Peking, for example, has great meaning in one sense because it saw the President of the United States for the first time visiting that capital of the People's Republic of China. But it has meaning primarily, not so much to our generation, or mine I should say, but to this younger generation that we see here in such great numbers. Because, let me tell you, imagine how dangerous the world would be if one-fourth of all the people of the world who live in the People's Republic of China, 10, 15 years from now had gathered enormous nuclear capability and had no communication with the United States of America. We could not allow that danger to continue to exist.

I am not suggesting, and no one should believe, that there are not differences in philosophy, and deep ones, that will remain between our Government and theirs as long as theirs is Communist and ours is free. I am not suggesting that we do not have differences in terms of interests, but I do say this: I say that when we look at the future of the world we have to learn to live in this world in a way in which nations with different philosophies and different interests can settle those differences at the conference table and will not be involved in a nuclear war, and we have made a great step in that direction by that trip to Peking.

The trip to Moscow had a similar purpose. There we had a communication with the Soviet Union. We had had some progress. But look at what has happened this year. Here again, let us understand what the situation is. The Soviet Union's government is a Communist government. Our philosophies are totally different.

They have different interests than we have in many parts of the world. That will continue. But again, imagine what we would leave to the younger generation had we not moved this year on that front. We would have gone down the road to an inevitable confrontation and a nuclear explosion, possibly, that would have destroyed civilization as we know it. I could not let that happen. You could not let it happen. That is why we went to Moscow. There we negotiated an historic number of agreements, agreements, for example, in the field of trade, agreements in the field of science, agreements in the field of space, and particularly those that you will remember, agreements to begin the limitation of nuclear arms.

But I again emphasize, it was only a beginning, just as the trip to Peking was a beginning. What we must do now is to go on from there and in going on from there what we must recognize is that just next month, for example, we are planning to meet with the leaders of the Soviet Union—our representatives—to negotiate the second round of arms limitation.

I am not suggesting that as a result of that meeting, any more than the first meeting, that all differences will disappear. But I do say this, and I say this as a message of hope to all of the wonderful young people here and your parents and your friends: that never since the end of World War II have the chances for peace for a whole generation been better than they are right today in the United States and in the world.

What we ask for is a chance to continue. What we ask for from the American people is a message to the leaders abroad, a message that the President of the United States, when he negotiates, has the sup-

port of the American people. We ask for that support in this election.

We also must recognize that in order to have these negotiations succeed to limit arms, in order for the United States to be able to play the role which we are destined to play, of building a peaceful world, it is vitally important that the President of the United States never be sent to the bargaining table with another country as the head of the second strongest nation in the world. We must remember that strength for the United States is vitally important to world peace.

I know there are those who say that we can cut our defenses so that we have the second strongest navy and the second strongest air force and the second strongest army and it doesn't really make any difference. But let me tell you, the day that happens peace and freedom will be in deadly jeopardy throughout the world. Let me say, keep America strong so that the President of the United States will represent a strong America and not a weak America.

Our thoughts, of course, turn also to our problems at home. We have moved forward to something we haven't had since President Eisenhower was President, and that is full prosperity without war and without inflation.

We have some way to go, but we now have the highest rate of growth of any industrial nation; we have the lowest rate of inflation of any of the great industrial nations. And we are going to continue on that road until Americans can have that opportunity that they have not had since 15 years ago when President Eisenhower was in the White House, and that is prosperity without war, without inflation.

We also ask you today for approval from my fellow Californians and for support in what we are doing in the field of fighting the rise in crime in this country and fighting dangerous drugs. It has to be done on all fronts, but one that is particularly important is in the appointment of judges to all the courts, and particularly to the Supreme Court.

Four years ago when I campaigned, I said that I would appoint judges who would recognize the necessity to strengthen the peace forces as against the criminal forces in this country. I have done so, but I have only had a beginning. We need 4 more years to strengthen the courts so we can have the peace forces strong, backed by the judges of this country, and if I could respectfully suggest you can help in this field, too.

I know that sometimes in recent years, in the late sixties, it became rather fashionable always to run down those who wore the uniform, whether it was a uniform serving their country abroad or the uniform of someone who was keeping our streets safe at home. Let me say: Back up the men on our peace forces in the United States, whether they are abroad or whether they are home. Give them the respect that they deserve.

There is one other great goal that I refer to today, and that is the goal of opportunity for all Americans. We in California feel so strongly about that because while we are the biggest State and the most populous State, we come from all the States and all the nations of the world. We believe in equal opportunity for everybody—an equal chance for the best education, an equal chance for good health, a chance for everybody to have a job, to go just as high as his talents will take him.

We want that. We can help in Washington in working toward that. We need your support to continue to develop that equal chance for every American, with ceiling unlimited as high as he or she wants to go.

And finally, may I say that as I look at this great crowd, I think of something else that we would like to leave during this next 4 years, something else in addition to peace which could last for a generation or longer, something in addition to prosperity without war and without inflation, to progress and opportunity for all Americans, and that is this:

I mentioned the fact that we have been to 50 States. Mrs. Nixon and I have traveled to 80 countries as Vice President and then as President. And in those travels as President of the United States I have visited four capitals that no President has ever been to before—Peking, Moscow, Bucharest, and Warsaw.

These were journeys for peace, but as those journeys took place, and as we saw those 80 countries, each time we came back to the United States and we saw this country, and we realized when we returned how very fortunate anyone is to live in the United States of America.

My fellow Californians, this is a great State, and this is a beautiful country. Oh, we have our problems, and we have those faults that we are trying to correct, but the wonder of it is, and the glory of it is that we have a system in which we can correct them in a peaceful way without resorting to violence, and that is the way we are going to do it.

I want you to know that as I look at America over these next 4 years and I think of your future, I believe that we have the chance—and this is our goal—to make the next 4 years the best 4 years in

America's history. That is what I ask for tonight.

Now, if I could close with one personal note, I mentioned a moment ago that the last rally of the 1960 campaign was here at Ontario. Tonight, as I drove through this crowd, I was thinking back to the first rally I ever attended or spoke to. It was in 1945, November. That is quite a few years ago, before most of this audience was born. But as I was thinking back to that, I thought of how good the people of California have been to us: First to the House of Representatives for two terms, then the United States Senate, and then 8 years as Vice President, out of office for a period of 8 years, then back in office again.

But I want you to know that looking back over those years, in victory, the people of California have enjoyed the victory with us. In defeat, they have stood by us, and we are most grateful for that. This year we look forward to a victory, but as we look forward to it, we know that we owe it to thousands, yes, millions of people in this State and across this Nation that we will never get a chance to thank personally.

Tonight, as I speak to you here in Ontario, I think you should know that this, of course, not only is the last rally of this campaign that I will speak to, it is the last time I will speak to a rally as a candidate in my whole life, and I want to say to all of you here who worked on this, to all of you who took the time to come, thank you very much for making it probably the best rally that we have ever had.

NOTE: The President spoke at 6:40 p.m. at a rally at Ontario International Airport. He spoke without referring to notes.

412   Radio Address: "The Birthright of an American Child." *November* 5, 1972

Good afternoon:

Next Tuesday, for the 47th time in our Nation's history, Americans will cast their ballots to choose a President for the next 4 years.

Daniel Patrick Moynihan, a former member of my Cabinet and a gifted observer of the American scene, has made the comment that "Elections are rarely our finest hours. This," he said, "is when we tend to be most hysterical, most abusive, least thoughtful about problems, and least respectful of complexity."

I think Americans want our democracy to meet a higher standard than that. We all want to make the election of 1972 one of our finest hours, and we have the opportunity to do so.

We need to recognize, first, that politics is not merely some kind of game to be played hard and played for keeps, with everyone defending his own interests as best he can. It is not just a competition in which one man or one party seeks to defeat another. It is not an auction in which the prize of office is awarded to the highest bidder for the favor of the voters.

Instead, in the highest sense, our democracy is a sacred trust which all of us who participate exercise together on behalf of those who cannot yet participate.

One American in three—over 69

million boys and girls, young men and women—will not be old enough to vote on Tuesday, but they will live for the rest of their lives with the consequences of the decision we, the voters, make. Additionally, during the 4 years of the next Presidential term, nearly 15 million newborn children will begin their lives in America—in a nation and in a world not of their making, but of our making.

I would like to spend a few minutes thinking with you this afternoon about the birthright we ought to guarantee for them. I would like to look beyond the election and focus on the things which I believe all Americans, no matter how they vote on Tuesday, will want their Nation to achieve in the 4 years between now and 1976.

The 10 goals in this birthright are not intended to be my campaign promises to you, for they are not something which any one man, by himself, could hope to deliver. To achieve them, all Americans must join hands and work together.

So we might think of these goals as campaign promises which America should make to itself, promises to be honored in the next 4 years, no matter who wins in the next 2 days.

First, let us give tomorrow's children the birthright of an America at peace in a world at peace—not peace with surrender, but peace with honor—not just an interlude between wars, but a time of lasting friendship and cooperation among all peoples, a time when mankind can unite in a new alliance against our common enemies—poverty, misery, and disease.

The recent breakthrough toward a negotiated settlement in Vietnam points to that kind of peace. So does the new relationship which the United States has begun to develop with the Soviet Union and the People's Republic of China. But there is much more to do—the further limitation of nuclear arms, the easing of tensions in Europe, the healing of tragic divisions in the Middle East, the continued strengthening of our alliances, the forging of new trade patterns and the continued development of our volunteer armed forces, which will be the indispensable linchpin of America's peace forces in the years ahead.

Peace, more than anything else, can enrich the lives of the children of the seventies. It is for their sake that we have worked so hard to give peace a chance and for their sake we must continue to do so.

Some of these new children will be girls, some will be boys. Some will be white, some black, some brown. Will discrimination and quotas limit their horizons? Let us resolve that they will not. As our second goal for the next 4 years, let us seek a more just America—an America in which every human being, regardless of race or religion, age or sex, wealth or national origin, enjoys equal rights before the law and unlimited opportunities for realizing his or her fullest potential.

Will the new children enjoy sound health, adequate nourishment, good medical care? Or will they have to contend with the hazards of a society where infant mortality is still higher than in numerous other countries of the world, and where cancer still strikes one American in four sometime during his lifetime?

Let us make our third goal a healthy America, where all our people enjoy steadily better health and increasing longevity, where hunger is unknown, and where deadly diseases and drug abuse are rapidly diminishing.

Through our plan for a comprehensive health program, our accelerated food assistance programs, our conquest-of-cancer efforts, and our total war against dangerous drugs, your Government today is committed to that kind of America for 1976.

Soon tomorrow's children will be ready to start school. Will their parents select the schools they attend? Will tax pressures force them, all of them, into public classrooms regardless of their preferences?

Let us assure each child, as the fourth part of his birthright, the chance to go to school in a well-educated America— in an educational system that calls each of us to excellence in all that we do, that brings the light of learning and the pride of useful skills to all who desire them, that preserves neighborhood schools and educational diversity, and that nurtures a new world renaissance in science, the arts, the humanities.

What about the homes in which these children grow up? Will their living standard be high? What about the careers which await them? What about the retirement years at the end of those careers?

Point five of the American birthright must be a secure and a prosperous America, where there are jobs for all who can work, a decent income with dignity for those who cannot work; where every dollar earned will buy a dollar's worth; where prudent government spending works for the people, with a fair tax system which does not force the people to work more for the government than they work for themselves.

We owe our children something better than steadily rising prices and ever-higher taxes to support welfare handouts. We owe them the kind of solid prosperity America has not had since the Eisenhower years of 1955 and 1956—when we had full employment without inflation and without war. We owe them a reform of the welfare system so that it will not be more profitable to go on welfare than to go to work. We must continue the progress of the last several years and reach those goals.

What about the quality of life in the cities and towns where tomorrow's children will live? What about the green earth around them?

Let us make the sixth article of their birthright a livable America—a nation whose urban and rural communities are growing in quality, order, and grace, a nation whose natural environment is restored and protected, with cleaner air and water, more parks and open spaces, wiser use of limited natural resources.

The 1970's have been called America's environmental decade. Through the mobilization of citizen concern and the massive support of government at every level, we are meeting that challenge. We are fighting the degradation of man's surroundings everywhere, from the inner city slum to the mountain wilderness, and we are in this fight to win.

Our seventh goal for the birthright of tomorrow's children must be an America free from fear, a country where the rule of law is supreme and the rate of crime is declining, where violence is replaced by peaceful change, where civility quiets the angry voices and where decency drives out moral decay. Here, too, we are making good progress, but we must do even better.

The last three articles of this birthright as we enter America's third century must deal with the conditions necessary for achieving all the other goals.

Our eighth goal must be a free and self-governed America, an America whose unique system of representative government—Federal, State, and local—is a better instrument of the people's will, a better servant of the people's needs, a better protector of the people's liberties in 1976 than at any time since the birth of our country in 1776.

To reach this high standard, sweeping reform will be needed, on the scale of a new peaceful American revolution. The sharing of the Federal revenue with our cities and States, which will begin less than 4 weeks from today, marks the first great step in starting the flow of power from Washington back to the people, where it belongs. We must keep the power flowing that way during the years ahead.

It was the genius of the people, not the mechanisms of government, that built America. That is why our ninth goal for 1976 must be a pluralist, open America, where government does not dominate, but liberates the individual, opening the way for a new surge of vitality, creative service, and civic responsibility on the part of private enterprise, voluntary institutions, and individual people across this land.

The tenth and last part of this American birthright, the most important aspect of all, is our children's right to be born into a great and a good America—a land where people's daily lives are guided by deep moral and spiritual principles, where families are close and strong, where patriotism flourishes without apology, where shared ideals forge unity out of diversity, and where the character of each individual and of the Nation as a whole measures up to the high hopes and the dreams which all mankind invests in America.

As your President during these past 4 years, I have visited every one of the 50 States, every region of the country, hundreds of American cities and towns, large and small. I know firsthand that the character of the American people measures up to the hopes of the world.

We can be proud that this land of ours is a great and a good country.

We can be proud of a democratic system in which the motive is not to grab for the spoils of victory, but to pass along a precious birthright to the generations who will come after us.

The choice of policies, of principles, and of candidates in this election is clearcut and momentous. I think the people understand what is at stake. I have confidence in their ability to make a wise decision. And whatever that decision is on Tuesday, I intend to support our elected leaders as I always have done, I intend to stand up for national unity as I have always done, because America is bigger than any one man or any one party.

In the midst of all the commotion of the final weekend before an election, I think it is vitally important to remind ourselves of the great American consensus which will continue to unite us next Wednesday morning, far more powerfully than any vote tallies might seem to divide us.

Carl Schurz, a German immigrant, who became a great American statesman, said 100 years ago: "Ideals are like stars; you will not succeed in touching them with your hands. But like the seafaring man on the desert of waters, you choose them as your guides, and following them you will reach your destiny."

The 10 birthright goals which I have outlined today embrace our Nation's timeless ideals. Let all Americans, of every party and political persuasion, take them as our guides on election day and every day throughout the next 4 years.

If we do this, then I believe that this election of 1972 will be remembered as one of America's finest hours, and that the next 4 years will be the 4 best years in America's first two centuries.

Thank you and good afternoon.

NOTE: The President spoke from a prepared text. His address was recorded at the Western White House, San Clemente, Calif., for broadcast at 4:40 p.m. on nationwide radio. Time for the broadcast was purchased by the Committee for the Re-Election of the President.

413   Remarks on Election Eve. *November 6, 1972*

Good evening:

Tomorrow, 100 million Americans will have an opportunity to participate in a decision that will affect the future of America and the future of the world for generations to come.

Regardless of how you vote, I urge each of you to vote. By your vote, you can make sure that this great decision is made by a majority of Americans eligible to vote, and not simply left to the minority who bother to vote.

I am not going to insult your intelligence tonight or impose upon your time by rehashing all the issues of the campaign or making any last-minute charges against our opponents.

You know what the issues are. You know that this is a choice which is probably the clearest choice between the candidates for President ever presented to the American people in this century.

I would, however, urge you to have in mind tomorrow one overriding issue, and that is the issue of peace—peace in Vietnam and peace in the world at large for a generation to come.

As you know, we have made a breakthrough in the negotiations which will lead to peace in Vietnam. We have agreed on the major principles that I laid down in my speech to the Nation of May 8. We

have agreed that there will be a cease-fire, we have agreed that our prisoners of war will be returned and that the missing in action will be accounted for, and we have agreed that the people of South Vietnam shall have the right to determine their own future without having a Communist government or a coalition government imposed upon them against their will.

There are still some details that I am insisting be worked out and nailed down because I want this not to be a temporary peace. I want, and I know you want, it to be a lasting peace. But I can say to you with complete confidence tonight that we will soon reach agreement on all the issues and bring this long and difficult war to an end.

You can help achieve that goal. By your votes, you can send a message to those with whom we are negotiating, and to the leaders of the world, that you back the President of the United States in his insistence that we in the United States seek peace with honor and never peace with surrender.

I will not go into the other issues tonight, except to say that as we move to peace, we will open doors to progress on many fronts here at home. It means that we can have something we haven't had since President Eisenhower was President 15 years ago—prosperity without war and without inflation.

It means we can have progress toward better education, better health—in all the areas that I have presented to the American people over these past 4 years.

It means that we can move toward a goal that every American wants: that is, opportunity for each person in this great and good land to go to the top in whatever particular activity he chooses regardless of his background.

Those, then, are the issues you will have in mind.

Let me say, finally, I want to thank you for the honor of serving as President for the past 4 years, and, regardless of your decision tomorrow, I can assure you that I shall continue to work for a goal that every American has: Let's make the next 4 years the best 4 years in America's history.

Thank you. Good evening.

NOTE: The President's remarks were recorded at the Western White House, San Clemente, Calif., for broadcast at 8:30 p.m. as part of a nationwide television program paid for by the Committee for the Re-Election of the President.

414   Remarks on Being Reelected to the Presidency. *November 7, 1972*

Good evening my fellow Americans:

Before going over to the Shoreham Hotel to address the victory celebration which is in process there, I wanted to take a moment to say a word to all of you in this very personal way, speaking from the Oval Office.

I first want to express my deep appreciation to every one of you, the millions of you who gave me your support in the election today, and I want to express my respect for millions of others who gave their support to Senator McGovern. I know that after a campaign, when one loses, he can feel very, very low, and his supporters as well may feel that way. And when he wins, as you will note when I get over to the Shoreham, people are feeling very much better.

The important thing in our process, however, is to play the game, and in the great game of life, and particularly the game of politics, what is important is that on either side more Americans voted this year than ever before, and the fact that you won or you lost must not keep you from keeping in the great game of politics in the years ahead, because the better competition we have between the two parties, between the two men running for office, whatever office that may be, means that we get the better people and the better programs for our country.

Now that the election is over, it is time to get on with the great tasks that lie before us. I have tried to conduct myself in this campaign in a way that would not divide our country, not divide it regionally or by parties or in any other way, because I very firmly believe that what unites America today is infinitely more important than those things which divide us. We are united Americans—North, East, West, and South, both parties—in our desire for peace, peace with honor, the kind of a peace that will last, and we are moving swiftly toward that great goal, not just in Vietnam, but a new era of peace in which the old relationships between the two super powers, the Soviet Union and the United States, and between the world's populous nation, the People's Republic of China, and the United States, are changed so that we are on the eve of what could be the greatest generation of peace, true peace for the whole world, that man has ever known.

This is a great goal, bigger than whether we are Democrats or Republicans, and it is one that I think you will want to work with me, with all of us, in helping to achieve.

There are other goals that go with that—the prosperity without war and without inflation that we have all wanted and that we now can have, and the progress for all Americans, the kind of progress so that we can say to any young American, whatever his background, that he or she in this great country has an equal chance to go to the top in whatever field he or she may choose.

I have noted, in listening to the returns a few minutes ago, that several commentators have reflected on the fact that this may be one of the great political victories of all time. In terms of votes that may be true, but in terms of what a victory really is, a huge landslide margin means nothing at all unless it is a victory for America. It will be a victory for America only if, in these next 4 years, we, all of us, can work together to achieve our common great goals of peace at home and peace for all nations in the world, and for that new progress and prosperity which all Americans deserve.

I would only hope that in these next 4 years we can so conduct ourselves in this country, and so meet our responsibilities in the world in building peace in the world, that years from now people will look back to the generation of the 1970's, at how we have conducted ourselves, and they will say, "God bless America."

Thank you very much.

NOTE: The President spoke at 11:54 p.m. in the Oval Office at the White House. He spoke without referring to notes. His remarks were broadcast live on radio and television.

415   Remarks at a Presidential Election Victory Rally. *November 8, 1972*

Mr. Vice President, Mrs. Agnew, all of our very distinguished guests here at the Shoreham Hotel, and the very distinguished audience listening on television and radio:

At Ontario, California, on Saturday night, at the conclusion of a speech to what was estimated as a crowd of 50,000, I said, "This is the last time I will ever be addressing a campaign rally as a candidate." It may be that that was the last campaign rally as a candidate, but this means tonight we still have a rally right here.

Now, let me briefly touch upon several significant things about this election. First—and this for me is rather unusual— I have never known a national election when I would be able to go to bed earlier than tonight.

Second, I want to say here to this great audience and to all of those who will be listening on television and radio, that I know from having been a candidate for Vice President, and a Vice President for 8 years, that this is always a team campaigning for office.

I want you to know that during the period of the last several weeks since the convention when I have had to be in Washington, for reasons that all of you could well understand, that I watched the Vice President as he carried the major burden of campaigning.

I watched with no concern, and considerable amusement, the attempts that were being made by some rather vicious heckling to get under his skin and get him to blow his cool. Let me say, the real test of a campaigner is to go through the fire of a campaign when he is taking all the heat. The Vice President has proved he is a great campaigner. I was going to say he can take it and he can dish it out, too.

I also would like to pay tribute to all of the other members of the team. I refer of course to our campaign chairman, Clark MacGregor, to John Mitchell, his predecessor, to Maurice Stans, our finance chairman, to all of the members of the Cabinet team who did such a magnificent job traveling through this country, to Representatives from the Congress, the House, the Senate, and the national Administration, who carried the story that we wanted to tell throughout the land. They were a great team.

I think they have been a great team over the past 4 years, and in this campaign, when you add up those States to what has been called a rather significant victory, they get a great deal of the credit, I can assure you.

I also want to pay tribute to another group that too often is overlooked. I wrote a book after the election defeat of 1960, and one of the chapters of that book dealt with the campaign of 1960. When you write a book, you are supposed to dedicate it to somebody, and, not being an ex-

pert at this sort of thing, I just put on the flyleaf of the dedication page in this book about the campaign of 1960—I dedicated it, "To Pat. She also ran."

I want all of you to know tonight how very grateful we should be to the wives of our Cabinet members, to the distaff members, as sometimes—I guess, we can still call them that in these days when you have to be very careful about how you describe people—but in any event, at least shall we say to our First Ladies, and they are always our First Ladies in our own families. I am simply very, very proud of all of them.

I can summarize how I feel about all of our campaign in this way: Our speakers throughout campaigned hard. Our speakers throughout campaigned clean. They campaigned on the issues. I am proud of the campaign they have put on, and it showed in the results.

Something else was new in this campaign. All of us know, of course, about those young voters. I recall at the convention that we were told by some of the enthusiasts there at our convention that the predictions were wrong that because of the overwhelming youth vote that was going to go against us that we had a very, very hard row to hoe if we were to win this election.

Let me say, based on the results I have seen today, we have accomplished what was thought to be the impossible. We not only won a majority of the votes of America, but we won a majority of the votes of young Americans.

All of you should know that one who stands in this position with 4 years ahead must think of what he wants for those 4 years. We want, of course, many things. We want to do the very best job we can for all the country, for all people in our society. We want to have in mind, too, the fact that in this election it was very unusual in another respect. It was not region against region. It was not one age group against another age group. It was not party against party. I think we can be proud of the fact that as we look at our majority, which is a very large majority, it comes from all of America.

Let us remember that in these next 4 years we are not going to work for one group against another. We are dedicated to work for all Americans to make this a greater country.

To those millions of Democrats and independents who supported us as well as, of course, to the Republicans who supported us in overwhelming numbers, they have, you have, our deep appreciation. To all those who worked so hard— our appreciation. I will never be able to thank all of you personally, not even get all the letters out that I would like. But I know what you did and I know how much you contributed.

I would simply like to leave one final thought with you, perhaps in a personal sense. No one knows before the votes are counted how it is going to come out. No one really would have predicted after our convention that we were going to win this kind of a victory. Now, at the present time I noticed some of the commentators are referring to the fact that it may be the greatest victory in American political history. Let me tell you, I have two reactions to that. Of course, it is great on election night to think that we have won a victory, but this will be a great victory depending upon what we do with it. In other words, we win elections not simply for the purpose of beating the other party or the other person, but to get the oppor-

tunity to do good things for our country. The next 4 years will be the time that we will try to make ourselves worthy of this victory.

I will simply say in that connection, it was a great victory but the greater the victory, the greater the responsibility, the greater the opportunity. We are going to try to meet it, dedicating ourselves to those great goals that I have discussed at such great length throughout this campaign and will in the next 4 years—building that world of peace, of real peace with honor throughout the world, and building at home, not only peace at home but the new prosperity and the progress for all Americans that is so close to our hearts.

Finally, on that personal note, about 30 days ago, when I was sitting in the Lincoln Sitting Room late at night trying to get some materials ready for a National Security Council meeting the next morning, Tricia dropped into the room around 10:30 or 11:00. She was going out to dedicate a dam or something at a nonpolitical affair. She was trying to get some suggestions about remarks. I find that whenever I make suggestions of remarks to Tricia or Julie or Eddie Cox they always can do better without any suggestions, but I made a couple. Then, before she left the room, she turned and said, "You know, Daddy, did you ever stop to think that this is your last campaign?" I said, "Yes, I have."

As I think of what she said that night, I simply want to say from the bottom of my heart, thanks for making our last campaign the very best one of all.

Thank you.

NOTE: The President spoke at 12:25 a.m. in the Regency Room of the Shoreham Hotel. He spoke without referring to notes. His remarks were broadcast live on radio and television.

416   Statement on the Death of Representative Frank T. Bow of Ohio.   *November* 13, 1972

I HAVE been deeply saddened to learn of the death of Representative Frank Bow of Ohio. In over 20 years of outstanding service in the Congress, Frank Bow earned respect as a man of energy, principle, and dedication. As ranking minority member of the House Appropriations Committee, he was a strong voice for fiscal responsibility, repeatedly taking his stand against excessive Government spending.

I hardly need to add that as President, I found in Frank Bow a staunch friend and supporter—a man whose loyalty never wavered and whose commitment was always total. His loss will be felt by his colleagues in the Congress, and by all Americans who value the example of a life well spent in the public service. Mrs. Nixon and I extend our heartfelt condolences to Frank Bow's family and many friends.

NOTE: Representative Bow, 71, died at Bethesda Naval Hospital. He served in the United States House of Representatives from 1951 until his death.

Richard K. Cook, Deputy Assistant to the President for Congressional Relations, represented the President at funeral services in Canton, Ohio, on November 15, 1972.

417   Memorandum About the "Zero-In On Federal Safety" Program.   *November* 15, 1972

Memorandum for Heads of Federal Departments and Agencies:

In 1971, I initiated the "Zero-In On Federal Safety" Program to replace "Mission Safety 70." The value of the "Zero-In" program was clearly demonstrated during that year when the frequency rate of disabling injuries dropped by nine percent over 1970. The 1971 rate of 6.0 disabling injuries per million man-hours worked is in fact the lowest ever achieved in the Federal Government.

This downward trend must be continued.

In an effort to obtain greater benefits from this program and to carry out our responsibility under the Occupational Safety and Health Act of 1970, I am extending the program of "Zero-In On Federal Safety" through December, 1973. In addition, we must develop a concerted effort to reduce occupational health hazards which may be present in Government workplaces.

Each agency is hereby directed to establish means to meet these objectives. The Secretary of Labor will outline a suggested program for all agencies to follow. Specific guidelines and materials will be provided through the Occupational Safety and Health Administration of the Department of Labor.

It is my sincere hope that you will continue to give your fullest support to the "Zero-In On Federal Safety" program during 1973. Through its effective implementation, the Federal Government—as the Nation's largest employer—will set an example for all.

RICHARD NIXON

NOTE: The memorandum was posted for the press.

418   Letter to Ambassador Gerard C. Smith on the Opening of the Second Round of Strategic Arms Limitation Talks in Geneva.   *November 21, 1972*

Dear Mr. Ambassador:

Three years ago you and your colleagues embarked on one of the most critical negotiations in our history. At that time there was little assurance that we could find common ground for discussion, let alone agreement on issues that had not been fully faced in the post-war period and that affected the vital security of the United States and the Soviet Union. The successful conclusion of the agreements signed on May 26 was a milestone not only in Soviet-American relations, but in the larger effort to create a more peaceful world.

These agreements, important as they are, cannot be a cause for complacency. We have taken the first step and the foundation for new agreements has been created. Now you face a task which in many respects is even more complex and more difficult, for both sides will now be obligated to make long term commitments, in a permanent agreement, to a stable strategic relationship for this decade and beyond.

In my letter to you three years ago [1] I

observed that no one could foresee the outcome of the negotiations, but I also expressed my conviction that arms control was in the mutual interest of our country and of the Soviet Union. We have learned in the last three years that such mutual interests do, in fact, exist. The achievement of the SALT agreements, as well as the Basic Principles governing our relations with the USSR, lead me to believe that your current efforts will meet with new success.

As you and your Soviet colleagues begin a new round of discussions, you have with you the hopes of all the American people—and indeed the hopes of all mankind.

Sincerely,

RICHARD NIXON

[The Honorable Gerard Smith, Director, Arms Control and Disarmament Agency, Washington, D.C. 20451]

NOTE: The letter was dated November 20, 1972, and the text was released November 21 at Camp David, Md. Ambassador Smith, Chairman of the United States delegation to the strategic arms limitation talks, read the letter at the opening session of the talks at the Soviet Mission in Geneva on November 21.

[1] See 1969 volume, Item 444.

419   Telephone Conversation With President Félix Houphouet-Boigny of the Ivory Coast.   *November 27, 1972*

PRESIDENT HOUPHOUET-BOIGNY. Mr. President, the inauguration of our land station for communications, following the

example set by your great country, gives me the occasion to reiterate our gratitude for the contribution you have made to our development, and the inauguration of the Kossou Dam last week in the presence of your personal representative [1] gave a visible demonstration of the personal interest that you have shown in our development. The people of Ivory Coast will never forget this.

I also wish to avail myself of this opportunity to express our appreciation for your persistent search for a peace that is real, just, and lasting, and I express the aspirations of all people in voicing the hope that these efforts will be successful, that you will have good help and the protection of the Everlasting.

PRESIDENT NIXON. Mr. President, I greatly appreciate the opportunity to talk to you personally by telephone through this historic new satellite communication. While I have not had the opportunity of meeting you personally, my wife still speaks of her very warm memories of the wonderful welcome she received when she was in Ivory Coast last year.

On my own visit to Ivory Coast during the 1960's, I was enormously impressed by the economic progress, by the tremendous development of your country. Mrs. Nixon reported to me—and other friends like Edgar Kaiser, who was recently in your country—that the Ivory Coast is one of the finest examples in the world of a new country making great economic progress under dynamic leadership of its President.

---

[1] On November 18, 1972, Edgar F. Kaiser of Lafayette, Calif., and John F. Root, United States Ambassador to the Ivory Coast, represented President Nixon at the dedication of the Kossou hydroelectric dam.

I can assure you, Mr. President, that during the remainder of my term of office, these next 4 years, that you can always count on not only the United States Government to cooperate with your Government for progress for both of our people, but you can count on my personal interest in your country and in your own success, because peace, greater opportunity, progress, justice for all people in the world, wherever they may live, is our common goal. I look forward to working with you toward the achievement of that goal, not only in your country but in the great continent of Africa and all over the world.

PRESIDENT HOUPHOUET-BOIGNY. Thank you, Mr. President.

PRESIDENT NIXON. Mr. President, I hope to have the opportunity at some time to meet with you personally during my second term in office.

PRESIDENT HOUPHOUET-BOIGNY. I will be very happy to respond to your invitation.

PRESIDENT NIXON. Thank you very much. Give our best wishes for the Christmas season and the New Year to all of your people.

PRESIDENT HOUPHOUET-BOIGNY. Thank you. We have the same fervent wishes for you and your family.

PRESIDENT NIXON. Thank you. *Merci beaucoup.*

NOTE: The telephone call began at 11:12 a.m. The President spoke from Camp David, Md. President Houphouet-Boigny spoke in French, and his remarks were translated by an interpreter.

The conversation inaugurated communications satellite service for the Ivory Coast via its first ground station near Abidjan.

420 Letter Accepting the Resignation of George W. Romney as Secretary of Housing and Urban Development. *November 27, 1972*

Dear George:

Your resignation as Secretary of Housing and Urban Development is a source of special regret to me, even though we have discussed your desire to leave the Cabinet for several months. I am grateful that you have agreed to serve until confirmation of a successor, and I accept your resignation effective at that time.

As a member of the Cabinet, you have contributed enormously not only of your time and energies, but also of that profound concern for the public good that has been the mark of your life and your career. Yours has been one of the most difficult assignments in the government, and you have handled it with great dedication and skill. Despite the bleak prospects which confronted the housing industry in 1969, your creative and determined actions have helped not only to set all-time records in housing production in each of the last two years, but also to energize a rebounding economy.

Your record is remarkable also for your forthrightness in pointing out the deficiencies in the untried housing programs that you were called upon, when taking office, to administer; for the innovative ways in which you worked to re-shape other HUD programs to reverse central city decay; for the programs you set in motion to modernize the housing industry, and for your establishment of mechanisms to stabilize the industry through a steadier and broader flow of mortgage funds. In addition, I have been particularly impressed by your success in decentralizing your department's operations, and bringing them closer to the communities and people they are meant to serve.

As you know, I share your concern with the need to encourage private problem-solving, and so to reduce the public temptation to expand the role of government beyond its proper limits. I also have great respect for your long and distinguished record of stimulating private and voluntary action. Thus, although I shall greatly miss having you as a member of the Administration, I am confident that in your private capacity you will continue to play a vital and constructive role in achieving the goals that we seek for America as we approach the Nation's 200th anniversary.

It has been a great personal pleasure to work with you during these past four years. Pat joins me in extending to you and Lenore our warmest good wishes, and in the hope that we will continue to see both of you often in the years ahead.

Sincerely,

RICHARD NIXON

[Honorable George W. Romney, Secretary of Housing and Urban Development, Washington, D.C. 20410]

NOTE: Secretary Romney's letter of resignation, dated November 9, 1972, and released with the President's letter at Camp David, Md., read as follows:

Dear Mr. President:

In submitting my resignation from the Cabinet, I want to thank you for the privilege of serving the nation under your great leadership. The experience has been a rewarding and invaluable one that, among other things, has deepened my understanding of our country's political processes.

As you know from our several in-depth discussions during the past year, my experience in public service has convinced me that inherent limitations in those political processes make the achievement of fundamental reform too dependent upon a crisis.

This results primarily from the essential but limited function of political parties and their candidates. Their basic function is to compete for the responsibility to govern. To win in this competition they must win elections. To do this they tend to avoid specific positions concerning, and discussion of, "life and death" issues in their formative and controversial stage for fear of offending uninformed voters and thus losing votes. As a result, elections and candidates seldom focus adequately on those vital issues concerning which the electorate must be knowledgeable if needed reform is to occur without a crisis.

To remedy this deficiency, the nation needs a coalition of concerned citizens dedicated to defining such issues, assembling the relevant, provable facts, identifying the alternate solutions or solution, and communicating their findings to the people. Such a body of truth seekers and communicators could create an enlightened electorate so that the parties and their candidates would find it to their advantage to seek voter support on the basis of the real issues rather than appealing to public and frequently superficial concerns of the moment.

Additionally, there is urgent need to stimu-late voluntary and private problem solving in American life if the role of government is to be kept within the limits that will continue constitutional government that vests ultimate power and responsibility in the people themselves.

As concerned as I am, I would like to be free to join others in organizing nationally for such purposes. I am convinced there is too much at stake to continue to risk our national future on achieving needed reform through successfully surviving the crisis solution process and the ever increasing reliance for problem solving on governmental action.

It is for these reasons that I submit my resignation as Secretary of the Department of Housing and Urban Development, to be effective at your pleasure. I believe I can be more helpful to you and the nation in such an effort. I am grateful for the encouragement you have given me with respect to this future activity.

Fortunately for all of us, your re-election by an historic margin opens up the opportunity not only to establish a generation of peace but to achieve actions as fundamental domestically as those you are achieving internationally.

With gratitude, admiration and prayerful support of your efforts.

Respectfully,

GEORGE ROMNEY

[The President, The White House]

421   Remarks on Plans for the Second Term. *November 27, 1972*

Ladies and gentlemen:

As you have been here at Camp David for the past 2 weeks, I know that you would like somewhat an evaluation of what has happened up to this time and some projection as to the future, so that you can know how to cover our activities between now and the time the Congress reconvenes.

I have had the opportunity over the past 2 weeks to meet now with all the members of the Cabinet and with all of the senior members of the White House Staff. All of those meetings, as you know, have taken place at Camp David.

The decisions with regard to the members of the next Cabinet will be announced beginning tomorrow. They will be announced over a period of time, and I think that all of the announcements will be concluded before the 15th of December. As far as the order in which they are announced, you should draw no connotations from that, because that depends in some instances upon whether we have completed the Congressional consultation which is necessary when Cabinet appointments are being made, and also, in other cases, whether we have completed the evaluation of appointments to the sub-Cabinet. Those appointments, as you will note as time goes on here during the next 2 or 3 weeks, become increasingly important in our plans for the operations of the Cabinet and, particularly, its relationship with the White House Staff.

I think a word would be in order as to why we do have you at Camp David, why these meetings could not have taken place in the comfort of the White House press room and, for that matter, the Oval Office.

I thought it would be interesting to recap for you in a moment the times that I have been here and why we will be using Camp David for activities of this type and other major decisions that will be made by the Administration over the next 4 years.

Looking over the past 4 years, I have written most of my major speeches here—the speech of November 3, the speech of May 8 with regard to the bombing and mining of Haiphong. A number of the major decisions have been made at Camp David, the August 15 economic decision in 1971, for example, the major budget meeting of this year, the budget for the next fiscal year, will be held this Thursday at Camp David.

The reason for that is not that the facilities here are any better than those at the White House—as a matter of fact I suppose the White House facilities in some respects, even for members of the Cabinet who come here, might be better—but the reason is that I find, and each indi-

vidual, of course, who holds the position which I hold must work in the way that it best fits his own patterns, I find that getting away from the White House, from the Oval Office, from that 100 yards that one walks every day from the President's bedroom to the President's Office or the extra 50 yards across to the EOB, getting away gives a sense of perspective which is very, very useful.

I developed that pattern early in the Administration and am going to follow it even more during the next 4 years. We know that in all walks of life, even in the case of you ladies and gentlemen of the press, that one constantly has the problem of either getting on top of the job or having the job get on top of you.

I find that up here on top of a mountain it is easier for me to get on top of the job, to think in a more certainly relaxed way at times—although the work has been very intensive in these past 2 weeks as it was before the other great decisions that have been made here—but also in a way in which one is not interrupted either physically or personally or in any other way and can think objectively with perception about the problems that he has to make decisions on.

As far as the Cabinet members are concerned, I asked them to do exactly the same thing over these past 2 weeks or 2½ weeks since the election. I asked each of them to leave his office or his home for a period of time to think about his department, to think also about his own role in Government, and then have a discussion with me with regard to how we could do a better job over the next 4 years than we have done over the past 4 years.

It has been interesting to note that each member of the Cabinet, virtually to a man, has said that having that opportunity, as a matter of fact being directed to take that opportunity, proved to be valuable. Each has come back with recommendations for reorganization of his own department, each has come back with recommendations for very significant cuts in expenditures and significant cuts in personnel, which had not been considered possible in the prior budget rundown which took place about a month ago. And each, of course, had had an opportunity to think of his own role, what he would want it to be, in the period ahead.

Now, with regard to the members of the Cabinet and what decisions you may expect as to those announcements, let me—without divulging what any of the decisions are now because they will be made over the next couple of weeks—let me tell you what generally has been the pattern.

Some members of the Cabinet—Secretary Laird, Secretary Romney, of course, come to mind—had indicated before the election that they desired to leave Government after their first 4 years. Those desires, of course, we have accepted, but with regret, because I would like to say that I consider every member of the Cabinet a valuable member of our team. I consider each one of them one who is a very valuable public servant, and every one of them, even those who have left, has been given the opportunity to remain in Government service in some very high capacity.

But as I have indicated, some had made the decision, and that decision has been respected, to leave Government service. Others felt that they could better serve by changing their position, by moving from one Cabinet position to another Cabinet position, or from a Cabinet position to another position in another area of Government with similar responsibility.

Without divulging what the eventual decision with regard to his future is, a good example of this is Caspar Weinberger, the Director of OMB. I remember, when he first took the job as Budget Director, he said that no one should be a Budget Director for more than 2 years, because by that time he wears himself out and he is unable to look at the job objectively from that time on. Mr. Weinberger will leave that position. I have prevailed upon him to accept another position. That will be one of the announcements that will be made in the course of the next few days.

But that same pattern repeated itself in a variety of ways with other members of the Cabinet and of the White House Staff as I talked to them.

A word, too, with regard to the White House Staff. Several changes will be made. I felt from the beginning that it was important that the White House establish the example for the balance of the Government in terms of cutting down on personnel, doing a better job with fewer people. Consequently, while there will be cuts in personnel across the Government, throughout the departments, the biggest cuts will be made in the White House Staff itself.

We have been able to do that for a number of reasons, but the most fundamental one is that we are going to put greater responsibility on individual Cabinet members for various functions that previously have been that of the White House Staff.

The White House Staff has rather grown like Topsy. It has grown in every administration. It is now time to reverse that growth to do a more effective job, by bringing the Cabinet members into closer contact with the White House, of course, with the President himself. This will become more apparent as the various appointments are announced and as our plans on reorganization are announced.

The other point that I should make is that there has been some speculation to the effect that there is a move here on the top of this mountain to, as a result of the rather significant victory of November 7, reach out and grasp a lot of power and draw it into the White House and to the executive department. Exactly the opposite is the case.

What we are trying to do is to find a way to make our Government more responsive to people, and the way to make it more responsive to people across this country is not to concentrate more and more power in one office, but to have that power given to and delegated to, where it possibly can, to responsible members of the Administration team in the Cabinet, in the White House, or in other agencies of the Government.

I think a final point that I might make has to do with the reasons for changing at all. I have covered this in an interview I gave immediately after the election, but I might elaborate on it for just a moment with you ladies and gentlemen here at Camp David.

My study of elections in this country, and of second terms particularly, is that second terms almost inevitably are downhill; not always—for example, in Woodrow Wilson's case, he had a very significant first term on the domestic scene, and then the war, World War I, came along in the second term. No one would have known what would have happened in the second term had that crisis not come along.

But generally speaking, whether they are Democratic administrations or Republican administrations, the tendency is for an administration to run out of steam after the first 4 years, and then to coast, and usually coast downhill. That is particularly true when there is what you call a landslide victory. As I have put it to some of my closest colleagues, generally when you think of a landslide, you are submerged by it and you also think in terms of a landslide pushing you downhill.

What I am trying to do is to change that historical pattern. The only way that historical pattern can be changed is to change not only some of the players but also some of the plays, if I may use the analogy to sports. What I am suggesting here is that when a new administration comes in, it comes in with new ideas, new people, new programs. That is why it has vitality and excitement. That is why oftentimes it has change which is very helpful to the country, and progress.

A second administration usually lacks that vitality. It lacks it not because the men and the women in the administration are any less dedicated, but because it is inevitable when an individual has been in a Cabinet position or, for that matter, holds any position in Government, after a certain length of time he becomes an advocate of the status quo; rather than running the bureaucracy, the bureaucracy runs him.

It has been my conviction for years that elected officials in this country too often become prisoners of what we would call the bureaucracy which they are supposed to run. This is no reflection on the bureaucracy. There are millions of dedicated people working for government throughout this country who are not elected officials or people who are appointed by the elected officials.

It is, however, simply a statement of fact that it is the responsibility of those who are elected to the highest office in this land to see to it that what they consider to be the directions that the people want them to follow are followed out and not that they simply come in and continue to go along doing things as they have been done in the past.

I do not consider the election of November 7, 1972, despite the rather massive majority, to have been simply an approval of things as they were. I do not consider that election to have been an endorsement of the status quo. That is completely contrary to the American tradition. This is not a standstill country. It is a go-ahead country. That is our tradition from the beginning. The American people are never satisfied with things as they are. The American people want change. In my view, as I have often stated, I think they want change that works, not radical change, not destructive change, but change that builds rather than destroys. It is that kind of change that I have tried to stand for, and I will continue to work for over these next 4 years.

But when we look at the election of 1972, we must recognize that it came after a year of very significant change: the Moscow summit, the Peking summit, and in the domestic field—while we had many disappointments—the revenue sharing, which will have such a massive effect on the relationships between Federal and State governments. But after that year of '72 in which we had had very significant change internationally and to a lesser extent on the domestic front, the American

people, in voting, I think, for the present Administration, were not voting to stand still but to go ahead with that kind of imaginative change.

So, I think you can expect the next Administration to be one that will have some new players. We will have some new plays, although we will consider this to be not a game, but very, very serious public business.

But we feel that we have a mandate, a mandate not simply for approval of what we have done in the past, but a mandate to continue to provide change that will work in our foreign policy and in our domestic policy, change that will build a better life, that will mean progress at home toward our great goals here, just as we have been making progress in the field of international affairs.

I will conclude simply by saying that Ron Ziegler will make the announcements here from Camp David. I will be here, of course, at the Camp, meeting with a number of sub-Cabinet people and others over the next 2 weeks, and as those announcements are made, you will have the opportunity to talk to each of the members of the Cabinet and the sub-Cabinet and to interview them.

Of course, those who have to come up for confirmation, and there will be several in that category, will not be able to answer any questions except in a very general sense.

With regard to specific names, I think it would be well to remove from the speculation two names I have noticed in the press. I did meet, as you know, with Governor Connally and with Governor Rockefeller. I believe that Governor Connally and Governor Rockefeller would be very valuable members of any Cabinet.

After discussions with them, I found that each would prefer at this time not to take a full-time Cabinet or Government position. However, I am glad to say that each has agreed to continue to serve on the Foreign Intelligence Advisory Board, and each has agreed to undertake special part-time assignments—Governor Connally in the field of international economic affairs where he has particular experience and capability, and Governor Rockefeller in the field of domestic affairs where he is undertaking some very intensive and very important research work in the development of our urban policies.

Thank you.

NOTE: The President spoke at 3:03 p.m. in the helicopter hangar at Camp David, Md. He spoke without referring to notes.

Subsequent White House announcements of personnel changes in the executive branch for President Nixon's second term are printed in Appendix E.

On November 8, 1972, the President had held meetings at the White House with members of the Cabinet and of the White House Staff to discuss the structuring of the executive branch for his second term.

422 Statement About the Death of Neil H. McElroy. *December 1, 1972*

WITH the death of Neil H. McElroy, the United States has lost an outstanding citizen, the American people have lost a dedicated public servant, and I have lost a valued friend and associate.

Neil McElroy served his country in many ways. He was a highly successful executive, an active civic and community leader, a strong and resourceful Secretary of Defense in the Eisenhower Administration, and—most recently—a very effective chairman for the President's Commission on School Finance.

To all of his undertakings, he brought the gifts of high character and keen intelligence. Mrs. Nixon and I are deeply grateful for his life and deeply saddened by his death. We extend our profound sympathy to the members of his family.

NOTE: Mr. McElroy, 68, died of cancer at Holmes Hospital in Cincinnati, Ohio, on November 30, 1972. He joined The Procter & Gamble Company in 1925 and served as chairman of the board 1959–71, and as chairman of the executive committee of the board 1971–72. He was Secretary of Defense 1957–59, and Chairman of the President's Commission on School Finance 1970–72.

The statement was released at Key Biscayne, Fla.

Secretary of Health, Education, and Welfare Elliot L. Richardson represented the President at funeral services in Cincinnati on December 3, and delivered a letter from the President to the McElroy family.

423 Message to the Crew of Apollo 17 Following Launch of the Spacecraft. *December 7, 1972*

WITH the final mission of the Apollo lunar exploration series man completes another step in his quest for knowledge of his universe and of himself. Those who come after will stand on the shoulders of the men of Apollo and their dedicated support team.

I wish you good luck and Godspeed.

RICHARD NIXON

NOTE: The message was made available to the press.

On December 5, 1972, the President had telephoned crew members Capt. Eugene A. Cernan, USN, Comdr. Ronald E. Evans, USN, and Dr. Harrison H. Schmitt at the Kennedy Space Center to extend his best wishes to them on their mission.

424   Statement Announcing Freeze on Hirings and Promotions in the Executive Branch.   *December* 11, 1972

I HAVE repeatedly made clear that it is my firm intention to hold down unnecessary Federal spending so that our people can be spared the higher prices and/or higher taxes that such spending inevitably generates. No Federal programs, no matter how attractive they may be individually, can have a higher priority than the protection of the purchasing power of all the people.

The budget I will send to the Congress in January will constitute a plan for keeping Federal spending under effective control, while providing responsible appropriations for all worthy programs.

We cannot wait until January, however, to begin action on one vital part of that plan: There is an urgent need for us to act now to keep the Federal bureaucracy from becoming too large, and thus too expensive, too unwieldy, and too unresponsive. Accordingly:

—I am today imposing a freeze on all new civilian hirings and on all civilian and military promotions by executive branch agencies.

—This freeze is effective at once and will remain in effect until the new budget is transmitted to the Congress in January.

—When the budget is transmitted, the freeze will be relaxed, but only to the extent permitted by the revised

spending goals for fiscal year 1973 as set forth in the budget.

Exceptions to the freeze order will only be permitted in cases where the actions are essential to preserve human life and safety, to protect property, to preserve the continuity of government, or for emergency situations—such as the need for the Postal Service to hire temporary help to meet the Christmas mail rush. All exceptions will have to be approved on a case-by-case basis by the Office of Management and Budget.

I do not expect this freeze to interfere in any way with plans for revitalizing the Federal Government. It will also have no effect on employees' eligibility for step increases, or on the scheduled comparability pay raise for Federal employees at the turn of the year.

My aim is to prevent unnecessary and wasteful growth of the Federal budget. Otherwise, we shall spurn the best chance we have had in more than 20 years to achieve prosperity without war and without inflation. I will not miss this opportunity.

NOTE: On the same day, the White House released a transcript of remarks by Secretary of the Treasury George P. Shultz announcing decisions reached by the President on economic stabilization and Federal spending. After his opening statement, Secretary Shultz and Caspar W. Weinberger, Director, Office of Management and Budget, answered questions for reporters. The question-and-answer session was included in the White House press release. Secretary Shultz's remarks are printed in the Weekly Compilation of Presidential Documents (vol. 8, p. 1752).

The text of a letter from Director Wein-

berger to the heads of departments and agencies about the freeze on hirings and promotions in the executive branch was also released by the White House and is printed in the Weekly Compilation of Presidential Documents (vol. 8, p. 1753).

425   Statement on Signing Executive Order Transferring Operations of the Office of Intergovernmental Relations to the Domestic Council. *December* 14, 1972

I HAVE today signed an Executive order [11690] transferring the operations of the Office of Intergovernmental Relations, which I established in 1969 to operate under the immediate supervision of the Vice President, to the Domestic Council, which has been the focal point for domestic policy formulation since it came into being 2½ years ago under Reorganization Plan No. 2 of 1970.

This action, which I am taking at Vice President Agnew's recommendation based on his extensive experience in intergovernmental relations, will facilitate improved two-way communication and coordination between the Federal Government and State and local governments. The Vice President, who acts as Vice Chairman of the Domestic Council, will still be closely informed about the views and concerns of Governors, State legislators, mayors, and county officials across the country and will, of course, continue to participate in all Domestic Council decisions.

Under the supervision of Kenneth R. Cole, Jr., Executive Director, the Domestic Council will assume the following new responsibilities and functions under the change effected today:

—to act as my principal point of contact with the executive and legislative officials of State and local government;

—to encourage closer cooperation between the various Federal agencies and their State and local counterparts;

—to keep the Federal Executive continuously aware of the views of State and local officials and to serve as a clearinghouse through which specific difficulties can be resolved;

—to work closely with the Advisory Commission on Intergovernmental Relations;

—to provide State and local officials with guaranteed access to the highest offices of the Federal Government— especially those offices having a direct impact on intergovernmental relations;

—to strengthen existing channels of communication and to create new channels among all levels of government;

—to transfer more decisionmaking authority to the Federal regional offices, and to facilitate an orderly transfer of appropriate functions to State and local government; and

—to provide the President with a more versatile domestic policy arm and give State and local government a direct role in the development of our domestic policy initiatives.

As a further step toward increasing intergovernmental involvement in the Federal domestic policy formulation process,

I shall also appoint Mr. Cole to the Advisory Commission on Intergovernmental Relations.

I expect this streamlining action within the Executive Office of the President to contribute significantly to our objective of achieving a stronger and better balanced Federal system in the United States during the next 4 years.

426   Statement Following Lift-Off From the Moon of the Apollo 17 Lunar Module.   *December* 14, 1972

AS THE Challenger leaves the surface of the Moon, we are conscious not of what we leave behind, but of what lies before us. The dreams that draw humanity forward seem always to be redeemed if we believe in them strongly enough and pursue them with diligence and courage. Once we stood mystified by the stars; today we reach out to them. We do this not only because it is man's destiny to dream the impossible, to dare the impossible, and to do the impossible, but also because in space, as on Earth, there are new answers and new opportunities for the improvement and the enlargement of human existence.

This may be the last time in this cen-

tury that men will walk on the Moon. But space exploration will continue, the benefits of space exploration will continue, the search for knowledge through the exploration of space will continue, and there will be new dreams to pursue based on what we have learned. So let us neither mistake the significance nor miss the majesty of what we have witnessed. Few events have ever marked so clearly the passage of history from one epoch to another. If we understand this about the last flight of Apollo, then truly we shall have touched a "many-splendored thing."

To Gene Cernan, Jack Schmitt, and Ronald Evans, we say God speed you safely back to this good Earth.

427   Statement on Receiving Necessary Ratifications of the International Telecommunications Satellite Organization's Definitive Agreements.   *December* 15, 1972

I NOTE with special satisfaction today that the number of ratifications necessary to bring the INTELSAT definitive agreements into force has been fulfilled. This marks an historic milestone in international communications, with consequences

ranging far into the future. All of the partner-members can take great satisfaction from the progress of this unique multinational venture for the peaceful use of outer space.

With its volume of traffic constantly increasing and with more new earth-stations being inaugurated each year, the global communications satellite system is helping to bring the peoples of the world closer together. It is our hope that the closing of communications gaps will greatly enhance understanding among nations.

We can now look forward to the day when nations around the world will be linked together for instantaneous communications. The implications of this development are enormous, presaging improved international relations in the political, economic, cultural, and scientific spheres.

I am pleased to congratulate the partner-members of INTELSAT and to express my confidence in the continued growth and expanding usefulness of this system.

NOTE: The texts of the agreements are printed in Treaties and Other International Acts Series (TIAS 7532).

On the same day, the White House released a fact sheet on INTELSAT and the agreements.

428 Message to the Congress on Federal Civilian and Military Pay Increases. *December 15, 1972*

To the Congress of the United States:

In accordance with the provisions of section 5305 of title 5, United States Code, I hereby report on the comparability adjustment I have ordered for the Federal statutory pay systems in January 1973.

The American system of career civil service is based on the principle of rewarding merit. As President I have a special appreciation of the contribution that the service makes to our Nation, and I am pledged to continue striving to make it an even more effective, responsive part of our Government. One way of achieving this is to maintain a salary scale for civil servants that is just and comparable to that received by equivalent individuals in the private sector.

The adjustment I have ordered is based on recommendations submitted to me by the Director of the Office of Management and Budget and the Chairman of the Civil Service Commission, who serve jointly as my "agent" for Federal pay. Their report, which is enclosed, compares Federal salaries with average private enterprise salaries as shown in the 1972 *National Survey of Professional, Administrative, Technical, and Clerical Pay*, and recommends a 5.14 percent increase in Federal salaries in order to achieve comparability with the private sector.

The report of the Advisory Committee on Federal Pay, which I appointed under the provisions of section 5306 of title 5, is also enclosed. The Advisory Committee generally agreed with the recommendations of the Director of OMB and the Chairman of the Civil Service Commission and endorsed their plans for studies and further refinements in the pay comparison process. However, the Advisory Committee also recommended that in addition to the 5.14 percent increase, an extra pay adjustment of approximately .36 percent be granted to make up for the three-month delay of this pay adjustment that was necessitated this year by the Economic Stabilization Act Amendments of 1971. Since such an increase would result in paying Federal employees higher salaries than comparable private enterprise employees as shown by the annual Bureau of Labor Statistics Survey, I have concluded that such additional increase would be neither fair nor justifiable.

Also transmitted is a copy of an Executive order promulgating the adjustments of statutory salary rates to become effective on the first day of the first pay period beginning on or after January 1, 1973.

Concurrent with the issuance of this Executive order adjusting pay for civil servants, I have also signed an Executive order providing a pay increase of 6.69 percent in the basic pay of members of our uniformed services. This Executive order complies with section 8 of Public Law 90–

207 (81 Stat. 654), which provides that whenever the rates of the General Schedule of compensation for Federal classified employees are adjusted upwards, there shall immediately be placed into effect a comparable upward adjustment in the basic pay of members of the uniformed services.

RICHARD NIXON

NOTE: The text of the message was released by the White House on December 15, 1972, in connection with the signing of Executive Order 11691, adjusting the rates of pay for certain statutory pay systems, and Executive Order 11692, adjusting the rates of monthly basic pay for members of the uniformed services. Since the 92d Congress was in adjournment, the message was not transmitted until January 9, 1973, after the opening of the first session of the 93d Congress.

429   Statement About the Space Program. *December* 19, 1972

THE SAFE return of the command module "America" marks the end of one of the most significant chapters in the history of human endeavor. In October 1958, this Nation set about sending men into a hostile, unknown environment. We had little idea what lay before us, but there was new knowledge to be gained and there was a heritage of meeting historical challenge—the challenge of greatness— to be sustained. Project Mercury, begun in 1958, taught us that man could survive and work in space. In 1961, President Kennedy voiced the determination of the United States to place a man on the Moon. We gained the understanding and the technology to embark on this great mission through Project Gemini, and we accomplished it with the Apollo lunar exploration series. In 1969, for the first

time, men from the planet Earth set foot on the Moon.

Since the beginning of Apollo, nine manned flights have been made to the Moon. Three circled that nearest neighbor in the universe, six landed and explored its surface. We have barely begun to evaluate the vast treasure store of extraterrestrial data and material from these voyages, but we have already learned much and we know that we are probing our very origins. We are taking another long step in man's ancient search for his own beginnings, pressing beyond knowledge of the means of human existence to find, perhaps, the meaning of human existence.

Nor is this great work ending with the return of Gene Cernan, Jack Schmitt, and Ron Evans from the Moon today.

Rather it has barely begun. As Sir Isaac Newton attributed his accomplishments to the fact that he stood "upon the shoulders of Giants," so Newton himself is one of the giants upon whose shoulders we now stand as we reach for the stars. The great mathematician once wrote: "I do not know what I may appear to the world; but to myself I seem to have been only like a boy playing on the seashore, and diverting myself in now and then finding a smoother pebble or a prettier shell than ordinary, whilst the great ocean of truth lay all undiscovered before me." I believe we have finally moved into that great ocean, and we are trying now to understand what surrounds us.

The making of space history will continue, and this Nation means to play a major role in its making. Next spring, the Skylab will be put into orbit. It will be aimed not at advancing the exploration of deep space, but at gaining in space new knowledge for the improvement of life here on Earth. It will help develop new methods of learning about the Earth's environment and the Earth's resources, and new methods of evaluating programs aimed at preserving and enhancing the resources of all the world. It will seek new knowledge about our own star, the Sun, and about its tremendous influence on our environment. Scientists aboard the Skylab will perform medical experiments aimed at a better knowledge of man's own physiology. Also, they will perform experiments aimed at developing new industrial processes utilizing the unique capabilities found in space. Skylab will be our first manned space station. It will be in use for the better part of a year, permitting the economy of extended usage, and laying the groundwork for further space stations.

Economy in space will be further served by the Space Shuttle, which is presently under development. It will enable us to ferry space research hardware into orbit without requiring the full expenditure of a launch vehicle as is necessary today. It will permit us to place that hardware in space accurately, and to service or retrieve it when necessary instead of simply writing it off in the event it malfunctions or fails. In addition, the Shuttle will provide such routine access to space that for the first time personnel other than trained astronauts will be able to participate and contribute in space as will nations once excluded for economic reasons.

The near future will see joint space efforts by this Nation and the Soviet Union in an affirmation of our common belief that the hopes and the needs that unite our people and all people are of greater consequence than the differences in philosophy that divide us.

Finally, we will continue to draw knowledge from the universe through the use of unmanned satellites and probes.

We cannot help but pause today and remember and pay homage to those many men and women—including those who made the ultimate sacrifice—whose hopes, whose energies, skill, and courage enabled the first man to reach the Moon and who now have seen with us perhaps the last men in this century leave the Moon. But the more we look back the more we are reminded that our thrust has been forward and that our place is among the heavens where our dreams precede us, and where, in time, we shall surely follow.

Though our ancestors would have called the deeds of Apollo miraculous, we do not see our age as an age of miracles. Rather, we deal in facts, we deal in scientific realities, we deal in industrial capacity, and technological expertise, and in the belief that men can do whatever they turn their hands to. For all this, however, can we look at the record of 24 men sent to circle the Moon or to stand upon it, and 24 men returned to Earth alive and well, and not see God's hand in it?

Perhaps, in spite of ourselves, we do still live in an age of miracles. So if there is self-congratulation, let it be tempered with awe, and our pride with prayer, and as we enter this special time of spiritual significance, let us reserve a moment to wonder at what human beings have done in space and to be grateful.

NOTE: The President telephoned Astronauts Cernan, Schmitt, and Evans aboard the U.S.S. *Ticonderoga* in the Pacific, following splashdown of the Apollo 17 command module "America," to express his personal congratulations on the successful completion of their mission.

430   Statement on the Death of Harry S Truman. *December* 26, 1972

HARRY S TRUMAN will be remembered as one of the most courageous Presidents in our history, who led the Nation and the world through a critical period with exceptional vision and determination.

Our hopes today for a generation of peace rest in large measure on the firm foundations that he laid.

Recognizing the new threat to peace that had emerged from the ashes of war, he stood boldly against it with his extension of aid to Greece and Turkey in 1947—and the "Truman Doctrine" thus established was crucial to the defense of liberty in Europe and the world. In launching the Marshall Plan, he began the most farsighted and most generous act of international rebuilding ever undertaken. With his characteristically decisive action in Korea, he made possible the defense of peace and freedom in Asia.

He was a fighter who was at his best when the going was toughest. Like all political leaders, he had his friends and his opponents. But friends and opponents alike were unanimous in respecting him for his enormous courage, and for the spirit that saw him through whatever the odds. Whether in a political campaign or making the great decisions in foreign policy, they recognized and admired him—in a description he himself might have appreciated the most—as a man of "guts."

Embroiled in controversy during his Presidency, his stature in the eyes of history has risen steadily ever since. He did what had to be done, when it had to be done, and because he did the world today is a better and safer place—and generations to come will be in his debt.

It is with affection and respect that a grateful Nation now says farewell to "the man from Independence"—to its thirty-third President, Harry S Truman.

NOTE: Former President Harry S Truman, 88, died after a long illness at Research Hospital in Kansas City, Mo.

The statement was released at Key Biscayne, Fla.

On December 27, 1972, the President and Mrs. Nixon placed a wreath at President Truman's bier in the Truman Library in Independence, Mo. They later called at the Truman home to express their sympathy.

431   Proclamation 4176, Announcing the Death of Harry S Truman.   *December 26, 1972*

By the President of the United States of America a Proclamation

To the People of the United States:

It is my sad duty to announce officially the death of Harry S Truman, thirty-third President of the United States, on December 26, 1972.

Throughout his long career in public service, Harry S Truman was known as a man of forthrightness and integrity. He served with distinction in the United States Senate; and when the death of President Franklin Delano Roosevelt thrust him suddenly into the Presidency in April of 1945 at one of the most critical moments of our history, he met that moment with courage and vision. His far-sighted leadership in the postwar era has helped ever since to preserve peace and freedom in the world.

Confronted during his Presidency with a momentous series of challenges, his strength and spirit proved equal to them all. His fortitude never wavered, and his faith in America never flagged.

President Truman had a deep respect for the office he held and for the people he served. He gave himself unstintingly to the duties of the Presidency while he held it, and in the years afterward he honorably supported and wisely counseled each of his successors.

The Nation to which he gave so much will honor his memory in admiration and respect, and the other countries for which he helped keep freedom alive will remember his name with gratitude.

Now, Therefore, I, Richard Nixon, President of the United States of America in tribute to the memory of President Truman, and as an expression of public sorrow, do hereby direct that the flag of the United States be displayed at half-staff at the White House and on all buildings, grounds, and Naval vessels of the United States for a period of thirty days from the day of his death. I also direct that for the same length of time the representatives of the United States in foreign countries shall make similar arrangements for the display of the flag at half-staff over their Embassies, Legations, and other facilities abroad, including all military facilities and stations.

I hereby order that suitable honors be rendered by units of the Armed Forces under orders of the Secretary of Defense on the day of the funeral.

I do further appoint December 28, 1972 to be a National Day of Mourning throughout the United States. I recommend that the people assemble on that day in their respective places of worship, there to pay homage to the memory of President Truman and to seek God's continued blessing on our land and on this His servant. I invite the people of the world who share our grief to join us in this solemn observance.

In Witness Whereof, I have hereunto set my hand this 26th day of December, in the year of our Lord nineteen hundred seventy-two, and of the Independence of the United States of America the one hundred ninety-seventh.

Richard Nixon

note: On the same day, the President signed Executive Order 11693 providing for the closing of Government departments and agencies on December 28, 1972.

432   Statement About the Death of Lester B. Pearson.
December 28, 1972

LESTER B. PEARSON, former Prime Minister of Canada, will be remembered as one of the 20th century's most untiring and effective workers in the cause of world peace. For four decades, as diplomat, statesman, and Nobel Peace Prize laureate, he gave unstintingly of himself in the service of Canada and the world community. The record of his accomplishments as an outstanding postwar leader has few equals.

Canada has lost a great leader. We in the United States have lost a firm friend. The world has lost a great statesman and a wise counselor. His life illustrates in a profound way how much one man, by virtue of hard work, high principle, and a sympathetic understanding of his fellow man, can accomplish in the cause of peace and freedom.

As one who has had the privilege of knowing Lester Pearson for two decades, and who has counted him a friend, I shall miss him greatly.

NOTE: Mr. Pearson, 75, died of cancer in Ottawa, Canada, on December 27, 1972. Mr. Pearson was President of the seventh session of the United Nations General Assembly 1952–53, recipient of the 1957 Nobel Peace Prize, and Prime Minister of Canada 1963–68.

Adolph W. Schmidt, United States Ambassador to Canada, officially represented the President at funeral services on December 31, when Vice President Spiro T. Agnew and the official party were unable to land at the Ottawa airport because of icy runway conditions.

Appendix A—Additional White House Releases

NOTE: This appendix lists those releases which are neither printed as items in this volume nor listed in subsequent appendixes. If the text of a release was printed in the Weekly Compilation of Presidential Documents, the page number is indicated below. Page references are to Volume 8 of the Compilation:

Appendix A

Appendix A

Appendix A

A–4

Appendix A

Appendix A

A–7

Appendix A

Appendix A

Appendix A

Appendix A

Appendix A

Appendix A

Appendix B—Additional White House Announcements

NOTE: This appendix lists those items of general interest which were announced to the press during 1972 but which are not noted elsewhere in this volume. A special series of announcements concerning the President's decisions on personnel changes for his second term is printed in Appendix E.

January

1 The President went with Mrs. Nixon to Andrews Air Force Base where the First Lady departed for her visits to Liberia, Ghana, and the Ivory Coast.

3 Ambassador Gerard C. Smith, head of the United States delegation to the strategic arms limitation talks, met with the President before leaving for the next session of the SALT negotiations in Vienna.

3 Clarence C. Hoffman of Minneapolis, chosen by the American Trucking Associations as Driver of the Year, was greeted by the President at the White House.

3 The President greeted three members of the American Hospital Association: Stephen M. Morris, association president; John W. Kauffman, president-elect; and Jack A. L. Hahn, immediate past president.

3 The President met with Henry Ford II, chairman of the National Center for Voluntary Action, to discuss the Center's programs.

7 The President sent congratulatory letters to Robert T. Stafford on his election as United States Senator from Vermont and to Richard W. Mallary, elected to succeed Mr. Stafford in the House of Representatives.

10 The President met with Arthur A. Fletcher, executive director of the United Negro College Fund, to present a personal contribution to the fund.

10 Members of the Committee on the Health Services Industry met with the President to discuss their work in assisting the Cost of Living Council.

January

13 The President attended the swearing in of John E. Sheehan as a member of the Board of Governors of the Federal Reserve System at a ceremony in the Oval Office at the White House.

13 The President met with Edwin M. "Jiggs" Fauver who is retiring this month as Chief of the White House Travel and Telegraph Services.

13 Members of the fifth-grade class of Ascension Academy, Alexandria, Va., called on the President at the White House. The President had received a birthday card from the class and wanted to express his appreciation personally.

19 The President announced the promotion of Tom C. Korologos to Deputy Assistant to the President and the appointment of Wallace H. Johnson as Special Assistant to the President, for assignment to Congressional relations duties with the United States Senate.

20 Terence Cardinal Cooke, Archbishop of New York, met with the President at the White House.

20 The President and Mrs. Nixon honored members of the Cabinet at a dinner marking the third anniversary of the President's inauguration.

21 The President announced that he has asked John S. D. Eisenhower, former United States Ambassador to Belgium and son of the late President, to head a delegation to the funeral of King Frederik IX of Denmark.

January

22 The President has written to Clifford H. Buck, president of the United States Olympic Committee, expressing good wishes for the 1972 Winter Olympic Team in Sapporo, Japan.

24 Mayor Frank L. Rizzo of Philadelphia met with the President to discuss Federal-city relationships.

26 Prime Minister Barend W. Biesheuvel of the Netherlands met with the President at the White House.

26 The President met with the Quadriad—Secretary of the Treasury John B. Connally, Chairman Herbert Stein of the Council of Economic Advisers, Director George P. Shultz of the Office of Management and Budget, and Chairman Arthur F. Burns of the Board of Governors of the Federal Reserve System—at the White House.

26 Representative Page Belcher of Oklahoma and Secretary of Agriculture Earl L. Butz met with the President at the White House to discuss agricultural and rural development matters.

28 Dr. Rainer Barzel, leader of the Christian Democratic Union of the Federal Republic of Germany, paid a courtesy call on the President at the White House.

28 Ambassador Yitzhak Rabin of Israel called on the President to present the first volume of the Encyclopedia Judaica.

31 Joseph M. A. H. Luns, Secretary General of the North Atlantic Treaty Organization, met with the President at the White House.

31 Brig. Gen. James D. Hughes, Military Assistant to the President, who is being reassigned to other duties, met with the President at the White House. During the meeting, the President presented him with his second star as major general and the Distinguished Service Medal.

31 Guilford Dudley, Jr., who has recently retired as United States Ambassador to Denmark, called on the President at the White House.

February

1 The President transmitted to the Senate for advice and consent to ratification the Convention on the Taking of Evidence Abroad in Civil or Commercial Matters.

1 The Apollo 15 astronauts called on the President to report on their recent 16-day goodwill mission to Poland and Yugoslavia.

1 Fifteen Boy Scouts and Explorers presented the Scouts' annual report to the President in a ceremony at the White House.

1 At the President's suggestion, beginning February 5, Ambassador George H. Bush, U.S. Permanent Representative to the United Nations, will visit Sudan, Kenya, Zambia, Zaïre, Gabon, Nigeria, and Chad. He will carry a message from the President to the head of state of each country.

1 The President hosted a dinner at the White House for Republican Governors.

2 Newly elected Representative Richard W. Mallary of Vermont met with the President at the White House.

2 Former Speaker of the House John W. McCormack called on the President at the White House.

3 Senate Majority Leader Mike Mansfield breakfasted with the President at the White House.

3 The President transmitted to the Senate for advice and consent to ratification the convention between the United States and Norway for the avoidance of double taxation and the prevention of fiscal evasion with respect to taxes on income and property.

3 The President accorded the personal rank of Ambassador to Joseph Martin, Jr., of the District of Columbia, during the period he serves as the United States Representative or Alternate Representative at meetings of the Conference of the Committee on Disarmament in Geneva.

February

3 The President transmitted to the Senate for advice and consent to acceptance an amendment to the Statute of the International Atomic Energy Agency.

3 Soviet poet Yevgeny Yevtushenko met with the President at the White House.

7 The President received a telephone call from President Alejandro A. Lanusse of Argentina.

7 The President met with 30 U.S. attorneys from key cities of the Nation who were in Washington for a discussion of the drug problem and related enforcement matters.

7 Ambassadors Moulaye el Hassan of Mauritania and Witold Trampczynski of Poland presented their credentials to the President in ceremonies at the White House.

8 The President hosted a reception for participants in the United States Jaycees Governmental Affairs Leadership Seminar being held in Washington February 6–9.

9 The President has asked Secretary of Transportation John A. Volpe to be his personal representative at funeral services for former Secretary of Commerce Sinclair Weeks.

10 In letters to the President of the Senate and the Speaker of the House, the President forwarded proposed legislation to authorize appropriations for the United States Arms Control and Disarmament Agency for 2 years after the expiration of the current authorization on June 30, 1972.

11 At Key Biscayne, Fla., the White House announced that the President welcomes a new agreement between the United States and the Soviet Union for a cooperative program in the field of health. Letters of agreement signed in Washington and Moscow established a U.S.-U.S.S.R. Joint Committee for Health Cooperation and recommended research on cancer, heart disease, and the environmental health sciences as the initial areas for the program.

February

14 Senators Howard H. Baker, Jr., Bill Brock, Robert C. Byrd, Robert P. Griffin, and John G. Tower and Representatives Thomas N. Downing, Norman F. Lent, and Tom Steed met with the President at the White House to discuss school busing.

14 Ambassador Slaheddine El Goulli of Tunisia called on the President at the White House.

14 Senator James L. Buckley of New York met with the President to report on his recent trip to eight Asian nations.

16 The President transmitted to the Senate for advice and consent to ratification a partial revision of the radio regulations (1959) relating to space telecommunications, with a final protocol, dated at Geneva, July 17, 1971.

29 The President met separately with the bipartisan leadership of the Congress and with the Cabinet to report on his visit to the People's Republic of China. Prior to his meeting with the leadership, the President informed Senators Mike Mansfield and Hugh Scott that Premier Chou En-lai had suggested that since they had expressed interest in visiting the People's Republic, he would invite them for a visit at a mutually convenient time.

March

6 Members of the Cabinet Committee on Education who have been studying the matter of school busing met with the President. Joining in the meeting were key black Presidential appointees, including Samuel C. Jackson and Samuel J. Simmons, Assistant Secretaries of Housing and Urban Development; William H. Brown III, Chairman, Equal Employment Opportunity Commission; James E. Johnson, Assistant Secretary of the Navy; Samuel R. Pierce, Jr., General Counsel, Department of the Treasury; and Robert J. Brown, Special Assistant to the President.

March

7 The President met with the Troika—Secretary of the Treasury John B. Connally, Chairman Herbert Stein of the Council of Economic Advisers, and Director George P. Shultz of the Office of Management and Budget—at the White House.

8 The President transmitted to the Senate for advice and consent to ratification the Treaty on Extradition between the United States of America and the Republic of Argentina.

8 A portrait of the President painted by Norman Rockwell was unveiled at the National Portrait Gallery. Tricia Nixon Cox represented her father at the ceremony.

10 George Meany, president, AFL–CIO, breakfasted with the President in the Family Dining Room at the White House. They were joined by George P. Shultz, Director, Office of Management and Budget, and Henry A. Kissinger, Assistant to the President for National Security Affairs.

10 Members of the Cabinet Committee on Education met with the President to discuss the school busing situation. Also participating were several attorneys from outside the government, for consultation on legal and constitutional aspects.

13 The President and Mrs. Nixon have decided that the pandas which are a gift from the People's Republic of China to the people of the United States will be housed at the National Zoological Park in Washington, D.C.

13 Ronald S. Berman, Chairman, National Endowment for the Humanities, met with the President at the White House.

13 Grover E. Murray, president, and John R. Bradford, dean of the College of Engineering, Texas Technological University, Lubbock, Tex., called on the President to present an invitation to address the annual convention of the American Association of Engineers to be held at Texas Tech in June. They were accompanied by Representative George H. Mahon of Texas.

March

14 Nassir Assar, Secretary-General of the Central Treaty Organization, paid a courtesy call on the President at the White House.

14 Wes H. Bartlett, president of Kiwanis International, called on the President at the White House. He was accompanied by Senator Jack Miller of Iowa.

14 Miss Debbie Wright, this year's "Maid of Cotton," called on the President at the White House. She was accompanied by Representative George H. Mahon of Texas.

14 Luci Johnson Nugent and her son, Patrick Lyndon, talked with the President in his office during their visit at the White House with Tricia Nixon Cox.

15 The President transmitted to the Senate for advice and consent to ratification the Universal Copyright Convention as revised at Paris on July 24, 1971, together with two related protocols.

16 In an announcement made simultaneously in Moscow, the White House stated that the President's official visit to the Soviet Union would begin on May 22, 1972.

17 Members of the Citizens' Advisory Council on the Status of Women met with the President to present their report entitled "Women in 1971" (Government Printing Office, 61 pp.).

20 The President met with members of the Cabinet Committee on International Narcotics Control for a report on their activities.

21 Members of the General Advisory Committee on Arms Control and Disarmament, chaired by John J. McCloy, met with the President at the White House for a review of United States negotiating positions in the strategic arms limitation talks and a presentation of the Committee's recommendations before the resumption of the talks in Helsinki on March 28. Ambassador Gerard C. Smith, head of the United States delegation to the talks, later met with the President for discussions and instructions prior to his return to the Helsinki negotiations.

March

21 Vice President Manea Manescu of Romania, who is also Chairman of the Economic Council of Romania, met with the President at the White House. They discussed economic matters, including the President's determination of March 16 that will enable the Overseas Private Investment Corporation to extend its programs to Yugoslavia and Romania.

21 Winners of the White House News Photographers Association contest met with the President at the White House.

23 The President has announced transfer of the old San Francisco Mint from the General Services Administration to the Department of the Treasury for restoration and for use by the Federal Government and the public. Dedicated in 1874 and declared a National Historic Landmark in 1961, the mint will now include an educational and historical museum as well as the Bureau of the Mint's Numismatic Service Division and data processing department.

23 Marshall Green, Assistant Secretary of State for East Asian and Pacific Affairs, and John H. Holdridge, Senior Staff Member, National Security Council, called on the President to report on their trip to 13 Asian countries where they met with officials to discuss the President's trip to China.

27 Ambassadors Dusan Spacil of Czechoslovakia, Angel Sagaz of Spain, and Zuhayr Mahmud al-Mufti of Jordan presented their credentials to the President in ceremonies in the East Room at the White House.

27 Members of the Advertising Council, Inc., were greeted by the President and Mrs. Nixon at a reception in the East Room at the White House.

28 King Hussein I of Jordan met with the President at the White House. In the evening, His Majesty attended a dinner hosted by the President at the White House.

March

28 The President transmitted to the Senate for advice and consent to ratification the Treaty on the Swan Islands between the United States and Honduras. The treaty provides for the recognition by the United States of the sovereignty of Honduras over the Swan Islands. The two Governments also agreed to establish a cooperative meteorological program on the islands.

28 Kevin Heald, 1972 Poster Child of the National Association for Retarded Children, met the President at the White House. Kevin is 6 years old and lives in Cedar Rapids, Iowa. He was accompanied by Calvin Hill, fullback of the Dallas Cowboys professional football team and the association's national sports chairman.

30 Ann Landers, national education crusade chairman of the American Cancer Society, and Mike Finamore, a 20-year-old leukemia victim from Glen Ridge, N.J., called on the President to launch the 1972 Cancer Crusade. The President presented Mr. Finamore with the society's annual Courage Award.

30 Frank E. Fitzsimmons, president of the International Brotherhood of Teamsters, met with the President at the White House.

April

3 The White House announced that Secretary of State William P. Rogers will visit Western Europe on the President's behalf early in May to consult with allied nations preparatory to the summit conference in Moscow. Secretary Rogers will visit the United Kingdom, France, the Federal Republic of Germany, Italy, Iceland, and Luxembourg, and will consult with NATO allies collectively at a special meeting of the North Atlantic Council in Brussels.

4 The President met with representatives of the Prisoner of War Committee of the Young Lawyers Section of the American Bar Association to thank them for their work in providing legal assistance to families of prisoners of war and those missing in action.

April

4 The White House announced that Secretary of Agriculture Earl L. Butz will visit the Soviet Union April 9–12. Secretary Butz will be returning the visit to the United States of the Soviet Minister of Agriculture, V. V. Matskevitch, last December. The Secretary will participate in the April 10 opening session of talks concerning the possibility of additional sales of U.S. grains and feedstuffs to the U.S.S.R.

4 John H. Chafee who is resigning as Secretary of the Navy met with the President at the White House.

4 French Ambassador Charles Lucet paid a farewell call on the President at the White House.

5 The White House announced plans for Dr. Theodore H. Reed, Director of the National Zoological Park, to leave on April 6 for Peking to deliver the two musk oxen which are being presented to the Chinese people. The two pandas which are being given in return to the American people will be brought back to Washington by Dr. Reed. Two Chinese advisers will come to the United States with the pandas to discuss their care and housing at the zoo.

7 The President announced transfer of 17 Federal properties to local governments for use as park and recreational facilities as part of the Legacy of Parks program. Included are lands in Florida, Iowa, Ohio, Washington, Wisconsin, Louisiana, California, Indiana, Michigan, Mississippi, New York, Puerto Rico, and Rhode Island.

10 Ambassador William J. Porter, head of the United States delegation to the Paris peace talks, met with the President at the White House before returning to Paris.

10 The President greeted approximately 250 members of the National Alliance of Businessmen at a reception at the White House. He also announced appointment of Gordon M. Metcalf as Chairman of the Alliance.

April

11 The President transmitted to the Senate for advice and consent to accession by the United States the Convention Establishing an International Organization of Legal Metrology, as amended.

11 The President transmitted to the Congress the budget for the District of Columbia for the fiscal year beginning July 1, 1972.

11 Senators Mike Mansfield and Hugh Scott met with the President to discuss their forthcoming visit to the People's Republic of China.

14 The President and Mrs. Nixon were guests of Prime Minister and Mrs. Pierre Elliott Trudeau at a gala performance in their honor at the National Arts Centre in Ottawa. The program featured the National Arts Centre Orchestra conducted by Mario Bernardi, and the Festival Singers of Canada.

17 The President met with Ambassador Witold Trampczynski of the Polish People's Republic. The Ambassador delivered an invitation to the President from Chairman of the Council of State Henryk Jablonski and Prime Minister Piotr Jaroszewicz to visit Poland following his visit to the Soviet Union and Iran at the end of May. The President has accepted the invitation with pleasure.

17 The President met with Donald B. Rice to thank him for his service as Assistant Director of the Office of Management and Budget. Mr. Rice has resigned to become president of the RAND Corporation.

17 The President went to the Capitol to attend an annual seafood luncheon hosted by Representative William M. Colmer of Mississippi.

19 The President has asked Vice President Agnew to act as his personal representative at the Okinawa Reversion Day ceremony in Tokyo on May 15. Other members of the delegation will be United States Ambassador to Japan Robert S. Ingersoll and the United States High Commissioner of the Ryukyu Islands, Lt. Gen. James B. Lampert.

April

20 Representative Cliffard D. Carlson, newly elected Member of the House of Representatives from Illinois, called on the President at the White House.

20 Members of the American Society of Newspaper Editors attending the society's annual meeting in Washington were guests of the President and Mrs. Nixon at a reception at the White House.

25 The President hosted a dinner for Members of Congress who are retiring from the Congress.

25 The White House announced that Henry A. Kissinger had been in Moscow April 20–24 to confer with Soviet leaders prior to the President's trip.

26 Minister of Foreign Affairs Yong Shik Kim of Korea met with the President at the White House.

26 The White House announced that the President had sent letters to the chairmen of six Congressional committees responsible for legislation outlined in the President's environmental message. The letters urged action on legislation in the areas of marine protection, noise control, toxic substances control, powerplant siting, ports and waterways safety, national land use policy, mined area protection, national resource lands management, and Federal environmental pesticide control.

26 The President met with Herbert F. DeSimone, Assistant Secretary of Transportation, who is resigning effective May 20.

29 Mrs. Nixon represented the President at the annual dinner of the White House Correspondents Association at the Washington Hilton Hotel.

May

1 In observance of National Secretaries Week, the President greeted a group of White House secretaries in the Rose Garden to thank them for their work in the White House.

May

1 Ambassador Gerard C. Smith, head of the United States delegation to the strategic arms limitation talks, met with the President and senior advisers at the White House. After the meeting, Press Secretary Ronald L. Ziegler announced that "the President has today directed Ambassador Smith to return to Helsinki with new instructions, which, together with the new instructions he is confident the Soviet representative will receive from his government, can lead to an agreement which is mutually acceptable to both sides."

1 The White House released the report of the emergency board created by Executive Order 11663 on March 31, 1972, to investigate the dispute between the carriers represented by the National Railway Labor Conference and certain of their employees represented by the Sheet Metal Workers' International Association (AFL–CIO).

2 The President participated in a White House swearing-in ceremony for Lt. Gen. Vernon A. Walters, USA, as Deputy Director of the Central Intelligence Agency.

2 Members of the Rebild Society of Denmark, an organization devoted to promoting Danish-American friendship, called on the President at the White House.

3 The President has designated Dr. Merlin K. DuVal, Assistant Secretary of Health, Education, and Welfare for Health and Scientific Affairs, to head the U.S. delegation to the 25th World Health Assembly in Geneva, Switzerland, from May 9–26, 1972.

4 The President met with L. Patrick Gray III, Acting Director of the FBI, and Mrs. Gray at the White House after attending funeral services for J. Edgar Hoover.

4 Frank E. Fitzsimmons, president of the International Brotherhood of Teamsters, and three vice presidents of the union called on the President at the White House.

4 Entertainer Ray Conniff met with the President in his office in the Executive Office Building.

May

4 The President has appointed John S. D. Eisenhower as his personal representative with the rank of Special Ambassador to the May 20 inauguration of President Chiang Kai-shek of the Republic of China.

4 The President transmitted to the Senate for advice and consent to ratification the protocol amending the Single Convention on Narcotic Drugs, 1961.

5 The President met with members of his Foreign Intelligence Advisory Board at the White House.

5 The President transmitted to the Senate for advice and consent to ratification the International Convention on the Establishment of an International Fund for Compensation for Oil Pollution Damage (Supplementary to the International Convention on Civil Liability for Oil Pollution Damage of 1969).

9 Senators Mike Mansfield and Hugh Scott had breakfast with the President and reported on their recent trip to the People's Republic of China.

9 The President and the First Lady hosted a reunion dinner for members of the Duke University Law School class of 1937.

11 Representatives Wilbur D. Mills and John W. Byrnes and Secretary of the Treasury John B. Connally had breakfast with the President and discussed tax reform.

11 Nikolai Patolichev, Minister of Foreign Trade of the Soviet Union, met with the President at the White House. Also participating in the meeting were Anatoly F. Dobrynin, the Soviet Union's Ambassador to the United States, Peter G. Peterson, Secretary of Commerce, Peter M. Flanigan, Assistant to the President for International Economic Affairs, and Henry A. Kissinger, Assistant to the President for National Security Affairs.

15 Brazilian Ambassador João Augusto de Araujo Castro called on the President at the White House to present a letter from President Emílio Garrastazú Médici.

May

15 Ambassadors Kifle Wodajo of Ethiopia, Jacques Kosciusko-Morizet of France, Sultan Mohammad Khan of Pakistan, and Andrés Aguilar of Venezuela presented their credentials to the President in ceremonies in the East Room at the White House.

15 The White House released the report of the emergency board created by Executive Order 11664 on March 31, 1972, to investigate the dispute between the Penn Central Transportation Company and certain of its employees represented by the United Transportation Union.

16 Enayet Karim, Chargé d'Affaires of Bangladesh, called on the President at the White House to deliver a message from Prime Minister Sheikh Mujibur Rahman which completed the formal exchanges establishing diplomatic relations at the embassy level.

16 Toma Granfil, Yugoslav Ambassador to the United States, called on the President at the White House.

16 John Cardinal Krol, Archbishop of Philadelphia, met with the President at the White House.

19 En route to the White House from Camp David, the President visited Gov. George C. Wallace of Alabama at Holy Cross Hospital in Silver Spring, Md., and Secret Service Agent Nicholas J. Zarvos at Walter Reed Army Medical Center in Washington.

19 The President announced the selection of the 1972 Presidential Scholars, 121 high school seniors chosen by the Commission on Presidential Scholars for outstanding academic achievement and leadership potential.

20 The President declared a major disaster in the State of Texas following heavy rains and flooding early this month. The President authorized use of Federal funds for relief and recovery efforts.

May

23 The President has announced the transfer of 2,273 acres of Federal land to State and local governments for park and recreational use under the Legacy of Parks program. Included are lands in California, Colorado, Connecticut, Georgia, Maryland, Massachusetts, Mississippi, Nevada, New Jersey, Texas, Washington, and Wisconsin.

June

2 The White House has announced the designation of offices in 12 departments and agencies to receive requests for declassification of material over 10 years old pursuant to Executive Order 11652 and the National Security Council directive of May 17, 1972.

3 The White House announced that Dr. Kissinger would visit Japan June 9-12 at the invitation of the Japan-U.S. Economic Council. During the visit, he would also meet with Prime Minister Eisaku Sato, Foreign Minister Takeo Fukuda, and Minister of International Trade and Industry Kakuei Tanaka.

5 After a meeting between the President and Secretary of the Treasury John B. Connally at Key Biscayne, Fla., the White House announced that Secretary Connally would undertake, on behalf of the President, a mission to a number of nations in South America and Asia. Departing on June 6, Secretary Connally, as the Special Representative of the President, will meet with chiefs of state and heads of government in Venezuela, Colombia, Brazil, Argentina, Bolivia, Peru, Australia, New Zealand, Singapore, South Vietnam, Cambodia, Malaysia, Bangladesh, India, Pakistan, Iran, and Afghanistan.

9 The President announced the transfer of 1,419 acres of Federal land to State and local governments for park and recreational use under the Legacy of Parks program. Included are lands in California, Hawaii, Iowa, Illinois, Kentucky, Missouri, New York, New Jersey, and Puerto Rico.

12 Ambassador Bui Diem of South Vietnam paid a farewell call on the President.

June

13 The President was represented by the Vice President at ceremonies in the East Garden in honor of the 1972 Presidential Scholars.

15 James C. Fletcher, Administrator, National Aeronautics and Space Administration, and the three members of the crew of Apollo 16 met with the President at the White House. They discussed the joint U.S.-U.S.S.R. space agreement, which was signed in Moscow on May 24, and reviewed progress toward a joint rendezvous and docking mission in 1975 and other future cooperation.

15 Prince Sultan ibn Abd al-Aziz Al-Saud, Minister of Defense and Aviation of Saudi Arabia, met with the President at the White House. Prince Sultan is visiting the United States as the guest of Secretary of Defense Melvin R. Laird.

15 The President transmitted to the Senate for advice and consent to ratification the International Convention on Tonnage Measurement of Ships, 1969, and the Convention on International Liability for Damage Caused by Space Objects.

21 The President met with the Quadriad—Secretary of the Treasury John B. Connally, Chairman Herbert Stein of the Council of Economic Advisers, Director George P. Shultz of the Office of Management and Budget, and Chairman Arthur F. Burns of the Board of Governors of the Federal Reserve System—at the White House. Following the meeting, the President met with Dr. Burns to discuss his trip, beginning June 24, to Peru, Argentina, Brazil, and Venezuela. Dr. Burns will meet with heads of the central banks and other financial leaders in the four countries.

21 The President has requested Secretary of State William P. Rogers, in addition to attending SEATO and ANZUS meetings in Canberra, Australia, on June 27-28 where he will brief the participants on the President's visits to the People's Republic of China and the Soviet Union, to make a visit to Indonesia, Bahrain, Kuwait, Greece, Romania, Hungary, and Yugoslavia.

June

22 The White House announced the creation of the National Committee for Employer Support of the National Guard and Reserve Forces, with James M. Roche, retired chairman of the board and chief executive officer of General Motors, as Chairman. The Committee will promote membership in the Guard and Reserve units and will focus its efforts on employers of members and potential members of the standby services.

22 John Cardinal Krol, Archbishop of Philadelphia, and John T. Gurash, chairman of the board of the Insurance Company of North America and head of a committee which conducted a survey of Catholic education in Philadelphia, met with the President at the White House to discuss parochial school financing.

22 The President met with executives of 29 independent broadcast organizations from across the Nation who were attending a White House briefing on the economy and the arms limitation treaty and interim agreement, as well as other topics.

22 The President hosted a reception at the White House for incumbent Republican Senators and Representatives.

23 House leaders Hale Boggs and Gerald R. Ford had breakfast with the President at the White House prior to their departure for the People's Republic of China.

23 The National Farm Family of the Year, Mr. and Mrs. Carlos D. Dixon and their three children, of Lonoke County, Ark., called on the President at the White House. They were selected in the second annual Farm Family of the Year contest sponsored by the Farmers Home Administration.

June

23 The President met at the White House with Henry A. Kissinger and Secretary of State William P. Rogers for a report on Dr. Kissinger's just-completed trip to the People's Republic of China and discussions of Secretary Rogers' upcoming trip around the world. The President and Dr. Kissinger then flew to Camp David for further discussions of the China trip and other foreign policy matters.

24 The President made a 2-hour helicopter tour of flood areas in Maryland and in southeastern Pennsylvania along the Susquehanna River and talked with flood victims and local officials at an evacuation center at the William Penn High School in Harrisburg, Pa.

24 The White House issued a joint statement on discussions between Henry A. Kissinger and officials of the People's Republic of China June 19–23.

26 The President met with 20 leaders of major veterans organizations who were attending a briefing at the White House on the arms limitation treaty and interim agreement and other foreign policy matters.

26 The President greeted 55 representatives of Polish-American communities throughout the country at a reception in the Blue Room. The representatives were in Washington for a Department of State briefing on United States-Polish relations and the President's recent trip to Warsaw.

26 The President presented the Distinguished Service Medal (Third Oak Leaf Cluster) to Gen. William C. Westmoreland, retiring Chief of Staff of the Army, in a ceremony in the Oval Office at the White House.

27 Republican members of the Senate Committee on Finance met with the President at the White House for discussions of revenue sharing, the debt ceiling bill, and welfare reform.

June

27 The President today transmitted to the Congress a proposed supplemental appropriation for fiscal year 1972 for $100 million for disaster relief. The funds would be used for relief to areas devastated by Tropical Storm Agnes and other major recent disasters.

27 The White House announced that Vice President Agnew, at the President's request, would leave on June 28 for a 2-day factfinding mission to check on conditions and disaster relief efforts in three of the hardest hit areas in the Northeast: Ellicott City, Md., Richmond, Va., and Elmira, N.Y.

27 The President and Mrs. Nixon hosted a reception in the Blue Room for 200 radio and television news anchormen and radio personalities and their wives who were attending briefings by Administration officials.

30 The President met with the Cost of Living Council and directed the Council to evaluate all steps which might be taken to insure adequate food supplies at reasonable prices. At his direction, Council members will meet with chain store and distribution groups, food processors, farmer and producer organizations, and international food exporters, and Secretary of Labor James D. Hodgson will meet with food industry labor organizations.

30 The President met at the White House with Ambassador Emil Mosbacher to express his appreciation for the efforts of the Ambassador and Mrs. Mosbacher during the Ambassador's tenure as Chief of Protocol. Ambassador Mosbacher's resignation is effective June 30.

July

1 The President met with leaders of six major vocational-educational organizations, the Vocational Industrial Clubs of America, National Advisory Council on Vocational Education, Office Education Association, Future Homemakers of America, Future Business Leaders of America, and Future Farmers of America.

July

1 The President has directed Secretary of Labor James D. Hodgson, Secretary of Commerce Peter G. Peterson, George A. Lincoln, Director, Office of Emergency Preparedness, and Anthony G. Chase, Deputy Administrator, Small Business Administration, to make a factfinding trip to the flood-stricken areas of New York and Pennsylvania to determine flood impact on jobs and business. Departing on Monday, July 3, they will visit Harrisburg and Wilkes-Barre, Pa., and the Corning-Elmira, N.Y., areas.

6 Maj. Gen. Alexander M. Haig, Jr., Deputy Assistant to the President for National Security Affairs, and Sir Robert Grainger Ker Thompson, British expert on Indochina, met with the President at the Western White House to report on their recent visits to South Vietnam.

6 The White House announced that the President has sent a message of congratulations to Japan's new Prime Minister, Kakuei Tanaka.

6 The President met at the Western White House with Clark MacGregor, who has resigned from the White House Staff, and William E. Timmons, who succeeds Mr. MacGregor as Assistant to the President for Congressional Relations.

7 The President met at the Western White House with George P. Shultz, Secretary of the Treasury and Chairman, Cost of Living Council, Virginia H. Knauer, Special Assistant to the President for Consumer Affairs and a member of the Council, and Herbert Stein, Chairman, Council of Economic Advisers. Secretary Shultz reported on his series of meetings with food industry representatives, and Dr. Stein discussed unemployment figures and the Wholesale Price Index.

7 French National Defense Minister Michel Debré and French Ambassador Jacques Kosciusko-Morizet met with the President at the Western White House.

July

7 Senator Hugh Scott of Pennsylvania reported to the President by telephone from Wilkes-Barre, Pa., on relief efforts following Tropical Storm Agnes.

7 House leaders Hale Boggs and Gerald R. Ford reported to the President by telephone from the airport on their return from the People's Republic of China.

12 Soviet Ambassador Anatoly F. Dobrynin met with the President at the Western White House.

15 The President attended memorial services for his aunt, Edith Timberlake, in Riverside, Calif.

17 The President met with Federal and State government representatives who were discussing action on the President's request to provide additional facilities for the beach at San Onofre State Park for public recreational use. The beach, located near the Western White House, was part of Camp Pendleton until the President directed, on March 31, 1971, that it be turned over to the State of California for public use.

17 Members of the executive committee of the International Brotherhood of Teamsters met with the President at the Western White House.

19 Henry A. Kissinger, Assistant to the President for National Security Affairs, met with the President at the White House to report on his session, earlier in the day in Paris, with Special Adviser Le Duc Tho and Minister Xuan Thuy of the North Vietnamese delegation to the Paris peace talks.

July

19 The White House announced that the President would send a message of condolence to Mrs. Samuel Z. Westerfield, Jr., on the death of her husband, the United States Ambassador to Liberia.

20 The President today announced the transfer of 12 parcels of Federal land to State and local governments for park and recreational use under the Legacy of Parks program. Included are lands in California, Florida, Idaho, Louisiana, Maryland, Mississippi, New York, Oregon, Puerto Rico, and Texas.

20 Armand Hammer, chairman of the board of the Occidental Petroleum Corporation, met with the President at the White House to discuss the recently signed assistance agreement between Occidental Petroleum and the Soviet Union.

21 Ambassadors Amos M. Dambe of Botswana, Abdullah Saleh Al-Mana of Qatar, Tran Kim Phuong of South Vietnam, U Lwin of Burma, and Harry Reginald Amonoo of Ghana presented their credentials to the President in ceremonies in the Blue Room at the White House.

21 The President has sent a telegram to President Georges Pompidou of France expressing his congratulations on the discovery and seizure of three heroin-producing laboratories by French anti-narcotics agents.

21 The President sent a letter to U.S. Civil Service Commission Chairman Robert E. Hampton requesting the Commission to review its procedures for recruiting, examining, and rating architects, artists, and designers for the Government.

July

24 Officials responsible for the domestic law enforcement aspects of the President's drug abuse prevention program met with the President at the White House to report on their activities during fiscal 1972.

25 The President met at the White House with representatives of the United States Conference of Mayors, the National League of Cities, the National Association of Counties, and the National Legislative Conference to discuss revenue sharing. Present at the meeting were Mayors Louie Welch of Houston, Sam Massell, Jr., of Atlanta, Moon Landrieu of New Orleans, Roman S. Gribbs of Detroit, Frank W. Burke of Louisville, Harry G. Haskell of Wilmington, Henry W. Maier of Milwaukee, John Driggs of Phoenix, Joseph Alioto of San Francisco, Wesley C. Uhlman of Seattle, Lee Alexander of Syracuse, Roy Martin of Norfolk, William Schaefer of Baltimore, Norman Mineta of San Jose, E. J. Garn of Salt Lake City, and Richard G. Hatcher of Gary; Gladys Spellman of Prince Georges County, Md., and State Representative John Conolly of Illinois.

26 Entertainer Johnny Cash, who was in Washington to testify before a Senate subcommittee on prison conditions, met with the President at the White House. Senator Bill Brock of Tennessee joined in the meeting.

28 Representatives Carl Albert, Hale Boggs, and Gerald R. Ford met with the President at the White House to discuss the report by Representatives Boggs and Ford on their recent trip to the People's Republic of China.

28 Brazilian Minister of Finance Antônio Delfim Netto met with the President at the White House to deliver a letter from President Emílio Garrastazú Médici. He was accompanied by Brazilian Ambassador João Augusto de Araujo Castro.

July

28 Mayor Jack D. Maltester of San Leandro, Calif., and John Gunther, executive director, United States Conference of Mayors, called on the President to present a medallion commemorating San Leandro's 200th anniversary.

28 David J. Mahoney, Chairman, American Revolution Bicentennial Commission, met with the President to present a status report on the Commission's plans.

28 The President transmitted to the Senate for advice and consent to ratification the Agreement Concerning Shrimp between the Government of the United States of America and the Government of the Federative Republic of Brazil.

28 The President attended a ceremony in the Cabinet Room for the signing of a Record of Discussions relating to the U.S.-U.S.S.R. Joint Commission on Scientific and Technical Cooperation. The document was signed by Dr. Edward E. David, Jr., Science Adviser to the President, who headed the U.S. delegation to the discussions in Moscow July 2–8. Soviet Ambassador Anatoly F. Dobrynin also attended the ceremony. The document was signed simultaneously in Moscow.

28 Sir Burk Trend, Secretary of the Cabinet of the United Kingdom, and the Earl of Cromer, British Ambassador to the United States, called on the President at the White House.

August

1 The President met with the president of the United States Jaycees, Samuel D. Weiner of New Martinsville, W. Va.

1 Entertainers Karen and Richard Carpenter met with the President at the White House to discuss their work in raising funds for cancer research. Karen is the national youth chairman of the American Cancer Society.

Appendix B

August

1 The President amended his major disaster declaration of June 10, 1972, for the State of Washington to include the severe storms which caused extensive damage to the fruit crop in Chelan and Douglas Counties from May 28 through June 17, 1972.

1 The President and the First Lady held a reception honoring members of the Presidential Protective Division of the United States Secret Service.

2 Henry A. Kissinger met with the President at the White House to report on his meeting in Paris on August 1 with Special Adviser Le Duc Tho and Minister Xuan Thuy of the North Vietnamese delegation to the Paris peace talks.

3 The President met with former professional football player Ollie Matson who has been nominated for membership in the Professional Football Hall of Fame.

4 The President went by helicopter to Assateague Island, Md., for a weekend stay.

7 Senator-designate Elaine Edwards of Louisiana met with the President at the White House. She was accompanied by her husband, Gov. Edwin W. Edwards, and Senator Russell B. Long.

7 Gen. Andrew J. Goodpaster, Supreme Allied Commander, Europe, met with the President at the White House for a general discussion of NATO developments and European affairs.

8 Miss Teenage America of 1972, Colleen Fitzpatrick of Lancaster, Ohio, called on the President at the White House.

8 Former heavyweight boxing champion Floyd Patterson called on the President at the White House.

August

8 Soviet Minister of Health Boris V. Petrovskiy paid a courtesy call on the President at the White House. Also present were Soviet Ambassador Anatoly F. Dobrynin and Secretary of Health, Education, and Welfare Elliot L. Richardson.

8 The President has designated five persons to be his personal representatives at the Summer Olympics in Munich, Germany, August 26 to September 10. They are Dr. Sammy Lee, chairman of the delegation, William A. Toomey, Malvin G. Whitfield, Rev. Robert E. Richards, and Patricia McCormick.

8 The President has authorized and instructed the Department of State to send $30 million in U.S. disaster relief assistance to the Philippines in the wake of floods there. The assistance will include emergency shipments of rice and flour valued at $24 million and a $6 million contribution from the Foreign Assistance Contingency Fund for emergency relief and rehabilitation needs.

8 The President hosted a dinner for the Cabinet at Camp David.

10 The President met with the Cost of Living Council for a first-year anniversary review of the new economic policy announced on August 15, 1971.

11 Secretary of Housing and Urban Development George W. Romney met with the President at the White House to report on his trip to Wilkes-Barre, Pa., to review his Department's flood relief efforts there after Tropical Storm Agnes.

11 The President signed an order designating the Administrator of Veterans Affairs to be a member of the Domestic Council. Administrator Donald E. Johnson met with the President at the White House to discuss the designation.

August

11 The President has designated Ambassador John A. McKesson III and John J. Louis, Jr., of Chicago, Ill., to serve as his personal representatives with the rank of Special Ambassador at ceremonies commemorating the 12th anniversary of the independence of the Gabon Republic at Libreville on August 16–17.

14 Ambassador William D. Eberle, Special Representative for Trade Negotiations, met with the President at the White House to report on his recent trip to Japan where he met with Prime Minister Kakuei Tanaka and other Japanese officials regarding trade matters.

14 Kenneth B. Keating, who has resigned as United States Ambassador to India, called on the President at the White House.

14 Economist Pierre Rinfret met with the President at the White House.

14 Mrs. Everett McKinley Dirksen, widow of the former Senate Minority Leader, called on the President to present a copy of her book about her husband.

14 Oral Roberts, chancellor of Oral Roberts University in Tulsa, Okla., called on the President at the White House.

14 Daniel P. Moynihan, former Counsellor to the President, met with the President at the White House.

19 Henry A. Kissinger, Assistant to the President for National Security Affairs, met with the President at Camp David to report on his trip to Paris, Saigon, and Tokyo.

21 The President went by helicopter from Camp David, Md., to Gettysburg, Pa., to visit Mrs. Dwight D. Eisenhower.

30 The President and Mrs. Nixon were guests at a reception for State and civic leaders at the home of Mrs. Clare Boothe Luce in Honolulu.

31 Ellsworth Bunker, United States Ambassador to Vietnam, met with the President in Honolulu.

September

3 The President sent a cable to Bobby Fischer congratulating him on winning the world's chess championship at Reykjavik, Iceland.

4 The President and Mrs. Nixon hosted a reception at their California home for reporters covering the Western White House.

7 James and John Roosevelt called on the President at the White House. They were accompanied by John B. Connally.

7 Representatives of the International Conference of Police Associations and the National Fraternal Order of Police met with the President at the White House.

7 Mickey Lolich of the Detroit Tigers professional baseball team called on the President at the White House.

7 Ambassadors Sadan Moussa Touré of the Republic of Guinea, Leo Tuominen of Finland, Telesphore Yaguibou of the Republic of Upper Volta, John M. Garba of Nigeria, and Arno Halusa of Austria presented their credentials to the President in ceremonies in the Blue Room at the White House.

8 Gen. Maraden Panggabean, Indonesian Minister of State, met with the President at the White House.

11 The Council on International Economic Policy met with the President at the White House to discuss trade relations with Europe.

11 Joseph DeSilva, of Los Angeles, Calif., secretary-treasurer of local 770 of the Retail Clerks International Association, called on the President at the White House.

11 Joseph R. Sanson, of Detroit, Mich., newly elected national commander of AMVETS, met with the President at the White House.

12 The Republican Congressional leadership and the Cabinet met with the President at the White House.

12 Representatives of the National League for Nursing met with the President at the White House.

September

12 Walter J. Hickel, former Governor of Alaska and former Secretary of the Interior, met with the President at the White House.

12 The President and the First Lady hosted a reception at the White House for members of the Republican National Committee, State Republican Chairmen, and Chairmen of State Committees for the Re-Election of the President.

14 Gov. Nelson A. Rockefeller met with the President at the White House.

14 The President met at the White House with a delegation of students from the Police Athletic League of Philadelphia who presented scrolls signed by 400,000 Philadelphia students pledging respect for law and authority, property, teachers, and the rights of others. They were accompanied by Philadelphia Mayor Frank L. Rizzo who met with the President following the presentation.

15 Entertainer Ray Charles met with the President at the White House.

15 Patrick E. Carr, of New Orleans, La., newly elected national commander of the Veterans of Foreign Wars, met with the President at the White House.

16 Henry A. Kissinger met separately with the President and Secretary of State William P. Rogers to report on his trip to the Federal Republic of Germany, the Soviet Union, the United Kingdom, and France. Dr. Kissinger had met with German leaders in Munich on September 9 and 10, en route to Moscow for meetings on September 10–14 with Soviet leaders to review the course of Soviet-American relations since the May summit. He had met with British officials in London on September 14 and 15 and then traveled to Paris where he met, on September 15, with the North Vietnamese representatives to the Paris peace talks and later with French President Georges Pompidou.

18 Terry Anne Meeuwsen, of De Pere, Wis., who was chosen to be Miss America of 1973, and Laurie Lea Schaefer, of Bexley, Ohio, who was Miss America of 1972, called on the President at the White House.

September

18 Jack O. Hicks, of La Rue, Ohio, newly elected national commander of the Disabled American Veterans, called on the President at the White House.

18 In a ceremony in the Oval Office at the White House, the President signed H.J. Res. 55, Public Law 92–422, authorizing a memorial in honor of the Seabees of the United States Navy to be erected on public grounds in the District of Columbia or its environs.

19 Stefan Olszowski, Polish Minister of Foreign Affairs, met with the President at the White House. He was accompanied by Witold Trampczynski, Polish Ambassador to the United States.

19 William P. Rogers, Secretary of State, and George H. Bush, U.S. Representative to the United Nations, met with the President at the White House for consultation prior to the opening of the 27th session of the United Nations General Assembly in New York later the same day.

19 Marian Scully, of Timahoe, County Cork, Ireland, called on the President at the White House. Miss Scully had greeted the President and Mrs. Nixon when they visited Ireland in October 1970.

19 National officers of the Reserve Officers Association of the United States called on the President at the White House.

19 The President approved a National Mediation Board recommendation to extend the reporting deadline from September 18 to October 30, 1972, for the emergency board created to investigate the dispute between the Long Island Rail Road Company and certain of its employees. The extension was agreed to by both parties. The emergency board was created by Executive Order 11679 of August 19, 1972.

23 During his visit to Texas, the President met with Texas Republican leaders at the San Antonio International Airport.

September

25 National officers of the Order of the American Hellenic Educational Progressive Association called on the President to present a gold medal commemorating the 50th anniversary of the Order of AHEPA.

25 The President met with a group of Republican candidates for national and State offices. They were: Mario D. Belardino of New York, Charles Conrad of California, Luther F. Hackett of Vermont, Dr. William R. Hunt of Pennsylvania, Martin A. Linsky of Massachusetts, Henry A. Povinelli of Connecticut, Wesley Powell and Meldrim Thomson, Jr., of New Hampshire, Joel Pritchard of Washington, and Edward Young of South Carolina.

25 Dr. Carl Hoffman, president of the American Medical Association, met with the President at the White House to report on his recent trip to the Soviet Union to review their medical program.

25 Thomas W. Gleason, president of the International Longshoremen's Association, called on the President at the White House.

26 Robert E. Merriam, Chairman of the Advisory Commission on Intergovernmental Relations, met with the President at the White House.

26 Joseph P. Tonelli, president of the United Papermakers International Union, called on the President at the White House.

26 The President met at the White House with a group of general presidents of building trades unions.

26 The President and the First Lady met with the British Ambassador to the United States, the Earl of Cromer, and the Countess of Cromer.

26 In a series of meetings at the Waldorf-Astoria Hotel in New York City, the President met with
   —a group of Jewish leaders from cities throughout the country,
   —leaders of the New York Committee for the Re-Election of the President, and
   —representatives of Democrats for Nixon from New York State.

September

27 In New York City, the President met at the Waldorf-Astoria Hotel with a group of approximately 200 New York State labor leaders, headed by Peter J. Brennan, president of the Building and Construction Trades Councils, AFL–CIO.

28 Henry A. Kissinger met with the President on board the Presidential yacht *Sequoia* to report on his meetings on September 26 and 27 in Paris with Special Adviser Le Duc Tho and Minister Xuan Thuy of the North Vietnamese delegation to the Paris peace talks.

29 French Minister of Foreign Affairs Maurice Schumann met with the President at the White House.

29 Sir Alec Douglas-Home, British Secretary of State for Foreign and Commonwealth Affairs, met with the President at the White House and was his guest at a working dinner in the evening.

October

2 Soviet Foreign Minister Andrei A. Gromyko met with the President at the White House and was the President's guest at a working dinner and for an overnight stay at Camp David.

2 Ambassadors Lombo Lo Mangamanga of Zaire, Anand Panyarachun of Thailand, Henri Raharijaona of the Malagasy Republic, Lloyd White of New Zealand, Philip J. Palmer of Sierra Leone, Paul Bomani of Tanzania, Douglas V. Fletcher of Jamaica, and Abdoulaye Diallo of Niger presented their credentials to the President in ceremonies in the Blue Room at the White House.

3 Joe L. Matthews, newly elected national commander of the American Legion, made a courtesy call on the President at the White House.

3 John Leyden, president of the Professional Air Traffic Controllers Organization, met with the President at the White House.

6 Pote Sarasin, Assistant Chairman of the Thai National Executive Council, met with the President at the White House.

October

6 Irish Minister of External Affairs Patrick J. Hillery called on the President at the White House.

6 Dr. L. V. Booth, president of the Progressive National Baptist Convention and a member of the board of Opportunities Industrialization Centers, met with the President at the White House.

6 Henry A. Kissinger and Maj. Gen. Alexander M. Haig, Jr., Assistant and Deputy Assistant to the President for National Security Affairs, met with the President to discuss General Haig's recent trip to South Vietnam to make a general assessment of the situation there.

9 Winston W. Marsh, president of the American Society of Association Executives, called on the President at the White House.

9 Sharon McLarty, of Amory, Miss., Miss National Teenage America of 1972, called on the President at the White House. She was accompanied by Senator James O. Eastland.

10 The Republican Congressional leadership and the Cabinet met with the President at the White House for a discussion of the proposed ceiling on Federal spending and other domestic matters.

10 Polish Ambassador Witold Trampczynski met with the President at the White House to receive a copy of a documentary film on the President's trip to Poland. The Ambassador received the film on behalf of Henryk Jablonski, Chairman of the Council of State.

10 The President and the First Lady hosted a reception in the East Room at the White House for State and national newspaper association officers and their wives.

12 Henry A. Kissinger met with the President at the White House immediately upon his return to Washington from 4 days of meetings in Paris with Special Adviser Le Duc Tho and Minister Xuan Thuy of the North Vietnamese delegation to the Paris peace talks.

October

13 Henry A. Kissinger and Maj. Gen. Alexander M. Haig, Jr., breakfasted with the President and Secretary of State William P. Rogers for a discussion of their meetings in Paris with North Vietnamese representatives.

13 The President met with the Pay Board in the Cabinet Room at the White House.

13 Representative Joe D. Waggonner, Jr., who will serve as the President's representative to the Bucharest Trade Fair October 15–18, met with the President at the White House.

13 The International Executive Board of the Utility Workers of America, AFL–CIO, met with the President at the White House.

13 Mrs. George Herman (Babe) Ruth, Bobby Thomson, and Ralph Branca called on the President at the White House.

14 The President met at the White House with a delegation of physicians from the People's Republic of China. They were beginning a 3-week tour of the United States, hosted by the Institute of Medicine of the National Academy of Sciences and the American Medical Association.

14 Timofey B. Guzhenko, Minister, Ministry of the Maritime Fleet of the Union of Soviet Socialist Republics, met with the President at the White House after signing, with Secretary of Commerce Peter G. Peterson, a major maritime agreement between the United States and the Soviet Union.

16 Gen. Creighton W. Abrams met with the President at the White House after being sworn in as Army Chief of Staff.

17 Mrs. Jeanne Squire, president, and Mrs. Lucille Shriver, director, National Federation of Business and Professional Women's Clubs, met with the President at the White House.

17 Dr. Carl A. Laughlin, president of the American Dental Association, called on the President at the White House.

October

18 Foreign Minister Masayoshi Ohira of Japan met with the President at the White House. They discussed the recent visit by Japanese Prime Minister Kakuei Tanaka to the People's Republic of China, as well as other matters relating to U.S.-Japanese relations and the general security situation in Asia.

19 Paul Hall, president of the Seafarers International Union of North America, Thomas W. Gleason, president of the International Longshoremen's Association, and Paul F. Richardson, president of Sea-Land Service, Inc., called on the President at the White House.

23 Henry A. Kissinger, Assistant to the President for National Security Affairs, met with the President at the White House to report on his trip to Paris, Saigon, and Phnom Penh. Dr. Kissinger had met in Paris with Minister Xuan Thuy of the North Vietnamese delegation to the Paris peace talks, and in Saigon had reviewed with President Nguyen Van Thieu the status of the Paris negotiations.

24 Henry A. Kissinger met with the President and Secretary of State William P. Rogers at the White House to discuss Vietnam peace negotiations.

24 The President met at the White House with the Policeman of the Year, Jake Miller of New Orleans, La., and ten police men and women who received honorable mention in the awards program.

27 The President met at the White House with a group of Spanish-speaking appointees serving in key positions in his Administration.

27 Prince Souvanna Phouma, Prime Minister of Laos, met with the President at the White House.

30 The President has received the report of Emergency Board No. 182, created to investigate a dispute between the Long Island Rail Road Company and certain employees represented by the Non-Operating Employees Conference Committee.

October

31 Gov. Nelson A. Rockefeller of New York met with the President at the White House.

31 The President directed the Secretary of the Treasury to implement a permanent exclusion order against imports of lightweight luggage which infringe on the patents of the Atlantic Products Corporation of Trenton, N.J.

November

1 John Cardinal Krol, Archbishop of Philadelphia, met with the President at the White House to discuss his recent trip to Poland.

3 Members of the Council on Environmental Quality met with the President at the White House.

3 Mayor Louis J. Tullio of Erie, Pa., met with the President at the White House.

7 The President and Mrs. Nixon voted at Concordia Elementary School in San Clemente, Calif., before returning to Washington.

21 The White House announced that Henry A. Kissinger would meet with Indonesian President Soeharto and Minister of Foreign Affairs Adam Malik in Brussels on November 22. Dr. Kissinger would then return to Paris following the meeting to continue discussions with the North Vietnamese representatives to the Paris peace talks.

22 The President has directed that regulations controlling the travel of U.S. ships and aircraft (Transportation Order T–2) be changed to permit both U.S. aircraft having a validated license from the Department of Commerce and U.S.-flag vessels to visit the People's Republic of China.

24 The White House announced that Henry A. Kissinger paid a courtesy call on French Minister of Foreign Affairs Maurice Schumann in Paris to thank the French Government for the courtesy extended during the Paris peace talks and to discuss the current talks.

November

25 Henry A. Kissinger, Assistant to the President for National Security Affairs, met with the President at the Waldorf-Astoria Hotel in New York City to report on his meetings in Paris with North Vietnamese representatives to the Paris peace talks which resumed on November 20.

29 Nguyen Phu Duc, Special Assistant to President Nguyen Van Thieu for Foreign Affairs, of South Vietnam met with the President at the White House.

29 The President met at the White House with black Administration appointees to thank them for their work and to discuss with them ways in which additional people of their caliber can be brought into the Administration.

30 The Joint Chiefs of Staff met with the President at the White House.

30 Nguyen Phu Duc, Special Assistant to President Nguyen Van Thieu for Foreign Affairs, met with the President at the White House for further discussions.

30 The White House announced that there would not be any further statement or announcement regarding U.S. troop levels in South Vietnam since the subject is being covered in the current negotiations.

30 Former Secretary of the Treasury John B. Connally met with the President and Secretary of the Treasury George P. Shultz at Key Biscayne, Fla., to discuss international economic matters.

December

2 Henry A. Kissinger met with the President at Key Biscayne for consultation prior to his departure for Paris to continue negotiations on the Vietnam situation.

5 Horacio Rivero, United States Ambassador to Spain, met with the President at the White House.

December

5 M. Harvey Taylor paid a courtesy call on the President at the White House. Mr. Taylor, who is 96 years old, was formerly Pennsylvania Republican State Chairman and a member and president pro tempore of the Pennsylvania State Senate. He was accompanied by Leroy S. Zimmerman, district attorney for Harrisburg, Pa.

5 The President attended a reception at Blair House honoring Californians serving in the Administration.

8 The President met with the Quadriad— Secretary of the Treasury George P. Shultz, Chairman Herbert Stein of the Council of Economic Advisers, Director Caspar W. Weinberger of the Office of Management and Budget, and Chairman Arthur F. Burns of the Board of Governors of the Federal Reserve System—at Camp David, Md.

12 W. Clement Stone, acting chairman of the National Center for Voluntary Action, met with the President at the White House to present a progress report on the Center's activities.

12 J. Willard Marriott, Sr., Chairman, and Jeb Stuart Magruder, Executive Director, of the 1973 Inaugural Committee, called on the President at the White House to present Inaugural License Plate No. 1.

14 Henry A. Kissinger met with the President at the White House to report on his meetings in Paris with North Vietnamese representatives to the Paris peace talks.

14 Senator Hugh Scott of Pennsylvania met with the President at the White House to discuss the upcoming legislative session and the reorganization of the executive branch for the second term.

16 The President and Mrs. Nixon hosted a dinner at the White House for members and former members of the Cabinet and top sub-Cabinet appointees.

December

19 Ambassadors Pheng Norindr of Laos, Alberto Quevedo Toro of Ecuador, Christo Zdravchev of Bulgaria, Abdel Aziz Al Nasri Hamza of Sudan, Nicolas Gonzalez Revilla of Panama, and John A. Sorokos of Greece presented their credentials to the President in ceremonies at the White House.

20 The President met with the labor members of the National Commission on Productivity who were meeting with officials at the White House.

22 Gen. Alexander M. Haig, Jr., Deputy Assistant to the President for National Security Affairs, met with the President and Henry A. Kissinger at Key Biscayne, Fla., to report on his recent trip to Southeast Asia where he met with President Nguyen Van Thieu of South Vietnam, Prime Minister Lon Nol of the Khmer Republic (Cambodia), Prince Souvanna Phouma of Laos, and Prime Minister Thanom Kittikachorn of Thailand.

December

23 The President sent a message to Gen. Anastasio Somoza Debayle, Supreme Chief of the Armed Forces of Nicaragua, expressing deepest sympathy to the Nicaraguan people following the earthquake which struck Managua.

24 The President spoke by telephone with General Somoza concerning U.S. efforts to assist the earthquake victims in Nicaragua.

30 The White House announced that negotiations between Henry A. Kissinger and Special Adviser Le Duc Tho and Minister Xuan Thuy of North Vietnam will be resumed in Paris on January 8, 1973. Technical talks between the experts of the two sides will be resumed on January 2. In a news briefing following the announcement, Deputy Press Secretary Gerald L. Warren stated, "The President has ordered that all bombing will be discontinued above the 20th parallel as long as serious negotiations are under way."

Appendix C—Presidential Documents Published in the Federal Register

[The texts of these documents are also printed in title 3A of the Code of Federal Regulations and in Volume 8 of the Weekly Compilation of Presidential Documents.]

PROCLAMATIONS

Appendix C

Appendix C

---

[1] Proclamation 4160 is printed in full on p. 946 of this volume as an example of the proclamations issued by President Nixon in 1972.

[2] Proclamation 4176 is printed in full on p. 1160 of this volume.

EXECUTIVE ORDERS

Appendix C

Appendix C

PRESIDENTIAL DOCUMENTS OTHER THAN PROCLAMATIONS AND EXECUTIVE ORDERS

Appendix D—Presidential Reports to the 92d Congress, Second Session

Subject	Published	Sent to the Congress	Date of White House release
Economic Report	H. Doc. 228	Jan. 27	Jan. 27
Department of Housing and Urban Development:			
6th annual	H. Doc. 239	Jan. 27	. . . .
7th annual	H. Doc. 338	Aug. 9	. . . .
Health Effects of Environmental Pollution	H. Doc. 241	Jan. 31	. . . .
National Endowment for the Humanities (6th annual)		Feb. 1	Feb. 1
Earthquake Insurance		Feb. 1	. . . .
Automotive Products Trade Act of 1965 (5th annual)		Feb. 1	. . . .
Uniform Relocation Assistance and Real Property Acquisition Policies Act of 1970 (1st annual)		Feb. 4 (H) Feb. 7 (S)	Feb. 4
Alaska Highway	H. Doc. 246	Feb. 8	Feb. 8
U.S. Arms Control and Disarmament Agency (11th annual)	H. Doc. 255	Feb. 10	. . . .
Federal Coal Mine Health and Safety Act of 1969 by Department of the Interior (1970)		Feb. 10	. . . .
Economic Stabilization Program:			
1st Quarterly		Feb. 11 (H) Feb. 14 (S)	Feb. 12
2d Quarterly		May 19 (H) May 22 (S)	May 20
3d Quarterly		Sept. 13	Sept. 13
4th Quarterly		Oct. 13	Oct. 13
National Growth, 1972 (1st biennial)		Feb. 29	. . . .
Special International Exhibitions (9th annual)		Mar. 6	. . . .
National Science Foundation (21st annual)	H. Doc. 188	Mar. 7	. . . .
U.S.-Japan Cooperative Medical Science Program under the International Health Research Act of 1960 (5th annual)	H. Doc. 189	Mar. 9	Mar. 9
Aeronautics and Space Report (1971)		Mar. 14	. . . .
Manpower Report (10th annual)	H. Doc. 192	Mar. 15	Mar. 15
International Coffee Agreement (1971)		Apr. 4	Apr. 4

Appendix D

Subject	Published	Sent to the Congress	Date of White House release
Communications Satellite Act of 1962 (9th annual)	H. Doc. 279	Apr. 5	. . . .
Corporation for Public Broadcasting (fiscal year 1971)		Apr. 10	. . . .
Office of Economic Opportunity (fiscal year 1971)	H. Doc. 280	Apr. 13	. . . .
National Science Board (4th annual)	H. Doc. 281	Apr. 13	Apr. 13
National Credit Union Administration (2d annual)		Apr. 24 (H) Apr. 25 (S)	. . . .
Natural Gas Pipeline Safety Act of 1968 (4th annual)		Apr. 25	. . . .
Availability of Government Services to Rural Areas (2d annual)	H. Doc. 287	May 2	. . . .
Job Evaluation Policy Act of 1970.		May 2	. . . .
World Weather Program (4th annual)		May 3	May 3
Civil Service Commission (fiscal year 1971)	H. Doc. 213	May 8	May 8
Federal Railroad Safety Act of 1970 (1st annual)		May 9	. . . .
National Advisory Council on Adult Education	H. Doc. 302	May 19 (H) May 22 (S)	. . . .
Communicable Disease Activities (fiscal year 1971)	H. Doc. 298	May 22 (H) May 23 (S)	. . . .
Occupational Safety and Health Act of 1970 (1st annual). .	H. Doc. 303	May 22 (H) May 23 (S)	May 22
Railroad Retirement Board (fiscal year 1971)	H. Doc. 227	June 7	. . . .
Five River Basin Commissions (fiscal year 1971) . . . . . Pacific Northwest River Basins Commission Souris-Red-Rainy River Basins Commission Great Lakes Basin Commission New England River Basins Commission Ohio River Basin Commission	H. Doc. 310	June 12	June 12
Hazardous Materials Control (2d annual)		June 16	. . . .
Commodity Credit Corporation (fiscal year 1971)		June 16	. . . .
Food for Peace Program under Public Law 480, 83d Congress (1971)	H. Doc. 318	June 29	. . . .
National Housing Goals (4th annual)	H. Doc. 319	June 29	. . . .
National Endowment for the Arts and National Council on the Arts (fiscal year 1971)		June 30	July 1
Comparability of Federal and Private Enterprise Salaries, joint annual report of the Director of the Office of Management and Budget and the Chairman of the Civil Service Commission	H. Doc. 332	Aug. 1	Aug. 1

Subject	Published	Sent to the Congress	Date of White House release
Urban Transportation, joint annual report of the Secretaries of Transportation and Housing and Urban Development	H. Doc. 331	Aug. 1	. . . .
Administration of Radiation Control for Health and Safety Act of 1968 (4th annual)	H. Doc. 334	Aug. 1	. . . .
National Advisory Council on Extension and Continuing Education (6th annual)	H. Doc. 335	Aug. 3	Aug. 3
Council on Environmental Quality (3d annual)		Aug. 7	. . . .
Progress Report on a Federal Interstate Compact for the Hudson River Basin		Aug. 9	. . . .
Surgeon General (15th and 16th annual)	H. Doc. 339	Aug. 10	. . . .
National Advisory Council on Economic Opportunity (5th annual)	H. Doc. 342	Aug. 15	. . . .
International Exposition on the Environment to be held in Spokane, Washington, in 1974		Aug. 15	Aug. 15
National Capital Housing Authority (fiscal year 1971)		Sept. 7	. . . .
Location of new Federal facilities in rural areas (2d annual)		Sept. 7	Sept. 7
United Nations (26th annual)	H. Doc. 297	Sept. 8	. . . .
Federal Ocean Program (1971)	H. Doc. 353	Sept. 11	. . . .
St. Lawrence Seaway Development Corporation (1971)	H. Doc. 354	Sept. 13	. . . .
National Traffic and Motor Vehicle Safety Act of 1966 and the Highway Safety Act of 1966 (1971)	H. Doc. 355	Sept. 13	Sept. 13
Federal Activities in Juvenile Delinquency, Youth Development and Related Fields (fiscal year 1971)		Sept. 18	. . . .
Foreign Assistance Program (fiscal year 1971)	H. Doc. 347	Sept. 19	. . . .
National Wilderness Preservation System (8th annual)	H. Doc. 357	Sept. 21	. . . .
Federal Coal Mine Health and Safety Act of 1969 by Department of Health, Education, and Welfare (2d annual)		Sept. 26	Sept. 26
Office of Economic Opportunity Grantee Annual Salary Report (fiscal year 1972)		Oct. 3	. . . .
International Educational and Cultural Exchange Program (fiscal year 1971)		Oct. 11	Oct. 11
National Corporation for Housing Partnerships (3d annual)		Oct. 13	. . . .

Appendix E—White House Announcements of Personnel Changes for the Second Term

NOTE: Speaking to reporters at Camp David on November 27, 1972 (Item 421), the President stated that his decisions on Cabinet officers for the second term would be announced by Press Secretary Ronald L. Ziegler in the next 2 or 3 weeks. This appendix carries the announcements, relating to Cabinet, sub-Cabinet, and White House Staff positions, as made by Mr. Ziegler in news briefings from November 28 to December 22, 1972.

Announcing New Assignments for the Second Term

November 28, 1972

The President intends to nominate Elliot Richardson, currently Secretary of Health, Education, and Welfare, to be Secretary of Defense succeeding Melvin Laird, who has long intended, as you know, to return to private life at the end of the first term.

The President is also announcing that Caspar Weinberger, currently Director of the Office of Management and Budget, will be nominated to succeed Elliot Richardson as Secretary of Health, Education, and Welfare.

The President has asked Roy Ash, who is president of Litton Industries, to succeed Caspar Weinberger as the Director of the Office of Management and Budget.

Elliot Richardson has served as Secretary of the Department of Health, Education, and Welfare since June of 1970 and has a distinguished career in government service. Mr. Richardson first joined the Administration in 1969 as Under Secretary of State. After a year and a half of highly respected service. Mr. Richardson was appointed Secretary of Health, Education, and Welfare. He is a lawyer and a former Lieutenant Governor and Attorney General of the State of Massachusetts.

Melvin Laird, as you know, became the Secretary of Defense as part of the President's original Cabinet, which was named in 1969. In accepting Secretary Laird's letter of resignation, the President said he looks back with a profound sense of pride on the years of dedicated service the Secretary has given his country and his handling of difficult decisions with enormous dedication and competence.

In announcing his intention to nominate Caspar Weinberger to be the new Secretary of Health, Education, and Welfare, the President is affirming his respect for both the organizational and creative skills Cap Weinberger will bring to the new post.

Cap Weinberger was named Deputy Director of the Office of Management and Budget when that office was created in July of 1970. In May 1972 the President appointed Cap Weinberger Director of the OMB. Mr. Weinberger is a former Chairman of the Federal Trade Commission. Before joining the FTC, he was Director of Finance for the State of California. Mr. Weinberger is an attorney and also served 6 years in the California State Legislature.

It was the energetic leadership of Roy Ash that steered the President's Advisory Council on Executive Organization, a council which many of you know was established in 1969 to undertake an exhaustive, critical review of the way the Government is operated.

Among the innovative reforms that resulted from the recommendations of the Council was the formation of the Office of Management and Budget. That office was formed following the Ash Council recommendation in July of 1970. It was formed, as the President said at that time, to bring better management and efficiency into the operation of the Government.

During the second term, President Nixon intends for the Office of Management and Budget to assume a new and expanded role. He intends for the Office of Management and Budget to undertake a comprehensive examination of all Government programs now in existence to determine whether they are actually meeting the purpose for which they were designated. The President feels the proven management skill and strong leadership of Roy

Ash is the right combination to direct the Office of Management and Budget with its expanded responsibilities.

These three announcements that the President is making today come at a time when an intensive review is being undertaken of the entire Government structure. They are part of the President's broad plan to bring fresh perspective and new vitality to the second 4 years of the Nixon Administration. President Nixon feels these three men will be strong members of an executive team which has, as the President says, a mandate to bring about constructive change, change that will work to build a better life for all Americans.

As President Nixon said, the next 4 years will be very exciting times for the Nation, both domestically and internationally. It is with full confidence and pleasure that he announces that these three people will be working with him to accomplish all that remains to be done.

Announcing Intention To Nominate a New Secretary of Labor

November 29, 1972

President Nixon has asked me to announce today his intention to nominate Peter Brennan for the Cabinet position of Secretary of Labor.

Peter Brennan has been president of the New York City and New York State Building and Construction Trades Councils for the past 15 years. The appointment of Peter Brennan will mark the first time since the early period of the Eisenhower Administration that a trade unionist has been named by a President to serve as the Government's highest labor official.

President Nixon feels that Peter Brennan is a man who exemplifies the best character and strength of America's working men and women. He is spirited, self-made, and, though he has worked at many different levels in organized labor, he has retained a unique sensitivity to the rank and file workingman. He has kept in touch with this combination of firm leadership, a strong sense of fairness, and special sensitivity to union and nonunion workers.

President Nixon feels that Peter Brennan is the right man to head a vital, responsive Department of Labor in the second term. Peter Brennan was born in New York City and worked his way through the ranks of the Painter's Union in New York City, starting as an apprentice shortly after graduation from Commerce High School.

Mr. Brennan was elected president of the New York City and New York State Building and Construction Trades Councils in 1957 and 1958. He, of course, will resign both posts upon confirmation as Secretary of Labor. Mr. Brennan is a vice president of the New York State AFL–CIO and a long-time associate of the national trade union leaders. Mr. Brennan has been instrumental in the cooperation of the building and construction trade unions with the Workers' Defense League to bring minorities into apprenticeship training programs.

Mr. Brennan and the President have known one another personally for the past several years. The President met with Peter Brennan and his executive council after Mr. Brennan led a parade of 150,000 building trade men, longshoremen, and other New York labor unions in support of the Administration's Vietnam policy in 1971. Over the past few years, President Nixon has met with Mr. Brennan off and on and consulted with him directly on labor matters.

Mr. Brennan will succeed James Hodgson, who has served in the Labor Department, as you know, for 4 years. He was appointed Secretary of Labor and has served as Secretary of Labor since July of 1970. Prior to that, he served as Under Secretary of Labor from 1969 through the period of 1970, prior to his appointment as Secretary of Labor.

Having served for 4 years in the Department of Labor, the Secretary expressed to the President that he desired to return to private life. However, in his discussions here at Camp David with President Nixon, the President asked the Secretary to consider assuming another high-level position within the Administration, specifically in the international area.

Secretary Hodgson's plans will be announced when they are set. He presently is considering assuming the new responsibility in the international area, together with other opportunities available to him in the private sector.

So Secretary Hodgson's plans will be announced when they are set, as I mentioned. President Nixon has expressed deep gratitude and admiration for the distinguished leadership James Hodgson has given the Department of Labor in his 4 years there. It has been a period marked by enormous strides in improving the relationship between labor and management, strides the President feels are due in large measure to the steady hand and calm understanding Secretary Hodgson has brought to the job of Secretary of Labor.

The President feels that Secretary Hodgson has made a pronounced and lasting contribution to the American workers and the Nation as a whole.

Announcing the President's Selections of Key Department of State Officials for the Second Term

November 30, 1972

You will recall that the President, in his remarks on Monday concerning new faces and new assignments among Cabinet members, made specific reference to the progress achieved in the field of foreign affairs during the past 4 years. He referred to his determination to continue that progress and to build on it during the next 4 years. In the interest of that continuity, the President has asked me to announce this morning that Secretary of State William P. Rogers will continue to serve as Secretary of State in the new Administration.

As you know, the Department of State, and particularly the Secretary himself, is deeply involved at the present time in a number of ongoing efforts of great importance to American foreign policy and world peace. Among them, of course, are the search for a settlement in the Middle East situation, the preparations for a European Security Conference, and for talks on mutual balanced force reductions in Europe.

The President feels Secretary Rogers has demonstrated outstanding abilities as a negotiator, and he, of course, will continue to play a central role in these efforts as the second term begins.

The President is also announcing this morning that he intends to make the following nominations for positions in the Department of State:

Kenneth Rush will be nominated to be Deputy Secretary of State. Mr. Rush, who is now Deputy Secretary of Defense, will succeed John N. Irwin.

William J. Casey will be nominated to be Under Secretary of State for Economic Affairs. Mr. Casey, who is now Chairman of the Securities and Exchange Commission, will be the first occupant of this newly created position of Under Secretary of State for Economic Affairs.

William J. Porter will be nominated to be Under Secretary of State for Political Affairs. Ambassador Porter, who is currently serving as the President's Personal Representative at the Paris meetings on Vietnam, will succeed U. Alexis Johnson.

Curtis W. Tarr will continue to serve as Under Secretary of State for Coordinating Security Assistance Programs.

Incidentally, in response to your earlier questions regarding the title of Kenneth Rush, who will be nominated as Deputy Secretary of State, a law signed on July 13, 1972, changed the title from Under Secretary to Deputy Secretary.

Q. That is the number two man, though?

MR. ZIEGLER. That is the second man in the State Department. But he is referred to as Deputy Secretary of State, consistent with the law signed July 13, 1972.

In reference to the individuals who are being nominated this morning, the President has asked me to make the following remarks:

Mr. Rush, as you know, has known the President since his student days at Duke Law School, where Mr. Rush was a member of the faculty at Duke. Since that time, Mr. Rush has had an outstanding career in industry. Prior to his service at the Department of Defense, Mr. Rush served with great distinction as Ambassador to West Germany, and played a most important role in negotiating the Berlin Agreement.

Mr. Casey is a lawyer, with considerable background and experience in international economic affairs. Mr. Casey's tenure as Chairman of the SEC has been marked by the kind of strong and innovative leadership which the President feels is essential for this new post of Under Secretary of State for Economic Affairs.

President Nixon has often indicated his concern that the United States be ready to meet and participate vigorously in the intensified international economic competition which lies ahead as the military competition of the past generation recedes. Economic relations, monetary issues, and trade will play a larger role than ever before in United States foreign policy during the next 4 years. Accordingly, President Nixon considers this appointment of Mr. Casey to be one of the most important appointments he is making for the new Administration.

Before his appointment to head the United States Delegation to Paris, Ambassador Porter was, as you know, United States Ambassador to Korea. He began his career in foreign service in 1937. His years of service in a variety of posts in Europe and Asia equip him admirably for the important new position he will be assuming.

Mr. Tarr was appointed to his present position in April of 1972, having previously served as Director of the Selective Service. For the previous decade, he was president of Lawrence College in Appleton, Wisconsin.

In appreciation of the distinguished service and contributions of Deputy Secretary Irwin and Under Secretary of State Alexis Johnson, and in line with the President's earlier comments concerning the desire of many top officials for a change of assignment, the President has asked both Deputy Secretary Irwin and Under Secretary Johnson to stay on in the Administration.

Alexis Johnson at the present time is the senior officer in the Foreign Service of the United States, both in personal rank and in the position he holds. He is the only Foreign Service officer who currently holds the rank of a Career Ambassador, the highest rank in the Foreign Service. To cap a career of exceptional distinction and dedication, the President will ask Under Secretary Johnson to accept a major new assignment commensurate with his special talents. Details of this assignment will be announced soon.

John Irwin has been asked by the President to take a high-level Ambassadorial post, and he is now considering this request.

Looking ahead, the President feels that the foreign policy initiatives of the past 4 years offer great promise for peace and understanding in the world, but he also believes that the realization of that promise will largely depend upon the conduct of our foreign policy during the second 4 years.

In that connection, he is delighted that Secretary of State Rogers can count on the support of this strong, new team at the next level of responsibility at the Department of State.

Announcing Continuation in the Second Term of Key Economic Policy Officials

December 1, 1972

The President has asked me to announce this morning that Secretary George Shultz will continue as Secretary of the Treasury as we start the second term of the Nixon Administration.

Secretary Shultz, as you recall, was one of the original members of President Nixon's Cabinet, serving first as Secretary of Labor. Then in 1970, when the Office of Management and Budget was formed, the President appointed George Shultz the first Director of the OMB.

Prior to joining the Administration, Secretary Shultz was dean of the Graduate School of Business at the University of Chicago, and he had also served several administrations here in Washington in an advisory capacity in the fields of economics and labor relations. It was during one such assignment for President Eisenhower, during the late 1950's, that Mr. Shultz's ability came to the attention of President Nixon. President Nixon, then Vice President of course, worked with George Shultz during the Eisenhower Administration.

The President has also requested that I announce today that Herbert Stein will remain as Chairman of the Council of Economic Advisers. Mr. Stein has agreed to stay on. Mr. Stein is the only present member of CEA who has served on the Council since the beginning of this Administration. He assumed the chairmanship in January of 1972. For 2 years prior to 1969, Mr. Stein was a senior fellow at the Brookings Institution, having come there after many years of distinguished service with the Committee for Economic Development.

With regard to the Council on International Economic Policy, which was instituted last year to coordinate affairs in this increasingly important area, the President wishes me to announce this morning that Peter Flanigan will retain his current responsibilities as Director of the Council on International Economic Policy in the second term.

Peter Flanigan, of course, has been a member of the White House Staff since the Inauguration, before which time he was in the investment banking business in New York, where he was a long-time personal friend and associate of the President.

There is one further organizational step in the area of economic policy which the President has decided to take. I will give you the basic announcement on this, and then Secretary Shultz, who is here this morning, will elaborate somewhat on the matter which I am about to outline for you.

As President Nixon outlined in some of his statements since the election, it is his aim, in recasting his Administration for the second term, to achieve better coordination in the formation and execution of policy. The President, you may also recall, in his remarks at Camp David on Monday spoke specifically of the delegation of more power to responsible members of the Administration's team in the Cabinet.

Pursuant to this goal, the President is naming Secretary Shultz as an Assistant to the President, in addition to continuing his present duties at the Treasury Department. In this capacity, it is the President's intention that Secretary Shultz will be the focal point and the overall coordinator of the entire economic policy decisionmaking process, both domestically and internationally.

He will, of course, work closely with the Council of Economic Advisers under Herb Stein, and the Council on International Economic Policy under Peter Flanigan. His duties as Assistant to the President will include chairing the new Cabinet-level Council on Economic Policy. The exact makeup of this the Secretary will give to you when he is here in a moment to brief you on his additional assignment.

Also, as a part of these new responsibilities, the Secretary will be available to the President for other assignments or special activities which the President may choose to ask Secretary Shultz to involve himself in.

Before going to your questions, and then to the more detailed briefing by Secretary Shultz, let me simply conclude by saying that President Nixon feels that, with the single exception of national security and defense, he has no higher obligation to the American people than that of providing the leadership to insure a healthy, prosperous economy in the United States, an economy which will make a better life not only for all Americans, but will contribute to a healthy economy throughout the world.

The President is determined to carry the very significant economic progress of his first term forward in the second term, a term which he anticipates will be a time of increasing challenges as well as increasing opportunities economically. The President is confident that the organizational changes which are announced today will enhance his ability to meet that objective, and he is gratified that a man such as George Shultz, who has the exceptional leadership capability which he has, will take charge of carrying out the new efforts in the second term.

[Following the Press Secretary's news briefing, Mr. Shultz spoke as follows:

This is the first time that I can remember that there has been any show of deference on the part of the Press Secretary. Something must have happened here. It is a new world, I will tell you. [*Laughter*]

I would first like to express my gratitude for the President's continued confidence in me and to say that I will be doing everything I possibly can, working as hard as I possibly can, to merit that continued confidence.

Let me first talk a bit about the Council in terms of the membership; second, a little about the mode of operation of the Council on Economic Policy as I would see it; and, third, about the arrangements for my own personal staffing on this as I at least anticipate it, recognizing that as with everything these matters evolve as they go along and develop as we try to do the sensible thing as we go along.

First of all, I think that you might say the primary membership of the Council on Economic Policy would be the Labor Department, Commerce Department, Agriculture Department, Transportation has a great play in this, and, especially when you come to international economic policy, the State Department, and within the Executive Office of the President.

In addition to the tremendous job that Mr. Ash will have as Director of the Office of Management and Budget in putting together the budget and working with the President in getting the priorities as expressed in the budget, he will also, of course, be a key member of the

Council on Economic Policy, as will the Chairman of the Council of Economic Advisers, the Director of the Council on International Economic Policy, and the Director of the Cost of Living Council. So that, you might say, is the primary membership, although, depending upon the nature of problems that are being addressed, other people might very well play an important role. It just depends upon the problem, which leads me to the second comment, that is, the mode of operation of the Council.

No doubt, there will be some meetings of the Council as a whole, but I would regard it more as a kind of working group and depending on the problem we are worrying about and working on, we will put together a working group that will develop policy and follow through on that problem.

In a sense, you could say that the Council on International Economic Policy on the one hand, and the Cost of Living Council, on the other, are examples of, you might say, continuing working groups that worry about essential aspects of policy. So, that is an initial thought about the mode of operation of the Council.

I might say that while I am the Chairman of the Council, the President will always be welcome and I know that he will want to come and take part in many of our meetings. He has expressed himself on many occasions before, but in the many discussions I have had with him, especially in the last 2 days, his interest in this and involvement in it, domestically and internationally, is very keen.

Third, in terms of personal arrangements—people always are interested in them—I will, of course, maintain my office as Secretary of the Treasury and carry out these responsibilities. I will also have an office in the White House and a very small staff to help me in carrying out the duties as Assistant to the President. My staff will be limited to the number of people that can get into the small amount of White House space that I have been able to bargain out of Mr. Haldeman. [*Laughter*] So, it will be a very small personal staff in working as Assistant to the President and working out of a White House office.

Well, those are some general comments. I will be glad to take your questions.]

Announcing the President's Decisions on Key White House Staff Positions for the Second Term

December 2, 1972

I have been getting a number of questions about key members of the White House Staff and what their intentions are. So, I can give you an up-date report on that this morning. This will not be complete because the planning for the second term is still underway. Some members of the White House Staff still are discussing their intentions with the President and others. The President has not made his final decisions on the operational organization of the White House Staff for the second term in its totality yet, but I can give you this basic rundown.

The President is pleased to announce that John D. Ehrlichman, Henry A. Kissinger, H. R. Haldeman, and William E. Timmons will continue in the second term as Assistants to the President. These men I have referred to will be remaining in basically the same positions that they currently hold.

Also, the President has asked me to announce this morning that Roy L. Ash, who has been named by the President to be Director of the Office of Management and Budget, will also have the title of Assistant to the President. This dual role parallels somewhat the new role that we announced for Secretary Shultz yesterday.

I think also that you are aware that Peter Flanigan is another individual who holds the position of Assistant to the President, in addition to his duties as Director of the Council on International Economic Policy.

Also, Herbert G. Klein will continue as Director of Communications for the Executive Branch in the second term.

I have also been asked to announce the names of some of the other key members of the President's staff who will hold essentially the same areas of responsibility they have held in the past. I should, however, note again that the President is proceeding with the planning for the organizational structure for the second term, the organizational structure of the White House Staff for the second term, and some of these positions could vary in the second term, but I can tell you at this time that remaining on the White House [Staff] in the roles which you are familiar with will be Leonard Garment, Special Consultant to the President, John Dean, Counsel to the President, Rose Mary Woods, Personal Secretary to the President. Also Special Assistants to the President Ray Price, Pat Buchanan, and Bill Safire will serve in the second term. Their roles will be changing somewhat, however, and as the President makes final decisions on the operational structure of the White House Staff we will be giving you more specifics on that.

I can also tell you this morning that Donald Rumsfeld, who has served in a number of top posts during the first term, most recently those of Counsellor to the President and Director of the Cost of Living Council, will be taking on a major new assignment in the next term at the President's request. The details of Don Rumsfeld's new position will be announced very soon.

I think it has also been general knowledge in Washington for some time now that Charles W. Colson, Special Counsel to the President, has long planned to return to private life at the end of the first term. However, the President has requested Mr. Colson to defer his departure and remain on the White House Staff during the transition period to assist in the planning for the second term. So, Mr. Colson will be staying on for 60 days or more.

Originally, Chuck wanted to leave at the end of December, and the President asked him to stay on for several months to assist in the planning for the second term. The President, of course, regrets the fact that Charles Colson will be leaving, but he understands that this was his plan. While he regrets Chuck is leaving the Administration, he is on the other hand pleased that Chuck will be in the Washington area after his departure from the Administration and will continue to be available for consultation.

I also believe that you know Harry Dent, Special Counsel to the President, has likewise intended to return to his law practice in South Carolina at the conclusion of the first term.

The President has reluctantly accepted his wish to do so. He, of course, wishes him well.

Bob Brown, who is also a Special Assistant to the President, is another member of the staff who has spoken many times to some of you about his intention to return to his business in North Carolina at the end of the first term. The President has accepted Bob's resignation with special regret.

In the case of both Harry Dent and Bob Brown, the President expresses his appreciation for all they have done as a part of the Administration, and their willingness to serve the President in whatever part-time capacity they can after their departure and return to, in the case of Harry Dent, South Carolina to his law practice, and in the case of Bob Brown, to his business in North Carolina.

I should emphasize to you at this point that the President's planning for the makeup of his personal staff in the second term is still going forward. We will have further announcements during the next couple of weeks regarding the various members of the staff who will be moving to new assignments, members of the staff who will be staying and some who have decided to leave the Administration after service for 4 years or more, and also further information on the operational structure when that is set. But I did want to provide you the information this morning on these key members of the White House Staff and what their intentions are and the decisions that have been made regarding their role in the second term.

I should tell you finally that in talking the other day to Robert Finch, who, as you know, is Counsellor to the President, I think it has already been announced by Bob that he intends to return to California at the end of this year. That has been a matter of record for some time. I think for several years now Bob has expressed his intention to leave Washington and return to California at the end of the first term. Bob mentioned to me that he will be holding a press conference in Washington next Tuesday to review his role and discuss his plans for California and also to discuss his future in California.

[In answer to a question following his remarks, Mr. Ziegler stated that he would be remaining as Press Secretary in the second term.]

Announcing Intention To Nominate a New United States Permanent Representative on the NATO Council

December 4, 1972

As we announced on Saturday, Donald Rumsfeld, who is a Counsellor to the President and Director of the Cost of Living Council, has been requested by the President to take on a major new assignment as we enter the second term. The President this morning asked me to announce his intention to nominate Mr. Rumsfeld to be the United States Permanent Representative on the North Atlantic Treaty Organization Council, succeeding Ambassador David Kennedy, who has expressed his desire to return to private life.

The position of Permanent Representative carries with it the rank of Ambassador. As most of you know, Mr. Rumsfeld has served with distinction in the President's Cabinet since early in the Administration. Before being asked by President Nixon to resign from the U.S. House of Representatives to become Director of the Office of Economic Opportunity and Assistant to the President in May of 1969, Don Rumsfeld had represented Illinois' 13th Congressional District for 6½ years.

Mr. Rumsfeld became Counsellor to the President in late 1970 and took on his additional duties as the Director of the Cost of Living Council on October 7, 1971. As Director, he has guided the successful Phase 2 portion of the President's economic stabilization program for the past 14 months.

President Nixon, from the very beginning of his Presidency, has attached the highest priority to strengthening and revitalizing this country's alliance with our Western European partners in the North Atlantic Treaty Organization. I think you all know that President Nixon regards the NATO ambassadorship as one of the most important diplomatic posts in Europe, as evidenced by the fact that Ambassador Kennedy has served in that post with great distinction.

Ambassador Kennedy is a long-time personal friend and associate of the President, and now, as a further mark of the fact that the President regards NATO as an extremely important diplomatic post, he is now selecting a man who has also been one of the President's closest advisers and personal associates to fill the post of Ambassador to the North Atlantic Treaty Organization Council.

The President feels that Mr. Rumsfeld's extensive and varied background in American domestic affairs will complement his ability as a negotiator and spokesman for United States interests in this new role, making him uniquely qualified to represent this country on the North Atlantic Treaty Organization Council at a time when the United States and Europe are increasingly interdependent economically and socially, as well as militarily.

In accepting the resignation of Ambassador Kennedy, another Chicagoan, as Don Rumsfeld is, and a long-time friend of the President's who has held several Cabinet posts since the beginning of the Administration, the President expressed his regret at the Ambassador's departure and his deep appreciation for Mr. Kennedy's important contribution to both domestic and foreign policy over the past 4 years as Secretary of Treasury, Ambassador at Large, and Ambassador to NATO.

The President asked the Ambassador to remain available to take on special assignments from time to time and to be available to assist further in the various negotiations on which he has worked during his tenure in Brussels. Ambassador Kennedy has agreed to do so.

Announcing Continuation in the Second Term of Secretary of the Interior and Intention To Nominate a New Secretary of Housing and Urban Development

December 5, 1972

I have two announcements to make this morning regarding the makeup of the President's Cabinet in the new Administration.

First, the President has asked me to announce that Secretary Rogers C. B. Morton will continue to serve as Secretary of the Interior. The wide-ranging responsibilities entrusted to the Department of the Interior in the 1970's, including conservation and management of the Nation's public lands, and restoring the country's natural beauty, requires strong and vigorous leadership. President Nixon feels that Secretary Morton has provided such leadership since he resigned from the Congress to take this assignment 2 years ago, and that he will continue to do so in the second term.

To fill the vacancy left by the resignation of Secretary George Romney, which we announced last Monday, the President has also asked me to announce today his intention to nominate James T. Lynn to be Secretary of Housing and Urban Development in the second-term Cabinet.

Mr. Lynn, as you know, is presently serving as Under Secretary of Commerce. He is a native of Cleveland, a veteran of naval service in World War II, and a graduate of Western Reserve University, with a law degree from Harvard. Mr. Lynn left the private practice of law in Cleveland to become General Counsel of the Department of Commerce in 1969, and was named by the President to be Under Secretary of Commerce in March of 1971. Mr. Lynn is 45 years old.

Repeatedly during the campaign this fall, and since the election, President Nixon has stressed his expectation that the next 4 years will afford an opportunity to make some of the same kind of dramatic progress in domestic affairs as we have made in international affairs during the past 4 years. Specifically, in his radio address on urban affairs on November 1, and then again in his message to the National League of Cities last week, President Nixon spoke of his conviction that what is often called the "urban crisis" can be turned into an "urban opportunity" if we have the right kind of public policies and leadership in this field.

The President feels that the Department of Housing and Urban Development made major strides in this direction under Secretary Romney's leadership, and he expects those strides to continue and accelerate under Mr. Lynn, whose impressive combination of youth and energy and outstanding management ability have been amply demonstrated during his service at the Department of Commerce.

So today we are announcing two Cabinet positions, the fact that Mr. Lynn will be nominated to fill the post of Secretary of HUD, and the fact that Secretary Morton will continue on with his responsibilities at the Department of the Interior.

Announcing Two Resignations From the Department of the Treasury

December 5, 1972

Last Friday, as you may recall, we announced that Secretary of the Treasury Shultz will be continuing in his present position into the second term, and we also announced the fact that he would be Chairman of the Council on Economic Policy and Assistant to the President.

Today I have two announcements that relate to the Department of the Treasury.

With reluctance and regret, the President has asked me to announce this afternoon that two other top officials of the Treasury Department have asked him to accept their resignations in order that they may return to private life. Those two gentlemen are Dr. Charls E. Walker, Deputy Secretary of the Treasury, and Eugene T. Rossides, Assistant Secretary of the Treasury for Enforcement, Tariff and Trade Affairs, and Operations.

Dr. Walker served as Assistant Secretary of the Treasury under Secretary Robert B. Anderson during the Eisenhower Administration from 1959 to 1961. He returned to the Department as number two man at the beginning of this Administration in 1969, first as Under Secretary and then in the new position of Deputy Secretary which was created earlier this year.

He has served the public interest with exceptional distinction, President Nixon feels, under three Secretaries of the Treasury. In accepting Dr. Walker's resignation, the President expressed his deep appreciation for the Deputy Secretary's numerous contributions to the policy successes of this Administration. Among the major pieces of legislation which Dr. Walker has successfully guided to passage have been the Tax Reform Act of 1969, the Revenue Sharing Act of 1972, the general revenue sharing bill which was signed in October, and legislation in the fields of student loans and minority enterprise.

The strong staff and vigorous administrative operation which the Treasury has built up over the past 4 years are largely to Dr. Walker's credit. Dr. Walker was instrumental in the developing of the President's new economic policies of August 1971, and has been a leading spokesman for those policies in literally hundreds of public forums over the past years.

President Nixon hopes to be able to continue drawing on the Deputy Secretary's counsel and expertise in the time ahead.

Assistant Secretary Eugene Rossides has been one of the ablest and most dedicated sub-Cabinet officials in the President's Administration since early 1969. In accepting with regret Mr. Rossides' decision to leave government service, the President indicated his gratitude for the Assistant Secretary's outstanding leadership in two fields which have commanded top importance in the efforts of this Administration, namely, law enforcement and international trade.

The Treasury Department's strong and effective role in combating the drug trade, organized crime, and air piracy during the past 4 years has been developed under the command of Assistant Secretary Rossides. Mr. Rossides has also been responsible for significant progress in the area of countervailing duties and anti-dumping regulations aimed at curbing unfair trade practices which can harm American interests in world markets.

The departure of both of these distinguished public servants, Deputy Secretary Walker and Assistant Secretary Rossides, is an occasion for gratitude for the services they have rendered to the Administration and the country over the past 4 years. So the President, with regret, is accepting the resignations of Dr. Walker and Eugene Rossides today.

I should add that the President will be meeting with Charls Walker later this week at Camp David, either tomorrow or Thursday. The President wants to meet with him further before he returns to private life. The President is pleased that Dr. Walker will be available to the President for counsel and his expertise in the time ahead.

Announcing the President's Decisions on Additional Personnel Changes for the Second Term

December 6, 1972

Continuing our announcements about the President's decision on key personnel at the Cabinet and sub-Cabinet levels, I have the following information to provide to you today:

President Nixon takes great pleasure in announcing that Secretary Earl Butz will be remaining as Secretary of Agriculture. Secretary Butz, as you remember, joined the Cabinet in December of 1971 after a distinguished career in both education and government service. President Nixon feels that considerable progress has been made in American agriculture during the past 4 years, both in terms of securing better rewards for the farmer through higher farm income, and also in terms of opening new markets for the American farmer around the world. The President looks to Secretary Butz to build on this solid base with continuing progress in the second term.

Also, this morning I have an announcement to make regarding the Department of Commerce. First, regarding Secretary Peterson, there has been a great deal of speculation over the past few weeks about Pete Peterson's plans.

Pete Peterson plans to return to private life. However, I should mention to you that in the course of the discussions that the President has held with Secretary Peterson over the last few weeks, there was considerable discussion regarding various assignments that Pete Peterson might undertake before returning to private life, as he plans to do.

Initially, there was some discussion that centered on establishing a Special Ambassadorship for Pete Peterson which would have been especially tailored to meet Pete Peterson's capabilities, and discussion in this regard centered on Pete Peterson assuming a special ambassadorship which would deal with foreign economic policy and foreign trade matters. This assignment, however, as it was discussed at the outset, would have required Pete Peterson to live in Europe. Pete Peterson felt, for personal reasons, that he could not assume a post which required him to live abroad.

However, the President does want the benefit of Pete Peterson's further views on international economic policy before he leaves the Administration. Therefore, I would like to announce today that Pete Peterson will be appointed the President's Special Representative. In that capacity, the President has asked Mr. Peterson to travel to Europe, to Japan, and other Asian countries besides Japan, and very likely to

Latin America. Following these visits which he will make, the President has asked him to make recommendations to the President on how the United States can better coordinate our economic policy with our major trading partners throughout the world.

The special assignment which I am referring to which Mr. Peterson will undertake before he returns to private life will be completed sometime in the spring. In the spring, the President will receive a very detailed and, I am sure, very thorough report, because that is the nature of all of Pete Peterson's work, on the matters of how we can better coordinate U.S. economic policy with our major trading partners.

So I did want to tell you that Mr. Peterson would be assuming the position as Special Representative to the President and will undertake this temporary assignment that I have referred to.

Succeeding Pete Peterson will be Frederick B. Dent, of Spartanburg, South Carolina. Mr. Dent has had an exceptionally distinguished career in industry and business. Mr. Dent became president of Mayfair Mills, a leading South Carolina textile firm, in 1947 at the age of 25, and has held that position ever since.[1] He has long been a leader in South Carolina civic affairs and has previously served in the Administration as a member of the Gates Commission, which made recommendations to President Nixon on the transition to an all-volunteer armed force.

President Nixon feels that Mr. Dent's wide knowledge of domestic and international business, and his proven executive ability, will make him an outstanding Secretary of Commerce.

Turning to the sub-Cabinet level, with regard to changes at the Treasury Department which we announced yesterday, President Nixon has asked me to announce his intention to nominate William E. Simon to be Deputy Secretary of the Treasury succeeding Charls Walker, who we announced yesterday would be returning to private life.

Also, the President intends to nominate Edward L. Morgan to be Assistant Secretary of the Treasury for Enforcement, Tariff and

---

[1] The White House Press Office later indicated that Mr. Dent joined Mayfair Mills in 1947 and became its president in 1958.

Trade Affairs, and Operations, succeeding Eugene Rossides. We announced the fact yesterday that Mr. Rossides would be returning to private life.

Mr. Simon, 45 years of age, lives in New Vernon, New Jersey, and is currently a partner in the New York investment banking firm of Salomon Brothers. Salomon Brothers specializes in the area of Government bonds and public finance. It is felt with his experience in this field, and his credentials as a young, forceful manager, that Mr. Simon is ideally suited to be second in command in the Department of the Treasury in a period when Federal, State, and local fiscal relationships are being transformed by revenue sharing, and also at a time when Secretary Shultz's new role as Assistant to the President for Economic Affairs will place increased departmental responsibilities on the Deputy Secretary of the Treasury.

Ed Morgan is well known, I think, to most of you, having played a key role in domestic affairs as a member of the White House Staff since the President's Inauguration in 1969. Ed Morgan first served as Deputy Counsel to the President, and then as Deputy Assistant to the President for Domestic Affairs and as Assistant Director of the Domestic Council. His additional duties at present include the post of Executive Director of the Cabinet Committee on Education and Vice Chairman of the Council of the Administrative Conference of the United States.

Before joining the White House Staff, Mr. Morgan had been in private law practice in Phoenix, Arizona. In asking Ed Morgan to take this new assignment, the President expressed his appreciation for Mr. Morgan's outstanding record here at the White House and **his expectation that Secretary Shultz's team** will be a strong team with Ed Morgan as a member of the Department of the Treasury.

Announcing Intention To Nominate a United States Ambassador to Italy and a New Secretary of Transportation

December 7, 1972

We are continuing today with the announcements relating to the makeup of the President's Cabinet in the second term.

I believe all of you are aware of the rumors that have been abroad in Washington now for quite some time to the effect that Secretary of Transportation John Volpe would be taking an important new assignment for the President at the conclusion of the first term. Today, President Nixon is gratified to announce his intention to nominate Secretary Volpe to be United States Ambassador to the Republic of Italy.

Secretary Volpe will succeed Graham A. Martin, a career Foreign Service officer, who has held the post since 1969. Ambassador Martin will be receiving another important assignment in the Administration in the second term.

When John Volpe takes up this key American diplomatic post in Rome, I think many of you are aware of the fact that he will be retracing a journey that brought his own parents to this country from Italy as penniless immigrants at the turn of this century. His remarkable career in business and public service, I believe, is also familiar to most of you here.

He started at the bottom of the construction trades as a hod carrier and rose to become Commissioner of Public Works for the State of Massachusetts, then Federal Highway Administrator in the Eisenhower Administration. Then he became a three-term Governor of the State of Massachusetts and most recently a member of President Nixon's Cabinet, and has served with great distinction in the President's Cabinet as Secretary of Transportation for the last 4 years.

As a member of President Nixon's Cabinet, Secretary Volpe has traveled to more than 20 countries on transportation policy matters and goodwill trips. He also accompanied the President on a state visit that President Nixon took to Italy in September of 1970.

During Secretary Volpe's term as Governor of Massachusetts, he helped to foster exchange relationships between the cities of Boston and Rome. For this and other contributions to Italian-American friendship, he was awarded the highest decoration which the Republic of Italy can confer on a foreign national.

John Volpe, when he assumes the post of Ambassador to the Republic of Italy, will be the first individual of Italian background ever to head the United States Mission in Rome. President Nixon is proud to be able to nominate as Ambassador to Italy a second-generation Italian-American whose own life story bears impressive witness to the close bonds between our two countries.

In requesting Secretary Volpe to accept the change of roles within the Administration, the President had warm praise for the job Secretary Volpe has done as Secretary of the Department of Transportation. When Secretary Volpe assumed his position in the Cabinet, the Department of Transportation was less than 2 years old. So the task of shaping the identity of the Department fell largely to Secretary Volpe from 1969 to the present time.

During this period, a number of steps have been taken to provide this country with a balanced transportation system which we will need in the future. The rail passenger service has been revitalized with the formation of Amtrak. The Urban Mass Transportation Act has brought about an eightfold increase in Federal funding for public transportation. The Airport and Airways Act has enhanced the outlook for air travel. The Interstate Highway System has been brought close to completion. And transportation safety has been improved under Secretary Volpe's leadership.

To carry out the efforts which Secretary Volpe started in the past 4 years, in the second term the President will nominate Claude Brinegar, of California, to succeed Secretary Volpe as Secretary of Transportation.

Those of you who are familiar with the top rank of business leadership in this country will recognize Mr. Brinegar's name as one of the most gifted, young executives in the United States today.

A member of the management team of the Union Oil Company of California for the past 20 years, Mr. Brinegar has served since 1968 as senior vice president of the company and as president of the Union 76 Division. Mr. Brinegar was educated at Stanford and completed his Ph. D. in economics in 1953. He is 45 years of age.

As we have said before, President Nixon anticipates that the years ahead will offer the opportunity for accelerated progress in America's domestic affairs. The President feels that transportation, in particular, is one area where such an opportunity exists. He is determined that the Federal role in the transportation field should be characterized by creative policies, aggressive management, and constructive co-operation between public and private sectors. He is convinced that Claude Brinegar is the right man to provide the leadership to make this happen.

The President welcomes the chance to bring a man of this caliber into the new Cabinet, and he looks forward to working closely with Secretary-designate Brinegar in the second term.

Incidentally, there is one fact that I know will come out sooner or later regarding Mr. Brinegar, so it was felt that we should make this clear today. The fact is that Mr. Brinegar, at some point in his life, lived a couple of years in the town of Yorba Linda, California. This came to light during the discussion the President had with Mr. Brinegar when they met here at Camp David. The President wanted to make sure that when the announcement was made, that we called attention to the fact that Mr. Brinegar did live for a period in the town in which the President was born, Yorba Linda, California.

Q. Did they meet there?

MR. ZIEGLER. No, they did not know one another. The President lived in Yorba Linda in 1913, and Mr. Brinegar lived there in 1958, so their paths did not cross, but the fact of the matter is that they do have an association there in relation to Yorba Linda.

Announcing the President's Decisions on Key Officials in the Departments of Justice and the Interior

December 8, 1972

We will continue now with the announcements that we have been making over the past few weeks in relation to the President's Cabinet. Today's announcements regard the President's Cabinet for the second term and also some sub-Cabinet posts as well, and relate to the Department of Justice and also to the Department of the Interior.

First, President Nixon is pleased to announce that Richard G. Kleindienst will continue to serve as Attorney General of the United States. Richard Kleindienst was sworn into office on June 12, 1972. The President feels he will provide a continuity of firm leadership for this vital department.

This Administration, as we have said before, has a top priority commitment to continue cutting down crime, narcotics, and other illegal activities in this country. Significant gains have been made in these areas during the last 4 years, and the President is directing that the Department of Justice continue to give emphasis to these areas in the second term.

Dick Kleindienst, as most of you know, has served in the Department of Justice from the beginning of President Nixon's first term, being appointed Deputy Attorney General on January 31, 1969, and serving in that position until John Mitchell left as Attorney General in June. Mr. Kleindienst at that time was nominated to become Attorney General.

We also have announcements today relating to other positions within the Justice Department. I am announcing at this time that the following members of the Justice Department will be leaving their posts:

Deputy Attorney General Ralph Erickson will be leaving his post and will be nominated to a high judicial post. President Nixon expresses his appreciation for the valuable service which Deputy Attorney General Ralph Erickson has provided during his term in that position.

David Norman, Assistant Attorney General of the Civil Rights Division, who also, I should say, will be nominated by the President for an important judicial position, will be leaving his position as Assistant Attorney General in the Civil Rights Division. He has served as Assistant Attorney General in the Civil Rights Division since August of 1971.

Jerris Leonard, Administrator of the Law Enforcement Assistance Administration since April of 1971, will be leaving that position and returning to private life and to the private practice of law.

Roger Cramton, Assistant Attorney General, Office of Legal Counsel, serving in that position since August of 1972, is returning to his profession of the teaching of law. He has been on leave for 2 years from the University of

Michigan Law School and will be returning to the University of Michigan Law School to continue his teaching profession.

Leo Pellerzi, Assistant Attorney General for Administration, is also leaving his post. The President takes specific note of the fact that he has contributed significantly to administrative reform in the Department of Justice during his time in office. He has been Assistant Attorney General for Administration since March of 1968.

President Nixon is also today announcing his intention to nominate Professor Robert H. Bork, of Yale Law School, to become Solicitor General. Professor Bork will succeed Erwin Griswold, whose intention to retire at the end of the current term of the U.S. Supreme Court has been known, I believe, for some time. Dean Griswold will be leaving the post of Solicitor General at the end of the term of the Court this spring or early summer.

Professor Bork will work under Solicitor General Griswold in the upcoming months in preparation for the assumption of the responsibilities of Solicitor General in the spring or early summer. Robert Bork will serve as Deputy Solicitor General during the period between January and spring or early summer.

Professor Bork has been on the faculty of the Yale Law School since 1962 in the major teaching areas of constitutional law and antitrust law. This year he served as a consultant to the Cabinet Committee on Education and participated in the drafting of the Administration's legislation relating to the busing of schoolchildren.

He is a native of Pittsburgh, where he was born in March of 1927. Professor Bork is a 1948 Phi Beta Kappa graduate of the University of Chicago and of its law school, where he received his law degree in 1953. Professor Bork was editor of the school's Law Review.

Prior to joining the Yale law faculty, Professor Bork was with a Chicago law firm specializing in antitrust and other major areas of litigation.

Also, I am announcing today the fact that the President will name Jewel Lafontant to accept a position in the Justice Department. The President has known Jewel Lafontant since 1952. She currently is serving on the United States delegation to the United Nations, and

comes highly recommended by Ambassador Bush.

President Nixon saw Jewel Lafontant at the meeting of the black appointees that was held at the White House a short time ago. At that time, the President had a discussion—actually following that meeting—with Jewel Lafontant and asked her if she would serve in this capacity in the second term, and it was worked out at that time. So I am announcing today that she will be assuming a position in the Justice Department in the Solicitor General's office, and will be named Deputy Solicitor General in the spring or early summer when Professor Bork assumes the position of Solicitor General.

In the period between the first of the year and early summer, she will be serving in the Solicitor General's office, preparing herself to assume the role of Deputy Solicitor General. She is a Chicago lawyer, a senior partner in the law firm of Stratford, Lafontant, Fisher & Malkin. She currently is serving as a U.S. Representative to the 27th Session of the United Nations General Assembly. She was appointed to that position in September.

She is a member of the United States Advisory Commission on International Educational and Cultural Affairs. She was a member from 1970 to 1972 of the Advisory Council for Minority Enterprise. She is a graduate of Oberlin College in Oberlin, Ohio. She graduated in 1943. She received her law degree from the University of Chicago in 1946.

Mrs. Lafontant has a son 14 years of age and lives in Chicago. She is 50 years old. She was an Assistant U.S. Attorney in Chicago from 1955 to 1958.

Q. Does she have the title of Ambassador right now?

MR. ZIEGLER. No. She does not carry the title of Ambassador. She carries the title of U.S. Representative to the 27th Session of the United Nations General Assembly.

I also have two announcements relating to the Department of the Interior. Harrison Loesch, Assistant Secretary for Public Land Management, will be leaving his post. Mr. Loesch has held the post of Assistant Secretary, Public Land Management, since April of 1969. Mr. Loesch has devoted many dedicated years to his responsibilities. The Administration and the President appreciate the great job he has done in the managing of public lands, and we are announcing today that he is returning to the private practice of law. He is moving on to other interests that he has. So Harrison Loesch will be leaving the position of Assistant Secretary for Public Land Management at the Department of the Interior.

Also, Louis R. Bruce, Commissioner of Indian Affairs in the Department of the Interior, will be leaving his post. He was appointed to his position in August of 1969.

Announcing Intention To Nominate Under Secretaries of the Interior and Transportation

December 9, 1972

I have several announcements to make today relating to sub-Cabinet positions.

The President will nominate Dr. John C. Whitaker to be Under Secretary of the Interior. He will succeed the late Dr. William T. Pecora. John Whitaker, since August of 1969, has served as Deputy Assistant to the President for the environment, natural resources, and energy policy. He has been involved in those areas, working on the Domestic Council staff.

He was Secretary of the Cabinet from January to August of 1969 and has long been involved, as you know, on the staff of President Nixon.

The President is highly pleased to be nominating a man with John Whitaker's impressive scientific and governmental experience for this very important position in the Department of the Interior. John Whitaker received his education at Georgetown University and at Johns Hopkins, where he earned his doctorate degree in geology in 1953. From 1953 until the time he joined the Administration, he pursued a career in geological exploration, geophysical surveying, and natural resources engineering in various parts of the country.

In the Administration, John Whitaker has coordinated policymaking for the President in such matters as the President's environmental policy messages to the Congress, the 1971 energy message to the Congress, and the reorganization plans creating the Environmental Protection Agency and the National Oceanic and Atmospheric Administration.

So John Whitaker will be nominated Under

Secretary of the Interior, succeeding the late Dr. William T. Pecora.

Moving to the Department of Transportation, the President will nominate Egil "Bud" Krogh, Jr., to be Under Secretary of Transportation, succeeding James M. Beggs. Mr. Beggs will return to private life, but he has agreed to serve as a consultant during the transition period.

Bud Krogh has been Deputy Assistant to the President for Domestic Affairs since November 1969. He also served as Assistant Director of the staff of the Domestic Council, where his policy responsibilities have included transportation, narcotics control, corrections and legal services, and liaison with the District of Columbia.

The President feels that Bud's fine performance in all of these assignments assures that he will play a strong and constructive role in advancing us toward a solution of the transportation problems which still face the Nation.

Bud Krogh holds a degree from Principia College, Elsah, Illinois, and the University of Washington in Seattle, where he received his law degree in 1968.

Incidentally, I should mention to you, in speaking of Bud Krogh, that he played a key role in the solution of the Capital's transportation problem, working very closely with the District of Columbia and with the Congress on the modern transit system which is now underway in the District of Columbia. So he has been involved extensively in dealing with transportation problems in his role at the White House, specifically, the District of Columbia transportation problem.

Announcing the President's Decisions on Key Agriculture Department Officials and Deputy Secretary of Defense

December 12, 1972

We have several announcements to make this morning regarding the sub-Cabinet for the second term concerning the Department of Agriculture. I have the following decisions to announce relating to the Department of Agriculture:

First, Under Secretary J. Phil Campbell, who has served very ably as second in command at the Department of Agriculture since the beginning of this Administration, will be remaining at the Department of Agriculture as Under Secretary.

Richard E. Lyng, Assistant Secretary for Marketing and Consumer Services, has decided to leave that position. President Nixon and Secretary Butz feel that Mr. Lyng's abilities are of great value to the Administration, and they have asked him to accept another top position at the Department of Agriculture and he is considering that request.

Thomas K. Cowden, Assistant Secretary for Rural Development and Conservation, will be resigning his post in order to take another important job within the Department of Agriculture. I should point out, as you will note in the biographical material, that Tom Cowden is 64 years old. Next June he will be 65 years old and requested another assignment, as he did not want to continue in the Assistant Secretary role through the next term. He plans to retire at some point next year.

Edward Shulman, General Counsel of the Department, is retiring from Government service. Edward Shulman is 65 years old and has been with the Department of Agriculture for 39 years. So he is retiring as General Counsel of the Department.

Q. Are we going to get biographies on all of them?

Mr. ZIEGLER. Yes. James V. Smith, Administrator of the Farmers Home Administration, has expressed his desire to return to private life. The President accepts Mr. Smith's resignation with regret.

Turning to the Department of Defense, the President has asked me to announce this morning that he intends to nominate William P. Clements, Jr., of Texas, to be Deputy Secretary of Defense in the new Administration. Mr. Clements will succeed Kenneth Rush, who will be leaving this position to become Deputy Secretary of State.

Mr. Clements has had a highly successful business career and is one of the most outstanding civic leaders of Dallas, Texas. At the present time he is chairman of the board of SEDCO, formerly known as Southeastern Drilling Co., Inc., of Dallas, Texas.

President Nixon believes that Mr. Clements' strong management and executive talents, as well as his wide knowledge of defense and na-

tional security affairs, will make him a very valuable member of Secretary Richardson's new team at the Department of Defense.

[The White House also announced that Carroll G. Brunthaver would remain as Assistant Secretary of Agriculture for International Affairs and Commodity Programs.]

Announcing the President's Further Decisions on Personnel for the Second Term

December 13, 1972

I do have several other announcements to make this morning regarding the makeup of the Administration in the second term.

Last Friday, as you recall, in announcing that Attorney General Kleindienst will be staying on at the Department of Justice, we also told you that his deputy, Ralph Erickson, will be leaving to accept a nomination in the Federal judiciary. Today the President is pleased to announce his intention to nominate Joseph T. Sneed, of North Carolina, to be Deputy Attorney General of the United States succeeding Mr. Erickson.

Mr. Sneed is widely respected in the legal profession as one of the most eminent professors of law in the United States today. At present, he is dean of the Duke Law School in Durham, North Carolina.

Before coming to Durham in 1971, he taught law for more than 20 years at Stanford, Cornell, and the University of Texas. He is active in a number of professional organizations and is a past president of the Association of American Law Schools.

President Nixon, as you know, feels the enforcement of the law and administration of justice are of the highest importance among the responsibilities which he owes to the American people, and he believes that Joseph Sneed can be of great assistance to him and to the Attorney General in carrying out these responsibilities. He welcomes Mr. Sneed as a member of the Administration.

The President today is also announcing that he is accepting with special regret the resignation of Frank Shakespeare as Director of the United States Information Agency. Mr. Shakespeare has expressed his desire to return to private life and will be announcing the details of his plans in private life in the near future.

In responding to Frank Shakespeare's decision, President Nixon expressed warm appreciation for the outstanding job he has done throughout the first term in helping to communicate United States policies and the American way of life to the world.

To succeed Mr. Shakespeare as Director of USIA, the President intends to nominate James Keogh. Mr. Keogh is well known to many of you, I think, from his key role here on the White House Staff as chief of writing and research and Special Assistant to the President during the first 2 years of this Administration.

Prior to 1969, Mr. Keogh had had a distinguished career in journalism, including long service with the Omaha World Herald in his home State of Nebraska, and later almost 20 years with Time magazine where he was executive editor. In 1968 he left that post as executive editor with Time to work for the President in the 1968 campaign.

Also, I am announcing this morning, on behalf of the President the fact that William H. Brown will continue as Chairman of the Equal Employment Opportunity Commission, a position to which he was designated by the President at the time he was sworn in as a member of the Commission in 1969. The EEOC, as you know, has recently received new powers to combat job discrimination of all types and has broadened its activities in this field during the last 4 years. The President feels that Chairman Brown has provided very effective leadership in this effort and he expects that leadership will continue in the new term.

Then, finally, I have one additional comment to make today on a personnel change relating to a news announcement that was made earlier this morning at the Department of the Interior by Secretary Morton. Secretary Morton announced this morning that he is naming Ronald H. Walker, who has been serving as Special Assistant to the President on the White House Staff, to become Director of the National Park Service succeeding George Hartzog whose resignation was announced last week.

Ron Walker, I think many of you know him, had the principal responsibility during the first term of supervising all Presidential travel, both foreign and domestic. In concurring with Secretary Morton's request to bring Mr. Walker over to Interior, where he previously served as Assistant to Secretary Hickel early in the Administration, the President had special thanks for the excellent service which Ron has rendered here at the White House.

The President attaches high importance to improving and expanding America's parklands. He is pleased that a man of Ron Walker's youth, energy, and proven abilities will be playing a key role in this effort during the period ahead.

———

Announcing the President's Additional Selections of Personnel for the Second Term

December 14, 1972

We have this morning several announcements to make regarding the various departments and changes which are being made in various departments. This morning's announcements relate to the Department of Labor, first.

The President has asked me to say that it is with deep appreciation for his services as Under Secretary that President Nixon accepts the resignation of Laurence H. Silberman. Larry Silberman has a number of options available to him both in public and private life and will be announcing his plans in the near future.

Larry Silberman, of course, has been Under Secretary of Labor for the last few years.

The President also accepts, with gratitude for their contributions, the resignations of Malcolm Lovell, Assistant Secretary of Labor for Manpower; Richard Grunewald, Assistant Secretary of Labor for Employment Standards; Geoffrey Moore, Commissioner of Labor Statistics; and George Guenther, Assistant Secretary for Occupational Safety and Health.

Finally, in relation to the Department of Labor, I think most of you are aware that Elizabeth Koontz has indicated her desire to return to private life. The President accepts her resignation with special regret and commends the service she has given in the Department.

The President is also announcing today that he has asked three officials of the Department of Labor to stay during the next Administration in the Department. Those officials are:

Michael Moskow, who is currently Assistant Secretary for Policy, Evaluation, and Research; W. J. Usery, Jr., who is Assistant Secretary for Labor-Management Relations; and Richard Schubert, who is the Department of Labor's Solicitor.

Finally, the President is announcing that four officials of the Administration will be remaining in their present positions for the second term: William Eberle will continue as the President's Special Representative for Trade Negotiations. As the President's chief trade negotiator, Bill Eberle will be a principal member of the Administration's team which manages foreign economic policy under George Shultz and Peter Flanigan.

Also continuing will be the two Deputy Special Representatives for Trade Negotiations, Harald B. Malmgren and William R. Pearce.

Then, finally, I would like to announce that Thomas S. Kleppe, a former Member of the Congress from North Dakota and a distinguished business executive, will continue as Administrator of the Small Business Administration.

We will have biographical material for you on all of the individuals that I referred to after the briefing.

Also, we are going to provide you, as soon as the briefing is over, information and some materials relating to the announcement I am about to give you. We will give you an Executive order and a statement by the President on the subject of intergovernmental relations and the Domestic Council.

As the statement will point out, the President is accepting the recommendation of the Vice President that the intergovernmental relations functions be transferred to the Domestic Council for improved communication and coordination between Federal and State and local governments. The functions which are outlined in the President's statement, which we will be giving you in a moment now, will be added to the Domestic Council responsibilities.

In that regard, President Nixon today is naming Kenneth R. Cole as Executive Director of the Domestic Council. We will be providing you a biography on Mr. Cole, who, as you know, has been Deputy Director of the Domestic Council. John Ehrlichman previously held

the title of Executive Director of the Domestic Council, but Ken Cole, in this responsibility, will have the day-to-day responsibilities of running the Domestic Council as the President wants John Ehrlichman to be available as Assistant to the President for additional responsibilities beyond being the President's chief domestic adviser. So Ken Cole will assume the responsibility of Executive Director of the Domestic Council.

Announcing Resignations of Certain Officials in the Departments of Health, Education, and Welfare and Transportation

December 15, 1972

The President has asked me to make the following announcements today pertaining to the Department of Health, Education, and Welfare, and the Department of Transportation.

As you know, Dr. Merlin K. DuVal, Assistant Secretary for Health and Scientific Affairs, has announced his intention to return to the University of Arizona to be vice president of medical affairs. The President is announcing today that he accepts Dr. DuVal's resignation with appreciation for his outstanding service in the Department.

President Nixon is also announcing today that he accepts the resignations of three other officials in the Department of Health, Education, and Welfare with gratitude for their contributions over the years of their service: Robert O. Beatty, Assistant Secretary for Public Affairs, who has been planning to return to his home State of Idaho for some time; John B. Martin, Commissioner of the Administration on Aging, who is returning to the private practice of law; and Dr. Jesse L. Steinfeld, Surgeon General, who has agreed to assist for a period during the transition and will then return to private life.

As most of you know, announcements have already been made by three key non-Presidential appointees at the Department with respect to their desire to return to private life. Those individuals are: Robert Q. Marston, Director of the National Institutes of Health; Vernon E. Wilson, Administrator, Health Services and Mental Health Administration; and

John D. Twiname, Administrator, Social and Rehabilitation Service.

The President also accepts today the resignations of two individuals who are administrators in the Department of Transportation: Douglas W. Toms, Administrator of the National Highway Traffic Safety Administration; and Carlos C. Villarreal, Administrator of the Urban Mass Transportation Administration.

All will be returning to private life. We have biographical information to provide to you on each of the individuals I have referred to.

Announcing Further Decisions on Personnel for the Second Term

December 18, 1972

We have several more announcements today relating to the makeup of the Administration in the second term, relating to some individuals who will be leaving Government to return to private life and others who will be receiving new areas of responsibility and others who will be staying.

The President has asked me to announce today the following resignations from the Department of Commerce. The President accepts with deep appreciation for his service the resignation of Dr. Harold C. Passer, Assistant Secretary for Economic Affairs, who will be returning to private industry, and Robert A. Podesta, Assistant Secretary for Economic Development, who will also be returning to private life. Dr. George Hay Brown, Director of the Bureau of the Census, has indicated that for personal reasons he wishes to return to private life. The President also accepts his resignation with sincere appreciation for his contribution.

In the Department of the Interior President Nixon is announcing that the resignations have been accepted of four officials whose service over the past years is greatly appreciated: Hollis M. Dole, Assistant Secretary for Mineral Resources; James R. Smith, Assistant Secretary for Water and Power Resources; Mitchell Melich, Solicitor for the Department of the Interior; and Ellis L. Armstrong, Commissioner of Reclamation, who also will be returning to private life.

There are some additional announcements

that I have to make regarding personnel changes on the White House Staff.

I believe that you will find in these a continuation of the pattern that some White House Staff members, as we have already indicated, will be staying, others will be returning to private life, while still others are moving to new positions or have moved to new positions in the Administration as we continue to make plans for the second term.

The President has already pointed out, as most of you have noted, that the Executive Office of the President will be reduced in numbers. We are working toward that objective and as time moves along you will note that changes will be made working toward the achievement of that objective. I have noted some stories that suggest we are making changes in many of the departments and reductions in departments, but not so much here at the White House. I can just assure you that the objective which the President outlined in relation to the White House will be met.

First, I would like to say that the President is very pleased to announce today that three members of his staff will be continuing on in the new Administration. They are Richard A. Moore, as Special Counsel to the President; Dwight L. Chapin, Deputy Assistant to the President; and Michael J. Farrell, Special Assistant to the President.

As we have made announcements before on the White House Staff, we have pointed out that as the new structuring that will take place in the White House evolves, the duties and responsibilities of some of the individuals who have been announced may expand or be altered somewhat. We are not prepared at this time to spell that out, but I did want to let you know, as we continue here, those individuals will be continuing.

The President is also announcing that he accepts with personal regret the resignations of four other members of the White House Staff: Brigadier General Robert L. Schulz, U.S. Army, retired, who has ably served President Nixon as liaison with former Presidents, will be leaving the staff. General Schulz formerly served as a top aide to the late President Eisenhower. President Nixon is extremely grateful for the quality of service that General Schulz has performed in this Administration. As most of you know,

General Schulz retired from the military in December of 1962. He plans to remain in Washington.

Also, the President accepts with personal regret the resignation of Desmond J. Barker, Jr., as Special Assistant to the President, who has served the President most effectively in a variety of assignments over the past few years. Des Barker will be returning to Utah and to private life.

George T. Bell, Special Assistant to the President, also will be returning to private life. George Bell has handled a wide-ranging variety of responsibilities. The President has commended George Bell for his competence and expresses appreciation both for his contribution to the Administration and for his friendship over the years.

Mark I. Goode, Special Assistant to the President, who has served as a consultant to the President, as most of you know, on communications matters, has expressed for some time that he intended to leave the Government after the first term. The President is accepting Mark's resignation with deep regret and, of course, wishes him, as he does the other individuals I have mentioned, well in their return to private life.

I should add that men like Mark Goode, of course, and others will be available and have said that they would be available to the President for consultations as we proceed in the second term.

Just as we are talking about the White House Staff, for the purpose of reminding you, others who served on the White House Staff in the first term and have now received new appointments and new responsibilities, of course, are Donald Rumsfeld, whom we announced would be nominated to become Ambassador to NATO; Ed Morgan, who is going to the Treasury Department; John Whitaker is going to the Interior Department; Bud Krogh to Transportation; and Ron Walker to the Interior Department.

Previously we have made the point that Harry Dent, for example, is returning to private life; Chuck Colson is returning to private life; Bob Brown and Bob Finch, we have also announced their plans to return to private life.

So I wanted to review that for you today because as we have been making announcements regarding the various departments, we are also proceeding with discussions with individuals on the White House Staff regarding their intentions and want to bring you up to date as to where we stand on that.

As President Nixon pointed out at Camp David, and this does not relate to individuals I referred to, but during this process of change that is taking place with new assignments being given and new responsibilities being given in some cases, and also taking into account the fact that some individuals plan to leave Government throughout this process, you will see a continuing reduction of the number of personnel within the Executive Office of the President.

Now, finally, President Nixon is very pleased to announce today that he will appoint Mrs. Anne Armstrong, who is cochairman of the Republican National Committee, to be Counsellor to the President. This appointment will be effective upon completion of her tenure as cochairman of the Republican National Committee. That takes place on January 19, 1973. The President expects that Mrs. Armstrong will bring an articulate voice and great creative energy to the highest councils of government. She will be a full member of the President's Cabinet, as previous Counsellors have been.

Anne Armstrong's counsel will include a wide range of domestic issues, among which will be an effective advocacy of increasing the role of women in government policymaking and government operations. But she will concentrate, of course, on other matters which the President will assign to her. We will give you biographical information on Anne Armstrong, as well as the others I have mentioned.

Just briefly, Mrs. Armstrong has been cochairman of the Republican National Committee since January of 1971 and has served as Republican committeewoman for Texas since 1968. She is married to Tobin Armstrong, also from Texas. She is the first woman Cabinet member since Mrs. Oveta Hobby held the post of Secretary of Health, Education, and Welfare in the Eisenhower Administration from 1953 to 1955.

Announcing Further Decisions on Personnel for the Second Term

December 19, 1972

The President has asked me to make several announcements today regarding further changes on the White House Staff for the second term, and also relating to the Administration. As I noted yesterday, I believe you will see in most of these a continuation of the pattern that many staff members are leaving to take other roles in the Government, and some are returning to private life.

Alexander P. Butterfield, Deputy Assistant to the President, will be named Administrator of the Federal Aviation Administration. In that post, he will succeed John Shaffer, who is returning to private life.

President Nixon has expressed to Alex Butterfield his deepest appreciation and highest regard for the service he rendered during the Administration. The President is confident that the high quality of service will be continued by Mr. Butterfield at the FAA.

Alex Butterfield, as Deputy Assistant to the President, has worked extremely close to the President on a day-to-day basis in the areas of appointments and other Presidential activities. Prior to joining the White House Staff, Alex Butterfield spent 20 years in the Air Force as a command pilot. We will be giving you a biography which spells out other details of Alex's background.

Now that I have been talking about a pattern, I have an announcement that departs from it and that is in the announcement of a new member of the White House Staff.

President Nixon is announcing today the appointment of William Baroody, Jr., to be Special Assistant to the President. William Baroody will succeed Chuck Colson, who was a Special Counsel to the President, and whom we previously announced would return to private life after assisting during the transition. Bill Baroody will take over Chuck Colson's responsibility for liaison with outside groups and special groups in the country.

Bill Baroody now is Assistant to Secretary of Defense Laird and served on Mel Laird's Congressional staff when the Secretary was a Member of the House of Representatives.

Q. Does the FAA post require Senate confirmation?

MR. ZIEGLER. Yes, it does.

President Nixon today is also announcing that he will nominate Frank Carlucci to be Under Secretary of the Department of Health, Education, and Welfare in the new Administration. Frank will succeed John G. Veneman, who has requested that his resignation be accepted by the President and has expressed a preference to return to private life.

The President has long been aware of Jack Veneman's desire at the end of this term to return to California and return to private life. In accepting Mr. Veneman's resignation, on Mr. Veneman's request, the President, of course, expresses regret that Mr. Veneman will be leaving, and praised his service as a deeply knowledgeable and very articulate spokesman for the Administration on the complex issues which HEW administers.

Frank Carlucci now is Deputy Director of the Office of Management and Budget. He formerly served as Director of the Office of Economic Opportunity. In selecting him for his new position at HEW, the President wanted a high caliber of leadership which Mr. Carlucci displayed in OMB, in OEO, and in such critical special assignments as coordinating the Pennsylvania flood relief efforts.

We have several other announcements to make this morning.

The President is announcing today, with a deep sense of personal regret, that he accepts the resignation of Harold Finger, Assistant Secretary for Research and Technology at the Department of Housing and Urban Development. Harold Finger was appointed in April of 1969 and has indicated to the President that he had a desire to return to private life at this time. President Nixon commends his excellent service in the Department and expresses gratitude for his contribution and support.

Yesterday we referred to other changes that were being made in the structure of the White House Staff. Some members of the White House Staff, as I pointed out at that time, are leaving the White House to assume other responsibilities in the Government, some are returning to private life, and some, of course, will be assuming new positions within the White House. But as this process continues, with individuals returning to private life or to other departments, you will see that the White House Staff and the Executive Office staff is moving to lower numbers. At some point here when this process is completed, I will be able to state to you the extent that the White House Staff has been reduced. I mentioned yesterday that the President intended to reduce the White House and Executive Office staff in the second term.

Continuing with announcements that relate to the White House Staff, first I would like to say that Bill Gifford, who was Special Assistant to the President, and who concentrated on the area of budget and management, is leaving the White House Staff to join George Shultz at the Treasury Department as an Assistant to the Secretary for Legislative Affairs.

Also, the President has asked me to express his sincere personal regret in accepting the resignation of John Nidecker of the White House Staff. John has expressed a desire to take another position in Government and the President appreciates his willingness to remain in the Administration in another important post which will be announced at a later time.

Q. What was his position?

MR. ZIEGLER. John Nidecker worked on the Congressional liaison staff.

Also, today I have been asked to tell you that four assistants in the office of Bill Timmons, who is an Assistant to the President for Legislative Affairs, will remain in their responsibilities. The four top assistants will be staying as Special Assistants for Legislative Affairs. They are: Richard Cook, Tom C. Korologos, Wallace Johnson, and Max Friedersdorf. Dick Cook and Tom Korologos will continue to serve as principal deputies for the House and the Senate respectively. We will have biographical information in just a moment.

Two other members of the White House Staff are also taking new positions, and I would like to give that information to you at this time.

Dan Kingsley, who served as Special As-

sistant to the President in the area of personnel and recruiting, is leaving the White House Staff and has joined the staff of the Inaugural Committee. Frank Herringer, a Staff Assistant who worked with Dan, and now with Fred Malek, is being nominated to be Administrator of the Urban Mass Transportation Administration at the Department of Transportation, so Frank will be leaving the White House Staff to assume the position as Administrator of the Urban Mass Transportation Administration at the Department of Transportation. Mr. Herringer will succeed Carlos Villarreal, who has served as the Administrator of the Urban Mass Transportation Administration since March of 1969. We have already announced previously that Carlos Villarreal would be leaving that post and returning to private life.

Frank Herringer has been a Staff Assistant in the White House since October of 1971, and as a deputy to Fred Malek he has been responsible for a wide range of personnel and management-related matters involving a number of major Government departments, including the Department of Transportation.

Announcing Further Decisions on Personnel for the Second Term

December 20, 1972

The President has asked me to make some additional announcements regarding the planning for the second term.

One of the most important new agencies of the Federal Government which has been created during this Administration is the Environmental Protection Agency. The EPA is beginning its third year of operation this month and throughout its entire existence one man has served as the Administrator of the Environmental Protection Agency, William Ruckelshaus.

The President has asked me to announce that Bill Ruckelshaus will continue in this key post as we begin the new term.

In reviewing the very active effective record of the EPA during its short lifetime so far, the President expressed his confidence that Mr.

Ruckelshaus will continue to be a strong force in the policymaking and enforcement areas of environmental protection.

As I mentioned to you yesterday, Bill Ruckelshaus was here at the White House yesterday and met with the President to discuss the Environmental Protection Agency in the second term. You may want to refer to that in your stories also.

The President also has asked me to announce today that he is accepting with great regret the resignation of Richard C. Van Dusen, Under Secretary of Housing and Urban Development. Mr. Van Dusen has served in this important post since the beginning of this Administration, and he indicated some time ago his plans to return to his private law practice in Detroit. Also I should mention to you that Dick Van Dusen was here at the White House yesterday and met with the President briefly so that they could have a chance to say goodby and for the President to wish him well before he departed HUD.

In accepting Dick Van Dusen's resignation, the President expressed gratitude and admiration for the outstanding job Mr. Van Dusen has done at HUD, particularly as a driving force in the decentralization of the Department. President Nixon believes Mr. Van Dusen's performance is a record of the finest service in the public interest and one that has won him the highest esteem from his colleagues and heartfelt appreciation of President Nixon.

The President is also accepting today the resignation of two other officials in the Department of Housing and Urban Development: Norman Watson, Assistant Secretary for Housing Management, and Eugene A. Gulledge, Assistant Secretary for Housing Production and Mortgage Credit. Both individuals plan to return to private life and the President expresses deep appreciation for their contribution and for their service.

Also today the President is announcing his intention to nominate Richard W. Roberts of Schenectady, New York, to be Director of the National Bureau of Standards in the Department of Commerce. He will succeed Lewis M. Branscomb, who resigned that position in 1972. We will have biographical information for you on that.

Announcing Further Decisions on Personnel for the Second Term

December 21, 1972

The President has asked me this morning to announce his intention to nominate Richard Helms to be Ambassador to Iran. Dick Helms will succeed Joseph Farland in that post, who will be returning to Washington to receive an assignment to another important position. So Dick Helms will be nominated by the President to be Ambassador to Iran, and Joseph Farland, the current Ambassador, will be returning to Washington to receive an assignment to another important post which we will announce in the near future.

The President is also designating James Schlesinger, currently Chairman of the Atomic Energy Commission, for nomination to succeed Mr. Helms as Director of Central Intelligence.

The President, as you know, met with Director Helms at Camp David on the 20th of November, shortly after the election. At that time, Director Helms reminded the President and discussed with the President the fact that the CIA had a general policy under his leadership of having officials retire when they reach the age of 60. Dick Helms, who will be 60 in March of next year, expressed the feeling that he should follow the same retirement policy which has been in effect at CIA.

The President and Director Helms talked about that for a period. The President requested that Dick Helms remain in Government and offered him the position which I have announced this morning. Dick Helms has accepted it.

The President, of course, has the greatest respect and deepest appreciation for the extremely able and devoted service which Mr. Helms has given to this country for more than a generation. As most of you know, he has been with the CIA since its beginning in 1947. Prior to that, he was a member of the Office of Strategic Services during World War II and has served as Deputy Director of the CIA and also Director of the CIA since 1966.

The President felt, as I said, that Mr. Helms should remain in Government service and is pleased that he has accepted the new position which I have referred to.

The President is also pleased that a man of James Schlesinger's background and ability is available to succeed Mr. Helms as Director of Central Intelligence. Mr. Schlesinger has been Chairman of the Atomic Energy Commission since August of 1971. Before that, he served in the Office of Management and Budget and in its predecessor organization, the Bureau of the Budget. As an Assistant Director of these units, he was responsible for national security and international programs.

Mr. Schlesinger came to the Federal Government in 1969 from the Rand Corporation, where he was director of strategic studies. Before that, he was a professor at the University of Virginia from 1955 to 1963. I should mention that Mr. Schlesinger met with the President at Camp David on November 21.

The President has also asked me to tell you this morning that he is accepting with very special regret the resignation of David Abshire as Assistant Secretary of State for Congressional Relations. Mr. Abshire plans to return to Georgetown University as chairman and executive director of the Center for Strategic and International Studies. The President commends his excellent performance and outstanding abilities, and is grateful for his service in the State Department over the past years.

The President also wanted to announce today that he has asked David Abshire to be his first appointee to the newly created Commission on the Organization of the Government for the Conduct of Foreign Policy, a commission which you are all familiar with.

The Commission to which David Abshire will be the first appointee was created by law on July 13, 1972, to make a broad review of the Government's foreign policy machinery. The President was grateful that Assistant Secretary Abshire has agreed to serve as a member. The Commission will ultimately be composed of 12 members, two public and two Government appointees of the President, four appointees of the President of the Senate, and four appointees of the Speaker of the House.

As I mentioned, the Commission was established by Public Law 92–352 on July 13, 1972, and is due to report its findings to the President and to the Congress by June 30, 1974.

Announcing Further Decisions on Personnel for the Second Term

December 22, 1972

We have several announcements for you today relating to the second term and the planning for the second term. Continuing the announcements we have made, or have been making, in recent days about key diplomatic posts and Ambassadorships in the second term, the President has asked me to announce that he intends to nominate John N. Irwin II, to be United States Ambassador to France, succeeding Arthur K. Watson, who returned to private life in October.

John Irwin has served with distinction as second in command of the United States Department of State for more than 2 years, having joined the Administration as Under Secretary of State in September of 1970 and assuming the title of Deputy Secretary when the name of that position was changed by statute last summer. John Irwin had previously served as a sub-Cabinet officer in the Defense Department as Assistant Secretary for International Security Affairs from 1958 to 1961.

We will have a complete biography of John Irwin available for you after the briefing, but I would like to say that the President, in asking John Irwin to undertake his new assignment overseas, commended him on the outstanding service he has rendered to the Administration and to the country during his tenure at the State Department. I think all of you know that the President considers the post of Ambassador to France one of the most important positions abroad, and one of the most important positions in Europe.

President Nixon considers Ambassador-designate Irwin to be extremely qualified to carry out these responsibilities.

Also today, the President has asked me to announce the fact that he is accepting with deep appreciation for his contributions the resignation of William W. Scranton as a member of the Price Commission. Governor Scranton has been a member of the Price Commission since its beginning in October of 1971. When Governor Scranton took on this new assignment, he indicated that he would serve for a period of only a year and that the time is up now. So the President has accepted with deep appreciation for his contribution to the Administration and to the country his resignation as a member of the Price Commission.

Finally, we have another announcement this morning with regard to a nomination which the President will make to the Senate early next year. This announcement regards an individual whose position does not make him a member of the President's Administration, strictly speaking, but which certainly makes him an important colleague and partner of the Administration.

I am referring to Mayor Walter E. Washington, the Mayor-Commissioner of the District of Columbia. The President is pleased to announce his intention to nominate Mayor Walter Washington to continue serving in his present post as the top official in the city of Washington for another 4-year term after his present term expires in February of 1973.

Walter Washington is the only man ever to have filled the post of Mayor-Commissioner, having been named to the job by President Johnson at the time it was created in 1967, and reappointed to a 4-year term by President Nixon in 1969. We will have, as I said, a complete biography on Mayor Walter Washington for you after the briefing.

Appendix F—Rules Governing This Publication

[Reprinted from the Federal Register, vol. 37, p. 23607, dated November 4, 1972]

TITLE 1—GENERAL PROVISIONS

Chapter 1—Administrative Committee of the Federal Register

PART 10—PRESIDENTIAL PAPERS

SUBPART A—ANNUAL VOLUMES

Sec.

10.1   Publication required.

10.2   Coverage of prior years.

10.3   Scope and sources.

10.4   Format, indexes, and ancillaries.

10.5   Distribution to Government agencies.

10.6   Extra copies.

AUTHORITY: 44 U.S.C. 1506; sec. 6, E.O. 10530, 19 FR 2709; 3 CFR 1954–1958 Comp. p. 189.

SUBPART A—ANNUAL VOLUMES

§ 10.1   *Publication required.*

The Director of the Federal Register shall publish, at the end of each calendar year, a special edition of the FEDERAL REGISTER called the "Public Papers of the Presidents of the United States." Unless the amount of material requires otherwise, each volume shall cover one calendar year.

§ 10.2   *Coverage of prior years.*

After consulting with the National Historical Publications Commission on the need therefor, the Administrative Committee may authorize the publication of volumes of papers of the Presidents covering specified years before 1957.

§ 10.3   *Scope and sources.*

(a) The basic text of each volume shall consist of oral statements by the President or of writings subscribed by him, and selected from—

(1) Communications to the Congress;

(2) Public addresses;

(3) Transcripts of news conferences;

(4) Public letters;

(5) Messages to heads of State;

(6) Statements released on miscellaneous subjects; and

(7) Formal executive documents promulgated in accordance with law.

(b) In general, ancillary text, notes, and tables shall be derived from official sources.

§ 10.4   *Format, indexes, and ancillaries.*

(a) Each annual volume, divided into books whenever appropriate, shall be separately published in the binding and style that the Administrative Committee considers suitable to the dignity of the Office of the President of the United States.

(b) Each volume shall be appropriately indexed and contain appropriate ancillary information respecting significant Presidential documents not printed in full text.

§ 10.5   *Distribution to Government agencies.*

(a) The Public Papers of the Presidents of the United States shall be distributed to the following, in the quantities indicated, without charge:

(1) *Members of Congress.* Each Senator and each Member of the House of Representa-

tives is entitled to one copy of each annual volume published during his term of office, upon his written request to the Director of the Federal Register.

(2) *Supreme Court.* The Supreme Court is entitled to 12 copies of each annual volume.

(3) *Executive agencies.* The head of each executive agency is entitled to one copy of each annual volume upon application to the Director.

(b) Legislative, judicial, and executive agencies of the Federal Government may obtain copies of the annual volumes, at cost, for official use, by the timely submission of a printing and binding requisition to the Government Printing Office on Standard Form 1.

§ 10.6 *Extra copies.*

Each request for extra copies of the annual volumes must be addressed to the Superintendent of Documents, to be paid for by the agency or official making the request.

INDEX

[Main references are to item numbers except as otherwise indicated]

Abel, I. W., 102 n.

ABM (antiballistic missile) systems. *See* Antiballistic missile (ABM) systems

Abortion, 142

Abrams, Gen. Creighton W., Jr., 103 [9], 129, 134 [2], 214 [6], 239 [11], App. B–18

Abshire, David M., App. E–24

Accidents. *See* Safety

Acree, Vernon D., App. A–17

ACTION

Associate Director, App. A–14, A–17

Deputy Director, App. A–6

Lead-based paint poisoning, 51 (p. 188)

Message to Congress on older persons, 100 (pp. 465, 482)

Acuff, Roy, 407

Adams, Henry, quoted, 372

Adams, John, quoted, 224

Addresses and remarks

Administration, second term plans, 421

Albuquerque, N. Mex., 409

American farmer, radio address, 377

American Legion, 54th annual national convention, 267

American Museum of Immigration, Liberty Island, N.Y., dedication, 321

Antiballistic missile treaty and interim agreement on strategic offensive arms

Ceremony marking entry into force, 334

Congressional briefing, 199

Transmittal to Congress, 196

Appointments and nominations. *See* Appointments and nominations

Ashland, Ky., 375

Atlanta, Ga., informal remarks after motorcade, 346

Austria, President's visit. *See under* Austria

Addresses and remarks—Continued

Bicentennial celebration of American independence, radio address to Nation, 224

Biological weapons convention, signing ceremony, 115

"Birthright of an American Child," radio address, 412

Blue Room at the White House, re-opening, 152

Brown, Robert J., dinner honoring, 31

Busing, address to Nation, 90

Campaign receptions

Northeast region, Pocantico Hills, N.Y., 365

Southern region, Atlanta, Ga., 347

Canada, President's visit. *See under* Canada

Chicago, Ill., 400

China, People's Republic of, President's visit. *See under* China, People's Republic of

Columbus Day dinner, 342

Congress, address to Joint Session at conclusion of trip to Austria, the Union of Soviet Socialist Republics, Iran, and Poland, 188

Connally Ranch, Floresville, Tex.

Dinner remarks, 315

Question-and-answer session with guests, 134

"Conversation with the President," CBS radio and television interview, 1

Crime, radio address, 350

Defense policy, radio address, 388

Distinguished Service Medal, presentation ceremony, 283

District of Columbia Metropolitan Police Department, 126

Drug abuse

Law enforcement activities, visit to New York City, 94

Radio address, 350

Index

[Main references are to item numbers except as otherwise indicated]

Index

[Main references are to item numbers except as otherwise indicated]

Index

[Main references are to item numbers except as otherwise indicated]

Index

Index

Index

Index

Index

Index

[Main references are to item numbers except as otherwise indicated]

Index

Index

[Main references are to item numbers except as otherwise indicated]

Index

Index

Index

Index

Index

Index

Index

Index

Index

Index

Index

[Main references are to item numbers except as otherwise indicated]

Index

Index

[Main references are to item numbers except as otherwise indicated]

Index

Index

[Main references are to item numbers except as otherwise indicated]

[Main references are to item numbers except as otherwise indicated]

Index

[Main references are to item numbers except as otherwise indicated]